COST ACCOUNTING

**The Robert N. Anthony/Willard J. Graham
Series in Accounting**

COST ACCOUNTING

Edward B. Deakin
The University of Texas at Austin

Michael W. Maher
The University of Michigan

1984

RICHARD D. IRWIN, INC.
Homewood, Illinois 60430

The diagram on the cover is a symbolic representation of the three major parts of cost accounting covered in this book.

 The computer terminal symbolizes *cost accounting systems.*

 The decision symbol denotes *differential costs for decision making.*

 The performance chart symbolizes *cost data for performance evaluation.*

Material from the Uniform CPA Examination Questions and Unofficial Answers, copyright © 1972, 1974, 1975, 1976, 1977, 1978, 1979, and 1981 by the American Institute of Certified Public Accountants, Inc., is reprinted (or adapted) with permission.

Material from the Certificate in Management Accounting Examinations, copyright © 1972, 1973, 1974, 1975, 1976, 1977, 1978, 1979, 1980, and 1981 by the National Association of Accountants, is reprinted and/or adapted with permission.

ISBN 0-256-02789-7

Library of Congress Catalog Card No. 83–80582

Printed in the United States of America

1 2 3 4 5 6 7 8 9 0 K 1 0 9 8 7 6 5 4

Preface

After reviewing the subject material in cost and managerial accounting both from an academic and a practical perspective, it became evident to us that cost accounting consists of three major topic areas:

Cost accounting systems.

Differential costs for decision making.

Cost data for performance evaluation.

These three areas are often distributed throughout different sections of cost and managerial accounting texts, thus giving the appearance that cost accounting is made up of diverse topical material with little cohesion. Our experience indicates that student response to the lack of structure has been generally negative. To overcome the criticisms about this lack of organization to the subject, this text is structured into parts that correspond to the three major topic areas.

Part 1 of the text deals with *cost accounting systems* including the flow of costs, job and process costing, cost allocation, and variable product costing. As the text is structured, students and instructors will find a comprehensive discussion of cost accounting systems in Part 1.

Part 2 of the text addresses the use of *differential costs for decision making*. In this part, we focus on the role of the accountant as a supplier of cost data for use in making decisions. This part includes cost estimation, cost-volume-profit analysis, differential costing for short- and long-run decisions, and capital investment analysis. Our approach is to show why differential cost concepts are important, how to identify costs that are differential, and how to use those differential costs in decisions.

Part 3 addresses the use of *cost data for performance evaluation* and control. Here we present the budget as the operating plan, and discuss the analysis of budget versus actual results, including flexible budgets, variance analysis, standard costs. Performance evaluation in decentralized organizations is also discussed in this part of the text.

These first three parts of the text emphasize the structure of cost accounting data systems and the use of the data in decision making and performance evaluation settings under conditions of certainty. Part 4 of the book introduces the problems that arise from conditions of uncertainty. Although some consideration of uncertainty appears in particular discussions in Parts 1 through 3, the more formal consideration of uncertainty is presented in this last part.

The organization of the book is designed to reflect the subareas of the subject. Yet it provides the instructor with flexibility in presentation to students. Courses that emphasize cost systems may use all of the chapters in Part 1 and perhaps a selection of other chapters. A course designed to emphasize decision making may skip all of Part 1 and include all of Part 2. In addition, the book is designed so any major part can follow the first two chapters:

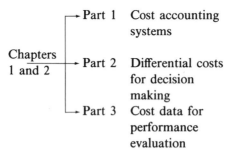

Chapters 1 and 2

Part 1 Cost accounting systems

Part 2 Differential costs for decision making

Part 3 Cost data for performance evaluation

We believe this text offers the opportunity to present a cohesive presentation of the subject matter of cost accounting with the flexibility to adapt to the emphasis called for by a particular course.

Cost accounting and other disciplines

Cost accounting has gone through dramatic changes in the past decade. As a result, a new look at the subject matter of cost accounting is needed. Developments in computer systems have reduced manual bookkeeping work. As a result, a discussion of cost systems can focus on the concepts that underlie the system rather than on details of bookkeeping. Our discussion of cost systems emphasizes cost flow concepts. We assume the computer is used to facilitate access to data and to use it. Our discussion of cost data analysis avoids tedious computations and focuses on the variables the manager should consider when using the outputs of data analysis programs.

Developments in such related disciplines as economics, behavioral sciences, statistics, and operations research have also had a major impact on cost accounting in recent years. At one time many cost accounting instructors spent a great deal of time teaching the basics of these related disciplines. The interesting accounting questions were necessarily deferred until students had a grasp of the analytical techniques.

A review of the subject coverage in these related disciplines revealed to us that the related discipline usually assumes cost data as given and then delves into the issues that are an integral part of the discipline itself. We follow the same approach in mirror image. We do not attempt to teach the technical aspects of related disciplines, such as statistics and operations research, except as they apply directly to the accounting data used in an analytical model. Instead, we focus on the *use* of cost data in decision models and on the *application* of techniques and concepts from other disciplines as they relate to cost accounting.

For example, in Chapter 13 we present cost analysis for multiple product decisions. One of the topics in the chapter shows how the results of product choice decisions can be affected by misapplication of full-absorption cost data in a multiple-product model. This chapter assumes that a student will have access to a computer for solution of complex linear programming problems, so we show how to interpret the input and output from the computer program. We discuss the aspects of linear programming as they relate to the cost analysis, but we do not attempt to teach the mechanics of linear programming.

As a result of this approach, we find there is more time available for the accounting questions that arise when attempting to apply quantitative techniques to managerial decision problems. Thus, students learn the interaction of quantitative methods with the accounting data system. In this way, the book emphasizes the comparative advantage of the accountant.

Student background

It is probably more important that students using this book have a tolerance for quantitative problem solving in an economic environment rather than having any specific set of prerequisites. We have strived to make cost accounting concepts as intuitive as possible. In this regard, a problem-solving orientation is very helpful for learning cost accounting just as it is for managing organizations.

We assume the book will be used in a cost or managerial accounting course in which students have had a minimum of one course in accounting principles or financial accounting. This prerequisite is especially useful for obtaining an orientation to accounting terminology and the financial reporting system. It is not necessary that students have had a previous course in managerial or cost accounting.

We assume users of the book have a knowledge of elementary algebra. Although previous coursework in statistics, operations research, computer sciences, and other similar disciplines is not required, we believe that such work can enrich the experience with this book because our emphasis on concepts and applications can help to synthesize and apply materials in these related disciplines.

There is ample material in the text to challenge students who have had previous courses in managerial accounting and in quantitative methods. The material in chapter appendixes and the variety of problems and cases can be used to enrich the course when students have an extensive background in accounting and related fields. Several course outlines have been provided in the instructor's manual to cover alternative course emphasis and intensity. In general, this book is packaged to provide maximum flexibility to instructors based on student background.

Learning by doing

We believe that cost accounting is best learned by applying the concepts, methods, and techniques to realistic problems. Our chapters emphasize the use of illustrations and examples. Many of these are drawn from our experience about the actual cost accounting problems faced in organizations. Each chapter begins with a brief statement of the chapter objectives. A set of key terms is provided at the end of each chapter together with self-study materials for review and instant feedback.

The remaining end-of-chapter material consists of questions, exercises, problems, and cases. Questions are designed to review in words the major concepts and issues in the chapter. Exercises are designed to test the application of specific points in the chapter to sets of numeric data. Problems integrate more than one point in a chapter and may integrate materials from other chapters. Cases require a more in-depth analysis of the issues, frequently combining verbal or written discussion with analysis of data. Cases may also integrate several parts of the book. Depending on the goals of the course and the background of the students, an instructor may assign any combination of questions, exercises, problems or cases. The materials in this section are not only numerous but diverse in order to provide an instructor with flexibility in assignments.

Acknowledgments

We are indebted to many people for their assistance and ideas. Robert N. Anthony was instrumental in developing this book. He provided helpful guidance and support on each of several revisions of drafts. He and Professor James S. Reece graciously permitted us to use several of their cases copyrighted by Osceola Institute.

We are particularly indebted to Professor Robert K. Mautz who helped get this book started. He wrote and edited a considerable portion of manuscript in the early stages of this book.

We are grateful for the comments of numerous reviewers. These include: Professors Robert N. Anthony, Wayne Bremser, Eugene Cominskey, Andrew DeMotses, Stanley Gartska, Lawrence Klein, Patrick McKenzie, Curtis Stanley, and John Tracy.

Many of our colleagues and mentors have provided stimulating ideas. These include: Professors Stephen Butler, Robert Colson, John Fellingham, Charles Huber, Robert Mautz, Kasi Ramanathan, and James Reece.

Numerous students have read the manuscript, worked problems, checked solutions, and otherwise helped us to write a teachable manuscript that is as error-free as possible. We are particularly grateful to Roger Baris, Janice Bershas, Amy Broman, Jongwook Cheh, Jean Lim, Keith McGarvey, Peter Tallian, Tom Terpstra, and Rajeev Vasudeva at the Universities of Chicago and Michigan. We are also grateful to the University of Texas students who class-tested this material. Particular thanks are due to Anthony Billings, Malcolm MacDonald, and Bruce MacKenzie-Graham for their comments and other support in developing this material.

We extend a special note of gratitude to Barbara Schmidt for her skillful typing of numerous drafts. Helen Maher provided many incisive comments in editing the manuscript and in typing early drafts. Cynthia Fostel used her unique blend of subject knowledge and editorial skill to improve the readability of the text.

We are grateful for permission to use problems and cases from numerous people and organizations. These include the Certificate in Management Accounting Examinations by the Institute of Management Accounting of the National Association of Accountants; the Uniform CPA Examinations by the American Institute of Certified Public Accountants; the President and Fellows of Harvard College; the Osceola Institute; Professor David Solomons; and l' Institut pour l' Etude des Methodes de Direction de l' Entreprise (IMEDE).

We extend special thanks to our families and colleagues who supported us in this endeavor.

We welcome comments from users.

Edward B. Deakin
Michael W. Maher

Contents

Part 3
Cost data for performance evaluation

17. The master budget 624

18. Using the budget for performance evaluation and control 674

COST ACCOUNTING

1

Cost
Accounting:
Its Nature and
Usefulness

This chapter presents an overview of the field of cost accounting and previews forthcoming chapters. In it, we examine the nature of cost accounting, who uses it, and how and why they use it. We explain how cost accounting relates to other fields, such as economics and financial accounting. Finally, we provide a brief outline of the book.

What is cost accounting?

Cost accounting is the subfield of accounting that *records, measures, and reports information* about costs. A cost is a *sacrifice of resources.* Costs are represented in the accounting system by outlays of cash, promises to pay cash in the future, and the expiration of the value of an asset. These include the cost of inventory, the costs of increasing sales volume, the costs saved from closing a branch office, and the like.

In this book, we identify two primary uses of cost information: *decision making and performance evaluation.* As shown in Illustration 1–1, cost accounting systems provide data for decision making and performance evaluation. Notice that the cost accounting system provides data for both managerial accounting and financial accounting. When costs are used inside the organization by managers to evaluate the performance of operations or personnel or as a basis for decision making, we say costs are used for managerial accounting purposes. When costs are used by outsiders, such as shareholders or creditors, to evaluate the performance of top management and make investment decisions about the organization, we say costs are used for financial accounting purposes. Further, cost accounting systems provide data for cost-based contracts, such as those used in contracts to provide medical service under Medicaid, and for tax purposes. In short, cost accounting systems provide data for multiple purposes.

This book focuses on cost accounting systems and on managerial uses of cost data for decision making and performance evaluation. That is, we focus on boxes I, II, and III in Illustration 1–1.

Illustration 1–1   **Relationship of cost accounting systems to uses of cost information**

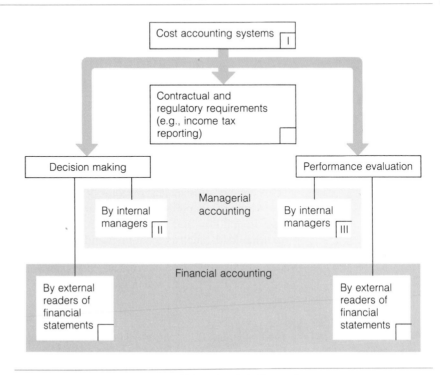

I, II, and III refer to parts of the book in which each topic is discussed.

Cost data for managerial purposes

Costs for decision making

Managers must often choose between two or more alternatives. Their decision is usually based on each action's financial consequences. Choosing among alternative actions is an important management activity in all organizations—large and small; profit making and not-for-profit; manufacturing, merchandising, and service. These calculations range from simple "back-of-the-envelope" figuring to complex computer simulation, but regardless of the complexity they are a necessary part of managing every organization.

One of the most difficult tasks in calculating such financial consequences is to estimate how costs (or revenues, or assets) will *differ* among the alternatives. For example, suppose the management of a department store is considering expanding its operations and store size to include several new product lines. As an alternative, the store could open a new outlet in a different location. The key is to determine which would be most profitable: remain the same size, expand operations in the current location, or open a new outlet. Using cost accounting techniques, the store can estimate differential costs; that is, how costs will differ for each alternative.

For example, suppose Jennifer's Sandwiche Shoppe has been open for lunch only, Monday through Friday, from 11 A.M. to 2 P.M. The owner-manager, Jennifer, is considering expanding her hours by opening Monday

Illustration 1-2 **Differential costs, revenues, and profits for one week**

	(1) Status quo Open 11 A.M.–2 P.M.	(2) Alternative Open 11 A.M.–2 P.M. and 5 P.M.–8 P.M.	(3) Difference (2) − (1)
Sales revenue	$1,100	$1,650[a]	$550
Costs:			
Food	500	750[a]	250
Labor	200	300[a]	100
Utilities	80	120[a]	40
Rent	250	250	—
Other	60	75[b]	15
Total costs	1,090	1,495	405
Operating profits	$ 10	$ 155	$145

[a] Fifty percent higher than status quo.
[b] Twenty-five percent higher than status quo.

through Friday evenings from 5 P.M. to 8 P.M. Jennifer figures her revenues, food costs, labor, and utilities would increase 50 percent, rent will remain the same, and other costs will increase by 25 percent if she opened in the evening. Jennifer's present and estimated future costs, revenues, and profits are shown in Columns 1 and 2 of Illustration 1–2. The differential costs, revenues, and profits are shown in Column 3 of Illustration 1–2. They are the differences between the data in Columns 1 and 2.

The analysis shows an increase in operating profits of $145 if the shop is opened in the evening. All other things being equal, Jennifer would therefore probably expand her hours. Note that only *differential* costs and revenues figured in the decision. Rent did not change, so it was not included.

Management accounting and GAAP In contrast to providing cost data for financial reporting to shareholders, cost data for managerial use (that is, within the organization) need not comply with generally accepted accounting principles (GAAP). Management is quite free to set its own definitions for cost information. Indeed, the accounting data used for external reporting may need to be modified to provide appropriate information for managerial decision making. For example, managerial decisions deal with the future, so estimates of future costs may be more valuable for decision making than the historical and current costs that are reported externally.

Costs for performance evaluation

An organization usually divides responsibility for specific functions among its employees. A maintenance group, for example, is responsible for maintaining a particular area of an office building, a K mart store manager is responsible for virtually all operations of the store, while the president of a company is responsible for the entire company. A responsibility center is a specific unit of an organization assigned to a manager who is held accountable for its operations and resources.

Consider the case of Jennifer's Sandwiche Shoppe. When Jennifer first opened her shop, she managed the entire operation herself. As the enterprise became more successful, she added a catering service. She then hired two managers: Sam to manage the shop and Carol to manage the catering service. Jennifer, as general manager, oversaw the entire operation.

Each manager is responsible for the revenues and costs of his or her department. Jennifer's salary, rent, utilities, and other costs are shared by both departments. Jennifer is directly responsible for these shared costs; the department managers are not.

Jennifer's organization has three responsibility centers as follows:

Responsibility center	Manager responsible	Responsible for
Entire organization	Jennifer, general manager	All of the organization's operations and resources, revenues, and costs
Sandwiche Shoppe	Sam, manager	Sandwiche Shoppe operations and resources (see Illustration 1–3 for revenues and costs)
Catering	Carol, manager	Catering operations and resources (see Illustration 1–3 for revenues and costs)

Illustration 1–3   **Responsibility centers, departmental costs and revenues**

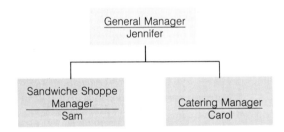

June 8–14

	Sandwiche Shoppe	Catering	Total
Sales revenue	$1,700	$1,100	$2,800
Department costs:			
Food	700	300	1,000
Labor[a]	300	500	800
Total department costs	1,000	800	1,800
Department margin	$ 700	$ 300	1,000
Utilities			150
Rent			250
Other			90
General manager's salary (Jennifer)			400
Operating profit			$ 110

[a] Includes department managers' salaries, but excludes Jennifer's salary.

Departmental income statements are shown in Illustration 1–3. Note that some costs—utilities, rent, other, and general manager's salary—are not considered departmental costs.

Budgeting   Managers in all organizations set financial goals for return on investment, cash balances, costs, earnings, and other performance indicators. Each responsibility center usually has a budget, which is a financial plan of the resources needed to carry out the center's tasks and meet financial goals. Estimates, as stated in budgets, help managers to decide if their goals can be achieved and, if not, what modifications will be necessary. At regular

Illustration 1–4   **Overview of the managerial process and the uses of cost accounting**

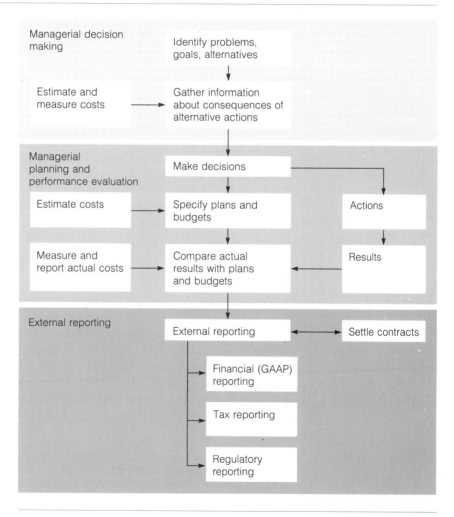

intervals of time, resources actually used are compared with the amount budgeted to assess the center's and the manager's performance. By comparing actual results with the budget plans, it is possible to identify the probable causes of variances from planned costs, profits, cash flows, and other financial targets. Managers can then take action to change their activities or revise their goals and plans. This process of planning and performance evaluation for responsibility centers is sometimes called *responsibility accounting.*

Overview

Illustration 1–4 presents a simplified overview of the two major uses of cost accounting for the managerial purposes discussed above plus the use of cost data for external reporting. Each time you are faced with an accounting problem, you should first ascertain the use of the data. Is it to value inventories in financial reports to shareholders? Is it to provide differential costs for a managerial decision? Is it to provide data for performance evaluation? Different needs require different kinds of accounting data.

Historical perspective

Although even the early Babylonians and Egyptians practiced cost accounting, the roots of modern cost accounting developed between 1880 and 1920.[1] During this period, companies began integrating production cost records with financial accounts, and standard cost systems emerged.

The 1920s and 1930s were especially eventful. Accounting for financial reports became subject to the regulations of the Securities and Exchange Commission (SEC) in 1934 and the Committee on Accounting Procedure of the American Institute of Certified Public Accountants (AICPA) in 1938. In addition, budgets became important tools for planning, cost control, and performance evaluation. Estimating and measuring costs for managerial decisions about alternative actions also became increasingly common. In his 1923 book, *The Economics of Overhead Costs,* J. M. Clark established the principle of different costs for different purposes. In recent years, this principle has been widely recognized and implemented by managerial accountants.

The content of cost accounting textbooks has reflected these changes over the years. In the early 1950s, cost accounting textbooks focused on procedures for measuring, recording, and reporting actual product costs for external purposes. This information applied almost exclusively to manufacturing companies. While product costing remains an important part of cost accounting, the emphasis now is on managerial uses and nonmanufacturing applications.

---

[1] See David Solomons, "The Historical Development of Costing," in *Studies in Cost Analysis,* ed. David Solomons (Homewood, Ill.: Richard D. Irwin, 1968), pp. 3–49; and James C. Stallman and T. Alan Russell, "Historical Development, Uses, and Challenges of Cost Accounting," in *The Managerial and Cost Accountant's Handbook,* ed. Homer A. Black and James Don Edwards (Homewood, Ill.: Dow Jones–Irwin, 1979), pp. 3–41.

The scope of cost accounting has broadened to include the application of mathematical and statistical techniques to cost analysis; consideration of how accounting affects managerial decision models employed in finance, economics, and operations management; and examination of the motivational impact of accounting.

The broad view of cost accounting that we take in this book is not clearly distinct from managerial accounting. However, in many organizations, cost accountants record cost data, while managerial accountants have the broader responsibility of operating the total internal accounting system.

While the traditional role of cost accounting to record full product cost data for external reporting and pricing remains strong, cost accounting for decision making and performance evaluation has gained importance in recent decades. Consequently, cost accountants must actively work with management to determine what accounting information is needed.

No longer restricted to manufacturing companies, cost accounting is now used in virtually every organization, including banks, fast-food outlets, professional organizations, hospitals, and government agencies. Because manufacturing operations present the most comprehensive, and perhaps the most complex, cost accounting situations, they are the settings of many of our examples and problems. Nonetheless, the concepts that we discuss can be applied to any organization.

Organizational environment

In most corporations, the controller is the chief accounting officer. In some firms, the controller has the rank of corporate vice president and reports directly to the company president. In others, the controller and the treasurer may both report to a financial vice president who is responsible for both accounting and financial affairs. The cost accounting function is typically the responsibility of the controller.

Illustration 1–5 shows an abbreviated version of the Du Pont Company's organization chart. The board of directors establishes policy. Officers of the company carry out that policy. Either the board chairperson or the president is designated chief executive officer. The *chief executive officer* (CEO) is responsible for supervising all officers of the corporation and thus is the top-ranking manager. Vice presidents are assigned responsibility over the individual divisions. They will usually appoint managers to supervise specified activities within their divisions.

The chain of authority that extends from the chief executive officer through successive levels of management to the workers who perform nonsupervisory tasks is called *line authority.* Line officers are responsible for activities directly related to the main goals of the organization.

Staff officers provide expert advice to line officers. The rise of highly specialized technical skills has led to *staff authority,* a recognition of the importance of technical expertise and judgment. A top staff person's authority may cross

Illustration 1–5   **Partial organization chart, E. I. Du Pont De Nemours & Company**

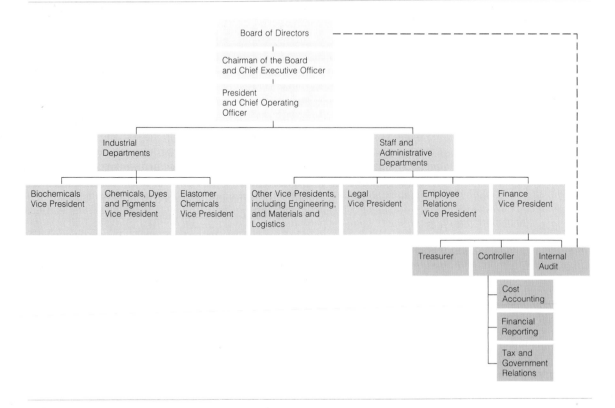

line distinctions in the company (for instance, from one division to another), but it is limited to questions related to the staff member's specialized knowledge. Du Pont's legal officer has no line authority in any corporate division. Nonetheless, no division can enter into a major contract that has not been reviewed by the legal staff. In a similar vein, the controller is the staff expert on accounting matters.

The office of controller

As the chief accounting officer, the controller is responsible for both external and internal accounting reports. External reports include published financial statements and reports to taxing authorities like the Internal Revenue Service and regulatory bodies like the Securities and Exchange Commission (SEC).

Internally, the controller is responsible for supplying management with accounting data for planning, performance evaluation, and decision making and for overseeing the company's internal control system. In addition, the controller maintains all cost and other accounting records, including inventories, receivables, payables, and fixed asset accounts. Most of these duties require the use of electronic data processing. In some cases, the controller supervises data processing operations, but frequently data processing is an independent department reporting to the financial vice president or another staff vice president.

In many organizations, the *internal audit department* provides a variety of auditing and consulting services, including auditing internal controls, auditing data for internal use, and assisting outside auditors in their examination of external financial reports.

The internal audit manager sometimes reports directly to the controller. However, because the controller's recordkeeping role may conflict with the audit function, the audit manager may report directly to the controller's superior (as at Du Pont) and is often given authority to communicate to the audit committee of the board of directors.

The office of treasurer

The corporate treasurer is primarily responsible for managing liquid assets (cash and short-term investments) and handling credit reviews and collection of receivables. The treasurer usually conducts business with banks and other financial sources and oversees public issues of stock and debt. In most cases, the treasurer focuses on financial problems while the controller concentrates on operating problems.

Professional environment

The accounting profession includes many kinds of accountants—external auditors, consultants, controllers, internal auditors, tax experts, and so forth. Because accounting positions carry great responsibility, accountants must be highly trained and well informed about new developments in their field. As a result, special organizations and certification programs have been established to serve accountants' needs and the public interest.

Organizations

Numerous organizations have arisen to keep accounting professionals aware of current issues. Most of these organizations have journals that help keep professional accountants up to date. Some of these organizations are listed below.

The *Financial Executive Institute* is an organization of financial executives such as controllers, treasurers, and financial vice presidents. It publishes a monthly periodical, *Financial Executive,* and a number of studies on accounting issues.

The *National Association of Accountants* is open to anyone who works in management accounting. It publishes the journal *Management Accounting* and numerous policy statements and research studies on accounting issues. It also sponsors the Certificate in Management Accounting (CMA) program.

The *Institute of Internal Auditors* is an organization of internal auditors.

It publishes a periodical called the *Internal Auditor* and numerous research studies on internal auditing. It also sponsors the Certificate in Internal Auditing program.

The *Association of Government Accountants* is an organization of federal, state, and local government accountants. It publishes the *Government Accountant's Journal.*

Certifications

Anyone who wishes to be licensed as a Certified Public Accountant (CPA) must pass an examination that includes questions on cost accounting, as well as other questions on accounting practice, theory, law, and auditing. We have included samples of CPA examination cost accounting questions in this book.

In 1972, a **Certificate in Management Accounting (CMA)** program was established to recognize educational achievement and professional competence in management accounting. The examination, educational, and experience requirements are similar to those for CPA certification, but they are aimed at professionals in management and cost accounting.[2] We have included a large number of problems from CMA examinations in this book.

Parallel examinations and certifications are given in Canada by the Society of Industrial Accountants and the Certified General Accountants Association.

Cost Accounting Standards Board

The *Cost Accounting Standards Board* (CASB) was set up by the U.S. Congress in 1970 to establish uniform cost accounting standards for U.S. defense contractors. The CASB's primary purpose was to avert disputes between the U.S. government and defense contractors about the allocation of costs in cost-based government contracts. The CASB was terminated in 1980, but its rules and standards are still used in numerous federal government purchases.[3]

Costs and benefits of accounting

How much accounting information will suffice? Managers often complain that they never have all the facts they need. More data could usually be provided to decision makers, but at a cost. For example, one division of National Steel Company recently installed a standard cost system that cost

---

[2] For more information about the CMA examination, write to the Institute of Management Accounting, 570 City Center Building, Ann Arbor, Michigan 48104. For more information about the CPA examination write to the American Institute of Certified Public Accountants, 1211 Avenue of the Americas, New York, New York 10036.

[3] For more details about the Cost Accounting Standards Board, see Gary F. Bulmash and Louis I. Rose, "The Cost Accounting Standards Board," in *The Managerial and Cost Accountant's Handbook,* ed. Homer A. Black and James Don Edwards (Homewood, Ill.: Dow Jones–Irwin, 1979), pp. 1231–60.

several million dollars. Management could justify the expenditure for more accounting because it believed that the system would help control costs and increase the efficiency of operations, thereby saving the company much more than it cost.

The question of how much accounting information will suffice can be resolved by evaluating costs and benefits of accounting information. In practice, it is especially difficult to measure the benefits of accounting systems. In deciding to install the standard cost system, the management of National Steel could be certain of only some of the costs and very few of the benefits of the system. Future benefits and costs can never be known with certainty. Nonetheless, accounting for managerial uses must, in principle, meet **cost-benefit requirements.**

The analysis of costs and benefits requires considerable cooperation between the users of accounting information and accountants. Users are more familiar with the benefits of the data, and accountants are more familiar with the costs. Such cooperation is shown in Illustration 1–6, where users identify their decision-making needs and demand data from accountants, who develop information systems to supply the data when it is cost-benefit justified. In practice, the process sometimes works in reverse. Accountants sometimes report data that users do not use. But if accountants and users interact, they eventually settle on a cost-benefit-justified supply of accounting data that meets users' needs.

Accounting theoreticians are working on solutions to the difficult problem of determining the optimal cost-benefit-justified accounting data system. We present some of these developments in Chapter 26, "The Economics of Information." Throughout this book, we assume that both users and accountants

Illustration 1–6   **Interaction between users and accountants**

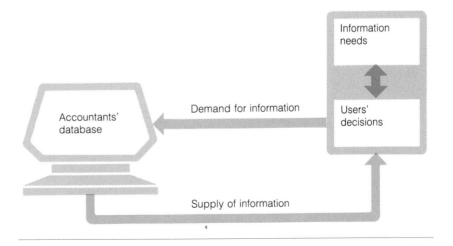

assess the costs and benefits of information in deciding whether to change an accounting system, whether to prepare a special report, and so forth.

How does cost accounting relate to other fields of study?

Cost accounting interfaces with many other fields of study. Consequently, you will discover concepts in this book that are discussed in other books also. One of the primary uses of cost accounting—valuing inventory and cost of goods sold for external reporting to shareholders—is part of financial accounting. Cost accounting is closely related to microeconomics. Some think of differential cost analysis, in particular, as a form of applied microeconomics. Cost accounting provides data for use in decision models for finance, operations management, and marketing. Cost accounting also relates to motivation and behavior because it is used in planning and performance evaluation. Finally, tools from statistics, mathematics, and computer sciences are used to perform cost analyses.

As noted earlier, this book focuses on three subjects: (1) cost accounting systems, (2) costs for managerial decision making, and (3) costs for managerial performance evaluations. These subjects correspond with the following chapters:

1. Cost accounting systems Chapters 3 and 4 provide the fundamental concepts, flow of costs, and cost allocation concepts on which the rest of the book is based.

Chapters 5 through 9 describe the design of accounting systems, cost accumulation in different kinds of organizations, allocation of costs to products, and a comparison of inventory valuation for managerial accounting and for financial accounting purposes.

2. Costs for managerial decision making Chapters 10 through 14 take a managerial perspective. Here we are primarily concerned with the estimated impact of managerial decisions on costs. The focus is on short-term operating decisions. For example, how will costs (as well as revenues and profits) be affected by an increase in volume? By closing a store? By developing a new product line?

Chapters 15 and 16 cover the use of cost accounting in long-term capital investment decisions. We discuss cash flow estimation and include tax effects of capital investment decisions.

3. Costs for managerial performance evaluation Chapters 17 through 21 discuss how managers use cost accounting to plan and budget their activities and to evaluate performance.

Chapters 22 and 23 discuss the use of cost accounting in managing decentralized organizations.

4. Cost accounting in an uncertain environment Chapters 24 through 26 cover some important advanced topics, including decision making under uncertainty, variance investigation models, and economics of information.

Summary

This chapter provides an overview of cost accounting. Cost accounting is the subfield of accounting that records, measures, and reports information about costs.

This book discusses cost accounting systems and the use of cost accounting in its two primary managerial uses: decision making and performance evaluation. In decision making, cost accounting is used by managers to assess financial consequences of alternative actions. In performance evaluation, accounting is used by managers to assign responsibility for costs and to measure employee performance.

The focus of cost accounting has moved from an emphasis on inventory and cost of goods sold valuation for external financial reporting to an emphasis on cost uses for managerial purposes in recent years. While cost accounting still provides data essential for external financial reporting, it has also recently achieved an important role in management.

Like any other service, product, or system in an organization, cost accounting is subject to economic cost-benefit evaluation. Perfectly accurate and complete accounting information, even if possible to obtain, would almost certainly be too costly to justify. The benefits of cost accounting information are usually derived by the managers who use it. Determination of the costs and benefits of accounting information requires cooperation between the users of information and the accountants who supply it.

Terms and concepts

The following terms and concepts should be familiar to you after reading this chapter:

Budget

Certificate in Management
    Accounting (CMA)

Controller

Cost

Cost accounting

Cost Accounting Standards Board
    (CASB)

Cost-benefit requirements

Costs for decision making

Costs for performance evaluation

Differential costs

Financial accounting

Generally accepted accounting
    principles (GAAP)

Managerial accounting

Responsibility center

Questions   1–1.   Column 1 lists several types of decision categories. Column 2 contains a list
                         of accounting costs and a corresponding letter. Place the letter of the accounting
                         cost that would be appropriate in the blank next to each decision category.

Column 1

_____ Analysis of divisional performance.
_____ Costing for income tax purposes.
_____ Determining how many units to pro-
           duce in the coming week.

Column 2

A. Costs for inventory valuation.
B. Costs for decision making.
C. Costs for performance evalua-
      tion.

1–2.   A manager once remarked, "All I need are the differential costs for decision
       making—don't bother me with information about any other costs. They aren't
       relevant for decision making." Comment on the manager's remarks.

1–3.   You are considering sharing your living quarters with another person. What
       costs would you include in setting a fair basis for splitting the cost with
       that other person? What costs would differ if another person were to move
       in with you?

1–4.   Would you support a proposal to develop a set of "generally accepted" account-
       ing standards for performance evaluation? Why or why not?

1–5.   The telephone company has established discounts for off-peak use of long-
       distance telephone services. A discount of 35 percent is offered for calls placed
       in the evenings during the week, and a discount of 60 percent is offered for
       late-night and weekend calls. Given that the telephone company would proba-
       bly not be profitable if these discounts were offered all the time, explain what
       cost considerations may have entered into management's decision to offer
       the discounts.

1–6.   A critic of the expansion of the role of the accountant has stated, "The control-
       ler should have enough work filling out tax forms and the paperwork required
       by the bureaucracy without trying to interfere with management decision
       making. Let's leave that role to those more familiar with the decision models
       employed by management." Comment.

1–7.   You are considering whether to purchase a new car to replace your present
       car. Being strictly rational in an economic sense, which of the following costs
       would you include in making your decision:

   a. Cost of the present car.
   b. Trade-in value of your present car.
   c. Maintenance costs on the present car.
   d. Maintenance costs on the new car.
   e. Fuel consumption on the present car.
   f. Fuel consumption on the new car.
   g. Cost of parking permits, garage rental, and similar "storage costs."
   h. Liability insurance on the present car.
   i. Liability insurance on the new car.
   j. Property and collision insurance on the present car.
   k. Property and collision insurance on the new car.
   l. Changes in the relative frequency of your friends' saying: "Let's use
         your car since it's newer," and the related costs of using the new car.
   m. Annual time depreciation on the present car.

    n.   Annual time depreciation on the new car.

    o.   Financing costs of the present car.

    p.   Financing costs for the new car.

You should be able to give reasons why each element should or should not be included in your analysis. (Hint: Which costs will be differential, that is, will be different if the new car is purchased?)

1–8. Why would the controller have an interest in the structure of an organization and in knowing the distinction between line and staff functions?

1–9. It is common practice for the internal auditor to report to the same person who is responsible for preparation of the accounting reports and the maintenance of accounting records. Why might such a supervisory relationship be established and what procedures might be installed to minimize the extent of conflict.

1–10. For a corporation organized according to the organization chart in Illustration 1–5, what potential conflicts might arise between production managers and the controller's staff? How might these potential conflicts be resolved with a minimum of interference from the chief executive officer?

1–11. What certifications are available to a person in an accounting career?

1–12. One of your colleagues commented, "I want to be a CPA. Why should I take cost accounting?" Indeed, why should a potential CPA study cost accounting?

1–13. What is the difference between the controller and the treasurer?

1–14. Roger Farley has just been named chief executive officer of a medium-size high technology company. Roger completed an M.B.A. degree a few years ago and has risen rapidly through the ranks of the organization, having started in the budgeting section of the controller's office. He has been so impressed with the importance of budgeting that he has proposed to create a new vice president position to coordinate the budgeting function since, as he had noted, it was often difficult for a mere "supervisor" to obtain the complete cooperation of other division managers in the budgeting function.

Comment on the proposed new position and suggest other ways that Farley might accomplish his objectives with less potential for conflict.

1–15. Marlene McHarris has recently been appointed the chief executive officer of a diversified corporate organization. The company has been organized along functional lines similar to Illustration 1–5. However, there are three separate manufacturing divisions, each dealing with somewhat different products and markets. Each manufacturing division has been headed by an assistant vice president with a vice president for manufacturing heading up all manufacturing operations. The manufacturing vice president is due to retire at the end of this year. The assistant vice presidents have proposed that a more efficient organization structure might be established if the company were to set up each manufacturing division as a more separate (decentralized) organization. As the vice president pointed out, "Each of these manufacturing divisions is sufficiently dissimilar that they would be better able to operate on their own. If each division had its own engineering and accounting staffs, there would be less need to cross division lines each time an engineering study or an accounting report were required. Moreover, the accounting sections could adapt their decision making and performance evaluation functions to the needs of the specific manufacturing divisions rather than treat them all alike."

As a recent college graduate, you have been asked to prepare some comments on the advantages and disadvantages of the proposal. Your supervisor is the present vice president and controller whose job is to coordinate the accounting activities for all three divisions.

Problems and cases

1–16. Identify costs for decision making

In your first day as a member of the controller's staff, you have been asked to report on a contemplated change in the equipment layout in the plant. The new layout is expected to result in a 10 percent reduction in labor costs, but no changes in any other costs. Last year, the costs of labor amounted to $7 per unit produced. Other costs amounted to $9 per unit produced. The company can sell as many units as it can manufacture. The company's union contract contains a provision for a 12 percent increase in labor costs for the coming year. In addition, analysis of other costs indicates that these costs may be expected to increase by 8 percent in the coming year.

Required:

Identify the costs that are differential for the decision to rearrange the plant. Specify any costs that you would need to know to make the decision even if the cost is not given in the problem.

1–17. Identify costs for decision making

Management of a division of a conglomerate company has been questioning whether operations in the division should be continued. The division has been operating at a "loss" for the past several years as indicated in the accompanying divisional income statement. If the division is eliminated, corporate overhead is not expected to change nor are any other changes expected in the operations or costs of other divisions.

Required:

What costs would be differential for the decision to discontinue operations in the division.

Divisional Income Statement

Sales revenue	$ 850,000
Costs:	
Advertising	35,000
Cost of goods sold	420,000
Administrative salaries	59,000
Selling costs	82,000
Building occupancy	181,000
Share of corporate overhead	96,000
Total costs	873,000
Net loss before income tax benefit	(23,000)
Tax benefit at 40% rate	9,200
Net loss	$ (13,800)

1–18. Cost concepts for different purposes

Lamar Manufacturing Corporation has just entered into an agreement to sell 20,000 units of product to a government agency this year at "cost plus 20 percent."

Lamar operates a manufacturing plant that can produce 60,000 units per year.

The company normally produces 40,000 units per year. The costs to produce 40,000 units are as follows:

	Total	Per unit
Materials	$ 480,000	$12
Labor	760,000	19
Supplies and other indirect costs that will vary with production	320,000	8
Building occupancy and other indirect costs that will not vary with production	440,000	11
Sales commissions and other variable marketing costs	80,000	2
Administrative costs (all fixed)	160,000	4
Totals	$2,240,000	$56

These data were supplied to the government agency as a basis for its evaluation of bids.

Based on the above data, company management expected to receive cash equal to $67.20 (that is, $56 × 120%) per unit for the units sold on the government contract. After completing 5,000 units, the company sent a bill (invoice) to the government for $336,000 (that is, 5,000 units at $67.20 per unit).

The president of the company received a call from the contracting agent for the government. The agent stated that the cost basis for the contract should be:

Materials	$12
Labor	19
Supplies, etc.	8
Total	$39

Therefore, the price per unit should be $46.80 (that is, $39 × 120%). Marketing costs are ignored because the contract bypassed the usual selling operation.

Required:

a. What was the conceptual basis for the costs used to prepare the invoice to the government?

b. What was the conceptual basis used by the government agent?

c. What price would you recommend? Why? (Note: You need not limit yourself to the costs selected by the company or by the government agent.)

2

Cost Concepts and Terminology

In this chapter, we introduce the fundamental concepts and terminology of cost accounting. You will discover that the term **cost** is ambiguous; it has meaning only in *specific context*. The adjectives that modify the term *cost* describe that context.

This chapter is outlined as follows. We begin with general concepts of the nature of cost. Then we discuss definitions of costs that are commonly used in describing cost accounting systems. Finally, we discuss additional cost concepts used in decision making and performance evaluation. We summarize the major cost definitions in Illustration 2–7 at the end of this chapter.

The nature of cost

A cost is a sacrifice of resources. In going about our daily affairs, we buy many different things—clothing, food, books, perhaps an automobile, a desk lamp, and so on. Each item has a price that measures the sacrifice we must make to acquire it. Whether we pay immediately or agree to pay at some later date, the cost is usually established by that price.

Measuring cost—that is, the sacrifice of resources—is sometimes more difficult than you might imagine. For example, consider the cost of a college education. College brochures often list the costs as amounts paid for tuition, fees, books, and (in some cases) board and room. The cost clearly includes cash sacrifices for tuition, books, and fees, but what about living costs? If these costs would be incurred whether or not a student attends college, one might argue that they are not costs of getting a college education.

Opportunity cost

Cash is not all that is sacrificed. Students also sacrifice their time. While there is no cash expenditure because of that time consumption, there is an opportunity cost. **Opportunity cost** is the *return* that could be realized from the *best foregone alternative use* of a resource. For example, many students give up other jobs to earn a college degree. Their foregone income is part of the cost of getting a college degree. This foregone income is the foregone return that could be realized from an alternative use of the scarce resource—time. Similarly, the opportunity cost of funds invested in a government bond is the foregone interest that could be earned on a bank certificate of deposit, assuming both securities were equal in risk and liquidity. And the opportunity cost of using a factory to produce a particular product is the sacrifice of profits that could be made by producing other products or by renting the factory to someone else. In each case, we assume that the foregone alternative use was the *best* comparable use of the resources given up.

Of course, no one can ever know all the possible opportunities available at any moment. Hence, some opportunity costs will undoubtedly not be considered. Accounting systems typically do not record opportunity costs, so they are sometimes incorrectly ignored in decision making.

Outlay cost

An outlay cost is a past, present, or future *cash outflow.* Outlay costs are usually contrasted with opportunity costs: outlay costs are recorded in the accounting records while opportunity costs are not.[1]

Consider the costs of occupying a building, for example. (These are often called *occupancy costs.*) Maintenance and utilities would be outlay costs. They would be recorded in the accounting records. Depreciation would also be recorded because it is an assignment of a portion of a *past outlay* of cash (to purchase the building) to a particular time period.

But suppose that there is an opportunity cost because the money to purchase the building could have been invested elsewhere. That opportunity cost is not usually recorded in the accounting records. Thus, the accounting records do not reflect all occupancy costs—only those that are identified by an outlay.

Cost and expenses

It is important to distinguish *cost* from *expense.* As previously discussed, a cost is a sacrifice of resources. An expense is a cost that is charged against revenue in an accounting period; hence, expenses are deducted from revenue in that accounting period. We use the term *expense* only when speaking of external financial reports.

The focus of cost accounting is on *costs,* not expenses. Generally accepted accounting principles (GAAP) and regulations such as the income tax laws specify when costs are to be treated as expenses. In practice, the terms *cost*

---

[1] There is evidence that people give greater weight to outlay costs than to opportunity costs. In one study, when subjects were told that the opportunity costs and outlay costs of education were equal, the outlay costs had a stronger effect on their decisions. R. Thaler, "Toward a Positive Theory of Consumer Choice," *Journal of Economic Behavior and Organization* 1 (1980), pp. 39–60. For some research in this area, see A. Tversky and D. Kahneman, "Judgment under Uncertainty: Heuristics and Biases," *Science,* 1974, pp. 1124–31; and S. Becker, J. Ronen, and G. Sorter, "Opportunity Costs—An Experimental Approach," *Journal of Accounting Research* (1974), pp. 317–29.

and *expenses* are sometimes used synonymously. We use the term *cost* in this book unless we are dealing with an income measurement issue under GAAP.

We shall relate much of our analysis and discussion to income statements. This makes it easier to see where the specific object of our analysis fits into an organization's total performance. Unless otherwise stated, we assume these income statements are prepared for *internal* management use, not for external reporting. We will focus on operating profit, which for internal reporting purposes is the excess of operating revenues over operating costs of generating those revenues. This figure differs from net income, which is operating profit adjusted for interest, income taxes, extraordinary items, and other adjustments required to comply with GAAP and other regulations.

While cost accounting provides cost data for external reporting, it does not deal specifically with the preparation of financial statements. To distinguish the amounts that might be reported internally from those reported externally, we reserve the term *net income* for external reporting.

Period costs versus product costs

Cost accounting requires a classification of costs into product or period categories. Product costs are costs that can be more easily attributed to *products,* while all other costs are period costs. The annual rent of an office building and the salary of a company executive are period costs. The cost of purchased merchandise for resale and related transportation-in costs are examples of product costs.

Cost of inventory

We now discuss product costing for measuring the value of inventory. The product costs assigned to inventory are carried in the accounts as assets. When the goods are sold, the costs of goods sold become period costs.

Cost of a product sold in merchandising

Consider the cost of items offered for sale in a merchandising organization like a supermarket, clothing store, or furniture store. In such companies, no manufacturing activity takes place; the items purchased are sold in the same condition they are received. Merchants do not incur additional costs to alter the form or nature of the products they acquire.

Even in such a basic cost accounting situation, the cost of the merchandise acquired for sale may include a number of individual costs. Besides the cost of the merchandise itself, the buyer may pay to transport the merchandise to the selling outlet, and insure it while it is in route.

For example, Masthead Clothing Stores had a beginning inventory of $125,000 on January 1. They purchased $687,000 during the year and had transportation-in costs of $26,000. During the year, they sold goods costing

Illustration 2–1

MASTHEAD CLOTHING STORES
Income Statement
For the Year Ended December 31

Sales revenue	$1,000,000
Cost of goods sold (see statement below) . . .	662,000
Gross margin	338,000
Marketing and administrative costs	200,000
Operating profit	$ 138,000

Cost of Goods Sold Statement
For the Year Ended December 31

Beginning inventory	$ 125,000ª
Cost of goods purchased:	
Merchandise cost	687,000
Transportation and other costs	26,000
Total cost of goods purchased	713,000
Cost of goods available for sale	838,000
Less cost of goods in ending inventory	176,000ª
Cost of goods sold	$ 662,000

ª Includes merchandise cost and the related transportation-in.

$662,000, including transportation-in. Sales revenue for the year was $1,000,000; marketing and administrative costs were $200,000. They had an ending inventory of $176,000 on December 31.

An income statement and a cost of goods sold statement are shown in Illustration 2–1. The term cost of goods sold is self-descriptive. It includes only the costs of the goods that were sold. It does not include the costs of selling the goods, such as the salaries of sales and delivery people. Nor does it include the cost of the facilities in which the sales are made. These are other costs of doing business. They are deducted from sales revenue as a period cost in the period when they are incurred.

Cost of a manufactured product

Now consider a manufacturing operation. The cost of a manufactured product includes all the costs of making it. The manufacturer purchases materials (for example, unassembled parts), hires workers to work on the material to convert it to a finished good, then offers the product for sale. For cost accounting purposes, three categories of manufacturing costs receive attention:

1. Direct materials from which the product is made. (From the point of view of a manufacturer, purchased parts are included in direct materials.) Direct materials are also called raw materials.
2. Direct labor of workers who transform the materials into a finished product.
3. All other costs of transforming the materials to a finished product, often

referred to in total as manufacturing overhead. Some examples of manufacturing overhead are:

a. *Indirect labor,* the cost of workers who do not work directly on the product, yet are required for the factory to operate, such as supervisors, janitors, maintenance workers, inventory storekeepers.

b. *Indirect materials,* such as lubricants for the machinery, polishing and cleaning materials, repair parts, and light bulbs, which are not a part of the finished product but are necessary to manufacture the product.

c. *Other manufacturing costs,* such as depreciation of the factory building and equipment, taxes on the factory assets, insurance on the factory building and equipment, heat, light, power, and similar expenses incurred to keep the factory operating.

Although we use the term *manufacturing overhead* in this book, other common synonyms used in practice are factory burden, factory overhead, burden, factory expense, and the unmodified word *overhead.*

Stages of production	There are three stages in which materials might exist in a manufacturing company at any time. The company may have *direct materials* that have not yet been put into production. There is also likely to be uncompleted work on the production line, which accountants refer to as work in process. And there may be finished goods that have been completely processed and are ready for sale. Because material in each of these stages has incurred costs, a cost accounting system will include three different inventory accounts: Direct Materials Inventory, Work in Process Inventory, and Finished Goods Inventory.

Each inventory account is likely to have a beginning inventory amount, additions (debits) and withdrawals (credits) during the period, and an ending inventory based on the units still on hand.

For example, Electron Manufacturing makes calculators. The activity in each of the company's three inventory accounts for a current year is described below:

Direct materials inventory

The company's direct materials inventory on hand January 1 was $400,000; purchases during the year were $1,600,000; ending inventory on December 31 was $360,000; and cost of direct materials put into production during the year was $1,640,000. A schedule of direct materials costs would appear as follows:

Beginning direct materials inventory, January 1	$ 400,000
Add purchases during the year	1,600,000
Direct materials available during the year	2,000,000
Less ending direct materials inventory, December 31	360,000
Cost of direct materials put into production	$1,640,000

Work in process inventory

The Work in Process Inventory account had a beginning balance on January 1 of $580,000. Costs incurred during the year were $1,640,000 in direct materials from the schedule of direct materials costs, $3,240,000 in direct labor costs, and $2,850,000 in overhead. The $7,730,000 sum of these last three items is the *cost of manufacturing* incurred during the year.

Adding the beginning work in process inventory to the $7,730,000 gives the total cost of work in process for the year. The $620,000 ending work in process inventory on December 31 is deducted to arrive at the *cost of goods finished* during the year. These events are summarized in the following schedule of cost of goods manufactured:

Beginning work in process inventory, January 1		$ 580,000
Manufacturing costs during the year:		
Direct materials	$1,640,000	
Direct labor	3,240,000	
Manufacturing overhead	2,850,000	
Total manufacturing costs incurred during the year		7,730,000
Total costs of work in process during the year		8,310,000
Less ending work in process inventory, December 31		620,000
Cost of goods manufactured during the period		$7,690,000

Finished goods inventory

The amount of work finished during the period and transferred from the production department to the finished goods storage area is added to the beginning inventory of finished goods as items available for sale. The beginning and ending finished goods inventory balances were $1,145,000 and $2,260,000, respectively. Cost of goods manufactured, or finished, by production and transferred out of work in process inventory was $7,690,000. Cost of goods sold was $6,575,000. A schedule of these costs follows:

Beginning finished goods inventory, January 1	$1,145,000
Cost of goods manufactured (finished) during the year	7,690,000
Cost of goods available for sale during the year	8,835,000
Less ending finished goods inventory, December 31	2,260,000
Cost of goods sold	$6,575,000

Note that the cost of goods finished during the year was carried forward from the Work in Process Inventory account.

Cost of goods manufactured and sold statement

As part of its internal reporting system, Electron Manufacturing prepares a cost of goods manufactured and sold statement. This statement is shown in Illustration 2–2. It incorporates and summarizes the information from the previous schedules.

Income statement　　In addition to the manufacturing costs noted above, Electron Manufacturing incurred marketing and administrative costs of $1,200,000 and had sales revenue of $10,000,000. The income statement is shown in Illustration 2–2.

Illustration 2–2

ELECTRON MANUFACTURING
Income Statement
For the Year Ended December 31

Sales revenue	$10,000,000
Cost of goods sold (see statement below)	6,575,000
Gross margin	3,425,000
Marketing and administrative costs	1,200,000
Operating profit	$ 2,225,000

Cost of Goods Manufactured and Sold Statement
For the Year Ended December 31

Beginning work in process inventory, January 1			$ 580,000
Manufacturing costs during the year:			
Direct materials:			
Beginning inventory, January 1	$ 400,000		
Add purchases	1,600,000		
Direct materials available	2,000,000		
Less ending inventory, December 31	360,000		
Direct materials put into process		$1,640,000	
Direct labor		3,240,000	
Manufacturing overhead		2,850,000	
Total manufacturing costs incurred during the year			7,730,000
Total costs of work in process during the year			8,310,000
Less ending work in process inventory, December 31			620,000
Cost of goods manufactured during the year			7,690,000
Beginning finished goods inventory, January 1			1,145,000
Finished goods inventory available for sale			8,835,000
Less ending finished goods inventory, December 31			2,260,000
Cost of goods manufactured and sold			$6,575,000

If you compare Illustrations 2–1 and 2–2, you will see that product costing in a manufacturing setting is more complex than product costing in merchandising. As a result, we devote a substantial amount of discussion to cost flows and product costing in a manufacturing setting in later chapters. Many of the product costing concepts used in manufacturing can be applied to merchandising and service organizations, too.

Prime costs and conversion costs

The sum of *direct materials* and *direct labor* is called **prime cost**. We think of manufacturing as the *conversion* of direct materials into a finished product. Thus, the sum of *direct labor* and *manufacturing overhead* is called **conversion cost**.

Illustration 2–3 summarizes the relationship between conversion costs, prime costs, and the three elements of manufactured product cost—direct materials, direct labor, and manufacturing overhead.

Nonmanufacturing costs

Nonmanufacturing costs are composed of two elements: marketing costs and administrative costs. **Marketing costs** are the costs required to obtain customer orders and provide customers with finished products. These include advertising, sales commissions, shipping, and marketing departments' building occupancy costs, among others. **Administrative costs** are the costs required to manage the organization and provide staff support. They include executive and clerical salaries; costs such as legal, finance, data processing, and accounting; and building occupancy for administrative personnel costs.

Nonmanufacturing costs are expensed in the period incurred for financial

Illustration 2–3   **Components of manufactured product cost**

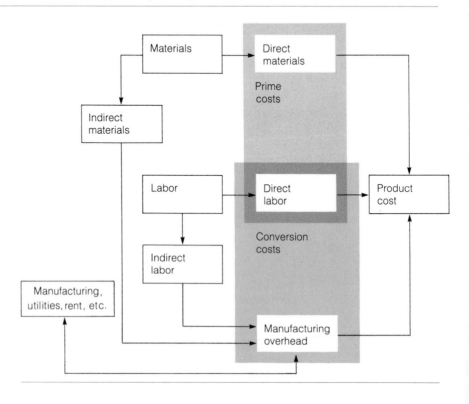

accounting, so they are considered *period* expenses for *financial* accounting purposes.

It is sometimes difficult to distinguish between manufacturing costs and nonmanufacturing costs. For example, are the salaries of factory administrators manufacturing or nonmanufacturing costs? What about the rent of factory offices? There are no clear-cut classifications, so companies usually set their own guidelines and follow them consistently.

Direct versus indirect costs

Earlier we distinguished between *direct* and *indirect* labor costs. *Direct* labor costs are the costs of the workers who transform direct materials into finished products, while *indirect* labor costs are the costs of workers who are needed to operate the factory but do not work directly on a product.

Any cost that can be directly related to a cost object is a direct cost of that cost object. Those that cannot are indirect costs. A cost object is any end to which a cost is assigned—for example, a unit of inventory, a department, or a product line.

Accountants use the terms *direct cost* and *indirect cost* much as a nonaccountant might expect. The only difficulty is that a cost may be direct to one cost object and indirect to another. For example, the salary of a supervisor in a manufacturing department is a direct cost of the department but an indirect cost of the individual items produced by the department. So whenever someone refers to a cost as either direct or indirect, you should immediately ask, "Direct or indirect with respect to what cost object? Units produced? A department? A division?" (When we use the terms *direct* and *indirect* to describe *direct labor, direct materials, indirect materials,* and *indirect labor,* the cost object is the unit being produced.)

Indirect costs are sometimes referred to as common costs. When indirect costs result from the sharing of facilities (buildings, equipment) or services (data processing, maintenance staff) by several departments, some method must frequently be devised for assigning a share of those costs to each user. The process of assignment is referred to as cost allocation. The allocation of indirect costs pervades cost accounting. We discuss implications of allocating common costs throughout this book.

Joint costs

A joint cost occurs when a single process contributes to the production of several different outputs. This can happen in many settings—in particular, lumber, oil refining, and meat processing. Suppose, for example, that a log is processed into three different products—two grades of lumber and chipboard. The log would be considered a joint cost of the lumber and chipboard, and some fraction of its cost would be allocated to each cost object—lumber and chipboard.

Differential costs

Decision making involves estimating costs of alternative actions. **Differential costs** are costs that change in response to a particular course of action. In estimating differential costs, the accountant wants to determine which costs will be affected by an action and how much they will change.

Fixed versus variable costs

Suppose the contemplated action is a change in the volume of activity. Management might ask questions like:

How much will our costs decrease if the volume of production is cut by 1,000 automobiles per month?

How much will our costs increase if we increase meal servings by 200 meals per day?

Between 1979 and 1982, Chrysler Corporation reduced its break-even point (where revenues equal costs) from 2.2 million units to 1.2 million units. What cost reductions occurred to accomplish this?

To answer questions like these, we need to know which costs are **variable costs** that will change with the volume of activity and which costs are **fixed costs** that will not change. Estimating the behavior of costs—which are fixed and which are variable—is very important for managerial purposes.

Consider a fast-food fried chicken operation. Which costs are variable? Which fixed? Suppose the outlet now serves 300 meals per day, but management thinks they may increase to 400 meals per day. What happens to costs if the mix of meal sizes—buckets, boxes, and so forth—remains the same and no expansion of facilities is needed?

Variable costs include the cost of chicken, potatoes, soft drinks, and other meal components. Some labor would be variable because additional help would be needed to prepare meals and serve customers. Additional supplies would probably be needed, too.

Fixed costs would include most occupancy costs, such as rent on the building and the manager's salary.

Illustration 2–4 represents the fixed costs and variable costs of the fast-food chicken operation graphically. Total fixed costs remain constant over some range of an activity, while total variable costs increase with increases in the activity levels. We have used dotted lines to highlight the fact that these behavior assumptions are only valid within a particular range of activity called the **relevant range**.

Variable manufacturing costs typically include direct materials, direct labor, and some manufacturing overhead (for example, indirect materials, materials-handling labor, energy costs). Also, such nonmanufacturing costs as distribution costs and sales commissions are variable. Much of manufacturing overhead and many nonmanufacturing costs are usually fixed costs.

In merchandising, variable costs include the cost of the product and some marketing and administrative costs. In merchandising, all of a merchant's

Illustration 2-4   **Fixed costs and variable costs**

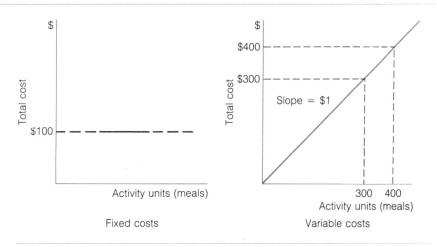

Fixed costs

Variable costs

product costs are variable; while in manufacturing, a portion of the product cost is fixed.

In service organizations (for example, consulting and auto repair), variable costs typically include direct labor, materials used to perform the service, and some overhead costs.

Two aspects of cost behavior complicate the task of classifying costs into fixed and variable categories. First, not all costs are strictly fixed or strictly variable. For example, electric utility costs may be based on a fixed minimum monthly charge plus a variable cost for each kilowatt-hour in excess of the specified minimum usage. Such a mixed cost has both fixed and variable components.

Second, the distinction between fixed and variable costs is only valid within specified volume limits. Capacity limits are usually maximum and minimum outputs that can be produced without altering the physical plant. If the capacity of operations is increased or decreased beyond the specified limits, a new estimate of cost behavior is required. For example, if the manager of the fried chicken outlet considers increasing the volume of meals from 300 per day to 2,000 per day, expanded facilities would be needed. Rent costs, utilities, and many other costs would then increase.

The significance of differential costs

Variable costs are costs that *change* in response to a change in *volume*. When volume changes within capacity limits, *differential* costs are usually assumed to be the *variable* costs. So-called fixed costs could be differential costs, too, if management considers increases (decreases) in volume such that an increase (decrease) in capacity is necessary. Consider the following situation in which the manager of the fried chicken outlet considers expanding capacity.

Illustration 2–5   **Differential cost analysis**

	(1)	(2)	(3) Difference
	Status quo	Alternative	(2) minus (1)
Number of meals per day	300	2,000	1,700
Sales revenue	$600[a]	$4,000[a]	$3,400
Costs:			
Variable	300[b]	2,000[b]	1,700
Fixed	100	1,200	1,100
Total costs	400	3,200	2,800
Operating profit	$200	$ 800	$ 600

[a] At $2 per meal.
[b] At $1 per meal.

Suppose the capacity of the fried chicken outlet is to be expanded to allow an increase in volume from 300 meals to 2,000 meals per day. (For simplicity, assume that an average meal consists of a small bucket of chicken, some potatoes, and one soft drink.) For current operations, the average variable cost per meal is $1 and fixed costs per day are $100. When volume is expanded, the average variable cost per meal will remain at $1, while fixed costs are expected to increase to $1,200 per day, partly because of the increased cost of rent incurred because of the expanded capacity. The average sales price per meal before and after the increase in volume is estimated at $2. The analysis of differential costs and revenues is shown in Illustration 2–5.

Column 3 indicates the differential costs, revenues, and operating profits. Note that differential costs include both variable costs and fixed costs in this example.

If the expansion to the fried chicken outlet required an additional investment in assets, the increase in profits must also justify any costs of the increased investment in assets.

The concept of differential cost is similar to *incremental* cost, except that differential cost refers to both cost decreases (decremental costs) and cost increases (incremental costs). Differential analysis considers all costs, revenues, assets, and nonfinancial variables affected by actions. While managerial accountants are skilled in many aspects of business, they have a comparative advantage over other staff and line personnel in their ability to estimate and analyze differential costs. Thus, we focus on estimating differential costs in this book. Of course, cost analysis is rarely the *sole* basis for decision making. Qualitative factors are also considered before decisions are made. However, the cost analysis is usually quite important.

Sunk costs   A sunk cost is an expenditure made in the past that *cannot be changed.* Sunk costs in and of themselves are not differential costs even though people sometimes act as if the sunk costs were relevant. For example, a clothing store has 15 pairs of slacks that cost the retailer $20. No slacks have been sold at the regular price of $39.95, and they cannot be returned to the manufacturer. The manager of the store knows that he can sell the slacks at $15 per pair, but he refuses to take a loss on them. The manager states, "I've got $20 apiece in these slacks. How can I afford the loss?" The $20 expenditure per pair of slacks is a sunk cost. It is not affected by the sale of the product. Consequently, the $20 is not relevant to the pricing decision. The store manager should ignore the sunk cost. The "loss" occurred when the market value of the slacks fell below the cost. The manager must act in the best way possible given the present and expected future conditions. If the expected future price is less than $15, the best the manager can do is take the loss now.

Most past expenditures are sunk costs. However, this does not mean that information about past expenditures is irrelevant. The store manager should ignore the cost of the slacks *now owned,* but information about the difficulty of selling the slacks for more than their cost is relevant for future decisions about buying that kind of merchandise. Also, the past cost is relevant for deriving the tax and book gain or loss on the eventual sale of the slacks.

Additional cost concepts used for performance evaluation	Most of the previously discussed cost concepts are used in performance evaluation. An additional important concept is assigning responsibility for costs is that of *controllability,* or who has control over the costs. By classifying costs as controllable or noncontrollable, managers are explicitly stating who has responsibility for them.
Controllable versus noncontrollable costs	A controllable cost is a cost that can be influenced or affected by a *particular manager* in the short run. A noncontrollable cost is a cost that cannot be influenced or affected by a *particular manager.* The manager of one responsibility center is usually not held responsible for the costs of another responsibility center because such costs are noncontrollable by the first manager. For example, the chief of a city police department is given a budgeted allowance for controllable costs, including salaries of departmental personnel and costs of operating automobiles. The chief is responsible for keeping actual costs within the budget limit. The chief of police is not held responsible for the costs of operating other departments (such as fire and sanitation) and administering the city because they are noncontrollable by the chief and the police department.

At increasingly higher organizational levels, more and more costs become controllable, as shown in Illustration 2–6. A cost is considered controllable at a specific level in an organization if the managers at that level can authorize the expenditure. For example, if only top management can authorize an advertising budget, then advertising costs would be controllable by top man-

Illustration 2–6   **Relation of cost control to organization level**

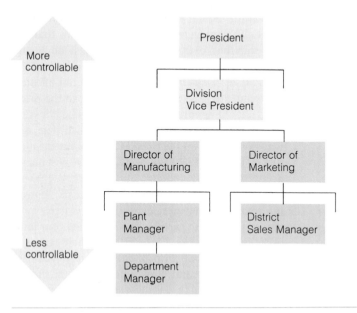

agement. Such costs would be noncontrollable for district sales managers. However, district sales managers would probably control employment terms for the sales personnel in their district. The costs related to the employment of sales personnel in a given district would be considered a controllable cost of the district manager. Of course, top management could also affect the employment terms of individual sales people so the costs related to the employment of individual sales personnel are also controllable by top management.

Full-absorption versus variable costing methods

In manufacturing organizations, the inventory values and cost of goods sold in external financial reports to shareholders are required by *generally accepted accounting principles* (GAAP) to include all manufacturing costs—direct materials, direct labor, and manufacturing overhead. Nonmanufacturing costs are *not* part of inventory values and cost of goods sold. This cost accounting system is known as **full-absorption costing.** (That is, units "fully absorb" all manufacturing costs.) Under full-absorption costing, all manufacturing costs, whether they are fixed or variable, are *product costs.*

An alternative method of deriving inventory values and cost of goods sold in manufacturing is known as *variable costing* (sometimes called *direct costing*). **Variable costing** does not "fully absorb" all manufacturing costs in units produced; instead, it only assigns units produced with the variable costs of manufacturing a good. The variable costs usually include direct materials, direct labor, and variable manufacturing overhead (for example, power to run machines, supplies). Fixed manufacturing overhead (for example, building occupancy costs) are treated as period costs under the variable costing system and not included in inventory values and cost of goods sold. Under variable costing, only variable manufacturing costs are product costs, while fixed manufacturing costs are *period costs.*

Whereas full-absorption costing is required for external reporting under GAAP and income tax laws, variable costing is often used for managerial decision making and performance evaluation.

Summary

The term *cost* is ambiguous when used alone; it has meaning only in a specific context. The adjectives used to modify the term *cost* describe that context.

Illustration 2–7 summarizes the definitions of the terms used in this chapter.

Illustration 2–7

Summary of definitions

Concept	Definition
Nature of Cost	
Cost	A *sacrifice* of resources.
Opportunity cost	The return that could be realized from the best foregone alternative use of a resource.
Outlay cost	Past, present, or near-future cash outflow.
Expense	The cost charged against revenue in a particular accounting period. We use the term *expense* only when speaking of external financial reports.
Cost Concepts for Cost Accounting Systems	
Product costs	Costs that can be more easily attributed to products; costs that are part of inventory.
Period costs	Costs that can be more easily attributed to time intervals.
Full-absorption costing method	All manufacturing costs—both fixed and variable—used in valuing inventory and deriving cost of goods sold.
Variable costing method	Only those variable manufacturing costs used in valuing inventory and deriving cost of goods sold.
Direct costs	Costs that can be directly related to a cost object.
Indirect costs	Costs that cannot be directly related to a cost object.
Common costs	Costs that are shared by two or more cost objects.
Additional Cost Concepts Used in Decision Making	
Variable costs	Costs that vary with the volume of activity.
Fixed costs	Costs that do not vary with volume of activity.
Differential costs	Costs that change in response to a particular course of action.
Sunk costs	Costs that result from an expenditure made in the past and cannot be changed by present or future decisions.
Additional Cost Concepts Used for Performance Evaluation	
Controllable costs	Costs that can be influenced or affected by a particular individual.
Noncontrollable costs	Costs that cannot be influenced or affected by a particular individual.

Each cost concept can be applied to specific managerial problems. For example, most managerial economic decisions rely on the concepts of differential costs. Product costing and inventory valuation use concepts related to full-absorption costing. Planning and performance evaluation are based on controllable cost concepts.

It is important to consider how use of these terms in cost accounting differs from common usage. For example, in common usage, a variable cost may vary with anything (geography, temperature, and so forth), while in cost accounting, variable cost relates solely to volume.

Terms and concepts

The following terms and concepts should be familiar to you after reading this chapter:

Administrative costs	**Manufacturing overhead**
Common costs	**Marketing costs**
Controllable cost	**Mixed cost**
Conversion cost	**Net income**
Cost	**Noncontrollable cost**
Cost allocation	**Operating profit**
Cost object	**Opportunity cost**
Cost of goods manufactured and sold statement	**Outlay cost**
	Period costs
Differential costs	**Prime cost**
Direct labor	**Product costs**
Direct materials	**Relevant range**
Expense	**Sunk cost**
Finished goods	**Variable costs**
Fixed costs	**Variable costing**
Full-absorption costing	**Work in process**
Joint cost	

Self-study problem

The following items appeared in the records of Shoreline Products, Inc., for a current year:

Accounts receivable	$ 183,000
Administrative costs	304,000
Capital stock	571,000
Depreciation—manufacturing	103,000
Direct labor	482,000
Finished goods inventory, January 1	160,000
Finished goods inventory, December 31	147,000
Heat, light, and power—plant	39,000
Insurance—manufacturing plant	48,000
Marketing costs	272,000
Miscellaneous manufacturing costs	12,000
Plant maintenance and repairs	40,000

Prepaid insurance, January 1	24,000
Property taxes—manufacturing	34,000
Direct materials purchases	313,000
Direct materials inventory, January 1	102,000
Direct materials inventory, December 31	81,000
Sales revenue	2,036,000
Supervisory and indirect labor	127,000
Supplies and indirect materials	14,000
Work in process inventory, January 1	135,000
Work in process inventory, December 31	142,000

Required:

Prepare an income statement with a supporting cost of goods manufactured and sold statement, using the full-absorption costing method.

Solution to self-study problem

SHORELINE PRODUCTS, INC.
Income Statement
For the Year Ended December 31

Sales revenue	$2,036,000
Cost of goods sold (see statement below) . . .	1,239,000
Gross margin	797,000
Less:	
Marketing costs	272,000
Administrative costs	304,000
Operating profit	$ 221,000

Cost of Goods Manufactured and Sold Statement
For the Year Ended December 31

Beginning work in process inventory, January 1			$ 135,000
Manufacturing costs during the year:			
Direct materials:			
Beginning inventory, January 1	$102,000		
Add purchases	313,000		
Direct materials available	415,000		
Less ending inventory, December 31	81,000		
Direct materials put into process		$334,000	
Direct labor		482,000	
Manufacturing overhead:			
Supervisory and indirect labor	127,000		
Supplies and indirect materials	14,000		
Heat, light, and power—plant	39,000		
Plant maintenance and repairs	40,000		
Depreciation—manufacturing	103,000		
Property taxes—manufacturing	34,000		
Insurance—manufacturing plant	48,000		
Miscellaneous manufacturing costs	12,000		
Total manufacturing overhead		417,000	
Total manufacturing costs incurred during the year			1,233,000
Total costs of work in process during the year			1,368,000
Less ending work in process inventory, December 31			142,000
Cost of goods manufactured during the year			1,226,000
Beginning finished goods inventory, January 1			160,000
Finished goods inventory available for sale			1,386,000
Less ending finished goods inventory, December 31			147,000
Cost of goods manufactured and sold			$1,239,000

Questions

2–1.   Contrast the meanings of the terms *cost* and *expense.*

2–2.   Identify the difference between product costs and period costs.

2–3.   Is cost of goods manufactured and sold an expense?

2–4.   Identify the similarities between the Direct Materials Inventory account of the manufacturer and the Merchandise Inventory account of the merchandiser. Are there any differences between the two accounts? If so, what are they?

2–5.   What are the three elements of product cost in a manufacturing operation? Describe each element briefly.

2–6.   "Prime costs are always direct costs and overhead costs are indirect." Comment on this statement.

2–7.   Unit costs represent the average cost of all units produced. If we want to know the cost to produce an additional quantity of product over and above the regular production level, why not simply multiply the unit average cost by the additional quantity to be produced?

2–8.   Compare the accounting for marketing and administrative costs in a manufacturing organization with the way those costs are treated in a merchandising organization.

2–9.   Must a manufacturing company use generally accepted accounting principles (GAAP) for its internal reporting? Why or why not?

2–10. Since historical costs are sunk (and, hence not directly useful for decision making purposes), why are accounting systems and reports based on historical costs?

Exercises

2–11. Compute manufacturing costs

The following balances appeared in the accounts of a manufacturing company during a current year:

	January 1	December 31
Direct materials inventory	$16,400	$ 18,300
Work in process inventory	19,100	17,700
Finished goods inventory	7,300	8,500
Direct materials used	–0–	86,600
Cost of goods sold	–0–	301,000

Required:

Compute the following:

a.   Cost of goods manufactured during the year.

b.   Manufacturing costs incurred during the year.

c.   Direct materials purchases during the year.

(Hint: Reconstruct a cost of goods manufactured and sold statement and fill in the missing data.)

2–12. Classify costs by function and behavior

For each of the following costs incurred in a manufacturing operation, indicate whether the costs would be fixed or variable (F or V) and whether they would be period costs or product costs (P or R, respectively). (Some costs might be product costs under full-absorption costing and period costs under variable costing.)

a. Plant security personnel.
b. Executive office security personnel.
c. Transportation-in costs on materials purchased.
d. Transportation-in costs on manufacturing equipment.
e. Assembly line workers' wages.
f. Supplies used in assembly work.
g. Property taxes on work in process inventories.
h. Sales taxes on equipment purchased.
i. Salaries of administrative staff.
j. Depreciation on factory building.
k. Overtime premium for assembly workers.
l. Factory heat and air conditioning.
m. Sales commissions.
n. Power to operate factory equipment.
o. Sales personnel office rental.
p. Depreciation on furniture for sales staff.
q. Production supervisory salaries.
r. Varnish used for finishing product.
s. Insurance on manufacturing plant.
t. Administrative personnel health insurance.
u. Controller's office supplies.

2–13. Estimate differential costs

CanDynamics Corporation manufactured 1,000 units of product last year and identified the following costs associated with the manufacturing activity (variable costs are indicated with V; fixed costs with F):

Direct materials used (V)	$25,200
Direct labor (V)	46,500
Supervisory salaries (F)	11,100
Indirect materials and supplies (V)	8,000
Plant utilities (other than power to run plant equipment) (F)	9,600
Power to run plant equipment (V)	7,100
Depreciation on plant and equipment (straight line, time basis) (F)	4,800
Property taxes on building (F)	6,500

Unit variable costs and total fixed costs are expected to remain unchanged next year.

Required:

Calculate the unit cost and the total cost if 1,200 units are produced.

2–14. Graph cost relationships

Refer to the information in Exercise 2–13. Based on that information construct a graph illustrating the relationship between fixed and variable costs.

2–15. Estimate costs and revenues in a cost-plus pricing setting

Bayside Appliances manufactures subassemblies for videorecorders which it sells to its primary contractor for $35.25 per unit. Last year, the company manufactured 10,000 subassemblies and incurred the following costs:

Direct materials	$36,000
Direct labor	19,000
Manufacturing overhead	82,000

Eighty percent of the overhead costs are fixed at a production volume of 10,000 subassemblies. This year, the buyer of the subassemblies has indicated that it will purchase 15,000 subassemblies and still allow the company to make the same gross margin percentage as last year. All of the cost elements are expected to remain unchanged. Full-absorption costing is used for the purposes stated in this problem.

Required:

Compute the total expected costs for the coming year and the unit price that the contractor will allow. (Note: There are no beginning or ending inventories. Round decimals to four places.)

2–16. Analyze the pricing impact of differences in cost estimates

Based on the information in Exercise 2–15 compute the following:

a. Allowed sales price if the buyer will purchase 30,000 subassemblies.
b. Allowed sales price if 15,000 units are to be purchased but the manufacturing overhead is 20 percent fixed and 80 percent variable.
c. Allowed sales price if 30,000 units are to be purchased but the manufacturing overhead is 20 percent fixed and 80 percent variable.

Given this information, what conclusions might be drawn concerning cost behavior patterns?

2–17. Prepare income statement

The following information has been gathered from the books of a manufacturing company during a current year:

Accounts receivable, January 1	$ 23,700
Administrative costs	42,100
Manufacturing building depreciation	25,000
Indirect materials and supplies	4,300
Sales commissions	13,200
Direct materials inventory, January 1	16,400
Direct labor	32,600
Direct materials inventory, December 31	17,000
Finished goods inventory, January 1	8,900
Finished goods inventory, December 31	7,100
Materials purchases	20,300
Equipment purchases	23,200
Work in process inventory, December 31	11,100
Supervisory and indirect labor	12,400
Property taxes, manufacturing plant	6,400
Plant utilities and power	21,500
Work in process inventory, January 1	13,200
Sales revenue	193,400

Required:

Prepare an income statement with a supporting cost of goods manufactured and sold statement.

2–18. Analyze income statement and cost data

Refer to the data in Exercise 2–17.

a. Would the sales commissions be handled differently if the company was a merchandising operation? If so, how?
b. If the above information is related to the manufacturing of 10,000 units of product, what are the unit prime costs? The unit depreciation?
c. Suppose the above information were to be used as a basis for estimating costs at another level of activity. At 8,000 units, what would the unit prime costs equal? The unit depreciation?

Problems and cases

For each of the following examples, find the unknown account balances for a current year:

2–19. Find the unknown account balances

Account	A	B	C	D	E
Direct materials inventory, January 1	*(a)*	$ 3,500	$ 16,000	$ 4,000	$ 22,500
Direct materials inventory, December 31	$ 3,600	2,900	14,100	6,200	*(i)*
Work in process inventory, January 1	2,700	6,720	82,400	6,280	*(j)*
Work in process inventory, December 31	3,800	3,100	76,730	6,280	42,600
Finished goods inventory, January 1	1,900	*(d)*	17,200	1,400	167,240
Finished goods inventory, December 31	300	4,400	28,400	2,300	Unknown
Purchases of direct materials	16,100	12,000	64,200	*(h)*	124,200
Cost of goods manufactured during this year	*(b)*	27,220	313,770	29,000	759,110
Total manufacturing costs	55,550	23,600	308,100	29,000	763,400
Cost of goods sold	56,050	27,200	302,570	28,100	*(k)*
Gross profit	*(c)*	16,400	641,280	6,700	937,300
Direct labor	26,450	3,800	124,700	11,600	*(l)*
Direct materials used	15,300	*(e)*	66,100	7,500	117,100
Manufacturing overhead	13,800	7,200	*(g)*	9,900	215,300
Sales revenue	103,300	*(f)*	943,850	34,800	1,679,950

2–20. Differential cost analysis for decision making

Rob Roberts has been working a summer job that pays $1,100 a month. The employer has offered to convert the job into a full-time position at $1,500 per month. Take-home pay is 70 percent of these amounts. In view of this offer, Rob is tempted not to return to school for the coming year. His friend Alice is trying to convince him to return to school. Rob remarks, "I've been talking to other friends and no matter how you figure it, school is extremely expensive. Tuition is about $2,200 per year. Books and supplies are another $300. Room and board will cost $3,700 a year even if I share a room. It costs $2,400 a year to keep up my car and clothing, and other incidentals amount to about $3,000 per year. I figure school will cost me the total of all these costs, which is $11,600 plus my lost salary of $18,000 per year. At $29,600 a year who can justify higher education?"

If you were Alice, how would you respond to Rob's remarks?

2–21. Cost bases for pricing decisions

Pat MacDonald, an independent engineer, has been invited to bid on a contract engineering project. Pat is not the only bidder on the project. Pat wants the bid only if it will return an adequate profit for the time and effort involved. The contract calls for 250 hours of Pat's time. The following cost data have been extracted from Pat's records and are believed to be relevant for the period covered by the contract:

	Per hour
Normal consulting rate	$100
Office costs, secretary, etc.	(38)
Travel, other variable costs	(22)
Normal "profit" per hour	$ 40
Billable hours (typical week)	30

The hourly rate for the office costs, secretary, etc., is based on a fixed cost of $1,140 per week divided by the 30 billable hours per typical week. However, these costs are fixed regardless of the number of hours Pat works per week. Under the contract, the travel and other expenses are expected to average about the same as for normal consulting.

Required:

Consider the "cost" that would be relevant for Pat's bid under each of the following independent situations and support your chosen cost basis:

a. Pat expects to be able to work on the contract during hours that would otherwise not be billable to other clients.
b. Pat would have to give up work for other clients to meet the time requirements under the contract. No ill will would be generated as a result of accepting the contract.
c. Pat believes that the contract would be the start of a long-term business relationship that could take up most of Pat's time. The initial bid would have to be close to the amount charged on subsequent projects. While Pat has the time now to take the project without giving up clients, eventually Pat would have to give up some other clients.

2-22. Prepare statements for a manufacturing operation

A manufacturing company has the following information in its books of account on December 31 of a current year:

Direct materials inventory, December 31	$ 85,000
Direct materials purchased during the year	360,000
Finished goods inventory, December 31	90,000
Indirect labor	32,000
Direct labor	400,000
Plant heat, light, and power	37,200
Building depreciation ($\frac{7}{8}$ is for manufacturing)	81,000
Administrative salaries	51,400
Miscellaneous factory costs	31,900
Marketing costs	37,000
Overtime premium on factory labor	12,100
Insurance on factory equipment	19,000
Transportation-out	1,600
Taxes on manufacturing property	13,100
Legal fees on customer complaint	8,200
Direct materials used	382,100
Work in process inventory, December 31	24,600

On January 1, the Finished Goods Inventory account had a balance of $80,000 and Work in Process Inventory account had a balance of $25,900. Sales revenue during the year was $1,625,000.

Required:

Prepare an income statement and cost of goods manufactured and sold statement.

2-23. Prepare projected statements based on past data

Assume that the statements of Shoreline Manufacturing Company (end of chapter self-study problem) were based on sales for 4,000 units. In the coming year, the following changes are expected:

1. Sales will increase to 4,800 units with a 5 percent increase in selling price.
2. No additional property or equipment will be required to meet increased demand.
3. Labor wage rates are expected to increase by 10 percent, and materials costs

are expected to increase by 15 percent before considering the increased volume.

4. Production will be increased by 20 percent (from 4,000 to 4,800 units) to meet the added demand.

5. Direct labor, direct materials, supplies, and indirect materials are variable costs. All other costs are fixed; that is, they do not change because of a change in production activity. (However, they may change because of price changes.)

6. Heat, light, power, and maintenance and repairs are expected to increase by 50 percent, regardless of volume. All other costs are expected to remain unchanged.

Required:

Prepare a report to indicate the total costs to be incurred in manufacturing activity during the coming year. (Round numbers to nearest whole dollar.)

2-24. Analyze effects of changes in cost categories using past data

Refer to the information in Problem 2–23. Assume that heat, light, power, repairs, and maintenance are fixed.

Required:

a. The unit prime costs for next year.
b. The unit prime costs for last year.
c. Unit fixed costs for this year.
d. Unit fixed costs for last year.
e. A brief statement concerning the differences in year-to-year unit costs.

2-25. Estimate most profitable operating level*

The following rate of production and sales data are given for a company division with a maximum capacity of 13,000 units and an unchangeable selling price of $4.50 per unit. The company is required by contract to keep the division operating and seeks to operate at the optimal level given these constraints. The manufacturing vice president has stated: "We should operate at 13,000 units since that level gives us the lowest unit cost."

	10,000	11,000	12,000	13,000
Variable manufacturing cost	$37,000	$40,800	$44,600	$48,400
Fixed manufacturing cost	9,000	9,000	9,000	9,000
Marketing costs	6,000	6,600	7,200	7,800
Administrative costs	6,000	6,000	6,200	6,400
Total costs	$58,000	$62,400	$67,000	$71,600
Unit cost	$5.80	$5.67	$5.58	$5.51

Required:

Determine the optimal level of output assuming that production must take place at one of the levels indicated in this schedule.

2-26. Analyze the costs at different demand levels†

Melville Corporation has determined that to increase its production beyond the current level of 10,000 units it will need to lease additional equipment and to pay overtime premiums to its employees. At the present level of operations of 10,000 units, fixed costs amount to $50,000 while variable costs equal $3 per unit. If an

---

* Adapted from W. J. Vatter, "Tailor-making Cost Data for Specific Uses," *National Association of (Cost) Accountants Bulletin (1954 Conference Proceedings).*

† Adapted from C. Purdy; R. K. Zimmer; and J. H. Grenell, "Costs in Relation to Pricing Products and Services," in *The Managerial and Cost Accountant's Handbook,* eds. Homer A. Black and James Don Edwards (Homewood, Ill.: Dow Jones–Irwin, 1979).

additional $20,000 in fixed costs are incurred per year, the company can produce an additional 10,000 units at a variable cost of $5 for the additional units. Management has determined that it cannot consider expanding the capacity unless the unit profit remains the same as at present. Thus, average cost must remain constant.

Required:

What minimum level of demand would be necessary before management would make the expansion?

2–27. Analyze the impact of a decision on income statements

You have been appointed manager of an operating division of HI-TECH, Inc., a manufacturer of products using the latest developments in microprocessor technology. Your division manufactures a special-purpose chip assembly, ZP-1. On January 1, 1984, you invested $1 million in automated processing equipment for chip assembly. At that time, your expected income statement was as follows:

Sales revenues	$3,200,000
Operating costs:	
Variable	400,000
Fixed (cash expenditures)	1,500,000
Equipment depreciation	300,000
Other depreciation	250,000
Total operating costs	2,450,000
Operating profits (before taxes)	$ 750,000

On October 25, 1984, you are approached by a sales representative from the Mammoth Machine Company. The company offers a new assembly machine at a cost of $1,300,000 which offers significant improvements on the manufacturing capabilities of the present equipment. The new equipment would be depreciated over three years with $100,000 in salvage value. Revenue from your department would be increased by 10 percent. Fixed cash expenditures could be reduced by 5 percent due to the more efficient machine. You will have to write off the cost of the old machine this year because it has no salvage value. Equipment depreciation in the income statement was for the old machine.

Your bonus is determined as a percentage of the operating profits before taxes from your division operations. Any equipment losses are included in computation of this bonus.

Required:

Ignore any effects on operations on the day of installation of the new machine. Assume the data given in your expected income statement would be realized in both 1984 and 1985.

a. Determine the difference in this year's income if the new machine is purchased and installed on December 31, 1984.
b. Determine the difference in next year's income if the new machine is purchased and installed on December 31, 1984.
c. Would you purchase the new machine?

2–28. Chris Collins' use of costs in decision making*

Chris Collins was supervisor of an assembly department in Dexter Electronics Company. In recent weeks, Collins had become convinced that a certain component, number S-36, could be produced more efficiently if certain assembly methods changes

---

* © Osceola Institute, 1979, with the generous permission of Professors Robert N. Anthony and James S. Reece.

were made. Collins had described this proposal to the company's industrial engineer, but the engineer had quickly dismissed Collins' ideas—mainly, Collins thought, because the engineer had not thought of them first.

Collins had frequently thought of starting a business, and felt that the ability to produce the S-36 component at a lower cost might provide this opportunity. Dexter's purchasing agent assured Collins that Dexter would be willing to buy S-36s from Collins if the price were 10–15 percent below Dexter's current cost of $1.65 per unit. Working at home, Collins experimented with the new methods, which were based on the use of a new fixture to aid in assembling each S-36. This experimentation seemed successful, so Collins proceeded to prepare some estimates for large-scale S-36 production. Collins determined the following:

1. A local toolmaker would make the new fixtures for a price of $500 each. One fixture would be needed for each assembly worker.
2. Assembly workers were readily available, on either a full-time or part-time basis, at a wage of $3.75 per hour. Collins felt that another 20 percent of wages would be necessary for fringe benefits. Collins estimated that on the average (including restbreaks), a worker could assemble, test, and pack 15 units of the S-36 per hour.
3. Purchased components for the S-36 should cost about $.85 per unit over the next year. Shipping materials and delivery costs would amount to approximately $.05 per unit.
4. Suitable space was available for assembly operations at a rental of $600 per month. A 12-month lease was required.
5. Assembly tables, stools, and other necessary equipment would cost about $300 per assembly worker.
6. Collins, as general manager, would receive a salary of $2,000 per month.
7. A combination office manager-bookkeeper was available for a salary of $900 per month.
8. Miscellaneous costs, including maintenance, supplies, and utilities, were expected to average about $325 per month.
9. Dexter Electronics would purchase between 400,000 and 525,000 units of S-36 a year, with 450,000 being Dexter's purchasing agent's "best guess." However, Collins would have to commit to a price of $1.40 per unit for the next 12 months.

Collins showed these estimates to a friend who was a cost analyst in another electronics firm. This friend said that all of the estimates appeared reasonable, but told Collins that in addition to the required investment in fixtures and equipment, about $70,000 would be needed to finance accounts receivable and inventories. The friend also advised buying enough fixtures and other equipment to enable producing the maximum estimated volume (525,000 units per year) on a one-shift basis (assuming 2,000 labor-hours per assembler per year). Collins thought this was good advice.

Required:

a. What are Collins' expected variable costs per unit? Fixed costs per month? What would the *total* costs per year of Collins' business be if volume was 400,000 units? 450,000 units? 525,000 units? (Limit yourself to *cash* costs; ignore depreciation of fixtures and equipment. Also, disregard any interest costs Collins might incur on borrowed funds.)

b. What is the average cost *per unit* of S-36 at each of these three volumes?

c. Re-answer Requirements *(a)* and *(b)* assuming that (1) Collins wanted to guarantee each assembly worker 2,000 hours of pay per year; (2) enough workers would be hired to assemble 450,000 units a year; (3) these workers could work overtime at a cost (including fringes) of $6.75 per hour; and (4) no additional fixed costs would be incurred if overtime were needed. (Do not use these assumptions for Requirement [d].)

d. Re-answer Requirements *(a)* and *(b),* now including depreciation as a cost. Assume the fixtures and other equipment have a useful life of six years, and that straight-line depreciation will be used.

e. Do you think Chris Collins should resign from Dexter Electronics and form the proposed enterprise?

Part 1

Cost
Accounting
Systems

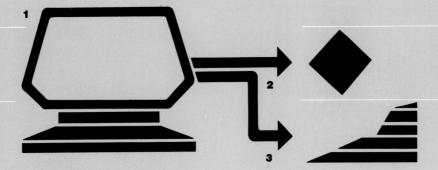

1. Cost accounting systems

3

Accounting for
Cost Flows:
Cost
Accumulation

To understand the cost accounting system for manufacturing, merchandising, and service organizations.

To see how costs are accumulated in the accounts, and how they are reported in the periodic financial statements.

In this chapter, we provide an overview of cost flows by showing how costs are accumulated in the accounting systems of merchandising, manufacturing, and service organizations. For now, we emphasize a broad perspective and reserve some of the more technical aspects of cost accumulation and allocation for later chapters.

Anyone who uses cost accounting information must understand the system that provides the data. Even people who are not cost accounting experts need to understand how the accounting system works if they are to use the information wisely and help design accounting systems that provide the data they want.

The general model

The essential purpose of any organization is to transform inputs into outputs. This activity for merchandising, manufacturing, and service organizations is shown in Illustration 3–1. These organizations share many *similarities*. All require labor and capital as inputs, and all transform them into a product for the market.

These organizations also differ from one another in many respects. The *differences* between these organizations are reflected in their accounting systems. A merchandising organization starts with a finished product and markets it. Because inventory is acquired in finished form, its cost is easily ascertained.

The accounting system for a manufacturing organization is more complex because direct materials are first acquired and then converted to finished products. As a result, to assign costs, it is necessary to relate materials, labor, and overhead to specific output. Thus, a manufacturer's accounting system focuses on work in process, which is the process of transforming materials into finished goods.

Service organizations are different from manufacturers and merchandisers because they have no inventory of goods (other than supplies). Costs are charged to responsibility centers for performance evaluation. In a public accounting firm, for example, costs are charged to the audit department,

Illustration 3–1   **Transformation of inputs to outputs**

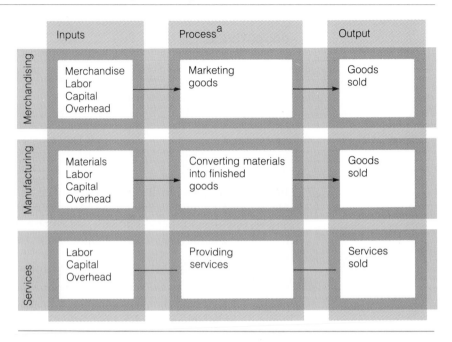

[a] The process refers to the major activity of the organization. Manufacturing and service organizations have marketing activities in addition to their major production activities.

the tax department, and so forth. Costs are also charged to jobs. Here is how a breakdown of professional service costs might look:

	Department	
Job	**Audit**	**Tax**
Mary Jones, tax return		$ 84
Dunkin Dozens, tax return and audit	$1,347	262
Gonzalez Manufacturing, Inc., audit	8,179	

This assignment of costs to jobs and departments helps managers control costs. It also facilitates performance evaluation. The manager of each department is held responsible for the costs of the department; the manager of each job is held responsible for the cost of the job.

Of the three kinds of operations, manufacturers require the most complex and comprehensive cost accounting system. All three need cost information for decision making and performance evaluation. But, in addition, manufacturers need product costing for inventory valuation and to measure cost of goods sold reported on external financial statements. Most also have service and merchandising activities whose costs must also be recorded.

Due to the complexity and comprehensiveness of manufacturing, we devote considerable attention to manufacturing problems in this text. Most of the concepts that we develop in a manufacturing context, however, can also be applied to merchandising and service operations.

Merchandising organizations

The flow of costs through the accounts in a merchandising operation is shown in Illustration 3–2. The top portion of the illustration deals with the purchase and sale of merchandise inventory. The Merchandise Inventory account shows the costs for which buyers are responsible. The cost of the units sold during the period is transferred to Cost of Goods Sold. The product cost in merchandising is simply the *acquisition cost plus* transportation-in costs (also called *freight-in*). This is not to minimize the difficulty of valuing inventory for financial reporting. Assumptions about inventory flow (for example, first-in, first-out [FIFO] versus last-in, first-out [LIFO]) and valuation decisions (for example, current cost versus historical cost) are needed. We merely point out that, all other things equal, valuing inventory is less complicated in merchandising than in manufacturing.

The Marketing and Administrative Costs account in the lower portion of Illustration 3–2 shows all the costs required to run the company and sell the merchandise. These costs can be thought of as the *value added* in

Illustration 3–2   **Flow of costs: Merchandising**

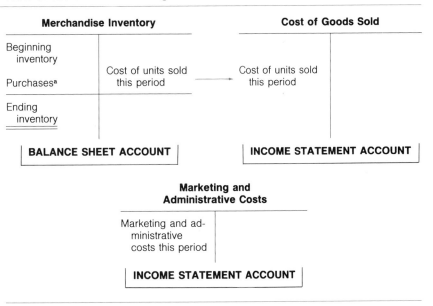

^a Includes transportation-in costs.

merchandising. A merchandising company adds value by acquiring products and distributing them to buyers in an efficient manner. Marketing and administrative costs are not added to the value of inventory, however. Some marketing and administrative costs are capitalized when incurred and expensed as depreciation (examples include buildings, display equipment, and other long-term assets). But most marketing and administrative costs are expensed for financial and tax-accounting purposes because they do not generate measurable tangible benefits for future periods.

The following example shows how costs would flow through the accounts in a merchandising operation. The journal and T-account entries present a standard model for accumulating costs in merchandising.

The Denim Shop sells one product: denim slacks. In April, The Denim Shop purchased 2,000 pairs of slacks at $9 each and sold 1,200 for $20 each. Transportation-in costs were $1 per pair. The Denim Shop had 100 pairs on hand on April 1 that had cost $7 per pair plus transportation-in of $1 per pair. No other merchandise was bought or sold during the month. The merchandise was sold on a FIFO basis. Marketing and administrative costs were $5,000. All transactions were on account.

The following entries were made to record these transactions:

(1)	Merchandise Inventory	18,000	
	Accounts Payable		18,000
	To record the purchase of 2,000 pairs of slacks at $9 per pair.		
(2)	Merchandise Inventory	2,000	
	Accounts Payable		2,000
	To record transportation-in of $1 per pair for 2,000 pairs of slacks.		
(3a)	Accounts Receivable	24,000	
	Sales Revenue		24,000
	To record the sales of 1,200 pairs of slacks at $20 per pair.		
(3b)	Cost of Goods Sold	11,800	
	Merchandise Inventory		11,800
	To record the cost of goods sold of 100 pairs of slacks from beginning inventory at $8 per pair (merchandise cost of $7 plus transportation-in of $1) and 1,100 pairs from current month purchases at $10 per pair (merchandise cost of $9 plus transportation-in of $1).		
(4)	Marketing and Administrative Costs	5,000	
	Accounts Payable		5,000
	To record marketing and administrative costs for April.		

The flow of costs is shown in Illustration 3–3 and the income statement in Illustration 3–4. The numbers in parentheses in Illustration 3–3 correspond to the numbers of the journal entries above.

Illustration 3–3
Merchandise cost flow

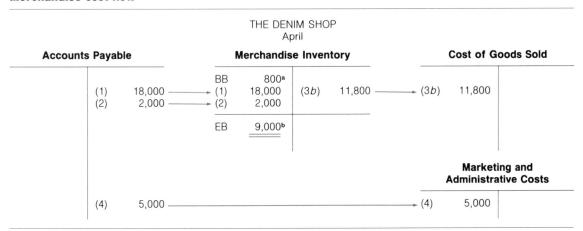

THE DENIM SHOP
April

Note: BB = beginning balance and EB = ending balance.
[a] Beginning inventory consists of 100 units at $8 ($7 purchase price plus $1 transportation-in).
[b] Ending inventory consists of 900 units at $10 each.
The 900 units is equal to the 100 units in beginning inventory plus the 2,000 units purchased and less the 1,200 units sold.
The $10 price per unit is the $9 purchase price plus $1 transportation-in.

Illustration 3–4

THE DENIM SHOP
Income Statement
For the Month Ended April 30

Sales revenue	$24,000
Cost of goods sold	11,800
Gross margin	12,200
Marketing and administrative costs	5,000
Operating profit	$ 7,200

Cost of Goods Sold Statement
For the Month Ended April 30

Beginning merchandise inventory	$ 800
Cost of goods purchased:	
Merchandise cost	18,000
Transportation-in	2,000
Cost of goods available for sale	20,800
Less cost of goods in ending inventory	9,000
Cost of goods sold	$11,800

In merchandising, performance evaluation and cost control are based on revenues and costs, which are usually accounted for by product line and department. For example, in a retail department store, costs are accumulated and reported for each major product line and department—sportswear, housewares, furniture, and so forth. Therefore, accounts like those in Illustration 3–3 would be provided for each department in a merchandising company.

Manufacturing organizations

The flow of costs in the transformation of direct materials into finished goods is shown in Illustration 3–5. The focal point is the Work in Process Inventory account. This account both *describes* the transformation of inputs into outputs and *accounts* for the costs incurred in the process. Manufacturing costs are accumulated in the left (debit) side of the Work in Process Inventory account. (This is referred to as cost accumulation.) When units are completed, their costs are credited to Work in Process inventory and debited to Finished Goods Inventory.

When a unit passes through Work in Process Inventory, it is charged with the full costs of manufacturing it: direct materials, direct labor, and manufacturing overhead. The full cost of manufacturing the unit is its inventory value under *full-absorption costing,* which is the method we use in this chapter. (Recall from Chapter 2 that an alternative method *variable costing excludes fixed manufacturing costs* in valuing inventory. We discuss the variable costing method in Chapter 9 and following chapters; for now, we use full-absorption costing.)

When the unit is sold, this full cost is expensed against revenue as cost of goods sold for financial and tax-accounting purposes. Full costs are also often used as input to product pricing, in contracts that call for cost-plus reimbursement, for long-range planning, in contracts based on prices, and in regulated industries where an organization's revenue is based on costs.

Costing for performance evaluation   Most companies have a separate Work in Process Inventory account for each department (for example, the assembly department, the finishing department) and for each product line. Department managers are held responsible for the costs incurred in their departments. The information also can aid department managers in their efforts to control costs.

We often hear about value added or conversion costs in manufacturing. Those are the direct labor and manufacturing overhead costs required *to convert* materials into finished goods. Companies often have little direct control over prices paid for direct materials or prices received for finished goods, particularly if they operate in purely competitive markets. A key factor for the success of such companies is how well they can control their conversion costs—direct labor and manufacturing overhead. Thus, companies monitor those costs closely in Work in Process Inventory.

The Direct Materials Inventory account is also useful for cost accountability. The purchasing department is responsible for obtaining materials at a good price. A comparison of the actual cost of materials purchased (shown on the left/debit side of Direct Materials Inventory) with budgeted costs

Illustration 3–5
Flow of costs: Manufacturing

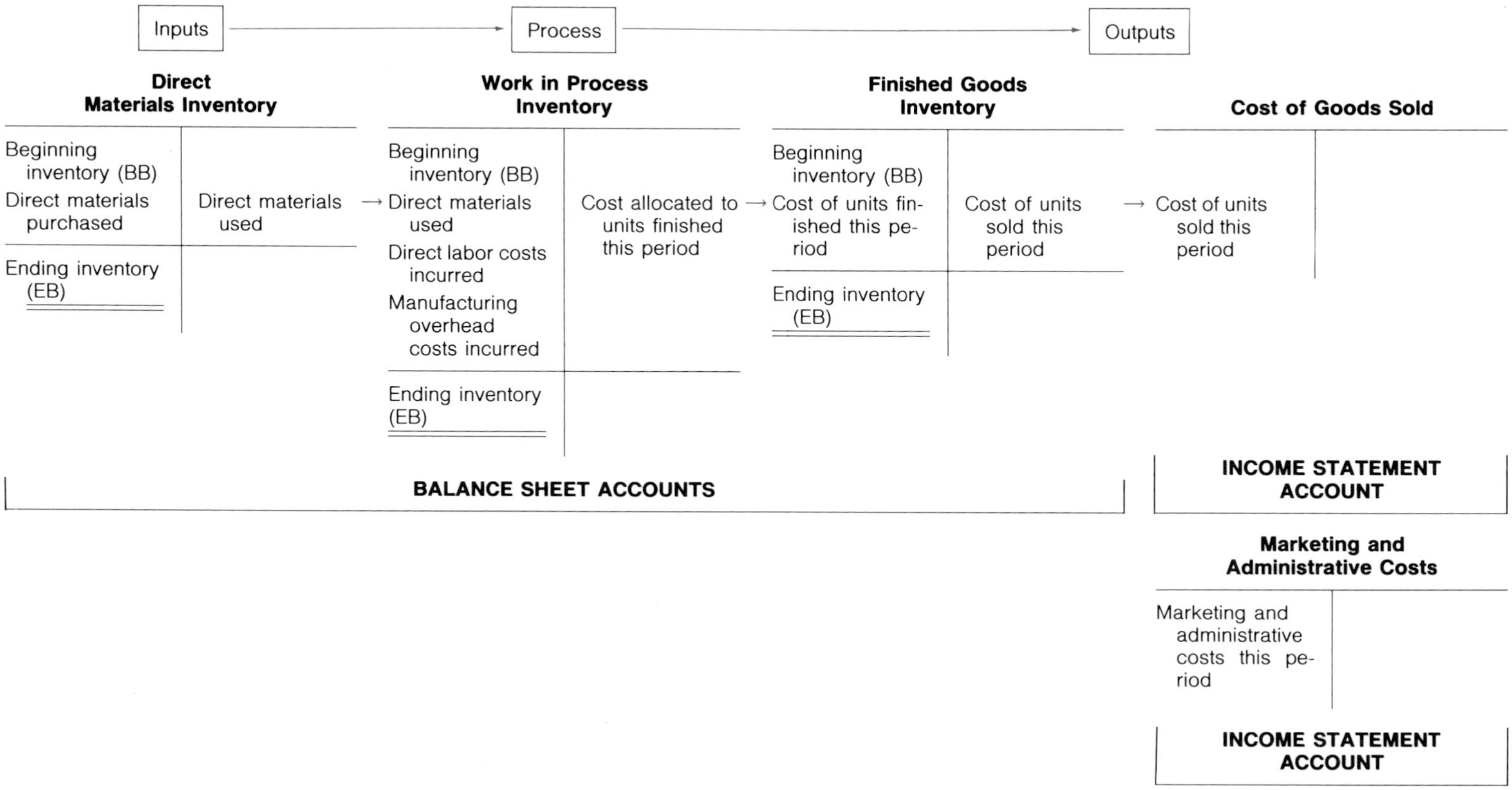

| Inputs | → | Process | → | Outputs |

Direct Materials Inventory

Beginning inventory (BB)
Direct materials purchased

Ending inventory (EB)

→ Direct materials used

Work in Process Inventory

Beginning inventory (BB)
→ Direct materials used
Direct labor costs incurred
Manufacturing overhead costs incurred

Ending inventory (EB)

Cost allocated to units finished this period →

Finished Goods Inventory

Beginning inventory (BB)
→ Cost of units finished this period

Ending inventory (EB)

Cost of units sold this period

Cost of Goods Sold

→ Cost of units sold this period

BALANCE SHEET ACCOUNTS

INCOME STATEMENT ACCOUNT

Marketing and Administrative Costs

Marketing and administrative costs this period

INCOME STATEMENT ACCOUNT

provides a measure of the purchasing department's performance in purchasing materials at a good price.

In short, accounting for costs in work in process inventory is very important for manufacturing companies. The cost data collected in that process can provide important information for many management purposes, and it is absolutely necessary for financial accounting. In the next section, we illustrate the process of product costing in manufacturing by showing a comprehensive example of cost flows through the accounts.

Accounting for the flow of costs in a manufacturing company

Nevada Instruments makes one product—a sophisticated calculator. On May 1, there were no beginning inventories of direct materials, work in process, or finished goods. During May, 10,000 units were manufactured and sold. Here is how the costs of manufacturing and selling those units are recorded:

Units produced	10,000
Units sold	10,000
Manufacturing costs:	
Direct materials purchased and used . . .	$120,000
Direct labor	80,000
Manufacturing overhead	240,000
Total manufacturing costs	$440,000
Marketing and administrative costs	$100,000
Sales revenue (10,000 units at $80)	800,000

We assume for this example that all costs and revenues are on account.

To illustrate the flow of costs through departments, assume Nevada Instruments has the following two manufacturing departments:

Department	Responsibility
Work in process—Assembly	To assemble calculators from direct materials
Work in process—Finishing	To inspect and package calculators

In addition, service departments such as purchasing, warehousing, and maintenance support manufacturing. The costs of operating these service departments are included in manufacturing overhead.

The manufacturing costs that were charged to the two departments are as follows:

	Assembly	Finishing	Source documents
Direct materials	$120,000	–0–	Materials requisition request
Direct labor costs	64,000	$16,000	Assignment of time between departments on time-cards
Manufacturing overhead	192,000	48,000	Many sources, including invoices and timecards
Totals	$376,000	$64,000	

The following journal entries describe Nevada Instruments' flow of costs for May. These entries correspond to the T-accounts in Illustration 3–6. Tracing the entries through the T-accounts will help you visualize the flow of resources through the company. Each entry summarizes the transactions for the month. (In practice, weekly or even daily entries would be made.)

(1) Direct Materials Inventory 120,000
    　　Accounts Payable .... 　　　　120,000
    To record the purchase of direct materials. This entry is made as materials are purchased.

(2) Work in Process Inventory—Assembly 120,000
    　　Direct Materials Inventory .... 　　　　120,000
    To record the requisition of direct materials for the production of 10,000 calculators. This entry is made when materials are sent to manufacturing.

(3) Work in Process—Assembly 64,000
    Work in Process—Finishing 16,000
    　　Wages Payable (or Accrued Factory Payroll) ..... 　　　　80,000
    To record costs of direct labor work in each manufacturing department. This entry is made when the payroll is computed—usually weekly.

(4) Manufacturing Overhead 240,000
    　　Accounts Payable .... 　　　　240,000
    To record manufacturing overhead costs. These costs are recorded as costs are incurred.

(5) Work in Process Inventory—Assembly 192,000
    Work in Process Inventory—Finishing 48,000
    　　Manufacturing Overhead .... 　　　　240,000
    To assign manufacturing overhead to each manufacturing department. This assignment is based on the actual costs incurred during the period. It usually takes place after all costs for the period have been recorded. (It is possible for entry (4) and entry (5) to be combined if the overhead costs are assigned to each manufacturing department when the costs are incurred.)

Illustration 3-6
Manufacturing Cost Flows

NEVADA INSTRUMENTS
May

BALANCE SHEET ACCOUNTS

Direct Materials Inventory

(1) 120,000	(2) 120,000 →

Work in Process Inventory—Assembly

(2) 120,000	(6) 376,000 →
(3) 64,000	
(5) 192,000	

Work in Process Inventory—Finishing

(6) 376,000	(7) 440,000 →
(3) 16,000	
(5) 48,000	

Finished Goods Inventory

(7) 440,000	(8b) 440,000 →

Cost of Goods Sold

(8b) 440,000	

Wages and Accounts Payable

	(1) 120,000
	(3) 80,000
	(4) 240,000
	(9) 100,000

Manufacturing Overhead

(4) 240,000	(5) 240,000

Accounts Receivable

(8a) 800,000	

Marketing and Administrative Costs

(9) 100,000	

Sales Revenue

	(8a) 800,000

INCOME STATEMENT ACCOUNTS

Note: Numbers in parentheses are journal entries in the text. Arrows show the flow of product from direct materials to cost of goods sold.

(6)	Work in Process—Finishing	376,000	
	Work in Process—Assembly		376,000
	To record the transfer of assembled units to the finishing department when units are transferred.		

(7)	Finished Goods Inventory	440,000	
	Work in Process Inventory—Finishing		440,000
	To record the transfer of finished units to the finished goods storage area. ($376,000 costs incurred in assembly and $64,000 added in finishing.)		

(8a)	Accounts Receivable	800,000	
	Sales Revenue		800,000
	To record the sale of goods.		

(8b)	Cost of Goods Sold	440,000	
	Finished Goods Inventory		440,000
	To record the cost of 10,000 calculators sold during the month.		

(9)	Marketing and Administrative Costs	100,000	
	Accounts Payable		100,000
	To record marketing and administrative costs when incurred.		

These entries describe the flow of costs from the acquisition of inputs through the sale of calculators. They represent the basic model of accounting for resource flows in manufacturing companies. To complete the operating cycle, we show the closing entry below.

Sales Revenue	800,000	
Cost of Goods Sold		440,000
Marketing and Administrative Costs		100,000
Retained Earnings		260,000
To close income statement accounts to Retained Earnings.		

The income statement for May is shown in Illustration 3–7.

Cost flows with inventory balances In the previous example, the total manufacturing costs are also the cost of goods sold because there are no

Illustration 3–7

NEVADA INSTRUMENTS
Income Statement
For the Month Ended May 31

Sales revenue	$800,000
Cost of goods sold[a]	440,000
Gross margin	360,000
Marketing and administrative costs	100,000
Operating profit	$260,000

As there were no beginning and ending inventories, the cost of goods sold is simply the sum of direct materials, direct labor, and manufacturing overhead costs for the month.

beginning or ending balances in the inventory accounts. In most situations, however, there are inventory balances. The relationship between manufacturing costs incurred and the cost of goods sold can be found from the following **basic inventory formula:**

$$
\begin{array}{ccccc}
\text{Beginning} & \text{Transfers-} & & \text{Transfers-} & \text{Ending} \\
\text{balance} + & \text{in} & = & \text{out} & + \text{balance} \\
\text{(BB)} & \text{(TI)} & & \text{(TO)} & \text{(EB)}
\end{array}
$$

Rearranging terms slightly, we have:

$$BB + TI - EB = TO$$

which is the basis for the flow of costs in Work in Process Inventory and Finished Goods Inventory accounts, as shown below:

Work in Process Inventory account	Finished Goods Inventory account	
BB		Beginning work in process inventory
+		plus
TI		Manufacturing costs incurred during the period
−		minus
EB		Ending work in process inventory
=		equals
TO	TI	Cost of goods manufactured during the period
	+	plus
	BB	Beginning finished goods inventory
	−	minus
	EB	Ending finished goods inventory
	=	equals
	TO	Cost of goods sold during the period

The following example demonstrates the flow of costs when there are inventory balances.

Assume the following facts apply to Nevada Instruments for July when the company manufactured 10,000 calculators and sold 9,000.

Production:	
Units produced	10,000
Direct materials purchased	$135,000
Direct materials used	125,000
Direct labor used:	
Assembly department	64,000
Finished department	16,000
Manufacturing overhead:	
Assembly department	192,000
Finishing department	48,000
Inventories:	
Beginning direct materials	10,000
Ending direct materials	20,000
Beginning work in process (all in assembly)	15,000

Ending work in process (all in assembly)	20,000
Beginning finished goods	30,000
Ending finished goods	52,000
Marketing and administrative costs	100,000
Sales:	
Units sold	9,000
Sales revenue ($80 per calculator)	$720,000

As in the previous example, we assume that all transactions were on account.

The flow of costs is shown in Illustration 3–8. (A good self-study technique is to make journal entries and demonstrate the flow of costs through T-accounts based on the above facts; then look at Illustration 3–8 to check your work.) Although some of the July amounts differ from those for May in the previous example, the basic structure of the entries is the same.

Illustration 3–9 presents Nevada Instruments' income statement for July and a cost of goods manufactured and sold statement with beginning and ending inventories.

If you compare Illustration 3–6 with 3–8 or Illustration 3–7 with 3–9, you will notice that the total manufacturing costs do not equal the cost of goods sold when some goods remain in inventory. Also, the cost of direct materials purchased does not equal the cost of direct materials used because some materials purchased remained in inventory.

It is easy to confuse *total manufacturing costs* with *cost of goods manufactured*. Think of *cost of goods manufactured* as *cost of goods finished*. This is the cost of goods completed and transferred to the finished goods storage area. They could have been *started* either in a previous period or in the current period. *Total manufacturing costs* are manufacturing costs incurred in the current period, without regard to when the goods are completed.

Managers of manufacturing departments are held accountable for costs incurred in their departments during the period. These are the manufacturing costs debited to Work in Process Inventory during the accounting period. Cost of goods sold reflects current period costs together with an adjustment for changes in inventory levels. If inventories increase, then some current period costs are deferred until that inventory is sold. If inventories decrease, cost of goods sold includes not only current period costs but the past costs related to the units sold from inventory. So for evaluating the performance of manufacturing managers, we do not look at cost of goods sold to assign responsibility for costs; we look at manufacturing costs charged to manufacturing departments.

Summary We have presented an overview of cost flows in manufacturing organizations in this section. The analysis presented here is the foundation of much of our work in subsequent chapters. In later chapters, for example, we build on the cost flow entries and T-accounts presented here for manufacturing companies. It is important to understand the cost flow analysis presented here before proceeding to subsequent chapters. We recommend that

Illustration 3–8
Flow of costs when there are inventory balances

NEVADA INSTRUMENTS
July

Direct Materials Inventory

BB	10,000		
(1)	135,000	(2)	125,000
EB	20,000		

Work in Process Inventory—Assembly

BB	15,000	(6)	376,000
(2)	125,000		
(3)	64,000		
(5)	192,000		
EB	20,000		

Work in Process Inventory—Finishing

BB	–0–	(7)	440,000
(6)	376,000		
(3)	16,000		
(5)	48,000		
EB	–0–		

Finished Goods Inventory

BB	30,000	(8b)	418,000
(7)	440,000		
EB	52,000		

Cost of Goods Sold

(8b)	418,000

Manufacturing Overhead

(4)	240,000	(5)	240,000

Wages and Accounts Payable

(1)	135,000
(3)	80,000
(4)	240,000
(9)	100,000

Marketing and Administrative Costs

(9)	100,000

Accounts Receivable

(8a)	720,000

Sales Revenue

(8a)	720,000

BALANCE SHEET ACCOUNTS

INCOME STATEMENT ACCOUNTS

Illustration 3–9

NEVADA INSTRUMENTS
Income Statement
For the Month Ended July 31

Sales revenue............................	$720,000
Cost of goods sold (see statement below)	418,000
Gross margin	302,000
Marketing and administrative costs	100,000
Operating profit	$202,000

Cost of Goods Manufactured and Sold
For the Month Ended July 31 Statement

Beginning work in process inventory, July 1........			$ 15,000
Manufacturing costs during the month:			
Direct materials:			
Beginning inventory, July 1	$ 10,000		
Add purchases	135,000		
Direct materials available	145,000		
Less ending inventory, July 31	20,000		
Direct materials put into process		$125,000	
Direct labor		80,000	
Manufacturing overhead		240,000	
Total manufacturing costs incurred			
during the month......................			445,000
Total costs of work in process during the month			460,000
Less ending work in process inventory, July 31 ...			20,000
Costs of goods manufactured during			
the month............................			440,000
Beginning finished goods inventory, July 1			30,000
Finished goods inventory available for sale			470,000
Less ending finished goods inventory, July 31			52,000
Cost of goods manufactured and sold			$418,000

you periodically refer to this overview as you work through subsequent chapters. This review will keep you in touch with the "big picture" when we develop the cost flow analysis in more detail.

Perpetual and periodic inventories

Inventories must be kept in every kind of organization. The **perpetual inventory** method requires an ongoing record of transfers-in and transfers-out. For example, in a factory, records are kept of all direct materials requisitioned and transferred to production departments. In a supermarket, specific goods and quantities are recorded for each sale. In a perpetual inventory system, an ongoing record of credits is made to the inventory account.

The **periodic** (or *physical*) **inventory** technique does not require an ongoing record of inventory transfers-out. Instead, the total transfers-out are derived from knowledge of beginning and ending inventories and transfers-in. Hence, any time management needs to know the cost of goods sold, a physical inventory must be taken.

For example, consider the sale of Brand XX tennis racquets at Martha's Sport Shop in March. Beginning inventory was 10 racquets, ending inventory was 15 racquets, and 40 racquets were purchased. The racquets are valued at $10 each.

From the accounting equation,

$$BB + TI = TO + EB$$

we solve for the unknown cost of goods sold, or TO,

$$TO = BB + TI - EB$$

Beginning inventory (10 racquets at $10)	$100
Ending inventory (15 racquets at $10)	150
Purchases (40 racquets at $10)	400

$$TO = \$100 + \$400 - \$150$$
$$TO = \$350$$

A perpetual inventory provides more data than a periodic inventory. For example, with a perpetual system, up-to-date inventory balances and cost of goods sold are always available. But with a periodic system, these data are only available after making a physical inventory count. Perpetual inventory is useful for control purposes, too, because the clerical record of transfers-out can be compared with a physical count to check for theft, spoilage, and other problems. However, the perpetual method requires more expensive data maintenance systems. After weighing the costs and benefits of the perpetual method, most organizations use it for larger, more valuable inventories. Periodically—say, every six months—they may take a physical inventory to check for shortages, theft, and clerical accuracy and to satisfy internal or external auditors. They use the periodic method for such things as office supplies and small merchandise.

Service organizations

Service organizations do not have input materials like manufacturers or merchandise inventory like merchandisers. Thus, service businesses, unlike manufacturers and merchandisers, do not need to account for inventories of finished goods.

However, most service organizations maintain a Work in Process Inventory account for internal use. Entered in this account is the cost of services performed for a customer but not yet billed. Labor and overhead are accumulated for each job, or "unit," much as they would be in a manufacturing company.

The flow of costs in service organizations is similar to the flow in manufacturing, as shown in Illustration 3–10. Input costs include the labor and overhead that are part of the service provided. Costs are usually collected by departments for performance evaluation purposes. In public accounting, con-

Illustration 3–10   **Flow of costs—service organization**

Accounts Receivable		Revenues	
Revenue from services performed	Collections on account		Revenue from services performed

Labor		Marketing and Administrative Costs	
Labor cost of services performed		Period costs	

sulting, and similar service organizations, costs are then charged to jobs or clients. As in manufacturing job shops, costs are collected by job for performance evaluation, to provide information for cost control, and to compare actual costs with past estimated costs for pricing of future jobs.

For example, consider the cost flows of a public accounting firm, Arthur Ross & Company. For the month of September, Arthur Ross & Company worked 200 hours for Client A and 700 hours for Client B. Ross bills clients at the rate of $80 per hour, while the labor cost for its audit staff is $30 per hour. The total number of hours worked in September was 1,000 (100 hours were not billable to clients), and overhead costs were $10,000. (Examples of unbillable hours are hours spent in professional training and meetings unrelated to particular clients.) Overhead is assigned to clients based proportionally on direct labor-hours; so Client A is assigned $2,000, Client B is assigned $7,000, and $1,000 remains unassigned. In addition, Arthur Ross & Company had $5,000 in marketing and administrative costs. All transactions are on account. Entries to record these transactions would be as follows.

(1)	Direct Labor—Client A	6,000	
	Direct Labor—Client B	21,000	
	Direct Labor—Unbillable	3,000	
	Wages Payable		30,000

To record labor costs for September and to assign direct labor costs to Client A (200 hours @ $30 = $6,000), Client B (700 hours @ $30 = $21,000), and unbilled (100 hours @ $30 = $3,000).

(2)	Unassigned Overhead	10,000	
	Accounts Payable		10,000

To record or accumulate overhead before it is assigned to clients.

(3)	Overhead—Client A	2,000	
	Overhead—Client B	7,000	
	Unassigned Overhead		9,000

To assign overhead costs for September to clients (that is, jobs).

(4) Marketing and Administrative Costs   5,000
        Accounts Payable   5,000
        To record marketing and administrative costs for Sep-
        tember.

(5) Accounts Receivable   72,000
        Revenue—Client A   16,000
        Revenue—Client B   56,000
        To record billings for services in September to Client
        A (200 hours @ $80 = $16,000) and to Client B (700
        hours @ $80 = $56,000).

Illustration 3–11 demonstrates cost flows through the T-accounts. The September income statement is presented in Illustration 3–12.

Summary

In this chapter, we discussed methods of recording and reporting cost flows in merchandising, manufacturing, and service organizations. The business of every organization is to transform inputs into outputs. Part of the accounting function for both external and internal purposes is to trace the flow of resources and account for them.

In *merchandising,* product costs are the purchase price of the merchandise plus the direct costs of obtaining it (for example, transportation-in costs) and making it ready for sale. This amount is used to value inventory for financial accounting and for decision making. For performance evaluation, costs are assigned to merchandising responsibility centers (for example, sporting goods, shoes, housewares).

In *manufacturing,* costs of inputs are accumulated in manufacturing (work in process) departments as production occurs. These departments are the basic responsibility centers in manufacturing, so the costs collected in those departments provide important information for performance evaluation and cost control. The information is also needed for full product costing. Thus, work in process inventory accounts are the focal point of accounting in manufacturing organizations.

There are two methods of accounting for inventories: perpetual and periodic. The perpetual method requires an ongoing record of transfers-out and inventory balances. The periodic method requires only a periodic (often monthly) count and valuation of inventory.

The costing systems of service organizations are similar to those of manufacturing with one important difference—there are usually no inventories of finished products. Like manufacturing, there are labor and overhead inputs. Many costing methods for manufacturing can be applied to service organizations if direct materials are omitted.

Illustration 3–11
Service cost flow

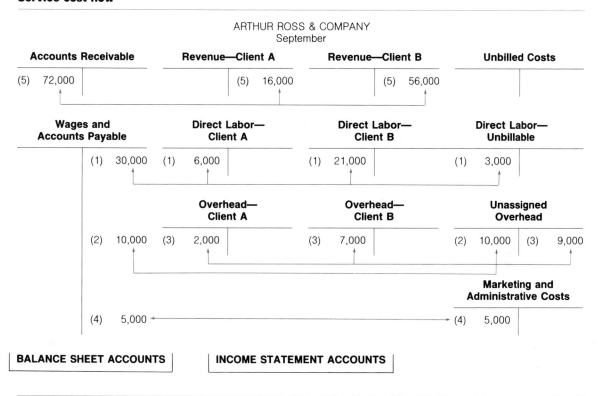

BALANCE SHEET ACCOUNTS   **INCOME STATEMENT ACCOUNTS**

Illustration 3–12

ARTHUR ROSS & COMPANY
Income Statement
For the Month Ended September 30

Revenue from service for clients		$72,000
Less costs of services to clients:		
Labor	$27,000	
Overhead	9,000	
Total costs of services to clients		36,000
Gross margin		36,000
Less other costs:		
Labor	3,000	
Overhead	1,000	
Marketing and administrative costs	5,000	
Total other costs		9,000
Operating profit		$27,000

Terms and concepts

The following terms and concepts should be familiar to you after reading this chapter:

Basic inventory formula	**Merchandising organization**
Conversion costs	**Periodic inventory**
Cost accumulation	**Perpetual inventory**
Full costs	**Service organizations**
Manufacturing organization	**Transportation-in costs**
Merchandise inventory	

Self-study problem

On January 1 of a current year Blazer Building Products has a beginning inventory of direct materials of $80,000. Work in process inventory at the start of the period amounts to $32,000 and finished goods inventory equals $75,000. The balance in cost of goods sold is zero. T-accounts showing these balances appear as follows:

Direct Materials Inventory	Work in Process Inventory
80,000	32,000

Finished Goods Inventory	Cost of Goods Sold
75,000	

During the year $22,000 of direct materials are purchased and $18,000 are transferred to the production area of the plant.

Direct labor costs of $17,500 are incurred, and $30,000 of overhead is incurred. All of the overhead costs are on account. Goods with a cost of $81,000 are completed and transferred to the finished goods warehouse. Additionally, goods costing $92,000 are sold at a price of $170,000. Marketing and administrative costs of $73,000 are incurred.

Required:

   a.   Prepare journal entries to show these events.
   b.   Prepare T-accounts to show the flow of costs.
   c.   Prepare an income statement and cost of goods manufactured and sold statement.

Solution to self-study problem

   a.   In journal entry form, these events are recorded as follows:

(1)	Direct Materials Inventory	22,000	
	Accounts Payable		22,000
	To record the purchase of materials.		
(2)	Work in Process Inventory	18,000	
	Direct Materials Inventory		18,000
	To record the transfer of materials to the production area.		

(3) Work in Process Inventory   17,500

       Wages Payable (or Accrued Factory Payroll) ..   17,500

       To record the distribution of payroll costs of direct labor.

(4) Manufacturing Overhead   30,000

       Accounts Payable   30,000

       To record manufacturing overhead costs incurred.

(5) Work in Process Inventory   30,000

       Manufacturing Overhead   30,000

       To assign manufacturing overhead to Work in Process Inventory.

(6) Finished Goods Inventory   81,000

       Work in Process Inventory   81,000

       To transfer the costs of goods completed to finished goods inventory.

(7) Cost of Goods Sold   92,000

       Finished Goods Inventory   92,000

       To recognize as a period cost the costs of the goods sold during the period.

(8) Marketing and Administrative Costs   73,000

       Accounts Payable   73,000

       To record marketing and administrative costs incurred during the period.

(9) Accounts Receivable   170,000

       Sales Revenue   170,000

       To record sales on account.

b. T-accounts to show the flow of costs:

Direct Materials Inventory

BB	80,000		
(1)	22,000	(2)	18,000
EB	84,000		

Work in Process Inventory

BB	32,000		
(2)	18,000		
(3)	17,500	(6)	81,000
(5)	30,000		
EB	16,500		

Finished Goods Inventory

BB	75,000		
(6)	81,000	(7)	92,000
EB	64,000		

Cost of Goods Sold

(7)	92,000

Wages and Accounts Payable

(1)	22,000
(3)	17,500
(4)	30,000
(8)	73,000

Manufacturing Overhead

(4)	30,000	(5)	30,000

Marketing and Administrative Costs

(8)	73,000

Accounts Receivable

(9)	170,000

Sales Revenue

(9)	170,000

c. **Statements:**

BLAZER BUILDING PRODUCTS
Income Statement
For the Year Ended December 31

Sales revenue	$170,000
Cost of goods sold (see statement below) . . .	92,000
Gross margin	78,000
Marketing and administrative costs	73,000
Operating profit	$ 5,000

BLAZER BUILDING PRODUCTS
Cost of Goods Manufactured and Sold Statement
For the Year Ended December 31

Beginning work in process inventory, January 1			$ 32,000
Manufacturing costs during the year:			
Direct materials:			
Beginning inventory, January 1	$ 80,000		
Add purchases	22,000		
Direct materials available	102,000		
Less ending inventory, December 31	84,000ᵃ		
Direct materials put into process		$18,000	
Direct labor		17,500	
Manufacturing overhead		30,000	
Total manufacturing costs incurred			
during year			65,500
Total costs of work in process during year			97,500
Less ending work in process inventory,			
December 31			16,500ᵇ
Cost of goods manufactured during			
the year			81,000
Beginning finished goods inventory, January 1			75,000
Finished goods inventory available for sale			156,000
Less ending finished goods inventory, December 31			64,000ᶜ
Cost of goods manufactured and sold			$ 92,000

ᵃ $84,000 = $102,000 − $18,000.
ᵇ $16,500 = $97,500 − $81,000.
ᶜ $64,000 = $156,000 − $92,000.

Questions

3–1. Differentiate between the processes used in a manufacturing operation and the processes used in a merchandising operation.

3–2. Why are there no inventories in a service organization?

3–3. Describe the three primary inventory accounts used by a manufacturer.

3–4. A merchandiser comments, "I perform services that add to the value of the products that I sell. My marketing staff facilitates economic efficiency by purchasing the right product, informing the consuming public of its availability, and distributing it in an efficient manner. Why shouldn't I be allowed to include my marketing and administrative costs as a part of the value of my inventory?" Reply to this comment.

3–5. What do we mean when we say, "After a unit has passed through Work in Process Inventory it has been charged with the 'full costs' of manufacturing"?

3–6. For what purposes would full cost data be used?

3–7. Why is the Work in Process Inventory account often considered the heart of the cost accounting system?

3–8. For each of the following accounts, indicate whether a balance in the account would be on the balance sheet or on the income statement:

Marketing Costs   Manufacturing Overhead
Direct Materials Inventory   Cost of Goods Sold
Accounts Receivable   Accumulated Depreciation
Work in Process Inventory   Sales Revenue
Finished Goods Inventory

3–9. For each of the following accounts indicate whether the account would be on the books of a service company, merchandiser, or manufacturer. Some accounts may appear on more than one organization type's books. Use "M" for a manufacturer, "R" for a merchandiser, and "S" for a service organization.

Cost of Goods Sold   Merchandise Inventory
Work in Process Inventory   Marketing Costs
Client Receivables   Finished Goods Inventory
Accounts Payable

3–10. What is the basic inventory formula? Explain each term and how the formula works.

Exercises

3–11. Flow of manufacturing costs— prepare journal entries

The following events took place at the Barton Manufacturing Corporation for the year 1984:

1. Purchased $80,000 in direct materials.
2. Incurred labor costs as follows:
    a. Direct labor, $42,000.
    b. Supervisory labor, $11,500 (part of manufacturing overhead).
3. Purchased manufacturing equipment for $67,200.
4. Other manufacturing overhead amounted to $80,500. This excludes supervisory labor.
5. Transferred 70 percent of the materials to the manufacturing assembly line.
6. Completed work on 60 percent of the goods in process. Costs may be assigned equally across all work in process.
7. Sold 90 percent of the completed goods.

There were no beginning balances in the inventory accounts. All dollars were handled on account.

Required:

Prepare journal entries to reflect these events.

3–12. Flow of manufacturing costs— prepare T-accounts

Refer to the data on the Barton Manufacturing Corporation in Exercise 3–11. Prepare T-accounts to show these events.

3-13. Prepare cost of goods sold statement

Refer to the data in Exercise 3–11, above. Prepare a cost of goods sold statement based on those data.

3-14. Prepare income statement for a merchandiser

High Plains Sales Corporation experienced the following events during a current year:

1. Incurred marketing costs of $197,000 on account.
2. Purchased $971,000 of merchandise.
3. Paid $26,000 in transportation-in costs.
4. Incurred $400,000 of administrative costs.
5. Took a periodic inventory on December 31 and learned that goods with a cost of $297,000 were on hand. This compared with a beginning inventory of $314,000 on January 1.
6. Sales revenue during the year was $1,850,000.

Required:

Prepare an income statement based on these data.

3-15. Analyze inventory flows—missing data

Fill in the missing item for the following inventories:

	(A)	(B)	(C)
Beginning balance	$40,000	?	$35,000
Ending balance	32,000	$16,000	27,000
Transferred in	?	9,000	8,000
Transferred out	61,000	11,000	?

3-16. Use T-accounts to trace inventory amounts—missing data

The following T-accounts represent data from a company's accounting records. Find the missing items represented by the ?'s.

Cost of Goods Sold

82,000	

Direct Materials Inventory

BB	?		
Purchases	18,000	Transferred out	21,000
EB	7,500		

Finished Goods Inventory

BB	46,500	
	?	
EB	?	

Work in Process Inventory

BB	6,000		
Materials	?		
Labor	17,000		58,600
Manufacturing overhead	?		
EB	9,700		

3-17. Prepare T-accounts from statements

The income statement and the cost of goods manufactured and sold statement for the Live Oak Manufacturing Company are reproduced below:

LIVE OAK MANUFACTURING COMPANY
Income Statement
For the Year Ended December 31

Sales revenue	$37,200
Cost of goods sold (see statement below)	25,700
Gross margin	11,500
Marketing costs	3,100
Administrative costs	2,700
Operating profit	$ 5,700

Cost of Goods Manufactured and Sold Statement
For the Year Ended December 31

Beginning work in process inventory, January 1			$ 1,200
Manufacturing costs during the year			
Direct materials:			
Beginning inventory, January 1	$1,300		
Add purchases	6,500		
Direct materials available	7,800		
Less ending inventory, December 31	1,700		
Direct materials put into process		$ 6,100	
Direct labor		12,400	
Manufacturing overhead		8,600	
Total manufacturing costs incurred during year . .			27,100
Total costs of work in process during the year			28,300
Less ending work in process inventory, December 31			1,800
Cost of goods manufactured during the year			26,500
Beginning finished goods inventory, January 1			5,200
Finished goods inventory available for sale			31,700
Less ending finished goods inventory, December 31			6,000
Cost of goods manufactured and sold			$25,700

Required:

Prepare T-accounts to show the flow of costs for the company. Assume that all dollar exchanges are on account.

3–18. Prepare journal entries from statement data

Using the statements for Live Oak Manufacutring Company, construct journal entries that would summarize the events disclosed in the statements.

3–19. Cost flows in a service organization

For the month of March, Conehead Consulting Group (CCG) worked 400 hours for Big Manufacturing, 100 hours for Little Manufacturing, and 200 hours for Retailers, Inc. CCG bills clients at the rate of $100 per hour, while labor cost is $40 per hours. The total number of hours worked in March were 800 hours, with 100 hours not billable to clients. Overhead costs, which were $12,000, are assigned to jobs (that is, clients) on the basis of direct labor-hours. Since 100 hours were not billable, some overhead will not be assigned to jobs. CCG had $6,000 marketing and administrative costs. All transactions are on account.

Required:

a. Show the flow of costs through T-accounts.
b. Prepare an income statement for CCG for the month ended March 31.

3–20. Service organization—journal entries

Prepare journal entries for the transactions in Exercise 3–19.

Problems and cases

3-21. Cost flows in service based industries*

White and Brite Dry Cleaners operates with five employees and the president, Hexter Strength. Hexter and one of the five employees attend to all the marketing and administrative duties. The remaining four employees work throughout the operation. White and Brite has four service departments: dry cleaning, coin washing and drying, special cleaning, and sewing repairs and altering. A timecard is marked, and records are kept to monitor the time each employee spends working in each department. When business is slow or when all is under control, there is idle time, and this is also marked on the timecard. (Note: It is necessary to have some idle time because White and Brite promises 60-minute service, and it is necessary to have available direct labor-hours to accommodate fluctuating peak demand periods throughout the day and the week.)

A summary of November operating data is as follows:

	Idle time	Dry cleaning	Coin washing and drying	Special cleaning	Sewing repairs and altering
Sales revenue		$2,625	$5,250	$2,000	$625
Direct labor (in hours)	25	320	80	125	90
Direct overhead:					
Cleaning compounds		$500	$250	$400	–0–
Supplies		125	200	175	$140
Electric usage		250	625	100	25
Rent		200	500	90	10

Other data:
1. The four employees working in the service departments all make $4 per hour.
2. The person in charge of marketing earns $1,000 per month, and Hexter earns $1,500 per month.
3. Indirect overhead amounted to $512 and is assigned to departments based on direct labor-hours used. Since there are idle hours, some overhead will not be assigned to a department.
4. In addition to salaries paid, marketing costs for such items as yellow page advertising, radio advertising, and special promotions totaled $400.
5. In addition to Hexter's salary, administrators costs amounted to $150.
6. All revenue transactions are cash and all others are on account.

Required:

a. Using T-accounts, show the flow of costs.
b. Prepare an income statement for White and Brite for the month of November. No inventories were kept.

3-22. Service organization—journal entries

Prepare journal entries for the November transactions in Problem 3-21.

3-23. T-accounts and income statements

Using T-accounts show the flow of costs for March for the Reham Company and then prepare an income statement for the month of March. All transactions are on account.

---

* Prepared by K. McGarvey.

	Balance, March 1	Balance, March 31
Direct materials inventory	?	$ 40,000
Work in process inventory	?	280,000
Finished goods	$100,000	80,000

Other information:

Direct labor costs	240,000
Manufacturing overhead	112,000
Material purchases	180,000
Direct materials put into process	200,000
Cost of goods sold	360,000
Marketing costs	100,000
Administrative costs	80,000
Sales on account	600,000

3–24. Analysis of accounts

Partially completed T-accounts and additional information for the Leaheim Company for the month of March are presented below:

Direct Materials Inventory

BB 3/1	1,000	
	4,000	
		3,200

Work in Process Inventory

BB 3/1	2,000
Direct labor	2,400
Manufacturing overhead	2,200

Finished Goods Inventory

BB 3/1	3,000	
	6,000	4,000

Cost of Goods Sold

During the month, sales were $8,000 and marketing and administrative costs were $1,600.

Required:

a. What was the amount of direct material issued to production during March?
b. What was the cost of goods manufactured during March?
c. What was the balance of the Work in Process Inventory account at the end of March?
d. What was the operating profit for March?

3–25. Find the missing items

Several items are missing from the following set of statements for a current year.

Income Statement
For the Year Ended December 31

Sales revenue	$246,700
Cost of goods sold	?
Gross margin	?
Marketing and administrative costs	32,400
Operating profit	$102,000

Cost of Goods Manufactured and Sold Statement
For the Year Ended December 31

Beginning work in process inventory, January 1, ...		$29,300
Manufacturing costs during the year:		
Direct Materials:		
Beginning inventory, January 1 . . . . $11,700		
Add purchases . . . . ?		
Direct materials available 64,100		
Less ending inventory, December 31 27,900		
Direct materials put into process	?	
Direct labor	?	
Manufacturing overhead	37,200	
Total manufacturing costs incurred during year .		?
Total costs of work in process during the year		?
Less ending work in process inventory, December 31 . .		17,400
Cost of goods manufactured during the year . . .		?
Beginning finished goods inventory, January 1		6,700
Finished goods inventory available for sale		124,800
Less ending finished goods inventory, December 31		?
Cost of goods manufactured and sold		?

Required: Find the missing items.

3–26. Prepare journal entries—manufacturing organizations

The following information has been gathered from the books of a manufacturing company:

Accounts receivable, January 1, 1984	$23,700
Administrative costs	42,100
Manufacturing building depreciation	25,000
Indirect materials and supplies	
taken from materials inventory	4,300
Marketing costs	13,200
Materials inventory, January 1, 1984	16,400
Direct labor	32,600
Transportation-in on materials	1,600
Materials inventory, December 31, 1984	17,000
Finished goods inventory, January 1, 1984	8,900
Finished goods inventory, December 31, 1984	7,100
Materials purchases	18,700
Equipment purchases	23,200
Work in process inventory, December 31, 1984	11,100
Supervisory salaries	12,400
Property taxes, manufacturing plant	6,400
Plant utilities and power	21,500
Work in process inventory, January 1, 1984	13,200
Sales revenue	193,400

All costs, except depreciation, are on account.

Required: Prepare journal entries to record the transactions during the current year. (Depreciation is recorded with a credit to Accumulated Depreciation and a debit to Manufacturing Overhead.)

3-27. Prepare T-accounts and income statements—manufacturing organizations

a. Use the data in Problem 3–26 and prepare T-accounts to show the flow of costs for this company.

b. Prepare an income statement and cost of goods manufactured and sold statement.

3-28. T-account analysis of cost flows

A manufacturing company has the following information in its books of account on December 31 of a current year:

Materials inventory, December 31	$85,000
Materials purchased during the year	360,000
Finished goods inventory, December 31	90,000
Indirect labor	32,000
Direct labor	400,000
Indirect materials and supplies	
(taken from materials inventory)	14,000
Factory heat, light, and power	37,200
Building depreciation (all manufacturing)	81,000
Administrative salaries	51,400
Miscellaneous factory costs	17,900
Marketing costs	37,000
Factory supervision	12,100
Insurance on factory equipment	19,000
Transportation-in on materials	1,600
Taxes on manufacturing property	13,100
Legal fees on customer complaint	8,200
Direct materials used	382,100
Work in process inventory, December 31	24,600

On January 1, the finished goods account had a balance of $80,000 and the Work in Process Inventory account had a balance of $25,900. All transactions are on account (except depreciation which is recorded with a debit to Manufacturing Overhead and a credit to Accumulated Depreciation). Sales equalled $1,625,000.

Required:

a. Prepare T-accounts to show these events and the flow of costs for the company.

b. Give the beginning direct materials inventory balance.

3-29. Prepare journal entries

Using the data in Problem 3–28, prepare journal entries to summarize the events.

3-30. Analyze cost flows and prepare statement

The following information applies to the A.B.C. Company for May:

Direct materials inventory, May 1	$18,000
Accounts payable, May 1	10,000
Work in process inventory, May 1	20,000

1. The accounts payable are for direct materials only. The balance on May 31 was $5,000. Payments of $135,000 were made during May.
2. The finished goods inventory as of May 31 was $22,000.
3. The cost of goods sold during the month was $1,104,000.
4. Total manufacturing costs for the month of May were $1,081,000.
5. There were 80,000 hours of direct labor worked during the month at a rate of $6.50 per hour.
6. Direct materials put into process amounted to $136,000.
7. There was no work in process inventory on May 31.

8. The gross margin for the month of May was $428,000, and the operating profit was $210,000.

Required:
Derive each of the following amounts and prepare an income statement and a statement of cost of goods manufactured and sold:

a. Ending inventory of direct materials on May 31.
b. Total overhead for May.
c. Cost of goods manufactured for May.
d. Finished goods inventory on May 1.
e. Total marketing and administrative costs for May.

**3–31. Reconstruct
missing data**

After a dispute concerning wages, Orville Arson tossed an incendiary device into the Sparkle Company's record vault. Within moments, only a few charred fragments were readable from the company's factory ledger, as shown below:

Direct Materials Inventory			Manufacturing Overhead	
BB 4/1	15,000			

Work in Process Inventory			Accounts Payable	
BB 4/1	4,500			
			EB 4/30	$9,000

Finished Goods Inventory			Cost of Goods Sold	
EB 4/30	11,000			

Sifting through ashes and interviewing selected employees has turned up the following additional information:

1. The controller remembers clearly that actual manufacturing overhead costs are recorded at $3 per direct labor-hour.
2. The production superintendent's cost sheets showed only one job in work in process inventory on April 30. Materials of $2,600 had been added to the job, and 300 direct labor-hours expended at $6 per hour.
3. The accounts payable are for direct materials purchases only, according to the accounts payable clerk. He clearly remembers that the balance in the account was $6,000 on April 1. An analysis of canceled checks (kept in the treasurer's office) shows that payments of $42,000 were made to suppliers during the month.
4. A charred piece of the payroll ledger shows that 5,200 direct labor-hours were recorded for the month. The employment department has verified that there are no variations in pay rates among employees (this infuriated Orville, who felt his services were underpaid).
5. Records maintained in the finished goods warehouse indicate that the finished goods inventory totaled $18,000 on April 1.
6. From another charred piece in the vault you are able to discern that the cost of goods manufactured for April was $89,000.

Required:

Determine the following amounts:

a. Work in process inventory, April 30.
b. Direct materials purchased during April.
c. Manufacturing overhead incurred during April.
d. Cost of goods sold for April.
e. Direct materials usage during April.
f. Direct materials inventory, April 30.

3–32. Reconstruct missing data

A hysterical Ima Dunce corners you in the hallway 30 minutes before her accounting class. "Help me, help me!" Ima pleads. "I woke up this morning and discovered that Fifo and Lifo (two pet German Shepherds) ate my homework and these shredded pieces are all that I have left!" Being a kind and generous soul, you willingly declare, "There is no need to fear! I am a real whiz at accounting and will be glad to help you." A relieved Ima Dunce hands you the following torn homework remnants.

Page 1

Direct labor-hours used	375
Direct labor rate — $5 per hour	
Direct materials purchased	$5,250
Direct materials beginning inventory	$1,400

Page 3

job remaining in ending work in process inventory:

Labor	$ 500
Direct materials	$1,300
Overhead	$ 200
nding work in process inventory	$2,000
Total revenue	$13,500
Gross margin	4,000
Marketing and administrative costs	
Operating profit	$1,000

Page 2

Actual manufacturing overhead	$750
ginning work in process inventory	$1,500
Cost of goods manufactured	$8,000
Ending finished goods inventory	$3,000
Cost of goods old	$9,500

Required:

a. Help Ima by determining the following:
   (1) Marketing and administrative costs.
   (2) Cost of goods sold.
   (3) Beginning finished goods inventory.
   (4) Direct materials used.
   (5) Ending direct materials inventory.
b. Prepare T-accounts to show the flow of costs.
c. Prepare an income statement.

4

Cost Allocation Concepts

OBJECTIVES
To understand the practical needs for assigning indirect costs to individual jobs,
    units, or organization segments.
To be familiar with the most common applications of cost allocations.
To understand the conceptual aspects of cost allocation including the pros and
    cons of allocations.

In this chapter, we discuss the concepts by which costs are assigned to jobs, departments, products, and other cost objects. This cost assignment process is called **cost allocation.** Unlike direct costs, allocated costs are indirect and, hence, common to two or more cost objects. If management wants to assign these costs to the individual cost objects, some method must be established to share the common costs. In this chapter, we present general principles for allocating costs, we examine reasons for making cost allocations, and we discuss how cost allocations can potentially mislead users of accounting information.

What is cost allocation?

A cost allocation is simply a proportional assignment of a cost to cost objects. For example, if two divisions share a facility that costs $15,000, that shared cost is referred to as a **common cost.** If we decide that cost should be shared based on, say, the number of employees in each division, then the number of employees is the **allocation base** and the divisions are the **cost objects.** Carrying this one step further, if 40 percent of the employees are in the first division, then that division is charged with 40 percent of the $15,000 cost, or $6,000. This $6,000 is the cost allocated to the first division. The remaining 60 percent, or $9,000, is allocated to the second division. All of the common costs are allocated to the divisions based on their proportional use of the allocation base. Hence, the full $15,000 has been allocated to the divisions based on the relative number of employees in each division.

There are numerous examples of cost allocation in organizations. Manufacturing overhead is a *common cost* that is usually allocated to each unit produced by a manufacturer. This allocation is required for financial reporting.

Multi-unit organizations often allocate headquarters' costs to individual branches. For example, an executive of K mart, a retail company with over 1,500 stores, told us: "Allocating corporate headquarters' costs to stores makes each store manager aware that these costs exist and must be covered by the individual stores for the company as a whole to be profitable." This allocation was used as an attention-getting device by management.

Depreciation of long-term assets is also a form of cost allocation. The purpose of depreciation is to allocate the original cost of the asset over the time periods that the asset helps generate revenues.

To describe how cost allocation works, consider the following example. Computerworld, Inc., sells microcomputers in two different markets: business and personal. Because the two markets have different requirements, the company has set up two divisions for handling the markets. Each division has its own separate sales staff and a separate area in the company store. However, because most hardware may be used for either business or personal applications, the company has a common showroom where the hardware is displayed. This common showroom reduces the investment that the company must make in computer systems for showroom display.

Computerworld, Inc., has established a system for evaluating the performance of each division. The company uses "divisional operating profits" as a performance measure. A bonus is assigned to each division based on the relative amount of operating profits earned by each division. This bonus is then shared by the division employees. The greater the profits in any division, the greater the bonus for the division. The greater the division bonus, the greater the bonus for each employee in the division.

The following information is available concerning last month's activities by the company:

	Business Division	Personal Division	Total
Sales revenue	$266,000	$121,800	$387,800
Cost of goods sold	159,600	73,080	232,680
Other costs traced directly to divisions	87,900	38,500	126,400
Division "operating profits" before showroom costs	$ 18,500	$ 10,220	$ 28,720
Number of units sold	28	42	70

Showroom costs, which amounted to $9,000 during the month, were common to both divisions. The company's management was trying to decide whether to allocate the showroom costs on the basis of the number of units sold or on the basis of sales revenue. The manager of the business division said, "The showroom is used to display *units* of hardware. We get more revenue per unit because of the nature of our separate operations. Therefore, the units should be used as the allocation base."

Following this argument, costs were allocated on the basis of units sold. The Business Division was charged with 28/70 times $9,000, or $3,600, for its share of the common costs. The Personal Division was charged with 42/70 times $9,000, or $5,400. The division operating profits, after the allocation of showroom costs, were:

Business Division: $14,900 = $18,500 − $3,600
Personal Division: $ 4,820 = $10,220 − $5,400

Any bonus would be split with 75.6 percent going to the Business Division $\left(.756 = \dfrac{\$14,900}{\$14,900 + \$4,820}\right)$ and 24.4 percent to the Personal Division $\left(.244 = \dfrac{\$4,820}{\$14,900 + \$4,820}\right)$. This example is a typical cost allocation problem. Later in this chapter, we continue the example and discuss other ways of allocating showroom costs and the impact of these alternatives.

The arbitrary nature of cost allocation

By definition, costs that are common to two or more cost *objects* are likely to be allocated to those cost objects on a somewhat arbitrary basis. This arbitrariness has led critics of cost allocation to claim that arbitrary cost allocations result in misleading financial reports and poor decisions. Despite these asserted problems, a recent study of corporate cost allocation found 84 percent of companies participating in the survey reported allocating common headquarters costs to divisions.[1] The study indicated that the primary managerial reason for cost allocation was to *remind responsibility center managers that common costs exist and had to be recovered by division profits.* While critics assert that cost allocations are arbitrary and misleading, others respond that considering the widespread practice of allocation, it must have some usefulness.

Cost allocation is an important topic in both financial and managerial accounting. Few accounting topics have evoked as much literature and debate.[2] No matter what career you choose, you will most likely encounter the use of allocations. They may be used to derive the performance measures by which you and your division are evaluated. Or they may be employed to determine costs in a contract between you or your employer and some other party. The method of allocation and its basis may be significant determinants of the value of the performance measure or the amount of the contract settlement.

The inherent arbitrariness of cost allocation implies that if there is no single method that is "absolutely right," then different people with an interest in the outcome of an accounting measurement may prefer one allocation method over another. Returning to the Computerworld example, the initial

[1] See J. M. Fremgren and S. S. Liao, *The Allocation of Corporate Indirect Costs* (New York: National Association of Accountants, 1981).

[2] Extensive discussions of cost allocation are presented in A. L. Thomas, *The Allocation Problem in Financial Accounting,* Studies in Accounting Research No. 3 (Sarasota, Fla.: American Accounting Association, 1969); A. L. Thomas, *The Allocation Problem: Part Two,* Studies in Accounting Research No. 9 (Sarasota, Fla.: American Accounting Association, 1974); and S. Moriarity, ed., *Joint Cost Allocations* (Norman: Center for Economic and Management Research, University of Oklahoma, 1981).

allocation of income for bonus sharing might be expected to lead to some questions by the Personal Divison.

Indeed, upon hearing about the Business Division manager's allocation proposal, the manager of the Personal Division suggested that the allocation was inappropriate. The Personal Division manager stated: "The Business Division people take a lot more time demonstrating each machine they sell. Indeed, I think they use the showroom facilities in roughly the same proportion as the dollar sales, not the number of units."

"If the costs are allocated on a sales basis, then the Business Division should be charged with $266,000/$387,800 times the $9,000 common showroom cost which comes to a charge of $6,173. We should be charged with the remaining $2,827. This is equal to our proportional share of sales, which is $121,800/$387,800 times $9,000."

Using the Personal Division manager's recommended cost allocation, the income for each division is:

$$\text{Business Division} \quad \$18,500 - \$6,173 = \$12,327$$
$$\text{Personal Division:} \quad \$10,220 - \$2,827 = \$\ 7,393$$

The Personal Division would receive 37.5 percent of the bonus, which equals $\dfrac{\$7,393}{\$12,327 + \$7,393}$. The Business Division would then receive the remaining 62.5 percent.

Upon hearing the debate between the two division managers, the company president stated: "Since there is no agreeable way to allocate showroom costs, we shall avoid the problem by *not allocating showroom costs.*" Unfortunately, that did not solve the problem of sharing the bonus. Omitting the allocation of showroom costs would result in splitting the bonus based on the division operating profit before showroom costs. Then the Business Division would receive $\dfrac{\$18,500}{\$10,220 + \$18,500}$, or 64.4 percent of the bonus. The Personal Division would have a 35.6 percent share computed as $\dfrac{\$10,220}{\$10,220 + \$18,500}$.

The shares of the bonus under each alternative are summarized as follows:

Allocation method and base	Business Division share	Personal Division share
Number of units	75.6%	24.4%
Sales revenue	62.5	37.5
No allocation	64.4	35.6

Although we cannot predict the outcome of how the bonus might ultimately be shared, the negotiation possibilities will probably require a resolution at the top-management level.

As the Computerworld example demonstrates, the cost allocation method, or lack thereof, can have a significant direct effect on the amounts paid to employees. Even when employee bonuses are not directly tied to operating profits, the profit performance of a division is a very important factor in determining pay and bonus amounts. It should come as no surprise that many managers and employees care about cost allocation methods. In fact, the method of cost allocation is frequently a controversial "hot" topic among managers in many organizations. The next section of the chapter describes the general methods of cost allocation used in many organizations.

Cost allocation methods

Outline of the process

The cost allocation process is comprised of three basic activities:

1. Accumulating the costs that relate to a product, department, or division (for example, manufacturing overhead in manufacturing overhead accounts or corporate headquarter's costs in accounts for corporate headquarters.)
2. Identifying the cost objects or recipients of the allocated costs (for example, a unit of product or a department).
3. Selecting a method for relating the costs that were accumulated to the cost objects.

The third activity is the most difficult because common costs cannot be directly associated with a single unit or department. The accountant must therefore find an indirect relationship between costs and cost objects that might serve as a meaningful allocation base. An analysis of past cost behavior may suggest such a relationship.

For example, we cannot usually trace manufacturing overhead to a *particular unit* produced. We can usually observe, however, that manufacturing overhead costs are higher in periods when more units are produced and lower in periods when fewer units are produced. Therefore, total manufacturing overhead costs are usually allocated equally to each unit produced in an accounting period. We cannot trace manufacturing overhead costs directly to a specific unit; therefore, each unit must share overhead equally.

Difficulties in selecting allocation bases

A basis of allocation cannot always be easily selected merely by examining the relationship between costs and cost objects. Consider, for example, the salary of the supervisor of Contractors, Inc., a house construction company. During the month of June, five different jobs were started and two were completed. There were no jobs in process at the beginning of the month. Each job benefited from the supervisor's planning and management, so his salary was a common cost of all five jobs. The company decided to allocate the supervisor's costs to the jobs for inventory valuation purposes at the end of June. What is the appropriate allocation method? The company considered the following alternatives:

1. Allocate the salary equally to each job.
2. Charge the entire salary to any one job (because as long as the supervisor works on at least one job, he must be paid a month's wages).
3. Allocate the salary in proportion to the cost of direct materials used on each job.
4. Allocate the salary on the basis of the direct labor-hours (or costs) on each job.
5. Require the supervisor to keep time records by job and allocate on the basis of the time spent on the job. (This alternative probably comes closest to allocating the supervisor's wages on a causal basis. However, it is costly to have a supervisor spending time filling out timecards instead of supervising.)

An argument could be made to support each of these allocation bases. Contractors, Inc., decided that Alternative 4 was preferable to Alternative 5 because it was an almost costless procedure and that it was preferable to Alternatives 1, 2, and 3 because most of the supervisor's time was spent supervising direct labor. This is an example of the reasoning that often takes place when accountants select allocation bases.

Typical allocation bases

Most common costs can be categorized into one of four groups. Certain bases of allocation are commonly associated with each.

1. *Labor-related common costs.* Labor-related common costs are usually allocated on the basis of number of employees, labor-hours, wages paid, or similar labor-related criteria. (See items 1 and 2 in Illustration 4–1).
2. *Machine-related common costs.* Machine-related common costs are usually allocated on the basis of machine-hours, current value of machinery and equipment, number of machines or similar machine-related criteria. (See items 3 through 6 in Illustration 4–1.)
3. *Space-related common costs.* Space-related common costs are usually allocated on the basis of area occupied, volume occupied, or similar space-related criteria. (See items 7 through 11 in Illustration 4–1.)
4. *Service-related common costs.* Service-related common costs may be allocated on the basis of quantity, value, time, and similar service-related criteria. (See items 12 through 16 in Illustration 4–1.)

These allocation bases are examples only. Common costs should be analyzed case by case to determine the most suitable allocation base.

Dual allocation rates

When two different relationships exist between a common cost and a cost object, two bases may be used to allocate common costs. Such an allocation is called a **dual rate** method. For example, a company may have purchased computer equipment based on projected demand for services. In addition

Illustration 4–1   **Typical allocation bases for common costs**

	Common cost	Typical allocation base
Labor related	1. Supervision	Number of employees Payroll dollars or labor hours
	2. Personnel services	Number of employees
Machine related	3. Insurance on equipment	Value of equipment
	4. Taxes on equipment	Value of equipment
	5. Equipment depreciation	Machine-hours, equipment value
	6. Equipment maintenance	Number of machines, machine-hours
Space related	7. Building rental	Space occupied
	8. Building insurance	Space occupied
	9. Heat and air conditioning	Space occupied, volume occupied
	10. Concession rental	Space occupied and desirability of location
	11. Interior building maintenance	Space occupied
Service related	12. Materials handling	Quantity or value of materials
	13. Laundry	Weight of laundry processed
	14. Billing and accounting	Number of documents
	15. Indirect materials	Value of direct materials
	16. Dietary	Number of meals

to purchase costs, there are costs incurred when the equipment is used. (These are mostly supplies and labor costs for computer operators.) Thus, there are two different relationships between the computer costs and the user departments: (1) capacity available to the user department and (2) current time usage.

Assume that the costs of renting the computer and other capacity costs are fixed costs, while the costs incurred for time usage are variable. Suppose the following rate is used to allocate costs:

$$\frac{\text{Rate per unit}}{\text{of time charged}} = \frac{\text{Variable cost}}{\text{per unit of time}} + \frac{\text{Fixed capacity costs}}{\text{Units of time}}$$

Hence, user departments will be charged for an "average" use of both time and capacity. Further, user departments who use a lot of time but do not need much capacity, subsidize user departments who need more capacity but do not use as much time.

An alternative method is to divide the computer costs into two separate components:

1. The fixed or capacity costs that are allocated on the basis of *capacity* demanded.

2.   The variable costs that are allocated on the basis of *time* used.

With this alternative, the costs assigned to individual departments reflect as closely as possible the relationship between the cost allocated and the factors that caused the company to incur the cost.

For example, Caucus Consulting rents a computer for $55,000 per month. This fee is based on the capacity of the equipment and has no relationship to actual usage. To operate the computer costs $250 per hour. Department A requested that it has access to 500 units of capacity, while Department B requested that it has access to 300 units of capacity. During the past month, Department A used 200 hours of computer time while Department B used 400 hours. Assuming these are the only two departments, how should the computer costs be allocated?

The firm first considered allocating costs on the basis of *time usage.* The cost allocation on the basis of time usage was:

Department A: $\dfrac{200 \text{ department hours used}}{600 \text{ total hours used}} \times \$205,000^a = \$\ \ 68,333$

Department B: $\dfrac{400 \text{ department hours used}}{600 \text{ total hours used}} \times \$205,000 \ = \ \underline{136,667}$

Total cost of the computer center $\underline{\underline{\$205,000}}$

---

a $205,000 = $55,000 + (200 hours + 400 hours) × $250

When this method was proposed, the manager of Department B argued, "My department is being charged for the monthly fixed rental fee on the basis of computer time used, but that monthly fee might have been lower if Department A had not demanded so much capacity."

To deal with this argument, the firm next allocated solely on the basis of *capacity demanded.* The resulting allocation was:

Department A: $\dfrac{\begin{array}{c}500 \text{ department units of} \\ \text{capacity requested}\end{array}}{\begin{array}{c}800 \text{ total units of} \\ \text{capacity requested}\end{array}} \times \$205,000 = \$128,125$

Department B: $\dfrac{\begin{array}{c}300 \text{ department units of} \\ \text{capacity requested}\end{array}}{\begin{array}{c}800 \text{ total units of} \\ \text{capacity requested}\end{array}} \times \$205,000 = \ \underline{\ \ 76,875}$

Total cost of the computer center $\underline{\underline{\$205,000}}$

When this method was proposed, the Department B manager was happy, but the Department A manager argued, "My department is being penalized because of our demand for capacity. We believe more costs should be allocated to Department B because they used 400 hours of computer time while we only used 200 hours."

The firm compromised by using a dual rate based on both capacity demanded and time usage. The resulting allocation was:

Department A: Capacity: $\frac{5}{8} \times \$55,000$	=	$ 34,375
Time: 200 hours × $250 per hour =		50,000
Total Department A		84,375
Department B: Capacity: $\frac{3}{8} \times \$55,000$	=	20,625
Time: 400 × $250 per hour	=	100,000
Total Department B		120,625
Total cost of the computer center		$205,000

Multiple-factor method

The dual basis method can be extended to include multiple factors. The multiple-factor method is often used when there are many relationships between common costs and cost objects.

Suppose, for example, that a manufacturing company wants to allocate corporate headquarters' costs to each of its plants. Some people might assert that these costs are related to the size of the payroll; others might argue these costs are related to the volume of business. Still others might argue that administrative costs are related to investment in assets. Actually, all three suggested bases are valid. In such cases, a company may use a **multiple-factor formula** that incorporates all of the factors in the allocation base. In this case, the percentage of the common cost to be allocated to a plant may be the arithmetic average of the following three percentages:

1. Percentage of payroll dollars in each plan to the total payroll dollars for both plants.
2. Percentage of volume in units in each plant to the total volume in both plants.
3. Percentage of the average gross book value of tangible assets of each plant to the total gross book value of tangible assets in both plants.

Assume the company has $282,000 in corporate headquarters' costs to apportion to the two plants and an analysis of the accounting and other records provides the following information:

Plant	Payroll dollars		Volume in units		Gross book value of tangible assets	
	Amount	Percent	Amount	Percent	Amount	Percent
1	$1,300	65	$6,750	75	$ 5,600	40
2	700	35	2,250	25	8,400	60
Totals	$2,000	100	$9,000	100	$14,000	100

The allocation to each plant would be computed as follows:

Plant	Fraction		Allocated cost	
1	$\frac{65\% + 75\% + 40\%}{3}$	$= 60\%$	$60\% \times \$282,000$	$= \$169,200$
2	$\frac{35\% + 25\% + 60\%}{3}$	$= 40\%$	$40\% \times \$282,000$	$= \underline{112,800}$
	Total allocated costs			$\underline{\underline{\$282,000}}$

The multiple-factor formula directs attention to the many relationships between common costs and cost objects. Thus, management may use this method to encourage employees to manage many factors relating common costs to cost objects.

In recent years, most state taxing authorities have used this "three-factor" formula approach to assign the income of a multistate business to the individual state for state income tax purposes. They presume the measures of assets, sales, and payrolls reflect the income generated in the states where the company operates.

Allocation of manufacturing overhead

Bases for applying manufacturing overhead to work in process

Manufacturing overhead costs are charged to units produced using a predetermined allocation base. Some common bases for allocation are direct material costs, direct labor costs, direct labor-hours, and machine-hours.

Direct materials costs may be an appropriate basis when overhead costs are closely related to the volume of materials handled. In an assembly area where many of the costs correspond to the quantity of materials used, it may be appropriate to assign overhead on the basis of direct materials costs.

Direct labor costs are often used as an allocation base when they seem to be related to overhead costs. When skilled workers use costly machinery and unskilled workers perform tasks that do not require similar capital investments, the use of rates based on direct labor may be appropriate. Such an allocation base would reflect the relationship between the higher overhead costs associated with skilled labor and the lower overhead costs associated with unskilled labor. Jobs that require more skilled labor would be charged a proportionately greater share of overhead.

Direct labor-hours are an appropriate allocation base when overhead costs do not vary among different wage classes of labor or when labor rates are influenced more by seniority or other factors that are unrelated to job skills.

Machine-hours may be a particularly appropriate basis of allocation when expensive or high power-consuming machinery is used. Computer installations normally charge their costs based on computer time used, and similar allocation bases may be appropriate in other situations.

Managers deciding how to allocate manufacturing overhead costs to jobs should examine both costs and benefits of alternative bases. For example, the costs of direct materials and direct labor for each job are readily available from the accounting records. It may be more costly to obtain data on the number of labor-hours or machine-hours used. Most companies use a labor-based allocation method. In this book, we use direct labor costs or direct labor-hours unless stated otherwise.

For example, a manufacturing company made 10,000 units of Product A in a month using 5,000 direct labor-hours and 20,000 units of Product B using 15,000 direct labor-hours. Total manufacturing overhead for the month was $50,000. How much manufacturing overhead is allocated to each unit produced in the company if direct labor-hours is the allocation base? The answer is computed as follows:

Step 1: Compute manufacturing overhead rate per labor-hour:
Rate = $50,000 ÷ (5,000 hours + 15,000 hours)
= $2.50 per hour

Step 2: Multiply rate times labor-hours per product:
Product A: $2.50 × 5,000 hours = $12,500
Product B: $2.50 × 15,000 hours = $37,500

Step 3: Divide total manufacturing overhead by units produced:
Product A: $12,500 ÷ 10,000 units = $1.25 per unit

Product B: $37,500 ÷ 20,000 units = $1.875 per unit

Allocations in cost-plus contracts

Cost allocations are often used for determining prices in "cost-plus-a-profit" contracts. Let us return to Computerworld, Inc., and change the situation such that Computerworld has only the Business Division with its sales of $266,000, cost of goods sold of $159,600, and other costs of $87,900. Computerworld has entered into a contract to supply 42 computers to a government agency on a cost-plus basis. The government agency will pay Computerworld a fee of $7,310 for the computers and will reimburse Computerworld for the "total cost" of supplying the computers. Does it make any difference if, or indeed how, we allocate the $9,000 in showroom costs to the government contract and other business?

Assume for this problem that the cost of goods sold under the contract is $73,080 and that other costs directly traceable to the contract total $38,500. If we do not allocate the showroom costs, then the revenue from the contract will equal $118,890 (that is, the $73,080 cost of goods sold plus the $38,500 direct costs plus the $7,310 fee). Total company operating profits will be:

	Regular business	Government contract	Total
Sales revenue	$266,000	$118,890	$384,890
Cost of goods sold	159,600	73,080	232,680
Direct costs	87,900	38,500	126,400
Showroom costs			9,000
Operating profit			$ 16,810
Number of units sold	28	42	70

However, if we allocate showroom costs to the contract based on, say, number of units sold, then the showroom costs allocated to the contract are $5,400 (= 42/70 × $9,000) plus the original $118,890 noted above, giving contract revenue of $124,290. Now total company operating profit becomes:

	Business	Contract	Total
Sales revenue	$266,000	$124,290	$390,290
Cost of goods sold	159,600	73,080	232,680
Direct costs	87,900	38,500	126,400
Allocated showroom costs	3,600[a]	5,400	9,000
Operating profit			$ 22,210

[a] $3,600 = $9,000 − $5,400

Notice how the company's total profit has increased because of the allocation of the common showroom costs. By transferring the $5,400 to the contract, the company's profit increases by the same amount.

If the method of allocation has not been specified in the contract, then the contracting agency may dispute the allocation, just as the manager of the Personal Division questioned the allocation in our earlier example. In this example, and in many similar situations, the allocation of costs has a clear impact on profits. Of course, under perfect competition, there will be other bidders who are willing to write a contract that does not reimburse them for any showroom costs. Hence, *in the long run,* these companies will not earn economic rents from their cost allocation method. However, if the parties to a contract have different ideas about what the "cost" is, there may be a dispute to resolve when it comes time to settle the contract.

The Cost Accounting Standards Board, which existed from 1971 to 1980, was established to develop uniform cost allocation principles for contractors and federal agencies to use in cost-plus contracts to minimize the disputes that were widespread in defense contracting.

Almost every cost-based regulation or contract requires allocation of common costs. These are the most common uses of cost allocation for external purposes. Cost allocations are rarely *required* for internal, managerial purposes, but they can be *useful* in many situations. For example, for a good or service to be independently profitable in the long run, it must cover both direct costs, like direct labor, and indirect costs allocated to it, like corporate headquarters' costs. Otherwise, it will be dropped from a company's portfolio of products, unless keeping it makes other products more profitable (for example, a loss leader). Consequently, indirect costs are often allocated to products to estimate the costs that must be covered in the long run.

Charging the cost of service departments to users

Virtually every organization has departments whose main job is to serve other departments. These include the laundry in a hospital, the computer center in a university, maintenance in a factory, security in a retail store, and so forth. Because the output of such **service departments** is not sold to outside customers, their costs must be covered by the revenue-generating departments inside the organization. Thus, the costs of departments that do not generate revenue are often allocated to departments that use their services as an attention-getting device. The allocation makes managers of such **user departments** aware that it is not enough to cover department costs for the organization as a whole to break even or make a profit. The following example tells why one actual company decided to allocate costs.

The Owens Company did not allocate the costs of its computer department to user departments. In 1982, top management noted that computer department costs had increased 400 percent over 1978 levels. While management acknowledged an increasing need for computer services within the company, they had not expected an increase of this magnitude.

Investigation showed that because departments were not charged for using the computer services, they treated the costs of computer services as if they were free. One of the top managers noted, "People were trying new software without any real need, just to see if it worked. Also, a lot of people were playing computer games during their breaks. User department managers had little or no incentive to worry about such things because they were not charged for use, or misuse, of the computer. We also found that the computer department was becoming a "gold-plate department" that offered the best possible service to users regardless of cost."

To deal with this problem, Owens Company started allocating computer department costs to user departments based on units of computer time and space and the amount of computer personnel time used. Each user department was given a fixed budget or allowance to spend on computer services. The user department manager's bonus and promotion prospects were negatively affected if the computer costs charged to the user department exceeded the budget.

As a result, departments began to use computer services only when the benefits were believed to exceed the costs. In addition, managers of user departments began to monitor computer department personnel to ensure that they would not be charged for wasted time.

Thus, allocating service department costs served two managerial purposes. First, user department managers had incentives to monitor service departments' costs. For example, when the computer department manager requested additional funds to purchase the latest technology hardware, user department managers challenged the need for this hardware.

Second, it stopped users from assuming that services have no cost. In theory, the user should use a service as long as the marginal benefit of a unit of service exceeds its marginal cost. Thus, the marginal cost of supplying a unit of service should be charged to the user to get the user to make the correct (economic) decision about how much of the service to use. Marginal costs are difficult to measure, however, so allocated costs are often used to estimate marginal costs.

Allocated costs can be misleading

When common costs are allocated, accounting records often make the cost appear as though it is a direct cost. For example, allocating some of factory rent to each unit of product would result in including the rent as part of the "unit cost," even though the total rent does not change with the manufacture of another unit of product. Cost data that includes allocated common costs may, therefore, be misleading if used incorrectly. The following example demonstrates the problem.

Electrodark, Inc., manufactures a line of electric equipment. Product A has a unit production cost of $80, made up of the following per unit costs:

Direct materials (variable cost)	$20
Direct labor (variable cost)	25
Variable manufacturing overhead	5
Total variable costs per unit	50

Fixed manufacturing overhead costs allocated to units:

$$\text{Unit cost} = \frac{\text{Fixed manufacturing cost per month}}{\text{Units produced per month}}$$

$$= \frac{\$600,000}{20,000 \text{ units}} = \underline{30}$$

Total unit cost used as the inventory value under full-absorption costing	$80

Electrodark has been asked to accept a special order for 1,000 units of Product A for $75 each. These units can be produced with capacity that is currently not being used. Marketing and administrative costs would not be affected by accepting the order. Accepting this special order would not affect the regular market for this product.

Marketing managers believed the special order should be accepted as long as the unit price of $75 exceeded the cost of manufacturing each unit. When the marketing managers learned from accounting reports that the inventory value was $80 per unit, their initial reaction was to reject the special order opportunity because, as one manager stated, "You are not going to be very profitable if it costs you more to make than your selling price!"

Fortunately, some additional investigation revealed the variable manufacturing cost to be only $50 per unit, and marketing management accepted the special order, which had the following impact on the company's operating profit:

Revenue from special order (1,000 units × $75 =)	$75,000
Variable costs of making special order (1,000 units × $50 =)	50,000
Contribution of special order to operating profit	$25,000

The moral of this example is that it is easy to incorrectly interpret costs and make incorrect decisions. In the example above, fixed manufacturing overhead costs had been allocated to units, most likely to value inventory for external financial reporting and tax purposes, which made the resulting unit cost of $80 appear to be the cost of producing a unit. Of course, only $50 was a variable cost of producing a unit, while the fixed costs of $600,000 per month would not be affected by the decision to accept the special order.

Cost accumulation and cost allocation

This chapter and Chapter 3 have discussed two key activities in cost accounting: cost accumulation and cost allocation. Costs are accumulated in accounts as transactions, such as the sale of goods or the purchase of an asset, take place. A transaction is a cost's *point of entry* into the organization. Once accumulated, or entered, costs are frequently assigned or allocated to units produced and other cost objects. You may think of cost accumulation as resulting from transactions with outsiders, while cost allocations are internal assignments of costs.

Costs are often accumulated by department for performance evaluation and then allocated to products for inventory valuation. For example, consider an assembly department that works on several different product lines. Direct materials, direct labor, and manufacturing overhead are accumulated in the assembly department and, as shown below, allocated to each product line.

Some costs are difficult to accumulate by responsibility center. Manufacturing overhead, for example, is often accumulated for several departments, then allocated to each department for responsibility costing, and then allocated to product lines to value inventory.

Summary

Cost allocation is the process of assigning common costs to two or more cost objects. Manufacturing overhead is common to units produced, for example, and is allocated to them to place a value on inventory and cost of goods sold for external financial reporting. Allocations of common costs to cost objects are often made on a somewhat arbitrary basis.

Cost allocation procedures are costly because they consume the time of accountants and decision makers. Thus, costs should not be allocated unless there is cost-benefit justification. A common reason for allocating costs is to satisfy external reporting requirements (for example, to value inventory on external financial reports). Cost allocations are rarely required for managerial purposes; however, under certain conditions they can be useful. Cost-plus contracts and cost-based rate regulations require allocations of common costs.

The cost allocation process involves (1) accumulating costs to be allocated, (2) identifying cost objects, and (3) selecting a basis for relating costs to cost objects. While any basis for allocating costs to cost objects is somewhat arbitrary, some common costs and related bases are:

1. Labor-related common costs—number of employees, labor-hours, wages paid, or other labor-related criteria.
2. Machine-related common costs—machine-hours, current value of machinery, number of machines, or other machine-related criteria.
3. Space-related common costs—area occupied, volume occupied, or other space-related criteria.
4. Service-related common costs—computer usage, service personnel time, or other service-related criteria.

Dual and multiple bases are often used for cost allocation when there is more than one relationship between a common cost and a cost object.

Cost allocation can be misleading, particularly if costs allocated for one purpose are used for another. For example, fixed manufacturing overhead is allocated to units to place a value on inventory for external financial reporting and tax purposes. It is too easy for decision makers to assume incorrectly that those unit values are the variable costs of manufacturing units.

Costs are accumulated as transactions occur. The accumulated costs are then allocated to various cost objects. Costs accumulate due to transactions with outsiders. Cost allocations are internal assignments of costs.

Terms and concepts

The following terms and concepts should be familiar to you after reading this chapter.

Allocation base   **Dual rate**

Common cost   **Multiple-factor formula**

Cost allocation   **Service departments**

Cost objects   **User departments**

Self-study problem

Dual Division Corporation operates its Uno and Duo divisions as separate cost objects. To determine the costs of each division, the company allocates common costs to the divisions. During the past month, the following common costs were incurred:

Computer services (80% fixed)	$254,000
Building occupancy	615,000
Personnel	104,000

The following information is available concerning various activity measures and service usages by each of the divisions:

	Uno	Duo
Area occupied	15,000 sq. ft.	40,000 sq. ft.
Payroll	$380,000	$170,000
Computer time	200 hrs.	140 hrs.
Computer storage	25 mbytes	35 mbytes
Equipment value	$175,000	$220,000
Contribution margin—before allocations	$439,000	$522,000

Required:

a. Allocate the common costs to the two departments using the most appropriate of the above allocation bases. For computer services use computer time only.

b. Allocate the common costs to the two departments using dual rates for the computer services.

Solution to self-study problem

a.

Cost	Allocation base	Allocated to Uno	Allocated to Duo
Computer services	Computer time	$\dfrac{200}{200 + 140} \times \$254{,}000$	$\dfrac{140}{200 + 140} \times \$254{,}000$
		$= \$149{,}412$	$= \$104{,}588$
Building occupancy	Area occupied	$\dfrac{15{,}000}{15{,}000 + 40{,}000} \times \$615{,}000$	$\dfrac{40{,}000}{15{,}000 + 40{,}000} \times \$615{,}000$
		$= \$167{,}727$	$= \$447{,}273$
Personnel	Payroll	$\dfrac{\$380{,}000}{\$380{,}000 + \$170{,}000} \times \$104{,}000$	$\dfrac{\$170{,}000}{\$380{,}000 + \$170{,}000} \times \$104{,}000$
		$= \$\ 71{,}855$	$= \$\ 32{,}145$
— Totals		$\$388{,}994$	$\$584{,}006$

Check: $254,000 + $615,000 + $104,000 = $388,994 + $584,006 = $973,000.

b.

Cost	Allocation base	Allocated to Uno	Allocated to Duo
Computer variable costs	Computer time	$\dfrac{200}{200 + 140} \times \$254{,}000 \times 20\%$	$\dfrac{140}{200 + 140} \times \$254{,}000 \times 20\%$
		$= \$\ 29{,}882$	$= \$\ 20{,}918$
Computer fixed costs	Computer storage	$\dfrac{25}{25 + 35} \times \$254{,}000 \times 80\%$	$\dfrac{35}{25 + 35} \times \$254{,}000 \times 80\%$
		$= \$\ 84{,}667$	$= \$118{,}533$
Building occupancy— per *(a)*		$= \$167{,}727$	$= \$447{,}273$
Personnel—per *(a)*		$= \$\ 71{,}855$	$= \$\ 32{,}145$
Totals		$\$354{,}131$	$\$618{,}869$

Check: $254,000 + $615,000 + $104,000 = $354,131 + $618,869 = $973,000.

Questions

4–1. If cost allocations are arbitrary and potentially misleading, should we assume that management is foolish for using information based on allocated costs?

4–2. What are some of the costs of cost allocation?

4–3. What are some of the benefits of cost allocation?

4–4. What principle is used to decide whether to allocate costs to cost objects.

4–5. One critic of cost allocation noted: "You can avoid the problem of arbitrary cost allocations by simply not allocating any common costs to other cost objects." What are your thoughts on this suggestion?

4–6. What do we mean when we say that common costs are not affected by the production of an additional unit of output. Isn't there some limit to the validity of this statement?

4–7. What are some management uses of information based on allocated costs?

4–8. List the three steps in the cost allocation process.

4–9. Is there a reasonable criterion for selecting the basis that is used to allocate costs? Explain your answer.

4–10. List the four broad categories of common costs and the usual basis for allocation of costs in each category. The basis may be expressed as an example or in broad terms.

4–11. A cost such as company headquarter's cost does not fit into any one of the broad categories of common costs. A cost such as this may be a result of a number of different causal factors. Is there a way to allocate such a cost? Describe the approach.

Exercises

4–12. Compute cost allocations

A company has two divisions that share the common costs of the company equipment service department. The following information is given concerning the equipment service department and the two other divisions:

Costs of the equipment service department, $48,500

Division	Service hours used this period	Value of equipment
A	460	$121,250
B	316	480,000

Required:

a. What is the service department cost that would be charged to each division using service hours as a basis for allocation?

b. What is the service department cost that would be charged to each division using value of equipment as a basis for allocation?

4–13. Dual rates for allocation

Using the data for the company in Exercise 4–12, determine the cost allocation if the fixed service department costs of $26,000 are allocated on the basis of value of equipment and the remaining costs (which are variable) are allocated on the basis of service hours used this period.

4–14. Compute rates for building use

Affiliated Retailers operates a department store in Enola, Pennsylvania. The store has 120,000 square feet. Each department in the store is charged with a share of the costs of the building. The following information is available concerning two of the departments in the store:

	Department	
	Fashion clothing	Furniture
Sales revenues	$700,000	$800,000
Cost of goods sold	370,000	380,000
Sales commissions, salaries, other direct expenses	210,000	240,000
Allocated administrative expenses	60,000	65,000
Net before building occupancy costs	$ 60,000	$115,000
Area occupied	10,000 sq. ft.	40,000 sq. ft.

The total building occupancy costs are $600,000 per year.

Required:

a. If area occupied is the basis for allocation of building occupancy costs, what is the operating profit or loss for each of these two departments?

b. Would you modify your answer to (a) if you learned that the fashion clothing department is located near the main entrance to the store and the furniture department is located in an upstairs, back corner of the store? How would you modify your answer?

4–15. Cost allocations using multiple factors

The Cost Accounting Standards Board has concluded that certain indirect costs that cannot be related to a government contract by any other manner are to be charged to the contract based on a three-factor formula. The three factors are property, payrolls, and all other costs charged to the contract. Each of these factors is entered into a fraction, the numerators of which are property, payroll, or all other costs charged to the contract and the denominators of which are the total property, payroll, and other costs incurred by the company. The three resulting fractions are summed, and the result divided by three. The result of this operation is the portion of these costs that are chargeable to the contract.

Stealthy Products, Inc., has a secret government contract. The company also engages in other activities. During the past year, it incurred $650,000 in costs chargeable to the government contract other than costs that must be charged based on the "three-factor formula." The company had incurred a total of $812,500 in the category of costs not covered by the formula.

In addition, Stealthy used $2,000,000 of its $3,000,000 in property for the government contract. Payrolls of employees engaged in the government contract amounted to $390,000 out of total payrolls of $468,000.

For the company, costs that are subject to the three-factor formula amount to $122,000.

Required:

How much of the $122,000 is chargeable to the government contract using the three-factor formula?

4–16. Dual rates for cost allocation

InanOut, Inc., has two primary operating departments: receiving and delivery. There are common costs for these two divisions as follows:

Personnel management	$28,000
Computer services	42,000
Property taxes on equipment	7,500

The above computer services costs are 75 percent fixed by the capacity of the computer equipment. The remaining 25 percent vary with the time usage.

Some additional data on the departments are:

	Receiving	Delivery
Number of employees	120	60
Space occupied	20,000 sq. ft.	15,000 sq. ft.
Value of equipment	$500,000	$300,000
Machine-hours used	12,000	8,000
Computer time used	40 hrs.	50 hrs.
Units produced	17,000	17,500
Computer capacity demanded	200 megabytes	100 megabytes

Required:

Prepare a schedule allocating the common costs to the two departments using dual rates for the computer costs.

4–17. Cost allocations—select appropriate base

For each of the types of common cost in the first column, select the most appropriate allocation base from the second column:

Common cost

Building utilities
Payroll accounting
Property taxes on personal property
Equipment repair
Quality control inspection

Allocation base

Value of equipment and inventories
Number of units produced
Number of employees
Space occupied
Number of service calls

Problems and cases

4–18. Cost allocation for rate-making purposes

Failsafe Insurance, Inc., is arguing for an increase in the allowed premiums from its insurance operations. Insurance rates in the jurisdiction in which Failsafe operates are designed to cover the operating costs and claims against the insurance policies written. As a part of Failsafe's operations, its agents collect commissions based on the premiums collected. Premiums collected are used to pay claims and to invest in a portfolio of securities. However, all sales commissions are charged against premium income. In addition, the administrative operation includes a division that is engaged in investment management. However, all administrative costs are charged against premium revenue in order to determine the income or loss from insurance operations. Failsafe claims that its insurance operations "just broke even" last year and that a rate increase is in order. In support of that contention, the following income statement (in millions) was submitted:

Premium revenue	$400
Operating costs:	
Claims	250
Administrative	70
Sales commissions	80
Total operating costs	400
Insurance profit (loss)	–0–
Investment income	30
Profit after investment income	$ 30

Further investigation reveals that approximately 20 percent of the premium revenues are invested for a period averaging one year. This is possible because under accrual accounting, claims are recorded before they are paid. In addition, 10 percent of the administrative costs are incurred by the investment management division. The state insurance commission (which sets insurance rates) believes that Failsafe's insurance activities should earn about 5 percent on its premium revenues.

Required:

a. If you were a consumer group, how would you present Failsafe's income statement?

b. If you were Failsafe management, what arguments would you present in support of the cost allocations included in the above income statement?

4–19. Cost allocation for travel reimbursement

Your company has a travel policy that reimburses employees for the "ordinary and necessary" costs of business travel. Quite often employees will mix a business trip with pleasure either by extending the time at the destination or by traveling from the business destination to a nearby resort or other personal destination. In such situations, an allocation must be made between the business and personal portions of the trip. However, the travel policy is unclear on the allocation method to follow.

Consider the following example:

An employee obtained an excursion ticket for $660 and traveled the following itinerary:

From	To	Mileage	Regular fare	Purpose
Washington, D.C.	Salt Lake City	1,839	$350	Business
Salt Lake City	Los Angeles	590	150	Personal
Los Angeles	Washington, D.C.	2,288	400	Return

Required:

Compute the business portion of the air fare and state the basis for the indicated allocation that would be appropriate according to each of the following independent scenarios:

a. Based on the maximum reimbursement for the employee.

b. Based on the minimum cost to the company.

c. Based on your recommendation.

4–20 Cost allocation for regulated utility pricing

Regulated utilities are generally permitted to charge users with the costs to service the specific class of users. Cost allocations are required to share common costs. For example, for an electric utility, common costs include costs of generating and distribution facilities. Variable costs, such as fuel costs, are normally considered direct.

Common costs are distributed on the basis of the capacity demanded by each class of user. Capacity may be measured in terms of peak use in a day or peak seasonal use. An alternative measure is to use average demand for allocating capacity charges. Average demand is the same as the actual use of electricity and, hence, is the usual basis for charging direct costs to users.

For example, Progressive Electric Company serves a three-county area. The area has two classes of users: (1) residential and (2) manufacturing. During the past year, the following data were generated:

User class	Daily peak use	Seasonal peak use	Average demand
Residential	50 million kwhr.	35 million kwhr.	15 million kwhr.
Manufacturing	25	20	18

The following costs were reported during the same period:

Facilities $3 million
Fuel   2 million

a. What are the three sets of rates per kilowatt-hour for each class of users under the alternative allocation systems?

b. What arguments might be raised supporting or opposing the alternatives by each user group?

4–21. Cost allocations in contracting

Idiograms, Inc., entered into a contract to produce certain units on a cost-plus basis. During the period of the contract, Idiograms had 280 of its 520 employees working on the contract exclusively. Idiograms paid $340,000 in wages to the contract-related employees. During the same time, it paid $480,000 in wages to its noncontract-related employees. Its labor-related overhead costs amounted to $275,000. Idiograms submitted the following invoice to the purchaser:

Materials costs	$ 645,306
Labor costs	340,000
Other overhead	260,000
Labor-related overhead (not included elsewhere)	148,077
Total costs	1,393,383
Agreed profit (20%)	278,677
Contract balance due	$1,672,060

Upon receipt of the invoice, the purchaser questioned the allocation of labor-related overhead noting that the costs seemed "out of line."

a. What basis did Idiograms use for the allocation of labor-related overhead costs?

b. What would be the effect on the contract balance due if Idiograms used the alternative basis suggested in the problem?

c. Is it possible to conclude which basis is "more appropriate"?

4–22. Determine state income tax allocations

MoIllCal, Inc., operates in three states: Missouri, Illinois, and California. The following information is available concerning the activities and taxing bases for each of the three states:

	Missouri	Illinois	California
Income tax rate	–0–	5%	7%
Basis for allocating income	—	Illinois sales over total sales	California sales, payroll, and property three-factor formula
Company sales occurring by state	—	$2.4 million	$1.8 million
Company payrolls by state	$2.6 million	.8	.6
Company property by state	1.2	.3	.5

Company headquarters are located in Missouri. Total company profits were $750,000 before state taxes.

Required:

What is the income tax liability due to each state?

4–23. Interaction of state taxes and contract costs

ArkFla, Inc., has two operating divisions. Fla Division operates entirely in Florida and engages exclusively in the manufacture and sale of commercial products. Ark Division operates exclusively in Arkansas and is engaged in the manufacture of military equipment. Prior to receiving a new defense contract, ArkFla, Inc., had the following distribution of property, payrolls, and sales between the two states:

	Arkansas	**Florida**
Property	$4.9 million	$ 5.6 million
Payrolls	1.2	1.6
Sales	7.4	11.7

Total income was $3 million. ArkFla received a government contract which required the addition of $1.0 million in property in Arkansas. Payroll in Arkansas was increased by $.9 million, and sales increased by $3.1 million. The contract added $300,000 to income.

Florida levies its 6 percent state income tax using the property, payrolls, and sales factors. No other elements in the factors for either state changed.

Required:

What effect, if any, did the defense contract have on the Florida tax liability?

4–24. Cost allocations in cost-plus pricing

Global Airlines is considering offering Business Class service on its transpacific routes. The problem Global faces is that it wants the Business Class service to provide an equivalent return to that which it obtains from its Economy service. The Business Class fare must be set in such a way that it will provide the same margin per seat as the Economy Class fare. Management has some question as to the appropriate way to assure that this objective will be met.

The published Economy Class fare is $800 one way. However, as noted by the revenue accounting manager, discount fares result in an average Economy Class fare of $500 one way.

Business Class service would incur a meal cost estimated at $45 per passenger. This compares with the Economy Class meal service cost of $25 per passenger.

For the space used for each seat in Business Class, it would be possible to fit in 1.5 Economy Class seats. Baggage handling, reservations, and similar incidental costs are estimated at $10 per passenger for the variable portion of those costs for either class. Fixed costs per flight (crew salaries, fuel, landing fees, etc.) are allocated $275 per passenger for either class.

Required:

What fare for Business Class would meet management's objectives?

4–25. Allocated costs and incentive contracts

Volume Sales Company has a highly competitive organization. Division managers (and division employees) receive a bonus if the division reports "above-average" returns for a year. Profits are determined using allocated common costs. Returns are measured by dividing profits by the investment into assets in each division.

The following profit and performance reports were prepared for the managers of Division X and Division Y (these are two of many divisions in the company):

	(in thousands)	
	Division X	**Division Y**
Sales revenue	$450	$600
Costs:		
Direct costs	200	300
Allocated costs	200	160
Division profit	$ 50	$140
Division investment base	$200	$560
Division return (Profit ÷ Investment base)	25%	25%

The average return for the company was also 25 percent.

The manager of Division X notes that allocated costs were distributed to each division on the basis of number of employees. She suggests that the allocated costs should be distributed on the basis of investment base because the allocated costs are predominently headquarters costs. In her view, the primary role of headquarters is to provide assets for the use of operating divisions. Had the costs been allocated on the basis of division investment, she calculated that Division X would have been charged with costs of $140 and Division Y with costs of $390.

The manager of Division Y argues that central management is really concerned with maintaining employee relations. The advantage to a large organization such as this one is that employees identify with the company not just with a division. He further asserts that the greater an employee's pay, the more the employee requires services of corporate headquarters. He therefore suggests that payroll costs be used as the basis for allocation of the common costs. If payroll costs were used, he calculated that Division X would be charged with $220 of allocated costs and Division Y with $135.

Required:

What suggestions do you have for the solution to the incentive compensation problem for Volume Sales Company?

4–26. Analyze data based on allocated costs

The Herbert Manufacturing Company manufactures custom-designed restaurant and kitchen furniture. Actual overhead costs incurred during the month are applied to the products on the basis of actual direct labor-hours required to produce the products. The overhead consists primarily of supervision, employee benefits, maintenance costs, property taxes, and depreciation.

Herbert Manufacturing recently won a contract to manufacture the furniture for a new fast-food chain. To produce this new line, Herbert Manufacturing must purchase more molded plastic parts for the furniture than for its current line. Through innovative industrial engineering, an efficient manufacturing process for this new furniture has been developed that requires only a minimum capital investment. Management is very optimistic about the profit improvement the new product line will bring.

At the end of October, the start-up month for the new line, the controller has prepared a separate income statement for the new product line. On a consolidated basis, the gross profit percentage was normal; however, the profitability for the new line was less than expected.

The president of the corporation is concerned that stockholders will criticize the decision to add this lower-quality product line at a time when profitability appeared to be increasing with the standard product line.

The results as published for the first nine months, for October, and for November are (in thousands):

	Fast-food furniture	Custom furniture	Consolidated
Nine months year to date:			
Gross sales	—	$8,100	$8,100
Direct material	—	2,025	2,025
Direct labor:			
Forming	—	758	758
Finishing	—	1,314	1,314
Assembly	—	558	558
Overhead	—	1,779	1,779
Cost of sales	—	6,434	6,434
Gross profit	—	$1,666	$1,666
Gross profit percentage	—	20.6%	20.6%
October:			
Gross sales	$400	$ 900	$1,300
Direct material	200	225	425
Direct labor:			
Forming	17	82	99
Finishing	40	142	182
Assembly	33	60	93
Overhead	60	180	240
Cost of sales	350	689	1,039
Gross profit	$ 50	$ 211	$ 261
Gross profit percentage	12.5%	23.4%	20.1%
November:			
Gross sales	$800	$ 800	$1,600
Direct material	400	200	600
Direct labor:			
Forming	31	72	103
Finishing	70	125	195
Assembly	58	53	111
Overhead	98	147	245
Cost of sales	657	597	1,254
Gross profit	$143	$ 203	$ 346
Gross profit percentage	17.9%	25.4%	21.6%

Ms. Jameson, cost accounting manager, stated that the overhead allocation based only on direct labor-hours is no longer appropriate. On the basis of a recently completed study of the overhead accounts, Jameson feels that only the supervision and employee benefits should be allocated on the basis of direct labor-hours and the balance of the overhead should be allocated on a machine-hour basis. In Jameson's judgment, the increase in the profitability of the custom design furniture is due to a misallocation of overhead in the present system.

The actual direct labor-hours and machine-hours for the past two months are shown below.

	Fast-food furniture	Custom furniture
Machine-hours:		
October:		
Forming	660	10,700
Finishing	660	7,780
Assembly	—	—
	1,320	18,480
November:		
Forming	1,280	9,640
Finishing	1,280	7,400
Assembly	—	—
	2,560	17,040
Direct labor-hours:		
October:		
Forming	1,900	9,300
Finishing	3,350	12,000
Assembly	4,750	8,700
	10,000	30,000
November:		
Forming	3,400	8,250
Finishing	5,800	10,400
Assembly	8,300	7,600
	17,500	26,250

The actual overhead costs for the past two months were:

	October	November
Supervision	$ 13,000	$ 13,000
Employee benefits	95,000	109,500
Maintenance	50,000	48,000
Depreciation	42,000	42,000
Property taxes	8,000	8,000
All other	32,000	24,500
Total	$240,000	$245,000

Required:

a. Reallocate the overhead for October and November using direct labor-hours as the allocation base for supervision and employee benefits. Use machine-hours as the base for the remaining overhead costs.

b. Support or criticize the conclusion that the increase in custom design profitability is due to a misallocation of overhead. Use the data developed in Requirement *(a)* to support your analysis.

(CMA adapted)

4–27. Discuss alternative allocation bases for retailer

Columbia Company is a regional office supply chain with 26 independent stores. Each store has been responsible for its own credit and collections. The assistant manager in each store is assigned the responsibility for credit activities including the collection of delinquent accounts because the stores do not need a full-time employee assigned to credit activities. The company has experienced a sharp rise in uncollectables the last two years. Corporate management has decided to establish a collections department in the home office to be responsible for the collection function companywide. The home office of Columbia Company will hire the necessary full-time personnel. The size of this department will be based upon the historical credit activity of all of the stores.

The new centralized collections department was discussed at a recent management meeting. A method to assign the costs of the new department to the stores has been difficult because this type of home office service is somewhat unique. Alternative methods are being reviewed by top management.

The controller identified the following four measures of services (allocation bases) that could be used:

1. Total dollar sales.
2. Average number of past-due accounts.
3. Number of uncollectible accounts written off.
4. One twenty-sixth of the cost to each of the stores.

The executive vice president stated that he would like the accounting department to prepare a detailed analysis of and the four service measures (allocation bases).

Required:

For each of the four measures of services (allocation bases) identified by the controller of Columbia Company:

(1) Discuss whether the service measure (allocation base) is appropriate to use in this situation.

(2) Identify the behavioral problems, if any, that could arise as a consequence of adopting the service measure (allocation base).

(CMA adapted)

4–28 Allocating costs to divisions

Darmen Corporation is one of the major producers of prefabricated houses in the home building industry. The corporation consists of two divisions: (1) Bell Division, which acquires the raw materials to manufacture the basic house components and assembles them into kits; and (2) Cornish Division, which takes the kits and constructs the homes for final home buyers. The corporation is decentralized, and the management of each division is measured by its income and return on investment.

Bell Division assembles seven separate house kits using materials purchased at the prevailing market prices. The seven kits are sold to Cornish for prices ranging from $45,000 to $98,000. The prices are set by corporate management of Darmen using prices paid by Cornish when it buys comparable units from outside sources. The smaller kits with the lower prices have become a larger portion of the units sold because the final house buyer is faced with prices that are increasing more rapidly than personal income. The kits are manufactured and assembled in a new plant just purchased by Bell this year. The division had been located in a leased plant for the past four years.

All kits are assembled upon receipt of an order from the Cornish Division. When the kit is completely assembled, it is loaded immediately on a Cornish truck. Thus, Bell Division has no finished goods inventory.

The Bell Division's accounts and reports are prepared on an actual cost basis. There is no budget and standards have not been developed for any product.

Bell Division's annual report is presented in Exhibit A. This report forms the basis of the evaluation of the division and its management by the corporation management.

Additional information regarding corporate and division practices is as follows:

1. The corporation office does all the personnel and accounting work for each division.
2. The corporate personnel costs are allocated on the basis of number of employees in the division.
3. The accounting costs are allocated to the division on the basis of total costs excluding corporate charges.
4. The division administration costs are included in factory overhead.
5. The financing charges include a corporate imputed interest charge on division assets and any divisional lease payments.

Exhibit A (4–28)

Bell Division
Performance Report
For the Year Ended December 31, 1984

	1984	1983	Increase or (decrease) from 1983 Amount	Percent change
Production data (in units)				
Kits started	2,400	1,600	800	50.0
Kits shipped	2,000	2,100	(100)	(4.8)
Kits in process at year-end	700	300	400	133.3
Increase (decrease) in kits in process at year-end	400	(500)	—	—
Financial data (in thousands)				
Sales	$138,000	$162,800	$(24,800)	(15.2)
Production costs of units sold:				
Direct material	32,000	40,000	(8,000)	(20.0)
Labor	41,700	53,000	(11,300)	(21.3)
Factory overhead	29,000	37,000	(8,000)	(21.6)
Costs of units sold	102,700	130,000	(27,300)	(21.0)
Other costs:				
Corporate charges for:				
Personnel services	228	210	18	8.6
Accounting services	425	440	(15)	(3.4)
Financing costs	300	525	(225)	(42.9)
Total other costs	953	1,175	(222)	(18.9)
Adjustments:				
Unreimbursed fire loss	—	52	(52)	(100.0)
Direct material losses due to improper storage	125	—	125	—
Total adjustments	125	52	73	(140.4)
Total deductions	103,778	131,227	(27,449)	(20.9)
Division profits	$ 34,222	$ 31,573	$ 2,649	8.4
Division investment	$ 92,000	$ 73,000	$ 19,000	26.0
Return on investment (Division profits ÷ Division investment)	37%	43%	(6)%	(14.0)

Required:

a. Discuss the value of the annual report presented for the Bell Division in evaluating the division and its management in terms of:
   (1) The accounting techniques employed in the measurement of division activities.
   (2) The manner of presentation.
   (3) The effectiveness with which it discloses differences and similarities between years.
   Use the information in the problem to illustrate your discussion.
b. Present specific recommendations you would make to the management of Darmen Corporation that would improve its accounting and financial reporting system.

(CMA adapted)

4–29. Cost allocation and decision making

At the end of 1984, the accounts showed that although the business as a whole was profitable, the sporting goods department of Pierre Wholesalers had shown a substantial loss. The income statement for the sporting goods department, shown here, reports on operations for 1984.

PIERRE WHOLESALERS COMPANY
Sporting Goods Department
Partial Income Statement for 1984

Sales revenue	$600,000	
Cost of goods sold	375,000	
Gross margin		$225,000
Costs:		
Direct labor and supervision	73,000	
Commissions of sales staff[a]	70,000	
Rent[b]	36,000	
State taxes[c]	8,000	
Insurance on inventory	14,000	
Administration and general office[d]	34,000	
Total costs		235,000
Loss before allocation of income taxes		$(10,000)

[a] All sales staff are compensated on straight commission at a uniform 6 percent of their sales.
[b] Rent is charged to departments on a square-foot basis. The company rents an entire building, and the sporting goods department occupies 15 percent of the building.
[c] Assessed annually on the basis of average inventory on hand each month.
[d] Allocated on basis of departmental sales as a fraction of total company sales.

Based on these results, management is considering closing the sporting goods department. Members of the management team agree that keeping the sporting goods department is not essential to maintaining good customer relations and supporting the rest of the company's business. Thus, eliminating the sporting goods department is expected to have no effect on the amount of business done by the other departments.

Required:

What action do you recommend to management of Pierre Wholesalers Company and why?

4–30. Allocation of fixed manufacturing overhead and decision making

Jenco, Inc., manufactures a combination fertilizer/weed-killer under the name Fertikil. This is the only product Jenco produces at the present time. Fertikil is sold nationwide through normal marketing channels to retail nurseries and garden stores.

Taylor Nursery plans to sell a similar fertilizer/weed-killer compound through its regional nursery chain under its own private label. Taylor has asked Jenco to submit a bid for a 25,000-pound order of the private brand compound. While the chemical composition of the Taylor compound differs from Fertikil, the manufacturing process is very similar.

The Taylor compound would be produced in 1,000-pound lots. Each lot would require 60 direct labor-hours and the following chemicals:

Chemicals	Quantity in pounds
CW-3	400
JX-6	300
MZ-8	200
BE-7	100

The first three chemicals (CW-3, JX-6, MZ-8) are all used in the production of Fertikil. BE-7 was used in a compound that Jenco has discontinued. This chemical was not sold or discarded because it does not deteriorate, and there have been adequate storage facilities. Jenco could sell BE-7 at the prevailing market price less $.10 per pound selling/handling expenses.

Jenco also has on hand a chemical called CN-5 which was manufactured for use in another product which is no longer produced. CN-5, which cannot be used in Fertikil, can be substituted for CW-3 on a one-for-one basis without affecting the quality of the Taylor compound. The quantity of CN-5 in inventory has a salvage value of $500.

Inventory and cost data for the chemicals which can be used to produce the Taylor compound are as follows:

Direct material	Pounds in inventory	Actual price per pound when purchased	Current market price per pound
CW-3	22,000	$ .80	$ .90
JX-6	5,000	.55	.60
MZ-8	8,000	1.40	1.60
BE-7	4,000	.60	.65
CN-5	5,500	.75	(salvage)

The current direct labor rate is $7 per hour. The manufacturing overhead rate is established at the beginning of the year and is applied consistently throughout the year using direct labor-hours (DLH) as the base. The predetermined overhead rate for the current year, based on a two-shift capacity of 400,000 total DLH with no overtime, is as follows:

Variable manufacturing overhead	$2.25 per DLH
Fixed manufacturing overhead	3.75
Combined rate	$6.00 per DLH

Jenco's production manager reports that the present equipment and facilities are adequate to manufacture the Taylor compound. However, Jenco is within 800 hours of its two-shift capacity this month before it must schedule overtime. If need be, the Taylor compound could be produced on regular time by shifting a portion of Fertikil production to overtime. Jenco's rate for overtime hours is one and one half the regular pay rate or $10.50 per hour. There is no allowance for any overtime premium in the manufacturing overhead rate.

Jenco's standard markup policy for new products is 25 percent of full manufacturing cost.

Required:

a. Assume Jenco, Inc., has decided to submit a bid for a 25,000-pound order of Taylor's new compound. The order must be delivered by the end of the current month. Taylor has indicated that this is a one-time order that will not be repeated.

Calculate the lowest price Jenco should bid for the order and not reduce its operating profit.

b. Without prejudice to your answer to Requirement *(a),* assume that Taylor Nursery plans to place regular orders for 25,000-pound lots of the new compound during the coming year. Jenco expects the demand for Fertikil to remain strong again in the coming year. Therefore, the recurring orders from Taylor will put Jenco over its two-shift capacity. However, production can be scheduled so that 60 percent of each Taylor order can be completed during regular hours or Fertikil production could be shifted temporarily to overtime so that the Taylor orders could be produced on regular time. Jenco's production manager has estimated that the prices of all chemicals will stabilize at the current market rates for the coming year and that all other manufacturing costs are expected to be maintained at the same rates or amounts.

Calculate the price Jenco, Inc., should quote Taylor Nursery for each 25,000-pound lot of the new compound assuming that there will be recurring orders during the coming year.

(CMA adapted)

4–31. Eastern Refineries, Ltd. (cost allocations in contract dispute)*

In 1977, American Oil Corporation and United Petroleum (two large integrated petroleum companies) entered into an agreement to construct and operate a petroleum fuels refinery in the Far East. A corporation named Eastern Refineries Limited was formed to operate the refinery. At the time the agreement was drawn up, American provided 70 percent of the capital while United provided 30 percent.

The sponsoring companies received capital stock in Eastern in proportion to the capital provided by them.

The Refinery A refinery processes crude oil through various heat, pressure, and chemical operations to extract as much gasoline from the crude as possible. Other products such as sulphur, kerosene, distillate fuels, and asphalt are produced as by-products. A certain quantity of fuel extracted from the crude is used to provide the heat necessary to operate the refinery as well as to provide heat and power for the refinery administrative and service support functions.

The original Eastern fuels refinery consisted of five principal processing units as diagrammed in Exhibit A. Crude oil was shipped to the refinery and piped to the crude splitter. This unit separates the crude oil into two products: (1) "overheads" which consist of the lighter fractions from the crude and (2) "bottoms" which contain the heavier fractions. Bottoms have relatively little energy content and are, therefore, usually sold as asphalt with very little further processing.

The overheads contain naphtha, a very light fraction; fuel oil, an intermediate product; and sulphur. The sulphur must be removed before the overheads can be

---

* CIPT Co. 1984.

processed into finished products. A desulphurization unit extracts the sulphur from the overheads. The remaining overhead flow is then distilled in the fractionator. The products with the lower boiling point (that is, the lighter fractions) vaporize as the temperature in the fractionator equals the boiling point of the respective fraction. The vaporized fractions are then cooled and return to their liquid state.

Naphtha, one of the lighter fractions, is used to make gasoline. With the use of heat and pressure in the reformer unit, naphtha is converted into gasoline. The remaining fractions are then directed to the catalytic cracker. This unit employs chemical and heat processes to convert some of the heavier materials from the fractionator into the more valuable naphthas. The naphthas from the catalytic cracker are then processed through the reformer in the same manner as the naphthas from the fractionator. The remaining output from the catalytic cracker is sold as distillate fuel products (such as kerosene, jet fuel, and heating oil).

Exhibit A (4–31)   **Flow of product through the eastern fuels refinery**

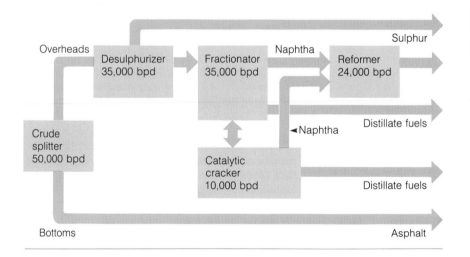

Refinery investment costs The costs to construct the initial refinery totaled $60 million. These initial costs were related to different units and support functions as follows (in thousands):

Unit	Investment cost
Crude splitter	$10,000
Desulphurizer	6,000
Fractionator	13,000
Catalytic cracker	15,000
Reformer	9,000
Administrative, support and other	7,000
Total	$60,000

The sponsoring companies entered into a contract for the processing of crude oil through the refinery. Each sponsor was permitted to utilize the refinery capacity to process crude oil in the same ratio as their equity investment. Thus, American was permitted to process 35,000 barrels per day (70 percent of 50,000 bpd capacity). The refinery did not take title to the crude it processed but rather acts as a processing service that receives the crude, processes it, and delivers the end products to each processor. To recover its costs, the refinery charges a processing fee to each of the sponsors. The processing fee consists of a variable charge based on the crude oil actually processed during a period plus a fixed charge based on the sponsor's share of refinery capacity.

Certain operating and cost data related to refinery processing during the years 1982 and 1983 are shown in Exhibit B.

Exhibit B (4–31)   **Summary operating and cost data (in thousands)**

	1982	1983
Crude processed (barrels):		
American	12,700	12,775
United	4,100	4,050
Total	16,800	16,825
Variable costs:		
American	$ 3,061	$ 2,965
United	1,008	954
Total	$ 4,069	$ 3,919
Fixed costs:		
American	$ 6,510	$ 6,447
United	2,790	2,763
Total	$ 9,300	$ 9,210
Products delivered:		
American:		
Gasoline (barrels)	6,126	6,103
Distillate Fuels (barrels)	2,780	2,759
Sulphur (tons)	16	16
Asphalt (barrels)	417	408
United:		
Gasoline (barrels)	2,362	2,376
Distillate Fuels (barrels)	591	597
Sulphur (tons)	7	8
Asphalt (barrels)	134	136

Expansion proposal American had been utilizing close to its share of capacity for several years. Indeed, to supply all of its customers in the market area served by this refinery, it was necessary to import finished distillate fuels from other, distant refining facilities. On occasion, to supply its customers, the company was required to purchase distillate fuels on the spot market.

As a result of market conditions, company management proposed that parts of the Eastern refinery be expanded. The expansion would provide additional distillate fuels for American's local needs and, in addition, would provide naphthas which could be transported to another American refinery for further processing. There would be a net reduction in the company's transportation costs from savings in distillate fuels transportation. As a result of this, and by eliminating the need to make spot market purchases, American management estimated it could obtain net after-tax cash savings of $2,500,000 in each of the estimated 20 years' life of the refinery expansion. The return on investment for the project was quite high because the project could utilize the tankage, wharf, and piping systems that were already in place at the refinery site.

According to the agreement between the sponsors of Eastern, any sponsor could request that the refinery company construct an expansion or modification to increase the maximum capacity of the refinery. If one of the sponsors proposed an expansion, it had to advise the other sponsor of the nature of the project, the estimated investment costs of the project together with an estimate of the fixed costs that would arise from the expansion. The other sponsor could elect to join in the project or could decline. If this sponsor declined participation, the expansion could still be conducted, but all of the investment costs would then be charged to the sponsor that proposed the expansion.

The agreement between the sponsors further provided that any such expansion would become a part of the refinery but that the sponsor who financed the expansion would receive the exclusive right to use the expansion. In addition, appropriate adjustments were to be made to the accounting procedures to reflect the existence of the expansion and to make certain that neither party was adversely affected by the expansion. The definition of "appropriate adjustments" was not specified in the agreement.

In 1982, American submitted a proposal to expand the crude splitter, desulphurizer, and fractionator. Summary data concerning the estimated incremental costs, investment required, and capacity expansions for the units are shown in Exhibit C. Information concerning American's estimated cash savings from the project were not disclosed because those data are proprietary.

Exhibit C (4–31)   **Proposal for expansion (dollars in thousands)**

Units to be expanded: Crude splitter
Desulphurizer
Fractionator

	Unit		
	Crude splitter	**Desulphurizer**	**Fractionator**
Incremental capacity	30,000 bpd	10,000 bpd	10,000 bpd
Projected costs of investment	$4,000	$800	$2,200
Projected incremental fixed costs (per year)	$ 300	$100	$ 150

After reviewing the proposal, United notified Eastern that it did not wish to participate. United objected to Eastern's construction of the proposed expansion on the grounds that they would suffer a reduced ability to compete with American should American obtain the proposed additional ability to produce distillate fuels.

American agreed to finance all of the costs of the expansion. The expansion was constructed for the investment costs shown in Exhibit C. The new units were placed in service at the start of 1984.

At the end of 1984 a report of operating and cost data was prepared. This report

Exhibit D (4–31)　　　　**Summary operating and cost data (in thousands)**

	1984
Crude processed (barrels):	
American	23,750
United	3,840
Total	27,590
Variable costs:	
American	$ 5,556
United	1,150
Total	$ 6,706
Fixed costs:	
American	$ 7,210
United	2,850
Total	$10,060
Products delivered:	
American:	
Gasoline (barrels)	6,128
Distillate (barrels)	6,320
Sulphur (tons)	25
Asphalt (barrels)	830
Naphthas (barrels)	3,975
United:	
Gasoline (barrels)	2,337
Distillate (barrels)	610
Sulphur (tons)	7
Asphalt (barrels)	133

is reproduced in Exhibit D. The fixed costs included $9,500,000 attributed to the original refinery plus $560,000 considered related to the expansion.

Upon receipt of this statement, United immediately objected to the allocation of fixed costs. In a memorandum to the board of directors of the refinery, United management stated:

> As you know, we objected to the expansion of this refinery because we believed such an expansion was not in the best interest of the refinery and would be harmful to our competitive position in the local market.
>
> Our agreement calls for the allocation of fixed costs on the basis of the maximum capacity of the Eastern refinery. Whereas we previously had 30 percent of that maximum capacity and paid 30 percent of the fixed costs, we now only have 18.75 percent of that capacity. However, you have charged us 28.3 percent of the total fixed costs. Our share of the fixed costs should not exceed 18.75 percent, and we request an immediate adjustment to our account.
>
> We note that under your allocation scheme our fixed costs per barrel amounted to $.74 this year, but the fixed costs allocated to American only amounted to $.30. This disparity clearly demonstrates that your method of allocation is incorrect.
>
> Finally, it is apparent that the wharf and related facilities that we helped construct is being utilized to a much greater extent now that American is processing a greater share of the refinery throughput. We believe that American should be required to reimburse us for the difference between our 30 percent investment in the wharf and our usage that this year only amounted to 13.9 percent.

We trust this matter can be resolved promptly at the next meeting of the board.

The chairman of the board of Eastern has directed this memorandum to the controller's office with the following comment:

The points raised in this letter will be discussed at next week's meeting of the board. It is imperative that we straighten this out at once. The points appear logical, and I hope that any error in your office can be corrected.

What is the amount by which they appear to have been overcharged? How would their method affect the economic viability of the expansion? What accounting principles did you use in arriving at your method of allocation?

Required:

The controller has asked you to prepare a draft of a response to the chairman of the board together with any supporting schedules or documents that would be required. Your response should address each of the points raised in the letter from United.

5

Job Costing

OBJECTIVES

To understand the way costs are assigned to goods or services in a job costing system.

This is the first of two chapters that present methods of accumulating and applying costs to products. Extending the overview of cost accumulation in Chapter 3, we discuss specific methods of calculating the cost of a unit produced. To make the analysis concrete, we focus on product costing methods when the units produced are called jobs.

Job costing versus process costing

There is a lot of variety in the nature of production activities just as in the accounting systems designed to record the activities. At the two ends of the spectrum are *job systems* and *process systems*. Each uses a different costing method. Job costing is used when units or batches of units are easily identifiable as separate units. In job costing, costs are traced to individual units or jobs, so each unit or job must be distinguishable from other units or jobs.

Organizations like print shops, custom home builders, and custom machines manufacturers use job systems. So do companies that produce on cost-based contracts, such as defense, highway, and dam construction contractors. Many nonprofit organizations use job costing to account for individual projects, such as rehabilitation or street repair programs. Some service organizations, such as CPA and consulting firms, use job costing to determine the cost of each job performed for each client.

For example, University Press recently published two books. One book was about 100 pages long; the other book was about 700 pages long. The 700-page book required more paper, more press time, and more editing than the 100-page book. An average cost per book (total costs divided by the two books published) would be meaningless; instead, each book is treated as a separate job to which costs of that job are assigned.

Job costing systems are also used when different product lines are manufactured. A furniture manufacturer may produce a batch of similar chairs, then a batch of tables, then a batch of chests, and so forth. Each batch can be treated as a job for accounting purposes.

Process systems are at the other end of the spectrum from job systems.

Process systems generally mass-produce a single, homogeneous product in a continuing process.

Process costing is used when identical units are produced through an *ongoing series* of *uniform production steps.* Process systems are used in manufacturing chemicals, grinding flour, refining oil, and assembling electronic calculators. Because individual units or batches of units are not readily identifiable, process costing systems differ from job costing systems. We discuss specific methods of accounting for process systems in Chapter 6.

Most organizations use job systems for some work and process systems for others. A house builder might use process costing for standardized homes with a particular floor plan. The same builder might use job costing when building a custom-designed home for a single customer. Honeywell, a high-technology company, uses process costing for most of their furnace thermostats and job costing for their specialized defense and space contracting work.

Accumulating costs for jobs

The accounting task in job costing is to measure the costs of producing each job. These costs are used for setting prices, bidding, controlling costs, and evaluating performance. Prospective customers almost always ask for estimates in advance, and they frequently award jobs on a competitive basis. Consequently, suppliers must be able to estimate costs very accurately if they are to compete and make a profit.

Source of data for job costing

In job operations, managers estimate and control costs by keeping separate records of costs for each job. The source document is some type of job cost record, called a job cost *sheet, card,* or *file.* Job costs files are used when accounting data are collected and stored by computer. Job costs sheets or cards are used when data are collected manually.

An example of a job cost record is shown in Illustration 5–1. This is a printout for Job No. 102 for Custom Manufacturing Company, which was started and finished in January. Note that this record shows detailed calculations for the direct materials, direct labor, and manufacturing overhead charged to the job.

As noted on the job cost record, the actual costs accumulated for the job are compared with estimated costs to evaluate employee performance in controlling costs and to provide information for negotiating for a price increase with the customer. The comparison of actual and estimated job costs also provides feedback on the accuracy of the cost estimation, which can be very important. In most job shops, the accuracy of job cost estimates can be the difference between a profitable organization and one that is bankrupt.

Illustration 5-1   **Job cost record**

Job number: 102   Customer: D. Bell
Date started: Jan 8   Date finished: Jan 26
Description: Manufacture custom equipment
              according to blueprint No. 48-102.

Assembly Department

| Direct Materials | | | Direct labor | | | Manufacturing overhead | |
Date	Requisition number	Cost	Date	Employee number	Cost	Date	Cost
Jan 8	102-A1	$23,000	Jan 8-14	88	$980	Jan 31	$52,000[a]
Jan 13	102-A2	$4,000	Jan 12-18	67	$720		
Jan 24	(return to storeroom)	($3,000)					

(Many more employees were added to this list. In total, $40,000 direct labor cost was incurred).

Total costs

Direct materials	$24,000	
Direct labor	$40,000	
Manufacturing overhead	$52,000[a]	$116,000

Transferred to finished goods inventory on   Jan 26

Total job costs:	Actual	Estimate
Direct materials	$24,000	$26,000
Direct labor	40,000	36,000
Manufacturing overhead	52,000[a]	46,800[a]
Total	$116,000	$108,800

Explain discrepancies between actual and estimated costs below:

Blueprint called for special parts that customer did not want. This reduced direct materials costs from the estimate. The replacement parts for the equipment required more finishing than the special parts did, so direct labor was higher than estimated. (As of January 31, we were negotiating with the customer for a price increase).

Note: Data and comments are assumed for purposes of this illustration.
[a] Actual manufacturing overhead was applied to the job after the end of January when actual overhead costs were known. Manufacturing overhead was estimated to be 130 percent of direct labor costs.

Recording job costs in the accounts

This section discusses methods of (1) obtaining materials, labor, and other items needed for production; and (2) accounting for the costs of production in job operations. Most companies with job operations follow these basic steps in accounting for job costs. We show the journal entries to record cost flows using Custom Manufacturing Company as an example.

Custom Manufacturing had one job in process on January 1—Job No. 101. After some minor work on Job No. 101, it was completed and shipped to a customer in January. The costs for the second job of Custom Manufacturing, Job No. 102, were presented on the job cost record in Illustration 5–1. Job No. 102 was started in January and moved to finished goods inventory on January 26. At January 31, it awaited shipment to a supplier. The third job, Job No. 103, was started in January and is still in process on January 31.

Beginning inventories Materials inventory on hand January 1 was $10,000. Beginning work in process inventory on January 1 was comprised of Job No. 101 which was in process on January 1.

The following costs had been incurred for Job No. 101 prior to January 1:

Direct materials	$14,000
Direct labor	22,000
Manufacturing overhead	25,000
Total	$61,000

Hence, the work in process inventory balance on January 1 was $61,000. There was no beginning finished goods inventory. These beginning balances are shown in Illustration 5–2.

Accounting for materials A company typically purchases, in advance, the materials that it commonly uses and stores them in materials inventory. Assume that in January, Custom Manufacturing purchased $60,000 of direct and indirect materials. This purchase was recorded as follows:

(1) Materials Inventory	60,000	
Accounts Payable		60,000

When the supplier sends an invoice or bill for the shipment, the payable is paid and recorded with a debit to Accounts Payable and a credit to Cash.

When materials are needed for a job or contract, the job supervisor or other authority requisitions them. The requested materials are removed from materials inventory and taken to the department where the job is being produced. The **materials requisition** form is next sent to the accounting department where it is the basis for the entry transferring materials from materials inventory to the job.

No materials were requisitioned for Job No. 101 in January. Job No.

Illustration 5–2
Cost flows through T-account—materials

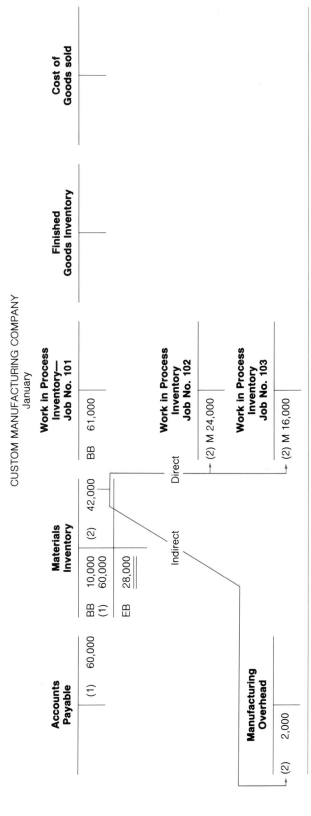

CUSTOM MANUFACTURING COMPANY
January

Note: BB = beginning balance; EB = ending balance; and M = materials. Numbers in parentheses correspond to journal entries presented in text.

102 had requisitions for materials totaling $27,000 and a return of $3,000 excess materials to materials inventory (see Illustration 5–1). The entries to record these transfers of direct materials are as follows:

(2a)	Work in Process Inventory—Job No. 102	27,000	
	Materials Inventory		27,000
	Per requisitions 102-A1 and 102-A2 (see Illustration 5–1).		
	Materials Inventory	3,000	
	Work in Process Inventory—Job No. 102		3,000
	Return of materials to materials inventory (see Illustration 5–1).		

Direct materials of $16,000 were requisitioned for Job No. 103, and recorded in entry 2b below.

Indirect materials   Materials inventory is also used for indirect materials and supplies that are not assigned to specific jobs but are charged to the Manufacturing Overhead account. For Custom Manufacturing, indirect materials requisitioned amounted to $2,000 in January, and recorded in entry 2b below.

(2b)	Work in Process Inventory—Job. No. 103	16,000	
	Manufacturing Overhead	2,000	
	Materials Inventory		18,000
	To record direct materials costs of $16,000 assigned to Job No. 103 and indirect materials costs of $2,000 charged to Manufacturing Overhead.		

Note that Illustration 5–2 presents the ending materials inventory balance, which can be found from the facts given above by solving the basic inventory formula:

$$\begin{array}{ccccccc} \text{Beginning} & + & \text{Transfers-} & = & \text{Transfers-} & + & \text{Ending} \\ \text{balance} & & \text{in} & & \text{out} & & \text{balance} \\ BB & + & TI & = & TO & + & EB \\ \$10,000 & + & \$60,000 & = & \$42,000 & + & EB \\ \$10,000 & + & \$60,000 & - & \$42,000 & = & EB \\ & & & & EB & = & \$28,000 \end{array}$$

Accounting for labor   Production workers are usually paid an hourly rate and account for their time each day on timecards, timesheets, or other records. The time record provides space for them to account for the hours spent on each job during the day. This time record is the basis for the company's payroll.

The total cost to the company includes gross pay plus the employer's share of social security taxes and employment taxes, employer's contribution to pension and insurance plans, and any other benefits that are paid for the employee by the company. In general, these costs range from about 15 percent to about 70 percent of the wage rate, depending on the fringe-benefit plans in effect at a company. It is common for companies to add these fringe-benefit costs to the wage rate to assign costs to jobs. For example, if a particular employee has a wage rate of $15 per hour and the additional costs to the employer for fringe benefits and payroll taxes are 30 percent of wages, then the cost of the employer's time to the company will be $19.50 per hour [= $15 + (.30 × $15)]. When we refer to a labor rate per hour in this book, we are referring to the cost to the company including an allowance for the employer's costs for fringe benefits and payroll taxes.

For example, the payroll department of Custom Manufacturing Company recorded accumulated costs of $110,000 for manufacturing employees. Of the $110,000 total, $80,000 was attributed to direct labor costs, including employee benefits and taxes. The $80,000 is charged to Work in Process Inventory and posted to the specific jobs worked on during the period. Based on timecards, Job No. 101 was charged with $10,000 in January, Job No. 102 with $40,000 as presented in the job cost record in Illustration 5–1, and Job No. 103 was charged with $30,000. The remaining $30,000 is indirect labor and charged to Manufacturing Overhead. This indirect labor includes the costs of supervisory, janitorial, maintenance, security, and timekeeping personnel, as well as idle time by direct labor employees and overtime premiums paid to direct laborers. The following entry was made to record labor costs in January.

(3)	Work in Process Inventory—Job No. 101	10,000	
	Work in Process Inventory—Job No. 102	40,000	
	Work in Process Inventory—Job No. 103	30,000	
	Manufacturing Overhead	30,000	
	Wages Payable (or Accrued Factory Payroll)		110,000
	To record direct labor costs of $80,000 assigned to jobs and indirect labor costs of $30,000 charged to Manufacturing Overhead.		

The flow of labor costs through the T-accounts is shown in Illustration 5–3.

Accounting for manufacturing overhead   Indirect manufacturing costs, including indirect materials and indirect labor, are usually accumulated in the Manufacturing Overhead account. Each department usually has its own manufacturing overhead summary account so each department manager can be held accountable for departmental overhead costs. This helps top management evaluate how well department managers control costs.

For example, in January, Custom Manufacturing had indirect materials costs of $2,000 and indirect labor costs of $30,000 charged to the Manufacturing Overhead account. Utilities and other costs were $46,000. An amortization of $7,000 representing the portion of prepaid taxes and insurance applicable to the period is included in the actual overhead, as is depreciation of $19,000. These items total $104,000 and represent the actual overhead incurred during the period. While these are called actual costs, some are allocated. For exam-

Illustration 5–3
Cost flows through T-accounts—labor costs

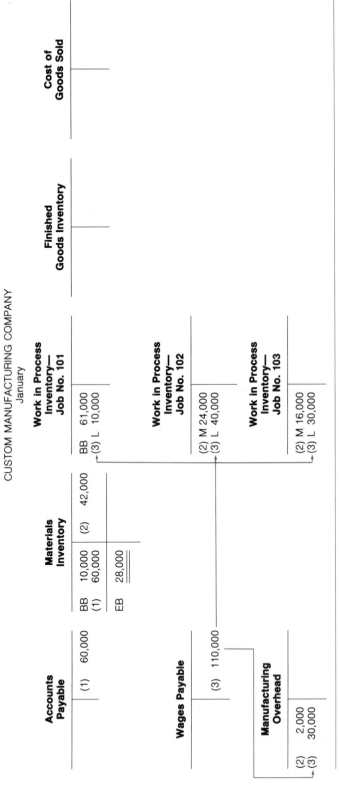

CUSTOM MANUFACTURING COMPANY
January

Accounts Payable

	(1) 60,000

Materials Inventory

BB	10,000	(2)	42,000
(1)	60,000		
EB	28,000		

Wages Payable

	(3) 110,000

Manufacturing Overhead

(2)	2,000	
(3)	30,000	

Work in Process Inventory— Job No. 101

BB	61,000	
(3) L	10,000	

Work in Process Inventory— Job No. 102

(2) M	24,000	
(3) L	40,000	

Work in Process Inventory— Job No. 103

(2) M	16,000	
(3) L	30,000	

Finished Goods Inventory

Cost of Goods Sold

Note: L = labor.

ple, depreciation is the cost of an asset allocated over time, and utilities at Custom are allocated between manufacturing and nonmanufacturing.

At the end of the month, Custom Manufacturing totals the actual manufacturing overhead costs incurred and applies them to jobs on the basis of direct labor costs incurred on each job. For January, the total manufacturing overhead costs incurred were $104,000 and direct labor costs were $80,000, so the overhead application rate was 130 percent of direct labor costs.

$$\frac{\text{Manufacturing overhead costs}}{\text{Direct labor costs}} = \frac{\$104,000}{\$80,000} = 130 \text{ percent}$$

The manufacturing overhead applied to each job in January was:

	Direct labor cost	Actual overhead rate	Manufacturing overhead applied
Job No. 101	$10,000	× 130 percent	= $ 13,000
Job No. 102	40,000	× 130	= 52,000
Job No. 103	30,000	× 130	= 39,000
Total	$80,000		$104,000

The journal entries to record manufacturing overhead were:

```
(4)  Manufacturing Overhead ..........................  72,000
         Accounts Payable ............................           46,000
         Prepaid Expenses ............................            7,000
         Accumulated Depreciation ....................           19,000
     To record actual manufacturing overhead costs other
     than indirect labor and indirect materials.

(5)  Work in Process Inventory—Job No. 101 .............  13,000
     Work in Process Inventory—Job No. 102 .............  52,000
     Work in Process Inventory—Job No. 103 .............  39,000
         Manufacturing Overhead ......................          104,000
     To record application of manufacturing overhead to jobs.
```

The flow of these costs through T-accounts is illustrated in Illustration 5–4.

Transfers to finished goods inventory When jobs are transferred out of production to the finished goods storage area, an entry is made transferring the costs of the jobs from the various work in process inventory accounts, to the Finished Goods Inventory account. For example, Custom Manufacturing completed Job No. 101 and Job No. 102 in January and transferred them to the Finished Goods Inventory account. The journal entry is:

Illustration 5–4
Cost flows through T-accounts—manufacturing overhead costs

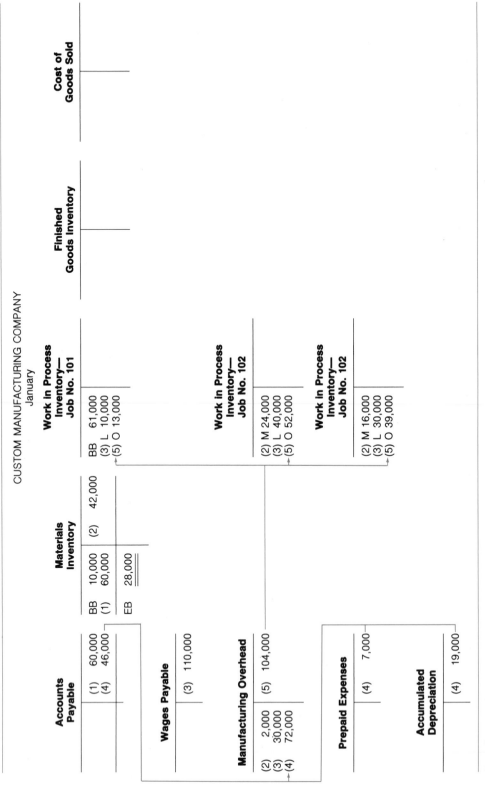

CUSTOM MANUFACTURING COMPANY
January

Accounts Payable

(1)	60,000
(4)	46,000

Wages Payable

(3)	110,000

Manufacturing Overhead

(2)	2,000	(5)	104,000
(3)	30,000		
(4)	72,000		

Prepaid Expenses

(4)	7,000

Accumulated Depreciation

(4)	19,000

Materials Inventory

BB	10,000	(2)	42,000
(1)	60,000		
EB	28,000		

Work in Process Inventory— Job No. 101

BB	61,000	
(3) L	10,000	
(5) O	13,000	

Work in Process Inventory— Job No. 102

(2) M	24,000	
(3) L	40,000	
(5) O	52,000	

Work in Process Inventory— Job No. 102

(2) M	16,000	
(3) L	30,000	
(5) O	39,000	

Finished Goods Inventory

Cost of Goods Sold

Note: O = manufacturing overhead.

(6) Finished Goods Inventory   200,000
            Work in Process Inventory—Job No. 101   84,000
            Work in Process Inventory—Job No. 102   116,000
        To transfer completed jobs to the finished goods storage
        area.

Note that the amount transferred includes costs incurred in both the current period and in previous periods. For example, the transfer for Job No. 101 includes both $61,000 from beginning work in process inventory and $23,000 of costs incurred in January to complete the job.

Transfer to cost of goods sold   When the goods are sold, they are transferred from the Finished Goods Inventory account to Cost of Goods Sold account. For example, Custom Manufacturing sold Job No. 101 in January for $120,000 on account. When the job was sold, the journal entry to record the cost of goods sold was:

(7) Cost of Goods Sold   84,000
            Finished Goods Inventory   84,000
        Accounts Receivable   120,000
            Sales Revenue   120,000

The flow of the costs of completed goods is shown in Illustration 5–5. The flow of all manufacturing costs, from the acquisition of materials to the final sale, are summarized in Illustrations 5–5 and 5–6.

Marketing and administrative costs

Marketing and administrative costs do not flow through Work in Process Inventory accounts. These costs are recorded in temporary accounts that are closed at the end of the accounting period. For example, Custom Manufacturing's marketing and administrative costs (all on account) were $10,000 in January. The entry to record these costs is:

Marketing and Administrative Costs   10,000
        Accounts Payable   10,000
    To record marketing and administrative costs incurred in January.

Completion of the operating cycle

Custom Manufacturing's income statement for January is shown in Illustration 5–7. The income statement and T-account flows can be related by cross-referencing many of the manufacturing costs from Illustrations 5–5 and 5–6. The temporary accounts (that is, income statement accounts) are usually closed only at the end of the year; but for illustrative purposes, we assume that Custom's accounts were closed for January to Retained Earnings. Assuming the jobs were sold for $120,000, the closing entry is:

Sales Revenue   120,000
        Cost of Goods Sold   84,000
        Marketing and Administrative Costs   10,000
        Retained Earnings   26,000
    To close temporary accounts.

Illustration 5–5
Cost flows through T-accounts—completed goods

CUSTOM MANUFACTURING COMPANY
January

Accounts Payable

(1)	60,000
(4)	46,000

Materials Inventory

BB	10,000	(2)	42,000
(1)	60,000		
EB	28,000		

Work in Process Inventory— Job No. 101

BB	61,000	(6)	84,000
(3) L	10,000		
(5) O	13,000		
	–0–		

Finished Goods Inventory

BB	–0–	(7)	84,000 → (7)
(6)	200,000		
EB	116,000		

Cost of Goods sold

84,000	

Wages Payable

(3)	110,000

Work in Process Inventory— Job No. 102

(2) M	24,000	(6)	116,000
(3) L	40,000		
(5) O	52,000		
	–0–		

Manufacturing Overhead

(2)	2,000	(5)	104,000
(3)	30,000		
(4)	72,000		

Work in Process Inventory— Job No. 103

(2) M	16,000	
(3) L	30,000	
(5) O	39,000	
EB	85,000	

Prepaid Expenses

(4)	7,000

Accumulated Depreciation

(4)	19,000

Illustration 5–6
Summary of cost flows

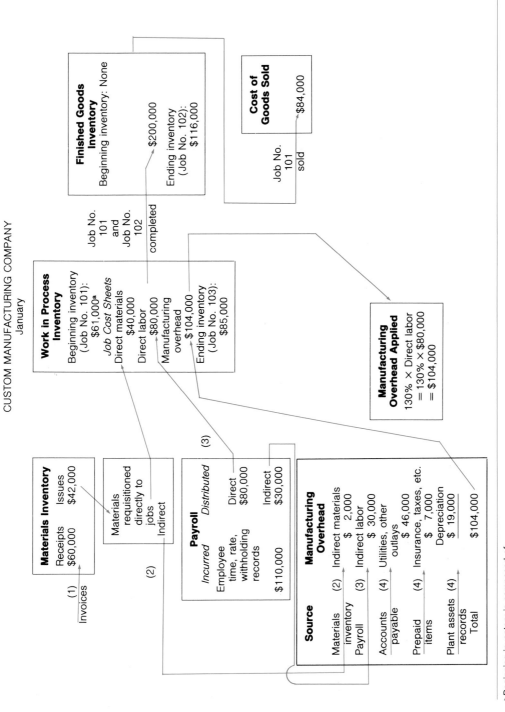

CUSTOM MANUFACTURING COMPANY
January

a Beginning inventory is composed of:

Direct material	$14,000
Direct labor	22,000
Manufacturing overhead	25,000
Total	$61,000

Illustration 5–7

CUSTOM MANUFACTURING COMPANY
Income Statement
For the Month Ended January 31

Sales revenue	$120,000
Cost of goods sold (see statement below) ..	84,000
Gross margin	36,000
Less marketing and administrative costs ...	10,000
Operating profit	$ 26,000

Cost of Goods Manufactured and Sold Statement
For the Month Ended January 31

Beginning work in process inventory, January 1			$ 61,000
Manufacturing costs during the month:			
Direct materials:			
Beginning inventory, January 1	$10,000		
Add purchases	60,000		
Materials available	70,000		
Less ending inventory, January 31	28,000		
Total materials used	42,000		
Indirect materials used	2,000		
Direct materials put into process		$ 40,000	
Direct labor		80,000	
Manufacturing overhead		104,000	
Total manufacturing costs incurred during the month			224,000[a]
Total costs of work in process during the month			285,000
Less work in process inventory, January 31 .			85,000
Cost of goods manufactured during the period			200,000[b]
Beginning finished goods inventory, January 1			–0–
Less ending finished goods inventory January 31			116,000
Cost of goods manufactured and sold			$ 84,000[c]

[a] This amount equals the total debits made to Work in Process Inventory in January.
[b] This amount equals the total debits to Finished Goods Inventory in January.
[c] This amount equals the total credits to Finished Goods Inventory in January.

Job costing in service organizations

Job operations are also found in service organizations, such as engineering, consulting, and accounting firms. The job costing procedure is basically the same in both service and manufacturing organizations, except that service firms use no direct materials.

Example Custom Engineering Company is an engineering consulting firm. Custom *Engineering* has the same cost data for January as Custom *Manufacturing,* but Custom Engineering *has no direct materials.* In addition, Custom Engineering has $2,000 in supplies in place of the $2,000 in indirect materials that Custom Manufacturing had. These supplies are purchased on account and shown on the debit side of the Service Overhead account.

Illustration 5–8
Cost flows through T-accounts—completed work

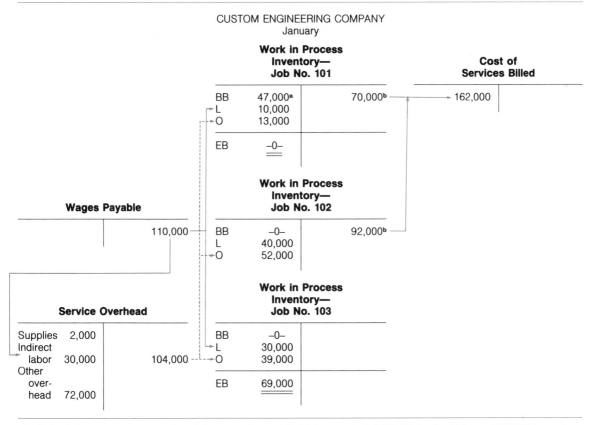

CUSTOM ENGINEERING COMPANY
January

[a] Beginning balance represents contract work in process but not billed. It is comprised of $22,000 for direct labor and $25,000 for service overhead incurred in previous period on Job No. 101.

[b] Job Nos. 101 and 102 were completed and billed in January.

Illustration 5–8 illustrates job costing in a service organization. It parallels Illustration 5–5 which shows cost flows for a manufacturing organization, except that direct materials costs have been deleted and some minor changes have been made in account titles. Also, we assume that the January 1 cost balance for Job No. 101 was $22,000 in direct labor and $25,000 in service overhead, for a total of $47,000. Job No. 102, which was completed in January, is assumed to have been billed in January.

Cost flows with multiple production departments

If a company had only one department, a single Manufacturing Overhead account and a single Work in Process Inventory account would suffice. But many manufacturing companies have several departments through which jobs pass in sequence. In each department, the job may accumulate direct material and direct labor costs, as well as manufacturing overhead. Thus, additions will be made to the job cost sheet as the order progresses from department to department.

Under such conditions, it is customary to establish a Work in Process Inventory account and a Manufacturing Overhead account for each department. As the job enters the first department in the process, it will be charged with some amount for direct materials. This will be recorded on the job cost record sheet and will also be charged to the department's Work in Process Inventory account. Time spent by direct laborers on the job in Department 1 and manufacturing overhead will also be charged on the job cost sheet and to Work in Process Inventory—Department 1.

When Department 1 has finished its work on an order, the job is forwarded to Department 2. At that time, an entry is made transferring the costs accumulated to date on the job cost sheet from Work in Process Inventory—Department 1 to Work in Process Inventory—Department 2. Costs transferred from previous manufacturing departments are called prior department costs.

Within Department 2, additional charges for materials, labor, and manufacturing overhead may be added. These costs are the responsibility of Department 2's manager. They will be recorded on the job cost sheet and charged to Work in Process Inventory—Department 2. When Department 2 has completed its work on a job, the total charges on the job to that point are transferred from Work in Process Inventory—Department 2 to the next department. If there are no subsequent departments, the total costs are transferred to Finished Goods Inventory. If jobs are sent directly from manufacturing to the customer, there may be no need for a Finished Goods Inventory account and the costs may be transferred directly to Cost of Goods Sold.

Example Assume the Custom Manufacturing Company described above has two production departments: cutting and assembly. All jobs pass through both departments. Assume January costs were incurred as follows in each department:

	Department		
	Cutting	**Assembly**	**Total**
Direct materials:			
Job No. 102	$21,000	$ 3,000	$24,000
Job No. 103	16,000	–0–	16,000
Direct labor:			
Job No. 101	–0–	10,000	10,000
Job No. 102	12,000	28,000	40,000
Job No. 103	30,000	–0–	30,000
Manufacturing overhead:			
Job No. 101	–0–	13,000	13,000
Job No. 102	15,600	36,400	52,000
Job No. 103	39,000	–0–	39,000

On January 1, Job No. 101 was in the assembly department. It was sold by the end of the month. On January 31, Job No. 103 was still in the cutting department.

Illustration 5–9 shows the flow of costs through the accounts when there are two production departments. (Illustration 5–9 is the same as Illustration 5–5, except Illustration 5–9 uses two departments whereas one department was assumed in Illustration 5–5.) Entry (6) in Illustration 5–9 shows the transfer of costs from the cutting department to assembly department.

This example assumes one overhead rate applies to both departments in the company; that is a company-wide overhead rate, 130% of direct labor costs, is used for both departments. An alternative is to use a separate overhead rate for each department, known as department overhead rates.

Use of predetermined overhead rates

In the Custom Manufacturing Company example, actual manufacturing overhead was applied to jobs after the end of the month; therefore, there was no difference between actual and applied overhead.

In reality, manufacturing overhead is often applied to jobs *before* the actual overhead is known. When this is done, a predetermined overhead rate is used to apply manufacturing overhead to jobs. This rate is usually established before the year in which it is to be used, and used for the entire year. This normalizes the application of manufacturing overhead to jobs; hence, the resulting product costs are called normal costs. The following chart shows that the only difference between *normal costing* and *actual costing,* which is the method used in the Custom Manufacturing example, is the rate used to apply overhead to jobs and other products.

	Product Costing method	
	Actual	**Normal**
Direct materials	Actual cost	Actual cost
Direct labor	Actual cost	Actual cost
Manufacturing overhead	Actual rate	Predetermined rate
	times	times
	Actual allocation base	Actual allocation base

Example Deluxe Manufacturing Company is exactly like Custom Manufacturing Company in every respect, except Deluxe Manufacturing uses an annual predetermined rate for applying manufacturing overhead to jobs. The predetermined rate is based on estimated direct labor costs.

Illustration 5–9
Cost flows through T-accounts—multiple departments

CUSTOM MANUFACTURING COMPANY

Accounts Payable

(1)	60,000
(4)	46,000

Materials Inventory

BB	10,000	(2)	42,000
(1)	60,000		
EB	28,000		

Wages Payable

(3)	110,000

Manufacturing Overhead—Cutting Department

(5a)	54,600	(5b)	54,600

Work in Process Inventory—Cutting Department— Job No. 102

BB	–0–	(6)	48,600
(2) M	21,000		
(3) L	12,000		
(5b) O	15,600		
EB	–0–		

Work in Process Inventory—Assembly Department Job No. 101

BB	61,000	(7)	84,000
(3) L	10,000		
(5c) O	13,000		
EB	–0–		

Work in Process Inventory—Assembly Department— Job No. 102

BB	–0–	(7)	116,000
(6) P	48,600		
(2) M	3,000		
(3) L	28,000		
(5c) O	36,400		
EB	–0–		

Finished Goods Inventory

(7)	200,000	(8)	84,000.

Cost of Goods Sold

(8)	84,000

Manufacturing Overhead	
(2) 2,000	(5a) 104,000
(3) 30,000	
(4) 72,000	

Manufacturing Overhead—Assembly Department	
(5a) 49,400	(5c) 49,400

Work in Process Inventory—Cutting Department— Job No. 103

BB	–0–
(2) M	16,000
(3) L	30,000
(5b) O	39,000
EB	85,000

Prepaid Expenses

(4) 7,000	

Accumulated Depreciation

(4) 19,000	

Note: P = costs of work done in prior departments; M = materials; L = labor; and O = manufacturing overhead charged to jobs during January.

Numbers in parenthese refer to journal entries to record the following transactions (transactions would not necessarily be in the following order):

(1) Purchase materials.
(2) Charge materials to jobs and to manufacturing overhead.
(3) Charge labor to jobs and to manufacturing overhead.
(4) Record additional overhead.
(5a), (5b), and (5c) Allocate overhead to departments, then to jobs.
(6) Transfer cost of work done on Job No. 102 in cutting department to assembly department.
(7) Transfer Job Nos. 101 and 102 to Finished Goods Inventory.
(8) Ship Job No. 101 to customer.

$$\text{Predetermined rate} = \frac{\text{Estimated manufacturing overhead for the year}}{\text{Estimated direct labor costs for the year}}$$

$$= \frac{\$1,200,000}{\$1,000,000}$$

$$= 120 \text{ percent}$$

Here is how Deluxe Manufacturing used its predetermined rate to charge manufacturing overhead to individual jobs. (Compare these with the manufacturing overhead charged to jobs at Custom Manufacturing in Illustration 5–5.)

	Actual direct labor costs	Predetermined overhead rate	Manufacturing overhead applied
Job number 101	$10,000	× 120%	= $12,000
Job number 102	40,000	× 120	= 48,000
Job number 103	30,000	× 120	= 36,000
Total	$80,000	× 120	= $96,000

By using a predetermined rate, Deluxe Manufacturing normalizes the overhead applied to jobs. Over the course of time, manufacturing overhead costs can be quite erratic. Preventive maintenance costs are often higher in months when activity is low. Utility costs in cold climates are higher in winter than in summer, and the opposite is true in warm climates. Idle time due to the installation of new equipment increases manufacturing overhead costs in some months. If Deluxe Manufacturing used actual costing, a job in a high-cost month would be assigned more overhead than an identical job in a low-cost month.

In addition, a company might not know its actual overhead costs until after the close of a fiscal year. Use of normal costs enables management to prepare financial statements based on good estimates of product costs in the interim.

Illustration 5–10 compares the flow of costs when manufacturing overhead is applied using actual costing and normal costing. Two accounts may be used to separate actual and applied overhead. At the end of an accounting period, the actual and applied accounts are closed. Usually this is not done until the end of the year when the books are closed. For illustrative purposes, however, we assume that Custom Manufacturing and Deluxe Manufacturing close their books for the month of January. The actual account is left with a zero balance under actual costing because all of the actual overhead is debited to Work in Process Inventory and credited to the Manufacturing Overhead account.

Under normal costing, however, the amount debited to the actual account (the actual manufacturing overhead) is unlikely to equal the amount applied. The reasons for this are discussed later in this chapter. The difference between

Illustration 5–10   **Comparison of manufacturing overhead cost flows using actual and normal costing methods**

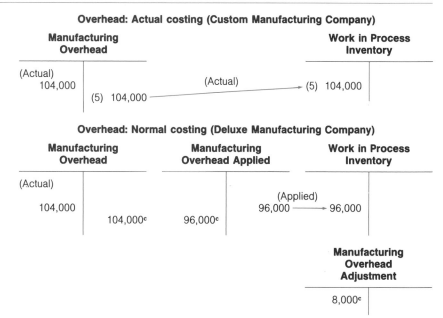

Overhead: Actual costing (Custom Manufacturing Company)

Manufacturing Overhead		Work in Process Inventory	
(Actual) 104,000		(5) 104,000	
	(5) 104,000		

Overhead: Normal costing (Deluxe Manufacturing Company)

Manufacturing Overhead		Manufacturing Overhead Applied		Work in Process Inventory	
(Actual) 104,000			96,000ᶜ	(Applied) 96,000 → 96,000	
	104,000ᶜ				

Manufacturing Overhead Adjustment	
8,000ᶜ	

ᶜ Refers to closing entry

the actual and applied manufacturing overhead is called a variance and is debited or credited to a *Manufacturing Overhead Adjustment* account. For example, the entry to account for overhead for Deluxe Manufacturing is:

Manufacturing Overhead Applied	96,000	
Manufacturing Overhead Adjustment	8,000	
Manufacturing Overhead		104,000

Underapplied overhead occurs when actual overhead exceeds applied overhead as for Deluxe Manufacturing. Underapplied overhead is shown as a *debit* to the Manufacturing Overhead Adjustment account. Overapplied overhead occurs when actual overhead is less than applied overhead. Overapplied overhead is shown as a *credit* to Manufacturing Overhead Adjustment.

Disposition of the manufacturing overhead adjustment   The manufacturing overhead adjustment is either (1) prorated to Work in Process Inventory, Finished Goods Inventory, and Cost of Goods Sold; or (2) assigned in total to Cost of Goods Sold.

If the adjustment is prorated to Work in Process Inventory, Finished Goods Inventory, and Cost of Goods Sold, then each job is, in effect, adjusted from the applied basis to approximate actual cost. For Deluxe Manufacturing, the status and cost of each job *before* prorating the overhead adjustment is shown at the top of Illustration 5–11. The adjustment will be assigned so that each account and job bears a share of the $8,000 manufacturing overhead adjustment proportional to the overhead applied to the account during the month as shown at the bottom of Illustration 5–11.

The following entry is made to record the adjustment:

Cost of Goods Sold	1,000	
Finished Goods Inventory	4,000	
Work-in-Process Inventory	3,000	
Manufacturing Overhead Adjustment		8,000

The adjusted balances of the Work in Process Inventory, Finished Goods Inventory, and Cost of Goods Sold accounts are exactly the same as if the actual costing method were used. (Note that Deluxe's adjusted account balances are the same as those for Custom Manufacturing shown in Illustration 5–5.)

Illustration 5–11
Proration of manufacturing overhead adjustment

DELUXE MANUFACTURING COMPANY
Cost of Jobs before Manufacturing Overhead Adjustment

Job no.	Beginning inventory	Direct materials	Direct labor	Manufacturing[a] overhead applied in January	Costs charged to jobs total	Status of job at end of month
101	$61,000	–0–	$10,000	$12,000	$ 83,000	Cost of Goods Sold
102	–0–	$24,000	40,000	48,000	112,000	Finished Goods Inventory
103	–0–	16,000	30,000	36,000	82,000	Work in Process Inventory
	$61,000	$40,000	$80,000	$96,000	$277,000	

Manufacturing Overhead Adjustment

Account	Manufacturing overhead applied in January	Percent of total overhead applied in January	Adjustment	Total costs assigned to jobs after prorating overhead adjustment[c]
Cost of Goods Sold	$12,000	12.5[b]	$1,000[c]	$ 84,000[d]
Finished Goods Inventory	48,000	50.0	4,000	116,000
Work in Process Inventory	36,000	37.5	3,000	85,000
	$96,000	100	$8,000	$285,000

[a] Applied at 120 percent of direct labor costs.

[b] 12.5% = $12,000 ÷ $96,000; 50.0% = $48,000 ÷ $96,000; 37.5% = $36,000 ÷ $96,000.

[c] Multiply the adjustment, which is $8,000, times the appropriate percent for each account. For example, $1,000 = 12.5% × $8,000.

[d] Add the adjustment to the account total before the overhead adjustment.

Many companies do not prorate the manufacturing overhead adjustment to inventories and Cost of Goods Sold; instead they transfer the entire adjustment to Cost of Goods Sold for both internal and external reporting. In a company with many kinds of products and inventories, proration can be complicated. If the amounts to be prorated are immaterial relative to inventory values and net income for external reporting, it may not be necessary to prorate for external reporting. For internal, managerial purposes, the overhead adjustment is usually not prorated because management focuses on the actual manufacturing costs incurred rather than on the amounts applied. Knowledge about the causes of differences between actual costs and the costs that were applied to jobs may, in some circumstances, suggest that management may need to revise overhead rates, impose new cost control procedures or take other actions.

The proration of the overhead adjustment to inventories and Cost of Goods Sold does not necessarily make the inventory values more accurate. Furthermore, any difference between actual and applied overhead will eventually be expensed (or contra-expensed) for external reporting purposes. Prorating the overhead adjustment merely defers expensing the portion allocated to inventories until those inventories are sold.

For external reporting, therefore, the difference between prorating the adjustment and assigning it in total to Cost of Goods Sold is a matter of timing. For managerial purposes, one must ask how useful it is to revalue work in process and finished goods inventories to actual cost. A large overhead adjustment may affect some cost control, performance evaluation, pricing, and other decisions, but if the adjustments are small, proration is probably not worthwhile.

Interim reporting   When normal costing is used and the overhead accounts are not closed monthly, there are two ways of reporting the balance in the Manufacturing Overhead Adjustment account on financial statements. It can either be (1) reported on the income statement, for example, as an adjustment to Cost of Goods Sold; or (2) carried on the balance sheet as an adjustment to inventory or as a deferred debit or credit. The first option treats the adjustment as a period cost, the second as a product cost. Management and accountants select the option they prefer and use it continuously for interim reporting consistency.

Sources of variance between actual and applied manufacturing overhead

Actual and applied manufacturing overhead are usually unequal when the normal costing method is used because normal costing uses *predetermined* instead of actual overhead rates. There are two basic reasons why actual and applied rates may not be equal.

The numerator reason   Actual overhead costs may turn out to be higher or lower than originally estimated due to unforeseen fluctuations in particular overhead costs. This affects the numerator of the formula used to calculate the predetermined overhead rate.

For example, assume the predetermined overhead rate for an organization was based on the assumption that manufacturing overhead would be $10,000 and direct labor costs would be $5,000. For illustrative purposes, we assume that all manufacturing overhead is a fixed cost, so it should remain the same regardless of activity levels.

$$\text{Predetermined rate} = \frac{\text{Estimated manufacturing overhead}}{\text{Estimated direct labor costs}}$$

$$= \frac{\$10,000}{\$5,000}$$

$$= 200 \text{ percent of direct labor costs}$$

Suppose the actual direct labor cost for the period was $5,000, as estimated, but the actual overhead turned out to be $12,000 instead of $10,000 (that is, the actual fixed costs exceeded the estimated fixed costs by $2,000). Consequently, manufacturing overhead would be $2,000 underapplied, as shown by the following T-accounts:

Manufacturing Overhead		Manufacturing Overhead Applied	
(Actual)			(Applied) 200% × 5,000 = 10,000
12,000			

Applied overhead does not equal actual overhead because overhead costs were higher than estimated in proportion to the direct labor costs.

The denominator reason   Actual volume of activity may turn out to be higher or lower than originally estimated. Fluctuations in the items in the denominator of the formula used to calculate the predetermined overhead rate may cause actual and applied overhead to differ.

For example, assume that as in the previous example, a company has a predetermined overhead rate of 200 percent based on estimates of $10,000 for overhead and $5,000 for direct labor costs. The actual overhead is $10,000 as estimated, but actual direct labor cost is only $3,750 because labor activity was 25 percent lower than estimated. As shown by the following T-accounts, actual overhead is $2,500 greater than applied:

Manufacturing Overhead		Manufacturing Overhead Applied	
(Actual)			(Applied) 200% × 3,750 = 7,500
10,000			

In this case, overhead was underapplied because direct labor costs were lower than estimated in proportion to overhead. Actual and applied overhead will be unequal whenever some (or all) manufacturing overhead costs are fixed and the estimate in the denominator base (for example, direct labor costs) does not equal the actual amount.

In later chapters we shall see that these **variances,** that is, differences, between actual and applied overhead may provide information useful for performance evaluation.

Summary

Most methods of producing goods and services can be classified into two general categories: job and process. Each requires a different costing system. Job costing is used when products are easily identifiable as individual units or batches of identical units. In job costing, costs are traced to each unit or job. Construction contractors, print shops, and consulting firms are likely to use job costing methods. Process costing is used by organizations that produce identical units through an ongoing series of uniform production steps. Oil refineries and chemical companies would use process costing methods. In process costing, costs for an accounting period are accumulated by department and spread evenly (or averaged) over all units produced in the period.

Job costing may require more recordkeeping than process costing, which may make it more expensive to use. But many organizations find that benefits of knowing the cost of each job justify the added cost of operating a job costing system. Job costing data can be used in bidding and pricing, controlling costs, and evaluating performance.

Our discussion of cost flows in the chapter is summarized by the flow of cost diagrams in Illustrations 5–5, 5–8, and 5–9.

The source document for job costing is the job cost record (also called a job cost sheet or card). Each job has a separate record on which its costs are accumulated. These records are used to value inventory for external financial reporting, for feedback on the accuracy of job cost estimations, and for evaluating how well costs were controlled on each job.

Manufacturing overhead is often applied to jobs before the actual overhead is known. A predetermined overhead rate is used instead of the actual overhead rate. This is known as normal costing. A comparison of actual costing and normal costing is presented below:

	Costing method	
	Actual	**Normal**
Direct materials	Actual cost	Actual cost
Direct labor	Actual cost	Actual cost
Manufacturing overhead	Actual rate times	Predetermined rate times
	Actual allocation base	Actual allocation base

When predetermined overhead rates are used, actual overhead rarely equals applied overhead. Overapplied or underapplied overhead may be charged in total to Cost of Goods Sold or prorated to goods in inventory and goods sold.

Some service organizations use job costing. Their methods often parallel those used in manufacturing, except service organizations do not have direct materials costs.

Terms and concepts

The following terms and concepts should be familiar to you after reading this chapter.

Actual costs	**Normal costing method**
Actual costing method	**Numerator reason**
Allocation basis	**Overhead adjustment**
Applied overhead	**Overapplied overhead**
Denominator reason	**Predetermined overhead rate**
Job costing	**Process costing**
Job cost record	**Prorated overhead adjustment**
Jobs	**Source document**
Materials requisition	**Underapplied overhead**
Normal costs	**Variance**

Self-study problem

Information on the Farawell Industrial Equipment Company, a job order company specializing in custom-built industrial equipment has been somewhat sketchy. Management wishes to determine various unknown balances and has hired you for assistance. The following data are available:

Account balances	January 1, 1984	December 31, 1984
Materials inventory	$205,000	$?
Work in process inventory	68,550	?
Finished goods inventory	31,000	65,000ª
Manufacturing overhead (actual)	–0–	247,000
Accounts payable—production materials	16,000	24,000
Cost of goods sold	–0–	769,650ª

ª Before prorating the overhead adjustment.

Accounts payable are for production materials, only. The Work in Process Inventory balances are supported by data in job cost records which relate to jobs in process at the balance sheet dates. On January 1, 1984, there were two jobs in process, as follows:

Date started	Job number	Direct materials	Direct labor
October 15, 1983	206	$14,200	$ 8,400
December 17, 1983	217	6,500	9,000
		$20,700	$17,400

On December 31, 1984, there was only one job in process, Job No. 372. However, the only available information on the job was the accumulated direct labor costs of $12,000 and direct materials of $21,900. Overhead is applied to jobs as a predetermined percentage of direct labor costs. The following additional information is available to you about events in 1984:

Payments made to suppliers in 1984	$342,000
Indirect materials issued from inventory	14,000
Direct labor costs incurred	140,000
Direct materials costs transferred to Finished Goods Inventory this period	403,800
Current period applied overhead in ending Finished Goods Inventory, December 31, 1984	30,000

Required:

a. T-accounts for the flow of costs detailed in this problem.

b. Materials purchased.

c. Direct materials issued to work in process inventory. (Hint: Consider how much was transferred out of work in process to finished goods.)

d. Materials Inventory account balance, December 31, 1984.

e. Overhead application rate.

f. Overhead applied to Work in Process Inventory account during 1984.

g. Over- or underapplied overhead.

h. Cost of the goods transferred to Finished Goods Inventory account during 1984.

i. Work in Process Inventory account, December 31, 1984.

j. Applied overhead in ending Work in Process Inventory account, December 31, 1984.

k. Proration of over- or underapplied overhead to Work in Process Inventory account, Finished Goods Inventory account and Cost of Goods sold account.

l. Balance in ending Work in Process Inventory account, December 31, 1984, after prorating overhead to inventory accounts and Cost of Goods Sold account.

Solution to self-study problem

a. We recommend setting up T-accounts before solving the problem, then recording the amounts in the accounts as you solve for each of the items below. Completed T-accounts are shown in Exhibit A.

For each of the items below, we use the basic accounting equation (also known as the basic inventory formula):

$$\text{Beginning balance} + \text{Transfers-in} = \text{Transfers-out} + \text{Ending balance}$$
$$\text{BB} + \text{TI} = \text{TO} + \text{EB}$$

Data given in the problem are indicated with an asterisk (*).

b. To find materials purchased, use the Accounts Payable account:

BB + TI (increases in accounts payable are materials purchased)
$$= \text{TO} + \text{EB}$$
$$\text{TI} = \text{TO} + \text{EB} - \text{BB}$$

Materials purchased (TI) = Payments to suppliers (TO) + Accounts payable, December 31, 1984 (EB) − Accounts Payable, January 1, 1984 (BB)

$$= \$342{,}000^* + \$24{,}000^* - \$16{,}000^*$$
$$= \$350{,}000$$

c. The Materials Inventory account has two unknowns; so to find direct materials issued, find the amount of direct materials transferred out of work in process inventory + Amount in ending work in process inventory (issued this period) − Amount in beginning work in process inventory (issued in a previous period).

Direct materials issued = Direct materials costs transferred to finished goods inventory + Direct materials in ending work in process inventory − Direct materials in beginning work in process inventory

$$= \$403{,}800^* + \$21{,}900^* - \$20{,}700^*$$
$$= \$405{,}000$$

d. To find Materials Inventory account balance on December 31, 1984, use the following formula:

$$BB + TI = TO + EB$$
$$BB + TI - TO = EB$$

Materials inventory, December 31, 1984 (EB) = Materials inventory, January 1, 1984 (BB) + Purchases (TI) − Direct materials issued (TO) − Indirect materials issued (TO)

$$= \$205{,}000^* + \$350{,}000^* - \$405{,}000^* - \$14{,}000^*$$
$$= \$136{,}000$$

e. Overhead application rate:

Work in process inventory, January 1, 1984 = Direct materials + Direct labor + Overhead applied

$$\$68{,}550^* = \$20{,}700^* + \$17{,}400^* + \text{Overhead applied}$$

Overhead applied = $\$68{,}550 - \$20{,}700 - \$17{,}400$
$$= \$30{,}450$$

Overhead application rate = Overhead applied ÷ Direct labor
$$= \$30{,}450 \div \$17{,}400^*$$
$$= 175\%$$

f. Overhead applied to work in process inventory = Direct labor costs incurred × Overhead application rate

$$= \$140{,}000^* \times 175\%$$
$$= \$245{,}000$$

g. Over- or underapplied overhead = Overhead applied − Actual manufacturing overhead

$$= \$245{,}000 - \$247{,}000^*$$
$$= -\$2{,}000 \qquad \text{(underapplied)}$$

h. To find the cost of goods transferred to the Finished Goods Inventory account, find TI to finished goods inventory:

$$BB + TI = TO + EB$$
$$TI = TO + EB - BB$$

Cost of goods transferred to finished goods inventory (TI) = Cost of goods sold (TO) + Finished goods, December 31, 1984 (EB) − Finished goods, January 1, 1984 (BB)

$$= 769,650* + \$65,000* - \$31,000*$$
$$= 803,650$$

i. To find the ending work in process inventory balance, use the Work in Process Inventory account:

$$BB + TI = TO + EB$$
$$BB + TI - TO = EB$$

Work in process inventory, December 31, 1984 (EB) = Work in process inventory, January 1, 1984 (BB) + Direct materials (TI) + Direct labor (TI) + Overhead applied (TI) − Cost of goods transferred to finished goods inventory (TO)

$$= \$68,550* + \$405,000 + \$140,000*$$
$$+ \$245,000 - \$803,650$$
$$= \$54,900$$

j. Applied overhead in ending work in process inventory = Direct labor in ending work in process inventory × 175%

$$= \$12,000* \times 175\%$$
$$= \$21,000$$

k. Prorationing of underapplied overhead:

$$\frac{\text{Total}}{\text{overhead applied}} = \frac{\text{Overhead applied}}{\text{in ending}}_{\text{work-in-process}}_{\text{inventory}} + \frac{\text{Overhead applied}}{\text{in finished}}_{\text{goods inventory}} + \frac{\text{Overhead applied}}{\text{to cost of}}_{\text{goods sold}}$$

$$\$245,000 = \$21,000 + \$30,000* + X$$
$$X = \$245,000 - \$21,000 - \$30,000$$
$$= \$194,000$$

Prorationing to:	Proportion of total (rounded)	Prorated amount
Ending work in process inventory	$21,000 ÷ $245,000 = 8.6%	$ 172 = .086 × $2,000
Ending finished goods inventory	$30,000 ÷ $245,000 = 12.2%	244 = .122 × $2,000
Cost of goods sold	$194,000 ÷ $245,000 = 79.2%	1,584 = .792 × $2,000
		$2,000

l. Balance in work in process inventory after prorationing = Work in process inventory, December 31, 1984 + Underapplied overhead prorated to work in process inventory

$$= \$54,900 + \$172$$
$$= \$55,072$$

Exhibit A   **Self-study problem—T-accounts**

Materials Inventory

BB 1/1	205,000*		14,000*
(b)	350,000	(c)	405,000
(d) EB 12/31	136,000		

Work in Process Inventory

BB 1/1	68,550*	(h)	803,650
(c)	405,000		
Given	140,000*		
(f)	245,000		
(i) EB 12/31	54,900		
(k) adj.	172		
(l) EB 12/31 after adj.	55,072		

Finished Goods Inventory

BB 1/1	31,000*		769,650*
(h)	803,650		
EB 12/ 31	65,000*		
(k) adj.	244		
EB 12/31 after adj.	65,244		

Cost of Goods Sold

	769,650*	
(k) adj.	1,584	

Accounts Payable

	342,000*	BB 1/1	16,000*
		(b)	350,000
		EB 12/31	24,000*

Manufacturing Overhead

EB 12/31	247,000*	247,000c

Manufacturing Overhead Applied

	245,000c	(f)	245,000

Manufacturing Overhead Adjustment

	2,000c	(k)	2,000

* Given in the problem.
The symbol for closing entry is c.

Questions

5–1. What are the characteristics of companies that are likely to be using a job order cost system?

5–2. What is the function of the *job cost record?*

5–3. What is the difference between the *Manufacturing Overhead* account and the *Manufacturing Overhead Applied* account?

5–4. On the first day on the job, a member of the management training program remarked: "The whole procedure of applying overhead and then spending a lot of time adjusting the inventory and cost of goods sold accounts back to the actual numbers looks like a complex solution to a simple problem. Why not simply charge the actual overhead to production and be done with it?" How would you reply to this comment?

5–5. The assignment of costs to departments and then to jobs is carried out partly for control purposes. Explain.

5–6. What methods, documents, and approvals are used to control materials inventories?

5–7. Why is control of materials important from a *managerial planning* perspective?

5–8. Labor fringe benefits and similar costs associated with the direct labor may be considered part of direct labor or part of manufacturing overhead. What are the justifications for each alternative treatment?

5–9. How is job costing in service organizations (for example, consulting firms) different from job costing in manufacturing organizations?

5–10. What are the *normal costs* of a product?

5–11. Why might differences between actual and applied manufacturing overhead not be prorated to inventories?

Exercises

5–12. Compute job order costs

On January 1, there were two jobs in process at the Bondview Printing Company. Details of the jobs are:

Job no.	Direct materials	Direct labor
A-15	$87	$32
A-38	16	42

Materials inventory at January 1 totaled $460, and $58 in materials were purchased during the month. A requisition for $8 in supplies was filled. On January 1, finished goods inventory consisted of two jobs: Job No. A-07 costing $196 and Job No. A-21 with a cost of $79. Both these jobs were sold during the month.

Also during January, Job Nos. A-15 and A-38 were completed. To complete Job No. A-15 required an additional $34 in direct labor. The completion costs for Job No. A-38 included $54 in direct materials and $100 in direct labor.

Job No. A-40 was started during the period but was not finished. A total of $157 of direct materials were brought from the storeroom during the period, and total direct labor costs during the month amounted to $204. Overhead has been applied at 150 percent of direct labor costs, and this relationship has remained fairly stable throughout the past few years.

Required:

Determine costs for Job Nos. A-15 and A-38 and balances in the January 31 inventory accounts.

5-13. Prepare journal entries for job order costs

Refer to the information in Exercise 5–12. Prepare the journal entries that would be required to represent the transactions discussed in the problem. In addition, prepare the journal entry to prorate any over- or underapplied overhead to the various inventory accounts if the overhead incurred for the month totaled $300.

5-14. Prepare journal entries for job order costs

The following transactions occurred at the March Production Company, a job order custom manufacturer:

1. Purchased $40,000 in materials.
2. Issued $2,000 in supplies from the materials inventory.
3. Purchased materials with a cost of $31,600.
4. Paid for the materials purchased in 1.
5. Issued $34,000 in materials to the production department.
6. Incurred wage costs of $56,000 which were debited to a temporary account called Payroll. Of this amount, $18,000 was withheld for payroll taxes and other similar liabilities. The remainder was paid in cash to the employees. (See transactions 7 and 8 for additional information about payroll.)
7. Recognized $28,000 in fringe benefit costs that were incurred as a result of the wages paid in 6. This $28,000 was debited to the temporary account called Payroll. Of this amount, $12,000 represents taxes payable while the remainder represents other liabilities for fringe benefits.
8. Analyzed the wage accounts and determined that 60 percent was direct labor, 30 percent indirect manufacturing labor, and 10 percent administrative and selling costs.
9. Paid cash for utilities, power, equipment maintenance, and other miscellaneous items for the manufacturing plant. The total amount was $43,200.
10. Paid $53,500 cash for new equipment.
11. Applied overhead on the basis of 175 percent of direct labor costs.
12. Recognized depreciation on manufacturing property, plant and equipment of $21,000.

Required:

a. Prepare journal entries to record the above transactions
b. The following balances appeared in the accounts of March Manufacturing Company:

	Beginning	**Ending**
Materials inventory	$74,100	
Work in process inventory	16,500	
Finished goods inventory	83,000	$ 66,400
Cost of goods sold		131,700

Prepare T-accounts to show the flow of costs during the period.

5-15. Under- or overapplied overhead

Refer to the information in Exercise 5–14 to answer the following questions:

a. What is the amount of over- or underapplied overhead?
b. If the current applied overhead in each of the inventory accounts and the Cost of Goods Sold account is as follows:

Work in process inventory	$ 8,820
Finished goods inventory	22,050
Cost of goods sold	57,330

Prepare a schedule to show the proration of the overhead.

5-16. Analyze accounting treatment of labor costs

Management of Absolute Limit Frame Company has been using a job order cost system and has been charging direct labor into production using the base labor rate only. All fringe benefits and payroll taxes are charged to overhead and included in the overhead allocation rate. For a current year, total direct labor costs charged to production amounted to $320,000. Overhead costs were applied at the rate of 200 percent of direct labor. Included in the overhead is $128,000 in fringe benefits related to direct labor wages. There are no overhead variances.

Information is also supplied on two jobs:

Job no.	Direct labor	Direct materials
379	$21,000	$16,000
396	17,000	26,000

Required:

a. What difference would it make if the direct labor fringe benefits were included in the direct labor charge rather than in applied overhead? Use the two illustrated jobs to demonstrate your conclusion.

b. Would your answer in (a) be changed if overhead were applied on the basis of 200 percent of direct materials cost, assuming direct materials costs were $320,000? Use the example job data to demonstrate your conclusions.

c. Briefly state the significance of your observations.

5-17. Estimate hours worked from overhead data

Terne Corporation had projected its overhead costs to total $660,000. Of this amount, it was estimated that $240,000 would represent fixed costs and the remainder would be variable. Direct labor was estimated to total 30,000 hours during the coming year, and the direct labor-hours would be used as a basis for the application of overhead. During the year, all overhead costs were exactly as planned and the direct labor costs per unit produced were also exactly as planned. However, there was $8,000 in overapplied overhead.

Required:

How many direct labor-hours were worked during the period? Show computations. (Hint: Compute the variable and fixed overhead rates per hour.)

5-18. Cost flows: T-accounts

Partially completed T-accounts and additional information for the XYZ Company for the month of March are presented below:

Materials Inventory

BB 3/1	1,000		
	4,000	3,200	

Work in Process Inventory

BB 3/1	2,000		
Direct labor	2,400		

Finished Goods Inventory

BB 3/1	3,000		
	6,000	4,000	

Cost of Goods Sold

Manufacturing Overhead

2,200	

Manufacturing Overhead Applied

Additional information

1. Labor wage rate was $12 per hour.
2. Manufacturing overhead is applied at $8 per direct labor-hour.
3. During the month, sales revenue was $8,000 and selling and administrative costs were $1,600.
4. The accounting period is one month long.

Required:

a. What was the amount of direct materials issued to production during March?
b. What was the amount of manufacturing overhead applied to products during March?
c. What was the cost of products completed during March?
d. What was the balance of the Work in Process Inventory account at the end of March?
e. What was the manufacturing overhead underapplied or overapplied during March?
f. What was the operating profit for March?

Problems and cases

5-19. Identify the missing items in the following set of T-accounts

Materials Inventory

BB 10/1	8,000		
	(a)	4,300	
EB 10/31	9,700	(b)	

Finished Goods Inventory

BB 10/1	14,200		
			(f)
EB 10/31	(g)		

Work in Process Inventory

BB 10/1	22,300		
	180,500		
	121,000		
	94,000	(e)	
EB 10/31	17,700		

Cost of Goods Sold

402,800	

Manufacturing Overhead Applied

	(d)

Wages Payable

		BB 10/1	124,300
162,000			(c)
			36,200
		EB 10/31	119,500

Manufacturing Overhead

121,000	
4,300	
36,200	
31,600	
3,200	

Accounts Payable—Materials Suppliers

	100,000

Accumulated Depreciation— Manufacturing Property, Plant, and Equipment

	BB 10/1	204,100
		(h)
	EB 10/31	235,700

Prepaid Insurance

BB 10/1	24,300	
		(i)
EB 10/31	21,100	

Required:

Compute the missing amounts indicated by the letters *(a)* through *(i)*.

5–20. Job order costing—prepare financial statements

The Helper Corporation manufactures one product and accounts for costs by a job order cost system. You have obtained the following information for the year ended December 31, 1984, from the corporation's books and records:

1. Total manufacturing cost added during 1984 (sometimes called cost to manufacture) was $1,000,000 based on actual direct material, actual direct labor, and applied manufacturing overhead on the basis of actual direct labor dollars.
2. Cost of goods manufactured was $970,000, also based on actual direct material, actual direct labor, and applied manufacturing overhead.
3. Manufacturing overhead was applied to work in process at 75 percent of direct labor dollars. Applied manufacturing overhead for the year was 27 percent of the total manufacturing cost added during 1984.
4. Beginning work in process inventory, January 1, was 80 percent of ending work in process inventory, December 31.

Required:

Prepare a formal cost of goods manufactured statement for the year ended December 31, 1984, for Helper Corporation. Show actual direct material used, actual direct labor, and applied manufacturing overhead. Show supporting computations in good form.

(CPA adapted)

5–21. Analyze overhead cost allocations in cost-plus contracting

Fargo Testing Corporation performs destructive testing to determine certain characteristics of industrial products. A recent test required burning plastics-based wall covering materials to assess the quantities and chemical composition of the smoke. Another job required applying stress to several chairs to determine whether they would meet load standards. Job control sheets are prepared to record the results of the tests as well as to maintain a record of costs. Customers are billed for jobs on a cost-plus basis.

Job cost data for the two jobs mentioned above are as follows:

	Job No. 486 wall covering	**Job No. 633 chair testing**
Direct materials	$21	$–0–
Direct labor	16 (1 hour)	64 (4 hours)
Overhead	24	96

Overhead is applied on the basis of company wide estimates of total overhead divided by total estimated direct labor costs for the company. The data used to prepare the current overhead estimates were prepared from the budget plan for this year. Selected data from that plan for two of the company's departments are:

Estimated cost item	**Burning chamber**	**Load testing area**
Variable overhead	$72,000	$ 8,000
Fixed overhead	64,000	84,000
Direct labor	34,000	118,000

During the current year, the company has noted a decrease in the jobs submitted which require use of the load testing area. Checking with other testing laboratories, management learned that the other companies were offering somewhat lower rates for this service. As a result, management has asked the controller's office to determine why the costs in the load testing section are out of line with the competition and to determine what the company overhead rate will have to be if, as expected, direct labor costs in the load testing area decrease to $61,000. Except for the impact of the volume change, no other costs are expected to change. The controller has asked for your help in preparing the cost estimates and in reviewing the costs in the load testing area to see where costs could be reduced.

Required:

Demonstrate your ingenuity in your reply to the controller. To illustrate your recommendations, show the impact on the recorded costs of Job Nos. 486 and 633.

5–22. Calculating departmental costs per patient day— overhead allocation.

The following data are available from the records of the Millvale General Hospital (in thousands):

Administrators' salaries	$ 250
Nursing staff salaries	1,400
Physicians	2,300
Other staff	800
Supplies, linens, similar materials	600
Other overhead	3,250

All costs have been allocated to the three departments in the hospital on the basis of patient days. A patient day is defined as one patient staying overnight in a department for one day. The departments and the patient days for each are listed below as they appear in the current year's budget:

	Department		
	Medical/ surgical	**Maternity**	**Psychiatric**
Thousands of patient days	36	12	14

Management of the hospital wishes to exercise better control over the costs for various services as well as to set rates for each type of service based on the hospital's costs of providing that service. To assist in this planning effort, information has been gathered on the proportion of various staff hours in the three departments as well as on the usage of supplies by each department. A report submitted to the controller showed this information as follows:

	Department		
	Medical/ surgical	**Maternity**	**Psychiatric**
Nursing staff	50%	30%	20%
Physicians	70	10	20
Other staff	40	20	40
Supplies, linens, similar materials	50	30	20

The hospital administrator would like to see how the different charged rates could be computed. Charge rates may be expressed in terms of patient days. Overhead costs that cannot be allocated directly may be allocated on the basis of physician time.

Required:

Prepare a report showing the costs per patient day *(a)* for the three departments combined and *(b)* for each department. Briefly explain why the cost per patient day is different in each department.

5–23. Comprehensive flow of job order costs

Pulsar Light Equipment Company assembles light and sound equipment for installation in various entertainment facilities. Each installation is designed according to the acoustical properties of the facility and the type of entertainment that management of the facility wishes to emphasize. An inventory of materials and equipment is on hand at all times so that installation may be started as quickly as possible. Special equipment is ordered as required. On September 1, the Materials and Equipment Inventory account had a balance of $48,000. A Work in Process Inventory account is maintained to record costs of installations not yet complete. There were two such jobs and details of the costs are as follows:

	Job No. B-46 Wheels and Spokes Country Music Hall	Job No. D-81 Stars Theater
Materials and equipment	$32,000	$95,000
Technician labor	6,500	9,700
Overhead (applied)	4,800	14,250

Overhead has been applied on the basis of the costs of materials and equipment installed. A 15 percent rate has been used, although the company has not conducted any studies that would determine the reasonableness of the allocation of overhead to jobs.

During September, two new installations were begun. Additional work was carried out on Job Nos. B-46 and D-81 with the latter job completed and billed to the Stars Theater. Details on the costs incurred on jobs this period are as follows:

	Job No. B-46	Job No. D-81	Job No. B-47	Job No. A-16
Materials and equipment	$3,200	$14,200	$17,000	$6,200
Technician labor (on account)	1,800	1,200	3,100	900

In addition to these costs, other events of the period included:

1. $25,000 payment received on Job No. B-43 delivered to customer in August.
2. Purchased materials and equipment for $18,700.
3. Billed Stars Theater $175,000 and received payment for $100,000 of that amount.
4. Payroll for indirect labor personnel totaled $1,300.
5. Issued supplies and incidental installation materials for current jobs. The cost of these items was $310.
6. Recorded overhead and advertising costs for the installation operation as follows (all cash except equipment depreciation):

Property taxes	$1,100
Showroom and storage area rental	1,350
Truck and delivery cost	640
Advertising and promotion campaign	1,200
Electrical inspections	400
Telephone and other miscellaneous	650
Equipment depreciation	900

Required:

a. Journal entries to record the flow of costs for the installation operation during September.
b. Amount of over- or underapplied overhead for the month.
c. Amount of over- or underapplied overhead to be prorated to Job No. D-81.
d. Inventory balances after prorating over- or underapplied overhead.

5-24. Job order costs for contracting

M-SP Industries, Inc., had a contract to produce a special order machine for the River Transport Company. To produce the machine, three processes were required and are labeled A, B, and C for convenience.

Information on the costs incurred in the three departments is as follows:

	Dept. A	Dept. B	Dept. C
Materials used	$6,200	$7,000	–0–
Direct labor cost	3,500	6,000	$8,000
Direct labor-hours	1,000	1,500	2,000
Machine-hours	100	50	500
Overhead allocation basis	$3 per direct labor-hour	150% direct labor cost	$14 per machine-hour

Management has become somewhat concerned about the complexities of this allocation method and about the impact of different cost allocations on the computed job costs. The estimated total overhead in each department and the estimated total overhead bases for this year are as follows:

	Dept. A	Dept. B	Dept. C
Estimated overhead	$240,000	$330,000	$140,000
Direct labor cost	280,000	220,000	120,000
Direct labor-hours	80,000	55,000	30,000
Machine-hours	10,000	1,500	10,000

One member of management suggested that a plantwide overhead rate be established based on direct labor cost. Another stated: "I understand from reading up on cost accounting that plantwide rates are not very useful. Rather, the rate should be departmentalized, but let's use one basis for each department."

The manufacturing vice president concluded the discussion by stating: "I'm not quite sure what the best approach would be in this circumstance. Let's ask the controller to give us some information on the alternatives and the effect on costs. Perhaps the River Transport job could be used as an example. I'll ask what that job would cost if a plantwide rate had been used on each basis. In addition, we can determine what that job cost would have been if departmentalized rates had been used. We can compare those costs to the ones that were actually charged to the job and discuss this further next week."

Required:

Prepare the report for the manufacturing vice president. Show computations.

5-25. Prorate overhead differences

Fermi Processing Corporation has a special order coating process that operates in two departments: surface preparation and application. Jobs enter the surface preparation department where chemical treatments clean the surface and prepare it chemically for the application of coatings. The coating takes place in the application department under carefully controlled conditions. The following cost and activity estimates were prepared for this year:

	Surface preparation	Application
Overhead costs	$190,000	$350,000
Direct materials	24,000	785,000
Direct labor	58,900	56,000
Machine-hours	16,000	40,000

During the year, work was performed on a number of job orders. Overhead in the surface preparation department was applied on the basis of $11.875 per machine-hour while overhead in the application department was applied at the rate of 44.59 percent of direct materials costs.

At the end of the year, the following balances appeared in the inventory accounts and Cost of Goods Sold account:

Work in Process Inventory—Surface Preparation:	
Direct materials	$ 3,720
Direct labor	2,945
Overhead applied	2,375
Work in Process Inventory—Application:	
Direct materials	28,000
Direct labor	2,800
Overhead applied	12,485
Finished Goods Inventory:	
Direct materials—surface preparation	2,800
—application	61,250
Direct labor—surface preparation	6,479
—application	11,760
Overhead applied—surface preparation	20,900
—application	27,311
Cost of Goods Sold:	
From last year's production	139,263
Direct materials—surface preparation	17,480
—application	695,750
Direct labor—surface preparation	49,476
—application	41,440
Overhead applied and prorated—surface preparation	150,100
—application	321,450

The overhead applied and prorated in the cost of Goods Sold account represents the applied overhead plus a debit or credit for any under- or overapplied overhead.

Required:

Determine the entry that would be required to prorate the over- or underapplied overhead assuming that the differences between actual overhead and applied overhead were due strictly to differences in the spending for the overhead items. (Volume was as planned.)

5–26. Find missing data in T-Accounts

The following T-accounts are to be completed with the missing information. Additional data appear after the accounts.

Materials Inventory		**Work in Process Inventory**	
EB 9/30 28,200		BB 9/1 16,300	
		Direct	
		Materials 43,100	

Finished Goods Inventory		**Cost of Goods Sold**	
EB 9/30 50,500			

Manufacturing Overhead		**Manufacturing Overhead Applied**	
(Actual)			132,000

Wages Payable		**Sales Revenue**	
			362,700

1. Materials of $56,800 were purchased during the month and the balance in the inventory account increased by $5,500.
2. Overhead is applied at the rate of 150 percent of direct labor cost.
3. Sales are billed at 80 percent over the normal cost of the jobs to which the sales relate.
4. The balance in Finished Goods Inventory decreased by $14,300 during the month.
5. Total credits to the Wages Payable account amounted to $101,000. All credits in this account are related to the manufacturing plant.
6. Factory depreciation totaled $24,100.
7. Overhead was underapplied by $12,540. All other charges for overhead incurred required payment in cash. Underapplied overhead is to be prorated.
8. The company has decided to allocate 25 percent of underapplied overhead to Work in Process Inventory, 15% to Finished Goods Inventory, and the balance to Cost of Goods Sold. Balances shown in T-accounts are before proration.

Required:

Complete the T-accounts.

5–27. Reconstruct missing data

Disaster struck the only manufacturing plant of the Complete Transaction Equipment Corporation on December 1. All the work in process inventory has been destroyed. A few records were salvaged from the wreckage and from a set of records located at the company's headquarters office. The loss is fully insured if adequate documentation can be supplied to the insurance company. The insurance company has also stated that it will pay the "normal" cost of the lost inventory since company policy states that seasonal and other nondirect costs should be apportioned to inventories on an annualized basis. Hence, the value of work in process inventory is made up of direct materials, direct labor, and applied overhead.

The following information about the plant appears on the October financial statements at the company's headquarters:

Materials inventory, October 31	$ 49,000
Work in process inventory, October 31	86,200
Finished goods inventory, October 31	32,000
Cost of goods sold through October 31	348,600
Accounts payable, materials suppliers on October 31	21,600
Manufacturing overhead through October 31	184,900
Payroll payable on October 31	–0–
Withholding and other payroll liabilities on October 31	9,700
Overhead applied through October 31	179,600

A quick count of the inventories on hand November 30 shows:

Materials inventory	$43,000
Work in process inventory	–0–
Finished goods inventory	37,500

The accounts payable clerk tells you that there are outstanding bills to suppliers of $50,100 and that cash payments of $37,900 have been made during the month to these suppliers.

The payroll clerk informs you that the payroll costs last month included $82,400 for the manufacturing section and that $14,700 of this was indirect.

At the end of November, the following balances were available from the main office:

Manufacturing overhead through November 30	$217,000
Cost of goods sold through November 30	396,600

You recall that each month there is only one requisition for indirect materials. **Among the fragments of paper you located the following pieces:**

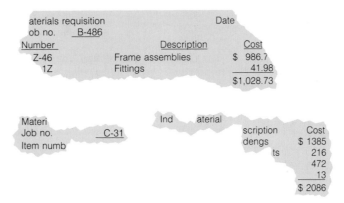

aterials requisition   Date
ob no.   B-486

Number	Description	Cost
Z-46	Frame assemblies	$ 986.7
1Z	Fittings	41.98
		$1,028.73

Materi
Job no.   C-31
Item numb

Ind   aterial

	scription	Cost
	dengs	$ 1385
	ts	216
		472
		13
		$ 2086

You also learn that during the month the overhead was overapplied by $1,200.

Required:

Determine the "normal" cost of the work in process inventory lost in the disaster.

5–28. Overhead assignment

Tastee-Treat Company prepares, packages, and distributes six frozen vegetables in two different size containers. The different vegetables and different sizes are prepared in large batches. The company employs an actual cost job order costing system. Manufacturing overhead is assigned to batches by a predetermined rate on the basis of direct labor-hours. The manufacturing overhead costs incurred by the company during two recent years (adjusted for changes using current prices and wage rates) are as follows:

	Year 1	Year 2
Direct labor-hours worked	2,760,000	2,160,000
Manufacturing overhead costs incurred (adjusted for changes in current prices and wage rates):		
Indirect labor	$11,040,000	$8,640,000
Employee benefits	4,140,000	3,240,000
Supplies	2,760,000	2,160,000
Power	2,208,000	1,728,000
Heat and light	552,000	552,000
Supervision	2,865,000	2,625,000
Depreciation	7,930,000	7,930,000
Property taxes and insurance	3,005,000	3,005,000
Total overhead costs	$34,500,000	$29,880,000

Required:
    a. Tastee-Treat Company expects to operate at a 2,300,000 direct labor-hour level of activity in Year 4. Using the data from two recent years, calculate fixed and variable overhead rates Tastee-Treat should employ to assign manufacturing overhead to its products. (Hint: The variable rate can be found by comparing the change in costs to the change in hours.)

    b. Explain how the company can use the information it developed for calculating the overhead rate for:

      (1) Evaluation of product pricing decisions.

      (2) Cost control evaluation.

      (3) Development of budgets.

(CMA adapted)

5–29. Incomplete data—job costing

    The Quik Copy Publishing Company is a rapidly growing company that has not been profitable despite its increases in sales. You have been called in as a consultant to find ways of improving the situation. You believe the problem results from poor cost control and inaccurate cost estimation on jobs. To gather data for your investigation, you turn to the accounting system, and find it almost nonexistent. However, you piece together the following information for April:

1. Production:
    a. Completed Job No. 101.
    b. Started and completed Job No. 102.
    c. Started Job No. 103.
2. Inventory values:
    a. Work in process inventory

March 31:	Job No. 101—Direct materials	$1,000
	—labor	480 hours @ $10 = $4,800
April 30:	Job No. 103—Direct materials	$800
	—labor	520 hours @ $10 = $5,200

    b. Each job in work in process inventory was exactly one-half done in labor-hours; however, *all* of the direct materials necessary to do the entire job were charged to each job as soon as the job was started.

    c. There were no direct materials inventories or finished goods inventories at either March 31 or April 30.

3. Actual manufacturing overhead, $10,000.
4. Cost of goods sold (before adjustment for over- underapplied overhead):

Job number 101:	Materials	$ 1,000
	Labor	?
	Overhead	?
	Total	$15,400
Job number 102:	Materials	?
	Labor	?
	Overhead	?
	Total	?

5. Overhead was applied to jobs using a predetermined rate per labor-hour. The same rate had been used since the company began operations. Over- underapplied

overhead is written off each month as an expense (not charged to Cost of Goods Sold).

6. All direct materials were purchased for cash and charged directly to Work in Process Inventory at the point of purchase. Direct materials purchased in April amounted to $2,300.

7. Direct labor costs charged to jobs in April amounted to $16,000. All labor costs were the same per hour for April for all laborers.

Required:

Trace the flow of costs through the system highlighting the following figures:

a. The cost elements (that is, material, labor, and overhead) of cost of goods sold, *before* adjustment for over- underapplied overhead, for *each job sold*.

b. The value of each cost element (that is, material, labor, and overhead) for each job in work in process inventory at April 30.

c. Over- underapplied overhead for April.

5–30. E-Z Printing Company (job costing for pricing and performance evaluation)*

Deborah Carr, founder and president of E-Z Printing Company was worried. The company was doing more business than ever before—sales were at an annual rate of about $625,000 a year, but operating profit had decreased slightly during recent months and the ratio of income to sales had dropped sharply. Ms. Carr wondered what had gone wrong and what she could do about it. She called in her chief (and only) accountant, Gene Hockman, and asked him to find out what was happening.

E-Z Printing did a general printing business on a customer order basis. Ms. Carr set the price to be charged for each job. When possible, she waited until the work was done and then quoted a price equal to 140 percent of the cost of the paper stock used, plus $25 for each labor-hour. Straight-time wage rates in the past, adjusted for recent wage rate increases, had averaged about $8 an hour, and this formula seemed to provide an adequate margin to cover overhead costs and provide a good profit. No attempt was made to modify these prices for seasonality, even though business was usually slow in the winter months and heavy in the spring and fall.

Most of E-Z Printing's work was done on the basis of predetermined contract prices. In bidding on these jobs, Ms. Carr applied her standard pricing formula to her own estimates of the amount of labor and paper stock the job would require. She prided herself on her ability to make these estimates, but she sometimes quoted a price that was higher or lower than the formula price, depending on her judgment of the market situation.

The company's production procedures were fairly simple. When a customer's order was received, it was assigned a production order number and a production order was issued. The material to be printed, known as the customer's copy, was given to a copy editor who indicated on the copy the sizes and styles of type that should be used. The editor sometimes made changes in the copy, usually after telephoning the customer to discuss the changes.

Once the customer's material had been copy-edited, it was sent to the composing room, where it was set in type. A proof copy was printed by hand and returned to the copy editor, who checked the printed copy against the original. Any errors in the proof were indicated in the margin, and the marked proof was sent to the customer for approval. At this point, the customer might decide to make changes in the copy,

---

* © 1968 by l'Institut pour l'Etude des Methodes de Direction de l'Enterprise (IMEDE), Lausanne, Switzerland, under the title Tipografia Stanca S.p.A. This case was revised and updated in 1984.

and these changes, as well as corrections of type-setting errors, were made as soon as the corrected proof was returned to the composing room.

In some cases, a second proof was sent to the customer for his/her approval, but at E-Z Printing most orders were sent to the pressroom as soon as the customer's corrections had been made and the second proof had been approved by the copy editor.

At this point, the order was ready for production on one of the presses in the pressroom. Printing instructions were contained in the production order, which specified the particular press to be used; the number of copies to be printed; the color, size, style, weight, and finish of the stock or paper to be used; and similar details. Copies were then printed, bound, and packaged for delivery to the customer.

An order could take as little as one day in the copy-editing and composing-room stages or as long as several weeks. Printing, binding, and packaging seldom took more than two days except on very large production runs of multipage booklets.

E-Z Printing's before-tax profit had fluctuated between 13 and 15 percent of net sales. The interim profit report for the first half of 1984 came as a shock to Ms. Carr. Although volume was slightly greater than in the first half of 1983, profit was down to 8.8 percent of sales, an all-time low. The comparison, with all figures expressed as percentages of net sales, was as follows:

	Jan. 1–June 30	
	1984	**1983**
Net sales	100.0%	100.0%
Production costs	77.6	72.3
Selling and administrative costs	13.6	13.9
Profit	8.8	13.9

Mr. Hockman knew that the company's problem must be either low prices or excessive costs! Unfortunately, the cost data already available told him little about the cost-price relationship for individual jobs. E-Z's operating costs were classified routinely into 20 categories, such as salaries, pressroom wages, production materials, depreciation, and so forth. Individual job cost sheets were not used, and the cost of goods in process was estimated only once a year, at the end of the fiscal year.

Detailed data were available on only two kinds of items: paper stock issued and labor time. When stock was issued, a requisition form was filled out, showing the kind of stock issued, the quantity, the unit cost, and the production order number. Similar details were reported when unused stock was returned to the stockroom.

As for labor, each employee directly engaged in working on production orders filled in a time sheet each day, on which (s)he recorded the time (s)he started on a given task, the times (s)he finished it or moved on to other work, and (in the case of time spent directly on a specific production order) the order number. His/her department number and pay grade were recorded on the time sheet by the payroll clerk.

Mr. Hockman's first step was to establish some overall cost relationships. Employees, for example, fell into three different pay grades, with the following regular hourly wage rates:

Grade	Rate
1	$12
2	8
3	6

These rates applied to a regular workweek of 40 hours a week. For work in excess of this number of hours, employees were paid an overtime premium of 50 percent of their hourly wage. Overtime premiums were negligible when the work load was light, but in a normal year they averaged about 5 percent of the total amount of hourly wages computed at the regular hourly wage rate. In a normal year, this was approximately 40 cents a direct labor-hour.

In addition to their wages, the employees also received various kinds of benefits, including vacation pay, health insurance, and old-age pensions. The cost of these benefits to E-Z Printing amounted to about 70 percent of direct labor cost, measured at regular straight-time hourly rates. The overtime premiums didn't affect the amount of fringe benefits paid or accrued.

Mr. Hockman estimated that all other shop overhead costs—that is, all copy department, composing room, and pressroom costs other than direct materials, direct labor, overtime premiums, and employee benefits on direct labor payrolls—would average $4 a direct labor-hour in a normal year.

Armed with these estimates of general relationships, Mr. Hockman proceeded to determine the costs of several recent production orders. One of these was Job No. A-467. This was received for copy editing on Monday, April 3, and delivered to the customer on Friday, April 7. Ms. Carr had quoted a price of $1,800 on this job in advance, on the basis of an estimate of $480 for paper stock costs and 45 direct labor-hours. All actual requisitions and time records relating to Job No. A-467 are included in the lists in Exhibits A and B. (To save space, some of the details shown on the requisitions and time tickets have been omitted from these tables.)

Required:

a. Diagram or explain to your own satisfaction the flow of actual material, labor, and overhead costs to Job No. A-467.

b. Develop a costing rate or rates for labor costs, to be used to charge a job cost sheet or Factory Overhead account for an hour of labor time. You must decide whether to use a single rate for all pay grades or a separate rate for each. You must also decide whether to include various kinds of fringe benefit costs in the

Exhibit A (5–30)   **Partial list of material requisitions (for the week of April 3–7)**

Req. no.	Job. no.	Amount[a]
4058	A-467	$300
R162	A-469	(20)
4059	A-467	60
4060	A-442	6
R163	A-455	(10)
R164	A-472	(8)
4060	A-467	36
R165	A-465	(12)
4062	A-467	96
4063	A-471	320
4064	A-473	264
4065	A-458	22
R-166	A-467	(32)
4066	A-481	176

[a] Amounts in parentheses are returned materials.

Exhibit B (5–30)   **Partial summary of labor time sheets (for the week of April 3–7)**

Employee no.	Pay grade	Dept.	Job no.[a]	Hours
14	2	Copy	A-463	6.6
14	2	Copy	A-467	1.4
15	1	Copy	A-467	3.3
15	1	Copy	—	2.7
15	1	Copy	A-467	8.8
18	3	Press	A-467	4.0
18	3	Press	A-472	4.6
22	1	Composing	A-455	3.8
22	1	Composing	A-467	8.4[b]
22	1	Composing	—	1.5
23	2	Press	A-458	3.4
23	2	Press	A-467	4.7[b]
23	2	Press	—	1.1
23	2	Press	A-459	2.5
24	2	Copy	A-470	7.4
28	1	Press	A-467	7.0
28	1	Press	A-458	1.0
31	3	Press	—	8.0
33	1	Composing	A-471	7.6
33	1	Composing	A-472	4.2
40	2	Press	A-469	3.6
40	2	Press	A-467	4.9
40	2	Press	—	0.2
43	1	Press	A-467	3.5
43	1	Press	A-481	5.8

[a] A dash indicates time spent on general work in the department and not on any one job.

[b] Employee No. 22 worked six hours of overtime during the week, none of them on Job No. A-467, while Employee No. 23 worked eight hours of overtime, including four hours spent on Job No. A-467.

labor costing rates or to regard these as overhead. Also consider the propriety of using the same overhead rate throughout the year.

c. Prepare a job order cost sheet for Job No. A-467 and enter the costs that would be assigned to this job, using the costing rates you developed in the answer to (b).

d. What conclusions might Mr. Hockman have reached on the basis of his analysis of this order? What suggestions would you make to Ms. Carr?

e. What could be the advantages of developing costs for each job? Do you think these advantages would be great enough to persuade Ms. Carr to hire an additional clerk for this purpose at an annual cost of about $20,000?

5–31. Huron Automotive Company (plantwide versus department overhead rates)*

Sandy Bond, a recent business school graduate who had recently been employed by Huron Automotive Company, was asked by Huron's president to review the company's present cost accounting procedures. In outlining this project to Bond, the president had expressed three concerns about the present system: (1) its adequacy for purposes

* © Osceola Institute, 1979, with the permission of Professors Robert N. Anthony and James S. Reece.

of cost control, (2) its accuracy in arriving at the true cost of products, and (3) its usefulness in providing data to judge supervisors' performance.

Huron Automotive was a relatively small supplier of selected automobile parts to the large automobile companies. Huron competed on a price basis with larger suppliers that were long established in the market. Huron had competed successfully in the past by focusing on parts that, relative to the auto industry, were of small volume and hence did not permit Huron's competitors to take advantage of economies of scale. For example, Huron produced certain parts usable only in four-wheel-drive vehicles.

Bond began the cost accounting study in Huron's carburetor division, which accounted for about 40 percent of Huron's sales. This division contained five production departments: casting and stamping, grinding, machining, custom work, and assembly. The casting and stamping department produced carburetor cases, butterfly valves, and certain other carburetor parts. The grinding department prepared these parts for further machining and precision ground those parts requiring close tolerances. The machining department performed all necessary machining operations on standard carburetors; whereas the custom work department performed these operations (and certain others) on custom carburetors, which usually were replacement carburetors for antique cars or other highly specialized applications. The assembly department assembled and tested all carburetors, both standard and custom.

Thus, custom carburetors passed through all five departments and standard carburetors passed through all departments except custom work. Carburetor spare parts produced for inventory went through only the first three departments. Both standard and custom carburetors were produced to order; there were no inventories of completed carburetors.

Bond's investigation showed that with the exception of materials costs, all carburetor costing was done based on a single, plantwide direct labor-hour rate. This rate included both direct labor and factory overhead costs. Each batch of carburetors was assigned its labor and overhead cost by having workers charge their time to the job number assigned the batch, and then multiplying the total hours charged to the job number by the hourly rate. Exhibit A shows how the July hourly rate of $17.61 was calculated.

Exhibit A (5–31)   **Calculation of plantwide labor and overhead hourly rate (month of July)**

	Dollars	Hours
Labor:		
Casting/stamping	$ 17,064	2,528
Grinding	11,984	2,140
Machining	61,400	7,675
Custom work	25,984	3,712
Assembly	92,142	15,357
Total labor	208,574	31,412
Overhead	344,589	
Total labor and overhead	$553,163	

$$\text{Hourly rate} = \frac{\$553,163}{31,412} = \$17.61 \text{ per hour}$$
$$(= \$6.64 \text{ labor}$$
$$+ \$10.97 \text{ overhead})$$

It seemed to Bond that because the average skill level varied from department to department, each department should have its own hourly costing rate. With this approach, time would be charged to each batch *by department;* then the hours charged by a department would be multiplied by that department's costing rate to arrive at a departmental labor and overhead cost for the batch; and finally these departmental costs would be added (along with materials cost) to obtain the cost of a batch.

Bond decided to see what impact this approach would have on product costs. The division's accountant pointed out to Bond that labor hours and payroll costs were already traceable to departments. Also, some overhead items, such as departmental supervisors' salaries and equipment depreciation, could be charged directly to the relevant department. However, many other overhead items, including heat, electricity, property taxes and insurance, would need to be allocated to each department if the new approach were implemented. Accordingly, Bond determined a reasonable allocation basis for each of these joint costs (for example, cubic feet of space occupied as the basis of allocating heating costs), and then used these bases to recast July's costs on a departmental basis. Bond then calculated hourly rates for each department, as shown in Exhibit B.

Exhibit B (5–31)   **Proposed departmental labor and overhead hourly rates**

Department	Labor rate per hour	Overhead per hour	Total cost per hour
Casting/stamping	$6.75	$ 9.83	$16.58
Grinding	5.60	9.42	15.02
Machining	8.00	19.58	27.58
Custom work	7.00	12.71	19.71
Assembly	6.00	6.65	12.65

In order to have some concrete numbers to show the president, Bond decided to apply the proposed approach to three carburetor division activities: production of model CS-29 carburetors (Huron's best-selling carburetor), production of spare parts for inventory, and work done by the division for other departments in Huron. Exhibit C summarizes the hourly requirements of these activities by department. Bond then costed these three activities using both the July plantwide rate and the pro forma July departmental rates.

Exhibit C (5–31)   **Direct labor-hour distribution for three carburetor division activities**

Department	CS-29 carburetors (per batch of 100)	Spare parts for inventory (per typical month)	Work for other departments (per typical month)
Casting/stamping	21 hrs.	304 hrs.	674 hrs.
Grinding	12	270	540
Machining	58	1,115	2,158
Custom work	—	—	—
Assembly	35	—	—
Total	126 hrs.	1,689 hrs.	3,372 hrs.

Upon seeing Bond's numbers, the president noted that there was a large difference in the indicated cost of CS-29 carburetors as calculated under the present and proposed methods. The present method was therefore probably leading to incorrect inferences about the profitability of each product, the president surmised. The impact of the proposed method on spare parts inventory valuation was similarly noted. The president therefore was leaning toward adopting the new method, but told Bond that the supervisors should be consulted before any change was made.

Bond's explanation of the proposal to the supervisors prompted strong opposition from some of them. The supervisors of the outside departments for which the carburetor division did work each month felt it would be unfair to increase their costs by increasing charges from the carburetor division. One of them stated:

> The carburetor division handles our department's overflow machining work when we're at capacity. I can't control costs in the carburetor division, but if they increase their charges, I'll never be able to meet my department's cost budget. They're already charging us more than we can do the work for in our own department, if we had enough capacity, and you're proposing to charge us still more!

Also opposed was the production manager of the carburetor division:

> I've got enough to do getting good quality output to our customers on time, without getting involved in more paperwork! What's more, my department supervisors haven't got time to become bookkeepers, either. We're already charging all of the divisions's production costs to products and work for other departments; why do we need this extra complication?

The company's sales manager also did not favor the proposal, telling Bond:

> We already have trouble being competitive with the big companies in our industry. If we start playing games with our costing system, then we'll have to start changing our prices. You're new here, so perhaps you don't realize that we have to carry some low-profit—or even loss—items in order to sell the more profitable ones. As far as I'm concerned, if a product *line* is showing an adequate profit, I'm not hung up about cost variations among items *within* the line.

When Bond reported this opposition to the president, the president replied:

> You're not telling me anything that I haven't already heard from unsolicited phone calls from several supervisors the last few days. I don't want to cram anything down their throats—but I'm still not satisfied our current system is adequate. Sandy, what do you think we should do?

Required:

a. Using the data in the exhibits, determine the cost of a 100-unit batch CS-29 carburetors, spare parts, and work done for other departments under both the present and proposed methods.

b. Are the cost differences between the two methods significant? What causes these differences?

c. Suppose that Huron purchased a new machine costing $400,000 for the custom work department. Its expected useful life is five years. This machine would reduce machining time and result in higher quality custom carburetors. As a result, the department's direct labor-hours would be reduced by 30 percent, and this extra labor would be transferred to departments outside the carburetor division. About 10 percent of the custom work department's overhead is variable with respect to direct labor-hours. Using July's data:

(1) Calculate the plantwide hourly rate (present method) if the new machine were acquired. Then calculate indicated costs for the custom work department in July, using both this new plantwide rate and the former $17.61 rate.

(2) Calculate the hourly rate for the custom work department only (Proposed method), assuming the machine were acquired and the proposed costing procedure were adopted. Then calculate indicated costs for the custom work department in July, using both this new rate and the former $19.71 rate.

(3) Under the present costing procedures, what is the impact on indicated custom carburetor costs if the new machine is acquired? What is this impact if the proposed costing procedures are used? What inferences do you then draw concerning the usefulness of the present and proposed methods?

d. Assume that producing a batch of 100 model CS-29 carburetors requires 126 hours, distributed by department as shown in Exhibit C, and $875 worth of materials. Huron sells these carburetors for $32 each. Should the price of a CS-29 carburetor be increased? Should the CS-29 be dropped from the product line? (Answer using both the present and the proposed costing methods.)

e. Assume that Huron also offers a model CS-30 carburetor that is identical to a CS-29 in all important aspects, including price, but is preferred for some applications because of certain design features. Because of the CS-30's relatively low sales volume, Huron buys certain major components for the CS-30 rather than making them in-house. The total cost of purchased parts for 100 units of model CS-30 is $1,800; the labor required per 100 units is 12, 7, 17, and 35 hours, respectively, in the casting/stamping, grinding, machining, and assembly departments. If a customer ordered 100 carburetors and said that either model CS-29 or CS-30 would be acceptable, which model should Huron ship? Why? (Answer using only the proposed costing method.)

f. What benefits, if any, do you see to Huron if the proposed costing method is adopted? Consider this question from the standpoint of (1) product pricing, (2) cost control, (3) inventory valuation, (4) charges to outside departments, (5) judging departmental performance, and (6) diagnostic uses of cost data. What do you conclude Huron should do regarding the proposal?

6

Process Costing

OBJECTIVES
To understand the accounting system used to record costs in continuous process
    operations.
To understand the alternative methods of accounting for costs in a process
    operation.
To be familiar with the treatment of spoiled units or other goods lost in production.

In this chapter, we continue our discussion of product costing methods by focusing on process costing. **Process costing** is used when identical units are produced through an *ongoing series* of *uniform production steps.* We also discuss ways of accounting for spoilage.

Companies that manufacture products in a continuous process, such as chemical-blending, petroleum, and steel-making operations, find it necessary to identify costs per unit for inventory valuation, cost estimation, and performance evaluation purposes. However, when items are produced through continuous processing, it is impossible to separate output into individual jobs. In job operations, costs are accumulated for two cost objects: *departments* and *jobs.* In process costing, costs are accumulated by department and then allocated evenly to units produced. (The term *process costing* is short for *product costing in continuous process systems.)*

What process costing does

Process costing assigns the manufacturing costs incurred in each department to the units that have been produced in that department. This is done on a period basis, typically by the month. Each unit that passes through a department that month is charged equally for the same amount of work.

This presents problems because the production process usually does not terminate at the end of the month (or other accounting period). Further, a department's operating costs may change from month to month. Thus, in any department, at the end of a period, there may be partly processed units that when finally finished will have incurred part of their production costs in one month and part in another. Illustration 6–1 shows the different classes of units that might be found in the Work in Process Inventory account during a month.

The equivalent unit concept

To allocate costs to physical units worked on in the same department in different periods, the equivalent unit concept is used. Under this system, if

Illustration 6–1   **Work in process inventory—manufacturing department 1**

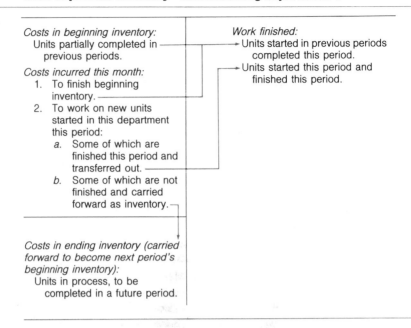

two units were started at the beginning of a month and each was 50 percent finished at the end of the month, the cumulative work done on the two partial units would be considered as equivalent to the work done on one whole unit. Thus, for process costing purposes, the two units would be one equivalent unit. The equivalent unit concept is diagrammed in Illustration 6–2. This concept is not limited to manufacturing. For example, university administrators often count the number of students in a department in terms of "full-time equivalents." One student who takes two courses when the full-time course load is five courses would be a "40 percent full-time equivalent" student.

Assigning costs to units

Assume that Department A had no beginning or ending inventory in August. Every unit it produced was started and completed during the month. If Department A started and completed 50 units during August, we would say the amount of work it produced was 50 equivalent units.

During August, $5,000 in costs were incurred in Department A. To determine the cost per unit, we divide the cost incurred by the equivalent units produced.

$$\text{Unit cost} = \frac{\text{Cost incurred}}{\text{Equivalent units}}$$

$$= \frac{\$5,000}{50 \text{ units}}$$

$$= \underline{\$100} \text{ per unit}$$

Illustration 6–2   **Equivalent unit concept**

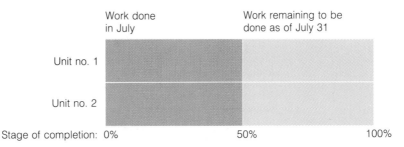

Unit no. 1 and unit no. 2, each 50 percent completed in July, would be equivalent to one whole unit produced in July.

Incomplete units in beginning inventory   In October, assume that Department A had beginning inventory but no ending inventory. On October 1, Department A had 12 units on hand, which the department manager estimated were two-thirds finished. Fifty units were completed during the month. There was no ending inventory on October 31.

The 50 completed units are composed of two groups:

1. Twelve units in process and two-thirds finished at the beginning of October.
2. Thirty-eight units started and finished in October.

The 12 units in the beginning inventory were already two-thirds finished. Therefore they required the equivalent of only four units of work to reach completion (12 units $\times$ $\frac{1}{3}$ = 4). Thus, the total equivalent units produced in Department A during October would be as follows:

Work necessary to complete beginning inventory (12 units $\times$ $\frac{1}{3}$ =)	4
Work necessary to start and finish 38 units	38
Equivalent whole units of work done	42

If the costs incurred in Department A in October were $3,780, the unit cost would be:

$$\text{Unit cost} = \frac{\text{Cost incurred}}{\text{Equivalent units}}$$

$$= \frac{\$3,780}{42 \text{ units}}$$

$$= \underline{\$90} \text{ per unit}$$

Incomplete units in beginning and ending inventories   In December, assume that Department A had both beginning inventory and ending inventory. On December 1, there were 12 units in beginning inventory that were two-thirds finished. During the month, 50 units were completed including the 12 units in beginning inventory, and another 15 units remained in process, one-third completed, on December 31. The equivalent units would be:

Work necessary to complete beginning inventory (12 units × ⅓ =)	4
Work necessary to start and finish 38 units	38
Work performed on ending inventory of 15 units (15 units ⅓ =)	5
Equivalent whole units of work done	47

If the costs incurred in Department A in December were $5,170, the unit cost of work done this period would be:

$$\text{Unit cost} = \frac{\text{Cost incurred}}{\text{Equivalent units}}$$

$$= \frac{\$5,170}{47 \text{ units}}$$

$$= \underline{\$110} \text{ per unit}$$

(These calculations assume the first-in, first-out [FIFO] method of assigning costs to units which will be discussed in detail in the following sections.)

This is the basic procedure for assigning costs to units in a process costing system. These steps are summarized in Illustration 6–3.

Illustration 6–3   **Procedure for allocating a department's costs to units (FIFO method)**

1. Recognize three possible classes of units:
    a. Work partly finished at beginning of period.
    b. Work started and finished this period.
    c. Work partly finished at end of period.
2. Estimate equivalent whole units of work done on each class during the period.
3. Add the equivalent whole units for the three classes to get the total equivalent units for work performed.
4. Divide the period's total department costs by total equivalent finished units of work performed to calculate the cost per unit for the period.

Methods of allocating process costs

All costs transferred into a department (or Work in Process Inventory account), whether as beginning inventory or new work during the period, must be assigned to either ending Work in Process Inventory or costs transferred out. The two most commonly used allocation methods are: (1) FIFO and (2) weighted average.

FIFO costing separates the costs of beginning inventory from the costs associated with current period work. Using this method, we identify a period's equivalent units produced and relate them to that period's costs.

Weighted-average costing combines the costs and equivalent units of a period with the costs and equivalent units in beginning inventory. That is, beginning inventory costs and current period costs are grouped together to determine product costs. As a result, it is difficult to identify current period activity and current period costs that may be important to evaluate the current period's performance. For this reason, the FIFO method is widely used even though the weighted average is easier to compute. Details of the FIFO method are discussed first in this chapter. The discussion of the weighted-average method follows the FIFO presentation.

FIFO process costing

FIFO process costing separates the costs and equivalent units of the current period from those of previous periods that are in beginning inventory. As noted before, the costs of the current period relate to three different activities:

1. Work necessary to complete the beginning inventory.
2. Work done on units started and completed during the period.
3. Work done on units not finished during the period.

All items of cost in a process are rarely incurred at the same time. For example, direct materials are often added at discrete points, while direct labor and manufacturing overhead costs tend to accumulate continuously. If direct labor and manufacturing overhead are proportionally related, as is often the case, they are usually combined for product costing purposes. Combined direct labor and manufacturing overhead are referred to as **conversion costs.**

For example, in Illustration 6–4, direct materials are added at only two specific points in the process, while conversion costs are applied evenly

Illustration 6–4   **Addition of direct materials and conversion costs to a manufacturing process**

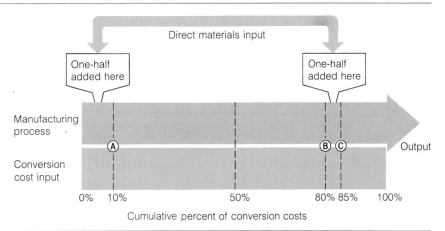

throughout. At point A of the process, units are 50 percent complete in terms of direct materials, but only 10 percent complete in terms of conversion costs. At point B, units are still only 50 percent complete in direct materials, but 80 percent complete in conversion costs. At point C, 100 percent of direct materials have been added, but only 85 percent complete in conversion costs.

Flow of direct materials costs

Assume Chemicals, Inc., has just one work in process department—blending. The production data and the flow of units for the blending department are presented in Illustration 6–5. The 4,500 units in beginning inventory on April

Illustration 6–5   **Data for blending operation**

CHEMICALS, INC.
Blending Operation
April

	Units[a]	Direct materials Costs	Direct materials Percent of processing completed	Conversion costs: Direct labor and manufacturing overhead Costs	Conversion costs: Direct labor and manufacturing overhead Percent of processing completed
Beginning work in process inventory, April 1	4,500	$ 1,625	10	$ 3,100	60
Costs incurred in April	—	56,252	—	25,944	—
Transfers-out to finished goods inventory	13,600	?	100	?	100
Ending work in process inventory, April 30	1,900	?	30	?	20

[a] These are whole units, some of which may be only partially completed.

Diagram of unit flows

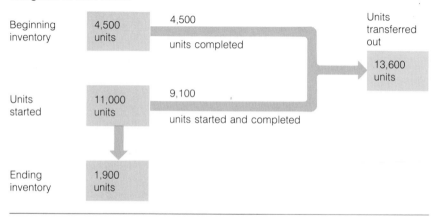

1 had 10 percent of total direct materials added in previous periods. They would require the remaining 90 percent of direct materials to be added during the current period for completion. Thus, 4,050 (90% × 4,500 units) equivalent units could have been produced with the direct materials added this period.

Units that are both started and completed during the period are worked on 100 percent during the period, so their finished unit equivalency equals their actual number. The blending department started and completed 9,100 units of product during April, which is 9,100 equivalent whole units. In total, 13,600 units were transferred to finished goods inventory (9,100 + 4,500).

The equivalent units in ending inventory are calculated by multiplying the number of units in the ending inventory times the percent of direct materials added. Thirty percent of the direct materials costs had been added to the 1,900 units in the ending inventory according to Illustration 6–5, so the equivalent units of work in ending inventory would be 570 units (1,900 units × 30%).

With FIFO process costing, the activity of the current period is isolated and measured in terms of the equivalent whole units that could have been produced during the period with the same effort. A summary of the equivalent unit computations of direct materials for Chemicals, Inc., is as follows:

1.	To complete beginning inventory	4,500 units × 90% = 4,050
2.	Started and completed	9,100 units × 100% = 9,100
3.	To start ending inventory	1,900 units × 30% = 570
	Total work in April	13,720

Assume the direct material costs debited to Work in Process Inventory for April were $56,252. The equivalent units produced were 13,720, so the unit direct materials cost for April would be:

$$\text{Unit cost} = \frac{\text{Cost incurred in April}}{\text{Equivalent units produced in April}}$$

$$= \frac{\$56,252}{13,720 \text{ units}}$$

$$= \$4.10 \text{ per unit}$$

The direct materials costs in ending work in process (WIP) inventory on April 30 is simply the unit cost of $4.10 times the 570 equivalent units in ending inventory:

$$\text{Direct materials in ending WIP inventory} = 570 \text{ units} \times \$4.10 = \$2,337$$

Costs transferred out are a little more difficult to calculate. We think it is easiest to consider three kinds of costs transferred out:

1. Costs in beginning inventory from work done in a previous period: $1,625.
2. Work done in the current period (April) to complete beginning inventory.

This is $4.10 per unit times 4,050 equivalent whole units required to complete beginning inventory. So the cost to complete beginning inventory is $4.10 × 4,050 units = $16,605.

3. Costs of units started and completed in the period, which is $4.10 per unit times 9,100 units started and completed, or $37,310.

These calculations of direct materials cost flows are summarized in Illustration 6–6.

Illustration 6–6   **Direct materials cost flows (FIFO method)**

CHEMICALS, INC.
Blending Operation
April

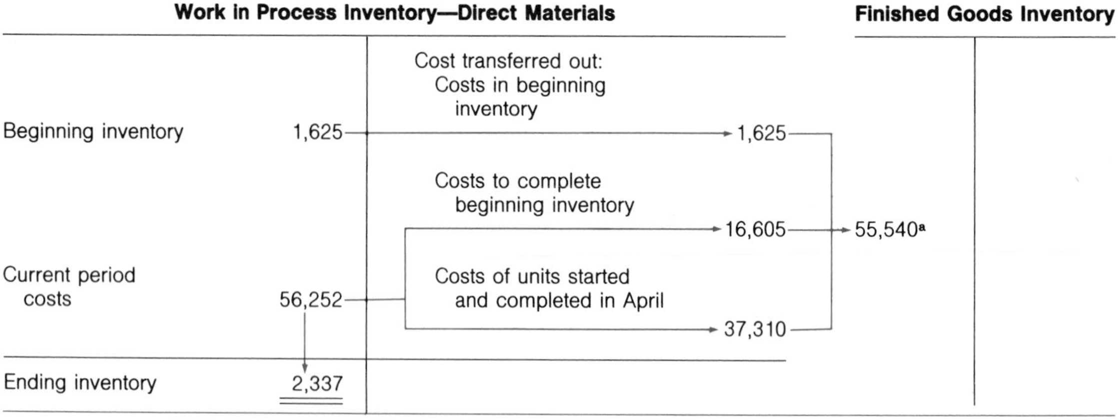

Work in Process Inventory—Direct Materials			Finished Goods Inventory
		Cost transferred out: Costs in beginning inventory	
Beginning inventory	1,625	→1,625	
		Costs to complete beginning inventory	
		→16,605	→55,540ª
Current period costs	56,252	Costs of units started and completed in April	
		→37,310	
Ending inventory	2,337		

ª Total costs transferred out of Work in Process Inventory—Direct Materials.

Flow of conversion costs

Equivalent units for conversion costs are calculated the same way as equivalent units for direct materials. As shown in Illustration 6–5, the 4,500 units in beginning inventory at Chemicals, Inc., needed 40 percent of conversion costs to complete, 9,100 units were started and finished in April, and the 1,900 units in ending inventory were 20 percent completed in terms of conversion costs. The equivalent unit computations for conversion costs are:

1. To complete beginning inventory	4,500 units × 40% =	1,800
2. Started and completed during the period	9,100 units × 100% =	9,100
3. To start ending inventory	1,900 units × 20% =	380
Total work in April		11,280

We know from the facts in Illustration 6–5 that the conversion costs debited to Work in Process Inventory—Conversion Costs for April were $25,944. Dividing this by the 11,280 equivalent units computed above gives the following unit conversion cost for April:

$$\text{Unit cost} = \frac{\text{Costs incurred in April}}{\text{Equivalent units produced in April}}$$

$$= \frac{\$25,944}{11,280}$$

$$= \$2.30 \text{ per unit}$$

The conversion cost component of the work in process inventory at April 30 is:

$$\frac{\text{Conversion costs in}}{\text{ending WIP inventory}} = 380 \text{ equivalent units} \times \$2.30 = \$874$$

Costs transferred out of the blending department's Work in Process Inventory—Conversion Costs are:

1. Costs in beginning inventory from work done in a previous period: $3,100.
2. Work done in the current period to complete beginning inventory:

$$1,800 \text{ equivalent units} \times \$2.30 = \$4,140$$

3. Cost of units started and completed in the period:

$$9,100 \text{ equivalent units} \times \$2.30 = \$20,930$$

Illustration 6–7 summarizes the flow of conversion costs for the blending department of Chemicals, Inc.

Illustration 6–7   **Conversion cost flows (FIFO method)**

CHEMICALS, INC.
Blending Operation
April

Work in Process Inventory—Conversion Costs			Finished Goods Inventory
		Costs transferred out:	
		Costs in beginning inventory	
Beginning inventory	3,100	3,100	
		Costs to complete beginning inventory	
		4,140	28,170[a]
Current period costs	25,944	Costs of units started and completed in April	
		20,930	
Ending inventory	874		

[a] Total cost transferred out of Work in Process Inventory—Conversion Costs.

Separate accounts for each cost incurred at different stages In the blending department of Chemicals, Inc., direct materials and conversion costs are applied to the manufacturing process at different stages, so there are separate accounts for each. In general, separate accounts are maintained for each product cost component that enters the process at a significantly different time.

Cost of production reports The computations for equivalent units and a summary of the flow of units are usually included in a cost of production report. Illustration 6–8 shows the portion of the cost of production report that would be prepared about the flow of units through the blending department. The second part of the report, which accounts for costs, is shown in Illustration 6–9. Managers often use the data in cost of production reports for performance evaluation and other decisions. For example, the cost information in Illustration 6–9 can be compared against budgets to see how actual costs correspond to estimated costs. The data can also be used to assign costs to inventory and cost of goods sold for financial reporting.

Summary of FIFO process costing FIFO process costing isolates current period activity and current period costs from previous period costs carried forward in a department's beginning inventory. Equivalent finished units computed under FIFO represent only the current period's activity. When the department's costs are divided between the costs to be transferred to a subse-

Illustration 6–8   **Cost of production report (FIFO method)**

Schedule of Equivalent Units–CHEMICALS, INC.
Blending Operation
April

	Units in production	Equivalent units	
		Direct materials	Conversion costs
Beginning inventory	4,500		
This period:			
To complete beginning inventory		4,050	1,800
Started and completed	9,100	9,100	9,100
Subtotal (equivalent units transferred out)	13,600	13,150	10,900
Ending inventory	1,900	570	380
Totals	15,500	13,720	11,280

Additional data:
1. Beginning inventory was 10 percent complete with respect to materials and 60 percent complete with respect to conversion costs.
2. During the period, 11,000 units were started (9,100 started and completed plus 1,900 started but not completed).
3. Ending inventory was 30 percent complete with respect to materials and 20 percent complete with respect to conversion costs.

Illustration 6–9   **Cost of production report (FIFO method)**

Schedule of Cost Flows—CHEMICALS, INC.
Blending Operations
April

	Totals	Direct materials	Conversion costs
Costs to be accounted for:			
Beginning inventory	$ 4,725	$ 1,625	$ 3,100
Current costs	82,196	56,252	25,944
Total to be accounted for	$86,921	$57,877	$29,044
Costs per equivalent unit:			
Materials		$4.10	
Conversion costs			$2.30
Cost assignment:			
Transferred out:			
From beginning inventory	$ 4,725	$ 1,625	$ 3,100
Current period	78,985	53,915[a]	25,070[b]
Total transferred out	83,710	55,540	28,170
Ending inventory	3,211	2,337[c]	874[d]
Total costs accounted for	$86,921	$57,877	$29,044

Additional computations:

[a] $53,915 = 13,150 equivalent units of materials transferred out at $4.10 per EU = $16,605 + $37,310 (Illustration 6–6).

[b] $25,070 = 10,900 equivalent units of conversion costs transferred out at $2.30 per EU = $4,140 + $20,930 (Illustration 6–7).

[c] $2,337 = 570 equivalent units in the ending inventory at $4.10 per EU.

[d] $874 = 380 equivalent units in the ending inventory at $2.30 per EU.

quent department (or finished goods inventory) and the costs to be included in ending inventory, the costs of the beginning inventory are transferred out first. Current period costs are then assigned to the finished units transferred out and those remaining in the ending inventory.

Weighted-average process costing

In contrast to FIFO costing, weighted-average costing combines beginning inventory costs and current period costs in computing product costs. These combined costs are assigned to goods transferred out and to ending inventory.

Weighted-average equivalent whole units   With weighted-average costing, equivalent whole units are simply the number of completed units transferred out plus the equivalent whole units in ending inventory. It does not matter how many units resulted from current period work or had been carried in beginning inventory.

We use the data from the blending department at Chemicals, Inc., and assume the weighted-average method had been used. Illustration 6–5 provided the following data about stages of completion of units for each cost category:

		Direct materials		Conversion costs	
	Units	Costs	Percent of processing completed	Costs	Percent of processing completed
Work in process:					
Beginning inventory	4,500	$ 1,625	10	$ 3,100	60
Costs incurred in April	—	56,252	—	25,944	—
Transfers-out	13,600	?	100	?	100
Ending inventory	1,900	?	30	?	20

We assume beginning inventory is the same under both FIFO and weighted average for our illustrative purposes.

Direct materials   If Chemicals, Inc., used weighted-average costing, the equivalent units for direct materials would be:

1. Equivalent units in beginning inventory	(10% × 4,500)	450
2. Equivalent units to complete beginning inventory	(90% × 4,500)	4,050
3. Units started and completed during current period	(100% × 9,100)	9,100
4. Equivalent units in ending inventory	(30% × 1,900)	570
Total equivalent whole units (beginning inventory plus current period production)		14,170

Alternative methods   There are two other ways to calculate weighted-average equivalent units:

1. Add the equivalent whole units in beginning inventory to our previous FIFO calculations of equivalent whole units:

$$\frac{450 \text{ in beginning inventory } + \ 13,720 \text{ in}}{\text{current period work (from FIFO calculations)}} = 14,170 \text{ equivalent units}$$

2. Or add the total completed units transferred out to the equivalent units in ending inventory:

$$13,600 \text{ transferred out} + (30\% \times 1,900 \text{ in ending inventory})$$
$$= 13,600 + 570$$
$$= 14,170$$

Since the three methods are mathematically equivalent, you can use whichever one you prefer. Indeed, you can use one to check the results of another.

Conversion costs   The computation of equivalent units for conversion costs is:

1. Equivalent units in beginning inventory	(60% × 4,500)	2,700
2. Equivalent units to complete beginning inventory	(40% × 4,500)	1,800
3. Units started and completed during current period	(100% × 9,100)	9,100
4. Equivalent units in ending inventory	(20% × 1,900)	380
Total equivalent units (beginning inventory plus current period work)		13,980

Direct materials cost flows   Using weighted-average costing, the blending department's total direct materials costs for April were:

Direct materials costs in beginning work in process inventory	$ 1,625
Direct materials costs incurred this period	56,252
Total costs to be accounted for	$57,877

The direct materials cost per equivalent unit is:

$$\text{Unit cost} = \frac{\text{Total costs}}{\text{Total equivalent whole units}}$$

$$= \frac{\$57,877}{14,170 \text{ equivalent units}}$$

$$= \underline{\$4.08447} \text{ per equivalent unit}$$

Using weighted-average costing, the direct materials component of the 13,600 units transferred out is $55,549 (13,600 × $4.08447). The direct materials component of the 570 equivalent units in ending inventory is $2,328 (570 × $4.08447). Illustration 6–10 shows the direct materials cost flows through the T-accounts, and Illustration 6–11 summarizes the cost calculations as they might appear in a cost of production report. (Compare the cost flows in Illustration 6–10 with those in Illustrations 6–6 and 6–7 to see how much more recordkeeping and computing are required by FIFO.)

Conversion cost flows   At Chemicals, Inc., the total conversion cost flows for April were:

Conversion costs in beginning work in process inventory	$ 3,100
Conversion costs incurred this period	25,944
Total costs to be accounted for	$29,044

The weighted-average conversion cost per equivalent unit is:

$$\text{Unit cost} = \frac{\text{Total costs}}{\text{Total equivalent whole units}}$$

$$= \frac{\$29,044}{13,980 \text{ equivalent units}}$$

$$= \$2.07754 \text{ per equivalent unit}$$

Illustration 6–10   **Cost flows using weighted-average costing**

CHEMICALS, INC.
Blending Operation
April

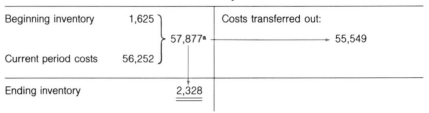

Work in Process Inventory—Direct Materials

Beginning inventory	1,625		Costs transferred out:
		57,877ª	55,549
Current period costs	56,252		
Ending inventory		2,328	

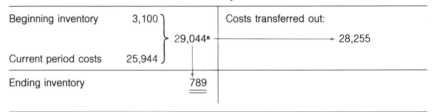

Work in Process Inventory—Conversion Costs

Beginning inventory	3,100		Costs transferred out:
		29,044ª	28,255
Current period costs	25,944		
Ending inventory		789	

ª Total costs to be accounted for.

The conversion cost component of the 13,600 units transferred out is $28,255 (13,600 $\times$ $2.07754), while the conversion cost component of the 380 equivalent units in ending inventory is $789 (380 $\times$ $2.07754). These cost flows and calculations are summarized in Illustrations 6–10 and 6–11.

Summary of weighted-average process costing Weighted-average process costing does not separate beginning inventory from current period activity. Unit costs are a weighted average of the two, whereas under FIFO process costing unit costs are based on current period activity only.

Illustration 6–12 compares the unit costs, costs transferred out, and ending inventory values under the two methods for Chemicals, Inc. Note that in this example costs per unit are lower under weighted average than under FIFO because the unit costs in beginning inventory are lower than current period unit costs. Thus, the lower unit costs in beginning inventory decrease the weighted-average unit cost.

While either weighted average or FIFO cost is acceptable for assigning costs to inventories and cost of goods sold for external reporting, the weighted-average method has been criticized for masking current period costs. Thus, using weighted-average costing, the unit costs reported for April are based not only on April's costs but also on previous periods' costs that were in April's beginning inventory as well. Whether this obscuring of current period

Illustration 6–11   **Cost of production report (weighted-average costing)**

CHEMICALS, INC.
Blending Operation
April

Status of units:	Units in production	Equivalent units Direct materials	Conversion costs
Transferred out	13,600	13,600	13,600
Ending inventory	1,900	570	380
Totals	15,500	14,170	13,980

Costs to be accounted for:	Totals	Direct materials	Conversion costs
Beginning inventory	$ 4,725	$ 1,625	$ 3,100
Current period	82,196	56,252	25,944
Totals	$86,921	$57,877	$29,044

Cost per equivalent unit:

$$\frac{\$57,877}{14,170 \text{ EU}} = \$4.08447 \text{ per EU} \qquad \frac{\$29,044}{13,980 \text{ EU}} = \$2.07754 \text{ per EU}$$

Cost assignment:

	Totals	Direct materials	Conversion costs
Transferred out	$83,804	$55,549[a]	$28,255[b]
Ending inventory	3,117	2,328[c]	789[d]
Totals	$86,921	$57,877	$29,044

Additional computations:
[a] $55,549 = 13,600 EU × $4.08447 per EU.
[b] $28,255 = 13,600 EU × $2.07754 per EU.
[c] $2,328 = 570 EU × $4.08447 per EU.
[d] $789 = 380 EU × $2.07754 per EU.

costs is important depends on the extent to which managers' decisions require knowledge of period unit costs. If computational and recordkeeping costs are about the same under both FIFO and weighted average, which we believe is generally the case if both are computerized, then FIFO costing has a slight advantage.

Accounting for prior department costs

Our discussion so far has assumed a single department. Usually products pass through a series of departments, however. As the product passes from one department to another, its costs must follow.

In principle, the units transferred out of one department and into another

Illustration 6–12   **Comparison of FIFO and weighted-average methods**

CHEMICALS, INC.
Blending Operation
April

		FIFO	Weighted average
Direct materials	Unit cost	$4.10	$4.08447
	Costs transferred out	$55,540	$55,549
	Ending inventory	2,337	2,328
Conversion costs	Unit cost	$2.30	$2.07754
	Costs transferred out	$28,170	$28,255
	Ending inventory	874	789
Total product costs	Unit cost	$6.40	$6.16201
	Costs transferred out	$83,710	$83,804
	Ending inventory	3,211	3,117

Note: Beginning inventory values were assumed to be the same under FIFO
and weighted average.

are the equivalent of direct materials for the receiving department. The costs of those units, which are called **prior department costs,** or transferred-in costs, are similar to the costs of direct materials put into process at the start of production in that department. Prior department costs are entered as a separate item on the receiving department's cost of production report. Equivalent whole units are computed for the costs transferred in. These units are 100 percent complete in terms of prior department costs.

Assume that on April 1, the blending department of Chemicals, Inc., had 4,500 units in beginning inventory with prior department costs of $10 per unit. During the month, 11,000 units were transferred in with prior department costs of $11 per unit. This information is summarized below:

	Prior department cost per unit	Number of units	Stage of completion
Units in beginning inventory	$10	4,500	100%
Units transferred in during April	11	11,000	100
Units transferred in and out during April	?	9,100	100
Units in ending inventory	?	1,900	100

Illustration 6–13 shows the flow of prior department costs through T-accounts using FIFO. Illustration 6–14 shows the cost of production report with prior department costs, in addition to the direct materials and conversion costs previously discussed.

Illustration 6–13
Prior department cost flows (FIFO method)

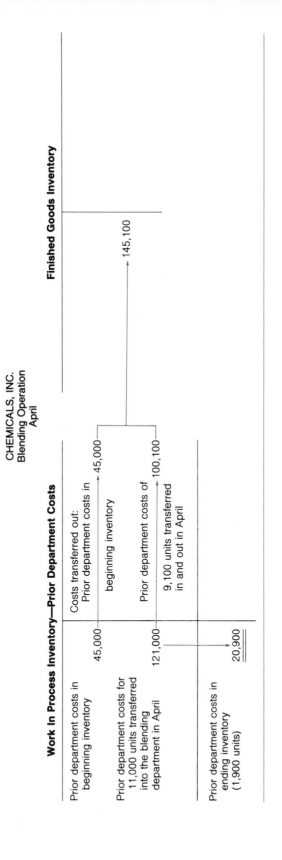

CHEMICALS, INC.
Blending Operation
April

Work In Process Inventory—Prior Department Costs

Prior department costs in beginning inventory	45,000	Costs transferred out: Prior department costs in beginning inventory → 45,000
Prior department costs for 11,000 units transferred into the blending department in April	121,000	Prior department costs of 9,100 units transferred → 100,100 in and out in April
Prior department costs in ending inventory (1,900 units)	20,900	

Finished Goods Inventory

→ 145,100

Illustration 6–14   **Cost of production report (FIFO method)**

CHEMICALS, INC.
Schedule of Cost Flows—Blending Operation

	Total costs	Prior department costs	Direct materials	Conversion costs
Costs to be accounted for:				
Beginning inventory	$ 49,725	$ 45,000	$ 1,625	$ 3,100
Current costs	203,196	121,000	56,252	25,944
Total to be accounted for	$252,921	$166,000	$57,877	$29,044
Equivalent units:				
1. To complete beginning inventory		–0–	4,050[b]	1,800[b]
2. Started and completed		9,100[a]	9,100[b]	9,100[b]
3. To start ending inventory		1,900[a]	570[b]	380[b]
Total equivalent whole units of production this period		11,000[a]	13,720[b]	11,280[b]
Current costs per equivalent unit		$11.00[a]	$4.10	$2.30
Cost assignment:				
Transferred out:				
From beginning inventory	$ 49,725	$ 45,000	$ 1,625	$ 3,100
Current period	179,085	100,100[c]	53,915	25,070
Total transferred out	228,810	145,100	55,540	28,170
Ending inventory	24,111	20,900[d]	2,337	874
Total costs accounted for	$252,921	$166,000	$57,877	$29,044

Note: This schedule is a modification of Illustration 6–9. The data used here for direct materials and conversion costs were taken from that illustration.

[a] Given in text of chapter.

[b] Previously calculated in the chapter.

[c] 9,100 of the units started in April were completed in April at $11; 9,100 × $11 = $100,100.

[d] 1,900 units in ending inventory on April 30 at $11; 1,900 × $11 = $20,900.

Responsibility for prior department costs

An important issue for performance evaluation is: Should a department manager be held accountable for *all* costs charged to the department? The answer is usually no. A department and its people are usually evaluated on the basis of costs *added by* the department relative to the good output from the department. Prior department costs are often excluded in comparing actual department costs with a standard or budget. We discuss this point more extensively in later chapters on performance evaluation, but we raise it here to emphasize that different information is needed for different purposes. Assigning costs to units for inventory valuation requires that prior department costs be *included* in department product cost calculations. However, assigning costs to departments for performance evaluation usually requires that prior department costs be *excluded* from departmental costs.

Changes in the measuring unit

In some manufacturing processes, the unit of measure in one department may be different from that in another. For example, in logging operations, logs are measured in volumetric terms as they enter the mill. Veneers are peeled from the logs and measured in area. Dimension lumber is measured in board feet. To minimize confusion under such circumstances, it is common for each department to use a measuring system that corresponds to the *units used to measure its outputs.*

For example, a veneer operation would use the area of veneer as its basis for measurement. If the veneer department received whole logs from another department, the physical units used for recording those logs would be the area of veneer the department expected to peel from the logs.

Spoilage

Some units of direct material may be lost during production. If the loss is a normal part of the production operation (such as that due to evaporation, chemical reactions, normal waste, or expected defective items), the reported number of units of product put into process may be adjusted to reflect the normal loss. Thus, units of product started is expressed in terms of expected or actual units of good output. The computation results in an increased cost per finished unit that has the effect of averaging the normal losses over the good units.

For example, suppose a department started 3,000 units. These units cost $24,000 for materials and conversion costs. It produced only 2,500 units of good output and lost 500 units. Thus, it would record 2,500 units produced at a cost of $9.60 per unit ($24,000 ÷ 2,500 good units = $9.60).

An alternative practice would be to record the 3,000 units at their cost of $8 per unit ($24,000 ÷ 3,000 units). At the end of the period, the $4,000 cost of the 500 lost units would be assigned to work-in-process inventory, finished goods inventory, or cost of goods sold depending on where the good units are. For example, if 1,000 of the good units are in ending finished goods inventory and the remaining 1,500 good units were sold, the entry would be:

Finished Goods Inventory—Lost Unit Costs . . . $1,600 \left(= \frac{1,000}{2,500} \times \$4,000 \right)$

Cost of Goods Sold—Lost Unit Costs . . . . $2,400 \left(= \frac{1,500}{2,500} \times \$4,000 \right)$

    Work in Process Inventory—Lost
      Unit Costs   4,000

Assuming there were no beginning inventories and these were the only costs incurred, both methods result in the same value of finished goods inventory and cost of goods sold. The flow of costs is diagrammed in Illustration 6–15.

Abnormal spoilage

If units are lost for unusual or abnormal reasons, the debit in the journal entry is made to an account such as Abnormal Spoilage Costs, which writes off the costs for the period. Whereas *normal* lost units or normal spoilage

Illustration 6-15
Cost flows for normal lost units

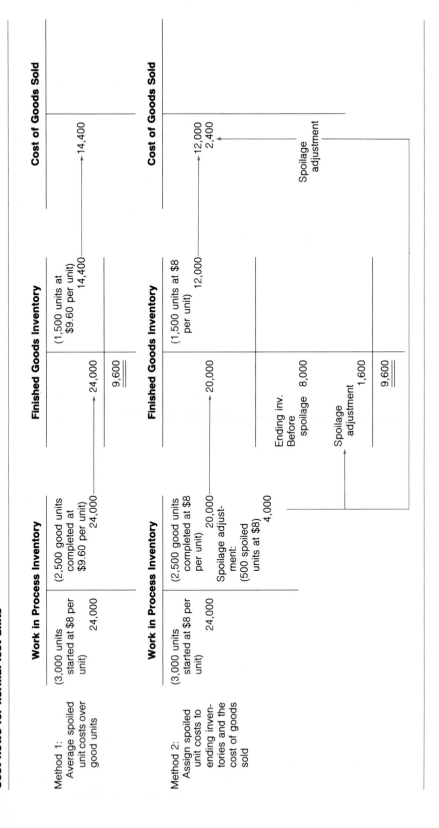

Work in Process Inventory

Method 1:
Average spoiled
unit costs over
good units

(3,000 units
started at $8 per
unit)   24,000

(2,500 good units
completed at
$9.60 per unit)
             24,000

Finished Goods Inventory

(1,500 units at
$9.60 per unit)
             14,400

             24,000

             9,600

Cost of Goods Sold

             14,400

Work in Process Inventory

Method 2:
Assign spoiled
unit costs to
ending inven-
tories and the
cost of goods
sold

(3,000 units
started at $8 per
unit)   24,000

(2,500 good units
completed at $8
per unit)
             20,000

Spoilage adjust-
ment:
(500 spoiled
units at $8)
             4,000

Finished Goods Inventory

(1,500 units at $8
per unit)
             20,000

Ending inv.
Before
spoilage   8,000

Spoilage
adjustment
             1,600

             9,600

Cost of Goods Sold

             12,000

             2,400

Spoilage
adjustment

is usually treated as a *product* cost, *abnormal* lost units or spoilage is treated as a *period* cost. For the example, if the 500 lost units were lost due to abnormal reasons, the journal entry to record the transfer of costs out of Work-in-Process would be:

Finished Goods Inventory	20,000	
Lost Unit Cost	4,000	
Work in Process Inventory		24,000

The Lost Unit Cost account would be a period expense and would appear in the income statement.

With this method, cost of goods sold would be stated at the $8 per unit cost excluding the abnormal lost unit costs. Thus, the balance in the Cost of Goods Sold account would be $12,000.

T-accounts to represent this flow are shown in Illustration 6–16.

Systems choice: Job costing versus process costing

In job costing, costs are collected for each unit produced, as discussed in Chapter 5. For example, a print shop collects costs for each order, a defense contractor collects costs for each contract, and a custom home builder collects costs for each house. In process costing, costs are accumulated in a department for an accounting period (for example, a month), then spread evenly, or averaged, over all units produced that month. Process costing assumes each unit produced is relatively uniform. A comparison of cost flows under each method is demonstrated by the following example.

Assume Marmaduke Manufacturing Company makes a customized product. In June, three jobs were started and completed (there were no beginning inventories). The manufacturing cost of each job was:

Job No. 10	$16,000
Job No. 11	12,000
Job No. 12	14,000
Total	$42,000

Job No. 10 was sold; hence, the cost of goods sold in June would be the cost of Job No. 10—$16,000. This flow of costs is shown in the top part of Illustration 6–17.

Suppose Marmaduke Manufacturing Company had used process costing. For convenience, assume each job is defined to be a single unit of product. Total manufacturing costs were $42,000, so each "unit" would be assigned a cost of $14,000. One unit was sold; hence, the cost of goods sold under process costing would be the *average cost* of all three jobs—$14,000. This flow of costs is shown in the bottom part of Illustration 6–17.

Note that with process costing, Marmaduke Manufacturing Company does not maintain a record of the cost of each unit produced. Process costing has less detailed recordkeeping; hence, if a company was choosing between job and process costing, it would generally find that recordkeeping costs are lower under process costing. Of course, process costing does not provide

Illustration 6–16

Work in Process Inventory			
(3,000 units at $8 per unit)	24,000	(2,500 units at $8 per unit)	20,000
		(500 units at $8 per unit)	4,000

Finished Goods Inventory	
20,000	(1,500 units at $8 per unit) 12,000

Cost of Goods Sold	
12,000	

Lost Unit Cost

4,000	

Illustration 6–17
Comparative flow of costs: Job and processing costing

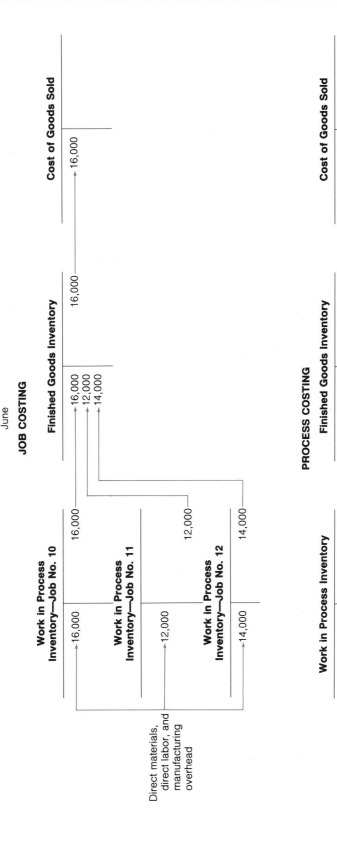

MARMADUKE MANUFACTURING COMPANY
June

JOB COSTING

Work in Process Inventory—Job No. 10	Finished Goods Inventory	Cost of Goods Sold
→16,000 16,000→	→16,000 16,000→	→16,000

Work in Process Inventory—Job No. 11		
→12,000 12,000→	→12,000	

Work in Process Inventory—Job No. 12		
→14,000 14,000→	→14,000	

Direct materials, direct labor, and manufacturing overhead

PROCESS COSTING

Work in Process Inventory	Finished Goods Inventory	Cost of Goods Sold
→42,000 42,000→	→42,000 14,000ᵃ→	→14,000

Direct materials, direct labor, and manufacturing overhead

ᵃ $14,000 = \dfrac{1\ \text{job}}{3\ \text{jobs}} \times \$42,000$

as much information as job costing because it does not maintain a record of the cost of each unit produced. Hence, the choice of process versus job costing systems involves a comparison of the costs and benefits of each system.

A cost-benefit comparison of job and process costing

Consider a house builder. Under job order costing, the costs must be accumulated for each house. If lumber is sent on a truck for delivery to several houses, it is not sufficient to record the total lumber issued, records must be kept of the amount delivered to, and subsequently returned from, each house. If laborers work on several houses, they must keep track of the time spent on *each* house. Process costing, however, simply requires recording the total costs incurred on all jobs. For the home builder, process costing records the average cost of all houses built. A custom home builder would probably use job order costing. A developer might consider each development a job, but use process costing for houses within each development.

Under process costing, the actual cost incurred for a particular unit is not reported. If all units are homogeneous, this loss of information is probably minimal. Is it important for Texas Instruments to know whether the cost of the 10,001st TI Business Analysis II calculator is different from the 10,002d? Probably not; particularly if the unit cost is calculated primarily to value inventory for external financial reporting. Cost control and performance evaluation will take place by department, not by unit produced, in process systems. For companies making relatively small, homogeneous units, the additional benefits of job costing would not justify the additional recordkeeping costs.

What if recordkeeping costs were equal under job and process systems for the units in a product line? Then we would say that job systems are better because they provide all of the data that process systems do, plus more. As a general rule, job systems are usually more costly than process systems, however. Thus, managers and accountants must decide whether there are enough additional benefits (for example, from better decisions) from knowing the actual cost of each unit, which is available in a job costing system to justify additional recordkeeping costs. For companies producing relatively large, heterogeneous items, the additional benefits of job costing usually justify the additional recordkeeping costs.

Comprehensive example, including FIFO, weighted average, prior department costs, and spoilage

This section presents a comprehensive process costing example.[1] Dexter Production Company manufactures a single product through a two-department manufacturing process—machining department and finishing department. In the production process, materials are added to the product in both departments. Normal spoilage occurs in the finishing department, and the spoiled units are not detected until units are completed and inspected. Dexter allocates production costs to spoiled units. These costs are then charged to Finished Goods Inventory because all units finished during the period are in Finished

---

[1] This example was adapted from a CPA examination.

Illustration 6–18
Comprehensive example—facts

	Machining department	Finishing department
Physical flow of units:		
Beginning inventory	–0–	20,000
Transferred in	–0–	60,000
Started in production	80,000	–0–
Transferred out	60,000	60,000
Ending inventory	20,000	18,000
Spoiled units	–0–	2,000

	Machining department	Finishing department	
	Ending inventory	Beginning inventory	Ending inventory
Percentage completion:			
Direct materials	100%	100%	100%
Direct labor	50	50	70
Overhead	25	50	70
Prior department costs	Not applicable	100	100

	Machining department	Finishing department
Beginning inventory costs:		
Direct materials	–0–	$ 28,000
Direct labor	–0–	24,000
Overhead	–0–	3,500
Prior department costs	–0–	118,000
Current costs:		
Direct materials	$240,000	90,000
Direct labor	140,000	161,500
Overhead	65,000	32,300

Goods Inventory. The information given in Illustration 6–18 appears in the company's records for October's activity.

The cost of production report for Dexter using FIFO costing is shown in Illustration 6–19 for the machining department.

Sixty thousand units valued at $360,000 are transferred into the finishing department. Using FIFO costing, the cost of production report for the finishing department is shown in Illustration 6–20.

The journal entry Dexter would use to record spoilage costs under the FIFO approach is:

Finished Goods Inventory—Spoilage Costs	21,000	
Work in Process Inventory—Finishing Department (prior department costs)		12,000
Work in Process Inventory—Finishing Department (direct materials)		3,000
Work in Process Inventory—Finishing Department (direct labor)		5,000
Work in Process Inventory—Finishing Department (manufacturing overhead)		1,000

Illustration 6–19
Cost of production report (FIFO method)—machining department

DEXTER PRODUCTION COMPANY
Machining Department

	Units of product	Equivalent units		
		Direct materials	Direct labor	Overhead costs
Status of units:				
Beginning inventory	–0–			
This period:				
To complete beginning inventory		–0–	–0–	–0–
Started and completed	60,000	60,000	60,000	60,000
Equivalent units transferred out	60,000	60,000	60,000	60,000
Ending inventory	20,000	20,000	10,000	5,000
Totals	80,000	80,000	70,000	65,000

		Direct materials	Direct labor	Overhead costs
Cost per equivalent unit:				
Costs		$240,000	$140,000	$65,000
Equivalent units		÷80,000	÷70,000	÷65,000
Cost per equivalent unit		=$3.00	=$2.00	=$1.00

	Total costs	Direct materials	Direct labor	Overhead costs
Cost assignment:				
Transferred out:				
From beginning inventory	–0–	–0–	–0–	–0–
Current period:				
Direct materials (60,000 × $3)		$180,000		
Direct labor (60,000 × $2)			$120,000	
Overhead (60,000 × $1)				$60,000
Total transferred out	$360,000			
Ending inventory:				
Direct materials (20,000 × $3)		60,000		
Direct labor (10,000 × $2)			20,000	
Overhead (5,000 × $1)				5,000
Total	85,000			
Totals	$445,000	$240,000	$140,000	$65,000

The cost flows from this example when FIFO costing is used are summarized in Illustration 6–21.

If the weighted-average method was used, the cost of production report would appear as in Illustration 6–22. The cost of production report for the machining department is the same under FIFO and weighted average because there is no beginning inventory in that department.

Illustration 6–20
Cost of production report (FIFO method)—finishing department

DEXTER PRODUCTION COMPANY
Finishing Department

		Equivalent units			
	Units of product	Prior department costs	Direct materials	Direct labor	Overhead costs
Status of units:					
Beginning inventory	20,000				
This period:					
To complete beginning inventory		–0–	–0–	10,000	10,000
Started and completed	40,000	40,000	40,000	40,000	40,000
Transferred out	60,000	40,000	40,000	50,000	50,000
Spoiled units	2,000	2,000	2,000	2,000	2,000
Ending inventory	18,000	18,000	18,000	12,600	12,600
Totals	80,000	60,000	60,000	64,600	64,600
Cost per equivalent unit:					
Costs		$360,000[a]	$ 90,000[b]	$161,500[b]	$32,300[b]
Equivalent units		÷60,000	÷60,000	÷64,600	÷64,600
Cost per equivalent unit		=$6.00	=$1.50	=$2.50	=$.50

Cost assignment:	Total costs	Prior department costs	Direct materials	Direct labor	Overhead costs
Transferred out:					
From beginning inventory	$173,500	$118,000	$ 28,000	$ 24,000	$ 3,500
Current period:					
Prior department costs (40,-000 × $6)		240,000			
Direct materials (40,-000 × $1.50)			60,000		
Direct labor (50,000 × $2.50)				125,000	
Overhead (50,000 × $.50)					25,000
Total from current period	450,000				
Spoiled units:					
(2,000 × $6)		12,000			
(2,000 × $1.50)			3,000		
(2,000 × $2.50)				5,000	
(2,000 × $.50)					1,000
Total	21,000				
Ending inventory:					
(18,000 × $6)		108,000			
(18,000 × $1.50)			27,000		
(12,600 × $2.50)				31,500	
(12,600 × $.50)					6,300
Total	172,800				
Totals	$817,300	$478,000	$118,000	$185,500	$35,800

[a] Prior department costs of the 60,000 units transferred in this period.
[b] Current costs.

Illustration 6-21 Cost flows through T-accounts (FIFO method)

DEXTER PRODUCTION COMPANY

Work in Process Inventory—Machining Department

Beg. inv.
M	-0-
L	-0-
O	-0-
T	-0-

Current period (80,000 units started)
M	240,000
L	140,000
O	65,000
T	445,000

Costs transferred out to the finishing department:
M	180,000
L	120,000
O	60,000
T	360,000

End. inv. (100%) (20,000 units) (50%) (25%)
M	60,000
L	20,000
O	5,000
T	85,000

Work in Process Inventory—Finishing Department

Beg. inv. (20,000 units)
M	(100%)	28,000
L	(50%)	24,000
O	(50%)	3,500
P	(100%)	118,000
T		173,500

Current period costs (60,000 units transferred from machining)
M	90,000
L	161,500
O	32,300
P	360,000
T	643,800

End. inv. (18,000 units)
M	(100%)	27,000
L	(70%)	31,500
O	(70%)	6,300
P	(100%)	108,000
T		172,800

Costs transferred out: 173,500

Costs in beg. inv.: 173,500

Costs to complete beg. inv.
M	-0-
L	25,000ᵃ
O	5,000ᵃ
P	-0-
T	30,000

Costs of 40,000 units started and completed in October:
M	60,000
L	100,000
O	20,000
P	240,000
T	420,000

Costs of 2,000 units spoiled in October:
M	3,000
L	5,000
O	1,000
P	12,000
T	21,000

Finished Goods Inventory

623,500
21,000

Note: M = direct materials, L = direct labor, O = manufacturing overhead, P = prior department costs, T = total costs. Percentages in parentheses are stages of completion.

ᵃ Equivalent units to complete beginning inventory times current period costs:
  L: 50% × 20,000 units × $2.50 = $25,000
  O: 50% × 20,000 units × $.50 = $5,000

ᵇ Spoiled units are assumed to come from current period's costs, not beginning inventory.

Illustration 6–22
Weighted-average cost flows—finishing department

DEXTER PRODUCTION COMPANY
Finishing Department

	Units of product	Equivalent units			
		Prior depart-ment costs	Direct materials	Direct labor	Overhead costs
Status of units:					
Transferred out[a]	60,000	60,000	60,000	60,000	60,000
Spoiled units	2,000	2,000	2,000	2,000	2,000
Ending inventory	18,000	18,000	18,000	12,600	12,600
Totals	80,000	80,000	80,000	74,600	74,600
Cost per equivalent unit:					
Costs:					
From beginning inventory		$118,000	$ 28,000	$ 24,000	$ 3,500
Current period		360,000	90,000	161,500	32,300
Total		$478,000	$118,000	$185,500	$35,800
Equivalent units		÷80,000	÷80,000	÷74,600	÷74,600
Cost per equivalent unit		=$5.9750	=$1.4750	=$2.4866	=$.4799

	Total costs	Prior depart-ment costs	Direct materials	Direct labor	Overhead costs
Cost assignment:					
Transferred out:					
(60,000 × $5.9750)		$358,500			
(60,000 × $1.4750)			$ 88,500		
(60,000 × $2.4866)				$149,196	
(60,000 × $.4799)					$28,794
Total	$624,990				
Spoiled units:					
(2,000 × $5.9750)		11,950			
(2,000 × $1.4750)			2,950		
(2,000 × $2.4866)				4,973	
(2,000 × $.4799)					960
Total	20,833				
Ending inventory:					
(18,000 × $5.9750)		107,550			
(18,000 × $1.4750)			26,550		
(12,600 × $2.4866)				31,331	
(12,600 × $.4799)					6,047
Total	171,478				
Totals	$817,301[b]	$478,000	$118,000	$185,500	$35,801[b]

[a] Includes units transferred out from beginning inventory.
[b] Amount different from comparable total in Illustration 6–20 because of rounding.

The journal entry to record spoilage under weighted average is:

Finished Goods Inventory—Spoilage adjustment	20,833	
Work in Process Inventory—Finishing Department (prior department costs)		11,950
Work in Process Inventory—Finishing Department (direct materials)		2,950
Work in Process Inventory—Finishing Department (direct labor)		4,973
Work in Process Inventory—Finishing Department (manufacturing overhead)		960

Summary

Process costing is used when it is not possible or practical to identify costs with specific lots or batches of product. The two most common methods of process costing are first-in, first-out (FIFO) costing and weighted-average costing. FIFO costing separates current period costs from the beginning inventory costs. The weighted-average method makes no distinction between beginning inventory and current period costs. As a result, weighted-average computations are simpler. However, the FIFO method is potentially more informative because it keeps separate track of current and previous period costs.

Illustration 6–23 summarizes the steps required to allocate costs to units. In comparing weighted-average and FIFO methods, note the importance of matching costs with units. Weighted-average costing includes beginning inventory (that is, work done in a previous period) in computing both equivalent units and unit costs, while FIFO costing *excludes* beginning inventory in computing equivalent units and unit costs.

Costs are usually applied to products at different times in the production process. Costs applied at the same time are usually grouped together for computational purposes. For example, if direct labor and manufacturing overhead are applied at the same time, they are combined into one category—conversion costs. Companies typically have three distinct categories of costs: direct materials, conversion costs, and prior department costs. The latter are costs transferred in from previous departments which, conceptually, are a type of direct materials to the receiving department.

Sometimes inputs and outputs are measured differently. When this is the case, the input units are typically redefined into the way output units are measured.

When units are spoiled in production, a common practice is to spread all costs, including costs incurred on the spoiled units, over the *good units* produced. An alternative is to remove the spoiled units from work in process (that is, credit Work in Process Inventory) and charge them to inventories and cost of goods sold. If the spoilage or lost units are not a normal part of production, then they are typically written off as a period expense for external financial reporting purposes.

Process costing systems accumulate costs for each production department;

Illustration 6–23   **Summary of steps for assigning process costs to units**

FIFO

1. *Equivalent units.* Determine equivalent units of production *this period* by adding:
   a. Work *this period* on units in beginning inventory.
   b. Work on units started and completed this period.
   c. Work on units started this period and in ending inventory.

2. *Unit cost.* Divide the total current period costs by the total equivalent units to obtain *this period's* unit cost.

3. *Costs transferred out.* Costs transferred out are the sum of:
   a. Cost of partly finished units in beginning inventory. These costs were incurred in a previous period and are transferred out in total.
   b. The current period unit cost times current period equivalent units transferred out.

4. *Ending inventory.* Costs assigned to ending inventory are the product of the current period unit cost and the number of current period equivalent units in ending inventory.

Weighted average

1. *Equivalent units.* Determine equivalent units of production this period *plus* those in beginning inventory. A shortcut method is to add:
   a. Total units transferred out.
   b. Equivalent units in ending inventory.

2. *Unit cost.* Divide the total current period costs plus costs in beginning inventory by total equivalent units to obtain a weighted average unit cost.

3. *Costs transferred out.* Costs transferred out are the product of the unit cost times the total units transferred out.

4. *Ending inventory.* Costs assigned to ending inventory are the product of the unit cost times the number of equivalent units in ending inventory.

however, they do not maintain separate records of costs for each unit produced. Thus, when comparing job costing and process costing systems, companies generally find that job costing provides more data but has greater recordkeeping costs. Managers and accountants must decide whether the additional data available under job costing justifies the higher recordkeeping costs. For companies in which relatively homogeneous units are produced in a continuous process, cost-benefit analysis generally favors process costing.

Terms and concepts

The following terms and concepts should be familiar to you after reading this chapter.

Abnormal spoilage

Conversion costs

Cost of production report

Equivalent unit

First-in, first-out (FIFO) costing

Good output

Lost units

Normal spoilage

Prior department costs

Process costing

Weighted-average costing

Self-study problem No. 1

FlyinFast, Inc., manufactures racquetball racquets. The process requires two manufacturing departments: frames and strings. Racquets are formed in the frames department using aluminum tubing, handle materials, and frame decorations. The completed frames are sent to the strings department where the racquets are stringed and packaged for shipment to sporting goods stores. Six thousand frames were transferred to the strings department this month.

Because the racquets are manufactured in such large numbers, the company uses a process cost accounting system to assign costs to racquets. The following information is available for FlyinFast manufacturing activities of the strings department during the past month:

	Units	Prior department costs	Direct materials	Conversion costs
Physical flow:				
Beginning inventory	1,000	100% complete	60% complete	75% complete
Ending inventory	2,700	100% complete	80% complete	45% complete
Costs incurred:				
Beginning inventory	—	$ 7,100	$ 600	$ 420
Current costs		43,200	2,500	6,475

Required:

Assume no units were lost or spoiled until you get to Requirements (e) and (f).

a. Prepare a schedule showing the equivalent production in the strings department if FIFO process costing were used.

b. Use a T-account to show the cost flows in the strings department under FIFO.

c. Prepare a schedule showing equivalent production in the strings department using weighted-average process costing.

d. Use a T-account to show cost flows in the strings department using weighted-average costing.

e. Assume that at the end of the stringing process, normal spoilage occurred. This was due to bending of the frames caused by tension produced at the end of the stringing process. Normal spoilage amounted to 100 units, and consequently the number of good units in ending inventory is 2,600. Recompute the equivalent units using both the FIFO method and the weighted-average method of process costing. Finish with a journal entry which removes the units from Work in Process Inventory and charges two thirds of their costs to Finished Goods Inventory and one third to Cost of Goods Sold.

f. Independent of your work for (e), assume that there were 140 units of abnormal spoilage, which occurred at the end of the stringing process, leaving inventory at the end of the month of 2,560 units. Recompute the equivalent units using both the FIFO method and weighted-average method of process costing. Finish with a journal entry that removes the units from Work in Process Inventory and charges abnormal spoilage to Abnormal Spoilage Expense.

Solution to self-study problem No. 1

a. Equivalent units—FIFO:

	Prior depart-ment costs	Direct materials	Conversion costs
To complete beginning inventory	–0–	400 (40%)[a]	250 (25%)[a]
Started and completed	3,300[b]	3,300[b]	3,300[b]
Ending inventory	2,700[c]	2,160 (80%)[c]	1,215 (45%)[c]
Equivalent work this period	6,000	5,860	4,765

[a] These percentages equal one minus the precent complete given in the problem.

[b] Beginning inventory + Current work − Ending inventory = Transferred out = 1,000 + 6,000 − 2,700 = 4,300. Of the 4,300 units transferred out, the first 1,000 are assumed to have come from the beginning inventory because we are using FIFO.

[c] Given in the problem.

b. See page 208.

b. Cost flows—FIFO:

Work in Process Inventory—Strings Department

Beginning inventory:			To Finished Goods			
Prior department			Inventory:			
costs	7,100[a]		From beginning			
Materials	600[a]		inventory		8,120	
Conversion costs	420[a]		From this period's			
Total beginning			costs:			
inventory		8,120	Prior department			
This period's costs:			costs	23,760[b]		
Prior department			Materials	1,578[c]		
costs included			Conversion costs	4,824[d]		
in units			Total trans-			
transferred into			ferred from			
this department			this period's			
this period	43,200[a]		costs		30,162	
Materials used			Total trans-			
this period	2,500[a]		ferred to			
Conversion costs			Finished			
incurred this			Goods			
period	6,475[a]		Inventory		38,282[e]	
Total costs						
incurred						
this period		52,175				
Total costs						
to be						
accounted						
for		60,295[e]				
Ending inventory:						
Prior department						
costs (43,200 −						
23,760)	19,440[f]					
Materials (2,500 −						
1,578)	922[f]					
Conversion costs						
(6,475 − 4,824)	1,651[f]					
Total ending						
inventory		22,013[e]				

[a] Given in the problem.

[b] Prior department costs transferred to Finished Goods Inventory:

$$\frac{\$43,200}{6,000 \text{ EU}} \times 3,300 \text{ units} = \$23,760$$

[c] Materials costs transferred to Finished Goods Inventory:

$$\frac{\$2,500}{5,860 \text{ EU}} \times (400 + 3,300) \text{ units} = \$1,578$$

[d] Conversion costs transferred to Finished Goods Inventory:

$$\frac{\$6,475}{4,765 \text{ EU}} \times (250 + 3,300) \text{ units} = \$4,824$$

[e] Of the $60,295 total costs to be accounted for, $38,282 were transferred to Finished Goods Inventory and $22,013 remained in ending Work in Process Inventory.

[f] These amounts may be found by subtracting costs transferred out from this period's costs (see calculations in parentheses), or they may be found by multiplying the equivalent unit cost times the equivalent units in ending inventory, as follows:

$$\text{Prior department costs: } \frac{\$43,200}{6,000 \text{ EU}} \times 2,700 \text{ units} = \$19,440$$

$$\text{Direct materials: } \frac{\$2,500}{5,860 \text{ EU}} \times (2,700 \times .80) = \$922$$

$$\text{Conversion costs: } \frac{\$6,475}{4,765 \text{ EU}} \times (2,700 \times .45) = \$1,651$$

c. Equivalent units—weighted average:

	Prior department costs	Direct materials	Conversion costs
Units transferred out	4,300	4,300	4,300
Ending inventory	2,700	2,160	1,215
	7,000	6,460	5,515

d. Cost flows—weighted average:

Work in Process Inventory—Strings Department

Prior department costs:			To Finished Goods Inventory:	
Beginning inventory	7,100		Prior department costs:	
Current	43,200		$(50,300 \div 7,000) \times 4,300 = 30,899$	
Total		50,300	Materials:	
			$(3,100 \div 6,460) \times 4,300 =$	2,063
Materials:			Conversion costs:	
Beginning inventory	600		$(6,895 \div 5,515) \times 4,300 =$	5,376
Current	2,500		Total transferred to	
Total		3,100	Finished Goods	
Conversion costs:			Inventory	38,338[a]
Beginning inventory	420			
Current	6,475			
Total		6,895		
Total costs to be accounted for		60,295[a]		

Ending inventory:			
Prior department costs (50,300 − 30,899)	19,401		
Materials (3,100 − 2,063)	1,037		
Conversion costs (6,895 − 5,376)	1,519		
Total ending inventory		21,957[a]	

[a] Of the $60,295 total costs to be accounted for, $38,338 were transferred to Finished Goods Inventory and $21,957 remained in ending Work in Process Inventory.

e.

Equivalent units—FIFO

	Units of product	Prior department costs	Direct materials	Conversion costs
To complete beginning inventory	1,000	–0–	400 (40%)	250 (25%)
Started and completed	3,300	3,300	3,300	3,300
Transferred out	4,300	3,300	3,700	3,550
Spoiled units	100	100	100	100
Ending inventory	2,600	2,600	2,080 (80%)	1,170 (45%)
Totals	7,000	6,000	5,880	4,820

Cost assignment—FIFO

	Total costs	Prior department costs	Direct materials	Conversion costs
Transferred out:				
From beginning inventory	$ 8,120	$ 7,100	$ 600	$ 420
From current period:				
Prior department costs				
$\left(3,300 \times \dfrac{\$43,200}{6,000}\right)$		23,760		
Direct materials				
$\left(3,700 \times \dfrac{\$2,500}{5,880}\right)$			1,573	
Conversion costs				
$\left(3,550 \times \dfrac{\$6,475}{4,820}\right)$				4,769
Total	30,102			
Spoiled units:				
$\left(100 \times \dfrac{\$43,200}{6,000}\right)$		720		
$\left(100 \times \dfrac{\$2,500}{5,880}\right)$			43	
$\left(100 \times \dfrac{\$6,475}{4,820}\right)$				134
Total	897			
Ending inventory:				
$\left(2,600 \times \dfrac{\$43,200}{6,000}\right)$		18,720		
$\left(2,080 \times \dfrac{\$2,500}{5,880}\right)$			884	
$\left(1,170 \times \dfrac{\$6,475}{4,820}\right)$				1,572
Total	21,176			
Totals	$60,295	$50,300	$3,100	$6,895

Note: Direct materials and conversion cost figures are rounded to the nearest dollar.

Journal entry—FIFO:

Finished Goods Inventory	598	
Cost of Goods Sold	299	
Work in Process Inventory—Strings Department:		
Prior departmental costs		720
Direct materials		43
Conversion costs		134

Total spoilage = $897.

Amount assigned to Finished Goods Inventory per problem requirement is $598 (= ⅔ × $897). The remaining $299 (= ⅓ × $897) is assigned to Cost of Goods Sold.

Equivalent units—weighted average:

	Units of product	Prior department costs	Direct materials costs	Conversion costs
Transferred out	4,300	4,300	4,300	4,300
Spoiled units	100	100	100	100
Ending inventory	2,600	2,600	2,080 (80%)	1,170 (45%)
Totals	7,000	7,000	6,480	5,570

Cost assignment—weighted average:

	Total costs	Prior department costs	Direct materials costs	Conversion costs
Transferred out:				
$\left(4{,}300 \times \dfrac{\$50{,}300}{7{,}000}\right)$		$30,899		
$\left(4{,}300 \times \dfrac{\$3{,}100}{6{,}480}\right)$			$2,057	
$\left(4{,}300 \times \dfrac{\$6{,}895}{5{,}570}\right)$				$5,323
Total	$38,279			
Spoiled units:				
$\left(100 \times \dfrac{\$50{,}300}{7{,}000}\right)$		719		
$\left(100 \times \dfrac{\$3{,}100}{6{,}480}\right)$			48	
$\left(100 \times \dfrac{\$6{,}895}{5{,}570}\right)$				124
Total	891			
Ending inventory:				
$\left(2{,}600 \times \dfrac{\$50{,}300}{7{,}000}\right)$		18,683		
$\left(2{,}080 \times \dfrac{\$3{,}100}{6{,}480}\right)$			995	
$\left(1{,}170 \times \dfrac{\$6{,}895}{5{,}570}\right)$				1,448
Total	21,126			
Totals	$60,296	$50,301	$3,100	$6,895

Journal entry—weighted average:

Finished Goods Inventory	594	
Cost of Goods Sold	297	
Work in Process Inventory—Strings Department:		
Prior departmental costs		719
Direct materials		48
Conversion costs		124

Total: $891.

Finished Goods Inventory: ⅔ × $891 = $594.

Cost of Goods Sold: ⅓ × $891 = $297.

f.

Equivalent units—FIFO:

	Units of product	Prior department costs	Direct materials	Conversion costs
To complete beginning inventory	1,000	–0–	400 (40%)	250 (25%)
Started and completed	3,300	3,300	3,300	3,300
Transferred out	4,300	3,300	3,700	3,550
Abnormal spoilage	140	140	140	140
Ending inventory	2,560	2,560	2,048 (80%)	1,152 (45%)
Totals	7,000	6,000	5,888	4,842

Cost assignment—FIFO:

	Total	Prior department costs	Direct materials	Conversion costs
Transfered out from beginning inventory	$ 8,120	$ 7,100	$ 600	$ 420
Current period costs:				
$\left(3,300 \times \frac{\$43,200}{6,000}\right)$		23,760		
$\left(3,700 \times \frac{\$2,500}{5,888}\right)$			1,571	
$\left(3,550 \times \frac{\$6,475}{4,842}\right)$				4,747
Total		30,078		
Abnormal spoilage:				
$\left(140 \times \frac{\$43,200}{6,000}\right)$		$ 1,008		
$\left(140 \times \frac{\$2,500}{5,888}\right)$			$ 59	
$\left(140 \times \frac{\$6,475}{4,842}\right)$				$ 187
Total	$ 1,254			
Ending inventory:				
$\left(2,560 \times \frac{\$43,200}{6,000}\right)$		18,432		
$\left(2,048 \times \frac{\$2,500}{5,888}\right)$			870	
$\left(1,152 \times \frac{\$6,475}{4,842}\right)$				1,541
Total	20,843			
Totals	$60,295	$50,300	$3,100	$6,895

Journal entry—FIFO:

Abnormal Spoilage Cost:	1,254	
Work in Process Inventory—Strings Department:		
Prior departmental costs		1,008
Direct materials costs		59
Conversion costs		187

Equivalent units—weighted average:

	Units of product	Prior department costs	Direct materials costs	Conversion costs
Transferred out	4,300	4,300	4,300	4,300
Abnormal spoilage	140	140	140	140
Ending inventory	2,560	2,560	2,048 (80%)	1,152 (45%)
Totals	7,000	7,000	6,488	5,592

Cost assignment—weighted average:

	Total	Prior department	Direct materials	Conversion costs
Transferred out:				
$\left(4,300 \times \dfrac{\$50,300}{7,000}\right)$		$30,899		
$\left(4,300 \times \dfrac{\$3,100}{6,488}\right)$			$2,054	
$\left(4,300 \times \dfrac{\$6,895}{5,592}\right)$				$5,302
Total	$38,255			
Abnormal spoilage:				
$\left(140 \times \dfrac{\$50,300}{7,000}\right)$		1,006		
$\left(140 \times \dfrac{\$3,100}{6,488}\right)$			67	
$\left(140 \times \dfrac{\$6,895}{5,592}\right)$				173
Total	1,246			
Ending Inventory:				
$\left(2,560 \times \dfrac{\$50,300}{7,000}\right)$		$18,395		
$\left(2,048 \times \dfrac{\$3,100}{6,488}\right)$			$ 979	
$\left(1,152 \times \dfrac{\$6,895}{5,592}\right)$				$1,420
Total	20,794			
Totals	$60,295	$50,300	$3,100	$6,895

Journal entry—weighted average:

Abnormal Spoilage Cost	1,246	
Work in Process Inventory:		
Prior department costs		1,006
Direct materials		67
Conversion costs		173

Self-study problem No. 2

Compute a cost for spoiled units

A company using the weighted-average costing method maintains a Spoilage Expense account for spoiled goods. This account is charged with the cost of units spoiled in process. Each unit spoiled is considered 80 percent complete with respect to conversion costs and 100 percent complete with respect to materials at the time of spoilage.

The accounting records show the following information for the activities in the Work in Process Inventory account:

Beginning inventory:
| Direct materials | $14,800 |
| Conversion costs | 21,650 |

Current period:
Direct materials	43,100
Conversion costs	79,220
Units transferred out	18,200
Units spoiled	2,300

Ending inventory:
Physical count	6,400
Percent of completion:	
Direct materials	40%
Conversion costs	25%

Required:

Compute the costs to be assigned to the spoiled units.

Solution to self-study problem No. 2

First, compute the equivalent units:

	Direct materials	Conversion costs
Transferred out	18,200	18,200
Spoiled 2,300 units	2,300 (100%)	1,840 (80%)
Ending inventory 6,400 units	2,560 (40%)	1,600 (25%)
Totals	23,060 EU	21,640 EU

Next, compute the total costs:

Beginning inventory	$14,800	$ 21,650
Current costs	43,100	79,220
Total costs	$57,900	$100,870

Next, compute costs per equivalent unit:

$57,900 ÷ 23,060 EU = $2.5108 per EU
$100,870 ÷ 21,640 EU = $4.6613 per EU

Then, multiply by the equivalent units spoiled:

| Direct materials | $2.5108 × 2,300 EU = $5,775 |
| Conversion costs | 4.6613 × 1,840 EU = $8,577 |

The total spoiled unit cost is $14,352 (= $5,775 + 8,577).

Questions

6–1. A manufacturing company has records of its current activity in work in process inventory and of its ending work in process inventory. However, the record of its beginning inventory has been lost. Express in equation form the data that would be needed to compute the beginning inventory.

6–2. If costs change from one period to another, costs that are transferred out of one department under FIFO process costing will include units with two different costs. Why?

6–3. Management of a company that manufactures small appliances is trying to decide whether to install a job order or process costing system. The manufacturing vice president has stated that job order costing gives them the best control because it is possible to assign costs to specific lots of goods. The controller, however, has stated that job order costing would require too much recordkeeping. Is there another costing system that might meet the manufacturing vice president's control objectives? Explain.

6–4. What are two ways to compute the number of units started and completed during a period?

6–5. Why are equivalent units computed for process costing? What is the distinction between equivalent units under FIFO and equivalent units under the weighted-average method?

6–6. Farleigh O. Tuvit is a new member of the controller's staff in the same company as you. Farleigh has just completed a report that urges the company to adopt the LIFO method for inventory accounting. The controller is concerned about the recommendation because the cost records are maintained on a FIFO basis. Indeed, the controller has not even heard of using LIFO for process cost accounting. Can you suggest how the controller might resolve the problem?

6–7. It has been said that prior department costs behave similarly to direct materials costs. Under what conditions are the costs similar. What differences arise that require the costs to be treated separately?

6–8. While examining the cost records of a company, you note that while the costs have changed from one period to another, the cost per equivalent unit transferred in to a subsequent department is the same as the cost per equivalent unit transferred out of the previous department. What does this tell you about the cost system in use?

6–9. A company wants to use weighted-average costing because it is simple to apply. However, the company also wishes to be able to monitor its costs. Is it possible to monitor cost trends using weighted average?

6–10. Describe methods for handling lost units in a process that expects certain losses due to shrinkage, evaporation, or other inherent characteristics of the process?

Exercises

6–11. Inventory flows, equivalent units—FIFO costing

For each of the following independent cases, determine the information requested (assume FIFO):

a. Beginning inventory amounted to 1,000 units. There were 4,500 units started and completed this period. At the end of the period, there were 3,000 units in inventory that were 30 percent complete. Using FIFO costing, the equivalent production for the period was 5,600 units. What was the percentage of completion of the beginning inventory?

b. The ending inventory had a value of $8,700 for conversion costs. There were 4,200 equivalent units required to complete the beginning inventory and 6,000 units started and completed. The ending inventory represented 1,000 equivalent units of work this period. FIFO costing is used. What was the total incurred for conversion costs this period?

c. There were 500 units in the beginning inventory that were 40 percent complete with respect to materials. During the period, 4,000 units were transferred out. The ending inventory consisted of 700 units that were 70 percent complete with respect to materials. How many units were started and completed during the period?

d. At the start of the period, there were 4,000 units in the work in process inventory. There were 3,000 units in the ending inventory and during the period, 9,500 units were transferred out to the next department. Materials and conversion costs are added evenly throughout the production process. FIFO costing is used. How many units were started this period?

6-12. Inventory flows, equivalent units—weighted-average costing

For each of the following cases, determine the units or equivalent units requested (assume weighted-average):

a. There were 8,200 units in the beginning inventory that were 40 percent complete with respect to conversion costs. During the period, 7,000 units were started. There were 6,500 units in the ending inventory that were 20 percent complete with respect to conversion costs. How many units were transferred out?

b. The beginning inventory consisted of 2,000 units with a direct materials cost of $14,200. The equivalent work represented by all of the direct materials costs in the Work in Process Inventory account amounted to 9,000 units. There were 3,000 units in ending inventory that were 20 percent complete with respect to materials. The ending inventory had a direct materials cost assigned of $4,500. What was the total materials costs incurred this period?

c. The Work in Process Inventory account had a beginning balance of $1,900 for conversion costs on items in process. During the period, $18,100 in conversion costs were charged to the account. Also during the period $19,200 in costs were transferred out. There were 400 units in the beginning inventory, and 4,800 units were transferred out during the period. How many equivalent units are in the ending inventory?

d. There were 2,100 units transferred in to the department during the period. The direct materials costs amounted to $2,520. The 3,200 units transferred out were charged to the next department at an amount that included $3,360 for direct materials costs. The ending inventory was 25 percent complete with respect to direct materials and had a cost of $630 assigned to it. How many units are in the ending inventory?

6-13. Compute equivalent units—FIFO and weighted-average methods

A company's records show the following information concerning the work in process in a manufacturing plant:

1. Beginning inventory, 6,000 units (30 percent complete—materials; 40 percent complete—conversion costs).
2. Transferred out, 17,000 units.
3. Ending inventory (10 percent complete—materials; 5 percent complete—conversion costs).

4. Started this month, 21,000 units.

a. Compute the equivalent units with respect to materials and conversion costs using the FIFO method.
b. Compute the equivalent units with respect to materials and conversion costs using the weighted-average method.

6–14. Compute costs per equivalent unit— FIFO method

The beginning work in process inventory showed a balance of $48,240. Of this amount, $16,440 arose from direct materials costs, and the balance was from conversion costs. There were 8,000 units in the beginning inventory that were 30 percent complete with respect to both direct materials and conversion costs.

During the period, 17,000 units were transferred out and 5,000 remained in the ending inventory. The units in the ending inventory were 80 percent complete with respect to direct materials and 40 percent complete with respect to conversion costs.

Costs incurred during the period amounted to $126,852 for direct materials and $219,120 for conversion. The FIFO method is used for inventory accounting purposes.

Compute the cost per equivalent unit for direct materials and for conversion costs.

6–15. Compute equivalent units and assign costs—FIFO method

The following data are presented in the accounting records for a company's manufacturing operations:

Item	Direct materials	Conversion costs	Total
Beginning inventory	$16,200	$13,100	$ 29,300
Current work	45,440	47,190	92,630
Totals	$61,640	$60,290	$121,930

During the period, the units that were transferred out included 6,400 equivalent units of current period work for direct materials and 6,700 equivalent units of current work for conversion costs. The ending inventory consisted of 2,000 units that were 35 percent complete with respect to direct materials and 55 percent complete with respect to conversion costs.

a. Compute the costs per equivalent unit for direct materials and conversion cost.
b. What are the costs transferred out and the costs assigned to the ending work in process inventory?

6–16. Assign costs— weighted-average method

A company uses the weighted-average method for accounting for its work in process inventories. The accounting records show the following information:

Beginning inventory (WIP):	
Direct materials	$ 360
Conversion costs	108
	$ 468

Debits to WIP this period:	
Direct materials	$3,714
Conversion costs	2,258

Quantity information is obtained from the manufacturing records and includes the following:

Beginning inventory	300 units
Percent of completion:	
Direct materials	60%
Conversion costs	30%
Current period units started	2,000 units
Ending inventory	600 units
Percent of completion:	
Direct materials	40%
Conversion costs	20%

Required:

a. Compute the cost per equivalent unit for direct materials and for conversion costs.

b. Determine the costs to be assigned to the ending work in process inventory.

Problems and cases

6–17. Compute manufacturing costs in several inventory accounts

The Jorcano Manufacturing Company uses a process cost system to account for its Product D. Production begins in the fabrication department where units of direct material are molded into connecting parts. After fabrication is complete, the units are transferred to the assembly department. There is no material added in the assembly department. After assembly is complete, the units are transferred to the packaging department where the units are prepared for shipping. After the units are ready for shipment, they are moved to the loading dock.

At the end of the period, the following inventory of Product D is on hand in the various locations around the plant:

1. No unused direct material or packing material.
2. Fabrication department: 300 units, one-third complete with respect to direct materials and one-half complete with respect to conversion costs.
3. Assembly department: 1,000 units, two-fifths complete with respect to conversion costs.
4. Packaging department: 100 units, three-fourths complete with respect to packing material and one-fourth complete with respect to conversion costs.
5. Loading dock: 400 units.

The direct materials entered in process in the fabrication department had a cost of $1.30 per equivalent unit of fabrication department output.

Required:

a. The direct materials costs in each of the inventory accounts.

b. The number of equivalent units of fabrication department labor in all inventories.

c. The number of equivalent units of assembly department conversion costs in all inventories.

(CPA adapted)

6–18. Compute equivalent units—FIFO and weighted average

The following information appears in the records of the Furlong Production Company:

Work in process inventory—molding department

Beginning inventory:		
Transferred-in costs	$ 4,800	3,000 units
Direct materials	1,080	20% complete
Conversion costs	600	25% complete

Current work:

Transferred-in costs	10,850	7,000 units
Direct materials	18,585	
Conversion costs	6,764	

The ending inventory is comprised of 1,000 units that are 45 percent complete with respect to direct materials and 65 percent complete with respect to conversion costs.

Required:

a. Compute the costs per equivalent unit using the FIFO method.
b. Compute the costs per equivalent unit using the weighted-average method.
c. Indicate whether the current period costs have increased, decreased, or remained the same compared to the period costs reflected in the beginning inventory.

6–19. Compute equivalent units— spoiled units omitted

Welgel, Inc., has a chemical process which incurs a 10 percent spoilage loss due to the nature of the chemical process. During the current period, liquid chemical which would be expected to result in 5,000 units of output was added to the process. There were 2,000 units that were 90 percent complete at the start of the period. All spoilage occurs between the 50 percent and 60 percent completion stage of the process. Materials and conversion costs are incurred at the same rate in the process. The ending inventory was 20 percent complete and consisted of 1,000 units before expected spoilage losses.

Required:

Compute the equivalent good units of work done this period. (Hint: Convert all units to equivalent units of good output.)

6–20. FIFO process costing

Mercantile Recovery Corporation has devised a process for converting garbage into liquid fuel. While the direct materials costs are zero, the operations requires the use of some direct labor and overhead. The company employs a process costing system and wishes to keep track of the production and costs of each period. At the start of the current period, there were 1,000 units in the work in process inventory. These units were 40 percent complete and were carried at a cost of $420.

During the month, costs of $18,000 were incurred. There were 9,000 units started during the period, and there were 500 units still in process at the end of the period. The ending units were 20 percent complete

Required:

a. Prepare a cost of production report to reflect these activities.
b. Show the flow of costs through T-accounts.

6–21. FIFO costing with multiple departments and changes in output unit measurements

(Requires solution of Problem 6–20.) Mercantile Recovery Corporation (from Problem 6–20) has a second department that blends the liquid fuel from the first department with ethanol to generate a liquid fuel with a higher octane content. Due to evaporation during the process, the input quantities will equal 105 percent of the output quantities. The company expresses all input units in terms of the equivalent output that can be obtained after allowing for the evaporation losses. Consequently, all beginning and ending inventory figures are stated in units of expected good output.

At the start of the month, there were 800 units in process that were 50 percent complete with respect to the addition of ethanol and 75 percent complete with respect to conversion costs. The costs of the beginning inventory are itemized as follows:

Transferred-in costs	$926
Ethanol	76
Conversion costs	150

During the period, the units received from the first department were put into production. Costs of $3,000 were incurred for ethanol, and costs of $5,000 were incurred for conversion. The ending inventory consisted of 900 units that were 20 percent complete with respect to the addition of ethanol and 30 percent complete with respect to conversion costs.

Required:

a. Prepare a cost of production report for the period.
b. Show the flow of costs through T-accounts.

6–22. FIFO process costing—two departments

Mellovar Chemical Company manufactures a blended chemical, X-9, for use as a wood preservative. Two chemicals (A and C) are mixed in the blending department and allowed to cure. After the curing period, the blend is sent to the distillation unit where heat processes extract the preservative. The company uses a FIFO system for accounting for work in process costs.

During the month, the following information appeared in the company records:

	Department	
Item	Blending	Distillation
Work in process inventory— start	3,000 liters	7,000 liters
Percentage of completion:		
Direct materials	30%	20%
Conversion costs	25%	40%
Ending inventory	4,000 liters	5,000 liters
Percentage of completion:		
Direct materials	40%	30%
Conversion costs	30%	60%
Units started during the period	?	11,000 liters
Units transferred out	?	?
Beginning inventory costs:		
Direct materials	$ 900	$ 840
Conversion costs	900	2,660
Transferred-in costs	–0–	16,100
Ending inventory costs:		
Direct materials	1,520	1,080
Conversion costs	1,380	2,625

The items marked with a question mark were not readily obtainable from the company records. There is no change in unit measurement between departments; all quantities are measured in liters. There are no losses in either department.

Required:

a. Prepare a cost of production report for the blending and distillation departments.
b. Show the flow of costs through T-accounts.

6–23. Normal and abnormal spoilage— FIFO

Refer to the information presented for the Mellovar Chemical Company in Problem 6–22. Assume the following:

1. 9,500 units were transferred out of the distillation department.
2. Prior department costs of units transferred in to distillation are $23,100.
3. It is expected that normal spoilage amounts to 30 percent of all units that are transferred into distillation. Any other unaccounted for units are assumed to be abnormal spoilage since a physical inventory confirmed the ending inventory and the units that were transferred in were counted at that time.

4. Normal spoilage occurs during the first 10 percent of the distillation process.
5. All spoilage costs are removed from Work in Process Inventory and charged to Abnormal Spoilage Costs or to Finished Goods Inventory (for normal spoilage) at the end of the accounting period.
6. Carry all calculations to three (3) decimal places, if necessary.
7. Mellovar Chemical Company uses FIFO process costing.

Required:

a. Prepare a cost of production report and a schedule of cost flows for the distillation department accounting for all normal and abnormal spoilage.
b. Prepare the journal entry that is consistent with item 5 above.

6–24. Cost of production report—weighted-average method

Spirit Processing Corporation uses the weighted-average method for its cost accounting. The company's books show the following balances:

	Units	Costs
Work in Process Inventory	300,000	$ 660,960
Finished Goods Inventory	200,000	1,009,800

Work in process inventory is 50 percent complete with respect to conversion costs. Materials are added at the beginning of the manufacturing process, and overhead is applied at the rate of 60 percent of the direct labor costs. There was no finished goods inventory at the start of the period. The following additional information is also available:

	Units	Costs Direct materials	Costs Direct labor
Beginning inventory (80% complete as to labor)	200,000	$ 200,000	$ 315,000
Units started	1,000,000		
Current costs		1,300,000	1,995,000
Units completed	900,000		

Required:

a. Prepare a cost of production report for Spirit Processing Company.
b. Show the adjusting journal entry required to reconcile the difference between recorded and actual ending balances of Work in Process Inventory and Finished Goods Inventory. Adjust Cost of Goods Sold for any difference.

(CPA adapted)

6–25. Equivalent unit computations—FIFO costing with spoiled units

Poole, Inc., produces a chemical compound by a continuous chemical process in two departments (A and B). The process functions as follows:

The chemical compound requires one kilogram of Chemical X and one kilogram of Chemical Y. One kilogram of Chemical X is processed in Department A and transferred to Department B for further processing. In Department B, one kilogram of Chemical Y is added when the process is 50 percent complete. When the processing is complete, the product is transferred to finished goods inventory.

Normal spoilage occurs in Department A. Five percent of Chemical X is lost in the first few seconds of processing. No spoilage occurs in Department B.

Conversion costs occur uniformly throughout the process. Poole's unit of measure for work in process is equivalent kilograms of good output. Chemical Y may or may not be in the inventories depending on the stage of processing.

The company records show the following information for the current month:

	Department A	Department B
Units in process at start	8,000 kg.	10,000 kg.
Stage of completion	75%	30%
Started or transferred in	50,000 kg.	?
Transferred out	46,500 kg.	?
Stage of completion of ending inventory	33⅓%	20%
Total equivalent units of direct materials added in Department B		44,500

Required:

Prepare the equivalent units computations for a cost of production report for Poole's chemical processing operation.

(CPA adapted)

6–26. FIFO process costing, overhead allocation

Zeus Company has two production departments (fabricating and finishing) and three cost centers for costs incurred to support manufacturing operations. In the fabricating department, polyplast is prepared from miracle mix and bypro. In the finishing department, each unit of polyplast is converted into six tetraplexes and three uniplexes.

The services represented by the costs accumulated in the service cost centers are provided to both producing departments. Service department costs are allocated to producing departments as follows:

Service cost	Allocation base
Building occupancy	Space occupied
Timekeeping and personnel	Number of employees
Other	50% to fabricating
	50% to finishing

Both production departments use process costing systems. All inventories are costed on a FIFO basis. The following data were taken from the fabricating department's records for the current month:

Quantities of polyplast:	
On hand at start of month	3,000
Started during the month	25,000
Transferred to finishing	19,000
Lost in process	3,000

Costs of work in process:	
Beginning inventory:	
Direct materials	$ 13,000
Conversion costs	39,000
Current period costs:	
Direct labor	154,000
Direct production overhead	132,000

The direct production overhead does not include any allocation of service costs. The service costs for the month were:

Building occupancy	$45,000
Timekeeping and personnel	27,500
Other	39,000

Utilization of service cost center allocation bases were as follows:

	Space occupied	Number of employees
Fabricating	75,000	135
Finishing	37,500	90
Totals	112,500	225

Additional inventory data for the fabricating department are:

Percentage of completion:
  Beginning of month   66⅔% materials   50% conversion
  End of month   100% materials   75% conversion

Materials inventory:

	Miracle mix		Bypro	
	Quantity	**Amount**	**Quantity**	**Amount**
Beginning inventory	62,000	$62,000	265,000	$18,550
Purchases:				
12th of the month	39,500	49,375		
20th of the month	28,500	34,200		
Fabricating usage	83,200		50,000	

Required:

a. Prepare a cost of production report for the fabricating department for the month. Include the supporting schedules necessary to explain your computations.
b. Show the flow of costs through T-accounts.

(CPA adapted)

6-27. Overhead cost allocation, FIFO process costing

Malcolm Company engages in continuous processing of cereals for bulk sales and uses FIFO process costing to account for its manufacturing costs. This costing method is used because costs are quite volatile due to the price volatility of commodities. The cereals are processed through one department. Overhead is applied on the basis of direct labor costs. The application rate has not changed over the period covered by the problem. The Work in Process Inventory account showed the following balances at the start of the current period:

Direct materials	$32,750
Direct labor	65,000
Overhead applied	81,250

These costs were related to 26,000 units that were in the process at the start of the period.

During the period, 30,000 units were transferred to Finished Goods Inventory. Of the units finished this period, 70 percent were sold. The costs charged to Finished Goods Inventory are allocated to Cost of Goods Sold based on the average costs of the period. No distinction is made in Finished Goods Inventory of the costs to complete beginning Work in Process Inventory and the costs of goods started and completed this period.

The equivalent units this period with respect to materials was 25,000. Of these units, there were 5,000 equivalent units with respect to materials in the ending work in process inventory. Materials costs incurred during the period totaled $75,100.

Conversion costs of $321,750 were charged into process in connection with the 31,250 equivalent units of work done this period with respect to these costs. The ending inventory consisted of a number of units which had 11,000 equivalent units of conversion costs of work on it as of the end of the period.

The balance in the Manufacturing Overhead account at the end of the period was $165,000.

Prepare T-accounts to show the flow of costs in the system. Any difference between actual and applied overhead of the period should be prorated to inventories and to cost of goods sold.

6–28. Weighted-average process costing with shrinkage

West Corporation is a divisionalized manufacturing company. A product called Aggregate is manufactured in one department of the California Division. Aggregate is transferred upon completion to the Utah Division at a predetermined price where it is used in the manufacture of other products.

Direct materials are added at the beginning of the process. Labor and overhead are added continuously throughout the process. Normal shrinkage of 10 to 14 percent, all occurs at the beginning of the process. In the California Division, all departmental overhead is charged to the departments, and divisional overhead is allocated to the departments on the basis of direct labor-hours. The divisional overhead rate for 1986 is $2 per direct labor-hour.

The following information relates to production during November 1986:

1. Work in process inventory, November 1 (4,000 pounds—75 percent complete):

Direct materials	$22,800
Direct labor at $5 per hour	24,650
Departmental overhead	12,000
Divisional overhead	9,860

2. Direct materials:

Inventory, November 1, 2,000 pounds	$10,000
Purchases, November 3, 10,000 pounds	51,000
Purchases, November 18, 10,000 pounds	51,500
Released to production during November, 16,000 pounds	

3. Direct labor costs at $5 per hour, $103,350.
4. Direct departmental overhead costs, $52,000.
5. Transferred to Utah Division, 15,000 pounds.
6. Work in process inventory, November 30, 3,000 pounds, 33⅓ percent complete.

The FIFO method is used for materials inventory valuation, and the weighted-average method is used for work in process inventories.

Prepare a cost of production report for the department of California Division producing Aggregate for November 1986 which presents:
a. The equivalent units of production by cost factor of Aggregate (for example, direct material, direct labor, and overhead).
b. Calculates the equivalent unit costs for each cost factor of Aggregate.
c. The cost of Aggregate transferred to the Utah Division.
d. The cost of abnormal shrinkage, if any.
e. The cost of the work in process inventory at November 30, 1986.

[Hint: Shrinkage is treated like spoilage.]

(CMA adapted)

6–29. Comprehensive job costing with equivalent units

The Custer Manufacturing Corporation, which uses a job order cost system, produces various plastic parts for the aircraft industry. On October 9, 1984, production was started on Job No. 487 for 100 front bubbles (windshields) for commercial helicopters.

Production of the bubbles begins in the fabricating department where sheets of plastic (purchased as raw material) are melted down and poured into molds. The molds are then placed in a special temperature and humidity room to harden the plastic. The hardened plastic bubbles are then removed from the molds and hand-worked to remove imperfections.

After fabrication the bubbles are transferred to the testing department where each bubble must meet rigid specifications. Bubbles that fail the tests are scrapped and there is no salvage value.

Bubbles passing the tests are transferred to the assembly department where they are inserted into metal frames. The frames, purchased from vendors, require no work prior to installing the bubbles.

The assembled unit is then transferred to the shipping department for crating and shipment. Crating material is relatively expensive, and most of the work is done by hand.

The following information concerning Job No. 487 is available as of December 31, 1984 (the information is correct as stated):

1. Direct materials charged to the job:
a. One thousand square feet of plastic at $12.75 per square feet was charged to the fabricating department. This amount was to meet all plastic material requirements of the job assuming no spoilage.
b. Seventy-four metal frames at $408.52 each were charged to the assembly department.
c. Packing material for 40 units at $75 per unit was charged to the shipping department.
2. Direct labor charges through December 31 were as follows:

	Total	Per unit
Fabricating department	$1,424	$16
Testing department	444	6
Assembly department	612	12
Shipping department	256	8
	$2,736	

3. Differences between actual and applied manufacturing overhead for the year ended December 31, 1984, were immaterial. Manufacturing overhead is charged to the four production departments by various allocation methods, all of which you approve.

Manufacturing overhead charged to the fabricating department is allocated to jobs based on heat-room hours; the other production departments allocate manufacturing overhead to jobs on the basis of direct labor dollars charged to each job within the department. The following reflects the manufacturing overhead rates for the year ended December 31, 1984.

Rate per unit

Fabricating department $.45 per hour
Testing department   .68 per direct labor dollar
Assembly department   .38 per direct labor dollar
Shipping department   .25 per direct labor dollar

4. Job No. 487 used 855 heat-room hours during the year ended December 31.
5. Following is the physical inventory for Job No. 487 as of December 31:

Fabricating department:

    a. Fifty square feet of plastic sheet.
    b. Eight hardened bubbles, one-fourth complete as to direct labor.
    c. Four complete bubbles.

Testing department:

    a. Fifteen bubbles which failed testing when two fifths of testing was complete. No others failed.
    b. Seven bubbles complete as to testing.

Assembly department:

    a. Thirteen frames with no direct labor.
    b. Fifteen bubbles and frames, one-third complete as to direct labor.
    c. Three complete bubbles and frames.

Shipping department:

    a. Nine complete units, two-thirds complete as to packing material, one-third complete as to direct labor.
    b. Ten complete units; 100 percent complete as to packing material; 50 percent complete as to direct labor.
    c. One unit complete for shipping was dropped off the loading docks. There is no salvage.
    d. Twenty-three units have been shipped prior to December 31.
    e. There was no inventory of packing materials in the shipping department at December 31.

6. Following is a schedule of equivalent units in production by department for Job No. 487 as of December 31.

CUSTER MANUFACTURING CORPORATION
Schedule of Equivalent Units in
Production for Job No. 487
December 31

| | | **Fabricating department** | | |
| | | **Bubbles (units)** | | |
	Plastic (sq. ft.)	**Materials**	**Labor**	**Overhead**
Transferred in from direct materials	1,000	—	—	—
Production to date	(950)	95	89	95
Transferred out to other departments	—	(83)	(83)	(83)
Spoilage	—	—	—	—
Balance at December 31	50	12	6	12

| | **Testing department (units)** | | |
| | **Bubbles** | | |
	Transferred in	**Labor**	**Overhead**
Transferred in from other departments	83	—	—
Production to date	—	74	74
Transferred out to other departments	(61)	(61)	(61)
Spoilage	(15)	(6)	(6)
Balance at December 31	7	7	7

| | **Assembly department (units)** | | | |
	Transferred in	**Frames**	**Labor**	**Over-head**
Transferred in from direct materials	—	74	—	—
Transferred in from other departments	61	—	—	—
Production to date	—	—	51	51
Transferred out to other departments	(43)	(43)	(43)	(43)
Balance at December 31	18	31	8	8

| | **Shipping department (units)** | | | |
	Transferred in	**Packing material**	**Labor**	**Over-head**
Transferred in from direct materials	—	40	—	—
Transferred in from other departments	43	—	—	—
Production to date	—	—	32	32
Shipped	(23)	(23)	(23)	(23)
Spoilage	(1)	(1)	(1)	(1)
Balance at December 31	19	16	8	8

Required:

Prepare a schedule for Job No. 487 of ending inventory costs for *(a)* direct materials by department, *(b)* work in process by department, and *(c)* cost of goods shipped. All spoilage costs are charged to cost of goods shipped.

(CPA adapted)

Allocating Service Department Costs

To understand the specific problem of allocating costs of a service that is shared by two or more other departments.

To be familiar with the three general methods for allocating service department costs.

Most departments in an organization fall into one of two categories: (1) departments that directly produce and market the organization's output, and (2) departments that support or supply services to other departments. The latter are *indirectly* involved in producing and marketing the organization's output, but their primary function is to provide services to other departments. Hence, they are called service departments. This chapter discusses methods of allocating service department costs to departments that receive those services.

Nature of service departments

Service *departments* differ from service organizations such as hospitals and city governments. Service organizations, merchandising organizations, and manufacturing organizations all have production or marketing departments *and* service departments. The former are directly involved in producing or marketing a service (for example, the intensive care unit in a hospital); the latter are support departments (such as the hospital laundry). Examples of production or marketing and service departments are:

Organization	Service department	Example of a production or marketing department
Manufacturing plant	Maintenance	Assembly
Retail store	Data processing	Sportswear
Hospital	Laundry	Intensive care unit
City government	Motor pool	Patrol units of the police department

The terms manufacturing and production are not synonomous—*production* is broader than *manufacturing*. In this book, when we refer to *manufacturing* departments, we specifically mean *production* departments in organizations that manufacture goods, such as an assembly department. An example of a

Illustration 7–1   **Service and user departments**

Service Department provides service to the final user department.

Service Department A provides service to Service Department B, which provides service to the final user department.

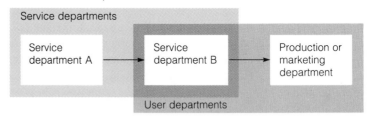

production department in a service organization would be the tax department of a public accounting firm.

Service departments are sometimes called intermediate cost centers, while production or marketing departments would be the final cost centers.

Further, we refer to any department that provides a service to another department as a service department and any department that uses the services of a service department as a user department. Service departments include centralized computer services, legal and accounting departments, and cost centers such as building occupancy which include building maintenance and repairs as well as other shared occupancy costs. User departments include (1) *production* or *marketing* departments, or (2) other *service* departments as shown in Illustration 7–1.

Rationale for charging the cost of service departments to users

Why do companies allocate service department costs to user departments? One reason in manufacturing companies is to allocate the cost of manufacturing service departments to units produced. This is required under generally accepted accounting principles (GAAP) for external financial reporting.

For example, suppose a company has one service department that provides services to two user departments that manufacture the company's two products: Product A and Product B. The service department's costs are $10,000 for the month of November. These costs are allocated 60 percent to Production Department A and 40 percent to Production Department B. (Methods of deriving allocation percentages are discussed later in this chapter; for now, assume the percentages are given.) Production Department A has direct costs

Illustration 7–2   **Allocation of service department costs to production departments**

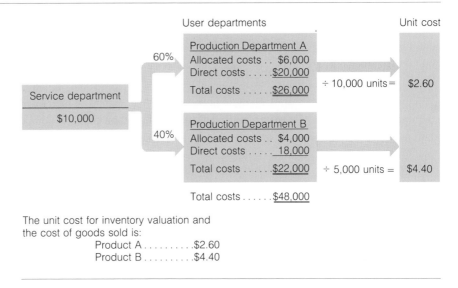

The unit cost for inventory valuation and
the cost of goods sold is:
Product A $2.60
Product B $4.40

of $20,000. It manufactured 10,000 units of Product A in November. Production Department B has direct costs of $18,000. It manufactured 5,000 units of Product B in November. As shown in Illustration 7–2, service department costs are first allocated to the production departments using the services. Then, direct plus allocated costs of those production departments are assigned to units produced.

Methods of allocating service department costs

In this section, we describe three methods of allocating service department costs: the direct method, the step method, and the simultaneous solution method. To make each method easier to understand, we use a comprehensive example. While our example is of a manufacturing company, keep in mind that the same methods can be used in nonmanufacturing organizations.

Assume Dunhill Products has three service departments: product engineering department (S1), building occupancy department (S2), and factory supervision department (S3). Costs are accumulated in these departments and allocated to two manufacturing departments and one marketing department: Manufacturing Department 1 (P1), Manufacturing Department 2 (P2), and the Marketing Department (P3). All six departments share the same building.

Dunhill Products allocates costs to Manufacturing Departments 1 and 2 for two purposes: (1) to value inventory for external financial reporting, and (2) to encourage department managers to monitor each other's costs; that is, *cross-department monitoring*. These are the manufacturing overhead costs for Dunhill Products. (In previous chapters, we simply called these costs "manufacturing overhead" without regard to which service department was responsible for them.) Costs are allocated to marketing only to encourage cross-department monitoring because marketing does not produce inventory.

Each service department is an *intermediate cost center* where costs are accumulated as incurred and then distributed to other cost centers. At Dunhill Products, product engineering (S1) costs are distributed on the basis of engineering staff time required by the user department. Building occupancy (S2) costs are distributed on the basis of area occupied by the user department. And factory supervision (S3) costs are distributed on the basis of the user department's manufacturing labor costs.

Allocation bases

Illustration 7–3 shows the basis of allocating costs for each service department and the proportions of costs allocated to user departments. For example,

Illustration 7–3   **Bases for service department cost allocations**

DUNHILL PRODUCTS
Product Engineering (S1)

Allocation base: Product engineering labor-hours worked in each user department.

User department	Product engineering labor-hours used	Proportion of total
Manufacturing Department 1 (P1)	14,000	.20
Manufacturing Department 2 (P2)	56,000	.80
Marketing (P3)	–0–	–0–
Totals	70,000	1.00

Building Occupancy (S2)

Allocation base: Area (square footage) in each user department.

User department	Square footage	Proportion of total
Manufacturing Department 1 (P1)	80,000	.32
Manufacturing Department 2 (P2)	60,000	.24
Marketing (P3)	60,000	.24
Product engineering (S1)	20,000	.08
Factory supervision (S3)	30,000	.12
Totals	250,000	1.00

Factory Supervision (S3)

Allocation base: Annual payroll dollars of user departments.

User department	Payroll dollars	Proportion of total
Manufacturing Department 1 (P1)	$360,000	.45
Manufacturing Department 2 (P2)	240,000	.30
Marketing (P3)	–0–	–0–
Product engineering (S1)	120,000	.15
Building occupancy (S2)	80,000	.10
Totals	$800,000	1.00

product engineering costs are allocated on the basis of engineering labor-hours worked for each user department. During the period, product engineering worked 14,000 hours for Manufacturing Department 1 and 56,000 hours for Manufacturing Department 2. Thus, 20 percent of product engineering costs are allocated to Manufacturing Department 1 $\left(20\% = \dfrac{14{,}000 \text{ hours}}{14{,}000 + 56{,}000 \text{ hours}}\right)$ and 80 percent to Manufacturing Department 2. Identical methods are used to derive the percentages for allocating building occupancy and factory supervision costs. (Percentages are shown in Illustration 7–3).

Methods of allocating costs are discussed next.

The direct method

The direct method allocates costs directly to the final user of a service, ignoring intermediate users. Illustration 7–4 shows the flow of costs and the allocations to be recognized for the departments when the direct method is used. The direct costs of departments are first accumulated in service departments. These are shown in parentheses on the debit side of the service department accounts. Then, service department costs are allocated to the manufacturing

Illustration 7–4
Flow of cost allocations—direct method

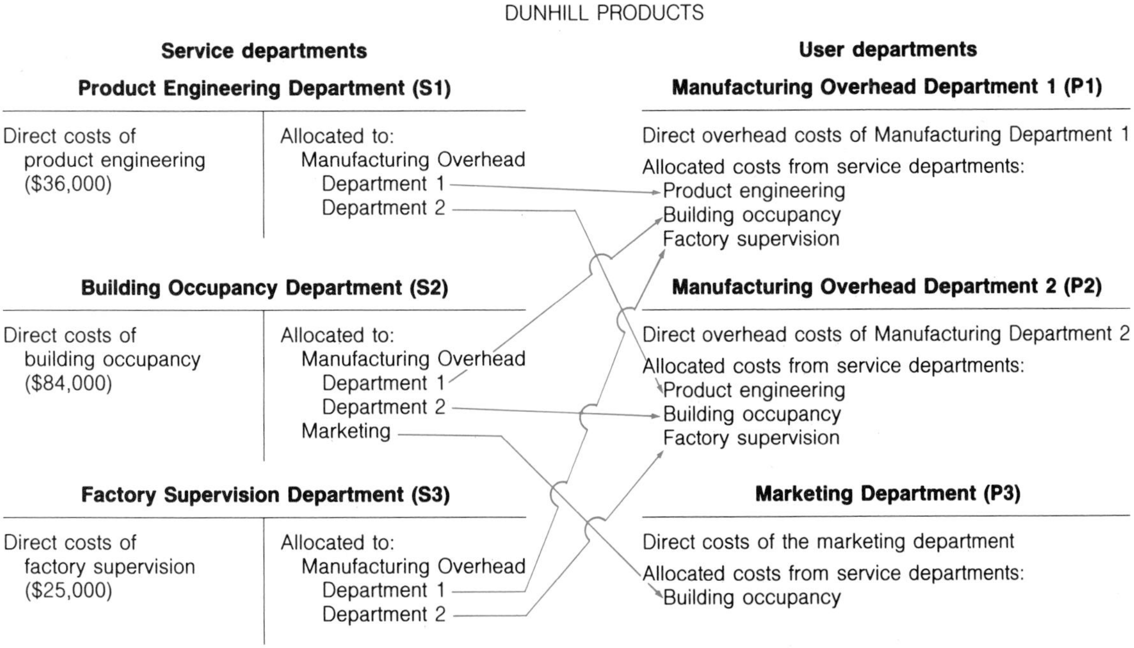

DUNHILL PRODUCTS

Illustration 7–5   **Cost allocation computations—direct method**

Service Department	This month's department costs	Proportion chargeable to		
		Manufacturing Department 1 (P1)	Manufacturing Department 2 (P2)	Marketing Department (P3)
Product engineering (S1)	$36,000	.2	.8	–0–
Building occupancy (S2)	84,000	.4	.3	.3
Factory supervision (S3)	25,000	.6	.4	–0–

Direct method cost allocation:

From		To		
Service Department	Amount	Manufacturing Department 1 (P1)	Manufacturing Department 2 (P2)	Marketing Department (P3)
Product engineering (S1)	$ 36,000	$ 7,200	$28,800	–0–
Building occupancy (S2)	84,000	33,600	25,200	$25,200
Factory supervision (S3)	25,000	15,000	10,000	–0–
Total allocated	$145,000	$55,800	$64,000	$25,200

Additional computations:
    Product engineering: $7,200 = .2 × $36,000 (P1)
                          $28,800 = .8 × $36,000 (P2)
    Building occupancy: $33,600 = .4 × $84,000 (P1)
                          $25,200 = .3 × $84,000 (P2) and (P3)
    Factory supervision: $15,000 = .6 × $25,000 (P1)
                          $10,000 = .4 × $25,000 (P2)

and marketing departments. There are no allocations between service departments. Thus, the building occupancy costs and the factory supervision costs that are attributable to the product engineering department are not allocated to product engineering. Likewise, the factory supervision costs that are related to the building occupancy function and the costs of the building space occupied by the factory supervision activity are not allocated to their respective service departments.

The use of the direct method of cost allocation at Dunhill Products is discussed below and shown in Illustration 7–5. Assume the accounting records show that costs of $36,000, $84,000, and $25,000 are accumulated in each service department S1, S2, and S3 respectively. Costs are allocated directly to Manufacturing Department 1 (P1), Manufacturing Department 2 (P2), and marketing (P3)—hence the name *direct* method.

Allocate product engineering department costs   Product engineering department costs of $36,000 are allocated to P1, P2, and P3 based on the product engineering labor-hours used by P1, P2, and P3. According to the facts given in Illustration 7–3, P1 used 20 percent and P2 used 80 percent of the total product engineering labor-hours. The marketing department did not use any product engineering labor-hours. Hence, the allocation of product engineering department costs is simply:

P1	20% × $36,000 =	$ 7,200
P2	80 × 36,000 =	28,800
Total	100%	$36,000

Allocated building occupancy department costs Building occupancy department costs are distributed to P1, P2, and P3 in the same ratio as the proportions of the square footage occupied by those departments alone. That is, the square footage proportions for P1, P2, and P3 based on data given in Illustration 7–3 are:

P1	.32
P2	.24
P3	.24
Total	.80

When these are scaled to 100 percent, we have:

P1	40% =	.32/.80
P2	30 =	.24/.80
P3	30 =	.24/.80
Total	100%	

These proportions are used to allocate building occupancy department costs as shown in Illustration 7–5.

Allocate factory supervision department costs Similar calculations are made for factory supervision department costs that are allocated on the basis of labor dollars. The labor dollar proportions for P1, P2, and P3 are (see Illustration 7–3):

P1	.45
P2	.30
P3	.00
Total	.75

When these are scaled to 100 percent, we have:

P1	60% =	.45/.75
P2	40 =	.30/.75
P3	0 =	–0–/.75
Total	100%	

These proportions are used to allocate factory supervision department costs as shown in Illustration 7–5.

Once these proportions are computed, the allocation proceeds with the cost distribution shown in Illustration 7–5. The $36,000 product engineering costs are allocated $7,200 (or 20 percent) to Manufacturing Overhead—Department P1, and $28,800 (or 80 percent) to Manufacturing Overhead—Department P2. The total allocated ($7,200 + $28,800) equals the total costs in the product engineering intermediate cost center ($36,000).

Similar allocations are made for the other two service cost centers. As a result of these allocations, the total service department costs charged to Manufacturing Department 1 are $55,800; to Manufacturing Department 2, $64,000; and to marketing, $25,200.

Limitations of the direct method   The direct method has been criticized because it ignores services provided by one service department to another. If one purpose of cost allocation is to encourage cross-department monitoring, then the direct method falls short because it ignores the costs service departments themselves incur when they use other service departments. An attempt to remedy this problem has resulted in the *step method* of allocating service department costs.

The step method

The step method recognizes services provided to other service departments. Allocations usually begin from the service department that has provided the greatest proportion of its total services to other service departments, or that services the greatest *number* of other departments. Once an allocation is made *from* a service department, no further allocations are made *to* that department. Hence, a service department that provides services to another service department and also receives services from that department will have only one of these two reciprocal relationships recognized. For example, when the step method is used at Dunhill Products, costs are allocated from factory supervision department to building occupancy department, but not vice versa as discussed below.

An analysis of service usage among service departments at Dunhill Products indicates that factory supervision supplies 25 percent of its services to other service departments while building occupancy supplies 20 percent of its services to other service departments. (See Illustration 7–3.) Product engineering provides no services to other service departments. Hence, the rank ordering for step allocation is:

Order	Service department
1	Factory supervision (S3)
2	Building occupancy (S2)
3	Product engineering (S1)

Allocating factory supervision department costs   Factory supervision costs would be allocated to all service departments that made use of factory supervision's services, whereas building occupancy's costs would be allocated only to those service departments that rank below it in the allocation order. Recall that under the step method, once a service department's costs have been allocated to other departments, no costs can be allocated back to it. The computation of service department costs allocated to other service departments at Dunhill Products is shown in Illustration 7–6.

Factory supervision department costs are charged to user departments based on the total labor dollars recorded for each. The distribution results in 15 percent of the $25,000 in factory supervision department costs being charged to product engineering, 10 percent to building occupancy, 45 percent to Manufacturing Department 1, and the remaining 30 percent to Manufacturing Department 2 (based on Illustration 7–3).

Illustration 7–6
Cost allocation computations—step method

DUNHILL PRODUCTS

Service department	This month's department costs	Proportion chargeable to—					
		S3	S2	S1	P1	P2	P3
Factory supervision (S3)	$ 25,000	–0–	.10	.15	.45	.30	–0–
Building occupancy (S2)	84,000	–0–	–0–	.09[a]	.37[a]	.27[a]	.27[a]
Product engineering (S1)	36,000	–0–	–0–	–0–	.20	.80	–0–
	$145,000						

Step method allocation:

	Cost allocation to—[b]					
	S3	S2	S1	P1	P2	P3
Direct service department costs	$ 25,000	$ 84,000	$ 36,000			
Factory supervision (S3)	$(25,000)	2,500	3,750	$11,250	$ 7,500	–0–
Building occupancy (S2)		$(86,500)	7,785	32,005	23,355	$23,355
Product engineering (S1)			$(47,535)	9,507	38,028	–0–
Total costs allocated				$52,762	$68,883	$23,355

[a] Factory supervision excluding building occupancy's share of the allocation base remaining:
  .09 = .08 ÷ (1.00 − .12), rounded
Similarly,
  .37 = .32 ÷ (1.00 − .12), rounded
and
  .27 = .24 ÷ (1.00 − .12), rounded
[b] Additional computations:
  Factory supervision (S3):
    $2,500 = .10 × $25,000; $3,750 = .15 × $25,000; etc.
  Building occupancy (S2):
    $86,500 = $84,000 + $2,500 (allocated costs from S3)
    $7,785 = .09 × $86,500; $32,005 = .37 × $86,500; etc.
  Product engineering (S1):
    $47,535 = $36,000 + $3,750 + $7,785 (Allocated costs from S2)
    $9,507 = .20 × $47,535; $38,028 = .80 × $47,535
  Proof:
    $25,000 + $84,000 + $36,000 = $52,762 + $68,883 + $23,355

Allocating building occupancy department costs   In determining the allocation of building occupancy department costs (second in the allocation order), the step method ignores the area occupied by factory supervision department because costs have already been allocated from that department. As a result, the portion of building occupancy department costs to be allocated to product engineering is determined by taking the 20,000 square feet used by product engineering and dividing by the 220,000 square foot basis (250,000 total square feet less the 30,000 occupied by factory supervision). The result is approximately 9 percent.

The total costs to be allocated from building occupancy is the sum of the direct costs ($84,000) plus the allocated costs ($2,500 from factory supervision). Therefore, the transfer to product engineering is 9 percent of $86,500, which equals $7,785. Similar computations are made for the other departments as shown in Illustration 7–6.

The flow of costs under the step method is diagrammed in Illustration 7–7.

Notice that Illustration 7–7 differs from Illustration 7–4, which showed cost flows using the direct method, because some costs flow from one service department to another. In addition, the costs allocated *from* service departments include not only the direct costs of the service departments but costs allocated *to* the service departments as well.

The step method may result in more equitable allocations than the direct method because it recognizes that service departments use other service departments. However, it does not recognize reciprocal services—for example, that building occupancy and factory supervision both provide and use each other's services. The simultaneous solution method of service department cost allocation deals with this problem. The step method is *not necessarily* better than the direct method when both costs and benefits are taken into account. A company that already uses the direct method may find it uneconomical to switch methods, especially if the only purpose of cost allocation is to value inventory for external financial reporting.

The simultaneous solution method

With the simultaneous solution method, the costs of each production, marketing, and service department are written in equation form:

$$\text{Total costs} = \frac{\text{Direct costs of}}{\text{the department}} + \frac{\text{Costs to be allocated}}{\text{to the department}}$$

The system of equations is then solved simultaneously using matrix algebra.[1] By solving all of the equations simultaneously, we provide for all interservice department allocations. This method is sometimes called the *reciprocal services*

---

[1] The use of matrix algebra in accounting is explained in detail in J. K. Shank, *Matrix Methods in Accounting* (Reading, Mass.: Addison-Wesley, 1972).

Illustration 7-7
Flow of cost allocations—step method

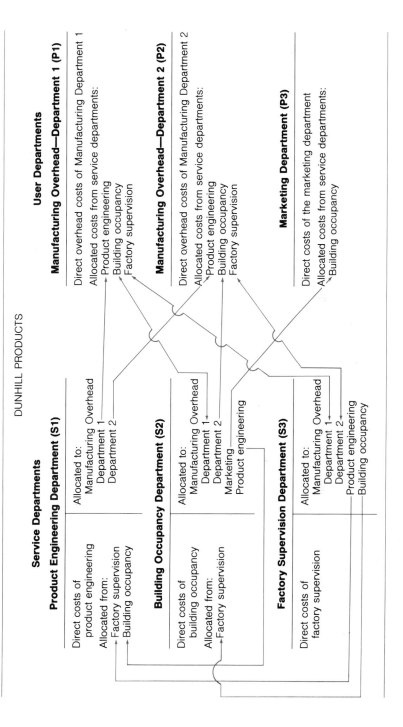

DUNHILL PRODUCTS

Service Departments

Product Engineering Department (S1)

Direct costs of product engineering

Allocated from:
→ Factory supervision
→ Building occupancy

Building Occupancy Department (S2)

Direct costs of building occupancy

Allocated from:
→ Factory supervision

Allocated to:
Manufacturing Overhead
  Department 1
  Department 2
Marketing
Product engineering

Factory Supervision Department (S3)

Direct costs of factory supervision

Allocated to:
Manufacturing Overhead
  Department 1
  Department 2
  Product engineering
  Building occupancy

Allocated to:
Manufacturing Overhead
  Department 1
  Department 2

User Departments

Manufacturing Overhead—Department 1 (P1)

Direct overhead costs of Manufacturing Department 1

Allocated costs from service departments:
  Product engineering
  Building occupancy
  Factory supervision

Manufacturing Overhead—Department 2 (P2)

Direct overhead costs of Manufacturing Department 2

Allocated costs from service departments:
  Product engineering
  Building occupancy
  Factory supervision

Marketing Department (P3)

Direct costs of the marketing department

Allocated costs from service departments:
  Building occupancy

method because it accounts for cost flows in both directions among service departments that provide services to one another.

The flow of costs using the simultaneous solution method of service departments costs is shown in Illustration 7–8. Note that the simultaneous solution method accounts for the reciprocal services between the building occupancy and factory supervision departments. The step method accounted for only one direction of services—from factory supervision to building occupancy, but not vice versa.

Simultaneous solution method using matrix algebra when there are three or more service departments The mathematical details of the simultaneous solution method when there are three (or more) service departments are presented in the appendix to this chapter. Generally, a computer is used to solve this allocation problem. For comparative purposes, we present the costs allocated to the production and marketing departments using the simultaneous solution method for Dunhill Products:

Department	Allocated costs
Manufacturing department 1 (P1)	$ 53,661
Manufacturing department 2 (P2)	70,328
Marketing (P3)	21,011
Total allocated costs	$145,000

Simultaneous solution method using linear algebra when there are only two service departments When there are only two service departments, linear algebra can be used to solve the allocation problem. To show how this works, we present a different example from the one previously used in this chapter.

Assume a company has two service departments, S1 and S2, and three production departments, P1, P2, and P3, with the following direct costs and allocation percentages:

Department	Direct costs	Percent of costs allocated to:				
		S1	S2	P1	P2	P3
S1	$ 79,000	—	30%	30%	30%	10%
S2	26,000	10%	—	15	15	60
	$105,000					

The two service departments' costs may be expressed in equation form as:

$$S1 = \$79{,}000 + .1\ S2 \qquad \text{Equation (1)}$$
$$S2 = \$26{,}000 + .3\ S1 \qquad \text{Equation (2)}$$

Illustration 7–8
Flow of cost allocations—simultaneous solution method

DUNHILL PRODUCTS

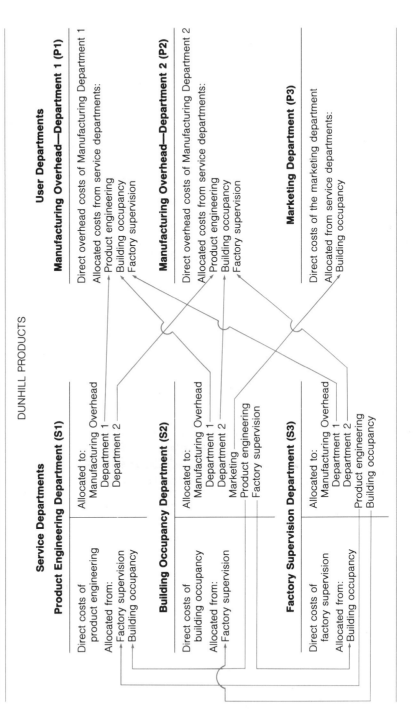

Service Departments

Product Engineering Department (S1)

Direct costs of
product engineering

Allocated from:
- Factory supervision
- Building occupancy

Building Occupancy Department (S2)

Direct costs of
building occupancy

Allocated from:
- Factory supervision

Allocated to:
Manufacturing Overhead
- Department 1
- Department 2
- Marketing
- Product engineering
- Factory supervision

Allocated to:
Manufacturing Overhead
- Department 1
- Department 2

Factory Supervision Department (S3)

Direct costs of
factory supervision

Allocated from:
- Building occupancy

Allocated to:
Manufacturing Overhead
- Department 1
- Department 2
- Product engineering
- Building occupancy

User Departments

Manufacturing Overhead—Department 1 (P1)

Direct overhead costs of Manufacturing Department 1

Allocated costs from service departments:
- Product engineering
- Building occupancy
- Factory supervision

Manufacturing Overhead—Department 2 (P2)

Direct overhead costs of Manufacturing Department 2

Allocated costs from service departments:
- Product engineering
- Building occupancy
- Factory supervision

Marketing Department (P3)

Direct costs of the marketing department

Allocated from service departments:
- Building occupancy

These yield two equations with two unknowns that can be solved by substitution.

Substituting Equation (2) into Equation (1) gives:

$$S1 = \$79,000 + .1(\$26,000 + .3\ S1)$$
$$S1 = \$79,000 + \$2,600 + .03\ S1$$

Collecting terms and solving:

$$.97\ S1 = \$81,600$$
$$S1 = \underline{\underline{84,124}}$$

Now substituting this value for S1 back into Equation (2) gives:

$$S2 = \$26,000 + .3(\$84,124)$$
$$S2 = \$26,000 + \$25,237$$
$$S2 = \underline{\underline{\$51,237}}$$

Thus, costs are simultaneously allocated between the two service departments. The values for S1 ($84,124) and S2 ($51,237) are then used as the total costs of the service departments that are to be allocated to the production departments. The allocations are:

		Allocated to					
		P1		P2		P3	
From	Total cost	Dollars	Percent	Dollars	Percent	Dollars	Percent
S1	$84,124	$25,237	30	$25,237	30	$ 8,412	10
S2	51,237	7,686	15	7,686	15	30,742	60
Totals		$32,923		$32,923		$39,154	

Computations:

For P1 and P2	For P3
S1: $25,237 = (.3) × $84,124;	$8,412 = (.1) × $84,124
S2: $7,686 = (.15) × $51,237;	$30,742 = (.6) × $51,237

The total costs allocated to the production departments amounts to $105,000 (= $32,923 + $32,923 + $39,154), which equals the costs to be allocated from the service departments ($79,000 + $26,000 = $105,000).

Comparison of methods

There are two ways to compare these three service—department allocation methods. The first is to examine how each allocates costs to departments receiving services. As shown in Illustration 7–9, only the simultaneous solution method allocates costs to all departments receiving services from other departments.

The second way to compare these three methods is to examine the costs each ultimately allocates to manufacturing and marketing departments, as

Illustration 7–9 **Comparison of services provided with departments receiving costs for each cost allocation method**

DUNHILL PRODUCTS

		Departments receiving costs under each method		
Service department	Services provided to:	Direct method	Step method	Simultaneous solution method
Product engineering (S1)	P1	P1	P1	P1
	P2	P2	P2	P2
Building occupancy (S2)	S1	None[a]	S1	S1
	S3	None[a]	None[a]	S3
	P1	P1	P1	P1
	P2	P2	P2	P2
	P3	P3	P3	P3
Factory supervision (S3)	S1	None[a]	S1	S1
	S2	None[a]	S2	S2
	P1	P1	P1	P1
	P2	P2	P2	P2

[a] These are user departments receiving services, but costs are not allocated to them under the indicated method.

shown in Illustration 7–10. Each method allocates the same total cost—$145,000. The difference is in the amounts allocated to manufacturing and marketing departments. The major factor affecting these allocations is the distribution of building occupancy costs. Under the direct method, the use of the building by other service departments is ignored. This results in a higher charge to the marketing department (and less costs allocated to production) because that department makes no use of the other service departments. As the utilization of the building by other service departments is recognized, the allocation to marketing decreases.

As a general rule, when there are interservice department activities to which costs can be assigned, the allocations to manufacturing and marketing

Illustration 7–10 **Comparison of dollar amounts allocated under each cost allocation method**

DUNHILL PRODUCTS

	Allocated service costs		
Department	Direct method	Step method	Simultaneous solution
Manufacturing Department 1 (P1)	$ 55,800	$ 52,762	$ 53,661
Manufacturing Department 2 (P2)	64,000	68,883	70,328
Marketing (P3)	25,200	23,355	21,011
Totals	$145,000	$145,000	$145,000

departments will differ under each method. If there are no interservice department activities, then all three methods will give identical results.

<table>
<tr><td>

Issues in allocating service department costs

</td><td>

It is usually advisable to allocate costs on a cause-and-effect basis. If this is not practical, the most reasonable basis possible should be found. By establishing a cause-and-effect relationship for the allocation of costs, service department managers can trace costs to their cause. Moreover, managers of user departments have an incentive to limit their use if the costs of the service center are allocated on a cause-and-effect basis. For example, in the early days of data processing, companies often charged an hourly rate for computer usage. No charge was made for support services such as programming. This encouraged users to request programming time because it carried no cost. The programmers were kept very busy and frequently engaged in programming activities that offered only marginal benefits. This represented a substantial cost to the computer services department that it was unable to pass on to user departments except through increases in hourly rates. The hourly rates then became so high that departments found it uneconomical to use the programs they had commissioned.

</td></tr>
</table>

Thus, when the basis of cost allocations does not reflect cause and effect, cost control becomes difficult because departments tend to make excessive demands for underpriced services. Moreover, evaluation of the computer services department is difficult because its output is measured in terms of computer hours while its costs are a function of both computer hours and programmer hours. Identifying the effect of each factor on total costs is made more difficult by a cost allocation system that ignores programmer hours.

In this case, more detailed cost allocations are needed, but in other cases, more detail does not provide more benefit. When costs cannot be directly related to production activities, production managers have no control over them and need relatively little information about them. Hence, an aggregate allocation both reduces the cost of allocating costs and reduces the time spent by production managers in sifting through excessive and unnecessary detail.

For example, many companies own or lease a building that houses both manufacturing and nonmanufacturing activities. The costs of the building lease or depreciation, property taxes, heat, air conditioning, light, water, repairs, security, maintenance, and similar costs occur as part of the overall building operation and cannot be directly associated with a specific activity within the building. The activities in individual cost centers have so little effect on overall building costs that their managers do not need item-by-item details of the building occupancy costs charged to their departments. A single line item, "Building occupancy costs," is usually sufficient. Better control may be obtained by accumulating the total building costs in a centralized cost center, so the building supervisor can be apprised of the detailed cost item and held responsible for controlling them.

The determination of how detailed a cost allocation should be is like other managerial decisions—it should be made on a cost-benefit basis. Cost allocation is, in itself, a costly procedure. If the benefits from increasing the detail of cost allocation are minimal, then more detailed cost allocations are probably not economically wise.

Allocating fixed service department costs

Although the allocation of variable service department costs can be useful for charging user departments, the allocation of fixed costs can have unintended effects. For example, the top administrators of Southwest University observed that faculty and staff were using the university's WATS (Wide Area Telephone Service) so much that the lines were seldom free during the day.[2] WATS allowed the university unlimited toll-free service within the United States. The fixed cost of WATS was $10,000 per month, variable cost per call was zero.

The top administrators learned that there was an average usage of 50,000 minutes per month on the WATS line, so they initially allocated the $10,000 monthly charged to callers (that is, departments) at a rate of $.20 per minute (= $10,000 ÷ 50,000 minutes). Now that they were being charged for the use of WATS, department heads discouraged their faculty and staff from using the telephone. Hence, the number of minutes used on WATS dropped to 25,000 per month, which increased the rate to $.40 per minute (= $10,000 ÷ 25,000). This continued until the internal cost allocation per minute exceeded the normal long-distance rates, and the use of WATS dropped almost to zero. Southwest University's total telephone bill increased dramatically.[3] The top administrators subsequently compromised by charging a nominal fee of $.10 per minute. According to the University's chief financial officer, "The $.10 per minute charge made us aware that there was a cost to the WATS service, albeit a fixed cost. The charge was sufficiently low, however, so as not to discourage bona fide use of WATS."

Moral The moral of the cost allocation story is as follows: Service department costs allocations are common in all types of organizations. Costs are allocated for a variety of reasons—for example, to satisfy regulatory, external financial reporting requirements; to meet contract requirements; to encourage

---

[2] This example is based on one given by Jerold L. Zimmerman, "The Costs and Benefits of Cost Allocations," *The Accounting Review,* July 1979, pp. 510–11.

[3] The solution to this problem is not necessarily zero. According to Zimmerman (1979), the correct price to charge users is ". . . the cost imposed by forcing others who want to use the WATS line to either wait or place a regular toll call . . . this cost varies between zero (if no one is delayed) to, at most, the cost of a regular toll call if a user cannot use the WATS line" (p. 510). The necessary procedure to implement such a pricing system is very difficult and costly. Zimmerman suggests that fixed allocations could be a simplified way of approximating the results of the more complicated theoretically correct pricing systems.

cross-department monitoring of costs; to make user department personnel aware of costs incurred by service departments. Costs allocated for one purpose usually have unexpected side effects. Hence, cost allocations should be made much like doctors prescribe medicine—"with an eye on the side effects."

Summary

Costs are accumulated in a department largely for performance evaluation purposes—that is, to make the department manager (and other personnel) responsible for controlling department costs. When a department provides services and support to other departments rather than producing or marketing the organization's output, its costs are often allocated to the departments it services. Hence, the service department is *directly* responsible for its own costs, and user departments are *indirectly* responsible for service department costs. This makes user department personnel aware of service department costs, and it can give them incentives to help control service department costs. We call this *cross-department monitoring.*

In addition, manufacturing service department costs are allocated to production departments for external financial reporting purposes—for example, to value inventory and cost of goods sold. Thus, there are two principal reasons for allocating service department costs:

1. *Cross-department monitoring,* which is a reason for service department allocation in all organizations.
2. *To value inventory and cost of goods sold* in manufacturing companies for external financial reporting.

Service department costs are allocated to user departments as follows:

1. Departments that provide and use each other's services are identified. At Dunhill Products, for example, Manufacturing Department 1 used the services of all three service departments.
2. Allocation bases are established. (Production engineering's costs were allocated to user departments based on the engineering labor-hours worked in each user department.)
3. One of three methods of allocating service department costs is selected:
   a. Direct method,
   b. Step method, or
   c. Simultaneous solution method.

The direct method allocates costs directly to production and marketing departments. Only production and marketing departments are recognized as user departments—other service departments are not.

The step method recognizes some, but not all, service departments as user departments. Costs are allocated in steps, usually beginning with an allocation from the service department that provides the greatest portion of its services to other service departments, and continuing until all costs are allocated to production and marketing departments. Once an allocation is made *from* a service department, no more costs can be allocated *to* it.

The simultaneous solution method simultaneously allocates costs to all departments that receive services. Unlike the step and direct methods, all interservice department allocations are recognized. This method has not been widely used because the mathematics are perceived as difficult and the procedure is very time consuming if done manually. With the widespread use of computers, we expect use of the simultaneous solution method to increase.

Cost allocations are often made for multiple reasons. Sometimes an allocation made for one purpose will have unexpected effects elsewhere. Consequently, it is wise to consider all of the effects of cost allocation.

Terms and concepts

The following terms and concepts should be familiar to you after reading this chapter.

Direct method	**Service departments**
Final cost center	**Service organizations**
Intermediate cost center	**Simultaneous solution method**
Manufacturing	**Step method**
Production department	**User department**

Self-study problem

T. Schurt & Company manufactures and sells T-shirts for advertising and promotional purposes and wholesales T-shirts with various designs for general sale. The company has two manufacturing operations: shirtmaking and printing. When an order for T-shirts is received, the shirtmaking department obtains the materials and colors requested and has the shirts made in the desired mix of sizes. The completed shirts are then sent to the printing department where the custom labels or designs are prepared and embossed on the shirts.

To support the manufacturing activity, the company has a building that houses the two manufacturing departments as well as the sales department. A payroll department has been established to handle the details of recordkeeping for employee wages and salaries as well as for issuing payroll checks. Finally, a design and patterns staff has been hired to develop shirt patterns, label designs, and, on occasion, to draw illustrations for the company's advertising. To aid in cost control, the company accumulates the costs of these support functions in separate service cost centers: (1) building occupancy, (2) payroll accounting, and (3) design and patterns.

During the current period, the direct costs incurred in each of the departments are as follows:

Shirtmaking (P1)	$210,000
Printing (P2)	140,000
Selling (P3)	80,000
Building occupancy (S1)	45,000
Payroll accounting (S2)	20,000
Design and patterns (S3)	10,000

Building occupancy costs are allocated on the basis of the number of square feet of each user department. Payroll accounting costs are allocated on the basis of the number of employees. The design and pattern costs are charged to departments on the basis of the number of designs requested by each department. For the current period, the following table summarizes the usage of services by other service cost centers and other departments:

	S1	S2	S3	P1	P2	P3
Building occupancy (S1) (square feet)	—	8,100	3,900	27,000	36,000	6,000
Payroll accounting (S2) (employees)	3	—	6	30	15	6
Design and patterns (S3) (designs)	—	—	—	15	40	5

Required:

a. Determine the total costs in each of the three "producing" departments using the direct method for service cost allocations.

b. Compute the cost allocations and total costs in each producing department using the step method.

Solution to self-study problem

To facilitate solution, express the usage of services in percentage terms:

Service center			Used by			
	S1	S2	S3	P1	P2	P3
S1	—	.100	.049	.333	.444	.074
S2	.050	—	.100	.500	.250	.100
S3	—	—	—	.250	.667	.083

a. Direct method:

Usage of services by producing departments only:

Service center	Used by		
	P1	P2	P3
S1	.391[a]	.522	.087
S2	.588[b]	.294	.118
S3	.250	.667	.083

[a] .391 = .333 ÷ (.333 + .444 + .074); .522 = .444 ÷ (.333 + .444 + .074), etc.

[b] .588 = .500 ÷ (.500 + .250 + .100), etc.

Allocation:

From	Amount	To		
		P1	P2	P3
S1	$45,000	$ 17,595[a]	$ 23,490	$ 3,915
S2	$20,000	11,760[b]	5,880	2,360
S3	$10,000	2,500[c]	6,670	830
Allocated costs		31,855	36,040	7,105
Direct costs		210,000	140,000	80,000
Total costs		$241,855	$176,040	$87,105

[a] $17,595 = $45,000 × .391; $23,490 = $45,000 × .522; $3,915 = $45,000 × .087.

[b] $11,760 = $20,000 × .588; $5,880 = $20,000 × .294; $2,360 = $20,000 × .118.

[c] $2,500 = $10,000 × .25; $6,670 = $10,000 × .667; $830 = $10,000 × .083.

b. Step method:

Order of allocation: S2, S1, S3.

Usage of services by producing departments and service cost centers excluding reciprocal allocations:

Service center	Used by				
	S1	S3	P1	P2	P3
S2	.050	.100	.500	.250	.100
S1	—	.054[a]	.370[a]	.494[a]	.082[a]
S3	—	—	.250	.667	.083

[a] .054 = .049 ÷ (.049 + .333 + .444 + .074) = .049 ÷ .900.
.370 = .333 ÷ .900; .494 = .444 ÷ .900, (rounded);
.082 = .074 ÷ .90.

Allocation:

From	Amount	To				
		S1	S3	P1	P2	P3
S2	20,000	$1,000[a]	$2,000[a]	$ 10,000	$ 5,000	$ 2,000
S1	46,000[b]	(1,000)	2,484[b]	17,020[b]	22,724	3,772
S3	14,484[c]		(4,484)	3,621[c]	9,661	1,202
	Total allocated costs			30,641	37,385	6,974
	Direct costs of P1, P2 and P3			210,000	140,000	80,000
	Total costs			$240,641	$177,385	$86,974

[a] $1,000 = $20,000 × .050; $2,000 = $20,000 × .10, etc.
[b] $46,000 = $45,000 direct costs + $1,000 allocated from S2. $2,484 = $46,000 × .054; $17,020 = $46,000 × .370; etc.
[c] $14,484 = $10,000 direct costs + $4,484 allocated from S1 and S2. $3,621 = $14,484 × .250; etc.

Appendix: The simultaneous solution method using matrix algebra[4]

The simultaneous solution method requires that cost relationships be written in equation form. The method then solves the equations for the total costs to be allocated to each department. The direct costs of each department are typically included in the solution. Thus, for any department, we can state the equation:

$$\text{Total costs} = \text{Direct costs} + \text{Allocated costs}$$

The total costs are the unknowns that we attempt to derive.

For example, let's assume the direct overhead costs of the departments at Dunhill Products Company are:

Product engineering (S1)	$ 36,000
Building occupancy (S2)	84,000
Factory supervision (S3)	25,000
Manufacturing Department 1 (P1)	500,000
Manufacturing Department 2 (P2)	270,000
Marketing (P3)	185,000

[4] For a more detailed discussion of matrix algebra see J. K. Shank, *Matrix Methods in Accounting* (Reading, Mass.: Addison-Wesley, 1972).

Using the information in Illustration 7–3, the total costs of Manufacturing Department 1 (P1) may be expressed as:

$$\text{Total costs} = \text{Direct costs} + \text{Allocated costs}$$
$$P1 = \$500{,}000 + 20\% \ S1 + 32\% \ S2 + 45\% \ S3$$

Similar equations are constructed for each of the other production departments.

$$P2 = \$270{,}000 + 80\% \ S1 + 24\% \ S2 + 30\% \ S3$$
$$P3 = \$185{,}000 + \quad 0 \quad S1 + 24\% \ S2 + \ 0 \quad S3$$

And for the service departments, the equations are:

$$S1 = \$36{,}000 + \quad 8\% \ S2 + 15\% \ S3$$
$$S2 = \$84{,}000 \qquad\qquad\quad + 10\% \ S3$$
$$S3 = \$25{,}000 + 12\% \ S2$$

Now we have a set of equations that express the total costs of each department as a function of direct costs and allocated costs.

Setting the equations in matrix form

To set the equations up in matrix form for solution, the terms are rearranged so that direct costs are on the right-hand side of the equation and all unknowns are on the left side. Each equation is expanded to include all of the departments in the system.

For example, the cost equation of Manufacturing Department 1 (P1) is rearranged as:

$$1 \ P1 + 0 \ P2 + 0 \ P3 = .20 \ S1 + .32 \ S2 + .45 \ S3 + \$500{,}000$$
$$1 \ P1 + 0 \ P2 + 0 \ P3 - .20 \ S1 - .32 \ S2 - .45 \ S3 = \$500{,}000$$

This is repeated for all production and service departments. The results are:

$$1 \ P1 + 0 \ P2 + 0 \ P3 - .20 \ S1 - .32 \ S2 - .45 \ S3 = \$500{,}000$$
$$0 \ P1 + 1 \ P2 + 0 \ P3 - .80 \ S1 - .24 \ S2 - .30 \ S3 = \ 270{,}000$$
$$0 \ P1 + 0 \ P2 + 1 \ P3 - \ 0 \ S1 - .24 \ S2 - \ 0 \ S3 = \ 185{,}000$$
$$0 \ P1 + 0 \ P2 + 0 \ P3 + \ 1 \ S1 - .08 \ S2 - .15 \ S3 = \ 36{,}000$$
$$0 \ P1 + 0 \ P2 + 0 \ P3 - \ 0 \ S1 + \ 1 \ S2 - .10 \ S3 = \ 84{,}000$$
$$0 \ P1 + 0 \ P2 + 0 \ P3 - \ 0 \ S1 - .12 \ S2 + \ 1 \ S3 = \ 25{,}000$$

Each equation may be interpreted as follows: The costs in any department before allocation (the right-hand side) equals the costs after allocation (the P terms) less the allocations that are to be charged to the service departments (the S terms with negative coefficients).

Reforming the system of equations in matrix notation saves repetition of all of the symbols for the unknowns and results in the following system of matrices and vectors:

$$\begin{bmatrix} 1 & 0 & 0 & -.20 & -.32 & -.45 \\ 0 & 1 & 0 & -.80 & -.24 & -.30 \\ 0 & 0 & 1 & 0 & -.24 & 0 \\ 0 & 0 & 0 & 1 & -.08 & -.15 \\ 0 & 0 & 0 & 0 & 1 & -.10 \\ 0 & 0 & 0 & 0 & -.12 & 1 \end{bmatrix} \times \begin{bmatrix} P1 \\ P2 \\ P3 \\ S1 \\ S2 \\ S3 \end{bmatrix} = \begin{bmatrix} \$500,000 \\ 270,000 \\ 185,000 \\ 36,000 \\ 84,000 \\ 25,000 \end{bmatrix}$$

To solve for the vector of unknowns (that is, the P's and S's), matrix algebra is used. If the matrix is labeled **A,** the vector of unknowns **X,** and the vector of direct costs **B,** the matrix form of the equation may be summarized as:

$$AX = B$$

To solve for **X,** we multiply both sides by the inverse of **A,** which is noted **A**$^{-1}$. This gives:

$$X = A^{-1}B$$

Computing the inverse of a matrix is tedious without the use of a computer or hand calculator with matrix capabilities. In this book, the inverse of any required matrices will be computed and presented as needed.

Taking the inverse of **A** and placing the results in the order:

$$X = A^{-1}B$$

We obtain:

$$\begin{bmatrix} P1 \\ P2 \\ P3 \\ S1 \\ S2 \\ S3 \end{bmatrix} = \begin{bmatrix} 1 & 0 & 0 & .20 & .3984 & .5198 \\ 0 & 1 & 0 & .80 & .3587 & .4559 \\ 0 & 0 & 1 & 0 & .2429 & .0243 \\ 0 & 0 & 0 & 1 & .0992 & .1599 \\ 0 & 0 & 0 & 0 & 1.0121 & .1012 \\ 0 & 0 & 0 & 0 & .1215 & 1.0121 \end{bmatrix} \times \begin{bmatrix} \$500,000 \\ 270,000 \\ 185,000 \\ 36,000 \\ 84,000 \\ 25,000 \end{bmatrix}$$

Carrying out the indicated multiplication, we obtain the solution for P1:

$$\begin{aligned} P1 &= (1)(\$500,000) + (0)(\$270,000) + (0)(\$185,000) \\ &\quad + (.20)(\$36,000) \\ &\quad + (.3984)(\$84,000) + (.5198)(\$25,000) \\ &= \$553,661 \end{aligned}$$

And carrying out similar matrix multiplication operations for the other rows of **A**$^{-1}$**B,** we obtain the solution vector:

$$\begin{bmatrix} P1 \\ P2 \\ P3 \\ S1 \\ S2 \\ S3 \end{bmatrix} = \begin{bmatrix} \$553,661 \\ 340,328 \\ 206,011 \\ 48,330 \\ 87,546 \\ 35,509 \end{bmatrix} \quad \begin{array}{l} \text{Manufacturing Department 1} \\ \text{Manufacturing Department 2} \\ \text{Marketing} \\ \text{Product engineering} \\ \text{Building occupancy} \\ \text{Factory supervision} \end{array}$$

The first three elements of this solution vector represent the total direct and allocated costs for P1, P2, and P3, respectively. The last three elements represent not only the total costs for each service department but also the costs that have passed through these departments because of the allocation procedure.

To determine the allocated costs in P1, P2, and P3, the direct costs are subtracted from the total costs in the solution vector. In the example, the allocated costs using the simultaneous solution method are:

Department	Allocated cost		Total cost		Direct cost
Manufacturing Department 1	$ 53,661	=	$553,661	−	$500,000
Manufacturing Department 2	70,328	=	340,328	−	270,000
Marketing	21,011	=	206,011	−	185,000
Total allocated cost	$145,000				

As a result of the allocation, a total of $145,000 has been allocated from the service departments to the operating departments. All of the interrelationships among service departments have been taken into account in this allocation.

Appendix self-study problem

Using the data provided in the T. Schurt & Company example, which is the self-study problem at the end of the chapter, compute the cost allocation and total costs for each producing department using the simultaneous solution method.

Solution to appendix self-study problem

Simultaneous solution method:

Step 1. Construct the cost equations.

$$P1 = \$210,000 + .333\ S1 + .500\ S2 + .250\ S3$$
$$P2 = \$140,000 + .444\ S1 + .250\ S2 + .667\ S3$$
$$P3 = \$80,000 + .074\ S1 + .100\ S2 + .083\ S3$$
$$S1 = \$45,000 \qquad\qquad + .050\ S2$$
$$S2 = \$20,000 + .100\ S1$$
$$S3 = \$10,000 + .049\ S1 + .100\ S2$$

Step 2. Arrange the cost equations to place the coefficients in one section, and the direct costs on the right-hand side of the equation.

$$1\ P1 + 0\ P2 + 0\ P3 - .333\ S1 - .500\ S2 - .250\ S3 = \$210,000$$
$$0\ P1 + 1\ P2 + 0\ P3 - .444\ S1 - .250\ S2 - .667\ S3 = 140,000$$
$$0\ P1 + 0\ P2 + 1\ P3 - .074\ S1 - .100\ S2 - .083\ S3 = 80,000$$
$$0\ P1 + 0\ P2 + 0\ P3 + 1.000\ S1 - .050\ S2 - .000\ S3 = 45,000$$
$$0\ P1 + 0\ P2 + 0\ P3 - .100\ S1 + 1.000\ S2 - .000\ S3 = 20,000$$
$$0\ P1 + 0\ P2 + 0\ P3 - .049\ S1 - .100\ S2 + 1.000\ S3 = 10,000$$

Step 3. Use the information in Step 2 to construct a matrix of coefficients, a vector of unknowns, and a vector of direct costs.

$$
\begin{bmatrix}
1 & 0 & 0 & -.333 & -.500 & -.250 \\
0 & 1 & 0 & -.444 & -.250 & -.667 \\
0 & 0 & 1 & -.074 & -.100 & -.083 \\
0 & 0 & 0 & 1 & -.050 & 0 \\
0 & 0 & 0 & -.100 & 1 & 0 \\
0 & 0 & 0 & -.049 & -.100 & 1
\end{bmatrix}
\times
\begin{bmatrix}
P1 \\ P2 \\ P3 \\ S1 \\ S2 \\ S3
\end{bmatrix}
=
\begin{bmatrix}
\$210,000 \\ 140,000 \\ 80,000 \\ 45,000 \\ 20,000 \\ 10,000
\end{bmatrix}
$$

Step 4. Invert the matrix **A** using a computer or other electronic assistance and enter the result into the format $X = A^{-1}B$.

$$
\begin{bmatrix}
P1 \\ P2 \\ P3 \\ S1 \\ S2 \\ S3
\end{bmatrix}
=
\begin{bmatrix}
1 & 0 & 0 & .3997 & .5450 & .2500 \\
0 & 1 & 0 & .5109 & .3422 & .6670 \\
0 & 0 & 1 & .0894 & .1128 & .0830 \\
0 & 0 & 0 & 1.0050 & .0503 & 0 \\
0 & 0 & 0 & .1005 & 1.0050 & 0 \\
0 & 0 & 0 & .0593 & .1030 & 1
\end{bmatrix}
\times
\begin{bmatrix}
\$210,000 \\ 140,000 \\ 80,000 \\ 45,000 \\ 20,000 \\ 10,000
\end{bmatrix}
$$

Step 5. Multiply the vector of direct costs by the first three rows of the matrix of A^{-1} to obtain the total costs for each of the three producing departments.

$$
\begin{aligned}
P1 &= 1 \times \$210,000 + .3997 \times \$45,000 + .5450 \times \$20,000 \\
&\quad + .2500 \times \$10,000 \\
&= \$210,000 + \$17,987 + \$10,900 + \$2,500 \\
&= \underline{\underline{\$241,387}}
\end{aligned}
$$

$$
\begin{aligned}
P2 &= 1 \times \$140,000 + .5109 \times \$45,000 + .3422 \times \$20,000 \\
&\quad + .6670 \times \$10,000 \\
&= \$140,000 + \$22,990 + \$6,844 + \$6,670 \\
&= \underline{\underline{\$176,504}}
\end{aligned}
$$

$$
\begin{aligned}
P3 &= 1 \times \$80,000 + .0894 \times \$45,000 + .1128 \times \$20,000 \\
&\quad + .0830 \times \$10,000 \\
&= \$80,000 + \$4,023 + \$2,256 + \$830 \\
&= \underline{\underline{\$87,109}}
\end{aligned}
$$

And check to see that this total: $241,387 + $176,504 + $87,109 equals $505,000 equals $210,000 + $140,000 + $80,000 + $45,000 + $20,000 + $10,000.

Questions

7–1. "Direct Materials" are considered direct with respect to both the manufacturing department using the materials and to the product. However, "indirect materials" cannot be associated directly with a specific job or product but may be related directly to the manufacturing department where the indirect materials are used. Explain the concepts "direct" and "indirect" in this setting.

7–2. What are the reasons for establishing service departments as intermediate cost objectives?

7–3. Why would the manager of an operating department not need reports that include the details of the cost items that comprise the operating department's share of the cost of building occupancy?

7–4. What argument(s) could be given in support of the simultaneous solution method as the preferred method for distributing the costs of service departments?

7–5. Under what conditions would the results obtained from using the direct method of allocation be the same as the results from using either other method? Why?

7–6. Consider a company with two producing departments and one service department. The service department distributes its costs to the producing departments on the basis of number of employees in each department. If the costs in the service department are fixed, what effect would the addition of employees in one department have on the costs allocated to the other department? Comment on the reasonableness of the situation.

7–7. Compare and contrast the direct method, the step method, and the simultaneous solution method of allocating costs.

7–8. The manager of an operating department just received a report of costs and has made the following comment with respect to the costs allocated from one of the service departments: "This charge to my division does not seem right. The service center installed equipment with the capacity to handle the maximum demand for services and some departments have substantially greater demand maximums than we do. Yet, because the costs of this service center are allocated based on the usage of services in each period, we are paying for excess capacity of other departments when other departments cut their usage levels." How might this manager's problem be solved?

7–9. What criterion should be used to determine the order of allocation from service departments when the step method is used. Explain why.

7–10. (Appendix.) The inverse of the matrix **A** in the cost allocation example can be subdivided into four submatrices in the following form:

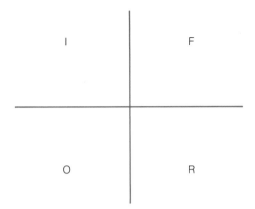

The partitions are established by drawing a line below the last row of coefficients that are related to producing departments (that is, row three in the Appendix example) and a vertical line to the right of the last column of coefficients for producing departments (that is, between the third and fourth columns in the Appendix example). Examine the elements of each of these submatrices and consider how the elements are used in the matrix multiplication to determine the allocation of costs. Give an explanation of the functions of each of these submatrices.

Exercises

7–11. Cost allocations, direct method

Thermal Corporation has two producing departments and two service departments labeled P1, P2, S1, and S2, respectively. Direct costs for each department and the proportion of service costs used by the various departments are as follows:

Cost center	Direct costs	Proportion of services used by			
		S1	S2	P1	P2
P1	$90,000				
P2	60,000				
S1	20,000	—	.80	.10	.10
S2	30,000	.20	—	.50	.30

Required:

Compute the allocation of service center costs to operating departments using the direct method

7–12. Cost allocations—step method

Using the data for the Thermal Corporation (Exercise 7–11), use the step method to allocate the service costs using:

a. The order of allocation recommended in the text.
b. The allocations made in the reverse of the recommended order.

7–13. (Appendix) Cost allocations— simultaneous solution

Using the data for the Thermal Corporation (Exercise 7–11), use the simultaneous solution method to allocate the service costs. Assume that the matrix A^{-1} is equal to:

$$\begin{bmatrix} 1 & 0 & .5952 & .6190 \\ 0 & 1 & .4048 & .3810 \\ 0 & 0 & 1.1905 & .2381 \\ 0 & 0 & .9524 & 1.1905 \end{bmatrix}$$

7–14. Cost allocations— simultaneous solution method—establish equations

A company is attempting to determine if elimination of a service department and replacement of that department's services with an outside supplier would be feasible. The center under consideration for elimination is labeled S1.

During the past month, the following costs were incurred in the three operating departments and two service departments in the company:

P1	$230,000
P2	615,000
P3	790,000
S1	124,000
S2	109,000

The usage of services by other departments is as follows:

Service cost center	User department				
	P1	P2	P3	S1	S2
S1	.30	.20	.10		.40
S2	.20	.15	.55	.10	

Required

Set up the equations needed to express the cost relationships as a system of simultaneous linear equations.

7–15. Cost allocations—direct method

Meridian Box Company has two service departments (maintenance and general factory administration) and two operating departments (cutting and assembly). Management has decided to allocate maintenance costs on the basis of the area in each department and general factory administration costs on the basis of labor-hours worked by the employees in each of their respective departments.

The following data appear in the company records for the current period:

	General factory administration	Maintenance	Cutting	Assembly
Area occupied (square feet)	1,000	—	1,000	3,000
Labor-hours	—	100	100	400
Direct labor costs (operating departments only)			$1,500	$4,000
Service department direct costs	$1,200	$2,400		

Required:

Use the direct method to allocate these service department costs to the operating departments.

7–16. Cost allocation—step method

Using the data for the Meridian Box Company, allocate the service department costs using the step method.

7–17. Cost allocation—simultaneous solution method

Using the data for the Meridian Box Company, allocate the service department costs using the simultaneous solution method. Matrix algebra is not required because there are only two service departments.

Problems and cases

7–18. Cost allocation—step method with three service departments

Oakland Corporation operates two producing departments: painting and polishing in its automotive refinishing operations. To facilitate control and accounting, the company has established three service departments for its plant: building occupancy, payroll accounting, and equipment maintenance. The accumulated costs in the three service departments were $180,000; $250,000; and $132,000, respectively. The company has decided that the building occupancy costs should be distributed on the basis of square footage used by each production and service department. The payroll accounting costs are to be allocated on the basis of number of employees while equipment maintenance costs are to be allocated on the basis of the dollar value of the equipment in each department. The use of each basis by all of the other departments during the current period is as follows:

Allocation base	Building occupancy	Payroll accounting	Equipment maintenance	Painting	Polishing
			Used by		
Building area	5,000	15,000	10,000	180,000	45,000
Employees	9	5	6	35	50
Equipment value (in thousands)	$12	$240	$35	$624	$324

The direct costs of the painting department included $475,000 in direct materials, $650,000 in direct labor, and $225,000 in overhead. In the polishing department, the direct costs consisted of $820,000 in direct labor and $145,000 in overhead.

Required:

Using the step method, determine the allocated costs and the total costs in each of the two producing departments.

7-19. Cost allocation: Comparison of dual and single rates

High Skies Airlines operates a centralized computer center for handling the data processing needs of its reservation, scheduling, maintenance, and accounting divisions. The costs associated with the use of the computer are charged to the individual departments on the basis of time usage. Due to recent increased competition in the airline industry, the company has decided it is necessary to make a more accurate allocation of costs so that it can price its services competitively and profitably. During the current period, the usage of data processing services and the storage capacity required for each of the divisions were as follows (in thousands):

Division	Time usage	Storage capacity
Reservations	2,500	15,000
Scheduling	1,700	6,000
Maintenance	6,300	2,100
Accounting	5,000	1,900

During the period, the costs of the computer center amounted to $3,525,000 for time usage and $2,500,000 for storage related costs.

Required:

Determine the allocation to each of the divisions using:

a. A single rate based on time usage.
b. Dual rates based on time usage and capacity usage.

Round all decimals to three places.

7-20. Allocation for economic decisions and motivation

Bonn Company recently reorganized its computer and data processing activities. The small installations located within the accounting departments at its plants and subsidiaries have been replaced with a single data processing department at corporate headquarters responsible for the operations of a newly acquired large-scale computer system. The new department has been in operation for two years and has been regularly producing reliable and timely data for the past 12 months.

Because the department has focused its activities on converting applications to the new system and producing reports for the plant and subsidiary managements, little attention has been devoted to the costs of the department. Now that the department's activities are operating relatively smoothly, company management has requested that the departmental manager recommend a cost accumulation system to facilitate cost control and the development of suitable rates to charge users for service.

For the past two years, the departmental costs have been recorded in one account. The costs have then been allocated to user departments on the basis of computer time used. The following schedule reports the costs and charging rate for 1984.

Data Processing Department
Costs for the Year ended December 31, 1984

1.	Salaries and benefits	$ 622,600
2.	Supplies	40,000
3.	Equipment maintenance contract	15,000
4.	Insurance	25,000
5.	Heat and air conditioning	36,000
6.	Electricity	50,000
7.	Equipment and furniture depreciation	285,400
8.	Building improvements depreciation	10,000
9.	Building occupancy and security	39,300
10.	Corporate administrative charges	52,700
	Total costs	$1,176,000
	Computer hours for user processing*	2,750
	Hourly rate ($1,176,000 ÷ 2,750)	$428

* Use of Available Computer Hours

Testing and debugging programs	250
Set up of jobs	500
Processing jobs	2,750
Downtime for maintenance	750
Idle time	742
	4,992

The department manager recommends that the department costs be accumulated by five activity centers within the department: systems analysis, programming, data preparation, computer operations (processing), and administration. He then suggests that the costs of the administration activity should be allocated to the other four activity centers before a separate rate for charging users is developed for each of the first four activities.

The manager made the following observations regarding the charges to the several subsidiary accounts within the department after reviewing the details of the accounts:

1. Salaries and benefits—records the salary and benefit costs of all employees in the department.
2. Supplies—records punch-card costs, paper costs for printers, and a small amount for miscellaneous other costs.
3. Equipment maintenance contracts—records charges for maintenance contracts; all equipment is covered by maintenance contracts.
4. Insurance—records cost of insurance covering the equipment and the furniture.
5. Heat and air conditioning—records a charge from the corporate heating and air conditioning department estimated to be the incremental costs to meet the special needs of the computer department.
6. Electricity—records the charge for electricity based upon a separate meter within the department.
7. Equipment and furniture depreciation—records the depreciation charges for all owned equipment and furniture within the department.
8. Building improvements—records the amortization charges for the building changes required to provide proper environmental control and electrical service for the computer equipment.
9. Building occupancy and security—records the computer department's share of the depreciation, maintenance, heat, and security costs of the building; these costs are allocated to the department on the basis of square feet occupied.
10. Corporate administrative charges—records the computer department's share of

the corporate administrative costs. They are allocated to the department on the basis of number of employees in the department.

Required:

a. For each of the 10 cost items, state whether or not it should be distributed to the five activity centers, and for each cost item which should be distributed, recommend the basis upon which it should be distributed. Justify your conclusion in each case.

b. Assume the costs of the computer operations (processing) activity will be charged to the user departments on the basis of computer hours. Using the analysis of computer utilization shown as a footnote to the department cost schedule presented in the problem, determine the total number of hours that should be employed to determine the charging rate for computer operations (processing). Justify your answer.

(CMA adapted)

7–21. Cost allocation: step method with analysis and decision making

O-Hi-O Corporation has been reviewing its operations to determine if there are any additional energy saving projects that might be carried out. The company's Intermac plant has its own electric generating facilities. The electric generating plant is powered by the production of some natural gas wells that the company owns and that are located on the same property as the plant. A summary of the usage of service department service by other service departments as well as by the two producing departments at the plant are summarized as follows:

| Service cost center | Natural gas production | Used by electric generating | | | Production department | |
		Fixed costs	Variable costs	Equipment maintenance	No. 1	No. 2
Natural gas production	—	—	.40	—	.10	.50
Electric generating:					.30	.50
Fixed costs	.10	—	—	.10	.55	.30
Variable costs	.10	—	—	.05	.50	.15
Equipment maintenance	.20	.10	.05	—		

Direct costs in the various departments and the labels used to abbreviate the department in the calculations are as follows (in thousands):

Department	Direct costs	Label
Natural gas production	$ 35	S1
Electric generation:		
Fixed costs	15	S2
Variable costs	40	S3
Equipment maintenance	24	S4
Production department		
No. 1	300	P1
No. 2	220	P2

At the present time, the company is allocating the costs of service departments to production departments using the step method. A review of the published electric utility rates by the local power company indicates that the power company would charge $80,000 per year for electric costs. Management rejected switching to the public utility on the grounds that its rates would cost more than the present company owned system.

Required:

a. Indicate the costs of electric service that management used to prepare the basis for its decision to continue generating power internally.

b. Prepare an analysis for management to indicate the costs of the company's own electric generating operations. Use the cost allocation technique that is most appropriate.

c. The costs of the natural gas production are based on the company's own costs to discover and develop the producing field. Would your answer in (b) change if the company could realize $29,000 per year from the sale of the natural gas now used for electric generating? (Assume no selling costs.)

7-22. (Appendix) Cost allocation and analysis of applied overhead.

White Paper Packaging Corporation prepares cardboard cartons according to customer orders. The company uses a job order cost system because the orders are sufficiently different from one customer to another. The company has two producing departments: printing and folding. Box cardboard is received in the printing department. There it is cut to the appropriate size and imprinted with the customer's specified advertising or other information. Printed cardboard is then transported to the folding department where special equipment folds and glues the boxes. When the boxes are completed, they are delivered to the warehouse for shipment to customers. Normally, the boxes are considered finished when they are ready for final assembly by the customer. That is, the company ships the boxes in a flat form with appropriate creases so that all the customer need do is set the box up and fold in the bottom and top.

The producing departments are serviced by three service areas: materials handling, payroll accounting, and building occupancy. Materials-handling costs are allocated based on direct materials used by each department. Payroll accounting costs are allocated based on total employees in each department, while dual allocation rates are used for building occupancy costs. The fixed building costs are allocated on the basis of department area, while the variable costs are allocated on the basis of labor costs.

During the current month, the following information is available concerning the direct costs and the usage of various allocation bases by each of the departments:

Department	Direct costs	Building area	Labor costs	Number of employees
Materials handling (S1)	$245,000	.25	.10	.08
Payroll accounting (S4)	90,000	.10	.07	—
Building occupancy:				
Fixed costs (S2)	128,000	—	.05	.07
Variable costs (S3)	49,000	.05	—	.03
Painting (P1):				
Direct materials	975,000			
Direct labor	430,000			
Overhead	650,000	.25	.35	.37
Folding (P2):				
Direct materials	65,000			
Direct labor	480,000	.35	.43	.45
Overhead	615,000			

Overhead is applied to production on the basis of 200 percent of direct labor costs in the departments. In painting, 30 percent of the direct overhead was fixed, while in folding, 80 percent of the direct overhead was fixed. Materials-handling costs are considered variable, and payroll accounting costs are considered fixed for analytic purposes.

Estimated labor costs for the period were $575,000 in painting and $450,000 in folding. While the allocated fixed costs were as anticipated, budgeted fixed costs in the painting department were $195,000 and in folding the costs were budgeted at $396,000.

Required:

Determine the applied overhead in each of the producing departments. The first two rows of the matrix $\mathbf{A}^{-1}$ are as follows:

P1	P2	S1	S2	S3	S4
1	0	.938	.560	.507	.499
0	1	.062	.440	.493	.501

7–23. Job order costing with service department cost allocations

WX Service Company operates a job order shop with two producing departments: Department A and Department B. Jobs are started in Department A and then move to Department B. When the work is finished in Department B, the jobs are immediately sold. The company also has two service departments, W and X, which perform support services for the producing departments. In addition, Departments W and X perform services for each other.

Overhead in Department A is applied to jobs on the basis of prime costs (that is, total direct materials, and direct labor). Overhead in Department B is applied on the basis of direct labor costs. For this period, the estimated overhead and estimated activity levels for applying overhead were as follows:

Department A:	Estimated overhead	$66,000
	Estimated prime costs	44,000
Department B:	Estimated overhead	33,000
	Estimated direct labor	30,000

During the month, direct materials and direct labor costs were incurred on jobs as follows:

	Job No. 22	Job No. 28	Job No. 36
Department A:			
Prime costs	$26,000	$13,200	$8,200
Department B:			
Direct materials	16,350	7,100	900
Direct labor	12,000	18,000	–0–

The balances of other departmental costs in the accounts for the service and producing departments (before allocation of service department costs) are as follows:

Department W	$11,300
Department X	14,000
Department A	46,300
Department B	21,500

The use of services by other departments was as follows:

	Used by			
Services of:	W	X	A	B
W	—	20%	30%	50%
X	40%	—	45	15

The company uses the step method for service cost allocation. Jobs No. 22 and No. 28 were completed during the period and were sold. Job No. 36 is in Department B.

Required:

a. What was the current period cost on Job Nos. 22 and 28 that was transferred to Cost of Goods Sold?

b. If actual overhead had been charged to Job No. 28, what amount of current period costs would have been transferred to Cost of Goods Sold for that job?

7-24. Cost allocation and decision making

The Promotion Department of the Doxolby Company is responsible for the design and development of all promotional materials for the corporation. This includes all promotional campaigns and related literature, pamphlets, and brochures. Top management is reviewing the effectiveness of the promotion department to determine if the department's activities could be managed better and more economically by an outside promotion agency. As a part of this review, top management has asked for a summary of the promotion department's costs for the most recent year. The following cost summary was supplied:

Promotion Department
Costs for the Year Ended November 30, 1978

Direct department costs	$257,500
Charges from other departments	44,700
Allocated share of general	
Administrative overhead	22,250
Total costs	$324,450

The direct department costs consist of those costs that can be traced directly to the activities of the promotion department such as staff and clerical salaries including related employee benefits, supplies, etc. The charges from other departments represent the costs of services that are provided by other departments of Doxolby at the request of the promotion department. The company has developed a charging system for such interdepartmental uses of services. For instance, the "in-house" printing department charges the promotion department for the promotional literature printed. All such services provided to the promotion department by other departments of Doxolby are included in the "Changes from Other Departments." General administrative overhead is comprised of such costs as top-management salaries and benefits, depreciation, heat, insurance, property taxes, etc. These costs are allocated to all departments in proportion to the number of employees in each department.

Required:

Discuss the usefulness of the cost figures as presented for the promotion department of Doxolby, Inc., as a basis for a comparison with a bid from an outside agency to provide the same type of activities as Doxolby's own promotion department.

(CMA adapted)

7-25. Allocate service department costs—direct and step methods

The Parker Manufacturing Company has three service departments (general factory administration, factory maintenance, and factory cafeteria), and two production departments (fabrication and assembly). A summary of costs and other data for each department prior to allocation of service department costs for the year ended June 30, 1984, are as follows:

	General factory adminis- tration	Factory mainte- nance	Factory cafe- teria	Fabrication	Assembly
Direct material costs	–0–	$65,000	$91,000	$3,130,000	$ 950,000
Direct labor costs	$90,000	82,100	87,000	1,950,000	2,050,000
Manufacturing overhead costs	70,000	56,100	62,000	1,650,000	1,850,000
Direct labor-hours	31,000	27,000	42,000	562,500	437,500
Number of employees	12	8	20	280	200
Square footage occupied	1,750	2,000	4,800	88,000	72,000

The costs of the general factory administration department, factory maintenance department, and factory cafeteria are allocated on the basis of direct labor-hours, square footage occupied, and number of employees, respectively. Round all final calculations to the nearest dollar.

Required:

a. Assuming that Parker elects to distribute service department costs directly to production departments without interservice department cost allocation, what would be the amount of factory maintenance department costs allocated to the fabrication department?

b. Assuming the same method of allocation as in (a), what would be the amount of general factory administration department costs allocated to the assembly department?

c. Assuming that Parker elects to distribute service department costs to other service departments (starting with the service department with the greatest total costs) as well as the production departments, what would be the amounts of factory cafeteria department costs allocated to the factory maintenance department? (Note: Once a service department's costs have been allocated, no subsequent service department costs are allocated back to it.)

d. Assuming the same method of allocation as in (c), what would be the amount of factory maintenance department costs allocated to the factory cafeteria?

(CPA adapted)

7–26. Allocate service department costs using direct and simultaneous solution methods

(Note: Matrix algebra is not required for this problem. An algebraic equation can be set up for the costs of each of the two service departments and solved by substitution.)

Barrylou Corporation is developing departmental overhead rates based upon direct labor-hours for its two production departments—molding and assembly. The molding department employs 20 people, and the assembly department employs 80 people. Each person in these two departments works 2000 hours per year. The production related overhead costs for the molding department are budgeted at $200,000, and the assembly department costs are budgeted at $320,000. Two service departments—repair and power—directly support the two production departments and have budgeted costs of $48,000 and $250,000, respectively. The production departments' overhead rates cannot be determined until the service departments' costs are properly allocated. The following schedule reflects the use of the repair department's and power department's output by the various departments.

	Department			
	Repair	**Power**	**Molding**	**Assembly**
Repair hours	0	1,000	1,000	8,000
Kilowatt-hour	240,000	0	840,000	120,000

Required:

a. Calculate the overhead rates per direct labor-hour for the molding department and the assembly department using the direct allocation method to charge the production departments for service department cost.

b. Calculate the overhead rates per direct labor-hour for the molding department and the assembly department using the simultaneous solution method to charge service department costs to each other and to the production department.

(CMA adapted)

7–27. Patient's Hospital (cost allocation, step method, and simultaneous solution)*

The annual costs of hospital care under the medicare program amount to $20 billion per year. In the medicare legislation, Congress mandated that reimbursement to hospitals would be limited to the costs of treating medicare patients. Ideally, neither nonmedicare patients nor hospitals would bear the costs of medicare patients nor would the government bear costs of nonmedicare patients. Given the large sums involved, it is not surprising that cost reimbursement specialists, computer programs, publications, and other products and services have arisen to provide hospital administrators with the assistance needed to obtain an appropriate reimbursement for medicare patient services.

Hospital departments may be divided into two categories: (1) revenue producing departments and (2) nonrevenue producing departments. This classification is simple, but useful. The traditional accounting concepts associated with "service department cost allocation" while appropriate to this context, lead to a great deal of confusion in terminology since all of the hospital's departments are considered to be rendering services.

Costs of revenue producing departments are charged to medicare and nonmedicare patients on the basis of actual usage of the departments. These costs are relatively simple to apportion. The costs of nonrevenue producing departments are somewhat more difficult to apportion. The approach to finding the appropriate distribution of these costs begins with the establishment of a reasonable basis for allocating nonrevenue producing department costs to revenue producing departments. Statistical measures of the relationships between departments must be ascertained. The cost allocation bases listed in Exhibit A have been established by medicare regulations as acceptable for cost reimbursement purposes. The regulated order of allocation must be used for medicare reimbursement even though the general rule may call for another order.

Exhibit A (7–27)   **Bases for allocating nonrevenue department costs to revenue-producing departments**

Nonrevenue cost center	Basis for allocation
Depreciation—buildings	Square feet in each department
Depreciation—movable equipment	Dollar value of equipment in each department
Employee health and welfare	Gross salaries in each department
Administrative and general	Accumulated costs by department
Maintenance and repairs	Square feet in each department
Operation of plant	Square feet in each department
Laundry and linen service	Pounds used in each department
Housekeeping	Hours of service to each department
Dietary	Meals served in each department
Maintenance of personnel	Number of departmental employees housed
Nursing administration	Hours of supervision in each department
Central supply	Costs of requisitions processed
Pharmacy	Costs of drug orders processed
Medical records	Hours worked for each department
Social service	Hours worked for each department
Nursing school	Assigned time by department
Intern/resident service	Assigned time by department

* © 1982 by CIPT Co.

A hospital may then use either a simultaneous solution method to the cost allocation problem or they may use the "step-down" or step method. If the step-down method is used, the order of departments for allocation is the same order as that by which the departments are listed in Exhibit A. Thus, depreciation of buildings is allocated before depreciation of movable equipment. Cost centers must be established for each of these nonrevenue producing costs that are relevant to a particular hospital's operations.

In the past year, the hospital reported the following departmental costs:

Nonrevenue producing:
Laundry and linen	$ 250,000
Depreciation—buildings	830,000
Employee health and welfare	375,000
Maintenance of personnel	210,000
Central supply	745,000

Revenue producing:
Operating room	$1,450,000
Radiology	160,000
Laboratory	125,000
Patient rooms	2,800,000

Percentage usage of services by one department from another department were as follows:

From	Laundry and linen	Depreciation buildings	Employee health and welfare	Maintenance of personnel	Central supply
Laundry and linen	—	.05	.10	–0–	–0–
Depreciation—buildings	.10	—	–0–	.10	–0–
Employee health and welfare	.15	–0–	—	.05	.03
Maintenance of personnel	–0–	–0–	–0–	—	.12
Central supply	.10	–0–	–0–	.08	—

	Operating rooms	Radiology	Laboratory	Patient rooms
Laundry and linen	.30	.10	.05	.40
Depreciation—buildings	.05	.02	.02	.71
Employee health and welfare	.25	.05	.04	.43
Maintenance of personnel	.36	.10	.08	.34
Central supply	.09	.04	.03	.66

The proportional usage of revenue producing department services by medicare and other patients was as follows:

	Medicare	Other
Operating rooms	25%	75%
Radiology	20	80
Laboratory	28	72
Patient rooms	36	64

Required:

a. Determine the amount of the reimbursement claim for medicare services using the step-down method of allocation.

b. (Optional). With the assistance of a computer, determine the claim for medicare services using the simultaneous solution method.

Allocating
Joint Costs

OBJECTIVES

To understand the nature of joint costs and how they are assigned to products.
To be familiar with the drawbacks of joint cost allocations.

A joint cost occurs when a single process contributes to the production of several different outputs. For example, a log may produce lumber, chipboard, and pulp. The production of these three joint products from a single input results in joint costs. The problem in such cases is whether and how to allocate the joint cost of the input to the multiple outputs.

For example, Illustration 8–1 diagrams the flow of costs incurred to process logs by the Sacramento-Sierra Company. These costs include direct materials, direct labor, and manufacturing overhead. As the logs are processed, two products emerge: lumber and chipboard. The stage of processing where the two products are separated is called the split-off point. Costs incurred in processing prior to the split-off point are called joint costs. This chapter shows how those joint costs can be allocated to products.

Joint cost allocation methods

There are three major methods of allocating joint costs: (1) the *relative sales value method*, (2) the *physical quantities method*, and (3) the *replacement method*.

Relative sales value method

With the relative sales value method, joint costs are allocated based on the proportion of the sales value of each product at the split-off point. Use of the relative sales value method requires a reliable measure of the sales value of each product at the split-off point.

If the joint products can be sold at the split-off point, the market value or sales price may be used for this allocation. However, if the products require further processing before they are marketable, then it is necessary to estimate the sales value at the split-off point. Usually the sales value is estimated by taking the sales value after further processing and deducting those added processing costs to arrive at the net realizable value at the split-off point. This net realizable value is then used as the measure of sales value at the

Illustration 8–1   **Diagram of joint cost flows**

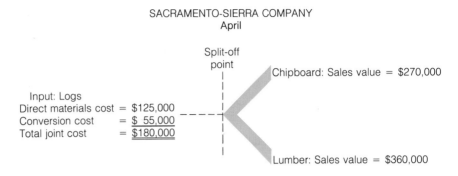

SACRAMENTO-SIERRA COMPANY
April

split-off point. In either case, joint costs are then allocated to the products in proportion to their relative sales values at the split-off point.

For example, the Sacramento-Sierra Company produces lumber and chipboard. Direct materials (that is, logs) cost $125,000 and conversion costs are $55,000 for a total of $180,000 in April. Lumber and chipboard have a total sales value of $630,000 at the split-off point. Chipboard has sales value of $270,000, or 42.857 percent of the total while lumber's value is $360,000, or 57.143 percent of the total.

The cost allocation would follow the proportional distribution of relative sales value:

To chipboard:
$$\left[\frac{\$270,000}{\$630,000}\right] \times \$180,000 = \$\ 77,143$$

To lumber:
$$\left[\frac{\$360,000}{\$630,000}\right] \times \$180,000 = \underline{\ \ 102,857}$$
$$\underline{\underline{\$180,000}}$$

A condensed statement of margins at split-off point is shown in Illustration 8–2.

Note that the margins as a percentage of sales are 71.43 percent for *both* products. This demonstrates an important concept of the relative sales value method—namely, that revenue dollars from any joint product are assumed to make the same percentage contribution at the split-off point as the revenue dollars from any other joint product. This approach implies a matching of input costs with revenues generated by each output.

Illustration 8–3 shows the flow of these allocated costs through T-accounts. Note that logs are materials held in Direct Materials Inventory until they are allocated to Work in Process Inventory.

Illustration 8–2   **Gross margin computations using relative sales value method**

SACRAMENTO-SIERRA COMPANY
April

Item	Chipboard	Lumber	Total
Sales value	$270,000	$360,000	$630,000
Less allocated joint costs	77,143	102,857	180,000
Gross margin	$192,857	$257,143	$450,000
Gross margin as a percent of sales	71.43[a]	71.43[a]	71.43[a]

[a] 71.43 = $192,857 ÷ $270,000 = $257,143 ÷ $360,000 = $450,000 ÷ $630,000.

Illustration 8–3   **Flow of costs using relative sales (value method)**

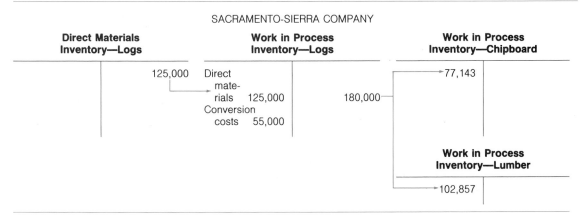

SACRAMENTO-SIERRA COMPANY

Estimating relative sales value

Not all joint products can be sold at the split-off point. Further processing may be required before the product is marketable. When no sales values exist for the outputs at the split-off point, the sales values must be estimated. Usually the relative sales values at the split-off point are estimated by taking the sales value of each product at the first point at which it can be marketed and deducting the processing costs that must be incurred to get there from the split-off point. The resulting *net realizable value* is used for joint cost allocation in the same way as an actual market value at the split-off point.

Suppose the management of Sacramento-Sierra finds the market for chipboard has changed such that it is more profitable to sell laminated chipboard than to sell plain chipboard. Additional processing to laminate the chipboard costs $20,000 before it can be marketed for $330,000. Lumber can still be marketed at the split-off point for $360,000. Illustration 8–4 diagrams the process.

Illustration 8–5 shows the allocation of the $180,000 joint cost to laminated chipboard and lumber if the laminated chipboard is manufactured.

Illustration 8-4 **Flow of costs—further processing beyond split-off point**

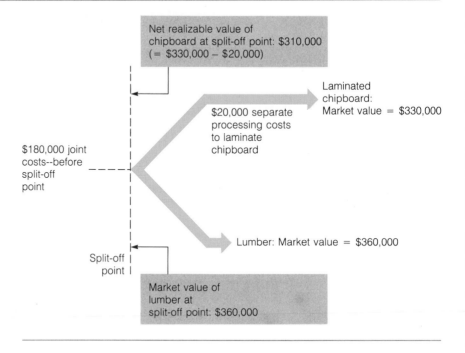

Illustration 8-5 **Relative sales value method using estimated net realizable value for laminated chipboard**

SACRAMENTO-SIERRA COMPANY

Item	Laminated chipboard	Lumber	Total
Sales value	$330,000	$360,000	$690,000
Less additional process costs to point of marketability	20,000	–0–	20,000
Estimated relative sales value at split-off point	310,000	360,000	670,000
Allocation of joint costs:			
$\left[\dfrac{\$310,000}{\$670,000}\right] \times \$180,000$	83,284		
$\left[\dfrac{\$360,000}{\$670,000}\right] \times \$180,000$		96,716	180,000
Margin	$226,716	$263,284	$490,000
Margin as a percent of sales	73.134	73.134	73.134

Physical quantities method

The **physical quantities method** is often used when output product prices are highly volatile, when much processing occurs between the split-off point and the first point of marketability, or when product prices are not available. This latter situation may arise in cost-based regulated pricing situations or in contract situations.

With the physical quantities method, joint costs assigned to products are based on a physical measure. This might be volume, weight, or any other common measure of physical characteristics. Many companies allocate joint costs incurred in producing oil and gas on the basis of energy equivalent (BTU content). They use this method because oil and gas are often produced simultaneously from the same well, the products are typically measured in different physical units (gas by thousand cubic feet (mcf.), oil by barrel). Moreover, the price of most gas is regulated so that relative market values are artificial. However, the common measure of quantity and the perceived value of the products is the relative energy content.

For example, assume that relative market values at the split-off point are not available at Sacramento-Sierra Company and that for every $180,000 of joint costs in processing logs we obtain 1,400 units of chipboard and 1,960 units of lumber. The allocation of joint costs using these physical quantity measures is shown in Illustration 8–6.

As long as the physical measures reflect economic values, this method of assigning costs may provide a reasonable basis for joint cost allocation. However, there are many cases where an allocation based on physical quantities would not accurately reflect economic values. For example, gold is often found in copper deposits. The physical quantities of gold may be small, yet their value may be significant. If the joint costs of mining the ore that contains the gold and copper were to be allocated to the output products on the basis of weight, the resulting product costs would not reflect a matching of costs with economic values.

The replacement method

The **replacement method** for joint cost allocation is widely used in industries where management can change output proportions. In petroleum refining

Illustration 8–6   **Physical quantities method**

SACRAMENTO-SIERRA COMPANY
April

Item	Chipboard	Lumber	Total
Output quantities	1,400 units	1,960 units	3,360 units
Joint allocation:			
$\left[\frac{1,400}{3,360}\right] \times \$180,000$	$75,000		
$\left[\frac{1,960}{3,360}\right] \times \$180,000$		$105,000	$180,000

and chemical processing, for example, the same input can be converted into numerous mixes of output. The replacement method is used when an output proportion is changed from a previously established mix.

For example, assume that Sacramento-Sierra Company had used the physical quantities method to allocate the $180,000 joint cost of log processing as follows:

$$\text{Chipboard, 1,400 units:} \quad \frac{1,400}{1,400 + 1,960} \times \$180,000 = \$75,000$$

$$\text{Lumber, 1,960 units:} \quad \frac{1,960}{1,400 + 1,960} \times \$180,000 = \$105,000$$

One day management decides to change this output mix to produce more chipboard. They find chipboard can be increased by 100 units if lumber is reduced by 80 units. They find it is also necessary to change the processing method in a way that adds $2,470 to the joint costs of processing logs.

Before the change in output mix, the unit cost of chipboard was $53.57 (= $75,000 ÷ 1,400 units), and the unit cost of lumber was $53.57 (= $105,000 ÷ 1,960). The cost of the 80 units of lumber that would be given up to produce the additional 100 units of chipboard would be $4,286 (= $53.57 × 80 units). This amount would be added to the costs of chipboard together with the additional $2,470 in processing costs. The costs of lumber would be credited with the $4,286. This would result in the cost allocation shown in Illustration 8–7. Illustration 8–8 diagrams these cost flows in the accounts.

Note that the unit cost of lumber remains $53.57, but the unit cost of chipboard increases from $53.57 to $54.50. Thus, the product that increases in volume is charged with the additional cost. The unit cost is left unchanged, however, for the product whose volume is decreased.

Illustration 8–7   **Replacement method**

SACRAMENTO-SIERRA COMPANY

Product	(1) Units	(2) Cost	(3) Cost[a] per unit
Chipboard (initial allocation)	1,400	$ 75,000	$53.57
Replacement cost of lumber used to produce chipboard	100	4,286	
Additional processing costs		2,470	
Totals	1,500	$ 81,756	54.50
Lumber (initial allocation)	1,960	$105,000	53.57
Replacement cost of lumber used to produce chipboard	(80)	(4,286)	53.57
Totals	1,880	$100,714	53.57

[a] Rounded to two decimal places. Column (3) = Column (2) ÷ Column (1).

Illustration 8–8   **Replacement method**

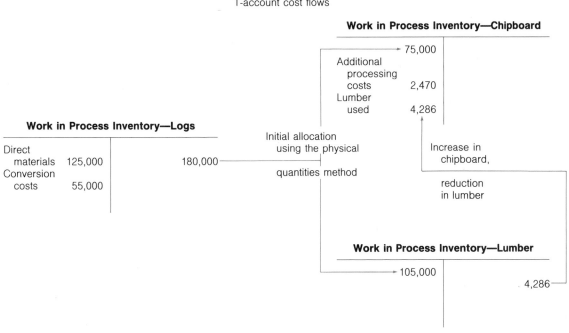

SACRAMENTO-SIERRA COMPANY
T-account cost flows

Work in Process Inventory—Chipboard

	75,000	
Additional processing costs	2,470	
Lumber used	4,286	

Work in Process Inventory—Logs

| Direct materials | 125,000 | 180,000 |
| Conversion costs | 55,000 | |

Initial allocation using the physical quantities method

Increase in chipboard, reduction in lumber

Work in Process Inventory—Lumber

| | 105,000 | 4,286 |

In summary:

1. The replacement method is used *after* joint costs are allocated to output products using another method (for example, the physical quantities method or the relative sales value method).

2. The replacement method is used when management decides to change a previously determined product mix.

   a. For the output that is *decreased,* product costs are reduced (that is, credited to Work in Process Inventory) by the number of units decreased times the unit cost of those units.

   b. For the output that is increased, product costs are increased (debited to Work in Process Inventory) by the sum of the amount of costs removed from the product that was decreased and additional processing costs that are required to change the output mix.

3. The replacement method is only used when a previously established product mix is changed so that one output is increased and another is decreased.

4. The cost of the input is assumed to be the same both before and after the change in product mix.

Comments on joint cost allocation methods

Due to the nature of joint production processes, it is not possible to separate the portion of joint costs attributable to one product or another on any direct-charge basis. As a result, if allocated joint costs are used for decision-making purposes, they should be used only with full recognition of their limitations. As long as the method used for allocation reasonably reflects the relative economic benefits obtained from the jointly produced outputs, the method is usually considered acceptable for financial reporting purposes, for cost-based regulation, and for contracts based on costs (for example, to determine executive bonuses).

Inventory valuation of joint products using estimated sales values

Some companies prefer to value their inventory of jointly produced outputs based on the estimated sales value at the split-off point of each output rather than on any allocation of joint costs. For example, using this approach, Sacramento-Sierra Company would value its inventory as:

	Inventory value if no additional processing beyond split-off point[a]	Inventory value if additional processing beyond split-off point required for chipboard[b]
Chipboard	$270,000	$330,000 − 20,000 = $310,000
Lumber	360,000	360,000

[a] Based on data from Illustration 8–2.
[b] Based on data from Illustration 8–4.

A modification of this is to reduce the net realizable value by an allowance for the normal profit that would be earned on the subsequent processing and sale of the outputs. Otherwise, the stated inventory values would include anticipated but unearned profits. From our perspective, either approach is acceptable as long as the users understand how inventory values are derived.

Processing decisions and joint costs

Many companies have opportunities to sell partly processed products at various stages of production. Management must decide whether it is more profitable to sell the output at an intermediate stage or to process it further. In such a sell-or-process-further decision, the relevant data to be considered are (1) the selling price of the intermediate product and (2) the additional costs of processing further.

Suppose Sacramento-Sierra Company can sell Chipboard for $270,000 at the split-off point or process it further to make laminated chipboard. The additional processing costs are $20,000, and the revenue from laminated chipboard would be $330,000. Should the company sell chipboard or process it

Illustration 8–9   **Income statements for sell or process—further decisions**

Item	Sell	Process further	Additional revenue and costs from processing further	
Revenues:				
From chipboard	$270,000	$330,000	$60,000	
From lumber	360,000	360,000	—	
Total revenues	630,000	690,000	60,000	
Less costs:				
Joint costs	(180,000)	(180,000)	—	
Separate processing of chipboard	–0–	(20,000)	(20,000)	
Margin	$450,000	$490,000	$40,000	net gain from processing further

further? As indicated in earlier examples, the revenue from lumber is $360,000, and the joint cost of processing logs is $180,000.

As shown in Illustration 8–9, the profit will be greater by $40,000 if chipboard is processed further. It is important to note that *the allocation of the joint costs between chipboard and lumber is irrelevant.* The $60,000 additional revenue from processing beyond the split-off point justified the expenditure of $20,000 for additional processing, regardless of the way joint costs are allocated.

Accounting for by-products

By-products are outputs from a joint production process that are relatively minor in quantity and/or value when compared to the main products. For example, sawdust and wood chips are by-products of lumber production and kerosene is a by-product of gasoline production. You may have seen advertisements for carpet and cloth mill ends at low prices. These are often by-products of textile production.

The usual objective of by-product accounting is to reflect the economic relationship between the by-products and the main products with a minimum of recordkeeping for inventory valuation purposes. Two common methods of accounting for by-products are:

Method 1).   The net realizable value from sale of the by-product is deducted from the cost of the main product.

Method 2).   The net realizable value from sale of the by-product is treated as other income.

Assume that By-Product Company has a production process that yields Output C as the main product and Output D as the by-product. The sale value of C is $200,000, while the sales value of D is $1,100. Processing costs up to the split-off point are $80,000. These costs are like joint costs,

Illustration 8–10   **Accounting for by-products**

BY-PRODUCT COMPANY

	Accounting method[a]	
	(1)	**(2)**
Sales revenue from		
Output C	$200,000	$200,000
Other income	–0–	800[b]
Total revenue	200,000	200,800
Cost of sales:		
Total production costs	80,000	80,000
Less by-product:		
Net realizable value	800[b]	
Adjusted cost of sales	79,200	80,000
Gross margin	$120,800	$120,800

[a] Description of accounting methods:
1. The net realizable value of the by-product is deducted from the cost of the main product.
2. The net realizable value from the sale of the by-product is treated as other income.

[b] $800 is the net realizable value of the by-product ($1,100 selling price minus $300 separate costs to process the by-product).

but they are not allocated between Output C and Output D—they are *all* allocated to Output C, the main product.

Also assume Output D requires $300 additional costs of processing to make it salable; hence, Output D's net realizable value is $800 ($1,100 − $300). The two methods of accounting for the by-product, Output D, are shown in Illustration 8–10. The flow of costs through T-accounts using Method 1 is shown in Illustration 8–11.

Whereas we have indicated two methods of accounting for by-products, there are many alternative methods used by companies. By-products are relatively minor products, by definition, hence, alternative methods of accounting for by-products are not likely to have a material effect on the financial statements for either internal or external reporting.

Scrap

Our discussion so far has assumed that the secondary or by-product output has a positive net realizable value—that is, that its sales value exceeds the costs of further processing and marketing. If an output net realizable value is negative, it is usually considered *scrap,* and it is disposed of at minimum cost. The cost of scrapping an output is usually debited to Manufacturing Overhead.

Why allocate joint costs?

Joint costs are allocated for many reasons. A major reason in manufacturing companies is that joint costs must be allocated to value inventory and compute

Illustration 8–11   Accounting for by-products

BY-PRODUCT COMPANY
Flow of costs[a]

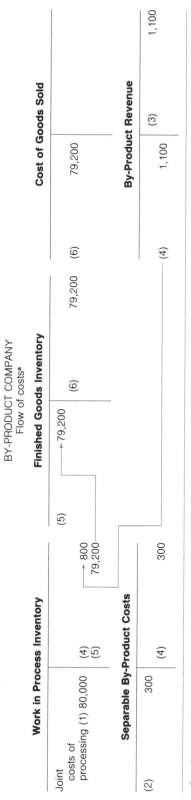

Work in Process Inventory

Joint costs of processing (1) 80,000		(4)	800
		(5)	79,200

Separable By-Product Costs

(2)	300	(4)	300

Finished Goods Inventory

(5)	79,200	(6)	79,200

Cost of Goods Sold

(6)	79,200	

By-Product Revenue

(4)	1,100	(3)	1,100

[a] Cost flows are shown using Method 1 in the text. According to this method, the net realizable value of the by-product is deducted from the production costs of the main product. Journal entries:

(1) Work in Process Inventory 80,000
       *Direct Materials Inventory ......   } 80,000
       *Direct Labor ....
       *Manufacturing Overhead ....
    * Credit to these accounts assumed for illustrative purposes.

(2) Separable By-product Costs   300
       *Direct Labor ....   } 300
       *Manufacturing Overhead ....
    * Credit to these accounts assumed for illustrative purposes.

(3) *Accounts Receivable 1,100
       By-product Revenue   1,100
    * Debit to this account assumed for illustrative purposes.

(4) By-product Revenue 1,100
       Separable By-product Costs ...   300
       Work in Process Inventory   800
    To deduct the net realizable value of the by-product from the cost of the main product.

(5) Finished Goods Inventory 79,200
       Work in Process Inventory   79,200

(6) Cost of Goods Sold 79,200
       Finished Goods Inventory   79,200

(7) *Accounts Receivable 200,000
       Sales Revenue (from main product)   200,000
    * Debit to this account assumed for illustrative purposes.

the cost of goods for external financial reporting under generally accepted accounting principles (GAAP). But there are many other reasons, too.

Joint cost allocations are useful in valuing inventory for insurance purposes. Should a casualty loss occur, the insurance company and the insured must agree on the value of the lost goods. One factor to be considered in arriving at a settlement is the cost of the material destroyed. If joint or by-products are destroyed, material and processing costs must be divided between the goods destroyed and those not destroyed.

Cost allocations can also be helpful in pricing cost of goods sold for measuring executive performance. Many companies compensate executives and other employees, at least partly, on the basis of departmental or division earnings for the year. When a single raw material is converted into products sold by two or more departments, the cost of that raw material must be allocated to the products concerned.

When companies are subject to rate regulation, the allocation of joint costs can be a significant factor in determining the regulated rates. Crude oil and natural gas are usually produced out of a common well. In recent years, energy price policies and gas utility rates have been based in part on the allocation of the joint costs of crude oil and natural gas.

In each of these cases, opposing interests are involved. For example, neither the insurance company nor the insured wishes to pay more or receive less than is "fair." Executives and employees will object to a cost of goods sold figure that they feel is overstated against them and understated for another department. Buyers and sellers of regulated products or services are both affected by pricing and neither wishes to give the other an advantage. When the allocation of costs can impinge on the financial fortunes of opposing parties, both sides review the allocation method critically.

Of course, any cost allocation method contains an element of arbitrariness. No allocation method can be beyond dispute. Consequently, methods of allocation must be clearly stated before they are implemented.

Summary

Joint cost allocations arise from the need to allocate common costs to two or more products manufactured from a common input. The usual objective of joint cost allocation is to relate the economic sacrifice (costs) of the inputs to the economic benefits received. Since there is no direct way to do this for joint products, approximations are necessary. The three methods of joint cost allocation distribute joint costs based on relative sales value, physical measures of relative output, or replacement cost for changes in output mix. While all three methods are acceptable for financial reporting purposes, care must be exercised before attempting to use the data for decision or policy-making purposes.

The relative sales value method allocates joint costs to products in proportion to their relative sales values. If additional processing is required beyond the split-off point before the product can be sold, an estimate of the net realizable value can be derived at the split-off point by subtracting the additional processing costs from the sales value that is known.

The physical quantities method allocates joint costs to products in proportion to a physical measure (for example, volume or weight).

The replacement method is used when an output proportion is changed from a previously established mix. For the output that is decreased, product costs are reduced by the number of units decreased times their unit cost. These costs, plus any additional processing cost needed to change the product mix, are added to the cost of the output being increased.

Management must often decide whether to sell products at split-off points or process them further. Joint cost allocations are usually irrelevant for these decisions.

By-products are relatively minor outputs from a joint production process. The two approaches most commonly used to account for by-products are to reduce the cost of the main product by either the net realizable value (sales value minus by-product processing costs) of the by-product, or to treat the net realizable value of the by-product as other income.

Terms and concepts	The following terms and concepts should be familiar to you after reading this chapter:

By-products	**Physical quantities method**
Joint costs	**Relative sales value method**
Joint products	**Replacement method**
Net realizable value	**Split-off point**

Self study problem	Ferguson Confections Company purchases cocoa beans and processes them into cocoa butter, cocoa powder, and cocoa shells. The standard yield from each 100-pound sack of unprocessed cocoa beans is 20 pounds of butter, 45 pounds of powder, and 35 pounds of shells. The butter must be molded and packed before it can be sold. The further processing costs $.15 per pound, but the resulting processed butter can be sold for $1.25 per pound. The powder can be sold for $.90 per pound at the split-off point. The shells, which are considered a by-product, sell for $.04 per pound. The company estimates net realizable values at the split-off point if no market price is available at that point.

The costs of the cocoa beans is $15 per hundred pounds. It costs $37 in labor and overhead to process each 100 pounds of beans up to the split-off point.

Required:	*a.* Assuming that the shells are recorded as other income at the time they are sold, compute the allocated joint cost of the butter and powder produced from 100 pounds of cocoa beans using the relative sales value method.

b. Assuming that the shells are recorded as other income at the time they are sold, compute the allocated joint cost of the butter and powder produced from each 100 pounds of cocoa beans using the physical quantities (pounds) method.

c. If the net realizable value of the shells is entered as a credit to the primary manufacturing costs at the time the shells are recovered and if the relative sales value method is used for joint cost allocation, what would be the allocation of the joint costs to the main products?

d. Suppose that powder could be processed further at a cost of $.70 per pound and the resulting product sold as instant cocoa for $1.50 per pound. Should the company sell the powder or the instant cocoa?

Solution to self-study problem

a. The joint costs to be allocated amount to $52—the total of the $15 in direct materials costs and the $37 in conversion costs.

Since the butter must be processed further, the sales value at split-off is approximated by deducting the additional processing costs ($.15 per pound) from the sales value at the first point of marketability (which is $1.25 per pound). The resulting sales value for butter is $1.10 per pound (computed as $1.25 less $.15) multiplied by the 20 pounds obtained per 100 pounds of beans. The total sales value for butter, then, is $22 (which is $1.10 per pound times 20 pounds).

The relative sales value of the powder is $40.50 which is the product of the selling price of $.90 per pound times the standard yield of 45 pounds per hundred pounds of input.

The allocation follows:

To cocoa butter:

$$\frac{\$22}{\$22 + \$40.50} \times \$52 = \underline{\underline{\$18.304}}$$

To cocoa powder:

$$\frac{\$40.50}{\$22 + \$40.50} \times \$52 = \underline{\underline{\$33.696}}$$

This results in an allocation of the total cost of $52 (which is $18.304 + $33.696) to the two products.

b. Since there is a total of 65 pounds of output of major products (20 pounds of beans and 45 pounds of butter) at the split-off point, the allocation is:

To cocoa butter:

$$\frac{20}{20 + 45} \times \$52 = \underline{\underline{\$16.00}}$$

To cocoa powder:

$$\frac{45}{20 + 45} \times \$52 = \underline{\underline{\$36.00}}$$

resulting in an allocation of the total $52 to the two products.

c. If the net realizable value of the shells is considered a reduction in the costs to be allocated, then the allocation would proceed as in part *(a)*, but using $50.60 (which is $52.00 less $1.40) as the cost to be allocated. This results in the following allocation:

To cocoa butter:

$$\frac{\$22}{\$22 + \$40.50} \times \$50.60 = \underline{\underline{\$17.8112}}$$

To cocoa powder:

$$\frac{\$40.50}{\$22 + \$40.50} \times \$50.60 = \underline{\underline{\$32.7888}}$$

As with the other methods, this too results in a full allocation of the $50.60 (that is, $17.8112 + $32.7888 = $50.60).

d. The company should sell the powder without further processing. Each pound processed further incurs an opportunity cost of $.90 in lost revenue from the sale of powder plus an incremental processing cost of $.70 per pound for a total cost of $1.60 per pound. However, the sales value of the instant cocoa is only $1.50 per pound. This is less than the economic cost to produce it.

Questions

8–1. What is the objective of joint cost allocation?

8–2. Why would a number of accountants express a preference for the relative sales value method of joint cost allocation?

8–3. What are the circumstances that would lead one to prefer a physical quantities method for joint cost allocation?

8–4. Since the replacement cost method attempts to cost joint products on an opportunity cost basis, should it not be used as the primary method for joint cost allocation? Why or why not?

8–5. Why are joint costs irrelevant in the sell or process further decision?

8–6. The chapter indicated that joint costs were not generally useful for decision-making purposes, but rather were used mostly for financial reporting, inventory valuation, and regulatory purposes. Under what conditions might the method of joint cost allocation impact on other decisions?

8–7. It has been stated that when using the relative market value method for joint cost allocation, it is not important that management actually plan to sell the output at the split off point. Why is that so?

8–8. What is the difference between joint products, by-products, and scrap?

8–9. For external financial reporting purposes, is it possible to avoid the problem of allocating joint costs? If so, how?

8–10. A company presently extracts phosphorus from certain ores that also contain traces of other minerals. Management has been asked to enter a contract to process uranium yellowcake (a semiprocessed ore) as a joint product. None of its present production would need to be given up to produce the yellowcake. Since uranium ores cannot be sold on an open market, what costs should management assign to the yellowcake for deciding whether to accept the contract?

8–11. How does the problem of joint cost allocation compare to the problem of the allocation of the building occupancy costs in a facility that is shared by several operating departments?

Exercises

8-12. Joint cost allocation, relative sales value method

A company processes Chemical DX-1 through a pressure treatment operation. After the process is complete, there are two outputs: L and T. The monthly costs of processing DX-1 amount to $45,000 for materials and $160,000 for conversion costs. This processing results in outputs that sell for a total of $455,000. The sales revenue from L amounts to $273,000 of the total.

Required:

Compute the costs to be assigned to L and T in a typical month using the relative sales value method.

8-13. Estimating relative sales value

Brazos Corporation operates an ore processing plant. A typical batch of ore that is run through the plant will yield three refined products: lead, copper, and manganese. At the split-off point, the intermediate products cannot be sold without further processing. The lead from a typical batch will sell for $20,000 after incurring additional processing costs of $8,000. The copper is sold for $40,000 after additional processing costs of $1,000. The manganese yield sells for $30,000 but requires additional processing costs of $6,000. The costs of processing the raw ore, including the ore costs, amount to $55,000 per batch.

Required:

Use the relative sales value method to allocate the joint processing costs.

8-14. Joint cost allocations using physical quantity measures

Riverside Plant Protein Corporation uses organic materials to produce fertilizers for home gardens. Through its production processes, the company manufactures a high-nitrogen fertilizer (with the trade name Hi-Nite) and a high phosphorus fertilizer (with the trade name Hi-Bloom). A by-product of the process is methane that is used to generate power for the company's operations. The fertilizers are sold either in bulk to nurseries or in individual packages for home consumers. The unit prices to nurseries are significantly less than the cost to home consumers. In addition, the proportion of each fertilizer sold to each consumer varies from one month to the next. As a result, it is not feasible to use a relative sales value approach for joint cost allocation. Rather, the company chooses to allocate the costs on the basis of the relative units of output.

Last month 500,000 units of input were processed at a total cost of $120,000. The output of the process consisted of 100,000 units of Hi-Nite, 200,000 units of Hi-Bloom, and 300,000 cubic feet of methane. The by-product methane would have cost $1,200 had it been purchased from the local gas utility. These costs are considered a reduction in the manufacturing overhead for the main products, and expensed separately.

Required:

What is the share of the joint costs to be assigned to each of the main products?

8-15. Joint costing, solve for unknowns

O'Connor Company manufactures Product J and Product K from a joint process. For product J, 4,000 units were produced having a sales value at the split-off point of $15,000. If Product J were processed further, the additional costs would be $3,000 and the sales value would be $20,000. For Product K, 2,000 units were produced having a sales value at split-off of $10,000. If Product K were processed further, the additional costs would be $1,000 and the sales value would be $12,000. Using the relative sales value at split-off approach, the portion of the total joint product costs allocated to Product J was $9,000.

Required:

Compute the total joint product costs.

(CPA adapted)

8-16. Replacement method

Valley Cane Company processes sugar cane into various output products. The outputs from the first stage of the process consist of two grades of sugar: refined and turbinado. In a typical month, $218,000 in sugar cane are processed and $325,000 in labor and overhead are incurred. A standard output mix consists of 40 percent refined sugar and 60 percent turbinado. Engineering studies assign 55 percent of the joint processing costs to the refined sugar.

If the processing temperature is increased, the yield of refined sugar can be increased by 20 percent (that is, from 40 percent of the initial output to an amount equal to 48 percent of the initial output). However, processing costs are increased 7.5 percent when this is done, and 15 percent of the original yield of turbinado is lost. The replacement cost is to be estimated on the basis of actual costs, not net realizable values.

Required:

Compute the costs that would be assigned to the additional refined sugar.

8-17. Sell or process further

Deep Forest Mills, Inc., operates a sawmill facility. With the present operation, the company accounts for the bark chips that result from the primary sawing operation as a by-product. The chips are sold by the truckload to another company at a cost of $5 per hundred cubic feet. Normally the sales revenue from this bark comes to $450,000 per month, although in some months as little as $170,000 might be realized. According to the company's accounting manual, the bark is charged to inventory at a "cost" of $2.20 per hundred cubic feet.

The company can rent equipment that will size the chips and bag them for sale as horticultural bark. Approximately 20 percent of the bark will be graded "large" and will sell for $15 per hundred cubic feet. About 65 percent will be graded "medium" and will sell for $8 per hundred cubic feet. The remainder will be called mulch and will sell for $1 per hundred cubic feet.

The costs of the grading equipment and the personnel to operate the equipment will amount to $260,000 per month, and is fixed regardless of the quantities of bark processed.

Required:

Should the company sell the bark or process it further (assuming a typical month)?

8-18. Accounting for by-products

A company engages in a manufacturing process that uses one input product (W) to produce three outputs (H, O, and A). Outputs H and O are considered main products. Output A is a by-product. During a recent month, the following events occurred:

1. Produced and sold 200 units of H and 100 units of O. Produced 25 units of A.
2. Recorded sales revenue of $35,000 from sales of H and O. The cost of sales before accounting for the by-product was $18,000.
3. Incurred $125 to process the 25 units of A to completion. These costs are charged (debited) against any credits for by-products as these costs are incurred.
4. Received $570 in revenue from the sale of 10 units of A.

Required:

Prepare a statement showing in parallel columns the gross margin (which is sales revenue plus or minus other income and cost of goods sold) that would be reported under each of the methods of by-product accounting described in the text.

Problems and cases

A company manufactures products A, B, and C from a joint process. Additional data are as follows:

8–19. Find missing data

	Product			
	A	**B**	**C**	**Total**
Units produced	8,000	4,000	2,000	14,000
Joint costs	$ 72,000	*a*	*b*	$120,000
Sales value at split-off	*c*	*d*	$30,000	200,000
Additional costs to process further	14,000	$10,000	6,000	30,000
Sales value if processed further	140,000	60,000	40,000	240,000

Required:

Determine the values for the lettered spaces.

(CPA adapted)

8–20. Find missing data

A clerk at the Hargis Corporation prepared a diagram showing the flow of materials and costs through the company's processing operation. However, certain pieces of data are missing from the diagram. You learn some additional information as follows:

1. Each of the three output products can only be sold at the end of all processing.
2. Joint costs are allocated estimating the relative sales value at split-off.
3. Costs of processing in each branch of the diagram are noted directly above the horizontal line for that branch.
4. Allocated joint costs are shown in parentheses on the diagonal line for the related branch of the process.
5. Relative sales values at split-off are shown on the diagonal line for the related branch of the process.
6. Letters represent missing data. If the letters are in parentheses, the missing data item is a cost. If the letter is not in parentheses, the missing data item is a sales value.
7. Total joint costs for the first process are $99. These are allocated to (b) and (c).

The diagram appears as follows:

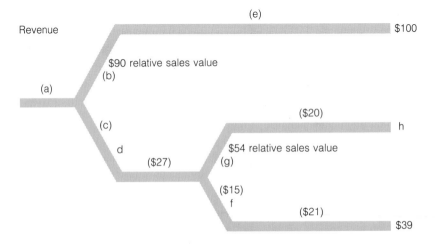

Provide amounts for each letter. (Hint: Start with a, then solve for f, then for d.)

8–21. Joint costing in a process costing context

Harrison Corporation produces three products: Alpha, Beta, and Gamma. Alpha and Gamma are main products while Beta is a by-product of Alpha. Information on the past month's production processes are given as follows:

1. In Department I, 110,000 units of raw material Rho are processed at a total cost of $120,000. After processing in Department I, 60 percent of the units are transferred to Department II and 40 percent of the units (now unprocessed Gamma) are transferred to Department III.
2. In Department II, the materials received from Department I are processed at a total additional cost of $38,000. Seventy percent of the units become Alpha and are transferred to Department IV. The remaining 30 percent emerge as Beta and are sold at $2.10 per unit. The selling costs for the Beta amount to $8,100.
3. In Department III, the Gamma is processed at an additional cost of $165,000. A normal loss of units of Gamma occurs in this department. The loss is equal to 10 percent of the units of good output. The remaining good output is then sold for $12 per unit.
4. In Department IV, Alpha is processed at an additional cost of $23,660. After this processing, the Alpha can be sold for $5 per unit.

Required: Prepare a schedule showing the allocation of the $120,000 joint cost between Alpha and Gamma using the relative sales value approach. Revenue from sales of by-products should be credited to the manufacturing costs of the related main product.

(CPA adapted)

8–22. Find maximum input price

Rambling Rose Corporation produces two joint products from its manufacturing operation. Product J sells for $37.50 per unit while Product M sells for $15.80 per unit. In a typical month, 19,000 input units are processed. Four thousand of these units become Product J after an additional $37,500 of processing costs are incurred. The remaining units are processed at a cost of $20,000. After processing these latter units, shrinkage amounting to 20 percent of the good output occurs. The good output is Product M. Product M could be sold before this further processing at a price of $12 per unit.

The joint process operates with all variable costs. In a typical month, the conversion costs amount to $114,075. Materials prices are volatile and, if prices are too high the company will simply stop production.

Required: Determine the maximum price the company should pay for the materials.

8–23. Effect of by-product versus joint cost accounting

Meadowlark Company processes input Q into three outputs: Eta, Phi, and Tau. The Eta accounts for 70 percent of the relative sales value at the split-off point while the Phi accounts for 25 percent. The balance is accounted for by the Tau. The joint costs amount to $159,050. If Tau is accounted for as a by-product, its relative sales value at split-off of $9,900 would be credited to the joint manufacturing costs and used as a basis for the inventoriable cost of the Tau.

Required: Determine the allocated joint costs for the three outputs if the Tau is accounted for as a joint product and if the Tau is accounted for as a by-product.

8–24. Joint costing— replacement method, break-even considerations

In refining crude oil, three primary classes of products are obtained: (1) gasolines; (2) distillates such as jet fuel, heating oil, and diesel fuel; and (3) residual fuel. Due to marketing considerations, a primary objective of the refining process is to obtain as much gasoline from the oil as possible. While some gasoline can be obtained with relatively little processing, obtaining greater yields of gasoline requires the use of catalytic processes under high pressures and temperatures. In addition to the characteristics of the refining process, a major determinant of the quantity of gasoline obtainable from a barrel of crude oil is the initial gravity of the oil. Certain heavy oils, while plentiful and relatively inexpensive, have yielded fairly low quantities of gasoline.

Great Lands Refining Company has developed a new process for obtaining more gasoline from heavy crude oils. Without the new process, the typical yield from heavy crudes is 60 percent gasoline, 22 percent distillates, and 18 percent residual. With the new process, the yield of gasoline would rise to 65 percent, distillates would decrease to 20 percent, and residual would decrease to 15 percent. Since the decrease in residual and distillate output could be made up through the use of coal and other nonpetroleum fuels, the company believes its process would be beneficial to the energy situation.

To obtain the increased yields, the variable costs of processing a barrel of crude oil would increase from $2 to $3. The refinery that would process this crude has a daily capacity of 50,000 barrels. The capacity would be unchanged by the process, but the fixed costs of the refinery would increase from $200,000 per day to $240,000 per day. The cost of a barrel of heavy crude is $30.

Joint processing costs are first allocated using engineering estimates of the "refining effort" to obtain the standard mix of each product. Under the present system, 60 percent of the refining effort is considered applicable to gasoline, 22 percent to distillates, and 18 percent to residual fuels. Any change in the product output would be charged into the accounts using the replacement method.

A standard barrel of oil contains 42 U.S. gallons. The refiner's gasoline price is $1.10 per gallon, while the price of distillates is $1 per gallon and the price of residual fuels is $.82 per gallon.

All figures can be reported in terms of the cash and income flows from one day's operations. For simplicity, assume there is no loss of mass in refining and the refinery operates at 100 percent capacity.

Required:

a. Use the replacement method to determine the cost of the increased gasoline production on a per barrel basis.

b. *(Optional)* What is the daily production level that is required to break even under the present system and what will it be if the new process is installed?

8–25. Effect of cost allocation on pricing and internal versus external buy decisions

Indio Agresearch is a large farm cooperative with a number of agriculture related manufacturing and service divisions. As a cooperative, the company pays no federal income taxes. The company owns a fertilizer plant which processes and mixes petrochemical compounds into three brands of agricultural fertilizer: Greenup, Maintane, and Winterizer. The three brands differ with respect to selling price and with respect to the proportional content of basic chemicals.

The fertilizer manufacturing division transfers completed product to the cooperative's retail sales division at a transfer price based on the costs of each type of fertilizer plus a markup.

The manufacturing division is completely automated so that the only costs incurred are costs of the petrochemical feedstocks plus overhead that is all considered fixed. The primary feedstock costs $2 per pound. Each 100 pounds of feedstock can produce either of the following mixtures of fertilizer:

	Output schedules (in pounds)	
	A	**B**
Greenup	50	60
Maintane	30	10
Winterizer	20	30

Production is limited to the 800,000 kilowatt-hours monthly capacity of the dehydrator. Due to different chemical makeup, each brand of fertilizer requires different usage of the dehydrator. Dehydrator usage in kilowatt-hours per pound of product is:

Product	**Kilowatt-hour usage per pound**
Greenup	32
Maintane	20
Winterizer	40

Monthly fixed costs are $75,000. At the present time, the company is producing according to output schedule A. Joint production costs including fixed overhead are allocated to each product on the basis of weight.

The fertilizer is packed into 100-pound bags for sale in the cooperative's retail stores. The manufacturing division charges the retail stores the allocated costs plus a 50 percent markup. The sales price for each product charged by the cooperative's retail sales division is as follows:

	Sales price per pound
Greenup	$10.50
Maintane	9.00
Winterizer	10.40

Selling expenses amount to 20 percent of the sales price.

Identical chemical fertilizers may be acquired by the retail division from other manufacturers and wholesalers at the following prices per pound:

Greenup	$7.50	7.21
Maintane	6.80	7.21
Winterizer	7.70	7.21

The manager of the retail division has complained that the price charged for Maintane is excessive and that he would prefer to purchase Maintane from another supplier.

The manager of the manufacturing division argues that the processing mix was determined based on a careful analysis of the costs of each product compared to the prices charged by the retail division. As was noted previously in setting the production schedule, a certain amount of Maintane must be produced. It is not reasonable to allow the retail division to purchase from the outside because of the manufacturing division would then be left with Maintane on hand that would have to be sold to outsiders. After selling and delivery expenses, the manufacturing division would only realize $6.30 per pound which, as the manufacturing division manager notes, is less than cost.

Required:

a. Assume joint production costs including fixed overhead are allocated to each product on the basis of weight. What is the allocated cost per pound of each product given the current production schedule?

b. Assume joint production costs including fixed overhead are allocated to each product on the basis of net realizable value. What is the allocated cost per pound of each product given the current production schedule?

c. Assume joint production costs including fixed overhead are allocated to each product on the basis of weight. Which of the two production schedules produces the higher operating profit to the firm as a whole? What is the maximum monthly operating profit that can be obtained by the firm?

d. Would your answer to part *(c)* be different if joint production costs including fixed overhead are allocated to each product on the basis of net realizable value? If so by how much?

8–26. Joint cost allocation and product profitability

Prednose Refining Company receives Chemical Z which it processes into Chemical A and Chemical B. The Chemical Z costs $30,000 per tankcar load. The process is such that Chemical Z is heated for 12 hours, at the end of which time there are 40,000 gallons of Chemical A with a market value of $10,000 and 20,000 gallons of Chemical B with a market value of $65,000. The cost of the heat process is $7,200.

Required:

a. If the Chemical Z costs and the heat process costs are to be allocated on the basis of gallons of output, what cost would be assigned to each product?

b. If the Chemical Z costs and the heat process costs are allocated on the basis of the value of the output, what cost would be assigned to each product?

c. Can you determine which product is more profitable? Explain why or why not.

9

Variable Costing

OBJECTIVES
To know the differences between variable costing and full absorption costing.
To understand the different uses for the information derived from each of these
    two types of cost systems.

Our discussion of inventory valuation methods thus far has been based on
the external reporting requirement that inventory in manufacturing companies
be valued using *full-absorption costing* (sometimes called absorption costing).
In this chapter, we introduce an alternative method, *variable costing* (sometimes called direct costing). Under **full-absorption costing,** all manufacturing
costs—fixed and variable—are assigned to units produced. Under **variable
costing,** only variable manufacturing costs are assigned to units produced.
Fixed manufacturing costs are written off as period expenses.[1]

In this chapter, we compare full-absorption and variable costing. We examine the differences that arise in cost flows through T-accounts and income
statements between the two methods. We also discuss the uses for which
the two methods are appropriate.

**Variable versus
full-absorption
costing**

This section presents a numerical comparison of variable and full-absorption
costing. Assume the facts shown for Stonewall Manufacturing for the months
of January and February shown in the chart on page 292.

---

[1] Recall from Chapter 2 that variable manufacturing costs vary with the volume of production,
while fixed costs remain the same despite changes in production volume within a relevant range
of activity. We explore the distinction between fixed and variable costs in more depth in Chapters
10 and 11.

	January	February
Units:		
Beginning inventory	–0–	100
Production	1,000	1,000
Sales	900	1,100
Ending inventory (all units are finished at the end of the period—		
there is no work in process inventory)	100	–0–
Costs:		
Variable manufacturing costs (per unit produced):		
Direct materials	$ 10	$ 10
Direct labor	5	5
Variable manufacturing overhead	3	3
Fixed manufacturing costs (per month)	8,000	8,000
Variable marketing costs (per unit sold)	2	2
Fixed marketing and administrative costs (per month)	12,000	12,000
Price per unit sold	45	45

Illustration 9–1 presents the flow of manufacturing costs through T-accounts in January for both full-absorption and variable costing. For now, we use **actual costing;** that is, actual direct materials, direct labor, and manufacturing overhead costs are debited to Work in Process Inventory. (Later in the chapter, we use **normal costing,** which is like actual costing except that manufacturing overhead is debited to Work in Process Inventory using a predetermined rate.)

Note that while total actual costs incurred are the same under both full-absorption and variable costing, fixed manufacturing costs are debited to Work in Process Inventory under full-absorption costing, but not under variable costing. As a consequence, the amounts in Work in Process Inventory and Finished Goods Inventory are higher under full-absorption costing.

Under full-absorption costing, the inventory value is:

$$\begin{array}{ccc}
\dfrac{\text{Number}}{\text{of units}} & \times & \left(\dfrac{\text{Variable manufacturing}}{\text{cost per unit}} + \dfrac{\text{Fixed manufacturing}}{\text{cost per unit}} \right) \\[2ex]
100 \text{ units} & \times & \left(\$18 + \dfrac{\$8,000 \text{ fixed manufacturing costs}}{1,000 \text{ units}} \right) \\[2ex]
= \quad 100 & \times & (\$18 + \$8) \\
= \quad \$2,600 & &
\end{array}$$

Under variable costing, the inventory value is:

$$\begin{array}{ccc}
\dfrac{\text{Number}}{\text{of units}} & \times & \dfrac{\text{Variable manufacturing}}{\text{cost per unit}} \\[2ex]
100 \text{ units} & \times & \$18 \\[1ex]
= \quad \$1,800 & &
\end{array}$$

Fixed manufacturing costs are treated as **product costs,** and therefore assigned to each unit under full-absorption costing. Under variable costing,

Illustration 9–1
Variable and full-absorption costing comparison: Flow of manufacturing costs

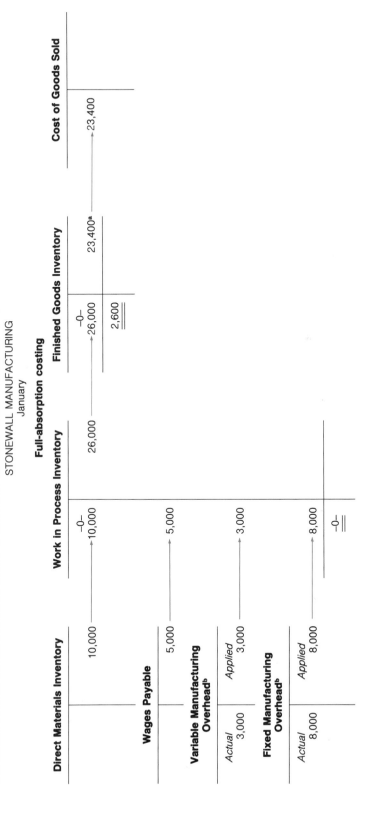

STONEWALL MANUFACTURING
January

Full-absorption costing

Illustration 9–1 (concluded)

Variable costing

Direct Materials Inventory

10,000	10,000

Work in Process Inventory

–0–	
10,000	18,000
5,000	
3,000	
–0–	

Finished Goods Inventory

–0–	
18,000	16,200
1,800	

Variable Cost of Goods Sold

16,200	

Wages Payable

	5,000

Variable Manufacturing Overhead[b]

Actual	Applied
3,000	3,000

Fixed Manufacturing Overhead (period expense)

8,000	

[a] $23,400 = \left[\dfrac{900}{1,000}\right] \times \$26,000 = 900 \times (\$8 + 18) = 900 \times \$26$

[b] We have placed actual and applied overhead in the same account with actual costs as debits and applied costs as credits. This was done for convenience in presentation. An alternative is to place actual overhead in one account and applied overhead in another account. Both methods are used in practice.

they are treated as period costs and thus are expensed in the period incurred. The total manufacturing costs incurred and expensed under the two systems are shown in Illustration 9–2.

Note that *all* manufacturing costs must be either expensed or inventoried under both methods. The key difference is the breakdown between costs expensed and costs inventoried. Also note the source of difference between the two methods. *Variable* manufacturing costs are treated as product costs under both methods, and marketing and administrative costs are treated as period expenses under both methods. The source of the difference is the treatment of fixed manufacturing costs. Fixed manufacturing costs are treated as product costs under full-absorption costing and as period expenses under variable costing.

Effect on profits

As shown in Illustration 9–3, the $800 higher profit in January under full-absorption costing is exactly the difference in the amount of costs inventoried under the two methods. Full-absorption inventories $800 of fixed manufacturing costs that are expensed under variable costing. Hence, under full-absorption, costs expensed are $800 lower and operating profits are $800 higher than under variable costing. Under full-absorption, the expensing of $800 of fixed manufacturing costs is deferred until the period when the units are sold.

As a general rule, under full-absorption costing, *when units produced exceed units sold* in a period, a portion of the period's fixed manufacturing costs are not expensed in that period. Under variable costing, however, all of the period's fixed manufacturing costs are expensed. Thus, when production ex-

Illustration 9–2   **Manufacturing costs incurred, expensed, and inventoried**

STONEWALL MANUFACTURING
January

	Manufac-turing costs incurred		Manufac-turing costs expensed		Increase in inventory
Full-absorption costing:					
Variable manufacturing costs	$18,000	=	$16,200[a]	+	$1,800[b]
Fixed manufacturing costs	8,000	=	7,200[c]	+	800[d]
Total	$26,000	=	$23,400		$2,600
Variable costing:					
Variable manufacturing costs	$18,000	=	$16,200[a]	+	$1,800[b]
Fixed manufacturing costs	8,000	=	8,000	+	–0–
Total	$26,000	=	$24,200	+	$1,800

[a] $16,200 = 900 units sold × $18 variable cost per unit.
[b] $ 1,800 = 100 units inventoried × $18 per unit.
[c] $ 7,200 = 900 units sold × $\dfrac{\$8,000 \text{ fixed manufacturing cost}}{\$1,000 \text{ units produced}}$

$\quad$ = 900 units × $8.
[d] $ 800 = 100 units inventoried × $8 per unit.

Illustration 9–3   **Variable and full-absorption costing comparison: Income statements**

STONEWALL MANUFACTURING
January

Full-absorption costing

Sales revenue	$40,500c
Cost of goods sold	23,400
Gross margin	17,100
Marketing and administrative costs	13,800a
Operating profit	$ 3,300

Variable costing

Sales revenue	$40,500c
Less:	
Variable cost of goods sold	16,200
Variable marketing and administrative costs	1,800b
Contributing margin	22,500
Less:	
Fixed manufacturing costs	8,000
Fixed marketing and administrative costs	12,000
Operating profit	$ 2,500

a Fixed costs + variable costs = $12,000 + ($2 × 900 units sold) = $13,800.

b $2 × 900 units sold = $1,800.

c $45 × 900 units sold = $40,500.

ceeds sales, fewer fixed manufacturing costs are expensed, and *operating profits are higher* under full-absorption than under variable costing.

On the other hand, if units sold exceed units produced, then more fixed manufacturing costs are expensed under full-absorption costing, so operating profits are lower under full-absorption than under variable costing. We show this case in Illustration 9–4, which presents Stonewall Manufacturing's cost flows for February. The company produced 1,000 units in February and sold 1,100 units, including 100 units from inventory. In this case, full-absorption costing (FAC) expenses more fixed manufacturing costs than does variable costing (VC), because full-absorption now expenses the fixed manufacturing costs that were deferred from January.

A summary of our analysis of manufacturing costs is shown in Illustration 9–5. Note that manufacturing costs expensed equals costs incurred *plus the decrease in inventory*. In Illustration 9–2, note that in January, manufacturing costs expensed equaled costs incurred *minus the increase in inventory*.

Illustration 9–6 compares full-absorption costing (FAC) and variable costing (VC) at Stonewall Manufacturing for January and February. It presents some important results. First, operating profits for the two-month period is the same under both methods—$10,000. This occurs because the company had no units in inventory at either the beginning or end of the period in question. Operating profits were higher under full-absorption costing in January, however, because units produced exceeded units sold. The reverse was true in February.

Illustration 9–4
Variable and full-absorption costing comparison: Flow of manufacturing costs

STONEWALL MANUFACTURING
February

Full-absorption costing

Direct Materials Inventory	Work in Process Inventory	Finished Goods Inventory	Cost of Goods Sold
10,000	–0– 10,000 →	Bal. 2,600 → 26,000	→ 28,600
		28,600	
		–0– ═══	

Wages Payable

5,000 →

Variable Manufacturing Overhead

Actual	Applied
3,000	3,000 →

Fixed Manufacturing Overhead

Actual	Applied
8,000	8,000 →

Work in Process Inventory (continued):
26,000

5,000 →

3,000 →

8,000 →

–0–
═══

Illustration 9–4 (concluded)

Variable costing

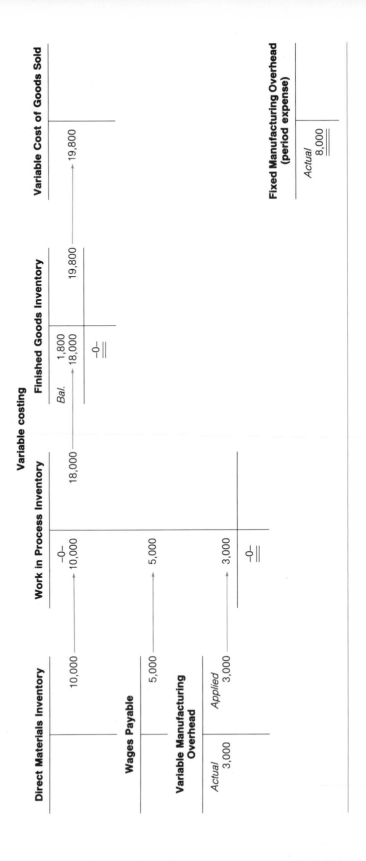

Direct Materials Inventory

10,000	

Wages Payable

	5,000

Variable Manufacturing Overhead

Actual	Applied
3,000	3,000

Work in Process Inventory

–0–	
10,000	18,000
5,000	
3,000	
–0–	

Finished Goods Inventory

Bal. 1,800	
18,000	19,800
–0–	

Variable Cost of Goods Sold

19,800	

Fixed Manufacturing Overhead (period expense)

Actual	
8,000	

STONEWALL MANUFACTURING
February

	Manufac- turing costs expensed		Manufac- turing costs incurred		Decrease in inventory
Full-absorption costing:					
Variable manufacturing costs	$19,800[a]	=	$18,000	+	$1,800[b]
Fixed manufacturing costs	8,800[c]	=	8,000	+	800[d]
Total	$28,600	=	$26,000	+	$2,600
Variable costing:					
Variable manufacturing costs	$19,800[a]	=	$18,000	+	$1,800[b]
Fixed manufacturing costs	8,000	=	8,000	+	–0–
Total	$27,800	=	$26,000	+	$1,800

[a] $19,800 = 1,100 units sold × $18 variable cost per unit.

[b] $ 1,800 = 100 units from inventory × $18 variable cost per unit.

[c] $ 8,800 = 1,100 units sold × $\dfrac{\$8,000}{1,000 \text{ units produced}}$

$= 1,100 \times \$8.$

[d] $ 800 = 100 units from inventory × $8 variable cost per unit.

STONEWALL MANUFACTURING
January and February

Full-absorption costing

	January	February	Total
Sales revenue	$40,500	$49,500	$90,000
Cost of goods sold	23,400	28,600	52,000
Gross margin	17,100	20,900	38,000
Marketing and administrative costs	13,800[a]	14,200[b]	28,000
Operating profits	$ 3,300	$ 6,700	$10,000
Change in finished goods inventory	+$ 2,600[c]	–$ 2,600	–0–

Variable costing

	January	February	Total
Sales revenue	$40,500	$49,500	$90,000
Less:			
Variable cost of goods sold	16,200	19,800	36,000
Variable marketing and administrative costs	1,800	2,200	4,000
Contribution margin	22,500	27,500	50,000
Less:			
Fixed manufacturing costs	8,000	8,000	16,000
Fixed marketing and administrative costs	12,000	12,000	24,000
Operating profits	$ 2,500	$ 7,500	$10,000
Change in finished goods inventory	+$ 1,800[c]	–$ 1,800	–0–

[a] $12,000 + ($2 × 900 units sold) = $13,800.

[b] $12,000 + ($2 × 1,100 units sold) = $14,200.

[c] From Illustration 9–2.

Second, the difference in operating profits between the two costing methods (FAC > VC by $800 in January, VC > FAC by $800 in February) equals the differences in the changes in Finished Goods Inventory account. (FAC inventory increased by $2,600, while VC inventory increased by $1,800 in January; FAC inventory decreased by $2,600, while VC inventory decreased by $1,800 in February.)

Third, the difference in operating profits equals the difference in fixed manufacturing costs expensed under the two systems.

In general, when the *inventory of manufactured goods does not fluctuate from period to period,* that is, production volume equals sales volume, operating profits are usually the same under both methods. If production volume equals sales volume, the profit figures will differ only if the fixed manufacturing costs per unit differ in beginning and ending inventory.

Important assumptions   There are three important assumptions to note before leaving this discussion. First, our example assumes that only a portion of manufacturing overhead is fixed. In fact, some or all of direct labor might be fixed as well. This occurs when direct labor costs are neither reduced when production volume decreases nor increased when production volume increases. If direct labor is fixed, it is treated as a *product* cost under full-absorption costing and a *period* cost under variable costing, just like fixed manufacturing overhead in our example.

Second, while our example has assumed that Finished Goods are the only inventory, the results hold for Work in Process Inventory, too. That is, fixed manufacturing costs would be part of Work in Process Inventory under full-absorption costing, but they would not be under variable costing.

Third, this entire discussion refers only to manufacturing costs, which are the only costs inventoried. It does *not* refer to marketing and administrative costs, which are not part of inventory.

Predetermined rates for manufacturing overhead

In the previous example, we compared full-absorption costing with variable costing when manufacturing overhead is applied to units produced after actual overhead costs are known. When manufacturing overhead is applied using a *predetermined* rate, the mechanics of comparison become a little more difficult, but the effects of the different costing methods on calculated profits remain the same as previously discussed.

For example, assume Stonewall Manufacturing decided to use *normal costing* with predetermined manufacturing overhead rates of $1.75 per actual direct labor-hour for variable manufacturing overhead and $3.50 per direct labor-hour for fixed manufacturing overhead. In both January and February, each unit required an average of two direct labor-hours to make; hence, you can also think of overhead as applied at the rate of $3.50 per unit produced for *variable* manufacturing overhead and $7 per unit produced for *fixed* manufacturing overhead. These rates were used for both January and February.

Illustration 9–7 shows the flow of manufacturing costs for January under

Illustration 9–7
Variable and full-absorption costing comparison: Flow of manufacturing costs using predetermined overhead rates

STONEWALL MANUFACTURING
January

Full-absorption costing

Direct Materials Inventory

10,000

Work in Process Inventory

-0-
10,000

5,000

3,500

→ 25,500

Finished Goods Inventory

25,500

22,950

2,550[a]

Cost of Goods Sold

22,950

Wages Payable

5,000

Variable Manufacturing Overhead

Actual
3,000

500[c]

Applied
$1.75 × 2
hours
per unit
× 1,000
units = 3,500

Fixed Manufacturing Overhead

Actual
8,000

Applied
$3.50 × 2
hours
per unit
× 1,000
units = 7,000
1,000[d]

7,000

-0-

Overhead Adjustment

1,000[d]

500[c]

Illustration 9–7 (concluded)

Variable costing

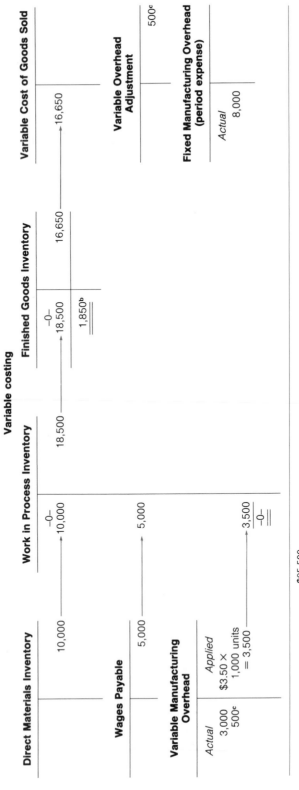

Direct Materials Inventory

10,000

Wages Payable

5,000

Variable Manufacturing Overhead

Actual	Applied
3,000	$3.50 ×
500ᶜ	1,000 units
	= 3,500
	3,500
–0–	

Work in Process Inventory

–0–
10,000

5,000

3,500

18,500

–0–

Finished Goods Inventory

–0–
18,500

16,650

1,850ᵇ

Variable Cost of Goods Sold

16,650

Variable Overhead Adjustment

500ᶜ

Fixed Manufacturing Overhead (period expense)

Actual
8,000

ᵃ $2,550 = 100 units left in inventory × $25,500 / 1,000 units produced .

ᵇ $1,850 = 100 units left in inventory × $18,500 / 1,000 units produced .

ᶜ This entry closes the Variable Manufacturing Overhead account.

ᵈ This entry closes the Fixed Manufacturing Overhead account.

both variable and full-absorption costing. (Recall that 1,000 units were produced, 900 were sold in January.) By comparing Illustration 9–7 with Illustration 9–1, you will see that actual and applied manufacturing overhead are
no longer equal. To keep the analysis from becoming overly complex, we
assume that the overhead adjustment is written off as a period cost, not
prorated to inventories and cost of goods sold.

Illustration 9–8 compares full-absorption and variable costing when predetermined overhead rates are used.

Illustration 9–8   **Variable and full-absorption costing comparison using predetermined**
overhead rates: Comparative income statements

STONEWALL MANUFACTURING
January and February

Full-absorption costing

	January	February	Total
Sales revenue	$40,500	$49,500	$90,000
Less:			
Cost of goods sold	22,950[a]	28,050[c]	51,000
Overhead adjustment	500[b]	500[d]	1,000
Gross margin	17,050	20,950	38,000
Marketing and administrative costs	13,800	14,200	28,000
Operating profits	$ 3,250	$ 6,750	$10,000
Change in finished goods inventory	+ $ 2,550	− $ 2,550	–0–

Variable costing

	January	February	Total
Sales revenue	$40,500	$49,500	$90,000
Less: Variable cost of goods sold	16,650[e]	20,350[f]	37,000
Add: Overapplied variable overhead	500	500[g]	1,000
Less: Variable marketing and			
administrative costs	1,800	2,200	4,000
Contribution margin	22,550	27,450	50,000
Less:			
Fixed manufacturing costs	8,000	8,000	16,000
Fixed marketing and administrative costs	12,000	12,000	24,000
Operating profits	$ 2,550	$ 7,450	$10,000
Change in finished goods inventory	+ $ 1,850	− $ 1,850	$ –0–

[a] $22,950 = 900 units sold × $25.50 cost per unit.

[b] The $500 underapplied overhead is the net result of $1,000 underapplied fixed manufacturing overhead
and $500 overapplied variable manufacturing overhead.

[c] $28,050 = 1,100 units sold × $25.50 cost per unit. It also equals the cost of producing 1,000 units,
or $25,500, plus the $2,550 cost of the 100 units sold from beginning Finished Goods Inventory.

[d] The underapplied overhead is the same in February as in January because all production quantities
and costs are the same in February as in January.

[e] $16,650 = 900 units sold × $18.50 cost per unit.

[f] $20,350 = 1,100 units sold × $18.50 cost per unit. It also equals the variable cost of producing 1,000
units, or $18,500, plus the $1,850 cost of the 100 units sold from beginning Finished Goods Inventory.

[g] Overapplied variable overhead is the same in February as in January because all production quantities
and costs are the same in both months.

The use of **predetermined overhead rates** instead of actual costs usually does not have much effect on the relationship between full-absorption and variable costing. For example, a comparison of Illustration 9–6 (actual costing using actual overhead) with Illustration 9–8 (normal costing using predetermined overhead rates) shows two key similarities:

1. The conceptual difference between full-absorption costing and variable costing is the same whether actual or normal overhead costs are used. Differences in operating profits occur because fixed manufacturing costs are inventoried under full-absorption costing but not under variable costing.

2. When all inventory is sold at the end of a period, total operating profits are the same under all methods. For example, in Illustration 9–6 and 9–8, operating profits for the entire period—January and February— are $10,000, whether actual or normal overhead rates, and whether full-absorption or variable costing are used.

Algebraic comparison of variable and full-absorption costing[2]

This section presents an algebraic comparison of full-absorption and variable costing. The basic concepts are the same as those presented earlier in this chapter; but instead of comparing full-absorption and variable costing using income statements and T-accounts, we use algebra here.

Basic models

The algebraic definition of operating profit under full-absorption (actual) and variable costing follows the notation shown below. The numbers for each equation are based on our previous example—Stonewall Manufacturing— for January.

Notation

X^s = actual volume sold—superscript s designates *sales* volume (900 units for Stonewall Manufacturing in January).

X^p = actual volume produced—superscript p designates *production* volume (1,000 units for Stonewall Manufacturing in January).

P = actual unit selling prices ($45).

$VMfg$ = actual *unit* variable *manufacturing* costs ($18 = $10 direct materials + $5 direct labor + $3 variable manufacturing overhead).

$FMfg$ = actual *total* fixed *manufacturing* costs per *month* ($8,000).

VMk = actual *unit* variable *marketing* costs ($2).

---

[2] This section was inspired by D. DeCoster and K. Ramanathan, "An Algebraic Aid in Teaching Differences Between Direct Costing and Full-Absorption Costing Models," *The Accounting Review,* October 1973, pp. 800–801. It may be skipped without loss of continuity.

$FMkAd$ = actual *total* fixed *marketing* and *administrative* costs per month ($12,000).

π_{fa} = operating profit under full-absorption costing.

π_v = operating profit under variable costing.

Variable costing profit equation

$$\pi_v = PX^s - VMfgX^s - VMkX^s$$
$$- FMfg - FMkAd$$
$$= (\$45 \times 900 \text{ units}) - (\$18 \times 900 \text{ units}) - (\$2 \times 900 \text{ units})$$
$$- \$8,000 - \$12,000$$
$$= \$2,500$$

which is the same as the variable costing operating profit shown in Illustration 9–6.

Full-absorption costing profit equation

$$\pi_{fa} = PX^s - \left(VMfg + \frac{FMfg}{X^p} \right) X^s$$
$$- VMkX^s - FMkAd$$
$$= (\$45 \times 900 \text{ units}) - \left[\left(\$18 + \frac{\$8,000}{1,000 \text{ units}} \right) \times 900 \text{ units} \right]$$
$$- (\$2 \times 900 \text{ units}) - \$12,000$$
$$= \$3,300$$

which is the same as the full-absorption costing operating profit shown in Illustration 9–6.

Source of the difference in operating profits

The only difference between the two equations above is the treatment of fixed manufacturing overhead. Under variable costing, $FMfg$ is deducted to arrive at operating profit, while under full-absorption costing, $\left(\frac{FMfg}{X^p} \right) X^s$ is deducted. Hence, the difference is:

$$FMfg - \left(\frac{FMfg}{X^p} \right) X^s = \$8,000 - \left(\frac{\$8,000}{1,000 \text{ units}} \times 900 \text{ units} \right)$$
$$= \$8,000 - (\$8 \times 900 \text{ units}) = \$800$$

That is, variable costing deducts $800 more in deriving operating profits, hence its operating profits are $800 lower in January. It is important to note that if $X^p = X^s$, the fixed manufacturing costs deducted would be the same under both methods.

A similar analysis can be made in February. For variable costing:

$$\pi_v = PX^s - VMfgX^s - VMkX^s - FMfg - FMkAd$$
$$= (\$45 \times 1{,}100 \text{ units}) - (\$18 \times 1{,}100 \text{ units}) - (\$2 \times 1{,}100 \text{ units})$$
$$- \$8{,}000 - \$12{,}000$$
$$= \underline{\$7{,}500}$$

which is also shown in Illustration 9–6.

For full-absorption costing:

π_{fa} = Sales revenue − Cost of goods sold for units produced in January − Cost of goods sold for units produced in February − Marketing and administrative costs

$$= (\$45)(1{,}100 \text{ units}) - \underbrace{\left(\$18 + \frac{\$8{,}000}{1{,}000}\right) 100 \text{ units}}_{\substack{\text{Cost of goods sold for} \\ \text{units produced in} \\ \text{January}}}$$

$$- \underbrace{\left(\$18 + \frac{\$8{,}000}{1{,}000}\right) 1{,}000 \text{ units}}_{\substack{\text{Cost of goods sold} \\ \text{for units produced} \\ \text{in February}}} - (\$2 \times 1{,}100 \text{ units})$$

$$- \$12{,}000$$
$$= \underline{\$6{,}700}$$

which is also shown in Illustration 9–6.

Debate over variable versus full-absorption costing

Debates about the desirability of full-absorption costing versus variable costing have gone on for decades.[3] For the most part, differences of opinion stem from the search for a "conceptually superior" method of valuing inventory and measuring income in external financial statements. Our perspective is much different. *We are not as concerned about selecting a "true" measure of inventory value or net income as we are with selecting the cost measure that is most appropriate for decision making,* after taking into account the

---

[3] For example, see C. Horngren and G. Sorter, "Direct Costing for External Reporting," *The Accounting Review,* January 1961; and J. Fremgen, "The Direct Costing Controversy—an Identification of Issues," *The Accounting Review,* January 1964.

costs and benefits of alternative costing methods. The most appropriate cost measure will usually be situation specific—it will depend on the nature of the decision, the nature of costs, the tastes of decision makers, and many other factors. The following discussions present advantages of each costing method—variable costing and full-absorption costing—for different uses by decision makers.

Advantages of variable costing, disadvantages of full-absorption costing	**Variable costing requires breakdown of manufacturing costs into fixed and variable components** Many managerial decisions require a breakdown of costs into variable and fixed components. The variable costing method is consistent with this breakdown. The full-absorption costing method is not; it treats fixed manufacturing costs as if they were unit (that is, variable) costs. Also, note that more data are presented under variable costing than under full-absorption in Illustration 9–6. Variable costing presents fixed and variable cost breakdowns and contribution margins.

Managers usually prefer to plan and control variable costs on a unit basis and fixed costs on a period basis. For example, managers plan and control the amount of direct materials and direct labor required to make a unit of output or the number of hours required to perform a job. Building rent, property taxes, and other fixed costs are planned and controlled per week, month, or year. It seldom makes much managerial sense to refer to rent costs as an amount per *unit* produced. Rather rent would be referred to as an amount per *month*.

Criticism of "unit fixed cost" under full-absorption costing Treating fixed costs as unit costs can be misleading. A unit fixed cost is a function of not only the amount of fixed costs but also the volume of activity.

For example, a plant manager observed that maintenance costs, which were fixed, had decreased from $12 per unit of output in May to $10 per unit in August. She was on her way to congratulate the maintenance department manager for the cost reduction when she stopped in the plant controller's office. There she learned that maintenance costs had *increased* from $12,000 in May to $18,000 in August. Meanwhile volume had increased from 1,000 units in May to 1,800 units in August. This explained the decrease in unit costs from $12 (= $12,000 ÷ 1,000 units) to $10 (= $18,000 ÷ 1,800 units).

The plant manager knew maintenance costs were supposed to be fixed. They should not have increased when volume increased. When she investigated further, she found that the maintenance department manager had hired several temporary employees to cover for a major absenteeism problem that occurred in August.

The moral of this story is that the conversion of fixed manufacturing costs to unit costs, which is done under full-absorption costing, can be misleading. Managers frequently find it necessary to convert the "unitized" fixed manufacturing cost (that is, the $12 and $10 per unit in the previous example) back to the original total for decision making purposes.

Variable costing removes the effects of inventory changes from income measurement   Another advantage of variable costing is that it removes the effects of inventory changes from income measurement. For example, under full-absorption costing, a company could increase its reported profits by building up inventory or decrease them by reducing inventory.

For example, Full Products, Inc., uses full-absorption costing to value inventory. After seeing the Period 1 financial statements shown in the bottom part of Illustration 9–9, the board of directors fired the president and hired a new one, stating, "Whatever else you do, increase profits in Period 2."

Illustration 9–9   **Profit improvement program**

FULL PRODUCTS, INC.

Facts

	Period 1	Period 2
Sales units	100,000	100,000
Production units	100,000	200,000
Selling price per unit	$ 10	$ 10
Variable manufacturing cost per unit	5	5
Fixed manufacturing costs per period	400,000	400,000
Fixed manufacturing costs per unit		
produced	4	2
Marketing and administrative costs		
per period	100,000	100,000

Income Statements
(full-absorption costing method)

	(1) Period 1	(2) Period 2
Sales	$1,000,000	$1,000,000
Cost of goods sold	900,000[a]	700,000[b]
Gross margin	100,000	300,000
Marketing and administrative costs	100,000	100,000
Operating profits	–0–	$ 200,000

[a] $900,000 = 100,000 units sold × ($5 + $4) manufacturing costs per unit.
[b] $700,000 = 100,000 units sold × ($5 + $2) manufacturing costs per unit.

The new president promptly stepped up production from 100,000 units to 200,000 units, as shown in Column 2 of Illustration 9–9. Operating profits increased from $0 in Period 1, to $200,000 in Period 2, and the new president collected a generous bonus.

Was Full Products, Inc, more profitable in Period 2? No; in fact, the company had 100,000 additional units in inventory to carry and sell. The apparent increase in profits is solely due to the deferral of fixed manufacturing cost under full-absorption costing by increasing ending inventory. Variable costing would expense the entire $400,000 of fixed manufacturing costs in Period 2 despite the increase in inventory. Thus, the Period 2 operating profits would have been zero under variable costing—the same as in Period 1.

In short, variable costing tends to fit managerial decision models better than full-absorption costing does. In subsequent chapters in this book, when we discuss uses of accounting information for managerial decision making, planning, and performance evaluation, we assume the company uses variable costing for internal purposes unless otherwise stated.

Advantages of full-absorption costing, disadvantages of variable costing

Neither the Financial Accounting Standards Board (FASB) nor the Internal Revenue Service (IRS) has recognized variable costing as *generally acceptable* in valuing inventory for external reports and tax purposes. The Internal Revenue Service defines inventory cost to include: (1) direct materials and supplies entering into or consumed in connection with the product, (2) expenditures for direct labor, and (3) indirect expenses incident to and necessary for the production of the particular item. Indirect expenses necessary for production would include fixed manufacturing costs. Thus, the most obvious advantage of full-absorption costing is that it complies with FASB pronouncements and tax laws.

Finally, proponents of full-absorption costing contend that this method recognizes the importance of fixed manufacturing costs. They hold that all manufacturing costs are costs of the product. Further, they argue, companies that build up inventories in anticipation of further increases in sales are penalized under variable costing—they should be allowed to defer fixed manufacturing costs until the goods are sold, just as they defer variable manufacturing costs.

In practice, companies may prepare *both* variable and full-absorption costing income statements depending on how such information is used. Variable costing reports can be used for internal purposes while full-absorption reports are prepared for external use. Preparation of many kinds of reports based on alternative accounting methods is possible at rapid speed and low cost with appropriately programmed computer equipment.

A second advantage of full-absorption costing is that it does not require a breakdown of manufacturing costs into fixed and variable components. While some manufacturing costs may fall neatly into fixed or variable categories, others do not. Supervision, indirect labor, and utilities, for example, are seldom either entirely fixed or entirely variable. Hence, variable costing may be more costly to implement than full-absorption costing. Like other accounting system choices, the costs and benefits of each method should dictate the best course of action in specific situations.

Comparative income statement formats

Traditional income statement formats do not lend themselves to variable costing because fixed and variable costs are not separated. The format used with variable costing is known as the contribution margin format. The variable costing income statements in this chapter use the variable costing format. For comparative purposes, the two formats are shown in Illustration 9–10. These two statements are based on the January-February totals from Illustration 9–6.

If income statements are used to make decisions involving changes in volume, the contribution format can be very helpful. Managers can often understand relationships between prices, costs, and volume better with the contribution margin format than with the traditional approach. Further, the contribution margin format presents more information—namely, the break-down of costs into fixed and variable portions.

Note the difference between the *contribution margin* and the *gross margin* in Illustration 9–10. The total contribution margin is $50,000 and represents the differential net revenue available to meet fixed costs and operating profits. The contribution margin ratio represents the fraction of each revenue dollar that is contributed towards fixed costs and profits. For the illustration, this amount would be 55.6 percent, which is $\frac{\$50,000}{\$90,000}$.

On the other hand, the gross margin is the difference between revenues and manufacturing costs, regardless of whether those manufacturing costs are fixed or variable. The gross margin represents the net revenues that remain after the deduction of manufacturing costs and, hence, are used for nonmanu-facturing costs and operating profits. Sometimes a gross margin ratio is computed. However, the gross margin ratio does not indicate what would happen if revenues were to increase due to volume increases with a corresponding increase in unit production.

Illustration 9–10
Income statement formal comparison: Traditional and contribution margin format

STONEWALL MANUFACTURING

Traditional format	January–February Total	Contribution margin format	January–February Total
Sales revenue	$90,000	Sales revenue	$90,000
Cost of goods sold	52,000	Less:	
Gross margin	38,000	Variable cost of goods sold	36,000
Marketing and administrative costs	28,000	Variable marketing and administrative costs	4,000
Operating profit	$10,000	Contribution margin	50,000
		Less:	
		Fixed manufacturing costs	16,000
		Fixed marketing and administrative costs	24,000
		Operating profit	$10,000

The terms *contribution margin* and *gross margin* are often used inter-changeably, but they are not the same. The only time they would be mathematically equal is when all variable costs are manufacturing costs and all fixed costs are nonmanufacturing costs. We know of very few examples of this situation.

Summary

This chapter compares full-absorption costing with variable costing. Manufacturing companies use full-absorption costing for external reporting to comply with generally accepted accounting principles (GAAP) and income tax laws; both of which require that product costs include fixed and variable manufacturing costs. Our previous discussion of full product costing in Chapters 3 through 8 assumed work in process and finished goods inventories were valued using full-absorption costing.

With variable costing, only variable manufacturing costs are inventoriable, while fixed manufacturing costs are treated as period costs. Many manufacturing companies use variable costing for internal reporting because it is consistent with the cost-behavior assumptions used in managerial decision making.

In the remaining chapters in this book, we focus on cost analysis for decision making. Hence, we assume variable costing is used for internal managerial purposes, while full-absorption costing is used for external financial reporting.

Illustration 9–11   **Summary comparison of full-absorption costing (FAC) and variable costing (VC)**

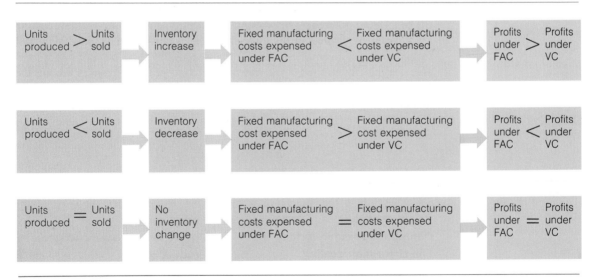

Note: These relationships assume the unit costs of inventory do not change from period to period.

Illustration 9–12   **Treatment of overhead in four costing methods: full-absorption, variable, actual, and normal**

Treatment of fixed manufacturing costs

	Product cost	**Period cost**
Actual overhead assigned to units	Actual, full-absorption	Actual, variable
Predetermined overhead rates	Normal, full-absorption	Normal, variable

Treatment of manufacturing overhead

The key difference between the two methods is the treatment of fixed manufacturing costs—full-absorption costing "unitizes" them and treats them as product costs, while variable costing treats them as period costs. Thus, operating profits will differ under each method if units produced and sold are not the same, as shown in Illustration 9–11.

The use of predetermined manufacturing overhead rates (that is, *normal* costing) may give a different unit cost to inventory than does actual costing. Consequently, operating profits may be different under the two systems. But the *conceptual* differences between full-absorption costing and variable costing are the same regardless of the form of overhead rate—namely, fixed manufacturing costs are inventoried under full-absorption costing but not under variable costing. Illustration 9–12 reviews the conceptual differences among the four methods. The self-study problem at the end of the chapter presents a numerical application.

Terms and concepts

The following terms and concepts should be familiar to you after reading this chapter.

Actual costing	**Period costs**
Contribution margin format	**Predetermined overhead rates**
Full-absorption costing	**Product costs**
Normal costing	**Variable costing (or direct costing)**

Self-study problem No. 1

Unit costs under various costing methods: Actual, normal, variable, and full-absorption

Dunn Enterprises produced 84,000 units in 1985 and sold 76,000 units. Costs incurred that year were:

Direct materials	$462,000
Direct labor	315,000
Variable manufacturing overhead	105,000
Fixed manufacturing overhead	400,000
Variable marketing and administrative costs	50,400
Fixed marketing and administrative costs	200,600

Historically Dunn Enterprises applied variable manufacturing overhead at $.40 per labor dollar and fixed manufacturing overhead at $1.20 per labor dollar. There were no beginning inventories in 1985.

Required:

Calculate the amount added to the finished goods inventory using:
a. Actual/variable costing.
b. Actual/full-absorption costing.
c. Normal/variable costing.
d. Normal/full-absorption costing.

Solution to self-study problem No. 1

	Actual	Normal
Full-absorption costing:		
Direct materials	$ 5.50	$ 5.50
Direct labor	3.75	3.75
Variable manufacturing overhead	1.25	1.50
Fixed manufacturing overhead	4.76	4.50
Total	$15.26	$15.25
Variable costing:		
Direct materials	$ 5.50	$ 5.50
Direct labor	3.75	3.75
Variable manufacturing overhead	1.25	1.50
Total	$10.50	$10.75

Ending inventory:
a. $10.50 × 8,000 = $84,000
b. $15.26 × 8,000 = $122,080
c. $10.75 × 8,000 = $86,000
d. $15.25 × 8,000 = $122,000

Self-study problem No. 2

Cash flows through T-accounts and income statement preparation

Barton Chemicals produces a line of extra-strength paint remover. During 1985, the company produced 8,000 barrels and sold 7,500 barrels at a price of $60 per barrel. The costs incurred were as follows:

Direct materials	$ 24,000
Direct labor	80,000
Variable manufacturing overhead	19,200
Variable marketing and administrative costs	24,800
Fixed manufacturing overhead	120,000
Fixed marketing and administrative costs	110,000

There were no beginning inventories in 1985.

Required:
    a. Using T-accounts, trace the manufacturing cost flows under variable costing.
    b. Using T-accounts, trace the manufacturing cost flows under full-absorption costing.
    c. Prepare an income statement for 1985 using the variable costing approach.
    d. Prepare an income statement for 1985 using the full-absorption costing approach.

Solution to self-study problem No. 2

BARTON CHEMICALS

a.

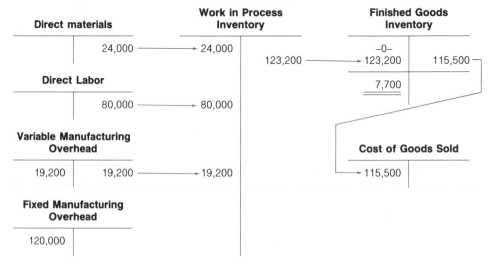

b.

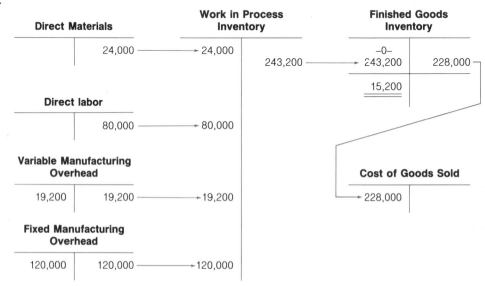

c.

Sales revenue	$450,000
Less:	
Variable cost of goods sold	115,500
Variable marketing and administrative costs ...	24,800
Contribution margin	309,700
Less:	
Fixed manufacturing overhead	120,000
Fixed marketing and administrative costs	110,000
Operating profit	$ 79,700

d.

Sales revenue	$450,000
Cost of goods sold	228,000
Gross margin	222,000
Less:	
Variable marketing and administrative costs ...	24,800
Fixed marketing and administrative costs	110,000
Operating profit	$ 87,200

Questions

9–1. Describe the key difference between full-absorption costing and variable costing.

9–2. How are marketing and administrative costs treated under variable costing? Under full-absorption costing?

9–3. Under what circumstances do you find operating profit under variable costing equal to full-absorption costing profits? When are variable costing profits smaller? When are they greater?

9–4. What are the advantages of variable costing? What are some of the criticisms advanced against it?

9–5. How can a company using full-absorption costing manipulate profits without changing sales?

9–6. Describe comparative inventory changes under both variable costing and full-absorption costing when—
    a. Sales volume exceeds production volume.
    b. Production volume exceeds sales volume.

Exercises

9–7. Comparative impact of full-absorption and variable costing on unit costs and profits

Milton, Inc., produces a single product that sells for $14.40. In 1983, Milton produced 80,000 units and sold 72,000 units. There was no beginning or ending work in process inventory that year.

Manufacturing costs and marketing and administrative costs for 1983 were as follows:

	Variable	Fixed
Direct materials	$280,000	—
Direct labor	200,000	—
Manufacturing overhead	80,000	$180,000
Marketing and administrative costs	69,120	120,000

Required:

a. Compute the unit product cost for 1983 under variable costing.

b. What would Milton's operating profit be for 1983 using the variable costing method?

9–8. Comparison of cost flows under full-absorption and variable costing

In 1984, Wyandotte Product incurred the following costs for its line of sewage pumps:

	Variable	Fixed
Direct materials	$500,000	—
Labor	475,000	$100,000
Supplies	80,000	—
Depreciation	—	70,000
Repairs and maintenance	40,000	120,000
Other manufacturing	30,000	40,000
Marketing and administrative costs	40,000	110,000

100,000 units were produced and 80,000 units sold that year.

Required:

a. Using T-accounts, trace the manufacturing cost flows under the variable costing approach.

b. Using T-accounts, trace the manufacturing cost flows under the full-absorption costing approach.

9–9. Comparison of full-absorption and variable costing on income statements

Refer to Exercise 9–8. Assume the selling price of sewage pumps is $20 each.

Required:

a. Present the income statement based on variable costing for 1984.

b. Present the income statement based on full-absorption costing for 1984.

c. Explain the difference in the operating profits.

9–10. Cost flows

Okanagan Products manufactures Ogo Pogos, a line of stuffed toys. Variable manufacturing overhead is applied at the rate of $1.20 per labor-hour, and fixed manufacturing overhead at a rate of $1.80 per labor-hour. Actual costs incurred in 1984 were as follows:

Direct materials	$ 50,000
Direct labor (at $4.20 per hour)	126,000
Actual variable overhead	40,000
Variable marketing and administrative costs	45,000
Actual fixed overhead	52,000
Fixed marketing and administrative costs	28,000

In 1984, 25,000 units were produced and 23,800 units sold at a selling price of $20 each.

Required:

a. Using T-accounts, trace the cost flows under the variable costing approach.

b. Using T-accounts, trace the cost flows under the full-absorption costing approach.

9–11. Income statements

Refer to Exercise 9–10 assuming that Okanagan Products charge over- or underapplied overhead to Cost of Goods Sold:

Required:

a. Prepare an income statement for 1984 using the variable costing approach.

b. Prepare an income statement for 1984 using the full-absorption costing approach.

9–12. Income statements: Analyze profit performance

Eaton's Enterprises released the following figures from its records for 1984 and 1985:

	1984	1985
Sales units	240,000	240,000
Production units	240,000	400,000
Selling price per unit	$20	$20
Variable manufacturing cost per unit	$12	$12
Annual fixed manufacturing cost	$1,200,000	$1,200,000
Variable marketing and administrative costs	$1.25	$1.25
Fixed marketing and administrative costs	$420,000	$420,000

Required:

a. Prepare income statements for 1984 and 1985 using full-absorption costing.
b. Prepare income statements for 1984 and 1985 using variable costing.
c. Comment on the different operating profit figures. Did profits really improve in any particular year?

9–13. Comparison of full-absorption and variable costing— income statement formats

Consider the following facts:

	Year 1	Year 2
Sales volume	50,000 units	150,000 units
Production volume	100,000 units	100,000 units
Selling price	$8 per unit	$8 per unit
Variable manufacturing costs	$5 per unit	$5 per unit
Fixed manufacturing costs	$100,000	$100,000
Nonmanufacturing costs (all fixed)	$ 50,000	$ 50,000

Required:

Prepare comparative income statements using the contribution margin format for the variable costing, and the traditional format using full-absorption costing.

9–14. Comparison of full-absorption and variable costing using the algebraic method—Part I

Assume the following data about actual prices, costs, and volume for Derivation Company for the first quarter:

Selling price	$5 per unit
Variable manufacturing costs	$3 per unit
Fixed manufacturing costs	$100,000 for the quarter
Marketing and administrative costs (fixed and variable combined)	$30,000 for the quarter
Sales volume	100,000 units for the quarter
Production volume	120,000 units for the quarter

There were no beginning inventories.

Required:

a. Using the algebraic method, derive the difference in operating profits between variable costing and full-absorption costing.
b. What is the inventory value at the end of the first quarter under (1) full-absorption costing and (2) variable costing?

9–15. Comparison of full-absorption and variable costing using the algebraic method—Part II

Refer to the information given in Exercise 9–14. Assume it is now the second quarter of the same year as in Exercise 9–14 and the volumes in the second quarter are as follows:

Sales volume	100,000 units
Production volume	100,000 units

Costs and prices remain the same in the second quarter as in the first quarter.

Required:

Using the algebraic method show the difference, if any, in operating profit between variable costing and full-absorption costing. (You may assume either LIFO or FIFO inventory flows.)

9–16. Comparison of full-absorption and variable costing using the algebraic method—Part III

Refer to the information given in Exercise 9–14. Assume it is now the third quarter of the same year and the volumes in the third quarter are as follows:

Sales volume	100,000 units
Production volume	80,000 units

Variable costs and selling price per unit remain the same in the third quarter as in the first quarter, as do quarterly fixed costs.

Required:

Using the algebraic method, show the difference in operating profits between variable costing and full-absorption costing. (You may assume either a FIFO or LIFO inventory flow.)

Problems and cases

Vagabond Products uses the following unit costs for one of the products it manufactures:

9–17. Solve to derive income statement amounts

Direct materials	$78.00
Direct labor	49.40
Manufacturing overhead:	
Variable	15.60
Fixed (based on 5,000 units per month)	13.00
Marketing and administrative costs:	
Variable	10.40
Fixed (based on 5,000 units per month)	7.28

In 1984, there were 1,000 units in beginning Finished Goods Inventory; 5,500 units were produced; and 6,500 units sold at $200 per unit. There was no beginning nor ending Work in Process Inventory. Actual costs for 1984 were as estimated. Over- or underabsorbed overhead is expensed to Cost of Goods Sold.

Required:

a. Prepare an income statement for 1984 using variable costing.

b. Would reported operating profits be more, less, or equal if full-absorption costing was used? Prove it with an income statement using full-absorption costing.

9–18. Comprehensive full-absorption and variable costing comparison

Kensington Company manufactures a single product with the following costs:

Selling price	$	5.00 per unit
Variable manufacturing costs (direct materials and direct labor)		3.00 per unit
Fixed manufacturing costs, based on a normal production volume of		
100,000 units per month (all manufacturing overhead is fixed)		1.00 per unit
Marketing and administrative costs (all fixed)		50,000 per month

Beginning inventory is valued at $4 per unit under full-absorption costing and at $3 per unit under variable costing.

Required:

The president of Kensington wants an analysis on the effect of variations in sales and production units. To help you he has included a chart for you to complete (all numbers in thousands). Complete the chart and comment on the results.

		S = P			S > P			S < P		
Units	Sales	100	80	110	115	90	125	90	75	100
	Production	100	80	110	100	80	110	100	80	110
	Sales Revenue									
Full-absorption Costing	Cost of goods sold (full-absorption)									
	Over (under) absorbed overhead									
	Marketing and administration									
	Operating profit									

Variable Costing	Cost of goods sold (variable)									
	Fixed manufacturing costs									
	Fixed marketing and administration									
	Operating profit									

9–19. Missing data

After a dispute with the company president, the controller of the Lance Company resigned in January 1985. At that time, his office was converting the internal reporting system from full-absorption to variable costing. You have been called in to prepare financial reports for the year 1984. Your investigation reveals that a considerable amount of data are missing, but you piece together the following information.

1. From the production department, you learn that the company manufactures valves that pass through one department. All materials are added at the beginning of production, and processing is applied evenly throughout the department. There is no spoilage.
2. From "sales" you learn that 90,000 units were sold at a price of $20 each during 1984.
3. From various sources you determined that variable manufacturing overhead was $330,000 and fixed manufacturing overhead was $210,000 for 1984. Nonmanufacturing costs (all fixed) were $280,000.
4. In one of the former controller's desk drawers you discover the draft of a report with the following information:
   a. "To improve our present accounting system we will be adopting the normal costing approach for both internal and external reporting in 1984. We will write off over- or underabsorbed overhead as part of cost of goods sold in 1984 rather than allocate it to inventories."
   b. "Direct unit costs remained the same in 1984 as in previous years: $4 per unit for materials cost and $2 per unit for direct labor. Variable overhead will be applied at a rate of $1.50 per direct labor dollar, and fixed overhead at $1 per direct labor dollar."
   c. "110,000 units were transferred from work in process inventory to finished

goods inventory. 120,000 units of materials were purchased and 115,000 units requisitioned to work in process inventory."

d. Inventory summary (in units):

	January 1, 1984	December 31, 1984
Work in process inventory	10,000 (40% complete)	15,000 (20% complete)
Finished goods inventory	No records	30,000
Direct materials	No records	10,000

Required:

a. Show the flow of whole units, including units started in work in process inventory, transferred to finished goods, and sold. Be sure to include both beginning and ending inventories.

b. Show the flow of manufacturing costs during the year, including beginning and ending inventories using full-absorption normal costing.

c. Prepare income statements using:
   (1) Full-absorption actual costing.
   (2) Full-absorption normal costing.
   (3) Variable actual costing.
   (4) Variable normal costing.
   Lance Company uses the weighted-average method of inventory valuation.

9–20. Conversion of variable to full-absorption costing

The S. T. Shire Company uses variable costing for internal management purposes and absorption costing for external reporting purposes. Thus, at the end of each year financial information must be converted from variable costing to full-absorption costing in order to satisfy external requirements.

At the end of 1984, it was anticipated that sales would rise 20 percent the next year. Therefore, production was increased from 20,000 units to 24,000 units to meet this expected demand. However, economic conditions kept the sales level at 20,000 units for both years.

The following data pertain to 1984 and 1985:

	1984	1985
Selling price per unit	$30	$30
Sales (units)	20,000	20,000
Beginning inventory (units)	2,000	2,000
Production (units)	20,000	24,000
Ending inventory (units)	2,000	6,000
Underabsorbed variable overhead	5,000	4,000

Variable cost per unit for 1984 and 1985:

Labor	$ 7.50
Materials	4.50
Variable overhead	3.00
	$15.00

Annual fixed costs for 1984 and 1985 (budgeted and actual):

Production	$ 90,000
Selling and administrative	100,000
	$190,000

The overhead rate under full-absorption costing is based upon practical plant capacity which is 30,000 units per year. Under- or overabsorbed overhead is taken to cost of goods sold.

Required:

a. Present the income statement based on variable costing for 1985.
b. Present the income statement based on full-absorption costing for 1985.
c. Explain the difference, if any, in the operating profit figures. Give the entry necessary to adjust the book figures to the financial statement figure, if one is necessary.
d. The company finds it worthwhile to develop its internal financial data on a variable cost basis. What advantages and disadvantages are attributed to variable costing for internal purposes?
e. There are many who believe that variable costing is appropriate for external reporting, and there are many who oppose its use for external reporting. What arguments for and against the use of variable costing are advanced for its use in external reporting?

(CMA adapted)

9–21. Comparison of full-absorption to variable costing with product mix

Witches Brew Corporation operates a processing plant in West Covina, California, that manufactures two grades of witches brew. The high-test (HT) grade sells for $26 per quart, while the low-grade (LG) sells for $14 per quart. A dispute broke out between the members of the coven concerning the sales effort that should be devoted to each of the products. Six members felt that greater emphasis should be placed on the high-test grade since it offered a greater profit per quart. Six members voted to increase sales of the low-grade brew since it required half of the labor to manufacture and labor was in short supply. You have been hired by the 13th member of the group to advise on the appropriate selling emphasis.

You have been able to conjure up the following information from the accounting records:

	HT	LG
Unit costs:		
Direct materials	$2	$1
Direct labor	4	2
Variable manufacturing overhead	3	3
Fixed manufacturing overhead	1	4
Variable marketing and administrative costs	7	2
Fixed marketing and administrative costs	4	3
Inventories and production data:		
Beginning inventory	1,000 qts.	2,000 qts.
Ending inventory	3,000 qts.	1,000 qts.
Sales this past month	7,000 qts.	12,000 qts.
Normal production	8,000 qts.	10,000 qts.
Minimum production	5,000 qts.	5,000 qts.

The minimum production requirements are established by the type of brewing equipment and cannot be changed. The maximum production is determined by the shortage of skilled gnomes. The total direct labor costs per month cannot exceed $52,000. There have been no cost changes in the past millenium. FIFO inventory flows are assumed.

a. Prepare a variable costing income statement for last month (ignore taxes).
b. Prepare a full-absorption costing income statement for last month (ignore taxes).
c. For the low-grade brew only, prepare a reconciliation between the operating profits in *(a)* and *(b)*.
d. Prepare your recommendation to the 13th member of the coven of the optimal mix of products and the total coven profit that would be earned with your recommended product mix. Ignore changes in inventories for this part!

9–22. Variable costing operating profit and reconciliation with full absorption

The Sierra Corporation employs a full-absorption costing system for its external reporting as well as for internal management purposes. The latest annual income statement appears as follows:

Sales revenue		$415,000
Cost of goods sold:		
Beginning inventory	$ 22,000	
Cost to manufacture	315,000	
Ending inventory	(86,000)	
Cost of goods sold		251,000
Gross margin		164,000
Marketing costs		83,000
Administrative costs		49,800
Operating profit before taxes		31,200
Income taxes		14,500
Operating profit after taxes		$ 16,700

Company management is somewhat concerned that although they are showing adequate income, there has been a shortage of cash to meet operating costs. The following information has been provided to you to assist management with its evaluation of the situation:

Statement of Cost of Goods Manufactured

Direct materials:		
Beginning inventory	$ 16,000	
Purchases	62,000	
Ending inventory	(22,000)	$ 56,000
Direct labor		125,100
Manufacturing overhead:		
Variable		39,400
Fixed (including depreciation of $30,000)		94,500
Cost of goods manufactured		$315,000

There are no work in process inventories. Management reports that it is pleased that this year manufacturing costs are 70 percent variable compared to last year when these costs were only 45 percent variable. This, management notes, provides more insurance against volume declines. While 80 percent of the marketing costs are variable, only 40 percent of the administrative costs are considered variable.

a. Prepare a variable costing income statement for the year.
b. Reconcile the difference between the full-absorption costing statement given in

the problem to the variable costing statement in part *(a)*. Use operating profit before taxes.

c. Assuming no change in inventories, compute the sales level that would be required to earn operating profits of $33,200.

9–23. Full-absorption versus variable costing

You have been given the following information concerning the All Fixed Company.

1. Sales: 10,000 units per year at a price of $46 per unit.
2. Production: 15,000 units in 1987; 5,000 units in 1988.
3. There was no beginning inventory in 1987.
4. Annual production costs are all fixed and equal $225,000 per year.
5. Ending finished goods inventory in 1987 was one third of that year's current production.
6. Annual marketing and administrative costs are $140,000 per year.

Required:

a. Prepare a full-absorption costing income statement.
b. Prepare a variable costing income statement.
c. Prepare a reconciliation of full-absorption operating profit to variable costing operating profit for 1987 and 1988.

9–24. Effect on net operating profit with changes in production and costing method

The X. B. Company uses an actual cost system to apply all production costs to the units produced. While the plant has a maximum production capacity of 40,000,000 units, only 10,000,000 units were produced and sold during 1985. There were no beginning or ending inventories.

The X. B. Company income statement for 1985 is as follows:

X. B. COMPANY
Income Statement
For the Year Ending December 31, 1985

Sales (10,000,000 units at $3)		$30,000,000
Cost of goods sold:		
Variable (10,000,000 at $1)	$10,000,000	
Fixed	24,000,000	34,000,000
Gross margin		(4,000,000)
Marketing and administrative costs		5,000,000
Operating profit (loss)		$ (9,000,000)

The board of directors is concerned about this loss. A consultant approached the board with the following offer: "I agree to become president for no fixed salary. But I insist on a year-end bonus of 10 percent of operating profit (before considering the bonus)." The board of directors agreed to these terms, and the consultant was hired.

The new president promptly stepped up production to an annual rate of 30,000,000 units. Sales for 1986 remained at 10,000,000 units.

The resulting X. B. Company income statement for 1986 is presented below.

X. B. COMPANY
Income Statement
For the Year Ending December 31, 1986

Sales (10,000,000 units at $3)		$30,000,000
Cost of goods sold:		
Cost of goods manufactured:		
Variable (30,000,000 at $1)	$30,000,000	
Fixed	24,000,000	
Total cost of goods manufactured	54,000,000	
Less ending inventory:		
Variable (20,000,000 at $1)	20,000,000	
Fixed $\left(\frac{20}{30} \times 24,000,000\right)$	16,000,000	
Total inventory	36,000,000	
Cost of goods sold		18,000,000
Gross margin		12,000,000
Marketing and administrative costs		5,000,000
Operating profit before bonus		7,000,000
Bonus.		700,000
Operating profit after bonus		$ 6,300,000

The day after the statement was verified, the president took his check for $700,00 and resigned to take a job with another corporation. He remarked, "I enjoy challenges. Now that X. B. Company is in the black, I'd prefer tackling another challenging situation." (His contract with his new employer is similar to the one he had with X. B. Company.)

Required:

a. As a member of the board of directors, comment on the 1986 income statement.

b. Using variable costing, what would operating profit be for 1985? For 1986? What are the inventory values? (Assume all marketing and administrative costs are fixed.)

c. Using T-accounts, show the flow of costs under full-absorption costing and under variable costing for 1986. (Assume there is no work in process inventory at the end of 1986.)

d. At what sales level would the outside executive be indifferent to the product costing approach used to determine his bonus? Why?

e. At what sales level would the outside executive prefer variable costing to full-absorption costing?

f. What would 1986 operating profit (loss) be if X. B. Company used full-absorption normal costing with a fixed manufacturing overhead rate of $2.40 $\left(\frac{\$24,000,000 \text{ fixed manufacturing costs}}{10,000,000 \text{ estimated unit sales}}\right)$? Prepare both an income statement and a T-account diagram of cost flows.

9–25. Comparative income statements and solving for unknowns

A client has requested your help in analyzing the operating of one of her divisions, the Wheeler Division. "I don't understand this! I received this income statement yesterday from the Wheeler Division managers (see Exhibit A), but one of our internal auditors came across this other one (see Exhibit B). The second statement shows a lower net income! I think something strange is going on here. It looks like the division managers are sending me this first statement (in Exhibit A) that makes them look good, while they're hiding the second statement (in Exhibit B) which shows what's really going on. I want you to look into this for me."

Required:

a. Units sold in August.

b. *Expected* and *actual* production in August.

c. *Beginning* and *ending* inventory in August.

d. Reconcile (assume FIFO flow of units):

(1) Actual fixed costs incurred in August $

    Add:

    Deduct:

    Fixed costs expensed under full-absorption costing $ _____

(2) Components of fixed costs expensed under full-absorption:

    Through cost of sales $

    Other (identify)

          Total $ _____

e. Summarize the transactions for the month in journal entry or T-account form for both units and dollars. Show the difference between full-absorption and variable costing in your summary. Use one summary account, Other Assets and Liabilities, for transactions that are not specifically identified with an account. Use one inventory account for both work in process and finished goods.

Exhibit A (9–25)

Wheeler Division
Income Statement
August

Sales revenue	$1,200,000
Cost of goods sold	800,000
Overabsorbed overhead	50,000
Gross margin	450,000
Selling and administrative costs	200,000
Operating profit	$ 250,000

Notes:

(1) Fixed manufacturing costs applied at predetermined rate of $2 per unit.

(2) No under- or overabsorbed overhead is prorated to inventories.

(3) Ending inventory is $640,000.

Exhibit B (9–25)

Wheeler Division
Income Statement
August

Sales revenue	$1,200,000
Cost of goods sold	600,000
Fixed costs	300,000
Gross margin	300,000
Selling and administrative costs	200,000
Operating profit	$ 100,000

9–26. Comprehensive problem on process costing, variable costing, and full-absorption costing

Whitaker Corporation manufactures Jink, which is sold for $20 per unit. Harsh (a direct material) is added before processing starts, and labor and overhead are added evenly during the manufacturing process. Actual costs per unit of Jink for 1984 are:

Harsh, 2 pounds	$3.00
Labor	6.00
Variable manufacturing overhead	1.00
Fixed manufacturing overhead	1.10

These costs have remained the same for several periods. Inventory data for 1984 follows:

	Units	
	January 1	**December 31**
Harsh (pounds)	50,000	40,000
Work in process inventory	10,000 (½ processed)	15,000 (⅓ processed)
Finished goods inventory	17,000	12,000

During 1984, 220,000 pounds of Harsh were purchased and 230,000 pounds were transferred to work in process inventory. Also, 110,000 units of Jink were transferred to finished goods inventory. Actual fixed manufacturing overhead during the year was $121,000. FIFO is used for inventory flows. Marketing and administrative costs were $145,000 for the year.

Required:

a. Determine the number of equivalent units produced for both materials (Harsh) and conversion costs.

b. Determine the work in process and finished goods inventories (in dollars) under (1) full-absorption costing and (2) variable costing on January 1, 1984, and December 31, 1984.

c. Prepare comparative income statements for 1984—full-absorption and variable costing.

d. Prepare a reconciliation of full-absorption to variable costing that compares the fixed manufacturing costs deducted from revenue (that is, expensed) under each method.

9–27. Incomplete records

On December 31, 1983, a fire destroyed the bulk of the accounting records of Malox Company, a small one-product manufacturing firm. In addition, the chief accountant mysteriously disappeared. You have the task of reconstructing the records for 1983. The general manager has said that the accountant had been experimenting with both full-absorption costing and variable costing on an actual costing basis.

The records are a mess, but you have gathered the following data for 1983:

1.	Sales	$450,000
2.	Actual fixed manufacturing costs incurred	66,000
3.	Actual variable manufacturing costs per unit for 1983 and for units in inventory on January 1, 1983	3
4.	Operating profit, full-absorption costing basis	60,000
5.	Notes receivable from chief accountant	14,000
6.	Contribution margin	180,000
7.	Direct material purchases	175,000
8.	Actual marketing and administrative costs (all fixed)	21,000
9.	Gross margin	81,000

You also learn that full-abosrption costs per unit in beginning finished goods inventory equals the 1983 full-absorption production cost per unit.

a. Prepare a comparative income statement on a full-absorption and variable costing basis.
b. Determine the number of units sold.
c. Determine the full-absorption cost per unit.
d. Determine the number of units produced.
e. Reconcile the operating profit under variable costing with that under full costing, showing the exact source of the difference.

9–28. Comparative income statements

Management of Bicent Company uses the following unit costs for the one product it manufactures:

	Projected cost per unit
Direct material (all variable)	$30.00
Direct labor (all variable)	19.00
Manufacturing overhead:	
Variable cost	6.00
Fixed cost (based on 10,000 units per month)	5.00
Nonmanufacturing:	
Variable cost	4.00
Fixed cost (based on 10,000 units per month)	2.80

The projected selling price is $80 per unit. The fixed costs remain fixed within the range of 4,000 to 16,000 units of production.

Management has also projected the following data for the month of June:

	Units
Beginning inventory	2,000
Production	9,000
Available	11,000
Sales	7,500
Ending inventory	3,500

Prepare a projected income statement for June for management purposes under *each* of the following product-costing methods:

a. Full-absorption costing with all variances charged to cost of goods sold each month.
b. Variable costing.

Supporting schedules calculating inventoriable production costs per unit should be presented in good form. Ignore income taxes.

(CPA adapted)

9–29. Evaluate full-absorption and variable costing

The vice president for sales of Huber Corporation has received the income statement for November. The statement has been prepared using variable costing and is reproduced below. The firm has just adopted a variable costing system for internal reporting purposes.

HUBER CORPORATION
Income Statement
For the Month of November
(in thousands)

Sales revenue $2,400
Less variable cost of goods sold   1,200
Manufacturing margin   1,200
Less fixed manufacturing costs at budget . . .   600
Gross margin   600
Less fixed nonmanufacturing costs   400
Operating profits before taxes . . . . $ 200

The controller attached the following notes to the statements.

1. The unit sales price for November averaged $24.
2. The unit manufacturing costs for the month were:

Variable cost $12
Fixed cost   4
Total cost $16

The unit rate for fixed manufacturing costs is a predetermined rate based upon a normal monthly production of 150,000 units.

3. Production for November was 45,000 units in excess of sales.
4. The inventory at November 30 consisted of 80,000 units.

Required:

a. The vice president for sales is not comfortable with the variable cost basis and wonders what the operating profit would have been under the prior full-abosrption cost basis.
   (1) Present the November income statement on a full-absorption cost basis.
   (2) Reconcile and explain the difference between the variable costing and the full-absorption costing operating profit figures.
b. Explain the features associated with variable cost profit measurement that should be attractive to the vice president for sales.

(CMA adapted)

9–30. Comprehensive case on full-absorption versus variable costing*— Landau Company

In early August, Terry Silver, the new marketing vice president of Landau Company, was studying the July income statement. Silver found the statement puzzling: July's sales had increased significantly over June's, yet income was lower in July than in June. Silver was certain that margins on Landau's products had not narrowed in July, and therefore felt that there must be some mistake in the July statement.

When Silver asked the company's chief accountant, Meredith Wilcox, for an explanation, Wilcox stated that production in July was well below standard volume because of employee vacations. This had caused overhead to be underabsorbed, and a large unfavorable volume variance had been generated, which more than offset the added gross margin from the sales increase. It was company policy to charge all variances to the monthly income statement, and these production volume variances would all wash out by year's end, Wilcox had said.

Silver, who admittedly knew little about accounting, found this explanation to be "Incomprehensible. With all the people in your department, I don't understand why you can't produce an income statement that reflects the economics of our business.

---

* © Osceola Institute, 1979.

In the company that I left to come here, if sales went up, profits went up. I don't see why that shouldn't be the case here, too."

As Wilcox left Silver's office, a presentation at a recent National Association of Accountants meeting came to mind. At that meeting, the controller of Winjum Manufacturing Company had described that firm's variable costing system, which charged fixed overhead to income as a period expense and treated only variable production costs as inventoriable product costs. Winjum's controller had stressed that, other things being equal, variable costing caused income to move with sales only, rather than being affected by both sales and production volume as was the case with full absorption costing systems.

Wilcox decided to recast the June and July income statements and balance sheets using variable costing. (The income statements as recast and as originally prepared, and the related balance sheet impacts, are shown in Exhibit A.) Wilcox then showed these statements to Terry Silver, who responded, "Now that's more like it! I *knew* July was a better month for us than June, and your new 'variable costing' statements reflect that. Tell your boss [Landau's controller] that at the next meeting of the executive committee I'm going to suggest we change to this new method."

At the next executive committee meeting, Silver proposed adoption of variable costing for Landau's monthly internal income statements. The controller also supported this change, saying that it would eliminate the time-consuming efforts of allocating fixed overhead to individual products. These allocations had only led to arguments between operating managers and the accounting staff. The controller added that since variable costing segregated the costs of materials, direct labor, and variable overhead from fixed overhead costs, management's cost control efforts would be enhanced.

Exhibit A (9–30)   **Effects of variable costing**

LANDAU COMPANY
Income Statements
June and July

	June		July	
	Full absorption costing	Variable costing	Full absorption costing	Variable costing
Sales revenues	$865,428	$865,428	$931,710	$931,710
Cost of goods sold at standard . .	484,640	337,517	521,758	363,367
Standard gross margin	380,788	527,911	409,952	568,343
Production cost variances:[a]				
Labor	(16,259)	(16,259)	(11,814)	(11,814)
Material	12,416	12,416	8,972	8,972
Overhead volume	1,730	—	(63,779)	—
Overhead spending[b]	3,604	3,604	2,832	2,832
Actual gross margin	382,279	527,672	346,163	568,333
Fixed production overhead	—	192,883	—	192,883
Marketing and administrative	301,250	301,250	310,351	310,351
Income before taxes	81,029	33,539	35,812	65,099
Provision for income taxes	38,894	16,099	17,190	31,248
Net income	$ 42,135	$ 17,440	$ 18,622	$ 33,851

[a] Parentheses denote unfavorable (debit) variances.

[b] Also known as the overhead "price" variance.

Impact on Balance Sheets

The only asset account affected by the difference in accounting method was inventories; on the liabilities and owners' equity side, only Accrued Taxes and Retained Earnings were affected.

	As of June 30		As of July 31	
	Full costing	**Variable costing**	**Full costing**	**Variable costing**
Inventories	$1,680,291	$1,170,203	$1,583,817	$1,103,016
Accrued taxes	450,673	205,831	467,863	237,079
Retained earnings	3,112,980	2,847,734	3,131,602	2,881,585

Silver also felt that the margin figures provided by the new approach would be more useful than the present ones for comparing the profitability of individual products. To illustrate the point, Silver had worked out an example. With full costing, two products in Landau's line, numbers 129 and 243, would appear as follows:

Product	Standard production cost	Selling price	Unit margin	Margin percent
129	$2.54	$4.34	$1.80	41.5
243	3.05	5.89	2.84	48.2

Thus Product 243 would appear to be the more desirable one to sell. But on the proposed basis, the numbers were as follows:

Product	Standard production cost	Selling price	Unit margin	Margin percent
129	$1.38	$4.34	$2.96	68.2
243	2.37	5.89	3.52	59.8

According to Silver, these numbers made it clear that Product 129 was the more profitable of the two.

At this point, the treasurer spoke up. "If we use this new approach, the next thing we know you marketing types will be selling at your usual markup over *variable* costs. How are we going to pay the fixed costs *then?* Besides, in my 38 years of experience, it's the lack of control over long-run costs that can bankrupt a company. I'm opposed to any proposal that causes us to take a myopic view of costs."

The president also had some concerns about the proposal. "In the first place, if I add together the June and July profit under each of these methods, I get almost $61,000 with the present method, but only $51,000 under the proposed method. While I'd be happy to lower our reported profits from the standpoints of relations with our employee union and income taxes, I don't think it's a good idea as far as our owners and bankers are concerned. And I share Sam's [the treasurer's] concern about controlling long-run costs. I think we should defer a decision on this matter until we fully understand all of the implications."

Required:

a.   Critique the various pros and cons of the variable costing proposal that were presented in the meeting. What arguments would you add?

b.   Should Landau adopt variable costing for its monthly income statements?

Part 2

Differential Costs for Decision Making

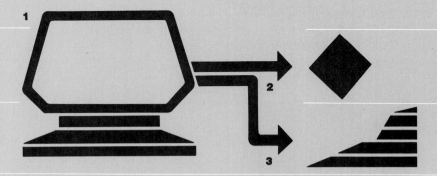

1. Cost accounting systems

2. Differential costs for decision making

10

Cost Estimation

OBJECTIVES
To understand methods of estimating costs.
To see how costs can be divided into fixed and variable portions.

Accounting systems are designed primarily to record and report costs that have been incurred in the past. However, it is important that management also be able to estimate future cost behavior. For example, in deciding among alternative actions, it is helpful to have a good estimate of the probable costs that would result from each choice. Management needs to know the costs that are likely to be incurred under normal operating conditions and how they might vary if conditions change. This chapter discusses methods of estimating costs.

Among the most frequently asked questions that require cost estimates are:

What will the costs be if we increase activity by 10 percent over the present level?

How can future overhead application rates be determined with maximum reliability?

How will costs change if specific labor- or energy-saving devices are installed?

What effect will a change in materials specifications have on our product costs?

How much cash will we need to pay our operating costs in the coming week, month, or year?

What bid should we enter on this contract?

What profit contribution can we expect if the organization performs as expected for the period?

In most cases, the controller's staff is called upon to prepare the estimates needed to answer these questions.

Methods of cost estimation

An *estimate* is a considered judgment about future events that takes into account past experience and probable changes in circumstances and conditions. Business conditions, like life in general, are subject to unanticipated changes. Future costs are uncertain at best, no matter how carefully they have been estimated.

Several approaches to cost estimation are in current use. The most common are:

1. Account analysis.
2. Engineering estimates.
3. Scattergraph and high-low estimates.
4. Statistical methods (usually employing regression analysis).

Results are likely to differ from method to method. Consequently, more than one approach is often applied so that results can be compared. Because line managers bear ultimate responsibility for all cost estimates, they frequently apply their own best judgment as a final step in the estimation process, modifying the estimates submitted by the controller's staff. These methods, therefore, should be seen as ways of helping management to arrive at the best estimates possible. Their weaknesses as well as their strengths require attention.

We discuss each of the four estimation methods in this chapter. The discussion of regression methods centers on practical applications rather than on the underlying statistical theory. A brief overview of the theory and some important considerations for its application are discussed in the appendix to this chapter.

Account analysis

The account analysis approach calls for a review of each cost account used to record the costs that are of interest. Each cost is identified as either fixed or variable, depending on the relationship between the cost and some activity.

The relationship between the activity and the cost is extremely important. For example, in estimating the production costs for a specified number of units within the range of present manufacturing capacity, direct materials and direct labor costs would be considered variable, while building occupancy costs would be considered fixed.

Illustration 10–1 shows a typical schedule of estimated manufacturing overhead costs prepared for a particular production level by Estimators, Inc. The production process is assumed to produce 40 units per direct labor-hour. Management has initially considered a production level of 4,600 units. To attain this production level, 115 direct labor-hours (4,600 units ÷ 40 units per hour) are required. The variable manufacturing overhead may be expressed as a cost per direct labor-hour or as a cost per unit, depending upon management's preference.

Following this approach, each major class of manufacturing overhead costs is itemized. Each cost is then divided into its estimated variable and fixed components. Management considers building occupancy costs, for exam-

Illustration 10–1   **Cost estimation using account analysis, Estimators, Inc.**

| | Costs at 4,600 units of output (115 direct labor-hours) | | |
Account	Total	Variable cost	Fixed cost
Indirect labor	$ 321	$ 103	$ 218
Indirect materials	422	307	115
Building occupancy	615		615
Property taxes and insurance	51	40	11
Power	589	535	54
Equipment repairs and maintenance	218	119	99
Data processing	113	88	25
Quality inspections	187	187	
Personnel services	115	47	68
Totals	$2,631	$1,426	$1,205

ple, to be entirely fixed and classifies the costs of quality inspections as entirely variable. The other costs are mixed—they have some fixed and some variable elements. The fixed and variable components of each cost item may be determined on the basis of the experience and judgment of accounting or other personnel. Also, other cost estimation methods discussed later in this chapter might be used to divide costs into fixed and variable components.

The total costs for the coming period are the sum of the estimated total variable and total fixed costs. For Estimators, Inc., assume that accounting personnel have relied on judgments of a number of people in the company and estimated fixed costs to be $1,205 and the total variable costs to be $1,426, as shown in Illustration 10–1.

Since the variable costs are directly related to the quantity of expected production, the variable manufacturing overhead per unit may be stated as $.31 (= $1,426 ÷ 4,600 units). The general cost equation may be expressed as:

Manufacturing overhead = $1,205 per period + $.31 per unit of output

For 4,600 units:

$$\text{Manufacturing overhead} = \$1,205 + \$.31 \times 4,600$$
$$= \$1,205 + \$1,426$$
$$= \$2,631$$

Now, if management wanted to estimate the costs at a production level of 4,800 units, it would substitute that figure for the 4,600 units in the previous equation. This results in:

$$\text{Manufacturing overhead} = \$1,205 + \$.31 \times 4,800$$
$$= \$1,205 + \$1,488$$
$$= \$2,693$$

This is simpler than re-estimating all of the manufacturing overhead cost elements listed in Illustration 10–1 for the different activity levels that management might wish to consider. Moreover, management's attention is drawn to the variable cost amount as the cost that changes with each increment in unit volume.

The variable costs could also be expressed in terms of costs per direct labor-hour. Since 115 direct labor-hours are required to produce 4,600 units (at the 40 units per hour assumed in the illustration), the variable cost per direct labor-hour (DLH) would be:

$$\$1,426 \div 115 \text{ hours} = \underline{\underline{\$12.40 \text{ per DLH}}}$$

Account analysis is a useful way of estimating costs. It makes use of the experience and judgment of managers and accountants who are familiar with company operations and the way costs react to changes in activity levels. Account analysis relies heavily on personal judgment. This may be an advantage or disadvantage depending on the bias of the person making the estimate. Decisions based on cost estimates often have major economic consequences for the people making the estimates. Thus, these individuals may not be entirely objective. More objective methods are often used in conjunction with account analysis so that the advantages of multiple methods are obtained.

Engineering estimates

Engineering estimates of costs are usually made by measuring the work involved in a task. A detailed step-by-step analysis of each phase of each manufacturing process, together with the kinds of work performed and movements involved, is prepared. (This is sometimes part of a *time-and-motion* study.) The time it should take to perform each step is then estimated. These times are often available from widely published manuals and trade association documents.

The times required for each step in the process are summed to obtain an estimate of the total time involved, including an allowance for unproductive time. This serves as a basis for estimating direct labor costs. Engineering estimates of the materials required for each unit of production are usually obtainable from drawings and specifications sheets.

Other costs are estimated in a similar manner. For example, the size and cost of a building needed to house the manufacturing operation can be estimated based on area construction costs and space requirements. An estimate of the needed number of supervisors and support personnel can be based on an estimate of direct labor time.

One advantage to the engineering approach is that it can detail each step required to perform an operation. This permits comparison with other settings where similar operations are performed. It enables a company to review its manufacturing productivity and identify specific strengths and weaknesses.

Another advantage is that it does not require data from prior activities in the organization. Hence, it can be used to estimate costs for totally new activities.

A company that uses engineering estimates can often identify where "slack" exists in its operations. For example, if an engineering estimate indicates that 80,000 square feet of floor area are required for an assembly process but the company has been using 125,000 square feet, the company may find it beneficial to rearrange the plant to make floor space available for other uses.

A difficulty with the engineering approach is that it can be quite expensive to use because each activity is using engineering norms. Another consideration is that engineering estimates are often based on optimal conditions. Therefore, when evaluating performance, bidding on a contract, planning for expected costs, or estimating costs for any other purpose, it is wise to consider that the actual work conditions will be less than optimal.

Scattergraph and high-low estimates

One way to overcome some of the shortcomings of account analysis and engineering estimates is to observe past cost behavior in relation to a specified activity measure. If a company's operations have followed a discernible pattern in the past and are expected to continue that pattern in the future, it may be possible to use the relationship between past costs and activity to estimate future costs. Of course, if the relationship changes, it may be necessary to adjust the estimated costs accordingly.

Analysts must be careful when predicting future costs from past data. In many cases, the cost-activity relationship changes. Technological innovation, increased use of robots, more mechanized processes, and the like may make the past cost-activity relationships inappropriate for predictive purposes.

In other cases, the costs themselves change so dramatically that old cost data are almost worthless predictors of future costs. Manufacturers using copper and silver in recent years have found that past cost data are not very helpful for predicting future costs. While adjustments to the data may be made, the resulting cost estimates tend to lose their objectivity as the number of adjustments increases.

Relevant range of activity

When attempting to extrapolate from past observations, one must consider the relevance of past activity levels to anticipated future activity levels. Extrapolations beyond the upper and lower bounds of past observations are highly subjective. If, for example, the highest activity level observed in the past was 4,100 units per month and we wished to predict costs to manufacture 4,600 units per month, an estimate based on past data may be highly inaccurate, because the past data do not reflect experience with output over 4,100 units.

The limits within which a cost projection may be valid is the *relevant range* for that estimate. The relevant range would include only those activity levels for which the assumed cost relationships used in the estimate are considered to hold. Thus, when past data are used, the relevant range for the projection is usually between the upper and lower limits of the past activity levels for which data are available.

Although the use of past data for future cost estimation has limitations, there are many cases in which it works quite well. In many estimates, past data, even if outside the relevant range, are adequate representations of the cost relationships that are likely to hold in the future. Moreover, reliance on past data is relatively inexpensive. It may be the only readily available, cost-effective basis for estimating costs.

Past data do show the relationships that held in prior periods and, at the least, may be a meaningful starting point for estimating future costs as long as their limitations are recognized. In the remainder of this chapter, we discuss specific methods of using past data to estimate future costs.

Preparing a scattergraph

Plotting past costs against past activity levels is often a useful way of visually depicting cost-activity relationships. Such a plot, called a scattergraph, will also indicate any significant change in the relationship between costs and activity at different activity levels.

To prepare such a plot, we first obtain the relevant data. For example, if estimates of manufacturing overhead costs are to be based on direct labor-hours, we must obtain information about past manufacturing overhead costs and related past direct labor-hours.

Number of observations   The number of observations to include depends on the availability of the data, the variability within the data, and the relative costs and benefits of obtaining reliable data. A rule of thumb is to use three years of monthly data if the physical processes have not changed significantly within that time. If the company's operations have recently changed significantly, however, data that predate the change may not be useful. If cost and activity levels are highly stable, then a relatively short period (12 months or so) may be adequate.

Data for the past 15 months were collected for Estimators, Inc., to estimate variable and fixed manufacturing overhead. These data are presented and plotted on the scattergraph in Illustration 10–2. Once all the data points were plotted, a line was drawn to fit the points as closely as possible. The line was extended to the vertical axis on the scattergraph.

The slope of the line represents the estimated variable costs, and the intercept with the vertical axis represents the estimate of fixed costs. The slope is referred to as the variable cost because it represents the change in costs that occurs as a result of changes in activity. The intercept is referred to as the fixed cost because it represents the costs that would be incurred at a

Illustration 10–2   **Data and scattergraph for cost estimation, Estimators, Inc.**

Time period	Overhead costs	Direct labor-hours (DLH)
1	$2,107	62
2	2,040	62
3	2,916	120
4	2,322	71
5	1,896	50
6	2,471	95
7	3,105	142
8	2,316	86
9	2,555	112
10	2,780	136
11	2,061	85
12	2,910	103
13	2,835	96
14	2,715	101
15	1,986	53

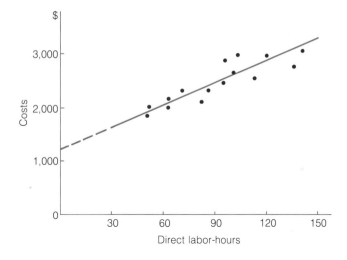

zero activity level given existing capacity *if the relationship plotted is valid from the data points back to the origin.* Note there are no observations of cost behavior around the zero activity level in this example, so the data do not indicate the costs that would occur when the activity level was zero. Rather, they provide an estimating equation useful within the relevant range. The slope and intercept may be measured using a ruler. However, preparing an estimate on this basis is subject to a good deal of error, especially if the points are scattered widely. Determination of the best fit is often a matter of "eyeball judgment." Consequently, scattergraphs are usually not used as the sole basis for cost estimates. Rather, they are used to illustrate the relationships between costs and activity levels and to point out any past data items that might be significantly out of line.

High-low cost estimation

If the cost relationships can be described by a straight line, any two points on a scattergraph may be used to prepare a cost-estimating equation. Typically, the *highest and the lowest activity points* are chosen—hence the name **high-low cost estimation.**

The slope of the total cost line, which estimates the increase of variable costs associated with an increase of one unit of production, may be estimated by the equation:

$$\text{Variable cost (per unit)} = \frac{\text{Cost at highest activity} - \text{Cost at lowest activity}}{\text{Highest activity} - \text{Lowest activity}}$$

The intercept is estimated by taking the total cost at either activity level and subtracting the estimated variable cost for that activity level.

$$\text{Fixed cost} = \frac{\text{Total cost at}}{\text{highest activity}} - \left[\frac{\text{Variable cost}}{\text{per unit}} \times \frac{\text{Highest activity}}{\text{stated in units}}\right]$$

or

$$\text{Fixed cost} = \frac{\text{Total cost at}}{\text{lowest activity}} - \left[\frac{\text{Variable cost}}{\text{per unit}} \times \frac{\text{Lowest activity}}{\text{stated in units}}\right]$$

Based on the data for Estimators, Inc., in Illustration 10–2, the highest activity level is 142 direct labor-hours. At this activity level, total manufacturing overhead costs are $3,105. The lowest activity level is 50 hours, with manufacturing overhead costs of $1,896. Substituting these data in the equation for variable cost yields:

$$\text{Variable cost per DLH} = \frac{\$3,105 - \$1,896}{142\ \text{DLH} - 50\ \text{DLH}}$$

$$= \frac{\$1,209}{92\ \text{DLH}}$$

$$= \$13.141\ \text{per DLH}$$

To obtain the fixed cost estimate, either the highest or lowest activity level and costs may be used.

$$\text{Fixed cost highest activity} = \$3,105 - \$13.141 \times 142\ \text{DLH}$$
$$= \$3,105 - \$1,866$$
$$= \$1,239$$

or

$$\text{Fixed cost lowest activity} = \$1,896 - \$13.141 \times 50\ \text{DLH}$$
$$= \$1,896 - \$657$$
$$= \$1,239$$

An estimate for the costs at any given activity level can be computed using the equation:

$$\text{Total cost} = \$1,239 + \$13.141 \times \text{specified DLH}$$

For the 115 hours required to produce 4,600 units, the total cost is:

$$\begin{aligned}
\text{Total cost} &= \$1,239 + \$13.141 \times 115 \text{ DLH} \\
&= \$1,239 + \$1,511 \\
&= \underline{\underline{\$2,750}}
\end{aligned}$$

Illustration 10–3 shows the construction of the high-low cost line and the cost estimate at 115 DLH for the data in this example. Note that the high-low method uses only two data points, while the scattergraph (Illustration 10–3) used many. Thus, the high-low method uses less information about cost behavior than the scattergraph does.

While the high-low method is easy to apply, care must be taken to assure that the two points used to prepare the estimates are representative of cost and activity relationships over the range of activity for which the prediction is made. The highest and lowest points could, however, represent unusual circumstances. When this happens, one should choose the highest and lowest points within the normal range of activity.

Both the scattergraph and high-low approaches can be used to derive cost estimates and graphically illustrate cost-activity relationships based on past experience. Whenever costs and activity levels can be plotted in two-dimensional space, the scattergraph is a useful visual display. We recommend using it in conjunction with other cost-estimation methods.

Illustration 10–3   **Diagram of high-low cost estimates, Estimators, Inc.**

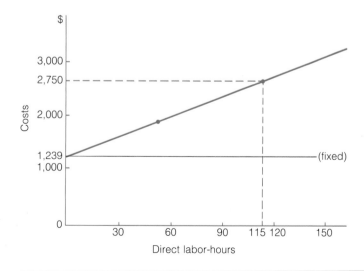

The high-low method should be used only as a rough guide. Since many handheld calculators have the ability to compute simple regression equations, we expect to see less and less use of the high-low method.

Statistical cost estimation (regression)

Regression techniques are designed to generate a line that best fits a set of data points. Because the regression procedure uses all data points, the resulting estimates have a broader base than estimates based only on high-low points.

In addition, regression techniques generate a number of additional statistics that under certain assumptions enable a manager to determine how well the estimated regression equation describes the relationship between costs and activities. The regression process also permits inclusion of more than one predictor. This latter feature may be useful when more than one activity affects costs. For example, variable manufacturing overhead may be a function of both direct labor-hours and the quantities of direct materials processed.

A comprehensive discussion of regression is not possible within the scope of this text. Many moderately priced hand calculators have regression capabilities, and most computers used in business and academia are equipped with regression programs. Therefore, we leave descriptions of these programs, and the assumptions on which regression analysis is based, to statistics and computer courses. Instead, we deal with regression techniques from the standpoint of accountants and managers as users of regression estimates already made for them.

A limited description of the use of regression programs for cost estimation follows. The appendix to this chapter discusses some of the more advanced technical considerations that may interest users of such programs.

Obtaining regression estimates

The most important step in obtaining regression estimates for cost estimation is to establish the existence of a logical relationship between activities that affect costs and the cost to be estimated. These activities are referred to as **predictors,** *X terms,* **independent variables,** or the *right-hand-side (RHS)* of a regression equation. The cost to be estimated may be called the **dependent variable,** the *Y term,* or the *left-hand-side (LHS)* of the regression equation.

Although regression programs will accept any data for the *Y* and *X* terms, entering numbers that have no logical relationship may result in misleading estimates. It is the accountant's responsibility to determine whether the activities are logically related to costs.

Assume, for example, that a logical relationship exists between direct labor-hours and manufacturing overhead costs for Estimators, Inc. Assume that a logical relationship also exists between direct materials costs and overhead costs. This latter assumption would be reasonable if the manufacturing process employed a substantial amount of materials and overhead costs included materials handling and storage. The data on manufacturing overhead costs, direct labor-hours, and direct materials costs for this process are presented in Illustration 10–4.

Illustration 10–4   **Data for regression estimation, Estimators, Inc.**

Overhead costs	Direct labor-hours	Direct materials costs
$2,107	62	$1,964
2,040	62	1,851
2,916	120	3,615
2,322	71	2,902
1,896	50	1,136
2,471	95	2,315
3,105	142	5,013
2,316	86	2,751
2,555	112	2,816
2,780	136	3,461
2,061	85	1,702
2,910	103	3,819
2,835	96	3,940
2,715	101	3,613
1,986	53	1,741

Estimators, Inc., first estimates costs using simple regression—or only one independent variable—to predict manufacturing overhead costs. They choose direct labor-hours, so past data on direct labor-hours would be entered as the X, or independent, variable. Past data on manufacturing overhead costs would be entered as the Y, or dependent, variable. The computer output giving the estimated relationship between direct labor-hours and manufacturing overhead for this situation is as follows:

Total manufacturing overhead = $1,334 + $12.373 per DLH

For cost estimation purposes, when reading the output of a regression program, the **intercept** term, $1,334, is an estimate of fixed costs. Of course, it should be used with caution because the intercept is outside of the relevant range of observations. The coefficient of the X term, in this example $12.373 per direct labor-hour, is an estimate of the variable cost per direct labor-hour. This is the **slope of the cost line.** The coefficients are often labeled b on the program output. Thus, the cost-estimation equation based on the regression results above would be:

Total costs = Intercept + b times DLH

Substituting 115 DLH into the equation yields:

$$\text{Total costs} = \$1,334 + (\$12.373 \times 115 \text{ DLH})$$
$$= \$1,334 + \$1,423$$
$$= \underline{\underline{\$2,757}}$$

This estimate of cost behavior is shown graphically in Illustration 10–5.

Illustration 10–5 **Scattergraph with regression estimated cost line, Estimators, Inc.**

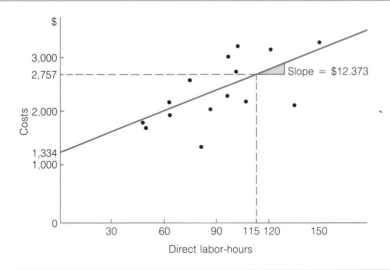

Correlation coefficients   In addition to the cost-estimating equation, the regression program provides other useful statistics. The **correlation coefficient** *(R)* is a measure of the proximity of the data points to the regression line. The closer R is to 1.0, the closer the data points are to the regression line. Conversely, the closer R is to zero, the poorer the fit of the regression line.

The **adjusted R-square** is the correlation coefficient squared and adjusted for the number of independent variables used to make the estimate. This adjustment to R-square recognizes that as the number of independent variables increases, R-square (unadjusted) increases. For example, if there are as many independent variables as there are observations, R-square (unadjusted) would be 1.0. The adjusted R-square is usually interpreted as the proportion of the variation in Y explained by the right-hand side of the regression equation; that is, by the X predictors.

For Estimators, Inc., the correlation coefficients, R-square and adjusted R-square, are:

Correlation coefficient *(R)*	.896
R-square	.802
Adjusted *R*-square	.787

Since the adjusted R-square is .787, it can be said that 78.7 percent of the changes in overhead costs can be explained by changes in direct labor-hours. For data drawn from accounting records (or for any real-world application), an adjusted R-square of .787 would be considered an exceptionally good fit.

The most commonly used regression technique is called *ordinary least squares regression.* With this technique, the regression line is computed so that the sum of the squares of the vertical distances from each point on the scattergraph to the regression line is minimized. Thus, as a practical consideration, it is important to beware of including data points that vary significantly from the usual. Because the regression program seeks to minimize squared differences, the inclusion of these extreme outliers may significantly affect the results. Consequently, organizations often exclude data for periods of such unusual occurrences as strikes, extreme weather conditions, and shutdowns for equipment retooling. A scattergraph often reveals such outliers so they can then be easily identified and omitted.

Regression with multiple predictors

While the prediction of overhead costs in the previous example, with its adjusted R-square of .787, was considered good, management may wish to see if a better estimate might be obtained using additional predictor variables. In such a case, they examine the nature of the operation to determine which additional predictors might be useful in deriving a cost-estimation equation.

Assume Estimators, Inc., has determined that direct materials costs may also affect manufacturing overhead. The results of using both direct labor-hours (X_1) and direct materials costs (X_2) as *predictors* of overhead (Y) were obtained using a computer program. The computer output from the program using direct labor-hours and direct materials costs yields the prediction equation:

$$\text{Manufacturing overhead costs} = \text{Intercept} + b_1X_1 + b_2X_2$$
$$= \$1,334 + \$4.359X_1 + \$.258X_2$$

where X_1 refers to direct labor-hours and X_2 refers to direct materials costs. (The intercepts in the simple and multiple regressions round to the same whole number by coincidence.) The statistics supplied with the output are:

Correlation coefficient (multiple R)	.976
Multiple R-squared	.952
Adjusted multiple R-squared	.944

The correlation coefficient (now expressed as *multiple R* because it is related to more than one predictor variable) for this regression is .976, and the adjusted multiple R-squared is .944. Both of these are an improvement over the results obtained when the regression equation included only direct labor-hours.

Improved results may be expected for two reasons. First, some overhead costs may be related to direct materials costs but not to direct labor-hours (for example, storeroom maintenance). Second, price changes could affect both overhead and direct materials costs but not direct labor-hours.

To prepare a cost estimate using this multiple regression equation requires not only the estimated direct labor-hours for the coming period but the direct materials costs as well. The additional data requirements for multiple regression models may limit their usefulness in many applications. Of course, in planning for the next period's production activity, companies will usually have already estimated direct materials costs and direct labor-hours and in such a situation the added costs of obtaining data may be quite low.

For example, Estimators, Inc., estimates its direct materials cost to be $.80 per output unit based on engineering estimates of materials needed and accounting estimates of direct materials costs. Production is estimated at 4,600 units, so direct materials costs of $3,680 (4,600 units × $.80 per unit) are expected in the coming period.

Substituting the 115 direct labor-hours and the $3,680 direct materials costs in the regression equation results in the following overhead estimate:

$$\text{Overhead} = \$1,334 + (\$4.359 \times 115) + (.258 \times \$3,680)$$
$$= \$1,334 + \$501 + \$949$$
$$= \$2,784$$

This estimate has the advantage of being based on two factors (direct labor and direct materials) that appear to be jointly affecting overhead costs. The correlation coefficient is higher for this equation than for the single predictor equation. However, an increase in R, alone, should not be the sole criterion for selecting a regression model.

Using the _b_'s as variable cost estimates

When using a simple linear regression, the intercept is often considered analogous to fixed costs and the slope to variable cost. Indeed, in many companies, regression estimates are used for estimating the fixed and variable components of manufacturing overhead for overhead application and analysis. Care should be exercised when doing this, however. For example, it is possible to have negative intercepts in empirical cost data, but it is highly unlikely that a company would have negative fixed costs.

If more than one predictor variable is used, as in Estimators, Inc.'s multiple regression above, the interpretation of the b's as variable costs is somewhat more hazardous. The assignment of coefficient values under regression is unstable if the predictor variables are correlated with one another. For the multiple regression of Estimators, Inc., the following correlation matrix was part of the computer output. It shows that the direct labor-hours and direct material dollars are highly correlated with one another (that is, a correlation of .832).

Variable	_b_
Direct labor-hours	4.359
Direct materials cost	.258

CORRELATION MATRIX:

	DLH	DMC
DLH	1.00	.832
DMC	.832	1.00

This means that there is overlapping explanatory power among the two predictors. This problem is referred to as **multicollinearity.** It does not affect the Y estimate, but rather it affects the interpretation of the contribution that each of the X's (that is, direct material dollars and direct labor-hours) is making to the prediction of Y.

Regression must be used with caution   A regression estimate is still only an estimate. Computerized statistical techniques sometimes have an aura of truth about them that is undeserved. In fact, a regression estimate may be little better than an eyeball estimate based on a scattergraph. Regression has advantages, however. It is objective; it provides a number of statistics not available from other methods; and it may be the only feasible method when more than one predictor is used.

Regression is so accessible that it can be used indiscriminately with unfortunate results. We recommend that users of regression (1) fully understand the methodology and its limitations; (2) specify the model, that is, the hypothesized relationship between costs and cost predictors; (3) know the characteristics of the data being used; and (4) examine a plot of the data.

Comparison of cost estimates

Each cost estimation method may yield a different estimate of the costs that are likely to result from a particular management decision. This underscores the advantages of using two or more methods to arrive at a final estimate. The different estimates of manufacturing overhead that resulted from the use of four different estimation methods for Estimators, Inc., are summarized in Illustration 10–6.

The figures are relatively close, but there are differences. While it is impossible to state which one is best, management may find that having all four alternatives gives the best indication of the likely range within which actual costs will fall. Moreover, by observing the range of cost estimates, management may be better able to determine whether more data need to be gathered. If decisions remain unchanged for all four cost estimates, then management may conclude that further information gathering is not warranted.

Illustration 10–6   **Summary of cost estimates, Estimators, Inc.**

Method	Total estimated costs	Fixed estimated costs	Estimated variable cost
Account analysis	$2,631	$1,205	$12.40 per DLH
High-low	2,750	1,239	$13.141 per DLH
Simple regression (DLH)	2,757	1,334	$12.373 per DLH
Multiple regression (DLH + DMCª)	2,784	1,334	$4.359 per DLH + $.258 per DMC

ª DMC = direct material costs.

Learning curves

The relationship between costs and independent variables is not always linear. A systematic nonlinear relationship has been found when employees gain experience performing a particular task. As their experience increases, their productivity improves and costs per unit decrease. Experience, or learning, obviously affects direct labor costs, but it also affects costs that are related to direct labor, like supervision and many others. In some cases, materials costs may be affected due to reductions in spoilage and waste.

The learning phenomenon often occurs when new production methods are introduced, when new products (either goods or services) are made, and when new employees are hired. For example, the effect of learning on the cost of aircraft manufacturing is well known. Manufacturers of products for the defense industry often develop and produce goods with cost-based contracts. These contracts may recognize the effect of learning by establishing a lower cost for the second item of an order than for the first, a lower cost for the fourth than for the second, and so forth.

For example, National Electronics, Inc., makes an electronic navigational guidance system that is used for spacecraft, aircraft, and submarines. The direct labor to make the system is subject to an 80 percent *cumulative learning curve.* This means that the unit *average* time required for two units is 80 percent of the time required for one unit; the unit *average* time for four units is 80 percent of the *average* time required per unit for two units; and so forth.

The first unit of a production batch, or run, of guidance systems is estimated to require 1,250 direct labor-hours. If the 80 percent cumulative learning curve is used, then the *average* for two units is estimated to be 1,000 hours (.80 × 1,250 hours), a total of 2,000 hours for both units. Thus, the second unit takes 750 hours to produce (750 = 2,000 − 1,250). Four units would take an average of 800 hours each (.80 × 1,000 hours), or a total of 3,200 hours. This means that a total of 1,200 hours (3,200 − 2,000) must be expended to produce the third and fourth units.

Mathematically, the learning curve effect can be expressed as:[1]

$$Y = aX^b$$

where

Y = *average* number of labor-hours required for X units
a = number of labor-hours required for the first unit
X = cumulative number of units produced
b = *index* of learning equal to the log of the learning rate divided by the log of 2; for the example with an 80 percent cumulative learning rate, $b = -.322$

---

[1] For more detail on accounting applications of learning curves, see F. P. Kollaritsch and R. B. Jordan, "The Learning Curve: Concepts and Applications," in *The Managerial and Cost Accountant's Handbook,* eds. H. A. Black and J. D. Edwards (Homewood, Ill.: Dow Jones-Irwin, 1979), pp. 971–1017; and W. J. Morse, "Reporting Production Costs that Follow the Learning Curve Phenomenon," *The Accounting Review,* October 1972, pp. 761–73.

Thus, the number of labor-hours from the National Electronics example could be derived as follows:

	Number of labor-hours			Computations
X	Average (Y)	Total	Marginal	
1	1,250	1,250	1,250	
2	1,000	2,000	750	$Y = 1{,}250 \times (2^{-.322}) = 1{,}000$
3	878	2,634	634	$Y = 1{,}250 \times (3^{-.322}) = 878$
4	800	3,200	566	$Y = 1{,}250 \times (4^{-.322}) = 800$
⋮	⋮	⋮	⋮	⋮
8	640	5,120		$Y = 1{,}250 \times (8^{-.322}) = 640$

Illustration 10–7   **Labor hours and volume graphs, National Electronics, Inc.**

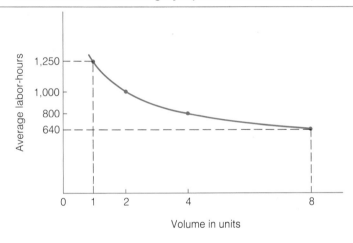

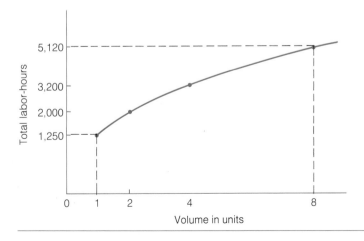

Illustration 10–7 presents the total and average labor-hours required for National Electronics, Inc. The curvilinear nature of the relationship between activity volume and labor-hours shows that the learning effects are large initially but become increasingly smaller as employees learn more about how to make the product.

The function

$$Y = aX^b$$

is curvilinear as shown in Illustration 10–7. The function is linear when expressed in logs because

$$\log Y = \log a + b \log X$$

so the function is linear when plotted on log-log paper as shown in Illustration 10–8. A good approximation of the average labor-hours required for X units can be obtained from a plot on log-log paper.

Assume that National Electronics, Inc., estimates the variable cost of producing each unit as follows:

Direct materials cost	$40,000 per unit
Direct labor	$20 per hour
Variable manufacturing overhead	$1,000 per unit plus 60 percent of direct labor costs

So the variable manufacturing cost per unit is estimated to be:

Unit No.	Direct materials	Direct labor	Variable manufacturing overhead	Total variable manufacturing cost of the unit
1	$40,000	$20 × 1,250 hours = $25,000	$1,000 + (.6 × $25,000) = $16,000	$81,000
2	40,000	$20 × 750 hours = $15,000	$1,000 + (.6 × $15,000) = $10,000	65,000
3	40,000	$20 × 634 hours = $12,680	$1,000 + (.6 × $12,680) = $8,608	61,288
4	40,000	$20 × 566 hours = $11,320	$1,000 + (.6 × $11,320) = $7,792	59,112

Applications of learning curves to accounting

The learning phenomenon applies to time, thus it could affect any costs that are a function of time. Hourly labor costs would be affected while straight piecework pay per unit would not. Any overhead costs that are affected by labor time would also be affected. For example, if 8 hours of supervisory labor are required for each 60 hours of worker time, reductions in worker time could result in a reduction in supervisory time if supervisory labor is a variable cost.

Whenever costs are estimated, the potential impact of learning should

Illustration 10–8   **Labor hours and volume—Log = log relationship**

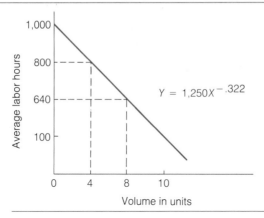

be considered. The learning phenomenon can affect costs used in inventory valuation, costs used in decision making, and costs used in performance evaluation.

Inventory valuation   Suppose production of a new product starts in January and continues through the year. The direct materials cost is $10 per unit throughout the year. Because of learning, the labor-hours (cost) per unit drops from 1 hour, at $16 per hour, in January to .25 hour in December. Manufacturing overhead, which is all fixed, is $8,000. The accountants estimate that 1,000 units will be produced in January, requiring 1,000 direct labor hours, so they apply this overhead to units at the rate of $8 per hour for inventory valuation. This same rate is (mistakenly) used throughout the year. In December of the same year, 1,000 units were produced, requiring 250 direct labor hours. Fixed manufacturing overhead was $8,000. As shown in Illustration 10–9, the overhead applied was at $8 per hour, but at only $2 per unit. The amount of overhead applied per unit should have been $8 per unit.

Decision making   A company is considering producing a new product. Fixed costs would be unaffected by the product. The variable cost of making and selling the first unit of the product is $40 per unit while the selling price is $38. At first glance, the product appears unprofitable because it doesn't even cover variable costs. However, because of learning, the variable cost will drop from $40 to $20 by the end of the first year of production, making it much more profitable.

Performance evaluation   First National Bank has developed labor time and cost standards for some of its clerical activities. These activities were subject to the learning curve phenomenon. The bank management observed

Illustration 10–9   **Effect of learning on inventory valuation**

		Unit inventory value	
		December	
	January	**Is**	**Should be**
Direct materials	$10	$10	$10
Direct labor	16 (= 1 hour × $16)	4 (= .25 hour × $16)	4
Manufacturing overhead applied	8 (= 1 hour × $8)	2 (= .25 hour × $8)	8
	$34	$16	$22

that time spent on these activities systematically exceeded the standard. Upon investigating the problem, management found high personnel turnover which meant the activities were carried out by inexperienced people. After changes were made in personnel policy, personnel turnover was reduced and the jobs were staffed with more experienced people. Hence, the time spent on clerical activities no longer exceeded standards.

Summary

Accurate cost estimation helps management to make informed decisions concerning the incurrence of future costs and how future costs may vary if conditions change. This chapter discusses four methods of cost estimation: (1) account analysis, (2) engineering estimates, (3) scattergraph and high-low estimates, and (4) statistical methods (usually employing regression analysis). Different methods of estimation are likely to produce different estimates of costs. Consequently, it is often desirable to use more than one approach and to permit management to apply its own best estimate to those arrived at by the controller's staff.

Account analysis calls for the identification of costs and judgment determination of whether a cost is fixed or variable in relation to the activity concerning which a decision is being made. Knowledge of the decision context and of the way an organization's costs relate to cost objects is very important. Once the fixed and variable portions are estimated, the total cost can be estimated by adding the fixed portion to the product of the variable portion per activity level and the activity level. The advantages of the method are its relative ease of application and its use of managerial experience and judgment. The disadvantage is that heavy reliance on judgmental decisions may cause estimates to be biased towards the decision makers personal biases or perceptions. Classification of cost behavior can be incorporated into the chart of accounts coding scheme to help facilitate future preparation of cost estimates.

Engineering estimates involve careful measurement of the actual cost-causing process. An engineer breaks the process into parts and compares what he observes to standards, specifications, and established scientific relationships. Based on these comparisons, the engineer is able to forecast what costs may be in the future given certain conditions. One form of the engineering approach to cost estimation is the time-and-motion study. The advantage of the engineering approach is that it can detail each step required to perform an operation. This provides a useful means of reviewing a company's total manufacturing process. Disadvantages are that the engineering approach is often quite expensive and that engineering estimates are often based on particular past conditions that may not occur in the future.

Scattergraphs and high-low estimates use past cost behaviors and their relation to some activity measure to estimate future costs given a specific activity level. This approach (and any other approach that uses past data) is limited to future estimates that are made within the relevant range of past activity levels. A scattergraph is a plotting of past costs along the vertical axis and of some activity measure along the horizontal axis. If the points fall into a roughly linear pattern, a line can be estimated to fit these points.

One method of determining the line is the high-low method. The high-low method takes the cost difference between the highest and lowest activity level and divides it by the difference in activity levels. This gives the slope of the line connecting the cost point at the highest activity level with the cost point at the lowest activity level. The slope represents the estimated variable cost per unit. Estimated fixed cost is determined by taking the total cost at either the highest or lowest activity level and subtracting from it the variable cost at that level. This approach is useful as an easy-to-apply method to derive cost estimates and to illustrate graphically cost behavior at different activity levels. It has the advantage of overcoming the subjectivity of the account analysis approach and the complexity of the engineering approach while still being simple to apply. Disadvantages include a tendency to project costs beyond the relevant range and the possibility of the highest and lowest points being unrepresentative of typical operating conditions.

The primary statistical method is called ordinary least squares regression. Like the scattergraph approach, past data are used, but unlike the high-low approach to estimating costs, all of the data points are used to estimate future variable and fixed costs at expected activity levels. In addition to cost estimates, regression is able to provide a number of additional statistics that aid in the estimate.

The focus of the regression portion of the chapter is on obtaining a basic understanding of the approach and the initial cost estimation from regression output provided by computers or calculators. Past data are plotted on a scattergraph and a mathematically determined line of best fit (minimal variation) is formed. Care must be used to exclude any unrepresentative outliers and to restrict cost estimates to the relevant range. It is also important to understand how independent variables (predictors) are used and how their relationship to the dependent variable (the cost to be estimated) helps to arrive at a regression equation. The correlation coefficient *(R)* and the adjusted *R*-square help to indicate the amount of the past cost variation that is explained by the predictors. Simple regression uses only one predictor while multiple regression uses more than one predictor to help explain a particular cost.

A common nonlinear relationship between costs and activity is the systematic relation between labor time and experience. This learning curve phenomenon implies that unit costs go down as more and more units are made (up to a point) because labor time per unit decreases. The potential impact of the phenomenon should be considered whenever costs are estimated.

Terms and concepts	The following terms and concepts should be familiar to you after reading this chapter.

Account analysis	**Independent variables**
Adjusted *R*-square	**Intercept and slope of cost line**
Correlation coefficient	**Learning curves**
Dependent variable	**Learning phenomenon**
Engineering estimates	**Predictors**
Estimate	**Regression**
Fixed cost	**Scattergraph**
High-low cost estimation	**Variable cost**

Note: The self-study problem(s) for this chapter follows the Appendix.

Appendix: Technical notes on regression	This appendix discusses some of the practical implementation and technical problems that often arise when regression analysis is used.
Practical implementation problems	Computers and hand-held calculators have greatly simplified regression analysis and made it available to more people. Consequently, this method has been increasingly used and potentially misused. In particular, people may be tempted to enter many variables into a regression model without careful thought to their validity. The results can be disastrous.

Some of the more common problems with using simple (one-predictor) regression estimates include: (1) attempting to fit a linear equation to nonlinear data, (2) failing to exclude outliers, and (3) including predictors with apparent but spurious relationships.

Effect of nonlinear relationships   The effect of attempting to fit a linear model to nonlinear data is likely to be seen when a company is operating close to capacity limits. Close to maximum capacity, costs accelerate more rapidly than activity due to shift differentials and overtime premiums paid to employees, increased maintenance and repair costs for equipment, and similar factors. The linear cost estimate understates the slope of the cost line in the ranges close to capacity. This situation is shown in Illustration 10–10.

Illustration 10–10   **Effect of fitting a linear model to nonlinear data**

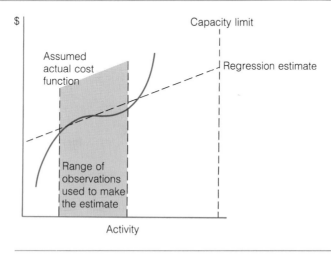

One way to overcome the problem would be to define a relevant range of activity up to, say, 80 percent capacity, and use the range for one set of cost-estimating regression equations. Another equation could be derived for the 81 percent to 100 percent capacity levels.

Another approach is to use nonlinear regression techniques to estimate the curve directly. However, nonlinear regression does not provide a constant variable cost estimate—the estimate is different at each level.

Effect of outliers   Because regression seeks to minimize the sum of the squared deviations from the regression line, observations that lie a significant distance away from the line may have an overwhelming effect on the regression estimates. Illustration 10–11 shows a case in which most of the data points lie close to a straight line, but due to the effect of one significant outlier, the computed regression line is a significant distance from most of the points.

This kind of problem can easily arise in accounting settings. Suppose a year's worth of supplies was purchased and expensed entirely in one month, or a large adjustment was made for underaccruing payroll taxes. The accounting records in such cases are clearly abnormal with respect to the activity measure. An inspection of a plot of the data can sometimes reveal this problem.

Illustration 10–11   **Effect of failure to exclude outliers**

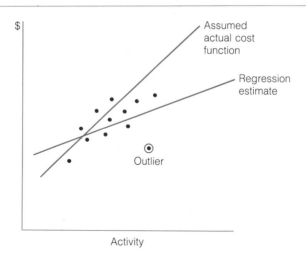

When an extreme outlier appears in a data set, scrutiny of the output from the regression equation will rarely identify it. Instead, a plot of the regression line on the data points is usually needed. If multiple predictors are used, an outlier will be even more difficult to find. The best way to avoid this problem is to examine the data in advance and eliminate highly unusual observations *before* running the regression.

Spurious relationships   It is sometimes tempting to feed the computer a lot of data and let the regression program "find" relationships among variables. This can lead to spurious relationships. For example, there may appear to be a relationship between Variable 1 and Variable 2, when, in fact, Variable 3, which was left out of the equation, explains the situation. Early medical studies that found an apparent relationship between smoking and heart disease were criticized because the relationship may have been spurious. Numerous other variables that may have been correlated with both smoking and heart disease, like the patient's diet and emotional characteristics, were left out.

It is important to have a good model for constructing regression equations. A cause-and-effect relation should exist between the predictor variable and the dependent variable. If such a relation does not exist, it is still possible to obtain a good fit and a regression estimate that, on the surface, appears significant. However, there is no assurance that the relation will continue into the future.

For example, there may be a good *statistical* relation between indirect labor costs and energy costs. One might create a regression equation using such a relation and find that the regression explains much of the change in indirect labor costs. However, there is no *logical* relation between the two costs. Both indirect labor and energy costs are driven by inflationary factors, but there is no cause-and-effect relationship between them.

Problems with correlation of the residuals

As previously discussed, a computed regression equation can be used to estimate a Y value for any set of X values. But care should be taken not to extrapolate beyond the set of data included in the regression. In addition, it is important that each observation be independent. The differences between the *estimated* Y values (found on the regression line) and the actual Y's should be randomly distributed. These differences are called residuals. If a residual is random, its expected value is zero for any observation.

If the residuals are not randomly distributed, the residual for any observation may be statistically related to the residual for another observation. The expected value for the residual is not zero. One such condition in which residuals are related to each other because observations are related to each other over time is known as *serial correlation* or *autocorrelation.* When the residuals are related to each other, the correlation coefficients and the presence of autocorrelation may be tested by using the Durbin-Watson statistic, which is usually provided on the output when regression is run on a computer. Another approach is to obtain a plot of the residuals over time from the regression program. If there is a pattern in the plotted residuals, then an autocorrelation problem exists. To cure the problem, it may be necessary to obtain additional predictor variables so that the reason for the correlation among residuals can be explained in the form of another variable in the model.

Confidence intervals for cost estimates

When making predictions about future costs, it is almost impossible to develop an estimate that will be exactly equal to the costs that are finally incurred. While it is not possible to eliminate all estimation error, it is possible to place bounds on an estimate so that a decision maker can know the range of likely costs. These bounds are usually expressed in the form of a *prediction interval,* sometimes called a confidence interval.

A prediction interval represents a range within which the actual cost is expected to fall a specified percentage of the time. Thus, a 95 percent prediction interval would represent a range within which the actual costs are expected to fall 95 percent of the time. The boundaries of a prediction interval are based on the assumption that the residuals from a regression are normally distributed. If this assumption holds, then the boundaries are equal to the predicted Y value plus or minus the standard error of the estimate of Y times the t-statistic for the specified prediction level. This may be expressed mathematically as:

$$Y \pm t \times SE_Y.$$

The t-statistic would be obtained from a table of Student's t that can be found in statistics textbooks or in most applications from a computer output. The wider the desired prediction interval, the larger the value of t, all other things equal.

The standard error of estimate (SE_Y) for a simple regression is

$$SE_Y = SE \sqrt{1 + \frac{1}{n} + \frac{(X' - \overline{X})^2}{\Sigma(X_i - \overline{X})^2}}$$

where

SE = the standard error of the regression
n = the number of observations
X' = the value of X for which the estimate is desired
$\overline{X}$ = the mean of the X values in the data set
X_i = the value of each X in the data set

The more distant the specified X value is from the mean, the wider the prediction interval.

For example, assume management of Estimators, Inc., had estimated the overhead costs for 115 direct labor-hours as follows:

$$Y = \$1,334 + \$12.373 \text{ per DLH}$$
$$= \$1,334 + \$12.373 \times 115 \text{ DLH}$$
$$= \$2,757$$

The computer output for the regression indicated a standard error for the regression of $182. The standard error of estimate for a Y based on 115 direct labor-hours is $192 computed as follows:

$$SE_Y = \$182 \times \sqrt{1 + \frac{1}{15} + \frac{(115 - 91.6)^2}{11,455.6}}$$
$$= \$182 \times \sqrt{1 + .06667 + .04780}$$
$$= \$182 \times 1.05568$$
$$= \$192$$

The computer would provide the information necessary to construct the prediction interval and, in many cases, would compute the interval itself. In this example, we obtain the following output from the computer (or from a statistics book for the t-statistic):

Standard error of the regression	$182
Standard error of estimate (115 hours)	$192
t-statistic for 95% confidence interval, $n = 15$; $n - 2 = 13$	2.160

The prediction interval is computed as:

$$\$2,757 \pm (\$192 \times 2.160) = \$2,757 \pm \$415$$

the upper limit of the prediction interval is

$$\$3,172 = \$2,757 + \$415$$

and the lower limit is

$$\$2,342 = \$2,757 - \$415$$

which means that we are 95 percent confident that the overhead will be between $2,342 and $3,172 when an activity level of 115 direct labor-hours is attained.

Heteroscedasticity

This prediction interval assumes that the standard deviation for the regression is constant over all of the values used in the regression equation. The variance in cost data may not be constant over all levels of costs. This condition is known as *heteroscedasticity*. When heteroscedasticity is present, prediction intervals will be incorrectly estimated.

To determine if heteroscedasticity is present, a plot of the residuals over different values of Y is needed. If the scatter of residuals is not constant over these Y values, the assumption of constant variance may be rejected. The problem may be cured by transforming the variables (X's and Y's) to their logarithms or square roots, or by constructing a regression with a new set of variables. Alternatively, one might adjust the confidence intervals at different activity levels.

In any event, the cost estimate itself is still the expected value for Y. The major practical problem is that the confidence intervals that might be constructed around Y are in error.

Prediction intervals for the *b*'s

In many cases, it may be desirable to determine if the b's are significantly different from zero. The t-statistic is used to test for the significance of b's.

To test whether the computed b is statistically different from zero, a t-statistic is computed. This t is simply the value of b divided by its standard error (SE_b). For the data used in the simple regression for Estimators, Inc., the t-statistic for the coefficient is

$$t = \frac{b}{SE_b}$$
$$= \frac{12.373}{1.703}$$
$$= 7.267$$

where the SE_b of 1.703 is given by the computer output. As a rule of thumb, a t of 2.0 or better may usually be considered significant. We reject the hypotheses that the regression results are due to chance and that the true value of b is zero.

To construct a 95 percent confidence interval around b, we would take the computed b and add or subtract the appropriate t value for the 95 percent confidence interval times the standard error of b. The confidence interval is:

$$b \pm t \times SE_b$$

The computer output for this example gives $SE_b = 1.703$

The value of t for a 95 percent confidence interval may be obtained from a table of t values in a statistics book.

$$t_{SE_b} = 2.160$$

Hence, the confidence intervals are:

$$b \pm 2.160 \times 1.703$$
$$= b \pm 3.678$$

With b equal to \$12.373, the upper limit would be:

$$\$16.051 \text{ (that is, } \$12.373 + \$3.678)$$

while the lower confidence limit would be:

$$\$8.695 \text{ (that is, } \$12.373 - \$3.678)$$

We would be 95 percent confident that the variable cost coefficient is between \$8.695 and \$16.051. These limits are quite wide. To narrow the limits, it is necessary to construct a better-fitting regression, if one can be constructed.

Self-study problem: Propylon Textiles*

Propylon, the wonder fabric of the 1980s, was the brain child of Henry Carr, scion of an old banking family. Pursuing his special interest in polymers as a chemistry graduate student, Carr had created a synthetic compound whose polymer threads were far superior to any of the synthetics in the textile industry. The fabric was crease resistant, wrinkle free, and it simulated the appearance and feel of natural fiber fabrics. Propylon took the world by storm when production began three years ago. In addition to its versatility, propylon is extremely strong and durable, heat resistant, and "breathes" like natural fibers.

By the second year, Propylon Textiles had reached its current production level with 10 product lines. Now after the third year of production, Natalie Martin, the controller, decided that the company had enough data to merit a detailed analysis of its overhead cost behavior.

The following monthly overhead costs were recorded for the previous two years:

---

* © Michael W. Maher, 1982. Prepared by Jean M. Lim under the supervision of Michael W. Maher.

Cost data for Propylon Textiles (in thousands)

Month, first year

	J	F	M	A	M	J	J	A	S	O	N	D	Two-year totals
Indirect materials	$ 22	$20	$ 23	$ 24	$ 22	$21	$20	$19	$19	$18	$18	$20	$ 503
Indirect labor	40	30	40	40	40	30	20	10	10	10	10	20	630
Lease	12	12	12	12	12	12	12	12	12	12	12	12	288
Utilities	9	9	8	8	8	7	8	7	8	8	9	9	206
Power	5	4	5	6	6	5	3	3	3	2	2	4	104
Insurance	1	1	1	1	1	1	1	1	1	1	1	1	24
Maintenance	20	6	6	6	6	6	20	6	6	6	6	6	200
Depreciation	2	2	2	2	2	2	2	2	2	2	2	2	72
Research and development	7	8	10	9	8	10	6	6	7	4	5	8	171
Total overhead	$118	$92	$107	$108	$105	$94	$92	$66	$68	$63	$65	$82	$2,198
Direct labor-hours	36.0	34.2	37.4	37.8	36.4	35.0	33.2	30.8	30.9	29.4	30.0	33.4	815.8 hours
Direct labor costs ($)	216.0	205.2	224.4	226.8	218.4	210.0	199.2	184.8	185.4	176.4	180.0	200.4	$4,997.4
Machine-hours	45.0	42.6	45.0	47.0	45.2	43.6	41.2	40.0	39.4	37.2	36.5	42.0	1,022.7 hours
Units produced	8.9	8.6	9.2	9.5	8.9	8.6	8.0	7.8	7.6	7.4	7.2	8.1	202.5 units

Month, second year

	J	F	M	A	M	J	J	A	S	O	N	D
Indirect materials	$21	$21	$ 23	$ 24	$24	$21	$ 22	$20	$19	$19	$21	$22
Indirect labor	20	30	40	50	30	30	30	20	10	10	30	30
Lease	12	12	12	12	12	12	12	12	12	12	12	12
Utilities	10	10	9	9	8	8	8	8	9	9	10	10
Power	5	5	6	7	6	4	5	4	2	2	5	5
Insurance	1	1	1	1	1	1	1	1	1	1	1	1
Maintenance	20	6	6	6	6	6	20	6	6	6	6	6
Depreciation	4	4	4	4	4	4	4	4	4	4	4	4
Research and development	6	8	1	9	8	8	7	7	7	5	8	9
Total overhead	$99	$97	$102	$122	$99	$94	$109	$82	$70	$68	$97	$99
Direct labor-hours	33.2	34.2	36.9	39.6	35.2	34.0	35.2	32.4	30.2	30.4	34.2	35.8
Direct labor costs ($)	207.5	213.7	230.6	247.5	220.0	212.5	220.0	202.5	188.7	190.0	213.7	223.7
Machine-hours	43.4	43.2	46.4	50.0	44.2	42.6	43.2	41.2	38.2	37.6	43.8	44.2
Units produced	8.4	8.6	9.1	9.8	8.9	8.4	8.7	8.1	7.7	7.5	8.6	8.9

You are a financial analyst at Propylon Textiles and have been asked by the controller to prepare a report on the firm's overhead cost behavior.

Exhibit A presents some computer output to help you with the analysis.

Exhibit A   **(SSP 1)**

SUBPROBLEM NO. 1:

Dependent variable = Overhead

Independent variables: DL hrs., DL cost, M hrs., units produced

R-square = .8935   R-square adjusted = .8710

Standard error of the regression[a] = 6.2190

Variable Name	No.	Estimated Coefficient	Standard Error[a]	T-Ratio[a] 19 DF
DL hrs.	1	3.1337	2.7705	1.1311
DL cost	2	.30600	.32961	.92839
M hrs.	3	.79964	2.0756	.38526
Units produced	4	−.09679	12.539	.00772
Intercept		−111.91	17.246	−6.4892

24 observations

Correlation matrix of coefficients:

Variable

1	.94063			
2	.93340	.96964		
3	.92895	.97321	.96158	
4	.93276	.98177	.97041	.97951
	1 DL hrs.	2 DL cost	3 M hrs.	4 units produced

SUBPROBLEM NO. 2:

Dependent variable = Overhead

Independent variable: DL hrs.

R-square = .8848   R-square adjusted = .8796

Standard error of the regression[a] = 6.0101

Variable Name	No.	Estimated Coefficient	Standard Error[a]	T-Ratio[a] 22 DF
DL hrs.	1	5.9676	.45910	12.999
Intercept		−111.27	15.654	−7.1079

24 observations

SUBPROBLEM NO. 3:

Dependent variable = Overhead

Independent variable: DL cost

R-square = .8712   R-square adjusted = .8654

Standard error of the regression[a] = 6.3538

Variable Name	No.	Estimated Coefficient	Standard Error[a]	T-Ratio[a] 22 DF
DL cost	2	.91426	.07493	12.201
Intercept		−98.789	15.657	−6.3096

24 observations

SUBPROBLEM NO. 4:

Dependent variable = Overhead

Independent variable: M hrs.

R-square = .8630   R-square adjusted = .8567

Standard error of the regression[a] = 6.5551

Variable Name	No.	Estimated Coefficient	Standard Error[a]	T-Ratio[a] 22 DF
M hrs.	3	4.9015	.41645	11.770
Intercept		−117.28	17.796	−6.5902
24 observations				

SUBPROBLEM NO. 5:

Dependent variable = Overhead

Independent variable: Units produced

R-square = .8700   R-square adjusted = .8641

Standard error of the regression[a] = 6.3834

Variable Name	No.	Estimated Coefficient	Standard Error[a]	T-Ratio[a] 22 DF
Units produced	4	23.799	1.9610	12.136
Intercept		−109.22	16.597	−6.5805
24 observations				

[a] Discussed in the chapter Appendix.

Required:

a. Using the account analysis method, calculate the monthly average for fixed costs and the variable cost rate per—

(1) Direct labor-hour.
(2) Machine-hour.
(3) Unit of output.

To help you, the comptroller has classified the various accounts as follows:

Account	Cost behavior
Indirect Materials	Variable
Indirect Labor	Variable
Lease	Fixed
Utilities	Fixed
Power	Variable
Insurance	Fixed
Maintenance	Fixed
Depreciation	Fixed
Research and Development	Fixed

b. Plot direct labor costs against total overhead. Are there any outliers? If so, determine possible causes.

c. Using the high-low method, identify the fixed and variable components for the following activity bases:

(1) Direct labor-hours.
(2) Direct labor costs.
(3) Machine-hours.
(4) Units of output.

Explain the apparent negative fixed costs.

d. (Appendix) Subproblem 1 in the computer output (Exhibit A) is a multiple linear regression with overhead as the dependent variable and direct labor-hours, direct labor costs, machine-hours, and units of output as independent variables. Explain the paradox between the high adjusted R^2 value and low t-statistics (labeled T-Ratio in the output).

e. Subproblems 2, 3, 4, and 5 in the computer output (Exhibit A) are simple linear regressions with overhead as the dependent variable and independent variables of direct labor-hours, direct labor costs, machine-hours, and units of output, respectively. Select the most appropriate activity base for overhead cost and explain your choice.

f. Plot indirect labor costs against direct labor-hours. What kind of cost behavior pattern do you observe?

g. Using the activity base selected in (e), sketch the overhead cost function. What does this overhead cost function tell you about the relationship between current production levels and capacity?

h. Verify the computer output in Exhibit A for Subproblems 1, 2, 3, 4, and 5 by entering the data in a computer or calculator.

Suggested solution to self-study problem

a.

Indirect materials	$ 503,000
Indirect labor	630,000
Power	104,000
Total variable costs	$1,237,000
Lease	$ 288,000
Utilities	206,000
Insurance	24,000
Maintenance	200,000
Depreciation	72,000
Research and development	171,000
Total fixed costs	$ 961,000

$$\text{Monthly fixed costs} = \frac{\$961,000}{24} = \$40,042$$

$$\text{Variable cost per DLH} = \frac{\$1,237,000}{815,800} = \$1.516$$

$$\text{Variable cost per machine-hour} = \frac{\$1,237,000}{1,022,700} = \$1.210$$

$$\text{Variable cost per unit produced} = \frac{\$1,237,000}{202,500} = \$6.11$$

b.

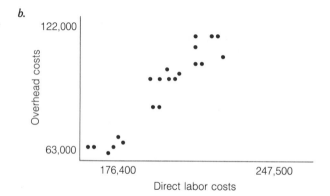

The first observation ($216,000; $118,000) appears to be an outlier. The most probable cause for the higher overhead cost is the relatively higher amount spent on maintenance that month. (Only 23 points are shown because 2 points are the same—namely, February and November of the second year.)

c. (1) Direct labor-hours:

$$V = \frac{\$122,000 - \$63,000}{39,600 - 29,400} = \underline{\underline{\$5.784}}$$

$$F = \$63,000 - \$5.784(29,400) = \underline{\underline{-\$107,050}}$$

(2) Direct labor costs:

$$V = \frac{\$122,000 - \$63,000}{247,500 - 176,400} = \underline{\underline{\$.830}}$$

$$F = \$63,000 - \$.830(176,400) = \underline{\underline{-\$83,412}}$$

(3) Machine-hours:

$$V = \frac{\$122,000 - \$63,000}{50,000 - 37,200} = \underline{\underline{\$4.609}}$$

$$F = \$63,000 - \$4.609(37,200) = \underline{\underline{-\$108,455}}$$

(4) Units of output:

$$V = \frac{\$122,000 - \$63,000}{9,800 - 7,400} = \underline{\underline{\$24.583}}$$

$$F = \$63,000 - \$24.583(7,400) = \underline{\underline{-\$118,914}}$$

The fixed costs appear to be negative because the estimate is made outside the relevant range. The implicit assumption of the above calculations is that unit variable costs are unchanged for all levels of production.

d. (Appendix) The independent variables are correlated to one another giving rise to the problem of multicollinearity. This causes large standard errors resulting in low t-statistics. Nevertheless, most of the variance in the dependent variable is explained by the fitted line, and hence the high adjusted R-square.

e. Based on the highest adjusted R-square and t-statistic, direct labor-hours would be the most appropriate activity base. Machine-hours may not be appropriate if processes for the various product lines are radically different. Since there are 10 product lines, units of output would not be a good activity base. In any event, statistical analysis alone is not sufficient for picking the activity base.

f.

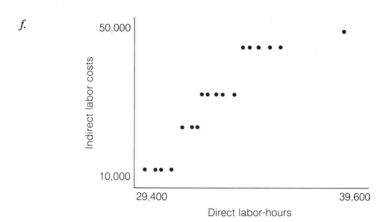

The costs are semifixed or step costs. Note that this is inconsistent with the controller's classification of these costs as "variable costs." (Not all 24 data points are presented because some points are the same in different months; February of the first year is the same as February of the second year, for example.)

g.

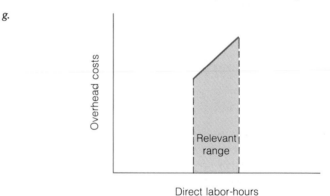

The steepness of the overhead function within the relevant range seems to imply that the firm is currently operating at capacity and is facing increasing marginal costs. In the long run, the company should seriously consider capacity expansion.

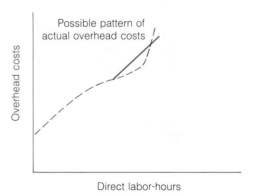

h. See output in Exhibit **A.**

Questions

10–1. Which method of cost estimation is not usually based on company records?

10–2. The following costs are labeled fixed or variable according to a typical designation in accounting. Identify the circumstances under which any of these costs would behave in a manner opposite to that listed:
  a. Direct labor—variable.
  b. Equipment depreciation—fixed.
  c. Utilities (with a minimum charge)—variable.
  d. Supervisory salaries—fixed.
  e. Indirect materials purchased in given sizes that become spoiled within a few days—variable.

10–3. What is the connection between the relevant range and the range of observations included in a data set for cost estimation purposes?

10–4. Why would a long-time executive prefer account analysis to statistical cost estimation methods?

10–5. If one simply wishes to prepare a cost estimate using regression analysis and enters data into a program to compute regression estimates, what problems might the person encounter?

10–6. When preparing cost estimates for account analysis purposes, should the costs be extracted from the historical accounting records?

10–7. How can one compensate for the effects of price instability when preparing cost estimates using high-low or regression techniques?

10–8. Under what conditions would engineering based cost estimates be preferred to other estimation techniques?

10–9. When using cost estimation methods based on past data, what are the trade-offs between gathering more data and gathering less?

10–10. The scatter diagram and the regression methods seem to go hand in hand. Why?

10–11. (Appendix) What considerations need to be included when constructing a confidence interval for a specific cost estimate *(Y)?*

10–12. What problems might arise when multiple independent variables are used?

10–13. (Appendix) A decision maker is interested in obtaining a cost estimate based on a regression equation. There are no problems with changes in prices, costs, technology, or relationships between activity and cost. Only one variable is to be used. What caveats might be in order if a regression is prepared for this purpose?

10–14. When using past data to predict a cost that has fixed and variable components, it is possible to have an equation with a negative intercept. Does this mean that at a zero production level the company will make money on its fixed costs? Explain.

Exercises

The accounting records of a company indicate the following manufacturing costs were incurred in the past year:

10–15 Account analysis cost estimation

Direct materials	$210,000
Direct labor	241,500
Manufacturing overhead	372,800

These costs were incurred to produce 70,000 units of product. Fixed manufacturing overhead amounts to $240,000.

For the coming year, the direct materials costs are expected to increase by 20 percent, excluding any effects of volume changes. Direct labor rates are scheduled to increase by 10 percent. Fixed manufacturing overhead is expected to increase 7.5 percent, and variable manufacturing overhead per unit is expected to remain the same.

Required:

a. Prepare a cost estimate for an activity level of 80,000 units of product.
b. Determine the costs per unit for last year and for this year.

10–16. High-low cost estimates

During the past five years, operations at a company have remained relatively stable. Over this time, the following data are available from the accounting records:

Item	Highest amount	Lowest amount
Marketing costs	$ 213,600	$ 129,300
Dollar sales	4,103,200	2,130,400

Required:

a. Use the high-low method to estimate the fixed and variable portion of the company's selling costs.
b. Estimate the selling costs for a sales volume of $3,750,000.

10–17. Using cost estimates in decisions

A company manager wishes to estimate the costs to make the packaging materials for the department's output rather than to purchase the packaging material from an outside supplier. A special machine will be required. The machine will be housed in some unused space in the company's existing production area. The machine can be rented at a cost of $200 per 40-hour week.

In addition, someone must operate the machine. The operator will be paid at a rate of $7.50 per hour. The machine can produce 100 units per hour.

The manager has prepared the following estimates of the costs per hundred units of packaging material manufactured in the company plant. These estimates are:

Direct materials	$14.20
Direct labor	7.50
Labor fringe benefits	2.00
Machine rental	5.00
Power to run machine	1.10
Other variable overhead	.35
Factory space costs	3.80
Total cost to make	$33.95

Comparing this amount to the purchase cost of $32 per hundred units, the manager concludes that the company should buy the units rather than make them.

Required:

Would your recommendation be the same as the manager's? Why or why not?

10–18. Interpreting regression data

The advertising manager of a company wanted to determine if the company's advertising program was successful. The manager used a pocket calculator to determine the relationship between advertising expenditures (the independent variable) and sales dollars. Monthly data for the past two years were entered into the calculator. The regression results indicated the following equation:

$$\text{Sales dollars} = \$845,000 - \$520 \times \text{Advertising}$$
$$\text{Correlation coefficient} = -.902$$

These results might imply that the advertising was reducing sales. The manager was about to conclude that statistical methods were so much nonsense when you walked in the room.

Required:

Help the manager. Why would there appear to be a negative relationship between advertising expenditures and sales?

10-19. Interpreting regression results

While preparing cost estimates of factory overhead, the controller suggested the use of regression analysis as one method of estimation. It was decided that the factory overhead could best be estimated using direct labor costs. Data were gathered for the past two years and entered into a regression program. The following output was obtained:

REGRESSION RESULTS:

Equation:
Intercept	$21,405
Slope	1.150

Statistical data:
Correlation coefficient	.872
R-square	.760
Adjusted R-square	.731

The company is planning on operating at a level that would call for direct labor costs of $24,000 per month for the coming year.

Required:

a. Use the regression output to write the overhead cost equation.
b. Based on the cost equation, compute the estimated overhead cost per month for the coming year.
c. Comment on the regression.

10-20. Interpreting regression data (Appendix)

The following output was obtained from a regression program that was used to estimate personnel department costs as a function of the number of employees in a company:

REGRESSION RESULTS:

Equation:
Personnel costs = $5,310 + $408 × Employees

Statistical data:
Correlation coefficient	.923
(R-squared)	.852
Adjusted R-square	.834
Standard error of slope	34.250
t-statistic for slope	11.912

Monthly data for the past two years were used to construct these estimates. Cost relationships are expected to be the same for the coming period.

Required:

a. Compute the estimated personnel costs for 28 employees.
b. Construct a 95 percent confidence interval for this cost prediction. The standard error of estimate is $582.30. (Use t = 2.074.)
c. Construct a 95 percent confidence interval for the slope coefficient. (Use t = 2.074.)

Problems and cases

10–21. Regression results—process costing

Management of Waverly Processing, Inc., has been attempting to obtain better cost estimates so that they can evaluate the company's operations in a more satisfactory manner. As a new management trainee, you recall some of the cost-estimation techniques discussed in cost accounting and suggest that these techniques may be useful in this situation.

The following data are given to you for analysis purposes:

Month	Equivalent production	Total overhead
1	1,425	$12,185
2	950	9,875
3	1,130	10,450
4	1,690	15,280
5	1,006	9,915
6	834	9,150
7	982	10,133
8	1,259	11,981
9	1,385	12.045
10	1,420	13,180
11	1,125	11,910
12	980	10,431

During the current month, the beginning work in process inventory contained 1,000 units that were 65 percent complete with respect to conversion costs. The manufacturing department transferred out 1,500 units this month. There were 1,200 units in the ending inventory, and these units were 30 percent complete with respect to conversion costs.

Using the above information, you go to the regression program in your computer and obtain the following output:

REGRESSION RESULTS:

Equation:
Intercept	$3,709
Slope	6.487

Statistical data:
Correlation coefficient (R)	.956
Adjusted R-square	.904

Required:

a. Use the high-low method to estimate the overhead cost function.
b. Use the regression method to estimate the overhead cost function.
c. Compute the equivalent units of production with respect to conversion costs for the current period.
d. Use the regression results to estimate the overhead costs for the current period.

10–22. Overhead cost estimation using high-low, scattergraph, and regression

The Franklin Plant of the Ramon Company manufactures electrical components. Plant management has been experiencing some difficulties with fluctuating monthly overhead costs. Management wants to be able to estimate overhead costs accurately to plan its operations and its financial needs. A trade association publication reports that for companies manufacturing electrical components, overhead tends to vary with direct labor-hours.

A member of the controller's staff proposed that the cost behavior pattern of these overhead costs be determined. It would then be possible to estimate overhead costs using direct labor-hours.

Another member of the accounting staff suggested that a good starting place for determining cost behavior patterns would be to analyze historical data.

Following this suggestion, monthly data were gathered on direct labor-hours and overhead costs for the past two years. It should be noted that there were no major changes in operations over this period of time.

The raw data are as follows:

Month number	Direct labor-hours	Overhead costs
1	20,000	$84,000
2	25,000	99,000
3	22,000	89,500
4	23,000	90,000
5	20,000	81,500
6	19,000	75,500
7	14,000	70,500
8	10,000	64,500
9	12,000	69,000
10	17,000	75,000
11	16,000	71,500
12	19,000	78,000
13	21,000	86,000
14	24,000	93,000
15	23,000	93,000
16	22,000	87,000
17	20,000	80,000
18	18,000	76,500
19	12,000	67,500
20	13,000	71,000
21	15,000	73,500
22	17,000	72,500
23	15,000	71,000
24	18,000	75,000

These data were entered into a computer regression program. The following output was obtained:

REGRESSION OUTPUT:

R-square	.9109
Coefficient of correlation	.9544
Coefficients of the equation:	
Intercept (slope)	39,859
Independent variable	2.1549

Required:

a. Use the high-low method to estimate the overhead costs of the Franklin Plant.

b. Prepare a scattergraph showing the overhead costs plotted against the direct labor-hours.

c. Use the results of the regression analysis to prepare the cost estimation equation and to prepare a cost estimate for 22,500 direct labor-hours.

d. Of the three methods, which one should be used for estimating overhead costs at the Franklin Plant? Explain.

(CMA adapted)

10–23. Cost estimates using account analysis, simple and multiple regression

Mountain View Outdoor Products Corporation has prepared a schedule of estimated overhead costs for the coming year. This schedule was prepared on the assumption that production would equal 80,000 units. Costs have been classified as fixed or variable according to the judgment of the controller.

The following overhead items and the classification as fixed or variable form the basis for the overhead cost schedule:

Item	Total cost
Indirect materials	$ 37,500 (all variable)
Indirect labor	194,200 ($171,000 fixed)
Building occupancy	236,420 (all fixed)
Power	27,210 (all variable)
Equipment depreciation	181,000 (all fixed)
Equipment maintenance	24,330 ($8,500 fixed)
Personal property taxes	14,100 ($6,350 fixed)
Data processing	11,220 ($9,470 fixed)
Techincal support	16,940 (all fixed)
Total estimated overhead	$742,920

In the past, the overhead costs have been related to production levels. However, price instability has led management to suggest that explicit consideration be given to including an appropriate price index in the cost equation. While management realizes that to estimate future costs using a regression model that includes both production and a price index as independent variables requires predicting a future value not only for production but for the price index as well, at least some recognition would be given to the dramatic price changes that have been experienced in the past few years. For cost estimation purposes, it is assumed that the next value of the index will be the same as the last period value of the index.

Following management instructions, data were gathered on past costs, production levels, and an appropriate price index. These data are:

Overhead costs	Production (units)	Price index
$718,480	62,800	89
735,110	72,800	90
768,310	93,400	93
717,670	56,900	95
715,960	58,800	98
726,880	69,000	100
753,420	87,000	101
777,640	98,000	103
720,410	59,200	103
718,100	62,600	106
736,800	73,100	108
714,220	60,400	113

There have not been any significant changes in operations over the period covered by these data nor are there any significant changes expected in the coming period.

When the data above were entered into a regression program using only the production level as the independent variable, the following results were obtained:

REGRESSION RESULTS:

Equation:
  Overhead = $626,547 + $1.504 × Production (units)

Statistical data:
    Correlation coefficient   .988
    R-squared   .976
    Adjusted R-square   .974

When both predictors were entered in the regression program, the following results were obtained:

MULTIPLE REGRESSION RESULTS:

Equation:
    Overhead = \$632,640 + (\$1.501 × Production) − (\$59.067 × Index)

Statistical data:
    Correlation coefficient (multiple R)   .988
    R-square   .976
    Adjusted R-square   .972

Correlation matrix:

	Production	Index
Production	1.00	−.087
Index	−.087	1.00

Required

a. Prepare a cost estimation equation using the account analysis approach.

b. Use the high-low method to prepare a cost estimate for the activity expected in the coming period.

c. Prepare a cost estimate using simple linear regression.

d. Use the multiple regression results to prepare an estimate of overhead costs for the coming period.

e. Comment on which method you think is most appropriate under the circumstances.

10–24. Simple regression—effect of data problems

The company you have recently started working for is preparing an estimate of its production costs for the coming period. The controller has already determined that direct materials costs amount to \$7.35 per unit and that direct labor costs amount to \$15.40. Overhead is to be applied on the basis of direct labor costs. However, estimation of total overhead is a somewhat more difficult problem.

The controller's office indicated that it estimated overhead costs at \$300 for fixed costs and \$12 per unit for variable costs. Your nemesis on the staff, Farleigh O. Tuvvit, has suggested that the company use the regression approach. Farleigh has already done the analysis on a home computer and reports that the "correct" cost equation is:

$$\text{Overhead} = \$883 + \$10.70 \text{ per unit}$$

Farleigh further reports that the correlation coefficient for the regression is equal to .82, and with 82 percent of the variation in overhead explained by the equation, it certainly should be adopted as the best basis for estimating costs.

When asked for the data used to generate the regression, Farleigh produces the following list:

Month	Overhead	Unit production
1	$4,762	381
2	5,063	406
3	6,420	522
4	4,701	375
5	6,783	426
6	6,021	491
7	5,321	417
8	6,133	502
9	6,481	515
10	5,004	399
11	5,136	421
12	6,160	510
13	6,104	486

The company controller is somewhat surprised that the cost estimates would be so different. You have, therefore, been given the task of checking out Farleigh's equation.

State your reasons for supporting or rejecting Farleigh's cost equation.

10–25. Multiple regression interpretation (Appendix)

Malibu Products Corporation molds fiberglass into automobile bodies that are replicas of antique cars. A major component of the company's overhead is the costs of handling materials used in the molding process. It was suggested at a recent meeting of the controller and the production vice president that past data be reviewed to see if a relationship could be found between the materials-handling costs and some predictor variable. The production vice president suggested that the quantity of materials be used. The controller suggested that the dollar value of the materials be used since the dollar value would explicitly include the effects of price fluctuations. It was also noted in the discussion that some of the materials-handling costs seem to vary with the number of shipments received in a month.

Data were gathered on materials-handling costs, weight of materials received, dollar value of receipts, and number of shipments. The data were gathered for the past 18 months. Eighteen months ago the semiautomated handling equipment that is in use today was installed. Prior to that time a manual system was in use.

The data appear as follows:

Materials-handling costs	Weight of materials	Dollar value of materials	Number of shipments
$606,000	2,425	$3,031,000	6
491,000	1,790	2,238,000	14
621,000	2,613	3,266,000	21
602,000	2,419	3,084,000	32
561,000	2,110	2,701,000	7
684,000	2,732	3,688,000	9
630,000	2,504	3,305,000	12
681,000	2,915	3,717,000	6
599,000	2,004	2,725,000	15
518,000	1,610	2,222,000	13
539,000	1,824	2,517,000	10
581,000	1,996	2,730,000	8
611,000	2,103	2,934,000	11
713,000	2,741	3,826,000	7
737,000	2,602	3,851,000	14
622,000	2,191	3,111,000	9
681,000	2,508	3,674,000	12
599,000	1,941	2,788,000	7

Based on these data, the following regressions are obtained:

REGRESSION 1: Materials-handling costs and weight of materials

Equation:
  Materials-handling costs = $271,610 + $150.80 × Weight

Statistical data:
Correlation coefficient	.863
R-square	.745
Standard error of slope	22.054
t-statistic for slope coefficient	6.838

REGRESSION 2: Materials-handling costs and value of materials

Equation:
  Materials-handling costs = $236,790 + .123 × Value

Statistical data:
Correlation coefficient	.975
R-square	.950
Standard error of slope	.007
t-statistic for slope coefficient	17.438

REGRESSION 3: Materials-handling costs and shipments

Equation:
  Materials-handling costs = $628,680 − $1127.8 × Shipments

Statistical data:
Correlation coefficient	.109
R-square	.012
Standard error of slope	2578.4
t-statistic for slope coefficient	−.437

After reviewing the above regressions, it was decided that a multiple regression including the dollar value of materials and the weight of materials might be more useful. The results of that regression were:

REGRESSION 4

Equation:
  Materials-handling cost = $251,760 + (.176 × Value) − ($78.50 × Weight)

Statistical data:
Correlation coefficient	.987	
R-square	.973	
Standard error of coefficients:		
Value	.0154	t-statistic 11.412
Weight	21.385	t-statistic −3.671

Correlation matrix:
	Weight	Value
Weight	1.00	.94
Value	.94	1.00

Required:

a. Prepare the cost estimate for handling 2,600 units of weight at a cost of $4,005,000 using each relevant regression.

b. Which regression would you recommend, if any? Why?

10–26. Regression analysis and loss prediction (Appendix)

The Johnstar Company makes an expensive chemical product. The costs average about $1,000 per unit of weight, and the material sells for $2,500 per unit of weight. Materials storage is extremely hazardous; therefore, a batch is made each day to fill customers' needs for the day. Failure to deliver the required quantity results in a shutdown for the customers with a corresponding cost penalty assessed against Johnstar. However, excess chemical on hand at the end of the day must be disposed of in costly, secure facilities.

The chemical increases in weight during processing, but the exact increase varies depending on temperature and pressure conditions as well as on the impurities present in the input materials. It is important for the company to know the final weight from any batch as soon as possible so that a new batch can be started should the expected final weight be smaller than required for customer needs.

A consultant was hired to advise the company on how to estimate the final weight of the product. The consultant recommended that the product be weighed after three hours and that the weight after three hours be used to predict the weight at the end of processing. Based on 20 processed batches, the following observations were made:

Batch no.	Weight at three hours	Final weight	Batch no.	Weight at three hours	Final weight
1	55 units	90 units	11	60 units	80 units
2	45	75	12	35	60
3	40	80	13	35	80
4	60	80	14	55	60
5	40	45	15	35	75
6	60	80	16	50	90
7	50	80	17	30	60
8	55	95	18	60	105
9	50	100	19	50	60
10	35	75	20	20	30

Data obtained from the regression analysis included the following:

R-square	.4126
Coefficient of correlation	.6424
Coefficients of the regression:	
Constant	28.6
Slope	1.008
Standard error of slope coefficient	.2834
t-statistic for slope	3.5559
Standard error of estimate	14.20 (for 70–72 units)

Required:

a. Use the results of the regression to calculate the estimate of the final weight of today's batch which at the end of three hours weighs 42 units.

b. (Statistics required) Customer orders for today total 68 units. The smallest batch that can be started must weigh at least 20 units at the end of three hours. What factors should be considered in deciding whether to start a new batch?

(CMA adapted)

10–27. Cost estimation—account analysis and regression methods* Bayview Manufacturing Company

(Computer required) The Bayview Manufacturing Company was in the process of preparing cost estimates for the coming year. The controller's staff prepared a preliminary income statement for the coming year based on an analysis of the various cost accounts and on a study of orders received by the company. The projected income statement appeared as follows:

---

* Adapted from a problem in "Report of the Committee on the Measurement Methods Content of the Accounting Curriculum," *Supplement to Volume XLVI of The Accounting Review* (1971).

Sales revenue		$3,000,000
Cost of sales:		
Direct materials	$1,182,000	
Direct labor	310,000	
Factory overhead	775,000	
Total cost of sales		2,267,000
Gross profit		733,000
Marketing costs		450,000
Projected operating profit		$ 283,000

Bayview produces three products: A, B, and C. A profit per unit for each product has been prepared by management and appears as follows:

	A	**B**	**C**
Sale price	$20.00	$10.00	$30.00
Less:			
Direct materials	7.00	3.75	16.60
Direct labor	2.00	1.00	3.50
Factory overhead	5.00	2.50	8.75
Marketing	3.00	1.50	4.50
Net unit profit	$ 3.00	$ 1.25	$ (3.35)

On the basis of this information, the planning committee decided that as few C should be produced as possible. Moreover, the company should emphasize the production of A, perhaps by engaging in a promotional campaign to increase the sale of A.

Before a final recommendation on the plan, the management planning committee asked the controller's office to make certain that these profit numbers were correct.

A review of the controller's recommendations indicated that the controller estimated that 20 percent of the overhead was variable and that 50 percent of the marketing costs were also variable.

Some additional data have been gathered from the accounting records.

First, the units are produced in two departments (molding and finishing). The following production rates indicate the times required to produce each unit in each department:

	A	**B**	**C**
Molding	2 per hour	4 per hour	3 per hour
Finishing	4 per hour	8 per hour	4/3 per hour

The direct labor cost and the overhead incurred in each department and for the company as a whole over the past 10 years is as follows:

Direct labor cost (in thousands)			Overhead cost (in thousands)		
Molding	**Finishing**	**Total**	**Molding**	**Finishing**	**Total**
$140	$170	$310	$341	$434	$775
135	150	285	340	421	761
140	160	300	342	428	770
130	150	280	339	422	761
130	155	285	338	425	763
125	140	265	337	414	751
120	150	270	335	420	755
115	140	255	334	413	747
120	140	260	336	414	750
115	135	250	335	410	745

Production cost relationships have not changed over this time period.

Information on the marketing costs for the past 10 years and the sales of products A, B, and C for the same period was obtained also. These data are:

	Sales (in thousands)			Marketing costs (in thousands)
Product A	**Product B**	**Product C**	**Total**	
$2,000	$400	$600	$3,000	$450
1,940	430	610	2,980	445
1,950	380	630	2,960	445
1,860	460	620	2,940	438
1,820	390	640	2,850	433
1,860	440	580	2,880	437
1,880	420	570	2,870	438
1,850	380	580	2,810	434
1,810	390	580	2,780	430
1,770	290	610	2,670	425

Required:

a. Comment on the use of the per unit profit measures for planning purposes.

b. Use regression estimates to determine if the estimates of fixed and variable overhead are reasonable.

c. Would you recommend the use of plantwide or departmental overhead rates? Why?

d. Prepare regression estimates of the fixed and variable component of marketing costs.

10–28. Regression cost estimation: cost of prediction error

The manager of the chemical processing division of Diamond Products Corporation, a small petrochemical company, is preparing a fixed price bid to process up to 800 units per month of certain feedstocks for a large farm cooperative. All of Diamond's customers have processing agreements which specify the allowed production and processing fee which Diamond can charge. Diamond receives the feedstocks, processes them, and then delivers the finished products to the contracting company.

Diamond incurs conversion costs in the process. Diamond's plant has a maximum capacity of 9,000 units per month. In a typical month, the usage is less than the full capacity and is expected to run at 7,300 units per month over the period of the contract with the cooperative. The manager knows that the cooperative can obtain similar processing elsewhere for a fee of $3.51 per unit. Any bid of $3.50 per unit or less will be accepted by the cooperative. A schedule of past production and processing costs is:

Month	Conversion costs	Production (units per month)
1	$23,840	7,300
2	25,714	7,615
3	21,375	6,410
4	24,163	7,130
5	27,332	8,120
6	21,163	6,110
7	23,143	7,040
8	27,582	8,340
9	23,913	7,280
10	23,708	7,045
11	25,315	7,610
12	26,862	8,030
13	27,439	8,150
14	23,840	7,115
15	24,988	7,580
16	23,100	6,960
17	24,189	7,320
18	24,631	7,540
19	25,917	7,880
20	23,711	7,210
21	22,324	6,510
22	23,684	7,130
23	28,790	8,410
24	25,446	7,830

The manager turns to the computer terminal and enters these data to obtain regression estimates of fixed and variable costs. The following results appear on the screen:

REGRESSION ANALYSIS:

Equation:
   $Y = \$868.433 + \$3.216X$

Statistical data:

Correlation coefficient	.980
R-square	.960
Adjusted R-square	.958
t-statistic for slope coefficient	22.847

After looking at the results, the manager prepares a bid of $3.50 for the processing. The manager's bid is forwarded to the controller's office for review and approval.

The controller notes the bid and the cost estimates. The controller expresses concern with the regression results because the fixed costs are lower than expected. The controller pulls out the cost report for the division and notes the following items which are believed to be fixed costs:

Building occupancy	$1,200
Utilities	450
Equipment depreciation	1,100

In addition, the controller makes note of the fact that there are a number of "mixed" costs in the chemical processing operation. Since the controller's estimate of fixed costs substantially exceeds the fixed cost estimate in the manager's regression equation, the controller asks the manager to explain the difference in the estimates.

The manager states that since the fixed costs will not change as a result of the contract, the fixed costs can be excluded from consideration.

Required:

a. Without the use of a computer, prepare an estimate of the fixed and variable costs that can be used to confirm or reject the manager's regression results.

b. (Computer required) Prepare your own regression estimate of fixed and variable costs.

c. If the manager had submitted a bid of $3.50 per unit for the 800 units per month to be processed, how much better or worse off would the company be compared to not submitting a bid? (That is, what is the cost of prediction error for this case?) Compute the amount on a monthly basis.

10–29. Regression analysis—multiple choice

Armer Company is accumulating data to be used in preparing its annual profit plan for the coming year. The cost behavior pattern of the maintenance costs must be determined. The accounting staff has suggested that regression be employed to derive an equation in the form of $y = a + bx$ for maintenance costs. Data regarding the maintenance hours and costs for last year and the results of the regression analysis are as follows:

	Hours of activity	Maintenance costs
January	480	$ 4,200
February	320	3,000
March	400	3,600
April	300	2,820
May	500	4,350
June	310	2,960
July	320	3,030
August	520	4,470
September	490	4,260
October	470	4,050
November	350	3,300
December	340	3,160
Sum	4,800	43,200
Average	400	3,600

Average cost per hour (43,200 ÷ 4,800) = $9

Intercept	684.65
b coefficient	7.2884
Standard error of the intercept	49.515
Standard error of the b coefficient	.12126
Standard error of the regression	34.469
R-square	.99724
t—value intercept	13.827
t—value b	60.105

Required:

a. In the standard regression equation of $y = a + bx$, the letter b is best described as the—
 (1) Independent variable.
 (2) Dependent variable.
 (3) Constant coefficient.
 (4) Variable coefficient.
 (5) Coefficient of determination.

b. The letter y in the standard regression equation is best described as the—
 (1) Independent variable.
 (2) Dependent variable.
 (3) Constant coefficient.

(4) Variable coefficient.

(5) Coefficient of determination.

c. The letter x in the standard regression equation is best described as the—

(1) Independent variable.

(2) Dependent variable.

(3) Constant coefficient.

(4) Variable coefficient.

(5) Coefficient of determination.

d. If the Armer Company uses the high-low method of analysis, the equation for the relationship between hours of activity and maintenance cost would be—

(1) $y = 400 + 9.0x$.

(2) $y = 570 + 7.5x$.

(3) $y = 3,600 + 400x$.

(4) $y = 570 + 9.0x$.

(5) Some equation other than those given above.

e. Based upon the data derived from the regression analysis, 420 maintenance hours in a month would mean the maintenance costs would be budgeted at—

(1) $3,780.

(2) $3,461.

(3) $3,797.

(4) $3,746.

(5) Some amount other than those given.

f. The coefficient of correlation for the regression equation for the maintenance activities is:

(1) $34.469 \div 49.515$.

(2) .99724.

(3) $\sqrt{.99724}$.

(4) $(.99724)^2$.

(5) Some amount other than those given above.

g. The percent of the total variance that can be explained by the regression equation is—

(1) 99.724%.

(2) 69.613%.

(3) 80.982%.

(4) 99.862%.

(5) Some amount other than those given above.

h. (Appendix) What is the range of values for the marginal maintenance cost such that Armer can be 95 percent confident that the true value of the marginal maintenance cost will be within this range? (Use $t = 2.23$.)

(1) $7.02–$7.56.

(2) $7.17–$7.41.

(3) $7.07–$7.51.

(4) $6.29–$8.29.

(5) Some range other than those given above.

(CMA adapted)

10–30. Learning curves

The Kelly Company plans to manufacture a product called Electrocal which requires a substantial amount of direct labor on each unit. Based on the company's experience with other products that required similar amounts of direct labor, management believes that there is a learning factor in the production process used to manufacture Electrocal.

Each unit of Electrocal requires 50 square feet of direct material at a cost of $30 per square foot for a total material cost of $1,500. The standard direct labor rate is $25 per direct labor-hour. Variable manufacturing overhead is assigned to products at a rate of $40 per direct labor-hour. The company adds a markup of 30 percent on variable manufacturing cost in determining an initial bid price for all products.

Data on the production of the first two lots (16 units) of Electrocal is as follows:

1. The first lot of eight units required a total of 3,200 direct labor-hours.
2. The second lot of eight units required a total of 2,240 direct labor-hours.

Based on prior production experience, Kelly anticipates that there will be no significant improvement in production time after the first 32 units. Therefore, a standard for direct labor-hours will be established based on the average hours per unit for units 17–32.

Required:

a. What is the basic premise of the learning curve?
b. Based upon the data presented for the first 16 units, what learning rate appears to be applicable to the direct labor required to produce Electrocal? Support your answer with appropriate calculations.
c. Calculate the standard for direct labor-hours that Kelly Company should establish for each unit of Electrocal.
d. After the first 32 units have been manufactured, Kelly Company was asked to submit a bid on an additional 96 units. What price should Kelly bid on this order of 96 units? Explain your answer.
e. Knowledge of the learning curve phenomenon can be a valuable management tool. Explain how management can apply the learning curve in the planning and controlling of business operations.

(CMA adapted)

10–31. Learning curves

The Xyon Company has purchased 80,000 pumps annually from Kobec Inc. The price has increased each year and reached $68 per unit last year. Because the purchase price has increased significantly, Xyon management has asked that an estimate be made of the cost to manufacture it in its own facilities. Xyon's products consist of stamping and castings. The company has little experience with products requiring assembly.

The engineering, manufacturing, and accounting departments have prepared a report for management that included the estimate shown below for an assembly run of 10,000 units. Additional production employees would be hired to manufacture the subassembly. However, no additional equipment, space, or supervision would be needed.

The report states that total costs for 10,000 units are estimated at $957,000 or $95.70 a unit. The current purchase price is $68 a unit so the report recommends a continued purchase of the product.

Components (outside purchases)	$120,000
Assembly labor[a]	300,000
Factory overhead[b]	450,000
General and administrative overhead[c]	87,000
Total costs	$957,000

Fixed overhead	50% of direct labor dollars
Variable overhead	100% of direct labor dollars
Factory overhead rate	150% of direct labor dollars

[a] Assembly labor consists of hourly production workers.

[b] Factory overhead is applied to products on a direct labor dollar basis. Variable overhead costs vary closely with direct labor dollars.

[c] General and administrative overhead is applied at 10 percent of the total cost of material (or components), assembly labor, and factory overhead.

Required:

a. Was the analysis prepared by the engineering, manufacturing, and accounting departments of Xyon Company and the recommendation to continue purchasing the pumps which followed from the analysis correct? Explain your answer and include any supportive calculations you consider necessary.

b. Assume Xyon Company could experience labor cost improvements on the pump assembly consistent with an 80 percent learning curve. An assembly run of 10,000 units represents the initial lot or batch for measurement purposes. Should Xyon produce the 80,000 pumps in this situation? Explain your answer.

(CMA adapted)

11

Cost-Volume-Profit Analysis

OBJECTIVES

To understand the relationship between the cost, volume, and revenue elements of the profit equation.

To see how that relationship may be used to assist management in its planning activities.

In this chapter, we discuss the use of cost-volume-profit (CVP) analysis for managerial decision making. Managers must understand the interrelationship of cost, volume, and profit for decision making. They rely on their cost accounting department to supply the information and analyses that aid them to anticipate and make sound decisions involving any of these three items.

During a gasoline shortage that hit the American automobile industry particularly hard, executives of one automobile company announced a price increase to reduce losses. Many observers were surprised that the company would raise prices when car sales were slumping and argued that the decision would further reduce the company's sales. The observers were correct in forecasting a decrease in the quantity of cars demanded at the higher price. But the auto executives had carried the analysis several steps farther and determined that increased prices would have a positive impact on the company's operating profits.

In making their decision, the executives needed to understand relationships between selling prices, sales volume, and costs. They also needed to understand which costs would vary with changes in volume and which costs would stay the same. Without this kind of analysis, they could not accurately determine the effect of price, volume, or cost changes on the company's operating profits.

Although their decision to raise prices in the face of decreasing demand struck some people as odd, these managers believed that the increase in price, coupled with an expected decrease in volume, would have little impact on total revenue. However, the total variable costs would be reduced with lower volume, so operating profits would be higher.

The profit equation

A simple relationship exists between total revenues *(TR)*, total costs *(TC)*, and operating profit *(π)*.

$$\text{Operating profit} = \text{Total revenues} - \text{Total costs}$$
$$\pi = TR - TC$$

Both total revenues and total costs are likely to be affected by changes in the quantity of output.[1] A statement of the profit equation that takes quantity of output into account adds useful information for examining the effects of revenue, costs, and volume on operating profits. Total revenue *(TR)* equals average selling price per unit *(P)* times the units of output *(X)*:

$$TR = PX$$

Total costs *(TC)* may be divided into a fixed component that does not vary with changes in output levels and a variable component that does vary. The fixed component is made up of total fixed costs *(F)* per period, while the variable component is the product of the average variable cost per unit *(V)* times the quantity of output *(X)*. Therefore, the cost function is:

$$TC = VX + F$$

Substituting the expanded expressions in the profit equation yields a more useful form, as follows:

$$\pi = TR - TC$$
$$\pi = PX - (VX + F)$$

Collecting terms, we have

$$\pi = (P - V)X - F$$

The contribution margin, *(P − V)*, shown in this version of the profit equation is the amount each unit sold *contributes* toward (1) covering fixed costs and (2) providing operating profits.

Note that *V* is the sum of unit *manufacturing costs* and unit *marketing and administrative* costs; *F* is the sum of total fixed *manufacturing costs,* fixed *marketing costs,* and fixed *administrative costs* for the period; and *X* refers to the number of units produced and sold during the period.

This model assumes *all* fixed costs are costs of the *period;* fixed manufacturing costs are not allocated to products and "unitized." Thus, the CVP model is consistent with variable costing but inconsistent with full-absorption costing.

For example, Sport Autos is an automobile dealership that carries one line of sports cars. During the month of February, Sport Autos purchased 20 sports cars and sold them at an average price of $15,000 each. Here is how the average variable cost of each car was determined:

Cost of each automobile to Sport Autos	$12,300
Dealer preparation costs	100
Sales commission	600
Average variable cost per car	$13,000

---

[1] Unless otherwise stated, we adopt the simplifying assumption that production volume equals sales volume so that changes in inventories may be ignored.

The fixed costs of operating the dealership for a typical month are $30,000. Using the profit equation, the results for February are:

$$\pi = (P - V)X - F$$
$$= (\$15,000 - \$13,000)20 \text{ cars} - \$30,000$$
$$= \$10,000$$

Although the $10,000 operating profit was derived algebraically, it could also be determined from an analysis of the flow of costs and the company's income statement for the month, as shown in Illustration 11–1.

Illustration 11–1   **Flow of costs, Sports Autos**

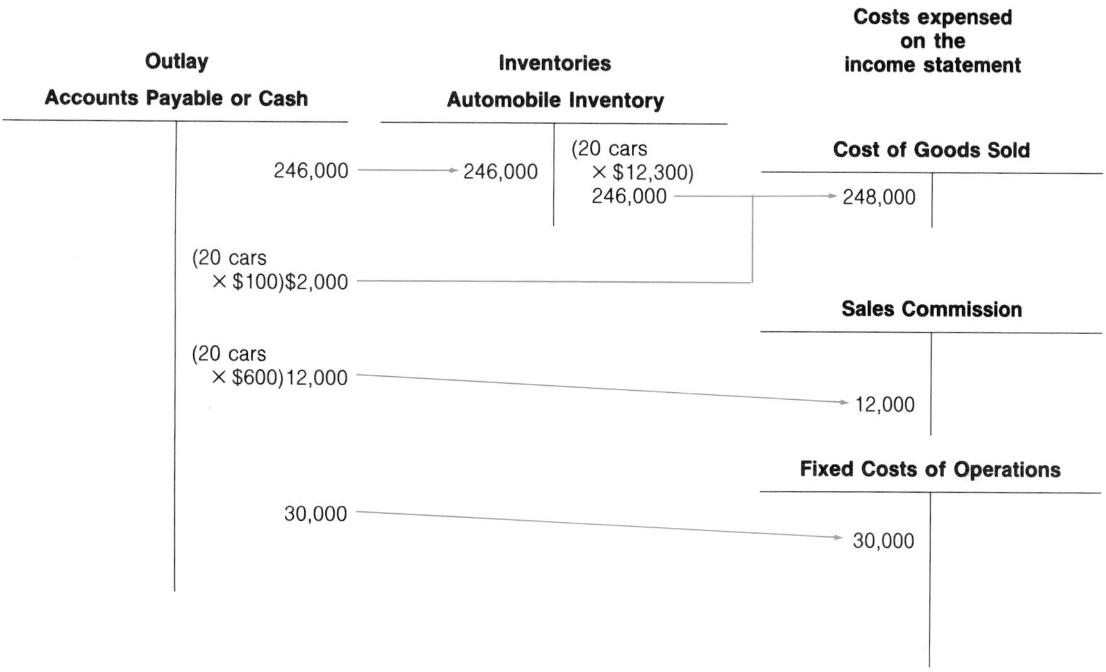

Outlay	Inventories	Costs expensed on the income statement
Accounts Payable or Cash	**Automobile Inventory**	

Cost of Goods Sold

246,000 → 246,000 | (20 cars × $12,300) 246,000 → | 248,000

(20 cars × $100)$2,000

Sales Commission

(20 cars × $600)12,000 → 12,000

Fixed Costs of Operations

30,000 → 30,000

SPORT AUTOS
Income Statement
February

Sales (20 cars at $15,000)	$300,000
Variable cost of goods sold	248,000
Variable selling costs	12,000
Contribution margin	40,000
Fixed costs	30,000
Operating profit	$ 10,000

Cost-volume-profit (CVP) relationships

The following example demonstrates how the profit equation can be used to find CVP relationships. Assume the manager of Sport Autos foresees a downturn in sales volume in March, but hopes for improvement in April. In fact, the manager has forecasted an operating profit of $0 for March, which is the break-even point where total revenue equals total costs. He forecasts $50,000 in operating profits for April. What volumes of sales will provide the expected operating profits? We start with the following profit equation:

$$\pi = TR - TC$$
$$= (P - V)X - F$$
$$= (\$15,000 - \$13,000)X - \$30,000$$

Setting operating profit equal to zero for March and to $50,000 for April, we find the required volumes:

For March:

$$\pi = (P - V)X - F$$
$$\text{If } \pi = \$0$$
$$\$0 = (\$15,000 - \$13,000)X - \$30,000$$
$$\$30,000 = \$2,000X$$
$$\frac{\$30,000}{\$2,000} = X$$
$$X = 15 \text{ cars}$$

For April:

$$\$50,000 = (\$15,000 - \$13,000)X - \$30,000$$
$$\$50,000 + \$30,000 = \$2,000X$$
$$\frac{\$80,000}{\$2,000} = X$$
$$X = 40 \text{ cars}$$

Thus, Sport Autos must sell 15 cars in March to break even and 40 cars in April to make the targeted operating profit of $50,000.

Equation for finding target volumes   In general, the equation for finding target volumes is:

$$\text{Target volume} = \frac{\text{Fixed costs} + \text{Target profit}}{\text{Contribution margin per unit}}$$

$$X = \frac{F + \pi}{P - V}$$

For April in the above example:

$$X = \frac{F + \pi}{P - V}$$

$$= \frac{\$30,000 + \$50,000}{\$15,000 - \$13,000}$$

$$= \frac{\$80,000}{2,000}$$

$$= \underline{\underline{40 \text{ cars}}}$$

Break-even point   The **break-even point** is a special case of the above equation where π is set equal to zero:

$$X = \frac{F}{P - V}$$

For March, in the above example:

$$X = \frac{F}{P - V}$$

$$= \frac{\$30,000}{\$15,000 - \$13,000}$$

$$= \underline{\underline{15 \text{ cars}}}$$

Illustration 11–2 presents these relationships in graphic form. Illustration 11–2 contains a number of elements that are explained below:

The *vertical axis* presents dollars (for example, revenue dollars, cost dollars).

The *horizontal axis* presents the volume of activity for a time period (for example, number of cars sold per month).

The *total revenue (TR)* line relates total revenue to volume (for example, if Sport Autos sells 40 cars in a month, its total revenue would be $600,000, according to the graph). The slope of *TR* is the price per unit, *P* (for example, $15,000 per car for Sport Autos).

The *total cost (TC)* line shows the total cost for each volume (for example, the total cost for a volume of 40 cars is $550,000 = [40 × $13,000] + $30,000). The intercept of the total cost line is the fixed cost for the period, *F* (for example, $30,000 for the month), and the slope is the variable cost per unit, *V* (for example, $13,000 per car).

The *break-even point* is the volume at which *TR* = *TC* (that is, the *TR* and *TC* lines intersect). Volumes lower than break-even result in an operating loss because *TR* < *TC;* volumes higher than break-even result in an operating profit because *TR* > *TC.* For Sport Autos, the break-even volume is 15 cars.

The amount of operating profit or loss can be read from the graph by measuring the vertical distance between *TR* and *TC.* For example, the vertical distance between *TR* and *TC* when *X* = 40 indicates π = $50,000.

Profit-volume model

For convenience, the cost and revenue lines are often collapsed into a single profit line. This summary version of CVP analysis is called profit-volume analysis.

Illustration 11–2   **CVP graph, Sport Autos**

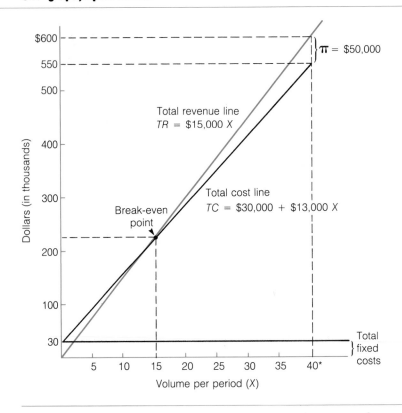

^{a} Note that the vertical distance between TR and TC at $x = 40$ is the target π for April: $50,000.

A graphic comparison of profit-volume and CVP relationships is shown in Illustration 11–3. Note that the slope of the profit-volume line equals the average unit contribution; the intercept equals the loss at zero volume, which equals fixed costs; and the vertical axis measures operating profit or loss.

Solving for unknowns

A major application of the CVP model is solving for unknowns. For example, suppose that after examining the figures just presented, Sport Autos' manager pointed out, "We cannot obtain 40 cars from the manufacturer to sell in April. If we can only get 30 cars to sell, can we still make $50,000 in April?" An answer can be obtained by holding outputs at 30 units, operating profits at $50,000, and solving for each of the other terms in the following profit equation:

$$\$50,000 = (P - V)30 \text{ cars} - F$$

Illustration 11–3   **Comparison of CVP and profit-volume graphs, Sport Autos**

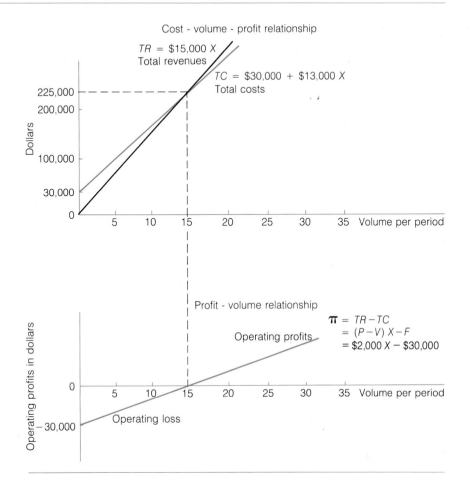

1. *Solve for contribution margin.*   Find the average contribution margin per unit required to cover Sport Autos' $30,000 fixed costs and provide operating profits of $50,000:

$$\$50,000 = (P - V)30 - \$30,000$$
$$\$80,000 = (P - V)30$$
$$(P - V) = \frac{\$80,000}{30}$$
$$= \underline{\underline{\$2,667}}$$

Thus, the average contribution margin per car must be $2,667 if Sport Autos is to make $50,000. The increase in the contribution margin from $2,000 to $2,667 must come from a price increase, a decrease in variable costs per unit, or a combination of the two.

2. *Solve for fixed cost.*   Holding the contribution margin per unit constant at $2,000, find the decrease in fixed costs that provides operating profits of $50,000 if 30 cars are sold:

$$\$50,000 = (\$15,000 - \$13,000)30 \text{ cars} - F$$
$$\$50,000 = \$60,000 - F$$
$$F = \underline{\underline{\$10,000}}$$

For Sport Autos to sell 30 cars while holding the unit contribution margin at $2,000 and to make operating profits of $50,000, a reduction in fixed costs from $30,000 to $10,000 would be required.

Managers can thus use CVP analysis to determine how to achieve profit goals by changing particular variables in the CVP equation.

CVP analysis provides a valuable tool for determining the impact of prices, costs, and volume on operating profits. An important part of management's job is to manage each factor that affects operating profits to improve profitability.

Margin of safety

Another calculation made from CVP analysis is the margin of safety. The margin of safety is the excess of projected (or actual) sales over the break-even sales level. The margin of safety formula is:

$$\text{Sales volume} - \text{Break-even sales volume} = \text{Margin of safety}$$

If Sport Autos sells 20 cars and its break-even volume is 15 cars, then its margin of safety is:

$$\text{Sales} - \text{Break even} = 20 - 15$$
$$= \underline{\underline{5 \text{ cars}}}$$

Sales volume could drop by five cars per month before a loss is incurred, all other things held constant.

The economist's profit-maximization model

The classical economist's profit-maximization model provides the foundation for CVP analysis. It assumes that management's goal is profit maximization, where profits are the difference between total revenues and total costs. Management's job is to determine and to take the most profitable actions possible.

In general, accountants accept the classical economist's model, but they make two simplifying assumptions:

1. In economics, *total revenue and total cost curves* are usually assumed to be nonlinear. The linearity simplifications are usually considered valid within some appropriate range of volume, termed the *relevant range*.
2. The opportunity cost of invested equity capital is usually excluded in the accountant's cost measures, while it is included in the economist's

model. Thus, in economic terms, the accountant's measurement of total costs is understated.

Despite these differences, decisions based on the accountant's model will probably not differ from decisions made using the economist's model as long as the alternatives being considered require the same invested equity capital. The break-even volume derived in the accountant's model, however, does not usually provide earnings to cover the opportunity cost of invested equity capital. However, the accountant's model could be formulated to include a cost of capital.

A comparison of accountants' and economists' assumptions about the behavior of costs and revenue is shown in Illustration 11–4. The solid lines represent accountants' assumptions about cost and revenue behavior, while the dashed lines designate economists' assumptions. Note the difference in assumptions about linearity as well as the systematically higher economists' costs because accounting costs do not include the opportunity cost of capital.

Simplifying assumptions about cost and revenue behavior

Strictly speaking, neither model is "correct," because both economists and accountants have made simplifying assumptions about cost and revenue behavior. The actual curves would be disjointed and would take into account inconsistencies such as sales discounts for certain customers, costs that are

Illustration 11–4   **Comparison of economists' and accountants' assumed cost and revenue behavior**

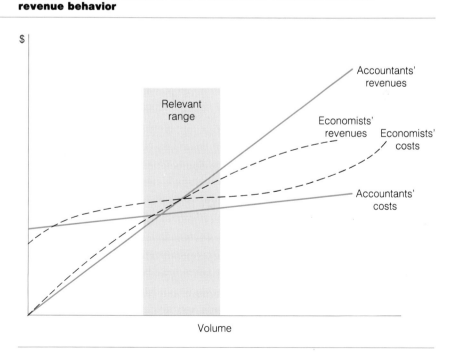

neither strictly fixed nor strictly variable, and so forth. However, a cost-benefit analysis of more "accurate" data about cost and revenue behavior may yield little additional benefit to decision makers. Indeed, it may not be feasible to obtain nonlinear cost data.

In short, while linear CVP models are simple, it may not be worthwhile to obtain more descriptive data about cost and revenue functions. This is particularly so if the analysis is used within the relevant range of volume.

Modifications of the basic model

CVP: Cash Flow analysis

Sometimes decision makers may be more interested in the impact of the volume of activity on cash or working capital than on accrual profits. They often want to know if it is possible to operate at a loss and still generate positive cash flows. This type of analysis may be particularly relevant in adverse economic times or when a company is phasing out part of its operations. So long as there are sufficient cash flows, it may be optimal to continue the operation, even though there is an accounting loss.

Both revenues and costs include noncash items. But the most significant noncash item tends to be depreciation, which is usually included in fixed costs. This classification is common because depreciation generally represents the allocation of the acquisition cost of plant and equipment (capacity) over time based on an estimate of their useful lives.

To see how noncash items can affect CVP analysis, suppose that the fixed costs of Sport Autos include depreciation of equipment and other assets of $4,000 per month and that this is the only noncash revenue or expense.

Illustration 11–5 compares cash flow and accrual profit-volume relationships. By substituting appropriate numbers into the profit equation, you can demonstrate that if Sport Autos operates at an accrual profit break-even volume each month, it will generate monthly net cash flows of $4,000. This is a short-run phenomenon only, of course. When the time comes to replace the depreciable assets, the need for a large cash outflow must be faced.

Depreciation also may be included in *variable costs* if it is based on the *units of production* of some asset and thus related to volume. A common example is the depreciation of a machine based on its usage. Also, the costs of oil or gas wells are usually depreciated over the number of units of oil or gas produced since the economic life of a wasting asset is dependent on the number of units of the resource rather than the age of the well.

Income taxes

Assuming that operating profits before taxes and taxable income are the same, income taxes may be incorporated into the basic model as follows:

After-tax operating profit = (Before-tax operating profit)(1 − tax rate)

If we let π_a designate after-tax operating profits, π_b designate before-tax operating profits, and t designate the tax rate, we have:

$$\pi_a = \pi_b(1 - t)$$

Illustration 11–5   **Comparison of short-run cash and accrual profit-volume relationships for Sport Autos**

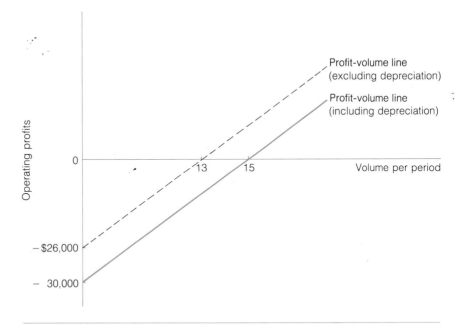

Note: The "cash break-even point" is found as follows:

$$X = \frac{\text{Fixed cash costs}}{\text{Cash contribution margin per unit}}$$
$$= \frac{\$30,000 - \$4,000 \text{ depreciation}}{\$15,000 - \$13,000} = \frac{\$26,000}{\$2,000} = 13 \text{ cars}$$

Substituting our earlier definition of operating profit, we obtain

$$\pi_a = [(P - V)X - F](1 - t)$$

Suppose that the manager of Sport Autos is interested in determining what volume is required to provide $50,000 in operating profit *after taxes* in April. $P = \$15,000$; $V = \$13,000$; $F = \$30,000$; and $t = .4$ (that is, an average tax rate for April of 40 percent). To find the required X that provides π_a of $50,000:

$$\pi_a = [(P - V)X - F](1 - t)$$
$$\$50,000 = [(\$15,000 - \$13,000)X - \$30,000](1 - .4)$$
$$\$50,000 = (\$2,000X - \$30,000)(.6)$$
$$\$50,000 = \$1,200X - \$18,000$$
$$\$68,000 = \$1,200X$$
$$\frac{\$68,000}{\$1,200} = X = 56\tfrac{2}{3} \text{ units}$$

Finding the break-even volume in dollars

Companies often measure volume in dollars rather than units. This is common when the CVP analysis deals with more than one product. If a company makes two products, it may be more meaningful to measure activity in dollars instead of units. As a practical matter, when CVP analysis is done for a single product, units are typically used to measure volume. When more than one product is involved, dollars are usually used.

When dollars are used, volume is no longer defined as X in the CVP model. Rather, volume is PX, where P is the unit price. Thus, instead of:

$$\pi = (P - V)X - F = PX - VX - F$$

we have

$$\pi = PX - \left(\frac{V}{P}\right)PX - F = \left(1 - \frac{V}{P}\right)PX - F$$

where V/P is the variable cost percentage of sales dollars, or variable cost ratio. Thus, the equation could be read:

$$\text{Operating profit} = \text{Sales revenue} - \left(\begin{matrix}\text{Variable cost} \\ \text{ratio}\end{matrix} \times \begin{matrix}\text{Sales} \\ \text{revenue}\end{matrix}\right) - \text{Fixed costs}$$

To find the break-even sales volume, set $\pi = 0$ and solve for PX as follows:

$$\pi = \left(1 - \frac{V}{P}\right)PX - F$$

$$0 = \left(1 - \frac{V}{P}\right)PX - F$$

$$\left(1 - \frac{V}{P}\right)PX = F$$

$$PX = \frac{F}{1 - \dfrac{V}{P}}$$

Or simply multiply both sides of the original break-even formula by P as follows:

Original formula for units:

$$X = \frac{F}{P - V}$$

Modified formula for dollars:

$$PX = \left(\frac{F}{P - V}\right)P$$

Since dividing the denominator by P is the same as multiplying the entire term by P, we obtain:

$$PX = \frac{F}{\dfrac{(P - V)}{P}}$$

The term $\dfrac{P - V}{P}$ is known as the contribution margin ratio.

The break-even sales amount for Sport Autos, first using the profit equation, is:

$$\pi = \left(1 - \frac{V}{P}\right)PX - F$$

$$0 = \left(1 - \frac{\$13,000}{\$15,000}\right)PX - \$30,000$$

$$= (1 - .8667)PX - \$30,000$$

$$= .1333PX - \$30,000$$

$$.1333PX = \$30,000$$

$$PX = \frac{\$30,000}{.1333} = \$225,000 \text{ (rounded)}$$

We can check this result by recalling that the break-even volume in units was 15 cars per month. If sold at a price of $15,000 each, the break-even volume measured in sales dollars is $225,000 (= 15 cars × $15,000).

The same result can be derived directly from the break-even formula:

$$PX = \frac{F}{1 - \dfrac{V}{P}}$$

$$= \frac{\$30,000}{1 - \dfrac{\$13,000}{\$15,000}} = \frac{\$30,000}{1 - .8667} = \$225,000$$

Finding target sales dollars   To consider a different example, suppose we want to find the break-even sales dollars for a management education course at a university. The tuition that 80 percent of the students pay is $1,000 each; while 20 percent of the students receive a discount and pay $800 each. The variable cost is $240 per student, and the fixed cost of the course is $10,000. What is the break-even point in tuition dollars?

$$PX = \frac{F}{1 - \dfrac{V}{P}}$$

$$= \frac{\$10,000}{1 - \left[\dfrac{240}{(.8 \times \$1,000) + (.2 \times \$800)}\right]}$$

$$= \frac{\$10,000}{1 - \left(\dfrac{\$240}{\$960}\right)}$$

$$= \frac{\$10,000}{.75}$$

$$= \$13,333$$

The course breaks even if tuition receipts amount to $13,333. Note that the variable cost ratio in this case is a *weighted average* based on the assumed product mix of 80/20 (20 percent of the students receive a discount). If the product mix were to change, the variable cost ratio would change and the break-even sales dollars would change.

Next, assume that the university has a target operating profit of $10,000 plus 10 percent of sales dollars for the management education course. From the original formula,

$$\pi = \left(1 - \frac{V}{P}\right)PX - F$$

we incorporate these profit goals as follows:

$$\$10,000 + .10PX = \left(1 - \frac{V}{P}\right)PX - F$$

Combining terms and solving for *PX* gives:

$$\$10,000 + .10PX = (1 - .25)PX - \$10,000$$
$$.10PX = .75PX - \$20,000$$
$$.10PX - .75PX = -\$20,000$$
$$.65PX = \$20,000$$
$$PX = \frac{\$20,000}{.65}$$
$$= \$30,769$$

Results:

Revenues	$30,769
Less variable costs (.25 × $30,769)	7,692
Fixed costs	10,000
Operating profits	$13,077

To check, $13,077 = $10,000 + (.10 × $30,769).

CVP analysis with semifixed costs

It is common for "fixed costs" to behave in a step fashion as follows:

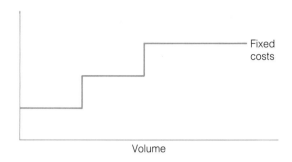

Suppose the managers of a manufacturing company are considering extending a factory's hours of operations to the evening hours. Assume the price, volumes, and costs would be as follows:

	Monthly production and sales	Total fixed costs	Variable cost	Price
Regular shift	0–10,000 units	$200,000	$15 per unit	$40 per unit
Evening shift	10,001–18,000 units	300,000	$15 per unit	$40 per unit

The CVP lines would be as follows:

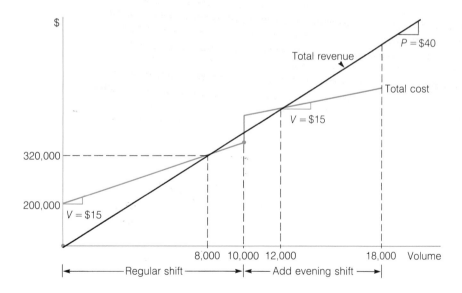

As indicated on the graph, if the company operates only one shift, its capacity is limited to 10,000 units. Adding the second shift increases the capacity to 18,000 units. Profits will increase if enough additional units can be sold.

The company would have two break-even points—one within each level of activity:

$$X = \frac{F}{P - V}$$

$$\text{Break-even } X \text{ (regular shift)} = \frac{\$200{,}000}{\$40 - \$15} = \underline{8{,}000 \text{ units}}$$

$$\text{Break-even } X \text{ (evening shift)} = \frac{\$300{,}000}{\$40 - \$15} = \underline{12{,}000 \text{ units}}$$

Should the company open the second shift, assuming all other things are the same except for the increase in each period's fixed costs and the increase in volume noted above? From the calculations shown below, and assuming the company can sell everything it makes, it is more profitable to operate with two shifts than with one.

	Regular shift only	Add evening shift
Volume in units	10,000	18,000
Sales revenue	$400,000 (=$40 × 10,000)	$720,000 (=$40 × 18,000)
Variable costs	150,000 (=$15 × 10,000)	270,000 (=$15 × 18,000)
Total contribution	250,000	450,000
Fixed costs	200,000	300,000
Operating profit	$ 50,000	$150,000

Multiproduct CVP analysis

We assumed that Sport Autos buys and sells only one line of sports cars. Many companies, of course, produce and/or sell many products from the same asset base.

Dual Autos sells two car models: Regular and Deluxe. The prices and costs of the two are:

	Regular	Deluxe
Average sales price	$12,000	$ 20,000
Less average variable costs:		
Automobile cost to dealer	(9,600)	(14,600)
Supplies used to prepare car for sale	(200)	(400)
Sales commission	(1,200)	(2,000)
Average contribution margin per car	$ 1,000	$ 3,000

Average monthly fixed costs are $36,000.

The profit equation presented earlier must now be expanded to consider the contribution of each product:

$$\pi = [(P_r - V_r)X_r] + [(P_d - V_d)X_d] - F$$

where subscript r designates the Regular model and subscript d designates the Deluxe model. Thus, the company's profit equation is:

$$\pi = (\$1,000X_r) + (\$3,000X_d) - \$36,000$$

The manager of Dual Autos has been listening to a debate between two of the sales personnel about the break-even point for the company. According to one, they have to sell 36 cars a month to break even. But the other claims that 12 cars a month would be sufficient. Who is right? The claim that 36 cars must be sold to break even is correct if *only* the *Regular* model is sold, while the claim that 12 cars need be sold to break even is correct if *only* the *Deluxe* model is sold. In fact, there are many break-even points. This is evident from Dual Auto's profit equation, which has two unknown variables. All possible break-even points for Dual Autos are listed in Illustration 11–6 (assuming, of course, that only *whole* autos can be sold).

Illustration 11–7 is a graphic presentation of the possible break-even volumes for Dual Autos. The break-even line in Illustration 11–7 is one of a family of lines known as **isoprofit,** or constant profit, lines. Operating profits are the same for any combination of product volumes on that line. The dashed line parallel to the break-even line shows the isprofit line for the various combinations of volumes that would provide $3,000 in operating profit.

Note in Illustration 11–7 that any combination of products to the right of the break-even line provides profits, while any combination to the left results in losses.

Illustration 11–6   **Combinations of break-even volumes for Dual Autos**

Regular model		Deluxe model		Total contribution for both models
Quantity	Total contribution	Quantity	Total contribution	
36	$36,000	0	$ –0–	$36,000
33	33,000	1	3,000	36,000
30	30,000	2	6,000	36,000
27	27,000	3	9,000	36,000
24	24,000	4	12,000	36,000
21	21,000	5	15,000	36,000
18	18,000	6	18,000	36,000
15	15,000	7	21,000	36,000
12	12,000	8	24,000	36,000
9	9,000	9	27,000	36,000
6	6,000	10	30,000	36,000
3	3,000	11	33,000	36,000
0	0	12	36,000	36,000

Illustration 11–7   **Illustration of possible break-even volumes for Dual Autos**

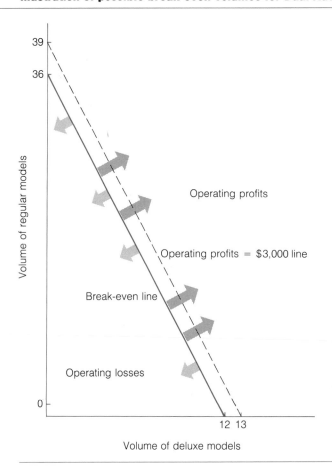

In general, the multiproduct CVP equation for n different products is:

$$\pi = (P_1 - V_1)X_1 + (P_2 - V_2)X_2 + \cdots + (P_n - V_n)X_n - F$$

CVP analysis of multiple products is *much* more complex than is analysis of a single product. As indicated in the Dual Autos example, even for a two-product company, the number of possible solutions is large because there are many combinations of product volumes that will yield a given profit. You can imagine the complications when hundreds of products are involved.

Simplifying   **Assuming a product mix**   To simplify matters, managers often assume
multiproduct CVP   a particular product mix.

For example, if the manager of Dual Autos would be willing to assume that the Regular and Deluxe models would be sold in a one-to-one ratio, the break-even point could be identified as 18 cars (9 regular models and 9 deluxe models).

Let X^* = the pairs of cars sold, such that

$$X^* = 1X_r + 1X_d$$

Given the following profit equation:

$$\pi = (\$1,000X_r) + (\$3,000X_d) - \$36,000$$

If $\pi = \$0$, then solving for X^* gives:

$$\$0 = (\$4,000X^*) - \$36,000$$
$$\$4,000X^* = \$36,000$$
$$X^* = \frac{\$36,000}{\$4,000}$$
$$= 9 \text{ pairs of cars}$$

This result means that Dual Autos must sell nine Regular *and* nine Deluxe model cars to attain the break-even point.

This problem can also be solved by using a weighted-average contribution margin per unit. When a company assumes a constant product mix, the contribution margin is the **weighted-average contribution margin** of all of its products.

For Dual Autos, the weighted-average contribution margin per unit

$$= (.5 \times \$1,000) + (.5 \times \$3,000)$$
$$= \$2,000$$

The multiple-product break even for Dual Autos can be determined from the break-even formula:

$$\pi = (\$2,000X) - \$36,000$$
$$\text{If } \pi = \$0$$
$$\$0 = (\$2,000X) - \$36,000$$
$$\$2,000X = \$36,000$$
$$X = \frac{\$36,000}{\$2,000}$$
$$= 18 \text{ cars}$$

where X refers to the break-even quantity. The product mix assumption means Dual Autos must sell nine Regular models and nine Deluxe models to break even.

Sensitivity analysis

Sensitivity analysis is any process that measures the impact of a change in a single variable or a combination of variables on profits or on some other decision variable. Because the results of multiproduct CVP analysis can be affected significantly by assumptions about product mix, sensitivity analysis should be used to enhance the results. Such analysis would consist of a series of calculations covering all possible changes in product mix within a range of reasonable probability.

If the assumption of Dual Autos' one-to-one ratio is changed to three (Regulars) to one (Deluxe), the break-even quantity increases:

$$\text{Weighted-average contribution margin} = .75(\$1,000) + .25(\$3,000)$$
$$= \underline{\underline{\$1,500}}$$

At break-even:

$$\$0 = (\$1,500X) - \$36,000$$
$$\$1,500X = \$36,000$$
$$X = \frac{\$36,000}{\$1,500}$$
$$= \underline{\underline{24 \text{ cars}}}$$

Of these 24 cars, three fourths (or 18) will be Regular models and 6 will be Deluxe models. To *check,* we can compute the profit as:

$$(18 \times \$1,000) + (6 \times \$3,000) - \$36,000 = \$0$$

which is, by definition, the break-even point.

On the other hand, if 70 percent of all sales are expected to be Deluxe models, the break-even quantity decreases, as shown below:

$$\text{Weighted-average contribution margin} = .3(\$1,000) + .7(\$3,000) = \$2,400$$

Now using the $2,400 margin in our formula,

$$\$0 = \$2,400X - \$36,000$$
$$\$2,400X = \$36,000$$
$$X = \frac{\$36,000}{\$2,400}$$
$$= 15 \text{ cars}$$

Of these 15 cars, 4.5 are Regular models and 10.5 are Deluxe. To *check,* we can compute the profit as:

$$(4.5 \times \$1,000) + (10.5 \times \$3,000) - \$36,000 = \$0$$

which, again, is the break-even point.

The impact of these three assumptions about product mix is demonstrated by the three profit-volume lines in Illustration 11–8. The slope of each profit-volume line is the weighted-average contribution margin of the two products.

Although we have used *break-even* quantities to demonstrate sensitivity to product-mix assumptions, the impact of these assumptions can be seen at other quantities as well. For example, Illustration 11–9 shows the operating profit for each product mix when sales volume equals 40 automobiles.

Illustration 11–8   **Impact of different assumptions about product mix, Dual Autos**

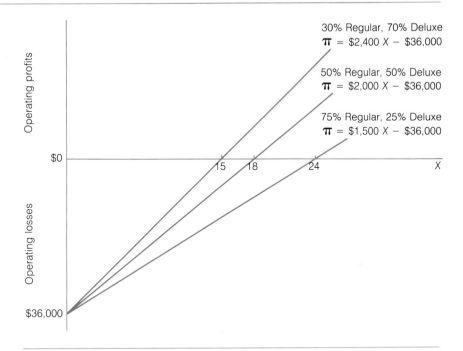

Illustration 11–9   **Impact of product mix on operating profits, Dual Autos**

		Quantity		
Mix	**Total cars**	**Regular**	**Deluxe**	**Operating profits**
30% Regular, 70% Deluxe	40	12	28	$60,000[a]
50% Regular, 50% Deluxe	40	20	20	44,000[b]
75% Regular, 25% Deluxe	40	30	10	24,000[c]

[a] $60,000 = (12 × $1,000) + (28 × $3,000) − $36,000
          = $12,000 + $84,000 − $36,000
[b] $44,000 = (20 × $1,000) + (20 × $3,000) − $36,000
          = $20,000 + $60,000 − $36,000
[c] $24,000 = (30 × $1,000) + (10 × $3,000) − $36,000
          = $30,000 + $30,000 − $36000

Common fixed costs in CVP analysis

Suppose that Dual Autos' total fixed costs of $36,000 can be attributed to the two products as follows:

Direct fixed costs:	
Regular model	$ 9,000
Deluxe model	9,000
Common fixed costs	18,000
Total fixed costs	$36,000

What is the break-even quantity for each product and for the company as a whole?

We compute the break-even volume for the Regular model:

$$X_r = \frac{F}{P - V} = \frac{\$9,000}{\$1,000} = \underline{\underline{9 \text{ cars}}}$$

and break-even volume for the Deluxe model:

$$X_d = \frac{F}{P - V} = \frac{\$9,000}{\$3,000} = \underline{\underline{3 \text{ cars}}}$$

If each product line just breaks even, the operating profit or loss for the company as a whole is:

$$
\begin{aligned}
&= (\$1,000 X_r) + (\$3,000 X_d) - \$36,000 \\
&= (\$1,000 \times 9) + (\$3,000 \times 3) - \$36,000 \\
&= \$18,000 - \$36,000 \\
&= -\underline{\underline{\$18,000}}
\end{aligned}
$$

Although the sale of nine Regular models and three Deluxe models would make each product appear to break even, the company would lose $18,000.

This demonstrates a common problem in applying CVP analysis. The volume required for a specific product to break even will not cover unassigned common costs.

One way of dealing with the problem is to allocate the common costs to the products. This permits a CVP analysis for each product. Of course, the results depend on the allocation method. In such cases, it is wise to perform sensitivity analysis with various allocation methods to discover any that might affect management decisions.

For example, Illustration 11–10 presents CVP analyses for Dual Autos, first assuming that the $18,000 in common fixed costs are allocated evenly to the two products, and then assuming that two thirds of the common fixed costs are allocated to the Deluxe model and one third to the Regular model. As you can see, changing the allocation of fixed costs changes the product mix required to break even or to a achieve a target level of operating profits for the company as a whole.

The break-even volumes shown in Illustration 11–10 are only two of many possible combinations. Allocating common fixed costs to products does not dispense with the product-mix problem. Nonetheless, it makes product-line CVP analysis possible, and it ensures that common fixed costs are not ignored. Because the allocation of common fixed costs is often arbitrary, we recommend performing sensitivity analysis on the allocation method before using the information for decision making.

Illustration 11–10

Impact of common fixed cost allocation method on break-even volume, Dual Autos

Allocation method A

	Regular	Deluxe
Direct fixed costs	$ 9,000	$ 9,000
Common fixed cost allocation	9,000	9,000
	$18,000	$18,000

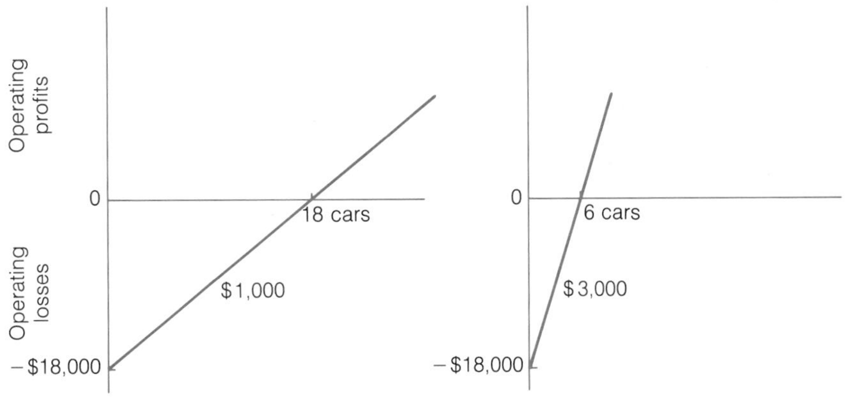

Allocation method B

	Regular	Deluxe
Direct fixed costs	$ 9,000	$ 9,000
Common fixed cost allocation	6,000	12,000
	$15,000	$21,000

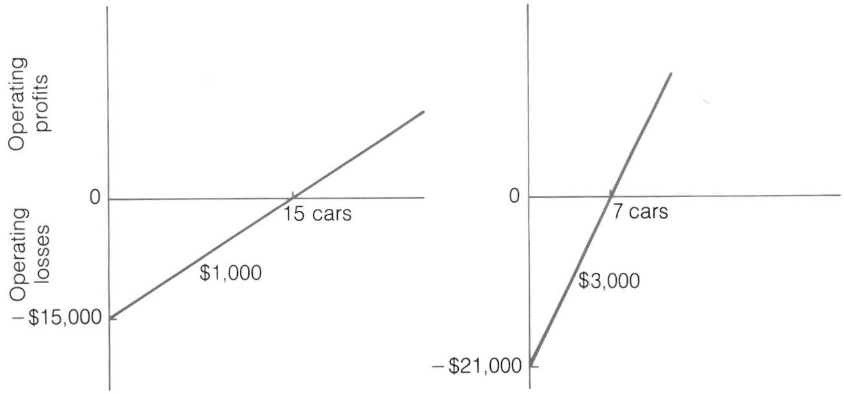

CVP analysis when there are inventory values	Suppose the management of Bloomington Products (BP) wants to use CVP analysis to analyze the impact of several sales volumes on operating profits. They provide the following expectations for next year:

Selling price per unit		$30
Cost classification	**Variable cost (per unit)**	**Fixed cost (per month)**
Manufacturing costs (the following amounts are assumed to apply both to beginning inventory and to units produced):		
Direct materials	$ 4	—
Direct labor	9	—
Manufacturing overhead	4	$306,000
Total manufacturing costs	17	306,000
Marketing and administrative costs	5	174,000
Total variable costs per unit	$22	
Total fixed costs per month		$480,000

Production volume	100,000 units
Sales volume	90,000 units
Beginning finished goods inventory	20,000 units
No work in process inventory is expected at either the beginning or end of the year.	

What operating profit will the company make if sales and production volume are as projected?

What is BP's break-even point?

To answer the first question, find π assuming all fixed manufacturing costs are treated as period costs, which is consistent with the *variable costing* method of valuing inventory:

$$\pi = (\$30 - 22)(90{,}000 \text{ units}) - \$480{,}000$$
$$= \$240{,}000$$

To answer the second question:

$$X = \frac{\$480{,}000}{\$8}$$
$$= 60{,}000 \text{ units sold}$$

Note that *the analysis is based on sales volume, not production volume.* Also note that the costs in the profit equation include both manufacturing and nonmanufacturing costs.

According to the profit equation, the total expected costs for the year are:

$$F + VX = \$480{,}000 + (\$22 \times 90{,}000 \text{ units})$$
$$= \$2{,}460{,}000$$

Are these all of the costs that are expected to be *incurred* during the year? No, these are only the year's fixed costs plus the variable costs associated with the units sold. There would be additional variable manufacturing costs incurred because of the excess of units produced over units sold. Costs incurred would amount to:

Fixed costs	Variable manufacturing costs	Variable marketing and administrative costs
$ 480,000	+ ($17)(100,000) units)	+ ($5)(90,000 units)
= 480,000	+ $1,700,000 + $450,000	
= 2,630,000		

The excess of costs incurred over costs in the profit equation, which is:

$$\$170,000 = \$2,630,000 - \$2,460,000$$

is the increase in inventory value under the variable costing method, which is:

$$\$170,000 = \$17 \text{ per unit times } 10,000 \text{ units increase in inventory.}$$

In short, when units produced and sold are not the same, costs shown in the profit equation will not equal costs incurred. The variable costs shown in the profit equation are the sum of the *variable manufacturing cost of goods sold* and the variable marketing and administrative costs of the period. The fixed costs in the profit equation are the total fixed costs expected to be incurred during the period.

Use of CVP for planning and performance evaluation

Once an estimate of CVP behavior has been derived, it can be used as a basis for planning and performance evaluation. Organizations often prepare plans that show expected revenue, costs, and operating profits at various volumes of activity. These are known as *flexible budgets.*

For example, recall that at Sport Autos V equals $13,000 and F equals $30,000. Based on these facts, the cost-volume line in Illustration 11–11 was developed. This **flexible budget line,** which shows the expected monthly costs at various levels of output, could be used as a flexible cost budget for Sport Autos.

Suppose that in November, 20 cars were sold, and the costs of these cars, including cost of goods sold, dealer preparation costs, sales commissions, and the fixed costs of running the dealership totaled $310,000. What were the expected costs for the month? By how much did actual costs vary from expected costs? From the cost-volume line in Illustration 11–11, we find expected costs of $290,000 (= $30,000 + [$13,000 × 20 cars] = $30,000 + $260,000). Actual costs exceeded expected costs by $20,000 (= $310,000 + $290,000).

Illustration 11–11   **Flexible cost budget based on the cost-volume line, Sport Autos**

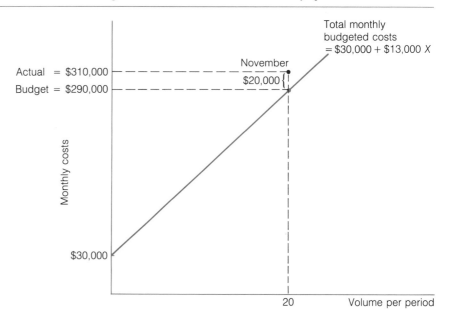

Suppose that Sport Autos' costs for the month of December were $530,000. Do these high costs reflect poor cost control or an unfavorable profit picture? Neither is necessarily the correct interpretation. The answer cannot be determined until we know December's volume. That is why a *flexible budget* is important. By definition, variable costs vary with volume; hence, if volume changes, total variable costs *should* change. In fact, if the volume in December was 40 cars, then $530,000 actual costs were lower than would be expected at that volume. This occurs because at 40 cars, we would expect to incur costs of $550,000 (= $30,000 fixed costs + [$13,000 × 40 cars] = $30,000 + $520,000). Actual costs were less than expected costs by $20,000.

The flexible budget is a very useful tool for evaluating how well employees and departments have performed compared to plans. We go into much more detail about the uses of flexible budgets in planning and performance evaluation, in Chapters 18 through 21.

Limitations and assumptions

Like any other tool, CVP analysis has limitations that make it more applicable to some decisions than to others. Some of these limitations and the impact they can have on the results of CVP analysis follow. As with any management information, the system is judged in terms of a cost-benefit test. Overcoming some of the listed limitations may not be cost justified.

Assumed and actual cost behavior

A linear CVP analysis assumes that:

1. Revenues change proportionately with volume.
2. Total variable costs change proportionately with volume.
3. Fixed costs do not change at all with volume.

One useful feature of CVP analysis is its simplicity in showing the impact of sales prices, costs, and volume on operating profits (or cash flows). But the cost of this simplicity is often a lack of realism. Some costs cannot be easily classified. Costs seldom behave in a neat linear fashion. CVP analysis is based on the assumption that within a specific range of activity, the linear expression approximates reality closely enough that the results will not be badly distorted.

Assumed linear relationships are more likely to be valid for short time periods (one year or less) and small changes in volume than for long periods and large changes in volume. Most fixed costs are only fixed in the short run. Over time, management may make decisions that change fixed costs. For example, during a recent downturn in the economy, a steel company announced the closing of two of the four blast furnaces in one of its plants. Many costs that were fixed while all four blast furnaces were operating (for example, supervisory salaries, product inspection costs, some maintenance and utilities costs) were temporarily eliminated.

Also, many nonvolume factors that would affect prices and costs (for example, limited capacity, technological changes, and input factor prices) are more likely to be constant over short time periods.

Assuming a constant product mix

As we saw earlier in the chapter with multiple products, a change in product mix can affect operating profits. Holding the product mix constant allows the analyst to focus on the impact of prices, costs, and volume on operating profits.

Recording costs as expenses

If the costs used in CVP analysis are not the same ones expensed in the financial statements, the resultant operating profit will not be the same. Discrepancies are usually caused by timing differences in the recognition of expenses.

The most common source of difference is the treatment of fixed manufacturing costs when production volume is not equal to sales volume. As discussed in Chapter 9, generally accepted accounting principles (GAAP) and income tax regulations require use of *full-absorption costing.* For financial statements, fixed manufacturing costs must be treated as product costs and expensed when the goods are sold. However, CVP analysis is like variable costing— *all* fixed costs, including fixed manufacturing costs, are treated as if they will be expensed during the period. Thus, while fixed manufacturing costs are treated as product costs for external financial reporting, they are treated as period costs for CVP analysis.

Summary

CVP analysis examines the impact of prices, costs, and volume on operating profits, as summarized in the profit equation:

$$\pi = (P - V)X - F$$

where

π = operating profits
P = average unit selling price
V = average unit variable costs
X = quantity of output
F = total fixed costs

CVP analysis is both a management tool for determining the impact of selling prices, costs, and volume on profits and a conceptual tool, or way of thinking, about managing a company. It helps management focus on the objective of obtaining the best possible combination of prices, volume, variable costs, and fixed costs.

An advantage of the CVP model is its simplicity. However, the price of such simplicity is a set of limiting assumptions that result in some loss of realism. When multiple products are analyzed, a constant product mix must be assumed or common costs must be allocated. Whenever assumptions are made, it is advisable to perform sensitivity analysis to determine whether (and how) the assumption affects decisions.

Terms and concepts

The following terms and concepts should be familiar to you after reading this chapter.

Break-even point   **Profit equation**
Contribution margin   **Profit-volume analysis**
Contribution margin ratio **Sensitivity analysis**
Cost-volume-profit (CVP) analysis **Variable cost ratio**
Isoprofit lines   **Weighted-average contribution**
Margin of safety   **margin**
Product mix

Self-study problem No. 1: Leonard Company

Given the following information for Leonard Company for April:

Sales	$180,000
Fixed manufacturing costs	22,000
Fixed marketing and administrative costs	14,000
Total fixed costs	36,000
Total variable costs	120,000
Unit price	$9
Unit variable manufacturing cost	5
Unit variable marketing cost	1

Required:

a. Operating profit when sales are $180,000 (as above).
b. Break-even quantity.
c. Quantity that would produce an operating profit of $30,000.
d. Quantity that would produce an operating profit of 20 percent of sales dollars.
e. Break-even sales quantity if unit variable costs are reduced by 10 percent per product unit, assuming no changes in total fixed costs.
f. Sales dollars required to generate an operating profit of $20,000.
g. Number of units sold in April.

Solution to self-study problem No. 1

a. $\pi = PX - VX - F$
$= \$180,000 - \$120,000 - \$36,000$
$= \$24,000$

b. Break-even $X = \dfrac{F}{P-V}$

$= \dfrac{\$36,000}{\$9 - \$6}$

$= 12,000$ units

c. $X = \dfrac{F + \text{Target } \pi}{P-V}$

$= \dfrac{\$36,000 + \$30,000}{\$9 - \$6}$

$= 22,000$ units

d. Target $\pi = .2PX$
$\pi = PX - VX - F$
$.2PX = PX - VX - F$
$.8PX - VX = F$
$(.8P - V)X = F$

$X = \dfrac{F}{(.8P - V)}$

$= \dfrac{\$36,000}{[(.8)(\$9) - \$6]}$

$= \dfrac{\$36,000}{\$1.20}$

$= 30,000$ units

e. $X = \dfrac{F}{P-V}$

$= \dfrac{\$36,000}{[\$9 - (.9)(\$6)]}$

$= \dfrac{\$36,000}{\$3.60}$

$= 10,000$ units

$$f. \quad PX = \frac{F + \text{Target } \pi}{1 - \dfrac{V}{P}} = \frac{F + \text{Target } \pi}{\dfrac{P - V}{P}}$$

$$= \frac{\$36{,}000 + 20{,}000}{1 - \dfrac{\$6}{\$9}} = \frac{\$36{,}000 + 20{,}000}{\dfrac{\$9 - \$6}{\$9}}$$

$$= \frac{\$56{,}000}{\dfrac{\$3}{\$9}}$$

$$= \$168{,}000$$

g. Units sold in April:

$$X = \frac{\$180{,}000}{\$9}$$

$$= 20{,}000 \text{ units}$$

Self-study problem No. 2: Multiproduct Company

Multiproduct Company produces these products with the following characteristics:

	Product I	Product II	Product III
Price per unit	$5	$6	$7
Variable cost per unit	3	2	4
Expected sales (units)	100,000	150,000	250,000

Total fixed costs for the company are $1,240,000.

Required:

Assuming the product mix would be the same at the break-even point, compute the break-even point in:

a. Units (total and by-product line).
b. Sales dollars (total and by-product line).

Solution to self-study problem No. 2

a. Compute weighted-average contribution margin:

Product mix	I 100,000 units	II 150,000	III 250,000	Total 500,000
	20%	30%	50%	100%

Weighted-average contribution margin $(P^* - V^*)$

$$.20(\$2) + .30(\$4) + .50(\$3) = \$3.10$$

Or

$$\frac{(100{,}000 \text{ units})(\$2) + (150{,}000)(\$4) + (250{,}000)(\$3)}{500{,}000} = \$3.10$$

$$X = \frac{\$1{,}240{,}000}{\$3.10} = 400{,}000 \text{ units}$$

b. To compute break-even sales dollars, find weighted-average price and variable costs:

$$P^* = (.20)(\$5) + (.30)(\$6) + (.50)(\$7)$$
$$= \$6.30$$
$$V^* = (.20)(\$3) + (.30)(\$2) + (.50)(\$4)$$
$$= \$3.20$$

$$\text{Break-even } PX = \frac{\$1,240,000}{1 - \dfrac{\$3.20}{\$6.30}} = \frac{\$1,240,000}{\dfrac{\$3.10}{\$6.30}}$$

$$= \frac{\$1,240,000}{.492 \text{ (rounded)}}$$

$$= \$2,520,000 \text{ (rounded to nearest \$1,000)}$$

(Check: 400,000 units × $6.30 = 2,520,000).

Product-line amounts:

	Total (100%)	Product I (20%)	Product II (30%)	Product III (50%)
Units	400,000	80,000	120,000	200,000
Units price	$6.30	$5	$6	$7
Sales dollars	$2,520,000	$400,000	$720,000	$1,400,000

Questions

11–1. Define the profit equation.

11–2. What are the components of total costs in the profit equation?

11–3. What is the meaning of the term *contribution margin?*

11–4. How does the total *contribution margin* differ from the *gross margin* that is often shown on companies' financial statements?

11–5. Compare cost-volume-profit (CVP) analysis with profit-volume analysis. How do they differ?

11–6. Is a company really breaking even if it produces and sells at the "break-even" point? What costs might not be covered?

11–7. What is usually the difference between CVP analysis on a cash basis and that on an accounting accrual basis? For a company having depreciable assets, would you expect the accrual break-even point to be higher, lower, or the same as the cash break-even point?

11–8. How is the profit equation expanded when multiproduct CVP analysis is used?

11–9. Is it possible to have many break-even points, and many alternative ways to achieve a target operating profit, when a company has multiple products?

11–10. Why is a constant product mix often assumed in multiproduct CVP analysis?

11–11. Define the contribution margin when a constant product mix is assumed in multiproduct CVP analyses.

11–12. When would the sum of the break-even quantities for each of a company's products not be the break-even point for the company as a whole?

11–13. What is the difference between economic "profits" and accounting "net income" or "operating profit"?

11–14. How can CVP analysis be used for planning and performance evaluation?

11–15. Name three common assumptions of linear CVP analysis.

11–16. Why might there be a difference between the operating profit calculated by CVP analysis and the net income reported in financial statements for external reporting?

11–17. Fixed costs are often defined as "fixed over the short-run." Does this mean they are not fixed over the long-run? Why or why not?

11–18. Why does the accountant use a linear representation of cost and revenue behavior in CVP analysis? How can this use be justified?

11–19. The following graph implies that profits increase continually as volume increases:

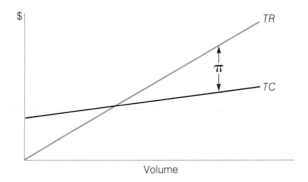

What are some of the factors that might prevent the increasing profits that are indicated when linear CVP analysis is employed?

11–20. Why would fixed costs tend not to be relevant for a typical CVP analysis? Under what circumstances might the fixed costs be relevant in CVP analyses?

11–21. CVP analysis is an oversimplification of the real-world environment. For this reason, it has little to offer a decision maker. Comment.

Exercises

11–22. A CVP graph

Identify each of the following on the graph below:

a. The total cost line.
b. The total revenue line.
c. The total variable costs area.
d. Variable cost per unit.
e. The fixed-costs area.
f. The break-even point.
g. The profit area (or volume).
h. The loss area (or volume).

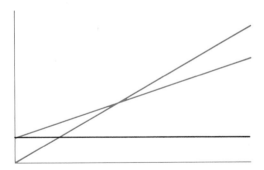

11-23. Profit-volume graph

Identify the places on the profit-volume graph indicated by the letters below:

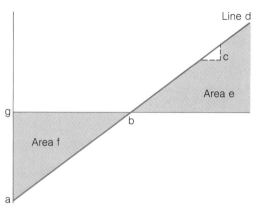

11-24. CVP analysis

The AJ Company produces one product with the following costs and revenues for the year:

Total revenues	$5,000,000
Total fixed costs	1,000,000
Total variable costs	3,000,000
Total quantity produced and sold	1,000,000 units

Required:

a. What is the selling price per unit?
b. What is the variable cost per unit?
c. What is the contribution margin per unit?
d. What is the break-even point?
e. What quantity of units is required for AJ Company to make an operating profit of $2,000,000 for the year?

11-25. CVP analysis with semifixed (step) costs

Shift Manufacturing Company manufactures and sells one product. The sales price of $10 remains constant per unit regardless of volume, as does the variable cost of $6 per unit. The company is considering operating at one of the following three levels of monthly operations:

	Volume range (Production and sales)	Total fixed costs
Level 1	0–16,000	$40,000
Level 2	16,001–28,000	72,000
Level 3	28,001–38,000	94,000

Required:

a. Calculate the break-even point(s).

b. If the company can sell everything it makes, should it operate at Level 1, Level 2, or Level 3? Support your answer.

11–26. CVP— sensitivity analysis

Alto, Inc., is considering introduction of a new product with the following price and cost characteristics:

Sales price	$	100 each
Variable cost		60 each
Fixed costs		200,000 per year

Required:

a. What quantity is required for Alto, Inc., to break-even?

b. What quantity is required for Alto, Inc., to make an operating profit of $100,000 for the year?

c. Assume the projected quantity for the year is 8,000 units for each of the following situations:

    (1) What will the operating profit be for 8,000 units?

    (2) What would be the impact on operating profit if the sales price decreases by 10 percent? Increases by 20 percent?

    (3) What would be the impact on operating profit if variable costs per unit decrease by 10 percent? Increase by 20 percent?

    (4) Suppose fixed costs for the year are 10 percent lower than projected, while variable costs per unit are 10 percent higher than projected. What would be the impact on operating profit for the year?

11–27. Multiple choice

Choose the *best* answer for each of the following questions:

a. If a firm has a negative contribution margin, to reach break even—

    (1) Sales volume must be increased.

    (2) Sales volume must be decreased.

    (3) Fixed cost must be decreased.

    (4) Fixed cost must be increased.

    (5) None of the above.

b. If total contribution margin is decreased by a given amount, operating profit would—

    (1) Decrease by the same amount.

    (2) Decrease by more than the given amount.

    (3) Increase by the same amount.

    (4) Remain unchanged.

    (5) None of the above.

c. The break-even point would be increased by—

    (1) A decrease in fixed costs.

    (2) An increase in contribution margin ratio.

    (3) An increase in variable costs.

    (4) A decrease in variable costs.

    (5) None of the above.

d. Given the following formulas, which one represents the break-even sales level in units?

P = selling price per unit; F = total fixed cost; V = variable cost per unit.

(1) $\dfrac{F}{P - V}$.

(2) $\dfrac{P}{F \div V}$.

(3) $\dfrac{F}{V \div P}$.

(4) $\dfrac{V}{SP - F}$.

(5) $\dfrac{P}{F - V}$.

e. Which of the following assumptions is *not* made in break-even analysis?
   (1) Volume is the only factor affecting cost.
   (2) No change between beginning and ending inventory.
   (3) The sales mix is maintained as volume changes.
   (4) All of the above are assumptions sometimes required in break-even analysis.

f. A company increased the selling price for its products from $1 to $1.10 a unit when total fixed cost increased from $400,000 to $480,000 and variable cost per unit remained the same. How would these changes affect the break-even point?
   (1) The break-even point in units would be increased.
   (2) The break-even point in units would be decreased.
   (3) The break-even point in units would remain unchanged.
   (4) The effect cannot be determined from the given information.

Problems and cases

11–28. CVP analysis over time

You have acquired the following data for the calendar years 1984 and 1985 for Celebration, Inc.:

	1984		1985		Dollar increase
Sales revenue	$750,000	100%	$840,000	100%	$90,000
Cost of goods sold	495,000	66	560,000	66⅔	65,000
Gross margin	$255,000	34%	$280,000	33⅓%	$25,000
Unit selling price	$10		$12		

Required:

Prepare a statement in good form which analyzes the variations in sales and cost of goods sold between 1984 and 1985.

(CPA adapted)

11–29. CVP— missing data

Freedom, Inc., management has performed cost studies and projected the following annual costs based on 40,000 units of production and sales:

	Total annual costs	Percent of total annual costs that is variable
Direct material	$400,000	100%
Direct labor	360,000	75
Manufacturing overhead	300,000	40
Selling, general, and administrative	200,000	25

Required:

a. Compute Freedom's unit selling price that will yield a projected 10 percent profit if sales are 40,000 units.

b. Assume that management selects a selling price of $30 per unit. Compute Freedom's dollar sales that will yield a projected 10 percent profit on sales assuming the above variable-fixed costs relationships are valid.

(CPA adapted)

11–30. Profit analysis with multiple products

Company BE produces two products, B and E, with the following characteristics:

	Product B	Product E
Selling price per unit	$5	$6
Variable cost per unit	3	2
Expected sales (units)	100,000	150,000

The total fixed costs for the company are $700,000.

Required:

a. What is the anticipated level of profits for the expected sales volumes?

b. Assuming the product mix would be the same at the break-even point, compute the break-even point in terms of each of the products.

c. If the product sales mix were to change to 4B:1E, what would the new break-even volume equal in terms of each of the products?

11–31. Profit computations at different activity levels

ElectroSol Systems, Inc., has been organized to manufacture and sell solar energy systems for installation in the Southwest. The marketing consultants for the company estimate that at a selling price of $3,000 per unit, the company should be able to sell 10,000 units per year. However, the company's financial advisor is of the opinion that a more likely sales level would be 7,000 units per year at the same sales price.

The company's controller estimates annual fixed costs will equal $12,000,000 and that the variable cost on each unit will be $1,600.

Required:

a. Determine the profit or loss at the 7,000-unit and 10,000-unit activity levels.

b. What is the break-even point?

c. What course of action would management be likely to take after receiving the results of this analysis?

11–32. CVP analysis of alternatives

Martell Corporation is a manufacturer of small home appliances. The company has idle facilities that would allow it to manufacture 50,000 hair dryers in the building currently used for small appliances. There is no alternative economic use of the idle facilities. However, Martell would have to spend $220,000 per year in equipment and administrative costs to get into the alternative line of business.

Should the company wish to produce additional hair dryers, it would be necessary to lease additional space and to purchase more equipment. The fixed costs that would be incurred per year to produce up to 160,000 hair dryers in excess of the 50,000 that can be produced in existing facilities would amount to $240,000 per year for a total of $460,000 fixed costs to provide a capacity for 210,000 hair dryers.

The company has been offered a contract to purchase 150,000 hair dryers per year by a large discount chain. The chain is willing to pay $5 per unit but must be assured of delivery of 150,000 units. Variable costs are estimated at $2 per unit.

The company estimates that it can sell up to 90,000 units through wholesalers at a price of $8 per unit. If the company sells through the wholesalers, it will not be required to produce any specific minimum quantity. However, the company expects to incur selling costs of $.25 more per unit for dryers sold to wholesalers.

Required:

Prepare a report showing the expected profit per year under these alternatives:

a. Sell to wholesalers using existing idle facilities only.
b. Sell to the chain store and to wholesalers (the new facilities must be acquired in this case).

11–33. CVP analysis and price changes

The Denton Manufacturing Company is concerned about the possible effects of inflation on its operations. Presently, the company sells 200,000 units at a unit price of $15. The variable costs of production are $8, and fixed costs amount to $1,120,000. The present profit level is $280,000. Production engineers have advised management that unit labor costs are expected to rise by 10 percent in the coming year and unit materials costs are expected to rise by 15 percent. Of the variable costs, 25 percent are from labor and 50 percent are materials. All other variable costs are expected to increase by 5%. Sales prices cannot increase more than 8 percent. It is also expected that fixed costs will rise by 2 percent as a result of increased taxes and other miscellaneous fixed charges.

The company wishes to maintain the same level of profits in real-dollar terms. It is expected that to accomplish this objective, profits will have to increase by 6 percent during the year.

Required:

a. Compute the volume of sales and the dollar sales level necessary to maintain the present profit level in nominal terms assuming the maximum price increase is implemented.
b. Compute the volume of sales and the dollar sales level necessary to attain the same profit level in real dollar terms assuming the maximum price increase is implemented.
c. If the volume of sales were to remain at 200,000 units, what price increase would be required to attain the same profit level in real-dollar terms?

11–34. Sensitivity analysis

Petersen Publishing Corporation is currently selling a line of executive education courses at a price of $90 per course. The company maintains office and publishing facilities at an annual fixed cost of $800,000 for office and administration and $720,000 for publishing operations. The variable costs of each course unit include $15 for promotion, $6 for administration and $12 for the published materials. At the present time, the company distributes 25,000 course units per year. Management is dissatisfied with the profitability of current operations and wishes to investigate the profit effects of several alternatives. The following questions have been raised by members of management in an attempt to evaluate the alternatives (each alternative should be considered independently).

Required:

a. What is the break-even level in terms of unit sales?
b. The company can hire an educational representative to sell the course material independently of current sales activity. Current sales would remain the same,

but the representative should be able to sell an additional 10,000 units at the $90 price. Promotion costs would amount to $20 per unit, and the representative would receive a commission of 25 percent of the sales price of each course unit. All other costs would remain unchanged. What is the profit effect of hiring the representative?

c. A publishing company has offered to produce the course materials at a price of $40 per course unit regardless of the number of course units. If this alternative is chosen, the fixed and variable costs of the current publishing operation would be eliminated. What is the profit effect of this alternative if sales remain at 25,000 units? If sales increase to 40,000 units?

11–35. CVP relationships with changes in cost structure

The Stockton Picket Fence Company manufactures prefabricated fence sections that sell at $6 per unit. The present facilities use an older model of semiautomated equipment. Variable costs are $4.50 per unit, and fixed costs total $300,000 per year.

An alternate semiautomated fence machine can be rented. This alternate machine would increase fixed costs to $550,000 per year, but variable costs would be reduced to $3.25 per unit.

Another fence machine supplier offers a fully automatic machine that would result in annual fixed costs of $800,000. However, the fully automatic machine would reduce the variable costs to $2 per unit.

There are no other costs or cash flows affected by the choice among these three alternatives.

Management is concerned about the break-even point for operations using each of these machines. Moreover, the sales volume for fence sections is quite erratic. Management is interested in the profit or losses that would occur with each type of equipment if the sales volume were 175,000 units and if the sales volume were 250,000 units.

Required:

Prepare a schedule showing the break-even point and the profit or loss obtainable for each equipment alternative at sales volumes of 175,000 and 250,000 units.

11–36. CVP analysis for fare pricing: Trans Western Airlines*

Trans Western Airlines is preparing to submit a proposal to its board of directors for air service between Phoenix, Arizona, and Las Vegas, Nevada. The route would be designed primarily to serve the recreation and tourist travelers that frequently travel between the two cities. By offering low-cost tourist fares, the airline hopes to persuade persons who now travel by other modes of transportation to switch and fly Trans Western on this route.

In addition, the airline expects to attract business travelers during the hours of 7 A.M. to 6 P.M. on Mondays through Fridays. The fare price schedule or tariff would be designed to charge a higher fare during business travel hours so that tourist demand would be reduced during those hours. The company believes that a business fare of $40 one way during business hours and a fare of $30 for all other hours would result in 50 percent business travel and 50 percent tourist travel each week.

To operate the route, the airline would need two 120-passenger jet aircraft. The aircraft would be leased at an annual cost of $2,800,000 each. Other fixed costs attributable to the Phoenix–Las Vegas route would amount to $900,000 per year. These fixed costs would not change regardless of the number of flights.

---

* © 1982 by CIPT Co., all rights reserved.

Operation of each aircraft requires a flight crew whose salaries are based primarily on the hours of flying time. The cost of the flight crew is approximately $300 per hour of flying time.

Aircraft maintenance and fuel costs are also a function of flying time. These costs are estimated at $110 per hour of flying time. Flying time between Phoenix and Las Vegas is estimated at 45 minutes each way.

The costs associated with processing each passenger amount to $7. This includes ticket processing and variable costs of baggage handling. Food and beverage service will be offered at no charge on flights during business hours. Food and beverage service is expected to break even through the charges levied for alcoholic beverages.

Required:

a. If five business flights and three tourist flights are offered each way every weekday, and 10 tourist flights are offered each way every Saturday and Sunday, what number of passengers must be carried on each flight to break even?

b. The board of directors requires an estimate of the load factor (or percentage of available seats occupied on a route) required to break even on a given route. What is the break-even load factor for this proposed route?

c. If Trans Western Airlines obtains authority to operate the Phoenix–Las Vegas route, its aircraft on that route will be idle between midnight and 6 A.M. The airline is considering offering a daily "Red Die" special that would leave Phoenix at midnight and would return by 6 A.M. The marketing division estimates that if the fare were no more than $15, at least 60 new passengers could be attracted to each one-way Red Die flight. Operating costs would be at the same rate for this flight, but additional advertising costs of $1,200 per week would be required for promotion of the service. Management wishes to know the minimum fare that would be required to break even on the Red Die special assuming the marketing division's passenger estimates are correct.

11–37. CVP analysis and profit targets

Martin Margolis Corporation is contemplating introducing a new line of cosmetic kits for skin care. The kits would sell for $12 each. The variable costs associated with each kit amount to $3. If the kits are to be introduced nationwide, the company will have to obtain acceptable profits on a test market basis. The fixed costs associated with producing the kits for the test market amount to $260,000 per year.

Required:

a. Compute the break-even point in units for test market sales.

b. If the desired profit level is $80,000 before tax, compute the sales level in units required to attain that profit level.

c. Assuming the tax rate is 45 percent and the desired profit level is $80,000 after tax, compute the required unit sales level.

11–38. CVP analysis with semifixed costs: Discovery Day Care Center*

Beverly Miller, director and owner of the Discovery Day Care Center, has a master's degree in elementary education. In the seven years she has been running the Discovery Center, her salary has ranged from nothing to $10,000 per year. "The second year," she says, "I made 62 cents an hour."

Her salary is what's left over after all other expenses are met.

Could she run a more profitable center? She thinks perhaps she could if she increased the student-teacher ratio, which is currently five students to one teacher. (Government

---

* © Michael W. Maher, 1984.

standards for a center like this set a maximum of 10 students per teacher.) However, she refuses to increase the ratio to more than six to one. "If you increase the ratio to more than 6:1, the children don't get enough attention. In addition, the demands on the teacher are far too great." She does not hire part-time teachers.

Beverly rents the space for her center in the basement of a church for $450 per month, including utilities. She estimates that supplies, snacks, and other nonpersonnel costs are $40 per student per month. She charges $190 per month per student. Teachers are paid $600 per month, including fringe benefits. There are no other operating costs. At present, there are 30 students and 6 teachers, in addition to Ms. Miller, who is not considered a teacher for this analysis.

Required:

a. What is the present operating profit per month of the Discovery Day Care Center before Ms. Miller's salary?

b. What is (are) the break-even point(s) assuming a student-teacher ratio of 6:1?

c. What would be the break-even point(s) if the student-teacher ratio was allowed to increase to 10:1?

d. Ms. Miller has an opportunity to increase the student body by six students. She must take all six or none. Should she accept the six students if she wants to maintain a maximum student-teacher ratio of 6:1?

e. Continuation of part (d). Suppose Ms. Miller accepts the six children. Now she has the opportunity to accept one more. What would happen to profit if she did, assuming she has to hire one more teacher.

11–39. R. A. Ro & Company

R. A. Ro & Company, maker of quality handmade pipes, has experienced a steady growth in sales for the past five years. However, increased competition has led Mr. Ro, the president, to believe that an aggressive advertising campaign will be necessary next year to maintain the company's present growth.

To prepare for next year's advertising campaign, the company's accountant has prepared and presented Mr. Ro with the following data for the current year, 1983:

Cost schedule

Variable costs:	
Direct labor	$ 8.00 per pipe
Direct materials	3.25 per pipe
Variable overhead	2.50 per pipe
Total variable costs	$13.75 per pipe
Fixed costs:	
Manufacturing	$ 25,000
Selling	40,000
Administrative	70,000
Total fixed costs	$135,000
Selling price, per pipe	$25.00
Expected sales, 1983 (20,000 units)	$500,000
Tax rate: 40%	

Mr. Ro has set the sales target for 1984 at a level of $550,000 (or 22,000 pipes).

Required:

a. What is the projected after-tax operating profit for 1983?

b. What is the break-even point in units for 1983?

c. Mr. Ro believes an additional selling expense of $11,250 for advertising in 1984, with all other costs remaining constant, will be necessary to attain the sales target. What will be the after-tax net income for 1984 if the additional $11,250 is spent?

d. What will be the break-even point in dollar sales for 1984 if the additional $11,250 is spent for advertising?

e. If the additional $11,250 is spend for advertising in 1984, what is the required sales level in dollars to equal 1983 after-tax operating profit?

f. At a sales level of 22,000 units, what is the maximum amount which can be spent on advertising if an after-tax operating profit of $60,000 is desired?

(CMA adapted)

11–40. Converting full-absorption costing income statements to CVP analysis

Pralina Products Company is a regional firm that has three major product lines—cereals, breakfast bars, and dog food. The income statement for the year ended April 30, 1984, is shown below; the statement was prepared by product line using full-absorption costing. Explanatory data related to the items presented in the income statement follow.

PRALINA PRODUCTS COMPANY
Income Statement
For the Year Ended April 30, 1984
(in thousands)

	Cereals	Breakfast bars	Dog food	Total
Sales in pounds	2,000	500	500	3,000
Revenue from sales	$1,000	$400	$200	$1,600
Cost of sales:				
Direct materials	330	160	100	590
Direct labor	90	40	20	150
Factory overhead	108	48	24	180
Total cost of sales	528	248	144	920
Gross margin	472	152	56	680
Operating costs:				
Selling costs:				
Advertising	50	30	20	100
Commissions	50	40	20	110
Salaries and related benefits	30	20	10	60
Total selling expenses	130	90	50	270
General and administrative costs:				
Licenses	50	20	15	85
Salaries and related benefits	60	25	15	100
Total general and administrative costs	110	45	30	185
Total operating costs	240	135	80	455
Operating profit before taxes	$ 232	$ 17	$ (24)	$ 225

Other data:

1. *Cost of sales.* The company's inventories of direct materials and finished products do not vary significantly from year to year. The inventories at April 30, 1984, were essentially identical to those at April 30, 1983.

Factory overhead was applied to products at 120 percent of direct labor dollars. The factory overhead costs for the 1983–1984 fiscal year were as follows:

Variable indirect labor and supplies	$ 15,000
Variable employee benefits on factory labor	30,000
Supervisory salaries and related benefits	35,000
Plant occupancy costs	100,000
	$180,000

There was no overapplied or underapplied overhead at year-end.

2. *Advertising.* The company has been unable to determine any direct causal relationship between the level of sales volume and the level of advertising expenditures. However, because management believes advertising is necessary, an annual advertising program is implemented for each product line. Each product line is advertised independently of the others.

3. *Commissions.* Sales commissions are paid to the sales force at the rates of 5 percent on the cereals and 10 percent on the breakfast bars and dog food.

4. *Licenses.* Various licenses are required for each product line. These are renewed annually for each product line.

5. *Salaries and related benefits.* Sales, and general and administrative personnel, devote time and effort to all product lines. Their salaries and wages are allocated on the basis of management's estimates of time spent on each product line.

Required:

a. The controller of Pralina Products Company has recommended that the company do a CVP analysis of its operations. As a first step the controller has requested that you prepare a revised income statement for Pralina Products Company that employs a product contribution margin format that will be useful in CVP analysis. The statement should show the profit contribution for each product line and the operating profit before taxes for the company as a whole.

b. The controller of Pralina Products Company is going to prepare a report that he will present to the other members of top management explaining CVP analysis. Identify and explain the following points that the controller should include in the report.

(1) The advantages which CVP analysis can provide to a company.

(2) The difficulties Pralina Products Company could experience in the calculations involved in CVP analysis.

(3) The dangers that Pralina Products Company should be aware of in using the information derived from the CVP analysis.

(CMA adapted)

11–41. CVP analysis with semifixed costs and changing unit variable costs

The Torous Company manufactures and sells one product. The sales price, $50 per unit, remains constant regardless of volume. Last year's sales were 12,000 units, and operating profits were −$40,000 (i.e., a loss). "Fixed" costs depended on production levels, as shown below. Variable costs per unit are 40 percent *higher* in Level 2 (night shift) than in Level 1 (day shift) because of additional labor costs due primarily to higher wages required to employ workers for the night shift.

	Annual production range (in units)	Annual total fixed costs
Level 1 (day shift)	0–15,000	$200,000
Level 2 (night shift)	15,001–25,000	364,000

Last year's cost structure and selling price are not expected to change this year. Maximum plant capacity is 25,000 units. The company sells everything it produces.

Required:

a. Compute the contribution margin per unit for last year for each of the two production levels.

b. Compute the break-even points for last year for each of the two production levels.

c. Compute the volume in units that will maximize operating profits. Defend your choice.

11–42. Bill French*

Bill French picked up the phone and called his boss, Wes Davidson, controller of Duo-Products Corporation. "Say, Wes, I'm all set for the meeting this afternoon. I've put together a set of break-even statements that should really make people sit up and take notice—and I think they'll be able to understand them, too." After a brief conversation about other matters, the call was concluded, and French turned to his charts for one last check-out before the meeting.

French had been hired six months earlier as a staff accountant. He was directly responsible to Davidson and, up to the time of this case, had been doing routine types of analysis work. French was an alumnus of a graduate business school and was considered by his associates to be quite capable and unusually conscientious. It was this latter characteristic that had apparently caused him to "rub some of the working guys the wrong way," as one of his co-workers put it. French was well aware of his capabilities and took advantage of every opportunity that arose to try to educate those around him. Wes Davidson's invitation for French to attend an informal manager's meeting had come as some surprise to others in the accounting group. However, when French requested permission to make a presentation of some break-even data, Davidson acquiesced. The Duo-Products Corporation had not been making use of this type of analysis in its planning or review procedures.

Basically, what French had done was to determine the level at which the company must operate in order to break even. As he phrased it:

The company must be able at least to sell a sufficient volume of goods so that it will cover all the variable costs of producing and selling the goods; further, it will not make a profit unless it covers the fixed, or nonvariable, costs as well. The level of operation at which total costs (that is, variable plus nonvariable) are just covered is the break-even volume. This should be the lower limit in all our planning.

The accounting records had provided the following information that French used in constructing his chart:

Plant capacity–2 million units.
Past year's level of operations–1.5 million units.
Average unit selling price–$1.20.
Total fixed costs–$520,000.
Average variable unit cost–$.75.

From this information, French observed that each unit contributed $.45 to fixed costs after covering the variable costs. Given total fixed costs of $520,000, he calculated that 1,155,556 units must be sold in order to break even. He verified this conclusion by calculating the dollar sales volume that was required to break even. Since the variable costs per unit were 62.5 percent of the selling price, French reasoned that 37.5 percent of every sales dollar was left available to cover fixed costs. Thus, fixed costs of $520,000 require sales of $1,386,667 in order to break even.

When he constructed a break-even chart to present the information graphically, his conclusions were further verified. The chart also made it clear that the firm was operating at a fair margin over the break-even requirements, and that the pretax profits accruing (at the rate of 37.5 percent of every sales dollar over break even) increased rapidly as volume increased (see Exhibit A).

Exhibit A (11-42)   **Break-even chart—total business**

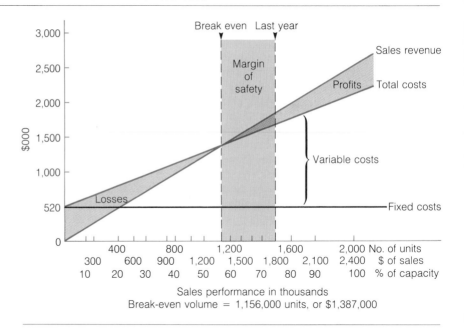

Sales performance in thousands
Break-even volume = 1,156,000 units, or $1,387,000

Shortly after lunch, French and Davidson left for the meeting. Several representatives of the manufacturing departments were present, as well as the general sales manager, two assistant sales managers, the purchasing officer, and two people from the product engineering office. Davidson introduced French to the few people whom he had not already met, and then the meeting got under way. French's presentation was the last item on Davidson's agenda, and in due time the controller introduced French, explaining his interest in cost control and analysis.

French had prepared enough copies of his chart and supporting calculations for everyone at the meeting. He described carefully what he had done and explained how the chart pointed to a profitable year, dependent on meeting the volume of sales activity that had been maintained in the past. It soon became apparent that some of the participants had known in advance what French planned to discuss;

they had come prepared to challenge him and soon had taken control of the meeting. The following exchange ensued (see Exhibit B for a checklist of participants with their titles):

Exhibit B (11–42) **List of participants in the meeting**

Bill French	Staff accountant
Wes Davidson	Controller
John Cooper	Production control
Fred Williams	Manufacturing
Ray Bradshaw	Assistant sales manager
Arnie Winetki	General sales manager
Anne Fraser	Administrative assistant to president

Cooper [production control]: You know, Bill, I'm really concerned that you haven't allowed for our planned changes in volume next year. It seems to me that you should have allowed for the sales department's guess that we'll boost sales by 20 percent, unit-wise. We'll be pushing 90 percent of what we call capacity then. It sure seems that this would make quite a difference in your figuring.

French: That might be true, but as you can see, all you have to do is read the cost and profit relationship right off the chart for the new volume. Let's see—at a million-eight units we'd. . . .

Williams [manufacturing]: Wait a minute, now!!! If you're going to talk in terms of 90 percent of capacity, and it looks like that's what it will be, you had better note that we'll be shelling out some more for the plant. We've already got okays on investment money that will boost your fixed costs by 10 thousand dollars a month, easy. And that may not be all. We may call it 90 percent of plant capacity but there are a lot of places where we're just full up and we can't pull things up any tighter.

Cooper: See, Bill? Fred is right, but I'm not finished on this bit about volume changes. According to the information that I've got here—and it came from your office—I'm not sure that your break-even chart can really be used even if there were to be no changes next year. Looks to me like you've got average figures that don't allow for the fact that we're dealing with three basic products. Your report here (see Exhibit C) on costs, according to product lines, for last year makes it pretty clear that the "average" is way out of line. How would the break-even point look if we took this on an individual product basis?

French: Well, I'm not sure. Seems to me that there is only one break-even point for the firm. Whether we take it product by product or in total, we've got to hit that point. I'll be glad to check for you if you want, but. . . .

Bradshaw [assistant sales manager]: Guess I may as well get in on this one, Bill. If you're going to do anything with individual products, you ought to know that we're looking for a big swing in our product mix. Might even start before we get into the new season. The "A" line is really losing out and I imagine that we'll be lucky to hold two thirds of the volume there next year. Wouldn't you buy that Arnie? [Agreement from the general sales manager.] That's not too bad, though, because we expect that we should pick up the 200,000 that we lose, and about a quarter million units more, over in "C" production. We don't see anything that shows much of a change in "B." That's been solid for years and shouldn't change much now.

Exhibit C (11–42)   **Product class cost analysis (normal year)**

	Aggregate	"A"	"B"	"C"
Sales at full capacity (units)	2,000,000			
Actual sales volume (units)	1,500,000	600,000	400,000	500,000
Unit sales price	$ 1.20	$ 1.67	$ 1.50	$ .40
Total sales revenue	1,800,000	1,000,000	600,000	200,000
Variable cost per unit	.75	1.25	0.625	.25
Total variable cost	1,125,000	750,000	250,000	125,000
Fixed costs	520,000	170,000	275,000	75,000
Profit.	155,000	80,000	75,000	–0–
Ratios:				
Variable cost to sales	.63	.75	.42	.63
Marginal income to sales	.37	.25	.58	.37
Utilization of capacity*	75.0%	30.0%	20.0%	25.0%

* Note: Each product requires the same amount of production capacity per unit.

Winetki [general sales manager]: Bradshaw's called it about as we figure it, but there's something else here too. We've talked about our pricing on "C" enough, and now I'm really going to push our side of it. Ray's estimate of maybe half a million—450,000 I guess it was—up on "C" for next year is on the basis of doubling the price with no change in cost. We've been priced so low on this item that it's been a crime—we've got to raise, but good, for two reasons. First, for our reputation; the price is out of line class-wise and is completely inconsistent with our quality reputation. Second, if we don't raise the price, we'll be swamped and we can't handle it. You heard what Williams said about capacity. The way the whole "C" field is exploding, we'll have to answer to another half million units in unsatisfied orders if we don't jack the price up. We can't afford to expand that much for this product.

At this point, Anne Fraser (administrative assistant to the president) walked up toward the front of the room from where she had been standing near the rear door. The discussion broke for a minute, and she took advantage of the lull to interject a few comments.

Fraser: This has certainly been enlightening. You clearly have a valuable familiarity with our operations. As long as you're going to try to get all the things together that you ought to pin down for next year, let's see what I can add to help you:

Number One: Let's remember that everything that shows in the profit area here on Bill's chart is divided just about evenly between the government and us. Now, for last year we can read a profit of about $150,000. Well, that's right. But we were left with half of that, and then paid our dividends of $50,000 to the stockholders. Since we've got an anniversary year coming up, we'd like to put out a special dividend of about 50 percent extra. We ought to retain $25,000 in the business, too. This means that we'd like to hit $100,000 profit *after* taxes.

Number Two: From where I sit, it looks as if we're going to have negotiations with the union again, and this time it's liable to cost us. All the indications are—and this isn't public—that we may have to meet demands that will boost our production costs—what do you call them here, Bill—variable costs—by 10 percent across the board. This may kill the bonus-dividend plans, but we've got to hold the line on past profits. This means that we can give that much to the union only if we can make it in added revenues. I guess you'd say that that raises your break-even point, Bill—and for that one I'd consider the company's profit to be a fixed cost.

Number Three: Maybe this is the time to think about switching our product emphasis. Arnie may know better than I which of the products is more profitable. You check me out on this Arnie—and it might be a good idea for you and Bill to get together on this one, too. These figures that I have (Exhibit C) make it look like the percentage contribution on line "A" is the lowest of the bunch. If we're losing volume there as rapidly as you sales folks say, and if we're as hard pressed for space as Fred has indicated, maybe we'd be better off grabbing some of that big demand for "C" by shifting some of the facilities over there from "A."

Davidson: Thanks, Anne. I sort of figured that we'd wind up here as soon as Bill brought out his charts. This is an approach that we've barely touched upon, but, as you can see, you've all got ideas that have got to be made to fit here somewhere. Let me suggest this: Bill, you rework your chart and try to bring into it some of the points that were made here today. I'll see if I can summarize what everyone seems to be looking for.

First of all, I have the idea that your presentation is based on a rather important series of assumptions. Most of the questions that were raised were really about those assumptions; it might help us all if you try to set the assumptions down in black and white so that we can see just how they influence the analysis.

Then, I think that John would like to see the unit sales increase taken up, and he'd also like to see whether there's any difference if you base the calculations on an analysis of individual product lines. Also, as Ray suggested, since the product mix is bound to change, why not see how things look if the shift materializes as he has forecast? Arnie would like to see the influence of a price increase in the "C" line; Fred looks toward an increase in fixed manufacturing costs of 10 thousand a month, and Anne has suggested that we should consider taxes, dividends, expected union demands, and the question of product emphasis.

I think that ties it all together. Let's hold off on our next meeting, fellows, until Bill has time to work this all into shape.

With that, the participants broke off into small groups and the meeting disbanded. French and Davidson headed back to their offices and French, in a tone of concern asked Davidson, "Why didn't you warn me about the hornet's nest I was walking into?"

"Bill, you didn't ask!"

Required:

a. What are the assumptions implicit in Bill French's determination of his company's break-even point?

b. On the basis of French's revised information, what does next year look like:

    (1)   What is the break-even point?

    (2)   What level of operations must be achieved to pay the extra dividend, ignoring union demands?

    (3)   What level of operations must be achieved to meet the union demands, ignoring bonus dividends?

   (4) What level of operations must be achieved to meet both dividends and expected union requirements?

  c. Can the break-even analysis help the company decide whether to alter the existing product emphasis?

  d. Calculate *each* of the three product's break-even points using the data in Exhibit C. Why is the sum of these three volumes not equal to the 1,155,556 units aggregate break-even volume?

  e. Evaluate Bill French's approach in developing and presenting his analysis.

12

Differential Costs

OBJECTIVES

To identify costs and revenues that change as a result of a decision.
To understand how to estimate the financial consequences of alternative
actions.

In this chapter, we discuss the use of cost analysis in making such short-run operating decisions as pricing, whether to make or buy products, and whether to drop or add a product line. Each decision requires the comparison of one or more proposed alternatives with the status quo. The task is to determine how costs, in particular, and profits, in general, will be affected if one alternative is chosen over another. This process is called differential analysis. Although decision makers are usually interested in *all* differences between alternatives, including financial and nonfinancial ones, we focus our attention on financial decisions that involve costs and revenues.

Differential analysis is the process of estimating the consequences of alternative actions that decision makers can take. Differential analysis is used for both short-run decisions like the ones we discuss in this chapter and the next, and for long-run decisions like those discussed in Chapters 15 and 16. Generally, the term **short run** is applied to decision horizons over which capacity will be unchanged—one year is usually used for convenience.

There is an important distinction between short-run and long-run decisions. Short-run decisions affect cash flow for such a short period of time that the time value of money is immaterial and hence ignored. Thus, the *amount* of cash flows is important for short-run analysis, but their *timing* is assumed to be unimportant. If an action affects cash flows over a longer period of time (usually more than one year), the time value of money is taken into account, as discussed in Chapters 15 and 16.

Differential costs versus variable costs	Differential costs are costs that change in response to alternative courses of action. Both **variable costs** and **fixed costs** may be differential costs. Variable costs are differential costs when a decision involves possible changes in volume. For example, a decision to close a plant would usually reduce variable costs and some fixed costs. All of the affected costs would be termed *differential costs*. On the other hand, if a machine replacement does not affect either the volume of output or the variable cost per unit, variable costs would not be differential costs.

As the illustrations in this chapter are presented, you will find that differential analysis requires an examination of the facts for each option that is relevant to the decision to determine which costs will be affected. Differential and variable costs have independent meanings and applications and should not be considered interchangeable.

Are historical costs relevant for decision making?[1]

You have probably seen retailers advertise their products for sale at prices below invoice cost. And you may have wondered how they could stay in business if they sold their products below cost. Of course, they could not stay in business if they consistently sold below cost. Retailers recognize, however, that the original cost of their merchandise is a sunk cost—a cost that has already been incurred and is *not differential* when it comes to holding versus selling merchandise.

For example, suppose that a clothing shop has 15 pairs of slacks that each cost the retailer $20. No slacks have been sold at the established price of $39.95, and the retailer believes they can only be sold if the price is reduced. In repricing, the retailer should disregard the original $20 per pair cost. A number of marketing and inventory control issues might be considered, but the historical cost is irrelevant.

Of course, if the slacks are sold for less than $20 per pair, the retailer's financial statement would show a loss. If the slacks were sold for $18 per pair, for example, the statement would be as follows:

Sale of slacks (15 pairs at $18)	$270
Cost of goods sold (15 pairs at $20)	300
Loss on sale	$ (30)

Decision makers are sometimes tempted to hold merchandise rather than sell it below cost in order to avoid showing a loss on their financial statements. In doing so, they may make a bad decision. If the merchandise is not sold immediately at a loss, it may be sold at a greater loss later, or it may have to be written off entirely if it cannot be sold at all. Under the circumstances, unless there is a possibility of a higher price later, the decision to sell now is the best.

The historical cost of an item is not always irrelevant, however. A decision to purchase an item for resale requires information about both its cost and its probable selling price. Nonetheless, once the merchandise *has been pur-*

---

[1] Many of the concepts presented in this chapter were developed by J. M. Clark in his classic work, *Studies in the Economics of Overhead Costs* (Chicago: University of Chicago Press, 1923). Clark developed the notion that costs that are relevant for one purpose are not necessarily relevant for another. If the term *sacrifice* is used to summarize the various meanings of cost, then it becomes clear that the sacrifices (costs) for one set of actions are not necessarily the same as those for another set of actions.

chased, the cash outlay (or promise to pay) has already occurred. The cost is *sunk,* and although it is relevant to income determination, it is irrelevant to subsequent marketing decisions.

Framework for decision making

Which costs are relevant depends on the decision under consideration. A framework for decision making, based on a company that receives a special order, is diagrammed in Illustration 12–1. First, each alternative is set forth as a branch of a decision tree. Second, the value of each alternative is determined. Third, the alternative with the highest value is chosen.

Illustration 12–1   **Framework for decision making**

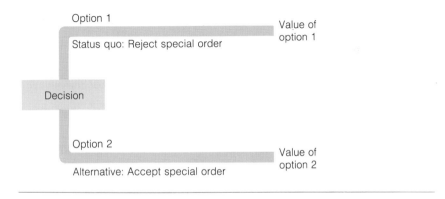

For example, Quick-Print uses a modern copy machine to make copies for walk-in customers. The machine is usually idle about two hours each day. On October 15, B. Onst, who is running for political office, asks Quick-Print to produce 10,000 copies of letters, speeches, memoranda, and other campaign materials to be ready on October 22. The candidate wants to pay only 8 cents per copy, even though the regular price is 10 cents per copy.

In deciding whether to accept the order, the owner of Quick-Print estimates the following operating data for the week in question:

Sales (100,000 copies at 10¢)	$10,000
Variable costs, including paper, maintenance, and usage payment to machine owner (100,000 copies at 6¢)	6,000
Total contribution margin	4,000
Fixed costs (operators, plus allocated costs of the print shop)	2,500
Operating profit	$ 1,500

To make the decision, the owner identifies the alternatives, determines the value of each alternative to the company, and selects the alternative with the highest value to the company.

The values of the alternatives are shown in Illustration 12–2. The best economic decision is to accept the order because the company will gain $200 from it. Fixed costs are not affected by the decision because they are not differential in this situation. Therefore, they are not relevant to the decision.

Illustration 12–2   **Analysis of special order, Quick-Print**

a. **Comparison of totals**

	Status quo: Reject special order	Alternative: Accept special order	Difference
Sales revenue	$10,000	$10,800	$800
Variable costs	(6,000)	(6,600)	(600)
Total contribution	4,000	4,200	200
Fixed costs	(2,500)	(2,500)	–0–
Operating profit	$ 1,500	$ 1,700	$200

b. **Alternative presentation: Differential analysis**

Differential sales, 10,000 at 8¢	$800
Less differential costs, 10,000 at 6¢	600
Differential operating profit (before taxes)	$200

The full-cost fallacy

The terms full cost or *full product cost* are used to describe a product's cost that includes both (1) the variable costs of producing and /or selling the product and (2) a share of the organization's fixed costs.[2] Sometimes decision makers use these full costs, mistakenly thinking they are variable costs.

For example, D. Facto, a Quick-Print employee, claims that accepting B. Onst's special order would be a mistake. "Since our variable costs are $6,000 and our fixed costs are $2,500, our total costs for the week without the special order are $8,500 for 100,000 copies. That works out to 8½ cents per copy, which is more than 8 cents per copy offered by Onst. We'd be losing ½ cent per copy!"

By considering fixed costs in the analysis, D. Facto is including irrelevant information. The fixed costs will be incurred whether the special order is accepted or rejected, so they should not bear on the decision. This is known as the full-cost fallacy because it is incorrect to assume that *all* costs are relevant to every decision. This is a common mistake in short-run decisions, in part because full product costs are emphasized and readily available in accounting records. However, even though all costs must be covered in the

---

[2] The relation between *full-cost* and *full-absorption cost* is discussed in Chapter 9.

long run or the company will fail, in the short run, it would be profitable to accept the order. While full product costs serve a wide variety of important purposes, they are not relevant to the kind of short-run operating decision described in the example above.

Differential fixed costs

In many short-run operating decisions, fixed costs remain unchanged because they are the costs of providing production capacity and capacity does not change in the short run. When short-run operating decisions do not involve a change in capacity, fixed costs remain unchanged and are therefore not differential.

In long-run decisions, however, fixed costs may be differential costs. For example, the addition of a new plant and new machines often involves differential fixed costs. Therefore, like variable costs, fixed costs must be carefully examined to determine if they are differential.

Cost analysis for pricing

The price-volume trade-off is derived from the market demand for a product. By definition, variable costs change with volume. If a change in price results in a change in volume, variable costs change too. Therefore:

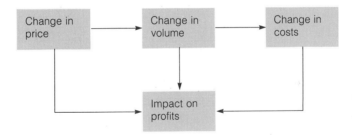

Thus, price-volume changes automatically involve changes in variable costs. The critical consideration for management is whether the joint effect of cost, price, and volume results in an increase or decrease in operating profits.

Cost-plus pricing   Some products are so unique that costs plus a specified allowance for profits provide the only available basis for pricing. Such products are sold under cost-plus contracts. In construction jobs, defense contracts, most custom orders, and many services, the cost of the product plays a significant role in determining its price.

An estimate of specific job costs is also an important guide for bidding on a job. If a bid price is too low compared to costs, the contract may be obtained, but the job will be performed at a loss. If a bid is considerably higher than costs, the contract will probably be lost.

Short-run and long-run differential costs for pricing

Sometimes the only way to sell a product is to cut its price. In such a case, the *minimum price is the differential cost that must be incurred to produce and/or sell the product.*

For example, Advent Manufacturing has a supply of products *on hand* that cost $4 each to manufacture. Selling them would require an additional $2 variable cost per unit. What is the *minimum* price Advent can charge? A quick answer might be $6 (manufacturing costs of $4 plus selling costs of $2). Actually, Advent can drop the price to $2, which is the differential cost to sell the products, and be no worse off than if it held the products unsold. Of course, the $2 is a *minimum* price; Advent's managers would prefer a higher price.

We observe theaters charging lower prices for matinee performances or airlines charging lower prices for certain kinds of passengers. These are examples of price discrimination to sell a product. Price discrimination exists when a product or service is sold at two or more prices that do not reflect proportional differences in marginal costs. If a seat would otherwise go unsold, airlines and theaters should be willing to sell it at a lower price, as long as the price exceeds the variable cost of filling the seat and does not decrease normal sales.

When used in pricing decisions, the differential costs required to sell and/or produce a product provide a floor. In the short-run, differential costs may be very low, as when selling one more seat on an already scheduled airline flight or allowing one more student into an already scheduled course in college.

In the long-run, however, differential costs are much higher. Returning to the airline example, long-run differential costs include the costs of buying and maintaining the aircraft, salaries for the crew, landing fees, and so forth. In the long run, these costs must be covered. To simplify this kind of analysis, the *full product costs* of making and/or selling a product are often used to estimate long-run differential costs. Hence, a common saying in business is: "I can drop my prices to just cover variable costs in the short run, but in the long run my prices have to cover full product costs."

Use of costs to determine legality of pricing practices

The Clayton and Sherman Anti-Trust Acts, the Robinson-Patman Act, and many state and local laws forbid certain pricing practices unless they are cost justified.[3] For example, predatory pricing to prevent or eliminate competition is illegal. A price that is below differential cost may be considered predatory.[4] Certain kinds of price discrimination among customers are also illegal, unless the discrimination is justified by actual differences in the costs

---

[3] See F. M. Sherer, *Industrial Market Structure and Economic Performance* (Boston: Houghton-Mifflin, 1980); and H. F. Taggart, *Cost Justification* (Ann Arbor: Michigan Business School, Division of Research, 1959).

[4] See P. Areeda and D. F. Turner, "Predatory Pricing and Related Practices under Section 2 of the Sherman Act," *Harvard Law Review* (February 1975), pp. 697–733.

of serving the different customers. While this is only a brief overview of the highly complex legal issues involved, it serves as a reminder of the necessity to maintain cost records to justify pricing practices.

Cost analysis for make-or-buy decisions

A make-or-buy decision is any decision in which a company decides whether to meet its needs internally or acquire goods or services from external sources. A restaurant that uses its own ingredients in preparing meals "makes," while one that serves meals from frozen entrees "buys." A steel company that mines its own iron ore and coal and processes the ore into pig iron "makes," while one that purchases pig iron for further processing "buys."

The make-or-buy decision is often part of a company's long-run strategy. Some companies choose to integrate vertically to control the activities that lead up to the final product. Other companies prefer to rely on outsiders for some inputs and specialize in only certain steps of the total manufacturing process.

Whether to rely on outsiders for a substantial quantity of materials depends on both differential cost comparisons and other factors that are not easily quantified, such as suppliers' dependability and quality control. Although make-or-buy decisions sometimes appear to be simple one-time choices, they are frequently part of a more strategic analysis in which top management makes a policy decision to move the company towards more or less vertical integration.

For example, the Better Homes Construction Company currently does its own site preparation and foundation work on the houses it builds. This work costs Better Homes $15,000 per house for labor, materials, and variable overhead. Should Better Homes consider buying site preparation and foundation work from an outside supplier? If satisfactory quality work could be subcontracted at anything below $15,000, Better Homes could save some of the money it now spends. The decision to buy would then provide a differential cost saving.

Make-or-buy decisions involving differential fixed costs

Net Minder Manufacturing produces tennis rackets. At the present time, it makes a cover for each racket at the following cost:

	Per unit	10,000 units
Costs that can be directly assigned to the product:		
Direct materials	$2.00	$20,000
Direct labor	1.00	10,000
Variable manufacturing overhead	.75	7,500
Fixed manufacturing overhead		2,500
Common costs allocated to this product line		15,000
		$55,000

This year's expected production is 10,000 units, so the full product cost is $5.50 ($55,000 ÷ 10,000 units).

Net Minder has received an offer from an outside supplier to supply any desired volume of covers at a price of $4.10 each. Here is the differential cost analysis that the accounting department prepared for management:

1. Differential costs are materials, labor, and variable overhead. These costs would definitely be saved if the covers are bought.
2. The direct fixed manufacturing overhead is the cost of leasing the machine for producing the covers. Although the machine cost is fixed for levels of production ranging from one unit to 20,000 units, it can be eliminated if we stop producing covers. Thus, although the machine cost is a fixed cost of producing covers, it is *differential* cost if we eliminate the product.
3. No other costs would be affected.

The accounting department also prepared cost analyses at volume levels of 5,000 and 10,000 units per year, as shown in Illustration 12–3. At a volume of 10,000 units, it is less costly for Net Minder to make the racket covers. But if the volume of racket covers needed drops to 5,000, Net Minder would save money by buying the racket covers.

Illustration 12–3   **Make-or-buy analysis, Net Minder Manufacturing**

	Status quo: Make product	Alternative: Buy product	Difference
a. 10,000 units			
Direct costs:			
Direct materials	$20,000	$41,000[a]	$21,000 higher
Labor	10,000	–0–	10,000 lower
Variable overhead	7,500	–0–	7,500 lower
Fixed overhead	2,500	–0–	2,500 lower
Common costs	15,000[d]	15,000[d]	–0–
Total costs	$55,000	$56,000	$ 1,000 higher

Differential cost *increase* by $1,000, so *reject* alternative to *buy.*

	Status quo: Make product	Alternative: Buy product	Difference
b. 5,000 units			
Direct costs:			
Direct materials	$10,000[b]	$20,500[c]	$10,500 higher
Labor	5,000[b]	–0–	5,000 lower
Variable overhead	3,750[b]	–0–	3,750 lower
Fixed overhead	2,500	–0–	2,500 lower
Common costs	15,000[d]	15,000[d]	–0–
Total costs	$36,250	$35,500	$ 750 lower

Differential cost *decrease* by $750, so *accept* alternative to buy.

[a] 10,000 units purchased at $4.10 = $41,000.

[b] Total variable costs reduced by half because volume was reduced by half.

[c] 5,000 units purchased at $4.10 = $20,500.

[d] These common costs remain unchanged for these volumes. Since they do not change, they could be omitted from the analysis.

This decision is sensitive to volume. To see why, consider only the costs that are affected by the make-or-buy decision: direct materials, direct labor, variable overhead, and fixed overhead. By setting the costs of making equal to the costs of buying, we find there is a unique volume at which Net Minder is indifferent (in terms of costs) between making and buying as shown below:

Make		Buy
Direct fixed manufacturing overhead	**Variable manufacturing costs**	**Costs to purchase covers**
$2,500 +	3.75X$ =	4.10X$

where X = the quantity of racket covers.
Solving for X:

$$\$2,500 + \$3.75X = \$4.10X$$
$$\$2,500 = \$.35X$$
$$\frac{\$2,500}{\$.35} = X$$
$$X = \underline{\underline{7,143}}$$

The result is shown graphically in Illustration 12–4. At a volume greater than 7,143, the preferred alternative is to make; at a volume less than 7,143, the preferred alternative is to buy.

Note the importance of separating fixed and variable costs for this analysis. Although determining which costs are differential usually requires a special analysis, the work can be made simpler if costs have been routinely separated into fixed and variable components in the accounting system. The previous analysis would not have been possible for Net Minder if overhead costs had not been separated into fixed and variable components.

Opportunity cost

Suppose Net Minder's volume is projected to be 10,000 covers. If volume is expected to be greater than 7,143 covers, the preceding analysis indicates that Net Minder should continue to produce the covers. However, that analysis has not considered the opportunity cost of the facilities being used to make racket covers. Opportunity costs are the foregone returns from not employing a resource in its best alternative use. Theoretically, determining opportunity cost requires consideration of every possible use of the resource in question. If Net Minder has no alternative beneficial use for its facilities, the opportunity cost is zero, in which case the previous analysis would stand.

But suppose that the facilities where covers are made could be used to assemble a cheaper version of the racket Net Minder presently produces. This cheaper version would provide a differential contribution of $4,000. If making rackets is the best alternative use of the facility, the opportunity

Illustration 12–4   **Graphical illustration of make-or-buy analysis**

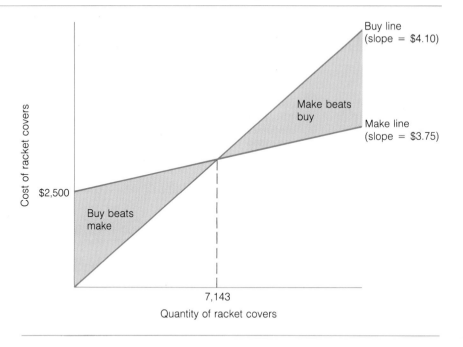

cost of using the facility to make covers is $4,000. In that case, Net Minder would be better off to buy the covers and use the facilities to make rackets, as shown in Illustration 12–5.

Almost without exception, determining opportunity cost is very difficult and involves considerable subjectivity. Opportunity costs are not routinely collected with other accounting cost data because they are not the result of completed transactions. They are possibilities only and must be estimated for each individual decision.

Some opportunity costs may be monetary, like the possible wages from the best job foregone; while others may be nonmonetary, like the status that accompanies certain occupations. Furthermore, if a benefit is foregone—and therefore never concretely existed—it is difficult to attach a realistic value to it.

Because they are so nebulous, opportunity costs are often omitted from decision-making analysis. It is easy to neglect them because they are not paid for and recorded in the accounts. Consequently, it is an accountant's responsibility to assist decision makers by reminding them that such costs exist. In general, opportunity costs occur whenever a scarce resource has multiple uses. Plants, equipment, money, time, and managerial talent all usually have opportunity costs. When a resource is not scarce or when a scarce resource can only be used in one way, opportunity costs are zero.

Illustration 12–5   **Make-or-buy analysis with opportunity cost of facilities, Net Minder Manufacturing**

	Status quo: Make product	Alternative: Buy product	Difference
a. **10,000 units**			
Total costs of covers from Illustration 12–3	$55,000	$56,000	$1,000 higher[a]
Opportunity cost of using facilities to make covers	4,000	–0–	4,000 lower[a]
Total costs, including opportunity cost	$59,000	$56,000	$3,000 lower[a]

Differential cost *decrease* of $3,000, so *accept* alternative to *buy.*

	Status quo: Make product	Alternative: Buy product, use facility to make rackets	Difference
b. **Another presentation**			
Total costs of covers from Illustration 12–3	$55,000	$56,000	$1,000 higher[a]
Less margin from use of facilities for making rackets	–0–	–4,000	4,000 lower[a]
Net cost	$55,000	$52,000	$3,000 lower[a]

Although the presentation is different, the result is still a $3,000 cost *decrease* if the alternative is accepted.

[a] These indicate whether the alternative is higher or lower than the status quo.

Whether such costs should be measured precisely or only approximately depends on the costs and benefits of the resulting information.

Adding and dropping product lines

Campus Bookstore hired a new general manager, a recent business school graduate, to improve its profit performance. As could be expected, the new manager asked to see the store's financial statements for the past year. The statements were prepared by product line for each of the store's three product categories: books, supplies, and general merchandise.

The statement that the manager received is presented in Illustration 12–6. It shows that the general merchandise department lost money during the third quarter of last year. "We could have increased operating profits from $6,000 to $13,000 for the quarter if we had dropped general merchandise," claimed the manager of the supplies department. "That department sold $120,000 worth of merchandise but cost us $127,000 to operate."

Although the economics of dropping the general merchandise line appeared favorable, the new manager asked an accountant to investigate which costs would be differential (that is, avoidable in this case) if that product line were dropped. According to the accountant:

Illustration 12–6

CAMPUS BOOKSTORE
Third-Quarter Product Line Financial Statement
(in thousands)

	Total	Books	Supplies	General merchandise
Sales revenue	$400	$200	$80	$120
Cost of goods sold (all variable)	300	160	45	95
Gross margin	100	40	35	25
Less fixed costs:				
Rent	18	6	6	6
Salaries	40	16	10	14
Marketing and administrative	36	12	12	12
Operating profit (loss)	$ 6	$ 6	$ 7	$ (7)

1. *All* variable cost of goods sold for that line could be avoided.
2. *All* salaries presently charged to general merchandise, $14,000, could be avoided.
3. *None* of the rent could be avoided.
4. Marketing and administrative costs of $6,000 could be saved.

The accountant prepared the differential cost and revenue analysis shown in Illustration 12–7 and observed the following:

1. Assuming the sales of the other product lines would be unaffected, sales would decrease by $120,000 from dropping the general merchandise line.
2. Variable cost of goods sold of $95,000 would be saved by dropping the product line.
3. Fixed costs of $20,000 ($14,000 in salaries and $6,000 in marketing and administrative expenses) would be saved.
4. In total, the lost revenue of $120,000 exceeds the total differential cost saving by $5,000. Thus, Campus Bookstore's net income for the third quarter would have been $5,000 *lower* if general merchandise had been dropped.

The discrepancy between the supplies manager's claim that operating profits would have *increased* by $7,000 and the accountant's finding that operating profits would have *decreased* by $5,000 stems from their basic assumptions. The supplies manager assumed that the entire $32,000 in fixed costs allocated to general merchandise were differential and would be saved if the product line were dropped. The accountant's closer examination revealed that only $20,000 of the fixed costs would be saved—thus, the $12,000 discrepancy.

This example demonstrates the fallacy of assuming that all costs presented on financial statements are differential. The financial statement presented in Illustration 12–6 was designed to calculate department profits, not to identify the differential costs for this decision. Thus, using operating profit calculated after all cost allocations, including some that were not differential to this

Illustration 12–7

CAMPUS BOOKSTORE
Differential Analysis
(in thousands)

	Status quo: Keep general merchandise	Alternative: Drop general merchandise	Differential: Increase (or Decrease) in operating profits
1. Sales revenue	$400	$280	$(120)
2. Cost of goods sold (all variable)	300	205	95
Contribution margin	100	75	(25)
3. Less fixed costs:			
Rent	18	18	–0–
Salaries	40	26	14
Marketing and administrative	36	30	6
4. Operating profits	$ 6	$ 1	$ (5)

decision, incorrectly indicated the product line should be dropped. General-purpose financial statements do not routinely provide differential cost information. Differential cost estimates depend on unique information that usually requires separate analysis. The bookstore statement, which was prepared on a contribution margin basis, clearly reveals the revenues and variable costs that are differential to this decision. But a separate analysis was required to determine which fixed costs are differential.

The opportunity cost of a product line   Keeping the general merchandise department may have an opportunity cost that we have not yet considered. Assume that the shelf space currently occupied by general merchandise could be used to increase the sale of books. The opportunity cost of retaining general merchandise is then measured by the probable foregone differential profits from the increased book sales. The accountant estimated the following figures to describe the substitution of increased book sales for general merchandise:

Drop general merchandise (from Illustration 12–7):	
Lost revenue	$120,000
Cost savings	115,000
Differential lost profit	$ 5,000
Add additional book sales:	
Additional book sales	$155,000
Less additional cost of books sold (all variable)	120,000
Contribution margin	35,000
Less additional fixed costs:	
Salaries	14,000
Marketing and administrative	4,000
Profit gained from additional book sales	$ 17,000

The analysis presented in Illustration 12–7 indicated that Campus Bookstore would lose $5,000 by eliminating general merchandise. However, given this additional information, an opportunity loss of $17,000 is incurred if the bookstore retains general merchandise and foregoes the opportunity to increase book sales. Based on these facts, Campus Bookstore is $12,000 (= $17,000 gained from additional book sales − $5,000 lost from dropping general merchandise) better off to drop the general merchandise department and increase book sales. Illustration 12–8 presents a summary analysis for all three options: status quo, eliminate general merchandise, and eliminate general merchandise and increase book sales.

Illustration 12–8

CAMPUS BOOKSTORE
Comparison of Three Alternatives
(in thousands)

	Status quo: Keep general merchandise[a]	**Alternative 1: Drop general merchandise**[a]	**Alternative 2: Drop general merchandise, increase book sales**
Sales revenue	$400	$280	$435 ($280 + 155[b])
Cost of goods sold (all variable)	300	205	325 ($205 + 120[b])
Contribution margin	100	75	110
Less fixed costs:			
Rent	18	18	18
Salaries	40	26	40 ($26 + 14[b])
Marketing and administrative	36	30	34 ($30 + 4[b])
Operating profit	$ 6	$ 1	$ 18
		Worst	Best

[a] These columns are taken directly from Illustration 12–7.

[b] These amounts are the increase in revenues and costs taken from the discussion in the text.

Summary

This chapter discusses *differential analysis.* Differential analysis determines *what* would differ and by *how much* if alternative actions are taken. Differential analysis is performed by comparing alternatives to the *status quo,* using the following model:

Status quo	**Alternative**	**Difference**
Revenue	Revenue	Change in revenue
less	less	less
Variable costs	Variable costs	Change in variable costs
equals	equals	equals
Total contribution	Total contribution	Change in total contribution
less	less	less
Fixed costs	Fixed costs	Change in fixed costs
equals	equals	equals
Status quo's profit	Alternative's profit	Change in profits

This chapter has focused on identifying and measuring differential costs, which are the costs that are different under different alternatives. Costs that are different under alternative actions are also known as **relevant costs.** Costs that do *not* differ are not relevant for determining the financial consequences of alternatives.

Terms and concepts	The following terms and concepts should be familiar to you after reading this chapter:

Differential analysis	**Price discrimination**
Differential costs	**Relevant costs**
Fixed costs	**Short run**
Full cost	**Special order**
Full-cost fallacy	**Sunk cost**
Make-or-buy decision	**Variable costs**
Opportunity costs	

Self-study problem No. 1

The following is a true story. An executive joins a tennis club and pays a $300 yearly membership fee. After two weeks of playing, the executive develops a "tennis elbow," but continues to play (in pain) saying, "I don't want to waste the $300!" Comment.

Solution to self-study problem No. 1

The $300 is a sunk cost and should be irrelevant to the executive. The executive should consider only the advantages and disadvantages of playing henceforth, including the pain, but the $300 should be ignored. (The executive later quit playing until his tennis elbow healed.)

Self-study problem No. 2

Visa Enterprises, Inc., has an annual plant capacity to produce 2,500 units. Its predicted operations for the year are:

Sales revenue (2,000 units at $40 each)	$80,000
Manufacturing costs:	
Variable	$24 per unit
Fixed	$17,000
Selling and administrative costs:	
Variable (commissions on sales)	$2.50 per unit
Fixed	$2,500

Should the company accept a special order for 400 units at a selling price of $32 each, which is subject to half the usual sales commission rate per unit? Assume no effect on regular sales at regular prices. What is the effect of the decision on the company's operating profit?

Solution to self-study problem No. 2

The special order should be accepted as shown by the following two alternative analyses:

	Status quo	Alternative	Difference
Sales revenues	$ 80,000	$ 92,800	$ 12,800
Variable costs	(53,000)	(63,100)	(10,100)
Contribution	27,000	29,700	2,700
Fixed costs	(19,500)	(19,500)	–0–
Operating profit	$ 7,500	$ 10,200	$ 2,700

Special order sales (400 × $32)		$12,800
Less variable costs:		
Manufacturing (400 × $24)	$9,600	
Sales commission (400 × $1.25)	500	10,100
Addition to company profit		$ 2,700

Self-study problem No. 3

Electronics, Inc., produces an electronic part that is used in guidance and navigation systems. Major customers are aircraft manufacturers.

The costs of the electronic part at the company's normal volume of 4,000 units per month are shown in Exhibit A.

Exhibit A (SSP 12–3)

Unit manufacturing costs:		
Variable materials	$200	
Variable labor	150	
Variable overhead	50	
Fixed overhead	120	
Total unit manufacturing costs		$520
Unit nonmanufacturing costs:		
Variable	150	
Fixed	140	
Total unit nonmanufacturing costs		290
Total unit costs		$810

The following questions refer only to the data given above. Unless otherwise stated, assume there is no connection between the situations described in the questions; each is to be treated independently. Unless otherwise stated, a regular selling price of $940 per unit should be assumed. Ignore income taxes and other costs that are not mentioned in Exhibit A or in a question itself.

a. *Price-volume analysis.* Market research estimates that volume would decrease to 3,500 units if the price were increased from $940 to $1,050 per unit. Assuming the cost behavior patterns implied by the data in Exhibit A are correct, would you recommend that this action be taken? What would be the impact on monthly sales, costs, and profits?

b. *Special order with opportunity costs.* On March 1, a contract offer is made to Electronics, Inc., by the federal government to supply 1,000 units to the Air

Force for delivery by March 31. Because of an unusually large number of rush orders from their regular customers, Electronics, Inc., plans to produce and sell 5,000 units during March, which will use all available capacity. If the government order is accepted, 1,000 units normally sold to regular customers would be lost to a competitor for this month only. The contract given by the government would reimburse the government's share of March variable manufacturing costs, plus pay a fixed fee of $140,000. There would be no variable nonmanufacturing costs incurred on the government's units. What impact would accepting the government contract have on March profits?

c. *Special order without opportunity costs.* How would your answer to (b) change if Electronics, Inc., had planned to produce and sell only 3,000 units in March; hence, they would not have lost sales to a competitor?

d. *Make or buy.* A proposal is received from an outside contractor who will make and ship 1,000 units per month directly to Electronics, Inc.'s customers as orders are received from Electronics, Inc.'s sales force. Electronics, Inc.'s fixed nonmanufacturing costs would be unaffected, but its variable nonmanufacturing costs would be cut by 20 percent for those 1,000 units produced by the contractor. Electronics, Inc.'s plant would operate at three fourths of its normal level, and total fixed manufacturing costs per month would be cut by 10 percent. Should the proposal be accepted for a payment to the contractor of $400 per unit? At what per-unit cost to the contractor would Electronics, Inc., be indifferent between making the product and buying from a contractor?

Solution to self-study problem No. 3

a. Raising this price would increase profits by $190,000.

	Status quo	Alternative	Difference
Price	$ 940	$ 1,050	—
Volume	4,000	3,500	—
Sales revenue	$3,760,000	$3,675,000	$ 85,000 lower
Variable costs	2,200,000	1,925,000	275,000 lower
Contribution	1,560,000	1,750,000	190,000 higher
Fixed costs	1,040,000	1,040,000	–0–
Profit	$ 520,000	$ 710,000	$190,000 higher

b. Accepting the special order would reduce profits by $250,000.

		Alternative			
	Status quo	Regular	Government	Total	Difference
Volume	5,000 regular	4,000	1,000	5,000	
Sales revenue	$4,700,000	$3,760,000	$540,000	$4,300,000	$400,000 lower
Variable costs	2,750,000	2,200,000	400,000	2,600,000	150,000 lower
Contribution	1,950,000	1,560,000	140,000	1,700,000	250,000 lower
Fixed costs	1,040,000			1,040,000	–0–
Profit	$ 910,000			$ 660,000	$250,000 lower

c. Accepting the order would increase profits by $140,000—the amount of the fee.
d. Using the outside contractor at a cost of $400 per unit would increase profits by $78,000 (= $478,000 increase in profit shown below − $400,000 paid to contractor).

	Status quo	Alternative	Difference
Sales revenue	$3,760,000	$3,760,000	$ −0−
Variable cost ignoring payment to contractor	2,200,000	1,770,000[a]	430,000 lower
Contribution	1,560,000	1,990,000	430,000 higher
Fixed costs	1,040,000	992,000[b]	48,000 lower
Profit	$ 520,000	$ 998,000	$478,000 higher

[a] $1,770,000 = (1,000 units × $120) + (3,000 units × $550).
[b] $992,000 = $560,000 nonmanufacturing costs
$\qquad$ + (.90 × $480,000) manufacturing costs
$\qquad$ = $560,000 + 432,000.

Electronics, Inc., would be indifferent between making and buying if the contractor charged $478 per unit, calculated as follows:

$$\text{Set status quo profit} = \text{Alternative profit}$$
$$\$520,000 = \$998,000 - \text{Payment to contractor}$$
$$\text{Payment to contractor} = \$998,000 - \$520,000$$
$$= \$478,000 \text{ for 1,000 units, or } \$478 \text{ per unit}$$

Self-study problem No. 4: Differential analysis, Justa Corporation

The Justa Corporation produces and sells three products. The three products, A, B, and C, are sold in a local market and in a regional market. At the end of the first quarter of the current year, the following income statement has been prepared:

	Total	Local	Regional
Sales revenue	$1,300,000	$1,000,000	$300,000
Cost of goods sold	1,010,000	775,000	235,000
Gross margin	290,000	225,000	65,000
Marketing costs	105,000	60,000	45,000
Administrative costs	52,000	40,000	12,000
Total mktg. & admin.	157,000	100,000	57,000
Operating profits..........	$ 133,000	$ 125,000	$ 8,000

Management has expressed special concern with the regional market because of the extremely poor return on sales. This market was entered a year ago because of excess capacity. It was originally believed that the return on sales would improve with time, but after a year, no noticable improvement can be seen from the results as reported in the above quarterly statement.

In attempting to decide whether to eliminate the regional market, the following information has been gathered:

	Products		
	A	**B**	**C**
Sales revenue	$500,000	$400,000	$400,000
Variable manufacturing costs as a percentage of sales revenue	60%	70%	60%
Variable marketing costs as a percentage of sales revenue	3	2	2

	Sales by markets	
Product	**Local**	**Regional**
A	$400,000	$100,000
B	300,000	100,000
C	300,000	100,000

All administrative costs and fixed manufacturing costs are common to the three products and the two markets and are fixed for the period. Remaining marketing costs are fixed for the period and separable by market. All fixed costs are based upon a prorated yearly amount.

Required:

a. Assuming there are no alternative uses for the Justa Corporation's present capacity, would you recommend dropping the regional market? Why or why not?

b. Prepare the quarterly income statement showing contribution margins by products.

c. It is believed that a new product can be ready for sale next year if the Justa Corporation decides to go ahead with continued research. The new product can be produced by simply converting equipment presently used in producing Product C. This conversion will increase fixed costs by $10,000 per quarter. What must be the minimum contribution margin per quarter for the new product to make the changeover financially feasible?

(CMA adapted)

Solution to self-study Problem No. 4

a. The regional market should not be dropped as this market not only covers all the variable costs and separable fixed costs but also gives net market contribution of $65,000 toward the common fixed costs.

$$\text{Sales} = \$300,000$$
$$\text{Variable manufacturing costs} = (.6 \times \$100,000) + (.7 \times \$100,000) + (.6 \times \$100,000)$$
$$= 190,000$$
$$\text{Marketing costs} = \$45,000$$

b. Quarterly income statement (in thousands):

	Product A	Product B	Product C	Total
Sales revenue	$500	$400	$400	$1,300
Less variable costs:				
Manufacturing	300	280	240	820
Marketing	15	8	8	31
Total variable cost	315	288	248	851
Contribution margin	185	112	152	449
Less fixed costs:				
Manufacturing				190
Marketing				74
Administrative				52
Total fixed costs				316
Operating profit				$ 133

c. The new product must contribute at least $162,000 (=$152,000 + $10,000) per quarter so as not to leave the company worse off when Product C is replaced.

Questions

12–1. One of your acquaintances notes: "This whole subject of differential costing is easy—variable costs are the only costs that are relevant." How would you respond?

12–2. When, if ever, are fixed costs differential?

12–3. What is the difference between a sunk cost and a differential cost?

12–4. Are sunk costs ever differential costs?

12–5. A manager in your organization has just received a special order that is "below cost." The manager points to the document and says: "These are the kinds of orders that will get you in trouble. Every sale must bear its share of the full costs of running the business. If we sell below our full cost, we'll be out of business in no time." Respond to this remark.

12–6. What factors should a company consider before dropping a division that shows an operating loss?

12–7. Why are opportunity costs often excluded from differential cost analyses?

12–8. Should opportunity costs be excluded from differential cost analyses? Why or why not?

12–9. If you are considering driving to a weekend resort for a quick break from school, what are the differential costs of operating your car for that drive?

12–10. If you are considering buying a second car, what are the differential costs of that decision? Are the differential costs in this question the same as in Question 12–9? Why or why not?

Exercises

12–11. Costs of special order

Boyer Company manufactures basketballs. The forecasted income statement for the year before any special orders is as follows:

	Amount	Per unit
Sales revenue	$4,000,000	$10.00
Manufacturing costs	3,200,000	8.00
Gross profit	800,000	2.00
Marketing costs	300,000	.75
Operating profit	$ 500,000	$ 1.25

Fixed costs included in the above forecasted income statement are $1,200,000 in manufacturing costs and $100,000 in marketing costs.

A special order offering to buy 50,000 basketballs for $7.50 each was made to Boyer. There will be no differential marketing costs if the special order is accepted.

Required:

What impact would acceptance of the special order have on operating profit?

(CPA adapted)

12–12. Costs in make-or-buy decisions

Cardinal Company needs 20,000 units of a certain part to use in its production cycle. The following information is available:

Cost to Cardinal to make the part:

Direct materials	$ 4
Direct labor	16
Variable overhead	8
Fixed overhead applied	10
	$38

Cost to buy the part from the Oriole Company	$36

If Cardinal buys the part from Oriole instead of making it, Cardinal could not use the released facilities in another manufacturing activity. Sixty percent of the fixed overhead applied will continue regardless of what decision is made.

Required:

What are the differential costs of the make-or-buy decision?

(CPA adapted)

12–13. Costs of distress sale

The Lantern Corporation has 1,000 obsolete lanterns that are carried in inventory at a manufacturing cost of $20,000. If the lanterns are remachined for $5,000, they could be sold for $9,000. If the lanterns are scrapped, they could be sold for $1,000.

Required:

What are the relevant costs of the optimal alternative? What is the optimal alternative?

(CPA adapted)

12–14. Costs for making versus buying

The Reno Company manufactures Part No. 498 for use in its production cycle. The cost per unit for 20,000 units of Part No. 498 are as follows:

Direct materials	$ 6
Direct labor	30
Variable overhead	12
Fixed overhead applied	16
	$64

The Tray Company has offered to sell 20,000 units of Part No. 498 to Reno for $60 per unit. Reno will make the decision to buy the part from Tray if there is a savings of $25,000 for Reno. If Reno accepts Tray's offer, $9 per unit of the fixed overhead applied would be totally eliminated.

Required:

Prepare a schedule to show the differential unit costs of the better alternative.

(CPA adapted)

12–15. Special order costs

The following data relate to a year's budgeted activity for Patsy Corporation, a single product company:

	Units
Beginning inventory	30,000
Production	120,000
Available	150,000
Sales	110,000
Ending inventory	40,000

	Per unit
Selling price	$5.00
Variable manufacturing costs	1.00
Variable marketing costs	2.00
Fixed manufacturing costs (based on 100,000 units)	.25
Fixed marketing costs (based on 100,000 units)	.65

Total fixed costs remain unchanged within a range of 25,000 units to total capacity of 160,000 units.

A special order is received to purchase 10,000 units to be used in an unrelated market. The sale would require production of 10,000 extra units.

Required:

What price per unit should be charged on the special order to increase operating profit by $9,000?

(CPA adapted)

12–16. Make or buy with alternate use for facilities

Golden, Inc., has been manufacturing 5,000 units of Part 10541 per month which is used in the manufacture of one of its products. At this level of production, the cost per unit of manufacturing Part 10541 is as follows:

Direct materials	$ 2
Direct labor	8
Variable overhead	4
Fixed overhead applied	6
Total	$20

Brown Company has offered to sell Golden 5,000 units of Part 10541 for $17 a unit. Golden has determined that it could use the facilities presently used to manufacture Part 10541 to manufacture Product RAC and generate an additional contribution margin per month of $8,000. Golden has also determined that one third of the fixed overhead applied will be saved even if Part 10541 is purchased from Brown, and Product RAC is made.

Required:

Prepare a schedule to show whether Golden should accept Brown's offer.

(CPA adapted)

12–17. Differential costs with effect on regular sales

P. B. Floyd, Inc., has operated a violin case manufacturing business since 1920. The regular price of violin cases is $40 each. Floyd's controller has prepared cost data on these cases based on a normal selling volume of 20,000 cases per year:

Direct materials	$ 7.50
Direct labor	8.00
Overhead	6.00 (75% fixed)
Marketing and administrative	4.00 (all fixed)
Total cost	$25.50

This week, the Ness Corporation moved into Floyd's market area. Ness instituted a media campaign designed to lure Floyd's customers. Indeed, Ness offered violin cases at one half of Floyd's selling price.

Floyd estimates that if he meets the Ness Corporation price, his volume will increase to 25,000 cases because people who previously were buying elsewhere would be induced to buy locally. However, if he does not meet Ness' price, Floyd's volume will fall to 4,000 cases per year.

Required:

Prepare a schedule to support the optimal decision for Floyd and to show the differential costs of the decision.

Problems and cases

12–18. Analyze rental decision

Heavy Products Division of Rentall, Inc., rents heavy equipment to construction firms that need extra equipment for short periods of time. Two types of equipment are rented: large earthmoving equipment and large cranes. Earthmoving equipment is generally rented by the month. Cranes are usually rented by the week.

The fees that Heavy Products charges for equipment are as follows:

	Charges		
	Per day	**Per week**	**Per month**
Earthmoving equipment	—	$1,000	$4,000
Cranes	—	1,250	5,000

Cost data prepared by the accounting department used to determine the prices for equipment are as follows:

	Annual cost	**Weekly cost per piece of equipment**
Estimated equipment cost:		
Supplies, gasoline, etc., and other miscellaneous costs	$190,000	$100
Department overhead (includes equipment depreciation and insurance, personal property taxes)	760,000	400
Company overhead (includes building depreciation and insurance, real estate taxes, utilities, maintenance department costs, administration, marketing, interest)	418,000	220

These calculations were based on a 250-workday and a 50-week year. Experience indicates that the earthmoving equipment is rented 80 percent of the available time and cranes only 60 percent of the available time.

Heavy Products received an offer from Dolores Construction Company to lease a new heavy crane for $30,000 for one year. Dolores would provide all supplies, but Heavy would be responsible for any necessary repairs.

Dolores plans to use the crane in another city. If a breakdown occurs, an outside repair company would be required. Based on studies of crane reliability, the outside repair cost for one year is estimated as:

Labor charges	$1,000
Parts	800
Total	$1,800

Labor costs incurred for outside service would be greater than internal costs because Heavy maintains its own repair crew on a fully staffed basis, year round. However, replacement parts costs would be the same.

Required:

Should Heavy Products lease the crane to Dolores? Show differential cost data to support your conclusion.

(CMA adapted)

12–19. Special order costs

Brike Company, which manufactures robes, has enough idle capacity available to accept a special order of 10,000 robes at $8 a robe. A predicted income statement for the year without this special order is as follows:

	Per unit	Total
Sales revenue	$12.50	$1,250,000
Manufacturing costs:		
Variable	6.25	625,000
Fixed	1.75	175,000
Total manufacturing costs . .	8.00	800,000
Gross profit	4.50	450,000
Marketing costs:		
Variable	1.80	180,000
Fixed	1.45	145,000
Total marketing costs	3.25	325,000
Operating profit	$ 1.25	$ 125,000

If the order is accepted, variable selling costs on the special order would be reduced by 25 percent because all of the robes would be packed and shipped in one lot. However, if the offer is accepted, management estimates that it will lose the sale of 2,000 robes at regular prices.

Required:

What is the net gain or loss from the special order?

(CPA adapted)

12–20. New product introduction—CVP considerations

Servo Gimmicks, Ltd. produces and sells new and unusual household products. The company recently received a proposal to manufacture a left-handed bottle opener. The product engineering department estimates that variable manufacturing costs for each unit will be:

Materials	$ .25
Labor	.50
Overhead	.30
Total	$1.05

Variable selling costs include $.55 for packaging and shipping. In addition, Servo allocates $.10 of common fixed costs to each unit sold. If Servo decides to sell the product, they will launch a media campaign on late night television. The media campaign will cost $450,000. Of course, Servo has a number of products, and if they don't produce the left-handed bottle opener, they will manufacture some other item. Servo estimates that any product they sell must contribute at least $500,000 to profits. This is an after-tax target.

The marketing department estimates that the optimal selling price for the product is $3.99.

Required:

If Servo's tax rate is 45 percent, how many left-handed bottle openers must be sold to meet the profit target? Show computations in good form.

12–21. Costs of new production department

The management of Bay Company is considering a proposal to install a third production department within its existing factory building. With the company's present production setup, direct materials are passed through Department I to produce Materials A and B in equal proportions. Material A is then passed through Department II to yield Product C. Material B is presently being sold "as is" at a price of $20.25 per pound. Product C has a selling price of $100 per pound.

The per pound standard costs currently being used by the Bay Company are as follows:

	Department I (Materials A and B)	Department II (Product C)	(Material B)
Prior department costs	$ —	$53.03	$13.47
Direct materials	20.00	—	—
Direct labor	7.00	12.00	—
Variable overhead	3.00	5.00	—
Fixed overhead:			
Direct	2.25	2.25	—
Allocated (⅔, ⅓)	1.00	1.00	—
	$33.25	$73.28	$13.47

These standard costs were developed by using an estimated production volume of 200,000 pounds of direct materials as the standard volume. The company assigns Department I costs to Material A and Material B in proportion to their net sales values at the point of separation, computed by deducting subsequent standard production costs from sales prices. Common fixed overhead costs of $300,000 are allocated to the two producing departments on the basis of the space used by the departments.

The proposed Department III would be used to process Material B into Product D. It is expected that any quantity of Product D can be sold for $30 per pound. Standard costs per pound under this proposal were developed by using 200,000 pounds of direct materials as the standard volume and are as follows:

	Department I (Materials A and B)	Department II (Product C)	Department III (Product D)
Prior department costs	—	$52.80	$13.20
Direct materials	$20.00	—	—
Direct labor	7.00	12.00	5.50
Variable overhead	3.00	5.00	2.00
Fixed overhead:			
Attributable	2.25	2.25	1.75
Allocated (½, ¼, ¼)	.75	.75	.75
	$33.00	$72.80	$23.20

Required:

If *(a)* sales and production levels are expected to remain constant in the foreseeable future, and *(b)* there are no foreseeable alternative uses for the available factory space, should the Bay Company install Department III and thereby produce Product D? Show calculations to support your answer.

(CMA adapted)

12–22. Differential costs and CVP analysis

You have been asked to assist the management of the Arcadia Corporation in arriving at certain decisions. Arcadia has its home office in Ohio and leases factory buildings in Texas, Montana, and Maine, all of which produce the same product. The management of Arcadia has provided you with a projection of operations for 1987, the forthcoming year, as follows:

	Total	Texas	Montana	Maine
Sales revenue	$4,400,000	$2,200,000	$1,400,000	$800,000
Fixed costs:				
Factory	1,100,000	560,000	280,000	260,000
Administration	350,000	210,000	110,000	30,000
Variable costs	1,450,000	665,000	425,000	360,000
Allocated home office costs	500,000	225,000	175,000	100,000
Total	3,400,000	1,660,000	990,000	750,000
Net profit from operations	$1,000,000	$ 540,000	$ 410,000	$ 50,000

The sales price per unit is $25.

Due to the marginal results of operations of the factory in Maine, Arcadia has decided to cease operations and sell that factory's machinery and equipment by the end of 1986. Arcadia expects that the proceeds from the sale of these assets would be greater than their book value and would cover all termination costs.

Arcadia, however, would like to continue serving its customers in that area if it is economically feasible and is considering one of the following three alternatives:

1. Expand the operations of the Montana factory by using space presently idle. This move would result in the following changes in that factory's operations:

	Increase over factory's current operations
Sales revenue	50%
Fixed costs:	
Factory	20
Administration	10

Under this proposal, variable costs would be $8 per unit sold.

2. Enter into a long-term contract with a competitor who will serve that area's customers. This competitor would pay Arcadia a royalty of $4 per unit based upon an estimate of 30,000 units being sold.

3. Close the Maine factory and not expand the operations of the Montana factory.

Required:

In order to assist the management of Arcadia Corporation in determining which alternative is more economically feasible, prepare a schedule computing Arcadia's estimated net profit from total operations that would result from each of the following methods:

a. Expansion of the Montana factory.
b. Negotiation of long-term contract on a royalty basis.
c. Shutdown of Maine operations with no expansion at other locations.

Note: Total home office costs of $500,000 will remain the same under each situation.

(CPA adapted)

12–23. Product-line elimination

U-Use-It, Inc., operates four rental departments: industrial equipment, small equipment, servingware, and trailers. The small equipment department rents items such as small tools, yard and garden equipment, kitchen equipment, etc. The items are rented by the hour or by the day. Because of the type of equipment rented, there are a large number of rentals with small dollar values for each rental.

The department employs three workers to issue and receive the equipment.

As noted in the following departmentalized income statement, the small equipment department is operating at a reported loss. Management is considering eliminating the department. If the department is eliminated, the costs of elimination would equal the liquidation value of any assets sold. The space occupied by the department would be reassigned to other departments. The costs marked V are variable, all others are fixed.

Approximately 10 percent of the repair parts from the maintenance department can be traced to small equipment. In addition, 48 percent of the labor costs in the maintenance department vary with the number of service calls. Employee benefits vary with direct labor in all departments. Equipment depreciation, equipment insurance, and personal property taxes are direct department costs.

Required:

Should U-Use-It eliminate the small equipment department? Show supporting computations.

(CMA adapted)

INCOME STATEMENT

		Rental departments				
	Company[a]	Industrial equipment	Small equipment	Servingware	Trailers	Maintenance department[a]
Sales revenue						
Rental sales	$ 4,000,000	$2,400,000	$240,000	$360,000	$1,000,000	$ 30,000
Costs:						
Direct labor (V)	434,400[b]	250,000	18,000	16,400	150,000	30,000
Employee benefits (V)	65,160[b]	37,500	2,700	2,460	22,500	4,500
Supplies, gasoline, etc. (V)	216,760[b]	150,000	5,000	6,760	55,000	1,200
Other miscellaneous costs (V)	24,590[b]	12,075	2,590	3,375	6,550	3,790
Equipment depreciation	790,000[b]	500,000	50,000	40,000	200,000	2,800
Equipment insurance	79,840[b]	56,000	2,560	1,280	20,000	160
Property taxes	212,250[b]	175,000	4,000	2,000	31,250	250
Building depreciation	57,000[b]	24,000	9,000	9,000	15,000	3,000
Building insurance	19,000[b]	8,000	3,000	3,000	5,000	1,000
Real estate taxes	47,500[b]	20,000	7,500	7,500	12,500	2,500
Utilities	28,500[b]	12,000	4,500	4,500	7,500	1,500
Repair parts	—	—	—	—	—	15,000
Maintenance[a]	65,700	16,425	32,850	5,475	10,950	$(65,700)
Administration	175,000	17,500	105,000	35,000	17,500	
Marketing	125,000	75,000	7,500	11,250	31,250	
Interest	400,000	240,000	24,000	36,000	100,000	
Total costs	2,740,700	1,593,500	278,200	184,000	685,000	
Net income before income taxes	1,259,300	$ 806,500	$ (38,200)	$176,000	315,000	
Income tax (40%)	503,720					
Net income	$ 755,580					
No. of rental invoices	15,000	1,500	9,000	3,000	1,500	
Square feet occupied	100,000	40,000	15,000	15,000	25,000	
Cost of equipment	$10,000,000	$7,000,000	$320,000	$160,000	$2,500,000	5,000
Assessed value of equipment	$ 5,000,000	$3,500,000	$160,000	$ 80,000	$1,250,000	$ 20,000
Service calls	1,500	375	750	125	250	$ 10,000

[a] Maintenance department dollar costs are allocated to rental departments on the maintenance cost line.
[b] These amounts do not include maintenance department costs.

12-24. Discontinuing product lines

The Scio Division of Georgetown, Inc., manufactures and sells four related product lines. Each product is produced at one or more of the three manufacturing plants of the division. See the product-line profitability statement for this year, which shows a loss for the baseball equipment line. A similar loss is projected for next year.

The baseball equipment is manufactured in the Evanston Plant. Some football equipment and all miscellaneous sports items also are processed through this plant. A few of the miscellaneous items are manufactured, and the remainder are purchased for resale. The item purchased for resale is recorded as materials in the records. A separate production line is used to produce the products of each product line.

The cost schedule presents the costs incurred at the Evanston Plant. Inventories at the end of the year were substantially identical to those at the beginning of the year.

The management of Georgetown, Inc., has requested a profitability study of the baseball equipment line to determine if the line should be discontinued. The marketing department of the Scio Division and the accounting department at the plant have developed the following additional data to be used in the study:

1. If the baseball equipment line is discontinued, the company will lose approximately 10 percent of its sales in each of the other lines.

EVANSTON PLANT
Product-Line Profitability
(in thousands)

	Football equipment	Baseball equipment	Hockey equipment	Miscellaneous sports items	Total
Sales revenue	$2,200	$1,000	$1,500	$500	$5,200
Cost of goods sold:					
Materials	400	175	300	90	965
Labor and variable overhead	800	400	600	60	1,860
Fixed overhead	350	275	100	50	775
Total	1,550	850	1,000	200	3,600
Gross profit	650	150	500	300	1,600
Marketing costs:					
Variable	440	200	300	100	1,040
Fixed	100	50	100	50	300
Corporate administration costs	48	24	36	12	120
Total	588	274	436	162	1,460
Contribution to corporation	$ 62	$ (124)	$ 64	$138	$ 140

2. The equipment now used in the manufacture of baseball equipment is quite specialized. It has a current salvage value of $105,000 and a remaining useful life of five years. This equipment cannot be used elsewhere in the company. If the equipment is sold, the proceeds would be invested at 10 percent per year.

3. The plant space now occupied by the baseball equipment line could be closed off from the rest of the plant and rented for $175,000 per year.

4. If the line is discontinued, the supervisor of the baseball equipment line will be released. In keeping with company policy, he would receive severance pay of $5,000.

EVANSTON PLANT
Cost Schedule
(in thousands)

	Football equipment	Baseball equipment	Miscellaneous sports items	Total
Materials	$100	$175	$ 90	$ 365
Labor	100	200	30	330
Variable overhead:				
Supplies	85	60	12	157
Power	50	110	7	167
Other	15	30	11	56
Subtotal	150	200	30	380
Fixed overhead:				
Suprevision[a]	25	30	21	76
Depreciation[b]	40	115	14	169
Plant rentals[c]	35	105	10	150
Other[d]	20	25	5	50
Subtotal	120	275	50	445
Total costs	$470	$850	$200	$1,520

[a] The supervision costs represent salary and benefit costs of the supervisors in charge of each product line.

[b] Depreciation cost for machinery and equipment is charged to the product line on which the machinery is used.

[c] The plant is leased. The lease rentals are charged to the product lines on the basis of square feet occupied.

[d] Other fixed overhead costs are the cost of plant administration and are allocated arbitrarily by management decision.

Required:

a. Should Georgetown, Inc., discontinue the baseball equipment line? Support your answer with appropriate calculations and qualitative arguments.

b. A member of the board of directors of Georgetown, Inc., has inquired whether the information regarding the discontinuance of product lines should be included in the financial statements on a regular monthly basis for all product lines. Draft a memorandum in response to the board member's inquiry. Your memorandum should (1) state why or why not this information should be included in the regular monthly financial statements distributed to the board and (2) detail the reasons for your response.

(CMA adapted)

12–25. Analyze alternative products

Ocean Company manufactures and sells three different products: Ex, Why, and Zee. Projected income statements by product line for the year are presented below:

	Ex	Why	Zee	Total
Unit sales	10,000	500,000	125,000	635,000
Sales revenue	$925,000	$1,000,000	$575,000	$2,500,000
Variable cost of units sold	285,000	350,000	150,000	785,000
Fixed cost of units sold	304,200	289,000	166,800	760,000
Gross margin	335,800	361,000	258,200	955,000
Variable nonmanufacturing costs	270,000	200,000	80,000	550,000
Fixed nonmanufacturing costs	125,800	136,000	78,200	340,000
Operating profit	$ (60,000)	$ 25,000	$100,000	$ 65,000

Production costs are similar for all three products. The fixed nonmanufacturing costs are allocated to products in proportion to revenues. The fixed cost of units sold is allocated to products by various allocation bases, such as square feet for factory rent and machine hours for repairs, etc.

Ocean management is concerned about the loss for product Ex and its considering two alternative courses of corrective action.

Alternative A. Ocean would purchase some new machinery for the production of product Ex. This new machinery would involve an immediate cash outlay of $650,000. Management expects that the new machinery would reduce variable production costs so that total variable costs (cost of units sold and nonmanufacturing costs) for product Ex would be 52 percent of product Ex revenues. The new machinery would increase total fixed costs allocated to product Ex to $480,000 per year. No additional fixed costs would be allocated to products Why or Zee.

Alternative B. Ocean would discontinue the manufacture of product Ex. Selling prices of products Why and Zee would remain constant. Management expects that product Zee production and revenues would increase by 50 percent. Some of the present machinery devoted to product Ex could be sold at scrap value that equals its removal costs. The removal of this machinery would reduce fixed costs allocated to product Ex by $30,000 per year. The remaining fixed costs allocated to product Ex include $155,000 of rent expense per year. The space previously used for product Ex can be rented to an outside organization for $157,500 per year.

Required:

Prepare a schedule analyzing the effect of Alternative A and Alternative B on projected total operating profit.

(CPA adapted)

12–26. Costs of a special order

Framar, Inc., manufactures automation machinery according to customer specifications. The company is relatively new and has grown each year. Framar has operated at 75 percent of practical capacity during the current year. The operating results for the most recent fiscal year are presented below.

FRAMAR INC.
Income Statement
(in thousands)

Sales revenue		$25,000
Less sales commissions		2,500
Net sales		22,500
Expenses:		
Direct material		6,000
Direct labor		7,500
Manufacturing overhead—variable:		
Supplies	$ 625	
Indirect labor	1,500	
Power	125	2,250
Manufacturing overhead—fixed:		
Supervision	500	
Depreciation	1,000	1,500
Corporate administration		750
Total costs		18,000
Net income before taxes		4,500
Income taxes (40%)		1,800
Net income		$ 2,700

Most of the management personnel had worked for firms in this type of business before joining Framar, but none of the top management had been responsible for overall corporate operations or for final decision on prices. Nevertheless, the company has been successful.

The top management of Framar wants to have a more organized and formal pricing system to prepare quotes for potential customers. Therefore, it has developed the pricing formula presented below. The formula is based upon the company's operating results achieved during the current year. The relationships used in the formula are expected to continue during the coming year. The company expects to operate at 75 percent of practical capacity during the current and coming years.

APA, Inc., has asked Framar to submit a bid on some custom designed machinery. Framar used the new formula to develop a price and submitted a bid of $165,000 to APA, Inc. The calculations to arrive at the bid price are given next to the pricing formula shown below.

Pricing formula

Details of formula	APA bid calculations
Estimated direct materials cost	$ 29,200
Estimated direct labor cost	56,000
Estimated manufacturing overhead calculated at 50% of direct labor	28,000
Estimated corporate overhead calculated at 10% of direct labor	5,600
Estimated total costs excluding sales commissions	$118,800
Add 25% for profits and taxes	29,700
Suggested price (with profits) before sales commissions	$148,500
Suggested total price equal suggested price divided by .9 to adjust for 10% sales commission	$165,000

Required:

a. Calculate the impact the order from APA, Inc., would have on Framar, Inc.'s net income after taxes if Framar's bid of $165,000 were accepted by APA.

b. Assume APA, Inc., has rejected Framar's price but has stated it is willing to pay $127,000 for the machinery. Should Framar, Inc., manufacture the machinery for the counter offer of $127,000? Explain your answer.

c. Calculate the lowest price Framar, Inc., can quote on this machinery without reducing its net income after taxes if it should manufacture the machinery.

d. Explain how the profit performance in the coming year would be affected if Framar, Inc., accepted all of its work at prices similar to the $127,000 counter offer of APA, Inc., described in Requirement (b)?

(CMA adapted)

12–27. Analyze special order

Nubo Manufacturing, Inc., is presently operating at 50 percent of practical capacity producing about 50,000 units annually of a patented electronic component. Nubo recently received an offer from a company in Yokohama, Japan, to purchase 30,000 components at $6 per unit, FOB Nubo's plant. Nubo has not previously sold components in Japan. Budgeted production costs for 50,000 and 80,000 units of output follow:

Units	50,000	80,000
Costs:		
Direct materials	$ 75,000	$120,000
Direct labor	75,000	120,000
Factory overhead	200,000	260,000
Total costs	$350,000	$500,000
Cost per unit	$7.00	$6.25

The sales manager thinks the order should be accepted, even if it results in a loss of $1 per unit, because he feels the sales may build up future markets. The production manager does not wish to have the order accepted primarily because the order would show a loss of $.25 per unit when computed on the new average unit cost. The treasurer has made a quick computation indicating that accepting the order will actually increase gross margin.

Required:

a. Explain what apparently caused the drop in cost from $7 per unit to $6.25 per unit when budgeted production increased from 50,000 to 80,000 units. Show supporting computations.

b. Explain why the conclusions of the production manager and the treasurer differ.

(CPA adapted)

12–28. Analyze alternative actions

Auer Company had received an order for a piece of special machinery from Jay Company. Just as Auer Company completed the machine, Jay Company declared bankruptcy, defaulted on the order, and forfeited the 10 percent deposit paid on the selling price of $72,500.

Auer's manufacturing manager identified the costs already incurred in the production of the special machinery for Jay as follows:

Direct materials used		$16,600
Direct labor incurred		21,400
Overhead applied:		
Manufacturing:		
Variable	$10,700	
Fixed	5,350	16,050
Nonmanufacturing		5,405
Total cost		$59,455

Another company, Kaytell Corporation, would be interested in buying the special machinery if it is reworked to Kaytell's specifications. Auer offered to sell the reworked special machinery to Kaytell as a special order for a net price of $68,400. Kaytell has agreed to pay the net price when it takes delivery in two months. The additional identifiable costs to rework the machinery to the specifications of Kaytell are as follows:

Direct materials	$ 6,200
Direct labor	4,200
	$10,400

A second alternative available to Auer is to convert the special machinery to the standard model. The standard model lists for $62,500. The additional identifiable costs to convert the special machinery to the standard model are:

Direct materials	$2,850
Direct labor	3,300
	$6,150

A third alternative for the Auer Company is to sell, as a special order, the machine as is (that is, without modification) for a net price of $52,000. However, the potential buyer of the unmodified machine does not want it for 60 days. The buyer offers a $7,000 down payment with final payment upon delivery.

The following additional information is available regarding Auer's operations:

1. Sales commission rate on sales of standard models is 2 percent while the sales commission rate on special orders is 3 percent. All sales commissions are calculated on net sales price (that is, list price less cash discount, if any).
2. Normal credit terms for sales of standard models are 2/10, net/30. Customers take the discounts except in rare instances. Credit terms for special orders are negotiated with the customer.
3. The application rates for manufacturing overhead and the nonmanufacturing costs are as follows:

Manufacturing:	
Variable	50% of direct labor cost
Fixed	25% of direct labor cost
Nonmanufacturing:	
Fixed	10% of the total of direct material, direct labor, and manufacturing overhead costs

4. Normal time required for rework is one month.
5. Auer normally sells a sufficient number of standard models for the company to operate at a volume in excess of the break-even point.

Auer does not consider the time value of money in analyses of special orders and projects when the time period is less than one year because the effect is not significant.

Required:

a. Determine the dollar contribution each of the three alternatives will add to the Auer Company's before-tax profits.
b. If Kaytell makes Auer a counter offer, what is the lowest price Auer Company should accept for the reworked machinery from Kaytell? Explain your answer.

(CMA adapted)

12–29. Analyze differential costs of new market

The Calco Corporation has been a major producer and distributor of molded and assembled plastic products for industrial use in its region for the past 20 years. Annual sales have averaged $60,000,000 for the past four years. Several times during this 20-year period the company has considered entering the consumer products market with items that could be manufactured in its facilities. Each time the product idea was sold to another company because Calco had no experience in the consumer markets, and its facilities were at or near full capacity.

Late last year the product engineering department presented a proposal to produce a plastic storage unit that was designed especially for the consumer market. The product was very well suited for the company's manufacturing process. No costly modification of machinery or molds would be required nor would operations in the assembly department have to be changed in any way. In addition, there was an adequate amount of manufacturing capacity available due to the recent expansion of facilities and a leveling of the sales growth in its industrial product lines.

The Calco management was receptive to this proposal. Although they had rejected consumer products in prior years, the arguments for the product were more persuasive this year—there was excess capacity, the products fit very well into the manufacturing process, and Calco's industrial markets appeared to be maturing. Therefore, entering the consumer market would give the company added opportunity to expand its sales.

The management is considering two alternatives for marketing the product. The first is to add this responsiblity to Calco's current marketing department. The other alternative is to acquire a small, new company named Jasco, Inc. Jasco was started by some former employees of a firm that specialized in marketing plastic products for the consumer market when they lost their jobs as a result of a merger. Jasco has not yet started operations.

Calco has never used independent distributors. Consequently, the management would prefer to acquire a distributor rather than merely enter into a contract for distribution of the product. The founders of Jasco are receptive to such an approach. In fact, Calco could acquire Jasco complete with personnel for a very nominal sum.

The manufacturing costs will be the same for either marketing alternative. The product engineering department has prepared the following estimates of the unit manufacturing costs for the new storage unit.

Direct materials	$14.00
Direct labor	3.50
Manufacturing overhead	10.00
Total	$27.50

The total overhead rate for all of Calco's manufacturing activities is $20 per hour. The rate is composed of $5 per hour for supplies, employee benefits, power, etc.; and $15 per hour for supervision, depreciation, insurance, taxes, etc.

Calco's marketing department has used their experience in the sale of industrial products to develop a proposal for the distribution of the new consumer product. The marketing department would be reorganized so that several positions that were scheduled for elimination now would be assigned to the new product. The marketing department's forecast of the annual financial results for its proposal to market the new storage units appears below.

Sales revenue (100,000 units at $45)	$4,500,000
Costs:	
Cost of units sold (100,000 units at $27.50)	2,750,000
Marketing costs:	
Positions that were to be eliminated	600,000
Sales commission (5% of sales)	225,000
Advertising program	400,000
Promotion program	200,000
Share of current marketing department's management costs	100,000
Total costs	4,275,000
Net income before taxes	$ 225,000

The Jasco founders also prepared a forecast of the annual financial results based upon their experience in marketing consumer products. The forecast presented below was based upon the assumption that Jasco would become part of Calco and be responsible for marketing the new storage unit in the consumer market.

Sales revenue (120,000 units at $50)	$6,000,000
Costs:	
Cost of units sold (120,000 units at $27.50)	3,300,000
Marketing costs:	
Personnel—sales	660,000
Personnel—sales management	200,000
Commissions (10%)	600,000
Advertising program	800,000
Promotion program	200,000
Office rental (the annual rental of a long-term lease already signed by Jasco)	50,000
Total costs	5,810,000
Net income before taxes	$ 190,000

Required:

Prepare a schedule of differential costs and revenues to assist management in deciding whether to enter the consumer market.

(CMA adapted)

12–30. Analyze short-term rental versus reimbursement policy

G & H Real Estate Agency is a moderate-sized company serving a metropolitan area of over one million people. G & H has 20 agents all of whom are free to list any kind of property from vacant land to commercial real estate anywhere in the greater metropolitan and surrounding three county area. Each agent travels extensively to cover the area served by G & H.

G & H requires all agents to be willing to travel throughout the entire area to list and sell property. To subsidize this travel requirement, the company has a reimbursement policy of $.25 per mile for all business-connected travel. The agents are responsible for all costs associated with the operation of their own automobiles. Last year the average mileage claimed by an agent was 50,000 miles. The number of miles driven are approximately the same each month, and the agents are reimbursed monthly.

The agents believe that $.25 per mile reimbursement is not unreasonable. However, they think that it is not adequate considering the wear and tear on the car and the inconvenience of the excessive amount of travel. Many agents believe that the amount of business related use is so great that two, and sometimes three, automobiles are required to meet their family needs. Further, the automobile used for business travel has to be traded in on an annual basis to avoid major repair costs.

Jack Golden, the president, believes that some of the arguments are legitimate. However, he also senses that some of the agents may have been claiming excess miles during the year. Golden is convinced that the annual mileage use would drop to 42,000 miles per year if the agents were not using their own cars. Therefore, he is considering an agency fleet of automobiles.

Golden asked both International Car Rental and a local automobile dealer, Aron Motor, to present proposals. The proposals are described below.

International Car Rental's proposal

International presented a lease arrangement with the following requirements:

1. G & H would rent 20 automobiles for an entire year at $66 per week per automobile and $.14 per mile.
2. When one of the 20 automobiles is in for service, International would provide a replacement at $7 per day and $.20 per mile. International would absorb all repair and maintenance costs. Normally, an automobile would be out of service only one day at a time, and each automobile can be expected to be out of service 12 days per year.
3. Cost of insurance is included in the weekly rental rate.
4. G & H would be required to purchase the gasoline for the automobiles at an average cost of $1.50 per gallon. International estimates that G & H should expect to get 21 miles per gallon.
5. International has agreed to collect the rental and mileage fees on a monthly basis.

Aron Motor's proposal

Aron offered a purchase-buy back arrangement with the following requirements:

1. G & H would buy 20 automobiles at $9,000 each. Aron would buy the automobiles back after one year at $4,000 each provided G & H subscribed to Aron's preferred customer maintenance and service plan.
2. G & H would have to bring each automobile in once every two months for preventive maintenance and service. The cost to G & H for each visit would be $50. Aron would provide a loaner automobile at no additional cost. Aron would accept responsibility for any additional repair and maintenance charges.
3. G & H would have to purchase insurance at a cost of $200 for each automobile. This would be paid at the beginning of the year.
4. G & H would purchase a new set of tires after six months at $125 per set.
5. G & H also would be responsible for the purchase of gasoline at an average cost of $1.50 per gallon. Aron states that because of proper maintenance, the automobiles will average 28 miles per gallon.
6. Aron requires that the purchase price of the automobiles be paid in full at the beginning of the year. However, the preventive maintenance service fee would be paid monthly.

Golden believes that this analysis does not require consideration of the time value of money. G & H's offices are open 300 days during the year.

Required:

Calculate an annual before-tax amount for—

a. The current reimbursement practice,
b. The proposal of International Car Rental, and
c. The proposal of Aron Motor.

which Jack Golden can use to compare the three alternatives. Based upon the before-tax data, which alternative should Golden accept?

(CMA adapted)

12–31. Incremental cost of special order

George Jackson operates a small machine shop. He manufactures one standard product available from many other similar businesses, and he also manufactures products to customer order. His accountant prepared the annual income statement shown below:

	Custom sales	Standard sales	Total
Sales revenue	$50,000	$25,000	$75,000
Materials	10,000	8,000	18,000
Labor	20,000	9,000	29,000
Depreciation	6,300	3,600	9,900
Power	700	400	1,100
Rent	6,000	1,000	7,000
Heat and light	600	100	700
Other	400	900	1,300
Total costs	44,000	23,000	67,000
Operating profit	$ 6,000	$ 2,000	$ 8,000

The depreciation charges are for machines used in the respective product lines. The power charge is apportioned on the estimate of power consumed. The rent is for the building space that has been leased for 10 years at $7,000 per year. The rent and heat and light are apportioned to the product lines based on amount of floor space occupied. All other costs are current expenses identified with the product line causing them.

A valued custom parts customer has asked Mr. Jackson if he would manufacture 5,000 special units for him. Mr. Jackson is working at capacity and would have to give up some other business in order to take this business. He can't renege on custom orders already agreed to, but he could reduce the output of his standard product by about one half for one year while producing the specially requested custom part. The customer is willing to pay $7 for each part. The material cost will be about $2 per unit and the labor will be $3.60 per unit. Mr. Jackson will have to spend $2,000 for a special device which will be discarded when the job is done.

Required:

a. Calculate and present the following costs related to the 5,000-unit custom order:
    (1) The differential cost of the order.
    (2) The full cost of the order.
    (3) The opportunity cost of taking the order.
    (4) The sunk costs related to the order.
b. Should Mr. Jackson take the order? Explain your answer.

(CMA adapted)

12–32. Hospital Supply, Inc.* (comprehensive differential costing case)

Hospital Supply, Inc., produced hydraulic hoists that were used by hospitals to move bedridden patients. The costs of manufacturing and marketing hydraulic hoists at the company's normal volume of 3,000 units per month are shown in Exhibit A.

Required:

The following questions refer only to the data given above. Unless otherwise stated, assume there is no connection between the situations described in the questions; each is to be treated independently. Unless otherwise stated, a regular selling price of $740 per unit should be assumed. Ignore income taxes and other costs that are not mentioned in Exhibit A or in a question itself.

a. What is the break-even volume in units? In sales dollars?
b. Market research estimates that volume could be increased to 3,500 units, which is well within hoist production capacity limitations, if the price were cut from $740 to $650 per unit. Assuming the cost behavior patterns implied by the data

---

* © Michael W. Maher, 1979.

Exhibit A **Costs per unit for hydraulic hoists**

Unit manufacturing costs:		
Variable materials	$100	
Variable labor	150	
Variable overhead	50	
Fixed overhead	120	
Total unit manufacturing costs		$420
Unit marketing costs:		
Variable	50	
Fixed	140	
Total unit marketing costs		190
Total unit costs		$610

in Exhibit A are correct, would you recommend that this action be taken? What would be the impact on monthly sales, costs, and income?

c. On March 1, a contract offer is made to Hospital Supply by the federal government to supply 500 units to Veterans Administration hospitals for delivery by March 31. Because of an unusually large number of rush orders from their regular customers, Hospital Supply plans to produce 4,000 units during March, which will use all available capacity. If the government order is accepted, 500 units normally sold to regular customers would be lost to a competitor. The contract given by the government would reimburse the government's share of March manufacturing costs, plus pay a fixed fee (profit) of $50,000. (There would be no variable marketing costs incurred on the government's units.) What impact would accepting the government contract have on March income?

d. Hospital Supply has an opportunity to enter a foreign market in which price competition is keen. An attraction of the foreign market is that demand there is greatest when demand in the domestic market is quite low; thus idle production facilities could be used without affecting domestic business.

   An order for 1,000 units is being sought at a below-normal price in order to enter this market. Shipping costs for this order will amount to $75 per unit, while total costs of obtaining the contract (marketing costs) will be $4,000. Domestic business would be unaffected by this order. What is the minimum unit price Hospital Supply should consider for this order of 1,000 units?

e. An inventory of 230 units of an obsolete model of the hoist remains in the stockroom. These must be sold through regular channels at reduced prices, or the inventory will soon be valueless. What is the minimum price that would be acceptable in selling these units?

f. A proposal is received from an outside contractor who will make and ship 1,000 hydraulic hoist units per month directly to Hospital Supply's customers as orders are received from Hospital Supply's sales force. Hospital Supply's fixed marketing costs would be unaffected, but its variable marketing costs would be cut by 20 percent for these 1,000 units produced by the contractor. Hospital Supply's plant would operate at two thirds of its normal level, and total fixed manufacturing costs would be cut by 30 percent. What in-house unit cost should be used to compare with the quotation received from the supplier? Should the proposal be accepted for a price (that is, payment to the contractor) of $425 per unit?

g. Assume the same facts as above in Requirement (f) except that the idle facilities would be used to produce 800 modified hydraulic hoists per month for use in hospital operating rooms. These modified hoists could be sold for $900 each, while the costs of production would be $550 per unit variable manufacturing expense. Variable marketing costs would be $100 per unit. Fixed marketing and manufacturing costs would be unchanged whether the original 3,000 regular hoists were manufactured or the mix of 2,000 regular hoists plus 800 modified hoists were produced. What is the maximum purchase price per unit that Hospital Supply should be willing to pay the outside contractor? Should the proposal be accepted for a price of $425 per unit to the contractor?

12–33. Sheridan Carpet Company (Differential analysis and pricing)*

Sheridan Carpet Company produced high-grade carpeting materials for use in automobiles and recreational vans. Sheridan's products were sold to finishers, who cut and bound the material so as to fit perfectly in the passenger compartment or cargo area (for example, automobile trunk) of a specific model automobile or van. Some of these finishers were captive operations of major automobile assembly divisions, particularly those that assembled the "top of the line" cars that included high-grade carpeting; other finishers concentrated on the replacement and van customizing markets.

Late in 1978, the marketing manager and the chief accountant of Sheridan met to decide on the list price for carpet number 104. It was industry practice to announce prices just prior to the January–June and July–December "seasons." Over the years, companies in the industry adhered to their announced prices through a six-month season unless significant unexpected changes in costs occurred. Sales of carpet 104 were not affected by seasonal factors during the two six-month seasons.

Sheridan was the largest company in its segment of the automobile carpet industry; its 1977 sales had been almost $30 million. Sheridan's salespersons were on a salary basis, and each one sold the entire product line. Most of Sheridan's competitors were smaller than Sheridan; accordingly, they usually awaited Sheridan's price announcement before setting their own selling prices.

Carpet 104 had an especially dense nap; as a result, making it required a special machine, and it was produced in a department whose equipment could not be used to produce Sheridan's other carpets. Effective January 1, 1978, Sheridan had raised its price on this carpet from $2.70 to $3.60 per square yard. This had been done in order to bring 104's margin up to that of the other carpets in the line. Although Sheridan was financially sound, it expected a large funds need in the next few years for equipment replacement and plant expansion. The 1978 price increase was one of several decisions made in order to provide funds for these plans.

Sheridan's competitors, however, had held their 1978 prices at $2.70 on carpets competitive with 104. As shown in Exhibit A, which includes estimates of industry volume on these carpets, Sheridan's price increase had apparently resulted in a loss of market share. The marketing manager, Mel Walters, estimated that the industry would sell about 630,000 square yards of these carpets in the first half of 1979. Walters was sure Sheridan could sell 150,000 yards if it dropped the price of 104 back to $2.70. But if Sheridan held its price at $3.60, Walters feared a further erosion in Sheridan's share. However, because some customers felt that 104 was superior to competitive products, Walters felt that Sheridan could sell at least 65,000 yards at the $3.60 price.

---

* © Osceola Institute, 1979.

Exhibit A (12–33)   **Carpet 104: Prices and production, 1976–1978**

Selling season*	Production volume (square yards)		Price (per square yard)	
	Industry total	Sheridan Carpet	Most competitors	Sherican Carpet
1976–1	549,000	192,000	$3.60	$3.60
1976–2	517,500	181,000	3.60	3.60
1977–1	387,000	135,500	2.70	2.70
1977–2	427,500	149,500	2.70	2.70
1978–1	450,000	135,000	2.70	3.60
1978–2	562,500	112,500	2.70	3.60

* 197x–1 means the first 6 months of 197x; 197x–2 means the second six months of 197x.

During their discussion, Walters and the chief accountant, Terry Rosen, identified two other aspects of the pricing decision. Rosen wondered whether competitors would announce a further price decrease if Sheridan dropped back to $2.70. Walters felt it was unlikely that competitors would price below $2.70, because none of them was more efficient than Sheridan, and there were rumors that several of them were in poor financial condition. Rosen's other concern was whether a decision relating to carpet 104 would have any impact on the sales of Sheridan's other carpets. Walters was convinced that since 104 was a specialized item, there was no interdependence between its sales and those of other carpets in the line.

Exhibit B contains cost estimates that Rosen had prepared for various volumes of 104. These estimates represented Rosen's best guesses as to costs during the first six months of 1979, based on past cost experience and anticipated inflation.

Exhibit B (12–33)   **Estimated cost of carpet 104 at various production volumes (first six months of 1979)**

	Volume (square yards)					
	65,000	87,500	110,000	150,000	185,000	220,000
Direct materials	$ .360	$ .360	$ .360	$ .360	$ .360	$ .360
Materials spoilage	.036	.035	.034	.034	.035	.036
Direct labor	.710	.685	.678	.666	.675	.690
Departmental overhead:						
Direct[a]	.098	.094	.091	.090	.090	.090
Indirect[b]	.831	.617	.491	.360	.292	.245
General overhead[c]	.213	.206	.203	.200	.203	.207
Factory cost	2.248	1.997	1.857	1.710	1.655	1.628
Selling and administrative[d]	1.461	1.298	1.207	1.112	1.076	1.058
Total cost	$3.709	$3.295	$3.064	$2.822	$2.731	$2.686

[a] Materials handlers, supplies, repairs, power, fringe benefits.

[b] Supervision, equipment depreciation, heat and light.

[c] Thirty percent of direct labor.

[d] Sixty-five percent of factory cost.

Required: *a.* What was the relationship (if any) between the 104 pricing decision and the company's future need for capital funds?

b. Assuming no intermediate prices are to be considered, should Sheridan price 104 at $2.70 or $3.60?

c. If Sheridan's competitors hold their prices at $2.70, how many square yards of 104 would Sheridan need to sell at a price of $3.60 in order to earn the same profit as selling 150,000 square yards at a price of $2.70?

d. What additional information would you wish to have before making this pricing decision? (Despite the absence of this information, still answer Requirement *(b)*!)

e. With hindsight, was the decision to raise the price in 1978 a good one?

13

Multiple-Product Decisions

OBJECTIVES

To understand the role of accounting data in making decisions when a company produces more than one output.

To understand how to apply linear programming techniques to this problem. To understand the sensitivity of linear programming results to cost data.

This chapter continues the discussion of differential cost analysis by explaining how differential costing is used to choose among multiple products.

Product-choice decisions

Choosing which products to manufacture and sell is a common managerial decision. Most companies are capable of producing a great variety of goods and services but are limited by capacity. Campus Bookstore, in Chapter 12, had to decide whether to use its limited space to sell general merchandise or to increase book sales. Due to a shortage of personnel, a small CPA firm may have to choose between performing work for client A or for client B. Students have to choose how to allocate their study time among their courses. An automobile manufacturer with limited production facilities must decide whether to produce compacts, full-size sedans, or some other model.

We usually think of product choices as short-run decisions because we have adopted the definition that in the short run, capacity is fixed, while in the long run, capacity can be changed. Thus, the automobile manufacturer may be able to produce both sedans and compacts in the *long run* by increasing capacity, and the CPA firm may be able to serve both Client A and Client B in the *long run* by hiring more professional staff. Nonetheless, in the short run, capacity limitations require choices.

For example, Glover Manufacturing makes two kinds of baseballs—hardballs and softballs. For now, assume that the company can sell all the baseballs it produces. Glover's cost and revenue information is presented in Illustration 13–1.

The profit-volume relationship for Glover's products is shown in Illustration 13–2. For instance, Glover Manufacturing can sell 250,000 hardballs or 250,000 softballs or any combination of hardballs and softballs totaling 250,000 to break even. The contribution margin of each product is the same, so the profit-volume relationship is the same regardless of the mix of products produced and sold.

Illustration 13–1   **Revenue and cost information, Glover Manufacturing**

	Hardballs	Softballs
Sales revenue per unit	$10.00	$9.00
Less variable costs per unit:		
Materials	4.00	2.50
Labor	1.50	2.00
Variable overhead	.50	.50
Contribution margin per unit	$ 4.00	$4.00

Fixed manufacturing costs: $800,000 per month.
Marketing and administrative costs (all fixed): $200,000 per month.

Illustration 13–2   **Profit-volume relationship assuming hardballs and softballs use equal scarce resources, Glover Manufacturing**

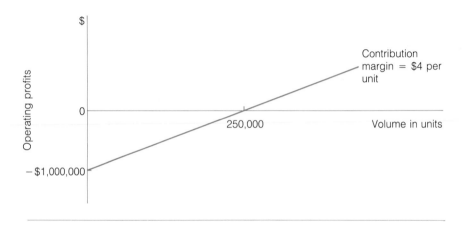

Product contribution margin with a single constrained resource

Recall that Glover Manufacturing can sell all of the baseballs it can produce. But should it produce hardballs or softballs? Without knowing either Glover's maximum production capacity or the amount of that capacity that is used by producing one product or the other, we might say that it doesn't matter because both products are equally profitable. But because capacity is limited, that answer would be incorrect if Glover uses up its capacity at a different rate for each product.

Suppose that Glover's capacity is limited to 7,200 machine-hours per month. (This limitation is known as a constraint.) Further, assume that machines may be used to produce either 30 hardballs per machine-hour or 50 softballs per machine-hour.

With a single constrained resource, the important measure of profitability is the contribution margin per unit of scarce resource used, *not* contribution margin per unit of product. In this case, softballs are more profitable than hardballs because softballs contribute $200 per machine-hour ($4 per soft-ball × 50 softballs per hour), while hardballs contribute only $120 per machine-hour ($4 per hardball × 30 hardballs per machine-hour). The hours required to produce one ball times the contribution per hour equals the contribution per ball.

$$\text{Hardballs: } \frac{1}{30} \text{ hours times \$120 per hour equals \$4 per hardball.}$$

$$\text{Softballs: } \frac{1}{50} \text{ hours times \$200 per hour equals \$4 per softball.}$$

For the month, Glover could produce 360,000 softballs (50 per hour × 7,200 hours) or 216,000 hardballs (30 per hour × 7,200 hours). If only softballs are produced, Glover's operating profit would be $440,000 (360,000 softballs times a contribution margin of $4 each minus fixed costs of $1,000,000). If only hardballs are produced, Glover's net *loss* would be $136,000 (216,000 hardballs times a contribution margin of $4 each minus $1,000,000). By concentrating on the product that yields the greater contribution per unit of scarce resource, Glover can maximize its profit.

Mathematical representation of the problem

The relationship between the usage of machine-hours to produce hardballs and softballs may be expressed as:

$$\left(\frac{1}{30}\right) H + \left(\frac{1}{50}\right) S \leq 7,200 \text{ machine-hours}$$

(To be precise, there are two more constraints that prevent negative production of either product. These are $H \geq 0$ and $S \geq 0$, but these are ignored in our discussion because negative production is not possible.)

The first term in the production expression reflects the fact that a hardball uses 1/30 hour of machine time. The second term indicates that each softball uses 1/50 hour of machine time. The third term or right-hand side constrains production time to 7,200 hours or less. Although it is possible to use fewer than 7,200 hours, that would indicate idle capacity. Hence, Glover is better off to use as many hours as possible. This point may also be shown mathematically, but we leave that to the operations researchers.

In short, the relationship between the product contribution margins and the constraints for Glover would be written as follows:

Objective function:
Maximize $4H + $4S

Constraints:

$$\text{Subject to } \left(\frac{1}{30}\right) H + \left(\frac{1}{50}\right) S \leq 7,200 \text{ hours}$$

The objective function states that the objective is to select the product mix that maximizes total contribution, given the unit contribution of hardballs is $4 and of softballs is $4. The constraint states that each hardball uses 1/30 of a machine-hour, each softball uses 1/50 of an hour and, in total, no more than 7,200 hours are available.

Graphic solution   Illustration 13–3 shows that relationship between production of each product and the amount of the scarce resources available. Glover Manufacturing can produce at any point along the line labeled "machine capacity," or at any interior point in the feasible production region. The feasible production region is the area in the graph bounded by the constraints on operating activities. In this case, production is bounded by zero on the low side and by 7,200 machine-hours on the high side.

The optimal solution must always be at a corner point. For example, if point 3 is, better than point 2, then it must also be better than any place on the *straight line* between points 2 and 3. Of course, if two corner points have the same total contribution, any point on a straight line between those

Illustration 13–3   **Single constraint, Glover Manufacturing**

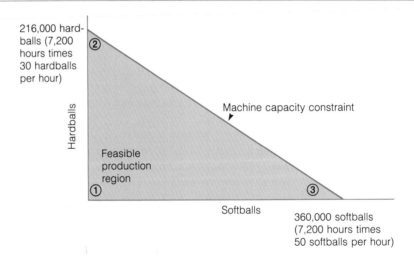

Corner point	Produce and sell		Total contribution margin	Fixed costs	Operating profits (loss)
	Hardballs	**Softballs**			
1	–0–	–0–	–0–	$1,000,000	$(1,000,000)
2	216,000	–0–	216,000 × $4 = $864,000	1,000,000	(136,000)
3	–0–	360,000	360,000 × $4 = $1,440,000	1,000,000	440,000

two corners would have the same total contribution as either corner point. However, by knowing that there can be no solution better than the solution at the optimal corner enables us to limit our search for the maximum profit combination to the corner points in the feasible region.

Because Glover can sell all it produces at a positive contribution margin for each product, it would prefer to produce as much as possible, which is at some point on the machine capacity line. Analysis of each **corner point** (that is, each corner of the feasible region) shows that it is optimal for Glover to produce and sell 360,000 softballs and no hardballs.

Glover's total contribution, and therefore total operating profit, is reduced for every hardball it produces. For example, the total contribution with production of 360,000 softballs is $1,440,000. To produce one hardball requires giving up 5/3 softballs, calculated as follows:

1. Start with the following constraint:

$$\left(\frac{1}{30}\right) H + \left(\frac{1}{50}\right) S \leq 7,200 \text{ machine-hours}$$

2. The choice requires no change in machine-hours, only a substitution of hardballs for softballs, so set $(1/30)H + (1/50)S = 0$
3. Now find the number of softballs given up for each hardball produced (the symbol Δ refers to "change"):

$$\left(\frac{1}{30}\right) \Delta H = -\left(\frac{1}{50}\right) \Delta S$$

$$\Delta H = -\frac{\left(\frac{1}{50}\right)}{\left(\frac{1}{30}\right)} \Delta S = -\left(\frac{5}{3}\right) \Delta S$$

4. Thus, every hardball produced requires giving up 5/3 softballs
5. Net effect on total contribution:

Contribution gained (one hardball × $4)	$4.00
Contribution lost (5/3 softballs × $4)	6.67
Net contribution lost per hardball produced	$2.67

This loss in contribution is referred to as the **opportunity cost** or **shadow price** of one additional hardball.

What is really sold?   In working with production constraints, it is often useful to think in terms of selling the service of the productive resources rather than selling units of product. For example, we can think of Glover as selling machine-hours, with each machine-hour contributing $200 if used to make softballs, $120 if used to make hardballs and $0 if not used at all.

Identifying differential costs

Notice that Glover Manufacturing's costs were divided into fixed and variable portions. By definition, the variable costs are differential with volume changes. In some companies, variable costs are not separated from fixed costs. This can lead to serious product-mix errors if fixed costs allocated to each unit of product are included when comparing the profitability of products. This error would result from treating fixed costs as differential costs.

For example, suppose that before any attempt was made to determine the optimal product mix for Glover Manufacturing, the accounting department had prepared the report in Illustration 13–4. As you can see, fixed and variable overhead costs are not separated. By applying overhead at 200 percent of labor, overhead *appears to vary with labor,* whereas we know that a substantial amount of the overhead is fixed. Based on this presentation, hardballs *appear* to be more profitable per unit of scarce resource than softballs, but in fact the opposite is true.

Accounting information is sometimes sent to personnel in operations and engineering who are unaware of the important but subtle distinction between *gross margin* and *contribution margin* that we have emphasized in this book. For example, suppose that the gross margin per unit from Illustration 13–4 is used instead of the contribution margin per unit from Illustration 13–1. Illustration 13–2 shows that there are two extreme production possibilities: 216,000 hardballs or 360,000 softballs. Using the gross margins from Illustration 13–4, production of 216,000 hardballs at $1.50 (total gross margin = $324,000) *appears* economically superior to production of 360,000 softballs at $.50 (total gross margin = $180,000).

Of course, we know that is wrong. As shown in Illustration 13–5, producing 216,000 hardballs and no softballs would result in a net loss of $136,000, while the correct product mix of 360,000 softballs and no hardballs provides operating profit of $440,000.

Thus, a common mistake in product-mix decisions stems from the failure to recognize which costs are differential. Fixed costs for different product mixes often do not differ in the short run. For purposes of valuing inventory for external reporting, however, fixed manufacturing overhead is assigned

Illustration 13–4   **Full costs of the product, Glover Manufacturing**

	Hardballs	Softballs
Sales revenue per unit	$10.00	$9.00
Less full manufacturing costs per unit:		
Materials	4.00	2.50
Labor	1.50	2.00
Overhead (applied at a rate of 200% of		
labor)[a]	3.00	4.00
Gross margin per unit	$ 1.50	$ .50

Marketing and administrative costs (all fixed): $200,000 per month.

[a] Any under- or overabsorbed overhead is written off as an expense of the period.

Illustration 13–5 **Comparison of product mix analyses, Glover Manufacturing**

	Gross margin method wrong decision: Produce all hardballs	Contribution margin method right decision: Produce all softballs
Sales revenue:		
Hardballs (216,000 × $10)	$2,160,000	
Softballs (360,000 × $9)		$3,240,000
Less variable manufacturing costs:		
Hardballs (216,000 × $6)	1,296,000	
Softballs (360,000 × $5)		1,800,000
Total contribution margin	864,000	1,440,000
Less fixed costs:		
Manufacturing	800,000	800,000
Marketing and administrative	200,000	200,000
Operating profit (loss)	$ (136,000)	$ 440,000

to units produced, thereby making fixed costs appear variable to the unsophisticated user of cost information. As in the other differential cost problems we have seen, it is important to determine which costs are *really differential* for decision making.

This is another example of a common problem in accounting. Costs that were assigned to units for one purpose (inventory valuation, in this case) could be inappropriately used for another purpose (product mix decisions, in this case).

Opportunity cost of resources

Opportunity cost is the loss from not taking the best foregone opportunity for the use of a resource. Machine capacity, or any other constraint, may have an opportunity cost.

For example, what is the opportunity cost to Glover Manufacturing of not having one more hour of machine capacity? First, assume that the increase in machine time would change neither fixed manufacturing nor fixed selling costs. With one more hour of machine time, Glover could produce 50 more softballs, as shown below:

Before: $(1/30)\ H + (1/50)\ S \leq 7{,}200$ machine-hours. If only softballs are produced:

$$\left(\frac{1}{50}\right) S = 7{,}200$$

$$S = \frac{7{,}200}{\left(\dfrac{1}{50}\right)}$$

$$= 360{,}000 \text{ softballs}$$

With one additional machine-hour and producing only softballs:

$$\left(\frac{1}{50}\right) S = 7{,}201$$

$$S = \frac{7{,}201}{\left(\dfrac{1}{50}\right)}$$

$$= 360{,}050 \text{ softballs}$$

With a unit contribution margin of \$4, production of 50 more softballs would add \$200 to profits. Thus, the opportunity cost of one hour of machine time is \$200. This opportunity cost is also known as a *shadow price*.

With this information, Glover's management can decide whether it is worthwhile to add machine time. If additional machine time can be leased for any amount less than \$200 per hour, for example, doing so would increase operating profits.

Multiple constraints

With one constraint, it is easy to see that Glover could maximize contribution by producing only softballs. But the situation becomes more complex when there are multiple constraints. Suppose that the sale of softballs is temporarily restricted so that only 200,000 can be sold during the next production period. Further, suppose that Glover cannot hold baseballs in inventory so everything produced must be sold in the same period. Now the constraints are:

(1) $\left(\dfrac{1}{30}\right) H + \left(\dfrac{1}{50}\right) S \leq 7{,}200$ machine-hours

(2) $\qquad\qquad\qquad\qquad S \leq 200{,}000$

These relationships are shown graphically in Illustration 13–6. Now to determine the optimal product mix, we find the monthly operating profit at each of the four corner points labeled. This optimal solution is to produce as many softballs as can be sold, 200,000, and use the remaining capacity to produce 96,000 hardballs.

As more constraints and products are added, solving for product mixes becomes more complex. Although it is possible to solve these problems by hand, they are typically solved by computer, as discussed in the following section.

Linear programming

The product choice problem is often much more complex than the two-product, two-constraint problems just presented for Glover Manufacturing. Companies often have many constraints and many choices. The method we

Illustration 13–6   **Product choice with multiple constraints, Glover Manufacturing**

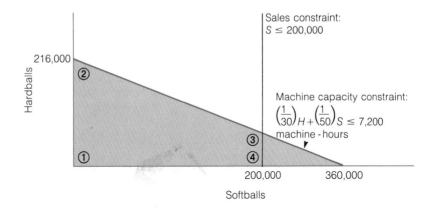

| | **Produce and sell** | | | | |
Corner point	Hardballs	Softballs	Total contribution margin	Fixed costs	Operating profit (loss)
1	–0–	–0–	–0–	$1,000,000	$(1,000,000)
2	216,000	–0–	216,000 × $4 = $864,000	1,000,000	(136,000)
3[a]	96,000	200,000	(96,000 × $4) + (200,000 × $4) = $1,184,000	1,000,000	184,000
4	–0–	200,000	200,000 × $4 = $800,000	1,000,000	(200,000)

[a] The volume at this corner point can be found by simultaneously solving for the machine and sales constraints.

$$\left(\frac{1}{30}\right)H + \left(\frac{1}{50}\right)S = 7{,}200 \text{ machine-hours}$$

$$S = \underline{\underline{200{,}000}}$$

$$\text{so } \left(\frac{1}{30}\right)H + \left(\frac{1}{50}\right)(200{,}000) = 7{,}200$$

$$\left(\frac{1}{30}\right)H + 4{,}000 = 7{,}200$$

$$\left(\frac{1}{30}\right)H = 3{,}200$$

$$H = \underline{\underline{96{,}000}}$$

used to find the optimal product mix for Glover Manufacturing is called **linear programming—graphic method.** The graphic method is a useful way to see how linear programming works, but it is impractical for complex problems with many choices and constraints.

A mathematical technique, known as the **linear programming—simplex method,** has been developed for solving complex product mix problems. This technique solves for corner solutions much as we did earlier in this chapter using graphs. Many computer software packages include the simplex method, or a variation of it for solving product-mix problems.

For the rest of this chapter, we assume product-mix decisions are solved on the computer. Our focus will be on setting up the problems so they can be entered into the computer and on interpreting the output, not on the mathematical procedures used to derive solutions.[1]

Comprehensive linear programming example

This section presents an example that we solved using the computer. We discuss how to set up the problem to enter it into the computer and how to interpret the results.

Assume that Hixon Company manufactures and sells three wood products—cabinets, labeled A; bookshelves, labeled B, and storage chests, labeled C. Each product must be processed through two departments—cutting, and assembly and finishing—before it is sold.

Illustration 13–7 presents data about product selling prices, costs, and the rate at which each product uses scarce resources. In addition to the information provided in Illustration 13–7, we learn that only 2,000 board feet of direct material can be obtained per week. The cutting department has 180 hours of labor available each week, and the assembly and finishing department has 240 hours of labor available each week. No overtime is allowed.

Hixon Company's contract commitments require it to make at least 100 units of Product A per week. Also, due to keen competition, no more than 100 units of Product B can be sold each week.

Fixed manufacturing overhead costs are estimated to be $1,500 per week. They are arbitrarily allocated to each unit at the rate of $5 per unit. Fixed

Illustration 13–7   **Hixon Company facts**

	Product A per unit	Product B per unit	Product C per unit
Selling price	$14.00	$18.00	$24.00
Direct labor cost	6.00	7.20	10.80
Direct material cost	.80	1.40	2.00
Variable overhead	1.52	2.00	2.96
Contribution margins	5.68	7.40	8.24
Fixed manufacturing overhead	5.00	5.00	5.00
Gross margins	$ .68	$ 2.40	$ 3.24
Material requirements in board feet per unit of output	4	7	10
Labor requirements in hours per unit of output:			
Cutting department	.30	.30	.40
Assembly and finishing department	.20	.30	.50

[1] More details on the mathematics of linear programming are available from books on operations research and quantitative methods. For example, see H. Bierman, C. Bonini, and W. Hausman, *Quantitative Analysis for Business Decisions,* 5th ed. (Homewood, Ill.: Richard D. Irwin, 1977).

manufacturing costs are unaffected by the product mix. Nonmanufacturing costs of $1,000 per week are fixed and unaffected by the product-mix decision.

Problem formulation

Hixon Company's product-mix decision problem can be solved using the linear programming technique. The constrained optimization problem is formulated as follows:

Maximize total contribution margin:

$$\$5.68A + \$7.40B + \$8.24C \qquad \text{Objective function}$$

Subject to the following constraints:

$$
\begin{array}{llll}
4A + & 7B + & 10C \le 2{,}000 \ \text{board feet} & \text{Direct material} \\
.30A + & .30B + & .40C \le \quad 180 \ \text{labor-hours} & \text{Cutting} \\
.20A + & .30B + & .50C \le \quad 240 \ \text{labor-hours} & \text{Assembly and finishing} \\
A & & \ge \quad 100 \ \text{units sold} & \text{Product A's sales} \\
& B & \le \quad 100 \ \text{units sold} & \text{Product B's sales}
\end{array}
$$

Using a linear programming computer package, we can obtain a solution for the above model. Illustration 13–8 shows how this problem was entered into the computer using a particular software package. The initial table in Illustration 13–8 is from the printout of the linear programming problem formulation. Illustration 13–9 shows the output. Most software packages present the output like the output in Illustration 13–9.

Solution

The Summary of Problem in Illustration 13–9 lists the linear programming (LP) solution to the optimization problem. The total contribution margin is maximized if Hixon Company produces 500 units of Product A and no units of Product B and Product C. The maximum total contribution obtainable under the present resource constraints is $2,840. Hence the operating profit realized from this production mix is $340 (= $2,840 − $1,500 fixed manufacturing costs − $1,000 fixed nonmanufacturing costs).

Opportunity costs

Product B and Product C have opportunity cost values of $2.54 and $5.96, respectively, as shown in Illustration 13–9. This opportunity cost or shadow price means that if we force Hixon, for example, to produce one unit of Product B, total contribution margin to the firm will be reduced by $2.54. This is because some production of the more profitable A will have to be given up to produce B. Similarly, the production of an additional unit of Product C would lower the contribution margin by $5.96.

Of the five constraints, only the direct material constraint has an opportunity cost attached to it. This opportunity cost figure shows us how total contribution margin changes as a result of a per unit change in the constraint.

Illustration 13–8   **Linear programming input,[a] Hixon Company**

ENTER THE NUMBER OF VARIABLES
3
ENTER THE NUMBER OF CONSTRAINTS
5
ENTER A 1 FOR MAXIMIZATION OR A 2 FOR MINIMIZATION
1

ENTER VARIABLE NAMES, ONE PER LINE
Prod A
Prod B
Prod C

ENTER CONSTRAINT NAMES, ONE PER LINE
Material
Cutting
Assembly
A sales
B sales

ENTER CONSTRAINT TYPES (< , > , or =), ONE FOR EACH CONSTRAINT
DO NOT SEPARATE WITH COMMAS
<<<><
ENTER 3 OBJECTIVE FUNCTION COEFFICIENTS, SEPARATED BY COMMAS
5.68,7.4,8.24
ENTER 5 CONSTRAINTS, 1 PER LINE (SEPARATE VALUES WITH COMMAS
AND ENTER THE RIGHT HAND SIDE VALUE AS THE LAST VALUE ON EACH LINE)
4,7,10,2000
.3,.3,.4,180
.2,.3,.5,240
1,0,0,100
0,1,0,100

INITIAL TABLE

			Product A	Product B	Product C
OBJ COEFF	MAXIMIZE		$5.68	$7.40	$ 8.24
CONSTRAINT		SOLUTION VALUES			
Material		2,000.	4.00	7.00	10.00
Cutting		180.	.30	.30	.40
Assembly		240.	.20	.30	.50
A sales		100.	1.00	—	—
B sales		100.	—	1.00	—

[a] Based on a program developed by Professor Robert Haessler, University of Michigan.

Thus, if we increase the direct material constraint from 2,000 board feet to 2,001 board feet, Hixon's contribution margin will increase by $1.42.

The other four constraints each have a solution value instead of an opportunity cost. This means that these constraints are not binding. The amounts shown under the heading Solution Values are the amounts of the scarce resources, or constraints, still available. For example, 30 labor-hours are still available in the cutting department; only 150 hours of the available

Illustration 13–9   **Linear programming output, Hixon Company**

SUMMARY OF PROBLEM:

SOLUTION VARIABLES	SOLUTION VALUES	NONSOLUTION VARIABLES	OPPORTUNITY COSTS
Prod A	500.	—	—
—	—	Prod B	$2.54
—	—	Prod C	5.96
—	—	Material	1.42
Cutting	30.	—	—
Assembly	140.	—	—
B sales	100.	—	—
A sales	400.	—	—

OPTIMAL VALUE OF SOLUTION IS $2,840

RANGES OF RIGHT-HAND-SIDE VALUES OF CONSTRAINTS

CONSTRAINT	LOWER LIMIT	UPPER LIMIT	INITIAL CONSTRAINT VALUE
Material	400.	2,400.	2,000
Cutting	150.	INF.	180.
Assembly	100.	INF.	240.
A Sales	NEG. INF.	500.	100.
B sales	–0–	INF.	100.

RANGES OF OBJECTIVE FUNCTION COEFFICIENTS

OBJECTIVE COEFFICIENT	LOWER BOUND	UPPER BOUND	INITIAL VALUE
Prod A	4.2286	PLUS INF.	5.6800
Prod B	NEG. INF.	9.9400	7.4000
Prod C	NEG. INF.	14.2000	8.2400

180 labor-hours were used. This unused scarce resource is sometimes known as *slack.* In the assembly and finishing department, 140 labor-hours are still available. For *B sales,* an additional 100 units could be produced and sold before the market constraint becomes binding. (Recall that no more than 100 units of B could be sold per week. The optimal solution is to sell no units of B.) Finally, for Product A, the solution value shows that optimal production of A exceeds the specified minimum by 400 units; that is, there is a "surplus" over the specified minimum.

Whereas binding constraints have an opportunity cost (for example, $1.42 per unit for direct materials), no opportunity cost is shown in the solution for the constraints that are not binding. For example, there is no opportunity cost for labor-hours in the cutting department because there is no value for having one additional hour, nor a loss for having one less hour.

Sensitivity analysis   All the parameters specified in this linear programming (LP) model are subject to some degree of estimation error. Decision makers need to know how much error can be tolerated before making a difference in the decision. Under the heading Ranges of Right-Hand-Side Values of Constraints in Illustration 13–9 we are given the upper and lower bound values of all the constraints in the linear programming model. For example, the direct material constraint has a lower bound value of 400 board feet and an upper bound value of 2,400 board feet. This means that beyond these parameters the direct material constraint will not be a binding constraint, all other things held constant.

If there is less than 400 board feet of direct material available, the company could not satisfy its constraint to make more than 100 units of A, because each unit of A requires 4 board feet. If more than 2,400 board feet of direct material were available, some constraint that is not now binding would become binding.

Labor-hours in the cutting department is not now binding. The constraint ranges tell us that if only 150 labor-hours were available, instead of the 180 hours now available, labor-hours would then be a binding constraint.

In short, outside of the ranges given, some other constraint(s) will be binding, resulting in a new product choice. The range of these right-hand-side values of constraints can be visualized as how far inward or outward a linear constraint can shift in a parallel fashion and still be a binding constraint.

Similarly, the Ranges of Objective Function Coefficients in Illustration 13–9 show how much the contribution margins of each of the products can increase or decrease before the optimal decision on the product mix changes. Hence, within the upper and lower bound values of the objective function coefficients, Hixon Company will choose to produce 500 units of Product A and none of the other two products.

Misspecification of the objective function

Suppose Hixon Company incorrectly specified its objective function using gross margins in the objective function instead of contribution margins. Based on the gross margins given in Illustration 13–7, this would result in the following formulation of the problem:

Maximize total gross margin:

$$\$.68A + \$2.40B + \$3.24C$$

Subject to the following constraints:

Material	$4A + 7B + 10C \leq 2{,}000$ board feet
Cutting	$.30A + .30B + .40C \leq 180$ hours
Finishing and assembly	$.20A + .30B + .50C \leq 240$ hours
A sales	$A \geq 100$ units
B sales	$B \leq 100$ units

The constraints are the same as those previously formulated.

The computer solution to this LP problem is given in Illustration 13–10. It is interesting to note that as a result of misspecifying the values of the objective function, Hixon Company will make a suboptimal production decision of manufacturing 100 units of Product A, 100 units of Product B, and 90 units of Product C. Now we compare this solution with the prior optimal solution in which contribution margins were used in the objective function.

	Gross margin method: Wrong decision			Contribution margin method: Right decision		
	Number of units	Unit contri- bution margin		Number of units	Unit contri- bution margin	
Total contribution:						
Product A	100	× $5.68	= $ 568.00	500	× $5.68	= $2,840
Product B	100	× 7.40	= 740.00			–0–
Product C	90	× 8.24	= 741.60			–0–
Total			$2,049.60			$2,840
Less fixed costs:						
Manufacturing			1,500.00			1,500
Nonmanufacturing			1,000.00			1,000
Operating profit (loss)			$ (450.40)			$ 340

The optimal value of the solution reported in the output of Illustration 13–10—$599.60—is a misleading number based on the assumption that fixed manufacturing costs are variable costs.

This model that maximized gross margins finds Product A relatively unattractive because of its low gross margin per unit of scarce resource. Illustration 13–7 shows that Product A is allocated a share of fixed costs that is relatively large compared to its other costs.

Removal of a binding constraint

Suppose Hixon Company has access to an unlimited supply of direct material. Then the optimal production mix for Hixon can be found using the LP formulation in Illustration 13–11. Without a materials constraint, the solution to the production decision problem is to produce 100 units of Product A, 100 units of Product B, and 300 units of Product C. Product A, which uses the least amount of material, is not as attractive as it was before because the supply of material is no longer a binding constraint.

This new optimum production point has a larger total contribution margin than the optimum obtained in Illustration 13–9 where availability of direct material was a binding constraint. The constraints that are now binding are the availability of labor in the cutting department, the size of the market for Product B, and the minimum required sales for Product A.

Illustration 13–10   **Linear programming output using gross margins instead of contribution margins, Hixon Company**

INITIAL TABLE

			Product A	Product B	Product C
OBJ COEFF	MAXIMIZE		$ .68	$2.40	$ 3.24
CONSTRAINT		SOLUTION VALUES			
Material		2,000.	4.00	7.00	10.00
Cutting		180.	.30	.30	.40
Assembly		240.	.20	.30	.50
A sales		100.	1.00	—	—
B sales		100.	—	1.00	—

SUMMARY OF PROBLEM:

SOLUTION VARIABLES	SOLUTION VALUES	NONSOLUTION VARIABLES	OPPORTUNITY COSTS
Prod A	100.	—	—
Prod B	100.	—	—
Prod C	90.	—	—
—	—	Material	$.324
Cutting	84.	—	—
Assembly	145.	—	—
—	—	B sales	.132
—	—	A sales	.616

OPTIMAL VALUE OF SOLUTION IS $599.60

Illustration 13–11   **Removal of a binding constraint, problem formulation, Hixon Company**

OBJECTIVE FUNCTION:	MAXIMIZE	$5.68A	+	$7.40B	+$8.24C
CONSTRAINT					
Cutting		.30A	.30B	.40C ≤ 180	
Assembly and finishing		.20A	.30B	.50C ≤ 240	
A sales		A		≥ 100	
B sales			B	≤ 100	

SUMMARY OF PROBLEM:

SOLUTION VARIABLES	SOLUTION VALUES	NONSOLUTION VARIABLES	OPPORTUNITY COSTS
Prod A	100.	—	—
Prod B	100.	—	—
Prod C	300.	—	—
—	—	Cutting	$20.60
Assembly	40.	—	—
—	—	B sales	1.22
—	—	A sales	.50

OPTIMAL VALUE OF SOLUTION IS $3,780

Note that the opportunity costs associated with the binding constraints on this new optimum are different from those presented in Illustration 13–9. The cutting department, which had an excess of 30 labor-hours before, now has an opportunity cost of $20.60 per unit of the scarce resource, labor hours.

Introducing an additional constraint

Now suppose that Hixon's contract commitments also require it to produce minimum of 100 units of Product C each week. Assume also that Hixon is once again facing a limited availability of direct material. The effect of an

Illustration 13–12 **Introducing an additional constraint, problem formulation, Hixon Company**

OBJECTIVE FUNCTION: MAXIMIZE $5.68A + $7.40B + $8.24C

CONSTRAINT

Material	4.0	+	7.0	+	10.0 ≤ 2,000.
Cutting	.30	+	.30	+	.40 ≤ 180.
Assembly	.20		.30		.50 ≤ 240.
A sales	A				≥ 100.
B sales			B		≤ 100.
C sales					C ≥ 100.

SUMMARY OF PROBLEM:

SOLUTION VARIABLES	SOLUTION VALUES	NONSOLUTION VARIABLES	OPPORTUNITY COSTS
Prod A	250.	—	—
—	—	Prod B	$2.54
Prod C	100.	—	—
—	—	Material	1.42
Cutting	65.	—	—
Assembly	140.	—	—
B sales	100.	—	—
A sales	150.	—	—
—	—	C sales	5.96

OPTIMAL VALUE OF SOLUTION IS $2,244

RANGES OF RIGHT-HAND—SIDE VALUES OF CONSTRAINTS

CONSTRAINT	LOWER LIMIT	UPPER LIMIT	INITIAL CONSTRAINT VALUE
Material	1,400.	2,866.6667	2,000.
Cutting	115.	INF.	180.
Assembly	100.	INF.	240.
A sales	NEG. INF.	250.	100.
B sales	–0–	INF.	100.
C sales	–0–	160.	100.

RANGES OF OBJECTIVE FUNCTION COEFFICIENTS

OBJECTIVE COEFFICIENT	LOWER BOUND	UPPER BOUND	INITIAL VALUE
Prod A	4.2286	PLUS INF.	$5.68
Prod B	NEG. INF.	9.94	7.40
Prod C	NEG. INF.	14.20	8.24

additional constraint on Hixon's optimal production decision can be seen in Illustration 13–12.

The Summary of Problem shows that Hixon's optimal product decision is to produce 250 units of Product A and 100 units of Product C. The total contribution margin is now only $2,244.

It is interesting to note that the opportunity costs of the nonsolution variables in Illustration 13–12 are identical to those in Illustration 13–9. The opportunity cost of an additional unit of direct material is $1.42, and the opportunity costs of producing additional units of Products B and C are $2.54 and $5.96, respectively. The reason for this can be seen in the Ranges of Right-Hand-Side Values of Constraints in Illustration 13–12. The lower limit for Product C's sales constraint is zero. Therefore, since the LP formulation in Illustration 13–9 falls within this range, the opportunity costs have remained unchanged.

Summary

This chapter presents the use of differential costing and linear programming models in making product choice decisions. The problem arises when there are limited amounts of resources that are being fully used and must be assigned to multiple products. The problem is to choose the optimal product mix within the constraints of limited resources.

The objective of product choice decisions is to maximize the contribution margin per unit of scarce resource used. For example, if the scarce resource is the limited number of hours a machine can operate per month, and the machine can make either of two products, the objective is to maximize the contribution per hour (or other unit of time) that each of the two products makes, then produce the product with the higher contribution margin per hour of machine time used.

Short-run product choice decisions assume fixed costs do not change regardless of product mix. It is important that product margins being optimized assume only variable costs change. Hence, product choice decisions use contribution margins, not gross margins.

Computerized linear programming models are widely used to derive the optimal product mix. Data are input to these models using objective functions that specify the contribution margin of each product, and constraints that indicate the amount of scarce resource each product uses. Provided the right data have been entered, the linear programming model then computes the contribution margin per unit of scarce resource for all products and all constraints (that is, scarce resources). The output indicates the mix of products and the quantity of each product to produce and sell that maximizes total contribution.

Terms and concepts

The following terms and concepts should be familiar to you after reading this chapter.

Constraints

Contribution margin per unit of scarce resource

Corner point

Feasible production region

Linear programming—graphic method

Linear programming—simplex method

Objective function

Opportunity cost

Product choice decisions

Shadow price

Self-study problem No. 1

Pacperson, Inc., manufactures two series of computer hardware: Twopack and Threepack. Data concerning selling prices and costs for each unit are as follows:

	Twopack	Threepack
Selling price	$1,000	$1,700
Materials	350	370
Direct labor	210	230
Overhead (80% fixed)	150	200
Gross margin	290	900
Marketing costs (variable)	80	240
Administrative costs (fixed)	60	80
Profit	$ 150	$ 580

Management has decided that at least 500 units of Twopack must be manufactured and sold each month. Likewise, at least 150 Threepack models must be manufactured and sold each month.

The company's production facilities are limited by machine capacity in the Assembly Control Section. Each Twopack model requires one-fourth hour in the Assembly Control Section. Each Threepack model, however, requires three-fourths hour in the assembly area. There is a total of 250 available hours per month in the Assembly Control Section. There are no other relevant constraints on production.

Required:

a. What is the appropriate objective function for these two products if management's objective is to maximize profits?

b. What equations would represent the constraints on the profitability from these two products?

c. Given the information in the problem, which product would management prefer to produce to maximize profits?

d. Graph the profit maximization problem and identify the feasible production region and corner points.

e. What is the optimal production schedule and the optimal contribution margin at that schedule?

f. What is the maximum price management would be willing to pay for one more hour of Assembly Control Section capacity?

g. What is the opportunity cost of each Twopack model? Why?

Solution to self-study problem No. 1

a. Determine the contributions for each product:

	Twopack	Threepack
Selling price	$1,000	$1,700
Variable costs:		
Materials	350	370
Direct labor	210	230
Variable overhead (20%)	30	40
Variable marketing	80	240
Total variable costs	670	880
Contribution margin	$ 330	$ 820

Maximize profit = $330 (Twopack) + $820 (Threepack)

b. Constraints:

$$\text{Twopack} \geq 500$$
$$\text{Threepack} \geq 150$$
$$\tfrac{1}{4}\ (\text{Twopack}) + \tfrac{3}{4}\ (\text{Threepack}) \leq 250$$

c. Contribution per assembly control hour:

$$\text{Twopack } \$330/.25 = \$1,320$$
$$\text{Threepack } \$820/.75 = \$1,093$$

The Twopack is preferred because it gives a greater contribution per hour.

d.

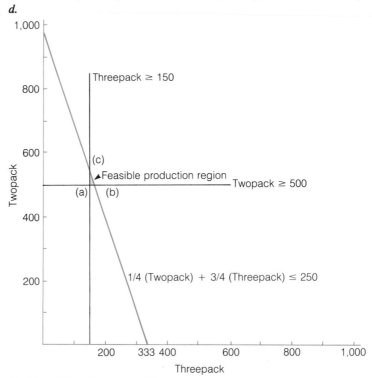

(a), (b), and (c) are the *corner points*.

e.

Points	Produce and sell Twopacks	Produce and sell Threepacks	Total contribution margin
a	500	150	$330(500) + $820(150) = $288,000
b	500	167[a]	$330(500) + $820(167) = $301,940
c	550[b]	150	$330(550) + $820(150) = $304,500

[a] ¼(500) + ¾ Threepack = 250, from assembly control constraint

$$\text{Threepack} = \frac{250 - \tfrac{1}{4}(500)}{\tfrac{3}{4}}$$

$$= 167$$

[b] ¼ Twopack + ¾(150) = 250, from assembly control constraint

$$\text{Twopack} = \frac{250 - \tfrac{3}{4}(150)}{\tfrac{1}{4}}$$

$$= 550$$

f. $1,320 plus the cost of assembly control time included in the objective function.

g. Zero. It is the product which management would prefer to produce.

Self-study problem No. 2: Yakima, Inc.*

Yakima, Inc., a rapidly expanding company, manufactures three lines of skis—Economy, Standard, and Deluxe. Currently faced with labor and machine capacity constraints, the company wants to select the optimal product mix in order to maximize operating profits. The following linear programming model of the problem was formulated and run on the computer:

Maximize: Total contribution margin $= 30X_1 + 23X_2 + 29X_3$

Subject to:
$$\text{Labor-hours} = 12X_1 + 10X_2 + 6X_3 \leq 40,000$$
$$\text{Machine-hours} = 8X_1 + 4X_2 + 10X_3 \leq 10,000$$

where:

$X_1 =$ Deluxe model
$X_2 =$ Economy model
$X_3 =$ Standard model

Using the computer output in Exhibit A, answer the questions below. Assume that all things are held constant in each case.

Required:

a. What is the optimal production level of the Economy model? The Standard model? The Deluxe model?

b. What would happen to the optimal value if the available capacity of the labor

---

* Prepared by Jean M. Lim under the supervision of Michael W. Maher.

constraint was decreased to 30,000 hours? If the machine-hours constraint was increased to 15,000 hours?

c. How much of the labor-hours resource is unused? How much of the machine-hours resource?

d. The Standard model shows an opportunity cost of $28.50. Explain the meaning of this value.

e. Show how the optimal value of $57,500 was computed. Show how the opportunity cost of $5.75 for the machine-hours constraint was computed.

f. Suppose an error in the data exists and $23 is not the correct contribution margin of the Economy model. What is the optimal production level of the Economy model if the correct unit contribution margin is $18? If it is $12? (Indicate if "unknown," given the available information.)

Exhibit A (SSP 13–2)   Initial table, Yakima, Inc.

			Deluxe	Economy	Standard
OBJ COEFF	MAXIMIZE		$30.	$23.	$29.
CONSTRAINT		SOLUTION VALUE			
Labor-hour		40,000.	12.	10.	6.
Machine-hour		10,000.	8.	4.	10.

SUMMARY OF PROBLEM:

SOLUTION VARIABLES	SOLUTION VALUES	NONSOLUTION VARIABLES	OPPORTUNITY COSTS
—	—	Deluxe	$16.00
Economy	2,500.	—	—
—	—	Standard	28.50
Labor-hour	15,000.	—	—
—	—	Machine-hour	5.75

OPTIMAL VALUE OF SOLUTION IS $57,500

RANGES OF RIGHT-HAND-SIDE VALUES OF CONSTRAINTS

CONSTRAINT	LOWER LIMIT	UPPER LIMIT	INITIAL CONSTRAINT VALUE
Labor-hour	25,000.	INF.	40,000.
Machine-hour	–0–	16,000.	10,000.

RANGES OF OBJECTIVE FUNCTION COEFFICIENTS

OBJECTIVE COEFFICIENT	LOWER BOUND	UPPER BOUND	INITIAL VALUE
Deluxe	NEG. INF.	46.00	30.
Economy	15.	PLUS INF.	23.
Standard	NEG. INF.	57.50	29.

Solution to self-study problem No. 2

a. Optimal production level for:
    (1) Economy model = 2,500 units.
    (2) Standard model = zero units.
    (3) Deluxe model = zero units.

b. *Labor constraint:* Total contribution remains the same since only 25,000 labor-hours are currently used.

Machine constraint: Total contribution increases by:

$$\$28,750 = \$5.75 \ (15,000 - 10,000)$$

c. 15,000 labor-hours unused. Zero machine-hours unused.

d. If a decision to produce one unit of the Standard model is made, total contribution margin will decrease by $28.50. Producing a unit of the Standard model means that 2½ units of the Economy model is foregone (see the relation between the Economy and Standard model in the binding machine constraint).

e. $57,500 = $23 × 2,500 units of the Economy model. Each additional machine hour allows production of .25 (= ¼) units of the Economy model. Since the Economy model has a unit contribution margin of $23, the value of one more unit of the scarce machine-hour resource is $5.75.

f. If the contribution margin = $18, 2,500 units of the Economy model will be produced, since the objective function coefficient is still within the relevant range (which is from $15 to plus infinity). If the contribution margin = $12, the optimal production level of the Economy model will be unknown, since the value of the objective function coefficient lies outside the relevant range.

Self-study problem No. 3*

This is a cost minimization problem.

Feeding livestock in the most economical manner possible is an important and continuous problem. In the livestock business, the animals have to receive certain nutrients, which are available in varying quantities in the commodities used.

Suppose the minimum nutrient requirement per day for each animal is 2 pounds of protein, 8 pounds of carbohydrates, and 6 pounds of roughage. Further suppose that there are four commodities available to feed: oats, corn, alfalfa, and linseed oil meal. The current prices and nutrient content for each commodity are:

	Price per pound	Amount of protein per pound	Amount of roughage per pound	Amount of carbohydrate per pound
Oats	$.015	–0–	.2	.1
Corn	.02	.2	.1	.3
Alfalfa	.01	.1	.4	.2
Linseed oil meal	.05	.5	.1	–0–

Required:

Your objective is to feed the animals at the lowest cost. However, your choice is subject to the constraints of providing at least the minimum amount of nutrients.

---

* Adapted from a problem by P. Marshall.

Solution to self-study problem No. 3

The problem is formulated as follows:

	Oats	Linseed oil meal	Corn	Alfalfa		Amount of resources
Protein	–0–	.5	.2	.1	≥	2.0 pounds
Roughage	.2	.1	.1	.4	≥	6.0 pounds
Carbohydrate	.1	–0–	.3	.2	≥	8.0 pounds
	$.015	$.05	$.02	$.01		Minimize cost of commodities

In this problem it has been possible to specify: The choices (the amount of each commodity to feed), the constraints (the minimum pounds of each nutrient required), and the objective (minimize the cost of feeding). It has also been possible to state the rates as constant over the entire range of choices; for example, every pound of oats has the same amount of protein and costs the same as every other pound of oats.

The computer solution to this minimization problem is given in Exhibit A. As can be seen from the Summary of Problem, the optimal solution will be to feed the livestock only alfalfa. In this case, the optimal amount is 40 pounds of alfalfa a day. All the other possible alternatives—oats, linseed oil meal, or corn—have opportunity costs attached to their use. Linseed oil meal, by far the most expensive choice, will cost the farmer $.05 for every additional pound used.

In the case of food requirement constraints, we find that only the carbohydrate constraint is binding. Forty pounds of alfalfa will provide the minimum 8 pounds of carbohydrates needed per day. The $.05 opportunity cost attached to the carbohydrate constraint means that every additional pound of carbohydrate needed will cost the farmer an additional $.05. The daily feed contains 2 pounds more protein and 10 pounds more roughage than the minimum required.

Exhibit A (SSP 13–3)   **Computer input**

```
ENTER THE NUMBER OF VARIABLES
4
ENTER THE NUMBER OF CONSTRAINTS
3
ENTER A 1 FOR MAXIMIZATION OR A 2 FOR MINIMIZATION
2

ENTER VARIABLE NAMES, ONE PER LINE
Oats
Linseed
Corn
Alfalfa

ENTER CONSTRAINT NAMES, ONE PER LINE
Protein
Roughage
Carbohydrate

ENTER CONSTRAINT TYPES (< , > , OR =), ONE FOR EACH CONSTRAINT
DO NOT SEPARATE WITH COMMAS
>>>
```

ENTER 4 OBJECTIVE FUNCTION COEFFICIENTS, SEPARATED BY COMMAS
.015,.05,.02,.01
ENTER 3 CONSTRAINTS, 1 PER LINE (SEPARATE VALUES WITH COMMAS
AND ENTER THE RIGHT-HAND-SIDE VALUE AS THE LAST VALUE ON EACH LINE)
0,0.5,0.2,0.1,2
0.2,0.1,0.1,0.4,6
0.1,0,0.3,0.2,8

INITIAL TABLE

			Oats	Linseed	Corn	Alfalfa
OBJ COEFF	MINIMIZE	—	.015	.05	.02	.01
CONSTRAINT		SOLUTION VALUE				
Protein		2.	—	.50	.20	.10
Roughage		6.	.20	.10	.10	.40
Carbohydrate		8.	.10	—	.30	.20

SUMMARY OF PROBLEM:

SOLUTION VARIABLES	SOLUTION VALUES	NONSOLUTION VARIABLES	OPPORTUNITY COSTS
—	—	Oats	$.01
—	—	Linseed	.05
—	—	Corn	.005
Alfalfa	40	—	—
CONSTRAINTS			
Protein	2.	—	—
Roughage	10.	—	—
—	—	Carbohydrate	.05

OPTIMAL VALUE OF SOLUTION IS $.40

RANGES OF RIGHT-HAND-SIDE VALUES OF CONSTRAINTS

CONSTRAINT	LOWER LIMIT	UPPER LIMIT	INITIAL CONSTRAINT VALUE
Protein	NEG. INF.	4.	2.
Roughage	NEG. INF.	16.	6.
Carbohydrate	4.	INF.	8.

RANGES OF OBJECTIVE FUNCTION COEFFICIENTS

OBJECTIVE COEFFICIENT	LOWER BOUND	UPPER BOUND	INITIAL VALUE
Oats	.005	PLUS INF.	.015
Linseed	–0–	PLUS INF.	.050
Corn	.015	PLUS INF.	.020
Alfalfa	–0–	.013	.010

Questions

13–1. If we want to maximize profit, why do we use unit contribution margins in our analysis instead of unit gross margins?

13–2. Management notes that the contribution from one product is greater than the contribution from a second product. Hence, they conclude that the company should concentrate on production of the first product. Under what, if any, conditions, will this approach result in maximum profits?

13–3. A company has learned that a particular input product required for its production is in limited supply. What approach should management take to maximize profits in the presence of this constraint?

13–4. What is the feasible production region?

13–5. Why are corner points on the feasible production region important for profitability analysis?

13–6. What do we mean by the opportunity cost of a resource?

13–7. Under what circumstances would fixed costs be relevant when management is making decisions in a multiproduct setting?

13–8. Describe how to compute the maximum price that a company would be willing to pay to obtain additional capacity for a scarce resource.

13–9. At what point does the opportunity cost of a constraint change?

13–10. What is the role of the accountant in the management decision process which uses linear programming models (or other mathematical programming techniques)?

Exercises

13–11. Formulate objective function

Thunderbird Productions, Inc., manufactures three products labeled A, B, and C. Data concerning the three products are as follows:

	A	B	C
Selling price	$40	$35	$50
Manufacturing costs:			
Materials	7	6	7
Direct labor	7	7	11
Overhead:			
Variable	3	3	6
Fixed	2	2	4
Total manufacturing	19	18	28
Gross profit	$21	$17	$22

Variable marketing costs equal 15 percent of the sales price of each product. Variable administrative costs are estimated at $1 per unit of product. Fixed administrative costs are allocated to each unit produced as follows: Product A, $3; Product B, $4; and Product C, $5.

Required:

What is the equation representing the objective function for the product-mix decision.

13–12. Analyze contributions under constrained conditions

Management of TutTut Jewelry Corporation has been reviewing its profitability and attempting to improve performance through better planning. The company manufactures three products in its jewelry line: necklaces, bracelets, and rings. Selected data on these items are:

	Necklaces	Bracelets	Rings
Selling price	$80	$60	$40
Contribution margin	35	25	20
Machining time required	.5 hour	.25 hour	.30 hour

The machining time is limited to 120 hours per month. Demand for each product far exceeds the company's ability to meet the demand. There are no other relevant production constraints.

At the present time, management produces equal quantities of each product. The production vice president has urged the company to concentrate on necklace production because that has the greatest margin. No bracelets or rings would be produced if this recommendation were followed.

Required:

a. If fixed costs are $5,000 per month, what profit will be obtained by following the production vice president's recommendation?

b. What is the maximum profit obtainable and what product or product combination must be sold to obtain that maximum?

13–13. Opportunity costs of additional capacity

Beldive Ltd. has formulated the following profit function:

$$\text{Profit} = \$12R + \$19S - \$20,000$$

where R and S are products and the $20,000 is the fixed costs for the company.

Production is limited by capacity in the Quality Control Section. The constraint for that section is formulated as

$$2R + 3S \leq 2,500$$

At present, each quality control unit as represented by the 2,500-unit constraint has a cost of $4.

A subcontractor has offered to perform quality control services at a cost of $7 per quality control unit.

Required:

Should the company utilize the services of the subcontractor? Show supporting calculations.

13–14. Formulate multiproduct choice problem

Milligan Company manufactures two models—small and large. Each model is processed as follows:

	Machining	**Polishing**
Small (S)	2 hours	1 hour
Large (L)	4 hours	3 hours

The time available for processing the two models is 100 hours per week in machining and 90 hours per week in polishing. The contribution margin is $5 for the small model and $7 for the large model.

Required:

Formulate the equations necessary to solve this product-mix problem.

(CPA adapted)

13–15. Solve multiple product-mix problem

The Random Company manufactures two products, Zeta and Beta. Each product must pass through two processing operations. All materials are introduced at the start of Process No. 1. There are no work in process inventories. Random may produce either one product exclusively or various combinations of both products subject to the following constraints:

	Process No. 1	Process No. 2	Contribution margin per unit
Hours required to produce one unit of:			
Zeta	1 hour	1 hour	$4.00
Beta	2 hours	3 hours	5.25
Total capacity in hours per day	1,000 hours	1,275 hours	

A shortage of technical labor has limited Beta production to 400 units per day. There are *no* constraints on the production of Zeta other than the hour constraints in the above schedule. Assume that all relationships between capacity and production are linear.

Required:

What is the contribution margin that would be obtained at the optimal product mix? Show computations in good form.

(CPA adapted)

13–16. Analyze constraints

Using the information for the Random Company in Problem 13–15 and assuming that the present Process 1 cost for each unit of Zeta is $2.35, what is the maximum price that Random would be willing to pay for an additional hour of Process 1 time?

13–17. Analyze limits on constraints

Using the information for the Random Company in Problems 13–15 and 13–16, how many additional units of Zeta would Random be willing to produce with the Process 1 hours that it would obtain assuming that it could obtain that processing time under the conditions indicated as profitable in Problem 13–16?

13–18. Product mix—graphic analysis

Jabba, Inc., manufactures two products, X and Y. Each product must be processed in each of two departments: assembling and finishing. The hours needed to produce one unit of product per department and the maximum possible hours per department follow:

Department	Production hours per unit		Maximum capacity in hours
	X	Y	
Assembling	2	2	500
Finishing	2	3	600

Other restrictions follow:
$X \geq 50$
$Y \geq 50$

The estimated gross margin on each product is $7 for *X* and $5 for *Y*. These gross margins include estimated fixed costs of $3 per unit. The total fixed costs are estimated at $320.

Required:

What is the optimal mix of output and what is the profit that would be obtained if the optimal mix were produced and sold.

13–19. Product mix—graphic analysis

The Hale Company manufactures Product A and Product B, each of which requires two processes, polishing and grinding. The contribution margin is $3 for Product

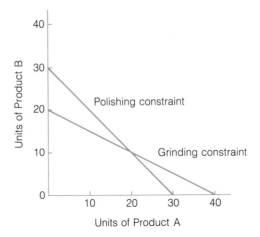

A and \$4 for Product B. The graph below shows the maximum number of units of each product that may be processed in the two departments.

Considering the constraints on processing, which combination of Product A and Product B maximizes the total contribution margin?

(CPA adapted)

13–20. Analyze constraints

Required:

Use the data in Problem 13–19 to answer the questions that follow.

a. What is the opportunity cost of requiring a minimum production of 25 units of A?

b. What is the opportunity cost of requiring a minimum production of 15 units of B?

c. What is the opportunity cost of relaxing the polishing constraint to allow production of 40 units of A, or 40 units of B, r some combination along a straight line that would connect those two production points?

d. What is the opportunity cost of relaxing the grinding constraint so that the company could produce 50 units of A or 25 units of B or some combination along a straight line that would connect those two production points?

Problems and cases

13–21. Analyze production under constraints

Leastan Company manufactures a line of carpeting which includes a commercial carpet and a residential carpet. Two grades of fiber—heavy duty and regular—are used in manufacturing both types of carpeting. The mix of the two grades of fiber differs in each type of carpeting, with the commercial grade using a greater amount of heavy-duty fiber.

Leastan will introduce a new line of carpeting in two months to replace the current line. The present fiber in stock will not be used in the new line. Management wants to exhaust the present stock of regular and heavy-duty fiber during the last month of production.

Data regarding the current line of commercial and residential carpeting are as follows:

	Commercial	Residential
Selling price per roll	$1,000	$800
Production specifications per roll of carpet:		
Heavy-duty fiber	80 pounds	40 pounds
Regular fiber	20 pounds	40 pounds
Direct labor-hours	15 hours	15 hours
Standard Cost per roll of carpet:		
Heavy-duty fiber ($3 per lb.)	$240	$120
Regular fiber ($2 per lb.)	40	80
Direct labor ($10 per DLH)	150	150
Variable manufacturing overhead (60% of direct labor cost)	90	90
Fixed manufacturing overhead (120% of direct labor cost)	180	180
Total standard cost per roll	$700	$620

Leastan has 42,000 pounds of heavy-duty fiber and 24,000 pounds of regular fiber in stock. All fiber not used in the manufacture of the present types of carpeting during the last month of production can be sold as scrap at $.25 a pound.

There are a maximum of 10,500 direct labor-hours available during the month. The labor force can work on either type of carpeting.

Sufficient demand exists for the present line of carpeting so that all quantities produced can be sold.

Required:

a. Calculate the number of rolls of commercial carpet and residential carpet Leastan Company must manufacture during the last month of production to exhaust completely the heavy duty and regular fiber still in stock.

b. Can Leastan Company manufacture these quantities of commercial and residential carpeting during the last month of production? Explain your answer.

c. (Computer required)   What is the maximum price the company would be willing to pay to obtain additional direct labor to use up the remaining fiber?

(CMA adapted)

13–22. Analyze alternative products

Excelsion Corporation manufactures and sells two kinds of containers—paperboard and plastic. The company produced and sold 100,000 paperboard containers and 75,000 plastic containers during the month of April. A total of 4,000 and 6,000 direct labor-hours were used in producing the paperboard and plastic containers, respectively.

The company has not been able to maintain an inventory of either product, due to the high demand; this situation is expected to continue in the future. Workers can be shifted from the production of paperboard to plastic containers and vice versa, but additional labor is not available in the community. In addition, there will be a shortage of plastic material used in the manufacture of the plastic container in the coming months due to a labor strike at the facilities of a key supplier. Management has estimated there will be only enough direct material to produce 60,000 plastic containers during June.

The income statement for Excelsion Corporation for the month of April is shown below. The costs presented in the statement are representative of prior periods and are expected to continue at the same rates or levels in the future.

EXCELSION CORPORATION
Income Statement
For the Month Ended April 30

	Paperboard containers	Plastic containers
Sales revenue	$220,800	$222,900
Less:		
Returns and allowances	6,360	7,200
Discounts	2,440	3,450
	8,800	10,650
Net sales	212,000	212,250
Cost of sales:		
Direct material cost	123,000	120,750
Direct labor	26,000	28,500
Indirect labor (variable with direct labor-hours)	4,000	4,500
Depreciation—machinery	14,000	12,250
Depreciation—building	10,000	10,000
Cost of sales	177,000	176,000
Gross profit	35,000	36,250
Nonmanufacturing expenses:		
Variable	8,000	7,500
Fixed	1,000	1,000
Commissions—variable	11,000	15,750
Total operating expenses	20,000	24,250
Income before tax	15,000	12,000
Income taxes (40%)	6,000	4,800
Net income	$ 9,000	$ 7,200

Required:

a. What is the contribution per unit of scarce resource?

b. What is the optimal product mix given the constraints in the problem?

(CMA adapted)

13–23. Multiple products—continue operations

Stac Industries is a multiproduct company with several manufacturing plants. The Clinton Plant manufactures and distributes two household cleaning and polishing compounds—regular and heavy duty—under the Cleen-Brite label. The forecasted operating results for the first six months of 1985, when 100,000 cases of each compound are expected to be manufactured and sold, are presented in the following statement.

CLINTON PLANT
Cleen-Brite Compounds
Forecasted Results of Operations
For the Six-Month Period Ending June 30, 1985
(in thousands)

	Regular	Heavy duty	Total
Sales revenue	$2,000	$3,000	$5,000
Cost of sales	1,600	1,900	3,500
Gross profit	400	1,100	1,500
Nonmanufacturing costs:			
Variable	400	700	1,100
Fixed[a]	240	360	600
Total nonmanufacturing costs	640	1,060	1,700
Income (loss) before taxes	$ (240)	$ 40	$ (200)

[a] The fixed nonmanufacturing costs are allocated between the two products on the basis of dollar sales volume on the internal reports.

The regular compound sold for $20 a case and the heavy duty sold for $30 a case during the first six months of 1985. The manufacturing costs by case of product are presented in the schedule at the top of the next column. Each product is manufactured on a separate production line. Annual normal manufacturing capacity is 200,000 cases of each product. However, the plant is capable of producing 250,000 cases of regular compound and 350,000 cases of heavy-duty compound annually.

	Cost per case	
	Regular	**Heavy duty**
Direct materials	$ 7.00	$ 8.00
Direct labor	4.00	4.00
Variable manufacturing overhead	1.00	2.00
Fixed manufacturing overhead[a]	4.00	5.00
Total manufacturing cost	$16.00	$19.00
Variable nonmanufacturing costs	$ 4.00	$ 7.00

[a] Depreciation charges are 50 percent of the fixed manufacturing overhead of each line.

The schedule below reflects the consensus of top management regarding the price-volume alternatives for the Cleen-Brite products for the last six months of 1985. These are essentially the same alternatives management had during the first six months of 1985.

Regular compound		**Heavy-duty compound**	
Alternative prices (per case)	**Sales volume (in cases)**	**Alternative prices (per case)**	**Sales volume (in cases)**
$18	120,000	$25	175,000
20	100,000	27	140,000
21	90,000	30	100,000
22	80,000	32	55,000
23	50,000	35	35,000

Top management believes the loss for the first six months reflects a tight profit margin caused by intense competition. Management also believes that many companies will be forced out of this market by next year and profits should improve.

Required:

a. What unit selling price should Stac Industries select for each of the Cleen-Brite compounds (regular and heavy duty) for the remaining six months of 1985? Support your selection with appropriate calculations.

b. Without prejudice to your answer to Requirement (a), assume the optimum price-volume alternatives for the last six months were a selling price of $23 and volume level of 50,000 cases for the regular compound and a selling price of $35 and volume of 35,000 cases for the heavy-duty compound.

(1) Should Stac Industries consider closing down its operations until 1986 in order to minimize its losses? Support your answer with appropriate calculations. (Stac could save none of its fixed costs by temporarily closing.)

(2) Identify and discuss the qualitative factors that should be considered in deciding whether the Clinton Plant should be closed down during the last six months of 1985.

(CMA adopted)

13–24. Analyze costs in a multiproduct setting

Bright Tubes, Inc., manufactures projection devices for large television screens. The devices come in two models: 48X and 60X, designed for screens with diagonal measurements of 48 and 60 inches, respectively. Data on sales prices and costs for each model are:

	48X	60X
Selling price	$140	$220
Variable costs:		
Materials	45	60
Other	40	45
Allocated fixed costs	20	50
Profit per unit	$ 35	$ 65

Allocated fixed costs are based on total monthly fixed costs of $140,000.

The only production limitation is on the availability of titanium oxide extruders (abbreviated TOEs) that are required for each projection tube. The 48X model requires 1 TOE, while the 60X model requires 2 TOEs. There are 4,000 TOEs available per month. Management has decided that it must sell at least 1,000 of each model per month to maintain a full product line.

Last month the company used a linear programming package with the profit function:

$$\text{Maximize profit} = \$35X + \$65Y$$

where X represented the 48-inch model and Y represented the 60-inch model. Product outputs, unit revenues and unit variable costs, and total fixed costs were exactly as planned.

Nonetheless, profit performance for last month was disappointing. You have been called in to help management analyze the cause for the poor performance last month and to help improve performance in the future.

Required:

a. What profit was earned last month?

b. What product mix would you recommend this month, and what profit would be expected with your recommended product mix? Show supporting calculations.

13–25. Analyze alternative actions with multiple products

Rienz Corporation manufactures two models: Average and Deluxe. The following data are derived from company accounting records for the two products for the past month:

	Average	Deluxe
Sales volume	1,000 units	800 units
Sales revenue	$135,000	$160,000
Manufacturing costs:		
Variable	25,000	40,000
Fixed	45,000	50,000
Marketing costs (all variable)	27,000	32,000
Administrative costs (all fixed)	20,000	25,000
Total costs	117,000	147,000
Division profit	$ 18,000	$ 13,000

Production is constrained by the availability of certain materials. Each Average model takes 10 kg. of these materials while each Deluxe model uses 15 kg. There are 22,000 kg. of materials available each month. Marketing constraints limit the number of Average models sold to 1,800 per month. Deluxe models are similarly limited to 1,200 per month.

The fixed manufacturing costs for each product would be eliminated if the product were no longer manufactured. However, administrative costs will not change with the elimination of either product.

Required:

What is the optimal product mix and what is the profit that would be earned at that product mix? Show computations in good form.

13–26. Formulate linear program

The Witchell Corporation manufactures and sells three grades, A, B, and C, of a single wood product. Each grade must be processed through three phases—cutting, fitting, and finishing—before it is sold.

The following unit information is provided:

	A	B	C
Selling price	$10.00	$15.00	$20.00
Direct labor	5.00	6.00	9.00
Direct materials	.70	.70	1.00
Variable overhead	1.00	1.20	1.80
Fixed overhead	.60	.72	1.08
Materials requirements in board feet	7	7	10
Labor requirements in hours:			
Cutting	$\frac{3}{6}$	$\frac{3}{6}$	$\frac{4}{6}$
Fitting	$\frac{1}{6}$	$\frac{1}{6}$	$\frac{2}{6}$
Finishing	$\frac{1}{6}$	$\frac{2}{6}$	$\frac{3}{6}$

Only 5,000 board feet of direct materials per week can be obtained. The cutting department has 180 hours of labor available each week. The fitting and finishing departments each have 120 hours of labor available each week. No overtime is allowed.

Contract commitments require the company to make 50 units of A per week. In addition, company policy is to produce at least 50 additional units of A, 50 units of B, and 50 units of C each week to actively remain in each of the three markets. Because of competition, only 130 units of C can be sold each week.

Required:

Formulate and label the objective function and the constraint functions necessary to maximize the contribution margin.

(CMA adapted)

13–27. Analyze results of linear program

(Computer required.) Use the information in Problem 13–26 to answer the questions that follow.

Required:

a. What is the optimal solution to the problem?
b. What is the contribution that would be earned at the optimal solution?
c. What is the maximum price management would be willing to pay for one additional board foot of lumber?

13–28. Analyze alternative products with differential fixed costs

Siberian Ski Company recently expanded its manufacturing capacity which will allow it to produce up to 15,000 pairs of cross-country skis of the mountaineering model or the touring model. The sales department assures management that it can sell between 9,000 and 13,000 of either product this year. Because the models are very similar, Siberian Ski will produce only one of the two models.

The following information was compiled by the accounting department:

	Model	
	Mountaineering	**Touring**
Selling price per unit	$88.00	$80.00
Variable costs per unit	52.80	52.80

Fixed costs will total $369,600 if the mountaineering model is produced but will be only $316,800 if the touring model is produced.

Required:

a. If Siberian could be assured of selling 12,000 of either model, which model would it sell? How much operating profit would be earned with sales of that product?

b. At what sales level, in units, would Siberian be indifferent regardless of the model it chooses to produce?

c. If Siberian faces a limitation on labor so that a maximum of 6,000 Mountaineering models or a maximum of 12,000 Touring models or some combination of models that would fall along that constraint can be produced, what is the optimal production schedule?

(CMA adapted)

13–29. Solve linear programming problem

(Computer required) Golden Company management wants to maximize profits on its three products: Ooh, Ahh, and Wow. The following information is available from the company accounting records:

	Ooh	**Ahh**	**Wow**
Sales price	$9	$8	$12
Manufacturing costs:			
Direct materials	2	1	3
Direct labor	3	2	2
Overhead	2	3	3
Selling and administrative costs	1	1	1
Profit per unit	$1	$1	$ 3

Analysis of selling and administrative costs indicate that 50 percent of those costs vary with sales. The remaining amount is fixed at $90,000.

Manufacturing overhead costs are based on machine-hours. A regression equation was computed based on the past 30 months of cost data. The equation was:

$$OVH = \$285,000 + \$.35 \, MHR$$

where OVH = overhead
MHR = machine-hours

The regression equation had an overall R-square of .85. The standard error for the intercept was $7,492 and for the slope was .07. Each Ooh requires .8 machine-hours. Each Ahh and Wow requires 1.2 machine-hours.

Each product requires usage of limited facilities. These time requirements in hours for each unit are:

	Ooh	**Ahh**	**Wow**
Preparation	.2	.1	.4
Molding	.1	.3	.5
Finishing	.3	.2	.1

There are 125,000 hours available in preparation; 85,000 hours in molding; and 70,000 hours in finishing.

Required:

a.   Formulate the above as a linear programming problem.

b.   Solve the problem and compute the profit at the optimal product mix.

13–30. Multiple-product choices, overtime considerations, input substitutions*

Jenco, Inc., manufactures a combination fertilizer/weed-killer under the name Fertikil. This is the only product Jenco produces at the present time. Fertikil is sold through normal marketing channels to retail nurseries and garden stores.

Taylor Nursery plans to sell a similar fertilizer/week-killer compound through it regional nursery chain under its own private label. Taylor has asked Jenco to submit a bid for a 25,000-pound order of the private brand compound. While the chemical composition of the Taylor compound differs from Fertikil, the manufacturing process is very similar.

The Taylor compound would be produced in 1,000-pound lots. Each lot would require 60 direct labor-hours and the following chemicals:

Chemicals	Quantity in pounds
CW-3	400
JX-6	300
MZ-8	200
BE-7	100

The first three chemicals (CW-3, JX-6, MZ-8) are all used in the production of Fertikil. BE-7 was used in a compound that Jenco has discontinued. This chemical was not sold or discarded because it does not deteriorate and there have been adequate storage facilities. Jenco could sell BE-7 at the prevailing market price less $.10 per pound selling/handling expenses.

Jenco also has on hand a chemical called CN-5 which was manufactured for use in another product that is no longer produced. CN-5, which cannot be used in Fertikil, can be substituted for CW-3 on a one-for-one basis without affecting the quality of the Taylor compound. The quantity of CN-5 in inventory has a salvage value of $500.

Inventory and cost data for the chemicals are as follows:

Direct materials	Pounds in inventory	Actual price per pound when purchased	Current market price per pound
CW-3	22,000	$ .80	$ .90
JX-6	5,000	.55	.60
MZ-8	8,000	1.40	1.60
BE-7	4,000	.60	.65
CN-5	5,500	.75	(salvage)

The current direct labor rate is $7 per hour. The manufacturing overhead rate is established at the beginning of the year and is applied consistently throughout the year using direct labor-hours as the base. The predetermined overhead rate for the current year, based on a two-shift capacity of 400,000 total direct labor-hours (DLH) with no overtime, is as follows:

Variable manufacturing overhead	$2.25 per DLH
Fixed manufacturing overhead	3.75 per DLH
Combined rate	$6.00 per DLH

* This problem can be assigned here or after Chapter 4 (see Problem 4–30). It is reproduced after both chapters for convenience.

Jenco's production manager reports that the present equipment and facilities are adequate to manufacture the Taylor compound. However, Jenco is within 800 hours of its two-shift capacity this month before it must schedule overtime. If need be, the Taylor compound could be produced on regular time by shifting a portion of Fertikil production to overtime. Jenco's rate for overtime hours is one and one half the regular pay rate, or $10.50 per hour. There is no allowance for any overtime premium in the manufacturing overhead rate.

Jenco's standard markup policy for new products is 25 percent of full manufacturing cost.

Required:

a. Assume Jenco, Inc., has decided to submit a bid for a 25,000-pound order of Taylor's new compound. The order must be delivered by the end of the current month. Taylor has indicated that this is a one-time order that will not be repeated. Calculate the lowest price Jenco should bid for the order and not reduce its operating profit.

b. Without prejudice to your answer to Requirement *(a)*, assume that Taylor Nursery plans to place regular orders for 25,000-pound lots of the new compound during the coming year. Jenco expects the demand for Fertikil to remain strong again in the coming year. Therefore, the recurring orders from Taylor will put Jenco over its two-shift capacity. However, production can be scheduled so that 60 percent of each Taylor order can be completed during regular hours or Fertikil production could be shifted temporarily to overtime so that the Taylor orders could be produced on regular time. Jenco's production manager has estimated that the prices of all chemicals will stabilize at the current market rates for the coming year and that all other manufacturing costs are expected to be maintained at the same rates or amounts.

Calculate the price Jenco, Inc., should quote Taylor Nursery for each 25,000-pound lot of the new compound assuming that there will be recurring orders during the coming year.

(CMA adapted)

13–31. Multiple product choice

Girth, Inc., makes two kinds of men's suede leather belts. Belt A is a high-quality belt while Belt B is of somewhat lower quality. The company earns a contribution margin of $7 for each unit of Belt A that is sold and $2 for each unit sold of Belt B. Each unit (belt) of type A requires twice as much manufacturing time as is required for a unit of type B. Further, if only Belt B is made, Girth has the capacity to manufacture 1,000 units per day. Suede leather is purchased by Girth under a long-term contract that makes available to Girth enough leather to make 800 belts per day (A and B combined). Each belt uses the same amount of suede leather. Belt A requires a fancy buckle, of which only 400 per day are available. Belt B requires a different (plain) buckle, of which 700 per day are available. The demand for the suede leather belts (A or B) is such that Girth can sell all that it produces.

Required:

a. Construct a graph to determine how many units of Belt A and Belt B should be produced to maximize daily profits.

b. Assume the same facts as above except that the sole supplier of buckles for Belt A informs Girth, Inc., that it will be unable to supply more than 100 fancy buckles per day. How many units of each of the two belts should be produced each day to maximize profits?

c. Assume the same facts as in Requirement *(b)* except that Texas Buckles, Inc., could supply Girth, Inc., with the additional fancy buckles it needs. The price would be $3.50 more than Girth, Inc., is paying for such buckles. How many, if any, fancy buckles should Girth, Inc., buy from Texas Buckles, Inc? Explain how you determined your answer.

(CMA adapted)

13–32. Selecting appropriate data for product-mix decisions

The Fiske Corporation manufactures and sells two products, A and B. The demand for both products exceeds current production capacity. The corporation has been unable to maintain an inventory of either product, or of Product B's primary direct material that presently is in short supply. Labor also is in short supply, but the existing force can be used for production of either of the two products. Data are available on the number of units of each product sold (net of returns) and on the number of direct labor-hours expended on each product. Machinery life is directly related to the number of units of each of the products manufactured.

The company utilizes a standard costing system and has determined that the standard unit cost of these products is as shown below:

	Product A	Product B
Direct materials	$1.000	$1.953
Direct labor	.375	.781
Factory overhead	.975	1.344
	$2.350	$4.078

Overhead shown on the standard cost sheets is obtained from the flexible budget shown below. This budget is based upon an assumption that 8,000 units of Product A and 6,400 units of Product B are being produced.

FISKE CORPORATION
Overhead Budget

	Fixed	Variable[a]	Total	Allocation to product A	Allocation to product B	Basis for allocation to product
Factory overhead:						
Indirect labor	$ 500		$ 500	$ 200	$ 300	Direct labor-hours
Depreciation:						
Machinery	5,000		5,000	2,000	3,000	Direct labor-hours
Building	7,200		7,200	4,000	3,200	Estimated number of units sold
Insurance—property and plant	800		800	300	500	Per unit sales price
Payroll taxes	95	$ 1,505	1,600	600	1,000	Per unit sales price
Utilities	500		500	200	300	Direct labor-hours
Supplies	800		800	500	300	Traced to product
Total factory overhead	14,895	1,505	16,400	7,800	8,600	
Administrative:						
Product A	429	2,500	2,929	2,929		
Product B	571	4,000	4,571		4,571	
Total administrative	1,000	6,500	7,500	2,929	4,571	
Marketing:						
Commissions		8,820	8,820	2,970	5,850	
Advertising	1,000		1,000	1,000		
Bad debts	500		500	300	200	
Total marketing	1,500	8,820	10,320	4,270	6,050	
Total overhead	$17,395	$16,825	$34,220	$14,999	$19,221	

[a] Based upon a projected production and sales volume of 8,000 units of Product A and 6,400 units of Product B.

Outside consultants have been engaged to determine an optimal product mix, and they currently are developing a linear programming model to determine how many units of each product to manufacture in order to maximize profit.

The following pro forma statement (in thousands) has been prepared for the month of April:

	Product A	Product B
Sales:		
A—8,000 units	$30.5	
B—6,400 units		$40.8
Gross sales	30.5	40.8
Less:		
Returns and allowances	.3	1.0
Discounts	.5	.8
Net sales	29.7	39.0
Cost of sales:		
Direct materials	8.0	12.5
Direct labor	3.0	5.0
Factory overhead	7.8	8.6
Total cost of sales	18.8	26.1
Gross margin	10.9	12.9
Operating expense:		
Administrative	2.9	4.6
Marketing	4.3	6.1
Total operating expense	7.2	10.7
Income from operations	3.7	2.2
Other:		
Interest revenue	.8	.5
Interest expense	(1.0)	(.8)
Total other	(.2)	(.3)
Operating profit before taxes . . .	3.5	1.9

Required:

For each of the numbered items below select the lettered answer that best indicates in what way the preceding financial data should be used in the determination of the optimal product mix. Assume that variable revenues and expenses are completely variable.

Answer choices

a. This aggregate dollar amount for the month divided by the aggregate number of units sold during the month should be used.

b. This aggregate dollar amount should be used.

c. This cost or revenue item should not be used.

d. This cost or revenue item should be included but amounts inappropriate for financial accounting purposes should be used.

e. The information given is insufficient to determine whether or not the item should be used.

Items to be answered

1. Sales.
2. Sales returns and allowances.
3. Sales discounts.
4. Direct materials.

5. Direct labor.
6. Indirect labor (fixed).
7. Depreciation—building.
8. Variable payroll taxes.
9. Utilities.
10. Supplies.
11. General and administrative expenses—variable.
12. General and administrative expenses—fixed.
13. Commissions on sales.
14. Advertising.
15. Bad debts expense.

(CPA adapted)

13–33. Formulate and solve linear program

The Elon Company manufactures two industrial products—X-10 which sells for $90 a unit and Y-12 which sells for $85 a unit. Each product is processed through both of the company's manufacturing departments. The limited availability of labor, material, and equipment capacity has restricted the ability of the firm to meet the demand for its products. The production department believes that linear programming can be used to routinize the production schedule for the two products.

The following data are available to the production department:

	Amount required per unit	
	X-10	Y-12
Direct material: Weekly supply is limited to 1,800 pounds at $12 per pound	4 pounds	2 pounds
Direct labor:		
Department 1—weekly supply limited to 10 people at 40 hours each at an hourly cost of $6	⅔ hour	1 hour
Department 2—weekly supply limited to 15 people at 40 hours each at an hourly rate of $8	1¼ hours	1 hour
Machine time:		
Department 1—weekly capacity limited to 250 hours	½ hour	½ hour
Department 2—weekly capacity limited to 300 hours	0 hours	1 hour

The overhead costs for Elon are accumulated on a plantwide basis. The overhead is assigned to products on the basis of the number of direct labor-hours required to manufacture the product. This base is appropriate for overhead assignment because most of the variable overhead costs vary as a function of labor time. The estimated overhead cost per direct labor-hour is:

Variable overhead cost	$ 6
Fixed overhead cost	6
Total overhead cost per direct labor-hour	$12

The production department formulated the following equations for the linear programming statement of the problem.

A = number of units of X-10 to be produced
B = number of units of Y-12 to be produced

Objective function to minimize costs:
Minimize $Z = 85A + 62B$

Constraints:
Material:
$4A + 2B \leq 1,800$ pounds
Department 1 labor:
$\frac{2}{3}A + 1B \leq 400$ hours
Department 2 labor:
$1\frac{1}{4}A + 1B \leq 600$ hours
Nonnegativity:
$A \geq 0, B \geq 0$

Required:

a. The formulation of the linear programming equations as prepared by Elon Company's production department is incorrect. Explain what errors have been made in the formulation prepared by the production department.
b. Formulate and label the proper equations for the linear programming statement of Elon Company's production problem.
c. (Computer required) Solve the linear program and determine the increase in the price of direct materials that would be required to change the product mix from that obtained in the optimal solution.

(CMA adapted)

13–34. Bayview Manufacturing Company (Linear programming and cost estimation)*

(Computer required) In November 1984, the Bayview Manufacturing Company was in the process of preparing its budget for 1985. As the first step, it prepared a pro forma income statement for 1984 based on the first 10 months' operations and revised plans for the last two months. This income statement, in condensed form was as follows:

Sales revenue		$3,000,000
Materials	$1,182,000	
Labor	310,000	
Factory overhead	775,000	
Selling and administrative	450,000	2,717,000
Net income before taxes		$ 283,000

These results were better than expected and operations were close to capacity, but Bayview's management was not convinced that demand would remain at present levels and hence had not planned any increase in plant capacity. Its equipment was specialized and made to its order; over a year's lead time was necessary on all plant additions.

---

* Based on "Report of the Committee on the Measurement Methods Content of the Accounting Curriculum," *Supplement to Volume XLVI of The Accounting Review* (1971), pp. 229–36. The original version of this problem was developed by Professor Carl Nelson.

Bayview produces three products; sales have been broken down by product, as follows:

100,000 of Product A at $20	$2,000,000
40,000 of Product B at $10	400,000
20,000 of Product C at $30	600,000
	$3,000,000

Management has ordered a profit analysis for each product and has available the following information:

	A	B	C
Material	$ 7.00	$ 3.75	$16.60
Labor	2.00	1.00	3.50
Factory overhead	5.00	2.50	8.75
Selling and administrative costs	3.00	1.50	4.50
Total costs	17.00	8.75	33.35
Selling price	20.00	10.00	30.00
Profit	$ 3.00	$ 1.25	$ (3.35)

Factory overhead has been applied on the basis of direct labor costs at a rate of 250 percent; and management asserts that approximately 20 percent of the overhead is variable and does vary with labor costs. Selling and administrative costs have been allocated on the basis of sales at the rate of 15 percent; approximately one half of this is variable and does vary with sales in dollars. All of the labor expense is considered to be variable.

As the first step in the planning process, the sales department has been asked to make estimates of what it could sell; these estimates have been reviewed by the firm's consulting economist and by top management. They are as follows:

A	130,000 units
B	50,000 units
C	50,000 units

Production of these quantities was immediately recognized as being impossible. Estimated cost data for the three products, each of which requires activity of both departments, were based on the following production rates:

	Product		
Department 1 (Molding)	2 per hour	4 per hour	3 per hour
Department 2 (Finishing)	4 per hour	8 per hour	4/3 per hour

Practical capacity in Department 1 is 67,000 hours and in Department 2, 63,000 hours; and the industrial engineering department has concluded that this cannot be increased without the purchase of additional equipment. Thus, while last year Department 1 operated at 99 percent of its capacity and Department 2 at 71 percent of capacity, anticipated sales would require operating both Department 1 and 2 at more than 100 percent capacity.

These solutions to the limited production problem have been rejected: (1) subcontracting the production out to other firms is considered to be unprofitable because of problems of maintaining quality, (2) operating a second shift is impossible because of a shortage of labor, and (3) operating overtime would create problems because a large number of employees are "moon-lighting" and would therefore refuse to work more than the normal 40-hour week. Price increases have been rejected; although they would result in higher profits this year, the long-run competitive position of the firm would be weakened resulting in lower profits in the future.

The treasurer then suggested that the Product C has been carried at a loss too long and that now was the time to eliminate it from the product line. If all facilities are used to produce A and B, profits would increase.

The sales manager objected to this solution because of the need to carry a full line. In addition, he maintains that there is a group of loyal customers whose needs must be met. He provided a list of these customers and their estimated purchases (in units) which total as follows:

A	80,000
B	32,000
C	12,000

It was impossible to verify these contentions, but they appeared to be reasonable and served to narrow the bounds of the problem, so the president concurred.

The treasurer reluctantly acquiesced, but maintained that the remaining capacity should be used to produce A and B. Because A produced 2.4 times as much profit as B, he suggested that the production of A (in excess of the 80,000 minimum set by the sales manager) be 2.4 times that of B (in excess of the 32,000 minimum set by the sales manager).

The production manager made some quick calculations and said the budgeted production and sales would be about:

A	104,828
B	42,344
C	12,000

The treasurer then made a calculation of profits as follows:

A	104,828 at $3.00	$314,484
B	42,344 at $1.25	52,930
C	12,000 at ($3.35)	(40,200)
		$327,214

As this would represent an increase of almost 15 percent over the current year, there was a general feeling of self-satisfaction. Before final approval was given, however, the president said that he would like to have his new assistant check over the figures. Somewhat piqued, the treasurer agreed, and at that point the group adjourned.

The next day the above information was submitted to you as your first assignment on your new job as the president's assistant.

Required:

Prepare an analysis showing the president what he should do.

Exhibits A and B contain information that you are able to obtain from the accounting system, which may help you to estimate an overhead cost breakdown into fixed and variable components different from that given in the case. (This analysis was required for Problem 10–27.)

Exhibit A (13–34)

	Direct labor cost (in thousands) Department			Overhead cost (in thousands) Department		
Year	1	2	Total	1	2	Total
1984	$140	$170	$310	$341	$434	$775
1983	135	150	285	340	412	762
1982	140	160	300	342	428	770
1981	130	150	280	339	422	761
1980	130	155	285	338	425	763
1979	125	140	265	337	414	751
1978	120	150	270	335	420	755
1977	115	140	255	334	413	747
1976	120	140	260	336	414	750
1975	115	135	250	335	410	745

Exhibit B (13–34)

	Sales (in thousands)				Marketing and administrative costs (in thousands)
Year	Product A	Product B	Product C	Total	
1984	$2,000	$400	$600	$3,000	$450
1983	1,940	430	610	2,980	445
1982	1,950	380	630	2,960	445
1981	1,860	460	620	2,940	438
1980	1,820	390	640	2,850	433
1979	1,860	440	580	2,880	437
1978	1,880	420	570	2,870	438
1977	1,850	380	580	2,810	434
1976	1,810	390	580	2,780	430
1975	1,770	290	610	2,670	425

14

Inventory
Management Costs

OBJECTIVES
To understand the role of cost data in inventory management decisions.
To understand models used for economic order quantity and safety-stock policy
  decisions.

In this chapter, we discuss how cost data are used in inventory management. Most companies use complex computer models to manage their inventories. But these models are all based on the fundamental models we introduce here. We present the classical economic order quantity (EOQ) model and the costs it should include. Then we examine the problem of stockouts and how to use cost data to determine the optimal safety-stock policy.

Importance of inventory management

Although costs must be controlled at all times, cost control seems to receive additional attention in adverse economic times or when interest rates are high. This phenomenon is highlighted in the following excerpts from an article in *The Wall Street Journal:*

> Businesses Aim for Stricter Controls As Slump Exposes Inventory Bulge
>
> Inventory control gains in importance when interest rates and inflation run high. That's because inflation raises the value of goods in inventory and high interest rates raise the cost of financing, cutting into current profits. Keeping the warehouse all but empty can cost future profits. Despite all the attention inventory has got in the past five years, however, keeping just the right amount of goods on hand has proved neither simple nor painless. . . .
>
> One of the most radical inventory-cutting programs has begun at Firestone Tire & Rubber Co. Firestone is overhauling its entire control system. When the company toted up $300 million in excess inventory [Firestone called in a] management consultant versed in computer [inventory management] systems.[1]

Inventory management activities can range from ensuring that there is an adequate selection of different sizes of clothing available in a retail store to stocking necessary replacement parts for commercial aircraft. The underlying principles are similar in both situations. The primary objective is to minimize the total costs of maintaining inventory.

Inventory-related costs include the costs of carrying inventory and the

---

[1] *The Wall Street Journal,* August 15, 1980, p. 15.

costs of replenishing goods that have been sold. As the number of units in inventory increases, the total annual carrying costs increase but the replenishment costs decrease. As we shall see, inventory management involves finding the minimum annual total of these two kinds of cost.

With carrying costs running at an annual rate from 15 percent to 40 percent of the value of an inventory, a $300 million excess inventory like Firestone's would result in unnecessary carrying costs of $45 million to $120 million per year. When such sums of money are at stake, inventory cost control can have a strong effect on profitability.

Inventory control models have been in use for some time. Operations research techniques and the advancement of computer systems have permitted the development of highly sophisticated inventory models. These models can monitor demand, forecast usage, calculate the most economic quantity to order, indicate when to order, and determine the optimal levels of inventory to keep on hand.[2]

Engineers and operations research specialists depend upon accountants for information about the costs that are relevant for use in these models.

Inventory costs

The goal in inventory cost control is to minimize total costs while maintaining the quantities of inventories needed for smooth operation. As already noted, some costs increase with the quantities of inventory on hand while other costs decrease.

Carrying costs increase with the quantity of inventory on hand. There are two classes of carrying cost: (1) *out-of-pocket costs* and (2) *cost of capital.* Out-of-pocket costs include such items as insurance on the value of the inventory, inventory taxes, annual inspections, obsolescence, and the like. The *cost of capital* is the opportunity cost of having funds in inventory rather than in other earning assets.

Ordering costs decrease with the quantity of inventory on hand. For example, given a constant usage rate, the greater the inventory on hand, the less frequently one must order; thus, the lower the ordering costs. An optimal inventory policy minimizes the sum of these two types of costs.

Inventory costs can be represented graphically as shown in Illustration 14–1.

The economic order quantity (EOQ) model

For analytical purposes, we divide inventory into two categories: (1) working inventory, which represents the units that are used in the normal course of operations; and (2) safety stock, which is the units that are kept on hand

---

[2] These models and their mathematical derivation are presented in operations research texts such as Frank S. Budnick, Richard Mojena, and Thomas E. Vollman, *Principles of Operations Research for Management* (Homewood, Ill.: Richard D. Irwin, 1977).

Illustration 14-1   **Economic lot size cost behavior**

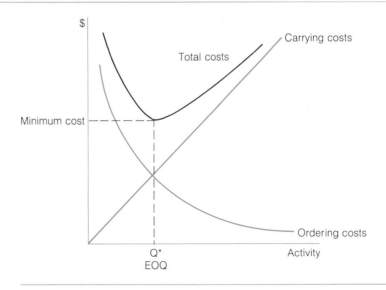

to protect against running out of inventory due to late deliveries, a speedup in production rates, and other similar factors.

Working inventory management   The cost-management problems for working inventory are to determine the optimal quantity to order and to decide when to place an order. These two decisions should be based on the carrying cost of the inventory and the costs to place an order. The inventory manager wants to know the point at which the total of these costs is minimized. We will next see how these costs are represented in the basic inventory models.

Carrying costs and ordering costs

Carrying costs are usually expressed in terms of the average number of units in the inventory. That is, in a given year, one would expect to incur carrying costs of:

$$\frac{Q}{2} \times S$$

where S is the cost to carry one unit in the inventory for one year and is comprised of out-of-pocket costs as well as cost of capital. The average inventory is presumed to be the average of the Q units that arrive at the start of the inventory cycle and the zero units that are left at the end. That is $(Q + 0)/2 = Q/2$.

Ordering costs are expressed as the product of the number of orders placed in a year times the cost to place one order. This function is:

$$\frac{A}{Q} = P$$

where A is the annual usage of the inventory item and P is the cost of placing one order. The term A/Q is the number of orders placed per year. This cost function decreases as Q increases.

The total inventory carrying and ordering cost is:

$$TC = \frac{QS}{2} + \frac{AP}{Q}.$$

This may be shown graphically as in Illustration 14–1, earlier in the chapter.

Note from the graph that the minimum total cost occurs at the point where the two cost functions are equal. This coincidence occurs in the most basic EOQ problem, but may not be generalized to more complex problems. For this problem, the optimal Q (labeled Q^*) is referred to as the economic order quantity or EOQ. It may be found by the equation:

$$Q^* = \sqrt{\frac{2AP}{S}}$$

If Q^* units are ordered each time and inventory usage and costs continue as planned, the inventory carrying and ordering costs will be at a minimum. Note how carrying costs increase with the quantity of inventory on hand, while ordering costs decrease with the quantity on hand. Inventory management seeks to minimize total costs and to identify the point Q^*, which is often referred to as the *economic order quantity* or *EOQ*. The total cost to maintain a given inventory level decreases in the range of zero to Q^* and then increases from Q^* to the maximum possible inventory level. To find Q^*, it is necessary both to construct the mathematical relationships for the cost functions and identify the elements of cost that should be included in each function. The first task is handled by operations research specialists; the second is the responsibility of cost accountants.

For example, Tri-Ply Company uses 25,000 units of Material Z per year in the manufacture of a specialty line of plywood laminates. The out-of-pocket costs for carrying Material Z are $2.50 per unit. Each unit costs $80, and the company's cost of capital is 25 percent. The cost to place an order for Material Z is $648. What is the optimal order size?

In this example, A = 25,000 units, P = $648, and S = $2.50 + $80 × 25% = $22.50. The optimal order size is:

$$Q^* = \sqrt{\frac{2 \times 25,000 \times \$648}{\$22.50}}$$
$$= \sqrt{1,440,000}$$
$$= 1,200 \text{ units}$$

Now, if Tri-Ply management follows the policy and orders 1,200 units each time, the annual costs of the inventory policy will be:

Carrying costs:

$$\frac{QS}{2} = \frac{1,200 \times \$22.50}{2} = \underline{\underline{\$13,500}}$$

Ordering costs:

$$\frac{AP}{Q} = \frac{25,000 \times \$648}{1,200} = \underline{\underline{\$13,500}}$$

so that total costs amount to $27,000 (that is, the $13,500 carrying costs plus $13,500 ordering costs). This is the minimum cost. Notice that total carrying costs equal total ordering costs, which is consistent with Illustration 14–1.

Applications

The EOQ model can also be used to compute the optimal (least-cost) production run. The costs to set up a production run are analogous to the ordering costs in the basic EOQ model. Carrying costs are the same as for the basic model.

For example, if the differential cost of setting up a production line to produce a specific type of item is $2,500, the demand for the item is 720,000 per year and the cost to carry each item in inventory is $1, then the economic production run size is:

$$Q^* = \sqrt{\frac{2 \times 720,000 \times \$2,500}{\$1}}$$

which equals 60,000 units.

While the EOQ model discussed here sets forth the principles for inventory-management models, actual applications are usually much more complex. Quite often the annual demand (or usage) variable changes from one order period to the next. In addition, rarely does a company order only one product from a given supplier. When multiple products are procured from one supplier, it may be possible to obtain ordering cost savings through ordering several items at one time. Inventory-management models are so complex that they are almost always computerized. A computer model can simultaneously consider the various products ordered from a vendor and estimate the optimal time to place an order for one or more of them.

Although more complex models will be encountered, the basic model contains the elements that a cost accountant must consider in developing an optimal inventory policy. In practice, management will employ more sophisticated computer software models to calculate and maintain an optimal inventory policy.

| **Relevant inventory costs** | Selecting the costs that are relevant to the EOQ is an application of *differential costing.* When preparing cost data for inventory models, we look at each cost and ask whether it will change with the number of: |

1. Units in inventory.
2. Units purchased.
3. Orders placed in a year.

For example, let's consider the costs obtained from Tri-Ply Company's records on a different inventory item. These costs are related to a specific inventory item:

Purchase price	$ 6.50 per unit
Transportation-in per unit	.50
Telephone call for order	11.00
Cost to unload a shipment	25.00 + $.15 per unit
Inventory taxes	.60 per unit per year
Costs to arrange for shipment of the material to the company	125.00
Salary of receiving dock supervisor (per month)	1,800.00
Insurance on inventory	.10 per unit per year
Warehouse rental	$12,000.00 per month
Average spoilage costs	1.30 per unit per year
Cost of capital	20% per year
Orders handled per month	600

Which of these items should be included in the EOQ computation? Using the three cost categories mentioned earlier, let's classify each item.

1. Costs that vary with the average number of units in inventory:

Inventory taxes	$ .60
Insurance on inventory	.10
Average spoilage costs	1.30
Total	$2.00

2. Costs that vary with the number of units purchased:

Purchase price	$6.50
Transportation-in	.50
Costs to unload	.15
Total	$7.15

    Total annual carrying costs per unit is the sum of the carrying costs from category 1, above, plus the cost of capital rate times the investment cost in category 2:

    $$\$.60 + \$.10 + \$1.30 + (20\% \times \$7.15) = \$2.00 + (20\% \times \$7.15)$$
    $$= \$3.43$$

3. Costs to place an order:

Costs of placing the order	$ 11.00
Unloading the shipment	25.00
Arranging for the shipment	125.00

    These three items total $161, which is the total ordering cost.

The other costs (warehouse rental and supervisor's salary) usually do not vary with the number of units in inventory, the number of units purchased, or the number of orders during the inventory planning horizon. Those costs are, therefore, irrelevant for this decision (although they may be important for long-range decision making).

Extensions on the basic EOQ model

The classical EOQ model may be extended to include other costs and considerations. The following examples show how inventory-management costs may be incorporated in some more complex settings.

Order size restrictions

Many companies will only accept orders for round lots such as even dozens, hundreds, tons, and the like. These restrictions are often related to assembly-line or packaging requirements. When there are restrictions on order size, computation of Q^* using the basic EOQ model will not necessarily provide an acceptable order quantity. If Q^* is not equal to one of the allowed order quantities, it is necessary to determine the total annual cost of ordering the two allowed quantities on either side of Q^*. In such cases, the optimal order size will be either Q^*, if allowed, or the allowed quantity closest to Q^* whether greater than or less. Drawing lines on a cost graph to show order size restrictions as shown in Illustration 14–2 demonstrates why the optimal alternative is limited to the choices mentioned.

Illustration 14–2   **EOQ with order size restrictions**

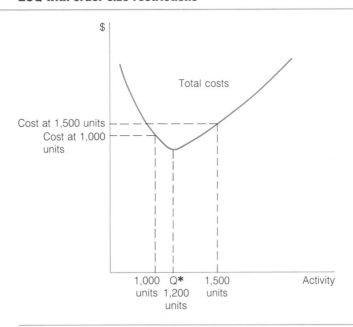

For example, suppose that the supplier of Material Z only accepts orders in round lots of 500 units. An order for 1,200 units would not be acceptable, but Tri-Ply could order 500, 1,000, or 1,500 units. The two order sizes, 1,000 units and 1,500 units, comprise the set from which the optimal order size is obtained. To determine which order size is optimal, the total annual costs for each alternative are examined.

If 1,000 units are ordered, then the annual inventory costs are $27,450. This is the sum of the carrying costs computed as:

$$\frac{QS}{2} = \frac{1,000 \times \$22.50}{2} = \$11,250$$

and the ordering costs:

$$\frac{AP}{Q} = \frac{25,000 \times \$648}{1,000} = \$16,200$$

If 1,500 units are ordered at a time, then the annual costs are $27,675, which is the sum of the carrying costs:

$$\frac{QS}{2} = \frac{1,500 \times \$22.50}{2} = \$16,875$$

and the ordering costs:

$$\frac{AP}{Q} = \frac{25,000 \times \$648}{1,500} = \$10,800$$

Therefore, the optimal policy, given the restrictions on order size, is to order 1,000 units each time.

Note that the difference in total costs between the two order sizes is relatively small ($225). In general, as long as the order quantity is relatively close to Q^*, the classical EOQ model is relatively insensitive to small changes in order quantities. If the actual order quantity is significantly different, however, the cost changes can be substantial. For example, at an order size of 500 units, the total costs increase to $38,025. Carrying costs of $22.50 per unit times 250 units = $5,625, and ordering costs for 50 orders (25,000/500) at $648 = $32,400. This computation highlights how the total costs change at different activity levels. Typically, they change very little for values close to Q^*. But as order size decreases, the total inventory-management costs increase rather rapidly. However, we highlight the point that the optimal inventory quantity will be at one of the two feasible order quantities adjacent to the initial Q^*.

Storage constraints   If there are constraints on the maximum number of units that may be stored and the computed value of Q^* is greater than the constraint, then the appropriate order size is the value of the constraint. This may be confirmed by inspect-

Illustration 14–3   **EOQ with storage limitations**

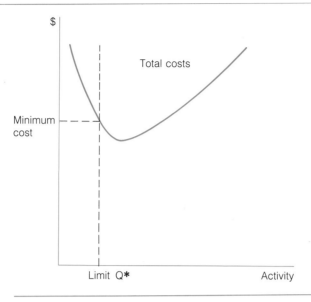

ing the cost function graph in Illustration 14–1 and drawing a constraint line anywhere between zero and Q^*. The minimum total cost is at the constraint. This may be seen from Illustration 14–3 which shows the constraint imposed on the inventory cost function.

When there are storage constraints, management may ask whether it is economically justifiable to obtain additional warehouse space to store the excess units. Suppose that Tri-Ply has a capacity constraint of 750 units. It could obtain additional warehouse space for $6,000 per year that would enable it to store the additional 450 units indicated by the economic lot size model. Should the company obtain the additional space?

To decide, they must look at the differential cost of the alternatives. If 750 units were ordered at a time (since this is the best that can be done with the constraint), the costs are:

Carrying costs:

$$\frac{QS}{2} = \frac{750 \times \$22.50}{2} = \underline{\underline{\$8,437.50}}$$

Ordering costs:

$$\frac{AP}{Q} = \frac{25,000 \times \$648}{750} = \underline{\underline{\$21,600}}$$

For a total cost of $30,037.50 (the sum of $8,437.50 + $21,600).

From the initial example, we know that the optimal inventory costs without the constraint are $27,000. The expected savings from the additional warehouse space are $3,037.50 (the difference between $30.037.50 and $27,000). Since the rental cost exceeds the expected savings, it is better to forego the rental and order in lots of 750 units.

This may also be formulated in the same manner as other differential cost problems. A comparison of the costs under the alternatives "Maintain present storage" and "Rent space" appears as:

Cost item	Maintain present storage	Rent space	Differential costs
Carrying costs (excluding space rental)	$ 8,437.50	$13,500.00	$5,062.50 higher
Ordering costs	21,600.00	13,500.00	8,100.00 lower
Space rental	–0–	6,000.00	6,000.00 higher
Total costs	$30,037.50	$33,000.00	$2,962.50 higher

This analysis yields the same results, namely that the differential costs of renting exceed the savings.

Quantity discounts

Suppliers often offer quantity discounts on purchases of materials, or shipping charges may be lower for bulk shipments. In such situations, the savings from ordering in larger lots may more than offset the incremental carrying costs. As a general rule, when quantity price breaks are available, the minimum EOQ will be the amount determined by the computation of Q^* without regard to price-break considerations. It may, however, be less costly to order a larger quantity to obtain the price break.

Assume the supplier of Material Z offers the following price breaks:

Number ordered	Discount
0–999	None
1,000–1,999	$1.00 per unit
2,000–4,999	1.50
5,000–9,999	1.75
10,000 and over	1.80

The optimal order quantity for Tri-Ply would either be 1,200 units—the optimal quantity ignoring the price breaks—or 2,000, 5,000, or 10,000 units. No other quantity is more economic than one of those four.

Tri-Ply management can analyze which of the four quantities is least costly if the price breaks are considered as *opportunity costs*. Foregoing the maximum available discount results in an opportunity cost equal to the difference between that maximum and the discount that Tri-Ply could obtain with its selected order policy. For example, if Tri-Ply orders in lots of 1,200 units, they obtain a discount of $1 per unit but forego the opportunity to obtain a $1.80 discount. If they order 1,200 units at a time, there is a foregone discount cost of $.80 on each unit ordered. Over the year, discounts of $20,000 would be lost. That is based on the 25,000 units ordered per year times the $.80 in lost discounts per unit.

In addition, the cost of capital for the inventory is reduced if they obtain a greater discount. The reduction in the cost of capital is the discount per unit times the cost of capital rate times the average number of units in inventory. Using a 20 percent cost of capital rate, this is $.80 × (1,200/2) × 20%, or $96 for Material Z ordered in lots of 1,200 instead of 10,000.

One way to analyze the EOQ when price breaks are available is to consider the total carrying cost, ordering cost, and foregone discount for the initial $Q*$ and the minimum quantities required to earn each additional price break. Such an analysis for Tri-Ply's purchases of Material Z is presented in Illustration 14–4.

Illustration 14–4   **Optimal order quantity with price breaks**

Order size	Carrying costs	Ordering costs	Foregone discount	Total costs
1,200	$ 13,500[a]	$13,500[b]	$20,000[c]	$ 47,000
2,000	$ 22,375[d]	$ 8,100[e]	$ 7,500[f]	$ 37,975 (Optimal)
5,000	$ 55,781[g]	$ 3,240[h]	$ 1,250[i]	$ 60,271
10,000	$111,500[j]	$ 1,620[k]	–0–	$113,120

Additional computations:

[a] $\$13,500 = \dfrac{1,200 \times (\$2.50 + 25\% \times \$80.00)}{2}$

assuming the $80 is net of the discount at this level.

[b] $\$13,500 = \dfrac{25,000}{1,200} \times \$648.$

[c] $\$20,000 = 25,000 \times (\$1.80 - \$1.00)$, where $1.80 is the maximum price break available.

[d] $\$22,375 = \dfrac{2,000 \times (\$2.50 + 25\% \times \$79.50)}{2}$

where $79.50 is $80 less the incremental $.50 discount.

[e] $\$8,100 = \dfrac{25,000}{2,000} \times \$648.$

[f] $\$7,500 = 25,000 \times (\$1.80 - \$1.50).$

[g] $\$55,781 \text{ (rounded)} = \dfrac{5,000 \times (\$2.50 + 25\% \times \$79.25)}{2}$

where $79.25 = $80.00 less the $.75 incremental discount.

[h] $\$3,240 = \dfrac{25,000}{5,000} \times \$648.$

[i] $\$1,250 = 25,000 \times (\$1.80 - \$1.75).$

[j] $\$111,500 = \dfrac{10,000 \times (\$2.50 + 25\% \times \$79.20)}{2}$

where $79.20 is $80 less the $.80 incremental discount.

[k] $\$1,620 = \dfrac{25,000}{10,000} \times \$648.$

The optimal order quantity, then, is the one with the lowest total cost, in this case, 2,000 units. Note the behavior of the carrying costs and ordering costs with changes in quantities and compare them to the patterns in Illustration 14–2. (Also note the portion of change in carrying costs resulting from the change in order quantity versus the change resulting from the reduction in cost of capital caused by the discounted price.)

Inventory management under uncertain conditions

So far we have considered only working inventory in our cost analyses. If usage rates and the time between order placement and order arrival (lead time) are known for certain, inventory management is simplified. Usage rates may vary due to unforeseen circumstances, and lead times may vary due to events beyond management's control. If an inventory item is used faster than anticipated or if lead time is longer than expected, a stockout may occur. Two kinds of stockouts are diagrammed in Illustration 14–5. In Case

Illustration 14–5

Inventory flows under uncertainty
Case A: Change in usage rate

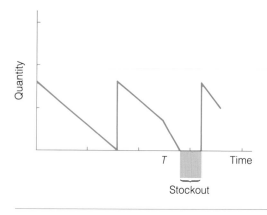

Case B: Change in time of arrival for new shipment

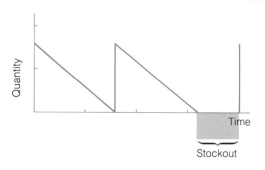

A, an order was placed at time T, but the rate of use increased. As a result, the inventory on hand was used up before the new shipment arrived. In Case B, the usage rate remained constant, but the new shipment did not arrive on time.

Stockouts can be costly Depending on the nature of the product, a stockout may require a special trip to pick up extra materials, the shutting down of operations until new materials can be obtained, or lost sales and customer ill will. Such added costs can be minimized by obtaining an optimal amount of *safety stock*. Had the company in the previous example maintained sufficient safety stock, then no stockout would have occurred. The situations from Illustration 14–5 are reproduced in Illustration 14–6 with the addition of safety stock. Now in Case A, the increased usage is satisfied from the

Illustration 14–6   **Inventory flows with safety stock**
Case A: Change in demand rate

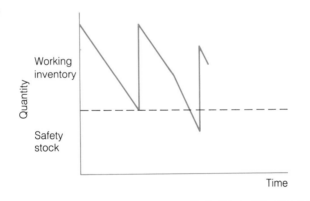

Case B: Change in lead time

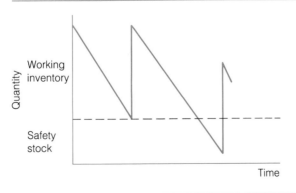

safety stock, and the new order replenishes both the safety stock and the working inventory. In Case B, the safety stock is used while awaiting the delayed arrival of the inventory order. Safety stock is replenished with subsequent orders.

Cost considerations for safety stock

Two costs must be considered in establishing an optimal safety stock policy: (1) the *cost to carry safety stock* and (2) the *cost of a stockout.*

The cost of carrying safety stock is the same as the cost of carrying working inventory. The full quantity of safety stock is the same as the average inventory of safety stock. Because the safety stock on hand at the start of the period should equal the safety stock on hand at the end of the period, the average of these two numbers is the full quantity of safety stock. Although safety stock may decrease from time to time as events require its use, these decreases are usually ignored.

Stockout costs require separate consideration. In the first place, the cost of one stockout is usually expressed in terms of the costs of alternative sources of supply, loss of customers or goodwill, and shutting down of operations over the stockout period. These opportunity costs are estimated from many data sources. Second, the number of stockouts is an expected value. The expected annual stockout cost is the product of the cost of one stockout times the number of orders placed per year times the probability of a stockout on any one order.

Returning to the original example for Tri-Ply Company's inventory of Material Z, let us consider that the company has a choice of alternative safety-stock levels, each of which will yield a different probability of a stockout. The staff has determined that there is a .5 probability of a stockout if no safety stock is maintained. A safety stock of 100 units would reduce the stockout probability to .3. If the safety stock is maintained at 250 units of Material Z, then there is a .05 probability of a stockout. Finally, a .01 probability of a stockout would be expected if the safety-stock level were 500 units. If the costs of one stockout are estimated at $3,200, the best choice of these four safety stocks is 250 units as shown by the analysis in Illustration 14–7.

Even with the optimal safety-stock level, there is a .05 probability of a stockout. Given that the company orders about 21 times a year (25,000 ÷ 1,200 ≈ 20.8), Tri-Ply can expect one stockout a year for Material Z (21 × .05 ≈ 1). But, it is more economical to incur this stockout cost than to maintain the additional safety stock. In reality, it is virtually impossible to eliminate stockouts. The problem in inventory management is to find the least-cost policy with respect to safety-stock levels and stockouts.

Similar cost analyses can be prepared if, for example, there are different stockout costs depending on the size of the stockout. The shortage of a few items that can be obtained by alternative transportation may result in incurring only the cost of the incremental transport charges, but one that

Illustration 14–7   **Cost analysis of safety-stock policies**

Safety stock	Carrying costs	Expected stockout costs	Total costs
0	$0 \times \$22.50$	$\dfrac{25,000}{1,200} \times .5 \times \$3,200$	
	$= \$0$	$= \$33,333$	$\$33,333$
100	$100 \times \$22.50$	$\dfrac{25,000}{1,200} \times .3 \times \$3,200$	
	$= \$2,250$	$= \$20,000$	$22,250$
250	$250 \times \$22.50$	$\dfrac{25,000}{1,200} \times .05 \times \$3,200$	
	$= \$5,625$	$= \$\ 3,333$	$8,958$ (Optimal)
500	$500 \times \$22.50$	$\dfrac{25,000}{1,200} \times .01 \times \$3,200$	
	$= \$11,250$	$= \$\ \ \ 667$	$11,917$

involves several hundred large items may not be so easily, or inexpensively, resolved.

Stockout costs as ordering costs   Since expected annual stockout costs vary directly with the number of orders placed in a year, stockout costs are an ordering cost. The problem in including these costs in the EOQ and safety-stock models is that the two models are interdependent. The cost per order used in the EOQ model depends on the optimal stockout probability. Discussion of some of the more complex problems in inventory management such as the joint solution to this problem is beyond the scope of this text. Our intention is to familiarize you with the nature of the problem and its implications for cost accounting.

Reorder point   Goods should be reordered when the quantity of inventory on hand has fallen to the sum of the usage over the lead time plus the safety stock. If an order is placed when the inventory has reached that level, the new shipment is expected to arrive when the total number of units on hand is equal to the safety stock—that is, the working inventory has fallen to zero.

For example, a safety stock of 250 has been chosen for Material Z. The lead time is six days, and the annual usage is 25,000 units. Assuming 220 working days per year, the reorder point for Material Z is 932 units. This is computed as:

$$\left[\frac{25,000}{220 \text{ days}} \times 6 \right] + 250 = 682 + 250$$

Illustration 14–8   **Reorder point**

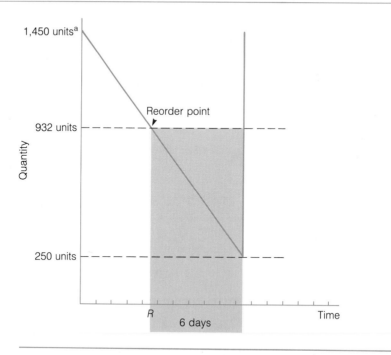

ᵃ 1,450 units = Q^* + safety stock = 1,200 units + 250 units.

When inventory falls to 932 units, an order should be placed for the optimal number of units (Q^* in the unconstrained problem or other cost-effective Q values in the presence of constraints). During the six days between order placement and order arrival, units are used at the rate of 113.64 per day (25,000 ÷ 220 is approximately 113.64). After six days, if all goes as planned, there will be approximately 250 units in inventory (the 932 units at reorder time less the 6 × 113.64 used during the lead time) when the new shipment of Q units arrives. This is diagrammed in Illustration 14–8. The reorder point is noted R. If an order is placed at that point in time, then 682 units will be used between the reorder time and the time when the new order arrives.

Summary   Adoption of an inventory management policy can be a source of significant cost savings to many organizations. The models are designed to determine the most economic order quantity (EOQ) under both constrained and unconstrained situations, the optimal level of safety stock, and the reorder point. Highly sophisticated computer models have been developed to monitor inventories. These models rely on a significant amount of data from the accountant in order to find the minimum cost of alternative inventory-management decisions. The costs that are relevant for these inventory-management decisions are those costs that will change with the decision. Thus, for example, in a EOQ decision, the accountant estimates the costs that will change with the number of units ordered. These include ordering costs and carrying costs. In a decision concerning safety-stock levels, the differential costs include the costs to carry the safety-stock and the stockout costs. The accountant performs a significant role in these decisions.

Terms and concepts	The following terms and concepts should be familiar to you after reading this chapter.

Carrying costs	**Ordering costs**
Economic order quantity (EOQ)	**Quantity discounts**
Economic production run	**Reorder point**
Expected annual stockout cost	**Safety stock**
Foregone discount cost	**Stockout**
Lead time	**Working inventory**

Self-study problem	Margolis Manufacturing Company is a customer of your bank. The president of the company was in your office earlier in the day to apply for an additional line of credit. Trying to help your client, you note that there is a substantial sum of money tied up in inventory. When you pointed this out to the company president, the response was:

"We can't afford to run out of stock. Therefore, our policy is to order as infrequently as possible and to keep as much safety stock on hand as can be stored in our warehouse. We order 5,000 units at a time just to make sure we don't run out."

As part of your analysis of the company's loan requirements, you call up the controller of the company for some further information. From the conversation, it appears that the company has a substantial quantity of one particular part in its warehouse. The controller relates the following information on this part:

Invoice cost	$ 120.00 .
Shipping charges	2.50 per unit + $175 per shipment
Inventory insurance	1.00 per unit per year
Annual costs to audit and inspect inventory	2.60 per unit + $5,000 per year
Warehouse utilities	980.00 per month
Warehouse rental	1,500.00 per month
Unloading costs for units received (paid to shipper)	.80 per unit
Receiving supervisor salary	1,760.00 per month
Processing invoices and other purchase documents	16.00 per order
Allowable order quantity 250 or multiples thereof.	

The company policy is to keep a safety stock of 3,000 units. Annual demand for the part is 45,000 units. The lead time for an order is 10 working days, and there are 250 working days per year for the plant. The controller indicated that if there is a stockout, it would be necessary to obtain the parts by special air courier at an additional cost of $8,100 per stockout. The probabilities of a stockout with various safety-stock levels are given as follows:

Safety stock	Probability of stockout
500	.25
1,000	.08
1,500	.02
2,000	.01

You estimate that the company's cost of capital is approximately 30 percent. You also know that the state has an inventory tax equal to 1 percent of the cost of items in inventory, which the state defines as the sum of the invoice price, shipping cost per unit, and the unloading costs. You assume for analysis purposes that a stockout probability of .02 would be reasonable for order cost determination in an optimal inventory policy.

Required:

a. What is the annual cost of the company's present inventory policy?
b. How many units should the company order at a time?
c. What is the optimal safety-stock level?
d. What is the annual cost of the optimal inventory policy identified in (b) and (c)?
e. What is the reorder point?

Solution to self-study problem

a. Annual costs:

   a. Investment costs:

Invoice price	$120.00
Shipping cost	2.50
Unloading	.80
Total investment costs	$123.30

   b. Carrying costs:

Cost of capital	$ 36.99 ($123.30 × 30%)
Insurance	1.00
Inventory tax	1.23 (1% × $123.30)
Audit and inspection	2.60
Total carrying costs	$ 41.82

Carrying costs per year:

Working inventory	5,000 units × ½ × $41.82 =	$104,550
Safety stock	3,000 units × $41.82 =	125,460
Total carrying costs		$230,010

Order costs:

Shipping	$175
Record processing	16
Stockout costs	Nil
Total	$191

Annual order costs:

$$\frac{45,000 \text{ units}}{5,000 \text{ per order}} \times \$191 = \$1,719$$

Total annual costs of the present inventory policy:
$231,729 which is $230,010 + $1,719

b. Economic order quantity (EOQ):

First, determine Q^* ignoring the order size restrictions:

Carrying costs *(S)*, $41.82 (per Requirement [*a*]).

Order costs *(P)*, $353.00 ($191 + .02 × $8,100).

$$Q^* = \sqrt{\frac{2 \times 45,000 \times \$353}{\$41.82}}$$

$$= \sqrt{759,684.36}$$

$$= \underline{872 \text{ units}}$$

Next, determine the annual costs at the next higher and lower allowable order quantity:

Quantity	Carrying costs	Order costs	Total costs
750	$\frac{750}{2} \times \$41.82$	$\frac{45,000}{750} \times \$353.00$	
	= $15,682.50	= $21,180.00	$36,862.50
1,000	$\frac{1,000}{2} \times \$41.82$	$\frac{45,000}{1,000} \times \$353.00$	
	= $20,910.00	= $15,885.00	$36,795.00

So that the optimal order quantity given the restrictions on order size is 1,000 units.

c. Optimal safety stock level:

Prepare a schedule showing the expected annual costs of each alternative safety stock quantity:

Safety stock quantity	Carrying costs	Expected stockout costs	Total costs
500	500 × $41.82	$\frac{45,000}{1,000} \times \$8,100 \times .25$	
	= $20,910	= $91,125	$112,035
1,000	1,000 × $41.82	$\frac{45,000}{1,000} \times \$8,100 \times .08$	
	= $41,820	= $29,160	$ 70,980
1,500	1,500 × $41.82	$\frac{45,000}{1,000} \times \$8,100 \times .02$	
	= $62,730	= $7,290	$ 70,020
			(Optimal)
2,000	2,000 × $41.82	$\frac{45,000}{1,000} \times \$8,100 \times .01$	
	= $83,640	= $3,645	$ 87,285

Therefore, the most economic safety-stock level would be 1,500 units with a total expected stockout and carrying cost of $70,020.

d. The total annual cost of the optimal inventory policy is computed as follows:

Costs of working inventory (per Requirement [b])	$36,795
Carrying costs of safety stock	62,730
	$99,525

This is a substantial savings over the present costs of $231,729 in Requirement (a) to this problem.

e. The reorder point is:

$$\text{Usage over lead time} + \text{Safety stock} = \frac{45,000}{250} \times 10 + 1,500$$
$$= 1,800 + 1,500$$
$$= 3,300 \text{ units}$$

Questions

14–1. Since the operations research specialists develop and maintain inventory models, why does the accountant become concerned with inventory policy decisions?

14–2. Why is the cost of capital included as a carrying cost of inventory?

14–3. In determining economic order quantities, the carrying cost per unit is divided by two. Why?

14–4. A staff accountant for Percolators, Inc., noted that the annual carrying cost for a specific inventory item is estimated at $28,500 while the annual order cost is estimated at $14,150. Does this information tell you anything about the relationship of the actual order quantity to the optimal order quantity? Explain.

14–5. In terms of the specifics of the costs associated with inventory policy, how does the concept of differential costs apply to the problem of inventory policy?

14–6. For each of the following costs, indicate whether the cost would be an out-of-pocket carrying cost (C), or a cost of placing an order (P). If the item does not qualify for any of these categories, note it as none of the above (N). Assume that wages vary with the level of work while salaries are fixed for a monthly or longer time period.
   a. Hourly fee for inventory audit.
   b. Salary of purchasing supervisor.
   c. Costs to audit purchase orders and invoices, on a per-order basis.
   d. Taxes on inventory.
   e. Stockout costs.
   f. Storage costs charged per unit in inventory.
   g. Fire insurance on inventory.
   h. Fire insurance on warehouse.
   i. Obsolescence costs on inventory.
   j. Shipping costs per shipment.

14–7. When constraints appear in an inventory problem, why is the optimal decision either Q^* or one of the alternatives adjacent to Q^*?

14–8. Supply labels for the lettered items in the following diagram of the quantities of an inventory item on hand over a recent time period:

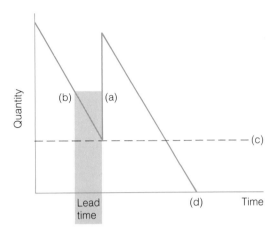

14–9. A company estimates that the lead time for a particular material is five days, but that the demand over lead time is uncertain. The distribution of demand over lead time is best approximated by the normal distribution (that is, a symmetric, bell-shaped curve). If there is a great number of possible values for the demand over lead time and if no safety stock is maintained, how frequently would a stockout be expected?

14–10. "Our company orders 5,000 units at a time just to make sure we don't experience a stockout." Comment on this statement.

14–11. Phenerome Corporation is a diversified company that has acquired a number of subsidiaries through mergers. The company is instituting an inventory control system which would incorporate economic inventory policy considerations. One of the company officers has noted that some subsidiaries use last-in, first-out (LIFO) for financial reporting and others use first-in, first-out (FIFO). The officer asks you: "These different inventory methods make it very difficult for us to prepare the corporate financials and our tax return. How will they affect operation of an inventory system since the investment costs will be different for the same item in a different subsidiary?"

Exercises

14–12. EOQ computation

One of the inventory items at a company has an investment cost of $38. The annual demand for the item is 32,500 units. It costs $215.50 to place an order for the material, and out-of-pocket storage costs amount to $4.80 per unit. The company cost of capital is 30 percent.

Required:

Determine the EOQ.

14–13. Analyzing inventory policy costs

A review of the inventories of a company indicates the following cost data for a given item:

Invoice price	$102.25 per unit
Processing invoices and other documents	21.45 per order + $1,475.80 per month
Permit fees for shipping	201.65 per truckload
Excise tax	4% of invoice price
Inventory tax	2% of the invoice price
Insurance on shipments	$ 1.50 per unit
Insurance on inventory	2.80 per unit
Warehouse rental	985.00 per month
Stockout costs	122.00 per order
Cost of capital	25%
Unloading—per truckload	$ 80.20 per order

Required:

Show the differential costs that would be included in an EOQ model.

14–14. Evaluating inventory policy costs

A company uses 1,500 units of Zeron per year. Each unit has an invoice cost of $222, including shipping costs and other investment costs. Because of the volatile nature of Zeron, it costs $860 for liability insurance on each shipment. The costs of carrying the inventory amount to $65 per item per year exclusive of a 20 percent cost of capital. Other order costs amount to $18 per order.

At present, the company orders 250 units at a time.

Required:

a. What is the annual cost of the company's current order policy?
b. What is the annual cost of the indicated economic order policy?

14–15. Economic order quantities with constraints

Percona Corporation uses a direct material, Zelda, in its production processes. The company uses 24,000 units of Zelda a year. The carrying costs of Zelda amount to $28.50 per unit, while order costs are $186.20 per order. The manufacturer of Zelda will only accept order in lots of even hundreds.

Required:

What is the optimal order quantity and the annual inventory costs given the restriction on order sizes?

14–16. Find missing data for EOQ

Goliard Company manufactures *Errantos,* a consumer product, in optimal production runs of 3,500 units 20 times per year. It is estimated that the setup costs (including nonproductive labor) amount to $717.50 for each batch. The company's cost of capital is 20 percent, and the out-of-pocket cost to store an Erranto for one year is $1.60.

Required:

Solve for the unknown inventory cost of an Erranto.

14–17. Evaluate safety-stock policy

Forest Products Corporation manufactures Maquis as one of its agricultural items. The manufacturing process requires several inputs including a nitrogen fixer, NFX. The company uses 39,000 units of NFX per year and orders in economic lot sizes of 2,600 units. The cost to carry a unit of NFX is $24.40. If there is a stockout, a carload of NFX must be purchased at retail from a local supplier. The retail price is $1,650 greater than the price from the regular supplier.

Looking at the past order records, it appears that certain safety-stock levels would result in stockouts according to the following schedule:

Safety-stock quantity	Probability of stockout
0	.50
150	.20
175	.05
250	.01

Required:

What level of safety stock would result in the least cost to the company?

14–18. Impact of quantity discounts on order quantity

Prescience Company uses 1,560 tankloads a year of a specific input material. The tankloads are delivered by rail to a siding on the company property. The supplier is offering a special discount for buyers of large quantities. The schedule is as follows:

Quantity ordered (tankloads)	Discount
1–19	–0–
20–79	2%
80–149	5
150 and over	6

Ordering costs amount to $400, and carrying costs are computed at 30 percent of the cost of the average inventory. Each tankload costs $1,500.

Required:

Compute the optimal order quantity. (Ignore the reduction in carrying costs arising from the discount.)

14–19. Impact of constraints on optimal order quantity with price breaks

Considering the situation in Exercise 14–18, suppose that the maximum storage capacity for the company is 100 tankloads. What would the optimal order quantity be? Demonstrate why.

14–20. EOQ analysis—multiple choice

a. The following information relates to the Henry Company:

Units required per year	30,000
Cost of placing an order	$400
Unit carrying cost per year	$600

Assuming that the units will be required evenly throughout the year, what is the EOQ?
(1) 200
(2) 300
(3) 400
(4) 500

b. Pierce Incorporated has to manufacture 10,000 blades for its electric lawn mower division. The blades will be used evenly throughout the year. The setup cost every time a production run is made is $80, and the cost to carry a blade in inventory for the year is $.40. Pierce's objective is to produce the blades at the lowest cost possible. Assuming that each production run will be for the same number of blades, how many production runs should Pierce make?
(1) 3
(2) 4
(3) 5
(4) 6

c. The Hancock Company wishes to determine the amount of safety stock that they should maintain for Product No. 135 that will result in the lowest cost. Each stockout will cost $75, and the carrying cost of each unit of safety stock will be $1. Product No. 135 will be ordered five times a year. Which of the following will produce the lowest cost?
(1) A safety stock of 10 units that is associated with a 40 percent probability of running out of stock during an order period.

(2) A safety stock of 20 units that is associated with a 20 percent probability of running out of stock during an order period.

(3) A safety stock of 40 units that is associated with a 10 percent probability of running out of stock during an order period.

(4) A safety stock of 80 units that is associated with a 5 percent probability of running out of stock during an order period.

d. The Polly Company wishes to determine the amount of safety stock that it should maintain for Product D that will result in the lowest cost.

The following information is available:

Stockout cost	$80 per occurrence
Carrying cost of safety stock	$2 per unit
Number of purchase orders	5 per year

The available options open to Polly are as follows:

Units of safety stock	Probability of running out of safety stock
10	50%
20	40
30	30
40	20
50	10
55	5

The number of units of safety stock that will result in the lowest cost is:

(1) 20

(2) 40

(3) 50

(4) 55

e. The Aron Company requires 40,000 units of Product Q for the year. The units will be required evenly throughout the year. It costs $60 to place an order. It costs $10 to carry a unit in inventory for the year. What is the EOQ?

(1) 400

(2) 490

(3) 600

(4) 693

(CPA adapted)

14–21. Determine optimal safety-stock levels

Wildridge Products, Inc., has expressed concern over the erratic delivery times for a critical product, Westovers. The company orders 3,000 at a time and has maintained a safety stock of 200 Westovers, but has been experiencing frequent stockouts and production delays. The plant operates 270 days per year. The company estimates that the lead time for Westovers is 5 days over which time 500 units will be used in production. The cost of storing a unit is $22 per year including capital costs. A stockout is estimated to cost $4,200 for each day that the company must wait for a shipment. Any time a stockout occurs, the company must wait until its sole supplier delivers these units.

Over the past several years, the lead times have been as follows:

Lead time (days)	Probability of lead time
9	.05
8	.15
6	.20
5	.40
4	.20

Other lead times have not occurred and may be ignored.

Required: Determine the most economic safety-stock level.

Problems and cases

14–22. Inventory policy cost evaluation

Astatic, Inc., is a wholesaler of Protoxid for industrial clients. Demand for Protoxid is stable at 350,000 units per year. Astatic orders the product from its supplier four times a year. An order is placed when the total Protoxid on hand amounts to 25,000 units. This represents a nine-day working supply plus safety stock. The company works 300 days per year. Recently, management of Astatic has expressed concern over the costs of carrying inventory and is seeking to evaluate the present inventory order and safety-stock policies.

As a part of the study, the following costs were identified with respect to Protoxid:

Invoice price	$ 32.92
Weight per unit	1.5 kg
Shipping charges	$ 1.05 per unit + $640 per truck + $.40 per kg.
Tax on each unit	1.80
Special packaging	3.65 ($1 is refunded on return of the shipping container).
Insurance on shipment	1.76 per unit—casualty insurance
	415.00 per shipment—liability bond
Processing order documents	183.00
Unloading operations	.82 per unit + $1,800 per week
Inspect and count for annual inventory	2.63 per unit
Rental of unloading equipment (1-day minimum rental— 200,000-unit daily capacity)	222.00 per day
Estimated obsolescence costs	1.35 per unit
Inventory record maintenance	.92 per unit + $2,200 per week
Inventory tax	3% of invoice price
Inventory insurance	15% of invoice price + $4,100 per month

The company estimates its cost of capital is 22 percent. In addition, a study was conducted on the costs of a stockout. The average stockout costs $5,400 due to the need to request special shipments from alternate suppliers. With various safety-stock levels, the probabilities of a stockout decrease as follows:

Safety stock	Probability of stockout
0	.5
7,000	.1
14,000	.02
21,000	.01

For determining optimal order quantity, a stockout probability per order of .02 may be assumed. Order sizes are restricted to round lots of 5,000. The company has the capacity to store 90,000 units.

Required:

a. What are the differential costs for inventory policy making?
b. What are the annual costs under the present order and safety-stock system?
c. What are the annual costs under the optimal order and safety-stock system?
d. What is the reorder point under the optimal order and safety-stock system?

14–23. Sensitivity of EOQ computations to changes in cost estimates

Retem & Company is instituting an economic order policy for its inventory. The following data are presented for one item in the inventory:

Annual usage	140,000 units
Storage costs	$7 per unit (out of pocket)
Cost of capital	30% on $62 investment per unit
Order costs	$490

Required:

a. What is the EOQ given these data?
b. What is the annual cost of following the order policy in requirement (a) if the cost of capital were 20 percent?
c. What is the EOQ and total annual costs if the cost of capital were 20 percent?

14–24. Inventory cycle analysis— multiple choice

Thoran Electronics Company began producing pacemakers last year. At that time, the company forecasted the need for 10,000 integrated circuits annually. During the first year, the company placed orders when the inventory dropped to 600 units so that it would have enough to produce pacemakers continuously during a three-week lead time. Unfortunately, the company ran out of this component on several occasions causing costly production delays. Careful study of last year's experience resulted in the following expectations for the coming year:

Weekly usage	Related probability of usage	Lead time	Related probability of lead time
280 units	.2	3 weeks	.1
180 units	.8	2 weeks	.9
	1.0		1.0

The study also suggested that usage during a given week was statistically independent of usage during any other week and usage was also statistically independent of lead time.

Required:

a. The expected average usage during a regular production week is:
   (1) 180 units.
   (2) 200 units.
   (3) 280 units.
   (4) 460 units.
   (5) Some usage other than those given above.
b. The expected usage during lead time is:
   (1) 840 units.
   (2) 400 units.
   (3) 360 units.

(4)   420 units.

(5)   Some usage other than those given above.

(CMA adapted)

14–25. Alternative order policy costs

The Committee for Human Improvement (CHI) is planning a fund-raising benefit. As part of the publicity and as a means of raising money, the committee plans to sell T-shirts with the CHI logo and a design commemorating the benefit event. However, since the committee has never held one of these benefits previously, there is no experience about the quantity of T-shirts to order.

You've been asked to volunteer your knowledge of cost accounting and provide the committee with some information on the cost of alternatives. The committee expects it can sell 500 shirts at a minimum, but will probably sell five times that amount. However, these numbers are very "soft." Since the committee is operating with limited funds, there is a desire to avoid undue risk in this T-shirt adventure.

After contacting several T-shirt manufacturers, you conclude that the best price structure is as follows:

Design logo and shirt	$75.00
Setup each production run	50.00
Cost per shirt:	
Orders of 1– 99	5.00
100– 499	3.00
500– 749	2.50
750– 999	2.25
1,000–1,999	2.00
2,000–2,999	1.90
3,000 and over	1.80

The shirts are expected to sell for $5 each. There are no costs to store the shirts since one of the committee members has volunteered storage space. However, unsold shirts are valueless.

Required:

Prepare an analysis of the costs of alternative T-shirt order policies for the committee. Since the sales volume is unknown, your report will have to focus on possible volumes. Use those suggested by the committee. Indicate to the committee the costs of each alternative and the differential or opportunity cost of selecting a less risky order size.

14–26. Estimate costs for optimal order policy

Mariposa Recreational Products Company produces roller skates for street use. The company has been so involved responding to the increased demand (now at 200,000 units per year) for its product that an adequate cost control system has not been installed. Recently, however, management has been directing its attention to this problem. A question has arisen concerning the EOQ for the sets of unassembled skate parts that are the company's direct materials.

The set of parts comes from one supplier and costs $16 per set. There is a charge of $1 per set for shipping from the manufacturer. When the parts arrive, they must be checked to make certain that each set is complete and that defective units are identified and returned to the manufacturer. The checking requires one-fourth hour per unit, and the labor rate for this activity is $6 per hour including variable fringe benefits. The same class of labor is required to check the inventory once a year as a part of the company's inventory management system. The checking requires an average of one-eighth hour per unit in inventory.

There is an inventory tax of $.62 per set of parts in inventory on February 28 each year. Insurance on the inventory amounts to $1.50 per unit. When placing an order, the company incurs out-of-pocket costs of $40 for bookkeeping and arranging transportation for the parts.

When the shipment arrives, a supervisor must review the documentation and determine the number of units in the shipment. This activity requires an incremental $35.00 of supervisory-related costs. A dockworker is also present to assist in unloading the shipment. This dockworker spends about $1\frac{2}{3}$ hours in this activity and is paid at the $6 labor rate. The parts manufacturer will only accept orders in lots of even hundreds.

The company estimates its cost of capital is 16 percent.

Required:

Determine the EOQ for sets of skate parts.

14–27. Sensitivity of economic order size models

After presenting the analysis for the Mariposa Recreational Products Corporation (Problem 14–26), you learn that the cost of supervision of unloading operations is not differential, but is part of the supervisor's salary and a fixed cost.

Required:

Demonstrate the effect that this discovery would have on the optimal order policy.

14–28. Determine optimal safety-stock levels

The Starr Company manufactures several products. One of its main products requires an electric motor. The management of Starr Company uses the EOQ model to determine the optimum number of motors to order. Management now wants to determine how much safety stock to keep on hand.

The company uses 30,000 motors annually at the rate of 100 per working day. The motors regularly cost $60 each. The lead time for an order is five days. The cost to carry a motor in stock is $10. If a stockout occurs, management must purchase motors at retail from an alternate supplier. The alternate supplier charges $80 per motor.

Starr Company has analyzed the usage during the past reorder periods by examining inventory records. The records indicate the following usage patterns during past reorder periods:

Usage during lead time	Number of times quantity was used
440	6
460	12
480	16
500	130
520	20
540	10
560	6
	200

Required:

Determine the least-cost safety-stock level and the total differential costs at that level.

(CMA adapted)

14–29. Determine optimal order quantity with price breaks and constraints

Weldone Supply offers discounts for quantity orders according to the following schedule:

Quantity	Discount
1– 999	None
1,000– 1,999	$1.00
2,000– 4,999	1.50
5,000– 9,999	2.00
10,000–19,999	4.00
20,000 and over	6.50

To decide whether to take advantage of the price-break system, you review your records and find that the order cost for this product is $400 and the carrying costs are $4. Usage amounts to 20,000 units per year. Your company has space to store up to 15,000 units. The cost of capital effect on the discount may be ignored.

Required:

Prepare a schedule showing the optimal order quantity.

14–30. Inventory costs versus costs for inventory management

Pointer Furniture Company manufactures and sells office furniture. To compete effectively in different markets, it produces several brands of office furniture. The manufacturing operation is organized by the item produced rather than by the furniture line. Thus, the desks for all brands are manufactured on the same production line. The desks are manufactured in batches. For example, 10 high-quality desks might be manufactured during the first two weeks in October and 50 units of a lower-quality desk during the last two weeks. Because each model has its own unique manufacturing requirement, the change from one model to another requires the factory's equipment to be adjusted.

Management of Pointer wants to determine the most economical production run for each of the items in its product lines. One of the cost parameters that must be determined before the model can be employed is the setup cost incurred when there is a change to a different furniture model. The accounting department has been asked to determine the setup cost for the desk (Model JE 40) in its junior executive line as an example.

The equipment maintenance department is responsible for all of the changeover adjustments on production lines in addition to the preventive and regular maintenance of all the production equipment. The equipment maintenance staff has a 40-hour workweek; the size of the staff is changed only if there is a change in the workload that is expected to persist for an extended period of time. The equipment maintenance department had 10 employees last year, and they each averaged 2,000 hours for the year. They are paid $9 an hour, and employee benefits average 20 percent of wage costs. The other departmental costs, which include such items as supervision, depreciation, insurance, etc., total $50,000 per year.

Two workers from the equipment maintenance department are required to make the change on the desk line for Model JE 40. They spend an estimated five hours in setting up the equipment. The desk production line on which Model JE 40 is manufactured is operated by five workers. During the changeover, these workers assist the maintenance workers when needed and operate the line during the one hour test run. However, they are idle for approximately 40 percent of the time required for the changeover.

The production workers are paid a basic wage rate of $7.50 an hour. Two overhead bases are used to apply the overhead costs of this production line because some of the costs vary in proportion to direct labor-hours while others vary with machine-hours. The overhead rates applicable for the current year are as follows:

	Based on direct labor-hours	**Based on machine-hours**
Variable	$2.75	$ 5.00
Fixed	2.25	15.00
	$5.00	$20.00

These department overhead rates are based upon an expected activity of 10,000 direct labor-hours and 1,500 machine-hours for the current year. This department is not scheduled to operate at full capacity because production capability currently exceeds sales potential at this time.

The estimated cost of the direct materials used in the test run totals $200. Salvage material from the test run should total $50. Pointer's cost of capital is 20 percent.

a. Prepare an estimate of Pointer Furniture Company's setup cost for desk Model JE 40 for use in the economic production run model. For each cost item identified in the problem, justify the amount and the reason for including the cost item in your estimate. Explain the reason for excluding any cost item from your estimate.

b. Identify the cost items which would be included in an estimate of Pointer Furniture Company's cost of carrying the desks in inventory.

(CMA adapted)

15

Capital Investment Cash Flows

OBJECTIVES

To understand methods of estimating cash flows for capital investment decision making including tax consequences of these decisions.

The most important decisions a company makes concern the acquisition of long-term assets. Because investment in long-term assets usually involves substantial sums of money and leaves funds at risk for long periods of time, the investment decision is important and risky. For this reason, companies pay a great deal of attention to capital investment decisions. With few exceptions, large investments in capital assets are made only with the approval of top management and/or the company directors. Extensive preliminary analyses are made of the assets to be acquired, the way they will complement the existing business, and how they will be acquired and financed.

While the final decision about asset acquisition is the responsibility of management, the capital investment models have been developed in accounting, engineering, and, more recently, in finance. Accountants have the very important role of estimating the amount and timing of the cash flows used in capital investment decision models.

In this chapter, we discuss the process of estimating future cash flows from capital investment projects. In Chapter 16, we discuss some of the different models used to evaluate the cash flows.

Analyzing cash flows	Capital investment models are based on the future cash flows expected from a particular asset investment decision. The amount and timing of the cash flows from an investment project determines the economic value of capital investment projects, regardless of the method of income reporting used in financial statements. The timing of those flows is important because cash received earlier in time has greater value than cash received later. As soon as cash is received, it can be invested in an alternative profit-making opportunity. Thus, there is an opportunity cost for the cash committed to any particular investment project. Because capital investment decision horizons extend over many years, the time value of money is often a significant factor.

To recognize the time value of money, the future cash flows associated with a project are adjusted to their present value using a predetermined discount rate. Summing the discounted values of the future cash flows and subtracting the initial investment yields the net present value of a project. This net present value represents the economic value of the project to the company at a given point in time. The decision models used for capital investments seek to optimize the economic value of a firm through optimizing the net present value of future cash flows.

For example, suppose an investor must choose between two very similar projects. Each project requires an immediate cash outlay of $10,000. Project 1 will return $14,000 at the end of two years, while Project 2 will return $14,000 at the end of three years. Clearly, the investor would prefer Project 1 over Project 2 because Project 1 will return the $14,000 one year earlier, and that amount would be available for reinvestment. Consequently, Project 1 has a higher net present value than Project 2.

Of course, the net present value alone does not indicate whether either project is worth the investment in the first place. That decision rests on a number of other factors. Will either project fit within the present organization? Does management have the expertise to operate the new business? What are the social and legal implications of the project? Is the project risk acceptable? While all of these questions are important, to simplify our examples, we assume that the projects we are comparing are of similar risk and are suitable investments. This allows us to focus on the analysis of cash flows from projects and how that analysis affects net present values.

Returning to the question of whether to invest in Project 1 or Project 2, we must determine if the net present value of the project is positive. If the net present value is positive, the project will earn a return greater than its discount rate. This rate is often referred to as the hurdle rate. If the project can earn its discount rate, it has passed the hurdle of the net present value criterion for investment decisions. Projects that do not meet the hurdle rate are rejected because the funds that would be invested in them can earn a higher rate in some other investment.

Distinguishing between revenues, costs, and cash flows

Sometimes there is a *timing difference* between revenue recognition and cash inflow, on the one hand, and the incurrence of a cost and the related cash outflow, on the other hand. When this occurs, it is important to distinguish cash flows from revenues and costs, and to note that capital investment analysis uses *cash flows, not revenues and costs.* For example, sometimes revenue from a sale is recognized on one date but not collected until a year later. In such cases, the cash is not available for other investment or consumption purposes until collected.

Net present value

The *net present value* of a project can be computed by using the equation:

$$NPV = \sum_{n=0}^{N} C_n \times (1 + d)^{-n}$$

where:

C_n = the cash to be received or disbursed at the end of time period n

d = the appropriate *discount rate* for the future cash flows

n = the time period when the cash flow occurs

N = the life of the investment, in years

Use of the equation with a calculator is probably the most efficient approach to computing net present values for most classroom and practical applications. Tables of net present value factors are in Appendix B to this chapter and may also be used to find present values. We use the equation in all chapter illustrations, computations, and discussions and round all printed factors to three decimals. Therefore, if we want to discount $20,000 for two years at 10 percent, we find the value of $(1.10)^{-2}$ by a power function in the calculator. In the calculator, the result of this computation is .826446281. Multiplying this amount by $20,000 yields the present value of $16,529. In this chapter, we would show our computations as:

$$\$20,000 \times (1+.10)^{-2} = \$20,000 \times .826$$
$$= \underline{\underline{\$16,529}}$$

We abbreviate the factor because it is simply an intermediate result. If you use the abbreviated factor or the factors from the present value tables, your answer will differ due to rounding. This should not cause alarm.

Applying present value analysis

Now, let's look at how present value analysis is used for capital investment decisions. As an example, consider the two projects mentioned earlier in the chapter. If the appropriate discount rate is 15 percent, then the net present value of each project may be computed as follows:

Project 1:
Cash inflow:	$14,000 \times (1+.15)^{-2}$	
	$= \$14,000 \times .756 = \$10,586$	
Cash outflow	$= -10,000$	
Net present value	$\underline{\underline{\$\quad 586}}$	

Project 2:
Cash inflow:	$14,000 \times (1+.15)^{-3}$	
	$= \$14,000 \times .658 = \$\ 9,205$	
Cash outflow	$= -10,000$	
Net present value	$\underline{\underline{\$\ (795)}}$	

The starting time for capital investment projects is assumed to be time 0. Therefore, any cash outlays required at the start of the project are not discounted. We will simply enter them at their full amount.

At a discount rate of 15 percent, Project 1 is acceptable and Project 2 is not. Project 1 will earn more than the required 15 percent return, while Project 2 will earn less.

You should check for yourself to see that at a 20 percent discount rate, the present values of both projects are negative. Therefore, if our required

Illustration 15–1   **Example net present value calculations**

Time	Net cash inflow or (outflow)	PV factor $(1 + d)^{-n}$ $d = 20$ percent	Net present value[a]
0	$(80,000)	1.000	$(80,000)
1	(9,000)	.833	(7,500)
2	31,200	.694	21,667
3	14,800	.579	8,565
4	(42,100)	.482	(20,303)
5	76,800	.402	30,864
6	79,600	.335	26,658
7	74,500	.279	20,792
8	61,100	.233	14,210
9	43,600	.194	8,450
10	(39,700)	.162	(6,412)
Net present value			$ 16,991

[a] Cash flow times factor may not equal net present value because factor is rounded to three places.

rate were 20 percent, neither project would meet the investment criterion. Alternatively, at 10 percent both projects have positive net present values and both would be acceptable.

Of course, the cash flows in most business investment opportunities are considerably more complex than our simplified examples, but the method for computing net present values remains the same.

Consider, for example, the cash flow pattern in Illustration 15–1. The cash flows can be either positive or negative in any year. This cash flow pattern is characteristic of a project that will begin with a pilot operation. If the pilot operation proves successful, full-scale facilities will be installed in Year 4. Operations will continue until Year 10, at which time costs will be incurred to dismantle the operation. Once the cash flows are determined, computation of the net present value is a mechanical operation. The critical problem for the accountant, however, is to estimate the expected future cash flows.

Estimating project cash flows

Estimating cash flows from an investment project is complicated by government tax policies to encourage capital investments. As a result, the cash flows from a project are best considered in four separate categories:

1. Investment outflows.
2. Periodic operating flows.
3. Depreciation tax shield.
4. Disinvestment flows.

Each category of cash flows requires distinct treatment and varies in tax consequences, opportunity costs, and other differential costs. The tax consequences are complicated so we will only discuss them in general here. Tax advice should be sought in any capital investment decision because the form of investment and financing can have a significant impact on the timing and amount of the project-related tax payments.[1] We will state some general assumptions about taxes and follow them in the chapter illustrations and problems unless otherwise stated.

Once the costs of a project have been converted to cash flows and categorized, it is possible to consider the tax and other consequences of the project. After all relevant factors have been considered, the net cash flow for each period in the life of the project can be scheduled and discounted.

Investment outflows

The primary outflow for most capital investments is the acquistion cost of the asset. In most cases, this cost can be easily determined. In other cases (particularly with leased assets), determining the acquisition cost may require additional analysis. (These problems are discussed in Chapter 16.) Acquisition costs may be incurred in Year 0 and in later years. In some cases, acquisition costs are incurred over periods of 10 to 20 years. All acquisition costs are listed as cash outflows in the years in which they are incurred.

investment tax credit For most business assets, a company is allowed a credit against its federal income tax liability based on the cost of an acquired asset. This investment tax credit is equal to 10 percent of the cost of most business assets as of this writing. As discussed later, the 1981 Economic Recovery Tax Act calls for depreciating most business furniture, fixtures, and equipment over five years. Automobiles and certain other assets qualify for a 6 percent investment tax credit and are depreciated over three years.

For example, a company has acquired several assets during the past year. A schedule of the investment costs of these assets and the related tax depreciation lives are:

Investment costs	Tax depreciation life
$1,400,000	3 years
2,500,000	5 years

The investment tax credit is computed as:

Investment costs	Rate	Tax credit
$1,400,000	6%	$ 84,000
2,500,000	10	250,000
Total investment tax credit		$334,000

---

[1] See R. M. Sommerfeld, *Federal Taxes and Management Decisions 1983–84 ed.* (Homewood, Ill.: Richard D. Irwin, 1983).

The tax credit is taken when the corporate tax return is filed. Because companies usually make estimated tax payments as the year goes on (much like you have taxes withheld from your earnings), tax credits are taken into account in the year of investment. While there are limitations on the credit, we will assume that this credit limitation does not affect the projects discussed in the chapter unless stated otherwise.

The 1982 tax act added a provision that the tax basis of property be reduced by one half of the amount of any investment tax credit claimed for it. The impact of this provision is discussed with other aspects of the tax shield from the write-off of investment costs later in this chapter.

Investment credit recapture   If an investment tax credit is claimed for an asset class but the asset is not held for the full term required for that asset class, part of the investment tax credit may be *recaptured*. That is, the amount must be paid to the Internal Revenue Service, but without interest or penalties. The amount to be recaptured depends upon the year of disposition and the property class. The following table shows the recapture percentages:

	Recapture percentages	
Year of disposition	**3-year property**	**All other property**
One full year after being placed in service	66	80
Second year	33	60
Third year	–0–	40
Fourth year	–0–	20
Fifth year	–0–	–0–

For example, if a company has claimed the full 10 percent credit on a $400,000 asset but discards the asset during the third year of the asset life, then 60 percent of investment tax credit is recaptured. This is computed as follows:

Credit claimed ($400,000 × 10%)	$40,000
Recapture percentage	60%
	$24,000

This $24,000 is a direct increase in the tax liability of the company in the year that the asset is disposed or taken out of service.

The investment tax credit is designed to subsidize companies that invest in capital assets by reducing investment costs.

Working capital commitments   In addition to the cash for purchase of long-term assets, many projects require additional funds for working capital needs (for example, to build up inventories). These cash flows often occur before the project is in operation.

Illustration 15–2   **Scheduling investment outflows, Marmaduke Company**

Year	Cash (outflow) or inflow	Remarks
0	$(500,000)	Initial investment
	50,000	Investment tax credit
	$(450,000)	Year 0 outflows
1	$(650,000)	Additional investment
	65,000	Investment tax credit
	(45,000)	Inventories
	(25,000)	Additional working capital requirement
	$(655,000)	Year 1 outflows

For example Marmaduke Company is considering a project that will require the outlay of $500,000 in Year 0. A further outlay of $650,000 will be required in Year 1. These outlays will qualify for the investment tax credit. The project will begin operation at the end of Year 1, at which time the company will be required to spend $45,000 on inventories for project operations. Also, the company estimated that an additional $25,000 will be required to meet other working capital needs (for example, average idle cash balances in bank accounts to handle cash transactions). The investment cash outflows and their timing are shown in Illustration 15–2.

The acquisition costs are shown at the time they are incurred. The related investment tax credits are scheduled at the same time. The outlays for working capital items are shown at the time those outflows occur.

Periodic operating flows

The primary reason for acquiring long-term assets is usually to generate positive periodic operating cash flows. These positive flows may result from such revenue-generating activities as new products, or they may stem from cost-saving programs. In either case, actual cash inflows and outflows from operating the asset are usually determinable in a straightforward manner. Often a schedule is prepared of the expected future operating characteristics of the asset together with its operating revenues and costs. As long as the revenues and costs are differential cash items, they are relevant for the capital investment decision. If the schedule includes costs that are not differential, however, it must be adjusted accordingly. A typical schedule of operating revenues and costs for a project is presented in Illustration 15–3.

The operating revenues and costs that represent differential cash flows are included in the differential cash flow column. Costs that do not involve cash (depreciation, depletion, and amortization) are excluded from the differential cash flow column. Allocations of fixed costs (such as corporate headquarters costs) are excluded because their total will not change; only their distribution among organization subunits will change. For example, if the project is acquired, the company does not expect that its administrative costs will increase by $38,700 (the $22,000 direct costs plus $16,700 indirect costs). The $16,700

Illustration 15–3   **Schedule of project revenues and costs (Year 1), Marmaduke Company**

Item	Amount[a]	Differential cash flow	Remarks
Project revenues	$420,000	$420,000	All cash
Prime costs	(135,000)	(135,000)	All cash
Manufacturing overhead:			
Indirect labor	(18,000)	(18,000)	All cash
Supplies	(6,500)	(6,500)	All cash
Allocated service department costs	(31,500)	(11,000)	$20,500 is an allocation of costs that will not change with this decision
Depreciation	(48,000)	–0–	Depreciation is not a cash flow
Other overhead	(29,200)	(29,200)	All cash
Selling commissions	(39,100)	(39,100)	All cash
Administration:			
Direct	(22,000)	(22,000)	All cash
Indirect	(16,700)	–0–	Allocation of fixed costs
Subtotals	$ 74,000	159,200	
Income tax on differential cash flows		(61,600)	Based on analysis of tax regulations
Net operating cash flow		$ 97,600	

[a] Based on fully allocated costs and financial accounting depreciation.

is an allocation used for internal performance evaluation and/or control purposes only.

If there are variable cash costs in other departments (for example, service departments) that change as a result of the project, however, then those service department costs should be included in the differential cash flow schedule. For this reason, $11,000 of allocated service department costs are included in the differential cash flow column.

Financing costs such as interest costs on loans, principal repayments, and payments under financing leases are typically excluded under the assumption that the financing decision is separate from the asset-acquisition decision. Under this assumption, the decision to acquire the asset is made first. If the asset-acquisition decision is favorable, then a decision will be made to select the best financing.

The income tax effects of the periodic cash flows from the project are also computed. Note that the tax effects are related to the project cash flows and not to the project profit computation. To analyze the net present value of the project, we want the *differential effect on our tax liability*. The income tax effect of depreciation is separate from the depreciation used for financial or internal reporting purposes. Therefore, any reductions in tax payments arising from depreciation are treated separately.

The steps carried out to compute the net operating cash flows for the project are repeated for each year in the project life. In some cases, the computations are simplified if the project is expected to yield identical cash flows for more than one year. In most practical contexts, however, the cash flows will differ from year to year, thus requiring a schedule that incorporates each year's cash flow projections.

Tax shield

To measure the income of an organization or one of its subunits, depreciation is used to allocate the cost of long-term assets over their useful lives. These depreciation charges are not cash costs and, thus, do not directly affect the net present values of capital investments. However, tax regulations permit depreciation write-offs that serve to reduce the required tax payment. The reduction in the tax payment is referred to as a **tax shield.** This tax shield is independent of the depreciation computed for income determination purposes and is based strictly on tax depreciation.

The tax allowances for depreciation is one of the primary incentives used by tax policy makers to promote investment in long-term assets. The faster an asset's cost can be written off for tax purposes, the sooner the tax reductions are realized and, hence, the greater the net present value of the tax shield. In recent years, tax depreciation has been accelerated to allow write-offs over very short-time periods regardless of an asset's expected life. To maximize present value, it is usually best to claim depreciation as rapidly as possible.

Straight-line depreciation   The predominant depreciation method for financial reporting has been the *straight-line method.* With this method, the cost of the asset, less any salvage value, is allocated equally to each year of the expected life of the asset.

Suppose that an asset has a depreciable base of $250,000, net of the investment tax credit adjustment. Assume the asset life for tax purposes is five years, and no salvage value. Straight-line depreciation of this asset for tax purposes will amount to $50,000 per year. This is computed as follows:

$$\text{Annual depreciation} = \frac{\text{Depreciable base} - \text{Salvage value}}{\text{Asset life}}$$

$$= \frac{\$250,000 - 0}{5 \text{ years}}$$

$$= \$50,000 \text{ per year}$$

The tax shield is equal to the reduction in the tax payment that arises if this depreciation method is used over the project life. Assuming a tax rate of 45 percent, the tax shield would result in a reduction in taxes of $22,500 per year ($50,000 × 45%).

Using a 20 percent discount rate, this tax shield has a present value of $67,289. Supporting computations are shown in Illustration 15–4.

Illustration 15–4   **Present value of straight-line depreciation tax shield**

Life: 5 years   Depreciation base: $250,000
Tax rate: 45%   Discount rate: 20%

Year	Depreci-ation	Tax shield	PV factor	Present value[a]
1	$ 50,000	$ 22,500	.833	$18,750
2	50,000	22,500	.694	15,625
3	50,000	22,500	.579	13,021
4	50,000	22,500	.482	10,851
5	50,000	22,500	.402	9,042
Totals	$250,000	$112,500		$67,289

[a] Cash flow times PV factor may not equal present value because PV factors are rounded to three places.

Accelerated cost recovery systems

To encourage capital investment, tax law permits the deduction of capital investment costs over a short period of time. The system of tax write-offs under this new set of rules is referred to as the **Accelerated Cost Recovery System** or **ACRS.** The depreciation write-off is specified for each of four asset categories. The actual useful life of an asset and its salvage value are ignored. The four categories are:

1. Three years: Automobiles, equipment used in research, light trucks.
2. Five years: Furniture, equipment, trucks, virtually all other personal property used in business.
3. Ten years: Public-utility property, railroad tank cars, certain real estate, boilers, and coal-conversion facilities.
4. Fifteen years: Most real estate.

Most assets can also be written off using the straight-line method instead of the ACRS. Natural resource assets are written off over the units of production from the property rather than over a time-based life.

ACRS specifies the percentage of the original cost, less half of any investment tax credit, that may be claimed in each year that the asset is owned. For three-year and five-year property, the percentages are:

Ownership year	Class of investment	
	Five years	Three years
1	15%	25%
2	22	38
3	21	37
4	21	—
5	21	—

Illustration 15–5   **Present value of ACRS tax shield**

ACRS life: 5 years   Depreciation basis $250,000
Tax rate: 45%   Discount rate   20%

Year	ACRS percent	Depreci- ation	Tax shield	PV factor	Present value[a]
1	15	$ 37,500	$ 16,875	.833	$14,063
2	22	55,000	24,750	.694	17,188
3	21	52,500	23,625	.579	13,672
4	21	52,500	23,625	.482	11,394
5	21	52,500	23,625	.402	9,494
Totals		$250,000	$112,500		$65,811

[a] Tax shield times PV factor may not equal present value because the PV factor is rounded to three places.

Let's assume that the $250,000 asset from Illustration 15–4 is classified as a five-year ACRS asset. The annual tax shield and the present value of that tax shield are computed in Illustration 15–5. Using the 20 percent discount rate and assuming no salvage value or scrap costs, the present value of the tax shield is $65,811.

In general, the sooner a depreciation write-off is taken for tax purposes, the greater its value to the investing company.

Disinvestment flows

The end of a project's life will usually result in some or all of the following flows:

1. Return of some working capital invested in the project (now a cash inflow).
2. Cash inflow or outflow from salvage of the long-term assets.
3. Tax consequences for any differences between salvage proceeds and the tax basis of the property.
4. Other cash flows, such as payments to environmental regulatory agencies.

These cash flows at the end of the life of the project are referred to as **disinvestment flows.**

Return of working capital   When a project ends, there are usually some leftover inventory, cash, and other working capital items that were used to support operations. These working capital items are then freed for use elsewhere. Therefore, at the end of a project's life, the return of these working capital items is shown as a cash inflow.

It is important not to double-count these items. Suppose that cash has been collected from a customer, recorded as a cash inflow to the company, but left in the project's bank account until the end of the project's life. It should not be counted again as a cash inflow at the end of the project.

The return of working capital is recorded as an inflow whenever it is freed for use in other organizational activities. If that does not occur until the end of the project's life, the cash inflow is included as part of disinvestment flows.

Salvage of long-term assets   Ending a project will usually require disposal of its assets. These are usually sold in secondhand markets. In some cases, more money is spent in disassembling the assets and disposing them than is gained from their sale. Any net outflows from disposal of a project's assets become tax deductions in the year of disposal. The *net salvage value* (sometimes negative) of an asset is listed as a cash inflow or outflow at the time it is expected to be realized (or incurred), regardless of the book value or tax basis of the asset.

In many cases, an asset will be traded in on a new asset rather than sold for cash. Should the trade-in value be used? One should include as a disinvestment flow the present value of the optimal decision at disposal. In practice, however, the estimated cash value from asset disposal is included in the capital budgeting analysis. Disposal usually occurs many years in the future, and the amount of the cash flows from disposal are usually small relative to total project cash flows, so the net present value computation is seldom very sensitive to changes in salvage terms. A project that will be acceptable only if the salvage terms are satisfactory may be a very questionable prospect to begin with.

Tax consequences of disposal   Any difference between the tax basis of project's assets (generally, the undepreciated balance) and the amount realized from project disposal results in a tax gain or loss. Therefore, a company's tax liability will be affected in the year of disposal. Tax laws on asset dispositions are complex, so tax advice should be sought well in advance of the proposed disposal date. In this chapter, we assume that any gains or losses on disposal are treated as ordinary income or losses.

Suppose that an asset is carried in the accounting records at a net book value of $70,000 and is salvaged for $30,000 cash. The tax basis of the asset is $10,000, and the tax rate is 45 percent. What are the cash flows from disposal of this asset?

First, the company receives the $30,000 as a cash inflow. They report a taxable gain of $20,000, which is the difference between the $30,000 proceeds and the $10,000 tax basis. This $20,000 gain is taxed at 45 percent, which results in a cash outflow of $9,000. The cash inflow on disposal is $21,000, the net of the $30,000 inflow and the $9,000 cash outflow.

As noted earlier, if the investment tax credit has been taken on an asset and the asset is taken out of service before the time required to earn the investment tax credit, part or all of the credit may be recaptured. Such **tax credit recapture** should be considered in determining disinvestment cash flows.

Other disinvestment flows The cessation of project operations may result in a number of costs that are not directly related to the sale of assets. It may be necessary to make severance payments to employees. Sometimes payments are required to restore the project area to its original condition. Some projects may incur regulatory costs when they are closed down. A cost analyst must inquire about the consequences of disposal to determine the costs that should be included in the disinvestment flows for a project.

Preparing the net present value analysis

Once the cash flow data have been gathered, they are assembled into a schedule that shows the cash flows for each year of the project's life. These flows may be classified into the four categories we just discussed:

1. Investment outflows.
2. Periodic operating flows.
3. Depreciation tax shield.
4. Disinvestment flows.

A summary schedule that shows the totals of the annual cash flows and the net present value of the project is prepared. This summary may be supported by as much detail as management deems necessary for making the investment decision.

For example, we have the following estimated data for an investment proposal for Mega-Projects Company:

Cash paid for long-term assets	
(40% paid in Year 0, balance in Year 1)	$250,000
Working capital requirements (Year 0)	50,000
Discount rate	25%
Marginal tax rate	45%
Project and ACRS life	5 years
Annual cash inflow from revenues	$198,500
Annual operating costs:	
Equipment depreciation	34,000
Building space usage costs	17,681
Prime costs	62,342
Taxes and insurance on equipment	
and inventory	18,200
Other variable overhead	6,076
Administrative costs:	
Direct	3,700
Other—allocated	12,155
Total estimated annual costs	$154,154

The building space-usage costs are an allocation of building costs that will not change if the project is undertaken. The allocated administrative costs are fixed management costs charged to projects for performance measurement purposes. The equipment is expected to have a salvage value of $105,000 at the end of Year 5. A schedule of the cash flows in each year of the project's life is given in Illustration 15–6.

Illustration 15–6   **Cash flow schedule with present value computations**

	Year					
	0	**1**	**2**	**3**	**4**	**5**
Investment outflows:						
Equipment cost	$(100,000)	$(150,000)				
Investment tax credit	10,000	15,000				
Working capital	(50,000)					
Net operating inflows[a]		59,500	$59,500	$59,500	$59,500	$ 59,500
Tax shield from depreciation[b]		16,031	23,512	22,444	22,444	22,444
Disinvestment:						
Return of working capital						50,000
Proceeds of disposal						105,000
Tax on gain[c]						(47,250)
Total cash flows	(140,000)	(59,469)	83,012	81,944	81,944	189,694
PV factor at 25%[d]		.800	.640	.512	.410	.328
Present values	$(140,000)	$ (47,575)	$53,128	$41,955	$33,564	$ 62,159

Net present value of project: $3,231

[a] Net operating cash flow (after tax):

Revenues		$198,500
Differential cash outflows:		
Prime costs	$(62,342)	
Taxes and insurance on equipment and inventory	(18,200)	
Other variable overhead	(6,076)	
Direct administrative costs	(3,700)	(90,318)
Revenues net of differential cash costs		108,182 (before taxes)
Income taxes on differential net cash flows		48,682 (at 45%)
Differential cash flows (after taxes)		$ 59,500

[b] Depreciation computations:
Using ACRS five-year life.
Tax basis = $237,500 = $250,000 × 95%.

Year	ACRS percent	Depreciation	Tax shield (at 45 percent)
1	15	$ 35,625	$ 16,031
2	22	52,250	23,512
3	21	49,875	22,444
4	21	49,875	22,444
5	21	49,875	22,444
Totals		$237,500	$106,875

[c] Gain is equal to salvage since the asset is fully depreciated for tax purposes. The tax is 45 percent of the gain, or 45% × $105,000 = $47,250.

[d] PV factor shown is rounded to three places. Present values are derived from unrounded PV computations.

Project costs include the equipment outlays in Year 0 and Year 1 with the related investment tax credit being claimed in the following years. The working capital requirements are shown as outflows in Year 0.

Annual cash flows are computed using the schedule of revenues and costs and adjusting for the costs that are not differential (building costs and allocated administrative costs) or that are not cash costs (depreciation). The net cash inflow of $108,182 is then reduced by the tax liability that is expected to arise in connection with this inflow at the 45 percent marginal tax rate. The after-tax cash inflow of $59,500 is shown for each year of the project's life.

Depreciation is computed using the five-year ACRS schedule. Salvage value is ignored, and the depreciable base is reduced by 5 percent, which is one half of the investment tax credit.

In the last year of the project, the disinvestment flows are given. These include the return of working capital and the proceeds from disposal of the asset. In addition, the tax consequences from selling the equipment for more than the zero tax basis are considered and the related $47,250 tax liability is included in the cash flow computations.

The net present value of the project is computed as the sum of the present values of each year's cash flow. The net present value of $3,231 indicates that the project is expected to earn at slightly better than the 25 percent used to discount the cash flows.

The schedule indicates the net cash flows in each year, thus assisting management in preparing its cash budgets for the life of the project. The net present value of each year's cash flow is presented for computational purposes and may not be required for management.

Inflation considerations in capital budgeting

When prices and costs are expected to change significantly over a project's life, it is important to consider their effects of those changes on project cash flows. In many cases, the cash flows will not change uniformly over the life of the project. Therefore, a careful analysis of each cost item may be necessary. Cash flows that will be received in the future will have a different real value than dollars received today due to changes in the purchasing power of those dollars. The actual dollars to be received are called **nominal dollars.**

The schedule of project cash flows can be adjusted to consider the nominal cash flows. The resulting nominal net cash flows are then discounted at a rate that recognizes inflation. This is the **nominal discount rate.** These adjustments compensate the company for the effects of inflation as well as for a return on capital.

Adjusting the discount rate

It is commonly accepted that the interest rate that the market demands includes elements of a return on capital as well as an adjustment for the effects of inflation. The discounting equation can be expanded to include the inflation element as a specific component:

$$[(1 + r)(1 + i)]^{-n}$$

where:

$r =$ the real return on capital required from now to period n
$i =$ the expected inflation rate between now and period n
$n =$ the number of the period in the future when the cash is to be received

The *real return* is the return on capital after adjustment for the effects of inflation. This equation may be used with a constant value for $i,$ or the value of i may be changed from one period to the next. In general, though, a constant inflation rate is assumed.

The terms within the brackets may be multiplied before the exponentiation operation. Subtracting 1 from the result of this multiplication gives the nominal discount rate for the project:

$$\text{Nominal rate} = (1 + r)(1 + i) - 1$$

In practice, the nominal discount rate implicitly considers the need to compensate for inflation. The schedule of cash flows is discounted using the nominal discount rate just as the value r was used earlier.

For example, a company has concluded that its projects should earn a real return of 12 percent and that the expected inflation rate over the project's life will be 10 percent per year. To find the nominal discount rate for present value, the following calculation is performed:

$$(1 + r)(1 + i) - 1 = (1.12)(1.10) - 1$$
$$= .232, \text{ or } 23.2\%$$

Management will probably discount the future cash flows using a 23.2 percent rate in the discounting equation:

$$(1 + d)^{-n} = (1.232)^{-n}$$

Adjusting future cash flows

The effects of inflation may be considered in the same four categories as the cash flows for capital investment projects.

Investment outflows Cash requirements for the initial investment may need to be adjusted if costs are not specified in a fixed-price contract and if costs are likely to change over the construction period. This is particularly common with projects that require several years to construct. The investment tax credit is also adjusted if any qualifying costs of the investment increase.

Working capital requirements often increase with the increased volume of nominal dollars. That is, more dollars are required to support the same level of activity. The investment in inventory generally will not change. The initial costs were incurred to procure a given quantity of inventory. Inventory may cost more to replace, but the replacement costs are included in period cash outflows.

For initial investment outlays, then, the inflation adjustment simply requires revising any outlays that are expected to change as a result of increasing costs and adjusting the investment tax credit. Any increases in working capital levels (other than inventory) are scheduled when they are required.

For example, consider the cash flows for Mega Projects Company in Illustration 15–6. Those flows ignored the effects of inflation. Now let's consider the impact of inflation on these flows. Suppose the equipment costs that were originally $100,000 in Year 0 and $150,000 in Year 1 are expected to increase by 8 percent per year (after Year 0). Of the $50,000 in working capital requirements, $40,000 is for cash and accounts receivable which must increase with the rate of inflation. How will an inflation rate of 10 percent per year affect the investment cash outflows?

1. Equipment cost: The Year 0 cost of $100,000 is unaffected. The Year 1 cost of $150,000 is increased by 8 percent, or $12,000, to $162,000 (that is, $8\% \times \$150,000 = \$12,000$).

2. Investment tax credit: The allowance in Year 1 is increased by 8 percent, or $1,200, to $16,200.

3. The initial cash outflow for working capital for noninventory items remains $40,000. In Year 1, however, working capital must be increased to $44,000 to keep up with the increased flow of nominal dollars (that is $40,000 $\times$ 1.10). Therefore, in Year 1 there will be a $4,000 cash outflow representing the additional commitment to working capital required by inflation.

In Year 2, an additional $4,400 will need to be added to working capital (that is, $44,000 \times 10\% = \$4,400$). In Year 3, working capital will need to be increased by $4,840; and in Year 4, the increase will be $5,324. There is no increase at the end of Year 5 because that is the end of the project's life and the working capital for noninventory items is returned at that time.

Net operating inflows   The inflows for each year are adjusted by multiplying the original amounts by $(1 + i)^n$. This restates the original cash inflow to the nominal dollars to be received in Year n. A similar computation is made for noninventory operating cash outflows.

Inventory complicates the matter somewhat because it is purchased in the year before it is sold. Thus, this year's cash outflow for inventory is for part of next year's cost of goods sold. Assuming FIFO inventory flows, this year's tax deduction for direct materials costs is based on last year's purchase of materials inventory.

Illustration 15–7 shows the adjustment from converting the no-inflation cash flows in Illustration 15–7 to the nominal flows. The net nominal flows are entered into the appropriate columns of the cash flow schedule in place of the original unadjusted cash flows.

Illustration 15–7　　　　**Inflation adjusted operating flows**

	Years *(n)*				
	1	**2**	**3**	**4**	**5**
Cash inflows from revenues[a]	$218,350	$240,185	$ 264,204	$ 290,624	$ 319,686
Cash outflows:					
Noninventory[b]	(88,350)	(97,185)	(106,904)	(117,594)	(129,353)
Inventory[c]	(11,000)	(12,100)	(13,310)	(14,641)	–0–
Net cash flows before taxes	119,000	130,900	143,990	158,389	190,333
Income taxes on cash flows at 45%[d]	(54,000)	(59,400)	(65,340)	(71,874)	(79,061)
Cash flows from operations	$ 65,000	$ 71,500	$ 78,650	$ 86,515	$ 111,272

Additional computations:

[a] $198,500 \times (1.10)^n$, $n = 1, \ldots, 5$.

[b] $[(\$62,342 - \$10,000) + 18,200 + 6,076 + 3,700] \times (1.10)^n = \$80,318 \times (1.10)^n$, $n = 1, \ldots, 5$.

[c] Inventory of $10,000 required for Year 1 was acquired as part of the Year 0 investment outflows. The cash outflows required to replace the inventory in Years 1 to 4 is $10,000 \times (1.10)^n$, $n = 1, \ldots, 4$.

[d] Taxes (assuming FIFO direct materials inventory) $= .45 \times$ (Revenues in Year n − Noninventory costs in Year n − Inventory purchases in Year $n - 1$)

Year 1: $.45 \times (\$218,350 - 88,350 - 10,000) = \$54,000$
　　2: $.45 \times (\$240,185 - 97,185 - 11,000) = \$59,400$
　　3: $.45 \times (\$264,204 - 106,904 - 12,100) = \$65,340$
　　4: $.45 \times (\$290,624 - 117,594 - 13,310) = \$71,874$
　　5: $.45 \times (\$319,686 - 129,353 - 14,641) = \$79,061$

Tax shield　Depreciation is based on the original cost of an asset. Hence, the tax shield from depreciation is only changed if the original investment costs change. Under conditions of continuing inflation, the value of the tax shield from depreciation declines relative to the other cash flows from the project. Since the tax shield does not increase with inflation when it is adjusted using a discount rate that recognizes inflation, its net present value decreases.

The tax basis for depreciation of the Mega-Project Company's new asset under inflation is 95 percent of the $262,000 cost, or $248,900. The ACRS tax shield is:

Year	ACRS percent	ACRS deduction	Tax shield[a]
1	15	$ 37,335	$ 16,801
2	22	54,758	24,641
3	21	52,269	23,521
4	21	52,269	23,521
5	21	52,269	23,521
		$248,900	$112,005

[a] Tax shield equals $.45 \times$ ACRS deduction.

Disinvestment flows Under conditions of inflation, disinvestment flows become more complex. The return of working capital will include all nominal cash and accounts receivable committed to the project. Therefore, the periodic cash outflows for working capital are summed and the total listed as a recovery at the end of the project's life.

The working capital returned in Year 5 includes the $40,000 initial outlay plus the outlays in Years 2 through 4 for a total return of $58,564 (which is $40,000 + $4,000 + $4,400 + $4,840 + $5,324). The inventory disposal results in saving the Year 5 costs of that inventory.

The proceeds from disposal of the long-term assets and their tax impact are also included in the disinvestment computation. Any difference between the proceeds on disposal as adjusted for inflation and the tax basis of the property is taxed.

For Mega-Projects Company, we assume that the market for used equipment similar to that used in the project is increasing at the rate of 7 percent per year. As a result, the proceeds from disposal are estimated as:

$$\$105,000 \times (1.07)^5 = \underline{\$147,268}$$

Since the asset has been fully depreciated for tax purposes, this entire amount is a gain, taxable at ordinary rates. The tax liability from the gain is:

$$45\% \times \$147,268 = \underline{\$66,271}$$

This amount is shown as an outflow in Year 5.

Summarizing the cash flows The adjusted cash flows for Mega-Project Company under inflation are summarized in the cash flow schedule in Illustration 15–8 as they were in Illustration 15–6 with no inflation considered. That is, all cash flows are scheduled and summed for each year of the project's life. In this case, however, yearly cash flows represent the amounts expected to be realized under certain inflation conditions.

The cash flows for the project are discounted using the 23.2 percent rate computed earlier, and the present values are shown for each year of the project's life. The net present value of the project is then computed. For this project, the net present value is $59,412.

Capital investment analyses sometimes incorrectly ignore the effect of inflation on cash flows, but increase their discount rate to reflect the changes in market rates of interest. These interest rates include inflationary expectations. On some projects, discounting the unadjusted cash flows with an inflation-adjusted interest rate can yield the opposite answer from what is optimal.

Taking explicit account of inflation in the cash flow analysis and the discount rate directly recognizes the effects of inflation on each project. In addition to the direct effect of inflation on cash flows from revenues and operating costs, the tax shield is worth less under inflation because it is

Illustration 15–8
Cash flow schedule adjusted for inflation with present value computations

	Year					
	0	**1**	**2**	**3**	**4**	**5**
Investment outflows:						
Equipment cost	$(100,000)	$(162,000)				
Investment tax credit	10,000	16,200				
Working capital:						
Noninventory	(40,000)	(4,000)	$ (4,400)	$ (4,840)	$ (5,324)	
Inventory	(10,000)					
Net operating inflows		65,000	71,500	78,650	86,515	$111,272
Tax shield from depreciation		16,801	24,641	23,521	23,521	23,521
Disinvestment:						
Return of working capital[a]						58,564
Proceeds on disposal						147,268
Tax on gain						(66,271)
Total cash flows	(140,000)	(67,999)	91,741	97,331	104,712	274,354
PV factor		.812	.659	.535	.434	.352
Present values[b]	$(140,000)	$ (55,194)	$60,442	$52,050	$ 45,452	$ 96,662

Net present value of project: $59,412

Nominal rate $= (1.12)(1.10) - 1 = .232 = 23.2\%$

[a] $58,564 = sum of cash released from working capital requirements = $40,000 + $4,000 + $4,400 + $4,840 + $5,324.

[b] Cash flow times PV factor does not equal present values because these PV factors are rounded.

based on the uninflated original cost of the asset.[2] Additional working capital requirements are needed to support the increased transaction flow in nominal dollars. Finally, in many real applications, the inflation rates for a specific project differ from general rates.

Post-audit of capital investment projects

Because capital investment projects are so important, companies commonly compare the cash flows that are actually realized from a project with the estimated flows in the original capital investment proposal. In that way, they hope to learn if the estimation process can be improved.

Some projects may improve reported accounting profits in the short run, but result in suboptimal net present values. When this occurs, it is necessary to identify the reasons for choosing a project that improves accounting profits

___

[2] The failure to index the depreciation tax shield to inflation has been criticized as creating disincentives to invest. For a summary of the issues, see M. Maher and T. Nantell, "The Tax Effects of Inflation: Depreciation, Debt, and Miller's Equilibrium Tax Rates," *Journal of Accounting Research* (Spring 1983).

rather than net present value. There may be rational explanations for such decisions, but management should critically evaluate those reasons.

A capital investment control program must consider more than initial project estimates. It must also determine if the capital investment decision-making process is operating well.

Summary

Capital investment planning involves a number of managerial and financial considerations. The accountant's role is to determine the amount and timing of relevant cash flows from the project. These cash flows are discounted back to the present to determine if the proposed project meets the established hurdle rate.

The net present value of a project is computed using the following equation:

$$\text{NPV} = \sum_{n=0}^{N} C_n \times (1 + d)^{-n}$$

where:

> C_n = cash flows at the end of time period n
> d = discount rate
> n = time period when the cash flow occurs
> N = total number of time periods in the project's life

The accountant's primary task is to estimate cash flows used in the net present value equation. These cash flows and their effects are:

1. Investment outflows:
    Acquisition cost ($-$).
    Investment tax credit ($+$).
    Working capital commitments ($-$).
2. Periodic operating flows, including:
    Period cash inflows ($+$) and outflows ($-$) before taxes.
    Income tax effect on inflows ($-$) and outflows ($+$).
3. Depreciation tax shield ($+$).
4. Disinvestment flows:
    Salvage value of long-term assets (usually $+$ unless there are disposal costs).
    Cash freed from working capital commitments ($+$).
    Investment tax credit recapture ($-$).
    Tax consequences of gain or loss on disposal ($-$ or $+$, respectively).
    Severance or relocation payments to employees, restoration costs, and the like (usually $-$).

Income taxes are an extremely important consideration, particularly due to regulations designed to encourage investment. The accountant may be the only analyst on the management team who understands the income tax effects. Improper treatment of tax effects may lead to suboptimal decisions.

Under conditions of inflation, the discount rate is usually adjusted to compensate for changes in price levels. The changes in cash flows that stem from inflation may also be included explicitly in the cash flow analysis.

Terms and concepts

The following terms and concepts should be familiar to you after reading this chapter.

Accelerated Cost Recovery System (ACRS)	Nominal discount rate
	Nominal dollars
Acquisition cost	Present value
Discount rate	Real return
Disinvestment flows	Tax credit recapture
Hurdle rate	Tax shield
Investment tax credit	Time value of money
Net present value	Working capital

Self-study problem

Melwood Corporation is considering the purchase of a small computer to automate its accounting and word processing systems. Management has been considering several alternative systems including a model labeled the P-25. The supplier of the P-25 has submitted a quote to the company of $7,500 for the equipment plus $2,400 for software. The equipment qualifies for the three-year ACRS tax treatment and the 6 percent investment tax credit. The software may be written off immediately for tax purposes. The company expects to use the new machine for four years and to use straight-line depreciation for financial reporting purposes. The market for used computer systems is such that Melwood would realize $1,000 for the equipment at the end of the four years. The software would have no salvage value at that time.

Melwood management believes that introduction of the computer system will enable the company to dispose of its existing accounting equipment. The existing equipment is fully depreciated for tax purposes and can be sold for an estimated $100.

Although the new system will not enable Melwood to reduce its work force, management believes that it will realize improvements in operations and benefits from the computer system that will be worth $8,000 per year before tax. Training costs of $6,000 are expected before the machine is installed so that employees can use the new machine. The training costs are immediately deductible for tax purposes.

Melwood uses a 15 percent discount rate for this investment and has a marginal income tax rate of 45 percent.

Required:
a. Prepare the schedule showing the relevant cash flows for the project.
b. Indicate whether the equipment meets Melwood's hurdle rate.

Solution to self-study problem

a.

MELWOOD CORPORATION

	Year				
	0	1	2	3	4
Investment:					
Equipment	$ (7,500)				
Tax credit at 6%	450				
Software ($2,400 × 55%)	(1,320)				
Old equipment ($100 × 55%)	55				
Training costs ($6,000 × 55%)	(3,300)				
Annual operating flows:					
($8,000 × 55%)		$4,400	$4,400	$4,400	$4,400
Tax shield[a]		819	1,244	1,211	
Disinvestment ($1,000 × 55%)					550
Cash flows	(11,615)	5,219	5,644	5,611	4,950
Discount factors at 15%		.870	.756	.658	.572
Present values	$(11,615)	$4,538	$4,268	$3,689	$2,830
Net present value	$ 3,710				

Additional computations:

[a] Tax shield:

Year	ACRS percent	Depreci- ation	Tax shield
1	25	$1,819	$ 819
2	38	2,764	1,244
3	37	2,692	1,211
		$7,275	$3,274

$7,275 = $7,500 − [1/2 × ($450)].

b.   With a positive net present cash flows of $3,710, the equipment meets the hurdle rate. The cost savings justify purchase of the equipment.

Appendix A: Computing net present values for constant cash flows

When periodic cash flows are expected to be equal over a period of time, a short-cut method may be used to compute the net present value of those cash flows. A series of level periodic payments is referred to as an annuity. The *present value of an annuity* may be obtained using the equation:

$$\text{Present value} = C_n \times \frac{1 - (1 + d)^{-n}}{d}$$

where:

d = the discount rate

n = the number of periods over which the periodic payment (C) will be received

For example, the present value of a series of six payments of $40,000 each at a discount rate of 25 percent is:

$$PV = \$40,000 \times \frac{1 - (1 + .25)^{-6}}{.25}$$
$$= \$40,000 \times 2.951424$$
$$= \$118,057$$

This amount may also be computed the long way by taking the present value of each year's cash flow as follows:

Year	Cash flow	PV factor	Present value
1	$40,000	.800	$ 32,000
2	40,000	.640	25,600
3	40,000	.512	20,480
4	40,000	.410	16,384
5	40,000	.328	13,107
6	40,000	.262	10,486
		2.952	$118,057

The sum of the present value factors for the six periods is the same within rounding as the computed factor for the six-year annuity. The present values computed under either method are the same. As with other present value calculations, the use of a calculator will be more efficient and will give more accurate answers than will use of the tables. A set of tables is given in Appendix B to this chapter.

Appendix B: Present value tables

The present values of $1 shown in Illustration 15–9 gives the present value of an amount received n periods in the future. It is computed using the equation $(1 + d)^{-n}$ as discussed in the chapter.

For example, to find the present value of $20,000 received 11 years from now at a discount of 16 percent, look over the 11-year row to the 16 percent column and find the relevant factor, .195. Multiply the $20,000 by this factor to obtain the present value of $3,900.

If you perform this same computation with a calculator, you will obtain the somewhat more precise answer of $3,908. The difference is due to rounding.

The present value of an annuity is the value of a series of equal periodic payments discounted at a stated rate. Illustration 15–10 gives a set of factors for present values of an annuity.

For example, to find the present value of a series of nine annual payments of $5,000 each at a discount rate of 18 percent, look across the nine-year row to the 18 percent column and find the factor, 4.303. Multiply the $5,000 times 4.303 to obtain the present value of those future payments, $21,515.

Illustration 15–11 provides the net present values for the text problems that are based on the recognition of inflation in the cash flow analysis.

Illustration 15–9 **Present value of $1**

Year	8%	10%	12%	14%	15%	16%	18%	20%	22%	24%
1	.926	.909	.893	.877	.870	.862	.847	.833	.820	.806
2	.857	.826	.797	.769	.756	.743	.718	.694	.672	.650
3	.794	.751	.712	.675	.658	.641	.609	.579	.551	.524
4	.735	.683	.636	.592	.572	.552	.516	.482	.451	.423
5	.681	.621	.567	.519	.497	.476	.437	.402	.370	.341
6	.630	.564	.507	.456	.432	.410	.370	.335	.303	.275
7	.583	.513	.452	.400	.376	.354	.314	.279	.249	.222
8	.540	.467	.404	.351	.327	.305	.266	.233	.204	.179
9	.500	.424	.361	.308	.284	.263	.225	.194	.167	.144
10	.463	.386	.322	.270	.247	.227	.191	.162	.137	.116
11	.429	.350	.287	.237	.215	.195	.162	.135	.112	.094
12	.397	.319	.257	.208	.187	.168	.137	.112	.092	.076
13	.368	.290	.229	.182	.163	.145	.116	.093	.075	.061
14	.340	.263	.205	.160	.141	.125	.099	.078	.062	.049
15	.315	.239	.183	.140	.123	.108	.084	.065	.051	.040

Year	25%	26%	28%	30%	32%	34%	35%	36%	38%	40%
1	.800	.794	.781	.769	.758	.746	.741	.735	.725	.714
2	.640	.630	.610	.592	.574	.557	.549	.541	.525	.510
3	.512	.500	.477	.455	.435	.416	.406	.398	.381	.364
4	.410	.397	.373	.350	.329	.310	.301	.292	.276	.260
5	.328	.315	.291	.269	.250	.231	.223	.215	.200	.186
6	.262	.250	.227	.207	.189	.173	.165	.158	.145	.133
7	.210	.198	.178	.159	.143	.129	.122	.116	.105	.095
8	.168	.157	.139	.123	.108	.096	.091	.085	.076	.068
9	.134	.125	.108	.094	.082	.072	.067	.063	.055	.048
10	.107	.099	.085	.073	.062	.054	.050	.046	.040	.035
11	.086	.079	.066	.056	.047	.040	.037	.034	.029	.025
12	.069	.062	.052	.043	.036	.030	.027	.025	.021	.018
13	.055	.050	.040	.033	.027	.022	.020	.018	.015	.013
14	.044	.039	.032	.025	.021	.017	.015	.014	.011	.009
15	.035	.031	.025	.020	.016	.012	.011	.010	.008	.007

Illustration 15–10

Present value of an annuity

Year	8%	10%	12%	14%	15%	16%	18%	20%	22%	24%
1	.926	.909	.893	.877	.870	.862	.847	.833	.820	.806
2	1.783	1.736	1.690	1.647	1.626	1.605	1.566	1.528	1.492	1.457
3	2.577	2.487	2.402	2.322	2.283	2.246	2.174	2.106	2.042	1.981
4	3.312	3.170	3.037	2.914	2.855	2.798	2.690	2.589	2.494	2.404
5	3.993	3.791	3.605	3.433	3.352	3.274	3.127	2.991	2.864	2.745
6	4.623	4.355	4.111	3.889	3.784	3.685	3.498	3.326	3.167	3.020
7	5.206	4.868	4.564	4.288	4.160	4.039	3.812	3.605	3.416	3.242
8	5.747	5.335	4.968	4.639	4.487	4.344	4.078	3.837	3.619	3.421
9	6.247	5.759	5.328	4.946	4.772	4.607	4.303	4.031	3.786	3.566
10	6.710	6.145	5.650	5.216	5.019	4.833	4.494	4.192	3.923	3.682
11	7.139	6.495	5.938	5.453	5.234	5.029	4.656	4.327	4.035	3.776
12	7.536	6.814	6.194	5.660	5.421	5.197	4.793	4.439	4.127	3.851
13	7.904	7.103	6.424	5.842	5.583	5.342	4.910	4.533	4.203	3.912
14	8.244	7.367	6.628	6.002	5.724	5.468	5.008	4.611	4.265	3.962
15	8.559	7.606	6.811	6.142	5.847	5.575	5.092	4.675	4.315	4.001

Year	25%	26%	28%	30%	32%	34%	35%	36%	38%	40%
1	.800	.794	.781	.769	.758	.746	.741	.735	.725	.714
2	1.440	1.424	1.392	1.361	1.331	1.303	1.289	1.276	1.250	1.224
3	1.952	1.923	1.868	1.816	1.766	1.719	1.696	1.673	1.630	1.589
4	2.362	2.320	2.241	2.166	2.096	2.029	1.997	1.966	1.906	1.849
5	2.689	2.635	2.532	2.436	2.345	2.260	2.220	2.181	2.106	2.035
6	2.951	2.885	2.759	2.643	2.534	2.433	2.385	2.339	2.251	2.168
7	3.161	3.083	2.937	2.802	2.677	2.562	2.508	2.455	2.355	2.263
8	3.329	3.241	3.076	2.925	2.786	2.658	2.598	2.540	2.432	2.331
9	3.463	3.366	3.184	3.019	2.868	2.730	2.665	2.603	2.487	2.379
10	3.571	3.465	3.269	3.092	2.930	2.784	2.715	2.649	2.527	2.414
11	3.656	3.543	3.335	3.147	2.978	2.824	2.752	2.683	2.555	2.438
12	3.725	3.606	3.387	3.190	3.013	2.853	2.779	2.708	2.576	2.456
13	3.780	3.656	3.427	3.223	3.040	2.876	2.799	2.727	2.592	2.469
14	3.824	3.695	3.459	3.249	3.061	2.892	2.814	2.740	2.603	2.478
15	3.859	3.726	3.483	3.268	3.076	2.905	2.825	2.750	2.611	2.484

Illustration 15–11

Present value tables for inflation problems

Year	18.80%	20.96%	23.20%	26.50%	28.80%	31.76%	39.08%
1	.842	.827	.812	.791	.776	.759	.719
2	.709	.683	.659	.625	.603	.576	.517
3	.596	.565	.535	.494	.468	.437	.372
4	.502	.467	.434	.391	.363	.332	.267
5	.423	.386	.352	.309	.282	.252	.192
6	.356	.319	.286	.244	.219	.191	.138
7	.299	.264	.232	.193	.170	.145	.099
8	.252	.218	.188	.153	.132	.110	.071
9	.212	.180	.153	.121	.103	.084	.051
10	.179	.149	.124	.095	.080	.063	.037
11	.150	.123	.101	.075	.062	.048	.027
12	.127	.102	.082	.060	.048	.037	.019
13	.107	.084	.066	.047	.037	.028	.014
14	.090	.070	.054	.037	.029	.021	.010
15	.075	.058	.044	.029	.022	.016	.008

Questions

15–1. What are the two most important factors (from an accounting standpoint) in the capital investment decision?

15–2. What is meant by the time value of money?

15–3. Given two projects with equal cash flows but different timings, how can we determine which (if either) project should be selected for investment (assuming no constraints on investment funds)?

15–4. What are the four types of cash flows related to a capital investment and why do we consider them separately?

15–5. For computing the investment tax credit, you conclude that either a three- or five-year life for the asset is appropriate, but there is no way to determine which life will occur. Which life would you use for the computation? Why?

15–6. Fatigue Corporation has a division that is operating at a $200,000 cash loss per year. The company cannot dispose of the division due to certain contractual arrangements it has made that require continued operation of the division. However, Fatigue has just received a proposal to invest in some new equipment for the division. If the equipment is purchased, the division will operate at a $40,000 cash loss per year. Is there any reason to consider acquisition of the equipment? Why or why not?

15–7. How do tax policies provide an incentive for capital investment?

15–8. Is depreciation included in the computation of net present values? Explain.

15–9. "Every project should bear its fair share of all of the costs of the company. To do otherwise would make present operations subsidize new projects." Comment.

15–10. Regardless of depreciation methods used, the total tax deduction for depreciation is the same. Why then would one be concerned about depreciation method for capital investment analysis?

15–11. What is the relationship between the desired real return to capital, the inflation rate, and the rate used to discount project cash flows under conditions of inflation?

15–12. Why might inflation be a disincentive to investment? Your response should be in terms of the impact of inflation on cash flows (that is, on the tax aspects of the question).

15–13. Describe the two ways of handling the liquidation of inventories at the end of a project's life?

15–14. Why would the investment in working capital increase over a project life under conditions of inflation while the investment in inventories would not?

Exercises

15–15. Compute net present values

A company is considering investment in a project that is expected to return the following cash flows:

Year	Net cash flow
1	$25,000
2	32,000
3	40,000
4	40,000
5	50,000
6	20,000

This schedule includes all cash flows from the project. The project will require an immediate cash outlay of $130,000.

Required:

a. What is the net present value of the project if the appropriate discount rate is 20 percent?

b. What is the net present value of the project if the appropriate discount rate is 12 percent?

15–16. Determine present value of investment outflows

A company is considering investing in a project that will require outlays as follows:

Year	Item	Amount
0	Engineering studies	$ 50,000
1	Project initiation (includes a $60,000 deposit to ensure performance)	175,000
2	Project construction	850,000
	Working capital	80,000
3	Return of deposits paid in Year 1	(60,000)

The 10 percent investment tax credit applies to all outlays except the working capital and the $60,000 of deposits that were paid out as part of project initiation outlays in Year 1. These performance deposits are returned in Year 3 after the construction contract terms have been fulfilled. The company has sufficient income from other sources to offset the investment tax credit.

Required:

Compute the net present value of these cash outlays if the appropriate discount rate is 18 percent.

15–17. Compute present value of tax shield—straight-line method

A company plans to acquire an asset at a cost of $210,000. The asset qualifies for a 10 percent investment tax credit. The asset will have a ten-year life and no estimated salvage value. Management has decided that the straight-line method will be used for tax depreciation for five years. A 22 percent discount rate is appropriate for this asset, and the company's tax rate is 40 percent.

Required:

Compute the present value of the tax shield.

15–18. Compute present value of tax shield—accelerated cost recovery system

Using the data in Exercise 15–17, compute the present value of the tax shield from depreciation assuming the asset qualifies for the three-year ACRS class and a six percent investment tax credit.

15–19. Compute present value of tax shield—accelerated cost recovery system

Using the data in Exercise 15–17, compute the present value of the tax shield from depreciation assuming the asset qualifies for the three-year ACRS class and a six percent investment tax credit.

15–20. Compute present value of cash flows with inflation considerations

A company has concluded that its cost of capital is 8 percent in real terms. The company is considering an investment in a project that will yield annual operating cash flows (before taxes) of $26,000 per year for seven years. At disinvestment, the costs of disposal will equal any liquidation value of the project. No additional working capital is required for the project. The project costs $120,000. It qualifies for treatment under the five-year ACRS and the 10 percent investment tax credit. The company's marginal tax rate is 40 percent.

Required:	a. Assuming no inflation, what is the net present value of this project? b. If inflation is expected to continue at a 10 percent rate, what is the present value of the project?
15–21. Present value of depreciation tax shield under inflation	Using the data in Exercise 15–17 and using a five-year ACRS life of the asset, what is the present value of the tax shield if the inflation rate is 8 percent? What is the present value of the tax shield if the inflation rate is 14 percent?

Problems and cases

15–22. Compute net present value

Essen Manufacturing Company is evaluating a proposal to purchase a new drill press as a replacement for a less efficient machine presently in use. The cost of the equipment, including delivery and installation, is $175,000. If the equipment is purchased, Essen will incur costs of $5,000 to remove the present equipment and revamp its service facilities. The full purchase price qualifies for the investment tax credit of 10 percent. Depreciation for tax purposes may be allowed over a five-year ACRS life. The present equipment has a book value of $100,000 and a remaining useful life of 10 years. It is being depreciated for book and tax purposes using the straight-line method over its actual life. However, the present equipment could be sold for only $40,000.

Management has provided you with the following comparative manufacturing cost data:

	Present equipment	New equipment
Annual capacity	400,000 units	500,000 units
Annual costs:		
Labor	$30,000	$25,000
Depreciation	10,000	17,500
Other (all cash)	48,000	20,000
Total annual costs	$88,000	$62,500

Both pieces of equipment are expected to have no salvage value at the end of 10 years. No changes in working capital are required with the purchase of the new equipment. The sales force does not expect any changes in volume of sales over the next 10 years. The company's cost of capital is 15 percent, and it marginal tax rate is 45 percent.

Required:

Prepare a schedule showing the net present value of the project.

(CPA adapted)

15–23. Impact of inflation on net present values

Management of Essen Manufacturing Company (Problem 15–22) has received your report on the estimated net present value of the new equipment. However, management is disturbed about their economist's report which indicates an expected inflation rate of 12 percent over the next 10 years.

Required:

Prepare a report indicating how this expectation would affect your computed net present values. Show supporting computations in good form.

15–24. Assess net present value of alternative projects

MacDonald & Company operates a diversified company with several operating divisions. Most of the divisions are profitable. However, Division M has consistently shown losses. Management is considering a proposal to purchase some new equipment for Division M which is designed to reduce labor and other operating costs. The division cannot be eliminated due to contractual agreements.

The latest division income statement appears as follows:

Revenues		$ 4,500
Costs:		
Direct materials	$1,250	
Direct labor	1,400	
Factory overhead:		
Indirect materials	200	
Indirect labor	350	
Utilities, taxes, etc.	600	
Depreciation	890	
Other	120	
Selling costs	450	
Administrative costs	380	
Total costs		5,640
Division contribution		$(1,140)

The costs are expected to continue in the future unless new equipment is purchased.

With the new equipment, direct labor is expected to be reduced by 40 percent. Depreciation will increase to $1,100 per year, but utilities are expected to decrease by $120. Other costs are expected to be reduced by $70 per year. The equipment will cost $10,000 and will qualify for the 10 percent investment tax credit. Salvage value of the equipment at the end of its seven-year useful life is expected to amount to $2,000. Tax depreciation would be available under the five-year ACRS life. Working capital can be permanently reduced by $110 if the new equipment is purchased.

Required:

If the company's cost of capital is 12 percent and its marginal tax rate is 40 percent, determine whether the new equipment should be purchased. Show supporting computations.

15–25. Compute present values

You are considering the purchase of a new car. If you purchase a car with a standard gasoline engine, you expect an average of 22 miles per gallon. If you purchase a diesel engine, you expect an average of 30 miles per gallon. Gasoline costs $1.30 per gallon, and diesel fuel costs $1.25 per gallon. The diesel engine will cost $500 more than the standard gasoline engine. However, when you trade the car in at the end of four years, it will be worth $150 more if it is equipped with a diesel engine.

Diesel engines do not require the $75 tune-up every 15,000 miles that the gasoline engines require. However, a diesel engine can involve other maintenance costs amounting to approximately $200 per year.

Your cost of capital is 14 percent.

Required:

Would you purchase the diesel or gasoline engine under each of the following independent situations (show supporting computations):

a. The car is strictly for personal use, and you plan to drive 10,000 miles per year.

b. The car is strictly for personal use, and you plan to drive 20,000 miles per year.

c. You are buying a fleet of cars for your company, thus all of the expenses are tax deductible. You can use a three-year ACRS life and recognize any gains or losses on disposal. The cars will be driven approximately 20,000 miles per year each. The marginal tax rate is 45 percent. Your company's after-tax cost of capital is 14 percent. The six percent tax credit applies.

15-26. Estimate maximum purchase price on subcontract*

Company Z has contracted to supply a governmental agency with 50,000 units of a product each year for the next five years. A certain component of this product can be either manufactured by Company Z or purchased from the X Corporation, which has indicated a willingness to enter into a subcontract for 50,000 units of the component each year for five years if the price offered is satisfactory. These alternative methods of procurement are regarded as equally dependable.

If Company Z decides to manufacture the component, it expects the following to occur:

1. A special-purpose machine costing $110,000 will have to be purchased. No other equipment or working capital will be required.
2. For tax purposes, this machine will be assumed to have a five-year ACRS life. Estimated salvage value at the end of five years is $10,000.
3. The investment tax credit will be 10 percent.
4. The manufacturing operation will require 1,000 feet of productive floor space. This space is available in a building owned by Company Z and will not be needed for any other purpose in the foreseeable future. The costs of maintaining this building (including repairs, utilities, taxes, and depreciation) amount to $2 per square foot of productive floor space per year.
5. Variable manufacturing costs—materials, direct labor, and so forth—are estimated to be 50 cents a unit.
6. Fixed factory costs other than those mentioned in 1 through 4—such as supervision and so forth—are estimated at $20,000 a year.
7. Income taxes are computed at the rate of 45 percent of taxable income or taxable savings.
8. The policy of Company Z is to subcontract if and only if the costs saved by manufacturing instead of subcontracting provide less than a 10 percent annual return on investment. For this purpose, return on investment is defined as the relationship between cost saving, after provision for income taxes, and the capital investment that will have to be made to permit Company Z to manufacture the component in its own plant.

Required:

What is the maximum price per unit that Company Z should be willing to offer to the X Corporation? Make explicit any assumptions that you believe to be necessary in solving the problem.

15-27. Compute net present value for manufacturing enterprise

Mariposa Recreational Products Corporation produces roller skates for street use. As a result of recent promotion of the sport, the company is considering expanding its present facilities to increase production by 35,000 units per year. The expansion will require an immediate outlay of $720,000 for the specialized equipment required for skate assembly. The company estimates the useful life of the project will be seven years. The company uses straight-line depreciation for book purposes, but will

---

* From Gordon Shillinglaw, Myron J. Gordon, and Joshua Ronen, *Accounting: A Management Approach* (Homewood, Ill.: Richard D. Irwin, 1979).

use a five-year ACRS schedule for tax purposes. Once the equipment is installed, it has no salvage value. The equipment will qualify for the investment tax credit.

The project requires an estimated cash and accounts receivable balance of approximately $80,000 which will be liquidated at the end of the project life. The project will also require $37,000 in working inventory and safety stock. These inventories will be liquidated at the end of last year of the project life.

The assembled skates sell for $29 wholesale per set. In addition to the costs of the unassembled parts, there is a cost of $6.50 per set for assembly labor, power, and other variable overhead. All variable overhead is included in the $6.50 charge, and all such variable overhead requires current cash outlays.

The fixed overhead of the factory and equipment amounts to $662,857 including the depreciation on the new equipment. Except for the equipment depreciation, all of these fixed overhead items require current cash outlays. All fixed overhead is included in this amount.

The company cost of capital is 16 percent, and this rate is applicable for investment evaluation purposes as well as representative of the cost of capital associated with the inventory. The company estimates that the tax rate applicable to the project income is 40 percent.

Required:

A schedule showing the net present value for the project with supporting details.

15–28. Compute present values

Hagerstown Glass Company is considering the purchase of some more efficient equipment for the manufacture of its quality line of glass tableware. Existing equipment with an original cost of $100,000 will be scrapped, and a salvage value of $8,000 is expected. The current book value of the existing equipment is $10,000. It is fully depreciated for tax purposes. The new equipment will cost $500,000. In addition, installation costs will amount to $40,000. While the equipment cost will qualify for the investment tax credit, the installation costs will not. Assume that the appropriate tax credit rate is 10 percent. The asset and installation costs would be depreciated on the five-year ACRS schedule.

The equipment will have a life of five years. At the end of its life, it will have no salvage value. The following data compare operations using the new equipment with present operations:

	New equipment	Old equipment
Annual capacity (units)	11,000	10,000
Price per unit	$ 55	$ 55
Variable costs per unit	20	35
Annual fixed costs	150,000	40,000
Depreciation (included in the annual fixed costs amount)	120,000	6,000

Demand is such that up to 15,000 units could be sold per year.

Required:

Determine the net present value of the project if the cost of capital is 25 percent and the marginal tax rate is 40 percent.

15–29. Present value computations

Wyle Company is considering a proposal to acquire new manufacturing equipment. The new equipment has the same capacity as the current equipment but will provide operating efficiencies in direct and indirect labor, direct material usage, indirect supplies, and power. Consequently, the savings in operating costs are estimated at $150,000 annually.

The new equipment will cost $300,000. The equipment dealer is certain that the equipment will be operational during the second quarter of the year it is installed. Therefore, 60 percent of the estimated annual savings can be obtained in the first year. Wyle will incur a one-time cost of $30,000 to transfer the production activities from the old equipment to the new equipment. No loss of sales will occur, however, because the plant is large enough to install the new equipment without interfering with the operations of the current equipment. The equipment dealer states that most companies use a five-year life when depreciating this equipment.

The current equipment has been fully depreciated and is carried in the accounts at zero book value. Management has reviewed the condition of the current equipment and has concluded that it can be used an additional five years. Wyle Company would receive $5,000 net of removal costs if it elected to buy the new equipment and dispose of its current equipment at this time.

Wyle currently leases its manufacturing plant. The annual lease payments are $60,000. The lease, which will have five years remaining when the equipment installation would begin, is not renewable. Wyle Company would be required to remove any equipment in the plant at the end of the lease. The cost of equipment removal is expected to equal the salvage value of either the old or new equipment at the time of removal.

The asset must be depreciated for tax purposes under the five-year ACRS schedule. Any gain or loss on disposal is taxed at ordinary income tax rates.

The company is subject to a 40 percent income tax rate and requires an after-tax return of at least 12 percent on any investment. The 10 percent tax credit applies.

Required:

a. Calculate the differential after-tax cash flows for Wyle Company's proposal to acquire the new manufacturing equipment.

b. Calculate the net present value of Wyle Company's proposal to acquire the new manufacturing equipment.

(CMA adapted)

15–30. Review and analyze a capital investment proposal

Wisconsin Products Company manufactures several different products. One of the firm's principal products sells for $20 per unit. The sales manager of Wisconsin Products has stated repeatedly that he could sell more units of this product if they were available. To substantiate his claim the sales manager conducted a market research study last year at a cost of $44,000. The study indicated that Wisconsin Products could sell 18,000 units of this product annually for the next five years.

The equipment currently in use has the capacity to produce 11,000 units annually. The variable production costs are $9 per unit. The equipment has a value for tax purposes of $60,000 and a remaining useful life of five years. The salvage value of the equipment is negligible now and will be zero in five years.

A maximum of 20,000 units could be produced annually on the new machinery which can be purchased. The new equipment costs $300,000 and has an estimated useful life of five years with no salvage value at the end of five years. Wisconsin Product's production manager estimated that the new equipment would provide increased production efficiencies that would reduce the variable production costs to $7 per unit.

Wisconsin Products Company uses straight-line depreciation on all of its equipment for tax purposes. The firm is subject to a 40 percent tax rate, and its after-tax cost of capital is 15 percent. The 10 percent investment tax credit applies to the new equipment.

The sales manager felt so strongly about the need for additional capacity that he attempted to prepare an economic justification for the equipment although this was not one of his responsibilities. His analysis, presented below and in the next column, disappointed him because it did not justify acquiring the equipment.

Required investment

Purchase price of new equipment		$300,000
Disposal of existing equipment:		
Loss of disposal	$60,000	
Less tax benefit (40%)	24,000	36,000
Cost of market research study		44,000
Total investment		$380,000

Annual returns

Contribution margin from product:	
Using the new equipment [18,000 × ($20 − 7)]	$234,000
Using the existing equipment [11,000 × ($20 − 9)]	121,000
Increase in contribution margin	113,000
Less depreciation	60,000
Increase in before-tax income	53,000
Income tax (40%)	21,200
Increase in income	31,800
Less 15% cost of capital on the additional	
investment required (.15 × $380,000)	57,000
Net annual return of proposed investment	
in new equipment	$ (25,200)

Required:

The controller of Wisconsin Product Company plans to prepare a discounted cash flow analysis for this investment proposal. The controller has asked you to prepare corrected calculations of—

a. The required investment in new equipment.
b. The recurring annual cash flows.

Explain the treatment of each item of your corrected calculations that is treated differently from the original analysis prepared by the sales manager.

(CMA adapted)

15–31. Capital investment analysis under inflation

Management of Excello Corporation is considering the purchase of energy saving equipment. The equipment has an invoice cost of $250,000. If purchased, the equipment would qualify for a special energy credit of 10 percent as well as for the regular investment tax credit. The energy credit reduces the depreciable base of the asset by five percent and is taken in the year of equipment acquisition.

The equipment has an expected useful life of seven years, at which time it will have a salvage value of $40,000. The equipment qualifies for five-year ACRS tax treatment. For income statement purposes, the company will depreciate the equipment on the straight-line basis over its useful life.

Present energy costs for the activities related to this equipment are $120,000 per year before taxes. The equipment will save 60 percent of these costs.

Working capital will be reduced by an estimated 5 percent of the initial year's after-tax cash energy cost savings. The working capital reduction will increase with inflation in future years until Year 7 when it is assumed that the company will have to restore the entire working capital savings.

The company's marginal tax rate is 40 percent, and its nominal cost of capital is 25 percent.

Required:

The net present value of the project if the expected inflation rate is 10 percent per year.

15–32. Estimate purchase price for a capital investment project

Transcontinental Oil Company is considering the purchase of some producing oil properties from Pan American Exploration Corporation. The properties have been producing for some time and are now at the point where further production is not worthwhile without the application of enhanced recovery equipment. Even with the enhanced recovery equipment, it is unlikely that the properties would be economically productive for more than six years.

The properties have to be acquired and paid for at the end of Year 0. If Transcontinental Oil Company decides to buy the properties, it will enter into a contract at date 0 to purchase the enhanced recovery equipment. However, the equipment cannot be installed until the end of Year 1. At that time, the contract calls for a payment of $1,450,000. For tax purposes, 40 percent of the Year 1 outlay could be deducted at the end of Year 1. The remaining 60 percent would have to be amortized on a units of production basis over the production from the properties in Years 2 through 6. The equipment purchase contract also has a provision which calls for the manufacturer of the enhanced recovery equipment to work over the wells at the end of Year 4. The contract specifies a payment of $1,500,000 to be made at that time for this service. All of the Year 4 payment would be deductible for tax purposes in Year 4.

The total acquisition cost for the properties has not yet been determined. For tax purposes, at least $825,000 of the property's value would have to be amortized over the total expected production of the properties. The balance, if any, would be immediately deductible according to the latest tax regulations. A special 10 percent investment tax credit would apply to all costs that are not immediately deductible. This tax credit would not reduce the depreciable base. Production expectations, per barrel prices of crude oil, and variable costs of production are as follows:

| | | Per barrel | |
Year	Expected production (thousand barrels)	Price	Variable costs
1	40	$35	$7
2	70	35	7
3	60	35	7
4	50	35	7
5	40	35	7
6	30	35	7

Both the per barrel prices of crude oil and variable costs are based on date 0 prices. It is expected that the value of the properties at the end of Year 6 will be zero due to environmental restoration requirements.

The tax rate for the company is 45 percent.

Required:

a. Ignoring the effects of inflation and assuming a desired after-tax rate of return of 10 percent, determine the maximum amount that Pan American could pay for Transcontinental.

b. If the after-tax rate of return is to be in *real* terms and the expected inflation rate is 6 percent per year, determine the maximum amount that could be paid by Pan American.

15–33. Capital investment analysis under inflation

Catix Corporation is a divisionalized company, and each division has the authority to make capital expenditures up to $200,000 without approval of the corporate headquarters. The corporate controller has determined that the cost of capital for Catix Corporation is 12 percent. This rate does not include an allowance for inflation, which is expected to occur at an average rate of 8 percent each year. Catix pays income taxes at the rate of 40 percent.

The Electronics Division of Catix is considering the purchase of an automated assembly and soldering machine for use in the manufacture of its printed circuit boards. The machine would be placed in service in early 1984. The divisional controller estimates that if the machine is purchased, two positions will be eliminated yielding a cost savings for wages and employee benefits. However, the machine would require additional supplies and more power would be required to operate the machine. The cost savings and additional costs in current 1983 prices are as follows:

Wages and employee benefits of the two positions eliminated ($25,000 each)	$50,000
Cost of additional supplies	3,000
Cost of additional power	10,000

The new machine would be purchased and installed at the end of 1983 at a net cost of $80,000. If purchased, the machine would be depreciated using a five-year ACRS life. The machine will become technologically obsolete in eight years and will have no salvage value at that time.

The Electronics Division compensates for inflation in capital expenditure analyses by adjusting the expected cash flows by an estimated price level index. The adjusted after-tax cash flows are then discounted using the appropriate discount rate.

The Plastics Division of Catix compensates for inflation in capital expenditure analyses by adding the anticipated inflation rate to the cost of capital and then using the inflation adjusted cost of capital to discount the project cash flows. The Plastics Division recently rejected a project with cash flows and economic life similar to those associated with the machine under consideration by the Electronics Division. The Plastics Division's analysis of the rejected project was as follows:

Net pre-tax cost savings	$37,000
Less incremental depreciation expenses	20,000
Increase in taxable income	17,000
Increase in income taxes (40%)	6,800
Increase in after-tax income	10,200
Add back noncash expense (depreciation)	20,000
Net after-tax annual cash inflow (unadjusted for inflation)	$30,200
Present value of net cash inflows using the sum of the cost of capital (12%) and the inflation rate (8%) or a minimum required return of 20%	$77,916
Investment required	(80,000)
Net present value	$ 2,084)

All operating revenues and expenditures occur at the end of the year. No changes are expected for working capital.

Required:

Prepare a schedule showing the expected future cash flows in nominal dollars. Also show the nominal net present value of the project.

(CMA adapted)

16

Capital
Investment
Models

OBJECTIVES

To understand some of the alternative methods for evaluating capital investment
   projects.

To see how capital investment analysis is applied to the decisions about financing
   assets.

When making capital investment decisions, management must consider other
factors besides the amount and timing of the cash flows. It must often make
some adjustment for differing levels of risk among projects. In addition,
management must usually consider a project's impact on divisional performance measures and on externally reported income. And it must choose
among a variety of financing methods. In this chapter, we discuss how management ranks competing projects given all these possible variations. We also
present some investment analysis models that managers use in addition to
the net present value discussed in Chapter 15.

   We now expand the analysis that we started in Chapter 15 and examine
how management actually selects the projects it will undertake. Let's consider
a new set of five investment projects with the net cash flows as indicated
in Illustration 16–1.

Illustration 16–1   **Cash flow schedules for alternative projects (in thousands)**

Year	Project A	B	C	D	E
0	$(425)	$(135)	$ (80)	$(170)	$ (90)
1	25	0	0	60	10
2	50	90	0	60	20
3	75	80	0	60	40
4	100	70	0	60	40
5	150	50	0	60	40
6	300	20	200	60	30
7	380	10	100	60	20
Totals	$ 655	$ 185	$ 220	$ 250	$ 110
Net present value (at 15%)	$ 88	$ 63	$ 44	$ 80	$ 23

Additional computations:

$88 = -\$425 + \$25 \times 1.15^{-1} + \$50 \times 1.15^{-2} + \$75 \times 1.15^{-3} + \$100 \times 1.15^{-4} + \$150 \times 1.15^{-5} + \$300 \times 1.15^{-6} + \$380 \times 1.15^{-7}$

$63 = -\$135 + \$90 \times 1.15^{-2} + \$80 \times 1.15^{-3} + \$70 \times 1.15^{-4} + \$50 \times 1.15^{-5} + \$20 \times 1.15^{-6} + \$10 \times 1.15^{-7}$

etc.

Using a 15 percent discount rate, each project has a positive net present value. Therefore, if funds were available, and if investment in one project did not exclude the possibility of investing in another project, all five projects would be chosen. However, there are often constraints on management's choice of projects.

For example, suppose management only had $450,000 to invest in these projects. Which projects, if any, would it select? Or, suppose that if Project B is selected, then Project C cannot be selected. Which project should then be chosen?

Effect of capital budget constraints

When capital investment opportunities are limited by *budget constraints,* management usually considers the summed net present values of all selected investments rather than the net present value of each investment alone. The existence of budget constraints that limit capital investment opportunities is usually a short-term phenomenon. In the long run, successful companies are usually able to raise funds for projects with positive net present values. Given budget constraints, though, and since all of these projects have positive net present values, they must be ranked to decide which is most desirable.

Net present value index method

The net present value index is often used for ranking purposes. This approach relates the net present value of a project to the dollars invested in it. The index is computed by dividing the net present value of a project by the initial investment. In equation form, we have:

$$\text{Net present value index} = \frac{\text{Project net present value}}{\text{Investment in project}}$$

So, for Project A in Illustration 16–1, the net present value index is:

$$\frac{\$88}{\$425} = \underline{\underline{.21}}$$

The net present value indexes for the other projects are:

$$
\begin{array}{lll}
\text{Project B} & .47 = \$63 \div \$135 \\
\text{Project C} & .55 = \$44 \div \$80 \\
\text{Project D} & .47 = \$80 \div \$170 \\
\text{Project E} & .26 = \$23 \div \$90 \\
\end{array}
$$

For investment choice purposes, projects are ranked by the amount of their net present value index. The greater the index amount, the more desirable the investment.

If it is possible to fund each project in part, rather than acquire the entire project, such as through partnership or joint venture arrangements, then by taking the projects in rank order, the maximum net present value could be obtained. Partial investments are common in real estate and natural resource projects. They are less common in manufacturing or other projects. Hence, the possibility of a partial investment may depend on the nature of the project.

In the example, the $450,000 is apportioned first to Project C, which costs $80,000 and has the greatest net present value index. Next selected are Project D, costing $170,000, and Project B, costing $135,000.

After making these three investments, $65,000 (that is, $450,000 — $80,000 — $135,000 — $170,000) is left for other projects. If we can fund a partial investment, we will invest the remaining $65,000 in Project E and obtain a 72.22 percent (that is, $65,000/$90,000) share in that project.

With this investment strategy, the net present value of the $450,000 investment is $203,611, which is the sum of the present values on Projects B through D plus 72.22 percent of the present value of Project E. No alternative strategy yields a higher net present value.

As a counter example, suppose we were to invest $425,000 in Project A and use the remaining $25,000 to acquire a 31.25 percent (that is, $25,000/$80,000) investment in Project C. The net present value from this combination is:

	Percent acquired	Net present value
Project A	100	$ 88,000
Project C	31.25	13,750 (that is, 31.25% × $44,000)
Total net present value		$101,750

This alternative offers a lower net present value than the one obtained using the present value index ranking method.

Indivisible investments

Of course, it may not be possible to acquire a partial interest in Project E. If the projects cannot be subdivided, their appropriate ranking becomes more complex. It may not be possible to invest the full $450,000. Any funds not invested in these projects would be expected to earn the cost of capital rate and, hence, have no net present value. The optimal solution to the project rank ordering could no longer be based entirely on the net present value index. Rather, we would have to consider the total present value of all selected projects however chosen.[1]

For the data in Illustration 16–1, the optimal ranking is to select Projects B, C, and D, which cost a total of $385,000 (total of $135,000 + $80,000 + $170,000). These three projects provide a combined net present value of

[1] The use of integer programming for this problem has been suggested in Richard H. Pettway, "Integer Programming in Capital Budgeting: A Note On Computations Experience," *Journal of Financial and Quantitative Analysis* (September 1973), pp. 665–72.

$187,000 (which is the sum of $63,000 + $44,000 + $80,000). The uninvested funds of $65,000 (the net of $450,000 − $385,000) will earn a net present value of zero because they are presumed to earn the cost of capital and no more. No other combination of projects costing an aggregate of $450,000 or less will provide a greater net present value for the company when partial investment in projects is not possible. In this example, the ranking is identical to the net present value index ranking, but this will not always be the case.

Mutually exclusive projects

In many cases, projects are **mutually exclusive.** That is, selecting one project precludes selecting another project. When this occurs, the project with the highest net present value is usually chosen. This selection technique is based on the assumption that unlimited capital is available. When investment funds are limited, net present value cannot be the sole basis of choice because selection of one project reduces the capital available for investment in other projects. The opportunity cost of the mutually exclusive project is, in part, the return that could be earned on the excluded project, rather than the cost of capital for the company as a whole.

For example, if Projects B and C from Illustration 16–1 are mutually exclusive and if investment funds are not limited, then the company prefers Project B. Investing in Project B results in a net present value of $63,000, whereas Project C yields a net present value of only $44,000. The critical assumption here is that the company has no better alternatives for the differential funds required for Project B. A comparison of differential investment and differential net present values shows the following:

	Project C	Project B	Differential
Initial cost	$80,000	$135,000	$55,000
Net present value	$44,000	$ 63,000	$19,000

The differential investment in Project B yields a differential net present value of $19,000. Now if the differential $55,000 could be invested in another project, for example, a new Project F, with a net present value greater than $19,000, the company would be better off selecting both Project C and the new Project F.

For example, if Project F costs $55,000 and has a net present value of $22,000, by investing in Projects C and F, the company obtains a net present value of $66,000 (which is the $44,000 from Project C plus $22,000 from Project F). This net present value is greater than the $63,000 from Project B. The increased present value is obtained with the same $135,000 investment.

Thus, when a company has limited capital and is unable to fund partial projects, the optimal set of projects is determined by considering the total net present value of all projects selected rather than the individual project net present values.

| **Other evaluation considerations** | Management considers factors other than net present values when making capital investment decisions. These factors may override the results of a pure present value analysis. We mention differences in the *riskiness* of projects, how well the project fits with other company projects, and the impact of projects on accounting income because these factors are frequently encountered by accountants. |

| **Differences in project risk** | There is often a correlation between the amount of risk a project entails and the return that can be earned from that project. If management uses net present values without adjustment for risk, high-risk projects with high expected returns may be the most commonly accepted. This outcome may be contrary to management intentions. Indeed, if management continues to accept riskier projects, overall company risk may increase. Its cost of capital will then increase to compensate lenders and investors for the greater risks. This will result in increasing the hurdle rate. |

To avoid this problem, management may require a higher rate of return from riskier projects. This risk premium is determined by analyzing the characteristics of a specific project and relating them to the company's other assets.[2] Management must be aware of the trade-offs between risk and return and select projects that meet predetermined objectives for overall company risk.

| **Portfolio considerations** | Investing in capital assets requires consideration of how they will fit with a company's existing *portfolio of assets.* New assets may be used to diversify away some risk for a company just as diversification of a securities portfolio may be used to reduce risk for an investor. For example, a company may acquire companies in other industries to avoid the business-cycle, technological, and political risks associated with its own industry. That is one reason why conglomerate mergers have become quite popular. |

The ways in which a specific investment can enhance a company's overall asset structure is another aspect of the capital investment decision. For example, in recent years companies that are significant energy users have acquired energy companies to assure themselves of a reliable energy supply. Brokerage firms have been merged with other kinds of financial institutions, such as credit card companies and retail stores, to diversify the services they can offer to their customers. These considerations extend beyond the accountant's domain, but they are significant for evaluating whether capital investment projects meet management's objectives.

---

[2] See, for example, J. C. VanHorne, *Fundamentals of Financial Management* (Englewood Cliffs, N.J.: Prentice-Hall, 1980).

Effects on income

Accounting measures of income are often used to evaluate organization performance and to measure compliance with contracts. For example, restrictive covenants in a loan agreement may require that a company maintain certain levels of working capital and retained earnings. Management will rarely select projects that have such an adverse effect on the working capital or other accounting numbers that the company no longer complies with contractual arrangements.

Management may also prefer to see growth in the income reported in the financial statements. In such cases, they will prefer projects that provide long-term growth over projects that show declining or level income trends.

For example, in Illustration 16–1, Project C has no net cash inflows for the first five years of its life. When depreciation is deducted from this zero cash flow to obtain net income for financial reporting, Project C shows net losses for its first five years. Management may decide to exclude Project C from consideration on this basis alone. To extend the example, a schedule of accounting income from each project is shown in Illustration 16–2. These accounting income data would be developed from sources other than those discussed in this chapter. As expected, Project C shows losses for the first five years.

Management may decide to select Project C in spite of the accounting losses because it yields a positive net present value as shown in Illustration 16–1. But management would be unlikely to place all of its capital investment funds in ventures like Project C unless the company had other sources of income, was particularly adventurous, or if management had incentives to maximize long-run payoffs instead of short-run accounting income. If the company had loan agreements or other contracts that required it to maintain certain net income levels, the early accounting losses from Project C could cause the company to default on its loan agreements and thus preclude it from staying in business long enough to earn the later rewards from Project C.

Externally required accounting income considerations for project investments may be considered a constraint by management on the company's

Illustration 16–2   **Accounting income from Projects A through E**

Year	Project A	B	C	D	E
1	(65)	(10)	(10)	20	0
2	5	80	(10)	30	10
3	45	70	(10)	40	10
4	70	40	(10)	50	20
5	150	20	(10)	50	30
6	330	10	220	40	30
7	120	(25)	50	20	10
Totals	$655	$185	$220	$250	$110

investment program. As such, it may be factored into a mathematical model such as a linear program for capital investment planning. Or management may simply include some accounting income requirements as additional hurdles for projects.

Evaluating financing alternatives

Once a project has been evaluated and found to have met all of the criteria for investment, a decision must be made about how to finance it. There are numerous variations in project financing that are designed to meet the specific needs of both borrower and lender. While investment and financing decisions are normally separated, some special financing opportunities may be linked to a specific capital investment. In these cases, the present value of the financing is usually included in the capital investment analysis.

The financial vice president has primary responsibility for managing the debt and equity of the company. Hence, the financing arrangements are made through the financial vice president's office.

The accountant is typically assigned responsibility for analyzing the cash flows under alternative financing arrangements. Such analysis will examine the tax effects of the alternatives as well as the differences in repayment terms and finance charges. The differential cash flows for each financing alternative may be scheduled and discounted to the present. The result is a net present value for each financing alternative. The financing alternative that requires the lowest present value cash payment is preferred, all other considerations being equal.

Lease versus borrow to buy

For example, Uni-Queue Company has decided to acquire an asset. They can either lease the asset for $15,000 per year during its five-year life or pay $70,000 for the asset and take out a loan for that amount. The loan is repayable at the rate of $14,000 per year on principal plus interest at 15 percent on each year's beginning loan balance. Both the lease and the loan are linked to the asset acquisition.

Under the proposed lease agreement, Uni-Queue is simply a lessee. They do not obtain the benefits of the investment tax credit or ACRS depreciation. At the end of the five years the asset is returned to the lessor.

On the other hand, if Uni-Queue Company purchases the asset, they obtain the benefit of the investment tax credit. For tax purposes, the equipment is classified under the five-year ACRS life. At the end of five years, management estimates that they could sell the asset for $15,000. All income taxes are at the company's ordinary tax rate of 45 percent. The company's cost of capital rate is 20 percent. We assume the risk to the company is the same whether the asset is acquired through lease or buy-borrow. Should management lease or borrow to buy?

To analyze this problem, we prepare a schedule of the differential cash flows for each financing alternative. We assume the periodic operating cash inflows generated by the project are the same whether the asset is leased or acquired through buying and borrowing. Hence, we ignore the operating cash inflows under both alternatives. The lease requires an annual outlay of $15,000, which is deductible for tax purposes, thus resulting in an after-tax cash outflow of $8,250 (computed as the $15,000 times 55 percent). The present value of this outflow may be found using the shortcut equation for a series of equal payments:

$$C \times \frac{1 - (1 + d)^{-n}}{d}$$

where:

$$\$(8,250) \times \frac{1 - (1.20)^{-5}}{.20} = \$(8,250) \times 2.991 = \underline{\underline{\$(24,673)}}$$

This present value of cash outlays is compared to the present value from borrowing to buy the asset.

The present value from buying the asset and borrowing the purchase amount requires consideration of four types of differential cash flows:

1. *Investment flows.*
2. *Periodic cash flows* (only those related to financing in this case).
3. *Tax shield.*
4. *Disinvestment flows.*

These are the same four categories that would be used to analyze cash flows when deciding whether to acquire the asset in the first place. The analysis for the data in this example is provided in Illustration 16–3.

The investment flows include the $70,000 outlay for the asset less the $70,000 in proceeds from the bank loan for a net of zero. The investment tax credit appears as a net cash inflow in Year 0 since that amount will be claimed as a credit against estimated taxes paid in that year.

The periodic cash flows represent the repayment of principal at $14,000 per year, based on $70,000 repaid equally over the five years. Interest is computed on the loan balance. Since interest is deductible for tax purposes, the amount shown for interest is equal to 55 percent (which is one minus the 45 percent tax rate) of the gross interest payment.

For Year 1, then, the net interest payment is:

$$\$70,000 \times 15\% \times 55\% = \underline{\underline{\$5,775}}$$

For Year 2:

$$\$(70,000 - \$14,000) \times 15\% \times 55\% = \underline{\underline{\$4,620}}$$

And so forth for Years 3 through 5. These calculations are detailed in Illustration 16–3.

Illustration 16–3   **Cash flow analysis for borrowing to buy**
Schedule of after-tax cash flows

	Year					
	0	**1**	**2**	**3**	**4**	**5**
Investment flows:						
Asset purchase	$(70,000)					
Loan	70,000					
Investment tax credit (ITC)	7,000					
Depreciation tax shield[a]		$ 4,489	$ 6,584	$ 6,284	$ 6,284	$ 6,284
Periodic flows:						
Loan repayment		(14,000)	(14,000)	(14,000)	(14,000)	(14,000)
Interest after tax[b]		(5,775)	(4,620)	(3,465)	(2,310)	(1,155)
Disinvestment flows:						
Salvage value						15,000
Tax on gain or loss on disposal[c]						(6,750)
Total cash flows	7,000	(15,286)	(12,036)	(11,181)	(10,026)	(621)
Present value factor		.833	.694	.579	.482	.402
Present values[d]	$ 7,000	$(12,738)	$ (8,358)	$ (6,470)	$ (4,835)	$ (250)
Net present value	$(25,651)					

Additional computations:

[a] Depreciation schedule:

Tax basis = $66,500 = $70,000 × 95%

Year	ACRS percent	Depreci- ation	Tax effect (45 percent)
1	15	$ 9,975	$ 4,489
2	22	14,630	6,584
3	21	13,965	6,284
4	21	13,965	6,284
5	21	13,965	6,284
Totals	100	$66,500	$29,925

[b] Interest calculation:

Year	Loan balance	Interest at 15 percent	After tax (1 − .45)
1	$70,000	$10,500	$ 5,775
2	56,000	8,400	4,620
3	42,000	6,300	3,465
4	28,000	4,200	2,310
5	14,000	2,100	1,155
Totals		$31,500	$17,325

[c] Salvage value	$15,000
Tax rate for this gain	45%
Tax on gain	$ 6,750

[d] Cash flow times present value factor does not equal present value because the present value factors shown here have been rounded to three places, while the present value is computed using the formula $(1 + d)^{-n}$, $n = 1, \ldots, 5$.

The tax shield is computed using the five-year ACRS tax life. For Year 1, the tax shield is:

$$(\text{Investment} - .5 \text{ ITC}) \times \text{ACRS percent} \times \text{Tax rate}$$

or:

$$\$70,000 \times 95\% \times 15\% \times .45 = \underline{\underline{\$4,489}}$$

For Year 2, the tax shield is:

$$\$70,000 \times 95\% \times 22\% \times .45 = \underline{\underline{\$6,584}}$$

The disinvestment flows include the $15,000 salvage value. Since the asset will be fully depreciated, there is a taxable gain on the full amount of the disposal proceeds. The tax on the gain is equal to the tax rate times the salvage value. This comes to $6,750 which is $15,000 times 45 percent. Since the asset will be held for five years, there will be no recapture of the investment tax credit.

The cash flows in each year are summed, and the net present value is computed by discounting the flows back to the present using the 20 percent cost of capital. The result is a present value for borrowing of $25,651. This amount indicates that the present value of the liability is greater than the $24,673 present value from leasing, so the preferred alternative is to lease. Of course the net present value of the entire project must be greater than or equal to zero or no investment will take place. In this situation, we first determined that the project had a positive net present value and then analyzed the financing alternatives. This two-step process is the one we understand managers usually follow when financing and investment decisions are independent.

Leasing and financing arrangements arise because of differences in the financial, risk, and tax situations of companies and investors. Leases and loan agreements therefore differ. This example should be viewed as a general guide to the approach that can be taken to evaluate alternatives in terms of the impact on cash flows and, hence, present values. Other circumstances may call for a different approach to the analysis.

Alternate capital investment models

Due to the complexity of the capital investment decision, one model of analysis is sometimes considered insufficient for evaluating investment proposals.[3] The most common models for assessing capital investment projects are:

1. Net present value.
2. Internal rate of return.

---

[3] Surveys of the use of capital investment models include V. B. Bavishi, "Capital Budgeting Practices at Multinationals," *Management Accounting* (August 1981), pp. 32–35; and J. Fremgen, "Capital Budgeting Practices: A Survey," *Management Accounting* (May 1973), pp. 19–25.

3. Payback.
4. Accounting rate of return.

We will discuss each of these alternative models in turn. Each model has its own advantages and may be encountered in certain decision settings. In a complex capital investment decision, it is likely that several alternative measures will be employed by management.

Net present value

As noted in the previous chapter, a project's net present value is computed by discounting its future cash flows to their equivalent value today. A discount rate must be selected for this computation. Finance texts recommend the use of a weighted-average cost of capital. With rapid changes in the value of money, some adjustment to book values is needed for determining the appropriate rate. Quite often companies adjust the rate to reflect inflationary effects. As noted in Chapter 15, the cash flows should also be adjusted for the effects of price-level changes. Some companies vary the rate to account for the differences in risk characteristics of different projects. Other companies use a rate that is determined as management's judgment of what a capital investment should earn. Whatever method is used for determining the discount rate, the end result is directed towards the objective of making the net present value an estimate of the economic value of the asset to the company.

Since the details of net present value calculations have been presented in Chapter 15, we will not repeat them here. Other alternative methods that we will discuss in more detail include internal rate of return, payback, and accounting rate of return. The first two of these are based on the same type of cash flow analysis which was presented in Chapter 15.

Internal rate of return

The internal rate of return or IRR is the rate of interest that a project is expected to earn over its life. If the internal rate of return were used as the cost of capital for discounting project cash flows, the net present value of the project would be exactly equal to zero. Thus, the IRR is that rate that makes the present value of project cash outflows equal to the present value of project cash inflows. This contrasts with the net present value method which employs a predetermined discount rate.

For example, consider Project A from Illustration 16–1. We know that the IRR from that project is in excess of 15 percent because the net present value is greater than zero. The IRR is the discount rate that equates the present value of Project A's cash inflows and outflows.

To compute the IRR, it is usually necessary to use a calculator, a computer program, or an iterative trial-and-error technique. For Project A, we know the rate is greater than 15 percent. Is it 20 percent? To find out, we discount the Project A cash flows using a 20 percent discount rate. As shown in Illustration 16–4, this results in a net present value of $(11,020). Since this

Illustration 16–4   **Trial-and-error approximation of internal rate of return**
                                          Basic data: Project A—Illustration 16–1 (in thousands)

		Discount rate			
Year	Cash flow	Step 1: 15 percent	Step 2: 20 percent	Step 3: 19.4 percent	Step 4: 19.3 percent
0	$(425.00)	$(425.00)	$(425.00)	$(425.00)	$(425.00)
1	25.00	21.74[a]	20.83[b]	20.94[c]	20.96[d]
2	50.00	37.81	34.72	35.07	35.13
3	75.00	49.31	43.40	44.06	44.17
4	100.00	57.18	48.23	49.20	49.37
5	150.00	74.58	60.28	61.81	62.07
6	300.00	129.70	100.47	103.54	104.06
7	380.00	142.86	106.05	109.84	110.48
Net present values		$ 88.18	$ (11.02)	$ (.54)	$ 1.24

Additional computations:
[a] $21.74 = $25 × 1.15^{-1}; $37.81 = $50 × 1.15^{-2}; etc.
[b] $20.83 = $25 × 1.20^{-1}; $34.72 = $50 × 1.20^{-2}; etc.
[c] $20.94 = $25 × 1.194^{-1}; $35.07 = $50 × 1.194^{-2}; etc.
[d] $20.96 = $25 × 1.193^{-1}; $35.13 = $50 × 1.193^{-2}; etc.

value is negative, the internal rate of return must be less than 20 percent. We then interpolate between the two interest rates based on the spread between the net present values as follows:

$$\frac{\$(11{,}020)}{\$11{,}020 + \$88{,}180} \times (20\% - 15\%) = \underline{(.56\%)}$$

This suggests that the internal rate of return is approximately .56 percent less than 20 percent. A rate of 19.4 percent results in a net present value of $(540), which indicates that rate is still too high. A rate of 19.3 percent yields a net present value of $1,240, which indicates that rate is too low. Therefore, we conclude that the internal rate of return is between 19.4 percent and 19.3 percent. While a calculator program could be used to produce a rate that is correct to several decimal places, whole percentages are usually sufficient and interpolations, for fractions of a percent are unnecessary.

Internal rate of return with constant cash flows   When the cash flows from a project are constant, it is possible to use the tables for present value of an annuity (Appendix B, Illustration 15–10 to Chapter 15) to find the approximate rate of return. Dividing the required investment by the annual net cash flow gives the factor for a project with a life equal to that of the project and an interest rate equal to the internal rate of return. All we need do is look across the row for number of periods until we come to the factor closest to our computed factor. The interest rate for the column of the table related to that factor is the approximate internal rate of return.

For Project D in Illustration 16–1, the factor is:

$$\frac{\$170,000}{\$60,000} = \underline{\underline{2.83}}$$

Which, for a seven-year project, is closest to the factor 2.802 in the column headed by an interest rate of 30 percent. Therefore, we estimate the IRR on this project as 30 percent.

Some questions with IRR   While the internal rate of return is widely used for project evaluations, it is sometimes considered inferior to net present value. Its primary disadvantage is its built-in assumption that net cash inflows are reinvested at the project's internal rate of return. By contrast, the net present value method assumes that the net cash inflows are invested at the cost of capital rate. If funds will be reinvested at the cost of capital, the IRR method will make a project whose rate of return is greater than the cost of capital appear more attractive than a similar project using the net present value approach.

In some cases, the differences between the assumptions in the IRR method and the present value method result in differences in the rankings of projects using each method. The present value index ranking may differ from the IRR ranking. The choice that management makes in such a situation will depend on management's objectives and evaluation of the assumptions underlying the two methods.

Multiple rates of return   An interesting problem arises in computing internal rate of return for cash flows that change sign more than once in the project life. This change in sign may occur if significant additional investment is required later in the life of the investment or if a significant cost is incurred when the project is abandoned. Such projects will have more than one internal rate of return. This problem is referred to as multiple rates of return.

IRR and performance evaluation   Many companies use internal rate of return to evaluate capital investments because they also use a measure of return on investment to evaluate performance. The differences between the net present value method and the internal rate of return are frequently inconsequential.

Payback

It is generally assumed that the longer a company's funds are tied up in an investment, the greater the risk to the company. In addition, there is a relationship between the speed of payback and the rate of return on a typical investment. For these reasons, companies often consider the length of time it takes to obtain a return of the investment in the project as a measure for project evaluation. The payback period is the number of years that will elapse before the original investment is repaid. As with most other capital investment models, cash flow data are used for this computation.

For example, using the data for Project B from Illustration 16–1, the payback period is:

Year	Net cash flow	Cash flow balance
0	$(135,000)	$(135,000)
1	–0–	(135,000)
2	90,000	(45,000)
3	80,000	35,000

A running balance of the net cash flow for the investment is maintained until the balance turns positive. For this project, the balance turns positive during the third year. The fraction of that third year that was required before the investment achieved payback is usually estimated by dividing the absolute value of the last negative balance in the balance column by the total cash flow in the payback year:

$$\frac{\text{Balance, end of Year 2}}{\text{Net cash flow, Year 3}}$$

or:

$$\frac{\$45,000}{\$80,000} = .5625$$

Project payback would then be stated as 2.5625 years, or approximately 2 years and 7 months. The fraction of a year computation is based on the assumption that the cash flows are received evenly throughout the payback year.

Shortcut payback computation   If a project has level cash flows throughout its life, the payback computation is simplified. The payback period may be computed in this case by dividing the project cost by the annual cash flow. For Project D from Illustration 16–1, the payback period is:

$$\frac{\$170,000}{\$60,000} = 2.83 \text{ years}$$

Payback reciprocal   When a project life is at least twice the payback period and the annual cash flows are approximately equal, the payback reciprocal may be used to estimate of the rate of return for the project.

Thus, for Project D from Illustration 16–1, the payback reciprocal is:

$$\frac{1}{2.83} = .35, \text{ or } 35\%$$

Programmed functions in calculators and computers are generally used to compute the rate of return directly. Therefore, use of the payback reciprocal approach is simply a rough, first-cut approximation.

Discounted payback   A method that recognizes the time value of money in a payback context is the discounted payback method. This method is used to compute the payback in terms of discounted cash flows received in the future. That is, the periodic cash flows are discounted using an appropriate cost of capital rate. The payback period is computed using the discounted cash flow values rather than the actual cash flows. If the discounted payback method were used for Project D from Illustration 16–1 and a 15 percent cost of capital rate was employed, the discounted payback period would be as shown in Illustration 16–5, which is a discounted payback period of four years.

Illustration 16–5   **Discounted payback method, Project D (dollars in thousands)**

Year	Cash flow	Discount factor[a]	Discounted cash flow	Balance
0	$(170)	—	$(170)	$(170)
1	60	.870	52	(118)
2	60	.756	45	(73)
3	60	.658	39	(34)
4	60	.572	34	–0–

[a] Discount factors rounded to three places.

Evaluation of payback methods   Payback approaches are generally easy to compute and, to the extent that risk and payback are correlated, give some measure of a company's risk exposure from a project. However, the payback period tells nothing about profitability. Thus, a project that returns the entire investment in Year 1 but results in no further cash flows appears better using the payback criterion than does a project that returns 50 percent of the investment cost per year for three years. With an investment of $100,000 and a cost of capital of 15 percent, a comparison of the net present value and payback period for these two projects is shown in Illustration 16–6. Clearly, Project 2 is the better choice when cash flows are considered. The payback method gives a misleading signal about the relative desirability of the two projects.

Thus, when using payback it is important to consider what will happen after the payback period is over. Managers often use payback as a screening device because it is easy (and therefore inexpensive) to use. The choice of the investment analysis model should be based on their costs and benefits compared to the alternative models. If decisions are sensitive to the decision

Illustration 16–6   **Comparison of net present value and payback periods**

	Project 1	Project 2
Investment cost	$100,000	$100,000
Annual cash flows:		
Year 1	$100,000	$ 50,000
Year 2	–0–	50,000
Year 3	–0–	50,000
Years 4 and after	–0–	–0–
Payback	1 year[a]	2 years[b]
Net present value at 15%	$ (13,043)[c]	$ 14,161[d]

Additional computations:

[a] One year = $100,000 cash return, Year 1 – $100,000 investment.

[b] Two years = $100,000 investment/$50,000 annual cash flow.

[c] $-13,043 = $-100,000 + $100,000 \times 1.15^{-1}$.

[d] $14,161 = $-100,000 + $50,000 \times 1.15^{-1} + $50,000 \times 1.15^{-2} + $50,000 \times 1.15^{-3}$.

model, then more care and expense is warranted than when decisions are the same regardless of the model used.[4]

Accounting rate of return

The accounting rate of return measures a project's rate of return in terms of accounting income however defined by management rather than in terms of cash flows. It relates the average accounting income from a project to the investment in the project and is computed using the following equation:

$$\text{Accounting rate of return} = \frac{\text{Average accounting income}}{\text{Investment}}$$

The accounting income for this computation is approximately equal to the sum of the average incremental cash flow from the project (C) less the average book depreciation (D). Investment may be based either on the *initial investment* or on the *average investment*. Average investment is usually assumed to equal one half of the difference between initial investment and salvage value. Incremental cash flows are usually approximated using revenues minus costs other than depreciation.

For example, consider Project D in Illustration 16–1. The project has an annual cash flow of $60,000 and an initial cost of $170,000. Assume that $154,000 of the investment cost is depreciable using a straight-line rate over the seven-year project life. This basis was determined by management's internal accounting procedures. Book depreciation is $22,000 per year (computed as $154,000/7 years). Average investment in the project is $85,000 which is one half of the original investment cost of $170,000.

[4] For a comparison of the impact of different capital budgeting models on decisions, see G. Sundem, "Evaluating Simplified Capital Budgeting Models Using a Time-State Preference Metric." *The Accounting Review* (April 1974), pp. 306–20.

The accounting rate of return *(R)* is:

$$R = \frac{C - D}{\frac{1}{2} \times I}$$

or:

$$\frac{\$60,000 - \$22,000}{\$85,000} = \underline{\underline{44.7\%}}$$

where:

    C = the average annual cash flow from the investment
    D = accounting depreciation
    I = the initial investment

The accounting rate of return may also be computed using the initial investment rather than the average investment. This estimate of the accounting rate of return is:

$$R = \frac{C - D}{I}$$

or:

$$\frac{\$60,000 - \$22,000}{\$170,000} = \underline{\underline{22.4\%}}$$

Since the accounting rate of return averages the cash flows to be received from a project and averages the depreciation, and since accounting rate of return ignores the time value of money, the method is rarely suitable for investment decision-making purposes. Sometimes management will constrain the investment decision to include only those projects that exceed a particular accounting rate of return in order to maintain particular financial accounting ratios. However, this method is considered inferior to a net present value evaluation if the objective is to maximize the long-run wealth of the organization.

Summary

When capital investment opportunities with positive net present values exceed capital budget constraints, the net present value index may be used to rank the projects. This index is calculated as follows:

$$\text{Net present value index} = \frac{\text{Project net present value}}{\text{Investment in the project}}$$

When partial investments are not possible, a ranking by net present value index may not indicate the optimal set of projects because there may be leftover, uninvested funds that have a positive net present value. Consequently, various combinations of projects must be evaluated to find the set of projects with the highest net present value.

Projects with high returns are not necessarily better than those with lower returns. If a high-return project entails greater risk, management will often use a higher discount rate. In addition, when investing in capital assets, management must consider how the new investment will fit with the company's portfolio of assets and its overall strategy. Sometimes projects with lower returns are accepted because they are more compatible with the company's long-range plans.

When financing arrangements are tied directly to an investment decision, the net present value of each package arrangement is usually calculated. For example, leasing is often a form of financing an asset, much like borrowing. Thus, it is appropriate to compare the cash flows under leasing with those under a borrow-to-buy arrangement.

Management may use more than one evaluation method for assessing capital investment projects. Internal rate of return expresses a projects return as an interest rate rather than as a net present value. Payback indicates how long a project will take to earn back its initial investment. Discounted payback indicates how long it will take to earn back the initial investment and the required cost of capital. Accounting rate of return shows a project's effect on accounting income. Each of these alternatives is frequently criticized as a primary means of investment analysis. But given the importance of capital investment decisions to most organization, use of more than one method may provide additional useful insights.

Terms and concepts

The following terms and concepts should be familiar to you after reading this chapter.

Accounting rate of return   Net present value index
Discounted payback method   Payback
Internal rate of return (IRR)   Payback period
Lease versus borrow to buy   Payback reciprocal
Multiple rates of return   Risk premium
Mutually exclusive

Self-study problem

Using the data from the Melwood Corporation (Chapter 15, self-study problem), compute the following alternative evaluation measures:

a. Present value index.
b. Internal rate of return.
c. Payback.
d. Payback reciprocal.
e. Discounted payback, using the 15 percent cost of capital rate.

f. Accounting rate of return on initial investment assuming straight-line book depreciation of equipment and software costs. Ignore the training costs, old equipment, and ITC in the computations.

Solutions to self-study problem

a. Present value index:

$$\frac{\text{Net present value}}{\text{Initial investment}} = \frac{\$3,709}{\$11,615} = \underline{\underline{31.9\%}}$$

b. Internal rate of return:

Because the net present value is positive at the 15 percent discount rate, we know the IRR must be greater than 15 percent. Trying several rates, we obtain:

			Rates	
Year	Cash flow	29 percent	30 percent	31 percent
0	$(11,615)	$(11,615)	$(11,615)	$(11,615)
1	5,219	4,046	4,015	3,984
2	5,644	3,392	3,340	3,289
3	5,611	2,614	2,554	2,496
4	4,950	1,788	1,733	1,681
		$ 225	$ (27)	$ (165)

So, the IRR is approximately 30 percent.

c. Payback:

Year	Cash flow	Balance
0	$(11,615)	$(11,615)
1	5,219	(6,396)
2	5,644	(752)
3	5,611	

$$2 \text{ years} + \frac{\$752}{\$5,611} = \underline{\underline{2.13 \text{ years}}}$$

d. Payback reciprocal:

$$1 \div 2.13 = 46.9\%$$

The life of the asset is less than twice the payback period; hence, the payback reciprocal may not be an accurate estimate of the internal rate of return. Compare this estimate with the estimate in Requirement *(b)* of this problem.

e. Discounted payback:

Year	Cash flow	Balance
0	$(11,615)	$(11,615)
1	4,538	(7,077)
2	4,267	(2,810)
3	3,689	—

$$2 \text{ years} + \frac{\$2,810}{\$3,689} = \underline{\underline{2.76 \text{ years}}}$$

f. Accounting rate of return:

$$\frac{\{ \$8,000 - [(\$7,500 + 2,400 - 1,000) \div 4 \text{ years}]\} \times (1 - .45)}{\$7,500 + 2,400}$$

$$= \frac{(\$8,000 - 2,225) \times .55}{\$9,900}$$

$$= \frac{\$3,176}{\$9,900}$$

$$= 32.17$$

Note: Software costs were written off immediately for tax purposes, but capitalized and included as part of the investment base for book purposes.

Questions

16–1. If there are no budget constraints, why would we invest in all projects with a positive net present value?

16–2. In the presence of budget constraints, what method is suggested for evaluating capital investment projects? Why?

16–3. When there are both budget constraints and investment indivisibilities, what method should be used for capital investment analysis? Why?

16–4. What is the appropriate method for choosing from among mutually exclusive projects? Why is the method appropriate?

16–5. There is a danger in relying entirely on net present value evaluations for projects. What is the danger?

16–6. Management must consider a number of factors in making a capital investment decision. What are some of the factors in addition to net present value?

16–7. Management often has a choice of financing alternatives for certain projects. How should the financing decision be handled?

16–8. What is the benefit of the use of payback for evaluating capital investment projects?

16–9. How can the payback method be improved to account for the effect of the time value of money?

16–10. Why would management use capital investment evaluation methods that are often criticized as inferior to net present value?

Exercises

16–11. Choosing from alternative investment possibilities

A company with limited investment funds and a cost of capital of 20 percent must choose among three competing capital investment projects with the following cash flow patterns (in thousands):

	Project		
Year	A	B	C
0	$(200)	$(350)	$(400)
1	50	80	70
2	90	190	150
3	100	250	270
4	100	120	200

The company has $600,000 available for investment.

Required:

How can the company optimally invest its $600,000 among the three projects assuming no other constraints on investment.

16–12. Effect of investment constraints on project selection

Using the same data as in Exercise 16–11, and assuming that the projects are not indivisible (that is, you must buy 100 percent of any project or else none of that project), determine the optimal investment policy for the company.

16–13. Effect of mutually exclusive projects

Using the same data as in Exercise 16–11, and assuming that Projects A and B are mutually exclusive, and that the projects are **not** indivisible, determine the optimal investment policy for the company.

16–14. Compute alternative project evaluation measures

A company is considering whether to invest in a project that costs $350,000 and will return $90,000 after tax for each of the next seven years. After that the asset will have no value.

Required:

Compute the following items for this project:

a. Payback.
b. Payback reciprocal.
c. Internal rate of return (using the tables).
d. Internal rate of return if the life is 12 years rather than 7.

16–15. Compute alternative investment evaluation measures

Branding Irons, Inc., is a manufacturer of western hats. The company has an opportunity to expand its production by purchasing a new automatic hat bander. The bander costs $200,000 and is fully depreciable for tax purposes using the straight-line method over a four-year life. The machine will have no salvage value. No additional working capital is required, and the machine will not qualify for the investment tax credit. The bander will result in cost savings of $80,000 per year. The company has a tax rate of 45 percent.

Required:

Compute the following investment evaluation measures for the bander:

a. Payback period.
b. Internal rate of return.
c. Accounting rate of return on the initial investment.

16–16. Present value of lease versus buy

The owner of Ruggles Company, a sole proprietorship, has determined that she should acquire some new energy saving equipment. If the equipment is acquired, it may either be leased or a special nonrecourse loan may be obtained for the total amount of the equipment purchase.

The lease calls for payments of $13,000 per year for eight years, whereas the loan calls for eight annual principal payments of $10,000 each plus 15 percent interest on the balance outstanding at the start of each year. Under the lease, the lessor obtains all tax benefits from equipment ownership.

The equipment, which cost $80,000, is depreciable under the five-year ACRS life. Moreover, the equipment qualifies for the investment tax credit. The equipment will have no value at the end of the project life (eight years).

Ruggles has a cost of capital rate of 20 percent and a marginal tax rate of 35 percent.

Required:

Determine whether Ruggles should lease or buy the asset. Show supporting data.

16–17. Effect of tax rates on the lease versus buy decision

If the marginal tax rate for Ruggles (Exercise 16–16) were 70 percent, would your decision in 16–16 remain the same? Show supporting data.

16–18. Capital investment analysis; alternative performance measures

Hazman Company plans to replace an old piece of equipment that has no book value for tax purposes and no salvage value. The replacement equipment would provide annual cash savings of $7,000 before income taxes. The equipment would cost $18,000 and would have no salvage value at the end of its five-year life. Hazman uses straight-line depreciation for both book and tax purposes. The company incurs a 40 percent marginal tax rate, and its after-tax cost of capital is 14 percent. Ignore the investment tax credit.

Required:

Compute the following performance measures for Hazman's proposed investment:

a. Payback period.
b. Payback reciprocal.
c. Accounting rate of return on average investment.
d. Net present value.
e. Present value index.
f. Internal rate of return.
g. Discounted payback.

(CMA adapted)

16–19. Alternate performance measures with ACRS tax shield

Using the data for Hazman Company in Exericse 16–18, assume you have just started working for Hazman. You recall that the 1981 Tax Act allows Hazman to use a five-year ACRS life for this equipment. Moreover, the equipment qualifies for a 10 percent tax credit.

Required:

Compute the following investment performance measures using the ACRS life and the investment tax credit:

a. Payback period.
b. Payback reciprocal.
c. Accounting rate of return on average investment ignoring the investment tax credit.
d. Net present value.
e. Present value index.
f. Internal rate of return.
g. Discounted payback.

16–20. Alternative capital investment measures

ABC Company is considering a capital investment proposal with an initial cost of $54,000. The asset is depreciated over a six-year period on the straight-line basis for both book and tax purposes. No salvage value is expected at the end of the asset life, and no investment tax credit is allowed. The before-tax cash inflow for the project is $20,000 per year. The income tax rate is 40 percent, and the company's cost of capital is 15 percent.

Required:

Compute the following:

a. Accounting rate of return on average investment.
b. Payback reciprocal.
c. Internal rate of return.

Problems and cases

16-21. Assess impact of tax policy

A provision of the Federal Tax Code permits a taxpayer to write off the first $5,000 in outlays for new capital equipment. However, if the taxpayer chooses to take the immediate write-off, the taxpayer loses the investment tax credit and the depreciation tax shield on that amount.

Assume that your company has acquired more than $5,000 in new capital equipment and now must decide whether to take the immediate write-off or whether to claim the investment tax credit and amortize the asset over a five-year ACRS life. Your company has an after-tax cost of capital of 20 percent and a marginal tax rate of 45 percent.

Required:

Prepare an analysis to show the following items for this decision:

a. Internal rate of return.
b. Net present value.
c. Payback period.
d. Optimal decision for the company.

16-22. Assess asset write-off versus capitalization

HighPotential Corporation has made a significant investment in new capital equipment during the past year. The company has invested over $5,000 in equipment that qualifies for the three-year ACRS write-off and the related 6 percent investment tax credit. The financial manager of HighPotential indicated that there is a tax policy that allows the company to write off the first $5,000 against current period income rather than take the tax credit and ACRS write-off. Your recommendation will be followed by the company. The company has a marginal tax rate of 45 percent and an after-tax cost of capital of 20 percent.

Required:

a. Compute the internal rate of return for the write-off.
b. Make your recommendation and offer supporting comments.

16-23. Compute alternate investment measures

Using the data from Wisconsin Products Company, Problem 15-30, compute the following alternative capital investment evaluation measures:

a. Payback.
b. Discounted payback.
c. Payback reciprocal.
d. Internal rate of return.
e. Accounting rate of return ignoring any tax consequences and based on average investment.

Comment on the differences among the alternative measures you have just computed.

16-24. Capital asset acquisition; lease or buy

Edwards Corporation produces and sells a wide range of products. The firm is considering adding a new stapler to one of its product lines. More equipment will be required to produce the new stapler. There are two alternative ways to acquire the needed equipment: (1) purchase equipment or (2) lease equipment.

The equipment can be purchased for $125,000. The equipment has no salvage value at the end of its useful life of five years.

Alternatively, the equipment can be acquired by a five-year lease for $40,000 annual rent. The lessor will assume all responsibility for taxes, insurance, and maintenance.

If purchased, the equipment would be financed as follows:

	Year-end payment		
Year	Interest	Principal	Total
1	$10,000	$21,307	$31,307
2	8,295	23,012	31,307
3	6,454	24,853	31,307
4	4,466	26,841	31,307
5	2,320	28,987	31,307

Engineering and management studies provide the following revenue and cost estimates (excluding lease payments and depreciation) for producing the new stapler:

	Equipment	
	Leased	Purchased
Unit selling price	$5.00	$5.00
Unit production costs:		
Materials	1.80	1.80
Conversion costs	1.65	1.65
Total unit production costs	3.45	3.45
Unit contribution margin	1.55	1.55
Estimated unit volume	40,000	40,000
Estimated total contribution margin	$62,000	$62,000
Other costs:		
Supervision	$16,000	$16,000
Taxes and insurance	—	3,000
Maintenance	—	3,000
Total	$16,000	$22,000

The machine qualifies for the five-year ACRS and the 10 percent tax credit if purchased.

The company uses an after-tax cost of capital of 10 percent. Its marginal tax rate is 40 percent. Assume all cash flows occur at year-end.

Required:

Should the company lease or buy the equipment?

(CMA adapted)

16–25. Assess capital investment project with alternative measures

The Baxter Company manufactures toys and other short-lived fad type items.

The research and development department came up with an item that would make a good promotional gift for office equipment dealers. Effort by Baxter's sales personnel has resulted in almost firm commitments for this product for the next three years. It is expected that the product's value will be exhausted by that time.

To produce the quantity demanded Baxter will need to buy additional machinery and rent additional space. It appears that about 25,000 square feet will be needed; 12,500 square feet of presently unused, but leased, space is available now. (Baxter's present lease with 10 years to run costs $3 a foot.) There is another 12,500 square feet adjoining the Baxter facility which Baxter will rent for three years at $4 per square foot per year if it decides to make this product.

The equipment will be purchased for about $900,000. It will require $30,000 in modifications, $60,000 for installation, and $90,000 for testing; all of these activities will be done by a firm of engineers hired by Baxter. All of the expenditures will be paid for on January 1, 1986, and all qualify for the six percent tax credit.

The equipment should have a salvage value of about $180,000 at the end of the third year. No additional general overhead costs are expected to be incurred.

The following estimates of revenues and costs for this product for the three years have been developed:

	1986	1987	1988
Sales	$1,000,000	$1,600,000	$800,000
Material, labor, and incurred overhead	400,000	750,000	350,000
Assigned general overhead	40,000	75,000	35,000
Rent	87,500	87,500	87,500
Depreciation	450,000	300,000	150,000
	977,500	1,212,500	622,500
Income before tax	22,500	387,500	177,500
Income tax (40%)	9,000	155,000	71,000
	$ 13,500	$ 232,500	$106,500

Required:

a. Prepare a schedule which shows the incremental, after tax, cash flows for this project. The equipment must be depreciated under the three-year ACRS for tax purposes.

b. If the company requires a two-year payback period for its investment, would it undertake this project?

c. Calculate the after-tax accounting rate of return for the project.

d. If the company sets a required rate of return of 20 percent after taxes, will this project be accepted?

(CMA adapted)

16–26. Sell or process further; cash flow evaluation; internal rate of return

Algonquin River Products Corporation is considering the investment in a new processing facility. The company extracts ores from an open-pit mine. During the year, 400,000 tons of ore are extracted. If the products from the extraction process are sold immediately upon removal of the dirt, rocks, and other impurities, a price of $65 per ton of ore can be obtained. The company has estimated that is extraction costs amount to 75 percent of the net realizable value of the ore.

Rather than sell all of the ore at the $65 price, it is possible to take 20 percent of the ore and process it further. The ore to be processed further would incur cash costs of $6 per ton in addition to the first processing costs. The processed ore would yield two products in equal proportion: A and B. One-half ton of Product A from processed ore would sell for $44, while one-half ton of Product B from processed ore would sell for $34.

To perform the additional processing, the company would install equipment costing $1,300,000. This equipment would qualify for the five-year ACRS and 10 percent ITC. At the end of the six-year project life, the equipment could be salvaged and the company would obtain $50,000 salvage proceeds.

The average inventory required would be 5,000 tons of ore. In addition, a cash balance of $45,000 would be needed to operate the additional process.

The company plans to obtain a loan for the project at an interest cost of 16 percent. The loan would be for the entire cost of the project including inventories and working capital. The company estimates its cost of capital at 20 percent and its marginal tax rate at 45 percent.

Required:

a. Prepare a schedule of the cash flows from the investment and indicate the net present value of the project.

b. What is the internal rate of return from the project?

Part **3**

Cost Data for Performance Evaluation

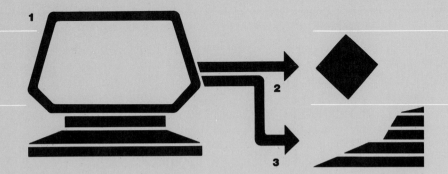

1. Cost accounting systems

2. Differential costs for
decision making

3. Cost data for
performance evaluation

17

The Master Budget

OBJECTIVES
To see the way the master budget is developed and how it fits into the overall
    plan for achieving organization goals.
To understand methods of acquiring budget data.
To compare the budgeting process in manufacturing and other organizations.

The use of budgeting in organizations was well stated by a controller who explained: "At our company, we view our master budget as a blueprint for operations, much like an architect's blueprint for the construction of a building. Like the architect's blueprint, our master budget helps us plan and coordinate activities, determine the means for achieving our goals, and establish some norms against which we can measure our performance. We consider our budget to be a comprehensive plan through which all levels of management formally indicate what they expect the future to hold. It expresses, in dollars, our plans for achieving company goals."

This chapter shows how a master budget is developed and how it fits into the overall plan for achieving organizational goals.

The overall plan

A master budget is part of an overall organizational plan made up of three components:

1. Organizational goals.
2. The strategic long-range profit plan.
3. The master budget (tactical short-range profit plan).[1]

Organizational goals

Organizational goals are the set of broad objectives established by management that company employees work to achieve. For example, the following quote is taken from internal documents of a manufacturing company in the paper industry: "Our long-range goal is to increase earnings steadily while maintaining our current share of market sales and maintain profitability within the top one third of our industry. We plan to achieve this goal while providing our customers with high-quality products and meeting our social responsibilities to our employees and the communities in which they live."

Such broad goals provide a philosophical statement that the company is

---

[1] For a more detailed description of these phases, see Glenn A. Welsch, *Budgeting: Profit Planning and Control* (Englewood Cliffs, N.J.: Prentice-Hall, 1976).

expected to follow in its operations. Many companies include statements of their goals in published codes of conduct and annual reports to stockholders.

Strategic long-range profit plan

While a statement of goals is necessary to guide an organization, it is important to detail the specific steps that will be taken to achieve them.[2] These steps are expressed in a long-range strategic plan. Because the long-range plans look into the intermediate and distant future, they are usually stated in rather broad terms. Strategic plans discuss the major capital investments required to maintain present facilities, increase capacity, diversify products and/or processes, and develop particular markets. For example, the previously mentioned paper company's strategies, as stated in their policy manual, included:

1. *Cost control.* Optimize contribution from existing product lines by holding product cost increases to less than the general rate of inflation. This will involve acquiring new machinery proposed in the capital budget as well as replacing our five least efficient plants over the next five years.
2. *Market share.* Maintain our market share by providing a level of service and quality comparable to our top competitors. This requires improving our quality control so that customer complaints and returned merchandise are reduced from a current level of 4 percent to 1 percent within two years.

Each strategy statement was supported by projected activity levels (sales volumes, aggregates costs, and cash flow projections) for each of the next five years. At this stage, the plans were not laid out in too much detail, but they were well thought out. Hence, the plans provided a general framework for guiding management's operating decisions.

The master budget (tactical short-range profit plan)

Long-range plans are achieved in year-by-year steps. The guidance is more specific for the coming year than it is for more distant years. The plan for the coming year is called the master budget. The master budget is also known as the *static budget,* the *budget plan,* or the *planning budget.* The income statement portion of the master budget is often called the profit plan. The master budget indicates the sales levels, production and cost levels, income, and cash flows that are anticipated for the coming year. In addition, these budget data are used to construct a budgeted statement of financial position (balance sheet).

Budgeting is a dynamic process that ties together goals, plans, decision making, and employee performance evaluation. The master budget and its relationship to other plans, accounting reports, and management decision-making processes is diagrammed in Illustration 17–1. On the left side are the organization goals, strategies, and objectives that set the long-term plan

---

[2] A classic discussion of organization goal setting is provided by James G. March and Herbert A. Simon in *Organizations* (New York: John Wiley & Sons, 1958).

Illustration 17–1   **Organizational and individual interaction in developing the master budget**

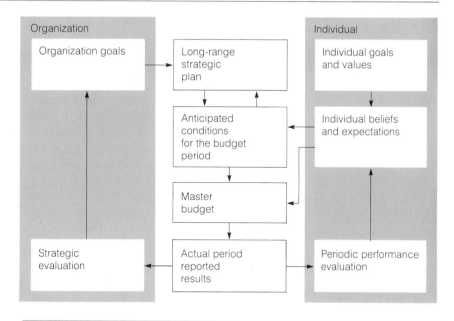

for the company. The master budget is derived from the long-range plan in consideration of conditions that are expected during the coming period. Such plans are subject to change as the events of the year unfold. Recently, the long-range plan for a U.S. automobile manufacturer called for development of several new product lines, but unfavorable short-run economic conditions required their postponement.

The human element in budgeting   The conditions anticipated for the coming year are based in part on individual manager's near-term projections. The individual's relationship to the budget is diagrammed on the right side of Illustration 17–1. Managers' beliefs about the coming period are affected by a number of factors, including their personal goals and values. Although budgets are often viewed in purely quantitative, technical terms, the importance of this human factor cannot be overemphasized.

Budget preparation rests on human estimates of an unknown future. People's forecasts are likely to be greatly influenced by their experiences with various segments of the company. For example, district sales managers are in an excellent position to project customer orders over the next several months, while market researchers are usually better able to identify long-run market trends and make macro forecasts of sales. One challenge of budgeting is to identify who in the organization is best able to provide the best information about particular topics.

Participative budgeting

The use of input from lower- and middle-management employees is often called participative or *grass roots* budgeting. The use of lower and middle managers in budgeting has an obvious cost—it is time consuming. But it also has some benefits. It enhances employee motivation and acceptance of goals, it provides information that enables employees to associate rewards and penalties with performance,[3] and it yields information that may not be otherwise obtainable.

A number of studies have shown that employees often provide inaccurate data when asked to give budget estimates. They may request more money than they need because they expect their request to be cut. And, employees who believe the budget will be used as a norm for evaluating their performance may provide an estimate that will not be too hard to achieve.

Thus, managers usually view the technical steps required to construct a comprehensive tactical budget plan in the context of the effect that people have on the budget and the effect that the budget will have on people. Ideally, the budget will motivate people and facilitate their activities so that organizational goals can be achieved.

Developing the master budget

While each organization is unique in the way it puts together its budget, all budgeting processes share some common elements. After organization goals, strategies, and long-range plans have been developed, work begins on the master budget. This is a detailed budget for the coming fiscal year, with some less-detailed figures for subsequent years. While budgeting is an ongoing process in most companies, the bulk of the work is usually done in the six months immediately preceding the beginning of the coming fiscal year. Final budget approvals from the chief executive and board of directors are made a month to six weeks before the beginning of the fiscal year.

To envision the master budgeting process, picture the financial statements most commonly prepared by companies: the income statement, the balance sheet, and the funds flow statement. Then imagine preparing these statements *before* the fiscal period. One modification to the set of traditional financial statements, however, is that many companies prepare a *cash flow budget* rather than a funds flow budget due to the importance of this information for cash management. Either can be prepared, but we'll restrict our discussion to the cash flow budget. We begin at the top of the budgeted income statement with a forecast of revenues for the budget period.

---

[3] See S. W. Becker and D. O. Green, "Budgeting and Employee Behavior," *The Journal of Business,* October 1962. A more comprehensive discussion of the behavioral effects of individuals and budget plans is presented by Don T. DeCoster in "An Intuitive Framework for Empirical Research in Participative Budgeting," in *Accounting Research Convocation,* ed. Gary John Previts (University, Ala.: University of Alabama Press, 1976). General discussions of behavioral aspects of budgeting are available in Anthony Hopwood, *Accounting and Human Behavior* (Englewood Cliffs, N.J.: Prentice-Hall, 1974); R. J. Swieringa and R. H. Moncur, *Some Effects of Participative Budgeting on Managerial Behavior* (New York: National Association of Accountants, 1975); and G. Hofstede, *The Game of Budget Control* (New York: Van Nostrand, 1967).

Sales forecasts

Forecasting sales is perhaps the most difficult aspect of budgeting because it involves considerable subjectivity. To reduce subjectivity and simultaneously gather as much information as possible, management often uses a number of different methods to obtain forecasts from a number of different sources.

Sales staff   Sales people are in the unique position of being close to the customers, and they may possess the best information in the company about customers' immediate and near-term needs. As previously indicated, however, they may be tempted to bias their sales forecasts if such forecasts are used as the norm for performance evaluation.

For example, Peter Jones is a district sales manager for the Hypo Manufacturing Company. For the coming budget year, he expects his district's sales to be $1,000,000, although they could drop as low as $800,000 or run as high as $1,200,000. His bonus at the end of next year will be 1 percent of the excess of actual sales over the sales budget. So if the budget is $1,000,000 and actual sales are also $1,000,000, he will receive no bonus.

However, if Peter provides a sales forecast that is too low, he will not be able to justify retaining his current number of employees. Further, if his sales forecasts are consistently much below the actual sales results or below what management thinks his district should be doing, he will lose credibility. Thus, Peter decides on a conservative but reasonable sales forecast of $900,000, which, he believes, will give him a high probability of getting a bonus and a low risk of losing his other objectives.

Of course, if Peter's performance were compared against a different set of norms, he would have different incentives. If, for instance, his bonus was a fixed percent of sales, he would have incentives to maximize sales. Then he would be motivated to make an optimistic sales forecast to justify obtaining a larger sales staff. Also, the high sales forecast would be used to estimate the amount of production capacity needed, thus ensuring that adequate inventory would be available to satisfy any and all customer needs. Of course, the managers and staff who receive forecasts usually recognize the subjectivity of the situation. As Peter's superior put it, "We've received sales forecasts from him for several years, and they're always a bit conservative. We don't ask him to revise his estimates. We simply take his conservatism into account when we put together the overall sales forecast."

Market research   To provide a check on forecasts from local sales personnel, management often turns to market researchers. This group probably does not have the same incentives that sales personnel have to bias the budget. Furthermore, researchers have a different perspective on the market. While they may know little about customers' immediate needs, they can predict long-term trends in attitudes, and the effects of social and economic changes on the company's sales, potential markets, and products.

The Delphi technique   The Delphi technique is another method that is employed to enhance forecasting and reduce bias in estimates. With this method, members of the forecasting group prepare individual forecasts and submit them anonymously. Each group member obtains a copy of all forecasts but is unaware of their sources. The group then discusses the results. In this way, differences between individual forecasts can be addressed and reconciled without involving the personality or position of individual forecasters. After the differences are discussed, each group member prepares a new forecast and distributes it anonymously to the others. These forecasts are then discussed in the same manner as before. The process is repeated until the forecasts converge on a single best estimate of the coming year's sales level.

Trend analysis   Trend analysis, which can range from a simple visual extrapolation of points on a graph to a highly sophisticated computerized time series analysis, may also be helpful in preparing sales forecasts.

Time series techniques use only past observations of the data series to be forecasted. No other data are included. This methodology is justified on the grounds that since all factors that affect the data series are reflected in the actual past observations, the past data are the best reflection of available information. This approach is also relatively economical because only a list of past sales figures is needed. No other data have to be gathered.

Forecasting techniques based on trend analysis often require long series of past data to derive a suitable solution. For example, the class of forecasting techniques called Box-Jenkins models[4] requires approximately 50 past observations to be used successfully. Generally, when these models are used in accounting applications, monthly data are required so that an adequate number of observations can be obtained.

Econometric models   Another forecasting approach is to enter past sales data into a regression model to obtain a statistical estimate of the projected sales, much like we used regression models to estimate costs in Chapter 10. These models often use observations from past data series, but the sales forecast is usually associated with relevant independent variables. For example, the predicted sales for the coming period may be related to such predictor variables as economic indicators, consumer-confidence indexes, back-order volume, and other internal and external factors that the company deems relevant. Advocates of these models contend that many relevant predictors can be included and that by manipulating the assumed values of the predictors, it is possible to examine a variety of hypothetical conditions and relate them to the sales forecast. This is particularly useful for performing sensitivity analysis, which we discuss later in this chapter.

Sophisticated analytical models for forecasting are now widely available. Most companies' computers have software packages that allow economical

---

[4] See G. E. P. Box and G. M. Jenkins, *Time Series Analysis, Forecasting and Control* (San Francisco: Holden Day, 1970); and D. Z. Williams, W. B. DeMoville, and L. D. Franklin, "Costs and Forecasting," in *The Managerial and Cost Accountant's Handbook,* ed. H. A. Black and J. D. Edwards (Homewood, Ill.: Dow Jones–Irwin, 1979).

use of these models. Nonetheless, it is important to remember that no model removes the uncertainty surrounding sales forecasts. Management has often found that the intuition of local sales personnel is a better predictor than sophisticated analysis and models. As in any management decision, cost-benefit tests should be used to determine which methods are most appropriate.

Comprehensive illustration   To make our discussion of the budgeting process more concrete, we'll develop the budget for the Hypo Manufacturing Company. We use a manufacturing example because it is the most comprehensive. The methods we discuss are also applicable to nonmanufacturing organizations.

Assume that Hypo's management went through the steps discussed above and arrived at the following sales budget for fiscal year 1985:

	Units	Price per unit	Total sales revenues
Estimated sales	6,400	$800	$5,120,000

The production budget

Production must not only meet current sales demand but must ensure that inventory levels are sufficient for activity levels expected during the budget period and into the following period. It is necessary, therefore, to determine the required inventory level for the beginning and end of the budget period. Once this is done, the production budget becomes an arithmetic exercise. The production level may be computed from the basic accounting equation (also known as the basic inventory formula):

$$\text{Beginning balance} + \text{Transfers-in} \equiv \text{Transfers-out} + \text{Ending balance}$$
$$\text{BB} + \text{TI} \equiv \text{TO} + \text{EB}$$

Adapting that equation to inventories, production, and sales, we have:

$$\text{Units in beginning inventory} + \text{Required production units} = \text{Budgeted sales units for the period} + \text{Units in ending inventory}$$

Rearranging terms to solve for *required production:*

$$\text{Required production units} = \text{Budgeted sales units for the period} + \text{Units in ending inventory} - \text{Units in beginning inventory}$$

This equation states that production is equal to the sales demand plus or minus an inventory adjustment. Production and inventory are assumed to be stated in equivalent finished units.

From the sales budget above, Hypo Manufacturing has projected sales of 6,400 units. Management estimates that there will be 900 units in the beginning inventory of finished goods. Based on management's analysis, the required ending inventory is estimated to be 1,000 units. We assume for simplicity that there is no beginning or ending work in process inventory. With this information, the budgeted level of production is computed as follows:

$$\frac{\text{Required}}{\text{production}} = \frac{6,400 \text{ units}}{\text{(sales)}} + \frac{1,000 \text{ units}}{\text{(ending inventory)}} - \frac{900 \text{ units}}{\text{(beginning inventory)}}$$

$$= \underline{\underline{6,500 \text{ units}}}$$

The production budget is then reviewed with management of the production facilities to ascertain whether the budgeted levels of production can be reached with the capacity available. If not, management may revise the sales forecast or consider ways of increasing capacity. If it appears that production capacity will exceed requirements, management may want to consider other opportunities for the use of the capacity.

One benefit of the budgeting process is that it facilitates the coordination of activities. It is far better to learn about discrepancies between the sales forecast and production capacity in advance so that remedial action can be taken. Lost sales opportunities due to inadequate production capacity or unnecessary idle capacity can thus be avoided.

Budgeted cost of goods manufactured and sold

Once the sales and production budgets have been developed and the efforts of the sales and production groups are coordinated, the budgeted cost of goods manufactured and sold can be prepared. The primary job is to estimate costs of direct materials, direct labor, and manufacturing overhead at budgeted levels of production.

Direct materials   Direct materials purchases needed for the budget period are derived from the basic accounting equation:

$$\frac{\text{Units in beginning}}{\text{materials inventory}} + \frac{\text{Required}}{\substack{\text{material} \\ \text{purchases}}} = \frac{\text{Materials to}}{\substack{\text{be used in} \\ \text{production}}} + \frac{\text{Ending}}{\substack{\text{materials} \\ \text{inventory}}}$$

The beginning and ending levels of materials inventory for the budget period are estimated, often with the help of an inventory control model, while the materials to be used in production are based on production requirements. Once these are known, the required material purchases can be found by rearranging the terms in the above equation to:

$$\frac{\text{Required}}{\substack{\text{material} \\ \text{purchases}}} = \frac{\text{Materials to}}{\substack{\text{be used in} \\ \text{production}}} + \frac{\text{Estimated}}{\substack{\text{ending} \\ \text{materials} \\ \text{inventory}}} - \frac{\text{Estimated}}{\substack{\text{beginning} \\ \text{materials} \\ \text{inventory}}}$$

Production at Hypo Manufacturing for the coming period will require two kinds of materials: Material R and Material S. For each unit of output, three units of R and five units of S are required. The beginning materials inventory is estimated to consist of 2,200 units of R and 4,000 units of S. The estimated ending inventory has been determined to equal 1,300 units of R and 4,600 units of S. The estimated cost for each unit of R is $10, and the estimated cost of each unit of S is $30. These costs are expected to remain constant during the coming budget period. Required production for the production budget is 6,500 units.

Computation of the required materials purchases in units of each material would be as follows:

$$\begin{matrix} \text{Required} \\ \text{material} \\ \text{purchases} \end{matrix} = \begin{matrix} \text{Materials to} \\ \text{be used in} \\ \text{production} \end{matrix} + \begin{matrix} \text{Estimated} \\ \text{ending} \\ \text{materials} \\ \text{inventory} \end{matrix} - \begin{matrix} \text{Estimated} \\ \text{beginning} \\ \text{materials} \\ \text{inventory} \end{matrix}$$

$$R = (6,500 \times 3) + 1,300 - 2,200$$
$$= \underline{\underline{18,600 \text{ units}}}$$

$$S = (6,500 \times 5) + 4,600 - 4,000$$
$$= \underline{\underline{33,100 \text{ units}}}$$

In dollar terms, this would amount to estimated purchases of $186,000 for R (18,600 input units × $10) and $993,000 for S (33,100 input units × $30).

These data are then assembled into a budgeted statement of cost of goods manufactured and sold. This statement is shown in Illustration 17–2.

Direct labor Estimates of direct labor costs are often obtained from engineering and production management. For Hypo Manufacturing, the direct labor costs are estimated as $146 per output unit produced. Thus, for 1985, the budgeted direct labor cost of production is 6,500 units × $146 = $949,000, which is also shown in Illustration 17–2.

Overhead Unlike direct materials and direct labor, which can often be determined from an engineer's specifications for a product, overhead is composed of many different kinds of costs with varying cost behaviors. Some overhead costs vary in direct proportion to production (variable overhead); some costs vary with production, but in a step fashion (e.g., supervisory labor); and other costs are fixed and will remain the same unless capacity or long-range policies are changed. Other costs do not necessarily vary with production, but they may be changed at management's discretion (some maintenance costs may be in this category).

Budgeting overhead requires an estimate based on production levels, man-

Illustration 17–2

HYPO MANUFACTURING COMPANY
Budgeted Statement of Cost of Goods Manufactured and Sold
For the Budget Year Ended December 31, 1985

Beginning inventory work in process			–0–
Manufacturing costs:			
Direct materials:			
Beginning inventory (2,200 R @ $10 + 4,000 S @ $30)	$ 142,000		
Purchases (18,600 R @ $10 + 33,100 S @ $30)	1,179,000		
Materials available for manufacturing	1,321,000		
Less: Ending inventory (1,300 R @ $10 + 4,600 S @ $30)	(151,000)		
Total direct materials costs		$1,170,000	
Direct labor		949,000	
Manufacturing overhead[a]		1,131,000	
Total manufacturing costs			$3,250,000
Deduct: Ending work in process inventory			–0–
Cost of goods manufactured			3,250,000
Add: Beginning finished goods inventory (900 units)[b]			450,000
Deduct: Ending finished goods inventory (1,000 units)[b]			(500,000)
Cost of goods sold			$3,200,000

[a] This figure is supported by the schedule of budgeted manufacturing overhead that is detailed in Illustration 17–3.

[b] Finished goods are valued at $500 per unit $\left(=\frac{\$3,250,000}{6,500 \text{ units produced}}\right)$ assuming FIFO. Hence beginning finished goods inventory is estimated to be $450,000 (= 900 units × $500), and ending finished goods inventory is estimated to be $500,000 (= 1,000 units × $500).

agement discretion, long-range capacity and other corporate policies, and external factors such as increases in property taxes. Due to the complexity and diversity of overhead costs, cost estimation techniques such as those described in Chapter 10 are frequently used. To simplify the budgeting process, costs are usually divided into fixed and variable components, with discretionary and semifixed costs treated as fixed costs within the relevant range.

Illustration 17–3

HYPO MANUFACTURING COMPANY
Schedule of Budgeted Manufacturing Overhead
For the Budget Year Ended December 31, 1985

Variable overhead needed to produce 6,500 units:		
Indirect materials and supplies	$ 38,000	
Materials handling	59,000	
Other indirect labor	33,000	$ 130,000
Fixed manufacturing overhead:		
Supervisor labor	175,000	
Maintenance and repairs	85,000	
Plant administration	173,000	
Utilities	87,000	
Depreciation	280,000	
Insurance	43,000	
Property taxes	117,000	
Other	41,000	1,001,000
Total manufacturing overhead		$1,131,000

The schedule of budgeted manufacturing overhead for Hypo Manufacturing is presented in Illustration 17–3. For convenience, after consultation with department management, the budget staff has divided all overhead into fixed and variable costs. Hypo Manufacturing can now determine the budgeted total manufacturing costs by adding the three components—materials, labor, and overhead. This total is $3,250,000, as shown in Illustration 17–2.

Completing the budgeted costs of goods manufactured and sold

We need only to include the estimated beginning and ending work in process and finished goods inventories to determine the required number of units produced—6,500. As previously indicated, there are no work in process inventories.[5] Finished goods inventories are as follows, assuming the cost per unit is estimated to be $500 in both beginning and ending inventory:

	Units	Dollars
Beginning finished goods inventory	900	$450,000
Ending finished goods inventory	1,000	500,000

Adding the estimated beginning finished goods inventory to the estimated cost of goods manufactured, then deducting the ending finished goods inventory, yields a cost of goods manufactured and sold of $3,200,000, as shown in Illustration 17–2.

This completes the second major step in the budgeting process: determining budgeted production requirements and the cost of goods manufactured and sold. Obviously, this part of the budgeting effort can be extremely complex in manufacturing companies. It can be very difficult to coordinate production schedules among numerous plants, some using other plants' products as their direct materials. It is also difficult to coordinate production schedules with sales forecasts. Misestimates of material availability, labor shortages, strikes, availability of energy, and production capacity often require reworking the entire budget.

Revising the initial budget   At this point in the budget cycle a first draft budget has been prepared. There is usually a good deal of coordinating and revising before the budget is considered final. For example, projected production figures may call for revised estimates of direct materials purchases and direct labor costs. Bottlenecks may be discovered in production that will hamper the company's ability to deliver a particular product and thus affect the sales forecast. The revision process may be repeated several times until a coordinated, feasible master budget evolves. No part of the budget is really

---

[5] If the company has beginning and ending work in process inventories, units are usually expressed as equivalent finished units, as discussed in Chapter 6 on process costing, and treated the way we have treated finished goods inventories. In most companies, estimates of work in process inventories are omitted from the budget because they leave a minimal impact on the budget.

formally adopted until the master budget is finally approved by the board of directors.

Marketing and administrative budget

Determining the appropriate budget for marketing and administrative costs is very difficult because management has much discretion in this area. For example, a company hired a new marketing executive who was famous for cost-cutting skills. The executive ordered an immediate 50 percent cut in the company's advertising budget, a freeze on hiring, and a 50 percent cut in the travel budget. The result—costs fell, and there was little immediate impact on sales. A year later, looking for new challenges, the executive moved on to another company. Soon afterwards, the executive's former employers noticed that sales were down because the company had lost market share to some aggressive competitors. Were the marketing executive's cost-cutting actions really in the best interest of the company? To this day, nobody can give a documented answer to that question because it is difficult to prove a causal link between the cost-cutting and the subsequent decrease in sales.

In another case, a company's president was the only one who used the corporate jet—and he used it only rarely. So the internal audit staff recommended selling it. The company president rejected the idea, saying, "One of the reasons I put up with the pressures and responsibilities of this job is because I enjoy some of its perquisites, including the corporate jet." Some costs that appear unnecessary, especially perquisites, are really part of the total compensation package and may, therefore, be necessary costs.

The budgeting objective here is to estimate the amount of marketing and administrative costs required to operate the company at its projected level of sales and production and to achieve long-term company goals. For example, the budgeted sales figures may be based on a new product promotion campaign. If production and sales are projected to increase, it is likely that an increase in support services—data processing, accounting, personnel, and so forth—will be needed to operate the company at the higher projected levels.

An easy way to deal with the problem is to start with a previous period's actual or budgeted amounts and make adjustments for inflation, changes in operations, and similar changes between periods. This method has been criticized and may be viewed as very simplistic, but it does have one advantage—it is relatively easy and inexpensive. As always, the benefits of improved budgeting methods must justify their increased costs.

At Hypo Manufacturing, each level of management submits a budget request for marketing and administrative costs to the next higher level, which reviews it and, usually after some adjustments, approves it. The budget is passed up through the ranks until it reaches top management. As shown in Illustration 17–4, the schedule of marketing and administrative costs is divided into variable and fixed components. In this case, variable marketing costs are those that vary with *sales* (not production). Fixed marketing costs are usually those that can be changed at management's discretion—for example, advertising.

Illustration 17–4

HYPO MANUFACTURING COMPANY
Schedule of Budgeted Marketing and Administrative Costs
For the Budget Year Ended December 31, 1985

Variable marketing costs:		
Sales commissions	$260,000	
Other marketing	104,000	
Total variable marketing costs		$ 364,000
Fixed marketing costs:		
Sales salaries	100,000	
Advertising	193,000	
Other	78,000	
Total fixed marketing costs		371,000
Total marketing costs		735,000
Administrative costs (all fixed):		
Administrative salaries	254,000	
Legal and accounting staff	141,000	
Data processing services	103,000	
Outside professional services	39,000	
Depreciation—building, furniture, and equipment	94,000	
Other, including interest	26,000	
Taxes—other than income	160,000	
Total administrative costs		817,000
Total budgeted marketing and administrative costs		$1,552,000

Budgeted income statement

According to the controller at Hypo Manufacturing, "At this point, we're able to put together the entire budgeted income statement for the period (Illustration 17–5), so we can determine our projected operating profits. By making whatever adjustments are required to satisfy generally accepted accounting principles (GAAP) for external reporting, we can project net income after income taxes and earnings per share. If we don't like the results, we

Illustration 17–5

HYPO MANUFACTURING COMPANY
Budgeted Income Statement
For the Budget Year Ended December 31, 1985

Budgeted revenues:		
Sales (6,400 units at $800)		$5,120,000
Costs:		
Cost of goods manufactured and sold (Illustration 17–2) ...	$3,200,000	
Marketing and administrative costs (Illustration 17–4)	1,552,000	
Total budgeted costs		4,752,000
Operating profit		368,000
Federal and other income taxes[a]		128,000
Operating profit after taxes		$ 240,000

[a] Computed by the company's tax staff.

go back to the budgeted income statement and, starting at the top, go through each step to see if we can increase sales revenues or cut costs. We usually find some plant overhead, marketing, or administrative costs that can be cut or postponed without doing too much damage to the company's operations."

Hypo's board of directors approved the sales, production, and marketing and administrative budgets and budgeted income statement as submitted. Note that the budgeted income statement also includes estimated federal and other income taxes that were obtained from the tax staff. We will not detail the tax estimation process because it is a highly technical area separate from cost accounting.

Cash budget

Although the budgeted income statement is a very important tool for planning operations, a company also needs cash to operate. Cash planning and the development of a cash budget are important to assure company solvency, maximize returns from cash balances, and determine whether the company is generating enough cash for present and future operations.

Preparing a cash budget requires that all revenues, costs, and other transactions be examined in terms of their effects on cash. The budgeted cash receipts are computed from the collections from accounts receivable, cash sales, sale of assets, borrowing, issuing stock, and other cash-generating activities. Disbursements are computed by counting the cash required to pay for materials purchases, manufacturing and other operations, federal income taxes, and stockholder dividends. In addition, the cash disbursements necessary to repay debt and acquire new assets must also be incorporated in the cash budget. Hypo Manufacturing's cash budget is shown in Illustration 17–6. The source of each item is indicated.

Budgeted balance sheets

Budgeted balance sheets, or statements of financial position, combine an estimate of financial position at the beginning of the budget period with the estimated results of operations for the period (from the income statements) and estimated changes in assets and liabilities. The latter results from management's decisions about optimal levels of capital investment in long-term assets (the capital budget), investment in working capital, and financing decisions. Decision making in these areas is, for the most part, the treasurer's function. We shall assume these decisions have been made and incorporate their results in the budgeted balance sheets. Illustration 17–7 presents Hypo Manufacturing's budgeted balance sheets at the beginning and end of 1985.

Master budget development in review

We have completed the development of a comprehensive budget for Hypo Manufacturing. A model of the budgeting process is presented in Illustration 17–8. Although we have simplified the presentation, you can still see that assembling a master budget is a complex process that requires careful coordination of many different organization segments.

Illustration 17–6

HYPO MANUFACTURING COMPANY
Cash Budget
For the Budget Year Ended December 31, 1985

Cash balance beginning of period[a]		$ 150,000
Receipts:		
Collections on accounts[a]	$5,185,000	
Sales of assets[a]	25,000	
Total receipts		$5,210,000
Less disbursements:		
Payments for accounts payable[a]	1,164,000	
Direct labor (Illustration 17–2)	949,000	
Manufacturing overhead requiring cash less noncash		
depreciation charges (Illustration 17–3)	851,000	
Marketing and administrative costs less noncash		
charges (Illustration 17–4)	1,458,000	
Payments for federal income taxes (per discussion		
with the tax staff)	252,000	
Dividends[a]	140,000	
Reduction in long-term debt[a]	83,000	
Acquisition of new assets[b]	320,000	
Total disbursements		$5,217,000
Budgeted ending cash balance (ties to Illustration 17–7)[c]		$ 143,000

[a] Estimated by the treasurer's office.
[b] Estimated by the treasurer's office, per the capital budget.
[c] Solved from the basic accounting equation:

$$BB + TI = TO + EB$$
$$\$150,000 + \$5,210,000 = \$5,217,000 + EB$$
$$EB = \$143,000$$

Key relationships: Sales cycle

Assembling the master budget demonstrates some key relations among sales, accounts receivable, and cash flows in the sales cycle. Advantages of understanding these relationships include the ability to solve for amounts that are unknown and to audit the master budget to ensure that the basic accounting equation has been correctly applied.

At Hypo Manufacturing, for example, the relationships among budgeted sales, accounts receivable, and cash receipts were as follows:

Sales	Accounts Receivable (Illustration 17–6)		Cash (Illustration 17–6)	
	BB 220,000		BB 150,000	
Illustrations	17–5 and 17–6	Illustrations	17–6 and 17–7	
5,120,000 →	5,120,000	5,185,000 →	5,185,000	
			25,000	5,217,000
	EB 155,000		EB 143,000	

Illustration 17–7

HYPO MANUFACTURING COMPANY
Budgeted Balance Sheets
For the Budget Year Ended December 31, 1985
(in thousands)

	Balance (January 1, 1985)	1985 Additions	1985 Subtractions	Balance (December 1985)
Assets				
Current assets:				
Cash	$ 150ª	$ 5,210ª	$ 5,217ª	$ 143ª
Accounts receivable	220*	5,120ᵇ	5,185ª	155*
Inventories	592ᶜ	3,259ᵈ	3,200ᵉ	651ᶠ
Other current assets	23*	100*	100*	23*
Total current assets	985	13,689	13,702	972
Long-term assets:				
Property, plant, and equipment	2,475*	320ª	300*	2,495*
Less: Accumulated depreciation	(850)*	(374)ᵍ	(275)*	(949)*
Total assets	$2,610	$13,635	$13,727	$2,518
Equities				
Current liabilities:				
Accounts payable	$ 140*	$ 1,179ʰ	$ 1,164ª	$ 155*
Taxes payable	156*	128ᵇ	252ª	32*
Current portion of long-term debt	83*	0*	83ª	0*
Total current liabilities	379	1,307	1,499	187
Long-term liabilities	576*	0*	0*	576*
Total liabilities	955	1,307	1,499	763
Shareholders' equity:				
Common stock	350*	0*	0*	350*
Retained earnings	1,305*	240ⁱ	140ª	1,405*
Total shareholders' equity	1,655	240	140	1,755
Total equities	$2,610	$ 1,547	$ 1,639	$2,518

* Estimated by personnel in the company's treasury department.

ª From cash budget (Illustration 17–6).

ᵇ From budgeted income statement (Illustration 17–5). Assumes all sales are on account.

ᶜ From budgeted statement of cost of goods manufactured and sold (Illustration 17–2), sum of beginning direct materials, work in process, and finished goods inventories ($142 + 0 + 450 = $592).

ᵈ From budgeted statement of cost of goods manufactured and sold (Illustration 17–2), sum of material purchases, direct labor, and manufacturing overhead ($1,179 + 949 + 1,131 = $3,259).

ᵉ From budgeted statement of cost of goods manufactured and sold (Illustration 17–2).

ᶠ From budgeted statement of cost of goods manufactured and sold (Illustration 17–2), sum of ending direct materials, work in process, and finished goods inventories ($151 + 0 + 500 = $651).

ᵍ Depreciation of $280 from schedule of budgeted manufacturing overhead (Illustration 17–3) plus depreciation of $94 from the schedule of budgeted marketing and administrative costs (Illustration 17–4) equals $374 increase in accumulated depreciation in 1985.

ʰ From budgeted statement of cost of goods manufactured and sold (Illustration 17–2). Accounts payable increases are assumed to be for materials purchases only.

ⁱ From budgeted income statement (Illustration 17–5), operating profits after taxes.

Illustration 17-8   **Assembling the master budget: manufacturing organization**

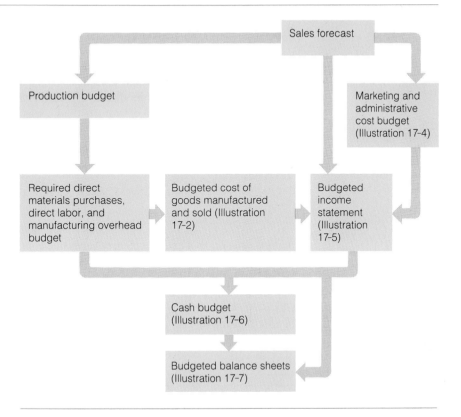

Sales are assumed to be on account. Note that the cash account and the cash budget in Illustration 17-6 are identical.

If an amount in the sales cycle is unknown, the basic accounting equation can be used to find the unknown amount. For example, suppose all of the amounts in the above diagram are known except ending cash balance and sales. Using the basic accounting equation;

$$BB + TI \equiv TO + EB$$

find sales from the Accounts Receivable account:

$$\$220,000 + TI \text{ (sales)} = \$5,185,000 + \$155,000$$
$$TI = \$5,185,000 + \$155,000 - \$220,000$$
$$= \$5,120,000$$

Find ending cash balance from the Cash account:

$$\$150,000 + (\$5,185,000 + \$25,000) = \$5,217,000 + EB$$
$$\$150,000 + \$5,185,000 + \$25,000 - \$5,217,000 = EB$$
$$EB = \$143,000$$

Budgeting in merchandising operations

While a manufacturing operation provides a good comprehensive example, budgeting is extensively used in other environments as well, as discussed in this and the following sections.

As in manufacturing, the sales budget in merchandising drives the operating budget. The major difference is that a merchandiser has no production budget. Instead, there is a merchandise purchases budget, much like the direct materials purchases budget in manufacturing. For example, at Stores, Inc., the purchases budget for a line of women's suits was determined at follows:

	Units	Dollars
Estimated sales for 1985	100	$20,000
Add estimated ending inventory	10	2,000
Deduct estimated beginning inventory	(15)	(3,000)
Required purchases	95	$19,000

As you can see, this budget requires extensive coordination between the managers responsible for sales and those in charge of buying. Because of the critical importance of timing and seasonality in merchandising, special attention is usually given to short-term budgets (for example, spring, summer, Christmas season budgets). The budget helps make formal an ongoing process of coordinating buying and selling. This coordination is critical to the success of merchandising enterprises.

Budgeting in service enterprises

A key difference in the master budget of a service enterprise is the absence of product or material inventories. Consequently, there is no need for a production budget, as in manufacturing, or a merchandise purchases budget, as in merchandising. Instead, service businesses need to carefully coordinate sales (that is, services rendered) with the necessary labor. Managers must ensure that personnel with the right skills are available at the right times.

The budget at David & Sons Company, a regional accounting firm, is developed around the three major services offered: audit, tax, and consulting. Projections of revenue are based on estimates of the number and kinds of clients the firm would service in the budget year and the amount of services requested. The forecasts stem primarily from services provided in previous years with adjustments for new clients, new services to existing clients, loss of clients, and changes in the rates charged for services.

Once the quantity of services (expressed in labor-hours) is forecast, the firm develops its budget for personnel. Staffing to meet client needs is a very important part of the budgeting process. As a partner of the firm put it, "If we overestimate the amount of services we'll provide, we may lose money because we have overstaffed. Our labor costs will be too high compared to our revenues. If we underestimate, we may lose business because we can't provide the services our clients need."

Budgeting in nonprofit organizations	The master budget has added importance in nonprofit organizations because it is usually a document that is used as a basis for authorizing the expenditure of funds. In many governmental units, the approved budget is a *legal* authorization for expenditure and the penalties for exceeding the authorized expenditures in the budget could be severe. This partially explains why a balanced budget takes on added importance in nonprofit organizations.[6]
Budgeting under uncertainty	Any projection of the future is uncertain. Recognizing this, managers often perform sensitivity analysis on their projections. This analysis is based on hypothetical questions, such as: What if labor costs are 10 percent higher (or lower) than projected? What if new health and safety regulations are passed that increase our costs of operations? What if our major supplier of direct materials goes bankrupt? By asking and answering such questions during the planning phase, management can discover the riskiness of various phases of its operations, and develop contingency plans.

As part of the budget plan at Hypo Manufacturing, for example, local managers were asked to provide three forecasts: their best estimate, an optimistic estimate (defined as "a 10 percent or less chance that conditions would be better than the optimistic estimate"), and a pessimistic estimate (defined as the situation where there is "a 10 percent or less chance that conditions would be worse"). The optimistic and pessimistic forecasts were not nearly so detailed as the best estimates, but they did highlight some potential problems and risks. From this analysis, top management learned that a major supplier of a distant plant was on the verge of bankruptcy. As a result, management developed relationships with other suppliers, increased the stockpiles of direct materials in the plant, and worked with the supplier to improve its financial position.

Top management at Hypo Manufacturing also learned that if all costs were as expected and the pessimistic forecast of sales came true, the company would suffer an operating loss. The primary reason for this would be a worsening of general economic conditions that would decrease demand for the company's products. This was important information to consider in making financial analyses. Further, management put an "early warning" system in place in which it carefully monitored such key economic variables as unemployment, consumer spending, gross national product, and the like. If these indicators signaled a downturn in the economy, management's contingency plan was to reduce production gradually so excess inventories would not build up

---

[6] For a further discussion of budgeting in government and other nonprofit organizations, see K. V. Ramanathan, *Management Control in Nonprofit Organizations* (New York: John Wiley & Sons, 1982); R. N. Anthony and R. E. Herzlinger, *Management Control in Nonprofit Organizations* (Homewood, Ill.: R. D. Irwin, 1980); and E. S. Lynn and R. J. Freeman, *Fund Accounting* (Englewood Cliffs, N.J.: Prentice-Hall, 1983).

Illustration 17–9 **Sensitivity analysis and contingency planning**

Sensitivity analysis "What if?"	Contingency planning "If, then."
	Status quo
Optimistic (Economic conditions	Increase discretionary costs
and sales better than expected.)	Increase production
Expected sales	Status quo
	Status quo
Pessimistic (Economic conditions	Reduce discretionary costs
and sales worse than expected.)	Curtail production

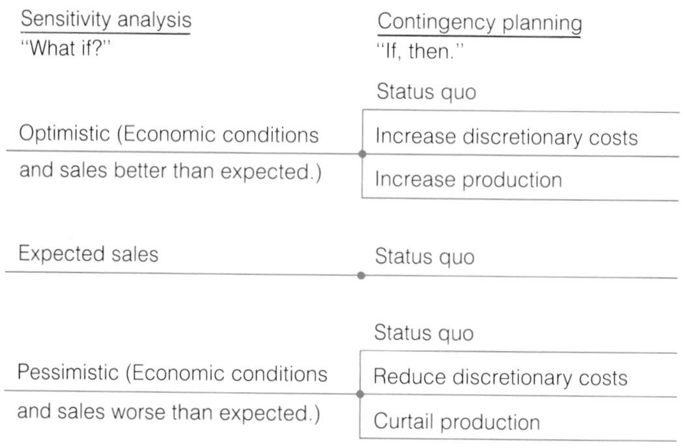

and to reduce discretionary spending on overhead, marketing, and administrative costs.

Illustration 17–9 provides an overview of sensitivity analysis and contingency planning. For each hypothesis in the sensitivity analysis, there is a choice of steps that can be taken. The procedure can be as simple as a diagram and a few notes on a piece of paper or as complex as a mathematical model incorporated into computerized formal planning models.[7] Of course, decisions about these models' degree of sophistication should be subject to cost-benefit analysis.

The incorporation of uncertainty into budget estimates can be quite useful. A major benefit of formal planning models is to explore many alternatives and options in the planning process. While it is beyond the scope of this book to go into details of formal corporate planning models, we think you can see how the budget plan can be integrated with formal planning models which set forth mathematical relationships among the operating and financial activities of an organization. The use of computer-based simulation models facilitates the asking of numerous "what if " questions which, as the number grows, become too difficult to deal with by hand.

Summary

This chapter has discussed and illustrated the budget process. The budget is part of the overall plan for achieving an organization's objectives. The master budget is a one-year (usually) plan that encompasses budgeted sales

---

[7] Chapter 24 discusses the use of mathematical models to deal with uncertainty.

and production, budgeted income statement, balance sheet, and cash flow statement, as well as supporting schedules.

The key to the budget is a good sales forecast because so many other parts of the budget depend on the sales forecast. The sales forecast is usually derived from multiple sources of data, including data provided by sales personnel and market researchers, and data from statistical analyses. Illustration 17–8 in the chapter shows how the rest of the master budget relates to the sales forecast.

Merchandising budgets are similar to manufacturing, except they have no production budget. Service organizations are similar, except they have no inventories. The budget is not only a planning tool, but also a legal authorization for expenditure in governmental units.

Budgeting under uncertainty involves making many forecasts, each representing a different possible set of circumstances. Sensitivity analysis ("what if") and contingency planning ("if, then") are used to derive a set of plans for each possible set of circumstances.

Terms and concepts	The following terms and concepts should be familiar to you after reading this chapter.

Budgeted balance sheets   **Participative budgeting**

Budgeting under uncertainty   **Production budget**

Cash budget   **Profit plan**

Delphi technique   **Sales forecasts**

Econometric models   **Sensitivity analysis**

Master budget   **Strategic long-range profit plan**

Organizational goals   **Trend analysis**

Self-study problem	Refer to the problem for Hypo Manufacturing Company in the chapter example. Assume the sales forecast was increased to 7,000 units with no change in price. The new target ending inventories are:

Finished goods   1,200 units
Material R   1,500
Material S   4,900

Payments for income taxes and income tax expense are proportional to operating profit before tax. Accounts receivable will increase by another $40,000 at this new sales level. Accounts payable will increase by an additional $2,000 at the new production level. Prepare a budgeted income statement, cost of goods manufactured and sold statement, administrative and selling cost budget, and cash budget for the coming year with this new data.

Solution to self-study problem

Exhibit A (SSP)

HYPO MANUFACTURING COMPANY
Budgeted Statement of Cost of Goods Manufactured and Sold
For the Budget Year Ended December 31, 1985
(prepared as of September 30, 1984)
(compare to Illustration 17–2)

Beginning work in process inventory			–0–
Manufacturing costs:			
Direct materials:			
Beginning inventory (Illustration 17–2) . . .	$ 142,000		
Purchases[a] (21,200 R @ $10 + 37,400 S @ $30)	1,334,000		
Materials available for manufacturing	1,476,000		
Less: Ending inventory (1,500 R @ $10 + 4,900 S @ $30)	(162,000)		
Total direct materials costs		$1,314,000	
Direct labor $\left(\$949,000 \times \dfrac{7,300}{6,500}\right)$		1,066,000	
Manufacturing overhead (Exhibit B) . . .		1,147,000	
Total manufacturing costs			$3,527,000
Deduct: Ending work in process inventory . . .			–0–
Cost of goods manufactured			3,527,000
Add: Beginning finished goods inventory			450,000
Deduct: Ending finished goods inventory[a]			(580,000)
Cost of goods sold			$3,397,000

[a] Additional computations:

Required production:

$$BB + Production = Sales + EB$$
$$900 + \quad P \quad = 7,000 + 1,200$$
$$ P \quad = 7,300$$

Material requirements:

$$R: \quad BB \ + Purchases = Production + EB$$
$$2,200 + \quad P \quad + (7,300 \times 3) + 1,500$$
$$ P \quad = 21,200$$

$$S: \quad BB \ + Purchases = Production + EB$$
$$4,000 + \quad P \quad = (7,300 \times 5) + 4,900$$
$$ P \quad = 37,400$$

Ending finished goods inventory (assuming FIFO):

$$\frac{\text{Ending units}}{\text{Units productted}} \times \text{Cost of goods manufactured} = \frac{1,200}{7,300} \times \$3,527,000$$
$$= \$580,000$$

Exhibit B (SSP)

HYPO MANUFACTURING COMPANY
Schedule of Budgeted Manufacturing Overhead
For the Budget Year Ended December 31, 1985
(prepared as of September 30, 1984)
(compare to Illustration 17–3)

Variable (based on production of 7,300 units):[a]		
Indirect materials and supplies	$ 43,000	
Materials handling....................................	66,000	
Other indirect labor..................................	37,000	$ 146,000
Fixed (same as for production of 6,500 units):		
Supervisor labor	175,000	
Maintenance and repairs	85,000	
Plant administration	173,000	
Utilities	87,000	
Depreciation	280,000	
Insurance	43,000	
Property taxes	117,000	
Other	41,000	1,001,000
Total manufacturing overhead		$1,147,000

[a] Additional computations:

$$\text{Indirect materials:} \quad \$38,000 \times \frac{7,300}{6,500} = \$43,000$$

$$\text{Materials handling:} \quad \$59,000 \times \frac{7,300}{6,500} = \$66,000$$

$$\text{Other indirect labor:} \quad \$33,000 \times \frac{7,300}{6,500} = \$37,000$$

Exhibit C (SSP)

HYPO MANUFACTURING COMPANY
Schedule of Budgeted Marketing and Administrative Costs
For the Budget Year Ended December 31, 1985
(prepared as of September 30, 1984)
(compare to Illustration 17–4)

Variable marketing costs:[a]		
Sales commissions	$284,000	
Other marketing	114,000	
Total variable marketing costs		$ 398,000
Fixed marketing costs:		
Sales salaries	100,000	
Advertising	193,000	
Other	78,000	
Total fixed marketing costs		371,000
Total marketing costs		769,000
Administrative costs (all fixed):		
Administrative salaries	254,000	
Legal and accounting staff	141,000	
Data processing services	103,000	
Outside professional services	39,000	
Depreciation—building, furniture, and equipment	94,000	
Insurance	26,000	
Taxes—other than income	160,000	
Total administrative costs		817,000
Total budgeted marketing and administrative costs		$1,586,000

[a] Additional computations:

$$\text{Sales commissions} = \$284,000 = \$260,000 \times \frac{7,000 \text{ units}}{6,400 \text{ units}}$$

$$\text{Other marketing} = \$114,000 = \$104,000 \times \frac{7,000 \text{ units}}{6,400 \text{ units}}$$

Exhibit D (SSP)

HYPO MANUFACTURING COMPANY
Budgeted Income Statement
For the Budget Year Ended December 31, 1985
(prepared as of September 30, 1984)
(compare to Illustration 17–5)

Budgeted revenues:		
Sales (7,000 units at $800)		$5,600,000
Budgeted expenses:		
Cost of goods manufactured and sold (Exhibit A)	$3,397,000	
Marketing and administrative costs (Exhibit C)	1,586,000	
Total budgeted costs		4,983,000
Budgeted operating profits		617,000
Federal and other income taxes[a]		215,000
Budgeted operating profits after taxes		$ 402,000

[a] Assumed proportional to operating profit:

$$\$128,000 \times \frac{\$617,000}{\$368,000} = \$215,000$$

Exhibit E (SSP)

HYPO MANUFACTURING COMPANY
Cash Budget
For the Budget Year Ended December 31, 1985
(prepared as of September 30, 1984)
(compare with Illustration 17–6)

Cash balance beginning of period		$ 150,000
Receipts:		
Collections on accounts[a]	$5,625,000	
Sales of assets (per management)	25,000	
Total receipts		5,650,000
Less disbursements:		
Payments for accounts payable[b]	1,317,000	
Direct labor (Exhibit A)	1,066,000	
Manufacturing overhead requiring cash less		
noncash depreciation charges (Exhibit B)	867,000	
Marketing and administrative costs less		
noncash charges (Exhibit C)	1,492,000	
Required payments for federal income taxes[c]		
(per discussion with the staff)	423,000	
Dividends and other distributions to shareholders		
(per management)	140,000	
Reduction in long-term debt	83,000	
Acquisition of new assets	320,000	
Total disbursements		5,708,000
Budgeted ending cash balance		$ 92,000

Additional computations:

[a] Collections on account per Illustration 17–6	$5,185,000
Additional sales ($5,600,000 − $5,120,000) (from Exhibit D and Illustration 17–5)	480,000
Less increase in receivables	(40,000)
	$5,625,000
[b] Payments on account per Illustration 17–6	$1,164,000
Additional materials purchases—per Exhibit A and Illustration 17–2	
($1,334,000 − $1,179,000)	155,000
Less increase in payables	(2,000)
	$1,317,000

[c] Payments on federal taxes are assumed to increase proportionately with the increase in budgeted operating profits from the text example to this one.

$$\left[\frac{\text{Budgeting operating profits in Exhibit D}}{\text{Budgeted operating profits in Illustration 17–5}} \right] \times \left[\begin{array}{c} \text{Budgeted tax} \\ \text{payments in} \\ \text{Illustration 17–6} \end{array} \right] = \frac{\$617,000}{368,000} \times \$252,000 = \$423,000$$

Questions

17–1. Explain the difference between strategic plans and the budget plan.

17–2. Why would more detail be included in a budget for the coming period than appears in a longer-range forecast?

17–3. The chief executive officer of Rigid Plastics Corporation remarked to a colleague, "I don't understand why other companies waste so much time in the budgeting process. I set our company goals, and everyone strives to meet them. What's wrong with that approach?" Comment on the executive's remarks.

17–4. What is the danger in relying entirely on middle management estimates of sales, costs, and other data used in budget planning?

17–5. Multigoal Corporation has established a bonus plan for its employees. An employee receives a bonus if the employee's subunit meets the cost levels specified in the annual budget plan. If the subunit's costs exceed the budget, no bonus is earned by employees of that subunit. What problems might arise with this bonus plan?

17–6. Why is it important to estimate inventory levels when estimating the production level required for a given sales forecast?

17–7. How can budgeting aid in the coordination of corporate activities?

17–8. Surveying the accounts payable records, a clerk in the controllers' office noted that expenses appeared to rise significantly within a month of the close of the budget period. The organization did not have a seasonal product or service to explain this behavior. Do you have a suggested explanation?

Exercises

17–9. Estimate sales revenues

Welcome Wedge Company manufactures a line of tools. Last year the company sold 500,000 Type A wedges at a price of $2 per unit. The company estimates that this volume represents a 20 percent share of the Type A wedge market. Marketing specialists have determined that as a result of the new advertising campaign and packaging, the company will increase its share of the market to 24 percent. The market itself is expected to increase by 5 percent. Due to changes in prices, the new price for the Type A wedge will be $2.15 per unit. This new price is expected to be in line with the competition.

Required:

Estimate the sales revenues for the coming year.

17–10. Estimate production levels

XiPhi, Inc., has just made its sales forecast for the coming period. The marketing department estimates that the company will be able to sell 480,000 units over the coming year. In the past, management has found that inventories of finished goods should be maintained at approximately three month's sales. The inventory at the start of the budget period is 27,000 units.

Required:

Estimate the production level required for the coming year.

17–11. Estimate cash disbursements

Terry Company is preparing its cash budget for the month of April. The following information is available concerning its inventories:

Inventories at beginning of April	$ 90,000
Estimated purchases for April	440,000
Estimated cost of goods sold for April	450,000
Estimated payments in April for purchases in March	75,000
Estimated payments in April for purchases prior to March	20,000
Estimated payments in April for purchases in April	75%

Required:

What are the estimated cash disbursements for inventories in April?

17–12. Estimate cash collections

The Fresh Company is preparing its cash budget for the month of May. The following information is available concerning its accounts receivable:

Estimated credit sales for May	$200,000
Actual credit sales for April	150,000
Estimated collections in May for credit sales in May	20%
Estimated collections in May for credit sales in April	70%
Estimated collections in May for credit sales prior to April	$ 12,000
Estimated write-offs in May for uncollectible credit sales	8,000
Estimated provision for bad debts in May for credit sales in May	7,000

Required:

What are the estimated cash receipts from accounts receivable collections in May?

(CPA adapted)

17–13. Estimate production and materials requirements

Vivid Colors Corporation manufactures a special line of graphic tubing items. For each of the next two coming years, the company estimates it will sell 150,000 units of this item. The beginning finished goods inventory contains 40,000 units. The target for next year's ending inventory is 20,000 units.

Each unit requires 5 feet of plastic tubing. The tubing inventory currently includes 100,000 feet of the required tubing. Materials on hand are targeted to equal three month's production. Any shortage in materials will be made up by the immediate purchase of materials.

Required:

Compute the production target and the materials requirements for the coming period.

17–14. Prepare a production budget

Eastern Forest Products Corporation manufactures floral containers. The controller is preparing a budget for the coming year and has asked for your assistance. The following data have been collected regarding costs and other factors related to container production:

Direct material specifications per container:
  1 pound Z-A styrene at $.40 per pound
  2 pounds Vasa finish at .80 per pound

Direct labor per container: ¼ hour at
$8.60 per hour

Overhead per container:

Indirect labor	$.12
Indirect materials	.03
Power	.07
Equipment usage cost	.36
Building occupancy	.19
Total overhead per unit	$.77

You learn that the equipment usage cost and building occupancy are fixed costs; these unit costs are based on a normal production of 20,000 units per year. Other overhead costs are variable. Plant capacity is sufficient to produce 25,000 units per year.

Labor costs are not expected to change during the year. However, the supplier of the Vasa finish has informed the company that a 10 percent price increase will be imposed at the start of the coming budget period. No other costs are expected to change.

During the coming budget period, the company expects to sell 18,000 units. Finished goods inventory is targeted to increase by 3,000 units to build for an expected sales increase the year after next. Production will take place evenly throughout the year. The inventory levels for Vasa finish and Z-A styrene are expected to remain unchanged throughout the year. There is no work in process inventory.

Required:

Prepare a production budget for the coming year.

17–15. Estimate administrative and selling budget

Your division of your company has just received its selling expense report for the past month. The report is reproduced below.

Item	Amount
Sales commissions	$135,000
Sales staff salaries	32,000
Telephone and mailing	16,200
Building rent	20,000
Heat, light, and water	4,100
Packaging and delivery	27,400
Depreciation	12,500
Marketing consultants	19,700

You have been asked to develop budgeted cost estimates for the coming year. Since this month is typical, you decide to prepare an estimated budget for a "typical month" in the coming year.

Some additional data that you uncover follows:

1. Sales volume is expected to increase by 5 percent.
2. Sales prices are expected to increase by 10 percent.
3. Commissions are based on a percentage of selling prices.
4. Sales staff salaries are scheduled to increase 8 percent in the middle of next year.
5. Building rent is based on a five-year lease that expires in three years.
6. Telephone and mailing expenses are scheduled to increase by 8 percent even with no change in sales volume. However, these costs are variable with the number of units sold, as are packaging and delivery costs.
7. Heat, light, and water are scheduled to increase by 12 percent.
8. Depreciation includes furniture and fixtures used by the sales staff. The company has just acquired an additional $19,000 in furniture that will be received at the start of next year and will be depreciated over a 10-year life using the straight-line method.
9. The marketing consultants expenses were for a special advertising campaign. The company runs these campaigns from time to time. During the coming year, the costs are expected to average $35,000 per month.

Required:

Prepare a budget for selling expenses for a typical month in the coming year.

17–16. Estimate cash disbursements

Serven Corporation has estimated its activity for June. Selected data from these estimated amounts are as follows:

Sales	$700,000
Gross profit (based on sales)	30%
Increase in trade accounts receivable during month	$ 20,000
Change in accounts payable during month	–0–
Increase in inventory during month	$ 10,000

Variable selling and administrative expenses (S&A) includes a charge for uncollectible accounts of 1 percent of sales.

Total S&A is $71,000 per month plus 15 percent of sales.

Depreciation expense of $40,000 per month is included in fixed S&A.

Required: On the basis of the above data, what are the estimated cash disbursements from operations for June?

(CPA adapted)

Problems and cases

17–17. Budgeting process: Behavioral issues

Springfield Corporation operates on a calendar year-basis. It begins the annual budgeting process in late August when the president establishes targets for the total dollar sales and net income before taxes for the next year.

The sales target is given to the marketing department where the marketing manager formulates a sales budget by product line in both units and dollars. From this budget sales quotas by product line in units and dollars are established for each of the corporation's sales districts.

The marketing manager also estimates the cost of the marketing activities required to support the target sales volume, and prepares a tentative marketing expense budget.

The executive vice president uses the sales and profit targets, the sales budget by product line, and the tentative marketing expense budget to determine the dollar amounts that can be devoted to manufacturing and corporate office expense. The executive vice president prepares the budget for corporate expenses and then forwards to the production department the product-line sales budget in units and the total dollar amount that can be devoted to manufacturing.

The production manager meets with the factory managers to develop a manufacturing plan that will produce the required units when needed within the cost constraints set by the executive vice president. The budgeting process usually comes to a halt at this point because the production department does not consider the financial resources allocated to be adequate.

When this standstill occurs, the vice president of finance, the executive vice president, the marketing manager, and the production manager meet together to determine the final budgets for each of the areas. This normally results in a modest increase in the total amount available for manufacturing costs while the marketing expense and corporate office expense budgets are cut. The total sales and net income figures proposed by the president are seldom changed. Although the participants are seldom pleased with the compromise, these budgets are final. Each executive then develops new detailed budget for the operations in his or her area.

None of the areas has achieved its budget in recent years. Sales often run below the target. When budgeted sales are not achieved, each area is expected to cut costs so that the president's profit target can still be met. However, the profit target is seldom met because costs are not cut enough. In fact, costs often run above the original budget in all functional areas. The president is disturbed that Springfield has not been able to meet the sales and profit targets. He hired a consultant with considerable experience with companies in Springfield's industry. The consultant reviewed the budgets for the past four years. He concluded that the product-line sales budgets were reasonable, and that the cost and expense budgets were adequate for the budgeted sales and production levels.

Required:

a. Discuss how the budgeting process as employed by Springfield Corporation contributed to the failure to achieve the president's sales and profit targets.

b. Suggest how Springfield Corporation's budgeting process could be revised to correct the problems.

c. Should the functional areas be expected to cut their costs when sales volume falls below budget? Explain your answer.

(CMA adapted)

17–18. Analyze budget planning process: Behavioral issues

RV Industries manufactures and sells recreation vehicles. The company has eight divisions strategically located to be near major markets. Each division has a sales force and two to four manufacturing plants. These divisions operate as autonomous profit centers responsible for purchasing, operations, and sales.

John Collins, the corporate controller, described the divisional performance measurement system as follows. "We allow the divisions to control the entire operation from the purchase of direct materials to the sale of the product. We, at corporate headquarters, only get involved in strategic decisions, such as developing new product lines. Each division is responsible for meeting its market needs by providing the right products at a low cost on a timely basis. Frankly, the divisions need to focus on cost control, delivery, and services to customers in order to become more profitable.

"While we give the divisions considerable autonomy, we watch their monthly income statements very closely. Each month's actual performance is compared with the budget in considerable detail. If the actual sales or contribution margin is more than 4 or 5 percent below the budget, we jump on the division people immediately. I might add that we don't have much trouble getting their attention. All of the management people at the plant and division level can add appreciably to their annual salaries with bonuses if actual net income is considerably greater than budget."

The budgeting process begins in August when division sales managers, after consulting with their sales personnel, estimate sales for the next calendar year. These estimates are sent to plant managers who use the sales forecasts to prepare production estimates. At the plants, production statistics, including direct material quantities, labor-hours, production schedules, and output quantities, are developed by operating personnel. Using the statistics prepared by the operating personnel, the plant accounting staff determines costs and prepares the plant's budgeted variable cost of goods sold and other plant expenses for each month of the coming calendar year.

In October, each division's accounting staff combines plant budgets with sales estimates and adds additional division expenses. "After the divisional management is satisfied with the budget," said Collins, "I visit each division to go over their budget and make sure it is in line with corporate strategy and projections. I really emphasize the sales forecasts because of the volatility in the demand for our product. For many years, we lost sales to our competitors because we didn't project high enough production and sales, and we couldn't meet the market demand. More recently, we were caught with large excess inventory when the bottom dropped out of the market for recreational vehicles.

"I generally visit all eight divisions during the first two weeks in November. After that the division budgets are combined and reconciled by my staff, and they are ready for approval by the board of directors in early December. The board seldom questions the budget.

"One complaint we've had from plant and division management is that they are penalized for circumstances beyond their control. For example, they failed to predict the recent sales decline. As a result, they didn't make their budget and, of course, they received no bonuses. However, I point out that they are well rewarded when they exceed their budget. Furthermore, they provide most of the information for the budget, so it's their own fault if the budget is too optimistic."

Required:

a. Identify and explain the biases the corporate management of RV Industries should expect in the communication of budget estimates by its division and plant personnel.

b. What sources of information can the top management of RV Industries use to monitor the budget estimates prepared by its divisions and plants?

c. What services could top management of RV Industries offer the divisions to help them in their budget development, without appearing to interfere with the division budget decisions?

d. The top management of RV Industries is attempting to decide whether it should get more involved in the budget process. Identify and explain the variables management needs to consider in reaching its decision.

(CMA adapted)

17–19. Prepare cash budget for service organization

The Triple-F Health Club (Family, Fitness, and Fun) is a nonprofit family oriented health club. The club's board of directors is developing plans to acquire more equipment and expand the club facilities. The board plans to purchase about $25,000 of new equipment each year and wants to begin a fund to purchase the adjoining property in four or five years. The adjoining property has a market value of about $300,000.

The club manager, Jane Crowe, is concerned that the board has unrealistic goals in light of its recent financial performance. She has sought the help of a club member with an accounting background to assist her in preparing a report to the board supporting her concerns.

The club member reviewed the club's records, including the cash basis income statements presented below. The review and discussions with Jane Crowe disclosed the additional information which follows the statement.

TRIPLE-F HEALTH CLUB
Statement of Income (Cash Basis)
For the Years Ended October 31
(in thousands)

	1984	1983
Cash revenues:		
Annual membership fees	$355.0	$300.0
Lesson and class fees	234.0	180.0
Miscellaneous	2.0	1.5
Total cash received	591.0	481.5
Cash costs:		
Manager's salary and benefits	$ 36.0	$ 36.0
Regular employees' wages and benefits	190.0	190.0
Lesson and class employee wages and benefits	195.0	150.0
Towels and supplies	16.0	15.5
Utilities (heat and light)	22.0	15.0
Mortgage interest	35.1	37.8
Miscellaneous	2.0	1.5
Total cash costs	496.1	445.8
Cash income	$ 94.9	$ 35.7

Additional information:

1. Other financial information as of October 31, 1984:
   a. Cash in checking account, $7,000.
   b. Petty cash, $300.
   c. Outstanding mortgage balance, $360,000.
   d. Accounts payable arising from invoices for supplies and utilities which are unpaid as of October 31, 1984, $2,500.
2. No unpaid bills existed on October 31, 1983.
3. The club purchased $25,000 worth of exercise equipment during the current fiscal year. Cash of $10,000 was paid on delivery and the balance was due on October 1 but has not been paid as of October 31, 1984.
4. The club began operations in 1978 in rental quarters. In October of 1980 it purchased its current property (land and building) for $600,000, paying $120,000 down and agreeing to pay $30,000 plus 9 percent interest annually on November 1 until the balance was paid off.
5. Membership rose 3 percent during 1984. This is approximately the same annual rate the club has experienced since it opened.
6. Membership fees were increased by 15 percent in 1984. The board has tentative plans to increase the fees by 10 percent in 1985.
7. Lesson and class fees have not been increased for three years. The board policy is to encourage classes and lessons by keeping the fees low. The members have taken advantage of this policy and the number of classes and lessons have grown significantly each year. The club expects the percentage growth experienced in 1984 to be repeated in 1985.
8. Miscellaneous revenues are expected to grow at the same percentage as experienced in 1984.
9. Operating expenses are expected to increase. Hourly wage rates and the manager's salary will need to be increased 15 percent because no increases were granted in 1984. Towels and supplies, utilities, and miscellaneous expenses are expected to increase 25 percent.

Required:

a. Construct a cash budget for 1985 for the Triple-F Health Club.
b. Identify any operating problem(s) that this budget discloses for the Triple-F health Club. Explain your answer.
c. Is Jane Crowe's concern that the board's goals are unrealistic justified? Explain your answer.

(CMA adapted)

17–20. Prepare budgeted profit plans for alternative market shares

The Barr Food Manufacturing Company is a medium-sized publicly held corporation, producing a variety of consumer food and specialty products. Current-year data were prepared as show below for the salad dressing product line using five months of actual expenses and a seven-month projection. These data were prepared for a preliminary 1984 budget meeting between the Specialty Products Division president, marketing vice president, production vice president, and the controller. The current-year projection was accepted as being accurate, but it was agreed that the projected income was not at a satisfactory level.

BARR FOOD MANUFACTURING COMPANY
Projected Income Statement
For the Year Ended December 31, 1983
(5 months actual; 7 months projected)
(in thousands)

Volume in gallons	5,000
Gross sales	$30,000
Transportation, allowances, discounts	3,000
Net sales	27,000
Less manufacturing costs:	
Variable	13,500
Fixed	2,100
Depreciation	700
Total manufacturing costs	16,300
Gross profit	10,700
Less costs:	
Marketing	4,000
Brokerage	1,650
Administrative	2,100
Research and development	500
Total costs	8,250
Operating profit	$ 2,450

The division president stated he wanted, at a minimum, a 15 percent increase in gross sales dollars and a before-tax profit for 1984 that is not less than 10 percent of gross sales. He also stated that he would be responsible for a $200,000 reduction in administrative costs to help achieve the profit goal.

Both the vice president—marketing and the vice president—production felt that the president's objectives would be difficult to achieve. However, they offered the following suggestions to reach the objectives.

1. Sales volume. The current share of the salad dressing market is 15 percent, and the total salad dressing market is expected to grow 5 percent for 1984. Barr's current market share can be maintained by a marketing expenditure of $4,200,000. The two vice presidents estimated that the market share could be increased by additional expenditures for advertising and sales promotion. For an additional expenditure of $525,000, the market share can be raised by 1 percentage point until the market share reaches 17 percent. To get further market penetration, an additional $875,000 must be spent for each percentage point until the market share reaches 20 percent. Any advertising and promotion expenditures beyond this level are not likely to increase the market share to more than 20 percent.
2. Selling price. The selling price will remain at $6 per gallon. The selling price is very closely related to the costs of the ingredients, which are not expected to change from last year.
3. Variable manufacturing costs. Variable manufacturing costs are projected at 50 percent of the net sales dollar (gross sales less transportation, allowances, and discounts).
4. Fixed manufacturing costs. An increase of $100,000 is projected for 1984.
5. Depreciation. A projected increase in equipment will increase depreciation by $25,000 over the 1983 projection.

6. Transportation, allowances, and discounts. The current rate of 10 percent of gross sales dollars is expected to continue in 1984.
7. Brokerage. A rate of 5 percent of gross sales dollars is projected for 1984.
8. Administrative costs. A $200,000 decrease in administrative costs from the 1983 forecast is projected; this is consistent with the president's commitment.
9. Research and development costs. A 5 percent increase from the absolute dollars in the 1983 forecast will be necessary to meet divisional research targets.

Required: The controller must put together a preliminary budget from the facts given. Can the president's objectives be achieved? If so, present the budget that best achieves them. If not, present the budget which most nearly meets the president's objectives.

(CMA adapted)

17–21. Cash budgeting, estimating collections on account

Varsity Company is preparing its cash budget for the month of May. The following information on accounts receivable collections is available from Varsity's past collection experience:

Current month's sales	12%
Prior month's sales	75
Sales two months prior to current month	6
Sales three months prior to current month	4
Cash discounts taken	2
Doubtful accounts	1

Credit sales are as follows:

May—estimated	$100,000
April	90,000
March	80,000
February	95,000

Required: What are the estimated accounts receivable collections for May?

(CPA adapted)

17–22. Prepare cash budget for nonprofit organization

United Business Education, Inc. (UBE), is a nonprofit organization that sponsors a wide variety of management seminars throughout the United States. In addition, it is heavily involved in research into improved methods of educating and motivating business executives. The seminar activity is largely supported by fees, and the research program from member dues.

UBE operates on a calendar-year basis and is in the process of finalizing the budget for 1986. The following information has been taken from approved plans that are still tentative at this time:

Seminar program:

Revenue. The scheduled number of programs should produce $12,000,000 of revenue for the year. Each program is budgeted to produce the same amount of revenue. The revenue is collected during the month the program is offered. The programs are scheduled so that 12 percent of the revenue is collected in each of the first five months of the year. The remaining programs, accounting for the remaining 40 percent of the revenue, are distributed evenly through the months of September, October, and November. No programs are offered in the other four months of the year.

Direct costs.   The seminar costs are made up of three segments:
1. Instructors' fees are paid at the rate of 70 percent of the seminar revenue in the month following the seminar. The instructors are considered independent contractors and are not eligible for UBE employee benefits.
2. Facilities fees total $5,600,000 for the year. They are the same for each program and are paid in the month the program is given.
3. Annual promotional costs of $1,000,000 are spent equally in all months except June and July when there is no promotional effort.

Research program:

Research grants.   The research program has a large number of projects nearing completion. The other main research activity this year includes the feasibility studies for new projects to be started in 1987. As a result, the total grant expense of $3,000,000 for 1986 is expected to be paid out at the rate of $500,000 per month during the first six months of the year.

Salaries and other UBE costs:

Office lease.   Annual amount of $240,000 paid monthly at the beginning of each month.
General administrative costs (telephone, supplies, postage, etc.). $1,500,000 annually or $125,000 a month.
Depreciation expense. $240,000 a year.
General UBE promotion.   Annual cost of $600,000, paid monthly.
Salaries and benefits:

Number of employees	Annual salary paid monthly	Total annual salaries
1	$50,000	$ 50,000
3	40,000	120,000
4	30,000	120,000
15	25,000	375,000
5	15,000	75,000
22	10,000	220,000
50		$960,000

Employee benefits amount to $240,000 or 25 percent of annual salaries. Except for the pension contribution, the benefits are paid as salaries are paid. The annual pension payment of $24,000, based on 2.5 percent of salaries (included in the total benefits and 25 percent rate), is due April 15, 1986.

Other information:

Membership income.   UBE has 100,000 members each of whom pays an annual fee of $100. The fee for the calendar year is invoiced in late June. The collection schedule is as follows.

July	60%
August	30
September	5
October	5
	100%

Capital expenditures. The capital expenditures program calls for a total of $510,000 in cash payments to be spread evenly over the first five months of 1986.

Cash and temporary investments at January 1, 1986, are estimated at $750,000.

Required:

a. Prepare a budget of the annual cash receipts and disbursements for UBE, Inc., for 1986.

b. Prepare a cash budget for UBE, Inc., for January 1986.

c. Using the information you developed in Requirement (a) and (b), identify two important operating problems of UBE, Inc.

(CMA adapted)

17–23. Estimate cash receipts using statistical forecasting model

Early in March, the Jackson City administrator presented a budget to the city council. This is four months prior to the start of the new fiscal year which begins July 1. Most of the important amounts must be estimated because the data upon which to base the final budget will (1) not be available until much closer to the end of the year or (2) are based upon estimates of events that occur in the next year.

The city revenues are a good example of the problem. The city obtains its cash revenues from four sources: property taxes, city income tax, parking fees and fines, and other revenues. The property taxes are based upon the assessed valuation of all the property in the city. The final assessment values for the fiscal year were not available until late May. The income taxes withheld depend upon the income earned next year by the residents of the city. The parking fees and fines depend, to a large extent, on the size of the population.

The city administrator added an estimate of the monthly cash receipts and disbursements for the next year to the budget material he presented to the council. The cash receipts were estimated using a cash forecasting model developed in the controller's department. The model was the result of statistical analysis of prior years results and is presented below:

$$C_i = mr_iA_t + \frac{(1 + l)T_{t-1}}{12} + \frac{(1 + G)P_{t-1}}{12} + \frac{(1 + G)R_{t-1}}{12}$$

where:

C_i = cash collected for the ith month (July = 1)
m = property tax rate per $1,000 of assessed valuation
r_i = percent of property tax collected in the ith month (July = 1)
A_t = the assessed valuation of property in year t (t = budget year) in thousands of dollars
l = inflation rate (decimal)
T = income taxes withheld from taxpayers
G = population growth (decimal)
P = parking fees and fines collections
R = other revenues collections

The assessed valuation in thousands of dollars, A_t, was estimated from the regression equation:

$$A_t = 50,000 + 1.05A_{t-1} + 3S$$

Where:

S = thousands of square feet of new construction since the last assessment

The numerical data shown below was available at the end of February when the budget for this fiscal year was constructed. The data for last fiscal year represents either actual figures or data that was projected for the entire year based upon the first eight months of last fiscal year. The data for this fiscal year represented either rates or amounts that would be experienced or were estimates of what was expected to be experienced.

Fiscal year

Last	Population (actual)	100,000 people
This	Population growth rate (estimated)	8%
Last	Assessed valuation (actual)	$600,000,000
Last	Square feet of new construction (projected)	30,000,000 sq. ft.
This	Property tax rate per $1,000 of assessed valuation (actual)	$25
Last	Income taxes withheld (projected)	$4,000,000
Last	Collections of parking fees and fines (projected)	1,000,000
Last	Other revenues collections (projected)	500,000
This	Inflation rate (estimated)	11% per year

The collection pattern for property taxes that has been experienced the past three years is shown below. City officials expected this pattern to persist in this fiscal year.

July	20%	January	1%
August	60	February	1
September	10	March	1
October	5	April	—
November	1	May	—
December	1	June	—

Required: Determine the estimate of the cash receipts for the month of August that the Jackson City administrator included in the budget material he presented to the city council in March. Use the cash forecasting model developed by the controller's department and the data available in February.

(CMA adapted)

17–24. Comprehensive budget plan

The C. L. Corporation appeared to be experiencing a good year. Sales in the first quarter were one-third ahead of last year, and the sales department predicted that this rate would continue throughout the entire year. Ruth Keenan, assistant controller, was asked to prepare a new forecast for the year and to analyze the differences from 1986 results. The forecast was to be based upon actual results obtained in the first quarter plus the expected costs of programs to be carried out in the remainder of the year. She worked with various department heads (production, sales, etc.) to get the necessary information. The results of these efforts are presented below.

C. L. CORPORATION
Expected Account Balances for December 31, 1987
(in thousands)

Cash	$ 1,200	
Accounts receivable	80,000	
Inventory (January 1, 1987)	48,000	
Plant and equipment	130,000	
Accumulated depreciation		$ 41,000
Accounts payable		45,000
Notes payable (due within one year)		50,000
Accrued payables		23,250
Common stock		70,000
Retained earnings		108,200
Sales		600,000
Other income		9,000
Costs of goods sold		
Manfacturing costs:		
Materials	213,000	
Direct labor	218,000	
Variable overhead	130,000	
Depreciation	5,000	
Other fixed overhead	7,750	
Marketing:		
Commissions	20,000	
Salaries	16,000	
Promotion and advertising	45,000	
Administrative:		
Salaries	16,000	
Travel	2,500	
Office costs	9,000	
Income taxes	—	
Dividends	5,000	
	$946,450	$946,450

Adjustments for the change in inventory and for income taxes have not been made. The scheduled production for 1987 is 450 million units, while the sales volume will reach 400 million units. Sales and production volume in 1986 was 300 million units. A full-absorption cost, FIFO inventory system is used. The company is subject to a 40 percent income tax rate. The actual financial statements for 1986 are presented below:

C. L. CORPORATION
Statement of Income and Retained Earnings
for the Year Ended December 31, 1986
(in thousands)

Revenue:			
Sales		$450,000	
Other income		15,000	$465,000
Expenses:			
Cost of goods manufactured and sold:			
Materials............................	$132,000		
Direct labor	135,000		
Variable overhead	81,000		
Fixed overhead	12,000		
		360,000	
Beginning inventory		48,000	
		408,000	
Ending inventory		48,000	360,000
Selling:			
Salaries		13,500	
Commissions		15,000	
Promotion and advertising		31,500	60,000
General and administrative:			
Salaries		14,000	
Travel		2,000	
Office costs		8,000	24,000
Income taxes		8,400	452,400
Operating profit			12,600
Beginning retained earnings			100,600
Subtotal			113,200
Less: Dividends			5,000
Ending retained earnings			$108,200

Required:

Prepare a budgeted income statement and balance sheet.

(CMA adapted)

17–25. Empire Glass Company (comprehensive budgeting case)*

Organization Empire Glass Company was a diversified company organized into several major product divisions. Each division was headed by a vice president who reported to the company's executive vice president, Landon McGregor. The Glass Products Division, the focus of this case, was responsible for manufacturing and selling glass food and beverage bottles.

McGregor's corporate staff included three financial people—the controller, chief accountant, and treasurer. The controller's department consisted of only two people— James Walker and his assistant, Ellen Newell. The market research and labor relations departments also reported in a staff capacity to McGregor.

All the product divisions were organized along similar lines. Reporting to each division vice president were staff members in the customer service and product research areas. Reporting in a line capacity to each vice president were also general managers of manufacturing and of marketing, who were respectively responsible for all the

---

* Copyright © 1964 by the President and Fellows of Harvard College. This case was prepared by David F. Hawkins as a basis for class discussion rather than to illustrate either effective or ineffective handling of an administrative situation. Reproduced by permission of the Harvard Business School.

Exhibit A (17–25)   **Top management and Glass Products management**

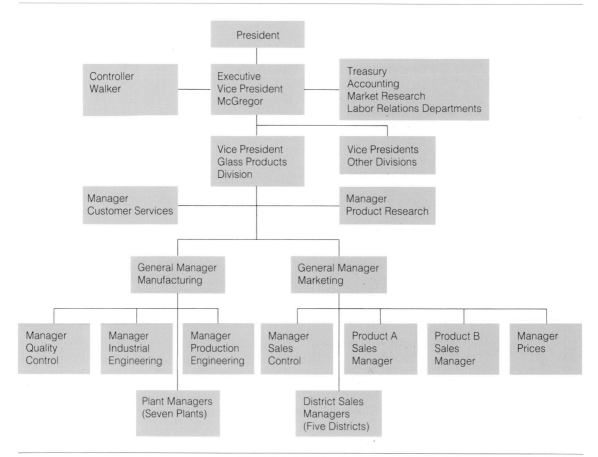

division's manufacturing and marketing activities. Both of these executives were assisted by a small staff of specialists. Exhibit A presents an organization chart of top management and of the Glass Product Division's management group. All corporate and divisional managers and staff were located in British City, Canada. Exhibit B shows the typical organization structure of a plant within the Glass Products Division. **Products and technology** Glass Products operated seven plants in Canada. Of their products, food jars constituted the largest group, including jars for products like catsup, mayonnaise, jams and jellies, honey, and instant coffee. Milk, beer, and soft-drink bottles were also produced in large quantities. A great variety of containers for wines, liquors, drugs, cosmetics, and chemicals were produced in smaller quantities.

Most of the thousands of different products, varying in size, shape, color, and decoration, were produced to order. According to Glass Products executives, the typical lead time between a customer's order and shipment from the plant was between two and three weeks.

The principal direct materials for container glass were sand, soda ash, and lime.

Exhibit B (17–25)   **Typical plant organization—Glass Products Division**

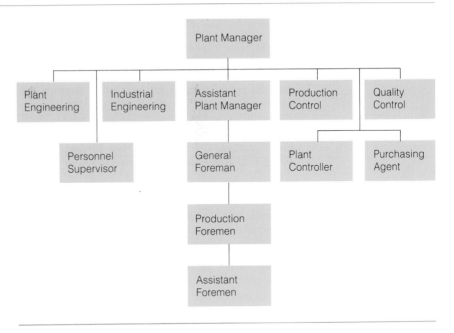

The first step in the manufacturing process was to melt batches of these materials in furnaces or "tanks." The molten mass was then passed into automatic or semiautomatic machines, which filled molds with the molten glass and blew the glass into the desired shape. The ware then went through an automatic annealing oven or lehr, where it was cooled slowly under carefully controlled conditions. If the glass was to be coated on the exterior to increase its resistance to abrasion and scratches, this coating—often a silicone film—was applied at the lehr. Any decorating (such as a trademark or other design) was then added, the product inspected again, and the finished goods packed in corrugated containers (or wooden cases for some bottles).

Quality inspection was critical in the manufacturing process. If the melt in the furnace was not completely free from bubbles and stones, or if the fabricating machinery was slightly out of adjustment or molds were worn, the rejection rate was very high. Although a number of machines were used in the inspection process, including electric eyes, much of the inspection was still visual.

Although glassmaking was one of the oldest arts, and bottles had been machine molded at relatively high speed for over half a century, Glass Products had spent substantial su.ns each year to modernize its equipment. These improvements had greatly increased the speed of operations and had substantially reduced the visual inspection and manual handling of glassware.

Most of the jobs were relatively unskilled, highly repetitive, and gave the worker little control over work methods or pace. The moldmakers who made and repaired the molds, the machine repairpersons, and those who made the equipment setup changes between different products were considered to be the highest classes of skilled workers. Wages were relatively high in the industry, in part because the plants were noisy and hot. Production employees belonged to two national unions, and bargaining was conducted on a national basis. Output standards were established for all jobs, but no bonus was paid to hourly plant workers for exceeding standard.

Marketing Over the years, Glass Products' sales had grown at a slightly faster rate than had the total glass container market. Until the late 1950s, the division had charged a premium for most of its products, primarily because they were of better quality than competitive products. Subsequently, however, the quality of the competitive products had improved to the point where they now matched the division's quality level. In the meantime, the division's competitors had retained their former price structure. Consequently, Glass Products had been forced to lower its prices to meet its competitors' lower market prices. According to one division executive:

> Currently, price competition is not severe, particularly among the two or three larger companies that dominate the glass bottle industry. Most of our competition is with respect to product quality and customer service. . . . In fact, our biggest competitive threat is from containers other than glass. . . ."

Each of the division's various plants shipped some products throughout Canada to some extent, although transportation costs limited each plant's market primarily to its immediate vicinity. While some of the customers were large and bought in huge quantities, many were relatively small.

Budgetary control system James Walker, Empire Glass Company controller for over 15 years, described the company's budgetary control system to a casewriter. Excerpts from that interview are reproduced below.

"To understand the role of the budgetary control system, you must first understand our management philosophy. Fundamentally, we have a divisional organization based on broad product categories. These divisional activities are coordinated by the company's executive vice president, while the head office group provides a policy and review function for him. Within the broad policy limits, we operate on a decentralized basis; each of the decentralized divisions performs the full management job that normally would be inherent in any independent company. The only exceptions to this are the head office group's sole responsibilities for sources of funds and labor relations with those bargaining units that cross division lines.

"Given this form of organization, the budget is the principal management tool used by head office to coordinate the efforts of the various segments of the company toward a common goal. Certainly, in our case, the budget is much more than a narrow statistical accounting device."

Sales budget "As early as May 15 of the year preceding the budget year, top management of the company asks the various division vice presidents to submit preliminary reports stating what they think their division's capital requirements and outlook in terms of sales and income will be during the next budget year. In addition, top management wants an expression of the division vice president's general feelings toward the trends in these items over the two years following the upcoming budget year. At this stage, head office is not interested in much detail. Since all divisions plan their capital requirements five years in advance and had made predictions of the forthcoming budget year's market when the budget estimates were prepared last year, these rough estimates of next year's conditions and requirements are far from wild guesses.

"After the opinions of the division vice presidents are in, the market research staff goes to work. They develop a formal statement of the marketing climate in detail for the forthcoming budget year and in general terms for the subsequent two years. Once these general factors have been assessed, a sales forecast is constructed for the company and for each division. Consideration is given to the relationship of the general economic climate to our customers' needs and Empire's share of each market. Explicitly stated are basic assumptions as to price, weather conditions, introduction of new products, gains or losses in particular accounts, forward buying, new manufacturing plants, industry growth trends, packaging trends, inventory carry-overs, and the development of alternative packages to or from glass. This review of all the relevant factors is followed for each of our product lines, regardless of its size and importance. The completed forecasts of the market research group are then forwarded to the appropriate divisions for review, criticism, and adjustments.

"The primary goal of the head office group in developing these sales forecasts is to assure uniformity among the divisions with respect to the basic assumptions on business conditions, pricing, and the treatment of possible emergencies. Also, we provide a yardstick so as to assure us that the company's overall sales forecast will be reasonable and obtainable.

"The division top management then asks the district managers what they expect to do in the way of sales during the budget year. Head office and the divisional staffs will give the district managers as much guidance as they request, but it is the sole responsibility of each district manager to come up with the district's forecast.

"After the district sales managers' forecasts are received by the divisional top management, the forecasts are consolidated and reviewed by the division's general manager of marketing, who may suggest revisions. The district managers know little of what's happening outside their territories; but at headquarters we can estimate the size of the whole market for, say, liquor, and each of our customer's market share. That's where the market research group's forecasts come in handy. Let me emphasize, however, that nothing is changed in the district manager's budget unless the district manager agrees. Then, once the budget is approved, nobody is relieved of responsibility without top management approval. Also, no arbitrary changes are made in the approved budgets without the concurrence of all the people responsible for the budget.

"Next, we go through the same process at the division and headquarters levels. We continue to repeat the process until everyone agrees that the sales budgets are sound. Then, each level of management takes responsibility for its particular portion of the budget. These sales budgets then become fixed objectives.

"I would say a division has four general objectives in mind in reviewing its sales budget:

1. A review of the division's competitive position, including plans for improving that position.
2. An evaluation of its efforts to gain either a larger share of the market or offset competitors' activities.
3. A consideration of the need to expand facilities to improve the division's products or introduce new products.
4. A review and development of plans to improve product quality, delivery methods and service."

Manufacturing budgets   "Once the division vice presidents, executive vice president, and company president have given final approval to the sales budget, we make a sales budget for each plant by breaking down the division sales budget according to the plants from which the finished goods will be shipped. These plant sales budgets are then further broken down on a monthly basis by price, volume, and end use. With this information available, the plants then budget their contribution, fixed expenses, and income before taxes. Contribution is the difference between gross sales, less discounts, and variable manufacturing costs. Income is the difference between contribution and fixed costs. It is the plant manager's responsibility to meet this budgeted *profit* figure, even if actual dollar sales drop below the budgeted level.

"Given the plant's sales budget, it is up to the plant manager to determine the fixed overhead and variable costs—at standard—that the plant will need to incur so as to meet the demands of the sales budget. In my opinion, requiring the plant managers to make their own plans is one of the most valuable things associated with the budget system. Each plant manager divides the preparation of the overall plant budget among the plant's various departments. First, the departments spell out the program in terms of the physical requirements, such as tons of direct material, and then the plans are priced at standard cost.

"The plant industrial engineering department is assigned responsibility for developing engineered cost standards. This phase of the budget also includes budgeted cost reductions, budgeted unfavorable variances from standards, and certain budgeted programmed fixed costs in the manufacturing area, such as service labor. The industrial engineer prepares this phase of the budget in conjunction with departmental line supervision.

"Before each plant sends its budget in to British City, a group of us from head office goes out to visit each plant. For example, in the case of Glass Products, Ellen Newell, assistant controller, and I, along with representatives of the division's manufacturing staffs, visit each of the division's plants. Let me stress this point: We do not go on these trips to pass judgment on the plant's proposed budget. Rather, we go with two purposes in mind. First, we wish to acquaint ourselves with the thinking behind the figures that each plant manager will send in to British City. This is helpful, because when we come to review these budgets with the top management—that is, the president and executive vice president—we will have to answer questions about the budgets, and we will know the answers. Second, the review is a way of giving guidance to the plant managers in determining whether or not they are in line with what the company needs to make in the way of profits.

"Of course, when we make our field reviews we do not know what each of the other plants is planning. Therefore, we explain to the plant managers that while their budget may look good now, when we put all the plants together in a consolidated budget the plant managers may have to make some changes because the projected profit is not high enough. When this happens, we tell the plant managers that it is not their programs that are unsound. The problem is that the company cannot afford the programs. I think it is very important that the plant managers have a chance to tell their story. Also, it gives them the feeling that we at headquarters are not living in an ivory tower.

"These plant visits are spread over a three-week period, and we spend an average of half a day at each plant. The plant managers are free to bring to these meetings any of their supervisors they wish. We ask them not to bring in anybody below the supervisory level—then, of course, you get into organized labor. During the half day we spend at each plant, we discuss the budget primarily. However, if I have time I like to wander through the plant and see how things are going. Also, I go over in great detail the property replacement and maintenance budget with the plant manager.

"About September 1, the plant budgets come into British City, and the accounting department consolidates them. Then, the division vice presidents review their respective division budgets to see if they are reasonable in terms of what the vice president thinks the corporate management wants. If the vice president is not satisfied with the consolidated plant budgets, the various plants within the division will be asked to trim their budgeted costs.

"When the division vice presidents and the executive vice president are satisfied, they will send their budgets to the company president. He may accept the division budgets at this point. If he doesn't, he will specify the areas to be reexamined by division and, if necessary, by plant. The final budget is approved at our December board of directors meeting."

Comparison of actual and standard performance   "At the end of the sixth business day after the close of the month, each plant wires to the head office certain operating variances, which we put together on what we call the variance analysis sheet. Within a half-hour after the last plant report comes through, variance analysis sheets for the divisions and plants are compiled. On the morning of the seventh business day, these reports are on the desks of top management. The variance analysis sheet highlights the variances in what we consider to be critical areas. Receiving this report as soon as we do helps us at head office to take timely action. Let us emphasize, however, we do not accept the excuse that plant managers have to go to the end of the month to know what happened during the month. They have to be on top of these particular items daily.

"When the actual results come into the head office, we go over them on the basis of exception; that is, we only look at those figures that are in excess of the budgeted amounts. We believe this has a good effect on morale. The plant managers don't have to explain everything they do. They have to explain only where they go off base. In particular, we pay close attention to the net sales, gross margin, and the plant's ability to meet its standard manufacturing cost. When analyzing sales, we look closely at price and mix changes.

"All this information is summarized on a form known as the Profit Planning and Control Report No. 1 (see Exhibit C). This document is backed up by a number of supporting documents (see Exhibit D). The plant PPCR No. 1 and the month-end trial balance showing both actual and budget figures are received in British City at the close of the eighth business day after the end of the month. These two very important reports, along with the supporting reports (PPCR No. 2–PPCR No. 11) are then consolidated by the accounting department to show the results of operations by division and company. The consolidated reports are distributed the next day.

Exhibit C (17–25) **Profit planning and Control Report No. 1**

MONTH					YEAR TO DATE		
Income Gain (+) or Loss (−) From						Income Gain (+) or Loss (−) From	
Prev. Year	Budget	Actual	Ref.		Actual	Budget	Prev. Year
			1	Gross Sales to Customers			
			2	Discounts & Allowances			
			3	Net Sales to Customers			
%	%		4	% Gain (+)/Loss (−)		%	%
				DOLLAR VOLUME GAIN (+)/ LOSS (−) DUE TO:			
			5	Sales Price			
			6	Sales Volume			
			6(a)	Trade Mix			
			7	Std. Variable Cost of Sales			
			8	Contribution Margin			
				CONTRIB. MARGIN GAIN (+)/ LOSS (−) DUE TO:			
			9	Profit Volume Ratio (P/V)*			
			10	Dollar Volume			
%	%	%	11	Profit Volume Ratio (P/V)*	%	%	%
			12	Budgeted Fixed Mfg. Cost			
			13	Fixed Manufacturing Cost-Transfers			
			14	Plant Income (standard)			
%	%	%	15	% of Net Sales	%	%	%
%	%	%	16	% Mfg. Efficiency	%	%	%
			17	Manufacturing Variances			
			18	Methods Improvements			
			19	Other Revisions of Standards			
			20	Material Price Changes			
			21	Division Special Projects			
			22	Company Special Projects			
			23	New Plant Expense			
			24	Other Plant Expenses			
			25	Income on Seconds			
			26				
			27				
			28	Plant Income (actual)			
%	%		29	% Gain (+)/Loss (−)		%	%
%	%	%	30	% of Net Sales	%	%	%
			36A				
				CAPITAL EMPLOYED			
			37	Total Capital Employed			
%	%	%	38	% Return	%	%	%
			39	Turnover Rate			

Plant	Division	Month	19 —— .

* The P/V ratio was defined to be: $\dfrac{\text{Price} - \text{Variable cost}}{\text{Price}}$.

Exhibit D (17–25)   **Brief description of PPCR No. 2–PPCR No. 11**

Report	Individual plant reports, description
PPCR No. 2	Manufacturing expense: Plant materials, labor, and variable overhead consumed. Detail of actual figures compared with budget and previous year's figures for year to date and current month.
PPCR No. 3	Plant expense: Plant fixed expenses incurred. Details of actual figures compared with budget and previous year's figures for year to date and current month.
PPCR No. 4	Analysis of sales and income: Part operating gains and losses due to changes in sales revenue, profit margins, and other sources of income. Details of actual figures compared with budget and previous year's figures for year to date and current month.
PPCR No. 5	Plant control statement: Analysis of plant direct material gains and losses, spoilage costs, and cost reduction programs. Actual figures compared with budget figures for current month and year to date.
PPCR No. 6	Comparison of sales by principal and product groups: Plant sales dollars, profit margin, and P/V ratios broken down by end product use (i.e., soft drinks, beer). Compares actual figures with budgeted figures for year to date and current month.

Report	Division summary reports, description
PPCR No. 7	Comparative plant performance, sales, and income: Gross sales and income figures by plants. Actual figures compared with budget figures for year to date and current month.
PPCR No. 8	Comparative plant performance, total plant expenses: Profit margin, total fixed costs, manufacturing efficiency, other plant expenses, and P/V ratios by plants. Actual figures compared with budgeted and previous year's figures for current month and year to date.
PPCR No. 9	Manufacturing efficiency: Analysis of gains and losses by plant in areas of materials, spoilage, supplies, and labor. Current month and year to date actuals reported in total dollars and as a percentage of budget.
PPCR No. 10	Inventory: Comparison of actual and budget inventory figures by major inventory accounts and plants.
PPCR No. 11	Status of capital expenditures: Analysis of the status of capital expenditures by plants, months, and relative to budget.

"In connection with the fixed cost items, we want to know whether the plants carried out the programs they said they would carry out. If they have not, we want to know why. Also, we want to know if they have carried out their projected programs at the cost they said they would.

"In addition to these reports, at the beginning of each month the plant managers prepare current estimates for the upcoming month and quarter on forms similar to the variance analysis sheets. Since our budget is based on known programs, the value of this current estimate is that it gets the plant people to look at their programs. Hopefully, they will realize that they cannot run their plants just on a day-to-day basis.

"If we see a sore spot coming up, or if the plant manager draws our attention to a potential trouble area, we may ask that daily reports concerning this item be sent to division top management. In addition, the division top management may send a division staff specialist—say, a quality control expert if it is a quality problem—to the plant concerned. The division staff members can make recommendations, but it is up to the plant manager to accept or reject these recommendations. Of course, it is well known throughout the company that we expect the plant managers to accept gracefully the help of the head office and division staffs."

Sales-manufacturing relations "If a sales decline occurs during the early part of the year, and if the plant managers can convince us that the change is permanent, we may revise the plant budgets to reflect these new circumstances. However, if toward the end of the year the actual sales volume suddenly drops below budget, we don't have much time to change the budget plans. What we do is ask the plant managers to go back over their budgets with their staffs and see where reduction of expense programs will do the least harm. Specifically, we ask them to consider what they may be able to eliminate this year or delay until next year.

"I believe it was Confucius who said: 'We make plans so we have plans to discard.' Nevertheless, I think it is wise to make plans, even if you have to discard them. Having plans makes it a lot easier to figure out what to do when sales fall off from the budgeted level. The understanding of operations that comes from preparing the budget removes a lot of the potential chaos that might arise if we were under pressure to meet a stated profit goal and sales declined quickly and unexpectedly at year end, just as they did last year. In these circumstances, we don't try to ram anything down the plant managers' throats. We ask them to tell us where they can reasonably expect to cut costs below the budgeted level.

"Whenever a problem arises at a plant between sales and production, the local people are supposed to solve the problem themselves. For example, a customer's purchasing agent may insist he wants an immediate delivery, and this delivery will disrupt the production department's plans. The production group can make recommendations as to alternative ways to take care of the problem, but it's the sales manager's responsibility to get the product to the customer. The sales force are supposed to know their customers well enough to judge whether or not the customer really needs the product. If the sales manager says the customer needs the product, that ends the matter. As far as we are concerned, the customer's wants are primary; our company is a case where sales wags the rest of the dog. Of course, if the change in the sales program involves a major plant expense that is out of line with the budget, then the matter is passed up to division top management for a decision.

"The sales department has the sole responsibility for product price, sales mix, and volume. They do not have direct responsibility for plant operations or profit. That's the plant management's responsibility. However, it is understood that the sales group will cooperate with the plant people whenever possible."

Motivation "There are various ways in which we motivate the plant managers to meet their profit goals. First of all, we only promote capable people. Also, a monetary incentive program has been established that stimulates their efforts to achieve their profit goals. In addition, each month we put together a bar chart which shows, by division and plant, the ranking of the various manufacturing units with respect to manufacturing efficience.* We feel the plant managers are fully responsible for variable manufacturing costs. I believe this is true, since all manufacturing standards have to be approved by plant managers. Most of the plant managers give wide publicity

---

* Manufacturing efficiency $= \dfrac{\text{Total standard variable manufacturing costs}}{\text{Total actual variable manufacturing costs}} \times 100\%.$

to these bar charts. The efficiency bar chart and efficiency measure itself is perhaps a little unfair in some respects when you are comparing one plant with another. Different kinds of products are run through different plants. These require different setups, and so forth, which have an important impact on the position of a plant. However, in general, the efficiency rating is a good indication of the quality of the plant managers and their supervisory staffs.

"Also, a number of plants run competitions within the plants that reward department heads based on their relative standing with respect to a certain cost item. The plant managers, their staffs, and employees have great pride in their plants.

"The number one item now stressed at the plant level is *quality*. The market situation is such that in order to make sales you have to meet the market price and exceed the market quality. By quality I mean not only the physical characteristics of the product but also delivery schedules. The company employee publications' message is that if the company is to be profitable, it must produce high-quality items at a reasonable cost. This is necessary so that the plants can meet their obligation to produce the maximum profits for the company in the prevailing circumstances."

The Future "An essential part of the budgetary control system is planning. We have developed a philosophy that we must begin our plans where the work is done—in the line organization and out in the field. Perhaps, in the future, we can avoid or cut back some of the budget preparation steps and start putting together our sales budget later than May 15. However, I doubt if we will change the basic philosophy. Frankly, I doubt if the line operators would want any major change in the system; they are very jealous of the management prerogatives the system gives them.

"It is very important that we manage the budget. We have to be continually on guard against its managing us. Sometimes, the plants lose sight of this fact. We have to be made conscious daily of the necessity of having the sales volume to make a profit. And when sales fall off and their plant programs are reduced, they do not always appear to see the justification for budget costs—although I do suspect that they see more of the justification for these cuts than they will admit. It is this human side of the budget to which we have to pay more attention in the future."

Required:

a. Describe each step of Empire's budget process from its start on May 15 until its final approval. Relate each step to the organization charts in Exhibits A and B.

b. Evaluate Empire's budgeting process. Have they related the budget to organizational goals? What incentives do participants have for biasing information?

18

Using the Budget for Performance Evaluation and Control

To understand the process for adjusting the budget to reflect actual conditions.
To know how differences between planned activity and actual activity are analyzed.

In Chapter 17, we described the development of the master budget as a first step in the budgetary planning and control cycle. In this chapter, we carry the process a step further to examine the use of the budget as a tool for performance evaluation and control. The master budget can be thought of as a blueprint for achieving the company's goals. The control process assures that the blueprint is followed; or if changes are required, that the best alternative is chosen.

The master budget includes operating budgets (for example, the budgeted income statement, the production budget, the budgeted cost of goods sold) and financial budgets (for example, the cash budget, the budgeted balance sheet). When management uses the master budget for control purposes, it focuses on the key items that must be controlled to ensure company success. Most such items are in the operating budgets, although some also appear in the financial budgets. In this chapter, we focus on the master budget income statement as a tool for controlling operations.

Flexible budgeting

A master budget presents a comprehensive view of anticipated operations. Such a budget is typically a static budget; that is, it is developed in detail for one level of anticipated activity. A flexible budget, by contrast, indicates budgeted revenues, costs, and profits for virtually all feasible levels of activities. Since variable costs and revenues change with changes in activity levels, these amounts are budgeted to be different at each activity level in the flexible budget.

For example, studies of past cost behavior in the machining department of the Greater Manufacturing Company indicate that the department expects to incur fixed costs of $500,000 per year and variable costs of $20 per unit produced. This cost function is graphed in Illustration 18–1. This is the same type of cost line that is used for cost-volume-profit (CVP) analysis discussed in Chapter 11. The expected activity level for 1985 is budgeted at 100,000 units. From the flexible budget line in Illustration 18–1, we find

Illustration 18–1

Comparison of master and flexible budget, machining department, Greater Manufacturing Company

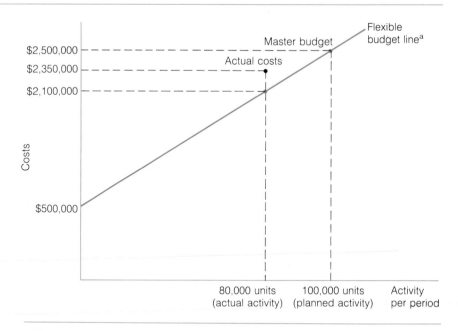

^a This is the cost line from cost-volume-profit analysis.

the budgeted costs at a planned activity of 100,000 units to be $2,500,000 [$500,000 + ($20 × 100,000 units)].

Suppose that actual costs are $2,350,000 for 1985. At first glance, one might assume that a good job of cost control was done because costs were $150,000 lower than the budget plan. But, in fact, only 80,000 units were actually produced instead of the 100,000 units originally planned. According to the flexible budget concept, the master budget must be adjusted for this change in activity. The adjusted budgeted costs for control and performance evaluation purposes would be $2,100,000 [$500,000 + ($20 × 80,000 units)]. Now it is clear that while costs are lower than planned, they are $250,000 higher than they should be, after *taking into account the level of activity in the department.*

The estimated cost-volume line in Illustration 18–1 is known as the flexible budget line because it shows the budgeted costs allowed for each level of activity. For example, if activity would increase to 120,000 units, budgeted costs would be $2,900,000 [$500,000 + ($20 × 120,000 units)]. If activity drops to 50,000 units, budgeted costs would drop to $1,500,000 [$500,000 + ($20 × 50,000 units)]. Whatever level of activity occurred during the period is entered into the flexible budget equation:

$$TC = F + VX$$

where:

TC = total budgeted costs for the period
F = fixed costs for the period
V = variable costs per unit
X = activity expressed as quantity of units

For the machining department at Greater Manufacturing:

$$TC = \$500,000 + \$20X$$

You can compare the master budget with the flexible budget by thinking of the master budget as an ex ante (before-the-fact) prediction of X (activity), while the flexible budget is based on ex post facto (after-the-fact) knowledge of the actual X.

Comparing budgets and results

A comparison of the master budget with the flexible budget and with actual results forms the basis for analyzing differences between plans and actual performance. The following example is used in this and subsequent chapters to illustrate the comparison of plans with actual performance.

The Boxx Company, a small manufacturing firm, makes wooden crates. Its master budget income statement is presented in Illustration 18–2. The format is consistent with variable costing, not full-absorption costing. We use this variable costing format for analyzing differences between actual and planned results because it separates fixed and variable costs.

Illustration 18–2   **Master budget, Boxx Company**

	Master budgets (based on 8,000 units)
Sales revenue (8,000 units at $20)	$160,000
Less:	
Variable manufacturing costs	80,000[a]
Variable marketing and administrative costs	8,000[b]
Contribution margin	72,000
Less:	
Fixed manufacturing costs	20,000
Fixed marketing and administrative costs	40,000
Operating profit	$ 12,000

The following estimates are used by Boxx Company to prepare the master budget:

Sales price	$ 20 per crate
Sales volume	8,000 crates
Production volume	8,000 crates
Variable manufacturing costs	$ 10 per crate
Variable marketing and administrative costs	1 per crate
Fixed manufacturing costs	20,000
Fixed marketing and administrative costs	40,000

[a] 8,000 budgeted units at $10 unit.
[b] 8,000 budgeted units at $1 per unit.

Illustration 18–3   **Flexible and master budget, Boxx Company (May)**

	Flexible budget (based on actual activity of 10,000 units)	Activity variance (based on variance in sales volume)	Master budget (based on 8,000 units sold)
Sales revenue	$200,000	$40,000 F	$160,000
Less:			
Variable manufacturing costsᵃ (at $10 per unit)	100,000	20,000 U	80,000
Variable marketing and administrative costs (at $1 per unit)	10,000	2,000 U	8,000
Contribution margin	90,000	18,000 F	72,000
Less:			
Fixed manufacturing costs	20,000	—	20,000
Fixed marketing and administrative costs	40,000	—	40,000
Operating profits	$ 30,000	$18,000 F	$ 12,000

ᵃ This can be thought of as "variable cost of goods sold."
U = "Unfavorable" variance.
F = "Favorable" variance.

The flexible budget, presented in Illustration 18–3, is based on *actual* activity. In May, 10,000 crates were actually produced and sold. The difference between operating profits in the master budget and operating profits in the flexible budget is called an *activity variance.* It is due to the 2,000 units difference between actual sales and planned sales. The $18,000 variance results from the 2,000 units difference times the $9 *budgeted* contribution margin per unit ($20 *budgeted* price − $11 *budgeted* variable costs). This difference can also be seen on the flexible budget profit-volume line in Illustration 18–4.

Favorable versus unfavorable variances

Note the use of F for favorable and U for Unfavorable besides each of the variances in Illustration 18–3. These terms describe the impact of the variance on the budgeted operating profits. A *favorable variance increases* operating profits, holding all other things constant. An *unfavorable variance decreases* operating profits, holding all other things constant. These terms are not intended to be used in a normative sense; thus, a favorable variance is *not necessarily good,* and an unfavorable variance is *not necessarily bad.*

An excellent case in point is the sales activity or volume variance in Illustration 18–3. Holding everything else constant, the 2,000 units increase in sales creates a favorable variance of $40,000 ($20 per unit budgeted price × 2,000 units) in sales. Is this really good? Perhaps not. Economic conditions may have been better than planned, which increased the volume demanded by

Illustration 18–4 **Flexible budget line, Boxx Company**

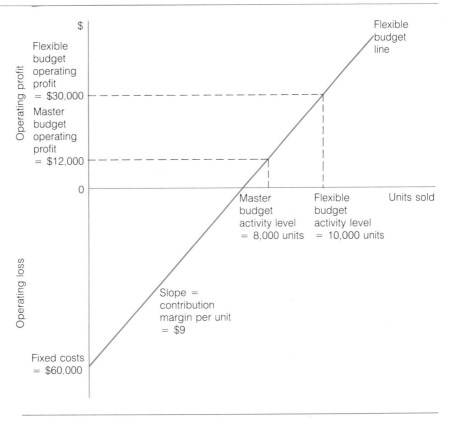

the market. Hence, perhaps, the 2,000-unit increase in sales volume should have been even greater taking everything into account.

Note that the variable cost variances are both labeled unfavorable. But this doesn't mean that they are bad for the company. Variable costs are expected to increase when volume is greater than planned.

Sales volume (activity) variance

The information in Illustration 18–3 has a number of uses. First, it isolates the increase in operating profits caused by the increase in activity from the master budget. Further, the resulting flexible budget shows budgeted sales, costs, and operating profits *after* taking into account the activity increase but *before* considering differences in *unit* selling prices, variable costs, and fixed costs from the master budget.

In general, we refer to this change from the master budget plan as an **activity variance.** When the change from the master budget to the flexible budget is due to changes in sales volume, the activity variance is also known as the **sales volume variance.**

Note the makeup of the $18,000 sales volume variance in Illustration 18–3. First, the difference between the master budget sales of $160,000 and the flexible budget sales of $200,000 (which is the estimated $20 unit sales price times the 10,000 units actually sold) is $40,000. This is based on the 2,000-unit increase in sales volume times the estimated $20 unit sales price. We use the *estimated* unit sales price instead of the *actual* price because we want to isolate the impact of the activity increase from changes in the sales price. We want to focus on the effects of volume alone. Thus, the sales amount in the flexible budget is *not the actual revenue* (actual price times actual volume) but the *estimated unit sales price times the actual number of units sold.* This permits us to isolate the effects of the difference between actual and expected sales volume. A sales price variance is also calculated, as discussed later in this chapter.

Comparing actual to the flexible budget

Assume the actual results for May are as follows:

	Actual
Sales price	$ 21 per crate
Sales volume	10,000 crates
Variable manufacturing costs	$105,440
Variable marketing and administrative costs	11,000
Fixed manufacturing costs	21,000 for May
Fixed marketing and administrative costs	44,000 for May

Now the actual results can be compared with both the flexible budget and the master budget as shown in Illustration 18–5. Column 1 is calculated from the facts presented above. Column 2 summarizes manufacturing variances (which are discussed in more detail in Chapter 19), and Column 3 shows marketing and administrative variances (which are discussed in more detail in Chapter 21). Costs have been divided into fixed and variable portions here and would be presented in more detail to the managers of centers having responsibility for them. Cost variances result from deviations in costs and efficiencies in operating the company. They are important for measuring productivity and helping to control costs.

Sales price variance   The sales price variance, Column 4, is derived from the *difference between the actual and budgeted selling price times the actual number of units sold* ($10,000 = [$21 − $20] × 10,000 units). Columns 5, 6, and 7 are carried forward from Illustration 18–3.

Variable manufacturing cost variances   Be careful to distinguish the variable cost variances in Columns 2 and 3, which are input variances, from

Illustration 18–5   Comparison of actual to budget, Boxx Company (May)

	(1) Actual (based on actual activity of 10,000 units sold)	(2) Manufacturing variances	(3) Marketing and administrative variances	(4) Sales price variances	(5) Flexible budget (based on actual activity of 10,000 units sold)	(6) Activity (sales volume) variance	(7) Master budget (based on a prediction of 8,000 units sold)
Sales revenue	$210,000	—	—	$10,000 F	$200,000	$40,000 F	$160,000
Less:							
Variable manufacturing costs	105,440	$5,440 U	—	—	100,000	20,000 U	80,000
Variable marketing and administrative costs	11,000	—	$1,000 U	—	10,000	2,000 U	8,000
Contribution margin	93,560	5,440 U	1,000 U	10,000 F	90,000	18,000 F	72,000
Less:							
Fixed manufacturing costs	21,000	1,000 U	—	—	20,000	—	20,000
Fixed marketing and administrative costs	44,000	—	4,000 U	—	40,000	—	40,000
Operating profits	$ 28,560	$6,440 U	$5,000 U	$10,000 F	$ 30,000	$18,000 F	$ 12,000

→Total variance from flexible budget = $1,440 U

→Total variance from master budget = $16,560 F

the variable cost variances in Column 6, which are part of the sales volume variance. Management *expects* the latter costs to be higher, in this case, because the sales volume is higher than planned.

Looking at Column 5, we see that variable manufacturing costs *should have been* $100,000 for a production and sales volume of 10,000 units, not $80,000 as expressed in the master budget in Column 7. We see from Column 1 that the actual variable manufacturing costs were $105,440, some $25,440 higher than the master budget, but only $5,440 higher than the flexible budget. Which number should be used to evaluate manufacturing cost control—the $25,440 variance from master budget or the $5,440 variance from the flexible budget?

The number that should be used to evaluate manufacturing performance is the $5,440 variance from the flexible budget. This points out a benefit of flexible budgeting. A superficial comparison of the master budget plan with the actual results would have indicated the variance to be $25,440. But, in fact, manufacturing is responsible for only $5,440, which is caused by deviation from production norms. We discuss the source of this $5,440 in more detail in Chapter 19.

Fixed manufacturing cost variance   The fixed manufacturing cost variance is simply the difference between actual and budgeted costs. Fixed costs are treated as period costs; they are not expected to be affected by activity levels within a relevant range. Hence, the flexible budget fixed costs equal the master budget fixed costs.

Marketing and administrative costs   Marketing and administrative costs are treated like manufacturing costs. Variable costs are expected to change as activity changes; hence, variable costs were expected to increase by $2,000 between the flexible and master budget, as shown in Illustration 18–5, because volume increased by 2,000 units. Comparing actual with flexible budget reveals $1,000 unfavorable marketing and administrative costs. Fixed marketing and administrative costs do not change as volume changes; hence, the flexible and master budget amounts are the same.

Units produced versus units sold

In the previous example, production volume and sales volume were equal. But the analysis becomes more complicated when the units sold are not the ones that were produced in the budget period.

Suppose that the 10,000 units Boxx Company sold in May per Illustration 18–5 had been produced in April and that 12,000 units were produced in May for sale in subsequent months. This has no effect on the activity variance because the master budget and flexible budget are based on *sales* volume. Thus, Columns 5, 6, and 7 of Illustration 18–5 remain unchanged. In addition, the sales price variance is based on units sold, so Column 4 remains the same. Generally, marketing and administrative costs are not affected by *pro-*

ducing 12,000 instead of 10,000 units, so we assume they do not change. This allows us to focus on Columns 1 and 2, which would change.

Assume that actual variable manufacturing costs are $10.544 *per unit* and fixed manufacturing costs are $21,000 *for the period.* This leaves the fixed manufacturing cost variance of $1,000 U unchanged. However, the variable manufacturing cost variance changes. In the month units are produced, the following variable manufacturing cost variances are computed:

$$\text{Units produced} \times [\text{Act. variable cost} - \text{Est. variable cost}] = \text{Variance}$$

Previous example (Illustration 18–5):

$$10,000 \times (\$10.544 - \$10.00) = \$5,440 \text{ U}$$

Present example:

$$12,000 \times (\$10.544 - \$10.00) = \$6,528 \text{ U}$$

The variable manufacturing cost variance for units *produced* in May is $6,528. This amount may be treated as a period cost and expensed in May, or it may be prorated to units sold and to units still in inventory. If prorated, all $6,528 would be charged to inventory in this case because the units produced in May are still in inventory at the end of May. Usually, the $6,528 variance due to May's production is written off in May and shown as a variance as illustrated in Illustration 18–6.

What about the units *sold* in May that were produced in April? If the 10,000 units produced in April had a variance of $.544 per unit, the variance on those units is $5,440. That variance was charged against April profits.

Note that the actual variable manufacturing costs of $106,528 in Illustration 18–6 are really a hybrid—$100,000 in flexible budget costs (based on 10,000 units produced last period and sold this period times $10 estimated cost per unit) plus the $6,528 variable manufacturing cost variance from the 12,000 units produced this period.

Reconciling full-absorption and variable costing

Now assume that Boxx Company produced 12,000 units and sold 10,000 units in May. Assume there was no beginning inventory on May 1, so the ending inventory on May 31 was 2,000 units. Using variable costing, the entire *fixed manufacturing cost* of $21,000 would be expensed, as shown in Illustrations 18–3 through 18–6. Such would not be the case, however, when full-absorption costing is used, and production and sales volume are not the same.

Using full-absorption costing, a portion of the fixed manufacturing costs would be allocated to the 2,000 units in ending inventory:

$$\frac{2,000 \text{ units}}{12,000 \text{ units}} \times \$21,000 = \underline{\underline{\$3,500}}$$

Thus, only $17,500 (= $21,000 − $3,500) of the actual fixed manufacturing

Illustration 18-6 Comparison of actual to budget, Boxx Company (May)

	(1) Actual (based on 10,000 units)	(2) Manufacturing variances	(3) Marketing and administrative variances	(4) Sales price variances	(5) Flexible budget (based on 10,000 units)	(6) Activity (sales volume) variance	(7) Master budget (based on 8,000 units)
Sales revenue	$210,000	—	—	$10,000 F	$200,000	$40,000 F	$160,000
Less:							
Variable manufacturing costs	106,528	$6,528 U	—	—	100,000	20,000 U	80,000
Variable marketing and administrative costs	11,000	—	$1,000 U	—	10,000	2,000 U	8,000
Contribution margin	92,472	6,528 U	1,000 U	10,000 F	90,000	18,000 F	72,000
Less:							
Fixed manufacturing costs	21,000	1,000 U	—	—	20,000	—	20,000
Fixed marketing and administrative costs	44,000	—	4,000 U	—	40,000	—	40,000
Operating profits	$ 27,472	$7,528 U	$5,000 U	$10,000 F	$ 30,000	$18,000 F	$ 12,000

Total variance from flexible budget = $2,528 U

Total variance from master budget = $15,472 F

costs are expensed in May using full-absorption costing. In this case, full-absorption operating profit would be $30,972 in May, or $3,500 higher than variable costing operating profit.[1] This difference in profits is due to the accounting system and not to managerial efficiencies. Care should be taken to identify the cause of such profit differences so that a variance due to accounting method is not misinterpreted as one due to operating activities. The budget planning and control methods presented in this book are based on the variable costing approach to product costing, unless otherwise stated.

Service and merchandising activities

The comparison of the master budget, the flexible budget, and actual results also can be used in service and merchandising organizations. The basic framework in Illustration 18–5 would be retained. Output would usually be defined as sales units in merchandising, but other measures are often used in service organizations. For example:

Organization	Units of activity
Public accounting, legal, and consulting firms	Professional staff hours
Laundry	Weight or pieces of clothing
Hospital	Patient days

Merchandising and service organizations focus on marketing and administrative costs to measure efficiency and to control costs. The key items to control are labor costs, particularly in service organizations, and occupancy costs per sales dollar, particularly in merchandising organizations.

Behavioral issues in budgeting

"You should only hold employees responsible for those things they can control" is sometimes claimed to be an important behavioral factor in designing accounting systems. This appeals to a sense of fairness that "the manager of the assembly department should not be charged with inefficiencies caused by the cutting department." Perhaps of more significance in an economic sense is the idea that holding employees responsible for only the things they can control reduces their risk. A well-established concept from the study of financial markets is that higher risk requires higher returns. In a similar fashion, risk-averse workers will demand a higher wage to assume greater risk, all other things equal. Flexible budgets can reduce risk to a worker, as demonstrated by the following example.

Assume that the manager of the repairs department has a budget of $100,000 for December. It turns out that machine time is low in December,

---

[1] Of course, as discussed in Chapter 9, if units sold exceed units produced, we expect the reverse to be true; that is, full-absorption operating profit would be lower than variable costing operating profit.

and repairs can be easily scheduled without overtime. As a result, the manager spends only $90,000 of the budget. However, suppose production increases during the month of January, and department personnel are working overtime to make the necessary repairs. Expenditures for the repairs department are $110,000 in January.

The manager of the repairs department believes performance is evaluated according to the budget and that his bonus, raises, promotions, and job could depend on meeting the budget. A risk-averse manager will prefer a system that adjusts the budget down to $90,000 in December, and up to $110,000 in January to reflect the changing levels of production, even though the average results for the two months are the same.

Current research has raised some questions about the admonition that "employees should only be held accountable for what they control." There may be situations in which both employers and employees are better off if employees are held accountable for more than just what they control. Further, few employers will ignore information about factors outside an employee's control that nevertheless affect the employee's performance.[2]

| Responsibility centers | Budgets for performance evaluation and cost control are typically organized around responsibility centers. Responsibility centers are organizational units for which someone has responsibility. For example, a business school within a university is often a responsibility center. The dean of the business school has a budgeted level of resources to work with, and is responsible to university officials for the way those resources are used to achieve the university's goals. Other examples are: |

Responsibility center	Person in charge	Responsible for
Company	Chief executive officer	All assets, equities, revenues, and costs of the company
Division	Division vice president	Divisional assets, equities, revenues, and costs
Plant	Plant manager	Plant production and costs
Department store	Store manager	Store's revenues and costs
Secretarial pool	Secretarial pool supervisor	Costs and secretarial production

[2] Extensive literature has been developed in recent years that deals with issues of risk sharing and incentives in organizations. While the work so far has been done in highly simplified analytical settings, and the results are difficult to generalize to organizations, some fundamental principles for incentive and control systems have been developed. For a review, see S. Baiman, "Agency Research in Managerial Accounting: A Survey," *Journal of Accounting Literature,* 1982.

Illustration 18–7   **Budget assigned to responsibility centers, Electronics, Inc.**

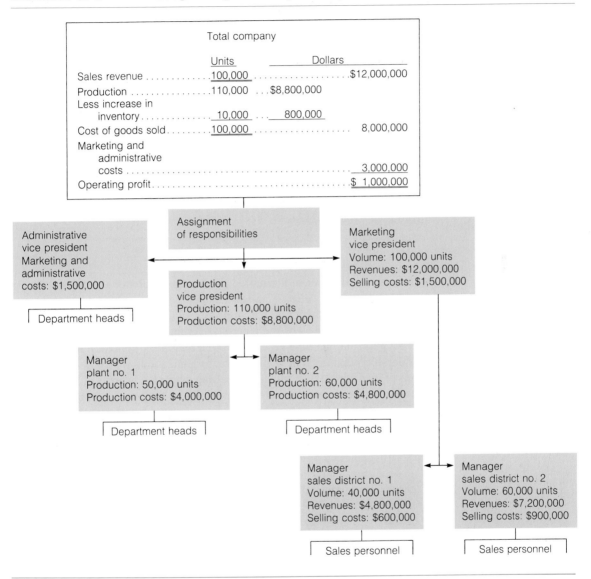

For example, the budget breakdown for Electronics, Inc., is shown in Illustration 18–7. Each of the three vice presidents—administrative, production, and marketing—is responsible for part of it. Based on accounting allocations, the marketing and administrative costs were divided equally between the marketing vice president and the administrative vice president. The administrative budget is subdivided into departments (data processing, accounting, personnel). The production budget is further divided among plant managers, who assign the budget to department heads (assembly, processing, quality control, warehousing). The marketing vice president assigned the marketing budget to the district sales managers.

Note that the production and marketing budgets both involve activity in units—units produced or units sold—while the administrative budget does not. This is one of the major difficulties in controlling marketing and administrative costs. It is difficult to relate these costs directly to changes in a company's sales and production. If the number of units sold increases 20 percent, should marketing and administrative cost increase the same amount? This is not an easy question to answer. Many companies, governmental units, and not-for-profit organizations have responded to this problem by trying to measure marketing and administrative activity. (We discuss some of these methods in Chapter 21.)

Zero-base budgeting

Many organizations have attempted to manage discretionary costs through a budgeting method called zero-base budgeting.[3] Numerous companies, including Texas Instruments, Xerox, and Control Data, and governmental units, including some agencies of the federal government, have implemented zero-base budgeting at one time or another. One reason the approach has attracted considerable popularity in public sector organizations is that it is seen as a means of managing expenditures in a setting where the benefits of the expenditures cannot be traced to the costs as easily as they can in manufacturing.

The novel part of zero-base budgeting is the requirement that the budgeting process start at zero, with all expenditures completely justified. This contrasts with the usual approach, in which a certain level of expenditures is allowed as a starting point, and the budgeting process focuses on requests for incremental expenditures. However, a strict zero-base approach has been found to be generally impracticable because of the massive amount of time required for implementation. Thus, many organizations that use zero-base budgeting in fact allow a floor that does not have to be justified in as much detail. In many organizations, this has been set at around 80 percent of the current level of expenditures. This floor is the lowest amount of money that would enable a responsibility center to continue its operations at a minimal level. Proposed increments of activity above this level are evaluated one by one in terms of costs and benefits.

---

[3] For more detailed information about zero-base budgeting, see P. Phyrr, *Zero-Base Budgeting* (New York: John Wiley & Sons, 1972); and J. Patillo. *Zero-Base Budgeting* (New York: National Association of Accountants, 1977). Also see R. Anthony and R. Herzlinger, *Management Control in Nonprofit Organizations* (Homewood, Ill.: Richard D. Irwin, 1980).

Summary

This chapter discussed and illustrated the use of the budgeted income statement for performance evaluation and control. The master budget income statement was compared with actual results. Differences, or variances, between actual results and the master budget were analyzed to determine why budgeted results did not occur.

The master budget is typically static; that is, it is developed in detail for one level of activity. A flexible budget recognizes that variable costs and revenues are expected to differ from the budget if the actual activity (for example, actual sales volume) differs from what was budgeted. A flexible budget can be thought of as the costs and revenues that would have been budgeted if the activity level had been correctly estimated in the master budget. The general relationship between actual, the flexible budget, and the master budget is shown below:

Actual	**Flexible budget**	**Master budget**
Actual costs and revenues based on actual activity	Costs and revenues that would have been budgeted if actual activity had been budgeted	Budgeted costs and revenues based on budgeted activity

Differences or variances between actual results and the flexible budget are differences between actual results and the budget that would have been prepared if activity had been accurately estimated. These variances include the sales price variance, manufacturing cost variances, and nonmanufacturing cost variances. Differences between the flexible and master budget results are due to the impact on revenues and costs of the difference between actual and budgeted volume.

When units produced and sold are not the same, a decision has to be made whether to prorate variances to units sold and those in inventory, or to write off the variance as a period cost.

Terms and concepts

The following terms and concepts should be familiar to you after reading this chapter.

Activity variance	**Responsibility centers**
Controllability	**Sales volume variance**
Financial budgets	**Static budget**
Flexible budget	**Variances**
Operating budgets	**Zero-base budgeting**

Self-study problem: Containers, Inc.*

In August, Containers, Inc., produced and sold 50,000 plastic minicomputer cases at a sales price of $10 each. (Budgeted sales were 45,000 units at $10.15.)

Budget:
  Standard variable costs per unit
    (that is, case) $4.00
  Fixed manufacturing overhead cost:
    Monthly budget $ 80,000
  Marketing and administrative:
    Variable $1.00 per case
    Fixed $100,000

Actual
  Actual manufacturing costs:
    Variable costs per unit $4.88
    Fixed overhead $ 83,000
  Actual marketing and administrative:
    Variable (50,000 @ $1.04 =)   52,000
    Fixed   96,000

Required:

Using variable costing, prepare a report comparing actual results with the flexible and master budgets for August. Include variances.

Solution to self-study problem

Comparison of actual to budget, Containers, Inc. (August), see page 691.

* This self-study problem continues through Chapters 19 and 20.

Comparison of actual to budget, Containers, Inc. (August)

	Actual (based on 50,000 units)	Manufacturing variances	Marketing and administrative variances	Sales price variances	Flexible budget (based on 50,000 units)	Activity (sales volume) variance	Master budget (based on 45,000 units)
Sales revenue	$500,000	—	—	$7,500 U	$507,500	$50,750 F	$456,750
Less:							
Variable manufacturing costs	244,000	$44,000 U	—	—	200,000	20,000 U	180,000
Variable marketing and administrative costs	52,000	—	$2,000[a] U	—	50,000	5,000 U	45,000
Contribution margins	204,000	44,000 U	2,000 U	7,500 U	257,500	25,750 F	231,750
Less:							
Fixed manufacturing costs	83,000	3,000 U	—	—	80,000	—	80,000
Fixed marketing and administrative costs	96,000	—	4,000 F	—	100,000	—	100,000
Operating profits	$ 25,000	$47,000 U	$2,000 F	$7,500 U	$ 77,500	$25,750 F	$ 51,750

Total variance from flexible budget = $52,500 U

Total variance from master budget = $26,750 U

[a] $2,000 = $.04 × 50,000 = ($1.04 − 1.00) 50,000 units.

Questions

18–1. What is a responsibility center?

18–2. Could some responsibility centers differ in the types of budget items they are accountable for? That is, might some responsibility centers be responsible only for costs, some only for revenues, some for both? Give examples.

18–3. Does a line worker avoid responsibility because he or she is not included formally in the responsibility reporting system? How can management keep control of the line worker's activities in the absence of formal budget control?

18–4. Budgets for governmental units are usually prepared one year in advance of the budget period. Expenditures are limited to the budgeted amount. At the end of the period, performance is evaluated by comparing budget authorizations with actual receipts and outlays. What management control problems are likely to arise from such a system?

18–5. "I don't understand why you accountants want to prepare a budget for a period that is already over. We know the actual results by then—all that other budget does is increase the controller's staff and add to our overhead." Comment on this remark.

18–6. "Last month we sold 1,000 fewer units than planned. Your performance report shows favorable activity variances for every variable manufacturing cost. I don't consider a drop in sales as a favorable event. How do you explain this?"

18–7. Why is a variable costing format more useful for performance evaluation purposes than an absorption costing format?

18–8. "All costs 'flex' with activity." True or false? Why or why not?

18–9. How will the performance measurement system differ when a company is using the LIFO inventory system from when a company is using the FIFO system?

18–10. What is zero-base budgeting and how does it differ from other budgeting practices?

Exercises

18–11. Compute revenue variances

High Vol Sales Corporation prepared a budget for the current year that called for sales of $28,500,000. At the end of the year, management noted that actual sales were $30,000,000. However, while the initial planned volume was 1,000,000 units, actual volume was 1,400,000 units. Production management has been complaining about the increased workload. Sales management has remarked, "Our volume is up, our sales revenue is up. . . . Let's be proud of the work our sales department is doing."

Required:

a. Analyze the reasons for the difference in sales revenue.

b. What do you think might be causing the increased revenue? (Show both the sales price and activity variances.)

18–12. Analyze contribution margin variances

PerkUp, Ltd. prepared a budget last period that called for sales of 7,000 units at a price of $12 each. The costs per unit were estimated to amount to $5 variable and $3 fixed. During the period, production was exactly equal to actual sales of 7,100 units. The selling price was $12.15 per unit. Variable costs were $5.90 per unit. Selling and administrative costs were all fixed at $15,000.

Required:

Prepare a performance report to show the difference between the actual contribution margin and the master budget.

18–13. Analyze changes in gross profit

Garfield Company, which sells a single product, provided the following data for calendar years 1986 and 1987:

	1986	1987
Sales volume	180,000 units	150,000 units
Sales revenue	$720,000	$750,000
Cost of goods sold	575,000	525,000
Gross profit	$145,000	$225,000

Required:

What impact did the changes in sales volume and changes in sales price have on the gross profit.

(CPA adapted)

18–14. Prepare budgets and derive variances

Peter Principals (a joint venture) provided the following information about its 1985 results:

	Actual	**Master budget**
Beginning inventory:		
Fixed costs	$ 12,000	$ 12,000
Variable costs	6,000	6,000
Current manufacturing costs:		
Variable	280,000	300,000
Fixed	600,000	540,000
Ending inventory:		
Variable	56,000	60,000
Fixed	120,000	108,000

There were 3,000 units in the beginning inventory. The master budget called for the production of 70,000 units; however, 65,000 were actually produced. Ending inventory contained 13,000 units. The company uses the FIFO inventory system.

Required:

a. Determine the budgeted and actual cost of goods sold (full-absorption costing).
b. Compute the manufacturing cost and activity variances (variable costing).

18–15. Prepare flexible budget data

The following information is provided concerning the operations of the Full Ton Company for the current period:

	Actual	**Master budget**
Sales volume	90 units	100 units
Sales revenue	$9,200	$10,000
Manufacturing cost of goods sold:		
Direct labor	1,420	1,500
Direct materials	1,200	1,400
Variable overhead	820	1,000
Fixed overhead	485	500
Cost of goods sold	3,925	4,400
Gross profit	5,275	5,600

	Actual	Master budget
Operating costs:		
Marketing costs:		
Variable	530	600
Fixed	1,040	1,000
Administrative costs:		
Variable	500	500
Fixed	995	1,000
Total operating costs	3,065	3,100
Operating profits	$2,210	$ 2,500

There are no inventories.

Required:

Prepare a flexible budget for the Full Ton Company.

(CPA adapted)

18–16. Analyze flexible budget data

Use the information for the Full Ton Company (Exercise 18–15) to prepare a performance report which will enable management to isolate the variances between master budget and actual results.

Problems and cases

18–17. Analyze activity variances— FIFO process costing

Fellite, Inc., manufactures foam padding for medical uses. The padding is produced in a continuous process. The company uses the FIFO process costing system for internal recordkeeping purposes. Since materials and conversion costs are added evenly throughout the process, it is not necessary to maintain separate account of materials and conversion costs for equivalent unit computations.

The master budget and actual results for the current period are reproduced as follows:

	Actual	Master budget
Physical count of units:		
Beginning work in process inventory	1,000 (80% complete)	1,000 (50% complete)
Transferred to next department	2,500 units	3,200 units
Ending inventory	800 (⅝ complete)	600 (⅔ complete)
Current period costs:		
Direct materials	$30,000	$32,500
Direct labor	24,600	27,000
Manufacturing overhead:		
Variable	16,200	14,500
Fixed	24,100	26,000

Required:

a. Compute the equivalent units of production this period. (Note: Equivalent unit computations are discussed in Chapter 6.).

b. Prepare a report showing the source of differences between master budget and actual results.

18–18. Compute master budget given actual data

Oleander Enterprises lost the only copy of the master budget for this period. Management wants to evaluate this period's performance, but feels they need the master budget to do so. Actual results for the period were:

Sales volume	120,000 units
Sales revenue	$672,000
Variable costs:	
Manufacturing	147,200
Marketing and administrative	61,400
Contribution margin	463,400
Fixed costs:	
Manufacturing	205,000
Marketing and administrative	113,200
Operating profit	$145,200

The company planned to produce and sell 108,000 units at a price of $5 each. At that volume, the contribution margin would have been $380,000. Variable marketing and administrative costs are budgeted at 10 percent of sales revenue. Manufacturing fixed costs are estimated at $2 per unit at the normal production level. Management note: "We budget an operating profit of $1 per unit."

Required:

a. Construct the master budget for the period.
b. Prepare a report comparing actual sales to the flexible budget and master budget.

18–19. Find missing data

	Actual 750 units	Manufacturing variances	Marketing and administrative variances	Sales price variance	Flexible budget (a)	Activity variance	Master budget 800 units
Sales revenue	$1,890			(b)	$2,025	(c)	(d)
Current manufacturing costs:							
Variable	(e)	$60 F			(f)	$38 F	(g)
Variable marketing and administrative	(h)		(i)		(j)	(k)	$216
Contribution margin	$1,180	(l)	(m)	(n)	(o)	(p)	(q)

Required:

Find the values of the missing items. Assume that sales volume equals production volume.

18–20. Adapt budget control concepts to research organization

The Argo Company has an extensive research program. The research activity is well organized. Each project is required to be broken down into its phases with the completion times and the cost of each phase estimated. The project descriptions and related estimates serve as the basis for the development of the annual research department budget.

The schedule below presents the costs for the approved research activities for a recent year. The actual costs incurred by projects or overhead category are compared to the approved activity and the variances noted on this same schedule.

The director of research prepared a narrative statement of research performance for the year to accompany the schedule. The director's statement follows the schedule.

ARGO COMPANY
Comparison of Actual with Budgeted Research Costs
(in thousands)

	Approved activity for the year	Actual costs for the year	(Over) under budget
Projects in progress:			
4–1	$ 23.2	$ 46.8	$(23.6)
5–3	464.0ª	514.8	(50.8)
New projects:			
8–1	348.0	351.0	(3.0)
8–2	232.0	257.4	(25.4)
8–3	92.8	—	92.8
Total research costs	1,160.0	1,170.0	(10.0)
General research overhead costs (allocated to projects in proportion to their direct costs):			
Administration	50.0	52.0	(2.0)
Laboratory facilities	110.0	118.0	(8.0)
Total	160.0	(170.0)	(10.0)
Allocated to projects	(160.0)	(170.0)	(10.0)
Balance	–0–	–0–	–0–
Total research costs	$1,160.0	$1,170.0	$(10.0)

ª Phases 3 and 4 only.

"The year has been most successful. The two projects, 4–1 and 8–1, scheduled for completion in this year were finished. Project 8–2 is progressing satisfactorily and should be completed next year as scheduled. The fourth phase of Project 5–3, with estimated direct research costs of $100,000 and the first phase of Project 8–3, both included in the approved activity for the year, could not be started because the principal researcher left our employment. They were resubmitted for approval in next year's activity plan."

Required:

From the information given, prepare an alternative schedule that will provide the management of Argo Company with better information than the existing schedule by which to judge the research cost performance for the given year. (Hint: separate direct from indirect costs.)

(CMA adapted)

18–21. Analyze performance

Persons Deli is planning to expand operations and, hence, is concerned that its performance reporting system may need improvement. The budgeted income statement for its Akron Persons Deli, which contains a delicatessen and restaurant operation is (in thousands):

	Delicatessen	Restaurant	Total
Gross sales	$1,000	$2,500	$3,500
Purchases	600	1,000	1,600
Hourly wages	50	875	925
Franchise fee	30	75	105
Advertising	100	200	300
Utilities	70	125	195
Depreciation	50	75	125
Lease cost	30	50	80
Salaries	30	50	80
Total	960	2,450	3,410
Operating profit	$ 40	$ 50	$ 90

The performance report that the company uses for management evaluation is as follows:

PERSONS RESTAURANT-DELI
Akron, Ohio
Net Income for the Year
(in thousands)

	Actual results				Over (under) budget
	Delicatessen	Restaurant	Total	Budget	
Gross sales	$1,200	$2,000	$3,200	$3,500	$(300)[a]
Purchases[b]	780	800	1,580	1,600	(20)
Hourly wages[b]	60	700	760	925	(165)
Franchise fee[b]	36	60	96	105	(9)
Advertising	100	200	300	300	—
Utilities[b]	76	100	176	195	(19)
Depreciation	50	75	125	125	—
Lease cost	30	50	80	80	—
Salaries	30	50	80	80	—
Total	1,162	2,035	3,197	3,410	(213)
Operating profit	$ 38	$ (35)	$ 3	$ 90	$ (87)

[a] There is no sales price variance.
[b] Variable costs. All other costs are fixed.

Required:

Prepare a schedule to indicate the flexible budget and relevant variances for the delicatessen department.

(CMA adapted)

18–22. Compare actual to budget with inventory adjustment

Partita Corporation prepared a budget for December 1985. The master budget appears as follows:

Sales revenue (9,000 units at $12)	$108,000

Cost of goods manufactured and sold:

Beginning finished goods inventory	$12,600	
Current manufacturing costs	39,400	
Ending finished goods inventory	(16,400)	
Cost of goods manufactured and sold		35,600
Gross profit		72,400
Marketing and administrative costs:		
Variable		24,300
Fixed		31,000
Operating profit before taxes		$ 17,100

Budgeted current manufacturing costs are all variable except for $8,100 in fixed costs. The ratio of variable to fixed costs in the current manufacturing costs also applies to beginning and ending inventory.

Actual results for the month were:

Sales revenues (8,700 units at $11.90)		$103,530
Cost of goods manufactured and sold:		
Beginning finished goods inventory	$12,600	
Current manufacturing costs	37,300	
Ending finished goods inventory	(16,442)	
Cost of goods manufactured and sold		33,458
Gross profit		70,072
Marketing and administrative costs:		
Variable		24,100
Fixed		31,600
Operating profit before taxes		$ 14,372

Assume FIFO. The ratio of fixed to variable costs in current manufacturing costs also applies to ending inventory. Actual fixed costs are $8,300 in December 1985.

Required:

Prepare an analysis to identify the causes for the difference between planned (master budget) profits and actual profits. All manufacturing cost variances are included in the current manufacturing costs listed in the actual income statement.

Hint: Change the format of the statements to show contribution margins.

18–23. Compare actual to budget with inventory adjustments

Wellston, Inc., prepared a comparison of its October master budget and actual results. The differences between the budget and actual were used as measures for evaluating performance during the period. The "performance statement" that was prepared follows (dollars in thousands):

	Actual	Master budget	Performance variance
Sales volume (units)	11,600	12,000	400 U
Sales revenue	$493	$498	$5 U
Cost of goods sold:			
Current manufacturing costs:			
Variable	302	306	4 F
Fixed	82	81	1 U
Deduct cost of goods added to the finished goods inventory:			
Variable	(62)	(61)	1 F
Fixed	(16)	(16)	
Cost of goods sold (net)	306	310	4 F
Gross profit	187	188	$1 U
Marketing and administrative costs:			
Variable	60	58	2 U
Fixed	90	92	2 F
Total marketing and administrative costs	150	150	—
Operating profit	$ 37	$ 38	$1 U

After reviewing these reports, the production manager noted: "We've certainly done our part to help out the company. If we could only get some more cooperation from the sales force, the bottom line would show some real improvement instead of this below-target performance."

Prepare a comparison of actual results and master budget, consistent with variable costing, that would be more helpful to Wellston management for evaluating October performance. Assume that the volume added to ending inventory was exactly as planned. Assume that the entire manufacturing variance was expensed for the month.

19

Manufacturing
Cost Variances

To understand how variances between planned and actual results can be analyzed by identifying the cause of the variance.
To be familiar with the management implications of variance analysis.

In management accounting, any deviation from a predetermined benchmark is a variance. In Chapter 17, we developed the master budget; and in Chapter 18, the flexible budget. We saw how the difference between the flexible budget and the master budget creates an activity variance, and how differences between actual results and the flexible budget create a number of other variances. In this chapter, we examine in detail how a specific group of variances—manufacturing cost variances—are developed, interpreted, and used.

Although the title of this chapter is "Manufacturing Cost Variances," the variances that we describe are used in nonmanufacturing organizations. Service organizations in particular can use the labor and overhead variances to assess efficiency and control costs. Labor standards and variances are used in many financial institutions such as banks to assess transaction and check-processing efficiency. Labor standards are also used in fast-food restaurants to assess efficiency in preparing and serving food.

Standard costs

A standard is a benchmark or norm. There are, for example, standards for admittance to school, standards for passing a course, standards for product safety. In accounting, the term *standard* is used in a similar fashion. A standard cost is the anticipated cost of producing and/or selling a unit of output; it is a predetermined cost assigned to goods produced. In this chapter, we are specifically concerned with the standard costs of *producing* a unit of output, that is, standard manufacturing costs.

Some clarifications

Standards versus budgets A standard cost is a *predetermined unit cost,* while a budget is a *financial plan.* Standard costs are often used to make up the financial plan. While in practice these terms are sometimes used interchangeably, standards usually refer to per unit amounts while budgets usually refer to totals.

Standard cost versus standard cost systems   Another potential source of confusion is the distinction between standard costs and standard cost systems. A standard cost system is an accounting system in which products are costed using standard costs instead of actual costs. We have postponed discussion of standard cost systems until Chapter 20, in part to emphasize that standard costs and manufacturing variances can be computed even if a formal standard cost accounting system is not used for product costing purposes.

In many companies, standards, like budgets, are developed and maintained "off the books." That is, they are not part of the formal accounting system. So when we discuss standard costs in this chapter, we are referring to standards developed to facilitate control of personnel and operations. Whether they are entered into the records to value inventory is another issue.

Sources of standard costs

The following description of the way standard costs are set is based on an interview with a controller in a manufacturing company. It is representative of the standard-setting process in most companies.

Variable manufacturing costs

Materials   A standard cost for every direct material used is computed by (1) examining current purchase prices and adjusting them for expected changes and (2) estimating the quantity of each direct material required to make each final product. The purchasing department helps us estimate how material prices will change. Our operations managers and industrial engineers help determine the quantities of materials needed to make our product.

Labor   Industrial engineers and operating managers estimate the number of direct labor-hours (or fractions of hours) required for each step of production by timing employees while they perform their duties. These hours are costed by accountants based on expected wage rates and fringe benefits during the period.

Variable overhead   Several years ago we began using regression analysis to estimate variable overhead rates. We ran actual variable overhead as the dependent variable and actual labor-hours as the independent variable for each production department. Each year we adjust the unit variable overhead rate based on feedback from production managers and accountants about changes in cost.

Budgeted fixed overhead

Production department managers and our accountants estimate the amount of fixed overhead that will be incurred in each production department, including service department costs (for example, maintenance) that have been allocated to the production department.

Review   All of these estimates are reviewed on a sample basis for reasonableness by our accounting staff and by our internal auditors. They are adjusted once a year to reflect changes.

Approvals   All standards are approved once a year by top management.

Despite the use of statistical techniques and industrial engineering methods for cost estimation, setting cost standards is more an art than a science.

Setting standards: An illustration

We will now illustrate how standard variable manufacturing cost variances are developed for the Boxx Company example that was introduced in Chapter 18. The standard variable manufacturing cost, which we called the *estimated cost* in Chapter 18, was $10 per crate.

Direct materials

Here is how the Boxx Company determines the standard price of the lumber it uses to make crates. The standard price reflects the price of the product delivered to Boxx Company, net of purchase discounts.

Direct materials: Standard price (per board foot)

Purchase price of lumber	$ .23
Shipping costs	.04
Less purchase discounts	(.02)
Standard price per board foot	$ .25

Note: A board foot is a quantity measure equal to the volume in a piece of lumber 12 by 12 inches and 1 inch thick.

Direct materials are purchased by the board foot, so the purchase price standard is expressed per *foot,* not per *crate.*

Direct material quantity standards are based on the quantity of direct material that should be used to make one unit under normal operating conditions. Each crate requires 9 board feet of lumber. One additional board foot of lumber is the allowance for waste in cutting the lumber to the proper size and constructing the crate.

Direct materials: Standard quantity (board feet)

Requirements per crate	9
Allowance for waste	1
Standard quantity per crate	10

The standard direct material cost per *crate* is then computed:

$$\text{\$.25 per board foot} \times \text{10 board feet per crate} = \underline{\text{\$2.50 per crate}}$$

Direct labor

Direct labor standards are based on a standard labor rate for the work performed and the standard labor-hours required. The standard labor rate includes not only wages earned but also fringe benefits, such as medical insurance and pension plan contributions, and taxes paid by the employer (for example, unemployment taxes and the employer's share of an employee's social security taxes).

Direct labor: Standard rate (price per hour)

Wage rate	$ 8.00
Employer's payroll taxes and fringe benefits	2.00
Standard rate	$10.00

Most companies develop one standard rate for each category of labor. We assume Boxx Company has only one category of labor.

Standard direct labor time is based on an estimate of the time required to perform each operation. For example, at Boxx Company, the amount of time required to make each crate—to cut the lumber to size, to assemble the crate, and to finish and inspect it—is estimated by timing each step and adding some time for personal needs and breaks. Sometimes a crate is assembled but later rejected when inspected, so an allowance is made for time spent on crates that will later be rejected. These estimates for each crate are as follows:

Direct labor: Standard time (hours)

Cutting department:	
Cutting	.08
Personal time	.01
Allowance for rejects	.01
Total cutting department	.10
Assembly department:	
Assembly	.24
Personal time	.04
Allowance for rejects	.02
Total assembly department	.30
Finishing and inspection department:	
Finishing and inspection	.08
Personal time	.01
Allowance for rejects	.01
Total finishing and inspection department	.10
Standard time per good crate completed	.50

For each good crate that is completed, the standard labor cost is:

$$\$10 \text{ per hour} \times .50 \text{ hours per crate} = \underline{\underline{\$5 \text{ per crate}}}$$

Variable manufacturing overhead

The first step in setting variable overhead standards is to select a *basis* that relates the cost to the product; that is, to determine x in the formula:

$$Y = a + bx$$

where:

$Y =$ estimated total overhead (the dependent variable)
$a =$ estimated fixed overhead
$b =$ estimated variable overhead rate per unit
$x =$ the independent variable(s) (usually an activity measure)

Either output or input measures of activity may be used for x. Boxx Company could develop a variable overhead rate per crate, which is an *output* measure, and apply that rate to each crate produced. Or it could apply overhead on the basis of standard direct labor-hours, which is an *input* measure.

Selecting activity measures for applying overhead

Output measures versus input measures of activity   Output measures of activity (for example, number of crates produced at Boxx Company, or number of automobiles produced in an automobile factory) sometimes work well as a basis for applying overhead—especially when a single product is completely produced in a single work operation. However, it becomes difficult to measure departmental activity in terms of output when the department works on multiple products and only a portion of the product is completed in each department. Hence, most companies find input measures, like direct labor-hours or direct labor costs, more practical.

If an input measure is used, its selection should be based on the following criteria:

1. *Causal relationship between the activity base and variable overhead costs.* An increase in the activity base should result in an increase in variable overhead costs. If an operation is labor intensive, labor-hours would probably be causally related to variable overhead. On the other hand, for a capital intensive operation, machine-hours could be the cause of variable overhead. As a product moves through several departments in a manufacturing operation, different activity bases may be used, as shown in the following diagram (the arrows refer to the movement of the product through various departments until it is finished):

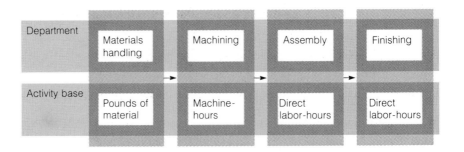

Department	Materials handling	Machining	Assembly	Finishing
Activity base	Pounds of material	Machine-hours	Direct labor-hours	Direct labor-hours

There is usually more than one cause of variable overhead, but to simplify matters, one independent variable is usually selected for a particular manufacturing department.

2. *Physical units versus dollars.* Physical units are often used for the activity base instead of dollars. If labor dollars are used, a contract settlement or other wage change could affect labor costs, but that does not necessarily mean that variable overhead costs would change.

3. *Cost-benefit constraints.* A model that specifies the relationship between variable overhead costs and their causes in so much detail that measures are precise could be quite costly. The benefits of such a complete model rarely justify its costs. Thus, a simplified model is usually preferred. For example, a simple regression model with one independent variable is often used in place of a multiple regression model, even though multiple regression may explain more variation in variable overhead. When examining variances between actual and standard costs, managers recognize that some variance is due purely to the infeasibility of setting perfect standards.

Boxx Company bases its variable overhead standards on standard direct labor-hours. A rate of $5 per direct labor-hour is used for each department. Estimates are made of variable manufacturing overhead, output, and standard labor-hours for each level of output for each department, as shown below:

	Department					
	Cutting		**Assembly**		**Finishing and inspection**	
Production output per month	Variable manufacturing overhead costs	Standard direct labor-hours	Variable manufacturing overhead costs	Standard direct labor-hours	Variable manufacturing overhead costs	Standard direct labor-hours
7,000 crates	$3,520	700	$10,480	2,100	$3,530	700
8,000 crates	4,050	800	12,080	2,400	4,100	800
9,000 crates	4,530	900	13,570	2,700	4,600	900
etc.						

Illustration 19–1   **Summary of standard costs, Boxx Company**

	(1) Standard input quantity	(2) Standard input price or rate	(1)×(2) Standard cost per crate
Direct materials (all charged to cutting department)	10 feet	$ .25 per foot	$ 2.50
Direct labor:			
Cutting department	.10 hours	$10 per hour	$1.00
Assembly department	.30	10	3.00
Finishing and inspection department	.10	10	1.00
Total direct labor	.50	10	5.00
Variable manufacturing overhead:			
Cutting department	.10	5	.50
Assembly department	.30	5	1.50
Finishing and inspection department	.10	5	.50
Total variable manufacturing overhead	.50	5	2.50
Total standard variable cost per crate			$10.00

These estimates and relationships are based on knowledge about prior period activities and costs, an estimate of how costs will change in the future, and a regression analysis in which overhead cost was the dependent variable and labor-hours the independent variable. After analyzing these estimates, the accountants decided to use $5 per standard labor-hour as the variable manufacturing overhead rate for each department because variable overhead averaged about $5 per standard direct-labor hour. (For example, in Cutting $\frac{\$3,520}{700} = \$5.03$ per hour.) In practice, different departments may have different rates. The standard direct labor quantity per crate is one-half hour; thus, the standard variable overhead rate per crate would be $2.50.

The variable manufacturing cost standards are summarized in a standard cost computer record or file. Illustration 19–1 presents the contents of such a file for Boxx Company.

Analysis of cost variances

General model

The conceptual cost variance analysis model compares actual input quantities and prices with standard input quantities and prices. *Both these actual and standard input quantities are for the actual output attained.* As shown in Illustration 19–2, a *price variance* and an *efficiency variance* can be computed for each variable manufacturing input. The actual costs incurred (Column 1) for the time period are compared with the standard allowed per unit times the number of good units of output produced (Column 3). This comparison provides the total variance for the cost or input.

In some companies, only the total variance is computed. In other companies, a more detailed breakdown into price and efficiency variances is made.

Illustration 19–2   **General model for analysis of variable manufacturing cost variances**

(1)

Actual

Actual input price (AP) times *actual* quantity (AQ) of input

(2)
Inputs at standard price

Standard input price (SP) times *actual* quantity (AQ) of input

(3)
Flexible production budget

Standard input price (SP) times *standard* quantity (SQ) of input allowed for actual output

(AP × AQ)	**(SP × AQ)**	**(SP × SQ)**

Price variance[a]
(1) minus (2):
(AP × AQ) − (SP × AQ)
= (AP − SP) × AQ

Efficiency variance[a]
(2) minus (3):
(SP × AQ) − (SP × SQ)
= SP × (AQ − SQ)

Total variance
(1) minus (3):
(AP × AQ) − (SP × SQ)

[a] The terms *price* and *efficiency* variances are general categories. While terminology varies from company to company, the following specific variance titles are frequently used:

Input	**Price variance category**	**Efficiency variance category**
Direct materials	Price (or purchase price) variance	Usage or quantity variance
Direct labor	Rate variance	Efficiency variance
Variable overhead	Spending variance	Efficiency variance

We shall avoid unnecessary complications by simply referring to these variances as either a "price" or "efficiency" variance.

Managers who are responsible for price variances may not be responsible for efficiency variances and vice versa. For example, purchasing department managers are usually held responsible for direct materials price variances while manufacturing department managers are usually held responsible for using the direct materials efficiently.

This breakdown of the total variance into price and efficiency components is facilitated by the middle term, Column 2, in Illustration 19–2. In going from Column 1 to Column 2, we go from *actual prices* (AP) times *actual quantity* (AQ) of input to *standard price* (SP) times *actual quantity* (AQ) of input. Thus, the price variance is calculated as:

$$\text{Price variance} = (\text{AP} \times \text{AQ}) - (\text{SP} \times \text{AQ})$$
$$= (\text{AP} - \text{SP})\text{AQ}$$

The efficiency variance is derived by comparing Column 2, standard price times actual quantity of input, with Column 3, standard price times standard quantity of input. Thus, the efficiency variance is calculated as:

$$\text{Efficiency variance} = (\text{SP} \times \text{AQ}) - (\text{SP} \times \text{SQ})$$
$$= \text{SP}(\text{AQ} - \text{SQ})$$

This general model may seem rather abstract at this point, but as we work examples, it will become more concrete and intuitive to you.

As we proceed through the variance analysis for each manufacturing cost input—direct materials, direct labor, variable manufacturing overhead, and fixed manufacturing costs—you will notice some minor modifications from the general model presented in Illustration 19–2. It is important to recognize that these are *modifications of one general approach* rather than a number of independent approaches to variance analysis. In variance analysis, a few basic methods can be applied with minor modifications to numerous business and nonbusiness situations.

Direct materials

Information about Boxx Company's use of direct materials for the month of May is presented below:

Standard costs: 10 board feet per crate @ $.25 per board foot = $2.50 per crate
Crates produced in May: 10,000
Actual materials used: 110,000 board feet @ $.264 per board foot = $29,040

Based on these data, the direct materials price and efficiency variances were calculated as shown in Illustration 19–3. Note that with a standard of 10 board feet per crate and 10,000 crates actually produced in May, Boxx Company expects to use 100,000 board feet to produce the 10,000 crates. Since each board foot has a standard cost of $.25, the standard materials cost allowed to make 10,000 crates is:

$$\text{Standard cost allowed to produce} = SP \times SQ$$
$$10{,}000 \text{ crates} = \$.25 \times (10 \text{ board feet} \times 10{,}000 \text{ crates})$$
$$= \underline{\underline{\$25{,}000}}$$

Note that Column 3 of Illustration 19–3 is called the flexible production budget. The flexible budget concept can be applied to production as well as to sales. The flexible budget in Chapter 18 was based on actual *sales* volume (that is, crates *sold*). The flexible budget in Illustration 19–2 is based on actual production volume (that is, crates *produced*).

Responsibility for direct materials variances The direct materials price variance shows that in May the prices paid for direct materials exceeded the standards allowed, thus creating an unfavorable variance of $1,540. Responsibility for this variance is usually assigned to the purchasing department. Reports to management would include an explanation of the variance—for example, failure to take purchase discounts, transportation costs higher than expected, different grade of direct material purchased, or changes in the market price of direct materials.

The explanation for the variance at Boxx Company was that home construction in the economy had increased significantly, thus driving the price

Illustration 19–3   **Direct materials variances, Boxx Company (May)**

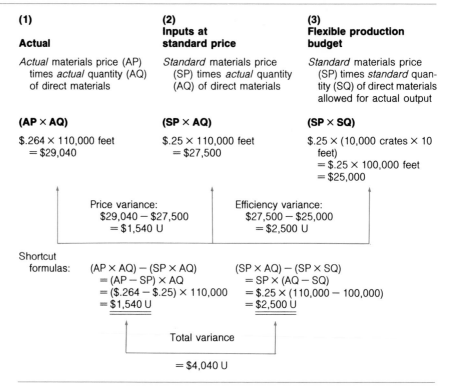

Note: To reconcile the difference between actual results and the flexible production budget, we can rearrange the analysis as follows:

Flexible budget	$25,000
Add: Unfavorable efficiency variance	2,500
Unfavorable price variance	1,540
Actual	$29,040

of lumber higher than expected. Further, prices were expected to continue climbing during the year. Based on this information, management decided to build up their inventory of lumber now to avoid even higher prices in the future. They also began market research to determine if they should increase sales prices for their crates.

Direct materials efficiency variances are typically the responsibility of production departments. In setting standards, an allowance is usually made for defects in direct materials, inexperienced workers, poor supervision, and the like. If actual materials usage is less than these standards, there is a favorable variance. If usage is in excess of standards, there is an unfavorable variance.

At Boxx Company, the unfavorable direct materials efficiency variance was attributed to the recent hiring of some inexperienced laborers who, in an effort to keep up with the production schedule, improperly measured and cut lumber to the wrong lengths. The cutting department manager claimed this was a one-time occurrence and foresaw no similar problems in the future.

Direct labor

To illustrate the computations of direct labor variances, assume for Boxx Company:

Standard costs: .50 hours per crate @ $10 per hour = $5 per crate
Crates produced in May: 10,000
Actual direct labor costs: Actual hours worked were 5,200, while the total actual labor cost was $49,920. Hence, the average cost per hour was $9.60 (= $49,920 ÷ 5,200 hours).

The computation of the direct labor price and efficiency variances is shown in Illustration 19–4.

Illustration 19–4

Direct labor variances, Boxx Company (May)

(1) **Actual**	**(2)** **Inputs at standard price**	**(3)** **Flexible production budget**
Actual labor price (AP) times *actual* quantity (AQ) of direct labor-hours used	*Standard* labor price (SP) times *actual* quantity (AQ) of direct labor-hours used	*Standard* labor price (SP) times *standard* quantity (SQ) of direct labor-hours allowed for actual output (i.e., 10,000 crates)
(AP × AQ)	**(SP × AQ)**	**(SP × SQ)**
$9.60 × 5,200 hours = $49,920	$10 × 5,200 hours = $52,000	$10 × (10,000 crates × .5 hours) = $10 × 5,000 hours = $50,000

Price variance:
$49,920 − $52,000
= $2,080 F

Efficiency variance:
$52,000 − $50,000
= $2,000 U

Shortcut formulas:

(AP × AQ) − (SP × AQ)
= (AP − SP) × AQ
= ($9.60 − $10) × 5,200
= $2,080 F

(SP × AQ) − (SP × SQ)
= SP × (AQ − SQ)
= $10 × (5,200 − 5,000)
= $2,000 U

Total variance
= $80 F

Note: Reconciling the difference between actual results and the flexible production budget, we obtain:

Flexible budget	$50,000
Add unfavorable efficiency variance	2,000
Less favorable price variance	(2,080)
Actual cost	$49,920

Direct labor price variance The direct labor price variance is caused by the difference between actual and standard labor costs per hour. Boxx Company's direct labor costs were less than the standard allowed, creating a favorable labor price variance of $2,080. The explanation given for Boxx Company's favorable labor price variance is that many inexperienced workers were hired in May. These inexperienced workers were paid a wage less than standard, thus reducing the *average* wage rate for all workers to $9.60.

In many companies, wage rates are set by union contract. If the wage rates used in setting standards are the same as those in the union contract, labor price variances will be nonexistent.

Labor efficiency variance The labor efficiency variance is a measure of labor productivity. It is one of the most closely watched variances because it is usually controllable by production managers. A financial vice president of a manufacturing company told us: "Direct materials are 57 percent of our product cost, while direct labor is only 22 percent. We only give direct materials variances a passing glance. But we carry out the labor efficiency variance to the penny; and we break it down by product line, by department, and sometimes by specific operation. Why? Because there's not much we can do about materials price changes, but there's a lot we can do to keep our labor efficiency in line."

Unfavorable labor efficiency variances have many causes. The workers themselves may be the cause. Poorly motivated or poorly trained workers will be less productive, whereas highly motivated and well-trained are more likely to generate favorable efficiency variances. Sometimes poor materials or faulty equipment can cause productivity problems. And poor supervision and scheduling can lead to unnecessary idle time.

Production department managers are usually responsible for direct labor efficiency variances. Scheduling problems may stem from other production departments that have delayed production. The personnel department may be responsible if the variance occurs because they provided the wrong kind of worker. The $2,000 unfavorable direct labor efficiency variance at Boxx Company was attributed to the inexperienced workers previously mentioned. Note that one event, such as hiring inexperienced workers, can affect more than one variance.

| **Variable manufacturing overhead** | To illustrate the computation of variable manufacturing overhead variances, assume for Boxx Company: |

Standard costs: .50 direct labor-hours per crate @ $5 per hour
  (variable manufacturing overhead rate) = $2.50 per crate
Crates produced in May: 10,000
Variable overhead costs in May: $26,480

The computation of the variable manufacturing overhead price and efficiency variances is shown in Illustration 19–5.

Illustration 19–5   **Variable overhead variances, Boxx Company (May)**

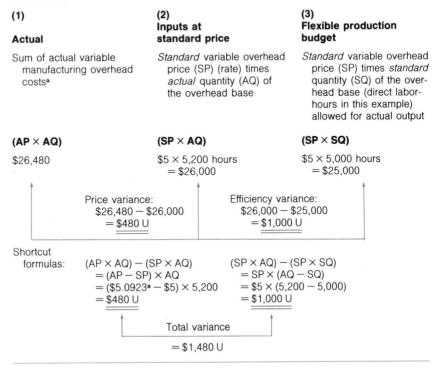

(1)

Actual

Sum of actual variable manufacturing overhead costs[a]

(2)
Inputs at standard price

Standard variable overhead price (SP) (rate) times *actual* quantity (AQ) of the overhead base

(3)
Flexible production budget

Standard variable overhead price (SP) times *standard* quantity (SQ) of the overhead base (direct labor-hours in this example) allowed for actual output

(AP × AQ)

$26,480

(SP × AQ)

$5 × 5,200 hours
= $26,000

(SP × SQ)

$5 × 5,000 hours
= $25,000

Price variance:
$26,480 − $26,000
= $480 U

Efficiency variance:
$26,000 − $25,000
= $1,000 U

Shortcut formulas:

(AP × AQ) − (SP × AQ)
= (AP − SP) × AQ
= ($5.0923[a] − $5) × 5,200
= $480 U

(SP × AQ) − (SP × SQ)
= SP × (AQ − SQ)
= $5 × (5,200 − 5,000)
= $1,000 U

Total variance
= $1,480 U

Note: Reconciling the difference between actual results and the flexible production budget, we obtain:

Flexible budget	$25,000
Add:	
Unfavorable efficiency variance	1,000
Unfavorable price variance	480
Actual cost	$26,480

[a] Total actual variable overhead costs can also be thought of as actual price (AP) times actual quantity (AQ). Divide the total actual variable overhead costs by the actual quantity of the variable overhead base:

$$AP = 26,480 \div AQ$$
$$= 26,480 \div 5,200 \text{ direct labor-hours}$$
$$= 5.0923$$

Variable manufacturing overhead price variances   The variable overhead standard rate was derived from a two-stage estimation: (1) an estimate of costs at various levels of activity and (2) an estimate of the relationship between those estimated costs and the basis which is direct labor-hours at Boxx Company. The price variance could have occurred because (1) actual costs—for example, machine power, materials handling, supplies, some indirect labor—were different from those expected. Also, (2) the price variance could occur because the relationship between variable manufacturing overhead costs and direct labor-hours is not perfect.

The variable overhead price variance actually contains some efficiency items as well as price items. For example, suppose utilities costs are higher than expected. One reason could be that utility rates are higher than expected; but an additional reason could be that kilowatt-hours (kwhr.) per labor-hour are higher than expected. Both would be part of the price variance because jointly they cause utility costs to be higher than expected. In some companies, these components of the variable overhead price variance are separated. This is commonly done for energy costs in heavy manufacturing companies, for example.

At Boxx Company, the unfavorable price variance for May was attributed to waste in using supplies and recent increases in rates charged for power to run the saws in the cutting department.

Variable overhead efficiency variance   The variable overhead efficiency variance must be interpreted carefully. It has nothing to do with the efficiency of *overhead* use. Rather, it is attributed to efficiency in using the base on which variable overhead is applied.

For example, at Boxx Company, variable overhead is applied on the basis of direct labor-hours. Thus, if there is an unfavorable direct labor efficiency variance because more direct labor-hours were used than allowed, there will be a corresponding unfavorable variable overhead efficiency variance. Boxx Company used 200 direct labor-hours more than allowed by the standard, resulting in the following dollar variances:

Direct labor efficiency: $10 × 200 hours = $2,000 U (Illustration 19–4)
Variable overhead efficiency: $5 × 200 hours = $1,000 U (Illustration 19–5)
Total direct labor and variable overhead efficiency variances: $15 × 200 hours = $3,000 U

Variable overhead is assumed to vary directly with the base

Thus, inefficiency in using the base (for example, direct labor-hours, machine-hours, units of output) is assumed to cause an increase in variable overhead. This emphasizes the importance of selecting the proper basis for applying variable overhead. Managers who are responsible for controlling the base will probably be held responsible for the variable overhead efficiency variance as well. Whoever is responsible for the $2,000 unfavorable direct labor efficiency variance at Boxx Company will probably be held responsible for the unfavorable efficiency variance, too.

Summary of variable manufacturing cost variances

The variable manufacturing cost variances are summarized in Illustration 19–6. Note that the total variable manufacturing cost variance is the same as that derived in Chapter 18. The analysis of cost variances in this chapter is just a more detailed analysis of the variable manufacturing cost variance that was derived in Chapter 18. (See Illustration 18–5.)

A summary of this kind is useful for reporting variances to high-level managers. It provides both an overview of variances and their sources. When used for reporting, the computations shown at the right of Illustration 19–6 are usually replaced with a brief explanation of the cause of the variance.

Illustration 19–6 **Variable manufacturing cost variance summary, Boxx Company (May)**

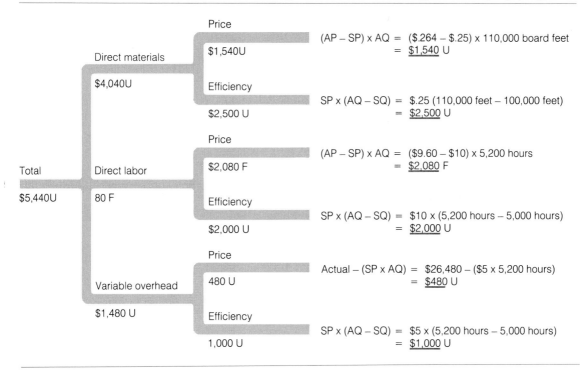

Price
Direct materials $1,540U
$4,040U

(AP – SP) x AQ = ($.264 – $.25) x 110,000 board feet
= $1,540 U

Efficiency
$2,500 U

SP x (AQ – SQ) = $.25 (110,000 feet – 100,000 feet)
= $2,500 U

Total

$5,440U

Price
Direct labor $2,080 F
80 F

(AP – SP) x AQ = ($9.60 – $10) x 5,200 hours
= $2,080 F

Efficiency
$2,000 U

SP x (AQ – SQ) = $10 x (5,200 hours – 5,000 hours)
= $2,000 U

Price
Variable overhead 480 U
$1,480 U

Actual – (SP x AQ) = $26,480 – ($5 x 5,200 hours)
= $480 U

Efficiency
1,000 U

SP x (AQ – SQ) = $5 x (5,200 hours – 5,000 hours)
= $1,000 U

Management may want more detailed information about some of the variances. This can be provided by extending each variance branch in Illustration 19–6 to show variances by product line, by department, or by other breakdowns.

Fixed manufacturing costs

In variance analysis, fixed manufacturing costs are treated differently from variable manufacturing costs. For illustrative purposes, we assume these fixed manufacturing costs are all overhead. Other manufacturing costs also may be fixed; if so, they can be treated the same way that we treat fixed manufacturing overhead. It is usually assumed that fixed costs are unchanged when volume changes, so the amount budgeted for fixed overhead is the same in both the master and flexible budgets. This is consistent with the variable costing method of product costing.

There are no input-output relationships for fixed overhead. Thus, there is no efficiency variance. The difference between the flexible budget and the actual fixed overhead is entirely due to changes in the costs that make up fixed overhead. Hence, the variance falls under the category of a price variance. (It is also called a spending or a budget variance.)

Illustration 19–7   **Fixed overhead variances, Boxx Company (May)**

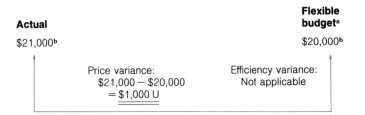

a For fixed costs, there is no difference between the flexible and master (or static) budget in Chapter 18.

b These amounts tie to Illustration 18–5 in Chapter 18 which presents an overview of the use of budgets for performance evaluation at Boxx Company.

The fixed manufacturing overhead in both the flexible and master budgets in Chapter 18 was $20,000. Assume the actual cost is $21,000. The variance analysis is shown in Illustration 19–7. Note that there is no calculation of the efficiency with which inputs are used. For performance evaluation, our computation of the fixed cost variance is the easiest of the variances with which we have worked so far. (Another variance, the production volume variance, is discussed in Appendix A to this chapter and in Chapter 20.)

Summary of manufacturing cost variances

Illustration 19–8 summarizes all of the manufacturing cost variances discussed in this chapter.

Comparison of actual to flexible production budget to master production budget

A comparison of actual results with the flexible and master budget was presented in Chapter 18 for *sales volume.* A similar comparison can be made for *production volume,* as shown in Illustration 19–9.

Now that the actual production costs, flexible budget amounts, and variances have been presented (see Columns 1, 2, 3, and 4 of Illustration 19–9), we can make the final comparison of budget to actual results. The master budget, which is shown in Column 6, is based on a projected or budgeted production of 8,000 crates, based on the information given in Chapter 18.

Materials variances when quantity purchased does not equal quantity used

So far we have assumed that Boxx Company used the same amount of direct materials that it purchased. Now we show how to calculate variances when the quantities purchased and used are not the same.

Recall the following facts from the Boxx Company example:

Standard costs: 10 board feet per crate @ $.25 per board foot = $2.50 per crate
Crates produced in May: 10,000
Actual materials used: 110,000 board feet @ $.264 = $29,040

Illustration 19-8   **Summary of manufacturing variance calculations, Boxx Company (May)**

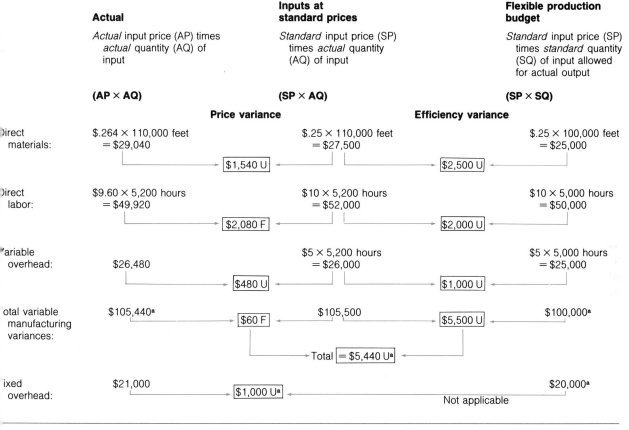

	Actual Actual input price (AP) times actual quantity (AQ) of input (AP × AQ)		Inputs at standard prices Standard input price (SP) times actual quantity (AQ) of input (SP × AQ)		Flexible production budget Standard input price (SP) times standard quantity (SQ) of input allowed for actual output (SP × SQ)
		Price variance		Efficiency variance	
Direct materials:	$.264 × 110,000 feet = $29,040	$1,540 U	$.25 × 110,000 feet = $27,500	$2,500 U	$.25 × 100,000 feet = $25,000
Direct labor:	$9.60 × 5,200 hours = $49,920	$2,080 F	$10 × 5,200 hours = $52,000	$2,000 U	$10 × 5,000 hours = $50,000
Variable overhead:	$26,480	$480 U	$5 × 5,200 hours = $26,000	$1,000 U	$5 × 5,000 hours = $25,000
Total variable manufacturing variances:	$105,440[a]	$60 F	$105,500	$5,500 U	$100,000[a]
		Total = $5,440 U[a]			
Fixed overhead:	$21,000	$1,000 U[a]		Not applicable	$20,000[a]

Numbers tie to Illustration 18-5, Chapter 18.

Illustration 19-9
Comparison of actual, flexible budget, and master budget for production activity, Boxx Company

	(1) Actual (based on production of 10,000 crates)	(2) Price variance	(3) Efficiency variance	(4) Flexible budget (based on production of 10,000 crates)	(5) Activity variance	(6) Master budget (based on production of 8,000 crates)
Variable manufacturing costs:						
Direct materials	$ 29,040	$1,540 U	$2,500 U	$ 25,000	$ 5,000 U	$ 20,000
Direct labor	49,920	2,080 F	2,000 U	50,000	10,000 U	40,000
Variable overhead	26,480	480 U	1,000 U	25,000	5,000 U	20,000
Subtotal	105,440	60 F	5,500 U	100,000	20,000 U	80,000
Fixed manufacturing overhead	21,000	1,000 U	Not applicable	20,000	–0–	20,000
Totals	$126,440	$ 940 U	$5,500 U	$120,000	$20,000 U	$100,000

Illustration 19–10   **Direct materials variances when quantities purchased and used are unequal, Boxx Company (May)**

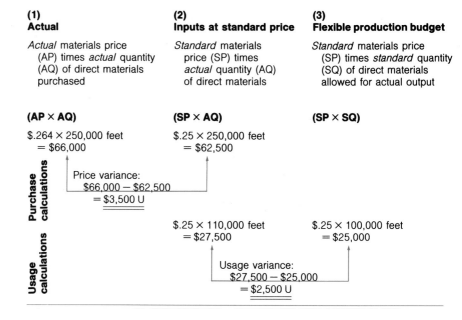

Now let's assume that 250,000 board feet were purchased in May at $.264 per board foot, 110,000 board feet were used, and there was no inventory on May 1.

The variance calculations are shown in Illustration 19–10. Note that the purchase price variance is different from the earlier example in the chapter because it is based on the materials purchased. The usage variance is the same as in the previous example because it is based on materials used, which is the same here as in the previous example.

How many variances to calculate?

We noted at the beginning of this chapter that every organization has its own approach to variance analysis, although virtually all are based on the fundamental model presented here. Because of the unique circumstances in each organization, we cannot generalize very much about which variances should be calculated. Managers and accountants in each organization should perform their own cost-benefit analysis to ascertain which calculations are justified.

In deciding how many variances to calculate, it is important to note the *impact* and *controllability* of each variance. When considering *impact,* we ask: "Does this variance matter? Is it so small that the best efforts to improve efficiency or control costs would have very little impact even if the efforts were successful?" If so, it's probably not worth the trouble to calculate and analyze. Hence, detailed variance calculations for small overhead items may not be worthwhile.

When considering the **controllability of a variance,** we ask: "Can we do something about it?" No matter how great the impact of the variance, if nothing can be done about the variance, then it is hard to justify spending resources to compute and analyze it. For example, materials purchase price variances are often high impact items. They are hard to control, however, because materials prices fluctuate due to market conditions that are outside the control of managers.

In general, high-impact, highly controllable variances should get the most attention, while low-impact, uncontrollable variances should get the least attention, as shown below:

Impact

		Low	High
Controllability	Low	Variances get the least attention	
	High		Variances get the most attention

Labor and materials efficiency variances are often highly controllable. With sufficient attention to scheduling, quality of employees, motivation, and incentives, these variances can often be dealt with effectively. An example of a high-impact, but hard-to-control, item for many companies has been the cost of energy. Many organizations, from airlines to taxicab companies to steel mills, have been able to do little about rising energy costs in the short run. Over time, of course, actions could be taken to reduce energy usage through acquisition of energy efficient equipment. In general, the longer the time interval, the greater the ability to control an item.

Management by exception and variance investigation

After variances have been computed and the initial analysis made, managers and accountants must decide which variances should be investigated. Because a manager's time is a scarce resource, some priorities must be set. This can be done through cost-benefit analysis. Only the variances for which the benefits of correction exceed the costs of follow-up should be pursued. In general, this is consistent with the "management by exception" philosophy that says, in effect, "Don't worry about what is going according to plan, worry about the exceptions."

But this is easier said than done. It may be almost impossible to predict either costs or benefits of investigating variances. So while the principle is straightforward, it is difficult to apply. In this section, we identify some characteristics that are important for determining which variances to investigate. In Chapter 25, we discuss statistical models for investigating variances.

Some problems are easily corrected as soon as they are discovered. When a machine is improperly set or a worker needs minor instruction, the investigation cost is low and benefits are very likely to exceed costs. This is often a usage or efficiency variance and is reported frequently—often daily—so immediate corrective action can be taken.

Some variances are not controllable in the short run. Labor price variances due to changes in union contract and overhead spending variances due to unplanned utility and property tax-rate changes may require little or no follow-up in the short run. Such variances sometimes prompt long-run action, such as moving a plant to a locale with lower wage rates and lower utility and property tax rates. In such cases, the short-run benefits of variance investigation are low, but the long-run benefits may be higher.

Data and timing problems   Many variances occur because of errors in recording, bookkeeping adjustments, or timing problems. A variance-reporting system (and the accounting department) can lose credibility if it contains bookkeeping errors and adjustments. For this reason, the accounting staff must carefully check variance reports before sending them to operating managers.

Updating standards	Standards are estimates. As such, they may not reflect the conditions that actually occur. This is especially likely to occur when standards are not updated and revised to reflect current conditions. If prices and operating methods are frequently changed, standards may be constantly out of date.

In many companies, standards are revised once a year. Thus, variances will occur because conditions change during the year but standards don't. When conditions change, but they are temporary and don't require a permanent revision of standards, some companies develop a planned variance. For example, an unexpected series of snowstorms curtailed activities much below normal in a steel plant in the Midwest. This affected the workers' productivity and created large unfavorable labor efficiency variances. In response, the accounting staff developed planned variances for a number of costs based on expected differences between actual costs and standard costs due to the snowstorms. For example, the January labor report for a particular department was as follows:

Item	Total efficiency variance	Planned efficiency variance	Unplanned efficiency variance
Direct labor—Department xx	$11,242 U	$9,100 U	$2,142 U

The department manager was not held responsible for the entire $11,242 U variance, but only the $2,142 U unplanned efficiency variance.

Behavioral issues in setting standards

Manufacturing personnel are often evaluated in terms of standard costs, so they have an interest in how difficult or easy the standards are to attain. These people often also have some input into setting standards. In fact, operating personnel are likely to be the best sources of information about appropriate standards in the company. But since the standards will be used to judge their performance, they have incentives to make the standards easily attainable.

As a manager of an assembly department put it, "The controller asked me how much time it will take to assemble Product 102x, and I told him two labor-hours per unit based on ideal conditions. Then he used that against me when it actually took two and one-half hours per unit. Now I add about 30 percent to the time I think it will take. That gives us some slack with still a chance to show a favorable variance."

Whether operating personnel actually bias the data they provide for setting standards, top management and the accounting staff recognize that operating personnel have *incentives* to do so. Thus, other sources of information, such as industry standards and estimates from other similar departments in the company, are often used for comparison. Operational auditors (people who audit the efficiency and/or effectiveness of operations) and outside consultants are often called in to check the reasonableness of standards. Information from one source provides a check on information from another source.

How "tight" should standards be? If standards are very loose, they can be met a large percentage of the time; if very tight, they can seldom, if ever, be met. Research indicates that standards at either extreme may not lead to the best employee performance.[1] The motivational problems of employees are similar to those of students. For example, if it is virtually impossible to improve your grade by studying hard for a test (that is, a tight standard), you may not be as motivated to study as hard as you would if you believed there was a good chance that studying would improve your grade. On the other hand, if you believe that you will get a good grade with minimal studying, you may not be inclined to study beyond that minimal level.

In general, the standards that seem to motivate best are moderately tight yet are perceived by employees as reasonable and attainable. This generalization may vary from situation to situation, of course.

Summary

This chapter discusses the computation and analysis of manufacturing cost variances. A variance is the difference between a predetermined standard and an actual result.

The model used for calculating variable manufacturing cost variances is based on the following diagram which divides the total variance between actual and standard into price and efficiency components.

---

[1] See Andrew C. Stedry, *Budget Control and Cost Behavior* (Englewood Cliffs, N.J.: Prentice-Hall, 1960); and Gary L. Holstrum, "The Effect of Budget Adaptiveness and Tightness on Managerial Decision Behavior," *Journal of Accounting Research* 9 (Autumn 1971), pp. 268–77.

(1) **Actual**	**(2)** **Inputs at standard price**	**(3)** **Flexible production budget**
Actual input price (AP) times *actual* quantity (AQ) of input	*Standard* input price (SP) times *actual* quantity (AQ) of input	*Standard* input price (SP) times *standard* quantity (SQ) of input allowed for actual output
(AP × AQ)	**(SP × AQ)**	**(SP × SQ)**

Price variance
(1) minus (2):
(AP × AQ) − (SP × AQ)
= (AP − SP) × AQ

Efficiency variance
(2) minus (3):
(SP × AQ) − (SP × SQ)
= SP × (AQ − SQ)

Total variance
(1) minus (3):
(AP × AQ) − (SP × SQ)

Fixed manufacturing costs have no efficiency variance. The price variance is simply the difference between actual fixed costs and the fixed costs in the flexible budget.

A key managerial question is: How many variances should be calculated and investigated? The answer depends on the impact and controllability of variances. In general, the greater the impact of a variance on profits and the more controllable it is, the easier it is to justify analysis of the variance.

Terms and concepts

The following terms and concepts should be familiar to you after reading this chapter.

Activity variance	**Standard cost**
Controllability of variance	**Standard cost system**
Efficiency variance	**Total variance**
Flexible production budget	**Usage variance**
Management by exception	**Variance**
Planned variance	**Variance investigation**
Price variance	

Self-study problem No. 1

During the past month, the following events took place at Containers, Inc.:

1. Produced and sold 50,000 plastic minicomputer cases at a sales price of $10 each. (Budgeted sales were 45,000 units at $10.15.)

2. Standard variable costs per unit (that is, case):

Direct materials: 2 pounds at $1	$2.00
Direct labor: .10 hours at $15	1.50
Variable manufacturing overhead: .10 hours at $5	.50
	$4.00 per case

3. Fixed manufacturing overhead cost:

Monthly budget	$ 80,000

4. Actual production costs:

Direct materials purchased: 200,000 pounds at $1.20	$240,000
Direct materials used: 110,000 pounds at $1.20	132,000
Direct labor: 6,000 hours at $14	84,000
Variable overhead	28,000
Fixed overhead	83,000

Required:

a. Compute the direct materials, labor, and variable manufacturing price and efficiency variances.
b. Compute the fixed manufacturing overhead price volume.

Solution to self-study problem No. 1

a. Production variances:

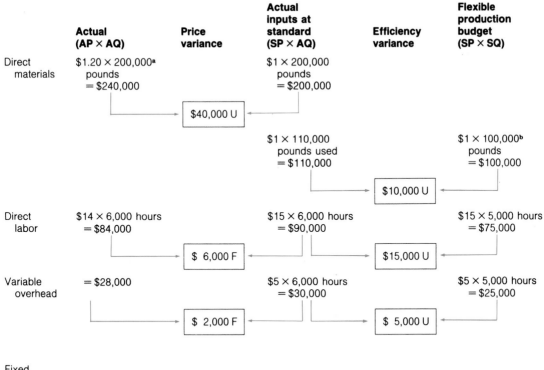

b.

ª Direct material pounds purchased.
ᵇ Standard direct materials pounds used in production per unit times units produced (2 pounds × 50,000 units).

The total variance between standard and actual is usually broken down by department for performance evaluation. This self-study problem breaks down variances for the Boxx Company example in the chapter.

Departmental materials variances All of the direct materials are charged to the cutting department of Boxx Company. Thus, all of the direct material efficiency variance of $2,500 U is assigned to the purchasing department.

Departmental labor variances To determine the departmental labor variances, we must know how much of the actual labor cost is charged to each department. This information is available from the payroll department as long as workers allocate their time to the departments they work in. At Boxx Company, the payroll department supplied the following information for May:

Department	Actual hours worked	Actual labor cost	Average cost[a] per hour
Cutting	1,200	$ 9,600	$ 8.00
Assembly	3,000	30,300	10.10
Finishing and inspection	1,000	10,020	10.02
		$49,920	

[a] Includes fringe benefits and taxes.

Departmental fixed overhead price variances Actual fixed overhead charged to each department may also be available from the accounting department. However, many of these costs are common to more than one department. For example, lease costs on a plant that contains several departments will have to be allocated to each department. Thus, many of the "actual" fixed overhead costs assigned to each department will often be allocated. For this reason, some companies do not include fixed overhead in departmental performance evaluation reports.

Boxx Company does break down fixed overhead by department, however. The actual and budgeted costs, and departmental price variances are as follows:

	Actual	Price variance	Flexible and master budget amount
Cutting department	$ 5,900	$ 100 F	$ 6,000
Assembly department	8,900	900 U	8,000
Finishing and inspection department	6,200	200 U	6,000
All departments	$21,000	$1,000 U	$20,000

Departmental variable overhead variances The actual variable overhead charged to each department is usually available from the accounting records. It usually includes both direct department costs and indirect costs that have been allocated to the department. This includes the costs of service departments. For Boxx Company, the actual costs for May were:

Cutting department	$ 5,800
Assembly department	14,980
Finishing and inspection department	5,700
Total	$26,480

Required:

Compute departmental direct labor and variable manufacturing overhead variances. Prepare a report that assigns manufacturing variances to each department.

Solution to self-study problem No. 2

The departmental labor variances are:

	Actual (AP × AQ)	(SP × AQ)	Flexible budget (SP × SQ)
Cutting department	$8 × 1,200 hours = $9,600	$10 × 1,200 hours = $12,000	$10 × 1,000 hours = $10,000

Price variance: = $2,400 F   Efficiency variance: = $2,000 U

Assembly department	$10.10 × 3,000 hours = $30,300	$10 × 3,000 hours = $30,000	$10 × 3,000 hours = $30,000

Price variance: = $300 U   Efficiency variance: = $0

Finishing and inspection department	$10.02 × 1,000 hours = $10,020	$10 × 1,000 hours = $10,000	$10 × 1,000 hours = $10,000

Price variance: = $20 U   Efficiency variance: = $0

All departments	Price variance: = $2,080 F	Efficiency variance: = $2,000 U

The departmental variable overhead variances are:

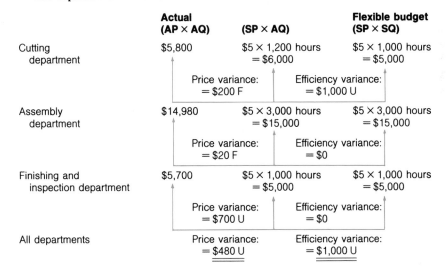

	Actual (AP × AQ)	(SP × AQ)	Flexible budget (SP × SQ)
Cutting department	$5,800	$5 × 1,200 hours = $6,000	$5 × 1,000 hours = $5,000

Price variance: = $200 F   Efficiency variance: = $1,000 U

Assembly department	$14,980	$5 × 3,000 hours = $15,000	$5 × 3,000 hours = $15,000

Price variance: = $20 F   Efficiency variance: = $0

Finishing and inspection department	$5,700	$5 × 1,000 hours = $5,000	$5 × 1,000 hours = $5,000

Price variance: = $700 U   Efficiency variance: = $0

All departments	Price variance: = $480 U	Efficiency variance: = $1,000 U

Departmental variance report

Variance	Purchasing	Cutting	Assembly	Finishing and inspection	Total
Materials:					
Price	$1,540 U				$1,540 U
Efficiency		$2,500 U			2,500 U
Labor:					
Price		2,400 F	$ 300 U	$ 20 U	2,080 F
Efficiency		2,000 U	–0–	–0–	2,000 U
Variable overhead:					
Price		200 F	20 F	700 U	480 U
Efficiency		1,000 U	–0–	–0–	1,000 U
Fixed overhead price		100 F	900 U	200 U	1,000 U
Totals	$1,540 U	$2,800 U	$1,180 U	$920 U	$6,440 U

Appendix A: Production volume variance[2]

Some companies use absorption costing for internal purposes. When this happens, fixed costs are added to the costs of units produced based on a predetermined fixed cost application rate. If the number of units produced differs from the number of units used to estimate the fixed cost per unit, a variance will arise. This variance is commonly referred to as a **production volume variance.** (It is also called a *capacity variance,* an *idle capacity variance,* or a *denominator variance.*)

Based on the example in the chapter, suppose management of the Boxx Company estimates that the company will produce 96,000 crates per year or, dividing by 12, a monthly average of 8,000 crates. If Boxx Company management used full-absorption costing, they would apply fixed overhead to production based on the formula:

$$\frac{\text{Estimated fixed overhead}}{\text{Estimated units}} = \frac{\$20,000}{8,000} = \$2.50 \text{ per unit}$$

If 10,000 units were actually produced during the period, $25,000 (= $2.50 × 10,000 units) of fixed overhead costs would have been charged into production. The production volume variance is the difference between the $25,000 applied fixed overhead and the $20,000 budgeted fixed overhead. Hence, in this situation there would be $5,000 favorable production volume variance. The variance is favorable because more overhead was applied than was budgeted—production was greater than the average monthly estimate. This variance is a result of the full-absorption costing system, it does not occur in variable costing.

---

[2] The production volume variance is also included in the Chapter 20 discussion of standard cost systems. It is discussed in this Appendix for the convenience of instructors and students who prefer to cover the production volume variance in the same chapter as other manufacturing variances.

Summary of overhead variances

The following diagram summarizes both variable and fixed overhead variances, based on facts given in the chapter and in this appendix:

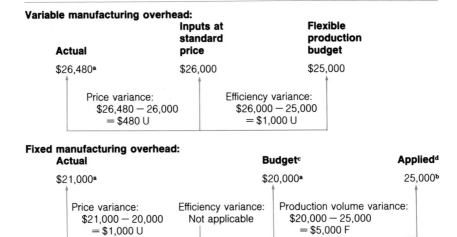

Variable manufacturing overhead:

Actual	Inputs at standard price	Flexible production budget
$26,480[a]	$26,000	$25,000

Price variance:
$26,480 − 26,000
= $480 U

Efficiency variance:
$26,000 − 25,000
= $1,000 U

Fixed manufacturing overhead:

Actual	Budget[c]	Applied[d]
$21,000[a]	$20,000[a]	25,000[b]

Price variance:
$21,000 − 20,000
= $1,000 U

Efficiency variance:
Not applicable

Production volume variance:
$20,000 − 25,000
= $5,000 F

[a] Amount given in chapter.
[b] Amount given in this appendix.
[c] This amount appears in both the master budget and the flexible budget.
[d] This is the amount of fixed manufacturing overhead debited to Work in Process Inventory under full-absorption costing.

Hence, with this method there are four overhead variances:

	Price	Efficiency	Production volume
Variable	$ 480 U	$1,000 U	Not applicable
Fixed	1,000 U	Not applicable	$5,000 F

This is sometimes called the *four-way* analysis of overhead variances.

Appendix B: Production mix-yield variances[3]

Often a mix of inputs is used in production. Chemicals, steel, fabrics, plastics, and many other products require a mix of direct materials, some of which can be substituted for each other without greatly affecting product quality.

The same holds for labor. Consider a consulting firm that has bid a job for 1,000 hours—300 hours of partner time at a cost of $60 per hour and 700 hours of staff time at a cost of $20 per hour. Due to scheduling problems, the partner spends 500 hours and the staff member spends 500 hours. If

---

[3] The mix variance is also discussed in another context in the presentation of marketing mix variances in Chapter 21.

the actual costs are $60 and $20 for partner and staff time, respectively, then there is no labor price variance. But even though the 1,000 hours time required was exactly what was bid, the job cost is $8,000 over budget, as shown below:

$$\text{Actual cost} = (500 \text{ hours} \times \$60) + (500 \text{ hours} \times \$20)$$
$$= \$30,000 + \$10,000$$
$$= \underline{\underline{\$40,000}}$$

$$\text{Budgeted cost} = (300 \text{ hours} \times \$60) + (700 \text{ hours} \times \$20)$$
$$= \$18,000 + \$14,000$$
$$= \underline{\underline{\$32,000}}$$

The $8,000 over budget results from the substitution of 200 hours of partner time at $60 for 200 hours of staff time at $20. The **mix variance** is the difference in labor costs per hour ($60 − $20 = $40) times the number of hours substituted (200): $40 × 200 hours = $8,000.

Two factors are important when considering mix variances. First, there is an assumed *substitutability of inputs*. While partner time may have been substitutable for staff time, the reverse may not have been true. Second, the prices must be different for a mix variance to exist. If the hourly costs of both partners and staff were the same, the substitution of hours would have no effect on the total cost of the job.

With this general concept in mind, we proceed with another example, using direct materials, which is a common application of mix variances in a production setting.

The Clean Chemical company makes a product—XZ—that is made up of two direct materials. The standard costs and quantities are:

Direct material	Standard price per pound	Standard number of pounds per unit of finished product
X	$4	5
Z	8	5
		10

The standard cost per unit of finished product is:

X: 5 pounds @ $4 = $20
Z: 5 pounds @ $8 = 40
  Total $60

During June, Clean Chemical had the following results:

Units produced	1,000 units of finished product
Materials purchased and used:	
Material X	4,400 pounds at $5
Material Z	5,800 pounds at $8
	10,200 pounds

Illustration 19-11   **Material variances, Clean Chemical (June)**

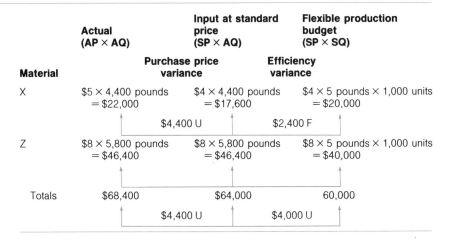

Material	Actual (AP × AQ)	Input at standard price (SP × AQ)	Flexible production budget (SP × SQ)
		Purchase price variance	Efficiency variance
X	$5 × 4,400 pounds = $22,000	$4 × 4,400 pounds = $17,600	$4 × 5 pounds × 1,000 units = $20,000
		$4,400 U	$2,400 F
Z	$8 × 5,800 pounds = $46,400	$8 × 5,800 pounds = $46,400	$8 × 5 pounds × 1,000 units = $40,000
Totals	$68,400	$64,000	60,000
		$4,400 U	$4,000 U

The two-way breakdown of variances, as shown in the text, gives the results shown in Illustration 19–11.

Our computation[4] of the mix variance breaks down the direct materials efficiency variance into two components: mix and yield. The mix variance measures the impact of substitution (Material Z appears to have been substituted for Material X), while the yield variance measures the input-output relationship holding the standard mix of inputs constant. Standards called for 10,000 pounds of materials. However, 10,200 pounds of input were required to produce 1,000 units of output; the overuse of 200 pounds is a physical measure of the yield variance.

To derive mix and yield variances, we define a new term: ASQ is the *actual amount of input used at the standard mix.*

Calculations for the three variances (price, mix, yield) for Clean Chemical are shown in Illustration 19–12. Note that the price variance remains unchanged while the sum of the mix and yield variances equals the efficiency variance in the two-way analysis of direct materials variances. In examining these calculations, recall that the standard proportions (mix) of direct materials are X = 50% and Z = 50%, while 10,200 pounds were used in total. Thus, ASQ for each material is:

X .5 × 10,200 pounds = 5,100 pounds
Z .5 × 10,200 pounds = 5,100
                         10,200

We have calculated the mix variance for each direct material to demonstrate its exact source. However, it is the *total* mix variance ($2,800 U) that is frequently used. In this example, the unfavorable mix is caused by a substitu-

---

[4] There are numerous alternative computations of mix variances. Each starts with the same total variance but breaks it down in a different manner.

Illustration 19–12   **Mix and yield variances, Clean Chemical (June)**

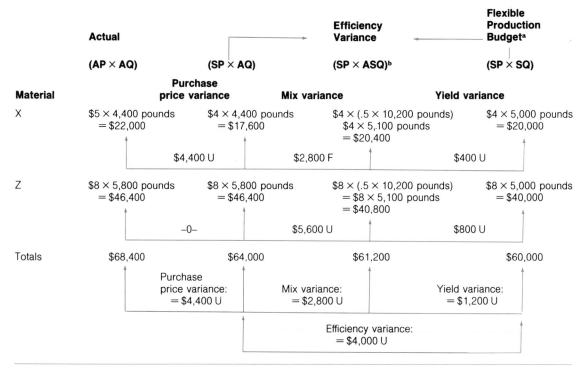

[a] Note that Columns 1 and 2 correspond with Columns 1 and 2 of the two-way analysis. Column 4 corresponds with Column 3 of the two-way analysis.

[b] ASQ = the actual amount of input used at the standard mix.

tion of the more expensive direct material Z for the less expensive direct Material X. To be precise the substitutions are:

Decrease in X:	700 pounds @ $4 = $2,800 decrease
Increase in Z:	700 pounds @ $8 = $5,600 increase
Net effect in pounds	–0–
Net effect in dollars	$2,800 increase

As previously indicated, the yield variance results from the overuse of 200 pounds. More precisely:

Material X: 100 pounds @ $4 =	$ 400 U
Material Z: 100 pounds @ $8 =	$ 800 U
Totals 200 pounds	$1,200 U

By separating the efficiency variance into its mix and yield components, we have isolated the pure mix effect by holding constant the yield effect, and we have isolated the pure yield effect by holding constant the mix effect.

Appendix self-study problem

Mix and yield variances Alexis Company makes a product, AL, from two materials: ST and EE. The standard prices and quantities are as follows:

	ST	**EE**
Price per pound	$2	$3
Pounds per unit of AL	10 pounds	5 pounds

In May, 7,000 units of AL were produced by Alexis Company, with the following actual prices and quantities of materials used:

	ST	**EE**
Price per pound	$1.90	$2.80
Pounds used	72,000	38,000

Required:

a. Compute materials price and efficiency variances.
b. Compute materials mix and yield variances.

Solution to appendix self-study problem

a. Price and efficiency variance:

		Actual	**Inputs at standard prices**	**Flexible production budget**
Quantities		Actual	Actual	Standard allowed
Costs		Actual	Standard	Standard
		(AP × AQ)	**(SP × AQ)**	**(SP × SQ)**
ST		($1.90 × 72,000)	($2 × 72,000)	($2 × 70,000[a])
EE		+ ($2.80 × 38,000)	+ ($3 × 38,000)	+ ($3 × 35,000[b])
Total		= $243,200	= $258,000	= $245,000

Price variance: $14,800 F   Efficiency variance: $13,000 U

b. Mix and yield variance:

Quantities	Actual	Actual	Actual	Standard allowed
Mix	Actual	Actual	Standard	Standard
Costs	Actual	Standard	Standard	Standard
ST		($2 × 72,000)	($2 × ⅔ × 110,000[c])	
EE		+ ($3 × 38,000)	+ ($3 × ⅓ × 110,000)	
Total	$243,200	= $258,000	= $256,667	$245,000
	(from above)	(from above)		(from above)

Price variance: $14,800 F   Mix variance: $1,333 U   Yield variance: $11,667 U

[a] 70,000 pounds = 7,000 units × 10 pounds per unit.

[b] 35,000 pounds = 7,000 units × 5 pounds per unit.

[c] Mix percentage ratio of ST pounds to total and EE pounds to total. For ST, $\frac{10}{10+5} = \frac{2}{3}$. For EE, $\frac{5}{10+5} = \frac{1}{3}$.

Appendix C: Alternative division of total variance into price and efficiency parts

In this chapter, we calculated each price variance based on actual quantity. That is:

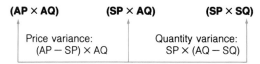

(AP × AQ)   **(SP × AQ)**   **(SP × SQ)**

Price variance: Quantity variance:
(AP − SP) × AQ   SP × (AQ − SQ)

But suppose that the order was reversed so that the quantity variance was calculated first and based on actual prices:

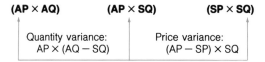

(AP × AQ)   **(AP × SQ)**   **(SP × SQ)**

Quantity variance: Price variance:
AP × (AQ − SQ)   (AP − SP) × SQ

Note that the two end points are the same, but the middle point is different.

The effect on variance calculations can be seen from the following if the following direct materials data from Boxx Company are used:

Standard costs: 10 board feet @ $.25 per board foot = $2.50 per crate
Crates produced in May: 10,000
Actual materials used: 110,000 board feet @ $.264 per board foot = $29,040

For this example, assume the quantity of board feet purchased equals the quantity used.

The calculation in the chapter was as follows:

(AP × AQ)   **(SP × AQ)**   **(SP × SQ)**

$.264 × 110,000 feet $.25 × 110,000 feet $.25 × 100,000 feet
= $29,040   = $27,500   = $25,000

Price variance: Quantity variance:
($.264 − $.25) × 110,000 $.25 × (110,000 − 100,000)
= $1,540 U   = $2,500 U

The alternative calculation is as follows:

(AP × AQ)   **(AP × SQ)**   **(SP × SQ)**

$.264 × 110,000 feet $.264 × 100,000 feet $.25 × 100,000 feet
= $29,040   = $26,400   = $25,000

Quantity variance: Price variance:
$.264 × (110,000 − 100,000)   ($.264 − $.25) × 100,000

= $2,640 U   = $1,400 U

Note that the *total* variance is the same in both cases—$4,040 U. However, the partition into price and efficiency variances is different. There are really three variances: a pure price variance ($1,400 in this case), a pure efficiency variance ($2,500), and a joint variance ($140 in this case). The joint variance

Illustration 19–13   **Graphic analysis of variance, direct materials, Boxx Company**

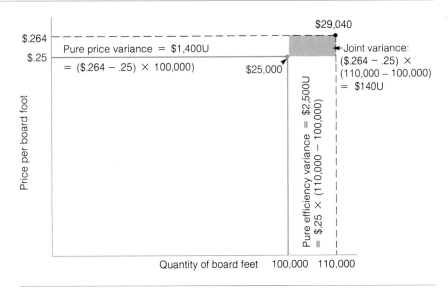

Note: The area inside the solid line represents the total standard costs allowed to make 10,000 crates. The area inside the dashed line represents the total actual costs incurred.

is part of the price variance in the first calculation and part of the efficiency variance in the second. The graph in Illustration 19–13 depicts these relationships.

Questions

19–1.   Why should management want to divide manufacturing cost variances into price and efficiency variances?

19–2.   What is the difference between a standard and a budget?

19–3.   What is the difference between a flexible budget and inputs priced at standard?

19–4.   The manager of the production division has just received a responsibility report that shows a substantial unfavorable variance for overtime premium. The manager objects to the inclusion of this variance because the overtime was due to the acceptance of a large rush order by the sales department. To whom should this variance be charged?

19–5.   Many companies set wage rates through negotiations with unions. Under these circumstances, how would a labor price variance arise that would be the responsibility of a line manager?

19–6.   One of the principles espoused by management is the idea that one should manage by exception. How can responsibility reporting systems and/or analysis of variances assist in that process?

19–7.   What are the three primary sources of variances for variable costs.

19–8.   Why are the variances for fixed costs different from the variances computed for variable costs?

19–9.   (Appendix A)   Would the production volume variance represent a difference is the cash outflows for the company when compared to budgeted cash outflows?

19–10. Why might management decision making be enhanced if materials price variances are recognized at the time of purchase rather than at the time of use?

Exercises

19–11. Direct labor variances

The master budget for a company called for direct labor costs of $14,000. These costs were to be incurred in the production of 21,000 units of output. The actual direct labor costs during the period amounted to $15,000. The standard hourly rate for labor is $8. Eighteen hundred hours were worked during the period, and 20,600 units were produced.

Required:

Compute the direct labor price and efficiency variances for the period.

19–12. Overhead variances

The following information is extracted from a responsibility report for a line manager:

	Actual	Master budget	Variance
Variable overhead	$31,850	$32,000	$ 150 F
Fixed overhead	48,420	49,600	1,180 F
Totals	$80,270	$81,600	$1,330 F

Additional information provided includes the master budget activity level of 16,000 units; actual output of 16,500 units; and knowledge that actual variable overhead was 96 percent of the standard for the input activity.

Required:

Compute the overhead price and efficiency variances.

19–13. Materials variances

A company has reported the following information concerning its direct materials:

Direct materials purchased (actual)	$413,265
Standard cost of materials purchased	407,391
Actual cost of materials used	78,264
Standard cost of materials used	74,193
Actual production	28,000 units
Standard direct materials cost per unit	$2.70

Required:

Compute the direct materials cost variances.

19–14. Reconcile flexible budget to actual

A responsibility report for a manufacturing division in a company contained the following information:

	Actual costs	Flexible budget
Direct labor	$217,650	$230,258
Factory overhead:		
Variable	193,400	201,475
Fixed	86,550	92,103

Actual production exceeded plans by 10 percent. The direct labor rate is $8 per hour, and 27,500 hours were used during the period. Variable and fixed overhead are charged on the basis of direct labor.

Required:

Reconcile the differences between flexible budget and actual costs for direct labor and the overheads.

19–15. Compute labor and overhead variances

The data below are related to the current month's activity of the Marilyn Corporation:

Actual total direct labor	$43,400
Actual hours worked	14,000
Standard hours allowed for actual output (flexible budget)	15,000
Direct labor price variance	1,400 U
Actual total overhead	32,000
Budgeted fixed costs	9,000
Master budget (normal) activity in hours	12,000
Actual fixed costs	9,100
Total overhead application rate per direct labor-hour	$2.25

Required:

Compute the labor and variable overhead price and efficiency variances, and the fixed overhead price variance.

(CPA adapted)

19–16. Materials variances

Information on Material Company's direct materials costs is as follows:

Actual quantities of direct materials used	20,000
Actual costs of direct materials used	$40,000
Standard price per unit of direct materials	$2.10
Flexible budget for direct materials	$41,000

Required:

a. What was Material Company's direct material price variance?
b. What was Material Company's direct materials efficiency variance?

(CPA adapted)

19–17. Overhead variances (Appendix A)

Information on Overhead Company's combined fixed and variable overhead costs is as follows:

Overhead applied	$80,000
Actual overhead	86,000
Flexible budget overhead	83,000
Master budget overhead	84,000

Required:

a. What is the amount of the over or underapplied overhead assuming full-absorption costing was used?
b. What is the production volume variance?

19–18. Direct labor

Lab Company reports the following direct labor information for Product CER for the month of October:

Standard rate	$6.00 per hour
Actual rate paid	$6.10 per hour
Standard hours allowed for actual production	1,500 hours
Labor efficiency variance	$600 U

Required:

What are the actual hours worked?

(CPA adapted)

19–19. Overhead variances

Hyperspace, Inc., shows the following overhead information for the current period:

Actual overhead incurred	$12,600 of which $3,500 is fixed
Budgeted fixed overhead	3,300
Standard variable overhead rate per direct labor-hour	$3
Standard hours allowed for actual production	3,500
Actual labor hours used	3,200

Required:

What are the variable overhead price and efficiency variance, and the fixed overhead price variance?

19–20. Production volume variance (Appendix A)

For the information given in Exercise 19–19, what is the fixed overhead production volume variance, assuming the normal hours allowed for budgeted production is 3,000 hours?

19–21. Direct materials

Information on Kennedy Company's direct materials cost is as follows:

Standard price per materials unit	$3.60
Actual quantity used	1,600
Standard quantity allowed for production	1,450
Materials price variance	$240 F

Required:

What was the actual purchase price per unit, rounded to the nearest cent?

(CPA adapted)

19–22. Manufacturing variances

The Hylab Company prepares its budgets on the basis of standard costs. A responsibility report is prepared monthly showing the differences between master budget and actual. Any variances are analyzed and reported separately. Materials price variances are computed at the time of purchase.

The following information relates to the current period:

Standard costs (per unit of output):

Direct materials, 1 kilogram @ $1 per kilogram	$ 1
Direct labor, 2 hours @ $4 per hour	8
Factory overhead:	
Variable (25% of direct labor cost)	2
Fixed (master budget 3,600 hours)	1 (based on direct labor-hours)
Total standard cost per unit	$12

Actual costs for the month:

Materials purchased	3,000 kilograms at $.90 per kilogram
Output	1,900 units using 2,100 kilograms of materials
Actual labor costs	3,200 hours at $5 per hour
Actual overhead:	
Variable	4,500
Fixed	1,800

Required:

a.   Compute the price and efficiency variances for the period.

b.   Compute the activity variance between the master budget and the flexible budget due to the difference in production volume.

19–23. Alternative variance calculations (Appendix C)

Based on the labor and variable overhead data given in Exercise 19–22, compute the labor and overhead variances using the method set forth in Appendix C to Chapter 19.

19–24. Materials mix and yield variances (Appendix B)

Starship Steel Company had the following direct materials data for its product:

Standard costs for one unit of output:
    Material A, 10 units of input at $100
    Material B, 20 units of input at $150

During August the company had the following results:

Units of output produced	2,000 units
Materials purchased and used:	
Material A	22,000 units at $90
Material B	39,000 units at $152

Required:

a. Compute materials price and efficiency variances.

b. Compute materials mix and yield variances.

19–25. Labor mix and yield variances (Appendix B)

Quicki-Burgers has two categories of direct labor: unskilled, which costs $8 per hour, and skilled, which costs $12 per hour. Management has established standards per "equivalent meal," which has been defined as a typical meal consisting of a sandwich, a drink, and a side order. Standards have been set as follows:

Skilled labor: 4 minutes per equivalent meal
Unskilled labor: 10 minutes per equivalent meal

During May, Quicki-Burger sold 30,000 equivalent meals and incurred the following labor costs:

Skilled labor: 1,600 hours	$19,000
Unskilled labor: 4,200 hours	37,000

Required:

a. Compute labor price and efficiency variances.

b. Compute labor mix and yield variances.

Problems and cases

19–26. Direct labor and variable overhead variance relationships

A company applies variable overhead on the basis of 150 percent of its direct labor costs. During the current period, actual variable overhead amounted to $10,150. There was a $900 favorable efficiency variance for variable overhead. There was a $725 unfavorable price variance for direct labor. During the period, 1,420 direct labor-hours were worked at a standard rate of $5 per hour.

Required:

Compute the price and efficiency variances and flexible production budget amounts for the direct labor and variable overhead.

19–27. Overhead variance relationships (Appendix A)

During the current period, a company reported a $50 unfavorable price variance for variable overhead and a $500 unfavorable price variance for fixed overhead. The variable overhead activity variance was $900 favorable. While the master budget called for $33,000 in variable overhead based on 11,000 direct labor-hours, only 10,600 hours were worked. Total overhead amounted to $54,350.

Required:

Compute the fixed overhead applied and all overhead variances, including the production volume variance.

19–28. Compute variances

Milner Manufacturing Company uses a job order costing system. It manufactures one product with a standard cost detailed as follows:

Direct materials, 20 meters at $.90 per meter	$18
Direct labor, 4 hours at $6 per hour	24
Factory overhead applied at five sixths of direct labor (the ratio of variable costs to fixed costs is 3 to 1)	20
Variable selling and administrative	12
Fixed selling and administrative	7
Total unit costs	$81

Standards have been computed based on a normal (master budget) activity level of 2,400 direct labor-hours per month.

Actual activity for the past month was as follows:

Materials purchased	18,000 meters at $.92 per meter
Materials used	9,500 meters
Direct labor	2,100 hours at $6.10 per hour
Total factory overhead	$11,100
Production	500 units

Required:

Prepare a table showing the actual costs, master budget, and all price, efficiency, and activity variances that can be computed from these data. (Some variances may be impossible to compute.)

(CPA adapted)

19–29. Find actual and budget amounts from variances

Bovar Company has just begun to manufacture a new electronic game with the trademark "Dandy." The company prepares its master budget on the basis of standard costs. The current standards per unit are as follows:

Direct materials, 6 kilograms at $1 per kilogram	$ 6
Direct labor, 1 hour at $4 per hour	4
Total overhead, 75% of direct labor	3
Total costs per unit	$13

The following data appeared in Bovar's records at the end of the past month:

Actual production	4,000 units	
Actual sales	2,500	

	Debit	Credit
Sales revenue		$50,000
Purchases (26,000 kilograms)	$27,300	
Materials price variance	1,300	
Materials efficiency variance	1,000	
Direct labor price variance	760	
Direct labor efficiency variance		800
Underapplied overhead	500	

The materials price variance is computed at the time of purchase.

Required:

Prepare a schedule showing the flexible production budget and actual costs together with all variances. The manufacturing overhead variances may be computed as though all of the manufacturing overhead costs were fixed.

(CPA adapted)

19–30. Variance computations with missing data

The following information is provided to assist you in evaluating the performance of the manufacturing operations of the Ashwood Company:

Units produced (actual)	21,000
Master budget:	
Direct materials	$165,000
Direct labor	140,000
Overhead	199,000
Standard costs per unit:	
Direct labor	$3.50 per hour × 2 hours per unit
Variable overhead	85% of direct labor
Actual costs:	
Direct materials	$188,700
Direct labor	140,000
Overhead	204,000

Variable overhead is applied on the basis of direct labor-hours. The efficiency variance for variable overhead was $1,870 F. Materials price variances are recorded at the time of use.

Required:

Prepare a table that will explain all differences between flexible budget and actual costs that can be explained with the above data.

19–31. Comprehensive variance problem

The Groomer Company manufactures two products, Florimene and Glyoxide, used in the plastics industry. The company prepares its master budget on the basis of standard costs. The current standards are as follows:

	Florimene	**Glyoxide**
Direct materials	3 kilograms at $1 per kilogram	4 kilograms at $1.10 per kilogram
Direct labor	5 hours at $4 per hour	6 hours at $5 per hour
Variable overhead (per direct labor-hour)	$3.20	$3.50
Fixed overhead (per month)	$20,700	$26,520
Expected activity (direct labor-hours)	5,750	7,800
Costs incurred for the month:		
Direct material	3,100 kilograms at $.90 per kilogram	4,700 kilograms at $1.15 per kilogram
Direct labor	4,900 hours at $3.80 per hour	7,400 hours at $5.10 per hour
Variable overhead	$16,170	$25,234
Fixed overhead	20,930	26,400
Units produced (actual)	1,000 units	1,200 units

Required:

Prepare a schedule showing actual costs, the flexible and master production budgets, together with all price, efficiency, and activity variances.

(CPA adapted)

19–32. Process costing variances

Alminex Mining Company uses a process costing system to account for the costs associated with ore benefication processes. Benefication is defined as the process by which the valuable components are extracted or converted from ores. For one of these processes, standards call for a yield of 5 percent nickel from a given quantity of ore. For cost accounting purposes, equivalent units are expressed in terms of tons of nickel obtained from a particular quantity of ore.

Because yields vary from one batch of ore to another, it is necessary to monitor materials variances carefully. A FIFO costing system is required.

The following inventories were on hand at the start of the month:

	Raw ore quantities	Standard cost
Unprocessed ore	2,100 raw ore tons	$23,100
Ore in process (i.e., work in process inventory):	600 raw ore tons	6,600
(100% complete for materials) (This ore had a nickel yield of 30T, which is exactly the 5% standard yield.)		19,200

During the month, 14,000 tons of unprocessed ore were put into production. In this and subsequent months, it was determined that the yield rate for this 14,000 tons of ore was 5.1 percent. 680 tons of nickel were sent out of the processing plant during the month. The ore on hand was 25 percent processed with respect to conversion costs at the end of the month, 60 percent at the beginning of the month.

The unprocessed ore entered into production this month had an average actual cost of $11.20 per ton. There was a $10,814 favorable price variance for conversion costs. Actual conversion costs totaled $1,062,986.

Required:

a. Equivalent units of production for the month in terms of tons of nickel for materials and conversion costs.

b. A cost of production report showing the value of units transferred out and the value of ending inventory.

c. Price and efficiency variances.

19–33. Process costing variances

Melody Corporation produces a single product known as jupiter. Melody uses the FIFO process costing method.

In analyzing production results, actual results are compared to the flexible budget and any variances are computed. The standard costs that form the basis for the budget are as follows:

Direct materials	1 kilogram at $10 per kilogram
Direct labor	2 hours at $4 per hour
Total overhead	2 hours at $1.25 per hour

Overhead applied during the current month amounted to $25,750.

Data for the month are presented below:

1. The beginning inventory consisted of 2,500 units that were 100 percent complete with respect to direct material and 40 percent complete with respect to conversion costs.

2. 10,000 units were started during the month.

3. The ending inventory consisted of 2,000 units that were 100 percent complete with respect to direct materials and 40 percent complete with respect to conversion costs.

4. Costs applicable to the current period production are as follows:

	Actual costs	Flexible budget
Direct materials (11,000 kilograms)	$121,000	$100,000
Direct labor (25,000 hours)	105,575	82,400
Factory overhead	31,930	30,000

Required:

Prepare a table showing the causes for the differences between actual costs and flexible budget.

19–34. Performance evaluation in service industries

Rock City Insurance Company estimates that its overhead costs for policy administration should cost $72 for each new policy obtained and $2 per year for each $1,000 face amount of insurance outstanding. The company set a budget of 5,000 new policies for the coming period. In addition, the company estimated that the total face amount of insurance outstanding for the period would equal $10,800,000.

During the period, actual costs related to new policies amounted to $358,400. A total of 4,800 new policies were obtained.

The cost of maintaining existing policies was $23,200. Had these costs been incurred at the same prices as were in effect when the budget was prepared, the costs would have amounted to $22,900. However, there was $12,100,000 in policies outstanding during the period.

Required:

Prepare a schedule to indicate the differences between master budget and actual costs for this operation.

19–35. Compute materials mix and yield variances (Appendix B)

The LAR Chemical Company manufactures a wide variety of chemical compounds and liquids for industrial uses. The standard mix for producing a single batch of 500 gallons of one liquid is as follows:

Liquid chemical	Quantity (in gallons)	Cost (per gallon)	Total cost
Maxan	100	$2.00	$200
Salex	300	.75	225
Cralyn	225	1.00	225
	625		$650

There is a 20 percent loss in liquid volume during processing due to evaporation. The finished liquid is put into 10-gallon bottles for sale. Thus, the standard material cost for a 10-gallon bottle is $13.

The actual quantities of direct materials and the respective cost of the materials placed in production during November were as follows:

Liquid chemical	Quantity (in gallons)	Total cost
Maxan	8,480	$17,384
Salex	25,200	17,640
Cralyn	18,540	16,686
	52,220	$51,710

A total of 4,000 bottles (40,000 gallons) were produced during November.

Required:

Calculate the total direct material variance for the liquid product for the month of November and then further analyze the total variance into a—

a. Material price variance.
b. Material mix variance.
c. Material yield variance.

(CMA adapted)

19–36. Compute labor mix and yield variances (Appendix B)

Landeau Manufacturing Company has a process cost accounting system. An analysis that compares the actual results with both a monthly plan and a flexible budget is prepared monthly. The standard direct labor rates used in the flexible budget are established each year at the time the annual plan is formulated and held constant for the entire year.

The standard direct labor rates in effect for the current fiscal year and the standard hours allowed for the output for the month of April are shown in the schedule below:

	Standard direct labor rate per hour	Standard direct labor-hours allowed for output
Labor class III	$8	500
Labor class II	7	500
Labor class I	5	500

The wage rates for each labor class increased under the terms of a new union contract. The standard wage rates were not revised to reflect the new contract.

The actual direct labor-hours worked and the actual direct labor rates per hour experienced for the month of April were as follows:

	Actual direct labor rate per hour	Actual direct labor-hours
Labor class III	$8.50	550
Labor class II	7.50	650
Labor class I	5.40	375

Required:

Calculate the dollar amount of the total direct labor variance for the month of April for the Landeau Manufacturing Company and analyze the total variance into the following components:

a. Direct labor rate variance.
b. Direct labor mix variance.
c. Direct labor performance (efficiency) variance.

(CMA adapted)

19–37. Comprehensive review of variances with missing data (Appendix B)

Merriweather Manufacturing Company is engaged in a chemical blending operation to produce certain industrial solvents. One solvent, Interno, is manufactured as a blend of three products: Alpha-28, Beta-32, and Gamma-07 (A, B, and G for short). This solvent is very active and must be shipped in special containers. In addition to the materials, the blending process requires three direct labor-hours per liter of solvent. Factory overhead is applied at the rate of 150 percent of direct labor costs.

You have been working for the Merriweather Manufacturing Company as a new management trainee in the controller's office. Today you had an opportunity to talk to the controller and advise him on the merits of your background and your education. The controller handed you some information on the last month's production of industrial solvents and asked you to analyze the variances for the product Interno. Confident in your abilities, you carried the computer printout with you as you left the office. Unfortunately, on the way home a gust of wind blew some of your papers away.

You were able to retrieve some of the information, but a good deal of it was torn or shredded.

At home, you have pieced together the following fragments from the computer printouts:

d costs per un

.500	1 Alpha	28 @ 5.00/1
.200	1 Beta	32 @10.00/
.400	1 Gamma	07 @
	tal	$ 8.30/lit

Expect

```
12,000  direct la
$80,000 fixed over
$71,500 variable ove
$4,000  container costs
```

ual costs

2,200	1 Alpha	28 @ 5.0
800	1 Beta	32 @ $11.20/1
1,000	1 Gamma	07 @ $ 9.10/1
4,010	containers	@ $ .95
Total materials		$ 32,979.50
direct labor		97,200.
variable ovh		61,700.
fixed overhead		80,960.

Varia

```
$ 755 Unf. Yie
   82 Fav. Mi
      nf. P
       . A
```

You also recall a discussion concerning the new direct labor rate of $9 per hour and how that rate had caused the production planning department to recommend a revaluation of the product line since certain products may not be profitable at this rate.

Required:

Defend your reputation with the controller and compute the variances for the solvent. (Hint: Separating the chemical inputs from the containers will make the solution more manageable.) If any variances cannot be computed, state why.

19–38. Racketeer, Inc.* (comprehensive overview of budgets and variances) (Appendix A)

"I just don't understand these financial statements at all!" exclaimed Mr. Elmo Knapp. Mr. Knapp explained that he had turned over management of Racketeer, Inc., division of American Recreation Equipment, Inc., to his son, Otto, the previous month. Racketeer, Inc., manufactures tennis rackets.

"I was really proud of Otto," he beamed. "He was showing us all the tricks he learned in business school and, if I say so myself, I think he was doing a rather good job for us. For example, he put together this budget for Racketeer, which makes it real easy to see how much profit we'll make at any sales volume (Exhibit A). As best as I can figure it, in March we expected to have a volume of 8,000 units and a profit of $14,500 on our rackets. But we did much better than that! We sold 10,000 rackets, so we should have made almost $21,000 on them."

"Another one of Otto's innovations is this standard cost system," said Mr. Knapp proudly. "He sat down with our production people and came up with a standard production cost per unit (see Exhibit B). He tells me this will tell us how well our production people are performing. Also, he claims it will cut down on our clerical work."

---

* © Michael W. Maher, 1982.

Exhibit A (19–38)   **Profit graph, Rackets, Racketeer, Inc.**

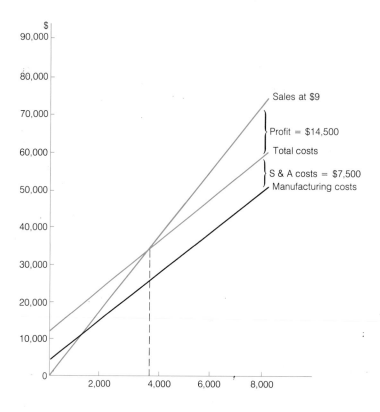

Exhibit B (19–38)   **Standard costs,[a] Racketeer, Inc.**

	Per racket
Raw material:	
Frame	$3.15
Stringing materials: 20 feet at 3¢ per foot	.60
Direct labor:	
Skilled ⅛ hour at $9.60 per hour	1.20
Unskilled ⅛ hour at $5.60 per hour	.70
Plant overhead:	
Indirect labor	.10
Power	.03
Supervision	.12[b]
Depreciation	.20[b]
Other	.15[b]
Total standard cost per frame	$6.25

[a] Standard costs are calculated for an estimated production volume of 8,000 units each month.

[b] Fixed costs.

Mr. Knapp continued, "But one thing puzzles me. My calculations show that we should have shown a profit of nearly $21,000 in March. However, our accountants came up with less than $19,000 in the monthly income statement (Exhibit C). This bothers me a great deal. Now I'm not sure our accountants are doing their job properly. It appears to me that they're about $2,200 short."

Exhibit C (19–38)

RACKETEER, INC.
Income Statement for March
Actual

Sales:	
10,000 rackets at $9	$90,000
Standard cost of goods sold:	
10,000 rackets at $6.25	62,500
Gross profit after standard costs	27,500
Variances:	
Material variance	(490)
Labor variance	(392)
Overhead variance	(660)
Gross profit	25,958
Selling and administrative expense	7,200
Net income	$18,758

"As you can probably guess," Mr. Knapp concluded, "we are one big happy family around here. I just wish I knew what those accountants are up to . . . coming in with a low net income like that."

Required:

Prepare a report for Mr. Elmo Knapp and Mr. Otto Knapp that reconcile the profit graph with the actual results for March. Show the source of each variance from the original plan (8,000 rackets) in as much detail as you can, and evaluate Racketeer's performance in March. Recommend improvements in Racketeer's profit planning and control methods.

Exhibit D (19–38)   Actual production data for March, Racketeer, Inc.

Direct materials purchased and used:	
Stringing materials	175,000 feet at 2.5¢ per foot
Frames	7,100 at $3.15 per frame
Labor:	
Skilled ($9.80 per hour)	900 hours
Unskilled ($5.80 per hour)	840 hours
Overhead:	
Indirect labor	$ 800
Power	250
Depreciation	1,600
Supervision	960
Other	1,250
Production	7,000 rackets

20

Standard Cost Systems

Virtually all companies use standards as a basis for evaluating performance. In some companies, standard costs replace actual costs in the accounting recordkeeping system. When this is done, products are costed at standard cost per unit of output instead of at actual cost. In this chapter, we discuss the characteristics of standard cost systems and demonstrate their flow of costs. The product costing emphasis of this chapter relates product costing concepts from Chapters 5 through 8 of this book to standard cost and variance concepts from Chapters 18 and 19.

Difference between standard costs and standard cost systems

There is a subtle but important distinction between the use of standard costs as the basis for variance analysis and performance evaluation, as discussed in Chapter 19, and the incorporation of those standards into the formal accounting system. While standard costs are an important part of the overall system that provides information for managerial decision making, they do not have to be formally entered into the accounting bookkeeping system to be used for performance evaluation. In short, we distinguish between *standard costs* and *standard cost systems;* the term standard cost system is used to describe a situation in which standard costs are part of the formal accounting recordkeeping system.

Advantages of a standard cost system

The use of standard costs instead of historical costs in the accounting records means that standard costs can be used for product costing as well as for performance evaluation. The use of standards instead of actual costs can greatly reduce the complexity of product costing for inventory valuation.

Under standard costing, the value of inventory is the number of units times the standard cost per unit. Cost flow assumptions such as FIFO and LIFO are unnecessary for all units that have the same standard costs. This reduces the clerical work needed to value inventories because records of the actual cost per unit are not kept. Every time a unit is produced, its standard cost is entered in the accounting records. At the end of the period, differences between the standard costs charged to production for all units and the actual costs of production are computed and analyzed.

For example, a sailboat manufacturer makes five models of small fiberglass sailboats. When the company used an actual product costing system, record-keeping was very detailed. According to the controller, "We kept track of the amount of direct materials and direct labor that went into each sailboat. Every worker had to keep track of the amount of time spent on *each sailboat*. We added a predetermined rate for variable and fixed overhead to give us the cost of each unit. We make about 50,000 sailboats each year, so you can imagine how much time was required by both operating people and accounting staff.

"We were already using standard manufacturing costs for budgeting and performance evaluation, so it was relatively easy to convert from an actual system to a standard system for product costing. Now we keep track of costs by department, by kind of input (direct material, direct labor, variable overhead, fixed overhead), and by product line. Operating people only allocate their time to departments and product lines. And we've saved a lot of time in keeping and checking records. We lost some data because we no longer know how much *each* sailboat costs. But we found that level of detail wasn't useful for management purposes and wasn't needed to value inventory."

The costs and benefits of using a standard rather than an actual costing system varies from company to company. The benefits of standard costing systems tend to increase with the amount of difficulty a company has in costing individual units of product. Thus, standard costing systems are often found in companies that use mass-production methods, particularly in conjunction with process costing. While standard costing systems may also be used in companies that make relatively large, heterogeneous units, they are relatively rare in that setting.

Standard costs are found in a variety of organizations, from banks to fast-food restaurants to manufacturing companies. Standard cost *systems* are most commonly used for manufacturing costs in manufacturing companies because they are used to value inventory.

While standard costing systems are especially useful as a method of product costing for inventory valuation, they can help improve standard costs for performance evaluation, too. When standards are part of the accounting system, they are likely to be given more attention by accountants and auditors who are concerned with their validity for product costing. A possible benefit of formalizing standard costs as part of a standard cost system is the ongoing monitoring and updating of standards to keep them current.

Standard cost flows

When a standard costing system is used, costs are transferred through the production process at standard. This means the entry debiting Work in Process

Inventory at standard cost could be made before actual costs are known. In process costing, units transferred between departments are valued at standard cost, while in job costing, standard costs are used to charge the job for its components. Actual costs are accumulated in accounts like accounts payable and factory payroll. Actual costs are compared with the total standard costs allowed for the output produced. The difference between the actual costs assigned to a department and the standard cost of the work done is the variance for the department.

Use of standards in the accounting system can facilitate the recording and transfer of costs from one department to another. Standard costs can be transferred with the physical flow of product, there is no need to wait until the actual cost data about the particular units become known.

For example, automobile repair shops charge customers for services at a predetermined (standard) hourly rate. In addition, these shops often use standard times for each task included on a repair order. If a shop is using this standard cost system and you take your car in for a tune-up, you will be billed the standard hours for that task times the standard hourly rate. This happens regardless of the actual time it takes to perform the tune-up and the actual cost of the labor used.

In the following sections, we discuss the flow of costs in a standard cost system, compare the actual and standard costs of work, and demonstrate how the variances are isolated in the accounting system. The variances are based on the calculations introduced in Chapter 19. Standard cost systems vary somewhat from company to company, so in reality, the method presented here is likely to be modified a bit to meet a company's specific needs.

The example in this chapter continues the Boxx Company example started in Chapter 18 and carried through Chapter 19. Illustration 20–1 summarizes the facts for Boxx Company. (We use the example from Chapter 19 in which direct materials purchases do not equal usage.)

Direct materials

Direct materials are purchased at their actual cost, but in a standard cost system they are often carried in direct materials inventory at the standard price per unit.[1] We assume that 250,000 feet are purchased and that 110,000 feet are used. The purchasing entry is:

Direct Materials Inventory	62,500	
Materials Price Variance	3,500	
Accounts Payable		66,000

To record the purchase of 250,000 board feet at the actual cost of 26.4 cents per foot and to record the transfer to Direct Materials Inventory at the standard cost per foot of 25 cents. To record the materials purchase price variance ($3,500 = (26.4¢ − 25¢) × 250,000 board feet).

---

[1] An alternative treatment is to carry materials at actual cost and then to charge materials into production at a standard price per unit.

Illustration 20–1
Cost data, Boxx Company

Actual production output in May: 10,000 crates
Variable cost data:

	Standards	Actuals	Variances Price	Variances Efficiency
Direct materials used	100,000 board feet allowed @ $.25 per board foot = $25,000	250,000 board feet purchased @ $.264 per board foot = $66,000 110,000 board feet @ $.264 per board foot = $29,040	250,000 feet × ($.264 − .25) = $3,500 U	(110,000 − 100,000 feet) × .25 = $2,500 U
Direct labor	5,000 hours @ $10 per hour = $50,000	5,200 hours @ $9.60 = $49,920	5,200 hours × ($10.00 − 9.60) = $2080 F	(5,200 − 5,000 hours) × $10.00 = $2,000 U
Variable manufacturing overhead (applied at $5 per standard direct labor-hour)	5,000 hours @ $5 = $25,000	= $26,480	$26,480 − ($5.00 × 5,200 hours) = $480 U	(5,200 − 5,000 hours) × $5.00 = $1,000 U

Fixed manufacturing overhead for the month (no standard or actual *unit* costs were calculated):

Budget	Actual
$20,000	$21,000

We refer to the cost of direct materials inventory as a standard cost because 25 cents per foot is the standard allowed per unit of input, but a word of caution is in order. This is the standard cost per unit of *input* (board feet), *not* the standard cost per unit of *output* (crates).

When materials are placed in production, Work in Process Inventory is debited for the standard quantity of input used at the standard cost per unit. The cutting department is allowed a standard of 100,000 board feet of lumber to make 10,000 crates at 25 cents per foot, but they actually used 110,000 board feet. The entry charging production for the standard cost of direct materials is:

Work in Process Inventory	25,000	
Materials Efficiency Variance	2,500	
Direct Materials Inventory		27,500

To record the requisition of 110,000 actual board feet at the standard cost per foot of 25 cents, and the charge to Work in Process Inventory at $2.50 per crate times 10,000 crates (or 25 cents per foot times 100,000 board feet allowed for 10,000 crates).

The materials price variance is usually the responsibility of the purchasing department, whereas the efficiency variance is usually the responsibility of the production departments.

Direct labor

Direct labor is credited to Accrued Payroll Accounts for the actual cost (including accruals for fringe benefits and payroll taxes) and charged to Work in Process Inventory at standard. The following entry is based on the facts about the standard costs allowed for Boxx Company as described in Chapter 19 and in Illustration 20–1:

Work in Process Inventory	50,000	
Labor Efficiency Variance	2,000	
Labor Price Variance		2,080
Accrued Payroll Accounts		49,920

To charge the production departments for the standard cost of direct labor at $10 per hour times 5,000 hours (10,000 crates times .50 hours allowed). To record the actual cost. To record the labor efficiency variance and the labor price variance.

Variable manufacturing overhead

Standard overhead costs are charged to production based on standard direct labor-hours per unit of output produced at Boxx Company. Overhead costs are often charged to production before the actual costs are known. This is demonstrated by the following sequence of entries:

1. Standard overhead costs are charged to production during the period. The credit entry is to an overhead applied account.
2. Actual costs are recorded in various accounts and transferred to an over-

head summary account. This accounting procedure is completed after the end of the period.

3. Variances are computed as the difference between the standard costs charged to production (overhead applied) and the actual costs (overhead summary).

This procedure is similar to that used to charge overhead to production using predetermined rates in normal costing.

Based on the data from Chapter 19 and Illustration 20–1, variable overhead is charged to production as follows:

Work in Process Inventory	25,000	
Variable Overhead Applied		25,000

Note that overhead is applied to work in process inventory on the basis of standard labor-hours *allowed.* As we shall see shortly, over- or underapplied overhead will represent a combination of the price and efficiency variances.

Actual variable overhead costs are recorded in various accounts and transferred to each department's variable manufacturing overhead account as follows:

Variable Overhead (Actual)	26,480	
Supplies Inventory		
Accrued Payroll—Indirect Labor		
Accounts Payable—Power		26,480
Maintenance Department		
Etc. (other accounts and service departments)		

These variable overhead variances are recorded by closing the applied and actual accounts as follows:

Variable Overhead Applied	25,000	
Variable Overhead Efficiency Variance	1,000	
Variable Overhead Price Variance	480	
Variable Overhead (Actual)		26,480

The flow of costs in the variable standard costing system for Boxx Company is given in Illustration 20–2.

As the units are transferred to Finished Goods Inventory, their *standard* cost is transferred from Work in Process Inventory to Finished Goods Inventory. The transfer to Finished Goods Inventory in Illustration 20–2 is based on the flow of completed units.

Likewise, Cost of Goods Sold is based on the standard cost of the units sold. In this case, we assume that 90 percent of the finished units have been sold.

Comparison of variable and full-absorption costing

We presented cost flows under variable costing in Illustration 20–2. Now we present standard cost flows under full-absorption costing.

Illustration 20–2
Standard cost flows—variable costing (Boxx Company)

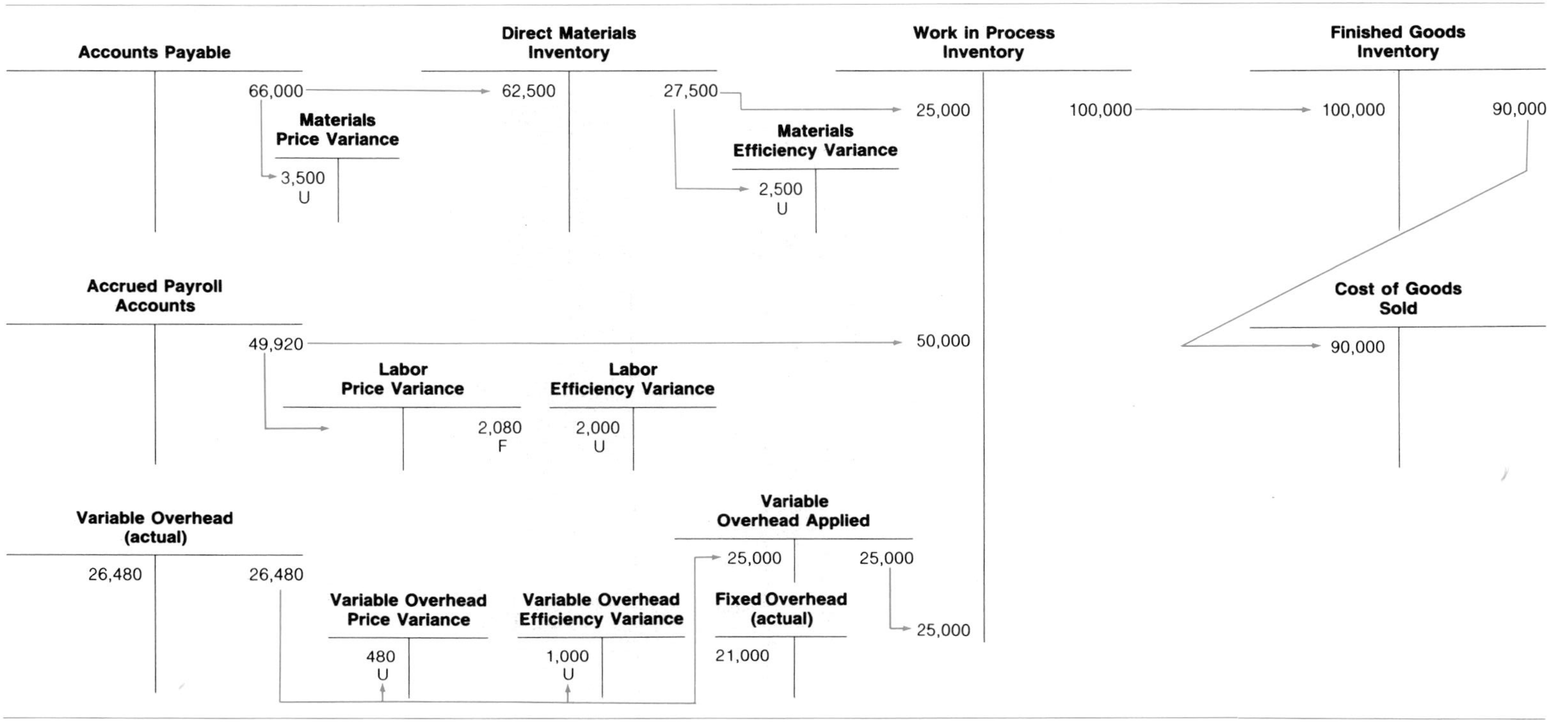

Fixed manufacturing costs and standard absorption costing

For variable costing and managerial decision-making purposes, we have assumed fixed manufacturing overhead is a period cost. Under full-absorption product costing using standard costs, a standard unit fixed manufacturing cost is derived.

Developing the standard unit cost for fixed manufacturing costs[2]

Like other standard costs, the fixed manufacturing standard cost is determined before the start of the production period. Unlike standard variable manufacturing costs, fixed costs are period costs. To convert them to product costs requires an estimation of not only the period cost but also the production volume for the period. The general formula is:

$$\frac{\text{Standard (or predetermined)}}{\text{fixed manufacturing overhead cost}} = \frac{\text{Budgeted fixed manufacturing cost}}{\text{Budgeted activity level}}$$

Assume that the estimated annual fixed manufacturing overhead at Boxx Company was $240,000 and the estimated production volume was estimated to be 96,000 crates (or 48,000 direct labor-hours.) Thus, Boxx Company would determine its annual rate as follows:

$$\text{Rate} = \frac{\$240,000 \text{ (budgeted fixed manufacturing cost)}}{96,000 \text{ crates (budgeted activity level for the year)}}$$
$$= \$2.50 \text{ per crate}$$

This rate is used to allocate fixed manufacturing costs to products. Each crate will be assigned $2.50 as the standard fixed manufacturing cost.

Entering fixed manufacturing overhead into Work in Process Inventory accounts

In Chapter 19, fixed costs were treated as period costs. In this section, we show how to treat fixed costs as product costs for inventory valuation. This allows us to use standard costing for full-absorption costing, as required for external financial reporting. Thus, fixed costs per period are now allocated to units.

At Boxx Company, fixed costs are charged to units at $2.50 per crate ($5 per *standard* direct labor-hour). Boxx Company produced 10,000 crates in May, for which 5,000 standard direct labor-hours are allowed at the rate of .5 hour per crate. Hence, the total fixed manufacturing overhead costs applied to production (that is, debited to Work in Process Inventory) amounted to $25,000 (= $2.50 × 10,000 crates or $5 × 5,000 hours). The actual and budgeted fixed manufacturing overhead costs were $21,000 and $20,000, respectively. An overall comparison of the actual, budgeted, and applied fixed manufacturing overhead follows.

As discussed in Chapter 19, the price variance is defined as the difference

---

[2] Material in this section is also discussed in Appendix A to Chapter 19.

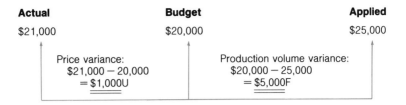

between actual ($21,000) and budgeted costs ($20,000). The production volume variance is now defined as the difference between budgeted costs ($20,000) and the amount applied or debited to Work in Process Inventory ($25,000).

Production volume variance

The production volume variance comes about because actual production is different from the estimated production volume. The difference for Boxx Company is caused by the production of 10,000 crates instead of the monthly budget of 8,000 $\left(= \dfrac{96,000 \text{ for the year}}{12 \text{ months}} \right)$. Consequently, production is charged with $25,000 (10,000 crates × $2.50 per crate) instead of $20,000 (8,000 crates × $2.50 per crate). The $5,000 difference is the production volume variance because it is caused by a deviation in production volume level (number of crates produced) from that estimated to arrive at the standard cost. If Boxx Company had projected 10,000 crates instead of 8,000 crates, the rate would have been $2 per crate $\left(= \dfrac{\$20,000}{10,000 \text{ crates}} \right)$. Thus, $20,000 (= $2 × 10,000 crates) would have been charged to production, and there would have been no production volume variance.

The production volume variance applies only to fixed costs and emerges because we are allocating a fixed period cost to units on a predetermined basis. It is unique to full-absorption costing. The benefits of calculating the variance for control purposes are questionable. While it signals a difference between expected and actual production levels, so does a production report of actual versus expected production quantities.

Price variance The production volume variance results from differences between the expected activity in the denominator of the formula used to determine the fixed manufacturing standard cost and the actual level of activity for a period. The *price variance* results from differences between the actual costs and those expected, as shown in the *numerator* of the same formula. Unlike the production volume variance, the price variance is commonly used for control purposes because it is a measure of differences between actual and budgeted period costs.

Entries Standard fixed overhead costs are charged to production based on standard direct labor-hours as shown in the following journal entries:

Work in Process Inventory	25,000	
Fixed Overhead Applied		25,000

(Fixed Overhead Applied equals Variable Overhead Applied
by coincidence in this example.)

Actual fixed overhead costs are recorded in various accounts and transferred to each department's fixed overhead account as follows:

Fixed Overhead (Actual)	21,000	
Building Depreciation		
Indirect Labor		
Heat		21,000
Plant Administration		
Etc. (other accounts and allocations from service departments)		

Fixed overhead variances are recorded by closing the applied overhead and actual overhead accounts as follows:

Fixed Overhead Applied	25,000	
Fixed Overhead Price Variance	1,000	
Fixed Overhead Production Volume Variance		5,000
Fixed Overhead (Actual)		21,000

The flow of costs using a standard full-absorption system is shown in Illustration 20–3. The differences between this and the flow of costs using a standard variable costing system, as shown in Illustration 20–2, are that in Illustration 20–3.

1. Fixed overhead costs are applied to Work in Process Inventory.
2. Fixed overhead variances are calculated as reconciling items for the difference between fixed overhead applied and actual fixed overhead costs.
3. The amounts transferred between Work in Process Inventory, Finished Goods Inventory, and Cost of Goods Sold are greater due to the inclusion of fixed overhead costs.

Under variable costing, the entire actual fixed manufacturing overhead of $21,000 would be expensed in the period. Under full-absorption costing, fixed manufacturing overhead travels through Work in Process Inventory and Finished Goods Inventory.

Transfer to Finished Goods Inventory and to Cost of Goods Sold

After production is completed in a department, units are transferred to subsequent Work in Process Inventory departments at standard cost. When all production work has been completed, units are transferred to Finished Goods Inventory and to Cost of Goods Sold at standard cost.

Finished Goods Inventory   This month 10,000 crates were finished and transferred to Finished Goods Inventory. After the crates have been finished and inspected, they are transferred to a finished goods storage area and recorded by the following entry:

Illustration 20-3
Standard cost flows—full absorption costing (Boxx Company)

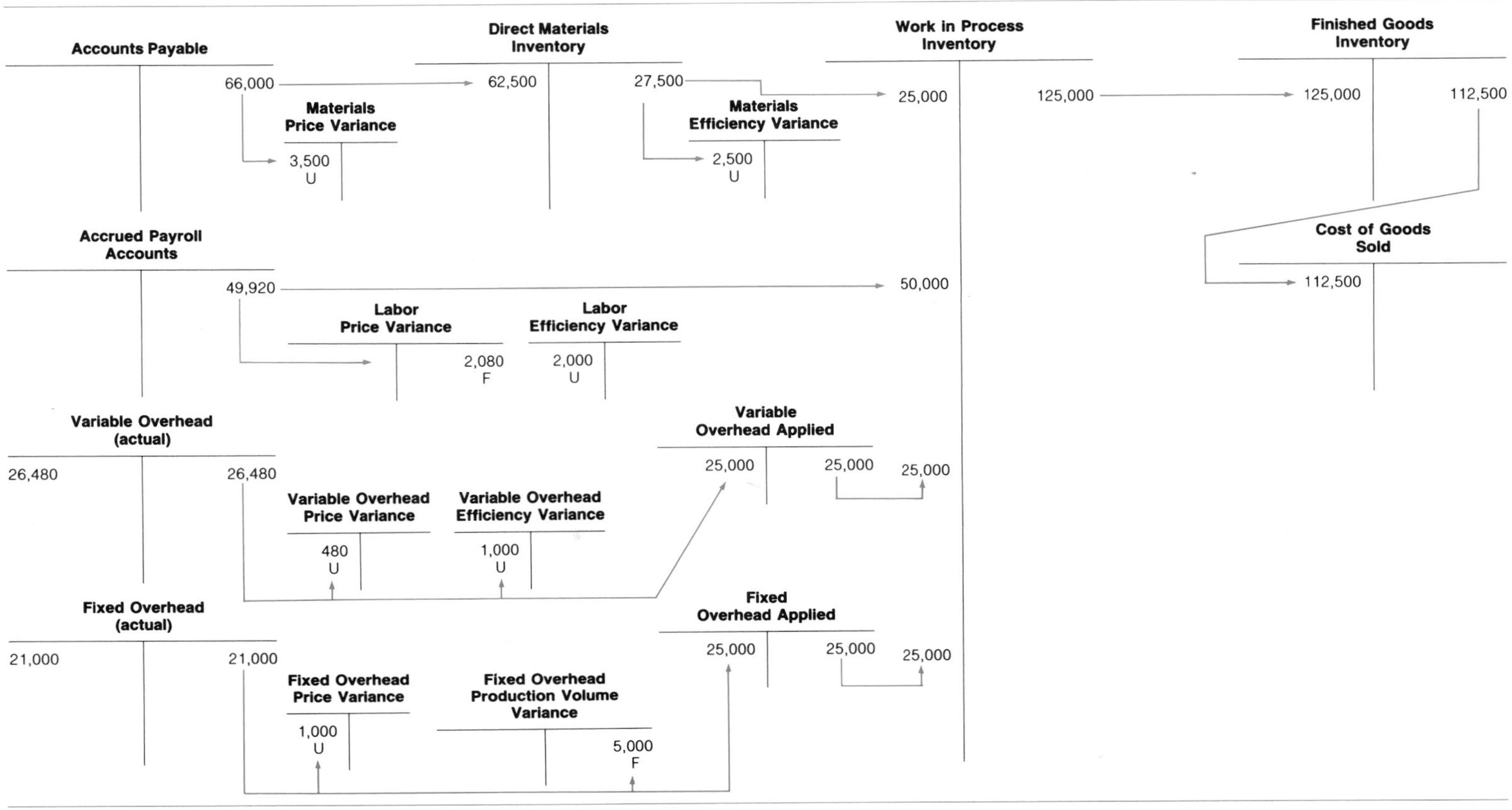

Accounts Payable

66,000

Materials Price Variance

3,500 U

Direct Materials Inventory

62,500 | 27,500

Materials Efficiency Variance

2,500 U

Work in Process Inventory

25,000 | 125,000

50,000

Finished Goods Inventory

125,000 | 112,500

Cost of Goods Sold

112,500

Accrued Payroll Accounts

49,920

Labor Price Variance

2,080 F

Labor Efficiency Variance

2,000 U

Variable Overhead (actual)

26,480

Variable Overhead Price Variance

480 U

Variable Overhead Efficiency Variance

1,000 U

Variable Overhead Applied

25,000 | 25,000

25,000

Fixed Overhead (actual)

21,000

Fixed Overhead Price Variance

1,000 U

Fixed Overhead Production Volume Variance

5,000 F

Fixed Overhead Applied

25,000 | 25,000

25,000

| Finished Goods Inventory . . . . | | 125,000 | |
| Work in Process Inventory . . . . | | | 125,000 |

To record the transfer of 10,000 completed crates at the following standard cost per crate:

Finishing and inspection department costs:

Direct labor	$ 1.00
Variable overhead	.50
Fixed overhead	.50
Total	2.00
Costs from cutting and assembly department	10.50
Total	$12.50

Cost of Goods Sold   During May, Boxx Company sold 9,000 of the crates it produced. This was recorded by the following entry:

| Accounts Receivable . . . . | 189,000 | |
| Sales Revenue . . . . | | 189,000 |

| Cost of Goods Sold . . . . | 112,500 | |
| Finished Goods Inventory . . . . | | 112,500 |

To record the sale of 9,000 crates at a price of $21 and a standard cost of $12.50 per crate.

A summary of these cost flows through T-accounts using a full-absorption standard costing system is shown in Illustration 20–3. A conceptual model is shown in Illustration 20–4.

Prorating standard cost variances

Although inventory may be valued at standard cost for internal reporting purposes, sometimes the standard costs must be adjusted to actual costs for contract settlements, taxes, and financial reporting purposes. This will usually require prorating the variances to each and every account that has been charged or credited with the specific standard cost that is now being adjusted to actual. When proration is complete, the balances in the inventory accounts closely approximate "actual" costs, and the variance accounts have no balances.

To illustrate the proration of variances, we use the Boxx Company example (Illustration 20–3) with the following changes: (1) we assume that at the end of the year only 80 percent of the standard costs incurred in production this period have been transferred to Finished Goods Inventory; (2) of the costs transferred to finished goods, 90 percent have been transferred to cost of goods sold; (3) there are no beginning inventories of direct materials; work in process, or finished goods. The variances for this example have been recorded in Illustration 20–5, but have not yet been prorated.

Materials variances

First, the materials price variance is prorated. *This variance is prorated to all accounts that contain current period materials costs at standard:* Direct Materials Inventory, Materials Efficiency Variance, Work in Process Inventory, Finished Goods Inventory, and Cost of Goods Sold. The relevant direct materials balances in each of these accounts are:

Ending Direct Materials Inventory	Materials Efficiency Variance	Ending Work in Process Inventory	Ending Finished Goods Inventory	Cost of Goods Sold	Total current material costs debited to Direct Materials Inventory
$35,000	+ $2,500	+ $5,000	+ $2,000	+ $18,000	= $62,500

These balances add up to the total materials costs at standard prices. The materials price variance of $3,500 U is prorated to each account in proportion to the account balance's percentage of the total materials costs at standard prices.

For each account, we have:

Account	(1) Standard cost in the account	(2) As a percent of total standard materials costs	Variance to be prorated Column 2 × $3,500
Materials Inventory	$35,000	56.0%	$1,960
Efficiency Variance	2,500	4.0	140
Work in Process Inventory	5,000	8.0	280
Finished Goods Inventory	2,000	3.2	112
Cost of Goods Sold	18,000	28.8	1,008
Total	$62,500	100.0%	$3,500

The journal entry to complete the prorating is:

Direct Materials Inventory	1,960	
Materials Efficiency Variance	140	
Work in Process Inventory	280	
Finished Goods Inventory	112	
Cost of Goods Sold	1,008	
Materials Price Variance		3,500

The variance is closed when the journal entry is made in the T-accounts, as shown in Illustration 20–6.

Materials efficiency variance For the materials efficiency variance, the variance to be prorated is now $2,640—that is, the original $2,500 plus the $140 that has been prorated from the Materials Price Variance account. The materials efficiency variance is prorated to the materials in ending Work in Process Inventory and Finished Goods Inventory and the materials in Cost of Goods Sold. These amounts are as follows, after adjusting for the materials price variance:

Work in Process Inventory	Finished Goods Inventory	Cost of Goods Sold	Total
($5,000 + $280)	+ ($2,000 + $112)	+ ($18,000 + $1,008)	= $26,400

Illustration 20–4
Overview of standard cost flows: Full-absorption costing

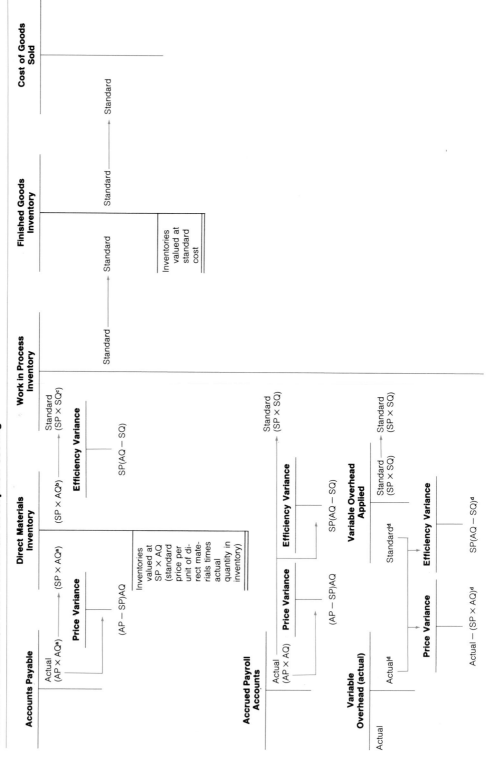

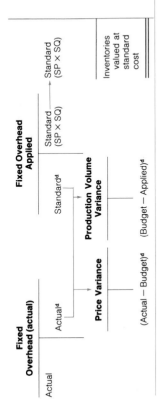

Fixed Overhead (actual)

Actual

Actual[d]

Price Variance

(Actual − Budget)[d]

Fixed Overhead Applied

Standard[d]

Standard (SP × SQ) ⟶ Standard (SP × SQ)

Production Volume Variance

(Budget − Applied)[d]

Inventories valued at standard cost

[a] Actual quantity of direct materials *purchased.*
[b] Actual quantity of direct materials *used.*
[c] Standard quantity of direct materials *used.*
[d] Closing entry.
AP = actual input cost per input unit.
SP = standard input unit price per input unit.
AQ = actual input quantity.
SQ = standard input quantity allowed for the actual output produced.

Illustration 20–5
Standard cost flows—full-absorption costing (Boxx Company)

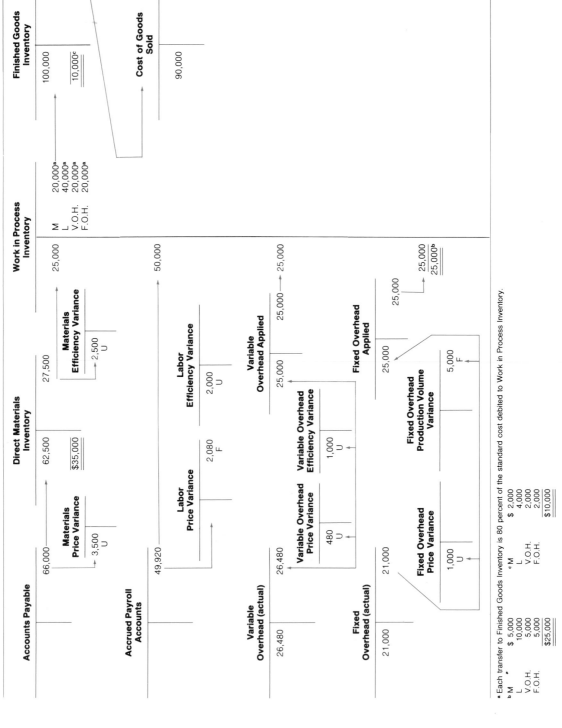

[a] Each transfer to Finished Goods Inventory is 80 percent of the standard cost debited to Work in Process Inventory.

[b]			[c]	
M	$ 5,000		M	$ 2,000
L	10,000		L	4,000
V.O.H.	5,000		V.O.H.	2,000
F.O.H.	5,000		F.O.H.	2,000
	$25,000			$10,000

Illustration 20–6
Standard cost flows—full-absorption costing Boxx Company prorated materials price variance

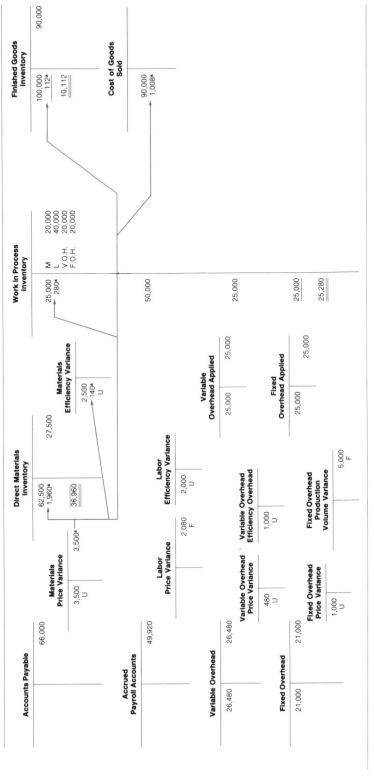

* Proration of materials price variance.

The variance is prorated as follows:

Account	(1) Cost in the account	(2) As a percent of total	Variance to be prorated Column 2 × $2,640
Work in Process Inventory	$ 5,280	20.0	$ 528
Finished Goods Inventory	2,112	8.0	211
Cost of Goods Sold	19,008	72.0	1,901
Total	$26,400	100.0	$2,640

The journal entry to record this prorating is:

Work in Process Inventory	528	
Finished Goods Inventory	211	
Cost of Goods Sold	1,901	
Materials Efficiency Variance		2,640

This variance is prorated in T-accounts in Illustration 20–7.

Instead of using the materials costs in each account after prorating the price variance, we could obtain the same prorating of the materials efficiency variance if we used the original materials balances before prorating the materials price variance ($5,000 in Work in Process Inventory, $2,000 in Finished Goods Inventory, and $18,000 in Cost of Goods Sold). This shortcut is often used in practice.

Labor and overhead variances

Labor and overhead variances are prorated among the current costs of labor and overhead respectively in ending Work in Process Inventory and Finished Goods Inventory, and Cost of Goods Sold. For Boxx Company, overhead is applied on the basis of direct labor; hence, the overhead costs in the inventory accounts will be proportional to the current period labor costs in those accounts. As a result, all of the labor and overhead variances can be combined and prorated proportionally to the labor cost balances in the inventories.

For the Boxx Company, the remaining variances are:

Labor price variance	$2,080 F
Labor efficiency variance	2,000 U
Variable overhead price variance	480 U
Variable overhead efficiency variance	1,000 U
Fixed overhead price variance	1,000 U
Fixed overhead production volume variance	5,000 F
Net total	$2,600 F

The labor cost balance in ending Work in Process Inventory is $10,000, which is the difference between the $50,000 debited to Work in Process Inventory and the $40,000 credited to Work in Process Inventory (see Illustration 20–6). The balance in Finished Goods Inventory is 10 percent of the $40,000 that was transferred to Finished Goods Inventory, or $4,000. The

Illustration 20–7
Standard cost flows—full-absorption costing Boxx Company modified example—prorated variances

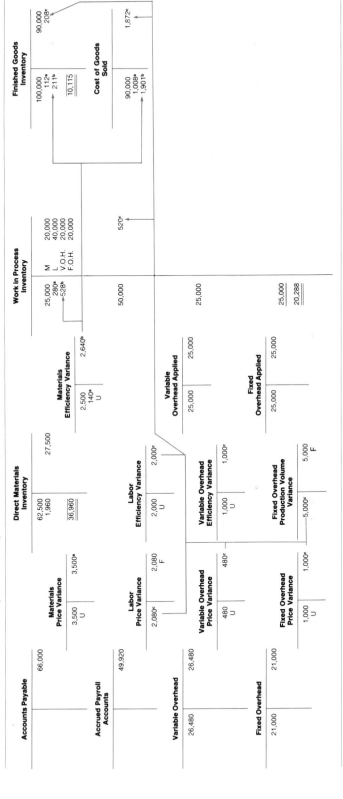

[a] Proration of materials price variance.
[b] Proration of materials efficiency variance.
[c] Proration of labor and overhead variances.

remaining $36,000 of current standard labor costs are in Cost of Goods Sold. Hence, the variances are prorated as follows:

Account	(1) Labor cost in the account	(2) As a percent of total	Variance to be prorated Column 2 × $2,600
Work in Process Inventory	$10,000	20.0	$ 520
Finished Goods Inventory	4,000	8.0	208
Cost of Goods Sold	36,000	72.0	1,872
		100.0	$2,600

The journal entry to close these variance accounts and to prorate the variance to inventories and cost of goods sold is (adjustments are credits to accounts because the net labor and overhead variance is favorable):

Labor Price Variance	2,080	
Production Volume Variance	5,000	
Labor Efficiency Variance		2,000
Variable Overhead Price Variance		480
Variable Overhead Efficiency Variance		1,000
Fixed Overhead Price Variance		1,000
Work in Process Inventory		520
Finished Goods Inventory		208
Cost of Goods Sold		1,872

Posting these entries to our T-accounts yields the results in Illustration 20–7. The inventory accounts and Cost of Goods Sold account now reflect an approximation of the actual cost of each inventory item. The variance accounts are closed.

Alternative treatment for variances

If the variances are relatively small, it may make little difference whether they are prorated or expensed as a period cost as a write-off to Cost of Goods Sold. Under the alternative treatment, all variances are closed, and the net variance is debited or credited to Cost of Goods sold or to a Summary of Variances Expense. For managerial purposes, we assume this is the method used and variances are not prorated, unless otherwise stated.

Comparison of unit inventory values under alternative costing methods

We have now completed the discussion of six alternative methods of valuing inventory in this book. They are:

	Actual costing	Normal costing	Standard costing
Variable costing	X	X	X
Full-absorption costing	X	X	X

The difference between variable and full-absorption costing is that full-absorption includes a share of fixed manufacturing costs in the unit cost, while variable costing does not. The difference between actual and normal costing is in the treatment of overhead. Normal costing uses predetermined overhead rates time an actual base while actual costing uses actual costs. Under standard costing, all manufacturing costs assigned to a unit are predetermined.

These differences are presented in Illustration 20–8. Illustration 20–9 presents a numerical comparison and contrast of these differences using data from the Boxx Company illustration.

Illustration 20–8   **Comparison of unit inventory values under alternative costing methods**

	Actual costing	Normal costing	Standard costing
Variable costing:			
Direct materials	Actual	Actual	Standard
Direct labor	Actual	Actual	Standard
Variable manufacturing overhead	Actual	Predetermined rate × Actual inputs or output	Standard rate × Standard inputs allowed for actual output
Fixed manufacturing overhead[a]	—	—	—
Full-absorption costing:			
Direct materials	Actual	Actual	Standard
Direct labor	Actual	Actual	Standard
Variable manufacturing overhead	Actual	Predetermined rate × Actual inputs or output	Standard rate × Standard inputs allowed for actual output
Fixed manufacturing overhead	Actual	Predetermined rate × Actual inputs or output	Standard rate × Standard inputs allowed for actual output

[a] Treated as a period cost in variable costing; not part of inventory.

Summary

This chapter describes cost flows using standard cost systems. We distinguish between the use of standard costs and the use of standard cost *systems* as follows: Standard costs are any estimated or predetermined costs used for any purpose, while a standard cost system uses the standard costs to place a value on inventory and the cost of goods sold. In standard cost systems, the standard costs are part of the accounting system; they replace actual costs in recording transactions between work in process production depart-

Illustration 20–9   **Comparison of unit inventory values under various costing systems, Boxx**
                               Company (May)

Facts
1. Actual production costs:

Direct materials: 110,000 board feet at $.264	$ 29,040
Direct labor: 5,200 hours at $9.60	49,920
Variable manufacturing overhead	26,480
Fixed manufacturing overhead	21,000
Total costs	$126,440

2. Predetermined overhead rates:
   Variable overhead $5 per direct labor-hour

   Fixed overhead rate per direct labor-hour

   $$= \frac{\text{Estimated annual fixed manufacturing costs}}{\text{Estimated standard direct labor-hours worked based on estimated number of crates produced}}$$

   $$= \frac{\$240,000}{48,000 \text{ hours}^a} = \$5 \text{ per direct labor-hour}$$

3. Standard variable manufacturing costs:

Direct materials: 10 board feet per crate at $.25	$ 2.50 per crate
Direct labor: .5 hours per crate at $10	5.00
Variable manufacturing overhead: .5 hour at $5	2.50
Total standard variable manufacturing costs	$10.00

4. Standard fixed manufacturing cost:
   .5 hour per crate times $5 per hour = $2.50 per crate

Comparison of inventory valuations:

	Actual costing		Normal costing		Standard costing	
	Total[b]	**Unit**[c]	**Total**[b]	**Unit**[c]	**Total**[b]	**Unit**[c]
Variable costing:						
Direct materials	$ 29,040	$ 2.904	$ 29,040	$ 2.904	$ 25,000	$ 2.50
Direct labor	49,920	4.992	49,920	4.992	50,000	5.00
Variable manu-facturing over-head	26,480	2.648	26,000[d]	2.60	25,000	2.50
Total	$105,440	$10.544	$104,960	$10.496	$100,000	$10.00
Full-absorption costing:						
Direct materials	$ 29,040	$ 2.904	$ 29,040	$ 2.904	$ 25,000	$ 2.50
Direct labor	49,920	4.992	49,920	4.992	50,000	5.00
Variable manu-facturing over-head	26,480	2.648	26,000[d]	2.60	25,000	2.50
Fixed manufactur-ing overhead	21,000	2.10	26,000[d]	2.60	25,000	2.50
Total	$126,440	$12.644	$130,960	$13.096	$125,000	$12.50

[a] Assumes annual production of 96,000 crates:

   96,000 crates × .5 standard direct labor-hours allowed per crate = 48,000 standard direct labor-hours

[b] Amount that would be charged to work in process in the month under each alternative costing method.

[c] Total divided by 10,000 crates produced in May.

[d] $5 per direct labor-hour times 5,200 direct labor-hours actually used.

Illustration 20–10 **Summary of variance proration**

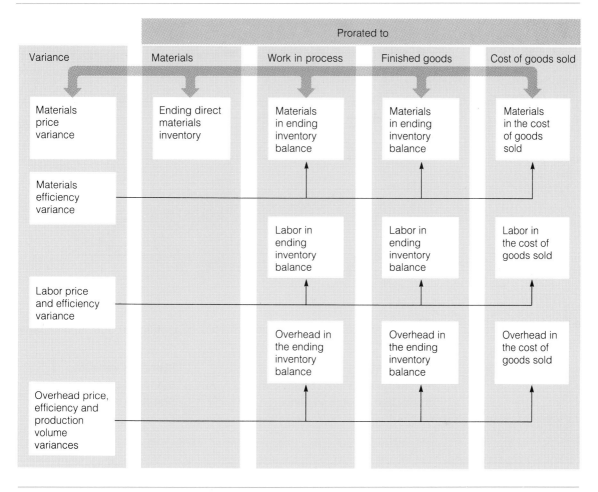

ments and in recording transactions between Work in Process Inventory and Finished Goods Inventory.

A major advantage of a standard system is that it reduces record keeping. Records of actual cost per unit are not kept. Instead, unit costs are standard costs. Many companies that manufacture with processes (for example, chemicals and petroleum) use standard cost systems because there is little benefit and great cost to record actual cost of each unit produced.

An overview of the standard cost system model is presented in Illustration 20–4. The basic idea is that costs are accumulated at actual cost in Accounts Payable, Accrued Payroll, and similar accounts. Costs are debited to Work in Process Inventory at standard cost. Standard costs are used to reflect the transfer of units between work in process departments, and from Work in Process Inventory to Finished Goods Inventory, and from Finished Goods Inventory to Cost of Goods Sold.

Manufacturing cost variances for a period are sometimes prorated among inventories and Cost of Goods Sold. This has the effect of restating Cost of Goods Sold and ending inventories to actual cost.

A summary of the way variances can be prorated is shown in Illustration 20–10.

We have presented the following six different methods of placing a cost value on inventory in this text:

	Actual costing	Normal costing	Standard costing
Variable costing	X	X	X
Full-absorption costing	X	X	X

Terms and concepts

The following terms and concepts should be familiar to you after reading this chapter.

Actual costing

Normal costing

Production volume variance

Prorating variances

Standard costing

Standard cost system

Self-study problem

(This is a continuation of a self-study problem from Chapters 18 and 19.)

1. Produced 50,000 and sold 40,000 plastic minicomputer cases at a sales price of $10 each. (Budgeted sales were 45,000 units at $10.15.)

2. Standard variable costs per unit (that is, case):

Direct materials: 2 pounds at $1	$2.00
Direct labor: .10 hours at $15	1.50
Variable manufacturing overhead: .10 hours at $5	.50
	$4.00 per case

3. Fixed manufacturing overhead cost:

Monthly budget		$80,000
Estimated monthly production		40,000 cases
	or	4,000 hours
Fixed overhead application rate		?

4. Actual production costs:

Direct materials purchased: 200,000 pounds at $1.20	$240,000	
Direct materials used: 110,000 pounds at $1.20	132,000	
Direct labor: 6,000 hours at $14	84,000	
Variable overhead	28,000	
Fixed overhead	83,000	

Required:

Use a standard full-absorption costing system to—

a. Record the transactions using journal entries.

b. Trace the transactions through T-accounts.

c. Prorate the variances.

Assume there is only one Work in Process Inventory account with no beginning or ending balance.

Solution to self-study problem

a.   (1)   Direct Materials Inventory 200,000

             Materials Price Variance 40,000

                Accounts Payable....................... 240,000

             To record the purchase of 200,000 pounds of materials at an actual cost of $1.20 per pound and to record the transfer to Direct Materials Inventory at the standard cost of $1 per pound.

   (2)   Work in Process Inventory 100,000

             Materials Efficiency Variance 10,000

                Direct Materials Inventory 110,000

             To record the requisition of 110,000 pounds of materials at the standard cost of $1 per pound and to charge Work in Process Inventory with the standard usage of 100,000 pounds of materials at the standard price.

   (3)   Work in Process Inventory 75,000

             Labor Efficiency Variance 15,000

                Labor Price Variance 6,000

                Accrued Payroll 84,000

             To charge Work in Process Inventory for the standard cost of direct labor at $15 per hour times 5,000 standard hours allowed and to record the actual cost of $14 per hour times the 6,000 hours actually worked.

   (4)   Work in Process Inventory 25,000

                Variable Overhead Applied 25,000

             To apply overhead to production at $5 per standard direct labor-hour times the 5,000 hours allowed.

   (5)   Variable Overhead (actual) 28,000

                Miscellaneous accounts (Cash, Accounts Payable, etc.) 28,000

             To record actual variable overhead.

   (6)   Variable Overhead Applied 25,000

             Variable Overhead Efficiency Variance 5,000

                Variable Overhead Price Variance 2,000

                Variable Overhead (actual) 28,000

To record variable overhead variances and to close the Variable Overhead Applied and Variable Overhead (actual) accounts

(7)　Work in Process Inventory 100,000
　　　　Fixed Overhead Applied 100,000
　　　To record fixed overhead at a standard cost of $20 per direct labor-hour times 5,000 standard hours
$$\left(\frac{\$80,000}{4,000\ \text{hours}}\right) = \$20 \text{ per hour}.$$

(8)　Fixed Overhead (actual) 83,000
　　　　Miscellaneous accounts (Cash,
　　　　　Accounts Payable, etc.) 83,000
　　　To record actual fixed overhead.

(9)　Fixed Overhead Applied 100,000
　　　Fixed Overhead Price Variance 3,000
　　　　Fixed Overhead Production
　　　　　Volume Variance 20,000
　　　　Fixed Overhead (actual) 83,000
　　　To record fixed overhead variances and to close the Fixed Overhead Accounts.

(10)　Finished Goods Inventory 300,000
　　　　Work in Process Inventory 300,000
　　　To record the transfer of 50,000 units of finished goods at the standard cost of $6 per unit.

(11)　Cost of Goods Sold 240,000
　　　　Finished Goods Inventory 240,000
　　　To record the sale of 40,000 units at a standard cost of $6 per unit.

b.

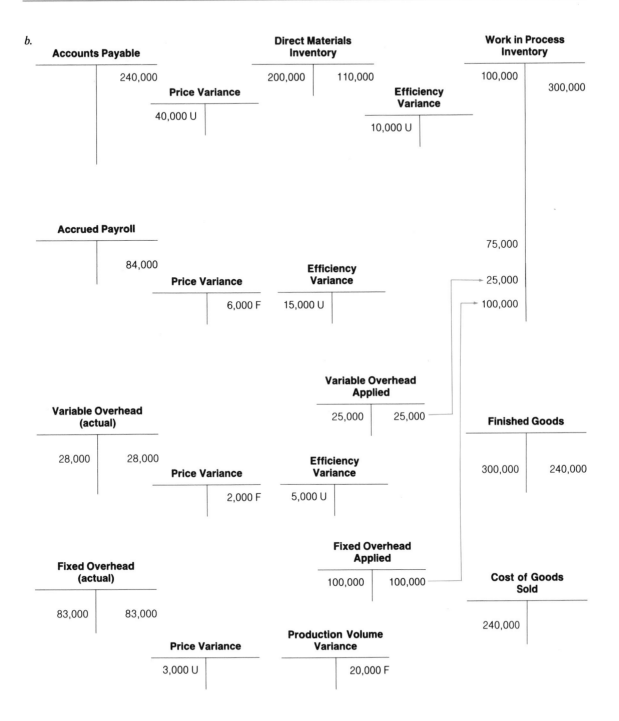

Accounts Payable	
	240,000

Price Variance	
40,000 U	

Direct Materials Inventory	
200,000	110,000

Efficiency Variance	
10,000 U	

Work in Process Inventory	
100,000	300,000

Accrued Payroll	
	84,000

Price Variance	
6,000 F	

Efficiency Variance	
15,000 U	

75,000

→ 25,000

→ 100,000

Variable Overhead Applied	
25,000	25,000

Variable Overhead (actual)	
28,000	28,000

Price Variance	
2,000 F	

Efficiency Variance	
5,000 U	

Finished Goods	
300,000	240,000

Fixed Overhead Applied	
100,000	100,000

Fixed Overhead (actual)	
83,000	83,000

Price Variance	
3,000 U	

Production Volume Variance	
	20,000 F

Cost of Goods Sold	
240,000	

c.

Prorate variances:

Materials price variance:

Account	(1) Cost in account	(2) Percent of total cost	Variance to be prorated (Column 2 × $40,000)
Direct Materials Inventory	$ 90,000	45	$18,000
Materials Efficiency Variance	10,000	5	2,000
Work in Process Inventory	–0–	—	—
Finished Goods Inventory	20,000	10	4,000
Cost of Goods Sold	80,000	40	16,000
	$200,000	100	$40,000

Materials efficiency variance:

Account	(1) Cost in account	(2) Percent of total cost	Variance to be prorated (Column 2 × $12,000ᵃ)
Work in Process Inventory	–0–	—	–0–
Finished Goods Inventory	$ 24,000	20	$ 2,400
Cost of Goods Sold	96,000	80	9,600
	$120,000	100	$12,000

Labor and overhead variances:

Labor price variance	$ 6,000 F
Labor efficiency variance	15,000 U
Variable overhead price variance	2,000 F
Variable overhead efficiency variance	5,000 U
Fixed overhead price variance	3,000 U
Fixed overhead production volume variance	20,000 F
Net total	$ 5,000 F

Account	(1) Cost in account	(2) Percent of total cost	Variance to be prorated (Column 2 × $5,000)
Work in Process Inventory	—	—	—
Finished Goods Inventory	$ 15,000	20	$ 1,000
Cost of Goods Sold	60,000	80	4,000
	$ 75,000	100	$ 5,000

ᵃ $12,000 equals $10,000 variance before proration plus $2,000 materials price variance prorated to materials efficiency variance.

Questions

20–1. What are the advantages of a standard cost system?

20–2. How do you distinguish between a standard cost and a standard cost system?

20–3. One manager was heard to remark, "We don't believe in using artificial numbers in our accounting system. Standard costing systems just make the readers fool themselves. We use normal costing instead—that gives us the true costs." Is the manager right? Comment.

20–4. Standard costing eliminates the need to compute equivalent units since all costs are transferred out at a standard amount. Do you agree? Why or why not?

20–5. What is the difference in the way labor and material costs are accounted for in a standard costing system versus the way overhead costs are accounted for?

20–6. How are variable overhead costs treated differently in a standard costing system from the treatment in a normal costing system?

20–7. How should variances be disposed of at the end of the year?

20–8. Why is it difficult to relate fixed costs to outputs from a production process?

20–9. "Just like price and efficiency variances, the production volume variance indicates whether a company has spent more or less than called for in the budget." Comment on this quote.

Exercises

20–10. Materials

Elgin Company purchased 20,000 units of Material A at a price of $1.30 per unit. During the month, 14,000 units of Material A were transferred to Work in Process Inventory. The standard cost of Material A is $1.38 per unit.

Required:

Prepare journal entries to record these transactions. There was no materials efficiency variance.

20–11. T-accounts for materials

Using the data on the Elgin Company's Material A, prepare T-accounts to show the flow of costs for these events.

20–12. Labor variances

Manor Lands, Inc., estimates its labor costs at $55 per unit of output. During the past month, 3,000 output units were manufactured. The total labor-hours allowed for this output amounted to 22,000 hours. The actual labor costs were $161,280. Actual labor-hours were 22,600.

Required:

Prepare T-accounts to show the flow of labor costs for these events.

20–13. Labor variances—journal entries

Prepare journal entries to record the labor costs for Manor Lands, Inc. (Exercise 20–12).

20–14. Overhead variance analysis

Standard Company has developed standard overhead costs based on a capacity of 180,000 direct labor-hours as follows:

Standard costs per unit:

Variable portion: 2 hours at $3	$ 6
Fixed portion: 2 hours at $5	10
	$16

During April, 85,000 units were scheduled for production; however, only 80,000 units were actually produced. The following data relate to April:

1. Actual direct labor cost incurred was $644,000 for 165,000 actual hours of work.
2. Actual overhead incurred totaled $1,378,000—$518,000 variable and $860,000 fixed.
3. All inventories are carried at standard cost.

Required:

Use T-accounts to show the recording of these overhead costs in Work in Process Inventory together with the related variances.

(CMA adapted)

20–15. Standard cost systems— overhead

Union Company uses a standard cost accounting system. The following overhead costs and production data are available for August 1981:

Standard fixed overhead rate per direct labor-hour	$ 1.00
Standard variable overhead rate per direct labor-hour	$ 4.00
Budgeted monthly direct labor-hours	40,000
Actual direct labor-hours worked	39,500
Standard direct labor-hours allowed for actual production	39,000
Overall overhead variance—favorable	$ 2,000
Actual variable overhead	$159,500

Required:

Show the flow of these overhead costs in T-account form.

(CPA adapted)

20–16. Overhead journal entries

Use the data in Exercise 20–15 and prepare journal entries to reflect the events of the month as they would appear in a standard cost system.

20–17. Overhead variance analysis— T-accounts

The following balances appeared in the accounts of the Rapid-Freeze Corporation:

Manfacturing
overhead $485,000
  Fixed portion: $210,000
  Variable portion: 275,000

Overhead applied: 465,836
  Fixed portion: $215,900
  Variable portion: 249,936

Fixed overhead was applied at the rate of $4.25 per direct labor-hour, and 48,000 hours were budgeted for the period. The company uses a standard costing system. The output attained during the period required 47,500 actual direct labor-hours.

Required:

Use T-accounts to show the flow of overhead costs and the overhead variances.

20–18. Prorate materials variances

Armadillo Corporation acquired 50,000 units of direct materials for $70,000. The standard cost of the materials was $1.30 per unit. During the month, 40,000 units of materials were used in a production process. Standard production would have required 42,000 units for the same number of outputs as were actually attained. Eighty percent of the units that used these materials were completed and transferred to Finished Goods Inventory. Seventy percent of these units that had been transferred to Finished Goods Inventory were sold this period.

a. Show the flow of costs for this information using a standard cost system.
b. Prorate the materials variances.

Problems and cases

20-19. Use T-accounts to show standard cost flows

Armando Corporation manufactures a product with the following standard costs:

Direct materials: 20 yards at $1.35 per yard	$27
Direct labor: 4 hours at $9 per hour	36
Factory overhead—applied at five sixths of direct labor. Ratio of variable costs to fixed costs: 2 to 1	30
Total standard cost per unit of output	$93

Standards are based on normal monthly production involving 2,400 direct labor-hours (600 units of output).

The following information pertains to the month of July:

Direct materials purchased: 18,000 yards at $1.38 per yard	$24,840
Direct materials used: 9,500 yards	
Direct labor: 2,100 hours at $9.15 per hour	19,215
Actual factory overhead	16,650

500 units of the product were actually produced in July and transferred to Finished Goods Inventory.

Required:

Show the flow of these costs in a standard cost system. Use T-accounts.

(CPA adapted)

20-20. Compute variances and use T-accounts to show standard cost flows

Juneau Trading Company manufactures a line of fur apparel. At the beginning of the period, there were 1,000 units in stock at a variable cost of $400 per unit. The full absorption cost of these units would be $450 each.

The plans for the coming period called for the following standards and activity:

Units produced and sold	2,000
Standard cost per unit:	
Direct materials	$175
Direct labor	200
Overhead	100 (60% variable)
Total	$475

During the period, 2,200 units were produced and 1,800 were sold. The following costs were incurred:

Direct materials	$360,000
Direct labor	412,000
Overhead:	
Variable	135,000
Fixed	81,000

Direct materials price variances are recorded at the time of purchase. No materials were purchased this period. Actual direct labor costs were 5 percent less per hour of labor than planned. Overhead costs are applied to production on the basis of direct labor. A standard costing system is used.

Required:

a. Prepare a table showing the differences between master budget and actual and explaining all variances.

b. Use T-accounts to show the flow of costs through the system, assuming FIFO.

20–21. Prorate variances

Use the data in Juneau Trading Company (Problem 20–20) and use T-accounts to show the prorationing of the standard cost variances.

20–22. Review variances, comprehensive standard cost problem (Extension of Problem 19–30.)

The following information is provided to assist you in evaluating the performance of the manufacturing operations at the Ashwood Company:

Units produced	21,000
Master budget:	
Direct materials	$165,000
Direct labor	140,000
Overhead	199,000

Standard costs per unit:
Direct labor: $3.50 per labor-hour × 2 hours per unit
Variable overhead: 85% of direct labor costs

Actual costs:	
Direct materials	$188,700
Direct labor	140,000
Overhead	204,000

Variable overhead is applied on the basis of the direct labor-hours allowed. The efficiency variance for variable overhead was $1,870 F. Materials price variances are recorded at time of use. There was a $4,000 production volume variance for fixed overhead. Actual materials usage priced at standard would have cost $8.50 per output unit.

Required:

a. Explain all differences between master budget and actual costs that can be explained with this information using a variable costing format. If there are any differences that cannot be explained, identify them and indicate what information is needed. (This requirement was required in Problem 19–30.)

b. Prepare T-accounts to show the cost flows that would arise from these events, using standard, full-absorption costing.

20–23. Comprehensive prorationing of variances

Based on the data for the Ashwood Company (Problem 20–22, above), use T-accounts to show how the variances would be prorated at the end of the period if 70 percent of the production had been transferred to Finished Goods Industry and if 90 percent of the completed production had been sold. All costs transferred out of Work in Process Inventory have been proportional to the standard costs per unit.

20–24. Standard costs and labor variances

Nanron Company has a process standard cost system for all its products. All inventories are carried at standard during the year. The inventories and cost of goods sold are adjusted for all variances considered material in amount at the end of the fiscal year for financial statement purposes. All products are considered to flow through the manufacturing process to finished goods and ultimate sale in a FIFO pattern.

The standard cost of one of Nanron's products manufactured in the Dixon Plant, unchanged from the prior year, is shown below.

Direct materials	$2
Direct labor (.5 direct labor-hour at $8)	4
Manufacturing overhead	3
Total standard cost	$9

There is no work in process inventory of this product due to the nature of the product and the manufacturing process.

The schedule below reports the manufacturing and sales activity measured at standard cost for the current fiscal year.

	Units	Dollars
Product manufactured	95,000	$855,000
Beginning finished goods inventory	15,000	135,000
Goods available for sale	110,000	990,000
Ending finished goods inventory	19,000	171,000
Cost of goods sold	91,000	$819,000

The manufacturing performance relative to standard costs both this year and last year were not good. The balance of the finished goods inventory, $140,800, reported on the balance sheet at the beginning of the year included a $5,800 adjustment for variances from standard cost. The unfavorable standard cost variances for labor for the current fiscal year consisted of a wage rate variance of $32,000 and a labor efficiency variance of $20,000 (2,500 hours at $8). There were no other variances from standard cost for this year.

Required:

Adjust the inventories and cost of goods sold to reflect the actual costs of this year's production.

(CMA adapted)

20–25. Revisions of standards

The Lenco Company employs a standard cost system as part of its cost control program. The standard cost per unit is established at the beginning of each year. Standards are not revised during the year for any changes in material or labor inputs or in the manufacturing processes. Any revisions in standards are deferred until the beginning of the next fiscal year. However, in order to recognize such changes in the current year, the company includes planned variances in the monthly budgets prepared after such changes have been introduced.

The following labor standard was set for one of Lenco's products effective July 1, 1979, the beginning of the fiscal year.

Class I labor: 4 hours at $6	$24.00
Class II labor: 3 hours at $7.50	22.50
Class V labor: 1 hour at $11.50	11.50
Standard labor cost per 100 units	$58.00

The standard was based upon the quality of material that had been used in prior years and what was expected to be available for the 1979–80 fiscal year. The labor activity is performed by a team consisting of four persons with Class I skills, three persons with Class II skills, and one person with Class V skills. This is the most economical combination for the company's processing system.

The manufacturing operations occurred as expected during the first five months of the year. The standard costs contributed to effective cost control during this period. However, there were indications that changes in the operations would be required in the last half of the year. The company had received a significant increase in orders for delivery in the spring. There were an inadequate number of skilled workers available to meet the increased production. As a result, the production teams, beginning in January, would be made up of more Class I labor and less Class II labor than the standard required. The teams would consist of six Class I persons, two Class II persons and one Class V person. This labor team would be less efficient than the normal team. The reorganized teams work more slowly so that only 90 units are produced in the same time period that 100 units would normally be produced. No direct materials will be lost as a result of the change in the labor mix. Completed units have never been rejected in the final inspection process as a consequence of faulty work; this is expected to continue.

In addition, Lenco was notified by its material supplier that a lower quality material would be supplied after January 1. One unit of direct material normally is required for each good unit produced. Lenco and its supplier estimated that 5 percent of the units manufactured would be rejected upon final inspection due to defective material. Normally, no units are lost due to defective material.

Required:

a. How much of the lower quality material must be entered into production in order to produce 42,750 units of good production in January with the new labor teams? Show your calculations.

b. How many hours of each class of labor will be needed to produce 42,750 good units from the material input? Show your calculations.

c. What amount should be included in the January budget for the planned labor variance due to the labor team and material changes? What amount of this planned labor variance can be associated with the (1) material change and (2) the team change? Show your calculations.

(CMA adapted)

20–26. Comprehensive review of materials and labor variances and standard cost flows

The Longhorn Manufacturing Corporation produces only one product, Bevo, and accounts for the production of Bevo using a standard cost system.

At the end of each year, Longhorn prorates all variances among the various inventories and cost of sales. Because Longhorn prices its inventories on the FIFO basis and all the beginning inventories are used during the year, the variances which had been allocated to the ending inventories are immediately charged to cost of sales at the beginning of the following year. This allows only the current year's variances to be recorded in the variance accounts in any given year.

Following are the standards for the production of one unit of Bevo: 3 units of item A at $1 per unit; 1 unit of item B at $.50 per unit; 4 units of item C at $.30 per unit; and 20 minutes of direct labor at $4.50 per hour. Separate variance accounts are maintained for each type of direct material and for direct labor. Direct material purchases are recorded initially at standard. Manufacturing overhead is applied at $9 per actual direct labor-hour and is not related to the standard cost system. There was no overapplied or underapplied manufacturing overhead at December 31, Year 1. After proration of the variances, the various inventories at December 31, Year 1 were valued as follows:

Direct material:

Item	Number of units	Unit cost	Amount
A	15,000	$1.10	$16,500
B	4,000	.52	2,080
C	20,000	.32	6,400
			$24,980

Work in process:

9,000 units of Bevo which were 100 percent complete as to items A and B, 50 percent complete as to item C, and 30 percent complete as to labor. The composition and valuation of the inventory follows:

Item	Amount
A	$28,600
B	4,940
C	6,240
Direct labor	6,175
	45,955
Overhead	11,700
	$57,655

Finished goods:

4,800 units of Bevo composed and valued as follows:

Item	Amount
A	$15,180
B	2,704
C	6,368
Direct labor	8,540
	32,792
Overhead	16,200
	$48,992

Following is a schedule of direct materials purchased and direct labor incurred for the year ended December 31, Year 2. Unit cost of each item of direct material and direct labor cost per hour remained constant throughout the year.

Purchases:

Item	Number of units or hours	Unit cost	Amount
A	290,000	$1.15	$333,500
B	101,000	.55	55,550
C	367,000	.35	128,450
Direct labor	34,100	4.60	156,860

During the year ended December 31, Year 2, Longhorn sold 90,000 units of Bevo and had ending physical inventories as follows:

Direct materials:

Item	Number of units
A	28,300
B	2,100
C	28,900

Work in process:

7,500 units of Bevo which were 100 percent complete as to items A and B, 50 percent complete as to item C, and 20 percent complete as to labor, as follows:

Item	Number of units or hours
A	22,900
B	8,300
C	15,800
Direct labor	800

Finished goods:

5,100 units of Bevo, as follows:

Item	Number of units or hours
A	15,600
B	6,300
C	21,700
Direct labor	2,050

There was no overapplied or underapplied manufacturing overhead at December 31, Year 2.

Required:

a. Prepare a schedule showing all materials and direct labor variances arising from activity in Year 2.

b. Use T-accounts to show the flow of materials and direct labor costs under the standard costing system in use.

(CPA adapted)

20–27. Racketeer (comprehensive cost flow problem)

Refer to the facts presented in Racketeer, Problem 19–38.

Required:

Using standard costing and full-absorption costing for Racketeer, present the flow of costs through accounts using journal entries and T-accounts.

20–28. Woodside Products, Inc.* (profit variance analysis)

Phil Brooks, president of Woodside Products, Inc., called Marilyn Mynar into his office one morning in early July 1979. Ms. Mynar was a business major in college and was employed by Woodside during her college summer vacation.

"Marilyn," Brooks began, "I've just received the preliminary financial statements for our 1979 fiscal year, which ended June 30. Both our board of directors and our shareholders will want, and deserve, an explanation of why our pretax income was virtually unchanged even though revenues were up by more than $175,000. The accountant is tied up working with our outside CPA on the annual audit, so I thought you could do the necessary analysis. What I'd like is as much of a detailed explanation of the $1,950 profit increase as you can glean from these data [Exhibit A]. I'd also like you to draft a statement for the next board meeting that explains the same $1,950 profit increase, but in a fairly intuitive, summary way. Of course, that doesn't mean 'don't use any numbers'!"

Required:

Prepare the detailed analysis of the $1,950 profit increase from fiscal 1978 to fiscal 1979 and draft an explanation for Woodside's board of directors, as requested by Phil Brooks. For the board's report, you may make any reasonable conjectures you wish as to what caused the variances you have calculated. For both years, assume that inventory was valued at $24 per unit. Assume also that none of the members

---

* Copyright Osceola Institute, 1979.

Exhibit A (20-28)

Operating Results
For the Years Ended June 30

1978		1979
$3,525,000	Sales revenues	$3,701,250
2,115,000	Cost of goods sold	2,310,450
1,410,000	Gross margin	1,390,800
902,400	Selling and administrative	881,250
$ 507,600	Income before taxes	$ 509,550

Other 1978 data

1. Sales = 88,125 units @ $40.
2. Cost of goods sold = 88,125 units @ $24.
3. Selling and administrative costs were $1.84 per unit variable selling cost plus $740,250 fixed S&A.
4. Production volume and sales volume were equal.
5. Production costs per unit were:

Materials	$ 9.60 (8 pounds at $1.20)
Direct labor	4.80 (.75 hours at $6.40)
Variable overhead	1.60 (per unit)
Fixed overhead	8.00 (based on long-term standard volume of 88,125 units)
	$24.00

Other 1979 data

1. Sales = 82,250 units @ $45.
2. Cost of goods sold includes 1979 production cost variances.
3. Selling and administrative costs were $2 per unit variable selling cost plus $716,750 fixed S&A.
4. Production volume was 81,100 units; standard volume was 88,125 units.
5. 626,200 pounds of material at $1.40 were consumed by production.
6. 64,860 direct labor-hours were worked at $6.90.
7. Actual variable overhead costs were $152,000.

of the board of directors has expertise in accounting calculations or terminology.

20-29. C. F. Church Manufacturing Company* (standard cost systems case)

C. F. Church Manufacturing Company was established in 1898 for the purpose of manufacturing toilet seats. The executives had devoted considerable effort to the development of a quality product, to widespread advertising of the product, and to the realization of economical manufacturing methods.

The manufacturing processes were quite simple. First, the seats were shaped out of wood at a branch plant. They were then shipped to the main plant, where they underwent the particular finishing processes required. Some units were sprayed with paint, but the best seats were coated with cellulose nitrate sheeting. After the seats were coated, the rough edges were filled and the seats were sanded, buffed, and polished. Finally, hinges and rubber bumpers were added, and the seats were packed for shipment. Most operations were performed by hand with the aid of small machines, such as paintspray guns and buffing wheels.

1. Accounting

Collection of material and labor cost   A major part of the work required in the cost system was the accumulation of data on actual and standard costs. The procedure used for materials was as follows. When an order for a particular style was started through the factory, the supervisor of the department that performed the first operation received a manufacturing order. On the basis of this order, the supervisor filled out a stores requisition slip for the necessary materials. Items listed on this requisition subsequently were priced, and their purchase cost was entered on the requisition by the cost department on a LIFO basis. (Inasmuch as direct material was purchased infrequently in large contract lots, this procedure was not difficult.) When seats were ready to be assembled and packed, the assembly department supervisor made out an assembly order (Exhibit A), which included a requisition for hinges, screws, bumpers, cartons, and fillers. These issues were also costed at LIFO. The totals of the requisition slips for the month served as the basis for credits to the respective materials inventory accounts and a debit to the Work in Process Inventory account for the cost of material put into process.

Exhibit A (20–29)

ASSEMBLY ORDER Nº 6291

Coated

Date __August__   Plate No. __2000__

Shipping Order No. _____

Work Order No. _____   Quantity __100__

Seats 2,000 – 917

Covers 2,000 – 917

Hinges 2,000

Special Instructions

FOR COST DEPT. ONLY	UNIT COST†		AMOUNT		✓
Material	5	51	551	00	
Labor		92	92	00	
Burden	1	90	190	00	
Total Cost	8	33	833	00	

REQUISITION Nº 6291

Hinges – Screws – Bumpers

Date __August__

DESCRIPTION	QUANTITY
Hinges 2,000	100
Screws 3/4 x 7	
Screws 5/8 x 7	
1 1/4 x 8	400
Brass Ferrules	200
Bar Bumpers	200
Tack Bumpers	200
Delivered by	

	UNIT COST*	AMOUNT	✓
Hinges			
Screws			
Screws			
Ferrules			
Bar Bumpers			
Tack Bumpers			

REQUISITION Nº 6291

Cartons – Fillers

Date __August__

DESCRIPTION	QUANTITY
Cartons 25	100
Fillers	200
800	
214	100
105	
Blocks	
Delivered by	

	UNIT COST*	AMOUNT	✓
Cartons			
Filler No. 1			
No. 105			
No. 800			
No. 214			
Blocks			

The direct labor debit to Work in Process Inventory was equally straightforward. Daily, each productive employee made out a time and production report (Exhibit B) on which he or she recorded the factory order number, the operation, the time spent on each operation, and the number of pieces that he or she had finished. A clerk in the payroll department entered the correct piece rate or hourly rate and made the proper extension. The total of the direct labor thus computed provided the credit to the Accrued Wages account and the debit (for direct labor) to Work in Process Inventory.

Standard overhead schedule (annual)   The debit to Work in Process Inventory for production overhead was based on annual estimates of the relation of overhead expenses to direct labor costs for each department. These annual estimates were made so that for each department there was available a schedule of standard overhead expenses at varying possible rates of capacity utilization. Exhibit C illustrates such a schedule for the coating department, Department No. 3.

The process used to prepare these schedules was as follows:

1. Determine 100 percent capacity of each department in terms of direct labor-hours and direct labor dollars by theoretically loading each unit of productive machinery and equipment with the number of workers required to operate it, together with the necessary productive employees on floor or bench work. Consider, however, the normal sales volume of different types of products and limitations as to type of equipment in any one department that affect the capacity of the plant as a whole. For example, output might be limited to the capacity of the coating and spraying departments.

2. Establish overhead expense allowances for each department, considering four general classifications: indirect labor, indirect supplies, fixed charges, and charges from nonproductive departments.

3. Base allowance for indirect labor and indirect supplies on the past year's experi-

Exhibit B (20–29)

FORM C-STR7918		C. F. CHURCH MFG. CO.						
		Time and Production			Date _August_ —			
Employee No. 3/3		Name						
Order No.	Oper. No.	TIME			Labor or Piece Rate	No. Pieces	Cost	✓
		Started	Finished	Elapsed				
2068	31	7:20	12:00	4.7	2.30	350	8 05	
2068	31	1:00	4:20	3.3	2.30	250	5 75	
								13 80

Exhibit C (20–29)
Overhead development, department No. 3 (coating)

	100%	95%	90%	85%	80%	75%	70%	65%	60%	50%	40%
Indirect labor:											
01 Supervision	775.00	775.00	775.00	775.00	775.00	775.00	775.00	775.00	775.00	775.00	775.00
08 General labor	625.00	595.00	565.00	535.00	505.00	470.00	440.00	405.00	375.00	315.00	250.00
10 Idle and lost time											
11 Guaranteed rate cost	375.00	356.00	338.00	319.00	300.00	281.00	263.00	244.00	225.00	188.00	150.00
16 Overtime bonus	100.00	100.00	95.00	95.00	90.00	85.00	80.00	75.00	50.00	25.00	25.00
19 Repairs and maintenance— M and E	175.00	175.00	165.00	165.00	160.00	160.00	160.000	150.00	150.00	100.00	100.00
Total indirect labor	2,050.00	2,001.00	1,938.00	1,889.00	1,830.00	1,771.00	1,718.00	1,649.00	1,575.00	1,403.00	1,300.00
Indirect supplies:											
31 Repairs and maintenance— M and E	25.00	25.00	25.00	25.00	25.00	20.00	20.00	20.00	15.00	15.00	10.00
35 Acetone and isotone	1,625.00	1,545.00	1,465.00	1,385.00	1,305.00	1,220.00	1,140.00	1,055.00	975.00	815.00	650.00
37 Sandpaper and sandbelts	11.00	10.00	10.00	9.00	9.00	8.00	8.00	7.00	7.00	5.00	4.00
38 Glue and cement	775.00	736.00	700.00	660.00	620.00	580.00	540.00	500.00	465.00	385.00	310.00
41 Consumable supplies	125.00	120.00	112.00	106.00	100.00	94.00	88.00	81.00	75.00	63.00	50.00
42 Loose and hand tools	50.00	48.00	45.00	43.00	40.00	38.00	35.00	33.00	30.00	25.00	20.00
46 Miscellaneous	15.00	14.00	14.00	13.00	12.00	11.00	10.00	9.00	9.00	7.00	6.00
Total indirect supplies	2,626.00	2,498.00	2,371.00	2,241.00	2,111.00	1,971.00	1,841.00	1,705.00	1,576.00	1,315.00	1,050.00

Fixed charges:											
65 Insurance—buildings and equipment	21.58	21.58	21.58	21.58	21.58	21.58	21.58	21.58	21.58	21.58	21.58
66 Insurance—L. and C	64.00	80.00	97.00	105.00	113.00	121.00	129.00	137.00	145.00	153.00	161.00
68 Power	11.00	14.00	16.00	18.00	19.00	21.00	22.00	23.00	24.00	26.00	27.00
69 Water	17.25	17.25	17.25	17.25	17.25	17.25	17.25	17.25	17.25	17.25	17.25
70 Taxes—city and town	28.68	28.68	28.68	28.68	28.68	28.68	28.68	28.68	28.68	28.68	28.68
71 Taxes—social security	212.00	265.00	318.00	345.00	371.00	398.00	424.00	450.00	477.00	504.00	530.00
72 Depreciation	81.25	81.25	81.25	81.25	81.25	81.25	81.25	81.25	81.25	81.25	81.25
73 Provision for vacations	725.40	725.40	725.40	725.40	725.40	725.40	725.40	725.40	725.40	725.40	725.40
78 Group insurance	112.70	112.70	112.70	112.70	112.70	112.70	112.70	112.70	112.70	112.70	112.70
80 Pensions	420.36	420.36	420.36	420.36	420.36	420.36	420.36	420.36	420.36	420.36	420.36
Total fixed charges	1,694.22	1,766.22	1,838.22	1,875.22	1,910.22	1,947.22	1,982.22	2,017.22	2,053.22	2,090.22	2,125.22
Total dept. expense	4,044.22	4,484.22	4,989.22	5,229.22	5,469.22	5,689.22	5,923.22	6,147.22	6,362.22	6,589.22	6,801.22
Charges from other departments	8,235.38	8,440.11	8,630.42	8,751.83	8,826.90	8,945.27	9,040.03	9,140.56	9,240.12	9,333.33	9,435.37
Total overhead expense	12,279.60	12,924.33	13,619.64	13,981.05	14,296.12	14,634.49	14,963.25	15,287.78	15,602.34	15,922.55	16,236.59
Direct labor dollars	3,750.00	4,687.00	5,625.00	6,094.00	6,562.00	7,031.00	7,500.00	7,969.00	8,437.00	8,906.00	9,375.00
Overhead rate	327%	276%	242%	229%	218%	208%	200%	192%	185%	179%	173%

ence, making adjustments if necessary for changes in wage rates and the prices of supplies. Compute these projections first for the 100 percent capacity determined above, and from this point use a sliding or graduated scale for the lower percentages of capacity. Give due recognition to the fact that some of these costs do not vary at all with production, that others vary in the same ratio as production, and that others, although not fixed, do not move proportionately with the rate of actual plant activity.

4. Prorate power expense according to the number of horsepower hours used and metered in the respective departments; water expense (after consideration is given to any special demands for water in particular departments) according to the number of employees; insurance, taxes, and depreciation with reference to the net book value of buildings and equipment. Charge directly to the department involved specific insurance that definitely can be assigned to an individual department, such as insurance on trucks in the shipping department or boiler indemnity for the steam department.

5. Distribute the total expense of nonproductive departments such as steam, general plant, shipping, and plant administration to the productive departments on the most logical basis: steam according to floor area, general plant and plant administration according to direct labor-hours, and shipping according to direct labor dollars. The estimated cost of defective work for the whole plant was distributed to operating departments on the basis of the expected distribution of direct labor dollars. This item of expense was included in the total of "Charges from other departments," shown at the bottom of Exhibit C.

6. Revise the standard overhead schedules only for a general increase or decrease in wage rates or material costs or an important change in the manufacturing processes.

Standard overhead rate   After the overhead expense schedule was prepared, executives estimated the percentage of capacity utilization expected during the coming year. The standard overhead rate was the rate shown on Exhibit C for the estimated percentage of capacity. For example, it was estimated that during the year the coating department would operate at an average of 80 percent of capacity. The standard overhead rate for the coating department was therefore 200 percent of direct labor, as shown at the bottom of the 80 percent column in Exhibit C. The other columns in Exhibit C were used for control purposes, as described below.

Actual overhead costs (monthly)   Actual overhead costs incurred during the month were debited to the Overhead account in the general ledger and to an appropriate detail account in an overhead subsidiary ledger. There was a detail account for each item listed in Exhibit C (supervision, general labor, and so forth) in each department. Service department and other overhead costs were allocated to the producing departments. At the end of the month, the amount of "absorbed overhead" (that is, overhead applied to Work-in-Process Inventory) was calculated by multiplying the overhead rate for each department by the actual direct labor cost of the department for the month. In the coating department, for example, the actual direct labor for August was $5,915.60, and this multiplied by 200 percent gave $11,831.20, the absorbed overhead. (Note that the rate used was the overhead rate determined annually, *not* the overhead rate under the column in Exhibit C that relates to the actual volume of the current month.)

The absorbed overhead for all departments was debited to Work in Process Inventory and credited to the Overhead clearing account. Any balance remaining in the

Overhead account (that is the net overhead variance) was then closed to Cost of Goods Sold. In August, for example, actual overhead was $45,914.98, absorbed overhead was $45,904.44, so $10.54 was debited to Cost of Goods Sold.

Standard product costs Deliveries from work in process to finished goods were recorded by completion in the factory of the assembly order (Exhibit A). On the lower left corner of that form there was space for the cost department to fill in the standard cost per unit and the total amount of standard cost for the order, and the total of these standard costs entries for a month was credited to the Work in Process Inventory account and debited to Finished Goods Inventory.

The standard costs per unit mentioned in the previous paragraph were prepared for each product in the form illustrated in Exhibit D. Because the lines on the standard

Exhibit D (20–29)

Standard Cost				
Date January 1			Plate No. 2000	
Description	**Material**	**Labor**	**Overhead**	**Total**
Receive woodwork	1.17	.004	.008	1.182
Insp. and hand sand		.012	.024	1.218
Bottom coat	.542	.038	.076	1.874
Trim T.B. and O.F. seats		.011	.022	1.907
Sand edges T.B.C.F. out		.003	.008	1.918
Sand edges T.B.C.F. in		.003	.008	1.929
Inspect		.012	.024	1.965
Top coat	.543	.079	.158	2.745
Shave		.010	.020	2.775
Sand edges—upright belt		.005	.014	2.794
Sand seats and covers		.039	.107	2.940
Inspect and file		.015	.030	2.985
Dope		.004	.008	2.997
Buff seats and covers		.108	.208	3.313
Inspect		.012	.024	3.349
Buff repairs		.044	.085	3.478
Trademark		.007	.014	3.499
Drilling		.004	.008	3.511
Total seat	2.255	.410	.846	3.511
Total cover no.	1.983	.399	.826	3.208
Total seat and cover	4.238	.809	1.672	6.719
Assemble		.032	.064	6.815
Cleanup polish		.033	.066	6.914
Seal end of carton		.006	.012	6.932
Inspect and wrap		.034	.068	7.034
Seat, label, and pack		.010	.020	7.064
Bar bumpers	.043			7.107
Tack bumpers	.019			7.126
Screws 1¼–8	.047			7.173
Hinge	1.04			8.213
Carton and filler 2—No. 1	.125			8.338
Total cost	5.512	0.924	1.902	8.338

cost sheets were arranged by successive operations, they showed the cumulative cost of a product at the completion of every operation as well as the final cost at which the product was delivered to finished goods inventory. For each operation and for the total cost there was a breakdown that showed separately the standard costs of materials, labor, and overhead. The method of arriving at these costs is described below.

Standard materials costs consisted of a predetermined physical amount per unit priced at the expected purchase price for each classification of raw stock or of finished parts stock. Standard labor costs for the various piece-rate operations were simply the current piece rates; in the case of daywork operations, they were the quotients obtained by dividing the daywork rate by an estimated attainable average output. Standard overhead costs were found by multiplying the departmental overhead rate selected for the year by the standard labor cost for the operation concerned. For example, the standard cost sheet for a style calling for a coated finish might show for an operation in the coating department a standard labor charge of $.079. As indicated above, operations in the coating department for the year were estimated to be at 80 percent of capacity, which for the coating department meant an overhead rate of 200 percent of productive labor. Thus, the standard overhead cost for the operation with a labor charge of $.079 was set at 200 percent of this amount, or $.158.

These standard product costs were used to price deliveries into finished stock, to cost work in process inventory, and to transfer production between accounts. Once the standard costs were prepared, it was expected that they would remain constant except for alterations necessary to reflect a significant change in the manufacturing process, a change in wage rates or in the price of materials, or the selection of a new normal volume that determined the unit allowance for overhead.

Variances   At the end of each month's accounting period, a physical inventory of direct materials, supplies, work in process, and finished goods was taken. For this inventory, direct materials and supplies were priced on the basis of LIFO purchase cost, and work in process and finished goods were priced according to the standard cost sheets described above. The difference between the inventory thus determined and the book balance of each inventory account was closed into Cost of Goods Sold. The most important of these differences was for work in process inventory.

A work in process statement (Exhibit E) was prepared each month. This report showed the beginning inventory at standard cost plus actual direct materials, actual labor, and actual absorbed overhead added during the period in each department. From this total cost figure, there were subtracted the actual deliveries to finished goods as indicated on the completed assembly orders, plus defects and less products transferred from Finished Goods Inventory back to Work in Process Inventory for reworking, all costed at standard cost. The resulting book value of work in process was compared with the figure obtained by valuing, at standard, the results of the physical inventory ($80,959.69). Any difference indicated by this comparison constituted the variance of actual cost from standard and was closed to Cost of Goods Sold. The physical inventory balance at standard constituted the debit to Work in Process Inventory at the beginning of the next month. If this Work in Process Inventory variance was large, its causes were investigated and action was taken accordingly.

A descriptive summary of the inventory accounts is given in Exhibit F.

Exhibit E (20–29)

Work in Process

Period Ending August		Order No. GENERAL				

Detail	Amount					
Balance from Last Period				158	597	19
DIRECT MATERIALS				76	338	21
DIRECT LABOR						
1 Varnish						
2 Spray	2	990	25			
3 Coating	5	915	60			
4 Filing		998	83			
5 Sanding	1	637	53			
6 Buffing & Polishing	6	175	78			
8 Assembling and Packing	4	788	60			
Total Direct Labor				22	506	59
OVERHEAD						
1 Varnish						
2 Spray	6	180	50			
3 Coating	11	831	20			
4 Filing	1	937	73			
5 Sanding	4	489	05			
6 Buffing & Polishing	11	888	76			
8 Assembling and Packing	9	577	20			
10 Shipping						
Total Overhead				45	904	44
TOTAL COST				303	346	43
Less Deliveries				222	386	74
BALANCE IN PROCESS at Std. Cost				80	959	69

DELIVERIES AT Std. Cost

Date		Amount		Date			Amount	Date			Amount	
8/31	Del.	220	876	63								
	Var.	1	259	07								
	Defect.		251	04								
	Net	222	386	74								

Exhibit F (20–29)   Summary of Entries to Inventory Accounts (August)

Direct Materials
(Several accounts according to nature of material)

Debits	Credits
$151,204 Balance	$76,318.21 Requisitions, priced at LIFO cost (debit to Work in Process Inventory).
$343,640.19 Purchases at invoice cost (credit to Accounts Payable).	$138.32 Adjustment to physical inventory (Dr. or Cr.).
$1,101.67 Materials salvaged from returned goods (credit to Cost of Goods Sold).	

A physical inventory of all direct materials was taken each month and the difference between inventory and book balance written off to Cost of Goods Sold.

Work in Process Inventory

Debits	Credits
$158,597.19 Balance	$220,894.24 Deliveries to finished goods at standard costs (debit to Finished Goods Inventory).
$76,318.21 Direct materials from requisitions priced at LIFO cost (credit to Direct Materials).	$251.04 Defective work, from defective work order (debit to Overhead).
$22,506.59 Direct labor from payroll summary (credit to Accrued Wages).	$1,259.07 Adjustment to physical inventory (Dr. or Cr.).
$20.00 Materials purchased not usually carried in inventory (credit to Accounts Payable).	
$17.61 Transfers from finished goods for reworking or alteration, at standard cost (credit to Finished Goods Inventory).	
$45,904.44 Absorbed overhead from overhead summary sheet (credit to Overhead).	

A physical inventory was taken of all work in process every month. This was priced and totaled according to standard costs at last operation performed; the difference between the inventory and balance in the Work in Process Inventory account, representing the cost variation, was written off to Cost of Goods Sold.

Finished Goods Inventory

Debits	Credits
$429,682.73 Balance	$400,954.09 Shipment at standard costs (debit to Cost of Goods Sold).
$220,894.24 Deliveries to finished goods at standard costs (credit to Work in Process Inventory).	$17.61 Transfers to work in process for reworking or alteration at standard cost (debit to Work in Process Inventory).

2. Control of overhead expenses

Budgeted overhead expenses   The company used the departmental overhead schedules to set targets for the supervisors who were responsible for incurring expenses.
A knowledge of the actual amount of direct labor for each productive department
made it a simple matter to determine which column of figures to use as the benchmark
for evaluating the spending performance of each supervisor. For example, the coating
department (Exhibit C) might be expected to operate, on the *average,* at 80 percent
of capacity; but in any one month the actual operations might vary considerably
from this average. Thus, if direct labor dropped to $7,031, the supervisor would be
expected to spend only $580 for glue and cement rather than the $620 allowable at
the average operating level. For nonproductive departments, the column selected
was the one that listed the expenses expected for the percentage of capacity nearest
the average operating level of all productive departments.

Comparison of actual and budget   The departmental comparisons of the actual
overhead expenses, by accounts, with the appropriate budgeted allowance for that
volume, are illustrated in the departmental budget sheet, Exhibit G. The August
budgeted expense figures for the coating department are based upon an output level
of 65 percent of capacity. This figure was arrived at by comparing the actual direct
labor expense for the month, amounting to $5,915.60, to the closest corresponding
direct labor expense, $6,094, which is under the 65 percent column shown on Exhibit
C. (Exhibit G is a standard form, and only those lines that are pertinent to the
operations of the coating department are filled in on the example shown.)

   Exhibit G also showed two items over which the supervisor had no control. Other
Overhead expenses was the total amount of fixed charges allocated to the department
on the basis of the percentage distributions described earlier. Defective Work was
the total amount of defective work budgeted ($600) and actual ($251.04) for the
entire plant, and it bore no relation to the work done in the coating department.
The amount allocated to each department for defective work was not shown on
Exhibit G because the basis of allocation was considered too arbitrary. The amounts
for both Other Overhead expenses and for Defective Work were shown in the Analysis
of Overhead Expenses principally as a matter of information for the supervisor. They
were not considered as being controllable by the supervisor.

   Each month the accounting department prepared Exhibit H, summarizing the
actual, budgeted, and absorbed overhead costs for each operating department. The
amount shown as Actual Expense was obtained by adding the Charges from Other
Departments to the other overhead items shown in Exhibit G (excluding defective
work). The Budgeted Expense was the total overhead for each department as shown
on the overhead development sheets (Exhibit C) at the applicable level of operations
(65 percent for the coating department in August).

   The amount of Absorbed Expense was computed by applying the *annual* overhead
rate to the direct labor in each productive department, as explained in the preceding
section.

   In the opinion of the management the entries in the column headed Loss or Gain
on Budget could be considered a measure of the effectiveness of departmental supervision, whereas the amount Over- or Underabsorbed was influenced both by efficiency
and by the volume of production.

   The departmental overhead budget constituted the point of real control over expenditures. At the end of each month, the president met with the cost accountant and

Exhibit G (20–29)

	Budget	Actual Expense	Over or Under Actual
C. F. CHURCH MFG. CO.			
HOLYOKE			
Analysis of Overhead Expenses			
DEPARTMENT #3 Coating		Month August	
INDIRECT LABOR			
01 Supervision	775.00	756.00	19.00
04 Truck Drivers & Helpers			
06 Shipping			
08 General Labor	405.00	171.22	233.78
09 Repair and Rework			
10 Idle and Lost Time		1.77	(1.77)
11 Guaranteed Rate Cost	244.00	28.14	215.86
16 Overtime Bonus	75.00	32.98	42.02
19 Repairs & Maint.	150.00	38.26	111.74
17 Vacations		46.00	(46.00)
21 Paid Holidays			
Total	1649.00	1074.37	574.63
INDIRECT SUPPLIES			
31 Repairs & Maint.	20.00	360.18	(340.18)
33 Repairs & Maint. Trucks			
35 Acetone & Isotone	1055.00	739.48	315.52
36 Buffing Compounds & Buffs			
37 Sandpaper & Sandbelts	7.00	9.60	(2.60)
39 Labels, Tape, etc., Glue & Cement	500.00	734.71	(234.71)
40 Shipping Cartons			
41 Consumable Supplies	81.00	55.54	25.46
42 Loose & Hand Tools	33.00	13.55	19.45
46 Miscellaneous	9.00	7.51	1.49
Total	1705.00	1920.57	(215.57)
OTHER OVERHEAD expenses:			
Insurance, power, taxes, social			
security, depreciation, group			
insurance & pension	1875.22	1472.46	402.76
DEFECTIVE WORK (memo)	600.00	251.04	348.96
DIRECT LABOR	6094.00	5915.60	178.40

the supervisors to discuss spending. At these meetings the supervisors were encouraged to discuss their performance as indicated by the budget report. When the system was first installed, the cost accountant did most of the talking, but with increasing familiarity with the costs for which they were responsible, each supervisor gradually became "cost conscious," and after a short time each supervisor knew approximately

Exhibit H (20–29)   **Overhead summary and statistics**

Plant—Holyoke   Period Ending—August 31

Dept. No.	Description	Direct Labor	Actual Expense	Budgeted Expense	(Loss) or Gain on Budget	Absorbed Expense	Over- or (Under-) absorbed
1							
2	Spray	2,990.25	6,464.64	7,103.64	639.00	6,180.50	(284.14)
3	Coating	5,915.60	12,829.53	13,981.05	1,151.52	11,831.20	(998.33)
4	Filing	998.83	2,590.83	2,190.20	(400.63)	1,937.73	(653.10)
4–I							
4–C							
4–5							
5	Sanding	1,637.53	3,907.74	5,243.47	1,335.73	4,489.05	581.31
6	Buffing	6,175.78	11,275.76	10,750.25	(525.51)	11,888.76	613.00
7							
8	Assemble and pack	4,788.60	8,846.48	8,998.58	152.10	9,577.20	730.72
9							
10							
11							
12							
14							
15							
	Total plant	22,506.59	45,914.98	48,267.19	2,352.21	45,904.44	(10.54)

what the monthly performance would be, even before seeing the budget comparison report.

The supervisor in charge of the coating department was particularly interested in controlling the overhead costs under his jurisdiction. Every month he discussed the analysis of overhead expenses with the factory manager and the cost accountant to evaluate with them the performance of his department. During the first week of September, he received the analysis of overhead expenses for August (Exhibit G), and he checked all the items carefully to learn if there were any costs out of line with his expectations for that month. He copied the August figures onto a sheet (Exhibit I) on which he had previously summarized the figures for recent months (except for July, which included a vacation shutdown). After he felt that he had a good idea of his cost position, he arranged for a meeting with the factory manager and the cost accountant to review the situation with them.

Required:

a. What are the major purposes of the standards developed by the company?

b. How does the company develop standard overhead rates? How often do you think they should be changed?

c. What steps are involved in the development of the standard cost sheet (Exhibit D)? How accurate do you judge the figures to be?

d. Try to explain fully the basis of each entry in Exhibit F. In particular, what are the possible causes of the $138.32 credit to Direct Materials, and the $1,259.07 credit to Work in Process Inventory labeled "adjustment to physical inventory" in Exhibit F?

Exhibit I (20–29)
Summary of performance in the coating department

	April Actual	April (Over) or Under	May Actual	May (Over) or Under	June Actual	June (Over) or Under	August Actual	August (Over) or Under
Indirect labor:								
01 Supervision	811	(36)	782	(7)	756	19	756	19
08 General labor	654	(119)	558	(23)	418	22	171	234
10 Idle and lost time	—	—	—	—	—	—	2	(2)
11 Guaranteed rate cost	313	6	154	165	50	213	28	216
16 Overtime bonus	63	32	45	50	37	43	33	42
19 Repairs and maintenance—machinery and equipment	89	76	30	135	35	125	38	112
17 Vacations	—	—	—	—	—	—	46	(46)
Total	1,930	(41)	1,569	320	1,296	422	1,074	575
Indirect supplies:								
31 Repairs and maintenance—machinery and equipment	5	20	85	(60)	176	(156)	360	(340)
33 Repairs and maintenance—trucks	—	—	—	—	—	—	—	—
35 Acetone and isotone	1,300	85	1,134	251	1,031	109	739	316
36 Buffing compounds and buffs	—	—	—	—	—	—	—	—
37 Sandpaper and sandbelts	10	(1)	14	(5)	5	3	10	(3)
39 Labels, tape, etc., glue and cement	575	85	462	199	182	358	735	(235)
40 Shipping cartons	—	—	—	—	—	—	—	—
41 Consumable supplies	66	40	116	(10)	48	40	56	25
42 Loose and hand tools	37	6	14	29	10	25	14	19
46 Miscellaneous	27	(14)	9	3	9	1	8	1
Total	2,020	221	1,834	407	1,461	380	1,922	(217)
Other overhead expenses: Insurance, power, taxes, social security, depreciation, group insurance, and pension	1,456	561	2,014	3	1,836	74	1,472	403
Defective work (memo)	391	209	656	(56)	594	6	251	349
Direct labor	7,812	157	8,024	(55)	6,599	(36)	5,916	178

e. Explain so as to distinguish them clearly from one another, the figures $12,829.53, $13,981.05, and $11,831.20 shown for the coating department on Exhibit H.

f. If you were the cost supervisor, what evaluation would you make of the performance of the coating department supervisor in controlling his overhead costs? About which items in Exhibits G–I would you be likely to question him?

g. How many dollars of the coating department variances reported in Exhibit H are attributable to "Charges from Other Departments"? Of what significance are these variances to *(a)* the coating department, and *(b)* the service departments that created these charges? Should they be included in the overhead summary and statistics report?

21

Revenue and Nonmanufacturing Cost Variances

OBJECTIVES

To understand the analyses made to compare budget plans and actual results for revenues and for nonmanufacturing costs.

In this chapter, we discuss variances for revenues and nonmanufacturing costs and how they are used to measure performance. The basic principles are the same as those presented in Chapters 18 through 20.

A variance is the difference between a predetermined norm and the actual results for a period. To illustrate the development of revenue and nonmanufacturing cost variances, we continue the example of Boxx Company. The basic facts about the Boxx Company are reviewed in Illustration 21–1. The overall comparison between Boxx Company's master budget, flexible budget, and actual costs, as originally presented in Chapter 18, is reproduced in Illustration 21–2.

Reporting on marketing performance

Like manufacturing managers, marketing managers are often evaluated on the basis of planned results versus actual outcomes. Marketing performance analysis, however, considers revenues as well as marketing costs. During the planning stage, standards are set for selling prices, marketing costs, and sales volume. The results of this planning activity are captured in the master budget for marketing.

During the period, sales transactions take place and costs are incurred by the marketing division. At the end of the period, the actual results are compiled. A flexible budget is also prepared that adjusts the master budget for the actual sales volume. The results are compared in a marketing performance report.

Illustration 21–1   **Boxx Company**

	Actual	Master budget
Sales price	$21 per crate	$20 per crate
Sales volume	10,000 crates	8,000 crates
Variable manufacturing costs	$10.544 per crate	$10 per crate
Variable marketing and administrative costs	$1.10 per crate	$1 per crate
Fixed manufacturing costs	$21,000	$20,000
Fixed marketing and administrative costs	44,000	40,000

Illustration 21-2
Comparison of actual to master budget

	(1) Actual (based on actual activity of 10,000 units sold)	(2) Manufacturing variances	(3) Marketing and administrative variances	(4) Sales price variances	(5) Flexible budget (based on actual activity of 10,000 units sold)	(6) Activity (sales volume) variance	(7) Master budget plan (based on a prediction of 8,000 units sold)
Sales revenue	$210,000	—	—	$10,000 F	$200,000	$40,000 F	$160,000
Less:							
Variable manufacturing costs	105,440	$5,440 U	—	—	100,000	20,000 U	80,000
Variable marketing and administrative costs	11,000	—	$1,000 U	—	10,000	2,000 U	8,000
Contribution margin	93,560	5,440 U	1,000 U	10,000 F	90,000	18,000 F	72,000
Less:							
Fixed manufacturing costs	21,000	1,000 U	—	—	20,000	—	20,000
Fixed marketing and administrative costs	44,000	—	4,000 U	—	40,000	—	40,000
Operating profits	$ 28,560	$6,440 U	$5,000 U	$10,000 F	$ 30,000	$18,000 F	$ 12,000

→ Total variance from flexible budget = $1,440 U

→ Total variance from master budget = $16,560F

A marketing performance report for the Boxx Company is presented in Illustration 21–3. This report is based on the data in Illustration 21–2, but contains greater detail for marketing activities. This allows marketing management to focus attention on costs and/or revenue items that contribute most significantly to variations from plans.

The marketing report differs from the manufacturing cost variance report in several other respects as well. It omits manufacturing variances and fixed manufacturing costs. Standard variable manufacturing costs are included in this report only because they are needed to derive the contribution margin, which is important for assessing marketing performance. The bottom line of the report is a marketing contribution to company profits rather than an operating profit. These differences arise because the report focuses on marketing and administrative management's responsibilities. Costs that are not controllable by marketing and administrative management are excluded.

Sales price and activity variances

Price and activity[1] variances for revenue are derived as shown in Illustration 21–4. The general technique is similar to the one used to derive manufacturing variances in Chapter 19.

Contribution margin variances

Decision makers sometimes find revenue activity variances inadequate or misleading if they do not take into account the variable costs of the products sold. For example, based on Illustration 21–4, it would not be correct to state that favorable sales results have increased operating profits by $50,000 ($10,000 favorable price variance plus $40,000 favorable activity variance), because the favorable *activity* variance is partly offset by the variable costs of the additional 2,000 crates produced and sold. The relevant additional cost is, of course, the extra variable costs incurred at this higher activity level.

A contribution margin variance can be used to combine the sales revenue effects and the variable costs of the additional units sold. The standard variable cost per unit is subtracted from the (actual or standard) unit sales price to provide the unit contribution margin. The resulting variance gives us the impact on profit from the changes in sales volumes. *Using the standard variable cost per unit, instead of actual, allows us to hold cost variances constant so that we can isolate the effect of sales volume on profits.*

The contribution margin variances for the Boxx Company are presented in Illustration 21–5. Note that this framework contains one modification. *"Actual" is not the actual total contribution margin but the actual revenue minus standard variable costs.* Note the sales price variance is the same, whether we use the revenue variance (Illustration 21–4) or the contribution margin variance (Illustration 21–5). However, the activity variance differs.

---

[1] This is also called a *sales volume variance.*

Illustration 21–3
Marketing performance report, Boxx Company

	Actual (10,000 units)	Marketing and administrative cost variances	Sales price variance	Flexible budget (10,000 units)	Activity variance	Master budget (8,000 units)
Sales revenue	$210,000	—	$10,000 F	$200,000	$40,000 F	$160,000
Less: Standard variable manufacturing costs	100,000			100,000	20,000 U	80,000
Variable marketing and administrative costs:						
Commissions	2,400	—		2,400		
Advertising	1,300	$ 200 U		1,100		
Packaging	6,100	900 U		5,200		
Other	1,200	100 F		1,300		
Subtotal	$ 11,000	$1,000 U		10,000		
Contribution margin	99,000	1,000 U	$10,000 F	90,000	2,000 U 18,000 F	8,000 72,000
Less: fixed marketing and administrative costs	44,000	4,000 U		40,000		40,000
Marketing and administrative profit contribution	$ 55,000	$5,000 U	$10,000 F	$ 50,000	$18,000 F	$ 32,000

Illustration 21–4

Revenue variances, Boxx Company (May)

Actual	**Flexible sales budget**	**Master sales budget**
Actual sales price (AP) times actual quantity (AQ) of units sold	Estimated or standard price (SP) times actual quantity (AQ) of units sold	Estimated or standard price (SP) times estimated or standard quantity (SQ) of units sold
AP × AQ	**SP × AQ**	**SP × SQ**
$21 × 10,000 crates = $210,000	$20 × 10,000 crates = $200,000	$20 × 8,000 crates = $160,000

Price variance:
$210,000 − $200,000

Activity variance:
$200,000 − $160,000

= $10,000 F   = $40,000 F

Total variance = $50,000 F

Shortcut
formulas:

$(AP \times AQ) - (SP \times AQ)$
$= (AP - SP) \times AQ$
$= (\$21 - \$20) \times 10,000$
$= \$10,000 \text{ F}$

$(SP \times AQ) - (SP \times SQ)$
$= SP \times (AQ - SQ)$
$= \$20 \times (10,000 - 8,000)$
$= \$40,000 \text{ F}$

Illustration 21–5

Contribution margin variances, Boxx Company (May)

"Actual"	**Flexible sales budget**	**Master sales budget**
[*Actual* sales price (AP) minus standard variable cost (SV)] times *actual* quantity (AQ)	[*Standard* sale price (SP) minus standard variable cost (SV)] times *actual* quantity (AQ)	[*Standard* sales price (SP) minus standard variable cost (SV)] times *standard* quantity (SQ) of units sold
(AP − SV) × AQ	**(SP − SV) × AQ**	**(SP − SV) × SQ**
($21 − $11) × 10,000 crates = $100,000	($20 − $11) × 10,000 crates = $90,000	($20 − $11) × 8,000 crates = $72,000

Price variance:
$100,000 − $90,000

Activity variance:
$90,000 − $72,000

= $10,000 F   = $18,000 F

Total variance = $28,000 F

Shortcut
formulas:

$[(AP - SV) \times AQ] - [(SP - SV) \times AQ]$
$= [(AP - SV) - (SP - SV)] \times AQ$
$= [(\$21 - \$11) - (\$20 - \$11)] \times 10,000$
$= \$10,000 \text{ F}$

$[(SP - SV) \times AQ] - [(SP - SV) \times SQ]$
$= (SP - SV) \times (AQ - SQ)$
$= (\$20 - \$11) \times (10,000 - 8,000)$
$= \$18,000 \text{ F}$

Sales incentives   Sales personnel are often given commissions or bonuses based on sales revenue. Suppose a salesperson has an opportunity to sell *one* of the following two products to a customer, *but not both:*

Revenue	Standard variable cost	Contribution margin
Product A: $100,000	$90,000	$10,000
Product B: $ 50,000	30,000	20,000

If the salesperson's commission is 2 percent of sales, he or she would clearly prefer to sell Product A, even though Product B provides a greater contribution to profits.

An alternative incentive plan would give the salesperson a commission based on contribution margin. If the salesperson's commission were 10 percent of contribution margin, *both* the salesperson and the company would benefit from the sale of Product B.

In general, it is best to tie employee incentives as close to organizational goals as possible. If the organizational goal is to maximize current sales, a commission based on sales makes sense. If the goal is current profit maximization, a commission based on contribution margins may be more appropriate.

Gross margin variances   Calculation of the contribution margin variance requires a breakdown of costs into fixed and variable portions. If this breakdown has not been made, a gross margin variance is sometimes calculated in place of the contribution margin variances. The basic approach is the same as for contribution margin variances except that the calculation is based on unit gross margin instead of a unit contribution margin.

Market share variance and industry volume variance

Managers frequently wonder whether the sales activity variance is due to general market conditions or to a change in the company's market share. The cause may be significant because of promotional strategies and/or pricing policies. At Boxx Company, for example, the marketing vice president wondered about the cause of the favorable activity variance of 2,000 units: "Our estimated share of the market was 20 percent. We projected industry sales of 40,000 crates, of which we would sell 8,000. We actually sold 10,000 crates. Was that because our share of the market went up from 20 percent to 25 percent (25% × 40,000 crates = 10,000 crates)? Or did we just hold our own at 20 percent, while the market increased to 50,000 crates (20% × 50,000 crates = 10,000 crates)?"

There are numerous sources of data available about industry volume (for example, trade journals, government census data). When these data are available, the activity variance could be divided into an industry volume variance and a market share variance. The industry volume variance tells how much of the sales activity variance is due to changes in industry volume. The market share variance tells how much of the activity variance is due to changes in market share. The market share variance is usually more controllable by the marketing department and is a measure of their performance.

The marketing vice president at Boxx Company learned that the favorable sales activity resulted from an improvement in both industry volume and market share. Industry volume went up from 40,000 units to 41,667, while market share went up from 20 percent to 24 percent. Hence the 2,000-unit favorable activity variance can be broken down into an industry effect and a market share effect, as shown in Illustration 21–6. Of the 2,000-unit increase in company volume, 333 crates, which is 20% of 1,667 units, is due to the increase in industry volume (holding market share constant), while 1,667 crates, which is 4% of 41,667 units, is due to an increased share of the market. Multiplying each figure by the *standard contribution margin* gives the impact of these variances on operating profits:

$$\text{Industry volume: } (\$20 - \$11) \times 333 \text{ crates} = \$\ 3{,}000 \text{ F}$$
$$\text{Market share: } \ \ \ (\$20 - \$11) \times 1{,}667 \text{ crates} = \$15{,}000 \text{ F}$$
$$\text{Total activity } \ \ \ (\$20 - \$11) \times 2{,}000 \text{ crates} = \$18{,}000 \text{ F}$$

Calculation of these variances is also shown in Illustration 21–7.

Use of the industry volume and market share variances enables management to separate that portion of the activity variance that coincides with changes in the overall industry from that which is specific to the company. Favorable market share variances indicate that the company is achieving better-than-industry-average volume changes. This can be very important information to a company sensitive about its market share.

Illustration 21–6

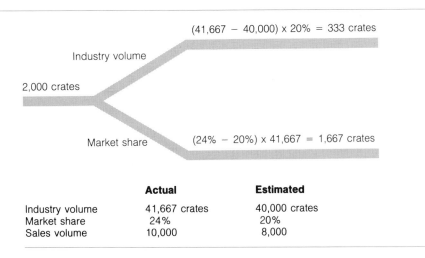

	Actual	Estimated
Industry volume	41,667 crates	40,000 crates
Market share	24%	20%
Sales volume	10,000	8,000

Illustration 21–7   **Industry volume and market share variances, Boxx Company (May)**

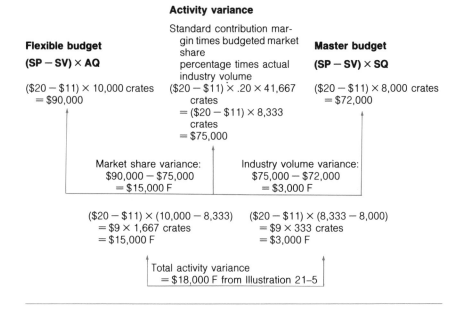

Activity variance

Flexible budget	Standard contribution margin times budgeted market share percentage times actual industry volume	Master budget
(SP – SV) × AQ		(SP – SV) × SQ
($20 – $11) × 10,000 crates = $90,000	($20 – $11) × .20 × 41,667 crates = ($20 – $11) × 8,333 crates = $75,000	($20 – $11) × 8,000 crates = $72,000

Market share variance:
$90,000 – $75,000
= $15,000 F

Industry volume variance:
$75,000 – $72,000
= $3,000 F

($20 – $11) × (10,000 – 8,333)
= $9 × 1,667 crates
= $15,000 F

($20 – $11) × (8,333 – 8,000)
= $9 × 333 crates
= $3,000 F

Total activity variance
= $18,000 F from Illustration 21–5

Sales mix variances

When a company sells multiple products, a sales mix variance is sometimes useful information. This is particularly so if the products are substitutes for each other. For example, an automobile dealer sells two kinds of cars: Super and Standard. For October, the estimated sales for the company were 1,000 cars: 500 Super models and 500 Standard models. The Super models were expected to have a contribution margin of $2,000 per car, while the Standard models were expected to have a contribution margin of $1,000 per car. Thus, the budgeted total contribution for October was:

Super: 500 at $2,000	$1,000,000	
Standard: 500 at $1,000	500,000	
Total contribution	$1,500,000	

When the results for October were tabulated, the company had sold 1,000 cars, and each model had provided the predicted contribution margin per unit. But the total contribution was a disappointing $1,200,000 because instead of the predicted 50–50 mix of cars sold, the mix was 20–80 (20 percent Super, 80 percent Standard), with the following results:

Super: 200 at $2,000	$ 400,000	
Standard: 800 at $1,000	800,000	
Total contribution	$1,200,000	

The $300,000 decrease from the budgeted contribution margin is called the *sales mix variance.* In this case, it occurred because 300 fewer Super models were sold (for a loss of 300 × $2,000 = $600,000), while 300 more Standard models were sold (for a gain of 300 × $1,000 = $300,000). The net effect is a loss of $1,000 in contribution margin for each Standard model that was sold instead of a Super model. (This emphasizes the importance of the substitutability assumption. If a store sells, among other things, jewelry and garden tractors, the mix variance would probably not be as useful as when comparing two different kinds of cars, or two kinds of garden tractors or two kinds of jewelry.)

Computation of sales mix variances

Assume Electron Company makes and sells two electronic games: Spacetrack and Earth Evaders. The estimated and actual results for the first quarter of the year were as follows:

	Spacetrack	Earth Evaders	Total
Standard sales price per unit	$20	$10	—
Actual sales price per unit	$21	$ 9	—
Standard variable cost per unit	$10	$ 5	—
Estimated sales volume	120,000	80,000	200,000
Estimated sales activity percentage	60%	40%	100%
Actual sales volume	140,000	140,000	280,000
Actual sales activity percentage	50%	50%	100%

A two-way analysis of contribution margin variance is shown in Illustration 21–8. This is the same approach that we presented in the section about contribution margin variances.

There are many ways to calculate sales mix variances. Each starts with the same total variance, but then breaks it down in a different manner. Our computation of the sales mix variances allows us to break down the sales activity variance into two components: sales mix and sales quantity. (Various terms are used here, including sales volume, pure sales volume, and pure sales quantity.) The *sales mix variance* measures the impact of substitution (it appears that Earth Evaders has been substituted for Spacetracks), while the sales quantity variance measures the variance in sales quantity, holding the sales mix constant.

Calculations for this example are presented in Illustration 21–9. The sales price variance is unaffected by our analysis, while the activity variance is broken down into the mix and quantity variances.

Source of the sales mix variance While we have calculated each product mix variance to show exact sources, the *total* mix variance ($140,000 U) is most frequently used. In this example, the unfavorable mix variance is caused

Illustration 21–8   **Contribution margin variances, Electron Company (first quarter)**

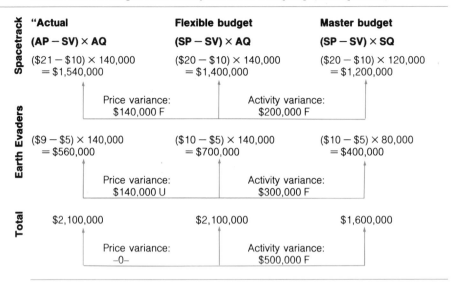

by the substitution of the lower-contribution Earth Evaders for the higher-contribution Spacetracks. To be precise, the substitutions are:

Decrease in Spacetracks:	28,000 @ $10 = $280,000 U	
Increase in Earth Evaders:	28,000 @ $5 = 140,000 F	
Net effect in units:	–0–	
Net effect in dollars		$140,000 U

The quantity variance results from the sale of 80,000 more units than expected. More precisely:

Spacetracks:	(168,000 − 120,000) × $10 = $480,000 F	
Earth Evaders:	(112,000 − 80,000) × $5 = 160,000 F	
Total quantity variance	80,000 units	$640,000 F

By separating the activity variance into its mix and quantity components, we have isolated the pure mix effect by holding constant the quantity effects, and we have isolated the pure quantity effect by holding constant the mix effect.

Nonmanufacturing cost variances

The computation of the activity variance in Illustration 21–2 includes a deduction of $2,000 for an increase in variable marketing and administrative costs:

$$\begin{array}{c}\text{Increase in variable}\\\text{marketing and}\\\text{administrative costs}\end{array} = \begin{array}{c}\text{Estimated (or}\\\text{standard) unit}\\\text{variable cost}\end{array} \times \left(\begin{array}{cc}\text{Actual sales} & \text{Master budget}\\\text{volume} & \text{sales volume}\end{array}\right)$$

$$\$1 \times (10{,}000 \text{ crates} - 8{,}000 \text{ crates}) = \underline{\underline{\$2{,}000 \text{ U}}}$$

Because the sales volume was higher than expected, these variable costs would be expected to increase. The increase in sales revenue that results from increased sales volume is at least partially offset by the increase in variable marketing and administrative costs.

The remaining variance is divided into fixed and variable portions as shown in Illustration 21–2.

$$\begin{array}{c}\text{Fixed marketing and}\\\text{administrative costs}\end{array} = \text{Actual} - \text{Budget}$$

$$= \$44{,}000 - \$40{,}000 = \underline{\underline{\$4{,}000 \text{ U}}}$$

Illustration 21–9 **Mix and quantity variances, Electron Company (first quarter)**

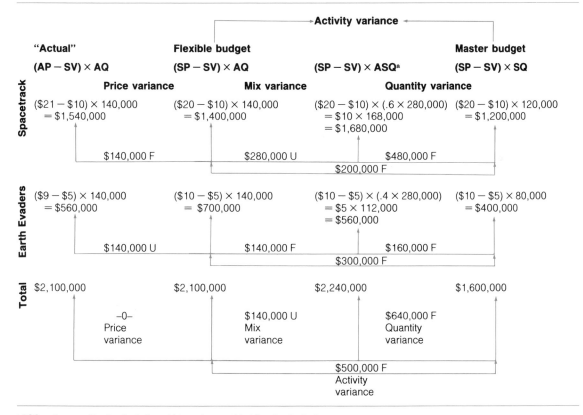

[a] ASQ = the quantity of units that would have been sold at the standard mix.

$$\begin{matrix}\text{Variable marketing and} \\ \text{administrative costs}\end{matrix} = \begin{pmatrix}\text{Actual unit} \\ \text{cost}\end{pmatrix} - \begin{matrix}\text{Standard} \\ \text{unit cost}\end{matrix} \times \begin{matrix}\text{Actual sales} \\ \text{volume}\end{matrix}$$

$$(\$1.10 - \$1.00) \times 10{,}000 \text{ crates} = \underline{\underline{\$1{,}000 \text{ U}}}$$

These variances are usually broken down by department, product line, and sales territory to provide more information about their causes and to assign responsibility for them.

Efficiency measures

In some cases, a price and efficiency variance can be used to analyze variable marketing and administrative costs. The key is to derive a reliable measure of activity that can be used as a basis for calculating an efficiency variance. Ideally, this requires some quantitative input that can be linked to output. In practice, one input is often linked to another input rather than directly to an output.

For example, in the accounts receivable department of a retail merchandiser, the personnel are expected to contact 10 delinquent customers per hour. The standard labor cost is $12 per hour including benefits. During July, 7,000 hours were worked, 65,000 contacts were made, and the average wage rate was $13 per hour. The price and efficiency variances are as shown:

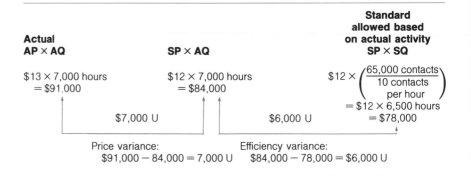

These calculations are very similar to the ones we used for manufacturing labor variances in Chapter 19. One important difference, however, is that we have not made the ideal linkage between the input measure of activity, which is customer contacts and the *output* measure, which is collections on accounts receivable. In some cases, this is possible, but often it is not. In this example, we expect 65,000 customer contacts to require 6,500 labor-hours, but we don't know how many customer contacts are required per dollar collected.

Variance analysis in non-manufacturing settings

The analysis of price and efficiency variances in nonmanufacturing settings is increasing. We find banks, fast-food outlets, hospitals, consulting firms, retail stores, and many others applying the variance analysis techniques that were discussed in Chapter 19 to their labor and overhead costs. The analysis requires some assumed relationship between inputs and outputs. Some examples are:

Department	Input	Output
Mailing	Labor-hours worked	Number of pieces mailed
Personnel	Labor-hours worked	Number of personnel changes processed
Food service	Hours worked	Number of meals served
Consulting	Billable hours worked	Customer revenues
Nursing	Labor-hours worked	Patients (of a particular care level) served
Check processing	Computer hours worked	Checks processed

Some of these attempts to measure efficiency are stretched a bit far. For example, suppose that a company evaluated an executive's efficiency based on the relationship between hours worked and the number of telephone calls handled. In this case, the linkage between number of telephone calls and company success would be tenuous at best. In general, jobs with routine tasks lend themselves to efficiency measures, while jobs with nonroutine tasks—like most administrative positions—do not.

Attempts to measure efficiency sometimes leads to employee resentment. In other cases, the measurement results in both better performance and better morale. Often, employee participation in the measurement process helps improve morale, while a top-down imposed measurement system provokes employee resentment.

Summary

Revenue variances are explained in terms of changes in activity and changes in price or contribution margin. If several products are sold, sales activity variance may be subdivided into a pure quantity and sales mix variance. Revenue variances may also be caused by market share or industry wide volume factors.

Marketing and administrative cost variances are analyzed in terms of price, efficiency, and activity components, much like manufacturing cost variances.

Terms and concepts

The following terms and concepts should be familiar to you after reading this chapter:

Activity variance	**Market share variance**
Contribution margin variance	**Revenue variance**
Gross margin variance	**Sales mix variance**
Industry volume variance	**Sales quantity variance**

Self-study problem No. 1*

Comprehensive revenue and nonmanufacturing cost variance analysis

Professors Shank and Churchill note that variances may be studied on several different levels. At one level, the difference between budgeted and actual results are considered. At the next level, activity variances are isolated. At the third level, the effects of price and efficiency variations are noted. For example, a company plans to sell 2,000 units of product at $5 per unit. Variable cost of sales are budgeted at $2 per unit and variable marketing and administrative costs at $1 per unit. Fixed manufacturing costs are estimated at $750 and fixed marketing costs at $250.

During the period, 2,100 units are sold at a price of $5.25 each. Variable cost of sales are $2.20. Variable marketing and administrative costs are $1.09. Fixed manufacturing costs are $730. Actual fixed marketing costs are $340.

Required:

Prepare an analysis of the revenue and marketing cost variances for these data.

Solution to self-study problem No. 1

	Actual (standard manufacturing)	Sales price variance	Marketing cost variance	Flexible budget (2,100 at $5)	Activity variance	Master budget (2,000 at $5)
Sales revenue	$11,025[a]	$525 F		$10,500	$500 F	$10,000
Variable cost of sales	(4,200)			(4,200)	200 U	(4,000)
Variable marketing and administrative costs	(2,289)[b]		$189 U	(2,100)	100 U	(2,000)
Contribution margin	4,536	525 F	189 U	4,200	200 F	4,000
Fixed costs marketing	(340)		90 U	(250)		(250)
M. & A. contribution to profit	$ 4,196	525 F	$279 U	$ 3,950	$200 F	$ 3,750

[a] 2100 @ $5.25 = $11,025.
[b] 2100 @ $1.09 = $2,289.

Self-study problem No. 2

Revenue mix analysis

Assume that the master budget has sales of 1,200 units of Product A and 800 units of Product B. Actual sales volumes were 1,320 of Product A and 780 of Product B. The expected contribution per unit of Product A was $1, and the expected contribution of Product B was $3.50.

Product A actually sold for 10 percent more than the expected price of $4 per unit. Product B sold for $6.688 per unit while the expected price was $6.50.

Required:

Prepare an analysis of the effect of changes in sales mix on contribution.

---

* Adapted from John K. Shank and Neil C. Churchill "Variance Analysis: A Management-Oriented Approach," *The Accounting Review,* October 1977, pp. 950–57.

Solution to self-study problem No. 2

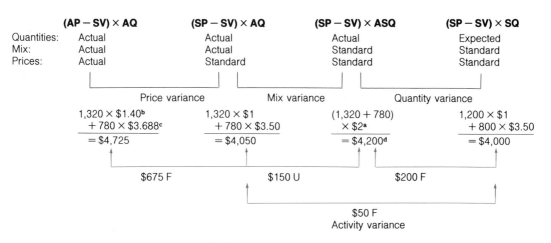

	$(AP - SV) \times AQ$	$(SP - SV) \times AQ$	$(SP - SV) \times ASQ$	$(SP - SV) \times SQ$
Quantities:	Actual	Actual	Actual	Expected
Mix:	Actual	Actual	Standard	Standard
Prices:	Actual	Standard	Standard	Standard

Price variance   Mix variance   Quantity variance

$1,320 \times \$1.40^b$ $\quad$ $1,320 \times \$1$ $\quad$ $(1,320 + 780)$ $\quad$ $1,200 \times \$1$
$+ 780 \times \$3.688^c$ $\quad$ $+ 780 \times \$3.50$ $\quad\quad \times \$2^a$ $\quad$ $+ 800 \times \$3.50$
$= \$4,725$ $\quad\quad = \$4,050$ $\quad\quad = \$4,200^d$ $\quad\quad = \$4,000$

$\$675$ F $\quad\quad\quad$ $\$150$ U $\quad\quad\quad$ $\$200$ F

$\$50$ F
Activity variance

[a] Weighted-average contribution: $\$2$ per unit $= \dfrac{\$4,000}{1,200 + 800}$

[b] "Actual" contribution margin of A $= \$4.40 - \$4.00 + \$1.00 = \$1.40$.

[c] "Actual" contribution margin of B $= \$6.688 - \$6.50 + \$3.50 = \$3.688$.

[d] Alternative computation: $(\$1 \times 2,100 \times .6) + (\$3.50 \times 2,100 \times .4) = \$4,200$.

Self-study problem No. 3

Industry effects on contribution

Insta-Pour Concrete, Inc., produces precast beams for highway and other bridge construction. The company's master budget called for sales of 20,000 beams which would have been 16 percent of the market in their market area. The contribution margin on each beam is $215. During the year, 21,000 beams were sold and a contribution margin of $4,620,000 was achieved using standard costs. The company's market share had increased to 22 percent of the total market.

Required:

Analyze the price, industry, and market share effects on the company's contribution.

Solution to Self-study problem No. 3

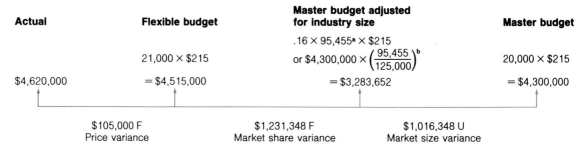

Actual	Flexible budget	Master budget adjusted for industry size	Master budget
		$.16 \times 95,455^a \times \$215$	
	$21,000 \times \$215$	or $\$4,300,000 \times \left(\dfrac{95,455}{125,000}\right)^b$	$20,000 \times \$215$
$\$4,620,000$	$= \$4,515,000$	$= \$3,283,652$	$= \$4,300,000$

$\$105,000$ F	$\$1,231,348$ F	$\$1,016,348$ U
Price variance	Market share variance	Market size variance

[a] $\dfrac{21,000}{.22} = 95,455$ estimated size of market during the period.

[b] $\dfrac{20,000}{.16} = 125,000$ estimated size of market at master budget preparation time.

Self-study problem No. 4

Analyze profit contribution of marketing activities

Purple Mountain Nursery sells landscape evergreens. The master budget called for sales of 250,000 trees at a price of $15 per tree. Variable costs to purchase trees were budgeted at $7 per tree. Variable marketing and administrative costs were estimated to cost $1.75 per tree. Fixed marketing and administrative costs were budgeted at $700,000.

During the year, 220,000 trees were sold at a price of $16 each. The variable purchase costs were $7, and variable marketing and administrative costs were $319,000. Fixed marketing and administrative costs were actually $735,000.

Required:

Analyze the causes for the change in profit.

Solution to self-study problem No. 4

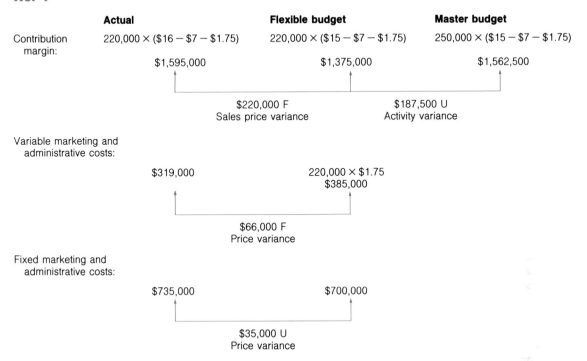

Questions

21–1.   Why would marketing management receive a performance report that included greater detail about the marketing costs?

21–2.   Why are variable manufacturing costs included in the marketing department's performance report? After all, those costs are incurred in the production departments.

21–3.   We normally deduct standard costs from the actual revenues when analyzing revenue variances. Why not use actual costs and actual revenues?

21–4.   The impact of changes in inventories is ignored in the marketing and administrative performance reports. Why is this so?

21–5.   Why is there no efficiency variance for revenues?

21–6.   The marketing manager of a company noted: "We had a favorable revenue activity variance of $425,000 yet company profits only went up by $114,000. Some part of the organization has dropped the ball—let's find out where the problem is and straighten it out." Comment on this remark.

21–7.   A production manager was debating with company management because production had been charged with a large unfavorable production volume variance. The production manager explained: "After all, if marketing had lined up sales for these units we would not have been forced to cut production. Marketing should be charged with the production volume variance, not production." Do you agree with the production manager? Why or why not?

21–8. What advantage does the industry volume variance approach offer for the analysis of contribution margin variances?

21–9. Could a small-loan company take advantage of the type of variance analysis discussed in this chapter to analyze the costs of processing loan payments? Give details to support your conclusion.

21–10. If there is no volume variance and no price variance, is there any need to compute a mix variance?

21–11. How could a CPA firm use the mix variance to analyze its revenues?

21–12. A company has three products that must be purchased in a single package. Is there any benefit to computing a sales mix variance under these circumstances?

Exercises

21–13. Compute revenue variances

On-the-Road Picnic Supplies manufactures and sells picnic coolers. The business is very competitive. The master budget for last year called for sales of 200,000 units at $9 each. However, as the summer season approached management realized that they could not sell 200,000 units at the $9 price. Rather, they would have to offer price concessions of $.50 per unit. At the end of the sales season, further price concessions were made. Actual results showed sales of 185,000 units at an average price of $8.35 each.

Required:

Compute the revenue variances for On-the-Road Picnic Supplies.

21–14. Analyze revenue variances

On-the-Road Picnic Supplies is trying to decide what to do in the coming year given the events that transpired last year (see Exercise 21–13). Management conducted a marketing survey which indicated that the company had two sales alternatives:

Sell 200,000 units at $8 each

or

Sell 165,000 units at $9.50 each

The company has variable costs of $3.65 per unit.

Required:

Compare the two alternatives and isolate the effect of volume and price differences on the two alternatives. Hint: Treat Alternative B as "master budget" and the other as "actual."

21–15. Compute marketing revenue and cost variances

Season-All, Inc., manufactures bulk artificial seasonings for use in processed foods. A seasoning called tryptich-aldehyde was budgeted to sell in 20 liter drums at a price of $48 per drum. The company expected to sell 150,000 drums. Variable manufacturing costs are $3.25 per drum. Variable marketing costs are $6.80 per drum.

During the year, 120,000 drums were sold at a price of $47.50. Variable manufacturing costs were $3.20 per drum, and variable marketing costs were $7.20 per drum.

Required:

Prepare an analysis of the marketing department's contribution margin for the period.

21–16. Analyze marketing cost variances

High Pressure Sales, Inc., uses telephone solicitation to sell products. The company has set standards that call for $450 of sales per hour of telephone time. Telephone solicitors receive a commission of 10 percent per dollar of sales. Other variable costs including costs of sales in the operation are budgeted to amount to 45 percent of sales volume. Fixed costs are budgeted at $411,500 per month. The number of sales hours per month are determined based on the number of days in a month less an allowance for idle time, scheduling, and other inefficiencies. This month, the company expected 180 hours of telephone calling time for each of 40 callers.

During the month, $2,700,000 of revenues were earned. Actual calling hours amounted to 7,050. The following marketing and administrative cost data for the period are provided below:

	Actual	Master budget
Cost of sales	$810,000	$972,000
Telephone time charges	32,200	32,400
Delivery services	161,100	194,400
Uncollectible accounts	121,500	145,800
Other variable costs	112,700	113,400
Fixed costs	409,000	411,500

Required:

Using sales dollars as a basis for analysis, compute the marketing cost variances for the period.

21–17. Efficiency measures for nonmanufacturing costs

Use the data for High Pressure Sales, Inc., to measure the efficiency of marketing operations for the month. Hint: Consider sales volume as an output measure and calling hours as an input.

21–18. Revenue mix variances

Gershwin, Rodgers, Bach & Hammerstein operate an accounting firm with partners and staff members. Each billable hour of partner time has a budgeted contribution of $100. Each billable hour of staff time has a budgeted contribution of $30. This month, the partnership budget called for 8,250 billable partner hours and 34,650 staff hours. Actual results were as follows:

Partner contribution: $855,000   9,000 hours
Staff contribution: $979,200   34,000

Required:

Compute the contribution margin variances (including the mix variance) for these data.

21–19. Revenue mix variances

Personna, Inc., sells two models of personal hair care kits. The Basic model has a contribution of $5.35 per unit while the Ultra model contributes $14.60 per unit. The master budget called for sales of 400,000 Basics and 180,000 Ultras during the current year. Actual results showed sales of 300,000 Basic with a contribution of $5.40 per unit and 200,000 Ultras with a contribution of $14.75 per unit.

Required:

Compute the revenue price, mix, and quantity variances for these data.

21–20. Relate revenue variances to industry standards

Oversea Airlines plans its budget and subsequently evaluates sales performance based on "revenue passenger miles." A revenue passenger mile is one paying passenger flying one mile. For this month, the company had estimated its revenues would amount to 20 cents per revenue passenger mile and that 40 million revenue passenger miles would be flown.

As a result of improvement in the economy, 43 million revenue passenger miles were flown this month. The price per revenue passenger mile averaged 20.3 cents. Subsequent analysis by management indicated that the industry had flown 7 percent more passenger miles this month than had been expected.

Required:

Isolate the price, industry, and market share effects on company revenues for the month.

Problems and cases

21–21. Revenue analysis using industry data and multiple product lines

Arsco Company makes three grades of indoor-outdoor carpets. The sales volume for the annual budget is determined by estimating the total market volume for indoor-outdoor carpet, and then applying the company's prior year market share, adjusted for planned changes due to company programs for the coming year. The volume is apportioned between the three grades based upon the prior year's product mix, again adjusted for planned changes due to company programs for the coming year.

Given below are the company budget for 1988 and the results of operations for 1988.

Budget

	Grade 1	Grade 2	Grade 3	Total
Sales—units (000 omitted)	1,000 rolls	1,000 rolls	2,000 rolls	4,000 rolls
Sales—dollars (in thousands)	$1,000	$2,000	$3,000	$6,000
Variable costs	700	1,600	2,300	4,600
Contribution margin	300	400	700	1,400
Manufacturing fixed cost	200	200	300	700
Product margin	$ 100	$ 200	$ 400	700
Marketing and administrative costs (all fixed)				250
Operating profit				$ 450

Actual

	Grade 1	Grade 2	Grade 3	Total
Sales—units	800 rolls	1,000 rolls	2,100 rolls	3,900 rolls
Sales—dollars (in thousands)	$810	$2,000	$3,000	$5,810
Variable cost	560	1,610	2,320	4,490
Contribution margin	250	390	680	1,320
Manufacturing fixed cost	210	220	315	745
Product margin	$ 40	$ 170	$ 365	575
Marketing and administrative costs (all fixed)				275
Operating profit				$ 300

Industry volume was estimated at 40,000 rolls for budgeting purposes. Actual industry volume for 1988 was 38,000 rolls.

Required:

Prepare an analysis to show the differences between master budget and actual that were due to price, volume, and industry effects.

(CMA adapted)

21–22. Revenue mix variances

Using the data for the Arsco Company (Problem 21–21), analyze the effect of changes in product mix on the revenue of the company.

21–23. Contribution margin variances

The Markley Division of Rosette Industries manufactures and sells patio chairs. The chairs are manufactured in two versions—a metal model and a plastic model of a lesser quality. The company uses its own marketing force to sell the chairs to retail stores and to catalog outlets. Generally, customers purchase both the metal and plastic versions.

The chairs are manufactured on two different assembly lines located in adjoining buildings. The division management and marketing department occupy the third building on the property. The division management includes a division controller responsible for the divisional financial activities and the preparation of reports explaining the differences between actual and budgeted performance. The controller structures these reports such that the marketing activities are distinguished from cost factors so that each can be analyzed separately.

The operating results for the first three months of the fiscal year as compared to the budget are presented in the next column. The budget for the current year was based upon the assumption that Markley Division would maintain its present market share of the estimated total patio chair market (plastic and metal combined). A status report had been sent to corporate management toward the end of the second month indicating that divisional operating profit for the first quarter would probably be about 45 percent below budget; this estimate was just about on target. The division's operating income was below budget even though industry volume for patio chairs increased by 10 percent more than was expected at the time the budget was developed.

Markley Division
Operating Results for the First Quarter

	Actual	Budget	Favorable (unfavorable) relative to the budget
Sale in units:			
Plastic model	60,000	50,000	10,000
Metal model	20,000	25,000	(5,000)
Sales revenue:			
Plastic model	$630,000	$500,000	$130,000
Metal model	300,000	375,000	(75,000)
Total sales	930,000	875,000	55,000
Less variable costs:			
Manufacturing (at standard):			
Plastic model	480,000	400,000	(80,000)
Metal model	200,000	250,000	50,000
Marketing:			
Commissions	46,500	43,750	(2,750)
Bad debt allowance	9,300	8,750	(550)
Total variable costs (except variable manufacturing variances)	735,800	702,500	(33,300)
Contribution margin (except variable manufacturing variances)	194,200	172,500	21,700
Less other costs:			
Variable manufacturing costs variances from standards	49,600	—	(49,600)
Fixed manufacturing costs	49,200	48,000	(1,200)
Fixed marketing administrative costs	38,500	36,000	(2,500)
Corporation offices allocation	18,500	17,500	(1,000)
Total other costs	155,800	101,500	(54,300)
Divisional operational profit	$ 38,400	$ 71,000	$ (32,600)

The manufacturing activities for the quarter resulted in the production of 55,000 plastic chairs and 22,500 metal chairs. The costs incurred by each manufacturing unit are presented below.

			Plastic Model	Metal model
Direct materials (stated in equivalent finished chairs):	**Quantity**	**Price**		
Purchases:				
Plastic	60,000	$5.65	$339,000	
Metal	30,000	$6.00		$180,000
Usage:				
Plastic	56,000	$5.00	280,000	
Metal	23,000	$6.00		138,000
Direct labor:				
9,300 hours at $6 per hour			55,800	
5,600 hours at $8 per hour				44,800
Manufacturing overhead:				
Variable:				
Supplies			43,000	18,000
Power			50,000	15,000
Employee benefits			19,000	12,000
Fixed:				
Supervision			14,000	11,000
Depreciation			12,000	9,000
Property taxes and other items			1,900	1,300

The standard variable manufacturing costs per unit and the budgeted monthly fixed manufacturing costs established for the current year are presented below.

	Plastic model	Metal model
Direct material	$5.00	$ 6.00
Direct labor:		
⅙ hour at $6 per direct labor-hour	1.00	
¼ hour at $8 per direct labor-hour		2.00
Variable overhead:		
⅙ hour at $12 per direct labor-hour	2.00	
¼ hour at $8 per direct labor-hour		2.00
Standard variable manufacturing cost per unit	$8.00	$10.00
Budgeted fixed costs per month:		
Supervision	$4,500	$3,500
Depreciation	4,000	3,000
Property taxes and other items	600	400
Total budgeted fixed costs for month	$9,100	$6,900

Variable marketing costs are budgeted to be six percent of sales dollars.

Required:

Explain the variance in Markley Division's *contribution margin* by calculating the:

Marketing price variance.

Marketing mix variance.

Marketing quantity variance.

(CMA adapted)

21–24. Analyze industry effects on contribution margins

Using the data for the Markley Division (Problem 21–23), analyze the extent to which the quantity variance can be explained in terms of industry and market share effects.

21–25. Analyze revenue variances

The following information has been prepared by a member of the controller's staff of Duo, Inc.:

DUO, INC.
Income Statement
For the Year Ended December 31,
(in thousands)

	Product AR-10		Product ZR-7		Total	
	Budget	**Actual**	**Budget**	**Actual**	**Budget**	**Actual**
Unit sales	2,000	2,800	6,000	5,600	8,000	8,400
Sales	$6,000	$7,560	$12,000	$11,760	$18,000	$19,320
Variable costs	2,400	2,800	6,000	5,880	8,400	8,680
Fixed costs	1,800	1,900	2,400	2,400	4,200	4,300
Total costs	4,200	4,700	8,400	8,280	12,600	12,980
Net profit	$1,800	$2,860	$ 3,600	$ 3,480	$ 5,400	$ 6,340

Required:

Analyze the above data to show the impact of price, quantity, and sales mix variances on net profit.

(CMA adapted)

21–26. Comprehensive review of variances, mix variances, analysis of differences between budget and actual

Sip-Fizz Bottling Company had prepared a sales and production budget for the 48-ounce bottle, 12-ounce can, and 10-ounce bottle units that the company produces and sells. Unit variable costs per case of soda are calculated as follows:

	Per case costs		
Ingredient	**48 ounce**	**12 ounce**	**10 ounce**
Syrup	$1.45	$1.00	$ .80
CO_2 gas	.02	.01	.01
Crown	.04	—	.04
Bottle	1.40		.30
Can		1.64	
Label	.07		
Total manufacturing cost	$2.98	$2.65	$1.15
Sales commission	.08	.14	.09
Advertising allowance	.08	.08	.08
Unit variable cost	$3.14	$2.87	$1.32

The advertising allowance is based on the number of cases sold. The selling price for the 48-ounce case is $5.40; for the 12-ounce case, $4.35; and for the 10-ounce case, $2.80. Sales for the month of November were forecasted at 70,000 cases of the 48-ounce bottles, 60,000 cases of 12-ounce cans, and 110,000 cases of the 10-ounce bottles. Fixed costs were estimated at $175,000.

During November, actual sales amounted to 80,000 cases of 48-ounce bottles, 50,000 cases of 12-ounce cans, and 120,000 cases of the 10-ounce bottles. Actual and budgeted selling prices were equal. Syrup costs were 10 percent greater than expected, but all other costs were at the same per unit amount as indicated above.

Total fixed costs amounted to $182,000, which are all other costs not explicitly identified above.

The company uses variable costing for internal reporting purposes. There were no beginning and ending inventories.

Required:

a. Determine the budgeted and actual operating profits.

b. Explain the difference between the budgeted and actual net operating profits in terms of the mix, price, and quantity variances during the period.

21–27. Dallas Consulting Group (Relate activity changes to industry effects)*

"I just don't understand why you're worried about analyzing our profit variance," said Dave Lundberg to his partner, Adam Dixon. Both Lundberg and Dixon were partners in the Dallas Consulting Group (DCG). "Look, we made $40,000 more profit than we expected (see Exhibit A). That's great as far as I am concerned," continued Lundberg. Adam Dixon agreed to come up with data that would help sort out the causes of DCG's $40,000 profit variance.

Exhibit A (21–27)

Budget and actual results

	Budget	Actual	Variance
Sales revenues	$630,000	$670,000	$40,000
Expenses:			
Salaries	460,000	460,000	—
Income	$170,000	$210,000	$40,000

DCG was a professional services partnership of three established consultants who specialize in cost reduction through the use of time-motion studies and through the streamlining of production operations by optimizing physical layout, manpower, and so on. In both of these areas, DCG consultants spend a great deal of time studying customers' operations.

The three partners each received fixed salaries that represented the largest portion of operating expenses. They were professors, and each used his or her university office for DCG business. DCG itself had only a post office box. All other DCG employees, primarily graduate students at the university, were also paid fixed salaries. No other significant operating costs were incurred by the partnership.

Revenues consisted solely of professional fees charged to customers for the two different types of services. Charges were based on the number of hours actually worked on a job. Thus, an increase in the actual number of hours worked on a job would cause a corresponding increase in revenue. Since all salaries were fixed, however, DCG's total operating expenses would not change.

Following the conversation with Lundberg, Dixon gathered the data summarized in Exhibit B. He took the data with him to Lundberg's office, and said, "I think I can identify several reasons for our increased profits. First of all, we raised the price for time-motion studies to $35 per hour. Also, if you remember, we originally estimated that the 10 consulting firms in the Dallas area would probably average about 15,000 hours of work each this year, so the total industry volume in Dallas would be 150,000 hours. However, a check with all of the local consulting firms indicates that the actual total consulting market must have been around 112,000 hours."

* Adapted from Robert Anthony and Glenn Welsch, *Fundamentals of Management Accounting,* 3d. ed. (Homewood, Ill.: Richard D. Irwin, 1980).

Exhibit B (21–27)   **Detail of revenue calculations**

Service[a]	Hours	Rate	Amount
Budget:			
A	6,000	$30	$180,000
B	9,000	50	450,000
	15,000		$630,000
Actual:			
A	2,000	35	70,000
B	12,000	50	600,000
	14,000		$670,000

[a] Service A = time-motion studies. Service B = consulting for production operations.

"This is indeed interesting, Adam," replied Lundberg. "This new data leads me to believe that there are several causes for our increased profits, some of which may have been negative. . . . Do you think you could quantify the effects of these factors in terms of dollars?"

Required: Use your knowledge of profit variance analysis to quantify this year's performance of DCG and explain the significance of each variance to Mr. Lundberg.

22

Decentralization and Performance Evaluation

To understand the reasons why organization structures vary from company to company.

To understand the role that accounting information plays in monitoring performance in complex organizations.

As organizations become large and complex, the manager's task grows increasingly difficult. A common rule of thumb is that one supervisor can usually manage about 10 subordinates. Consequently, managerial duties are delegated in all but very small organizations.

Accounting can play an important role in evaluating the performance of those who have been delegated organizational responsibility. The use of accounting for performance evaluation is often called **responsibility accounting.** Budgeting and variance analysis, as discussed in Chapters 17 through 21, are part of the responsibility accounting process. In this and the next chapter, we discuss the costs and benefits of decentralization, the structure of organizational units, and the accounting measures used to evaluate the performance of organizational units and their managers.

Conceptual framework	When authority is decentralized, a superior, whom we call a *principal,* delegates duties to a subordinate, whom we call an *agent.* We find **principal-agent relationships** in many settings, including:

Principals	Agents
Stockholders	Top management
Corporate (top) managers	Divisional managers
Taxi company owner	Taxicab drivers
Retail store manager	Department managers

Many aspects of both financial and managerial accounting have been developed to help monitor agency relations. Accounting information enables principals to evaluate agents' performance and make decisions about their future employment prospects. In addition, accounting information is used in employment contracts. Employee commissions and bonuses are often based on accounting performance measures.

Thus, accounting information has a motivating effect. Agents who know that accounting information is used in their evaluation have incentives to make themselves "look good" on that basis. Sometimes agents take actions to make themselves look good that are not in the best interests of their company.

For example, a farm implement manufacturing company paid its sales managers commissions based on their sales to dealers. During an adverse economic period, the sales managers pressured dealers to make purchases with the provision that the company would take back any equipment not sold in six months. Sales rapidly rose, and production management increased output to meet the increased demand. The salespeople were paid substantial bonuses for improved performance. In the meantime, the equipment sat in the dealers' showrooms. At the end of the six-month period, the dealers returned substantial quantities of equipment to the manufacturer. The accounting performance measure—sales to dealers—did not represent the more significant performance measure of sales to final purchasers. Hence, the commissions were paid even though the equipment was never sold to a final buyer.

The key issue facing every principal is how to develop a cost-justified performance evaluation system that captures the relevant performance measure. If information were costless, principals would always prefer more information to less.[1] But information is not costless; there are costs to produce the information, and managers incur costs to process the information so they can use it. Indeed, too much information can overwhelm a manager— leading to what is commonly referred to as information overload. So principals must balance the cost of obtaining more information about an agent against the benefits of being better able to make decisions about the agent for future employment prospects, and motivating the agent to take desired actions.

Goal congruence

When all members of an organization have incentive to perform in the common interest, total goal congruence exists. This occurs when the group acts as a team in pursuit of a mutually agreed-upon objective. Individual goal congruence occurs when individual's personal goals are congruent with organizational goals.

While total goal congruence is uncommon, there are cases in which a strong team spirit suppresses individual desires to act differently. Examples include some military units and some athletic teams. Many companies attempt to achieve this esprit de corps. According to students of the Japanese management style, Japanese managers have created a strong team orientation among workers that has resulted in considerable goal congruence.

In most American business settings, however, personal goals and organizational goals differ. Employees and employers have different opinions of how much risk employees should take, how hard employees should work, and so forth. Performance evaluation and incentive systems are designed to encour-

---

[1] See Steven Shavell, "Risk Sharing and Incentives in the Principal and Agent Relationships," *The Bell Journal of Economics* 10 (Spring 1979), pp. 55–73.

age employees to *behave* as if their goals were congruent with organizational goals. This results in behavioral congruence; that is, an individual *behaves* in the best interests of the organization, regardless of his or her own goals.

Such behavioral congruence is also common in education. Examinations, homework, and the entire grading process are parts of a performance evaluation and incentive system that encourages students to behave in a certain manner. Sometimes the system appears to encourage the wrong kind of behavior, however. For example, if the goal of education is to encourage students to learn, they might be better off taking very difficult courses. But if students' grades suffer when they take difficult courses, they may have an incentive to take easier courses. As a result, some students take difficult courses and learn more, while others take easier courses in an attempt to maximize their grade-point averages.

Problems of this kind occur in all organizations, whenever it is not in the employees' best interest to take actions that are in the organization's best interest. Consider the case of a plant manager who believes that a promotion and bonus will result from high plant operating profits. Short-run profits will be lowered if the production line is closed for much-needed maintenance, but the company may be better off in the long run. The manager must decide between doing what makes the manager look good in the short run and doing what is in the best interest of the company.

Although such conflicts cannot be totally removed, if they are recognized, they can be minimized. To deal with the problem described above, some companies budget maintenance separately. Others encourage employees to take a long-run interest in the company through stock-option and pension plans that are tied to long-run performance. Still others retain employees in a position long enough that any short-term counterproductive actions will catch up with them.

Organizational structure	Some organizations are very centralized: decisions are handed down from the top, and subordinates carry them out. The military is a good example of centralized authority. At the other extreme are highly decentralized companies in which decisions are made at divisional and departmental levels. In many conglomerates, operating decisions are made in the field, while corporate headquarters is, in effect, a holding company.

The majority of companies fall between these extremes. At General Motors, for example, operating units are decentralized while the research and development and finance functions are centralized.

Many companies begin with a centralized structure but become more and more decentralized as they grow. Consider the following example of a fast-food franchise that started with one hamburger stand.[2]

---

[2] This example is based on an actual company for which one of the authors was a consultant.

We had a counter and 10 stools when we started. When winter came, we had to take out two stools to put in a heating furnace, and almost went broke from the loss of revenue! But during the following year, I obtained the statewide franchise for a nationally known bar-b-que chain and I expanded my menu.

At first, I did a little of everything—cooking, serving, bookkeeping, and advertising. I hired one full-time employee. There was little need for any formal management-control system—I made all important decisions, and they were carried out. Soon we had eight stores. (Each outlet or location is called a "store.") I was still trying to manage everything personally. Decisions were delayed. A particular store would receive food shipments, but no one was authorized to accept delivery. If a store ran out of supplies or change, its employees had to wait until I arrived to authorize whatever needed to be done. With only one store, I was able to spend a reasonable amount of time on what I call high-level decision making—planning for expansion, arranging financing, developing new marketing strategies, and so forth. But with eight stores, all of my time was consumed with day-to-day operating decisions.

Finally, I realized that the company had grown too big for me to manage alone. So I decentralized, setting up each store just like it was an independent operation. Now each store manager takes care of day-to-day operating decisions. Not only has this freed my time for more high-level decision making but it also provides a better opportunity for the store managers to learn about management, and it gives me a chance to evaluate their performance for promotion to higher management positions, which I intend to create soon.

Advantages of decentralization

The larger and more complex an organization is, the greater the advantages of decentralization are. Some advantages of decentralization include:

1. *Faster response.* As described by the owner-manager of the fast food chain, local managers can react to a changing environment more quickly than can isolated top management. With centralized decision making, delays occur while information is transmitted to decision makers, and further delays occur while instructions are communicated to local managers.

2. *Wiser use of management's time.* The owner-manager of the fast food chain complained that there was too little time for high-level decision making. Top management usually has a comparative advantage over middle management in this area. If their time is consumed by day-to-day operating decisions, they will be forced to ignore important strategic decisions. Furthermore, local managers may be able to make better operating decisions because of their technical expertise and knowledge about local conditions.

3. *Reduction of problems to manageable size.* There are limits to the complexity of problems that humans can solve.[3] Even with the aid of comput-

---

[3] This is often called "bounded rationality." An excellent discussion is provided by Herbert A. Simon, "Rational Decision Making in Business Organizations," *The American Economic Review,* September 1979.

ers, some problems are too complex to be solved by a central management. By dividing large problems into smaller, more manageable parts, decentralization reduces the need to simplify.

4. *Training, evaluation, and motivation of local managers.* By decentralizing, managers receive on-the-job training in decision making. Top management can observe the outcome of local managers' decisions and evaluate their potential for advancement. By practicing with small decisions, managers learn how to make big decisions. Finally, ambitious managers are likely to be frustrated if they only implement the decisions of others and never have the satisfaction of making their own decisions and carrying them out. This satisfaction can be an important motivational reward for managers.

Disadvantages of decentralization

While there are many advantages of decentralization, there are also disadvantages. The major disadvantage is that local managers may make decisions that are not congruent with the preferences of top management and constituents of the organization (such as, stockholders). Thus, decentralized companies incur the costs of monitoring and controlling the activities of local managers. They incur the costs that result when local managers make decisions and take actions that are not in the best interests of the organization and are missed by the monitoring system.

A company must weigh the costs and benefits and decide on an economically optimal level of decentralization. One can assume that for organizations that are highly centralized, the disadvantages of decentralization outweigh the advantages, while the reverse is true for companies that are decentralized.

Organization of decentralized units

There are five basic kinds of decentralized units: standard cost centers, discretionary cost centers, revenue centers, profit centers, and investment centers.

Standard cost centers

In standard cost centers, managers are responsible for the cost of an activity for which there is a well-defined relationship between inputs and outputs. They are often found in manufacturing operations where the inputs—direct materials, direct labor, and overhead—can be specified for each output. The production departments of manufacturing plants are examples of standard cost centers. But the concept has been applied in nonmanufacturing settings too. In banks, for example, standards can be established for check processing, so check-processing departments might be standard cost centers. In hospitals, food services departments, laundries, and laboratories are often set up as standard cost centers.

Managers of standard cost centers are held responsible for the amount of inputs used to produce an output. Often the amount of output required will be determined by someone other than the cost center manager, such as the market place, top management, or the marketing department. A plant manager is often given a production schedule to meet as efficiently as possible. If the plant is operated as a standard cost center, manufacturing cost variances like those discussed in Chapter 19 will be used to help measure efficiency.

Discretionary cost centers

Standard cost centers require a well-specified relationship between inputs and outputs for performance evaluation. When managers are held responsible for costs but the input-output relationship is not well specified, a discretionary cost center is established. Legal, accounting, research and development, advertising, and many other administrative and marketing departments are usually discretionary cost centers. Discretionary cost centers are also common in government and other nonprofit organizations. Budgets are established for and used as a ceiling. Managers are usually evaluated on bases other than costs. However, there are usually penalties for exceeding the budget ceiling.

Revenue centers

Managers of revenue centers are typically responsible for marketing a product. Consequently, the manager is held responsible for revenue or contribution margin variances (see Chapters 18 and 21 for definitions of these variances). If pricing policy is set by top management, or if prices are otherwise beyond the revenue center manager's control, sales activity variances (including sales mix variance, if any) will be used to evaluate performance.

Profit centers

Managers of profit centers are held accountable for profits. They manage both revenues and costs, both production and sales volumes. Managers of profit centers have more autonomy than do managers of cost or revenue centers; thus, they sometimes have more status.

For example, a diversified company may organize its chemical manufacturing division as a cost center. However, if the company has its chemical operation organized so that chemical manufacturing and chemical marketing are both units within the Chemical Division, then the Chemical Division may be operated as a profit center. All revenues and costs of Chemical Division activities would be included in the performance evaluation basis. A profit center is evaluated based on a comparison of actual profits with planned profits. Profit variances are analyzed to support the evaluation decision.

Investment centers

Managers of investment centers have responsibility for profits and investment in assets. These managers have relatively large amounts of money with which to make capital budgeting decisions. For instance, in one company, the manager of a standard cost center cannot acquire assets that cost more than $5,000 without approval from a superior, but an investment center manager

Illustration 22–1   **Organization structure and responsibility centers**

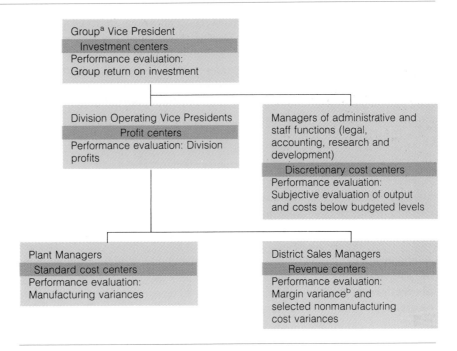

ᵃ "Group" refers to a group of divisions.

ᵇ Margin variances are based on the contribution margin (price minus variable cost) of the products sold.

can make acquisitions costing up to $500,000 without higher approval. Investment centers are evaluated using some measure of profits related to the invested assets in the center.

The use of responsibility centers

A survey of the Fortune 1,000 largest industrial companies provided some interesting results about the use of responsibility centers.[4] Of the 620 companies that responded to the survey, 95.8 percent had profit centers or investment centers and 74 percent had two or more investment centers. Investment centers were found in the majority of firms in all industries and for all sizes of companies with one exception: 56 percent of the companies in the smallest size category (sales less than $100 million) had no investment centers.

As depicted in Illustration 22–1, the form a responsibility center takes is closely related to its position in the organizational structure. For the company

[4] See James Reece and William Cool, "Measuring Investment Center Performance," *Harvard Business Review*, May–June 1978, pp. 28 ff.

shown, plant managers run standard cost centers and district sales managers operate revenue centers. Moving up the organization chart, we find that division managers who are in charge of both plant managers and district sales managers have responsibility for profits.

Of course, every company is organized uniquely (in some highly decentralized companies, manufacturing plants are profit centers, for example). However, it is generally true that a broader scope of authority and responsibility, hence profit or investment centers, are found at higher levels in an organization.

Performance measurement

We discussed performance measures for standard cost centers and revenue centers in Chapters 17 through 21. Here we examine performance measurement in discretionary cost centers, profit centers, and investment centers.

Performance measurement in discretionary cost centers

Discretionary costs that may include research and development, accounting systems, and similar costs are difficult to manage because their appropriate levels are difficult to determine. For the same reason, it is difficult to evaluate the performance of a discretionary cost center manager. Companies have tried numerous methods of determining appropriate relationships between discretionary costs and activity levels and comparison with other firms. But relating costs to activity levels remains primarily a matter of management judgment or discretion. Consequently, managers of discretionary cost centers are typically given a budget and instructed not to exceed it without higher-level authorization. In most governmental units, it is against the law to exceed the budget without obtaining authorization from a legislative body (Congress, the state legislature, the city council).

Such a situation can invite suboptimal behavior. Managers have incentives to spend all of their budgets, even if some savings could be achieved, to support their requests for the same or higher budgets in the following year. Furthermore, there is often no well-specified relationship between the quality of services and costs. (Would the quality of research and development go down 10 percent with a 10 percent cut in funds? Would crime increase 10 percent if police department funds were cut 10 percent?)

Ideally, we want to measure performance in a well-specified way, as we do when comparing actual inputs to standard inputs in a standard cost center. But it is very difficult and costly to measure the performance of the manager and workers in a discretionary cost center. Thus, it is also hard to provide incentives for employees to perform at the levels that best achieve organizational goals.

Consequently, the budgets of discretionary cost centers are often based on negotiation and agreement between the cost center manager and top management. The budget then becomes a constraint on cost center operations.

Cost center management is expected to perform as well as possible within the budget constraint. Top management often finds it pays to pick carefully discretionary cost center managers who are loyal to the organization and committed to help achieve its objectives. These managers can be given considerable freedom with a high probability that they will not intentionally suboptimize.

Cost cutting   Discretionary cost centers are prime targets for short-run cost cutting. It is easy to observe an immediate 10 percent cost savings, while the consequences may not be observed until the distant future, if ever. Therefore, when top management decides to cut costs, discretionary cost centers are often the first to be affected. On the other hand, when times are good, discretionary cost centers may receive a surplus of funds because of overoptimism about future prospects. As a result, managers of discretionary cost centers may try to build in some slack so that when funds are cut they can continue to provide at least minimal services. The manager of an accounting department put it this way: "When times are good, we spend a lot on employee training and recruiting, and we stock up on supplies and equipment. In tough times we can cut out the frills and use up the excess supplies and equipment. This carries us through without drastically hurting our level of services." Whether this is the best way to manage remains an open question.[5]

Performance measurement in profit centers

Decentralized organizations depend heavily on profit measures to evaluate the performance of decentralized units and their managers. Due to the difficulties of measuring profits, many companies have tried to use multiple measures of performance. In the early 1950s, General Electric proposed an extensive and innovative performance measurement system that evaluated market position, productivity, product leadership, personnel development, employee attitudes, public responsibility, and balance between short-range and long-range goals in addition to profitability. But even when a company uses a broad range of performance measures, accounting results continue to play an important role in performance evaluation. A commonly heard adage is that "hard" measures of performance tend to drive out "soft" measures. Nevertheless, no accounting measure can fully measure the performance of an organizational unit or its manager.

In profit centers, we encounter the usual problems related to measuring profits for the company as a whole plus an important additional one: How are the company's revenues and costs allocated to each profit center? A profit center that is totally separate from all other parts of the company

---

[5] See Michael Schiff and Arie Lewin, "The Impact of People on Budgets," *The Accounting Review,* April 1970, pp. 259–69; and James March and Herbert Simon, *Organizations* (New York: John Wiley & Sons, 1958), chaps. 5 and 6.

operates like an autonomous company. The profits of that kind of center can be uniquely identified with it.

But a completely independent profit center is a highly unusual case. Most profit centers have costs (and perhaps revenues) in common with other units. The profit center may share facilities with other units or use headquarters' staff services, for example. If so, a cost allocation question arises (see Chapters 4 and 7). While it is commonly accepted that profit centers should be allocated only the costs (and revenues) for which they are responsible, this principle is difficult to apply. In fact, the majority of companies do allocate uncontrollable common costs.

A related problem involves the transfer of goods between a profit center and other parts of the organization. Such goods must be priced so that the profit center manager has incentives to trade with other units when it is in the best interests of the organization. Chapter 23 discusses this transfer pricing problem in more detail.

There are no easy ways to determine how to measure performance in a profit center. Much is left to managerial judgment. Whatever the process chosen, its objective should be straightforward: measure employees' performance in ways that motivate them to work in the best interest of their employers and compare that performance to standards or budget plans.

Performance measurement in investment centers

Managers of investment centers are responsible for profits and investment in assets. They are evaluated on their ability to generate a sufficiently high return on investment to justify the investment in the division.

Relating profits to capital investment is an intuitively appealing concept. Capital is a scarce resource. If one unit of a company shows a low return, the capital may be better employed in another unit where the return is higher, or invested elsewhere, or paid to stockholders.

Relating profits to investment also provides a scale for measuring performance. For example, Investment A generated $200,000 in operating profits while Investment B generated $2,000,000. But Investment A required a capital investment of $500,000 while Investment B required an investment of $20,000,000. As you can see from the following calculation, return on investment (ROI) provides a different picture from operating profits.

		Investment	
		A	**B**
1.	Operating profits	$200,000	$ 2,000,000
2.	Investment	500,000	20,000,000
3.	Return on investment (1) ÷ (2)	40%	10%

Although ROI is a commonly used performance measure, it has its limitations. The many difficulties of measuring profits affect the numerator, while problems in measuring the investment base affect the denominator. Consequently, it is difficult to make precise comparisons among investment centers.

Measuring investment center assets and profits

Each company is likely to measure an investment center's operating profits and assets in somewhat different ways. For example, Reece and Cool found that 40 percent of the companies that had investment centers defined "investment center profits" consistently with the way net income is calculated for shareholder reporting. However, many companies did not assess income taxes, allocate corporate administrative costs, or allocate interest on corporate debt to investment centers.

Companies also differ in the assets that they assign to an investment center. Reece and Cool (1978) asked which assets were included in the calculation of an investment center's asset base and found the following assets were included by the indicated percentage of companies:

Asset	Percentage including
Cash	63
Receivables	94
Inventories	95
Land and buildings used solely by the investment center	94
Allocated share of corporate headquarter's assets	16

Most companies define an asset base that is easily understandable and approximates the assets that the investment center manager is accountable for. Including assets in the base encourages managers to manage those assets.

Choice of measure: ROI versus residual income

ROI evaluation is widely used in companies. However, the method is not without drawbacks. Some contend that if managers are encouraged to maximize ROI, they may turn down investment opportunities that are above the minimum acceptable rate for the corporation but below the rate their center is currently earning. For example, suppose that a corporation has a cost of capital of 15 percent. A division has an opportunity to make an additional investment that will return $400,000 per year for a $2,000,000 investment. The ROI for this project is 20 percent (which is $400,000 $\div$ $2,000,000), so the project qualifies at the corporate level in meeting ROI targets. Assuming the project meets all other corporate requirements, it should be accepted. However, the manager of the division in which the investment would take place may reject the investment if the division's ROI is greater than 20 percent. For example, suppose that the center currently earns:

$$ROI = \frac{\$1,000,000}{\$4,000,000} = 25\%$$

With the new investment, ROI would be:

$$ROI = \frac{\$1,000,000 + \$400,000}{\$4,000,000 + \$2,000,000} = 23.3\%$$

Because a comparison of the old and new returns would imply that performance had worsened, the center's manager might hesitate to make such an investment, even though the investment would have a positive benefit for the company as a whole.

An alternative is to measure **residual income** (RI). Residual income is defined as:

$$\text{Investment center operating profits} - [\text{Capital charge} \times \text{Investment center assets}]$$

where the capital charge is the minimum acceptable rate of return.

Using the numbers from the previous example, we can see the impact of the investment in additional plant capacity on residual income. Before the investment:

$$\begin{aligned}
RI &= \$1,000,000 - (.15 \times \$4,000,000) \\
&= \$1,000,000 - \$600,000 \\
&= \underline{\underline{\$400,000}}
\end{aligned}$$

The residual income from the additional investment in plant capacity is:

$$\begin{aligned}
RI &= \$400,000 - (.15 \times \$2,000,000) \\
&= \$400,000 - \$300,000 \\
&= \underline{\underline{\$100,000}}
\end{aligned}$$

Hence, after the additional investment, the residual income of the division will increase:

$$\begin{aligned}
RI &= (\$1,000,000 + \$400,000) - [.15 \times (\$4,000,000 + \$2,000,000)] \\
&= \$1,400,000 - (.15 \times \$6,000,000) \\
&= \$1,400,000 - \$900,000 \\
&= \underline{\underline{\$500,000}}
\end{aligned}$$

The additional investment in plant capacity *increases* residual income, appropriately improving the measure of performance.

Most managers recognize the weakness of ROI and take it into account when ROI is lowered by a new investment. This may partially explain why residual income does not dominate ROI as a performance measure. Moreover, residual income is not the net income reported to shareholders. Thus, it may be a less familiar concept for managers than operating profits or divisional net income. In addition, ROI is expressed as a percentage that can be compared with related percentages—like the cost of capital, the prime interest rate, and the Treasury bill rate. Most companies studied by Reece and Cool (1978) use ROI. Only 2 percent used residual income alone, while 28 percent used both ROI and residual income.

For the remainder of this section, we use ROI for illustrative purposes, but the issues we discuss apply equally to ROI and residual income.

Measuring the investment base

Three issues are frequently raised in measuring investment bases: (1) Should *gross* book value be used? (2) Should investment in assets be valued at historical cost or current value? and (3) Should investment be measured at the beginning or the end of the year? While no method is inherently right or wrong, some may have advantages over others. Further, it is important to understand how the measure of the investment base will affect ROI.

Gross book versus net book value Suppose that a company uses straight-line depreciation for a physical asset with a 10-year life and no salvage value.

The cost of the asset does not change; it is the same in Year 3 as in Year 1. Illustration 22–2 compares ROI under net book value and gross book value for the first three years. For simplicity, all operating profits before

Illustration 22–2

The impact of net book versus gross book value methods on ROI (in thousands)

Facts: Operating profits before depreciation (all in cash flows at end of year):
Year 1, $100; Year 2, $100; and Year 3, $100.

Asset cost at *beginning* of Year 1, $500. The only asset is depreciable, with a 10-year life and no salvage value. Straight-line depreciation is used. The straight-line rate is .1 per year. The denominator in the ROI calculations is based on *end*-of-year asset values.

Year	Net book value	Gross book value
1	$ROI = \dfrac{\$100^a - (.1 \times \$500)^b}{\$500^c - (.1 \times \$500)^d}$	$ROI = \dfrac{\$50^e}{\$500}$
	$= \dfrac{\$50}{\$450} = \underline{\underline{11.1\%}}$	$= \underline{\underline{10\%}}$
2	$ROI = \dfrac{\$100 - (.1 \times \$500)}{\$450 - (.1 \times \$500)}$	$ROI = \dfrac{\$50}{\$500}$
	$= \dfrac{\$50}{\$400} = \underline{\underline{12.5\%}}$	$= \underline{\underline{10\%}}$
3	$ROI = \dfrac{\$100 - (.1 \times \$500)}{\$400 - (.1 \times \$500)}$	$ROI = \dfrac{\$50}{\$500}$
	$= \dfrac{\$50}{\$350} = \underline{\underline{14.3\%}}$	$= \underline{\underline{10\%}}$

[a] The first term in the numerator is the annual cash operating profits.

[b] The second term in the numerator is depreciation for the year.

[c] The first term in the denominator is the beginning-of-year value of the assets used in the investment base.

[d] The second term in the denominator reduces the beginning-of-year value of the asset by the amount of current year's depreciation.

[e] $50 = $100 − ($500 × .1). Companies sometimes use only cash flows in the numerator.

depreciation in the computation are assumed to take place at the end of the year, and ROI is based on year-end value of the investment.

Note that the ROI increases each year under the net book value method even though no operating changes take place. This occurs because the numerator remains constant, while the denominator decreases each year as depreciation accumulates.

Critics contend that if these ROI numbers are used naively, investment center managers have incentives to postpone replacing assets longer than economically wise because their ROI will go down on replacement. In addition, the net book value method makes a center with old assets look better than a comparable center with new assets. As one manager told us: "The secret is to get into a center just after assets have been bought and run it until it's time to replace them. ROI is at a peak then because there is very little investment base. Then transfer to another center that has new assets. Of course, the poor fellow that follows you has to replace assets and watch ROI plummet." While such a strategy may work, we suspect the opportunities for such game playing are relatively few. Moreover, if top management is observant, a manager playing such a strategy should be detected after relatively few moves.

Historical cost versus current cost   The previous example assumed no inflation. Working with the same facts, assume that the current replacement cost of the asset increases 20 percent per year, as do operating cash flows. Illustration 22–3 compares ROI under historical cost and current cost.

Note that ROI increases each year under the historical cost methods even though no operating changes take place. This occurs because the numerator is measured in current dollars to reflect current cash transactions while the denominator and depreciation charges are based on historical cost. The current cost—gross book value method—reduces the effect by adjusting both the depreciation in the numerator and the investment base in the denominator to reflect price changes. Measuring current costs can be a difficult and expensive task, however, so there is a trade-off in the choice of performance measures.

We derived a level ROI in the current cost—gross book value—method because the asset and all other prices increased at the same rate. If inflation affecting cash flows in the numerator increases faster than the current cost of the asset in the denominator, then ROI will increase over the years until asset replacement under the current cost method. Of course, ROI will decrease over the years until asset replacement if the denominator increases faster than the numerator.

Although current cost may seem to be a superior measure of ROI, recall that there is no single right or wrong measure. In fact, Reece and Cool (1978) reported that 85 percent of the companies with investment centers used historical cost net book value. Furthermore, how the measure is used is more important than how it is calculated. All of the measures we have

Illustration 22–3 **The impact of historical cost versus current cost methods on ROI (in thousands)**

Facts: Operating profits before depreciation (all in cash flows at end of year):
Year, $100; Year 2, $120; and Year 3, $144.
Annual rate of price changes 20 percent.
Asset cost at *beginning* of Year 1, $500. The only asset is depreciable with 10-year life and no slavage value.
Straight-line depreciation is used; straight-line rate is .1 per year. The denominator in the ROI computation is based on *end*-of-year asset value.

	Historical cost		Current cost	
Year	**Net book value (1)**	**Gross book value (2)**	**Net book value (3)**	**Gross book value (4)**
1	$\text{ROI} = \dfrac{\$100^a - (.1 \times \$500)^b}{\$500^c - (.1^f \times \$500)^d}$ $= \dfrac{\$50}{\$450} = 11.1\%$	$\text{ROI} = \dfrac{\$50}{\$500}$ $= 10\%$	$\text{ROI} = \dfrac{\$100 - (.1 \times 1.2^e \times \$500)}{(1.2^e \times \$500) - (.1 \times 1.2^e \times \$500)}$ $= \dfrac{\$100 - \$60}{\$600 - \$60} = \dfrac{\$40}{\$540} = 7.4\%$	$\text{ROI} = \dfrac{\$100 - \$60}{(1.2 \times \$500)}$ $= \dfrac{\$40}{\$600} = 6.7\%$
2	$\text{ROI} = \dfrac{\$120 - (.1 \times \$500)}{\$500 - (.2^f \times \$500)}$ $= \dfrac{\$70}{\$400} = 17.5\%$	$\text{ROI} = \dfrac{\$70}{\$500}$ $= 14\%$	$\text{ROI} = \dfrac{\$120 - (.1 \times 1.2 \times \$600)}{(1.2 \times \$600) - (.2^f \times 1.2 \times \$600)}$ $= \dfrac{\$120 - \$72}{\$720 - \$144} = \dfrac{\$48}{\$576} = 8.3\%$	$\text{ROI} = \dfrac{\$120 - \$72}{(1.2 \times \$600)}$ $= \dfrac{\$48}{\$720} = 6.7\%$
3	$\text{ROI} = \dfrac{\$144 - (.1 \times \$500)}{\$500 - (.3^f \times \$500)}$ $= \dfrac{\$94}{\$350} = 26.9\%$	$\text{ROI} = \dfrac{\$94}{\$500}$ $= 18.8\%$	$\text{ROI} = \dfrac{\$144 - (.1 \times 1.2 \times \$720)}{(1.2 \times \$720) - (.3^f \times 1.2 \times \$720)}$ $= \dfrac{\$144 - \$86.4}{\$864 - \$259.2} = \dfrac{\$57.6}{\$604.8} = 9.5\%$	$\text{ROI} = \dfrac{\$144 - \$86.4}{(1.2 \times \$720)}$ $= \dfrac{\$57.6}{\$864} = 6.7\%$

[a] The first term in the numerator is the annual operating profits before depreciation.

[b] The second term in the numerator is depreciation for the year.

[c] The first term in the denominator is the beginning of the first year value of the assets used in the investment base.

[d] The second term in the denominator reduces the beginning-of-year value of the asset by the amount of current year's depreciation.

[e] This term (1.2) adjusts the beginning-of-year asset value to the end-of-year value (current value).

[f] This term reduces the net book value of the asset. The replacement cost is reduced by 10 percent for depreciation at the end of Year 1, by 20 percent at the end of Year 2, and by 30 percent at the end of Year 3.

presented can offer useful information. As long as the measurement method is understood, it can enhance performance evaluation.

Beginning, ending, or average balance An additional problem arises in measuring the investment base for performance evaluation. Should the base be the beginning, ending, or average balance? Using the beginning balance may encourage asset acquisitions early in the year to increase income for the entire year. Asset dispositions would be encouraged at the end of the year to reduce the investment base for next year. If end-of-year balances are used, similar incentives exist to manipulate purchases and dispositions. Average investments would tend to minimize this problem, although it may be more difficult to compute. In choosing an investment base, management must balance the costs of the additional computations required for average investment against the potential negative consequences of using the beginning or ending balances.

Comparing the performance of investment centers

A company is often tempted to compare the performance of its investment centers and even to encourage competition among them. The problems inherent in ROI measurement complicate such comparisons. In addition, investment centers may be in very different businesses. It is very difficult to compare the performance of a manufacturing center with the performance of a center that provides consulting service and has a relatively small investment base. Differences in the riskiness of investment centers should also be taken into account. We recommend comparing the performance of investment centers only if they are very similar.

When there are diverse investment centers, management will frequently establish target ROI's for the individual investment centers. The investment center will be evaluated by comparing the actual ROI with the target ROI. Such a comparison procedure is similar to the budget versus actual comparisons that are made for cost centers, revenue centers, and profit centers. It sometimes makes more sense to compare the ROI of an investment center with a company in the same industry than to compare it with other investment centers in its company.

Evaluating managers versus evaluating centers

The evaluation of a manager is not necessarily identical to the evaluation of the cost, profit, or investment center. As a general rule, managers are evaluated based on a comparison of actual results to targets. A manager who is asked to take over a marginal operation and turn it around may be given a minimal ROI target, consistent with the past performance of the division. If the manager meets or exceeds that target, the manager would be rewarded. However, it may be that even with the best management, a division cannot be turned around. Thus, it is entirely possible that the center would be disbanded even though the manager had received a highly positive evaluation.

Cost centers are usually evaluated by comparing the cost to produce internally with the cost to acquire the same product or service from the outside. Investment centers are usually evaluated by comparing the return earned by the investment center with the alternative use of funds that could be realized from liquidation of the investment center.

It is conceivable that there would be conflicts in the outcomes of an evaluation based on targeted performance with the results of an evaluation based on opportunity costs. This merely implies that the objectives for evaluating managers are different from the objectives of evaluating a center. Top management would like to reward the manager that performs well in an adverse situation but, conversely, should be willing to bail out of a bad operation if better use can be made of company resources.

Controllability concept Frequently we hear that the center or manager being evaluated should only be held accountable for those items that can be controlled by the manager or center. Thus, if central management decides that a particular operating center will sell a given number of units of output at a given price, the center manager has no control over that decision and, hence, should not be evaluated based on the results of operations as that decision affects the results. Of course, if central management is specifying output volumes and prices, then the organization is probably highly centralized. The various operating centers and managers would probably best be evaluated by comparing actual costs with budgeted costs and not evaluated on some measure of divisional profits. In other words, the managers and divisions would be evaluated based on the factors that they can control, namely, costs.

An interesting problem arises in implementing this concept in an ongoing problem. How does one evaluate the performance of a manager who takes over an existing division where the assets, operating structure, and markets are established prior to the manager's arrival at the helm? The new manager cannot control the fact that certain assets are on hand, nor can the new manager control the markets in which the division operates at the time the manager takes over. However, in time, the new manager can change all of these factors. As a general rule, evaluating the manager on the basis of performance targets, as suggested earlier in this chapter, overcomes this problem. The new manager establishes a plan for operating the division and works with top management to set targets for the future. Those targets are compared to actual results as the plan is enacted and the manager is evaluated based on those results. In short, the longer the manager is at the division, the more responsibility the manager takes for the success of the division.

Summary

Performance evaluation is usually based on a responsibility accounting system. The key factor in establishing a performance evaluation system is to encourage all segments of an organization to act to attain common organization goals. The evaluation system must be cost effective. There is a great diversity in organization structures ranging from highly centralized to highly decentralized organizations. We presume the degree of centralization is established to optimize the balance between the costs of decentralization and the benefits.

Organization subunits may be organized as standard cost centers, discretionary cost centers, revenue centers, profit centers, or investment centers. The basis for evaluation of each type of center is designed to capture the activities that are under the control of the center manager. Cost centers, revenue centers, and profit centers are usually evaluated based on a comparison of actual performance with budgeted goals. Investment centers are evaluated on the basis of the efficiency with which the assets employed in the center are used to generate profits. The usual form of measurement for investment centers is return on investment (ROI).

Managers are typically evaluated by comparing established performance targets with actual results. Centers are evaluated using an opportunity cost approach. Hence, a manager can excel in the management of a mediocre center, and, conversely, a manager could receive a poor evaluation in a highly profitable center. In general, top managers match the performance measurement system with the factors that are under the control of the center or of the manager of the center. This promotes evaluation based on the factors that the manager or center can use to impact results.

Terms and concepts

The following terms and concepts should be familiar to you after reading this chapter.

Behavioral congruence	Investment centers
Centralized	Principal-agent relationship
Controllability concept	Profit centers
Current cost	Residual income
Decentralized	Responsibility accounting
Discretionary cost centers	Responsibility centers
Discretionary costs	Return on investment (ROI)
Goal congruence	Revenue centers
Information overload	Standard cost centers

Self-study problem No. 1

The Mars Division of Hyperspace Company has assets of $1.4 billion, operating profits of $.35 billion, and a cost of capital of 30 percent.

Required:

Compute ROI and residual income.

Solution to self-study problem No. 1

$$ROI = \frac{\$.35 \text{ billion}}{1.4 \text{ billion}} = 25\%$$

$$RI = \$.35 \text{ billion} - (.30 \times \$1.4 \text{ billion})$$
$$= \$.35 \text{ billion} - .42 \text{ billion}$$
$$= -\$.07 \text{ billion (that is, a residual}$$
$$\text{``loss'' of \$70 million)}$$

Self-study problem No. 2

Current value versus historical cost

The E Division of E. T. Enterprises acquired depreciable assets costing $2,000,000. The cash flows from these assets for three years were as follows:

Year	Cash flow
1	$500,000
2	600,000
3	710,000

The current cost of these assets were expected to increase 25 percent per year. Depreciation of these assets for internal, managerial purposes was 10 percent per year; the assets have no salvage value. The denominator in the ROI calculation is based on *end*-of-year asset values.

Required:

Compute the ROI for each year under each of the following methods:

a. Historical cost, net book value.
b. Historical cost, gross book value.
c. Current cost, net book value.
d. Current cost, gross book value.

Solution to self-study problem No. 2

(a) and (b) historical cost:

Year	Net book value	Gross book value
1	$ROI = \dfrac{\$500{,}000 - (.10 \times \$2{,}000{,}000)^{a}}{\$2{,}000{,}000 - (.10 \times \$2{,}000{,}000)}$ $= \dfrac{\$300{,}000}{1{,}800{,}000} = 16.7\%$	$ROI = \dfrac{\$500{,}000}{\$2{,}000{,}000}$ $= 25\%$
2	$ROI = \dfrac{\$600{,}000 - (.10 \times \$2{,}000{,}000)}{1{,}800{,}000 - (.10 \times \$2{,}000{,}000)}$ $= \dfrac{\$400{,}000}{\$1{,}600{,}000} = 25\%$	$ROI = \dfrac{\$600{,}000}{\$2{,}000{,}000}$ $= 30\%$
3	$ROI = \dfrac{\$710{,}000 - (.10 \times \$2{,}000{,}000)}{1{,}600{,}000 - (.10 \times \$2{,}000{,}000)}$ $= \dfrac{\$510{,}000}{\$1{,}400{,}000} = 36.4\%$	$ROI = \dfrac{\$710{,}000}{\$2{,}000{,}000}$ $= 35.5\%$

(c) and (d) current cost:

Year	Net book value	Gross book value
1	$ROI = \dfrac{\$500{,}000 - (.10 \times 1.25^{b} \times \$2{,}000{,}000)}{(1.25 \times \$2{,}000{,}000) - (.10^{c} \times 1.25 \times 2{,}000{,}000)}$ $= \dfrac{\$500{,}000 - 250{,}000}{2{,}500{,}000 - 250{,}000} = 11.1\%$	$\dfrac{\$500{,}000}{\$2{,}500{,}000}$ $= 20\%$
2	$ROI = \dfrac{\$600{,}000 - (.10 \times 1.25 \times \$2{,}500{,}000)}{(1.25 \times \$2{,}500{,}000) - (.20^{c} \times 1.25 \times \$2{,}500{,}000)}$ $= \dfrac{\$600{,}000 - 312{,}500}{\$3{,}125{,}000 - 625{,}000} = 11.5\%$	$\dfrac{\$600{,}000}{\$3{,}125{,}000}$ $= 19.2\%$
3	$ROI = \dfrac{\$710{,}000 - (.10 \times 1.25 \times \$3{,}125{,}000)}{(1.25 \times \$3{,}125{,}000) - (.30^{c} \times 1.25 \times 3{,}125{,}000)}$ $= \dfrac{\$710{,}000 - 390{,}625}{\$3{,}906{,}250 - 1{,}171{,}875}$ $= \dfrac{\$319{,}375}{\$2{,}734{,}375} = 11.7\%$	$\dfrac{\$710{,}000}{\$3{,}906{,}250}$ $= 18.2\%$

[a] The first term in the numerator is annual cash flow; the second term in the numerator is annual depreciation; the first term in the denominator is the beginning-of-year net book value of the asset; the second term in the denominator reduces the beginning-of-year value by the amount of the current year's depreciation.

[b] This term increases asset value to replacement cost.

[c] This reduces the net book value of the asset by 10 percent after one year, by 20 percent after two years, and by 30 percent after three years.

Questions

22–1. Accounting is supposed to be a neutral, relevant, and objective measure of performance. Why would problems arise when applying accounting measures to performance evaluation contexts.

22–2. A company prepares the master budget by taking each division manager's estimate of revenues and costs for the coming period and entering the data into the budget without adjustment. At the end of the year, division managers are given a bonus if their division "profit" is greater than the budget. Do you see any problems with this system?

22–3. Is top management ever an agent in a principal-agency relationship as discussed in the chapter?

22–4. Is top management ever a principal in a principal-agency relationship as discussed in the chapter?

22–5. Sales managers in a company were paid on an incentive system based upon the number of units sold to ultimate buyers (that is, the units were not likely to be returned except if defective). How might that incentive system lead to dysfunctional consequences?

22–6. XYZ Division of Multitudenous Enterprises, Inc., produces and sells blank video disks. The division is evaluated based on income targets. The company uses the same measure of income for division performance evaluation as for external reporting. What problems, if any, can you envision in this performance evaluation system?

22–7. You overhear the comment, "This whole problem of measuring performance for segment managers using accounting numbers is so much hogwash. We pay our managers a good salary and expect them to do the best possible job. At least with our system there is no incentive to play with the accounting data." Does the comment make sense?

22–8. What are the advantages of using a ROI type measure rather than the absolute value of division profits as a performance evaluation technique?

22–9. Under what conditions would the use of ROI measures inhibit goal-congruent decision making by a division manager?

22–10. The chapter suggested there might be some problems in the use of residual income. Can you suggest what some of those problems might be?

22–11. Using historical costs of assets in the ROI denominator is a mismatch of current revenues and costs in the numerator with the denominator. This problem may be corrected by using current costs in the denominator. No changes need be made to the numerator. How do you feel about this suggestion?

22–12. Central management of Holdum, Inc., evaluated divisional performance using residual income measures. The division managers were ranked according to the residual income in each division. A bonus was paid to all division managers with residual income in the upper half of the ranking. The bonus amount was in proportion to the residual income amount. No bonus was paid to managers in the lower half of the ranking. What biases might arise in this system?

22–13. Parsed Phrases Corporation entered into a loan agreement that contained the provision that Parsed Phrases would be required to make additional interest payments if its net income fell below a certain dollar amount. Immediately after the agreement was signed, the FASB instituted a new accounting requirement that caused Parsed's income to fall below the requirements. Absent the accounting change, Parsed would have met the income requirement.

Required:

a. Should the pre-change or post-change income number be used to determine if Parsed should pay the additional interest charge? Why or why not?

b. Would your answer in *(a)* change if Parsed has entered into a management contract that provided that the new manager would be paid a bonus based on achieving certain income levels. However, after taking office, the accounting rules changed so that the manager could never achieve those agreed on income levels?

22–14. Management of Division A is evaluated based on residual income measures. The division can either lease or buy a certain asset. Would the performance evaluation technique have any impact on the lease or buy decision? Why or why not?

22–15. What impact does the use of gross book value or net book value in the investment base have on the computation of ROI?

Exercises

22–16. Compute residual income and ROI

Des Moines Division of The Iowa Corporation has assets of $1,400,000. During the past year, the division had profits of $250,000. Iowa Corporation has a cost of capital of 14 percent.

Required:

a. Compute the division ROI.

b. Compute the division residual income.

22–17. Impact of new project on performance measures

A division manager is considering the acquisition of a new asset that will add to her division's profit. The division is expected to earn $750,000 on assets of $2,700,000. The company cost of capital is 20 percent. The new investment has a cost of $450,000 and is expected to have a cash flow of $167,000 before depreciation considerations. The asset will be depreciated using the straight-line method over a six-year life. The new asset meets the company investment criteria. Division performance is measured using an investment base of the original cost of division assets.

Required:

a. What is the division ROI before acquisition of the new asset?

b. What is the division ROI after acquisition of the new asset?

22–18. Impact of leasing on performance measures

The division manager in Exercise 22–17, above, has the option of leasing the asset on a year-to-year lease. The lease payment would be $145,000 per year, and all depreciation and other tax benefits would accrue to the lessor.

Required:

What is the division ROI if the asset if leased?

22–19. Residual income measures and new project consideration

Consider the investment project detailed in Exercises 22–17 and 22–18.

Required:

a. What is the division's residual income before considering the project?
b. What is the division's residual income if the asset is purchased?
c. What is the division's residual income if the asset is leased?
d. Ignoring the tax benefits that might be associated with the purchase of the asset that will be lost by leasing the asset, the cost of the lease is estimated to equal 23 percent per year. Should the company lease the asset?

22–20. Compare historical cost, net book value to gross book value

The Raiders Division of Shark Company has just started operations. It purchased depreciable assets costing $1,000,000 that have an expected life of four years, after which the assets can be salvaged for $200,000. In addition, the division has $1,000,000 in assets that are not depreciable. After four years, the division will have $1,000,000 available from these assets. In short, the division has invested $2,000,000 in assets that will last four years, after which it will salvage $1,200,000. Assume the annual cash operating profits are $400,000. In computing ROI, this division uses *end*-of-year asset values in the denominator.

Required:

a. Compute ROI using net book value.
b. Compute ROI using gross book value.

22–21. Computations using beginning-of-year asset values

Assume the same facts as in Exercise 22–20, except the division uses *beginning*-of-year asset values in the denominator for computing ROI.

Required:

a. Compute ROI using net book value.
b. Compute ROI using gross book value.
c. If you worked Exercise 22–20, compare these results with 22–20. How different is the ROI computed using end-of-year asset values, as in 22–20, from the ROI using beginning-of-year values as in this exercise?

22–22. Compare current cost to historical cost

Assume the same facts as in Exercise 22–20, except all cash flows increase 10 percent at the end of the year. This has the following effect on the assets' replacement cost and annual cash flows:

End of year	Replacement cost	Annual cash flow
1	$2,000,000 × 1.1 = $2,200,000	$400,000 × 1.1 = $440,000
2	$2,200,000 × 1.1 = $2,420,000	$440,000 × 1.1 = $484,000
⋮	Etc.	Etc.

Required:

a. Compute ROI using historical cost gross book value.
b. Compute ROI using historical cost net book value.
c. Compute ROI using current cost gross book value.
d. Compute ROI using current cost net book value.

22–23. Assess depreciation effects on performance measurement
Required:

A division is considering acquisition of a new asset. The asset will cost $160,000 and have a cash flow of $70,000 per year (excluding depreciation) for each of the five years of the asset life.

a. What is the ROI for each year of the asset life if the division using beginning-of-year asset balances for the computation?
b. What is the residual income each year if the cost of capital is 25 percent?

22–24. Effects of current cost on performance measurements

A division acquired an asset with a cost of $200,000 and a life of four years. The cash flows from the asset considering the effects of inflation and ignoring depreciation effects were scheduled as:

Year	Cash flow
1	$ 60,000
2	90,000
3	125,000
4	150,000

The current cost of the asset is expected to increase at a rate of 25 percent per year, compounded each year. Performance measures are based on gross values.

Required:

a. What is the ROI for each year of the asset life using a historical cost approach?
b. What is the ROI for each year of the asset life if both the investment base and depreciation are based on the current cost of the asset at the start of each year?

22–25. Evaluate different division performance

The following data are available for two divisions in your company:

	East division	West division
Division profit	$ 75,000	$ 500,000
Division investment	200,000	2,000,000

The cost of capital for the company is 20 percent.

Required:

a. Which division had the better performance? Why?
b. Would your evaluation change if the company's cost of capital was 25 percent?

Problems and cases

22–26. Equipment replacement and performance measures

You have been appointed manager of an operating division of HI-TECH, Inc., a manufacturer of products using the latest microprocessor technology. Your division has $800,000 in assets and manufactures a special chip assembly. On January 2 of the current year, you invested $1 million in automated equipment for chip assembly. At that time your expected income statement was:

Sales revenues	$3,200,000
Operating costs:	
Variable	400,000
Fixed (all cash)	1,500,000
Depreciation:	
New equipment	300,000
Other	250,000
Division profit	$ 750,000

On October 25, you were approached by a sales representative from Mammoth Machine Company. Mammoth offers a new assembly machine at a cost of $1,300,000 which offers significant improvements over the equipment you bought on January 2. The new equipment would expand department output by 10 percent while reducing cash fixed costs by 5 percent. The new equipment would be depreciated for accounting purposes over a three-year life. Depreciation would be net of the $100,000 salvage value of the new machine. The new equipment meets your company's 20 percent cost of capital criterion. If you purchase the new machine, it must be installed prior to the end of the year. For practical purposes, though, you can ignore depreciation on the new machine because it will not go into operation until the start of next year.

The old machine must be disposed of to make room for the new machine. The old machine has no salvage value.

Your company has a performance evaluation and bonus plan based on ROI. The return includes any losses on disposals of equipment. Investment is computed based on the end-of-year balance of assets.

Required:

a. What is your division's ROI if the new machine is not acquired?

b. What is your division's ROI this year if the new machine is acquired?

c. If the new machine is required and operates according to specifications, what ROI would be expected for next year?

22–27. Evaluate trade-offs in return measurement

As a division manager of HI-TECH, Inc. (Problem 22–26), you are still assessing the problem of whether to acquire the Mammoth Manufacturing Company machine. You learn that the new machine could be acquired next year. However, if you wait until next year, the new machine will cost 15 percent more than this year's price. The salvage value would still be $100,000. No other costs or revenue estimates would be affected. You could have delivery any time after January 1 at the new price. Depreciation on the new and old machines would be apportioned on a month-by-month basis for the time each machine is in use. Fractions of months may be ignored.

Required:

a. When would you want to purchase the new machine if you wait until next year?

b. What are the costs that must be considered in making this decision?

22–28. Analyze performance report for decentralized organization

Bio-grade Products is a multiproduct company manufacturing animal feeds and feed supplements. The need for a widely based manufacturing and distribution system has led to a highly decentralized management structure. Each divisional manager is responsible for production and distribution of corporate products in one of eight geographical areas of the country.

Residual income is used to evaluate divisional managers. The residual income for each division equals each division's contribution to corporate profits before taxes less a 20 percent investment charge on a division's investment base. The investment base for each division is the sum of its year-end balances of accounts receivable, inventories, and net plant fixed assets (cost less accumulated depreciation). Corporate policies dictate that divisions minimize their investments in receivables and inventories. Investments in plant fixed assets are a joint division/corporate decision based on proposals made by divisional plant managers, available corporate funds, and general corporate policy.

Alex Williams, divisional manager for the Southeastern Sector, prepared the 1985 and preliminary 1986 budgets in late 1984 for his division. Final approval of the 1986 budget took place in late 1985 after adjustments for trends and other information developed during 1985. Preliminary work on the 1987 budget also took place at that time. In early October of 1986, Williams asked the divisional controller to prepare a report that presents performance for the first nine months of 1986. The report is reproduced in Exhibit A.

Exhibit A (22–28)

Bio-grade Products—Southeastern Sector
(in thousands)

	1986			1985	
	Annual budget	**Nine-month budget[a]**	**Nine-month actual**	**Annual budget**	**Actual results**
Sales	$2,800	$2,100	$2,200	$2,500	$2,430
Divisional costs and expenses:					
Direct materials and labor	$1,064	$ 798	$ 995	$ 900	$ 890
Supplies	44	33	35	35	43
Maintenance and repairs	200	150	60	175	160
Plant depreciation	120	90	90	110	110
Administration	120	90	90	90	100
Total divisional costs and expenses	1,548	1,161	1,270	1,310	1,303
Divisional margin	1,252	939	930	1,190	1,127
Allocated corporate fixed costs	360	270	240	340	320
Divisional profits	892	669	690	850	807
Cost of capital of divisional investment (20%)	420	321[b]	300[b]	370	365
Divisional residual income	$ 472	$ 348	$ 390	$ 480	$ 442
	Budgeted balance 12/31/86	**Budgeted balance 9/30/86**	**Actual balance 9/30/86**	**Budgeted balance 12/31/85**	**Actual balance 12/31/85**
Division investment:					
Accounts receivable	$ 280	$ 290	$ 250	$ 250	$ 250
Inventories	500	500	650	450	475
Plant fixed assets (net)	1,320	1,350	1,100	1,150	1,100
Total	$2,100	$2,140	$2,000	$1,850	$1,825
Cost of capital (20%)	$ 420	$ 321[b]	$ 300[b]	$ 370	$ 365

[a] Bio-grade's sales occur uniformly throughout the year.
[b] Imputed interest is calculated at only 15 percent to reflect that only nine months or three fourths of the fiscal year has passed.

Required:

a. Evaluate the performance of Alex Williams for the nine months ending September 1986. Support your evaluation with pertinent facts from the problem.

b. Identify the features of Bio-grade Products divisional performance measurement reporting and evaluating system which need to be revised if it is to reflect effectively the responsibilities of the divisional managers.

(CMA adapted)

22–29. Evaluate investment choice and performance measures

Amberina, Inc., operates several different semiautonomous divisions. A problem has recently arisen with respect to two divisions which process and sell plastics products. The Plastics Blending Division obtains feedstocks that it blends and, as a result of a joint process, splits into Phyrene and Extrene. The Plastics Blending Division processes the Phyrene further and sells the resulting product to the outside. The Extrene is sold to the Tools Division where it is molded into tool handles and sold.

In a typical year, $240,000 of costs are incurred in the blending of the feedstock. The Phyrene is processed further at a cost of $80,000 and is then sold to the outside at a price of $325,000. The Extrene is sold to the Tools Division at "cost plus 20 percent" where cost is determined on the basis of relative sales value at the split-off point. The Tools Division incurs an additional cost of $60,000 in molding the plastic and sells the resulting tool handles for $175,000.

The company's cost of capital is 15 percent. The Plastics Blending Division has assets of $240,000 while the Tools Division has assets of $120,000.

The Tools Division has learned that it could purchase the company that it is selling the handles to and, thus, obtain the ability to manufacture complete tools. The additional processing costs would amount to $61,000 per year and revenues would amount to $360,000. In addition, depreciation expenses would be incurred based on the amount spent to purchase the tool manufacturing company. The manufacturing company is asking $265,000 for its assets. These assets would be depreciated on a straight line basis for internal reporting purposes. Sum-of-the-years'-digits depreciation would be used for tax purposes. It is expected that the assets would have a useful life of five years with a salvage value of $77,500 at the end of the five years. In addition, $50,000 in working capital would be required to operate the tool manufacturing plant. Income taxes are 40 percent of net income.

Required:

The head of the Tools Division wants your assessment of the feasibility of the investment in terms of *(a)* net present value of the project, *(b)* the impact of the project on the Tools Division return on investment, and *(c)* the change in the sharing of costs of the Extrene which the manager of the Plastics Blending Division will be likely to demand if the project is installed. You may assume that if the tool manufacturing plant is acquired, there is no alternative market for the tool handles.

22–30. ROI and management behavior

The Notewon Corporation is a highly diversified company that grants its divisional executives a significant amount of authority in operating the divisions. Each division is responsible for its own sales, pricing, production, costs of operations, and the management of accounts receivable, inventories, accounts payable, and use of existing facilities. Cash is managed by corporate headquarters; all cash in excess of normal operating needs of the divisions is transferred periodically to corporate headquarters for redistribution or investment.

The divisional executives are responsible for presenting requests to corporate management for investment projects. The proposals are analyzed and documented at corporate headquarters. The final decision to commit funds to acquire equipment, to expand existing facilities, or for other investment purposes rests with corporate management. This procedure for investment projects is necessitated by Notewon's capital allocation policy.

The corporation evaluates the performance of division executives by the ROI measure. The asset base is composed of fixed assets employed plus working capital exclusive of cash.

The ROI performance of a divisional executive is the most important appraisal factor for salary changes. In addition, the annual performance bonus is based on the ROI results with increases in ROI having a significant impact on the amount of the bonus.

The Notewon Corporation adopted the ROI performance measure and related compensation procedures about ten years ago. The corporation did so to increase the awareness of divisional management of the importance of the profit/asset relationship and to provide additional incentive to the divisional executives to seek investment opportunities.

The corporation seems to have benefited from the program. The ROI for the corporation as a whole increased during the first years of the program. Although the ROI has continued to grow in each division, the corporate ROI has declined in recent years. The corporation has accumulated a sizable amount of cash and short-term marketable securities in the past three years.

The corporation management is concerned about the increase in the short-term marketable securities. A recent article in a financial publication suggested that the use of ROI was overemphasized by some companies with results similar to those experienced by Notewon.

Required:

a. Describe the specific actions division managers might have taken to cause the ROI to grow in each division but decline for the corporation. Illustrate your explanation with appropriate examples.

b. Explain, using the concepts of goal congruence and motivation of divisional executives, how Notewon Corporation's over emphasis on the use of the ROI measure might result in the recent decline in the corporation's return on investment and the increase in cash and short-term marketable securities.

c. What changes could be made in Notewon Corporation's compensation policy to avoid this problem? Explain your answer.

(CMA adapted)

22–31. Capitalize or expense decisions and performance measurement

Oil and gas companies inevitably incur costs on exploration ventures that are unsuccessful. These ventures are called "dry holes." There is a continuing debate over whether those costs should be written off as period expense or whether they should be capitalized as part of the "full" cost of finding profitable oil and gas ventures. PMX Drilling Company has been writing these costs off to expense as incurred. However, this year a new management team was hired to improve the "profit picture" of PMX's oil and gas exploration division. The new management team was hired with the provision that they would receive a bonus equal to 10 percent of any profits in excess of the 1985 base year profits of the division. However, no bonus would be paid if profits were less than 20 percent of end-of-year investment. The following information was included in the performance report for the division:

	1986	1985	Increase over base year
Sales revenues	$4,100,000	$4,000,000	
Costs incurred:			
Dry holes	–0–	800,000	
Depreciation and other amortization	780,000	750,000	
Other costs	1,600,000	1,550,000	
Division profit	$1,720,000	$ 900,000	$820,000
End of year investment	$8,100,000	$6,900,000	

During the year, the new team spent $1 million on exploratory activities, but $900,000 was spent on ventures that were unsuccessful. The new management team has included the $900,000 in the 1986 end-of-year investment base because they state, "You can't find the good ones without hitting a few bad ones."

Required:

a. What is the ROI for 1985 and 1986?
b. What is the amount of the bonus that the new management team is likely to claim?
c. If you were on the board of directors of PMX, how would you respond to the new management's claim for the bonus?

22–32. Evaluate performance evaluation system: Behavioral issues

The ATCO Company purchased the Dexter Company three years ago. Prior to the acquisition, Dexter manufactured and sold plastic products to a variety of customers. Dexter has since become a division of ATCO and now only manufactures plastic components for products made by ATCO's Macon Division. Macon sells its products to hardware wholesalers.

ATCO's corporate management gives the Dexter Division management a considerable amount of authority in running the division's operations. However, corporate management retains authority for decisions regarding capital investments, price setting of all products, and the quantity of each product to be produced by the Dexter Division.

ATCO has a formal performance evaluation program for the management of all of its divisions. The performance evaluation program relies heavily on each division's

ATCO COMPANY
Dexter Division
Income Statement
For the Year Ended October 31
(in thousands)

Sales revenue		$4,000
Costs and expenses:		
Product costs:		
Direct materials	$ 500	
Direct labor	1,100	
Factory overhead	1,300	
Total	2,900	
Less: Increase in inventory	350	2,550
Engineering and research		120
Shipping and receiving		240
Division administration:		
Manager's office	210	
Cost accounting	40	
Personnel	82	332
Corporate costs:		
Computer	48	
General services	230	278
Total costs and expenses		3,520
Divisional operating profit		$ 480
Net plant investment		$1,600
Return on investment		30%

return on investment. The income statement of Dexter Division provides the basis for the evaluation of Dexter's divisional management.

The financial statements for the divisions are prepared by the corporate accounting staff. The corporate general services costs are allocated on the basis of sales dollars and the computer department's actual costs are apportioned among the divisions on the basis of use. The net division investment includes division fixed assets at net book value (cost less depreciation), division inventory, and corporate working capital apportioned to the divisions on the basis of sales dollars.

Required:

a. Discuss the financial reporting and performance evaluation program of ATCO Company as it relates to the responsibilities of the Dexter Division.

b. Based upon your response to Requirement *(a),* recommend appropriate revisions of the financial information and reports used to evaluate the performance of Dexter's divisional management. If revisions are not necessary, explain why revisions are not needed.

(CMA adapted)

22–33. Divisional performance measurement: Behavioral issues

Divisional managers of SIU Incorporated have been expressing growing dissatisfaction with the current methods used to measure divisional performance. Divisional operations are evaluated every quarter by comparison with the static budget prepared during the prior year. Divisional managers claim that many factors are completely out of their control but are included in this comparison. This results in an unfair and misleading performance evaluation.

The managers have been particularly critical of the process used to establish standards and budgets. The annual budget, stated by quarters, is prepared six months prior to the beginning of the operating year. Pressure by top management to reflect increased earnings has often caused divisional managers to overstate revenues and/ or understate expenses. In addition, once the budget had been established, divisions were required to "live with the budget." Frequently, external factors such as the state of the economy, changes in consumer preferences, and actions of competitors have not been adequately recognized in the budget parameters that top management supplied to the divisions. The credibility of the performance review is curtailed when the budget can not be adjusted to incorporate these changes.

Top management, recognizing the current problems, has agreed to establish a committee to review the situation and to make recommendations for a new performance evaluation system. The committee consists of each division manager, the corporate controller, and the executive vice president who serves as the chairman. At the first meeting, one division manager outlined an Achievement of Objectives System (AOS). In this performance evaluation system, divisional managers would be evaluated according to three criteria:

1. Doing better than last year. Various measures would be compared to the same measures of the prior year.

2. Planning realistically. Actual performance for the current year would be compared to realistic plans and/or goals.

3. Managing current assets. Various measures would be used to evaluate the divisional management's achievements and reactions to changing business and economic conditions.

A division manager believed this system would overcome many of the inconsistencies of the current system because divisions could be evaluated from three different viewpoints. In addition, managers would have the opportunity to show how they would react and account for changes in uncontrollable external factors.

A second division manager was also in favor of the proposed AOS. However, he cautioned that the success of a new performance evaluation system would be limited unless it had the complete support of top management. Further, this support should be visible within all divisions. He believed that the committee should recommend some procedures which would enhance the motivational and competitive spirit of the divisions.

Required:

a. Explain whether or not the proposed AOS would be an improvement over the measure of divisional performance now used by SIU Incorporated.

b. Develop specific performance measures for each of the three criteria in the proposed AOS that could be used to evaluate divisional managers.

c. Discuss the motivational and behavioral aspects of the proposed performance system. Also, recommend specific programs that could be instituted to promote morale and give incentives to divisional management.

(CMA adapted)

22–34.—Change to more centralized organization structure: Behavorial issues

Greengrass Company is an established manufacturer and wholesaler of a broad line of lawn fertilizer and yard maintenance products. Greengrass Company has annual sales of approximately $100 million and has been a wholly owned subsidiary of a large conglomerate, KSU Corporation, for the past five years. Prior to that, it was an independent corporation with the stock controlled by the founding and managing family.

A. B. Cardwell, son of the founder, is currently the president of the company, but he is scheduled to retire in May of next year. His nephew, B. C. Cardwell, is currently executive vice president and has been heir apparent to the presidency ever since A. B. Cardwell became president.

Greengrass Company had maintained a pattern of increasing profits for many years. During the past three years, however profits have decreased significantly. Management has attributed this to reduced demand caused by cool, wet summers in the company's primary marketing area coupled with intense competitive activity.

Following his return from a week-long corporate management planning meeting, A. B. Cardwell called a staff meeting to discuss plans for next year's marketing season. At the close of the meeting, he announced that the KSU Board had named William Thoma to become president of Greengrass Company in May of next year. Cardwell explained that KSU's management was concerned with the subsidiary's slumping profits and had decided to assume a greater degree of control over Greengrass operations. Thoma's appointment was the first step in this direction. In addition, a new system of financial reporting to KSU management is to be installed.

Mr. Thoma's reputation was well known by the entire staff. He had been executive vice president of two other KSU-owned companies during the previous three years. In both cases, the companies had records of declining profits prior to his appointment. A significant management reorganization occurred in each of those companies within 12 months after his appointment. In each case, some members of senior management were given early retirement or released, depending upon their ages. Their replacements usually came from other KSU companies with which Thoma had been associated. While earnings did increase following the reorganizations, the entire "personality" of the companies was changed.

Required:

a. Discuss the ways the change to a more centralized organization and decision structure can be expected to influence the behavior of Greengrass managers.

b. Discuss the impact of William Thoma's selection as the new president on the behavior of Greengrass managers.

(CMA adapted)

22–35. Presenting cost information to production managers

Denny Daniels is production manager of the Alumalloy Division of WRT, Inc. Alumalloy has limited contact with outside customers and has no sales staff. Most of its customers are other divisions of WRT. All sales and purchases with outside customers are handled by other corporate divisions. Therefore, Alumalloy is treated as a cost center for reporting and evaluation purposes rather than as a revenue or profit center.

Daniels perceives the accounting department as a historical number generating process that provides little useful information for conducting his job. Consequently, the entire accounting process is perceived as a negative motivational device that does not reflect how hard or how effectively he works as a production manager. Daniels tried to discuss these perceptions and concerns with John Scott, the controller for the Alumalloy Division. Daniels told Scott, "I think the cost report is misleading. I know I've had better production over a number of operating periods, but the cost report still says I have excessive costs. Look, I'm not an accountant, I'm a production manager. I know how to get a good quality product out. Over a number of years, I've even cut the direct materials used to do it. But the cost report doesn't show any of this. Basically, it's always negative, no matter what I do. There's no way you can win with accounting or the people at corporate who use those reports."

Scott gave Daniels little consolation. Scott stated that the accounting system and the cost reports generated by headquarters are just part of the corporate game and almost impossible for an individual to change. "Although these accounting reports are pretty much the basis for evaluating the efficiency of your division and the means corporate uses to determine whether you have done the job they want, you shouldn't worry too much. You haven't been fired yet! Besides, these cost reports have been used by WRT for the last 25 years."

Daniels perceived from talking to the production manager of the Zinc Division that most of what Scott said was probably true. However, some minor cost reporting changes for Zinc had been agreed to by corporate headquarters. He also knew from the trade grapevine that the turnover of production managers was considered high at WRT, even though relatively few were fired. Most seemed to end up quitting, usually in disgust, because of beliefs that they were not being evaluated fairly. Typical comments of production managers who have left WRT are:

1. "Corporate headquarters doesn't really listen to us. All they consider are those misleading cost reports. They don't want them changed and they don't want any supplemental information."

2. "The accountants may be quick with numbers, but they don't know anything about production. As it was, I either had to ignore the cost reports entirely or pretend they are important even though they didn't tell how good a job I had done. No matter what they say about not firing people, negative reports mean negative evaluations. I'm better off working for another company."

A recent copy of the cost report prepared by corporate headquarters for the Alumalloy Division is shown below. Daniels does not like this report because he believes it fails to reflect the division's operations properly, thereby resulting in an unfair evaluation of performance.

Alumalloy Division
Cost Report
For the Month of April 1980
(in thousands)

	Master budget	Actual cost	Excess cost
Aluminum	$ 400	$ 437	$ 37
Labor	560	540	(20)
Overhead	100	134	34
Total	$1,060	$1,111	$ 51

Required:

Identify and explain three changes that could be made in the cost information presented to the production managers that would make the information more meaningful.

22–36. Empire Glass Company

Refer to Problem 17–25 which is the Empire Glass Company case (comprehensive budgeting and management control case).

Required:

Evaluate the strength and weaknesses of Empire's performance evaluation methods and organization structure. Should the plants continue to be profit/investment centers, or should they be cost centers? Why?

23

Transfer Pricing

To understand the use and computation of transfer prices in decentralized
    organizations.
To comprehend the behavioral issues involved in transfer pricing.

When goods or services are transferred from one unit of an organization to
another, the transaction is recorded in the accounting records. The value
assigned to the transaction is called the *transfer price*. Since this exchange
takes place inside of the organization, considerable discretion can be used
in putting a value on the transaction. Transfer prices are widely used for
decision making, product costing, and performance evaluation; hence, it is
important to consider the way those prices may be determined and the advantages and disadvantages of alternative transfer pricing methods.

Cost allocation and transfer pricing

Transfer pricing is commonly applied to the flow of costs in a manufacturing
organization. When goods are transferred from a production unit (work in
process) to a finished goods storage area, this transaction is recognized in
the accounts at cost. The cost may be actual, normal, or standard. The
value assigned to the transaction may differ depending on which of the three
costing methods is used.

The costs accumulated in the Work in Process Inventory account include
common costs allocated to the department as well as the direct costs of
the department. The value of the costs allocated and, hence, the value assigned
to the products in Work in Process Inventory depend in part on the basis
used to allocate the common costs.

If a service department, such as a maintenance department, provides services to production, marketing, or other user departments, the costs of that
service department are transferred to the user departments. Those costs may
be transferred to user departments by one of at least three different methods,
as discussed in Chapter 7.

So far in this book, we have discussed cost allocations without specifically
defining them as transfer prices. The cost allocations presented so far, which
describe the transfers of goods in process and the assignment of service department costs, have all been based on cost. Although the measure of cost and
the allocation method may vary among organizations, transfers are almost
always made at cost in centralized types of organizations.

Transfer pricing in decentralized organizations

In this chapter, we extend the discussion of cost allocation to include the use of market values as the basis of determining transfer prices. In addition, we present some of the effects of using transfer prices in a decentralized organization.

In decentralized organizations, responsibility for decision making rests at lower levels of the organization hierarchy. Relatively autonomous responsibility centers buy from and sell to each other. At General Motors, for example, it is common for one division to buy direct materials from a number of suppliers, including other divisions of General Motors. In effect, responsibility centers buy and sell from each other. The transfer price becomes a cost to the buyer and a revenue to the seller division. If the divisions are evaluated based on some measure of profitability that includes these transfer-price-based costs and revenues, then setting the transfer price can have an impact on the reported performance measures and, hence, the evaluation of each division's performance. Determining the appropriate transfer price can be important both to managers who are performance evaluators as well as to the managers whose performance is subject to such evaluation.

Recording a transfer

Division A of Shockless Power Company makes a motor that is purchased by Division B, which manufactures refrigerators. When the motors are sold or transferred, their cost becomes a part of the cost of goods sold for Division A. If they are sold to an outside buyer, the cash or receivable exchanged for the motors becomes revenue to Division A. Likewise, if Divison A transfers motors to Division B, some recognition of the transfer will be made on the books of Division A. If the motors are transferred at cost, then Division A would obtain no profit from the transfer. In a decentralized organization, the internal transfer is often priced at the market value of the goods transferred.

For example, let's assume that Division A can sell the motors or transfer them to Division B at a price of $50 per motor. The inventory cost of the motors is $40 each. This cost includes a variable manufacturing cost of $30 and allocated fixed manufacturing costs of $10 per motor. The transfer of 2,000 motors from Division A to Division B would be recorded on Division A's books as:

Receivable from Division B	100,000	
Sales Revenue		100,000
Cost of Goods Sold	80,000	
Finished Goods Inventory		80,000

With this entry, Division A would have a recorded gross margin of $20,000 from the transfer of motors to Division B.

On Division B's books, the receipt of the 2,000 motors from Division A would be recorded as

Direct Materials Inventory	100,000	
Payable to Division A		100,000

For evaluating the performance of each individual division, these costs and revenues would be used as the basis for profit measurement. However, for external financial reporting purposes, any interdivisional profits are eliminated to avoid double counting in the financial statements.

Recording the transfer of goods and services, whether using cost-based methods as discussed in Chapters 4 and 7, or market value methods as we discuss in this chapter, is a straightforward accounting procedure. The critical question is the value to be assigned to the transfer.

Setting transfer prices

The value placed on transferred goods and services is often used to coordinate the activities of various responsibility centers. The transfer price can be a device to motivate managers to act in the best interest of the company. Furthermore, transfer prices are important performance measures for responsibility centers because they represent a cost to the buyer and revenue to the seller. If the transfer price is indicative of the opportunity cost of the goods or services transferred, the price may make a better basis for such evaluation purposes than otherwise.

As might be expected, a conflict can arise between the company's interests and an individual manager's interests when transfer-price-based performance measures are used. The following example demonstrates such a conflict.

The production division of Ace Electronics Company was operating below capacity. The assembly division of the same company received a contract to assemble 10,000 units of a final product, XX–1. Each unit of XX–1 required one part, A-16, that was made by the production division. Both divisions are decentralized, autonomous investment centers and are evaluated based on operating profits and return on investment.

The vice president of the assembly division called the vice president in charge of the production division and made a proposal:

Assembly VP: Look Joe, I know you're running below capacity out there in your department. I'd like to buy 10,000 units of A-16 at $30 per unit. That will enable you to keep up your production lines.

Production VP: Are you kidding, Meg? I happen to know that it would cost you a lot more if you had to buy A-16's from an outside supplier. We refuse to accept less than $40 per unit which gives us our usual markup and covers our costs.

Assembly VP: Joe, we both know that your variable costs per unit are only $20. I realize I'd be getting a good deal at $30, but so would you. You should treat this as a special order. Anything over your differential costs on the order is pure profit. Look Joe, if you can't do better than $40, I'll have to go elsewhere. I have to keep my costs down, too, you know.

Production VP: The $40 per unit is firm. Take it or leave it!

The assembly division subsequently sought bids on the part and was able to obtain its requirements from an outside supplier for $38 per unit. The production division continued to operate below capacity. The actions of the two divisions cost the company $180,000. This amount is the difference between the price paid for the part from the outside supplier ($38) and the differential costs of producing in the assembly division ($20) times the 10,000 units in the order.

Although currently we cannot explain why the production VP would refuse such an order, we can surmise that competition between the two divisions for a share of bonus payments or other performance-based rewards may lead the production VP to expect a reduction in relative performance measures. This would occur if the assembly VP was to receive a windfall due to the bargain price paid for the transferred part. Research in this topic area is under way, and perhaps when complete, we will have a better understanding of the reasons for such behavior.

How can a decentralized organization avoid this type of cost? Although there is no easy solution to this type of problem, there are three general approaches to the problem:

1. Direct intervention,
2. Centrally established transfer price policies,
3. Negotiated transfer prices.

Each of these approaches has advantages and disadvantages. Each may be appropriate under different circumstances. In the next part of this section, we discuss these alternatives.

Direct intervention

Ace Electronic's top management could have directly intervened in this pricing dispute and ordered the production division to produce the A-16's and transfer them to the assembly division at a management-specified transfer price. If this were an extraordinarily large order, or if internal product transfers were rare, direct intervention may be the best available solution to the problem. It would induce division managers to make the decision that maximizes company profits but at the same time allows managers to maintain their autonomy. The risk in direct intervention is that top management will become swamped with pricing disputes and individual division managers will lose the flexibility and other advantages of autonomous decision making. Thus, direct intervention promotes short-run profits by minimizing the type of uneconomic behavior demonstrated in the Ace Electronics case, but there is a cost in reduced benefits from decentralization.

So long as the transfer pricing problems are infrequent, the benefits of direct intervention may outweigh the costs. However, if transfer transactions are common, direct intervention can be costly by requiring substantial top-management involvement in decisions that should be made at the divisional level. To avoid this problem, a company may establish a transfer pricing policy that encourages decentralized managers to make an economically optimal decision for the company without significantly reducing their autonomy.

Centrally established transfer price policies

A transfer pricing policy should allow divisional autonomy yet encourage managers to pursue corporate goals consistent with their own personal goals. Additionally, the use of transfer prices to determine the selling division's revenue and the buying division's cost should be compatible with the company's performance evaluation system. The two bases for transfer price policies are:

1. Market prices.
2. Cost.

Although variations exist in both alternative bases, the two may be considered to encompass the most widely discussed approaches to establishing transfer pricing policies. We discuss these approaches and their advantages and disadvantages in the following sections.

Market prices

External-based market prices are generally considered the best basis for transfer pricing. When there is a competitive market for the product, when there is little differentiation in the product, and when the prices are readily available, market prices work well as transfer prices. Indeed, a number of economic analyses indicate the superiority of market prices in certain theoretic settings.[1] An advantage to the use of market prices is that both the supplying and purchasing divisions can buy and sell as many units as they want at the market price. Managers of both supplying and purchasing divisions are indifferent between trading with each other or with outsiders. From the company's perspective, this is fine as long as the supplying unit is operating at capacity, which it would in such a market.

However, situations are rare in which such markets exist. Usually it costs more to acquire an item than can be realized from a sale. The difference is due to market transaction costs. Indeed, the very existence of two responsibility centers that trade with one another in one company tends to indicate that there may be advantages to not dealing with whatever market exists for transferred goods. For example, a common company framework may facilitate control of the internally supplied product quality or delivery reliability. Furthermore, costs of negotiating transactions can be reduced or eliminated when dealing internally. When such advantages exist, it is in the company's interest to create incentives for internal transfer. Top management may establish policies that direct two responsibility centers to trade internally

---

[1] A classic paper is by J. Hirshleifer, "On the Economics of Transfer Pricing," *Journal of Business,* July 1956. Also see J. Ronen and G. McKinney, "Transfer Pricing for Divisional Autonomy," *Journal of Accounting Research,* Spring 1970; and R. Swieringa and J. Waterhouse, "Organizational Views of Transfer Pricing," *Accounting, Organizations and Society,* May 1982.

unless they can show good reason why external trades are more advantageous. A variation on this approach may be an established policy that provides the buying division a discount for items purchased internally.

Complexities of market imperfections   Transfer pricing becomes more complex when suppliers and purchases cannot sell and buy all they want in perfectly competitive markets. Transaction costs create a spread between the price at which a division can sell a product and the price at which one can buy. Such differences may affect the economic value of the alternative to transfer or to deal with the outside. Moreover, if there is no unique outside price, then the transfer price is not uniquely defined. For example, should the divisions of Ace Electronics base a transfer price on the $40 regular sales price of the production division, the $20 marginal sales price of the production division (since they have idle capacity) or the $38 alternative price from the outside bidder?

In situations where the market is imperfect, generally an opportunity cost approach will be used to establish a range of transfer prices. For the selling division, the opportunity cost of transferring is the greater of:

1. The outside sales value of the transferred product.
2. The differential production cost for the transferred product.

For the buying division, the opportunity cost of acquiring by transfer is the lesser of:

1. The price that would be required to purchase from the outside.
2. The profit that would be lost from producing the final product if the transferred unit could not be obtained at an economic price.

A transfer is in the best economic interest of the company if the opportunity cost for the selling division is less than the opportunity cost for the buying division.

This approach can be illustrated using the Ace Electronics example. Because of its idle capacity, the production division could not sell any more of part A-16 to the outside; hence, the outside sales value was zero. The differential production costs were $20 per unit produced. Thus, the opportunity cost of producing each unit of A-16 internally is $20.

The assembly division must pay $38 to acquire the part from the outside. Since the buying division is willing to pay $38 for the part, we assume that their contribution margin from manufacturing their output unit is at least as great as this amount. Hence, the opportunity cost for the buying division is $38 per unit. Since the opportunity cost from the transfer ($20) is less than the opportunity cost of buying from the outside ($38), the optimal economic decision for the company is to transfer. What transfer price would encourage a transfer in this situation?

As long as the transfer price is greater than the opportunity cost of the selling division and less than the opportunity cost of the buying division, a transfer will be encouraged. In this situation, any transfer price in excess of $20 should encourage the production division to transfer. This will occur because the production division obtains a profit contribution equal to the difference between the transfer price and the differential cost of $20.

If the transfer price were $30, as initially suggested by the assembly division manager, then the production division would have a differential contribution of $10 per unit (which is the $30 price less the $20 differential cost). Unless the production division could negotiate a higher transfer price or find use for its idle capacity, it could do no better than this transfer.

The buying division should be willing to acquire the part by internal transfer so long as the transfer price for the part is no greater than $38. The buying division's operating profit per unit will increase by the difference between the outside purchase price and the internal transfer price. Thus, if the assembly division could obtain the part at $30 per unit, then the assembly division's operating profit would be greater by $8 per unit transferred.

From the first part of the example, we noted that the decision not to transfer cost the company $180,000 for the 10,000 units requested by the assembly division. If the transfer price were set at $30, then this $180,000 profit would be shared by the two divisions as follows:

Production division:

$$\$100,000 = 10,000 \text{ units} \times (\$30 - \$20)$$

Assembly division:

$$\$80,000 = 10,000 \text{ units} \times (\$38 - \$30)$$

Total:

$$\$180,000$$

Of course, if the production division were able to sell part A-16 to the outside for $40 per unit, or were able to use its resources to produce some other output that provided an equivalent revenue of $40 per unit of A-16, then its opportunity cost would be $40 and the transfer would not be in the economic interest of the company. For each unit transferred in this case, the production division would incur an opportunity cost of $40 per unit in lost sales revenue. At the same time, the assembly division would incur a cost of $40 for each unit transferred when they could acquire the unit on the outside for $38. The production division's operating profit would be the same, but the assembly division's operating profit would decrease by $20,000. That is:

Production division:

$$\$0 = 10,000 \times (\$40 - \$40)$$

Assembly division:

$$\$(20,000) = 10,000 \times (\$38 - \$40)$$

The question of interest is how management can use market-based prices to establish a transfer pricing policy that will induce the economically optimal decisions by decentralized managers.

Establishing a market price policy   To encourage transfers that are in the interest of the company, management may set a transfer pricing policy based on the use of market prices for the intermediate product, such as part A-16. As a general rule, a market-price-based transfer pricing policy contains the following guidelines:

1.   The transfer price is usually set at a discount from the cost to acquire the item on the open market.
2.   The selling division may elect to transfer or to continue to sell to the outside.

The first part of the policy induces the buying division to acquire from within the company. The discount is usually set so that the selling and buying divisions can share in the savings from avoiding the outside market transactions. With such a discount, the selling division and buying division would both be induced to transfer in normal circumstances.

For example, the typical solution to the Ace Electronics problem would have the production division sell to a wholesale market at the $40 price. The assembly division would probably be required to pay the wholesale price plus the wholesaler's markup. Let's say that the purchase price is $45. If management has established a transfer pricing policy that provides a 5 percent discount from the outside acquisition market price, then the transfer price would be $42.75, or 95 percent of $45. The assembly division would prefer to buy at that price due to the savings, and the production division would sell at that price because it exceeds the $40 they could obtain on the outside market. Under this policy, both divisions benefit from the transactions costs in the outside market.

An established policy will, most likely, be imperfect in the sense that it will not always work to induce the economically optimal outcome. However, as with other management decisions, the cost of any system must be weighed against the benefits of the system. Improving a transfer pricing policy beyond some optimal point will result in the costs of the system exceeding the benefits. As a result, management tends to settle for a satisfactory system rather than a perfect system. We can envision situations where such a transfer pricing policy as we have suggested will not work.

One such situation is when the opportunity cost of the transferred item is not the same as the outside market for the product. For example, Ace's production division might be able to use the capacity required for the transferred A-16's to manufacture some other part. The resources used to manufacture the other part yield an opportunity cost of $44 per equivalent unit of A-16. This could happen if the other part were more profitable than the

A-16. In this situation, the selling division would rather produce the alternate part, obtain the $44, and let the assembly division buy from the outside.

Another limitation on the use of the suggested management policy can arise when there are temporary fluctuations in market prices. If there is a temporarily depressed market for A-16, should the company permit the assembly division to buy from the outside while the production division faces possible layoffs or shutdown of operations? In this situation, management would probably intervene directly and require a transfer. Management would set a transfer price for internal recordkeeping purposes and, hopefully, modify its performance evaluations to recognize the benefits derived from the internal transfer.

A third limitation on the use of a market-based rule is that market prices are not always readily available. In this situation, the costs of implementing a market-based policy may be substantial. If the price of the item to be transferred is not widely quoted, bids may be needed from outside suppliers. Such suppliers will be unwilling to bid when they realize that the company will simply use the bid to set a transfer price rather than to seriously consider the offered goods.

Depending on the nature of the outside markets and the availability of information about market prices, management may elect to establish a transfer pricing policy based on cost rather than on market prices.

Cost-based transfer price policies

When external markets do not exist or are not available to the company or when information about external market prices is not readily available, companies may elect to use some form of cost-based transfer pricing system. The costs used may be based on full costing or variable costing, actual cost or standard cost. When cost alone is used for transfer pricing, the selling division cannot realize a profit on the goods transferred. This may be a disincentive to the selling division. Some companies overcome this problem by setting a transfer price on a cost-plus basis. The cost-plus price includes the allowed cost of the item plus a markup or other profit allowance. With such a system, the selling division obtains a profit contribution on units transferred and, hence, benefits if performance is measured on the basis of divisional operating profits.

Standard costs or actual costs   If actual costs are used as a basis for the transfer, any variances or inefficiencies in the selling division are passed along to the buying division. The problems of isolating the variances that have been transferred to subsequent buyer divisions becomes extremely complex. To promote responsibility in the selling division and to isolate variances within divisions, standard costs are usually used as a basis for transfer pricing in cost-based systems.

For example, if Ace Electronics used a cost-based transfer pricing system instead of a market-based system, a policy might be established that would result in Part A-16 having a transfer price equal to its full cost plus a 20 percent markup on cost. The variable cost of the part has already been given as $20. Assume that the appropriate share of fixed costs for the part is $15 per unit. The transfer price is $42 which equals 120 percent of the $35 full cost. If these costs are standard costs, then the assembly division will be charged $42 per unit regardless of actual operations in the production division. If the production division incurs a cost of $38 per unit due to price changes, inefficiencies, or other reasons, then the production division's operating profit per unit will fall by the $3 cost overrun. That is, production expected a profit of $7 per unit (which is $42 − $20 − $15). However, actual profits of the division are $4 per unit, which is the difference between the $42 transfer price and the $38 cost. The assembly division is still charged with the standard $42 cost regardless of what happens in the production division.

Now let's see what happens if actual costs are used. The transfer price policy is the same: 120 percent of cost. With the cost now at $38, the transfer price is $45.60 per unit, or 120 percent of $38. The assembly division gets charged not only with the $3 per unit cost overrun but also a $.60 profit per unit on that cost overrun. What happens to the production division? They obtain an increased profit from the cost overrun!

The assembly division expected a profit of $7 per unit based on the standard costs. Using actual cost, the transfer price is $45.60 while the production division's costs are $38 per unit. The production division's unit profit is now $7.60 which is $45.60 less $38. Such a policy can be a disincentive to cost control. Of course, management could assure that the assembly division would not obtain profits on cost overruns by fixing the plus portion of the cost-plus price at a percentage of standard costs or a stated monetary amount.

Other motivational aspects   When the transfer pricing rule does not give the supplier a profit on the transaction, motivational problems can arise. For example, if transfers are made at differential cost, the supplier makes no contribution towards profits on the transferred goods. Under these circumstances, the transfer price policy does not motivate the supplier to transfer internally because there is seldom, if ever, a profit from internal transfers. This situation can be remedied in several ways.

A supplier whose transfers are almost all internal is usually organized as a cost center. The center manager is normally held responsible for costs, not for revenues. Hence, the transfer price does not affect the manager's performance measures. In companies where such a supplier is a profit center, the artificial nature of the transfer price should be taken into consideration when evaluating the results of that center's operations.

A supplying center that does business with both internal and external customers could be set up as a profit center for external business when the manager has price-setting power and as a cost center for internal transfers when the manager does not have price-setting power. Performance on external business could be measured as if the center were a profit center, while performance on internal business could be measured as if the center were a cost center.

A dual transfer pricing system could be installed to provide the selling division with a profit, but charge the buying department with costs only. That is, the buyer could be charged the cost of the unit, however cost might be determined, and the selling division credited with cost plus some profit allowance. The difference could be accounted for by a special centralized account. This system would preserve cost data for subsequent buyer departments, and would encourage internal transfers by providing a profit on such transfers for the selling divisions.

We have assumed that supplier center managers are rewarded on the basis of some profit measurement. However, other bases of reward are possible to encourage internal transfers. For example, many companies recognize internal transfers and incorporate them explicitly in their reward systems. Other companies base part of a supplying manager's bonus on the purchasing center's profits. There are ways of creating incentives for managers to transfer internally in organizational settings where profit-based transfer prices would be disadvantageous. Management can choose from the cost-based pricing rules when such a policy would be cost beneficial.

Negotiated prices

An alternative to a centrally administered transfer pricing policy is to permit managers to negotiate the price for internally transferred goods and services. Under this system, the managers involved act much the same as the managers of independent companies. Negotiation strategies may be similar to those employed when trading with outside markets. The major advantage to negotiated transfer prices is that they preserve the autonomy of the division managers. However, the two primary disadvantages are that a great deal of management effort may be consumed in the negotiating process, and the final price and its implications for performance measurement may depend more on the manager's ability to negotiate than on other factors.

For example, in the Ace Electronics case, the manager of the production division is at a distinct disadvantage in the negotiating process. There is idle capacity in the production division; hence, the manager is faced with a choice of zero profits or whatever he might be able to get from the assembly manager. The assembly manager has the upper hand here. The assembly manager could offer anything over $20, and it would improve the absolute value of the production manager's profit measure. If the assembly manager offered $21 per unit, the production manager's profits would increase by $1 per unit. However, the assembly manager would show an extra profit of $17 per unit over what she could make if she bought the units at $38 from the outside supplier. Depending on the compensation system, the production manager could realize a reduction in compensation because his relative profitability would fall if he makes the transfer.

Current practices

In a survey of corporate practices, Vancil reported that nearly half of the 239 companies that reported their transfer pricing policies used a cost-based transfer pricing system. Thirty-one percent used a market-price-based system, and 22 percent used a negotiated system.[2] The results of this survey are summarized in Illustration 23–1.

Illustration 23–1

Transfer pricing practices

Method used	Percent	Number
Cost based:		
Variable cost based	4.6	11
Full cost based	25.5	61
Cost plus	16.7	40
Total cost based	46.8	112
Market based	31.0	74
Negotiated transfer prices	22.2	53
Total companies reporting their transfer pricing policy	100	239

SOURCE: R. Vancil, *Decentralization, Managerial Ambiguity by Design,* (Homewood, Ill.: Dow Jones-Irwin, 1979), p. 180. Results based on questionnaires mailed to 1,010 firms; there were 357 usable responses.

Summary

When companies transfer goods or services between divisions, a price is assigned to that transaction. This transfer price becomes a part of the recorded revenues and costs in the divisions involved in the transfer. As a result, the dollar value assigned to the transfer can have significant implications in measuring divisional performance. Transfer pricing systems may be based on direct intervention, market values, costs, or through negotiation among the division managers. The appropriate method depends on the markets in which the company operates and management's goals. In any event, top management usually tries to use transfer pricing systems to promote corporate goals without destroying the autonomy of division managers.

Terms and concepts

The following terms and concepts should be familiar to you after reading this chapter.

Cost-based transfer pricing
Dual transfer pricing
Market-based transfer pricing
Negotiated transfer price
Opportunity cost approach

Opportunity cost of acquiring by transfer
Opportunity cost of transferring
Transfer price

[2] Richard F. Vancil, *Decentralization, Managerial Ambiguity by Design* (Homewood, Ill.: Dow Jones-Irwin, 1979), p. 180.

<table>
<tr><td>**Self-study
problem No. 1**</td><td>The Peter Foote shoe company has two divisions: production and marketing. Production manufactures Peter Foote shoes which it sells to both the marketing division and to other retailers (the latter under a different brand name). Marketing operates several small shoe stores in shopping centers. Marketing sells both Peter Foote and other brands.</td></tr>
</table>

Some relevant facts for production are as follows:

Production is operating far below its capacity.

Sales price to outsiders	$28.50[a] per pair
Variable cost to produce	19.00[a] per pair
Fixed costs	$100,000 per month

[a] To keep the analysis from becoming unnecessarily complex, we assume Peter Foote makes one product line and each pair of shoes has the same variable cost and price as each other pair.

The following data pertain to the sale of Peter Foote shoes by marketing:

Marketing is operating far below its capacity.

Sales price	$40 per pair
Variable marketing costs	5% of sales price

Marketing has decided to reduce the sales price of Peter Foote shoes. The company's variable manufacturing and marketing costs are differential to this decision, while *fixed* manufacturing and marketing costs are not.

Required:

    a. What is the *minimum* price that can be charged for the shoes and still cover differential manufacturing and marketing costs?

    b. What is the appropriate transfer price for this decision?

    c. What if the transfer price was set at $28.50? What effect would this have on the minimum price set by the marketing manager?

Solution to self-study problem No. 1

    a. From the company's perspective the minimum price would be the variable cost of producing and marketing the goods. They would solve for this minimum price, P_C, (the subscript C means this is the minimum price that is in the *company's* best interest) as follows:

$$P_C = \$19 + .05P_C$$
$$P_C - .05P_C = \$19$$
$$.95P_C = \$19$$
$$P_C = \underline{\underline{\$20}}$$

The *minimum* price the company should accept is $20. If the company was centralized, we would expect that this information would be conveyed to the manager of marketing, who would be instructed not to set a price below $20.

    b. The transfer price that correctly informs the marketing manager about the differential costs of manufacturing is $19.

    c. If the production manager set the price at $28.50, the marketing manager would solve for the minimum price (which we call P_M for *Marketing's* solution):

$$P_M = \$28.50 + .05\,P_M$$
$$P_M - .05\,P_M = \$28.50$$
$$.95\,P_M = \$28.50$$
$$P_M = \underline{\underline{\$30}}$$

So the marketing manager sets the price in excess of $30 per pair. In fact, prices of $28, $25, or anything greater than $20 would have generated a positive contribution margin from the production and sale of shoes.

Self-study problem No. 2

How would your answer to self-study problem No. 1 change if the production division had been operating at full capacity?

Solution to self-study problem No. 2

If the production division had been operating at capacity, there would have been an implicit opportunity cost of internal transfers. Production would have foregone a sale in the wholesale market to make the internal transfer. The implicit opportunity cost to the company is the lost contribution margin ($28.50 − $19 = $9.50) from not selling in the wholesale market.

Thus, if production had sufficient sales in the wholesale market such that it would have had to forego those sales to transfer internally, the transfer price should have been:

$$\begin{matrix}\text{Differential cost} \\ \text{of production}\end{matrix} + \begin{matrix}\text{Implicit opportunity cost} \\ \text{to company if goods are} \\ \text{transferred internally}\end{matrix} = \$19 + \$9.50$$

$$= \$28.50$$

Marketing would have appropriately treated the $28.50 as part of *its* differential cost of buying and selling the shoes. When production was operating below full capacity (hence, the implicit opportunity cost of transferring to marketing was zero), the minimum price for the shoes was derived as follows:

$$P_M = \$19 + .05\,P_M$$
$$.95\,P_M = \$19$$
$$P_M = \$20$$

However, if production is operating at full capacity, the minimum price is:

$$P_M = \$28.50 + .05\,P_M$$
$$.95\,P_M = \$28.50$$
$$P_M = \$30$$

Questions

23–1. What are some of the bases for establishing a transfer price?

23–2. Why do transfer prices exist even in highly centralized organizations?

23–3.   What are some goals of a transfer pricing system in a decentralized organization?

23–4.   Why are market-based transfer prices considered optimal under many circumstances?

23–5.   What are the limitations to market-based transfer prices?

23–6.   What are the advantages of a centrally administered transfer price (that is, direct intervention)? What are the disadvantages of such a transfer price?

23–7.   Why do company often use prices other than market prices for interdivisional transfers?

23–8.   Division A has no external markets. It produces monofilament that is used by Division B. Division B cannot purchase this particular type of monofilament from any other source. What transfer pricing system would you recommend for the interdivisional sale of monofilament? Why?

23–9.   What is the basis for the minimum and maximum transfer prices recommended in the text?

23–10. Some have suggested that managers should negotiate transfer prices. What are the disadvantages of a negotiated transfer price system?

23–11. Describe the economic basis for transfer pricing systems.

Exercises

23–12. Evaluate transfer pricing system

A company permits its decentralized units to "lease" space to one another. Division X has leased some idle warehouse space to Division Y at a price of $1 per square foot per month. Recently, Division X obtained a new five-year contract that will increase its production sufficiently so that the warehouse space will no longer be idle. Division X has notified Division Y that the new rental price will be $3.50 per square foot per month. Division Y can lease space at $2 per square foot in another warehouse, but prefers to stay in the shared facilities. Division Y management states that it would prefer not to move. Division X figures it will lose the equivalent of $3 per square foot if it cannot use the space now used by Division Y.

Required:

Comment on the transfer pricing system. Include a recommendation on the appropriate action that should be taken. Your recommendation should also show the minimum transfer price for warehouse rental as well as the maximum transfer price.

23–13. Journal entries for transfer pricing

Terra Firma Construction Company has two operating divisions. A precast concrete division manufactures building parts out of concrete. These parts are shipped to building sites and assembled on the site. The company also has a site construction division that constructs buildings from the precast concrete parts. The precast concrete division transferred units that cost $800,000 to a construction site operated by the site construction division. The units were transferred at a price of $950,000.

Required:

a.   What journal entries would be required to record the transfer of the parts on the books of each division?

b.   What eliminations would be required when Terra Firma Construction Company prepares its external financial reports?

23–14. Evaluate transfer prices

Wellcome Enterprises is a diversified real estate company. Its brokerage division acts as an agent for buyers and sellers of real estate. Its leasing division rents and manages properties for others. Its maintenance division performs various contract services such as carpentry, painting, plumbing, and electrical work. The maintenance division has an estimated variable cost of $18 per labor-hour. Fixed costs for the maintenance division are $75,000 per month. This amounts to $7.50 per hour at normal capacity. The maintenance division usually charges $35 per hour for labor performed for outsiders. This rate is competitive with the rates charged by other maintenance companies. The leasing division has complained that it could hire its own maintenance staff at an estimated cost of $20 per hour (including prorated fixed costs).

Required:

a. What is the minimum transfer price that the maintenance division should obtain for its services?

b. What is the maximum price that the leasing division should pay?

c. Would your answer in (a) or (b) change if the maintenance division had idle capacity? If so, which answer would change and what would the new amount be?

23–15. Transfer pricing analysis

Mar Company has two decentralized divisions, X and Y. Division X has always purchased certain units from Division Y at $75 per unit. Because Division Y plans to raise the price to $100 per unit, Division X desires to purchase these units from outside suppliers for $75 per unit. Division Y's costs follow:

Y's variable costs per unit	$70
Y's annual fixed costs	$15,000
Y's annual production of these units for X	1,000 units

If Division X buys from an outside supplier, the facilities Division Y uses to manufacture these units would remain idle. What would be the result if Mar enforces a transfer price of $100 per unit between Divisions X and Y?

(CPA adapted)

23–16. Transfer pricing with imperfect markets

Selling division offers its product to outside markets at a price of $200. Selling incurs variable costs of $70 per unit and fixed costs of $50,000 per month based on monthly production of 1,000 units.

Buying division can acquire the product from an alternate supplier at a cost of $210 per unit. Buying division can also acquire the product from selling division for $200, but must pay $15 per unit in transportation costs in addition to the transfer price charged by selling division.

Required:

a. What are the costs and benefits of the alternatives available to selling and buying divisions with respect to the transfer of the selling division's product? Assume that selling can market all that it can produce.

b. How would your answer change if selling had idle capacity sufficient to cover all of buying's needs?

23–17. Transfer pricing with imperfect markets—ROI evaluation

Division S of S&T Enterprises has an investment base of $600,000. Division S produces and sells 90,000 units of a product at a market price of $10 per unit. Its variable costs total $3 per unit. The division also charges each unit with a share of fixed costs based on capacity production of 100,000 units per year. The fixed cost "burden" is computed at $5 per unit. Any production volume variance is written off to expense at the end of the period.

Division T wants to purchase 20,000 units from Division S. However, Division T is only willing to pay $6.20 per unit. The reason Division T can only pay the lower amount is that Division T has an opportunity to accept a special order at a reduced price. The order is only economically justifiable if Division T can acquire the Division S output at a reduced price.

Required:

a. What is the ROI for Division S without the transfer to Division T.
b. What is Division S's ROI if it transfers 20,000 units to Division T at $6.20 each?
c. What is the minimum transfer price for the 20,000 unit order that Division S would accept if Division S were willing to maintain the same ROI with the transfer as they would accept by selling their 90,000 units to the outside market?

Problems and cases

23–18. Transfer pricing—performance evaluation issues

The Ajax Division of Gunnco, operating at capacity, has been asked by the Defco Division of Gunnco Corporation to supply it with Electrical Fitting No. 1726. Ajax sells this part to its regular customers for $7.50 each. Defco, which is operating at 50 percent capacity, is willing to pay $5 each for the fitting. Defco will put the fitting into a brake unit that it is manufacturing on essentially a cost-plus basis for a commercial airplane manufacturer.

Ajax has a variable cost of producing fitting No. 1726 of $4.25. The cost of the brake unit as being built by Defco is as follows:

Purchased parts—outside vendors	$22.50
Ajax fitting—1726	5.00
Other variable costs	14.00
Fixed overhead and administration	8.00
	$49.50

Defco believes the price concession is necessary to get the job.

The company uses ROI and dollar profits in the measurement of division and division manager performance.

Required:

a. Consider that you are the division controller of Ajax. Would you recommend that Ajax supply fitting 1726 to Defco? (Ignore any income tax issues.) Why or why not?
b. Would it be to the short-run economic advantage of the Gunnco Corporation for the Ajax Division to supply Defco Division with fitting 1726 at $5 each? (Ignore any income tax issues.) Explain your answer.
c. Discuss the organizational and manager behavior difficulties, if any, inherent in this situation. As the Gunnco controller what would you advise the Gunnco Corporation president do in this situation?

(CMA adapted)

23–19. Evaluate profit impact of alternative transfer decisions

A. R. Oma, Inc., manufactures a line of men's perfumes and after-shaving lotions. The manufacturing process is basically a series of mixing operations with the addition of certain aromatic and coloring ingredients; the finished product is packaged in a company-produced glass bottle and packed in cases containing 6 bottles.

A. R. Oma feels that the sale of its product is heavily influenced by the appearance and appeal of the bottle and has, therefore, devoted considerable managerial effort to the bottle production process. This has resulted in the development of certain unique bottle production processes in which management takes considerable pride.

The two areas (that is, perfume production and bottle manufacture) have evolved over the years in an almost independent manner; in fact, a rivalry has developed between management personnel as to "which division is the more important" to A. R. Oma. This attitude is probably intensified because the bottle manufacturing plant was purchased intact 10 years ago, and no real interchange of management personnel or ideas (except at the top corporate level) has taken place.

Since the acquisition, all bottle production has been absorbed by the perfume manufacturing plant. Each area is considered a separate profit center and evaluated as such. As the new corporate controller you are responsible for the definition of a proper transfer value to use in crediting the bottle production profit center and in debiting the packaging profit center.

At your request, the bottle division general manager has asked certain other bottle manufacturers to quote a price for the quantity and sizes demanded by the perfume division. These competitive prices are:

Volume	Total price	Price per case
2,000,0000 eq. cases[a]	$ 4,000,000	$2.00
4,000,000	7,000,000	1.75
6,000,000	10,000,000	1.67

[a] An "equivalent case" represents six bottles each.

A cost analysis of the internal bottle plant indicates that they can produce bottles at these costs:

Volume	Total price	Cost per case
2,000,000 eq. cases	$3,200,000	$1.60
4,000,000	5,200,000	1.30
6,000,000	7,200,000	1.20

(Your cost analysts point out that these costs represent fixed costs of $1,200,000 and variable costs of $1 per equivalent case.)

These figures have given rise to considerable corporate discussion as to the proper value to use in the transfer of bottles to the perfume division. This interest is heightened because a significant portion of a division manager's income is an incentive bonus based on profit center results.

The perfume production division has the following costs in addition to the bottle costs:

Volume	Total cost	Cost per case
2,000,000 cases	$16,400,000	$8.20
4,000,000	32,400,000	8.10
6,000,000	48,400,000	8.07

After considerable analysis, the marketing research department has furnished you with the following price-demand relationship for the finished product:

Sales volume	Total sales revenue	Sales price per case
2,000,000 cases	$25,000,000	$12.50
4,000,000	45,600,000	11.40
6,000,000	63,900,000	10.65

Required:

a. The A. R. Oma Company has used market price transfer prices in the past. Using the current market prices and costs, and assuming a volume of 6,000,000 cases, calculate the income for—
 (1) The bottle division.
 (2) The perfume division.
 (3) The corporation.

b. Is this production and sales level the most profitable volume for—
 (1) The bottle division?
 (2) The perfume division?
 (3) The corporation?

Explain your answer.

(CMA adapted)

23–20. Transfer prices and tax regulations

ExIm, Inc., has two operating divisions in a semiautonomous organization structure. Division Ex is located in the U.S.A. It produces a part labeled XZ-1 which is an input to Division Im which is located in the south of France. Division Ex has idle capacity that it uses to produce XZ-1. The market price of XZ-1 domestically is $60. The variable costs are $25 per unit. The company's U.S. tax rate is 40 percent of income.

After paying the transfer price for each XZ-1 received from Division Ex, Division Im also pays a shipping fee of $15 per unit. Part XZ-1 becomes a part of Division Im's output product. The output product costs an additional $10 to produce and sells for an equivalent $115. Division Im could purchase Part XZ-1 from a Paris supplier at a cost of $50 per unit. The company's French tax rate is 70 percent of income. Assume French tax laws permit transferring at either variable cost or market price. Assume the U.S. division's income is taxed at 40%.

Required:

What transfer price is economically optimal for ExIm, Inc.?

23–21. Regulated product prices*

The state of Alaska receives a royalty equal to 12.5 percent of the value of the oil produced from state lands. The royalty is payable when the oil is produced. Because most Alaskan oil is located on the remote North Slope where there is no market for the oil, the transfer price for the oil is typically determined at the refinery gate in California. Transportation charges are deducted from the "California landed price" to arrive at an estimated price at the production point (that is, the North Slope). In January 1981, price controls were lifted for all crude oil produced after January 22, 1981. When the price controls were lifted, there was approximately 45 million barrels of oil in the Trans-Alaskan pipeline system that had been produced but had not yet been delivered to the refinery gate. The controlled price of Alaskan oil at

---

* © E. B. Deakin, 1981.

the refinery gate was $16 per barrel. The uncontrolled price was $34 per barrel. Transportation charges were $7 per barrel both before and after the lifting of price controls.

Required:

What is the appropriate transfer price (and, hence, value for royalty determination purposes) of the 45 million barrels in the pipeline at the decontrol date? Why?

23–22. Evaluate transfer price system

MBR, Inc., consists of three divisions that formerly were three independent manufacturing companies. Bader Corporation and Roach Company merged in 1975, and the merged corporation acquired Mitchell Company in 1976. The name of the corporation was subsequently changed to MBR, Inc., and each company became a separate division retaining the name of its former company.

The three divisions have operated as if they were still independent companies. Each division has its own sales force and production facilities. Each division management is responsible for sales, cost of operations, acquisition and financing of divisional assets, and working capital management. The corporate management of MBR evaluates the performance of the divisions and division managements on the basis of ROI.

Mitchell Division has just been awarded a contract for a product that uses a component that is manufactured by the Roach Division as well as by outside suppliers. Mitchell used a cost figure of $3.80 for the component manufactured by Roach in preparing its bid for the new product. This cost figure was supplied by Roach in response to Mitchell's request for the average variable cost of the component and represents the standard variable manufacturing cost and variable selling and distribution expense.

Roach has an active sales force that is continually soliciting new prospects. Roach's regular selling price for the component Mitchell needs for the new product is $6.50. Sales of this component are expected to increase. However, the Roach management has indicated that it could supply Mitchell with the required quantities of the component at the regular selling price less variable selling and distribution expenses. Mitchell's management has responded by offering to pay standard variable manufacturing cost plus 20 percent.

The two divisions have been unable to agree on a transfer price. Corporate management has never established a transfer price policy because interdivisional transactions have never occurred. As a compromise, the corporate vice president of finance has suggested a price equal to the standard full manufacturing cost (that is, no selling and distribution expenses) plus a 15 percent markup. This price has also been rejected by the two division managers because each considered it grossly unfair.

The unit cost structure for the Roach component and the three suggested prices are shown below.

Regular selling price	$6.50
Standard variable manufacturing cost	$3.20
Standard fixed manufacturing cost	1.20
Variable selling and distribution expenses	.60
	$5.00
Regular selling price less variable selling and distribution expenses ($6.50 − .60)	$5.90
Variable manufacturing plus 20% ($3.20 × 1.20)	$3.84
Standard full manufacturing cost plus 15% ($4.40 × 1.15)	$5.06

Required: a. Discuss the effect each of the three proposed prices might have on the Roach Division management's attitude toward intracompany business.

b. Is the negotiation of a price between the Mitchell and Roach Divisions a satisfactory method to solve the transfer price problem? Explain your answer.

c. Should the corporate management of MBR, Inc., become involved in this transfer price controversy? Explain your answer.

(CMA adapted)

23–23. Analyze transfer pricing data

MultiProduct Enterprises, Inc., has a decentralized organization that provides for management evaluation based on measures of division contribution. Divisions A and B operate in similar product markets. Division A produces a solid state electronic assembly that may be sold to the outside market at a price of $16 per unit. The outside market can absorb up to 140,000 units per year. These units require two direct labor-hours each.

If A modifies the units with an additional one half hour of labor time, the units can be sold to Division B at a price of $18 per unit. Division B will accept up to 120,000 of these units per year.

If Division B does not obtain 120,000 units from A, then Division B will purchase the needed units for $18.50 from the outside. Division B incurs $8 of additional labor and other out-of-pocket costs to convert the assemblies into a home digital electronic radio, calculator, telephone monitor, and clock unit. The unit can be sold to the outside market at a price of $45 each.

Division A has estimated that its total costs amount to $925,000 for fixed costs and $6 per direct labor-hour. Capacity in Division A is limited to 400,000 direct labor-hours per year.

Required: a. Total contribution margin to A if it sells 140,000 units to the outside.

b. Total contribution margin to A if it sells 120,000 units to B.

c. The costs to be considered in determining the optimal company policy for sales by Division A.

d. The annual contributions and costs for Divisions A and B under the optimal policy.

23–24. Analyze transfer pricing policy

PortCo Products is a divisionalized furniture manufacturer. The divisions are autonomous segments with each division being responsible for its own sales, costs of operations, working capital management, and equipment acquisition. Each division serves a different market in the furniture industry. Because the markets and products of the divisions are so different, there have never been any transfers between divisions.

The Commercial Division manufactures equipment and furniture that is purchased by the restaurant industry. The division plans to introduce a new line of counter and chair units that feature a cushioned seat for the counter chairs. John Kline, the division manager, has discussed the manufacturing of the cushioned seat with Russ Fiegel of the Office Division. They both believe a cushioned seat currently made by the Office Division for use on its deluxe office stool could be modified for use on the new counter chair. Consequently, Kline has asked Russ Fiegel for a price for 100-unit lots of the cushioned seat. The following conversation took place about the price to be charged for the cushioned seats.

Fiegel: John, we can make the necessary modifications to the cushioned seat easily. The direct materials used in your seat are slightly different and should cost about 10 percent more than those used in our deluxe office stool. However, the labor time should be the same because the seat fabrication operation basically is the same. I would price the seat at our regular rate—full cost plus 30 percent markup.

Kline: That's higher than I expected, Russ. I was thinking that a good price would be your variable manufacturing costs. After all, your capacity costs will be incurred regardless of this job.

Fiegel: John, I'm at capacity. By making the cushion seats for you, I'll have to cut my production of deluxe office stools. Of course, I can increase my production

Exhibit A (23–24)   **Office Division, standard costs and prices**

		Deluxe office stool		Economy office stool
Direct materials:				
Framing		$ 8.15		$ 9.76
Cushioned seat:				
Padding		2.40		—
Vinyl		4.00		—
Molded seat (purchased)		—		6.00
Direct labor:				
Frame fabrication	(.5 × $7.50/DLH)	3.75	(.5 × $7.50/DLH)	3.75
Cushion fabrication	(.5 × $7.50/DLH)	3.75		—
Assembly[a]	(.5 × $7.50/DLH)	3.75	(.3 × $7.50/DLH)	2.25
Manufacturing:				
Overhead	(1.5DLH × $12.80/DLH)	19.20	(.8DLH × $12.80/DLH)	10.24
Total standard cost		$45.00		$32.00
Selling price (30% markup)		$58.50		$41.60

[a] Attaching seats to frames and attaching rubber feet.

Exhibit B (23–24)   **Office Division, manufacturing overhead budget**

Overhead item	Nature	Amount
Supplies	Variable—at current market prices	$ 420,000
Indirect labor	Variable	375,000
Supervision	Nonvariable	250,000
Power	Use varies with activity; rates are fixed	180,000
Heat and light	Nonvariable—light is fixed regardless of production while heat/air conditioning varies with fuel charges	140,000
Property taxes and insurance taxes	Nonvariable—any change in amounts/rates is independent of production	200,000
Depreciation	Fixed-dollar total	1,700,000
Employee benefits	20% of supervision, direct and indirect labor	575,000
Total overhead		$3,840,000
Capacity in direct labor-hour		300,000
Overhead rate/direct labor hour		$12.80

of economy office stools. The labor time freed by not having to fabricate the frame or assemble the deluxe stool can be shifted to the frame fabrication and assembly of the economy office stool. Fortunately, I can switch my labor force between these two models of stools without any loss of efficiency. As you know, overtime is not a feasible alternative in our community. I'd like to sell it to you at variable cost, but I have excess demand for both products. I don't mind changing my product mix to the economy model if I get a good return on the seats I make for you. Here are my standard costs for the two stools and a schedule of my manufacturing overhead. [See Exhibit A for standard costs, and see Exhibit B for overhead schedule.]

Kline: I guess I see your point, Russ, but I don't want to price myself out of the market. Maybe we should talk to corporate to see if they can give us any guidance.

Required:

a. John Kline and Russ Fiegel did ask PortCo corporate management for guidance on an appropriate transfer price. Corporate management suggested they consider using a transfer price based upon variable manufacturing cost plus opportunity cost. Calculate a transfer price for the cushioned seat based upon variable manufacturing cost plus opportunity cost.

b. Which alternative transfer price system—full cost, variable manufacturing cost, or variable manufacturing cost plus opportunity cost—would be better as the underlying concept for an intra company transfer price policy? Explain your answer.

(CMA adapted)

23–25. Differential costing and transfer pricing decisions

National Industries is a diversified corporation with separate and distinct operating divisions. Each division's performance is evaluated on the basis of total dollar profits and return on division investment.

The WindAir Division manufactures and sells air-conditioner units. The coming year's budgeted income statement, based upon a sales volume of 15,000 units, appears below.

WindAir Division
Budgeted Income Statement
For the 1979–1980 Fiscal Year

	Per unit	Total (in thousands)
Sales revenue	$400	$6,000
Manufacturing costs:		
Compressor	70	1,050
Other direct materials	37	555
Direct labor	30	450
Variable overhead	45	675
Fixed overhead	32	480
Total manufacturing costs	214	3,210
Gross margin	186	2,790
Operating costs:		
Variable marketing	18	270
Fixed marketing	19	285
Fixed administrative	38	570
Total operating costs	75	1,125
Operating profit before taxes	$111	$1,665

WindAir's division manager believes sales can be increased if the unit selling price of the air conditioners is reduced. A market research study conducted by an independent firm at the request of the manager indicates that a 5 percent reduction in the selling price ($20) would increase sales volume 16 percent, or 2,400 units. WindAir has sufficient production capacity to manage this increased volume with no increase in fixed costs.

At the present time, WindAir uses a compressor in its units which it purchases from an outside supplier at a cost of $70 per compressor. The division manager of WindAir has approached the manager of the Compressor Division regarding the sale of a compressor unit to WindAir. The Compressor Division currently manufactures and sells a unit exclusively to outside firms which is similar to the unit used by WindAir. The specifications of the WindAir compressor are slightly different which would reduce the Compressor Division's direct material cost by $1.50 per unit. In addition, the Compressor Division would not incur any variable selling costs in the units sold to WindAir. The manager of WindAir wants all of the compressors it uses to come from one supplier and has offered to pay $50 for each compressor unit.

The Compressor Division has the capacity to produce 75,000 units. The coming year's budgeted income statement for the Compressor Division is shown below and is based upon a sales volume of 64,000 units without considering WindAir's proposal.

Compressor Division
Budgeted Income Statement
For the 1979–1980 Fiscal Year

	Per unit	Total (in thousands)
Sales revenue	$100	$6,400
Manufacturing costs:		
Direct materials	12	768
Direct labor	8	512
Variable overhead	10	640
Fixed overhead	11	704
Total manufacturing costs	41	2,624
Gross margin	59	3,776
Operating costs:		
Variable marketing	6	384
Fixed marketing	4	256
Fixed administrative	7	448
Total operating costs	17	1,088
Operating profit before taxes	$ 42	$2,688

Required:

a.   Should WindAir Division institute the 5 percent price reduction on its air-conditioner units even if it cannot acquire the compressors internally for $50 each? Support your conclusion with appropriate calculations.

b.   Without prejudice to your answer to Requirement (a), assume WindAir needs 17,400 units. Should the Compressor Division be willing to supply the compressor units for $50 each? Support your conclusions with appropriate calculations.

c.   Without prejudice to your answer to Requirement (a), assume WindAir needs 17,400 units. Would it be in the best interest of National Industries for the Compressor Division to supply the compressor units at $50 each to the WindAir Division? Support your conclusions with appropriate calculations.

(CMA adapted)

23–26. Shuman Automobiles, Inc. (evaluate use of responsibility centers and transfer pricing policy)*

Clark Shuman, part owner and manager of an automobile dealership, was nearing retirement and wanted to begin relinquishing his personal control over the business's operations. (See Exhibit A for current financial statements.) The reputation he had established in the community led him to believe that the recent growth in his business would continue. His long-standing policy of emphasizing new-car sales as the principal business of the dealership had paid off, in Shuman's opinion. This, combined with close attention to customer relations so that a substantial amount of repeat business was available, had increased the company's sales to a new high level. Therefore, he wanted to make organizational changes to cope with the new situation, especially given his desire to withdraw from any day-to-day managerial responsibilities. Shuman's three "silent partners" agreed to this decision.

Exhibit A (23–26)

Income Statement
For the Year Ended December 31

Sales of new cars			$3,821,873
Cost of new-car sales[a]		$3,156,401	
Sales remuneration		162,372	3,318,773
			503,100
Allowances on trade[b]			116,112
New cars' gross profit			386,988
Sales of used cars		2,395,696	
Cost of used-car sales[a]	$1,907,277		
Sales remuneration	91,564		
		1,998,841	
		396,855	
Allowances on trade[b]		61,118	
Used cars' gross profit			335,737
			722,725
Service sales to customers		347,511	
Cost of work[a]		256,984	
		90,527	
Service work on reconditioning:			
Charge	236,580		
Cost[a]	244,312	(7,732)	
Service work gross profit			82,795
			805,520
General and administrative expenses			491,710
Income before taxes			$ 313,810

[a] These amounts include overhead assignable directly to the department, but exclude allocated general dealership overhead.

[b] Allowances on trade represent the excess of amounts allowed on cars taken in trade over their appraised value.

---

* © Osceola Institute, 1979.

Accordingly, Shuman divided up the business into three departments: new-car sales, used-car sales, and the service department (which was also responsible for selling parts and accessories). He then appointed three of his most trusted employees managers of the new departments: Jean Moyer, new-car sales; Paul Fiedler, used-car sales; and Nate Bianci, service department. All of these people had been with the dealership for several years.

Each of the managers was told to run his department as if it were an independent business. In order to give the new managers an incentive, their remuneration was to be calculated as a straight percentage of their department's gross profit.

Soon after taking over as manager of new-car sales, Jean Moyer had to settle upon the amount to offer a particular customer who wanted to trade his old car as a part of the purchase price of a new one with a list price of $6,400. Before closing the sale, Moyer had to decide the amount he would offer the customer for the trade-in value of the old car. He knew that if no trade-in were involved, he would deduct about 15 percent from the list price of this model new car to be competitive with several other dealers in the area. However, he also wanted to make sure that he did not lose out on the sale by offering too low a trade-in allowance.

During his conversation with the customer, it had become apparent that the customer had an inflated view of the worth of his old car, a far from uncommon event. In this case, it probably meant that Moyer had to be prepared to make some sacrifices to close the sale. The new car had been in stock for some time, and the model was not selling very well, so he was rather anxious to make the sale if this could be done profitably.

In order to establish the trade-in value of the car, the used-car manager, Fiedler, accompanied Moyer and the customer out to the parking lot to examine the car. In the course of his appraisal, Fiedler estimated the car would require reconditioning work costing about $350, after which the car would retail for about $1,850. On a wholesale basis, he could either buy or sell such a car, after reconditioning, for about $1,600. The wholesale price of a car was subject to much greater fluctuation than the retail price, depending on color, trim, model, and so forth. Fortunately, the car being traded in was a very popular shade. The retail automobile dealer's handbook of used-car prices, the Blue Book, gave a cash buying price range of $1,375 to $1,465 for the trade-in model in good condition. This range represented the distribution of cash prices paid by automobile dealers for that model of car in the area in the past week. Fiedler estimated that he could get about $1,100 for the car "as is" (that is, without any work being done to it) at next week's auction.

The new-car department manager had the right to buy any trade-in at any price he thought appropriate, but then it was his responsibility to dispose of the car. He had the alternative of either trying to persuade the used-car manager to take over the car and accepting the used-car manager's appraisal price, or he himself could sell the car through wholesale channels or at auction. Whatever course Moyer adopted, it was his primary responsibility to make a profit for the dealership on the new cars he sold, without affecting his performance through excessive allowances on trade-ins. This primary goal, Moyer said, had to be "balanced against the need to satisfy the customers and move the new cars out of inventory—and there was only a narrow line between allowing enough on a used car and allowing too much."

After weighing all these factors, with particular emphasis on the personality of the customer, Moyer decided he would allow $2,135 for the used car, provided the customer agreed to pay the list price for the new car. After a certain amount of haggling, during which the customer came down from a higher figure and Moyer came up from a lower one, the $2,135 allowance was agreed upon. The necessary papers were signed, and the customer drove off.

Moyer returned to the office and explained the situation to Joanne Brunner, who had recently joined the dealership as accountant. After listening with interest to Moyer's explanation of the sale, Brunner set about recording the sale in the accounting records of the business. As soon as she saw the new car had been purchased from the manufacturer for $4,445, she was uncertain as to the value she should place on the trade-in vehicle. Since the new car's list price was $6,400 and it had cost $4,445, Brunner reasoned the gross margin on the new-car sale was $1,955. Yet Moyer had allowed $2,135 for the old car, which needed $350 repairs and could be sold retail for $1,850 or wholesale for $1,600. Did this mean that the new-car sale involved a loss? Brunner was not at all sure she knew the answer to this question. Also, she was uncertain about the value she should place on the used car for inventory valuation purposes. Brunner decided that she would put down a valuation of $2,135, and then await instructions from her superiors.

When Fiedler, manager of the used-car department, found out what Brunner had done, he went to the office and stated forcefully that he would not accept $2,135 as the valuation of the used car. His comment went as follows:

"My used-car department has to get rid of that used car, unless Jean (Moyer) agrees to take it over himself. I would certainly never have allowed the customer $2,135 for that old tub. I would never have given any more than $1,250, which is the wholesale price less the cost of repairs. My department has to make a profit too, you know. My own income is dependent on the gross profit I show on the sale of used cars, and I will not stand for having my income hurt because Jean is too generous towards his customers."

Brunner replied that she had not meant to cause trouble, but had simply recorded the car at what seemed to be its cost of acquisition, because she had been taught that this was the best accounting practice. Whatever response Fiedler was about to make to this comment was cut off by the arrival of Clark Shuman, the general manager, and Nate Bianci, the service department manager. Shuman picked up the phone and called Jean Moyer, asking him to come over right away.

"All right, Nate," said Shuman, "now that we are all here, would you tell them what you just told me?"

Bianci, who was obviously very worried, said: "Thanks Clark; the trouble is with this trade-in. Jean and Paul were right in thinking that the repairs they thought necessary would cost about $350. Unfortunately, they failed to notice that the rear axle is cracked, which will have to be replaced before we can retail the car. This will probably use up parts and labor costing about $265.

"Beside this," Bianci continued, "there is another thing that is bothering me a good deal more. Under the accounting system we've been using, I can't charge as much on an internal job as I would for the same job performed for an outside customer. As you can see from my department statement (Exhibit B), I lost almost 8,000 bucks on internal work last year. On a reconditioning job like this which costs out at $615, I don't even break even. If I did work costing $615 for an outside customer, I would be able to charge him about $830 for the job. The Blue Book gives a range of $810 to $850 for the work this car needs, and I have always aimed for about the middle of the Blue Book range. That would give my department a gross profit of $215, and my own income is based on that gross profit. Since it looks as if a high proportion of the work of my department is going to be the reconditioning of trade-ins for resale, I figure that I should be able to make the same charge for repairing a trade-in as I would get for an outside repair job."*

Exhibit B (23–26)

Analysis of Service Department Expenses
For the Year Ended December 31

	Customer jobs	Reconditioning jobs	Total
Number of jobs	2780	1051	3831
Direct labor	$106,930	$ 98,820	$205,750
Supplies	37,062	32,755	69,817
Department overhead (fixed)	31,558	26,067	57,625
	175,550	157,642	333,192
Parts	81,434	86,670	168,104
	256,984	244,312	501,296
Charges made for jobs to customers or other departments	347,511	236,580	584,091
Gross profit (loss)	90,527	(7,732)	82,795
General overhead proportion			57,080
Departmental profit for the year			$ 25,715

Messrs. Fielder and Moyer both started to talk at once at this point. Fiedler, the more forceful of the two, managed to edge out Moyer: "This axle business is unfortunate, all right; but it is very hard to spot a cracked axle. Nate is likely to be just as lucky the other way next time. He has to take the rough with the smooth. It is up to him to get the cars ready for me to sell."

Moyer, after agreeing that the failure to spot the axle was unfortunate, added: "This error is hardly my fault, however. Anyway, it is ridiculous that the service department should make a profit out of jobs it does for the rest of the dealership. The company can't make money when its left hand sells to its right."

At this point, Clark Shuman was getting a little confused about the situation. He thought there was a little truth in everything that had been said, but he was not sure how much. It was evident to him that some action was called for, both to sort out the present problem and to prevent its recurrence. He instructed Ms. Brunner, the accountant, to "work out how much we are really going to make on this whole deal," and then retired to his office to consider how best to get his managers to make a profit for the company.

A week after the events described above, Clark Shuman was still far from sure what action to take to motivate his managers to make a profit for the business. During the week, Bianci, the service manager, had reported to him that the repairs to the used car had cost $688, of which $320 represented the cost of those repairs that had been spotted at the time of purchase, and the remaining $368 was the

---

* In addition to the Blue Book for used car prices, there was a Blue Book which gave the range of charges for various classes of repair work. Like the used-car book, it was issued weekly, and was based on the actual charges made and reported by vehicle repair shops in the area.

cost of supplying and fitting a replacement for the cracked axle. To support his own case for a higher allowance on reconditioning jobs, Bianci had looked through the duplicate invoices over the last few months, and had found examples of similar (but not identical) work to that which had been done on the trade-in car. The amounts of these invoices averaged $805, which the customers had paid without question, and the average of the costs assigned to these jobs was $596. (General overhead was not assigned to individual jobs.) In addition, Bianci had obtained from Ms. Brunner, the accountant, the cost analysis shown in Exhibit B. Bianci told Shuman that this was a fairly typical distribution of the service department expense.

Required:

a. Suppose the new-car deal is consummated, with the repaired used car being retailed for $1,850, the repairs costing Shuman $688. Assume that all sales personnel are on salary (no commissions), and that departmental overheads are fixed. What is the dealership contribution on the total transaction (that is, new and repaired-used cars sold)?

b. Assume each department (new, used, service) is treated as a profit center, as described in the case. Also assume in (1) to (3) that it is known with certainty *beforehand* that the repairs will cost $688.

   (1) In your opinion, at what value should this trade-in (unrepaired) be transferred from the new-car department to the used-car department? Why?

   (2) In your opinion, how much should the service department be able to charge the used-car department for the repairs on this trade-in car? Why?

   (3) Given your responses to (1) and (2), what will be each of the three departments' contributions on this deal?

c. Is there a strategy in this instance that would give the dealership more contribution than the one assumed above (that is, repairing and retailing this trade-in used car)? Explain. In answering this question, assume the service department operates at capacity.

d. Do you feel the three profit center approach is appropriate for Shuman? If so, explain why, including an explanation of how this is better than other specific alternatives. If not, propose a better alternative and explain why it is better than three profit centers and any other alternatives you have considered.

23–27. Birch Paper Company (evaluate transfer pricing policy and use of responsibility centers)*

"If I were to price these boxes any lower than $480 a thousand," said James Brunner, manager of Birch Paper Company's Thompson Division, "I'd be countermanding my order for last month for our sales force to stop shaving their bids and to bid full cost quotations. I've been trying for weeks to improve the quality of our business, and if I turn around now and accept this job at $430 or $450 or something less than $480, I'll be tearing down this program I've been working so hard to build up. The division can't very well show a profit by putting in bids which don't even cover a fair share of overhead costs, let alone give us a profit."

Birch Paper Company was a medium-sized, partly integrated paper company, producing white and kraft papers and paperboard. A portion of its paperboard output was converted into corrugated boxes by the Thompson Division, which also printed and colored the outside surface of the boxes. Including Thompson, the company

---

* Copyright © 1957 by the President and Fellows of Harvard College. This case was prepared by William Rotch under the direction of Neil E. Harlan as a basis for class discussion rather than to illustrate either effective or ineffective handling of an administrative situation. Reprinted by permission of the Harvard Business School.

had four producing divisions and a timberland division, which supplied part of the company's pulp requirements.

For several years each division had been judged independently on the basis of its profit and ROI. Top management had been working to gain effective results from a policy of decentralizing responsibility and authority for all decisions except those relating to overall company policy. The company's top officials felt that in the past few years the concept of decentralization had been successfully applied and that the company's profits and competitive position had definitely improved.

Early in the year, the Northern Division designed a special display box for one of its papers in conjunction with the Thompson Division, which was equipped to make the box. Thompson's package design and development staff spent several months perfecting the design, production methods, and materials that were to be used; because of the unusual color and shape, these were far from standard. According to an agreement between the two divisions, the Thompson Division was reimbursed by the Northern Division for the out-of-pocket cost of its design and development work.

When the specifications were all prepared, the Northern Division asked for bids on the box from the Thompson Division and from two outside companies, West Paper Company and Erie Papers, Inc. Each division manager normally was free to buy from whichever supplier he wished, and even on sales within the company, divisions were expected to meet the going market price if they wanted the business.

At this time, the profit margins of converters such as the Thompson Division were being squeezed. Thompson, as did many other similar converters, bought its board, liner, or paper; and its function was to print, cut, and shape it into boxes. Though it bought most of its materials from other Birch divisions, most of Thompson's sales were to outside customers. If Thompson got the order from Northern, it probably would buy its linerboard and corrugating medium from the Southern Division of Birch. The walls of a corrugated box consist of outside and inside sheets of linerboard sandwiching the corrugating medium.

About 70 percent of Thompson's out-of-pocket cost of $400 a thousand for the order represented the cost of linerboard and corrugating medium. Though Southern Division had been running below capacity and had excess inventory, it quoted the market price, which had not noticeably weakened as a result of the oversupply. Its out-of-pocket costs on liner and corrugating medium were about 60 percent of selling price.

The Northern Division received bids on the boxes of $480 a thousand from the Thompson Division, $430 a thousand from West Paper, and $432 a thousand from Erie Papers. Erie offered to buy from Birch the outside linerboard with the special printing already on it, but would supply its own inside liner and corrugating medium. The outside liner would be supplied by the Southern Division at a price equivalent to $90 a thousand boxes, and would be printed for $30 a thousand by the Thompson Division. Of the $30, about $25 would be out-of-pocket costs.

Since this situation appeared to be a little unusual, William Kenton, manager of the Northern Division, discussed the wide discrepancy of bids with Birch's commercial vice president. He told the commercial vice president, "We sell in a very competitive market, where higher costs cannot be passed on. How can we be expected to show a decent profit and return on investment if we have to buy our supplies at more than 10 percent over the going market?"

Knowing that Brunner had on occasion in the past few months been unable to operate the Thompson Division at capacity, the commercial vice president thought it odd that Brunner would add the full 20 percent overhead and profit charge to his out-of-pocket costs. When he asked Brunner about this over the telephone, his answer was the statement that appears at the beginning of the case. Brunner went on to say that having done the developmental work on the box, and having received no profit on that, he felt entitled to a normal markup on the production of the box itself.

The vice president explored further the cost structures of the various divisions. He remembered a comment the controller had made to the effect that costs that for one division were variable could be largely fixed for the company as a whole. He knew that in the absence of specific orders from top management, Kenton would accept the lowest bid, namely, that of West Paper for $430. However, it would be possible for top management to order the acceptance of another bid if the situation warranted such action. And though the volume represented by the transactions in question was less than 5 percent of the volume of any of the divisions involved, other transactions could conceivably raise similar problems later.

Required:

Does the system motivate Mr. Brunner in such a way that actions he takes in the best interests of the Thompson Division are also in the best interests of the Birch Paper Company? If your answer is "no," give some specific instances related as closely as possible to the type of situation described in the case. Would the managers of other divisions be correctly motivated? What should the vice president do?

Part **4**

The Impact of Uncertainty on Cost Analysis

24

Decision Making under Uncertainty

OBJECTIVES
To understand the impact of uncertainty on decisions, particularly cost-volume-
 profit (CVP) decisions.
To be familiar with alternative ways of dealing with uncertainty.

In earlier chapters, the use of accounting data for decision making was based
on the implicit assumption of certainty. The real world, however, is characterized by uncertainty. Decisions must be made and actions taken without definite
knowledge of the results. For example, suppose that HyperMedical Engineering Company has developed a new device for modifying viral cells. Demand
for the product exceeds the company's present manufacturing capacity. HyperMedical Engineering's management could build a new plant, in which
case the capital budgeting techniques discussed in Chapters 15 and 16 would
be employed.

But, building a plant takes several years; moreover, competitors in the
biomedical engineering field may develop a similar product and, hence, cut
into HyperMedical's market. So to meet the immediate demand, management
is considering obtaining a new plant under a short-term lease to meet the
increased demand. The fixed lease payments for a new plant will result in
a step increase in costs similar to that diagrammed in Illustration 24–1.
The point A on the volume axis represents the current level of activity which
is also the full capacity of the old plant. Management expects that volume
will increase to the level represented by point B. If this happens, then the
profits at B will be sufficiently greater than the profits at A to warrant leasing
the new plant. However, the costs of operating the new plant result in a
step increase in the fixed costs. If management is certain that the number
of units represented by the point B on the volume axis will be sold with
the new plant, then the lease would be justified. Unfortunately, demand is
rarely known with certainty.

Suppose management expected profit from a demand increase to point
B, and went ahead with the lease. Management would be unpleasantly surprised if actual demand were less than expected.

Knowledge of the extent of uncertainty and the impact of that uncertainty
on decision outcomes is important information for decision making in an
uncertain world. In this chapter, we introduce the concepts used to deal
with uncertainty and illustrate how those concepts are applied to CVP analysis.

Illustration 24–1   **Effect of leased plant on CVP relationships**

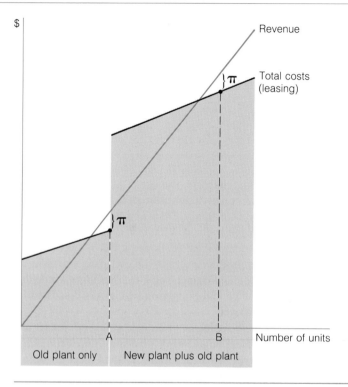

A is also the capacity of the old plant.

Dealing with uncertainty	There are six steps that we suggest be followed when dealing with decisions under uncertainty. These are:

1. Establish a set of mathematically quantified objectives.
2. Determine the set of actions that can be taken.
3. Estimate the various outcomes that are likely to occur after the decision.
4. Assign probabilities to those outcomes.
5. Compute the payoffs that are likely under each paired set of actions and outcomes.
6. Choose the action that is best in achieving objectives.

Use of this approach does not assure profitable operations, but it does provide a rational basis for decision making. In the long run, following this method can be expected to result in decisions that achieve established objectives.

Establishing objectives

Company management usually establishes objectives. In addition to maximizing profit, management may seek to avoid excessive risk, attain certain market shares, or introduce new products. Once the qualitative objectives are determined, they must be expressed in mathematical terms. This mathematical statement of management goals is called an objective function. An example of an objective function is the expression:

Maximize profit (π) where:

$$\pi = (P - V)X - F$$

This is the profit equation from Chapter 11. The term X represents the quantity sold per period, P is the price per unit, V represents the variable cost per unit, and F is the fixed costs per period.

If management wanted, they could extend this analysis to include more complex statements of objectives. For example, management may have different preferences for risk. A utility function that reflects management's attitude toward risk might be used instead of a profit equation. Management may face constraints in devising the profit plan. These constraints may also be incorporated in an uncertainty mode. We shall assume the profit equation above reflects management's objectives. More complex objective functions are discussed in the management science, statistics, and accounting literature.[1]

The role of cost data in an uncertain environment can be demonstrated using a linear profit function such as the CVP equation. Extensions to these more complex settings may be studied in operations research or statistics. No matter how complex the situation, the accountant's task is to provide the cost data that are relevant to the decision.

We can apply this approach to the problem faced by the management of HyperMedical Engineering. We will approach the problem in the suggested order and then discuss the results of the outcome of the analysis.

Determining the action set

Once objectives have been established, management must consider the alternative actions that may be taken to attain them. In our example, there may be several ways to meet the increased demand. As we noted, management might construct a new plant. Or it might subcontract for a certain amount of production. It might also purchase another company that is in the same business. Each action entails different amounts of profit and risk.

Management will consider each alternative as a possible way to meet its established objectives. Other alternatives would also be considered. For exam-

---

[1] For references in the accounting literature, see A. Charnes, W. Cooper, and Y. Ijiri, "Breakeven Budgeting and Programming to Goals," *Journal of Accounting Research,* Spring 1963; J. Hilliard and R. Leitch, "Cost-Volume-Profit Analysis under Uncertainty: A Log-Normal Approach," *The Accounting Review,* January 1975; J. Demski and G. Feltham, *Cost Determination: A Conceptual Approach* (Ames: Iowa State University Press, 1976); and J. Demski, *Information Analysis,* (Reading, Mass.: Addison-Wesley Publishing, 1980).

ple, management could ignore the increased demand and continue to produce at the same level as before. To simplify the discussion, we will assume that the only possibilities are to lease a new plant or to subcontract for the added demand.

Estimating outcomes

The outcome that will occur after the decision has been made is unknown and usually beyond the control of management. The external influences that affect the outcome are called exogenous factors. For example, in the HyperMedical example, management may expect that future demand for the product will continue to increase. But the level of future demand is affected by such factors as the state of the economy, competition, and technological change. When management makes its expansion decision, it cannot know the exact level of future demand because it cannot perfectly predict these exogenous factors.

Nevertheless, management can estimate the possibilities of specific **outcomes**. While HyperMedical's management may expect future demand to increase by 5,000 units next year, they may estimate that demand could increase by as much as 40,000 units. The 5,000-unit increase is considered much more likely than the 40,000 increase, but both are possibilities.

A set of mutually exclusive and collectively exhaustive outcomes is constructed to represent the possible future outcomes. As a practical matter, a small representative set of possibilities is usually chosen or else we assume the outcomes will follow a continuous distribution which may be analyzed through direct computation or some sampling method. In our example, the set of demand increases is 1,000, 2,000, 5,000, 10,000, and 40,000 units. In reality, demand increase *might* be 1,386 units or 61,903 units or any other number; but, to avoid excessive computations, the limited set is usually sufficient.

Assigning probabilities to outcomes

Now that we have the set of five estimated future demand levels, the next task is to think about each outcome, estimate how likely it is to occur, and evaluate the payoffs. In the decision literature, the term *payoff* is used to indicate the value of each outcome.

The probability of each demand level's occurrence is estimated statistically or by other means. Marketing studies may be conducted to evaluate future demand levels and the related **probabilities** that those levels will, in fact, occur. Past trends may be extrapolated using time series analyses when there is a sufficient reason to believe the trends will continue in the future. Management may use its own judgment based on knowledge of contract negotiations with potential buyers or other factors. Assessing these probabilities is always a subjective process even though mathematical models may yield results that are precise to the last unit of production. Because the future is uncertain, probability statements about the future are also uncertain. Nonetheless, management uses such probability assessments when their benefits exceed the cost of obtaining them.

HyperMedical management may realize that a 5,000-unit increase is more likely than a 40,000-unit increase, but more precision is needed to evaluate riskiness. Based on quantified data about future demand levels, management assesses the future increases in demand, and, based on experience and judgment, estimates the following set of probabilities:[2]

Increased future demand (units)	Probability
1,000	.10
2,000	.20
5,000	.50
10,000	.15
40,000	.05
Total	1.00

The set of probabilities may contain as few or as many demand levels as needed to obtain the desired degree of precision. The desired precision in the results will depend on the reliability of the data and the trade-off between the costs and benefits of gathering additional information. The probabilities must always sum to one, as they do here. It is assumed that the probabilities are independent of the decision. That is, whether HyperMedical leases a new plant or subcontracts, the set of probabilities for future demand levels will be the same.

Computing payoffs

The accountant must often compute the payoffs for each alternative and for each outcome. To do this, the costs that are likely for each level of activity and for each alternative action choice must be considered. This is a direct application of the concepts of differential costing that have been introduced earlier in this book. For example, assume that HyperMedical's management could subcontract any number of units at any time and obtain the profit function:

$$\pi = (\$8 - \$7)X_s$$

where

π = operating profit from subcontracting
X_s = quantity subcontracted

This equation indicates a $1 net profit per unit.

---

[2] See R. Libby, *Accounting and Human Information Processing* (Englewood Cliffs, N.J.: Prentice-Hall, 1981), for a discussion of behavioral probability estimation and revision.

Or, management could lease a new plant capable of producing 10,000 units with a profit function of:

$$\pi' = (\$8 - \$2)X_p - \$20,000$$

where

π' = operating profit from leasing
X_p = quantity produced and sold
$20,000 is the fixed cost

Management would only want to lease one plant and knows the base demand level.

The payoffs for each outcome under each alternative action are computed and tabled as:

Future demand	Payoffs	
	Subcontract	Lease plant
1,000	$ 1,000	$−14,000[a]
2,000	2,000	−8,000
5,000	5,000	10,000
10,000	10,000	40,000
40,000	40,000	70,000

Additional computations:
[a] $−14,000 = 1,000($8 − $2) − $20,000; $−8,000 = 2,000($8 − $2) − $20,000; etc.

At the 40,000-unit level, both manufacturing and subcontracting would be required since the plant can only produce 10,000 units. Manufacturing 10,000 at a profit of $40,000 plus subcontracting 30,000 (that is, 40,000 − 10,000) at a profit of $30,000 is necessary to obtain the $70,000 total.

To make its decision, HyperMedical's management computes the expected payoffs under each considered alternative action. The expected payoff for each action is the weighted sum of the payoffs for each outcome times the probability associated with that outcome. For subcontracting, the expected payoff is:

Demand level	Probability		Payoff at this level	Expected payoff
1,000	.10	×	$ 1,000	= $ 100
2,000	.20	×	2,000	= 400
5,000	.50	×	5,000	= 2,500
10,000	.15	×	10,000	= 1,500
40,000	.05	×	40,000	= 2,000
Expected payoff for subcontracting				$6,500

For the alternative to lease a new plant, the expected payoff is computed using the same method:

Demand level	Probability		Payoff at this level		Expected payoff
1,000	.10	×	$−14,000	=	$−1,400
2,000	.20	×	−8,000	=	−1,600
5,000	.50	×	10,000	=	5,000
10,000	.15	×	40,000	=	6,000
40,000	.05	×	70,000	=	3,500
Expected payoff for leasing					$11,500

Making the decision

The expected payoff levels are compared, and the alternative with the higher expected payoff is selected under the decision criterion established in Step 1. Since the expected payoff from leasing a new plant ($11,500) is greater than the expected payoff from subcontracting ($6,500), the data suggest that management should lease the new plant. This is only a suggestion. The decision is the responsibility of management, and management may elect to use other decision criteria. In the following section, we discuss some other decision criteria that managers use.

Loss minimization criteria

Although leasing the new plant yields the highest expected payoff, HyperMedical runs the risk of a loss if this alternative is chosen and if demand is only 1,000 or 2,000 units. Adding the probabilities of these two demand levels suggests that there is a .3 probability of a loss. If management finds this loss exposure too great, they may seek a less risky alternative. Given the information in the example, there is no risk of accounting loss from subcontracting. However, if demand reaches 5,000 or more units, there is an opportunity loss from subcontracting—a greater payoff could have been earned if the plant had been leased.

Management may establish risk minimization as its objective in Step 1. Risk minimization may be defined in terms of the probability of loss. Management may state its objectives in terms of loss minimization. For example, management may seek to minimize the maximum loss to which it would be exposed. This is called the minimax criterion. Or management may set some loss amount and a related expected value as a limit on risk. For example, the criterion could be: "Don't invest if there is more than a 30 percent probability of a loss."

The appropriate decision would be to subcontract to minimize the risk of an accounting loss. By subcontracting, the risk of loss is reduced to zero, but with leasing there is a .3 probability of loss. Therefore, to minimize the probability of loss, management would probably prefer subcontracting.

Why would management give up the incremental expected payoff just to eliminate the possibility of a loss? Recent research suggests that management may be constrained by contracts (such as loan agreements) that call for severe penalties if particular profit levels are not maintained. Under such circumstances, the losses that would be incurred if demand did not permit profitable operation of the leased plant would trigger other costs. Indeed, loan terms may be renegotiated, interest rates increased, or loans may be called. For these reasons, management may prefer risk minimization to payoff optimization for a specific proposal.

On the other hand, some managers would prefer the added risk because of the potential for greater profits should demand levels go higher than anticipated. Although we generally assume managers are risk averse, we realize that they differ in their risk preferences. Hence, a general rule for treating risky projects may not be applicable in a given circumstance.

Profit variability and risk

Another approach to comparing the risk of alternative projects is to measure the dispersion in returns from the alternatives. The standard deviation of the returns may be computed and used as a project risk measure.

The standard deviation for the payoff series is defined as:

$$ s = \sqrt{\sum_{j=1}^{n} (I_j - \bar{I})^2 P_j} $$

where:

n = number of observations
s = the standard deviation of the payoff series for each alternative
I_j = the computed payoff or income at each demand level
P = the probability of attaining that demand level
$\bar{I}$ = the expected payoff level

Illustration 24–2 shows the relationship of the standard deviation measure to the variability of outcomes. The distributions shown represent the probability distributions for the profits from each of two projects. Since Project A has a smaller standard deviation, it is considered less risky, all other things held constant.

For HyperMedical, the standard deviation for subcontracting is:

$$ s = \sqrt{[(\$1,000 - \$6,500)^2(.10)] + [(\$2,000 - \$6,500)^2(.20)] + [(\$5,000 - \$6,500)^2(.50)] + [(\$10,000 - \$6,500)^2(.15)] + [(\$40,000 - \$6,500)^2(.05)]} $$
$$ = \sqrt{\$3,025,000 + \$4,050,000 + \$1,125,000 + \$1,837,500 + \$56,112,500} $$
$$ = \sqrt{\$66,150,000} $$
$$ = \$8,133 $$

On the other hand, if HyperMedical leases the plant, the standard deviation of the payoff is:

$$ s = \sqrt{[(\$-14,000 - \$11,500)^2(.10)] + [(\$-8,000 - 11,500)^2(.20)] + [(\$10,000 - \$11,500)^2(.50)] + [(\$40,000 - \$11,500)^2(.15)] + [(\$70,000 - \$11,500)^2(.05)]} $$
$$ = \sqrt{\$65,025,000 + \$76,050,000 + \$1,125,000 + \$121,837,500 + \$171,112,500} $$
$$ = \sqrt{\$435,150,000} $$
$$ = \$20,860 $$

Illustration 24–2   **Payoff variability and standard deviation**

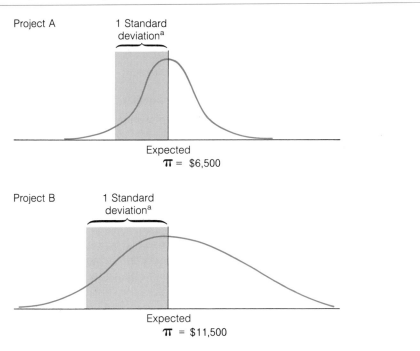

Project A

1 Standard deviation[a]

Expected
π = $6,500

Project B

1 Standard deviation[a]

Expected
π = $11,500

[a] Brackets indicate the relative standard deviations

Using this criterion, subcontracting results in a smaller standard deviation than leasing. Hence, subcontracting would be considered less risky if the standard deviation was used as the risk measure.

The standard deviation has some limitations as a risk measure. One disadvantage is that payoffs that exceed the expected value are treated the same as payoffs that are less than the expected value. Few would object to payoffs that exceed the mean. Yet, in our example, the greatest contribution to the standard deviation comes from the payoffs in excess of the mean. This would indicate that the risk is unbalanced. Leasing is riskier, but the risk is likely to result in greater payoffs.

A second difficulty with the use of a single project risk calculation such as standard deviation is that it ignores other company projects that may have offsetting effects. Portfolio theory has been developed in finance to consider the impact of a single project on a company's overall risk.

Finally, the standard deviation ignores the differences in the expected payoffs from projects. To compensate for this, the coefficient of variation (c.v.) may be computed. The c.v. is the *standard deviation of the project divided by the expected value of the project.* For the subcontracting alternative, the c.v. is:

$$\frac{\$8,133}{\$6,500} = 1.25$$

and for leasing the plant, the c.v. is:

$$\frac{\$20,860}{\$11,500} = 1.81$$

Scaling the standard deviation in this manner relates its value to the magnitude of the expected return. A lower c.v. may imply a lower level of relative risk. For the example, the c.v. is less for subcontracting. This suggests that subcontracting is less risky than leasing even when scaled for the difference in payoffs.

Risk evaluation—an indifference approach

Another way to evaluate two alternatives is to consider the point at which the advantage switches from one alternative to the other. For example, at small increases in demand, it would pay to subcontract; but at some point, the advantage switches from subcontracting to leasing. The switch occurs at the point where the two payoff equations are equal. Illustration 24–3 indicates the conceptual basis for this assertion.

Illustration 24–3   **Comparison of subcontracting profit with profit from leased plant**

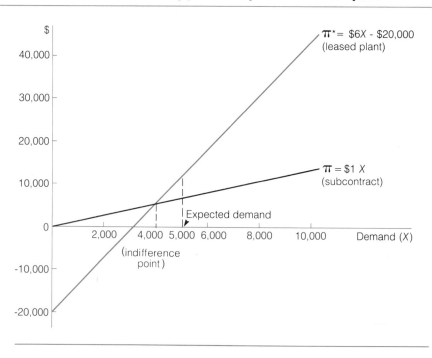

The diagram indicates that so long as the new demand is greater than 4,000 units, leasing will result in a greater profit than subcontracting. Management may consider the spread between expected demand (5,000 units) and the break-even quantity as a range of protection for its decision. Demand would have to be 1,000 units less than expected before management would have wished it had made the other decision. This indifference point is computed by finding the point where the two payoff functions are equal:

$$\pi = \pi^*$$
$$X(\$8 - \$7) = X(\$8 - \$2) - \$20,000$$
$$\$1X = \$6X - \$20,000$$
$$\$5X = \$20,000$$
$$X = \underline{\underline{4,000}}$$

Management can use this indifference approach to decide which alternative to use. If they are confident that the actual demand will exceed 4,000 by a substantial margin and by a significant probability, they will decide to lease the plant. But if the actual future demand is likely to be close to or less than 4,000 and management is risk averse, then they will probably subcontract. If management is risk seeking, they may choose to lease because of the greater potential reward. Later, as the actual demand becomes better known, the decision may be reviewed and changed if it is possible to do so.

CVP under uncertainties in prices and costs

Accountants also consider the impact of uncertainty on CVP analysis. Up to this point, we have assumed that only uncertainty in CVP analysis was the expected value of X, the quantity of units produced and sold. But in reality, any of the inputs to the profit equation are uncertain. Indeed, the probability of obtaining profit numbers that are equal to plans is very small. When all the variables in the CVP equation are uncertain, the same approach that was used for uncertainties in X is extended to the other variables.

Since the number of computations rapidly increases as the number of uncertain variables increases, computer assistance is usually required. A technique known as Monte Carlo analysis is used to sample from the distributions of each variable and to compute the profit for each sampled combination of selling price, variable cost, unit volume, and fixed costs, labeled P, V, X and F, respectively. The resulting expected profit and standard deviation can be used in exactly the same manner as when only X was uncertain.

To use Monte Carlo analysis, we must specify the distributions for each variable in the profit function. If we focus on the profit from leasing a new plant, we need to specify distributions for P, V, and F. The distribution for X that was obtained earlier will be used.

Let us assume the following distributions for the variables:

	Value	Probability
For *P*:		
	$7	.3
	8	.4
	9	.3
For *V*:		
	$1.50	.3
	1.75	.2
	2.00	.1
	2.50	.1
	3.00	.3
For *F*:		
	$18,000	.4
	20,000	.2
	22,000	.4

These data are entered into a computer program that uses random numbers to sample from the distributions and compute an expected profit as well as the standard deviation for that profit. In addition, the program may be designed to plot the different outcomes and their frequencies.

The results of using such a program for 1,000 iterations indicated an expected profit of $21,020 and a standard deviation of $52,794. These data would be used for decision making in the same way that the mean and standard deviation were used when only the quantity varied.

Illustration 24–4   **Monte Carlo simulation results for CVP analysis (in thousands of dollars)**

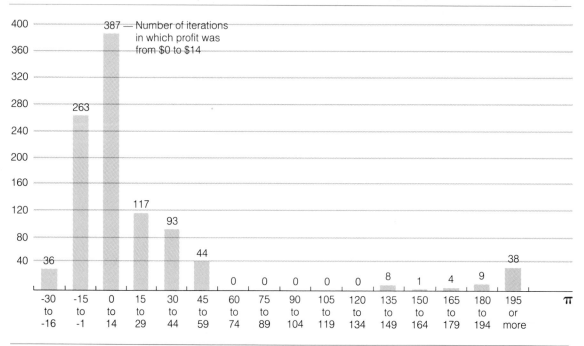

The plotted outcomes from this program are shown in Illustration 24–4. Note the concentration of outcomes at profit levels of $-15,000 to $15,000. Overall, it appears that the probable outcome would be a modest profit in the range of zero to $45,000. The very high profits occur infrequently. Further analysis of these higher profits and their likelihood might be conducted if management were risk seeking.

The advantage of using computer simulation is that the distribution of payoffs may be observed even with very complex interrelationships. Indeed, the Monte Carlo method could be extended to include prices, costs, and quantities for multiple products as well as interrelationships between the products. For example, if the price of one output increases more than 20 percent, consumers may switch to another alternative output. A computer simulation could be designed to include the switch when the specific round of the simulation indicated a 20 percent increase in price for the first output.

Summary

In the uncertainty that characterizes the real world, decision makers must consider the possibility that the outcome they expect from a decision may not be the outcome that actually occurs. Because of the potential difference between actual results and expectations, there is a risk in decision making. Managers assess the extent of risk for decision alternatives. A six-step process is suggested for risk assessment. The role of the accountant is oriented primarily to evaluating the differential costs and revenues from the set of likely outcomes. The expected value of each alternative decision and a measure of the risk of loss or variability for each alternative can be used to help make decisions that conform to management's risk preferences. Monte Carlo simulations may be used to analyze more complex profit relationships.

Terms and concepts

The following terms and concepts should be familiar to you after reading this chapter.

Coefficient of variation	**Payoffs**
CVP under uncertainty	**Probabilities**
Expected value	**Risk**
Minimax	**Risk minimization**
Monte Carlo	**Simulation**
Outcomes	**Standard deviation**

Self-study problem

Thunder Manufacturing Company produces a volatile chemical, Vapo, that must be sold in the month produced or else discarded. Thunder can manufacture Vapo itself at a variable cost of $40 per unit, or they can purchase it from an outside supplier at a cost of $70 per unit. Thunder can sell Vapo at $80 per unit. Production levels must be set at the start of the period and cannot be changed during the period. The production process is such that at least 9,000 units must be produced during the period. Thunder management must decide whether to produce Vapo or whether to purchase it from the outside supplier.

The possible sales of Vapo and their probabilities are:

Demand (units)	Probability
4,000	.4
7,000	.5
11,000	.1

Required:

a. The expected demand.
b. The expected profit from purchasing Vapo from an outside supplier and selling it.
c. The expected profit from manufacturing and selling.
d. The standard deviation from purchasing and selling.
e. The standard deviation from manufacturing and selling.
f. The coefficient of variation for each alternative.

Solution to self-study problem

a. Expected demand is 6,200 units, computed as:

Demand (units)	Probability	Expected demand (units)
4,000	.4	1,600
7,000	.5	3,500
11,000	.1	1,100
Expected demand		6,200

b. The expected profit from purchasing and selling would be equal to the unit contribution times the expected quantity or

$$(\$80 - \$70) \times 6,200 \text{ units} = \underline{\$62,000}$$

c. Even though the production cost is stated as a variable cost, since a minimum of 9,000 units must be produced, the cost is really fixed up to that point because of minimum production constraints. Units produced in excess of the 9,000 minimum would carry the variable cost of $40 each. The expected profit from manufacturing is:

Demand (units)	Probability	Manufacturing cost	Profit	Expected profit
4,000	.4	$360,000	$ (40,000)	$ (16,000)
7,000	.5	360,000	200,000	100,000
11,000	.1	440,000	440,000	44,000
Expected profit				$128,000

c. The standard deviation from purchasing and selling is:

$(I - \bar{I})$	$(I - \bar{I})^2 p$ (million)
$(4,000 - 6,200)$ ($\$10$)	$\$193.6$
$(7,000 - 6,200)$ ($\$10$)	32.0
$(11,000 - 6,200)$ ($\$10$)	230.4
	$\$456.0$

$$\$21,354 = \sqrt{\$456.0 \text{ million}}$$

d. The standard deviation from manufacturing and selling is:

$(I - \bar{I})$	$(I - \bar{I})^2 p$ million
$\$(-40,000 - \$128,000)$	$\$11,289.6$
$(200,000 - \$128,000)$	$2,592.0$
$(440,000 - \$128,000)$	$9,734.4$
Total	$\$23,616.0$

$$\$153,675 = \sqrt{\$23,616.0 \text{ million}}$$

e. The coefficient of variation for purchasing and selling is:

$$.344 = \frac{\$21,354}{\$62,000}$$

The coefficient of variation for manufacturing and selling is:

$$1.201 = \frac{\$153,675}{\$128,000}$$

Questions

24–1. What are the steps in decision making under uncertainty?

24–2. What is the role of the accountant in decision making under uncertainty?

24–3. The comment, "Since we can't know the future, there's not much point in doing all this elaborate analysis," is frequently heard. Respond to this comment.

24–4. Why do we limit the possible outcomes to discrete numbers such as 3,000 units or $500,000 in revenues when the actual numbers might be 3,129 units, $486,313 in revenue, or some similar odd number?

24–5. Why would management give up a lucrative payoff in exchange for a project with a smaller payoff, but with little or no risk of loss?

24–6. What is the coefficient of variation, and why is it important?

24–7. Discuss the use of the standard deviation as a risk measure.

24–8. How can CVP analysis be used to assess project risk?

24–9. What are the problems in applying simulation analysis to the assessment of risk?

Exercises

24–10. Estimate expected payoffs from alternative actions

Welcome Homes, Inc., is considering the alternatives to renovating a building and renting it or to purchasing a new building and renting it. The new rental market in the area is fairly stable. An investor can purchase a $10 million building with $2 million down and finance the balance. Assuming a three-year holding period, the project will have a net present value of $12 million.

Renovation property is somewhat riskier because the costs of the renovation add more uncertainty than with new construction. A typical renovation project may require the same $2 million down payment and financing of $8 million. However, after completion of the renovation, the project may have a different net present value than the new construction. Indeed, Welcome Homes' management has prepared the following schedule of outcomes for the renovation project:

Net present value (million)	Probability
$ 8	.2
11	.2
14	.3
16	.2
19	.1

To simplify the analysis, we assume there are no other possible outcomes from the renovation project.

Required:

What is the expected value of the renovation project?

24–11. Estimate risk measures

Using the data for Welcome Homes, Inc. (Exercise 24–10), estimate:

a. The standard deviation of the renovation alternative.
b. The risk of loss from the renovation decision.

24–12. Indifference analysis under uncertainty

Fanzole Corporation has a patent on a new medical device selling for $14 per unit. However, demand for the device is uncertain. The company can build its own manufacturing facilities and incur variable costs of $4 and fixed costs of $1,200,000 per year.

On the other hand, the company could hire a subcontractor who would meet the demand for a variable cost of $12 per unit and no fixed costs.

Required:

Ignoring risk, at what demand level would management be indifferent between the alternatives?

24–13. Estimate margin of safety

After further market analysis, Fanzole Corporation has obtained the following assessment of the demand levels and their probabilities:

Demand in thousands of units	Probability
50	.08
100	.25
150	.30
200	.27
250	.10

The cost and revenue data are the same as in Exercise 24–12. Assume there are no other possible demand outcomes.

Required:	What is the margin of safety for Fanzole Corporation's new medical device?

24–14. Estimate standard deviation of alternatives

Using the data for Fanzole Corporation, estimate the standard deviation for manufacturing and for subcontracting.

24–15. Assess impact of uncertainty

TimeDelay, Inc., has an opportunity to sell an asset for $15 million today. Alternatively, TimeDelay can use the asset in production for one month. If it is used, the expected profits and their probabilities are:

Profit	Probability
$ 8,000,000	.1
12,000,000	.2
15,000,000	.3
20,000,000	.4

The asset would be sold at the end of the month, and the present value of the sale is included in the profit computations.

Required:

a. The expected value of the production alternative.
b. The standard deviation of the production alternative.
c. The coefficient of variation for the production alternative.

Problems and cases

24–16. Expected value of sales

Jackston, Inc., manufactures and distributes a line of Christmas toys. The company had neglected to keep its doll house line current. As a result sales, have decreased to approximately 10,000 units per year from a previous high of 50,000 units. The doll house has been redesigned recently and is considered by company officials to be comparable to its competitors' models. The company plans to redesign the doll house each year in order to compete effectively. Joan Blocke, the sales manager, is not sure how many units can be sold next year, but she is willing to place probabilities on her estimates. Blocke's estimates of the number of units which can be sold during the next year and the related probabilities are as follows:

Estimated sales in units	Probability
20,000	.10
30,000	.40
40,000	.30
50,000	.20

The units would be sold for $20 each.

The inability to estimate the sales more precisely is a problem for Jackston. The number of units of this product is small enough to schedule the entire year's sales in one production run. If the demand is greater than the number of units manufactured, then sales will be lost. If demand is below supply, the extra units cannot be carried over to the next season and would be given away to various charitable organizations. The production and distribution cost estimates are listed below.

	Units manufactured			
	20,000	**30,000**	**40,000**	**50,000**
Variable costs	$180,000	$270,000	$360,000	$450,000
Fixed costs	140,000	140,000	160,000	160,000
Total costs	$320,000	$410,000	$520,000	$610,000

The company intends to analyze the data to facilitate making a decision as to the proper size of the production run.

Required:

Prepare a payoff table for the different sizes of production runs required to meet the four sales estimates prepared by Joan Blocke for Jackston, Inc. If Jackston, Inc., relied solely on the expected monetary value approach to make decisions, what size of production run would be selected?

(CMA adapted)

24–17. Analyze cost alternatives under uncertainty

The administrator for a large midwestern city continually seeks ways to reduce costs without cutting services. The administrator has asked all department heads to review their operations to determine if cost saving procedures can be implemented.

The Department of Streets is responsible for the proper functioning of the city's computerized traffic control system including the replacement of the 50,000 bulb units in the traffic lights. The department has kept detailed records regarding the failure rate of the bulb units over the past 18 months. The pattern of bulb failures that has been experienced is as follows:

Failure occurs within ___ quarter of replacement	**Probability**
First	.1
Second	.3
Third	.6

The Department of Streets has been replacing the bulb units as they have failed. The estimated cost to replace the bulb units, using this procedure, exclusive of the cost of the bulb unit, is $5.40 per unit.

The manager of the Department of Streets is considering replacing all of the bulb units at once, for example, at the beginning of every quarter, plus replacing bulbs as they fail. The manager estimates that the cost to replace all bulb units at once would be $1.40 per unit, exclusive of the cost of the bulb. The cost to replace each unit as it failed would still be $5.40 per unit.

Each bulb costs $1 regardless of the replacement procedure used.

Required:

a. Calculate the annual bulb and replacement cost to the Department of Streets if the present policy of replacing the bulb units as they fail is continued.

b. Calculate the estimated annual bulb and replacement cost if all bulb units are replaced when they fail and all bulb units are replaced on a regular basis at the beginning of:

(1) Every quarter.
(2) Every second quarter.
(3) Every third quarter.

Show your calculations for all three alternatives.

c. Why would there be such a large difference between the two estimated replacement costs per unit (replace as failure occurs, $5.40; replace all at once, $1.40). Explain your answer.

(CMA adapted)

24–18. Discuss simulation analysis

Fred Adamson manages a large door-to-door selling organization. The pattern of weekly sales is quite seasonal, but highly predictable. The typical annual pattern is shown below.

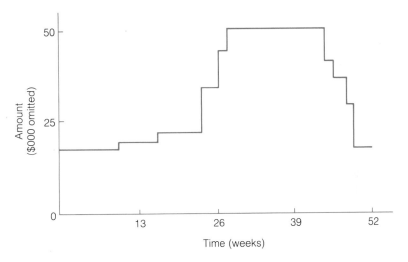

Adamson's most difficult problem is cash management. He often experiences either a cash shortage or has idle reserves. The cash outflows are not a problem because Adamson has a set payment schedule. The sales force is paid its 10 percent commission weekly, and Adamson's suppliers are paid five weeks after the sale.

The problem arises from Adamson's inability to predict accurately the cash collections from sales. All sales are made on account, and the customers are asked to remit their payments by mail within four weeks. If Adamson fails to receive the payment within eight weeks, he sends customers personalized form letters threatening legal action. Six percent of the payments are never received, but legal action is not actually taken due to its high cost.

Adamson has maintained collection experience records that have allowed him to specify a frequency distribution distribution for the collection lag. This frequency distribution is presented in the following schedule:

Collection lag (number of weeks from sale until actual collection)	Percentage of accounts
1	2
2	4
3	8
4	16
5	18
6	12
7	8
8	6
9	4
10	8
11	6
12	2
Uncollectible	6
	100

Adamson has discussed his cash management problem with a business acquaintance who is a consultant. The consultant has suggested that Adamson consider using simulation analysis.

Required:

a. Explain what is meant by *simulation analysis* and discuss why the computer is a useful tool in performing a simulation.

b. Explain why computer simulation would be an appropriate analysis technique for Fred Adamson to use in an attempt to solve his cash management problem.

c. Explain the basic structure of a simulation model that would address Fred Adamson's cash management problem.

(CMA adapted)

24–19. Analyze cost of changes in production facilities under uncertainty

(Understanding of the normal distribution is required for this problem.)

Racell Corporation is a food manufacturer that produces several different kinds of cereals. Krinkles, one of Racell's cereals, is packaged and sold in a 500-gram box. The filling equipment used to fill the boxes cannot be set precisely enough to guarantee that each box will contain exactly 500 grams. The volume by weight of cereal put in the boxes is normally distributed with a standard deviation of 12 grams. The filling equipment can be adjusted to vary the mean fill, but the standard deviation is constant. Management has specified that the filling equipment be set so that no more than three boxes out of 100 have less than 500 grams. If a box does contain less than 500 grams, the box is emptied and the contents are reentered into the filling process.

The manufacturer of the filling equipment being used by Racell has informed the company that an attachment is available that can improve the performance of the filling operation. The manufacturer estimates that the standard deviation of the filling operation for Krinkles can be reduced to 8 grams. The attachment would have to be replaced after 150,000 boxes were filled and would cost $1,500.

Racell sells 900,000 boxes of Krinkles annually. Krinkles are sold on the retail market for $1.35 a box; the wholesale price is $1.10 a box. The standard variable production cost is $.75 to produce 500 grams.

Required:

Should Racell Corporation acquire the attachment that would reduce the standard deviation of the filling process from 12 to 8 grams? Support your decision with appropriate calculations. Table of Z values is given.

Table of areas from mean to the number of standard deviations (Z) from mean for a normal distribution

Z	Area	Z	Area	Z	Area
1.0	.341	1.7	.455	2.4	.492
1.1	.364	1.8	.464	2.5	.494
1.2	.385	1.9	.471	2.6	.495
1.3	.403	2.0	.477	2.7	.497
1.4	.419	2.1	.482	2.8	.497
1.5	.433	2.2	.486	2.9	.498
1.6	.445	2.3	.489	3.0	.499

(CMA adapted)

24–20. CVP analysis under uncertainty

The Wing Manufacturing Corporation produces a chemical compound, Product X, which deteriorates and must be discarded if it is not sold by the end of the month during which it is produced. The total variable cost of the manufactured compound, Product X, is $50 per unit, and its selling price is $80 per unit. Wing can purchase the same compound from a competing company at $80 per unit plus $10 transportation per unit. Management has estimated that failure to fill orders would result in the loss of 80 percent of customers placing orders for the compound. Wing has manufactured and sold Product X for the past 20 months. Demand for the product has been irregular, and at present there is no consistent sales trend. During this period, monthly sales have been as follows:

Units sold per month	Probabilities
8,000	.25
9,000	.60
10,000	.15

In the production of Product X, Wing uses a primary ingredient, K-1. This ingredient is purchased from an outside supplier at a cost of $24 per unit of compound. It is estimated that there is a 70 percent chance that the supplier of K-1 may be shut down by a strike for an indefinite period. A substitute ingredient, K-2, is available at $36 per unit of compound, but Wing must contact this alternative source immediately to secure sufficient quantities. A firm purchase contract for either material must now be made for production of the primary ingredient next month. If an order were placed for K-1 and a strike occurred, Wing would be released from the contract and management would purchase the chemical compound from its competitor. Assume that 9,000 units are to be manufactured and all sales orders are to be filled.

Required:

a. Compute the monthly contribution margin from sales of 8,000, 9,000, and 10,000 units if the substitute ingredient, K-2, is ordered.

b. Prepare a schedule computing the average monthly contribution margin that Wing should expect if the primary ingredient, K-1, is ordered with the existing probability of a strike at the supplier. Assume that the expected average monthly contribution margin from manufacturing will be $130,000 using the primary ingredient and the expected average monthly loss from purchasing Product X from the competitor (in case of a strike) will be $45,000.

(CPA adapted)

24–21. Estimating contributions under uncertainty

Commercial Products Corporation requested your assistance in determining the potential loss on a purchase contract that will be in effect at the end of the year. The corporation produces a chemical compound that deteriorates and must be discarded if it is not sold by the end of the month during which it is produced.

The total variable cost of the manufactured compound is $25 per unit, and it is sold for $40 per unit. The compound can be purchased from a competitor at $40 per unit plus $5 transportation per unit. It is estimated that failure to fill orders would result in the complete loss of 8 out of 10 customers placing orders for the compound.

The cost of the primary ingredient used to manufacture the compound is $12 per unit of compound. It is estimated that there is a 60 percent chance that the primary ingredient supplier's plant may be shut down by a strike for an indefinite period. A substitute ingredient is available at $18 per unit of compound, but the corporation must contract immediately to purchase the substitute, or it will be unavailable when needed. A firm purchase contract for either the primary or the substitute ingredient must now be made with one of the suppliers for production next month. If an order were placed for the primary ingredient and a strike should occur, the corporation would be released from the contract and management would purchase the compound from the competitor. Assume 5,000 units will be produced or ordered.

The corporation has sold the compound for the past 30 months. Demand has been irregular, and there is no discernible sales trend. During this period, sales per month has been:

Units sold per month	Number of months[a]
4,000	6
5,000	15
6,000	9

[a] Occurred in random sequence.

Required:

a. For each of the following, prepare a schedule of the—
   (1) Probability of sales of 4,000, 5,000, or 6,000 units in any month.
   (2) Contribution to income if sales of 4,000, 5,000, or 6,000 units are made in one month, and 4,000, 5,000, or 6,000 units are manufactured for sale in the same month. Assume all sales orders are filled.
b. Should management order the primary or substitute ingredient during the anticipated strike period?

(CPA adapted)

24–22. Simulation (computer required)

Monte Carlo simulation is a method for analyzing CVP relationships under conditions of uncertainty, and under assumptions concerning the distribution of the sales, volume, and variable cost variables. This situation is somewhat unrealistic since most companies deal in more than one product. In addition, companies *seem* to face constraints in the allocation of resources among different product lines.

Excelsior Corporation has five products, named creatively enough as A, B, C, D, and E. Relevant data for these products are as follows:

Expected value of

Product	Price	Variable cost	Maximum sales	Expected sales
A	$15	$ 6	20,000	15,000
B	14	7	50,000	17,000
C	18	8	19,000	18,500
D	25	17	10,000	10,000
E	6	2	30,000	26,000

The standard deviation of each item in the list, except the sales limit, is equal to 25 percent of the expected value of the item. Aggregate sales of all products cannot exceed $1,500,000.

Required:

a. What is the expected sales volume and profit from all products?

b. Write a computer program to simulate the probabilistic behavior of each of the variables assuming that they are normally distributed. Run the simulation for 100 iterations. What is the expected sales volume and profit for all products? Prepare a graph of the profit data.

c. Expand the program to incorporate the maximum sales constraints. Using the same simulation data from (b) show the expected sales volume and profits.

d. Comment on the differences in results for each of the three items listed above.

25

The Variance Investigation Decision

OBJECTIVES

To be familiar with decisions about whether and when to investigate a variance.
To understand the concepts of statistical quality control as they relate to accounting
  variances.

Variances represent differences between planned results and actual performance. A variance may be caused by a change in output activity, a change in the efficiency with which inputs are used, or a change in the unit cost of an input. Variance analysis is important for performance evaluation and control as we discussed in Chapters 18 to 21. A substantial number of variances are usually included in any set of internal management reports, and managers don't have the time to investigate all of them. So, some method must be found to investigate only those variances that are expected to produce a benefit in excess of investigation costs.

In this chapter, we discuss how to determine which variances should be investigated. We also examine the costs associated with variance investigation decisions and how they may be minimized. These costs include the costs of conducting an investigation plus the costs of correcting the process if it needs correction. On the other hand, suppose we do not investigate a variance. Then if the process is out of control, we incur the costs of letting it continue out of control.

The investigation setting

Imagine that you are managing the employee benefits section of the Great Plains Corporation and are responsible for its operations. The employee benefits section is a cost center in the company's organization. Your compensation and your future with the company will be evaluated on the basis of the cost center's performance. The monthly report on your cost center has just arrived. It appears as follows:

GREAT PLAINS CORPORATION
Employee Benefits Section
Responsibility Report
(in thousands)

Cost item	Budget	Actual	Variance
Staff salaries	$155	$156	$ 1 U
Operator wages	137	151	14 U
Other wages	41	39	2 F
Communications	12	9	3 F
Utilities	39	48	9 U
Supplies	16	11	5 F
Maintenance and repairs	24	8	16 F
All other	80	85	5 U
Totals	$504	$507	$ 3 U

How do you decide which variances to investigate? This decision is similar to other management decisions whose objective is to minimize the net present value of expected costs. To make the decision, consider the costs associated with your decision alternatives. These alternatives may be restricted to:

1. Investigate the variance.
2. Do not investigate.

Intermediate decisions may also be made. For example, you may wait until you receive next month's report before investigating. Or, you might decide to conduct a very brief pilot study before deciding to carry on a full-fledged investigation. To minimize the complexity of our discussion, we will limit our consideration to the first two alternatives. Adding other choices makes the mathematics more complex, but the underlying approach is the same.

Essentially, you must consider the trade-offs between the costs of investigating and the costs of allowing the process to continue without investigation. You must determine the differential costs and a method for assessing the trade-offs.

Investigation decision costs

While the actual costs of the investigation decision depend on the specifics of the operation, some typical investigation costs include:

1. Opportunity costs of the time you spend tracking down the cause of a variance.
2. Opportunity costs of the time your staff spends in the investigation.
3. Costs to test equipment that may be out of adjustment.
4. Costs to shut down an operation while testing equipment.
5. Costs to restart or rearrange activities to increase efficiency.
6. Consulting fees of outside experts hired to examine operations.

For example, the costs to investigate the unfavorable variance in utilities costs may require an inspection tour of the operating area to check that lights and equipment are shut off when not in use. A more elaborate investigation might involve hiring a consulting firm to study utilities usage and suggest a conservation program.

If you don't investigate a variance, other costs may be incurred. Some possibilities include:

1. Costs of continued inefficient operations including inefficient use of labor, materials, and energy.
2. Costs of improperly adjusted equipment including failure to meet product specifications, damaged or defective goods, and hazardous operating conditions.

The utilities costs that might be incurred if no investigation were made would include any energy costs from equipment that was left on when not in use, costs of heat lost through leakage in walls or insulation, and loss of lighting power through inefficient fixtures, dirty light covers, and the like.

The purpose of investigating a variance is to save future costs. But costs can only be saved if your investigation uncovers a factor that can be adjusted. This does not always occur. Sometimes, a variance is just a random event or is beyond control. If the variance is a random event, investigating it will yield no benefits to offset your investigation costs. For example, there would be no benefit in discovering that a variance stemmed from an error in reading the utility meter that is offset in subsequent periods. If a variance is due to an increase in utility rates, then there is probably little management can do except adjust future budgets. Additional, but less direct actions might include taking steps to reduce future energy use.

Conceptual basis for investigation decisions

In earlier chapters, we suggested that the typical cost function could be expressed as:

$$Y = a + bX$$

where:

Y = the total cost
a = fixed cost
b = variable cost
X = activity in units of input or output.

In an uncertain world, we must add a term to this equation to represent the variability likely to arise in any cost setting. The new equation is:

$$Y = a + bX + e$$

and the new term, e, is the difference between what costs should be if they followed our equation and what actual costs are. This term is called the error term. It implies differences in costs due to random error. The key question that should be asked when a variance is observed is whether the variance is simply a value of e or whether the variance represents changes in *a, b,* or *X.* Managers prefer not to spend resources investigating variances that are just random events.

In deciding whether a variance investigation is likely to yield net benefits, a manager focuses on variances that are too large to have been caused by random events. The larger a cost variance, the less likely it was caused by random event. Generally, managers will use subjective judgment in deciding whether to investigate a variance. However, the statistical process formalizes the subjective process.

Statistical decision models

The statistical decision model for the variance investigation decision may be diagrammed as:

	Alternatives	
State	**Investigate**	**Do not investigate**
In control	*I*	0
Out of control	*C + I*	*L*

The two columns of the matrix represent the alternative management actions (Investigate, Do not investigate) and the two rows represent the unknown state of the process (In control, Out of control). Each cell represents a pairing of a decision alternative and a state of the process. The symbols in the cells represent the costs of each pairing.

For example, if we investigate the utilities cost variance, we incur an investigation cost *(I)* if the process is in control. Hence, the first cell in the matrix shows that *I* is the cost from the paired event "Investigate, In control." If the process is out of control and we investigate, our cost is the cost to correct *(C)* and the investigation cost *(I).* Thus, the cost in the first column of the second row of the matrix is *C + I.*

If we don't investigate and the process is in control, we incur zero costs. The zero is entered in the first row of the second column.

Finally, if we do not investigate and the process is out of control, we incur the cost (or loss) of letting the process stay out of control. This loss is labeled *L* and entered in the appropriate cell. Generally, variance investigation decisions are made on a periodic basis and are reviewed as each new report is issued. Therefore, if the process is out of control, subsequent variance reports will tend to signal this. The value of *L,* therefore, must be stated in terms of the costs that will be incurred until management intervenes and corrects the process. Some out-of-control processes may remain out of control only until the next report. Others can remain out of control for months or years. Computing *L,* then, involves considering these future management actions.

Since we don't know the state of the process when we make the investigation decision, the costs of each alternative is conditional on the probability that the alternative reflects the actual situation. The cost of each alternative, then, is an expected value. The manager chooses the alternative whose cost has the lower expected value.

Suppose that the costs to investigate the variance in utilities expense is $500. The costs to correct an out-of-control process is $1,000, and the cost of allowing the utilities to remain out of control for another period is $4,000. (Assume this is a short-term problem. If this were a long-term problem, the procedure would be the same but the amounts would be present values of future costs.) We enter each cost in the appropriate place in the decision matrix and derive a cost for each paired alternative/state outcome. This yields the following matrix:

	Alternative	
State	**Investigate**	**Do not investigate**
In control	$ 500	$ 0
Out of control	1,500	4,000

If the probability of being out of control is .3, which is the less costly alternative? To answer the question, we must compute the expected value of each alternative. If we investigate, the probability is .3 that we will obtain the benefits of correcting the out-of-control process and .7 (which is 1 − .3) that we will find nothing wrong. The expected cost of the investigation alternative is therefore:

$$.7 \times \$500 + .3 \times \$1,500 = \$350 + \$450$$
$$= \$800$$

The expected value of the alternative "Do not investigate" is computed similarly. Since the cost of the pair "Do not investigate, In control" is zero, that term will equal zero and is ignored. The expected cost of not investigating is the product of the probability of being out of control times the cost of being out of control. For this example,

$$.3 \times \$4,000 = \$1,200$$

Since the expected cost of an investigation is less than the expected cost of not investigating, the model suggests that the variance should be investigated.

Management policy and statistical theory

It is unlikely that management would employ this approach directly in an actual application. The cost and probability data are usually not available for the types of variance investigations encountered in typical monthly reporting settings. However, the statistical approach may be applied in principal;

relating the statistical decision theory approach to the manager's decision, therefore, requires some additional steps.

If we assume that the greater the variance, the greater the probability that it is caused by an out-of-control process, an investigation policy can be established that relates the variance amount to a probability of being out of control. At some probability, management is indifferent to whether an investigation is conducted or not. If the actual probability of being out of control as indicated by the dollar amount of the variance is greater than implied by our critical probability (p^*), it pays to investigate. Otherwise, the expected value of not investigating is greater. This critical probability is, in essence, a break-even point between two cost functions.

The expected costs of an out-of-control process (L) increase as the probability of being out of control increases. We can express the cost function for the out-of-control situation as Lp, where p is the probability of being out of control.

Likewise, the expected cost to correct an out-of-control process increases with the probability that the process is out of control. That is, if we investigate, as the value of p increases, so does the chance that we will discover and correct the out-of-control process. Hence, the cost of investigating is equal to I plus Cp.

If we diagram the relationship between the expected costs of investigating and not investigating, the point where the two cost functions are equal represents the critical value of p^*. This diagram is shown in Illustration 25–1.

Illustration 25–1   **Cost functions for variance investigation**

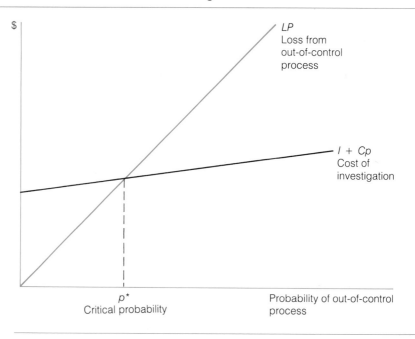

$ LP
Loss from
out-of-control
process

$I + Cp$
Cost of
investigation

p^*
Critical probability

Probability of out-of-control
process

To find p^*, we set the expected cost of investigating equal to the expected cost of not investigating and solve for the unknown p^*. We then must relate the variance data in the responsibility report to the probability of being out of control. If, as indicated by the variance report, that probability is greater than p^*, we initiate an investigation. Otherwise we do not.

The cost function for the decision to investigate may be obtained from the information used to compute the expected cost when the probability of being out of control was .3. If we replace the given probabilities with p^*, the cost of investigating is expressed:

$$(1 - p^*)I + p^*(I + C) = I - Ip^* + Ip^* + Cp^*$$
$$= I + Cp^*$$

The cost of not investigating is:

$$Lp^*$$

Setting the cost functions equal to each other and solving for p^* gives:

$$I + Cp^* = Lp^*$$
$$I = Lp^* - Cp^*$$
$$I = (L - C)p^*$$
$$p^* = \frac{I}{(L - C)}$$

Using this formula for the data given for our utility cost investigation problem, we obtain a critical probability of:

$$p^* = \frac{\$500}{\$4,000 - \$1,000}$$
$$= .16\tfrac{2}{3}$$

Therefore, as long as the probability of being out of control is greater than .16⅔, the expected investigation costs will be less than the expected costs of allowing the process to continue without investigation.

To check, should we investigate if the probability of being out of control is .15? By knowing the critical probability, we can immediately answer no. The following computations support this:

The expected cost of the investigation is:

$$(1 - .15) \times \$500 + .15 \times (\$1,000 + \$500) = \$425 + \$225$$
$$= \$650$$

The expected cost of not investigating is:

$$.15 \times \$4,000 = \$600$$

Hence, the model indicates that with an out-of-control probability of .15, the better alternative is not to investigate.

Relating statistical probabilities to variances

Knowing p^*, however, is only one basis for setting a variance investigation policy. Managers usually make a variance investigation decision based on the absolute monetary value of the variance itself. The additional steps to compute p^* are not carried out every time a manager receives a responsibility report. As a result, it is necessary to relate the magnitude of a variance to the probability that a process is out of control. Once this is accomplished, a policy may be set that states that a variance should be investigated if it exceeds the dollar value that is related to p^*.

Relating the dollar value of a variance to the probability that a process is out of control is not an easy task. Some authors suggest that the probability of being out of control is equal to the complement of the probability of being in control. That is, if the probability of being in control is .75, the probability of being out of control is .25 (which is $1 - .75$). This approach is computationally simple, but incorrect in most circumstances. This is because when we observe a variance, we don't know the source of the variance. The cost function under uncertainty from above was:

$$Y = a + bX + e$$

Observation of a variance may have come from a cost process represented by this equation. However, it may also have come some other cost process represented by (say):

$$Y = a + b'X + e$$

which is an out-of-control process. The idea that the in-control probability may be computed as the complement of the out-of-control probability is conditioned on the assumption that e would be zero in the out-of-control equation above.

To illustrate, consider the diagram of the random process that generates variances for in-control and out-of-control processes presented in Illustration 25–2.

If the process is in control, variances are generated due to the random nature of the process. That is, spending or usage may differ from plans purely as a result of random factors. Such variances might follow a normal distribution as in the top panel of Illustration 25–2. In such a case, the variance has an expected value (or mean) of $0. Nonetheless, some variances may be reported even though the process is in control.

The second panel of Illustration 25–2 shows the distribution of variances expected from an out-of-control process. If the process is out of control, we assume that there is a shift in costs to a higher level. The out-of-control process is also subject to random variation, as shown by the probability distribution.

Given a variance, we cannot know if the process is in or out of control. But we assess the probability that the process is out of control by referring to the two probability distributions. For example, Case 1 in Illustration 25–2 shows a $23,000 favorable variance. Looking at the distribution of an out-

Illustration 25–2　　**Relationship between in-control and out-of-control processes**

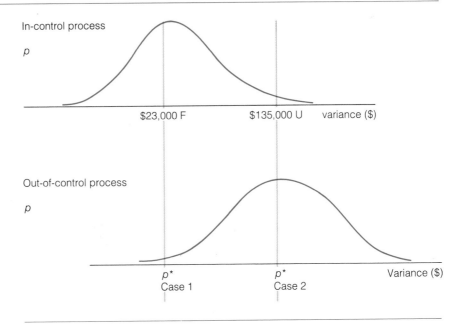

of-control process, it appears that there is a very small probability that a process with that variance would be out of control.

By contrast, Case 2 shows a variance of $135,000 U. The probability that this variance came from an in-control process is small, as shown by the location of that variance in the probability distribution in the first panel of Illustration 25–2. The probability that the $135,000 unfavorable variance came from an out-of-control process is higher, as shown in the second panel. The probability of being out of control is measured by looking at the relative probabilities of observing the variance from each of the two processes.

The probability of being out of control is not equal to the complement of the probability of being in control. However, the lower the probability that the process is in control, the greater the probability that the process is out of control. Therefore, if we find p^* on the out-of-control distribution, we can extend p^* to the distribution for the in-control process just as was done in Illustration 25–2.

The mathematical process for computing exact values for p^* in terms of an in-control process (rather than the out-of-control process) requires knowledge of the probability distribution for the out-of-control process and the use of Bayesian statistics. Since we are only presenting a conceptual basis for the role of p^* in the establishment of a variance investigation policy, we will not discuss the mathematical details.

Statistical quality control charts

In situations where there is a large number of units produced by some process, production engineering developed a method for sampling some of the units produced and comparing the samples to product specifications. If the sample fell within certain tolerances, the production process was considered in control and no further investigation conducted. However, if the sample was beyond some tolerance limits, an investigation was conducted to see if the process was out of control. The procedure is referred to as statistical quality control.

A familiar example of this method is the testing of the weight of cereal in a box of cereal. To make certain that the machines that fill the boxes are operating properly, several filled cereal boxes are pulled from the production line and weighed. If the weight of the cereal in the box is within certain limits, it is assumed that the machines filling the boxes are opearting properly.

It has been suggested that accounting data may be analyzed using statistical quality control methods to help management approach the variance investigation decision. With this method, the process that generates a cost variance is considered to have a mean of zero. If we know the standard deviation of the process that generates variances, we can set tolerance limits for variances. Those that fall within the tolerance limits are assumed to come from an in-control process, otherwise the variance is investigated.

Although we have assumed a zero mean for the variance, it is possible to adapt the method to a broader set of values for the variance. However, estimating the standard deviation of an accounting cost is usually more of a problem. Sometimes the standard deviation can be obtained as a part of a regression-based cost estimate (Chapter 10). In other cases, simulation techniques may be used to analyze the behavior of a process and the accounting data that would be generated from that process.

We usually assume that the in-control process is normally distributed, although other assumptions are possible. Assuming a zero mean, in the statistical quality control method, the variance is divided by the standard deviation for the variance. The result is a z-value. If the z-value is greater than 1.96, the probability that the variance came from an in-control process is less than .025. If the z-value is 2.56 or more, the probability that it came from an in-control process is no greater than .005.

For example, the variance in utilities costs for the employee benefits section of Great Plains was $9,000. If the standard deviation for that variance is $4,500, then the z-value is 2. That z-value is close enough to 1.96 for us to state that the probability of its coming from an in-control process is about .025.

When there are frequent observations of variances, it may be helpful to diagram the variances by their relationship to the in-control process. This may be done using statistical quality control charts. An example is reproduced in Illustration 25–3.

The chart is constructed by drawing a horizontal time line for the mean of the process. The vertical scale gives the values for the observations. For cereal weights, the scale could be grams. For accounting variances, the scale

Illustration 25–3   **Statistical quality control chart**

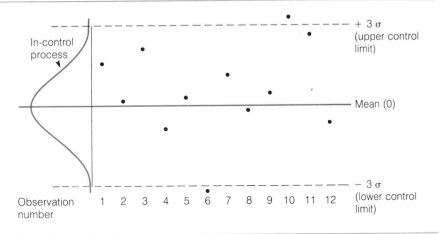

would be monetary amounts. The vertical scale could also be converted to z-values since any observed number when divided by its standard deviation gives a z-value. The specific scaling would be specified by the managers using the charts.

An **upper and lower control limit** is drawn on the chart at the observation values that are considered critical by management. An observation that falls within the control limits is considered acceptable; one that falls without is not. If the observation falls outside the control limits, the process is investigated. In the United States, the control limits are usually set at three standard deviations. Statisticians use the greek letter **sigma** (σ) for denoting the standard deviation of a population. Hence, control are frequently referred to as three-sigma or two-sigma control charts depending on how many standard deviations are used to set the control limits.

Using the observations in Illustration 25–3, we note that observations 6 and 10 fall outside the control limits. These observations would be investigated.

Control charts and variance investigation

The statistical quality control chart is based on engineering observations of repetitive processes. As a conceptual model, it is useful because if we can relate p^* to the in-control process and if we set the upper and lower control limits in terms of p^*, it is possible to construct control charts that illustrate observations that may need investigation. They provide a visual effect not possible from a numerical report. If we use the control chart to plot variances in a specific account over time, it may be possible to detect trends or other patterns in variances that would signal the need to investigate even if the control limits were not exceeded. For example, if a cost were relatively stable

Illustration 25–4   **Highlighting trends in variances with a statistical quality control chart**

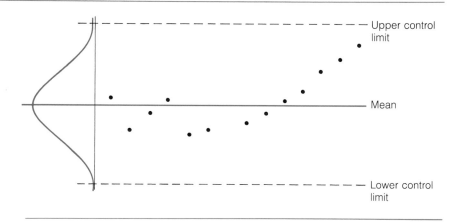

for several months and then began to show successively greater unfavorable variances, as in Illustration 25–4, a manager might decide to investigate the variance even though it falls within the control limits.

Management investigation policies

So far, we have assumed that a variance should be investigated only if the expected benefits from investigation outweigh the costs. This approach focuses on finding a critical probability of being out of control and relating the variance report data to that critical probability. As a practical matter, management usually sets an investigation policy based on some threshhold dollar or percentage limitation for variances. For example, a policy may be established that says:

> Investigate all variances that exceed $7,000 or are greater than 20 percent of the flexible budget amount for the specific cost item.

Such a policy is easy to implement, does not require extensive statistical analysis every period, and can be cost effective if its limits actually do approximate the amounts that would be obtained by a formal analysis of out-of-control probabilities.

If this policy were in effect for the employee benefits section of Great Plains, the following costs would be investigated based on the responsibility report earlier in the chapter:

Cost	Reason to investigate
Operator wages	Exceeds $7,000
Communications	Exceeds 20%
Utilities	Exceeds both limits
Supplies	Exceeds 20%
Maintenance and repairs	Exceeds both limits

Assuming that the limits have been established to approximate the investigations that would be conducted using the p^*-based minimum-cost approach, your investigations would be cost effective.

Summary

The decision to investigate variances is an important management decision because the investigation requires the use of scarce management resources, while letting a process continue out of control may result in waste. It is rare that all variances should be investigated. Many are caused by random processes. Conceptually, a variance may be a signal that a process is out of control. If the signal indicates that the probability of being out of control exceeds the critical point where it is more cost effective to investigate than not to investigate, management should conduct an investigation. It may be possible to compute this critical probability using statistical methods. An alternative approach is to use statistical quality control charts to monitor variances over time. However, managers usually establish an investigation rule based on the absolute amount of the variance or on the amount as a percentage of flexible budget. Such ad hoc rules are usually relatively easy to implement and, so long as they approximate the results that would occur with a more rigorous statistical analysis, they are probably cost effective.

Terms and concepts

The following terms and concepts should be familiar to you after reading this chapter.

Critical probability	**Out-of-control probability**
Error term	**Random event**
Expected value	**Sigma (σ)**
In-control probability	**Standard deviation**
Lower control limit	**Statistical quality control**
Mean	**Upper control limit**

Self-study problem

Wild and Crazy Lens Corporation has been experiencing problems controlling costs. A recent responsibility report for one of the company's divisions indicated the following (in thousands):

Item	Budget	Actual	Variance
Direct materials	$ 45	$ 39	$6 F
Direct labor	40	48	8 U
Overhead:			
Utilities	10	9	1 F
Property taxes	6	5	1 F
Supervision	8	6	2 F
Equipment repairs	7	10	3 U
Totals	$116	$117	$1 U

The division manager stated that there was no problem since the overall variance was less than 1 percent of total costs and that was close enough.

As a member of the controller's staff, you learn that the cost to investigate each variance is $1,250. If the process is out of control, it costs an estimated $1,000 to correct. However, if the process is out of control and stays out of control, the variance in next month's report is expected to be the same as this month's variance. If the variance appears next month, the process will be investigated and controlled. Hence, the only loss of delay is one month's variance.

Required:

a. What is the critical probability for investigating the direct labor variance?

b. Given the stated costs from the problem, which other variances would you investigate if you were responsible for these costs?

c. Can you suggest some possible causes for the variances that appear in this report?

Solution to self-study problem

a. If L is equal to the $8,000 variance, then the cost functions may be set up as:

$$Lp = I + Cp$$
$$\$8,000p = \$1,250 + \$1,000p$$
$$\$7,000p = \$1,250$$
$$p = .179$$

which is the critical probability.

b. The only other costs that would be investigated are those with unfavorable variances greater than $1,250. The only cost meeting this criterion is equipment repairs.

c. It appears that there is a significant drop in materials costs suggesting the possibility that substandard materials may have been purchased. If so, this may explain why labor costs have such a high variance and why equipment repair costs are substantially greater than budget. This section of the problem is designed to illustrate how management judgment enters the variance investigation decision process. A reveiw of the report and the given cost structure suggests that only unfavorable variances be investigated. However, it is likely that in this situation the unfavorable variances have a common cause. Management's experience would override any statistical analysis of the data.

Questions

25–1. Why doesn't management just investigate all unfavorable variances and forget about complex investigation rules?

25–2. What is the basic decision that management must make when considering whether to investigate a variance?

25–3. The cost function $Y = a + bX + e$ has been used in the chapter to describe the problem facing management when deciding whether to investigate a variance. How does this function illustrate the problem?

25–4. The larger a variance, the more likely management is to investigate it. What is the rationale for this?

25–5. Should favorable variances be investigated? Why or why not?

25–6. What is the role of the out-of-control probability in the variance investigation decision?

25–7. Under what conditions would statistical quality control charts be useful in a responsibility-reporting setting?

25–8. Management usually sets a variance investigation policy such as "Investigate all variances greater than $10,000 or 20 percent of the budgeted amount for the item." Why would management use such a rule when statistical rules give a more precise answer?

25–9. Why do we study statistical rules for variance investigation if they are not widely used by managers?

25–10. Alpha Corporation has implemented the use of statistical quality control charts in analyzing variances. The company has set upper and lower control limits equal to two standard deviations. Assuming that there are no out-of-control situations anywhere in the company, what is the probable proportion of variances that will be outside the control limits?

Exercises

25–11. Estimate critical probabilities

Required:

The cost of an investigation is $4,000. If the process is out of control, it will cost $9,000 to correct it. However, if the process stays out of control, the company expects it will cost $15,000 until the process is corrected.

What is the critical out-of-control probability?

25–12. Evaluate costs of variance investigation decision

Greensward, Inc., has observed an unfavorable variance of $25,000 in its direct materials usage. They estimate that this variance indicates that there is a .70 probability that the manufacturing process is out of control. The cost to investigate this variance necessitates shutting down operations at a cost of $8,000. If the process is out of control, repairs will be ordered costing an estimated $15,000. In addition, the production line will stay closed down during the repair process. The shutdown is estimated to cost $26,000.

If the process is out of control and is left out of control, the company expects that $45,000 in excess materials will be used between now and the time when the next variance report comes out. At that time, the variance would indicate a 1.0 probability that the process was out of control.

Required:

Indicate the expected costs of investigating and not investigating for this situation.

25–13. Investigating a process

A production manager of Wargames, Inc. is trying to determine if a particular production process is in control. The cost of investigation is $3,000, and if the process is out of control, it will cost the company $7,000 to correct the error. By correcting the error, the present value of the cost savings until the next scheduled routine intervention will be $20,000. The probability of the process being in control is .80, and the probability of the process being out of control is .20.

Required:

a. Should the process be investigated? Why or why not?

b. At what level of probability of the process being out of control would the manager be indifferent about whether to investigate?

(SMA adapted)

25–14. Investigating a process

An unfavorable variance of $20,000 was reported for a manufacturing process. If no investigation is conducted and the process is out of control, the present value of excess production costs that could be avoided over the remaining budget period is an estimated $10,000. The cost of conducting an investigation is expected to be $2,000; if the process were actually out of control, the cost of correction would be an additional $1,000. There is a .80 probability that the $20,000 variance was caused by random uncontrollable events.

Required:

a. Should the process be investigated?

b. At what probability level does the expected cost of investigating equal the expected cost of not investigating?

Problems and cases

25–15. Analyze costs and variances

The Clark Company has a contract with a labor union that guarantees a minimum wage of $500 per month to each direct labor employee having at least 12 years of service. One hundred employees currently qualify for coverage. All direct labor employees are paid $5 per hour.

The direct labor budget for 1985 was based on the annual usage of 400,000 hours of direct labor at $5, or a total of $2,000,000. Of this amount, $50,000 (100 employees × $500) per month (or $600,000 for the year) was regarded as fixed. Thus, the budget for any given month was determined by the formula $50,000 + $3.50 (direct labor-hours worked).

Data on performance for the first three months of 1985 follow:

	January	February	March
Direct labor-hours worked	22,000	32,000	42,000
Direct labor costs budgeted	$127,000	$162,000	$197,000
Direct labor costs incurred	110,000	160,000	210,000
Variance	17,000 F	2,000 F	13,000 U

The factory manager was perplexed by the results, which showed favorable variances when production was low and unfavorable variances when production was high, because he believed his control over labor costs was consistently good.

Required:

a. Why did the variances arise? Explain and illustrate, using amounts and diagrams as necessary.

b. Does this direct labor budget provide a basis for controlling direct labor cost? Explain, indicating changes that might be made to improve control over direct labor cost and to facilitate performance evaluation of direct labor employees.

(CPA adapted)

25–16. Costs of investigation

The Bilco Oil Company currently sells three grades of gasoline: regular, premium, and "regular plus," which is a mixture of regular and premium. Regular plus is advertised as being "at least 50 percent premium." Although any mixture containing 50 percent or more premium gas could be sold as "regular plus," it is less costly to use exactly 50 percent. The percent of premium gas in the mixture is determined by a valve in the blending machine. If the valve is properly adjusted, the machine provides a mixture that is 50 percent premium and 50 percent regular. If the valve is out of adjustment, the machine provides a mixture that is 60 percent premium and 40 percent regular.

Once the machine is started, it must continue until 100,000 gallons of "regular plus" have been mixed.

Cost data available:	
Cost per gallon—premium	32¢
—regular	30¢
Cost of checking the valve	$80
Cost of adjusting the value	$40

The probabilities of the valve's condition are estimated to be:

Event	Probability
In adjustment	.7
Out of adjustment	.3

Required

a. Should Bilco investigate the valve?
b. At what probability would Bilco be indifferent about whether to investigate?

(CMA adapted)

25–17. Issues in variance investigation— multiple choice

The folding department foreman must decide each week whether his department will operate normally the following week. He may order a corrective action if he feels the folding department will operate inefficiently; otherwise he does nothing. The foreman receives a weekly folding department efficiency variance report from the accounting department. A week in which the folding department operates inefficiently is usually preceded by a large efficiency variance. The graph below gives the probability that the folding department will operate normally in the following week as a function of the magnitude of the current week's variance reported to the foreman:

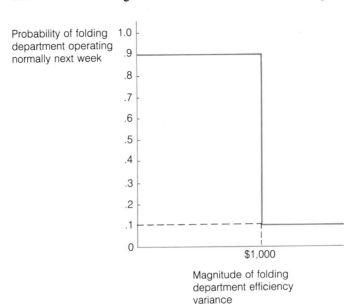

Required:

a. An efficiency variance of $1,500 this week means the probability of operating normally the following week is:
   (1) 0 percent.
   (2) 10 percent.
   (3) 90 percent.
   (4) 100 percent.

b. What are the possible relationships between the current efficiency variance and next week's operations?
   (1) Large variance followed by normal operation, large variance followed by inefficient operation, small variance followed by normal operation, and small variance followed by inefficient operation.
   (2) Large variance followed by normal operation, small variance followed by inefficient operation, and small variance followed by normal operation.
   (3) Large variance followed by inefficient operation, small variance followed by normal operation, and small variance followed by inefficient operation.
   (4) Large variance followed by 90 percent of normal operation, small variance followed by 10 percent of normal operation, large variance followed by inefficient operation, and small variance followed by inefficient operation.

c. If the foreman can determine for certain whether the folding department will operate normally next week and the cost of corrective action is less than the extra cost of operating the folding department inefficiently, then the best decision rule for the foreman to follow is:
   (1) If normal operations are predicted, do not take corrective action; if inefficient operations are predicted, take corrective action.
   (2) Regardless of the current variance, do not take corrective action.
   (3) If normal operations are predicted, take corrective action; if inefficient operations are predicted, do not take corrective action.
   (4) Regardless of the current variance, take corrective action.

d. The following cost information is relevant to the folding department foreman in deciding whether corrective action is warranted:

   $ 500 = cost of corrective action that will assure normal operation of folding department for the following week.

   $3,000 = excess cost of operating folding department inefficiently for one week.

   The foreman receives a report that the folding department efficiency variance is $600. The expected cost of not taking corrective action is:
   (1) $0.
   (2) $300.
   (3) $2,700.
   (4) $3,000.

(CPA adapted)

25–18. Control charts

Jean Auel was recently appointed controller for a medium-sized manufacturing firm. Her first assignment is to investigate whether material usage within the plant is under control. She recalls studying statistical quality control techniques in a management education course and decided to apply it to her investigation. She took the following two samples:

Sample number	Cost of each item			
1	$945	$876	$852	$941
2	822	943	949	782

The control limits specified are $880 ± $60.

Required:

a. Prepare a control chart using the designated control limits.

b. Comment on the results.

25–19. Control charts

An engineer for the Jordan Valley Tool Company specified that the diameter of a particular part should have tolerance limits of .352 and .356. J. Telleria, assistant to the controller, asked production personnel to sample these parts. A random sample of 20 parts had the following diameters:

Exhibit A

Number	Diameter
1	.351
2	.350
3	.353
4	.352
5	.359
6	.360
7	.362
8	.351
9	.353
10	.358
11	.355
12	.350
13	.353
14	.354
15	.353
16	.354
17	.355
18	.355
19	.356
20	.354

The standard deviation diameter for this type of part has been established as .354 and .003 respectively after several years of sampling. The Jordan Valley Tool top management has established a policy that variances outside of the two-sigma should be investigated by the accounting staff. Engineering and production personnel believe a process is in control as long as variances are within three standard deviations from the mean, however.

a.   Construct a control chart and plot the sample on it.

     b.   Are the present engineering tolerance limits currently attainable? If not, what alternatives are open to the company?

26

The Economics
of Information

OBJECTIVES
To understand the economic theory about why managers acquire information and
why they limit the amount of information they acquire.
To understand the economic consequences of using the wrong information in a
decision.

Managers are employed to make and implement decisions. The outcome
from such decisions is rarely known in advance with certainty. Hence, the
decision may result in a profit or a loss. Information is used to assist the
manager in making economic decisions. Cost accounting information is part
of the manager's available information set. While managers can obtain a
great deal of information to assist them in making a decision, at some point
the information gathering must end and the decision must be made. Determining this point is a decision that results in incurring costs to, hopefully, obtain
benefits. Hence, the decision to acquire information is an economic decision.

As providers of information, cost accountants are required to understand
the economics of the decision to acquire information. We assume in this
chapter that routine information, such as that required for external reporting,
will be gathered without an explicit economic analysis. Hence, in this chapter
we will focus on the economics of information used for special purposes
such as for decision making.

Some examples of risky management decisions that require cost information
include:

1. Choosing the price to set for a new product where the price must cover
   costs and provide an adequate profit.
2. Deciding whether an adequate profit could be earned by entering a new
   market.
3. Evaluating whether a new employee benefit would be cost effective.
4. Deciding to explore for natural resources.
5. Determining whether to finance the company through bank loans, public
   debt, or equity.

For each of these decisions, the net benefit to the company is affected by
events beyond the control of the decision maker. Information is used to
help management make more informed decisions.

Cost data and information economics

As discussed in earlier chapters, cost accounting differs from financial accounting in several ways. One major difference is that because the information is provided only to insiders, the user need not be limited by the rules for external reporting. Hence, the inside user can specify exactly the information to be provided for any given decision. The only limitation that the user faces is that information, like any good, is costly. At some point, the cost of additional information will exceed the benefit that can be expected from it. The conceptual basis for determining how much information to request is found in the field of information economics.

Consider the decision-making problem of a manager of WowZow Audio Corporation who is about to introduce a miniature cassette player into the market. This cassette player will fit entirely in the ear, thus eliminating the need for earphones and a cumbersome playing device. The product will be called an EarHear. The EarHear requires an investment of $7 million in plant and equipment. Assume, for simplicity, that there are only two possible outcomes from this decision:

1. The product is well accepted, costs and revenues are equal to expected levels, and the future cash flows will be worth a net present value of $20 million.
2. The product is a failure, and the total investment will be lost.

If you were the manager, would you invest the $7 million with this information? This problem is similar to other decision-making problems under uncertainty. Similarities with the approach in Chapter 24 appear here also, except in this chapter we focus on the acquisition of information rather than on the production decision.

Just knowing the possible outcomes is insufficient information on which to base this decision. The manager will seek information until the expected cost of that information exceeds its benefits.

Deciding whether the cost-benefit criterion has been met is usually a matter of personal judgment. The process of this judgment has been studied and is called **information economics.** Information economics is a highly analytical field of study. Briefly, information is deemed to meet the cost-benefit test if the expected value of a decision (net of the costs of the information) increases as a result of obtaining additional information. That is, the expected value of the decision must increase by more than the cost of the information obtained. The value assigned to different outcomes from a decision is called a payoff. Payoffs may be positive or negative.

The expected value criterion

Just knowing all of the possible payoffs from a decision may not be very useful for decision making. Some way must be found to aggregate the different outcomes. The usual approach is to obtain the expected value of each decision alternative. The expected value is the sum of each possible outcome times the probability of its occurrence.

Let's return to our example. The manager faces a possible gain (or payoff) of $20 million from the investment. Against this he runs the risk of losing the $7 million investment. Before investing in such a risky project, he would at least want to assess the relative probabilities of making $20 million versus losing $7 million. If the probability of making the $20 million is equal to .60, we can compute the expected value of the project:

Payoff (million)	Probability	Expected value (million)
$20	.60	$12
(7)	.40	(2.8)
Project expected value		$ 9.2

The expected value is the sum of the product of each possible outcome times the probability of that outcome. It represents the expectation from the project, not the actual outcome. Indeed, in this example, the actual outcomes are limited to either a $20 million positive payment or a $7 million loss.

Since the expected value of the project is positive, we will assume that the project is acceptable to the manager from the standpoint of maximizing company values. However, the project is risky. If the manager accepts this project, there is a significant (.40) probability that the company will suffer a $7 million loss. Can the manager do anything about that loss?

The opportunity loss concept

By making a decision to accept the project, there is a .4 chance that a loss will be incurred. The $2.8 million expected loss from the unfavorable outcome is referred to as an expected opportunity loss. The loss may never actually be realized, but there is a .4 chance that it will occur.

Now let's assume that the manager could acquire information that would make a perfect prediction of this project's success. Such information would be called perfect information. This information would provide the manager with perfect knowledge about the future. If the manager had such perfect knowledge, the project would be accepted only when the positive outcome was assured. This would occur with a .6 probability. Otherwise the manager would avoid the project and, at least, avoid the loss. Hence, with perfect knowledge, the outcome with the highest payoff for each known state would be selected. The expected value of the project would be the sum of the expected values for each outcome and its related best action:

Outcome (million)	Best action	Probability	Expected value (million)
$20	Invest	.60	$12
(7)	Avoid	.40	0
Expected value of project with perfect information			$12

Expected value of perfect information

With perfect knowledge about the future, the manager would be able to identify the 60 percent of the time when the new product would be successful. Under those circumstances, the manager would invest in the new product. The remaining 40 percent of the time, when the new product would fail, the manager would know not to invest. Hence, the manager could avoid the $7 million loss that was likely to occur 40 percent of the time.

The expected **value of perfect information** is the amount that could be saved with perfect knowledge about the future. That amount is also the difference between the $12 million expected value of the project with perfect information and the $9.2 million expected value of the project without perfect information. It is also the expected opportunity loss of the decision to invest. If the manager could obtain perfect information, the information would be worth up to $2.8 million. If the information cost is less than this, the manager's expected value would increase if the information were obtained.

Suppose a market research company can conduct a study of the product and its acceptance in a test market. The company will manufacture a sufficient quantity of the product for test-marketing purposes. As a result of this test, the manager will have perfect information about the outcome if the product is introduced to the general market. The total cost of the market research project is $1 million. This $1 million is an **information cost.** Should the manager pay for the market research and order the limited production run?

If the product will be successful, the market study will indicate this with absolute certainty. Therefore, with probability .6, WowZow Audio will obtain the $20 million payoff less the $1 million spent on the market study.

On the other hand, with probability .4, the market study will indicate that the product will not be successful. When this occurs, WowZow Audio will lose the $1 million cost of the market study, but no more.

The expected value of this decision with costly perfect information is:

Payoff (million)	Probability	Expected value (million)
$19	.6	$11.4
(1)	.4	(.4)
Project expected value		$11

This is, of course, exactly $1 million less than the expected value of the project with cost-free perfect information.

Perfect versus imperfect information

So far we have discussed the value of information that provides a perfect prediction. But since information about the future will probably be imperfect, why then do we consider the value of perfect information?

First, the value of perfect information provides an upper limit on the costs that should be incurred to obtain information for decision making. Second, the framework used to estimate the value of perfect information can also be used to estimate the value of imperfect information.

Imperfect information does not allow certain prediction of the outcome that will occur, but it allows us to revise our probabilities about the outcomes of a decision. The value of imperfect information is the increase in the expected value of the decision that arises from the ability to revise the probabilities. The value of imperfect information can be estimated using the technique called Bayesian statistics.

Now let's extend the example in the problem. We now assume that the marketing study and trial production run will provide imperfect information. The report can have two possible outcomes: a good report indicating that the product will be successful or a bad report showing that the product will fail. Since the study is an imperfect information source, a good report can occur even if the product will fail. Likewise, a bad report can occur even though the product would succeed. Nonetheless, use of the report may enable us to revise our initial probabilities and make a better decision. The initial probabilities are often referred to as prior probabilities, or priors.

Revising prior probabilities with information

In deciding to conduct the market research, the relevant criterion is whether the expected value of the project will increase sufficiently to cover the cost of the study. To test this, WowZow management must know how reliable the report will be. That is, if they receive a good marketing report, what is the probability that the product will actually be successful.

To conduct this analysis, some statistical notation is helpful. Using the symbol S to indicate a successful product and the symbol F to indicate a failure, we can note the prior probabilities as:

$$p(S) = .6$$
$$p(F) = .4$$

The next step is to find out the probabilities of obtaining a good report (G) or a bad report (B) given that the product will be successful. These are called conditional probabilities because they depend on the actual, unknown outcome. This information must be obtained from other sources, perhaps from the market research company or from management's judgment about similar past projects. For the example, we assume these probabilities are:

$$p(G|S) = .85$$
$$p(B|S) = .15$$

From similar sources, we must also obtain the probabilities of each report given that the product will fail:

$$p(G|F) = .20$$
$$p(B|F) = .80$$

This information is used to compute the probabilities of getting a good or bad report before the report is ordered. If the probabilities of each report type are known, the expected value of the project with the imperfect information can be computed. This information may be used to help decide whether to order the report. The difference in the value with the imperfect information and the value of the project without any information provides the maximum price we would be willing to pay for the imperfect information, assuming we follow the expected value criterion.

To obtain the probabilities of getting each kind of report, we add the probabilities of obtaining that report under each possible outcome. The probability of getting both a certain kind of report and a certain outcome is called a **joint probability.** In the example, the probability of getting a good report is equal to the sum of the joint probability of a good report when the outcome is success plus the probability of a good report when the outcome is failure. Thus, we multiply the probability of success times the probability of getting a good report when the outcome will be success. Then we multiply the probability of failure times the probability of getting a good report when the outcome will be failure. Then we add the results of these two multiplications. In notational form this is:

$$p(G) = p(S) \times p(G|S) + p(F) \times p(G|F)$$

Which for the example data yields:

$$p(G) = .6 \times .85 + .4 \times .2$$
$$= \underline{\underline{.59}}$$

We therefore have a .59 probability of getting a good report before contracting for the market study.

The probability of getting a bad report is equal to $1 - .59$, or .41. This may be verified by computing the probabilities of a bad report conditioned on both possible outcomes just as was done for the good report. The calculations are:

$$p(B) = p(S) \times p(B|S) + p(F) \times p(B|F)$$
$$= .6 \times .15 + .4 \times .8$$
$$= \underline{\underline{.41}}$$

Now, before we incur the cost of acquiring the report, we know the probability that we will obtain a good report or a bad report. This information is important because if the report is to have any impact on our decision, the different type of report must result in a change in our decision. That is, in this limited situation, if the report is good, then the investment meets the expected value criterion. If the report is bad, then the investment would not meet the criterion and, presumably, would be avoided. If we will take one action or the other regardless of the type of report, then the report has no value. Why spend resources on information that has no potential to change a decision?

Regardless of which report we receive, the project can still succeed or fail. Hence, after receiving the report we must make a decision whether to embark on the project. At this point, it is helpful to diagram the possible outcomes. A decision tree is useful for this purpose as shown in Illustration 26–1.

The first decision is whether to conduct the test. These are the two main branches of the decision tree. If we decide to conduct the test and, hence,

Illustration 26–1   **Decision tree for information evaluation**

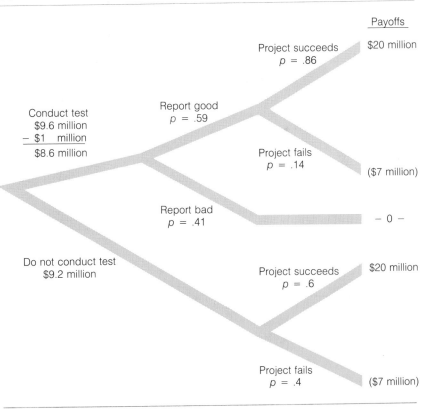

acquire the report, we must make the investment decision after receipt of the report. The decision will be based on the expected payoff from each outcome. To make the decision, we must know the probabilities of success or failure after receiving each kind of report. These probabilities are called posterior probabilities. In this example we ignore the possibility of investing in the project if the report is bad because the report outcome must affect our decision. We could extend the analysis to evaluate the expected payoff given a bad report. But, since a receipt of a bad report would preclude us from investing in the project, we enter a zero payoff for that outcome.

Prior to receiving the report, we were given the probability of project success as .6 and the probability of failure as .4. The expected value of the project absent the report is the second main branch in Illustration 26–1. Now we want to see if the expected value of the project is greater with the information in the report.

The objective of this analysis is to find out how the report will revise the initial probabilities (.6 for success and .4 for failure). This process of revising probabilities requires knowledge of the probabilities of success and failure given each type of report. These probabilities are known as **posterior probabilities.** They may be found using Bayes' theorem. If the report is good, the probability of success is estimated as:

$$p(S\,|\,G) = \frac{p(G\,|\,S) \times p(S)}{p(G)} = \frac{.85 \times .6}{.59} = \underline{\underline{.86}}$$

The posterior probability of failure given a good report is the complement of this amount, or .14.

The posterior probabilities when a bad report is received are computed in the same manner. For success, the probability is:

$$p(S\,|\,B) = \frac{p(B\,|\,S) \times p(S)}{p(B)} = \frac{.15 \times .6}{.41} = \underline{\underline{.22}}$$

The probability of failure given the bad report is then .78 which is the complement of the probability of success.

These posterior probabilities have been entered on the decision tree in Illustration 26–1 and are used to compute the expected value of the project with imperfect information.

Computing the value of imperfect information

The expected value of the decision to introduce the new product with imperfect information is obtained by computing the expected value of the project given each report. This is referred to as the conditional value of the decision given a certain report. That is, if we get a good report, we compute an expected value for the project conditioned on the good report. Multiplying that conditional value by the probability of obtaining that report gives us the expected value of the project after taking into account that a good report will only be received some fraction of the time. The expected value for the project is the sum of the expected values of each report outcome.

For the example, we have the following analysis to determine the expected value with a good report:

Outcome (million)	Posterior probability	Expected value (million)
$20	.86	$17.2
(7)	.14	(1)
Conditional value with good report		$16.2
Probability of good report		× .59
Expected value of product given the probability of a good report		$ 9.6

If the report is good, WowZow Audio would invest in the EarHear because the expected $16.2 million payoff is positive. Before we order the test market study, we have a .59 probability that the report will be favorable. Therefore, before ordering the study, we expect that the value of the joint outcome of a good report and the decision to go ahead with the product introduction will be $9.6 million.

Next we find the expected value of going ahead with the product introduction in the face of a bad report:

Outcome (million)	Posterior probability	Expected value (million)
$20	.22	$ 4.4
(7)	.78	(5.5)
Expected value of product after a bad report		$(1.1)

Since the expected value of product introduction would be negative after receiving a bad report, management of WowZow Audio would not introduce the product if a bad report were received. This is as we anticipated. Hence, the expected payoff would be zero.

The value of the decision to introduce the project with imperfect information is, then, the sum of the values of the decision for each report outcome. That is $9.6 million plus zero, or $9.6 million.

The value with imperfect information is compared to the value with no information. The increase represents the maximum that we would be willing to pay for the imperfect information. In this case, the difference is $.4 million (the $9.6 million − $9.2 million).

If the cost of the market study and trial production run were $1 million, the decision would be not to commission the study. Its cost exceeds the $.4 million benefit that can be expected from it.

Other considerations in information evaluation

Formal analysis of information needs provides a cost minimizing approach to the obtaining of information. However, it has frequently been said that management lacks sufficient prior information to compute the expected value of imperfect information. Hence, formal analysis is not possible. In other cases, a decision can be made without formal analysis. Before analyzing information value, a manager will ask the following questions:

1. Will the information make a difference?
2. How costly would the error be if action were taken without the information?

The first question asks if the information will possibly change the decision. The second asks about the cost of prediction error. Unless the information can be expected to make a difference and unless the value of the difference exceeds the cost of the information, the information should not be obtained.

Changing a decision with information

In the example, the imperfect market study and test production run had value because the decision involved a choice. If a bad report was received, management would avoid introducing the new product, and hence avoid the related loss. But if the receipt of a bad report would not deter introduction of the new product, the test study would have no value in this context. That is, regardless of the outcome of the study, the decision would not change. In such a case, there would be no economic reason to conduct the study. We invest in the project, period. No formal analysis of information value is needed.

Why would management proceed with a project when the outcome of a test study is negative? Several possibilities exist. In some cases, management may be required to proceed with the project due to legal requirements, contract obligations, or other imperatives. In this situation, the set of outcomes has been misspecified—any outcome that is based on avoiding the project is not possible. In other cases, the information may be so unreliable that a bad report would not dissuade management from proceeding with the project.

Let's modify the chapter example to demonstrate what happens if a bad report does not affect our decision. Suppose that after receipt of a bad report the conditional probabilities are:

$$p(S|B) = .35$$
$$p(F|B) = .65$$

This will change other probabilities, but we only focus on the expected value of the decision to invest in the project given the bad report. The value is now:

Payoff (million)	Probability	Expected value (million)
$20	.35	$7
(7)	.65	(4.55)
Project expected value		$2.45

Although the expected value of the project is now substantially less than we had initially expected, it is still positive. Since our decision rule is to accept projects with a positive expected value, the decision does not change in the face of a bad report. Since conducting the study would result in an information cost with no resulting benefit, we would not conduct the study.

Cost of prediction error

There is always the question of how much of a difference information makes in the decision making process. We have seen that information enables a manager to avoid certain losses. This may be expanded into the concept of the **cost of prediction error.** The cost of prediction error is the difference between the actual cost incurred based on the incorrect information and the cost that would be incurred with the correct information.

To illustrate the cost of prediction error, let's consider an inventory management example. One problem in inventory management is to minimize the total annual inventory policy cost, which is the annual cost of ordering and carrying inventory. The total inventory policy cost may be represented by the equation:

$$TC = \frac{QS}{2} + \frac{AP}{Q}$$

where

Q = quantity ordered at one time
S = cost to store one unit in inventory for a year
A = annual usage of the time
P = cost to place an order

The basic economic order quantity (EOQ) model (described in Chapter 14) may be used to find the order quantity needed to minimize inventory policy cost. The minimum total cost is obtained when:

$$Q = \sqrt{\frac{2AP}{S}}$$

Suppose that we used values of:

$$A = 50,000$$
$$P = \$20$$
$$S = \$.50$$

and obtained an optimal Q of:

$$2,000 = \sqrt{\frac{2 \times 50,000 \times \$20}{\$.50}}$$

Total costs for the year would be estimated as:

$$TC = \frac{2,000 \times .50}{2} + \frac{50,000 \times \$20}{2,000}$$
$$= \underline{\underline{\$1,000}}$$

After adopting the policy of ordering 2,000 units at a time and using that policy for a year, it becomes evident that there was an error in estimating the storage costs per unit *(S)*. Instead of \$.50, the actual storage costs were \$1.50. What was the cost of prediction error?

First, we find the optimal cost that would have been incurred had we used the correct storage cost. The new EOQ given the new storage cost information is:

$$1,155 = \sqrt{\frac{2 \times 50,000 \times \$20}{\$1.50}}$$

If we had the good fortune to realize that this was the optimal order quantity instead of the 2,000 that we used during the year, our inventory policy costs would have been:

$$TC^* = \frac{1,155 \times \$1.50}{2} + \frac{50,000 \times \$20}{1,155}$$
$$= \underline{\underline{\$1,732}}$$

However, based on our incorrect data, we followed an order policy of 2,000 units per year. As a result, we incurred inventory policy costs of:

$$TC = \frac{2,000 \times \$1.50}{2} + \frac{50,000 \times \$20}{2,000}$$
$$= \underline{\underline{\$2,000}}$$

The difference between the costs incurred under the actual policy and the costs under the optimal (hindsight) policy is \$268. This is the opportunity cost of having incorrect information at the start of the period and is sometimes referred to as the cost of prediction error. The amount reflects the most we could gain from the correct information given that \$1.50 was the actual storage cost per unit. Note that the expected \$1,000 inventory policy cost is not relevant. It formed the basis for the initial budget and will probably be used in traditional variance analysis. However, because the input data were incorrect, the budgeted results could not be attained.

In general, the cost of prediction error (\$2,000 − \$1,732) could be used to evaluate the prediction procedure. Any difference between $2,000 and actual costs would be the basis for evaluating operating managers since their activities were based on the EOQ policy of 2,000 units per order. However, whether this method is followed in practice is another question.

| **Management uses of information economics** | It is unlikely that management would routinely go through the formal analytical process described here to decide whether to gather information. Presumably this is because some of the probabilities are difficult to estimate (and further because managers may not be trained in the use of probability revision techniques). Furthermore, certain loan or employment contracts may require that studies be conducted or other data be gathered to assure that managers meet their stewardship obligations. However, it is probably true that in general, informal consideration is given to the economic usefulness of information for any given decision setting. Otherwise cost information would be demanded in unlimited quantities. When very large investments are incurred and when there is sufficient information to permit specification of the probabilities, formal analysis may be carried out. Indeed, petroleum exploration companies make wide use of the techniques described here. In their operations, they gather information about the probabilities of various amounts of recoverable oil or gas deposits in a given location. The costs to drill and install production facilities are so high that the benefits of gathering information exceed the costs. Moreover, there have been so many deposits explored that a sufficient data base exists to estimate probabilities. |

It is generally believed that managers acquire information only when it is economically efficient to do so. In an information economics sense, managers will acquire information when the expected value of a decision with information, net of any information costs, exceeds the expected value of that decision without information. The Bayesian revision formulation provides a formal analysis that is reasonably descriptive of the manager's information evaluation process, although the exact terms of the manager's revision process may differ from the Bayesian specifications.

The cost accountant, consultant, or other supplier of information understands that the commodity supplied (information) will only be purchased if required or if the user perceives it is economical. Understanding the process by which information has value should enable the buyer of information to relate its price to its value. The mathematics of information economics become very complex when the number of choices increases and when the decision includes other factors characteristic of a real-world setting. However, the concepts are based in the information economics model presented here. Presumably managerial accountants are hired because someone decides that managerial accounting information is economic in the sense discussed in this chapter.

Summary

Information is a product that may have value just as any other commodity. Management must make decisions concerning whether to gather information for decision making and other purposes. Information economics is the field of study that established the concepts used to formalize management's decisions about gathering information. The analytic approach suggests that the difference in expected value of a decision that results from the acquisition of information should be determined. If the information costs less than the difference in expected value, then it is economic to acquire the information. On a hindsight basis, it is sometimes possible to compare the profit that could have been attained with correct information and to compare that with the information actually used to set policy. The difference is referred to as the cost of prediction error. Although information economics models are complex and are infrequently used explicitly, the concepts behind the models serve as general guidelines to management decisions about the acquisition of information. After all, accountants are information producers and command a pecuniary reward for their services. If information had no value, what would become of accountants?

Terms and concepts

The following terms and concepts should be familiar to you after reading this chapter.

Conditional probabilities	**Payoff**
Cost of prediction error	**Perfect information**
Imperfect information	**Posterior probabilities**
Information cost	**Prior probabilities (priors)**
Information economics	**Value of imperfect information**
Joint probability	**Value of perfect information**
Opportunity loss	

Self-study problem: Soong's Soybean Products*

After several years of supplying tofu to several supermarket chains, the Soong family decided that it was time to diversify their operations in the light of increasing competition from other tofu manufacturers.

At a recent family conference, several members came up with new product ideas as possible alternatives to tofu. A dehydrated soybean protein was considered too low margin. Soybean jello, despite popularity within oriental communites, was rejected on the grounds that it was highly perishable and appealed only to a very small market segment.

Laura Soong, a recent biochemistry graduate, then suggested that they exploit the growing diet and health food market by introducing a soybean ice cream. "I've perfected it in the lab," she said. "It is low in cholesterol and has only one quarter

---

* © Jean M. Lim and Michael W. Maher, 1984.

the calories of regular ice cream. But more important, it tastes almost like the real thing!" She then provided her estimates of costs for the project.

Based on Laura's figures, David Soong, the family accountant, estimates that if sales are high, the total contribution margin from the product will be $300,000. If sales are low, the total contribution margin earned by the Soongs will be $50,000. Fixed costs for the project will be $150,000. David is uncertain as to what the probability distribution of sales would be. Hence, he attaches on a prior probability of .5 for high sales and .5 for low sales.

The Soong family can conduct a survey of various health food outlets to determine the true demand for the new product. The reliability of the survey is such that it will signal high sales 70 percent of the time when actual sales will be high, and signal low sales 90 percent of the time when actual sales will be low. The costs of such a survey are $20,000.

Required:

Assuming that the Soong family is risk neutral:

a. What action will they take without the survey?
b. Should the Soong family take the survey? What should their decision be?
c. How much will they be willing to pay for perfect information?

Solution to self-study problem

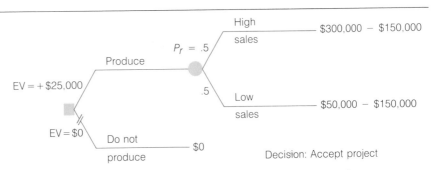

b. Let:

H = actual high sales state
L = actual low sales state
Y_H = survey signal for high sales state
Y_L = survey signal for low sales state
P_r = probability

$$Pr(Y_H|H) = .7$$
$$\therefore Pr(Y_L|H) = .3$$
$$Pr(Y_L|L) = .9$$
$$Pr(Y_H|L) = .1$$

$$Pr(Y_H) = Pr(Y_H|L)Pr(L) + Pr(Y_H|H)Pr(H)$$
$$= .1(.5) + .7(.5)$$
$$= .4$$

$$Pr(Y_L) = Pr(Y_L|L)Pr(L) + Pr(Y_L|H)Pr(H)$$
$$= .9(.5) + .3(.5)$$
$$= .6$$

$$Pr(H|Y_H) = \frac{Pr(Y_H|H)Pr(H)}{Pr(Y_H)}$$

$$= \frac{.7(.5)}{.4}$$

$$= .875$$

$$\therefore Pr(L|Y_H) = .125$$

$$Pr(H|Y_L) = \frac{Pr(Y_L|H)Pr(H)}{Pr(Y_L)}$$

$$= \frac{.3(.5)}{.6}$$

$$= .25$$

$$\therefore Pr(L|Y_L) = .75$$

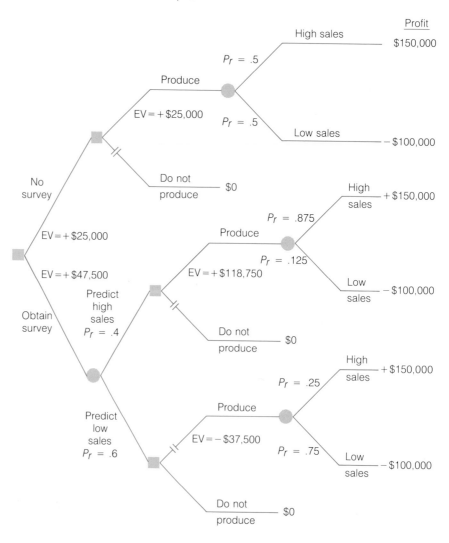

The Soong family should take the survey. The expected value of the project, less the cost of the survey, is:

$$\$47,500 - \$20,000 = \underline{\$27,500}$$

Without the survey, the expected value of the project is:

$$\underline{\$25,000}$$

c. Working through the Bayesian analysis in part *(b)*, assuming perfect information, we get:

$$Pr(Y_H) = .5$$
$$Pr(Y_L) = .5$$
$$Pr(H \mid Y_H) = 1.0$$
$$Pr(L \mid Y_L) = 1.0$$

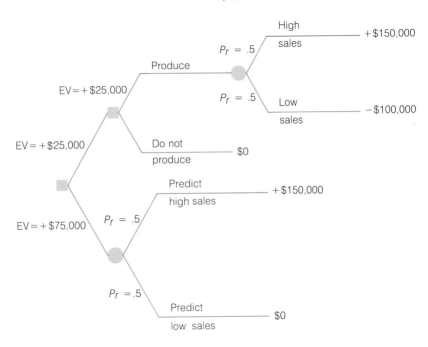

Expected value of perfect information $= \$75,000 - \$25,000$
$$= \underline{\$50,000}$$

Questions

26–1. A manager was overheard saying, "I want all the information before I make a decision. Get me all the information!" Comment on this quote.

26–2. Does information reduce the risk in a manager's decision?

26–3. Since no one can supply perfect information, why do we even consider the perfect information case?

26–4. "Imperfect information is worthless since it cannot predict the future with certainty." Comment on this quote.

26–5. Management has invested $8 million in a project. The payoffs from the project will either be zero or a present value of $20 million. Either event is equally likely. The original investment cost will be deducted in computing the profit from the project. Now management learns that it can obtain perfect information about the outcome from the project. What is the maximum value of that information for this investment project?

26–6. What are the limitations on the use of the information economics approach by management?

26–7. Management knows that if it purchases a report there is a good chance the results of the report will affect management's decision. Should management purchase the report or should they consider something in addition?

26–8. What is the difference between the value of information and the cost of prediction error?

26–9. When does a cost of prediction error arise?

Exercises

26–10. Computing expected values and finding probabilities

The ARC Radio Company is trying to decide whether or not to introduce as a new product a wrist "radiowatch" designed for shortwave reception of exact time as broadcast by the National Bureau of Standards. The "radiowatch" would be priced at $60 which is exactly twice the variable cost per unit to manufacture and sell it. The incremental fixed costs necessitated by introducing this new product would amount to $240,000 per year. Subjective estimates of the probable demand for the product are shown in the following probability distribution:

Annual demand (units)	Probability
6,000	.2
8,000	.2
10,000	.2
12,000	.2
14,000	.1
16,000	.1

Required:

a. What is the expected value of the demand for the product?

b. What is the probability that the demand for the product will be below the break-even point?

(CMA adapted)

26–11. Value of perfect information

Suppose an oil driller is faced with the following options:

State of nature	Probability	Payoff Drill	Don't drill
No oil	.7	−$100,000	–0–
Oil	.3	+ 150,000	–0–

The driller can obtain information from seismic tests that perfectly predicts whether or not oil will be found if drilling commences.

Required:

a. What action would the driller take without any information?
b. What action would the driller take with the perfect information?
c. What is the value of the perfect information?

26–12. Value of imperfect information—applying Bayes theorem

Refer to Exercise 26–11. Suppose the driller could not obtain perfect information but could obtain imperfect information from seismic tests that was accurate 80 percent of the time.

Required:

What is the value of the imperfect information? Should it be obtained?

26–13. Cost of prediction error

XXX Company estimates the following costs, prices, and volume for its single product:

Selling price	$ 200 per unit
Variable cost	150 per unit
Fixed costs	$1,000,000 per period
Sales volume	40,000 units

Based on this forecast, the company produced 40,000 units. Prices and costs were as expected, except sales were only 35,000 units. Due to the nature of the product, 5,000 units were scrapped for a net-of-salvage-cost revenue of $10,000.

Required:

Compute the cost of prediction error.

26–14. Value of perfect information

An owner-manager of a small company is trying to decide whether to accept a special order from a customer. This is a one-time order. Rejection of the order results in no present or future impact on profits. If the order is accepted, the increased revenue to the company will be $1,000,000. The costs of making the products for the special order are not known with certainty; but they are estimated to be either $800,000 or $1,200,000, depending on how much time is needed for its manufacture. Hence, acceptance of the order would result in a net gain of $200,000 *or* a net loss of $200,000, while rejection will produce neither gain nor loss.

The owner-manager regards the two production cost events as having the following probabilities: (1) there is a .6 probability that production costs will be low, hence, a $200,000 profit would be made on the order; (2) there is a .4 probability that production costs will be high, hence, a $200,000 *loss* would be incurred if the order is accepted. Consequently, the expected value of accepting the order is +$40,000 = (.6 × $200,000) + (.4 × $−200,000).

Suppose that *before* deciding whether to accept or reject the order, the owner-manager has the option of analyzing a set of special orders already in production, thereby gaining information that will aid in decision making. The cost of setting up the necessary accounting records and analyzing whatever data are reported are estimated to be $50,000.

The owner-manager is assumed to be risk neutral.

Required:

a. What is the best decision for the owner-manager before considering the information?
b. Assuming the information is perfect, what is the value of that information to the owner-manager? Should the information be obtained.

26–15. Value of imperfect information

Refer to Exercise 26–14. Suppose the information that the owner-manager can obtain is not perfect. Past experience for similar information indicates that such information is correct about 80 percent of the time; that is, when the information predicts low production costs, production costs turn out to be low 80 percent of the time and high 20 percent of the time. The relationship between high and low costs and the related information is summarized as follows:

P (*low costs* given information *predicts low costs*) = .80
P (*high costs* given information *predicts low costs*) = .20
P (*low costs* given information *predicts high costs*) = .20
P (*high costs* given information *predicts high costs*) = .80

Required:

a. What action would the owner-manager take if the imperfect information were obtained?

b. What is the value of the imperfect information?

26–16. Improving the accuracy of information

Refer to Exercise 26–15. Suppose the accuracy of the imperfect information could be improved as follows: For an additional cost of $10,000, the accuracy of the information could be improved from 80 percent to 90 percent.

Required:

Is it worthwhile to obtain the more accurate information?

26–17. Revising probabilities using Bayes theorem

Refer to Exercises 26–14 and 26–15. Suppose instead of the probabilities given in Exercise 26–16, the owner-manager receives information as follows:

P(Information signal/event)

For example, the owner-manager believes that if a low-cost event occurs, there is some probability P that the information would correctly detect it. Suppose such information would correctly identify high costs 70 percent of the time and correctly identify low costs 30 percent of the time. The costs of the information are $40,000.

Required:

Should this information be obtained? What is its value?

Problems and cases

26–18. Value of perfect information

Vendo Company operates the concession stands at the University football stadium. Records of past sales indicate that there are basically four kinds of football weather, that sales of hot dogs depend on the weather, and that the percentage of football games played in each kind of weather is as follows:

Weather	Percentage of game days	Hot dogs sold
Snow	10%	10,000
Rain	20	20,000
Clear/warm	40	30,000
Clear/cold	30	40,000

Hot dogs cost Vendo Company $.60 each and are sold for $1.00. Hot dogs unsold at the end of each game are worthless. Ignore income taxes.

Required:

a. Prepare a table with four rows and four columns showing the contribution margin from each of the four purchasing strategies of buying 10,000, 20,000, 30,000, or 40,000 hot dogs and the four weather conditions, snow, rain, clear/warm, and clear/cold.

b. Assuming that the chances of snow, rain, clear/warm, and clear/cold are 10 percent, 20 percent, 40 percent, and 30 percent, respectively, compute the expected contribution margin from each of the following purchasing strategies:

(1) Buy 10,000 hot dogs.

(2) Buy 20,000 hot dogs.

(3) Buy 30,000 hot dogs.

(4) Buy 40,000 hot dogs.

c. What is the optimal purchasing strategy in the absence of a weather forecast, and what is the expected contribution margin from following this strategy? (This answer will be the largest of the four expected payoffs computed in [b].)

d. If Vendo had a perfect weather forecast for each game, it would buy 10,000 hot dogs when snow is predicted, 20,000 when rain is predicted, 30,000 when clear/warm is predicted, and 40,000 when clear/cold is predicted. What is the expected average contribution margin per football game assuming the availability of a perfect weather forecast and that the four kinds of weather will occur in the frequencies 10, 20, 40, and 30 percent?

e. What is the expected dollar value to Vendo Company of a perfect weather forecast per football game? That is, what is the expected dollar value of the information from a perfect weather forecast?

(CMA adapted)

26–19. Value of perfect information

The Jessica Company has been searching for more formal ways to analyze its alternative courses of action. The expected value decision model was among those considered. In order to test the effectiveness of the expected value model a one-year trial in a small department was authorized.

This department buys and resells a perishable product. A large purchase at the beginning of each month provides a lower cost than more frequent purchases and also assures that Jessica Company can buy all of the item it wants. Unfortunately, if too much is purchased the product unsold at the end of the month is worthless and must be discarded.

If an inadequate quantity is purchased, additional quantities probably cannot be purchased. If any should be available, they would probably be of poor quality and be overpriced. Jessica chooses to lose the potential sales rather than furnish poor quality product. The standard purchase arrangement is $50,000 plus $.50 for each unit purchased for orders of 100,000 units or more. Jessica is paid $1.25 per unit by its customers.

The needs of Jessica's customers limit the possible sales volumes to only four quantities per month—100,000, 120,000, 140,000, or 180,000 units. However, the total quantity needed for a given month cannot be determined prior to the date Jessica must make its purchases. The sales managers are willing to place a probability estimate on each of the four possible sales volumes each month. They noted that the probabilities for the four sales volumes change from month to month because of the seasonal nature of the customers' business. Their probability estimates for December sales units are 10 percent for 100,000, 30 percent for 120,000, 40 percent for 140,000, and 20 percent for 180,000.

The following schedule shows the quantity purchased each month based upon the expected value decision model. The actual units sold and product discarded or sales lost are shown also.

	Quantity (in units)			Sales units lost
	Purchased	**Sold**	**Discarded**	
January	100,000	100,000	—	20,000
February	120,000	100,000	20,000	—
March	180,000	140,000	40,000	—
April	100,000	100,000	—	80,000
May	100,000	100,000	—	—
June	140,000	140,000	—	—
July	140,000	100,000	40,000	—
August	140,000	120,000	20,000	—
September	120,000	100,000	20,000	—
October	120,000	120,000	—	20,000
November	180,000	140,000	40,000	—

Required:

a. What quantity should be ordered for December if the expected value decision model is used?

b. Suppose Jessica could ascertain its customers' needs prior to placing its purchase order rather than relying on the expected value decision model. How much would it pay to obtain this information for December?

c. The model did not result in purchases equal to potential sales except during two months. Is the model unsuitable in this case or is this a characteristic of the model? Explain your answer.

(CMA adapted)

Glossary

The number in parentheses after each definition is the chapter(s) in which the term or concept is most extensively discussed.

Abnormal spoilage   Spoilage due to reasons other than the usual course of operations of a process. This may include goods spoiled as a result of error or as a result of casualty losses. (6)

Absorption costing   See *full-absorption costing.*

Accelerated cost recovery system (ACRS)   System in the tax law which specifies the tax depreciation allowed. (15)

Account analysis   The method of cost estimation that calls for a review of each account making up the total cost being analyzed. Each account is classified as fixed or variable based on the judgment of the classifier. (10)

Accounting rate of return   A measure of project returns using accounting concepts of income. (16)

Acquisition cost   Costs to purchase an investment or inventory item and to get it in place and in condition for use. (15)

Action set   The alternatives available to managers in a given decision setting. (24)

Activity variance   Variance due to changes in volume of sales or production. (18, 19, 21)

Actual costing   A system of accounting whereby overhead is assigned to products based on actual overhead incurred. (5, 9, 20)

Actual costs   Amounts determined on the basis of actual (historical) costs incurred. (5)

Adjusted R-square   The correlation coefficient in regression squared and adjusted for the number of independent variables used to make the estimate. (10)

Administrative costs   Costs required to manage the organization and provide staff support for organization activities. (2)

Allocation base   A measure that can be directly related to two or more cost objects and is considered to approximate the proportion of a common cost shared by two or more cost objects. For example, direct labor hours may be related to each unit produced. If direct labor hours are used to assign manufacturing overhead costs to products, then the direct labor hours are called the allocation base. (4)

Applied overhead Overhead assigned to a job or other cost object using an estimated overhead rate. (5)

Autocorrelation See *serial correlation.*

Basic accounting formula (Also known as the basic inventory formula.) Beginning balance plus transfers-in equals transfers-out plus ending balance. (3)

Behavioral congruence When individuals behave in the best interest of the organization regardless of their own goals. (22)

Break-even point The volume level where profits equal zero. (11)

Budget A financial plan of the resources needed to carry out tasks and meet financial goals. (1)

Budget plan Term for master budget. (17)

Budget variance A price variance for fixed costs. (19)

Budgeted balance sheets Statements of financial position that combine estimates of financial position at the beginning and end of the budget period with the estimated results of operations for the period and estimated changes in assets and liabilities. (17)

Budgeting under uncertainty Making many forecasts, each representing a different possible set of circumstances. (17)

By-products Outputs of joint production processes that are relatively minor in quantity and/or value. (8)

Carrying costs Those costs which increase with the number of units in inventory. (14)

Cash budget A period-by-period statement of cash on hand at the start of a budget period; expected cash receipts classified by source; expected cash disbursements classified by function, responsibility, and form; and the resulting cash balance at the end of the budget period. (17)

Centralized Refers to those organizations where decisions are made by a relatively small number of individuals at the high ranks of the organization. (22)

Certificate in Management Accounting A program established to recognize educational achievement and professional competence in management accounting. (1)

CMA Acronym for Certificate in Management Accounting. (1)

Coefficient of variation The standard deviation of a project divided by the expected value of the project. (24)

Common costs A synonym for indirect costs. Also, costs of shared facilities, products, or services. (2, 4)

Conditional probabilities Those likelihoods that depend on a specific result. (26)

Constraints Activities, resources, or policies that limit or bound the attainment of an objective. (13)

Contribution margin The difference between revenues and variable costs. (11)

Contribution margin format The outline of a financial statement which shows the contribution margin as an intermediate step in the computation of operating profits or income. (9, 11)

Contribution margin per unit of scarce resource Contribution margin per unit of a particular input with limited availability. (13)

Contribution margin ratio Contribution margin as a ratio of sales revenue. (11)

Contribution margin variance Variance based on contribution margins. (21)

Controllability concept The idea that managers should only be held responsible for costs or profits over which they have decision-making authority. (22)

Controllability of variance One rationale used in deciding whether a variance should be calculated, analyzed and investigated. (19)

Controllable cost A cost that can be affected by a manager in the short run. (2)

Controller The chief accounting officer in most corporations. (1)

Conversion costs The sum of direct labor and manufacturing overhead. (2, 3, 6)

Corner point A corner of the feasible production region in linear programming. (13)

Correlation coefficient A measure of the linear relationship between two or more variables such as cost and some activity measure. (10)

Cost A sacrifice of resources. (1, 2)

Cost accounting The subfield of accounting that records, measures, and reports information about costs. (1)

Cost Accounting Standards Board The federal governmental body set up to establish methods of accounting for costs by government defense contractors. (1)

Cost accumulation The process of adding costs to a cost object such as a job, department, or inventory account. (3, 5, 6)

Cost allocation The process of assigning indirect costs to cost objects. (2, 4, 7, 8)

Cost-based transfer pricing Transfer pricing policy based on full costing or variable costing, and actual cost or standard cost. (23)

Cost-benefit requirements The criterion that an alternative will be chosen if and only if the benefits from it exceed the costs. This criterion has been cited as a basis for evaluating cost data-gathering and reporting systems. (1)

Cost object Any end to which a cost is assigned. Examples include a product, a department, or a product line. (2, 4)

Costs for decision making Costs that are included in financial analysis by managers. See *differential costs*. (1)

Costs for performance evaluation Costs that are used in planning and performance evaluation analysis by managers. (1)

Cost of goods finished Cost of goods manufactured. (2, 3)

Cost of goods manufactured The cost of goods completed and transferred to the finished goods storage area. (2, 3)

Cost of goods sold The cost assigned to products sold during the period. (2, 3, 5, 6)

Cost of goods manufactured and sold statement Statement which incorporates and summarizes the information from the direct materials costs schedule, the cost of goods manufactured schedule, and the cost of goods sold schedule. (2, 3, 5)

Cost of prediction error The difference between the actual cost incurred based on incorrect information and the cost that would have been incurred with correct information. (26)

Cost-volume-profit (CVP) analysis Study of the interrelationships between cost and volume and how they impact on profit. (11)

Critical probability The probability of different outcomes which equalizes the value of the outcomes. (25)

Cross-department monitoring A reason for allocating costs, where it is hoped that managers of user departments have incentives to monitor the service department's costs. (7)

Current costs Cost to replace or rebuild an existing asset. (22)

CVP Cost-volume-profit.

CVP under uncertainty Consideration of the extent of uncertainty and the impact of that uncertainty on decision inputs and outcomes in cost-volume-profit decision analysis. (24)

Decentralized Refers to those organizations where decisions are spread out among divisional and departmental management rather than kept exclusively by higher management. (22)

Decremental costs Costs that decrease with a particular course of action.

Delphi technique Forecasting method where individual forecasts of group members are submitted anonymously and evaluated by the group as a whole. (17)

Denominator reason Differences between actual overhead costs and applied overhead caused by differences between actual activity and the activity used in the denominator of the formula used to compute the predetermined overhead rate. (5)

Dependent variable In a cost estimation context, the costs to be estimated from an equation. Also called the Y-term or the left-hand side (LHS) in regression. (10)

Differential analysis Process of estimating the consequences of alternative actions that decision makers can take. (12)

Differential costs Costs that change in response to a particular course of action. (1, 2, 12)

Direct costing A synonym for *variable costing*. (9)

Direct labor The cost of workers who transform materials into a finished product at some stage of the production process. (2)

Direct materials Those materials that can be feasibly identified with the product. (2)

Direct method A method of cost allocation that charges costs of service departments to user departments and that ignores any services used by other service departments. (7)

Discount rate An interest rate used to compute net present values. (15)

Discounted payback method A method of assessing investment projects that recognizes the time value of money in a payback context. (16)

Discretionary cost center An organization unit where managers are held responsible for costs, but the relationship between costs and outputs is not well established. (22)

Discretionary costs Costs that are difficult to relate to outputs. Examples include research and development, information systems, and some advertising. (22)

Disinvestment flows Cash flows that take place at the termination of a capital project. (15)

Dual rate method A method of cost allocation that separates a common cost into fixed and variable components and then allocates each component using a different allocation base. (4)

Dual transfer pricing Transfer pricing system where the buying department is charged with costs only, and the selling department credited with cost plus some profit allowance. (23)

Econometric models Statistical method of forecasting using regression models. (10)

Economic order quantity (EOQ) The number of units to order at one time to minimize total expected annual costs of an inventory system. (14)

Economic production run The number of units per batch in a production line that will minimize the expected annual costs of setting up production runs and storing the units produced. (14)

Efficiency variance A difference between budgeted and actual results arising from differences between the inputs that were expected per unit of output and the inputs that were actually used. (19, 20, 21)

Engineering estimates Cost estimates based on measurement and pricing of the work involved in a task. (10)

EOQ Abbreviation for economic order quantity. (14)

Equivalent units The amount of work actually performed on products with varying degrees of completion, translated to that work required to complete an equal number of whole units. (6)

Error term The unexplained difference between a prediction and actual outcomes. Sometimes called random error. (25)

Estimate A considered judgment about future events that takes into account past experience and probable changes in circumstances and conditions. (10)

Expected annual stockout cost The product of the cost of one stockout times the number of orders placed per year times the probability of a stockout in a year. A measure of the costs likely from running out of inventory at various times during the year. (14)

Expected opportunity loss A loss that may occur if certain unfavorable outcomes result after a decision has been implemented. (24)

Expected value The weighted average of all of the outcomes of a decision process. (24)

Expense A cost that is charged against revenue in an accounting period. (2)

Factory burden A synonym for manufacturing overhead. (2)

Factory overhead A synonym for manufacturing overhead. (2)

Favorable variances Variances that, taken alone, result in an addition to net income. (18)

Feasible production region The area in a graph of production opportunities bounded by the limits on production. (13)

Final cost center A cost center, such as a production or marketing department, from which costs are not allocated to another cost center. (7)

Financial accounting The preparation of financial statements and data for outsiders, primarily stockholders and creditors. (1)

Financial budget Refers to the budget of financial resources; for example, the cash budget and the budgeted balance sheet. (18)

Finished goods Product that has been completed and is in inventory awaiting sale. (2)

First-in, first-out (FIFO) costing The first-in, first-out inventory method whereby the first goods received are the first charged out when sold or transferred. (6)

Fixed costs Costs that are unchanged as volume changes within the relevant range of activity. (2, 10, 11)

Flexible budget A budget that indicates revenues, costs, and profits for different levels of activity. (18)

Flexible budget line The expected monthly costs at different levels of output. (11, 18)

Flexible production budget Standard input price times standard quantity of input allowed for actual output. (19)

Foregone discount The opportunity cost of ordering in a smaller lot size than that which receives the maximum quantity discount. (14)

Freight-in An alternative term for transportation-in.

Full-absorption costing A system of accounting for costs in which both fixed and variable manufacturing costs are considered product costs. (2, 9)

Full cost The sum of the fixed and variable costs of manufacturing a unit of product. (3, 12)

Full cost fallacy The assumption that fixed costs will vary with production. (12)

GAAP Acronym for generally accepted accounting principles.

Generally accepted accounting principles The rules, standards, and conventions that guide the preparation of financial accounting statements.

Goal congruence When all members of a group operate in concert toward a common set of objectives. (22)

Good output Units that are expected to be completed and suitable for further processing or for sale at the end of a production process. (6)

Gross margin The difference between sales revenues and manufacturing costs as an intermediate step in the computation of operating profits or net income. (3)

Gross margin variance Variances based on gross margins. (21)

Heteroscedasticity In multiple regression analysis, the condition of a variance that changes with the change in the dependent variable.

High-low cost estimation A method of estimating costs based on two cost observations, usually the costs at the highest activity level and costs at the lowest activity level. (10)

Hurdle rate The discount rate required by a company before it will invest in a project. (15)

Impact of a variance One rationale used in deciding whether a variance is important enough to compute, analyze and investigate. (19)

Imperfect information Information which may cause the recipient to revise the probabilities of certain decision outcomes. (26)

In-control probability The likelihood that a process is operating within specifications. (25)

Incremental costs Costs that increase in response to a particular course of action.

Independent variables The X-terms, or predictors, on the right-hand side of a regression equation. See *predictors*. (10)

Industry volume variance The portion of the sales activity variance that is due to changes in industry volume. (21)

Information cost Cost of obtaining information. (26)

Information economics A formal system for evaluating whether the cost-benefit test has been met for information. (26)

Information overload A characteristic of too much data. The intended user is overwhelmed by the quantity of data supplied. (22)

Intercept The point where a line crosses the vertical axis. In regression, this line is the regression line and the intercept is the constant term on the right-hand side of the equation. In cost estimation, the intercept is sometimes used as the fixed cost estimate. (10)

Intermediate cost center A cost center whose costs are charged to other departments in the organization. Intermediate cost centers are frequently service departments. (7)

Internal rate of return (IRR) The interest rate that equates the inflows and outflows from an investment project. (16)

Investment centers Organization subunits responsible for profits and for investment in assets. (22)

Investment tax credit A reduction in federal income taxes arising from the purchase of long-term assets. Usually treated as a reduction in investment cost for analytical purposes. (15)

IRR   Abbreviation for internal rate of return. (16)

Isoprofit lines   Family of constant profit lines where operating profits are the same for any combination of product volumes on each of those lines. (11)

Job costing   An accounting system that traces costs to individual units of output or to specific contracts, batches of goods, or jobs. (5)

Job cost record   The source document for entering costs under job costing. This is sometimes referred to as a job cost sheet, job cost file, or job card. (5)

Jobs   Units or batches of units that are easily distinguishable from other units or batches. (5)

Joint cost   A cost of a manufacturing process in which two or more outputs come from the process. (2, 8)

Joint probability   The probability of two or more events occurring. (26)

Joint products   Outputs from a common input and common production process. (8)

Lead time   The time between order placement and order arrival. (14)

Learning curve   The mathematical or graphic representation of the learning phenomenon. (10)

Learning phenomenon   A systematic relationship between the amount of experience in performing a task and the time required to carry out the task. (10)

Lease versus borrow to buy   Choice of financing the investment in an asset through either a lease or a purchase using borrowed funds. (16)

Line   Officers and other corporate employees directly responsible for activities related to the main goals of the organization.

Linear programming-graphic method   Graphic solution of a linear programming problem by selecting the best corner solution. (13)

Linear programming-simplex method   Solution of a linear programming problem using a mathematical technique. Used for solving complex product mix problems. (13)

Lost units   Goods that evaporate or otherwise disappear during a production process. (6)

Lower control limit   The minimum value of some observation which still indicates that the process is in control. (25)

Make-or-buy decision   A decision whether to acquire needed goods internally or to purchase them from outside sources. (12)

Management by exception   An approach to management requiring that reports emphasize the deviation from an accepted basing point, such as a standard, a budget, an industry average, or a prior-period experience. (18, 19)

Managerial accounting   The preparation of cost and related data for managers to use in performance evaluation or decision making. (1)

Manufacturing   Term used to describe production departments in organizations that manufacture goods, such as an assembly department. (7)

Manufacturing department   Production departments in organizations that produce goods.

Manufacturing organization   An organization characterized by the conversion of raw inputs into some other output products. (3)

Manufacturing overhead   All production costs except direct materials and direct labor. (2)

Manufacturing overhead adjustment   The difference between applied and actual overhead.

Margin of safety   The excess of projected or actual sales over the break-even sales level. (11)

Marginal costs   The economist's analog to differential costs and/or variable costs.

Market-based transfer pricing   Transfer pricing policy where (1) the transfer price is usually set at a discount from the cost to acquire the item on the open market and (2) the selling department may elect to transfer or to continue to sell to the outside. (23)

Market share variance   The portion of the sales activity variance arising from a change in the company's proportion of sales in the markets in which the company operates. (21)

Marketing costs   Costs to obtain customer orders and provide customers with the finished product. (2)

Master budget   The financial plan for the coming year or other planning period. (17)

Materials requisition   A form used to obtain materials from a storeroom. It is the source document for recording the transfer of materials to production. (5)

Matrix allocation   The simultaneous solution method of service department cost allocation.

Mean   The average of a series of data, sometimes referred to as the expected value. (24, 25)

Merchandise inventory   In a merchandising organization, the cost of goods acquired but not yet sold. (3)

Merchandising organization   An organization characterized by marketing goods or services rather than converting raw inputs into output. (3)

Minimax   The criterion to minimize the maximum loss from a decision. (24)

Mix variance   A variance which arises from a change in the relative proportion of outputs (a sales mix variance) or inputs (a materials or labor mix variance). (21)

Mixed cost   A cost that has both fixed and variable components.

Monte Carlo   A method of sampling from an assumed distribution function to obtain simulated observations of costs or other variables. (24)

Multicollinearity   Correlation between two or more independent variables in a multiple regression equation.

Multiple-factor formula An allocation formula used as an allocation base when a cost is considered not reasonably assignable on just one base. (4)

Multiple rates of return Problem arising when computing the internal rate of return for cash flows that change signs more than once in the project's life. It is possible, then, for such a project to have more than one internal rate of return. (16)

Mutually exclusive Term used in capital investment decisions to describe a situation where selection of one project precludes the selection of another. (16)

Negotiated transfer price System whereby the transfer prices are arrived at through negotiation between managers of buying and selling departments. (23)

Net income Operating profit adjusted for interest, income taxes, extraordinary and other items required to comply with GAAP and other regulations. (2)

Net present value Difference between the discounted future cash flows from a project and the value of the discounted cash outflows to acquire the project. (15)

Net present value index Ratio of the net present value of a project to the funds invested in the project. (16)

Net realizable value In joint cost allocation, the estimated value of a joint product that is not sold until further processing is conducted. (8)

Nominal discount rate A rate of interest that includes compensation for inflation. (15)

Nominal dollars Actual numerical count of money exchanged without adjusting for inflation. (15)

Noncontrollable cost A cost that cannot be changed or influenced by a given manager. (2)

Nonmanufacturing costs Administrative and marketing costs.

Normal costing A system of accounting whereby direct materials and direct labor are charged to cost objects at actual, and manufacturing overhead is applied. (5, 9, 20)

Normal costs Product cost amounts where actual direct materials and direct labor costs are assigned to products, but where manufacturing overhead is applied using a predetermined rate. (5)

Normal spoilage Spoiled goods that are a result of the regular operation of the production process. (6)

Numerator reason A difference between actual and applied overhead caused by differences between estimated overhead costs and actual overhead costs for the period. (5)

Objective function Mathematical statement of an objective to be maximized or minimized in a linear programming model. (13)

Operating budgets Refers to the budgeted income statement, the production budget, the budgeted cost of goods sold and supporting budgets. (18)

Operating profit The excess of operating revenues over the operating costs to generate those revenues. (2)

Opportunity cost   The lost return that could have been realized from the best foregone alternative use of a resource. (2, 12, 13)

Opportunity cost approach   Method of managerial performance evaluation based on a comparison of actual results to targets.

Opportunity loss   Loss from an unfavorable outcome. (26)

Ordering costs   Costs that increase with the number of orders placed for inventory. (14)

Ordinary least squares regression   A regression method that minimizes the sum of the squared distances of each observation from the regression line.

Organizational goals   Set of broad objectives established by management that company employees work to achieve. (17)

Outcomes   Possible results of a given action. (24, 26)

Outlay cost   A past, present, or future cash outflow. (2)

Outliers   Observations of costs at different activity levels (or similar phenomena) that are significantly different from other observations in the data series. (10)

Out-of-control probability   The probability that a process is not operating according to specifications. (25)

Overapplied overhead   The excess of applied overhead over actual overhead incurred during a period. (5)

Overhead   Usually refers to manufacturing overhead but is an ambiguous term when unmodified. (2)

Overhead adjustment   A debit or credit entry to change overapplied or underapplied overhead in total to cost of goods sold or to be prorated to goods in inventory and goods sold. (5)

Participative budgeting   A system for assembling the master budget using employees at all levels in the organization. (17)

Payback   One method of assessing capital investment projects using the rationale that there is a positive relationship between the speed of payback and the rate of return. (16)

Payback period   The time required to recoup an investment from the cash flows from the project. (16)

Payback reciprocal   One divided by the payback period in years. (16)

Payoff   The value of an outcome from a decision. (24, 26)

Perfect information   Information that predicts with complete accuracy the outcome which will occur from a decision. (26)

Period costs   Costs that can be more easily attributed to time intervals. (2, 9)

Periodic inventory   A method of inventory accounting whereby inventory balances are determined on specific dates (such as quarterly) by physical count rather than on a continuous basis. (3)

Perpetual inventory   A method of accounting whereby inventory records are maintained on a continuously updated basis. (3)

Physical quantities method   Joint cost allocation based on measurement of the volume, weight, or other physical measure of the joint products at the split-off point. (8)

Planned variance   Variances that are expected to arise if certain conditions affect operations. (19)

Planning budget   Another term for master budget. (17, 18)

Posterior probabilities   The probabilities that are obtained as a result of revising prior probabilities with additional conditional probability data. (26)

Predetermined overhead rate   An amount obtained by dividing total estimated overhead for the coming period by the total overhead allocation base for the coming period. It is used for applying overhead to cost objects in normal or standard costing systems. (5, 9)

Predictors   The variables on the right-hand side of a regression equation (the X-terms) used to predict costs or a similar dependent variable. They are activities that affect costs and costs to be estimated. (10)

Present value   The amounts of future cash flows discounted to their equivalent worth today. (15)

Price discrimination   Sale of products or services at different prices when the different prices do not reflect differences in marginal costs. (12)

Price variance   A difference between actual costs and budgeted costs arising from changes in the cost of inputs to a production process or other activity. (19)

Prime cost   The sum of direct materials and direct labor. (2)

Principal-agent relationships   The relationship between a superior, referred to as the principal, and a subordinate, called the agent. (22)

Prior department costs   Manufacturing costs incurred in some other department and charged to a subsequent department in the manufacturing process. These costs are related to goods transferred in from a department that is upstream in the manufacturing process. (6)

Prior probabilities (priors)   Initial probability estimates. (26)

Probabilities   Likelihoods that given outcomes will, in fact, occur. (24, 26)

Process costing   An accounting system that is used when identical units are produced through an ongoing series of uniform production steps. Costs are allocated by department and then allocated to units produced. (6)

Product choice decisions The product choice problem arises when there are limited amounts of resources that are being fully used and must be allocated to multiple products. The decision is to choose the optimal product mix. (13)

Product costs Those costs which can be attributed to products; costs that are part of inventory. For a manufacturer they include direct materials, direct labor, and manufacturing overhead. The manufacturing overhead attributed to products differs under the variable costing and the full-absorption costing systems. (2, 9)

Product mix A combination of outputs to be produced within the resource constraints of an entity. (11)

Production budget Production plan of resources needed to meet current sales demand and ensure adequate inventory levels. (17)

Production departments Departments in service, merchandising, or manufacturing organizations that generate goods or services which are ultimately sold to outsiders. (7)

Production volume variance A variance which arises because the quantity of outputs differs from the quantity used to assign fixed costs to units of output. (20)

Profit center An organization subunit responsible for profits because they manage revenues, costs, production, and sales volumes. (22)

Profit equation Operating profits equal total contribution margin less fixed costs. (11)

Profit plan The income statement section of the master budget. (17)

Profit-volume analysis A summary version of CVP analysis where the cost and revenue lines are collapsed into a single profit line. See *Cost-volume-profit analysis*. (11)

Purchase price variance The price variance based on the quantity of materials purchased.

Prorated overhead adjustment Assigning portions of overapplied or underapplied manufacturing overhead to goods in inventory and goods sold. (5)

Prorating variances Assigning portions of variances to the inventory and cost of goods sold accounts to which the variances are related. (20)

Quantity discounts Price reductions offered for bulk purchases. (14)

Random event An occurrence that is beyond the control of the decision maker or manager. (25)

Raw materials An alternative term for direct materials. (2)

Real discount rate The discount rate that compensates only for the use of money, not for inflation (also known as the *inflation adjusted rate*).

Real dollars Monetary measures that are adjusted for the effects of inflation so they have the same purchasing power over time.

Real return Return on capital after adjustment for the effects of inflation. (15)

Reciprocal allocation An alternative term for the simultaneous solution method of service department cost allocation. (7)

Regression Statistical procedure to determine the relationship between variables. (10)

Relative sales value method Joint cost allocation based on the proportional values of the joint products at the split-off point. The values may be based on actual sales prices or market values of the joint product, or they may be estimated from market values of a product generated with further processing of the joint product. (8)

Relevant costs Costs that are different under alternative actions. (12)

Relevant range The activity levels within which a given fixed cost will be unchanged even though volume changes. (2)

Reorder point The quantity of inventory on hand which triggers the need to order another lot of materials. (14)

Replacement method Joint cost allocation based on the change in costs arising from a change in the mix of outputs. (8)

Residual income The excess of actual profits over the profit targeted for an organization subunit. (22)

Responsibility accounting A system of reporting tailored to an organizational structure so that costs and revenues are reported at the level having the related responsibility within the organization. (22)

Responsibility center A specific unit of an organization assigned to a manager who is held accountable for its operations and resources. (1, 18, 22)

Return on investment (ROI) The ratio of profits to investment in the assets that generate those profits. (22)

Revenue center An organization subunit responsible for revenues and, typically, for marketing costs. (22)

Revenue variances Variances in prices and activity that affect sales or other revenues. (21)

Risk A decision setting in which the decision maker can calculate the probability that a given outcome will be associated with a particular course of action. (24)

Risk minimization A managerial objective to reduce the probability of loss. (24)

Risk premium Additional interest or other compensation required for risks in investments. (16)

Safety stock Inventory carried to protect against delays in delivery, increased demand, or other similar factors. (14)

Sales forecasts Estimation of future sales. (17)

Sales mix variance See *mix variance*. (21)

Sales price variance Variance arising from changes in the price of goods sold.

Sales quantity variance In multiproduct companies, a variance arising from the change in volume of sales, independent of any change in mix. (21)

Sales volume variance Variance arising from changes in the quantity of sales. (18)

Scattergraph   A plot of costs against past activity levels sometimes used as a rough guide for cost estimation. (10)

Sensitivity analysis   The study of the effect of changes in assumptions on the results of a decision model. (11, 17)

Serial correlation   In regression, the condition of a systematic relationship between the residuals in the equation. Sometimes referred to as autocorrelation. (10)

Service departments   An organizational subunit whose main job is to provide services to other subunits in the organization. (4, 7)

Service organizations   Organizations whose output product is a result of the performance of some activity rather than some physical product. (3)

Shadow price   Opportunity cost of an additional unit in a constrained multiple product setting. (13)

Short run   Period of time over which capacity will be unchanged. (11, 12)

Sigma   The number of standard deviations that a given observation is from the mean. (25)

Simplex method   A systematic method of evaluating corner points in linear programming. (13)

Simulation   A method of studying problems whereby a model of a system or operational process is subjected to a series of assumptions and variations in an effort to find one or more acceptable solutions. (24)

Simultaneous solution method   The method of service department cost allocation that recognizes all services provided by any service department, including services provided to other service departments. (7)

Slope of cost line   The angle of a line to the horizontal axis. In cost estimation the slope is usually considered the variable cost estimate. (10)

Source document   A basic record in accounting which initiates the entry of an activity in the accounting system. (5)

Special order   An order that will not affect other sales, and is usually a short run occurrence. (12)

Spending variance   Price variance. (19)

Split-off point   Stage of processing where two or more products are separated. (8)

Spoilage   Goods that are damaged, that do not meet specifications, or that are otherwise not suitable for further processing or sale as good output. (6)

Staff   A corporate group or employee with specialized technical skills, such as accounting or legal staff.

Standard cost   The anticipated cost of producing and/or selling a unit of output. (19)

Standard cost centers   An organization subunit where managers are held responsible for costs and where the relationship between costs and outputs is well defined. (22)

Standard costing A system of accounting whereby all manufacturing costs are charged to cost objects at standard cost. (19, 20, 21)

Standard cost system An accounting system in which products are costed using standard costs instead of actual costs. (20)

Standard deviation A measure of risk. It is computed as the square root of the sum of the squared differences between actual observations and the mean of the data series divided by one less than the number of observations. (24, 25)

Static budget Another term for *master budget.* (17)

Statistical quality control A method for evaluating a repetitive process to determine if the process is out of control. (25)

Step method The method of service department cost allocation that recognizes some interservice department services. (7)

Stockout Running out of inventory. (14)

Strategic long-range profit plan Statement detailing specific steps to be taken in achieving a company's organization goals. (17)

Sunk cost An expenditure made in the past that cannot be changed by present or future decisions. (2, 12)

Tax credit recapture Recapture of investment tax credit taken on an asset if the asset is taken out of service before the time required to earn the investment tax credit. (15)

Tax shield A deduction from taxable income based on the cost of an asset. It is sometimes referred to as tax depreciation. (15, 16)

Time value of money The concept that cash received earlier is worth more than cash received later. (15)

Total manufacturing costs Total costs charged to Work in Process in a given period.

Total variance The difference between total actual costs for the time period and the standard allowed per unit times the number of good units produced. (19)

Transfer price The price at which goods or services are traded between organization subunits. (23)

Transferred-in costs An alternative term for prior department costs.

Transportation-in costs The costs incurred by the buyer of goods to ship the goods from the place of sale to the place where the buyer can use the goods. (3)

Treasurer The corporate officer responsible for cash management and financing corporate activities.

Trend analysis Method of forecasting based on time series analysis. (17)

Underapplied overhead The excess of actual overhead over applied overhead in a period. (5)

Unfavorable variances Those variances which, taken alone, reduce operating profit or net income.

Upper control limit The maximum value which may be observed and still assume that a process is in control. (25)

Usage variance An alternative term for efficiency variance, usually related to materials used. (19)

User departments Organization subunits that use the services of service departments. (4, 7)

Value of information Value placed on information one could possibly obtain in a decision-making context. (1, 26)

Variable cost ratio Variable costs as a percentage of sales dollars. (11)

Variable costing A system of accounting for costs that only assigns products with the variable cost of manufacturing. (2, 9)

Variable costs Costs that change with a change in volume of activity. (2, 10, 11, 12)

Variances Differences between planned results and actual outcomes. (18, 19, 20, 21)

Variance investigation The next step taken if managers judge that the benefits of correction exceed the costs of follow-up. (19, 25)

Weighted-average contribution margin The contribution margin of all a company's products when a constant product mix is assumed. (11)

Weighted-average costing The inventory method that combines costs and equivalent units of a period with the costs and equivalent units in beginning inventory for product costing purposes. (6)

Work in process Uncompleted work on the production line. (2, 3)

Working capital Cash, accounts receivable, and other short-term assets required to maintain an activity. (15)

Working inventory Units kept on hand in the normal course of operations. (14)

X-terms The terms on the right-hand side of a regression equation, sometimes called the predictors or the independent variables. (10)

Y-term The dependent variable in a regression equation. In a cost context it is the costs being estimated from the X-terms. (10)

Zero-base budgeting A system of establishing financial plans beginning with an assumption of no activity and justifying each program or activity level. (18)

Supplementary Readings

These supplementary readings are additional academic and professional books and articles that extend the discussion in this book. These readings are listed alphabetically for each major part of this book. After the readings for each part is listed, there is a general category that lists readings covering more than one part of this book.

Introduction: Chapters 1 and 2

Anthony, R. N. "Cost Concepts for Control." *Accounting Review,* April 1957.

————. "Some Fruitful Directions for Research in Management Accounting." In *Accounting Research 1960–1970: A Critical Evaluation,* ed. N. Dopuch and L. Revsine. Champaign: Center for International Education and Research in Accounting, University of Illinois, 1973.

————. "A Case for Historical Costs." *Harvard Business Review* (November–December 1976), pp. 69–79.

Becker, S.; J. Ronen; and G. Sorter. "Opportunity Costs—An Experimental Approach." *Journal of Accounting Research* (1974), pp. 317–29.

Black, H., and J. Edwards, eds. *The Managerial and Cost Accountant's Handbook* (Homewood, Ill.: Dow Jones-Irwin, 1979).

Thalen, R. "Toward a Positive Theory of Consumer Choice." *Journal of Economic Behavior and Organization* 1 (1980).

Tversky, H., and D. Kahneman. "Judgment under Uncertainty: Heuristics and Biases." *Science* (1974), pp. 1124–31.

Part 1: Cost accounting systems (Chapters 3–9)

Baker, K. R., and R. E. Taylor. "A Linear Programming Framework for Cost Allocation and External Acquisition when Reciprocal Services Exist." *Accounting Review,* October 1979, pp. 784–90.

Capettini, R., and G. Salamon. "Internal versus External Acquisition of Services when Reciprocal Services Exist," *Accounting Review,* July 1977.

Churchill, N. "Linear Algebra and Cost Allocations: Some Examples." *Accounting Review,* October 1964, 894–904.

Cohen, S. I., and M. Loeb. "Public Goods, Common Inputs, and the Efficiency of Full Cost Allocations." *Accounting Review,* April 1982, pp. 336–47.

DeCoster, D., and K. Ramanathan. "An Algebraic Aid in Teaching Differences in Direct Costing and Full-Absorption Costing Models. *Accounting Review,* October 1973, pp. 800–801.

Fess, P., and W. Ferrara. "The Period Cost Concept for Income Measurement— Can It Be Defended?" *Accounting Review,* October 1961.

Fremgen, J. "The Direct Costing Controversy—An Identification of Issues," *Accounting Review,* January 1964.

Fremgen, J., and S. S. Liao. *The Allocation of Corporate Indirect Costs.* New York: National Association of Accountants, 1981.

Green, D. "A Moral to the Direct Costing Controversy?" *Journal of Business,* July 1960.

Hamlen, S. S.; W. A. Hamlen; and J. T. Tschirhart. "The Use of Core Theory in Evaluating Joint Cost Allocation Schemes." *Accounting Review,* July 1977, pp. 616–27.

Horngren, C., and G. Sorter. "Direct Costing for External Reporting." *Accounting Review,* January 1964.

Ijiri, Y. et al. "The Effect of Inventory Costing Methods on Full and Direct Costing." *Journal of Accounting Research,* Spring 1965.

Itami, H., and R. Kaplan. "An Activity Analysis Approach to Unit Costing with Multiple Interactive Products." *Management Science,* August 1980.

Jensen, D. "The Role of Cost in Pricing Joint Products: A Case of Production in Fixed Proportions." *Accounting Review,* July 1974, pp. 465–76.

—————. "A Class of Mutually Satisfactory Allocations." *Accounting Review,* October 1977, pp. 842–56.

Kaplan R., and G. L. Thompson. "Overhead Allocation via Mathematical Programming Models." *Accounting Review,* April 1971.

—————. "Variable and Self Service Costs in Reciprocal Allocation Models." *Accounting Review,* October 1973.

Manes, R. P.; S. H. Park; and R. Jensen. "Relevant Costs of Intermediate Goods and Services." *Accounting Review,* July 1982, pp. 594–606.

Moriarity, S., ed. "Joint Cost Allocation." *Proceedings of the University of Oklahoma Conference on Cost Allocations.* Norman, Okla.: Center for Economic and Management Research, 1981.

Sorter, G., and C. T. Horngren. "Asset Recognition and Economic Attributes—A Relevant Costing Approach." *Accounting Review,* July 1962.

Taggart, H. "Cost Justification under the Robinson-Patman Act." *Journal of Accountancy,* June 1956.

Thomas, A. "The Allocation Problem in Financial Accounting." *Studies in Accounting Research No. 3.* Sarasota, Fla.: American Accounting Association 1969.

—————. "The Allocation Problem: Part Two." *Studies in Accounting Research No. 9.* Sarasota, Fla.: American Accounting Association, 1974.

—————. *A Behavioral Analysis of Joint-Cost Allocation and Transfer Pricing.* Champaign, Ill.: Stipes Publishing, 1980.

Verrecchia, R. E. "An Analysis of Two Cost Allocation Cases," *Accounting Review,* July 1982, pp. 579–93.

Weil, R. "Allocating Joint Costs," *American Economic Review,* December 1968.

Williams, T. H., and C. H. Griffin. "Matrix Theory and Cost Allocation." *Accounting Review,* July 1964, pp. 671–78.

Zimmerman, J. L. "The Costs and Benefits of Cost Allocations," *Accounting Review,* July 1979, pp. 504–21.

Part 2: Differential costs for decision making (Chapters 10–16)

Abernathy, W. J., and K. Wayne. "Limits of the Learning Curve," *Harvard Business Review,* September–October 1974, pp. 109–19.

Areeda, P., and D. Turner. "Predatory Pricing and Related Practices under Section 2 of the Sherman Act." *Harvard Law Review,* February 1975, pp. 697–733.

Becker, S. W.; J. Ronen; and G. H. Sorter. "Opportunity Costs—An Experimental Approach," *Journal of Accounting Research,* Autumn 1974, pp. 317–29.

Benston, G. J. "Multiple Regression Analysis of Cost Behavior," *Accounting Review,* October 1966, pp. 657–72.

Bierman, H., Jr., and S. Smidt. *The Capital Budgeting Decision.* New York: Macmillan, 1980.

Bierman, H., Jr.; C. Bonini; and W. Hausman. *Quantitative Analysis for Business Decisions.* 5th ed. (Homewood, Ill.: Richard D. Irwin, 1977).

Blocher, E., and C. Stickney. "Duration and Risk Assessments in Capital Budgeting." *Accounting Review,* January 1979, pp. 180–88.

Bruns, W. J. "Accounting Information and Decision Making: Some Behavioral Hypotheses." *Accounting Review,* July 1968, pp. 469–480.

Buffa, E., and J. Miller. *Production-Inventory Systems: Planning and Control.* Homewood, Ill.: Richard D. Irwin, 1979.

Bump, E. A. "Effects of Learning on Cost Projections." *Management Accounting,* May 1974.

Charnes, A., W. W. Cooper; and Y. Ijiri. "Breakeven Budgeting and Programming to Goals." *Journal of Accounting Research,* Spring 1963.

Clark, J. M. *Studies in the Economics of Overhead Costs.* Chicago: University of Chicago Press, 1923.

Cohen, M., and R. Halperin. "Optimal Inventory Order Policy for a Firm Using the LIFO Inventory Costing Method." *Journal of Accounting Research,* Autumn 1980.

Comiskey, E. E. "Cost Control by Regression Analysis." *Accounting Review,* April 1966, pp. 235–38.

Davidson, S., and R. L. Weil, eds. *Handbook of Cost Accounting.* New York: McGraw-Hill, 1978, chap. 2.

Dillon, R. D. and J. F. Nash. "The True Relevance of Relevant Costs." *Accounting Review,* January 1978.

Dopuch, N. "Mathematical Programming and Accounting Approaches to Incremental Cost Analysis." *Accounting Review,* October 1963, pp. 745–53.

Dyckman, T. R. "The Effects of Alternative Accounting Techniques on Certain Management Decisions." *Journal of Accounting Research,* Spring 1964, pp. 91–107.

Ferrara, W. L. "Probabilistic Approaches to Return on Investment and Residual Income." *Accounting Review,* July 1977, pp. 597–604.

Friedman, L. A., and B. R. Neuman. "The Effects of Opportunity Costs on Project Investment Decisions: A Replication and Extension." *Journal of Accounting Research,* Autumn 1980, pp. 407–19.

Jensen, R. E. "A Multiple Regression Model for Cost Control: Assumptions and Limitations." *Accounting Review,* April 1967, pp. 265–73.

Kaplan, R. S. "Management Accounting in Hospitals: A Case Study." In *Accounting for Social Goals: Budgeting and Analysis of Non-Market Projects,* ed. J. L. Livingstone and S. Gunn. New York: Harper & Row, 1974.

Kelejian, H. H., and W. E. Oates, *Introduction to Econometrics.* New York: Harper & Row, 1981, especially chaps. 2–4.

Larcker, D. F. "The Perceived Importance of Selected Information Characteristics for Strategic Capital Budgeting Decisions." *Accounting Review,* July 1981, pp. 519–38.

Le Brone, H. "The Learning Curve: A Case Study." *Management Accounting,* February 1978.

Maher, M., and T. Nantell. "The Tax Effects of Inflation: Depreciation, Debt, and Miller's Equilibrium Tax Rates. *Journal of Accounting Research,* Spring 1983.

Miller, M., and C. Upton. "Leasing, Buying, and the Cost of Capital Services," *Journal of Finance,* June 1976.

Morse, W. J. "Reporting Production Costs that Follow the Learning Curve Phenomenon," *Accounting Review,* October 1972, pp. 761–73.

Pogue, G. "The Learning Curve and Unit Costs." *Management Accounting,* April 1983 (published in Great Britain).

Sommerfeld, R. *Income Taxes and Management Decisions.* Rev. ed. Homewood, Ill.: Richard D. Irwin, 1981.

Sundem, G. L. "Evaluating Simplified Capital Budgeting Models Using a Time-State Preference Metric." *Accounting Review,* April 1974, pp. 306–20.

Taggart, H. *Cost Justification.* Ann Arbor, Mich.: Michigan Business School, Division of Research, 1959.

Van Horne, J. C. *Financial Management and Policy.* 5th ed. Englewood Cliffs, N.J.: Prentice-Hall, 1980.

——. *Fundamentals of Financial Management.* Englewood Cliffs, N.J.: Prentice-Hall, 1980.

Weingartner, H. *Mathematical Programming and the Analysis of Capital Budgeting Problems.* Englewood Cliffs, N.J.: Prentice-Hall, 1962.

Wonnacott, R. J., and T. H. Wonnacott. *Econometrics.* New York: John Wiley & Sons, 1979.

Part 3: Cost data for performance evaluation (Chapters 17–23)

Abdel-Khalik, A. R., and E. Lusk. "Transfer Pricing—A Synthesis." *Accounting Review,* January 1974.

Ansari, S. L. "Behavioral Factors in Variance Control: Report on a Laboratory Experiment." *Journal of Accounting Research,* Autumn 1976, pp. 189–211.

Anthony, R., and R. Herzlinger. *Management Control in Nonprofit Organizations.* Rev. ed. Homewood, Ill.: Richard D. Irwin, 1980.

Anthony, R., and J. Dearden. *Management Control Systems.* 5th ed. Homewood, Ill.: Richard D. Irwin, 1984.

Anthony, R., and G. Welsch. *Fundamentals of Management Accounting.* 3d ed. Homewood, Ill.: Richard D. Irwin, 1980.

Argyris, C. *The Impact of Budgets on People.* New York: The Financial Executives Research Foundation, 1952.

Arrow, K. *Limits of Organization.* New York: W. W. Norton, 1974.

Atkinson, A. A. "Standard Setting in an Agency." *Management Science,* September 1978.

————. "Information Incentives in a Standard-Setting Model of Control." *Journal of Accounting Research,* Spring 1979, pp. 1–22.

Baiman, S., and J. S. Demski. "Variance Analysis Procedures as Motivation Devices." *Management Science,* August 1980, pp. 840–48.

————. "Economically Optimal Performance Evaluation and Control Systems." *Journal of Accounting Research,* Supplement 1980, pp. 184–220.

Benke, R., and J. Edwards. *Transfer Pricing: Techniques and Uses.* New York: National Association of Accountants, 1980.

Benston, G. "The Role of the Firm's Accounting System for Motivation." *Accounting Review,* April 1963.

Birnberg, J. G.; I. H. Frieze; and M. D. Shields. "The Role of Attribution Theory in Control Systems." *Accounting, Organizations and Society,* December 1977, pp. 189–200.

Blocher, E. "Performance Effects of Different Audit Staff Assignment Strategies." *Accounting Review,* July 1979.

Brown, C. "Human Information Processing for Decision to Investigate Cost Variances." *Journal of Accounting Research,* Spring 1981, pp. 62–85.

Brownell, P. "Participation in Budgeting, Locus of Control, and Organizational Effectiveness." *Accounting Review,* October 1981, pp. 844–60.

————. "Participation in the Budgeting Process—When It Works and When It Doesn't." *Journal of Accounting Literature,* Spring 1982.

Bruns, W. J., and J. Waterhouse. "Budgetary Control and Organization Structure." *Journal of Accounting Research,* Autumn 1975, pp. 177–203.

Burns, T. J., ed. *The Behavioral Aspects of Accounting Data for Performance Evaluation* (Columbus: College of Administrative Science, Ohio State University, 1970).

Cammann, C. "Effects of the Use of Control Systems." *Accounting, Organizations and Society,* November 1976, pp. 301–14.

Collins, F. "The Interaction of Budget Characteristics and Personality Variables with Budgetary Response Attitudes." *Accounting Review,* April 1978, pp. 324–35.

————. "Managerial Accounting Systems and Organizational Control: A Role Perspective." *Accounting, Organizations, and Society,* June 1982.

Cress, W. A Study of the Relationship between Budget-related Planning and Control Policies and Procedures and Firm Performance and Selected Firm Characteristics. Ann Arbor, Mich.: University Microfilms International, 1980.

Demski, J. S. "Optimal Performance Measurement." *Journal of Accounting Research*, Autumn 1972, pp. 243–58.

————. "Uncertainty and Evaluation Based on Controllable Performance." *Journal of Accounting Research*, Autumn 1976, pp. 230–45.

Demski, J. S., and G. A. Feltham. "Economic Incentives in Budgetary Control Systems." *Accounting Review*, April 1978, pp. 336–59.

Devine, C. "Observations on Internal Controls." In *Essays in Honor of William A. Paton*, ed. S. Zeff et al. Ann Arbor: University of Michigan, 1979.

Dittman, D., and P. Prakash. "Cost Variance Investigation: Markovian Control versus Optimal Control." *Accounting Review*, April 1979, pp. 358–73.

Dopuch, N., and D. F. Drake. "Accounting Implications of a Mathematical Programming Approach to the Transfer Price Problem." *Journal of Accounting Research*, Spring 1964.

Foran, M. F., and D. T. DeCoster. "An Experimental Study of the Effects of Participation, Authoritarianism, and Feedback on Cognitive Dissonance in a Standard Setting Situation." *Accounting Review*, October 1974, pp. 751–63.

Frank, W., and R. Manes. "A Standard Cost Application of Matrix Algebra." *Accounting Review*, July 1967, pp. 516–25.

Godfrey, J. T. "Short-Run Planning in a Decentralized Firm." *Accounting Review*, April 1971, pp. 282–97.

Gonedes, N. "Accounting for Managerial Control." *Journal of Accounting Research*, Spring 1970.

Gonik, J. "Tie Salesmen's Bonuses to Their Forecasts." *Harvard Business Review*, May–June 1978.

Groves, T., and M. Loeb. "Incentives in Divisionalized Firms." *Management Science*, March 1979, pp. 221–30.

Hirshleifer, J. "On the Economics of Transfer Pricing." *Journal of Business*, July 1956.

————. "Economics of the Divisionalized Firm." *Journal of Business*, April 1957.

Holstrum, G. L. "The Effect of Budget Adaptiveness and Tightness on Managerial Decision Behavior." *Journal of Accounting Research*, Autumn 1971, pp. 268–77.

Hopwood, A. G. "An Empirical Study of the Role of Accounting Data in Performance Evaluation. *Journal of Accounting Research*, Supplement 1972.

Ijiri, Y., J. C. Kinard; and F. B. Putney. "An Integrated Evaluation System for Budget Forecasting and Operating Performance with a Classified Budgeting Bibliography." *Journal of Accounting Research*, Spring 1968.

————. "Recovery Rate and Cash Flow Accounting." *Financial Executive*, March 1980, pp. 54–60.

Jacobs, F. H. "An Evaluation of the Effectiveness of Some Cost Variance Investigation Models." *Journal of Accounting Research*, Spring 1978, pp. 190–203.

Jennergren, L. Peter. "On the Design of Incentives in Business Firms—A Survey of Some Research." *Management Science,* February 1980.

Jiambalvo, J. "Performance Evaluation and Directed Job Effort: Model Development and Analysis in a CPA Firm Setting." *Journal of Accounting Research,* Autumn 1979, pp. 436–55.

————. "Measures of Accuracy and Congruence in the Performance Evaluation of CPA Personnel: Replication and Extensions." *Journal of Accounting Research,* Spring 1982, pp. 152–61.

Kanodia, C. "Risk Sharing and Transfer Price Systems under Uncertainty." *Journal of Accounting Research,* Spring 1979.

Kenis, I. "Effects of Budgetary Goal Characteristics on Managerial Attitudes and Performance." *Accounting Review,* October 1979, pp. 707–21.

Khandwalla, P. N. "The Effect of Different Types of Competition on the Use of Management Controls." *Journal of Accounting Research,* Autumn 1972, pp. 275–85.

Lawler, E., and J. Rhode. *Information and Control in Organizations.* Santa Monica, Calif.: Goodyear Publishing, 1976.

Lev, B. "An Information Theory Analysis of Budget Variances." *Accounting Review,* October 1969.

Lin, W. T. "Multiple Objective Budgeting Models: A Simulation." *Accounting Review,* January 1978, pp. 61–76.

Livingstone, J. "Organization Goals and Budget Process." *Abacus,* June 1975.

Loeb, M., and W. Magot. "Soviet Success Indicators and the Evaluation of Divisional Management," *Journal of Accounting Research,* Spring 1978.

Loomis, C. J. "How G E Manages Inflation." *Fortune,* May 4, 1981.

Lorange, P. *Corporate Planning: An Executive Viewpoint.* Englewood Cliffs, N.J.: Prentice-Hall, 1980.

Magee, R. "The Usefulness of Commonality Information in Cost Control Decisions," *Accounting Review,* October 1977.

Magee, R., and J. W. Dickhaut. "Effects of Compensation Plans on Heuristics in Cost Variance Investigations." *Journal of Accounting Research,* Autumn 1978, pp. 294–314.

————. "Equilibria in Budget Participation." *Journal of Accounting Research,* Autumn 1980, pp. 551–73.

Maher, M. W.; K. V. Ramanthan; and R. B. Peterson. "Preference Congruence, Information Accuracy, and Employee Performance: A Field Study." *Journal of Accounting Research,* Autumn 1979, pp. 476–503.

————. "Regulation and Controls: Firms' Response to the Foreign Corrupt Practices Act." *Accounting Review,* October 1981.

March, J., and H. Simon. *Organizations.* New York: John Wiley & Sons, 1958.

Merchant, K. A. "The Design of the Corporate Budgeting System: Influences on Managerial Behavior and Performance." *Accounting Review,* October 1981, pp. 813–29.

Merville, L. J., and J. W. Petty. "Transfer Pricing for the Multinational Firm." *Accounting Review,* October 1978.

Milani, K. "The Relationship of Participation in Budget-Setting to Industrial Supervisor Performance and Attitudes: A Field Study." *Accounting Review,* April 1975, pp. 274–84.

Mock, T. J. "The Value of Budget Information." *Accounting Review,* July 1973, pp. 520–34.

Neumann, B. R. "An Empirical Investigation of the Relationship between an AID Hospital Classification Model and Accounting Measures of Performance." *Journal of Accounting Research,* Spring 1979, pp. 123–39.

Onsi, M. "A Transfer Pricing System Based on Opportunity Cost." *Accounting Review,* July 1970, pp. 535–43.

————. "Factor Analysis of Behavioral Variables Affecting Budgeting Slack." *Accounting Review,* July 1973, pp. 535–50.

Otley, D. T. "Budget Use and Managerial Performance." *Journal of Accounting Research,* Spring 1978, pp. 122–49.

Owens, R. W. "Cash Flow Variance Analysis." *Accounting Review,* January 1980, pp. 111–16.

Reece, J. S., and W. R. Cool. "Measuring Investment Center Performance." *Harvard Business Review,* May–June 1978.

Rockness, H. O. "Expectancy Theory in a Budgeting Setting: An Experimental Examination." *Accounting Review,* October 1977, pp. 893–903.

Ronen, J. "Nonaggregation versus Disaggregation of Variances." *Accounting Review,* January 1974.

Ronen, J., and J. L. Livingstone. "An Expectancy Theory Approach to the Motivational Impacts of Budgets." *Accounting Review,* October 1975, pp. 671–85.

Ronen, J., and G. McKinney. "Transfer Pricing for Divisional Autonomy." *Journal of Accounting Research,* Spring 1970, pp. 99–112.

San Miguel, J. "The Behavioral Sciences and Concepts and Standards for Management Planning and Control." *Accounting, Organizations and Society,* November 1977, pp. 177–86.

Schiff, M., and A. Y. Lewin. "The Impact of People on Budgets." *Accounting Review,* April 1970, pp. 259–68.

Searfoss, D. G. "Some Behavioral Aspects of Budgeting for Control: An Empirical Study." *Accounting, Organizations and Society,* November 1976, pp. 375–85.

Seiler, R. E., and R. W. Bartlett. "Personality Variables as Predictors of Budget System Characteristics." *Accounting, Organizations and Society,* December 1975.

Shank, J., and N. Churchill. "Variance Analysis: A Management-Oriented Approach. *Accounting Review,* October 1977.

Shavell, S. "Risk Sharing and Incentives in the Principal and Agent Relationship." *Bell Journal of Economics,* Spring 1979.

Simon, H. "Rational Decision Making in Business Organizations." *The American Economic Review,* September 1979.

Solomons, D. *Divisional Performance Measurement and Control.* Homewood, Ill.: Richard D. Irwin, 1968.

Sorensen, J. E., and H. D. Grove. "Cost-Outcome and Cost-Effectiveness Analysis: Emerging Nonprofit Performance Evaluation Techniques. *Accounting Review,* July 1977, pp. 658–75.

Stedry, C., *Budget Control and Cost Behavior.* Englewood Cliffs, N.J.: Prentice-Hall, 1960.

Suver, J. D., and Helmer, F. T. "Developing Budgeting Models for Greater Hospital Efficiency." *Management Accounting,* July 1979.

Swieringa, R. J., and R. H. Moncur. "The Relationship Between Managers' Budget-Oriented Behavior and Selected Attitude, Position, Size, and Performance Measures." *Journal of Accounting Research,* Supplement 1972, pp. 194–209.

———. *Some Effects of Participative Budgeting on Managerial Behavior.* New York: NAA, 1975.

Swieringa, R. J., and J. H. Waterhouse. "Organizational Views of Transfer Pricing." *Accounting, Organizations and Society,* June 1982.

Thomas, A. L. "Transfer Prices of the Multinational Firm: When Will They Be Arbitrary?" *Abacus,* June 1971, pp. 40–53.

———. *A Behavioral Analysis of Joint-Cost Allocation and Transfer Pricing* (Champaign, Ill.: Stipes Publishing, 1980).

Vancil, R. F. *Decentralization: Managerial Ambiguity by Design.* Homewood, Ill.: Dow Jones-Irwin, 1979.

Watson, D., and J. Baumler. "Transfer Pricing: A Behavioral Context." *Accounting Review,* April 1975.

Welsch, G. A. *Budgeting: Profit Planning and Control,* Englewood Cliffs, N.J.: Prentice-Hall, 1978.

Williams, J. J. "Zero-Base Budgeting: Prospects for Developing a Semi-Confusing Budgeting Information System." *Accounting, Organizations and Society,* August 1981, pp. 153–64.

Wolk, H. I., and A. D. Hillman. "Materials Mix and Yield Variances." *Accounting Review,* July 1972, pp. 549–55.

Part 4: Accounting in an uncertain environment (Chapters 24–26)

Adar, Z.; A. Barnea; and B. Lev. "A Comprehensive Cost-Volume-Profit Analysis under Uncertainty." *Accounting Review,* January 1977.

Baiman, S., and J. Demski. "Variance Analysis Procedures as Motivational Devices." *Management Science,* August 1980, pp. 840–48.

Becker, S., and D. Green. "Budgeting and Employee Behavior. *Journal of Business,* October 1962.

Bierman, H.; L. E. Fouraker; and R. K. Jaedicke. "A Use of Probability and Statistics in Performance Evaluation." *Accounting Review,* July 1961, pp. 409–17.

Box, G., and G. Jenkins. *Time Series Analysis, Forecasting and Control.* San Francisco: Holden Day, 1970.

Charnes, A.; W. Cooper; and Y. Ijiri. Breakeven Budgeting and Programming to Goals." *Journal of Accounting Research,* Spring 1983.

Constantinides, G.; Y. Ijiri; and R. A. Leitch. "Stochastic Cost-Volume-Profit Analysis and a Linear Demand Function." *Decision Sciences,* June 1981.

Cushing, Barry. "Some Observations on Demski's Ex Post Accounting System." *Accounting Review,* October 1968, pp. 668–71.

DeCoster, D. "An Intuitive Framework for Empirical Research in Participative Budgeting." In *Accounting Research Convocation,* ed. G. Previts. University, Ala.: University of Alabama Press, 1976.

Demski, J. "An Accounting System Structured on a Linear Programming Model." *Accounting Review,* October 1967, pp. 701–12.

————. "Analyzing the Effectiveness of the Traditional Cost Variance Model." *Management Accounting,* October 1967, pp. 9–19.

————. "Some Observations on Demski's Ex Post Accounting System: A Reply." *Accounting Review,* October 1968, pp. 672–74.

————. "Decision-Performance Control." *Accounting Review,* October 1969, pp. 669–79.

————. *Information Analysis.* 2nd ed. Reading, Mass.: Addison-Wesley Publishing, 1980.

Demski, J., and G. Feltham. Cost Determination: A Conceptual Approach. Ames, Iowa: Iowa State University Press, 1976.

Dittman, D. A., and P. Prakash. "Cost Variance Investigation—Markovian Control of Markov Processes. *Journal of Accounting Research,* Spring 1978, pp. 14–25.

————. "Cost Variance Investigation: Markovian Control versus Optimal Control." *Accounting Review,* April 1979, pp. 358–73.

Dopuch, N.; J. Birnberg; and J. Demski. "An Extension of Standard Cost Variance Analysis." *Accounting Review,* July 1967, pp. 526–36.

Feltham, G. A. *Information Evaluation. Studies in Accounting Research No. 5.* Sarasota, Fla.: American Accounting Association, 1972.

————. "Cost Aggregation: An Information Economic Analysis." *Journal of Accounting Research,* Spring 1977, pp. 42–70.

Ferrara, W. L.; J. C. Hayya; and D. A. Nachman. "Normalcy of Profit in the Jaedicke-Robichek Model." *Accounting Review,* April 1972.

Hilliard, J. E., and R. A. Leitch. "Cost-Volume-Profit Analysis under Uncertainty: A Log Normal Approach. *Accounting Review,* January 1975, pp. 69–80.

————. "A Reply." *Accounting Review,* January 1976, pp. 168–71.

Ijiri, Y., and H. Itami. "Quadratic Cost Volume Relationship and Timing of Demand Information." *Accounting Review,* October 1973, pp. 724–37.

Jaedicke, R. K., and A. A. Robichek. "Cost-Volume-Profit Analysis Under Conditions of Uncertainty." *Accounting Review,* October 1964, pp. 917–26.

Johnson, G. L., and S. S. Simik. "Multiproduct C-V-P Analysis under Uncertainty." *Journal of Accounting Research,* Autumn 1971, pp. 278–86.

Kaplan, R. S. "Optimal Investigation Strategies with Imperfect Information." *Journal of Accounting Research,* Spring 1969, pp. 32–43.

————. "The Significance and Investigation of Cost Variances: Survey and Extensions." *Journal of Accounting Research,* Autumn 1975, pp. 311–37.

Lau, A. H., and H. Lau. "CVP Analysis under Uncertainty—A Log Normal Approach: A Comment." *Accounting Review,* January 1976, pp. 163–67.

Liao, M. "Model Sampling: A Stochastic Cost-Volume-Profit Analysis." *Accounting Review,* October 1975, pp. 780–90.

Libby, R. Accounting and Human Information Processing. Englewood Cliffs, N.J.: Prentice-Hall, 1981.

Lobo, G. J., and M. W. Maher. *Information Economics and Accounting Research.* Ann Arbor: Division of Research, Graduate School of Business Administration, University of Michigan, 1980.

Shih, W. "A General Decision Model for Cost-Volume-Profit Analysis under Uncertainty." *Accounting Review,* October 1979, pp. 687–706.

Sundem, G. L. "A Game Theory Model of the Information Evaluator and the Decision Maker." *Journal of Accounting Research,* Spring 1979, pp. 243–61.

General

These references cover more than one topic in cost accounting.

Albergo, H. "Building Better Controls in the Commercial Lending Function." *Management Accounting,* February 1980.

Arrow, K. J. *The Limits of Organization.* New York: W. W. Norton, 1974.

Ashton, R. H. "Deviation-Amplifying Feedback and Unintended Consequences of Management Accounting Systems." *Accounting, Organizations and Society,* November 1976, pp. 289–300.

Babson, S. M., Jr. "Profiling Your Productivity." *Management Accounting,* December 1981.

Baiman, S. "The Evaluation and Choice of Internal Information Systems within a Multiperson World." *Journal of Accounting Research,* Spring 1975, pp. 1–15.

————. "Agency Research in Managerial Accounting: A Survey." *Journal of Accounting Literature,* Spring 1982.

Bancroft, A., and R. Wilson. "Management Accounting for Marketing." *Management Accounting,* December 1979 (published in Great Britain).

Barrett, T. M. "Modular Data Base Accounting System for Marketing." *Management Accounting,* October 1980 (published in Great Britain).

Caplan, E. H., and J. Champoux. *Cases in Management Accounting: Context and Behavior.* New York: National Association of Accountants, 1978.

Chow, C. W., and Waller, W. S. "Management Accounting and Organizational Control." *Management Accounting,* April 1982 (white collar compensation, cost control and managerial accounting).

Cyert, R. M., and J. March. *Behavioral Theory of the Firm.* Englewood Cliffs, N.J.: Prentice Hall, 1963.

Davidson, S., and R. L. Weil, eds. *Handbook of Cost Accounting.* New York: McGraw-Hill, 1978.

Demski, J. S. *Information Analysis.* Reading, Mass.: Addison-Wesley Publishing, 1980.

Demski, J. S., and G. A. Feltham. *Cost Determination: A Conceptual Approach.* Ames, Iowa: Iowa State University Press, 1976.

Demski, J. S., and D. Kreps. "Models in Managerial Accounting." *Journal of Accounting Research,* Supplement 1982.

Dermer, J., and J. P. Siegel. "The Role of Behavioral Measures in Accounting for Human Resources." *Accounting Review,* January 1974, pp. 88–97.

Dopuch, N.; J. Birnberg; and J. Demski. *Cost Accounting.* 3d ed. New York: Harcourt Brace Jovanovich, 1982.

Drucker P. "Controls, Control and Management." In *An Introductory View of Management.* New York: Harper & Row, 1979, chap. 31.

Flamholtz, E. G. "The Impact of Human Resource Valuation on Management Decisions: A Laboratory Experiment." *Accounting, Organizations and Society,* August 1976, pp. 153–65.

Gillespie, J. F. "An Application of Learning Curves to Standard Costing." *Management Accounting,* September 1981.

Ginzberg, M. J. "An Organizational Contingencies View of Accounting and Information Systems Implementation." *Accounting, Organizations and Society,* December 1980, pp. 369–83.

Godfrey, J. T., and T. R. Prince. "The Accounting Model from an Information Systems Perspective." *Accounting Review,* January 1971, pp. 75–89.

Gow, E. "Direct Labour Effectiveness." *Management Accounting,* November 1979 (published in Great Britain).

Harrell, A. M., and H. D. Klick. "Comparing the Impact of Monetary and Nonmonetary Human Asset Measures on Executive Decision Making." *Accounting, Organizations and Society,* December 1980, pp. 393–400.

Harris, M., and A. Raviv. "Some Results on Incentive Contracts with Applications to Education and Employment, Health Insurance and Law Enforcement." *American Economic Review,* March 1978, pp. 20–30.

Haseman, W. D., and A. B. Whinston. "Design of a Multidimensional Accounting System." *Accounting Review,* January 1976, pp. 65–79.

Henrici, S. B. "How Deadly is the Productivity Disease?" *Harvard Business Review,* November–December 1981.

Hilton, R. W. "The Determinants of Cost Information Value: An Illustrative Analysis." *Journal of Accounting Research,* Autumn 1979, pp. 411–35.

Hilton, R. W.; R. J. Swieringa; and R. E. Hoskin. "Perception of Accuracy as a Determinant of Information Value." *Journal of Accounting Research,* Spring 1981, pp. 86–108.

Hopwood, A. *Accounting and Human Behavior.* Englewood Cliffs, N.J.: Prentice-Hall, 1976.

Horngren, C. T. *Cost Accounting: A Managerial Emphasis.* 5th ed. Englewood Cliffs, N.J.: Prentice-Hall, 1982.

Ijiri, Y. *Management Goals and Accounting for Control.* Skokie, Ill.: Rand McNally, 1965.

Itami, H. *Adaptive Behavior: Management Control and Information Analysis.* Sarasota, Fla.: American Accounting Association, 1977.

Ivison, S. "Productivity Measurement and the Accountant." *Management Accounting,* October 1982 (published in Great Britain).

Jaggi, B., and H. Lau. "Toward a Model for Human Resource Valuation." *Accounting Review,* April 1974, pp. 321–29.

Jensen, M. C., and W. H. Meckling. "Theory of the Firm, Managerial Behavior, Agency Costs and Ownership Structure." *Journal of Financial Economics,* October 1976, pp. 305–60.

Kaplan, R. S. "Application of Quantitative Models in Managerial Accounting: A State of the Art Survey." In *Management Accounting—State of the Art* (Robert Beyer Lecture Series). Madison: University of Wisconsin, 1977. Reprinted in *Accounting Journal,* Winter 1977–78.

———. *Advanced Management Accounting.* Englewood Cliffs, N.J.: Prentice-Hall, 1982.

MacIntyre, D. K. "Marketing Costs: A New Look." *Management Accounting,* March 1983.

Malkiel, B. G. "Productivity—The Problem behind the Headlines." *Harvard Business Review,* May–June 1979.

Mammone, J. L. "A Practical Approach to Productivity Measurement." *Management Accounting,* July 1980.

McConnell, C. R. "Why is U.S. Productivity Slowing Down?" *Harvard Business Review,* March–April 1979.

McNiven, M. A. "Plan for More Productive Advertising." *Harvard Business Review,* March–April 1980.

Mecimore, C. D., and Cornick, M. G. "Banks Should Use Management Accounting Models." *Management Accounting,* February 1982.

Morse, W. *Cost Accounting.* 2d ed. Reading, Mass.: Addison-Wesley Publishing, 1981.

Mullins, L. "Behavioural Implications of Management Accounting." *Management Accounting,* January 1981 (published in Great Britain).

O'Neill, J. A. "One Path through the Productivity Measurement Jungle." *Management Accounting,* January 1979 (published in Great Britain).

———. "Pitfalls in the Ratio Analysis of Productivity Change." *Management Accounting,* May 1980 (published in Great Britain).

Ouchi, W. "A Conceptual Framework for the Design of Organizational Control Mechanisms." *Management Science,* September 1979, pp. 833–48.

Palmer, J. *The Use of Accounting Information in Labor Negotiations.* New York: NAA, 1977.

Pfeffer, J. *Organizational Design.* Arlington Heights, Ill.: AHM Publishing, 1978.

Possett, R. W. "Measuring Productive Costs in the Service Sector." *Management Accounting,* October 1980.

Prakash, P., and A. Rappaport. "Information Interdependencies: System Structure Induced by Accounting Information." *Accounting Review,* October 1975, pp. 723–34.

Ramanthan, K. *Management Control in Nonprofit Organization.* New York: John Wiley & Sons, 1982.

Rayburn, L. G. "Marketing Costs—Accountants to the Rescue." *Management Accounting,* January 1981.

———. *Principles of Cost Accounting.* Rev. ed. Homewood, Ill.: Richard D. Irwin, 1983.

Rosenzweig, K. "An Exploratory Field Study of the Relationships between the Controller's Department and Overall Organizational Characteristics." *Accounting, Organizations and Society,* December 1981, pp. 339–54.

Ross, T. L., and R. J. Bullock. "Integrating Productivity of Measurement into a Standard Cost System," *Financial Executive,* October 1980.

Sheridan, T. J. "The Framework of Management Accounting in Banks." *Management Accounting,* March 1983 (published in Great Britain).

Shillinglaw, G., *Managerial Cost Accounting.* 5th ed. Homewood, Ill.: Richard D. Irwin, 1982.

Solomons, D., ed. *Studies in Cost Analysis.* 2d ed. Homewood, Ill.: Richard D. Irwin, 1968.

Spence, A. M. "The Economics of Internal Organization. An Introduction." *Bell Journal of Economics,* Spring 1976, pp. 163–72.

Spicer, B., and V. Ballew. "Management Accounting Systems and the Economics of Internal Organization." *Accounting, Organizations, and Society,* March 1983.

Steele, B., and G. Kalorkoti. "Measuring the Cost Effectiveness of Office Automation." *Management Accounting,* April 1983 (published in Great Britain).

Tiessen, P., and J. H. Waterhouse. "Towards a Descriptive Theory of Management Accounting." *Accounting, Organizations, and Society* (1983).

Tipgos, M. A., and Crum, R. P. "Applying Management Accounting Concepts to the Health Care Industry." *Management Accounting,* July 1982.

Tomassini, L. A. "Behavioral Research on Human Resource Accounting: A Contingency Framework." *Accounting, Organizations and Society,* August 1976, pp. 239–52.

———. "Assessing the Impact of Human Resource Accounting: An Experimental Study of Managerial Decision Preferences." *Accounting Review,* October 1977, pp. 904–14.

Williamson, O. *Markets and Hierarchies: Analysis and Antitrust Implications.* New York: Free Press, 1975.York: Free Press, 1975.

Index

This book has been set Video Comp, in 10 and 9 point Times Roman, leaded 2 points. Part numbers are 18 point Helvetica medium and part and chapter titles are 24 point Helvetica medium. The size of the type page is 36½ by 48 picas.